Critical values of the *t* Distribution

Degrees of Freedom	$t_{.100}$	$t_{.050}$	$t_{.025}$	$t_{.010}$	$t_{.005}$
1	3.078	6.314	12.706	31.821	63.657
2	1.886	2.920	4.303	6.965	9.925
3	1.638	2.353	3.182	4.541	5.841
4	1.533	2.132	2.776	3.747	4.604
5	1.476	2.015	2.571	3.365	4.032
6	1.440	1.943	2.447	3.143	3.707
7	1.415	1.895	2.365	2.998	3.499
8	1.397	1.860	2.306	2.896	3.355
9	1.383	1.833	2.262	2.821	3.250
10	1.372	1.812	2.228	2.764	3.169
11	1.363	1.796	2.201	2.718	3.106
12	1.356	1.782	2.179	2.681	3.055
13	1.350	1.771	2.160	2.650	3.012
14	1.345	1.761	2.145	2.624	2.977
15	1.341	1.753	2.131	2.602	2.947
16	1.337	1.746	2.120	2.583	2.921
17	1.333	1.740	2.110	2.567	2.898
18	1.330	1.734	2.101	2.552	2.878
19	1.328	1.729	2.093	2.539	2.861
20	1.325	1.725	2.086	2.528	2.845
21	1.323	1.721	2.080	2.518	2.831
22	1.321	1.717	2.074	2.508	2.819
23	1.319	1.714	2.069	2.500	2.807
24	1.318	1.711	2.064	2.492	2.797
25	1.316	1.708	2.060	2.485	2.787
26	1.315	1.706	2.056	2.479	2.779
27	1.314	1.703	2.052	2.473	2.771
28	1.313	1.701	2.048	2.467	2.763
29	1.311	1.699	2.045	2.462	2.756
30	1.310	1.697	2.042	2.457	2.750
40	1.303	1.684	2.021	2.423	2.704
60	1.296	1.671	2.000	2.390	2.660
120	1.289	1.658	1.980	2.358	2.617
∞	1.282	1.645	1.960	2.326	2.576

C.I.	80%	90%	95%	98%	99%

Critical Points of *Z* for Selected Levels of Significance

	Level of Significance α:	
	0.05	0.01
One-Tailed Test	+ or 1.645 −	+ or 2.326 −
Two-Tailed Test	+ and 1.96 −	+ and 2.576 −

Note: + or − means we use the positive value in the table for a right-hand-tailed test and the negative value for a left-hand-tailed test. In a two-tailed test, we use both the positive and the negative values.

Source: Tabular data from M. Merrington, "Table of Percentage Points of the *t*-Distribution," *Biometrika* 32 (1941) p. 300. Reproduced by permission of the *Biometrika* trustees.

COMPLETE BUSINESS
STATISTICS

THIRD EDITION

COMPLETE BUSINESS
STATISTICS

AMIR D. ACZEL
Bentley College

Ask Prof
To explain Block Design
Pg 485

**Irwin
McGraw-Hill**

Boston, Massachusetts   Burr Ridge, Illinois   Dubuque, Iowa
Madison, Wisconsin   New York, New York
San Francisco, California   St. Louis, Missouri

Irwin/McGraw-Hill

A Division of The **McGraw·Hill** *Companies*

© Richard D. Irwin, a Times Mirror Higher Education Group, Inc. company, 1989, 1993, and 1996

Minitab is a registered trademark of Minitab, Inc.

Irwin Book Team

Publisher: *Thomas E. Casson*
Senior sponsoring editor: *Richard T. Hercher, Jr.*
Associate editor: *Colleen A. Tuscher*
Developmental editor: *Wanda J. Zeman*
Senior marketing manager: *Brian Kibby*
Production supervisor: *Laurie Kersch*
Assistant manager, graphics: *Charlene R. Perez*
Project editor: *Beth Cigler*
Designer: *Larry J. Cope*
Cover designer: *Jeanne Muskat*
Compositor: *Interactive Composition Corporation*
Typeface: *11/13 Times Roman*
Printer: *Von Hoffmann Press, Inc.*

Library of Congress Cataloging-in-Publication Data

Aczel, Amir D.
    Complete business statistics/Amir D. Aczel.—3rd ed.
      p. cm.
    Includes bibliographical references and index.
    Student edition ISBN 0-256-13894-X
    Instructor's edition ISBN 0-256-20678-3
    1. Commercial statistics. 2. Statistics. I. Title.
HF1017.A26 1996
519.5—dc20   95–36381

Printed in the United States of America
    4 5 6 7 8 9 0 VH 2 1 0 9 8

To my father Captain E. L. Aczel and to the memory of my mother Miriam Aczel

PREFACE

evising a successful text as it moves into its third edition presented many challenges. I wanted to make sure to retain all of the features that users found attractive in a text of this kind and useful in their teaching, and yet add new ones to improve the book even further.

While maintaining completeness in the sense of covering as many important topics of business statistics as possible, some topics that were considered too advanced or specialized were somewhat reduced in coverage. These were in the chapter on forecasting and in the chapter on multivariate methods. On the other hand, some coverage was expanded in the quality control chapter in response to reviewer suggestions.

Many of the problems and some of the examples were renewed, replaced by new problems from business and economics literature. As always, only highest quality, interesting, and useful examples and problems were included.

As with the first edition of this book, I have tried to achieve several important goals. First, I wanted a book that really explained statistical thinking and the ideas of statistical inference rather than just giving formulas and examples as do many business statistics books. I also wanted to stress an intuitive understanding of statistical procedures and an understanding of what statistics is all about. For example, this book explains the logical principle behind the analysis of variance rather than just the computations. Once the student understands this principle, the complicated sums of squares suddenly make sense and the final result is not just a number—it is a complete picture of what the data are trying to tell us about an actual problem. As another example, this is one of very few statistics books at this level that actually explains the meaning of *degrees of freedom*.

My second goal was to write a book that is firmly rooted in the real world. I carefully chose exceptional problems and examples that I came across in actual business situations; in doing so, I drew on my experience in the field. I also chose a wide selection of real problems and examples from the fields of finance, management, transportation, tourism, accounting, public administration, economics, production, the fashion industry, advertising, and other areas. Many of the examples and problems originate in professional business literature; other problems are company-specific and originate in statistical consulting projects. Among these, I have also made an effort to mix international settings and situations.

My third goal was to present a wide range of statistical topics. I sought to write a *complete* book of business statistics, and I included several important topics that are avoided by other authors. This is the only book I know of at this level that includes a chapter on multivariate statistical methods.

After an introduction to descriptive statistics (Chapter 1), the book moves on to a thorough treatment of probabilistic reasoning and the concepts of probability theory—the basis for all of statistical inference. The book then provides the student with a detailed explanation of random variables, expected values, the variance, and the standard deviation. There is an entire chapter devoted to the normal distribution—including some optional advanced topics not commonly covered, as well as a wide range of problems demonstrating the usefulness of the normal probability model. Once the student is comfortable with probability and random variables, the ideas of sampling are carefully explained. Estimation and confidence intervals are next, followed by a very thorough discussion of statistical hypothesis testing. Hypothesis tests are explained at several different levels, including the philosophy behind a statistical hypothesis test, when and how tests should be conducted, and how to carefully interpret their results. This is one book that truly explains the meaning of statistical *significance.*

Every chapter in this book introduces the basics of the theory and then expands the discussion to include more advanced material. Chapter 11 on multiple regression, for example, contains many advanced topics. At the beginning undergraduate level, however, an instructor many choose the earlier sections, leaving out more complicated topics such as transformations. He or she is left with a thorough, clear, and easy-to-understand discussion of multiple regression models. The presentation is complete and includes a discussion of the *pitfalls* to avoid when conducting a regression analysis.

Books written specifically for an introductory course, however, often fail to discuss the perceived "difficult" topics in regression and other areas. This is one reason why statisticians so often encounter misuse of statistical methods and the consequent distortion of results and implications. This is especially true now that computers and software packages for statistical analysis are so prevalent that everyone has access to "statistics." It is now more important than ever before to teach business practitioners and others the *correct* use of statistics. Computing power should go hand in hand with—not replace—statistical reasoning, correct selection of a statistical model, careful evaluation of the underlying assumptions, and cautious interpretation of results. It is my hope that this book stresses these aspects of any analysis more completely and understandably than other statistics texts. It is, in fact, the development and implementation of new statistical software that made me realize just how important it is that we teach the advanced topics. When a microcomputer can be used to perform complicated multivariate analysis, statistical instruction that does not cover such topics is behind the times.

The book integrates theory and examples with use of the computer. The main computer package demonstrated is MINITAB. This package was chosen because it is very easy to use. Each chapter where data analysis is conducted contains a section on the use of the computer. MINITAB is explained in some detail to allow the student to use it with little or no prior preparation. Three other packages are explained and used in the book: SPSS, SYSTAT, and SAS.

Many people were helpful to me in preparing this book. I would like to thank Robert Fetter of Yale University for his many helpful comments and suggestions. I gratefully acknowledge the help of the following reviewers who contributed to the first edition: Michael Sklar, Emory University; John Sennetti, Texas Tech University; Jamie Eng, San Francisco State University; Chaim M. Ehrman, Loyola University of Chicago; Samuel Kotz, University of Maryland; Andrew Seila, University of Georgia; Paul Rubin, Michigan State University; Amitava Mitra, Auburn University; Randall Anderson, California State University; Charles Feinstein, University of Santa Clara; Peter Seagle, State University of New York—Albany; Michael Broida, Miami University of Ohio; Gary Franko, Siena College; Mary Sue Younger, University of Tennessee; Robert Des Jardines, University of North Carolina at Chapel Hill; Marvin Puterman, University of British Columbia; Ralph St. John, Bowling Green State University; Charles Warnock, Hong Kong University; Thomas Knowles, Illinois Institute of Technology; Donald Robinson, Illinois State University; and Peg Young, George Mason University.

I also thank the following reviewers of the second edition whose insightful comments helped to fine-tune the text and supplement package: Sung K. Ahn, Washington State University; James Behel, Harding University; Sherman Chottiner, Syracuse University; Chaim M. Ehrman, Loyola University; Nicholas Farnum, California State University, Fullerton; Stuart Kellog, University of Miami, Coral Gables; Brenda Masters, Oklahoma State University; G. Steven Rhiel, Old Dominion University; Don Robinson, Illinois State University; Marjorie Rubash, Bradley University; Amy Schmidt, Bentley College; Vincent Showers, Bradley University; Jay Sounderpandian, University of Wisconsin, Parkside; Ron Suich, California State University, Fullerton; Peter Westfall, Texas Tech University; Othmar Winkler, Georgetown University; and John Wong, Wichita State University.

I would like to thank the following reviewers who contributed to the third edition and offered many valuable comments and suggestions:

Kenneth D. Lawrence—New Jersey Institute of Technology

Duncan K. H. Fong—Penn State University

Sung K. Ahn—Washington State University

Thomas J. Page—Michigan State University

Ik-Whan G. Kwon—Saint Louis University

Supriya Lahiri—University of Massachusetts, Lowell

David M. Rocke—University of California, Davis

Paul Randolph—Texas Tech University

Burt Madden—University of Arkansas at Little Rock

James R. Schmidt—University of Nebraska, Lincoln

Martin R. Young—University of Michigan

I would like to thank the following colleagues, friends, and students who also helped with the project. I am most grateful to Erl Sörensen for countless suggestions, encouragement, and advice. James Zeitler of Bentley College has also been very helpful. I am grateful to my colleagues Dominique Haughton, Norm Josephy, Nick Teebagy, Andrew Stollar, Richard Fristensky, John Leeth, Scott Callan, Amy Schmidt, and Joseph Kane for many suggestions. I acknowledge help from students Harpreet Singh, Joseph Lessard, Jay Goldberg, Garrett Tight, and Karl Haase. I would also like to thank Frederick Mosteller, Harvard University; Arnold Zellner, University of Chicago; and Johannes Ledolter, University of Iowa, for helpful comments. I also thank Charles Saccardo, Michael Epelman, and John Taranto.

I would like to thank Bruce Powell of Richard D. Irwin, Inc., who first suggested that I write this book. Furthermore, I am indebted to my editor, Richard T. Hercher Jr., for all his help, encouragement, enthusiasm, and support throughout this project. I would also like to thank Colleen Tuscher, sponsoring editor; Wanda Zeman, developmental editor; Beth Cigler, project editor; Tom Whipple, copy editor; Larry Cope, designer; and many others of the highly professional staff at Irwin for all their help and hard work.

Among others, I am indebted to the *Biometrika* trustees for permission to reprint various statistical tables from *Biometrika* publications, and the American Marketing Association for permission to reprint many tables and other information from the *Journal of Marketing* and the *Journal of Marketing Research.* I would also like to acknowledge the New York Times Company for its kind permission to reprint several articles. Finally, I thank my wife Debra for all her help in editing the manuscript and for her many suggestions and ideas.

Amir D. Aczel

CONTENTS IN BRIEF

CONTENTS

Confidence Intervals   *207*

Hypothesis Testing   *242*

8 The Comparison of Two Populations   *314*

9 Analysis of Variance   *356*

10   Simple Linear Regression and Correlation   *415*

Multiple Regression 470

Time Series, Forecasting, and Index Numbers 566

13 Quality Control and Improvement   *599*

14 Nonparametric Methods and Chi-Square Tests   *622*

15 Bayesian Statistics and Decision Analysis   *700*

16 Multivariate Analysis   *752*

17 Sampling Methods   786

1

INTRODUCTION AND DESCRIPTIVE STATISTICS

1-1 INTRODUCTION

It is better to be roughly right than precisely wrong

—*Maynard Keynes*

You all have probably heard the story about Malcolm Forbes, who once got lost floating for miles in one of his famous balloons and finally landed in the middle of a cornfield. He spotted a man coming toward

Continued

him and asked, "Sir, can you tell me where I am?" The man said, "Certainly, you are in a basket in a field of corn." Forbes said, "You must be a statistician." The man said, "That's amazing, how did you know that?" "Easy," said Forbes, "your information is concise, precise, and absolutely useless!"[1]

The purpose of this book is to convince you that information resulting from a good statistical analysis is always concise, often precise, and never useless! The spirit of statistics is, in fact, very well captured by the quotation above from Keynes. This book should teach you how to be at least roughly right a high percentage of the time.

The word *statistics* is derived from the Italian word *stato,* which means "state," and *statista* refers to a person involved with the affairs of state. Therefore, *statistics* originally meant the collection of facts useful to the *statista.* Statistics in this sense was used in 16th-century Italy and then spread to France, Holland, and Germany. We note, however, that surveys of people and property actually began in ancient times.[2] Today, statistics is not restricted to information about the state but extends to almost every realm of human endeavor. Neither do we restrict ourselves to merely collecting numerical information, called *data.* Our data are summarized, displayed in meaningful ways, and analyzed. Statistical analysis often involves an attempt to generalize from the data. Statistics is a science—the science of information. Information may be *qualitative* or *quantitative.* To illustrate the difference between these two types of information, let's consider an example. ■

EXAMPLE 1-1   Realtors who help sell condominiums in the Boston area provide prospective buyers with the information given in Table 1–1. Which of the variables in the table are quantitative and which are qualitative?

SOLUTION   The asking price is a *quantitative* variable: it conveys a quantity—the asking price in dollars. The number of rooms is also a quantitative variable. The direction the apartment faces is a *qualitative* variable since it conveys a quality (east, west, north, south). Whether a condominium has a washer and dryer in the unit (yes or no), and whether or not heat is provided as part of the condo fee are also qualitative variables.

---

[1] From an address by R. Gnanadesikan to the American Statistical Association, reprinted in *American Statistician* 44, no. 2 (May 1990), p. 122.

[2] See Anders Hald, *A History of Probability and Statistics and Their Applications before 1750* (New York: Wiley, 1990), pp. 81–82.

TABLE 1-1　Boston Condominium Data

Asking Price	Number of Rooms	Direction Facing	Washer/Dryer?	Heated?
$168,000	2	E	Y	Y
$152,000	2	N	N	Y
$187,000	3	N	Y	Y
$142,500	1	W	N	N
$166,800	2	W	Y	N

A **quantitative variable** can be described by a number for which arithmetic operations such as averaging make sense. A **qualitative (or categorical) variable** simply records a quality. If a number is used for distinguishing members of different categories of a qualitative variable, the number assignment is arbitrary.

The field of statistics deals with **measurements**—some quantitative and some qualitative. The measurements are the actual numerical values of a variable. (Qualitative variables could be described by numbers, although such a description might be arbitrary; for example, $N = 1$, $E = 2$, $S = 3$, $W = 4$, $Y = 1$, $N = 0$.)

There are four generally used **scales of measurement,** listed here from weakest to strongest.

Nominal Scale.　In the **nominal scale** of measurement, numbers are used simply as labels for groups or classes. If our data set consists of blue, green, and red items, we may designate blue as 1, green as 2, and red as 3. In this case, the numbers 1, 2, and 3 stand only for the category to which a data point belongs. "Nominal" stands for "name" of category. The nominal scale of measurement is used for qualitative rather than quantitative data: blue, green, red; male, female; professional classification; geographic classification; and so on.

Ordinal Scale.　In the **ordinal scale** of measurement, data elements may be ordered according to their relative size or quality. Four products ranked by a consumer may be ranked as 1, 2, 3, and 4, where 4 is the best and 1 is the worst. In this scale of measurement we do not know how much better one product is than others, only that it is better.

Interval Scale.　In the **interval scale** of measurement, we can assign a meaning to distances between any two observations. The data are on an *interval* of numbers, and distances between elements can be measured in units. In August 1995, the Dow Jones average was 4610; in December 1991, it was 2914. These numbers are on an interval scale.

Ratio Scale.　The **ratio scale** is the strongest scale of measurement. Here not only do distances between paired observations have a meaning, but there is a meaning also to ratios of distances. Salaries are measured on a ratio scale: A salary of $50,000 is twice as large as a salary of $25,000. Such a comparison is not possible with temperatures, which are on an interval scale but not on a ratio scale (we can't say that 50°F is twice as warm as 25°F). The ratio scale contains a *meaningful zero* (0°F in temperature is not meaningful in this respect). The distinction between the interval and ratio scales, however, is not always immediately clear.

Samples and Populations

In statistics we make a distinction between two concepts: a population and a sample.

> The **population** consists of the set of all measurements in which the investigator is interested. The population is also called the **universe.**
>
> A **sample** is a subset of measurements selected from the population. Sampling from the population is often done randomly, such that every possible sample of *n* elements will have an equal chance of being selected. A sample selected in this way is called a **simple random sample,** or just a **random sample.** A random sample allows chance to determine its elements.

For example, Farmer Jane owns 1,264 sheep. These sheep constitute her entire *population* of sheep. If 15 sheep are selected to be sheared, then these 15 represent a *sample* from Jane's population of sheep. Further, if the 15 sheep were selected at *random* from Jane's population of 1,264 sheep, then they would constitute a *random sample* of sheep.

The definitions of sample and population are relative to what we want to consider. If Jane's sheep are all we care about, then they constitute a population. If, however, we are interested in all the sheep in the county, then all of Jane's 1,264 sheep are a sample of that larger population (although this sample would not be random).

The distinction between a sample and a population is very important in statistics.

Data and Data Collection

A set of measurements obtained on some variable is called a **data set**. For example, heart rate measurements for 10 patients may constitute a data set. The variable we're interested in is heart rate, and the scale of measurement here is a ratio scale. (A heart that beats 80 times a minute is twice as fast as a heart that beats 40 times a minute.) Our actual observations of the patients' heart rates, the data set, might be 60, 70, 64, 55, 70, 80, 70, 74, 51, 80.

Data are collected by various methods. Sometimes our data set consists of the entire population we're interested in. If we have the actual point spread for five football games, and if we are interested only in these five games, then our data set of five measurements is the entire population of interest. (In this case, our data are on a ratio scale. Why? Suppose the data set for the five games tells only whether the home or visiting team won. What would be our measurement scale in this case?)

In other situations data may constitute a sample from some population. If the data are to be used to draw some conclusions about the larger population they were drawn from, then we must collect the data with great care. A conclusion drawn about a population based on the information in a sample from the population is called a **statistical inference**. Statistical inference is an important topic of this book. To ensure the accuracy of statistical inference, data must be drawn randomly from the population of interest, and we must make sure that every segment of the population is adequately and proportionally represented in the sample.

Statistical inference may be based on data collected in surveys or experiments, which must be carefully constructed. For example, when we want to obtain information from people, we may use a mailed questionnaire, or a telephone interview, as a convenient instrument. In such surveys, however, we want to minimize any **nonresponse**

bias. This is the biasing of the results that occurs when we disregard the fact that some people will simply not respond to the survey. The bias distorts the findings, because the people who do not respond may belong more to one segment of the population than to another. In social research some questions may be sensitive—for example, "Have you ever been arrested?" This may easily result in a nonresponse bias, because people who have indeed been arrested may be less likely to answer the question (unless they can be perfectly certain of remaining anonymous). Surveys conducted by popular magazines often suffer from nonresponse bias, especially when their questions are provocative. What makes good magazine reading often makes bad statistics.

Suppose we want to measure the speed performance or gas mileage of an automobile. Here the data will come from experimentation. In this case we want to make sure that a variety of road conditions, weather conditions, and other factors are represented. Pharmaceutical testing is also an example where data may come from experimentation. Drugs are usually tested against a placebo as well as against no treatment at all. When designing an experiment to test the effectiveness of a sleeping pill, the variable of interest may be the time, in minutes, that elapses between taking the pill and falling asleep.

In experiments, as in surveys, it is important to **randomize** if inferences are indeed to be drawn. People should be randomly chosen as subjects for the experiment if an inference is to be drawn to the entire population. Randomization should also be used in assigning people to the three groups: pill, no pill, or placebo. Such a design will minimize potential biasing of the results.

In other situations data may come from published sources, such as statistical abstracts of various kinds or government publications. The published unemployment rate over a number of months is one example. Here, data are "given" to us without our having any control over how they are obtained. Again, caution must be exercised. The unemployment rate over a given period is not a random sample of any *future* unemployment rates, and making statistical inferences in such cases may be involved and difficult. If, however, we are interested only in the period we have data for, then our data do constitute an entire population, which may be described. In any case, however, we must also be careful to note any missing data or incomplete observations.

In this chapter, we will concentrate on the processing, summarization, and display of data—the first step in statistical analysis. In the next chapter, we will explore the theory of probability, the connection between the random sample and the population. Later chapters build on the concepts of probability and develop a system that allows us to draw a logical, consistent inference from our sample to the underlying population.

Why worry about inference and about a population? Why not just look at our data and interpret them? Mere inspection of the data will suffice when interest centers on the particular observations you have. If, however, you want to draw meaningful conclusions with implications extending beyond your limited data, statistical inference is the way to do it.

In marketing research, we are often interested in the relationship between advertising and sales. A data set of randomly chosen sales and advertising figures for a given firm may be of some interest in itself, but the information in it is much more useful if it leads to implications about the underlying process—the relationship between the firm's level of advertising and the resulting level of sales. An understanding of the true relationship between advertising and sales—the relationship in the population of advertising and sales possibilities for the firm—would allow us to predict sales for any level of advertising and thus to set advertising at a level that maximizes profits.

A pharmaceutical manufacturer interested in marketing a new drug may be required by the Food and Drug Administration to prove that the drug does not cause serious side effects. The results of tests of the drug on a random sample of people may then be used in a statistical inference about the entire population of people who may use the drug if it is introduced.

A bank may be interested in assessing the popularity of automatic teller machines. The machines may be tried on a randomly chosen group of bank customers. The conclusions of the study could then be generalized by statistical inference to the entire population of the bank's customers.

A quality control engineer at a plant making disk drives for computers needs to make sure that no more than 3% of the drives produced are defective. The engineer may routinely collect random samples of drives and check their quality. Based on the random samples, the engineer may then draw a conclusion about the proportion of defective items in the entire population of drives.

These are just a few examples illustrating the use of statistical inference in business situations. In the rest of this chapter, we will introduce the descriptive statistics needed to carry out basic statistical analyses. The next chapters will develop the elements of the inference from samples to populations.

PROBLEMS

1–1. A survey by an electric company contains questions on the following:
1. Age of household head.
2. Sex of household head.
3. Number of people in household.
4. Use of electric heating (yes or no).
5. Number of large appliances used daily.
6. Thermostat setting in winter.
7. Average number of hours heating is on.
8. Average number of heating days.
9. Household income.
10. Average monthly electric bill.
11. Ranking of this electric company as compared with two previous electricity suppliers.

Describe the variables implicit in these 11 items as quantitative or qualitative, and describe the scales of measurement.

1–2. Discuss the various data collection methods described in this section.

1–3. Discuss and compare the various scales of measurement.

1–4. The following table and explanatory notes are reprinted from the *Wall Street Journal*, March 22, 1995, pp. C19–23, and pertain to information on mutual funds.
  a. For each variable listed, state whether the variable is qualitative or quantitative and give its scale of measurement.
  b. Look at a current issue of the *Wall Street Journal* or a similar publication and select a random sample of mutual funds listed. Describe how you selected the random sample.

Explanatory Notes

What These Listings Provide. . .

		NASD DATA			LIPPER ANALYTICAL DATA				
Monday	Inv. Obj.	NAV	Offer Price	NAV Chg.	%Ret YTD	Max Initl Chrg.	Total Exp Ratio		
Tuesday	Inv. Obj.	NAV	Offer Price	NAV Chg.	——— Total Return ———				
					YTD	4 wk	1 yr	Rank	
Wednesday	**Inv. Obj.**	**NAV**	**Offer Price**	**NAV Chg.**	**———Total Return———**				
					YTD	**13 wk**	**3 yr***	**Rank**	
Thursday	Inv. Obj.	NAV	Offer Price	NAV Chg.	——— Total Return ———				
					YTD	26 wk	4 yr*	Rank	
Friday	Inv. Obj.	NAV	Offer Price	NAV Chg.	——— Total Return ———				
					YTD	39 wk	5 yr*	Rank	
							* Annualized		

Mutual fund data are supplied by two organizations. The daily Net Asset Value (NAV), Offer Price and Net Change calculations are supplied by the National Association of Securities Dealers (NASD) through Nasdaq, its automated quotation system. Performance and cost data are supplied by Lipper Analytical Services Inc.

Daily price data are entered into Nasdaq by the fund, its management company or agent. Performance and cost calculations are percentages provided by Lipper Analytical Services, based on prospectuses filed with the Securities and Exchange Commission, fund reports, financial reporting services and other soruces believed to be authoritative, accurate and timely. Though verified, the data cannot be guaranteed by Lipper or its data sources and should be double-checked with the funds before making any investment decisions.

Performance calculations, as percentages, assuming reinvestment of all distributions, and after all asset based charges have been deducted. Asset based charges include advisory fees, other non-advisory fees and distribution expenses (12b-1). Figures are without regard to sales, deferred sales or redemption charges.

INVESTMENT OBJECTIVE (Inv. Obj.)
Based on stated investment goals outlined in the prospectus. The Journal assembled 27 groups based on classifications used by Lipper Analytical in the daily Mutual Fund Scorecard and other calculations.

NET ASSET VALUE (NAV)
Per share value prepared by the fund, based on closing quotes unless noted, and supplied to the NASD by 5:30 P.M. Eastern time.

OFFER PRICE
Net asset value plus sales commission, if any.

NAV CHG.
Gain or loss, based on the previous NAV quotation.

TOTAL RETURN
Performance calcuations, as percentages, assuming reinvestment of all distributions. Sales charges aren't reflected. Percentages are annualized for periods greater than one year. For funds declaring dividends daily, calculations are based on the most current data supplied by the fund within publication deadlines. A YEAR TO DATE (YTD)

change is listed daily, with results ranging from 4 weeks to 5 years offered throughout the week.

MAXIMUM INITIAL SALES COMMISSION (Max Initl Chrg)

Based on prospectus; the sales charge may be modified or suspended temporarily by the fund, but any percentage change requires formal notification to the shareholders.

TOTAL EXPENSE RATIO (Total Exp Ratio)

Shown as a percentage and based on the fund's annual report, the ratio is total operating expenses for the fiscal year divided by the fund's average net assets. It includes all asset based charges such as advisory fees, other non-advisory fees and distribution expenses (12b-1).

RANKING (R)

Funds are grouped by investment objectives defined by the Wall Street Journal and ranked on longest time period listed each day. Performance measurement begins at either the closest Thursday or month-end for periods of more than one year. Gains of 100% or more are shown as a whole number, not carried out one decimal place. A = top 20%; B = next 20%; C = middle 20%; D = next 20%; E = bottom 20%.

e-Ex-distribution. f-Previous day's quotation. s-Stock split or divided. x-Ex-dividend.
p-Distribution costs apply, 12b-1 plan. r-Redemption charge may apply.
g-Footnotes x and s apply. l-Footnotes e and s apply. t-Footnotes p and r apply. v-Footnotes x and e apply.
z-Footnotes x, e, and s apply.
NA-Not available due to incomplete price, performance or cost data. NE-Deleted by Lipper editor; data in question. NL-No load (sales commission). NN-Fund doesn't wish to be tracked. NS-Fund didn't exist at start of period.
k-Recalculated by Lipper, using updated data. l-No valid comparison with other funds because of expense structure.

Mutual Fund Quotations

	Inv. Obj.	NAV	Offer Price	NAV Chg.	YTD	13 wks	3 yrs R
IncGro	G&I	14.88	NL	−0.04	+7.6	+8.6	+9.5 B
L Treas	BND	9.06	NL	−0.04	+5.8	+5.9	NS..
NatRes	SEC	9.69	NL	−0.04	+0.8	+2.3	NS..
NITFI	IDM	10.52	NL	...	+4.3	+4.8	+6.3 C
NITFL	GLM	11.20	NL	−0.01	+6.0	+6.6	+7.8 A
STreas	BST	9.74	NL	−0.01	+3.1	+3.2	NS..
Tg1995	BND	97.36	NL	+0.01	+2.2	+2.4	+6.6 D
Tg2000	BND	70.56	NL	−0.18	+5.9	+6.0	+9.2 A
Tg2005	BND	49.30	NL	−0.24	+7.0	+7.3	+11.3 A
Tg2010	BND	35.26	NL	−0.19	+6.9	+7.5	+11.7 A
Tg2015	BND	25.91	NL	−0.19	+7.5	+7.9	+11.5 A
Tg2020	BND	17.64	NL	−0.14	+8.4	+8.9	+11.7 A
TNote	BIN	10.01	NL	−0.01	+3.9	+3.9	+6.0 C
Utilin	SEC	9.09	NL	−0.07	+4.4	+3.1	NS ..
Babson Group:							
Bond L	BND	1.50	NL	...	+3.7	+4.0	+6.8 C
Bond S	BST	9.63	NL	...	+3.9	+4.1	+6.1 A
Enterp2	SML	16.60	NL	−0.05	+2.5	+6.7	+6.8 D
Enterp	SML	15.39	NL	−0.10	+1.6	+4.0	+9.2 C
Gwth	GRO	12.82	NL	+0.01	+7.1	+8.8	+8.6 B
Intl	ITL	14.98	NL	+0.01	−3.0	−1.5	+10.0 B
Shadw	SML	9.93	NL	...	+4.3	+5.4	+6.8 D
TaxFrL	GLM	8.57	NL	−0.01	+6.2	+6.9	+6.2 E
TaxFrS	STM	10.61	NL	−0.01	+3.0	+3.1	+4.6 C

UMB B	BIN	10.77	NL	−0.01	+4.3	+4.4	+5.7 D
UMB Hrt	SML	9.56	NL	−0.01	+3.9	+5.2	+5.6 E
UMB St	GRO	15.82	NL	−0.04	+5.4	+6.3	+8.1 C

Delaware Group:

TrendA p	CAP	12.59	13.36	−0.03	+7.1	+11.6	+9.6 B
ValueA p	CAP	19.18	20.35	−0.02	+1.6	+2.2	+7.4 C
DelcpA p	MID	24.17	25.64	+0.05	+6.6	+10.9	+4.8 E
DeclnA p	EQI	16.39	17.39	−0.01	+8.0	+9.0	+10.2 A
DecTRA p	EQI	13.01	13.80	−0.01	+8.6	+9.4	+10.0 B
DelawA p	S&B	18.16	19.27	0.03	+5.4	+6.7	+7.3 C
DelchA p	BHI	6.14	6.45	...	+3.9	+4.9	+8.4 D
DelchB t	BHI	6.14	6.14	...	+3.7	+5.1	NS ..
IntlEqA p	ITL	11.25	11.94	−0.01	−1.1	0.0	+9.2 C
TreasA p	BST	9.08	9.36	...	+2.8	+2.7	+4.4 C
TxUSA p	GLM	11.92	12.51	−0.01	+4.5	+5.1	+7.4 C
TxIntA p	...	10.18	10.49	−0.01	NA	NA	NA ..
TxInsA p	ISM	10.95	11.50	−0.01	+4.5	+4.9	+6.2 E
TxPaA p	MPA	8.23	8.64	−0.01	+5.0	+5.5	+6.8 D
UsGvtA p	MTG	7.79	8.18	−0.01	+3.6	+3.2	+4.5 E

Nuveen Funds:

MunBd	GLM	9.00	9.45	−0.01	+5.6	+6.1	+6.6 D
InsMun R	ISM	10.40	10.40	−0.02	+7.6	+8.5	+7.7 A
InsTxA	ISM	10.44	10.93	−0.02	+7.7	+8.6	NS ..
CA Ins R	ISM	10.24	10.24	−0.02	+7.8	+8.8	+7.1 C
CA Val R	MCA	10.14	10.14	...	+7.0	+7.6	+6.5 D
FL Val R	MFL	10.05	10.05	−0.01	+7.5	+8.3	+7.2 C
MA Ins R	DMA	10.10	10.10	−0.01	+6.5	+7.4	+7.3 B
MA Val R	DMA	9.56	9.56	−0.01	+6.4	+7.1	+7.4 A
MD Val R	SSM	9.91	9.91	−0.01	+7.2	+7.9	+6.7 D
MI Val R	SSM	10.18	10.18	−0.01	+7.4	+8.3	+7.8 A
NJ Val R	MNJ	9.93	9.93	−0.01	+5.3	+6.0	+7.2 B
NY Ins R	ISM	10.17	10.17	−0.02	+7.0	+7.8	+7.4 A
NY Val R	DNY	10.18	10.18	−0.01	+7.0	+7.7	+7.6 A
OH Val R	MOH	10.20	10.20	−0.01	+6.8	+7.6	+7.6 A
PA Val R	MPA	10.04	10.04	...	+7.6	+8.5	+7.3 C

Prudential Funds:

NichA	MID	12.69	13.36	+0.02	+5.8	+8.8	+8.0 C
NichB	MID	12.21	12.21	+0.01	+5.6	+8.5	+7.1 D
Adl A	BST	9.57	9.67	−0.01	+2.7k	+2.9k	NS ..
Adl B	BST	NA	NA	NA	NA	NA	NS ..
AllChsvA	S&B	11.03	11.61	−0.01	+3.5	+4.8	+7.6 C
AllStrA	S&B	11.33	11.93	...	+3.6	+4.0	+6.1 D
BlckGv	BST	9.31	9.60	−0.01	+2.4k	+2.6k	+3.5k D
CAInA B	MCA	10.10	10.41	...	+6.2	+7.1	+8.4 A
EqutA p	GRO	14.11	14.85	−0.01	+6.6	+8.5	+12.1 A
EurGr A	ITL	10.96	11.54	−0.05	+0.4	+1.6	NS ..
GlobA p	WOR	13.07	13.76	...	−3.0	−2.0	+11.4 B
GlobGnA	WOR	17.06	17.96	−0.05	−4.2	−1.8	+12.5 A
GlAstA	WBD	1.78	1.80	...	+2.2k	+0.1k	+1.7k D
GlobNatA	SEC	12.33	12.98	−0.05	+3.9	+5.1	+9.4 C
GIUtA	SEC	13.13	13.82	−0.01	+2.6	+2.3	+10.6 C

GNMAA	MTG	13.97	14.55	−0.03	+5.1k	+5.0k	+5.2k D
GVIncA p	MTG	8.61	8.97	−0.02	+5.1	+5.2	+6.0 B
GtOA p	SML	11.76	12.38	...	+4.3	+10.5	+9.6 C
HIYdA p	BHI	7.89	8.22	−0.01	+5.1k	+6.5k	+9.7k C
InVrA p	SEC	11.24	11.83	...	+3.4	+2.0	+6.8 D
MultA p	CAP	12.83	13.51	+0.01	+3.3	+2.9	+11.4 A
MuHIA	HYM	10.74	11.07	−0.01	+5.4	+6.2	+7.4 B

Quest For Value:

CA TE	MCA	10.48	11.00	−0.01	+6.9	+7.5	+6.9 C
Fund	CAP	12.33	13.05	−0.01	+10.1	+11.9	+9.9 B
GlEq	WOR	13.12	13.88	−0.05	+1.3	+2.5	+10.2 B
GrIncA	G&I	9.83	10.32	−0.04	+6.0	+7.4	+9.0 B
InvQln	BND	10.13	10.64	+0.02	+5.9	+5.8	+7.4 B
NatlTE	GLM	10.62	11.15	−0.02	+6.3	+6.9	+7.6 A
NY TE	DNY	10.55	11.08	−0.01	+6.2	+7.1	+7.7 A
Opport	S&B	20.01	21.17	−0.07	+9.3	+10.0	+11.5 A
OpportB	S&B	19.86	19.86	−0.07	+9.2	+9.9	NS ..
SmCap	SML	15.69	16.60	+0.01	−3.3	−0.1	+7.0 D
UsGov	BIN	10.99	11.54	...	+3.4	+3.7	+5.2 E
RBB GvtSc p	MTG	9.58	10.06	...	+4.0	+4.1	+5.8 C
Revest	G&I	9.95	NL	−0.01	+3.0	+6.3	NS ..

RSI Trust:

ActBd	MTG	27.42	27.42	−0.03	+4.8	+4.9	+7.0 A
Core	G&I	38.26	38.26	−0.11	+7.9	+9.1	+10.0 B
EmGr	SML	39.26	39.26	+0.01	+5.4	+12.3	+13.6 A
IntBd	BIN	26.40	26.40	+0.01	+4.3	+4.4	+5.7 D
IntlEq	ITL	34.67	34.67	...	−5.7	−4.6	+8.1 C
STIF	BST	18.78	18.78	...	+1.2	+1.3	+3.1 E
Value	G&I	27.68	27.68	+0.08	+6.5	+7.2	+6.5 D
Rainbw	CAP	4.76	NL	+0.04	+2.6	+4.4	−1.6 E
ReaGr	S&B	13.02	13.67	...	+2.4	+2.9	+0.6 E

1–5   Five ice cream flavors are rank-ordered by preference. What is the scale of measurement?

1–6.   What is the difference between a qualitative and a quantitative variable?

1–7.   A town has 15 neighborhoods. If you interviewed everyone living in one particular neighborhood, would you be interviewing a population or a sample from the town? Would this be a random sample? If you had a list of everyone living in the town, called **frame,** and you randomly selected 100 people from all the neighborhoods, would this be a random sample?

1–8.   What is the difference between a sample and a population?

1–9.   What is a random sample?

1–10.   For each tourist entering the United States, the U.S. Immigration and Naturalization Service computer is fed the tourist's nationality and length of intended stay. Characterize each variable as quantitative or qualitative.

1–11.   What is the scale of measurement for the color of a karate belt?

1–12.   An individual federal tax return form asks, among other things, for the following information: income (in dollars and cents), number of dependents, whether filing singly or jointly with a spouse, whether or not deductions are itemized, amount paid in local taxes. Describe the scale of measurement of each variable, and state whether the variable is qualitative or quantitative.

1-2 Percentiles and Quartiles

Given a set of numerical observations, we may order them according to magnitude. Once we have done this, it is possible to define the boundaries of the set. Any student who has taken a nationally administered test, such as the Scholastic Aptitude Test (SAT), is familiar with *percentiles*. Your score on such a test is compared with the scores of all people who took the test at the same time, and your position within this group is defined in terms of a percentile. If you are in the 90th percentile, 90% of the people who took the test received a score lower than yours. We define a percentile as follows.

> The *P*th **percentile** of a group of numbers is that value below which lie *P*% (*P* percent) of the numbers in the group. The position of the *P*th percentile is given by $(n+1)P/100$, where n is the number of data points.

Let's look at an example.

A large department store collects data on sales made by each of its salespeople. The data, number of sales made on a given day by each of 20 salespeople, are as follows:

EXAMPLE 1-2

9, 6, 12, 10, 13, 15, 16, 14, 14, 16, 17, 16, 24, 21, 22, 18, 19, 18, 20, 17

Find the 50th, 80th, and 90th percentiles of this data set.

First, let's order the data from smallest to largest:

SOLUTION

6, 9, 10, 12, 13, 14, 14, 15, 16, 16, 16, 17, 17, 18, 18, 19, 20, 21, 22, 24

To find the 50th percentile, we need to determine the data point in position $(n + 1)P/100 = (20 + 1)(50/100) = (21)(0.5) = 10.5$. Thus, we need the data point in position 10.5. Counting the observations from smallest to largest, we find that the 10th observation is 16, and so is the 11th. Therefore, the observation that would lie in position 10.5 (halfway between the 10th and 11th observations) is 16. Thus, the 50th percentile is 16.

Similarly, we find the 80th percentile of the data set as the observation lying in position $(n + 1)P/100 = (21)(80/100) = 16.8$. The 16th observation is 19, and the 17th is 20; therefore, the 80th percentile is a point lying 0.8 of the way from 19 to 20, that is, 19.8.

The 90th percentile is found as the observation in position $(n + 1)P/100 = (20 + 1)(90/100) = (21)(0.9) = 18.9$, which is 21.9.

Certain percentiles have greater importance than others because they break down the **distribution** of the data (the way the data points are distributed along the number line) into four groups. These are the quartiles. **Quartiles** are the percentage points that break down the data set into quarters—first quarter, second quarter, third quarter, and fourth quarter.

> The **first quartile** is the 25th percentile. It is that point below which lie 1/4 of the data.

Similarly, the second quartile is the 50th percentile, as we computed in Example 1–2. This is a most important point and has a special name—the *median*.

> The **median** is the point below which lie half the data. It is the 50th percentile.

We define the third quartile correspondingly:

> The **third quartile** is the 75th percentile point. It is that point below which lie 75 percent of the data.

The 25th percentile is often called the **lower quartile;** the 50th percentile point, the median, is called the **middle quartile;** and the 75th percentile is called the **upper quartile.**

EXAMPLE 1-3   Find the lower, middle, and upper quartiles of the data set in Example 1–2.

SOLUTION   Based on the procedure we used in computing the 80th and 90th percentiles, we find that the lower quartile is the observation in position $(21)(0.25) = 5.25$, which is 13.25. The middle quartile was already computed (it is the 50th percentile, the median, which is 16). The upper quartile is the observation in position $(21)(75/100) = 15.75$, which is 18.75.

> We define the **interquartile range** as the difference between the first and third quartiles.

The interquartile range is a measure of the spread of the data. In Example 1–2, the interquartile range is equal to Third quartile − First quartile = $18.75 - 13.25 = 5.5$.

PROBLEMS

1–13.   The following data are numbers of passengers on flights of Delta Air Lines between San Francisco and Seattle over 33 days in April and early May.

> 128, 121, 134, 136, 136, 118, 123, 109, 120, 116, 125, 128, 121, 129, 130, 131,
> 127, 119, 114, 134, 110, 136, 134, 125, 128, 123, 128, 133, 132, 136, 134, 129, 132

Find the lower, middle, and upper quartiles of this data set. Also find the 10th, 15th, and 65th percentiles. What is the interquartile range?

1–14.   The following data are annualized returns on a group of 15 stocks.

> 12.5, 13, 14.8, 11, 16.7, 9, 8.3, −1.2, 3.9, 15.5, 16.2, 18, 11.6, 10, 9.5

Find the median, the first and third quartiles, and the 55th and 85th percentiles for these data.

1–15.   The following data are scores on a management examination taken by a group of 22 people.

> 88, 56, 64, 45, 52, 76, 54, 79, 38, 98, 69, 77, 71, 45, 60, 78, 90, 81, 87, 44, 80, 41

Find the median and the 20th, 30th, 60th, and 90th percentiles.

1–16.   Following are the numbers of daily bids received by the government of a developing country from firms interested in winning a contract for the construction of a new port facility.

$$2, 3, 2, 4, 3, 5, 1, 1, 6, 4, 7, 2, 5, 1, 6$$

Find the quartiles and the interquartile range. Also find the 60th percentile.

1–17.   Find the median, the interquartile range, and the 45th percentile of the following data.

$$23, 26, 29, 30, 32, 34, 37, 45, 57, 80, 102, 147, 210, 355, 782, 1{,}209$$

1-3 Measures of Central Tendency

Percentiles, and in particular quartiles, are measures of the relative positions of points within a data set or a population (when our data set constitutes the entire population). The median is a special point, since it lies in the center of the data in the sense that half the data lie below it and half above it. The median is thus a measure of the *location* or *centrality* of the observations.

In addition to the median, there are two other commonly used measures of central tendency. One is the *mode* (or modes—there may be several of them), and the other is the *arithmetic mean,* or just the *mean.* We define the mode as follows.

The **mode** of the data set is the value that occurs most frequently.

Let us look at the frequencies of occurrence of the data values in Example 1–2, shown in Table 1–2. We see that the value 16 occurs most frequently. There are three data points with this value—more points than for any other value in the data set. Therefore, the mode is equal to 16.

The most commonly used measure of central tendency of a set of observations is the mean of the observations.

The **mean** of a set of observations is their **average**. It is equal to the sum of all observations divided by the number of observations in the set.

Let us denote the observations by $x_1, x_2, \ldots, x_n$. That is, the first observation is denoted by x_1, the second by x_2, and so on to the nth observation, x_n. (In Example 1–2 $x_1 = 6$, $x_2 = 9, \ldots,$ and $x_n = x_{20} = 24$.) The sample mean is denoted by $\bar{x}$.

Mean of a sample:

$$\bar{x} = \frac{\sum\limits_{i=1}^{n} x_i}{n} = \frac{x_1 + x_2 + \cdots + x_n}{n} \tag{1-1}$$

where Σ is summation notation. The summation extends over all data points.

When our observation set constitutes an entire population, instead of denoting the mean by $\bar{x}$ we use the symbol μ (the Greek letter mu). For a population, we use N as the number of elements instead of n. The population mean is defined as follows.

TABLE 1-2   Frequencies of Occurrence of Data Values in Example 1-2

Value	Frequency
6	1
9	1
10	1
12	1
13	1
14	2
15	1
16	3
17	2
18	2
19	1
20	1
21	1
22	1
24	1

Mean of a population:

$$\mu = \frac{\sum\limits_{i=1}^{N} x_i}{N} \qquad (1\text{--}2)$$

The mean of the observations in Example 1–2 is found as

$$\bar{x} = (x_1 + x_2 + \cdots + x_{20})/20 = (6 + 9 + 10 + 12 + 13 + 14 + 14 + 15$$
$$+ 16 + 16 + 16 + 17 + 17 + 18 + 18 + 19 + 20 + 21 + 22 + 24)/20$$
$$= 317/20$$
$$= 15.85$$

The mean of the observations of Example 1–2, their average, is 15.85.

Figure 1–1 shows the data of Example 1–2 drawn on the number line along with the mean, median, and mode of the observations. If you think of the data points as little balls of equal weight located at the appropriate places on the number line, the mean is that point where all the weights would balance. It is the *fulcrum* of the point-weights, as shown in Figure 1–1.

What characterizes the three measures of centrality, and what are the relative merits of each? The mean summarizes all of the information in the data. It is the average of all observations. The mean is a single point that can be viewed as the point where all the mass—the weight—of the observations is concentrated. It is the center of mass of the data. If all the observations in our data set were the same size, then (assuming the total is the same) each would be equal to the mean.

The median, on the other hand, is an observation (or a point between two observations) in the center of the data set. One-half of the data lie above this observation, and one-half of the data lie below it. When we compute the median, we do not consider the exact location of each data point on the number line; we only consider

FIGURE 1-1   Mean, Median, and Mode for Example 1-2

whether or not it falls in the half lying above the median or in the half lying below the median.

What does this mean? If you look at the picture of the data set of Example 1–2, Figure 1–1, you will note that the observation $x_{20} = 24$ lies to the far right. If we shift this particular observation (or any other observation to the right of 16) to the right, say, move it from 24 to 100, what would happen to the median? The answer is: absolutely *nothing* (prove this to yourself by calculating the new median). The exact location of any data point is not considered in the computation of the median, only its relative standing with respect to the central observation. *The median is resistant to extreme observations.*

The mean, on the other hand, is sensitive to extreme observations. Let us see what happens to the mean if we change x_{20} from 24 to 100. The new mean is

$$\bar{x} = (6 + 9 + 10 + 12 + 13 + 14 + 14 + 15 + 16 + 16 + 16 + 17 + 17$$
$$+ 18 + 18 + 19 + 20 + 21 + 22 + 100)/20$$
$$= 19.65$$

We see that the mean has shifted almost four units to the right to accommodate the change in the single data point x_{20}.

The mean, however, does have strong advantages as a measure of central tendency. *The mean is based on information contained in all the observations in the data set,* rather than being an observation lying "in the middle" of the set. The mean also has some desirable mathematical properties that make it useful in many contexts of statistical inference. In cases where we want to guard against the influence of a few outlying observations (called *outliers*), however, we may prefer to use the median.

EXAMPLE 1-4

Continuing with the condominium prices from Example 1–1, a larger sample of asking prices for two-bedroom units in Boston (numbers in thousand dollars, rounded to the nearest thousand) is

168, 152, 167, 155, 171, 165, 150, 177, 295

What are the mean and the median? Interpret their meaning in this case.

SOLUTION

Arranging the data from smallest to largest, we get

150, 152, 155, 165, 167, 168, 171, 177, 295

There are nine observations, so the median is the value in the middle, that is in the fifth position. That value is 167 thousand dollars.

To compute the mean, we add all data values and divide by 9, giving us 177.778 thousand dollars—that is, $177,778. Now notice some interesting facts. The value 295 is clearly an *outlier*. It lies far to the right, away from the rest of the data bunched together in the 150–177 range.

In this case, the median is a very descriptive measure of this data set: it tells us where our data (with the exception of the outlier) are located. The mean, on the other hand, pays so much attention to the large observation 295 that it locates itself at 177.8, a value larger than our largest observation, except for the outlier. If our outlier had been more like the rest of the data, say 175 instead of 295, the mean would be 164.4. Notice that the median does not change and is still 167. This is so because 175 is on the same side of the median as 295.

Sometimes an outlier is due to an error in recording the data. In such a case it should be removed. Other times there is a good reason for it being "out in left field" (actually right field in this case).

As it turned out, the condominium with asking price of $295,000 was quite different from the rest of the two-bedroom units of roughly equal square footage and location. This unit was located in a prestigious part of town (away from the other units, geographically as well). It had a large whirlpool bath adjoining the master bedroom, its floors were marble from the Greek island of Paros; all light fixtures and faucets were gold plated; the chandelier was Murano crystal. "This is not your average condominium," the realtor said, inadvertently reflecting a purely statistical fact in addition to the intended meaning of the expression.

The mode is less useful than either the mean or the median. The mode tells us our data set's most frequently occurring value. There may be several modes. In Example 1–2, our data would possess two modes if we had another data point equal to 18, for example. Of the three measures of central tendency, we are most interested in the mean.

If a data set or population is *symmetric* (that is, if one side of the distribution of the observations is a mirror image of the other) and if the distribution of the observations has only one mode, then the mode, the median, and the mean are all equal. Such a situation is demonstrated in Figure 1–2. Generally, when the data distribution is not symmetric, then the mean, median, and mode will not all be equal. The relative positions of the three measures of centrality in such situations will be discussed in Section 1–6.

In the next section, we discuss measures of variability of a data set or population.

PROBLEMS

1–18. Discuss the differences among the three measures of centrality.

1–19. Find the mean, median, and mode(s) of the observations in problem 1–13.

1–20. Do the same as problem 1–19 using the data of problem 1–14.

1–21. Do the same as problem 1–19 using the data of problem 1–15.

1–22. Do the same as problem 1–19 using the data of problem 1–16.

1–23. Do the same as problem 1–19 using the observation set in problem 1–17.

1–24. Do the same as problem 1–19 for the data in Example 1-1.

1–25. Find the mean and median offer price for the Delaware Group Funds in problem 1–4.

FIGURE 1–2   A Symmetrically Distributed Data Set

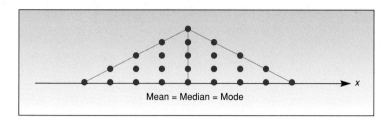

Mean = Median = Mode

1-4   Measures of Variability

Consider the following two data sets.

Set I: 1, 2, 3, 4, 5, 6, 6, 7, 8, 9, 10 ,11
Set II: 4, 5, 5, 5, 6, 6, 6, 6, 7, 7, 7, 8

Compute the mean, median, and mode of each of the two data sets. As you see from your results, the two data sets have the same mean, the same median, and the same mode, all equal to 6. The two data sets also happen to have the same number of observations, $n = 12$. But the two data sets are different. What is the main difference between them?

Figure 1–3 shows data sets I and II. The two data sets have the same central tendency (as measured by any of the three measures of centrality), but they have a different *variability*. In particular, we see that data set I is more variable than data set II. The values in set I are more spread out: they lie farther away from their mean than do those of set II.

There are several measures of **variability,** or **dispersion.** We have already discussed one such measure—the interquartile range. (Recall that the interquartile range is defined as the difference between the upper quartile and the lower quartile.) The interquartile range for data set I is 5.5, and the interquartile range of data set II is 2 (show this). The interquartile range is one measure of the dispersion or variability of a set of observations. Another such measure is the *range*.

> The **range** of a set of observations is the difference between the largest observation and the smallest observation.

The range of the observations in Example 1–2 is: Largest number − Smallest number = 24 − 6 = 18. The range of the data in set I is 11 − 1 = 10, and the range of the data in set II is 8 − 4 = 4. We see that, conforming with what we expect from looking at the two data sets, the range of set I is greater than the range of set II. Set I is more variable.

The range and the interquartile range are measures of the dispersion of a set of observations, the interquartile range being more resistant to extreme observations. There are also two other, more commonly used measures of dispersion. These are the *variance* and the square root of the variance—the *standard deviation*.

The variance and the standard deviation are more useful than the range and the interquartile range because, like the mean, they use the information contained in all the observations in the data set or population. (The range contains information only

FIGURE 1-3   Comparison of Data Sets I and II

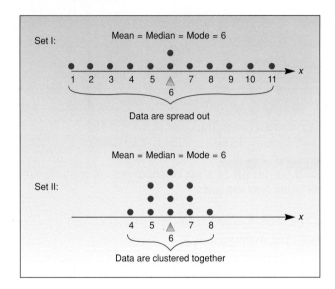

on the distance between the largest and smallest observations, and the interquartile range contains information only about the difference between upper and lower quartiles.) We define the variance as follows.

> The **variance** of a set of observations is the average squared deviation of the data points from their mean.

When our data constitute a sample, the variance is denoted by s^2, and the averaging is done by dividing the sum of the squared deviations from the mean by $n - 1$. (The reason for this will become clear in Chapter 5.) When our observations constitute an entire population, the variance is denoted by σ^2, and the averaging is done by dividing by N. (σ is the Greek letter sigma; we call the variance *sigma-squared*. The capital sigma is known to you as the symbol we use for summation, Σ.)

Sample variance:

$$s^2 = \frac{\sum\limits_{i=1}^{n} (x_i - \bar{x})^2}{n - 1}$$

(1–3)

Recall that $\bar{x}$ is the sample mean, the average of all the observations in the sample. Thus, the numerator in equation 1–3 is equal to the sum of the squared differences of the data points x_i (where $i = 1, 2, \ldots, n$) from their mean, $\bar{x}$. When we divide the numerator by the denominator $n - 1$, we get a kind of average of the items summed in the numerator. This average is based on the assumption that there are only $n - 1$ data points. (Note, however, that the summation in the numerator extends over all n data points, not just $n - 1$ of them.) This will be explained in section 5–5.

When we have an entire population at hand, we denote the total number of observations in the population by N. We define the population variance as follows.

Population variance:

$$\sigma^2 = \frac{\sum\limits_{i=1}^{N}(x_i - \mu)^2}{N} \qquad (1\text{-}4)$$

where μ is the population mean.

Unless noted otherwise, we will assume that all our data sets are samples and do not constitute entire populations; thus, we will use equation 1–3 for the variance, and not equation 1–4. We now define the standard deviation.

The **standard deviation** of a set of observations is the (positive) square root of the variance of the set.

The standard deviation of a sample is the square root of the sample variance, and the standard deviation of a population is the square root of the variance of the population.[3]

Sample standard deviation:

$$s = \sqrt{s^2} = \sqrt{\frac{\sum\limits_{i=1}^{n}(x_i - \overline{x})^2}{n-1}} \qquad (1\text{-}5)$$

Population standard deviation:

$$\sigma = \sqrt{\sigma^2} = \sqrt{\frac{\sum\limits_{i=1}^{n}(x_i - \mu)^2}{N}} \qquad (1\text{-}6)$$

Why would we use the standard deviation when we already have its square, the variance? The standard deviation is a more meaningful measure. The variance is the average squared deviation from the mean. It is squared because if we just compute the deviations from the mean and then average them, we get zero (prove this with any of the data sets). Therefore, when seeking a measure of the variation in a set of observations, we square the deviations from the mean; this removes the negative signs, and thus the measure is not equal to zero. The measure we obtain—the variance—is still a *squared* quantity; it is an average of squared numbers. By taking its square root, we "unsquare" the units and get a quantity denoted in the original units of the problem (e.g., dollars instead of dollars squared, which would have little meaning in most applications). The variance tends to be large because it is in squared units. Statisticians like to work with the variance because its mathematical properties

---

[3] A note about calculators: If your calculator is designed to compute means and standard deviations, find the key for the standard deviation. Typically, there will be two such keys. Consult your owner's handbook to be sure you are using the key that will produce the correct computation for a sample (division by $n - 1$) versus a population (division by N).

simplify computations. People applying statistics prefer to work with the standard deviation because it is more easily interpreted.

Let us find the variance and the standard deviation of the data in Example (1–2). It is convenient to carry out hand computations of the variance by use of a table. After doing the computation using equation 1–3, we will show a shortcut that will help in the calculation. Table 1–3 shows how the mean, $\bar{x}$, is subtracted from each of the values and the results are squared and added together. At the bottom of the last column we find the sum of all squared deviations from the mean. Finally, the sum is divided by $n - 1$, giving s^2, the sample variance. Taking the square root gives us s, the sample standard deviation.

By equation 1–3, the variance of the sample is equal to the sum of the third column in the table, 378.55, divided by $n - 1$: $s^2 = 378.55/19 = 19.923684$. The standard deviation is the square root of the variance: $s = \sqrt{19.923684} = 4.4635954$, or, using two-decimal accuracy,[4] $s = 4.46$.

If you have a calculator with statistical capabilities, you may avoid having to use a table such as Table 1–3. If you need to compute by hand, there is a shortcut formula for computing the variance and the standard deviation.

Shortcut formula for the sample variance:

$$s^2 = \frac{\sum_{i=1}^{n} x_i^2 - \left(\sum_{i=1}^{n} x_i \right)^2 / n}{n - 1} \qquad (1\text{–}7)$$

Again, the standard deviation is just the square root of the quantity in equation 1–7. We will now demonstrate the use of this computationally simpler formula with the data of Example 1–2. We will then use this simpler formula and compute the variance and the standard deviation of the two data sets we are comparing: set I and set II.

As before, a table will be useful in carrying out the computations. The table for finding the variance using equation 1–7 will have a column for the data points, x, and a column for the squared data points, x^2. Table 1–4 shows the computations for the variance of the data in Example 1–2.

Using equation 1–7, we find

$$s^2 = \frac{\sum_{i=1}^{n} x_i^2 - \left(\sum_{i=1}^{n} x_i \right)^2 / n}{n - 1} = \frac{5{,}403 - (317)^2/20}{19} = \frac{5{,}403 - 100{,}489/20}{19}$$

$$= 19.923684$$

The standard deviation is obtained as before: $s = \sqrt{19.923684} = 4.46$. Using the same procedure demonstrated with Table 1–4, we find the following quantities leading to the variance and the standard deviation of set I and of set II. Both are assumed to be samples, not populations.

---

[4] In quantitative fields such as statistics, there is always the problem of decimal accuracy. How many digits after the decimal point should we carry? This question has no easy answer; everything depends on the required level of accuracy. As a rule, we will use only two decimals, since this suffices in most applications in this book. In some procedures, such as regression analysis, it is recommended that more digits be used in computations (these computations, however, are usually done by computer).

TABLE 1-3   Calculations Leading to the Sample Variance in Example 1-2

x	$(x - \bar{x})$	$(x - \bar{x})^2$
6	$6 - 15.85 = -9.85$	97.0225
9	$9 - 15.85 = -6.85$	46.9225
10	$10 - 15.85 = -5.85$	34.2225
12	$12 - 15.85 = -3.85$	14.8225
13	$13 - 15.85 = -2.85$	8.1225
14	$14 - 15.85 = -1.85$	3.4225
14	$14 - 15.85 = -1.85$	3.4225
15	$15 - 15.85 = -0.85$	0.7225
16	$16 - 15.85 = 0.15$	0.0225
16	$16 - 15.85 = 0.15$	0.0225
16	$16 - 15.85 = 0.15$	0.0225
17	$17 - 15.85 = 1.15$	1.3225
17	$17 - 15.85 = 1.15$	1.3225
18	$18 - 15.85 = 2.15$	4.6225
18	$18 - 15.85 = 2.15$	4.6225
19	$19 - 15.85 = 3.15$	9.9225
20	$20 - 15.85 = 4.15$	17.2225
21	$21 - 15.85 = 5.15$	26.5225
22	$22 - 15.85 = 6.15$	37.8225
24	$24 - 15.85 = 8.15$	66.4225
	0	378.5500

TABLE 1-4   Shortcut Computations for the Variance in Example 1-2

x	x^2
6	36
9	81
10	100
12	144
13	169
14	196
14	196
15	225
16	256
16	256
16	256
17	289
17	289
18	324
18	324
19	361
20	400
21	441
22	484
24	576
317	5,403

Set I: $\Sigma\ x = 72$, $\Sigma\ x^2 = 542$, $s^2 = 10$, and $s = \sqrt{10} = 3.16$
Set II: $\Sigma\ x = 72$, $\Sigma\ x^2 = 446$, $s^2 = 1.27$, and $s = \sqrt{1.27} = 1.13$

As expected, we see that the variance and the standard deviation of set II are smaller than those of set I. While each has a mean of 6, set I is more variable. That is, the values in set I vary more about their mean than do those of set II, which are clustered more closely together.

The sample standard deviation and the sample mean are very important statistics used in inference about populations.

EXAMPLE 1-5

In financial analysis, the standard deviation is often used as a measure of *volatility* and of the *risk* associated with financial variables. The data below are exchange rate values of the British pound, given as the value of one U.S. dollar's worth in pounds. The first column of 10 numbers is for a period in the beginning of 1993, and the second column of 10 numbers is for a similar period in the beginning of 1995. During which period, of these two precise sets of 10 days each, was the value of the pound more volatile?

1993	1995
0.6666	0.6332
0.6464	0.6254
0.6520	0.6286
0.6522	0.6359
0.6510	0.6336
0.6437	0.6427
0.6477	0.6209
0.6473	0.6214
0.6507	0.6204
0.6536	0.6325

SOLUTION

We are looking at two *populations* of 10 specific days at the start of each year (rather than a random sample of days), so we will use the formula for the population standard deviation. For the 1993 period we get $\sigma = 0.005929$, while for the 1995 period we get $\sigma = 0.007033$. We conclude that during the 1995 ten-day period the British pound was more volatile than in the same period in 1993. Notice that if these had been random samples of days, we would have used the sample standard deviation. In such cases we might have been interested in statistical inference to some population.

PROBLEMS

1–26. Explain why we need measures of variability and what information these measures convey.

1–27 What is the most important measure of variability and why?

1–28. What is the computational difference between the variance of a sample and the variance of a population?

1–29. Find the range, the variance, and the standard deviation of the data set in problem 1–13 (assumed to be a sample).

1–30.   Do the same as problem 1–29 using the data in problem 1–14.

1–31.   Do the same as problem 1–29 using the data in problem 1–15.

1–32.   Do the same as problem 1–29 using the data in problem 1–16.

1–33.   Do the same as problem 1–29 using the data in problem 1–17.

1–5   Grouped Data and the Histogram

It often happens that data are grouped. This happened naturally in Example 1–2, where we had a group of three points with a value of 16 and three groups of two points (14s, 17s, and 18s). In other cases, especially when we have a large data set, the collector of the data may break the data into groups even if the points in each group are not equal in value. The data collector may set some (often arbitrary) group boundaries for ease of recording the data. When considering the salaries of 5,000 executives, for example, the data may be reported in the form: 1,548 executives in the salary range $60,000 to $65,000; 2,365 executives in the salary range $65,001 to $70,000; and so on. In this case, the data collector or analyst has processed all the salaries and put them into groups with defined boundaries. In such cases, there is a loss of information. We are unable to find the mean, variance, and other measures because we do not know the actual values. (There are, however, formulas that allow us to find the approximate mean, variance, and standard deviation. The formulas assume that all data points in a group are placed in the midpoint of the interval.) In this example, we would assume that all 1,548 executives in the $60,001–$65,000 *class* make exactly ($60,000 + $65,000)/2 = $62,500; we estimate similarly for executives in the other groups.

> We define a group of data values within specified group boundaries as a **class.**

When data are grouped into classes, we may also plot a frequency distribution of the data. Such a frequency plot is called a *histogram*.

> A **histogram** is a chart made of bars of different heights. The height of each bar represents the **frequency** of values in the class represented by the bar. Adjacent bars share sides.

We demonstrate the use of histograms in the following example. Note that a histogram is used only for measured, or ordinal, data.

Management of an appliance store recorded the amounts spent at the store by the 184 customers who came in during the last day of the big sale. The data, amounts spent, were grouped into categories as follows: $0 to less than $100, $100 to less than $200, and so on up to $600, a bound higher than the amount spent by any single buyer. The classes and the frequency of each class are shown in Table 1–5. The frequencies, denoted by $f(x)$, are shown in a histogram in Figure 1–4.

As you can see from Figure 1–4, a histogram is just a convenient way of plotting the frequencies of grouped data. Here the frequencies are *absolute frequencies*, or **counts** of data points. It is also possible to plot *relative frequencies*.

EXAMPLE 1–6

TABLE 1–5   Classes and Frequencies, Example 1–6

x Spending Class ($)	f(x) Frequency (number of customers)
0 to less than 100	30
100 to less than 200	38
200 to less than 300	50
300 to less than 400	31
400 to less than 500	22
500 to less than 600	13
	184

FIGURE 1–4   A Histogram of the Data in Example 1–6

The **relative frequency** of a class is the count of data points in the class divided by the total number of data points.

The relative frequency in the first class, $0 to less than $100, is equal to count/total = 30/184 = 0.163. We can similarly compute the relative frequencies for the other classes. The advantage of relative frequencies is that they are standardized: they add to 1.00. The relative frequency in each class represents the proportion of the total sample in the class. Table 1–6 gives the relative frequencies of the classes.

Figure 1–5 is a histogram of the relative frequencies of the data in this example. Note that the shape of the histogram of the relative frequencies is the same as that of the absolute frequencies, the counts. The shape of the histogram does not change; only the labeling of the $f(x)$ axis is different.

Relative frequencies—proportions that add to 1.00—may be viewed as probabilities, as we will see in the next chapter. Hence, such frequencies are very useful in statistics, and so are their histograms.

1–6   Skewness and Kurtosis

In addition to measures of location, such as the mean or median, and measures of variation, such as the variance or standard deviation, there are two attributes of a frequency distribution of a data set that may be of interest to us. These are *skewness* and *kurtosis*.

TABLE 1–6   Relative Frequencies, Example 1–6

x Class ($)	f(x) Relative Frequency
0 to less than 100	0.163
100 to less than 200	0.207
200 to less than 300	0.272
300 to less than 400	0.168
400 to less than 500	0.120
500 to less than 600	0.070
	1.000

FIGURE 1–5   A Histogram of the Relative Frequencies in Example 1–6

Skewness is a measure of the degree of asymmetry of a frequency distribution.

When the distribution stretches to the right more than it does to the left, we say that the distribution is *right-skewed*. Similarly, a *left-skewed* distribution is one that stretches asymmetrically to the left. Four graphs are shown in Figure 1–6: a symmetric distribution, a right-skewed distribution, a left-skewed distribution, and a symmetrical distribution with two modes.

Recall that a symmetric distribution with a single mode has mode = mean = median. Generally, for a right-skewed distribution, the mean is to the right of the median, which in turn lies to the right of the mode (assuming a single mode). The opposite is true for left-skewed distributions.

Kurtosis is a measure of the flatness (versus peakedness) of a frequency distribution.

Flat distributions are called *platykurtic*, and peaked distributions are called *leptokurtic*. Neutral distributions—not too flat and not too peaked—are called *mesokurtic*. Figure 1–7 shows two examples of kurtosis.

FIGURE 1–6   **Skewness of Distributions**

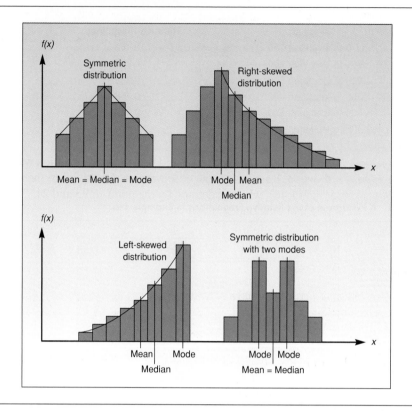

FIGURE 1–7   **Kurtosis of Distributions**

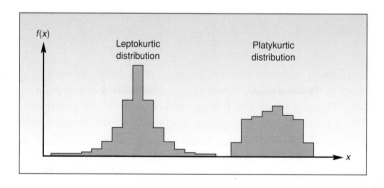

1–7   Relations between the Mean and the Standard Deviation

The mean is a measure of the centrality of a set of observations, and the standard deviation is a measure of their spread. There are two general rules that establish a relation between these measures and the set of observations. The first is called Chebyshev's theorem, and the second is the empirical rule.

Chebyshev's Theorem

A mathematical theorem attributed to Chebyshev establishes the following rules:

1. At least 3/4 of the observations in a set will lie within 2 standard deviations of the mean.
2. At least 8/9 of the observations in a set will lie within 3 standard deviations of the mean.

In general, the rule states that at least $1 - 1/k^2$ of the observations will lie within k standard deviations of the mean. (We note that k does not have to be an integer.) In Example 1–2 we found that the mean was 15.85 and the standard deviation was 4.46. According to rule 1 above, at least 3/4 of the observations should fall in the interval Mean $\pm\ 2s = 15.85 \pm 2(4.46)$, which is defined by the points 6.93 and 24.77. From the data set itself, we see that only one observation, 6, lies outside this range of values. Since there are 20 observations in the set, 19/20 are within the specified range, so the rule that at least 3/4 will be within the range is satisfied.

The Empirical Rule

If the distribution of the data is mound-shaped—that is, if the histogram of the data is more or less symmetric with a single mode or high point—then tighter rules will apply.

1. Approximately 68% of the observations will be within 1 standard deviation of the mean.
2. Approximately 95% of the observations will be within 2 standard deviations of the mean.
3. A vast majority of the observations (all of them, or almost all of them) will be within 3 standard deviations of the mean.

For the data set in Example 1–2, even though the distribution of the data set is not perfectly symmetric, the empirical rule holds approximately (especially its last two parts). The mean is 15.85 and the standard deviation is 4.46. The two points that are one standard deviation on either side of the mean are $15.85 - 4.46 = 11.39$ and $15.85 + 4.46 = 20.31$. We see that 14 out of our 20 data points lie within this range. This is 70% of our observations. The two points that lie 2 standard deviations on either side of the mean are $15.85 - 2(4.46) = 6.93$ and $15.85 + 2(4.46) = 24.77$. We see that 19 out of our 20 data points lie within this range, or 95.83% of our observations. The 3 standard deviation limits around the mean are 2.47 and 29.23. One hundred percent of our observations lie within this range.

PROBLEMS

1–34. Check the applicability of Chebyshev's theorem and the empirical rule for the data set in problem 1–13.

1–35. Check the applicability of Chebyshev's theorem and the empirical rule for the data set in problem 1–14.

1–36. Check the applicability of Chebyshev's theorem and the empirical rule for the data set in problem 1–15.

1–37. Check the applicability of Chebyshev's theorem and the empirical rule for the data set in problem 1–16.

1–38. Check the applicability of Chebyshev's theorem and the empirical rule for the data set in problem 1–17.

1-8   Methods of Displaying Data

In section 1–5, we saw how a histogram is used to display frequencies of occurrence of values in a data set. In this section, we will see a few other ways of displaying data, some of which are descriptive only. We will introduce frequency polygons, cumulative frequency plots (called *ogives*), pie charts, and bar charts. We will also see examples of how descriptive graphs can sometimes be misleading. We will start with pie charts.

Pie Charts

A **pie chart** is a simple descriptive display of data that sum to a given total. A pie chart is probably the most illustrative way of displaying quantities as percentages of a given total. The total area of the pie represents 100% of the quantity of interest (the sum of the variable values in all categories), and the size of each slice is the percentage of the total represented by the category the slice denotes. Pie charts are used to present frequencies for categorical data. The scale of measurement may be nominal or ordinal. Figure 1–8 is a pie chart of the geographical locations of the world's largest telecommunications companies.

Bar Graphs

Bar graphs (which use horizontal or vertical rectangles) are often used to display categorical data where there is no emphasis on the percentage of a total represented by each category. The scale of measurement is nominal or ordinal.

Graphs using horizontal bars and those using vertical bars are essentially the same. In some cases, it may be more convenient for the purpose at hand to use one versus the other. For example, if we want to write the name of each category inside the rectangle that represents that category, then a horizontal bar graph may be more convenient. If we want to stress the height of the different columns as measures of the quantity of interest, we would use a vertical bar graph. Figure 1–9 is an example of how a bar graph can be used effectively to display and interpret information.

Frequency Polygons and Ogives

A **frequency polygon** is similar to a histogram except that there are no rectangles, only a point in the midpoint of each interval at a height proportional to the frequency or relative frequency (in a relative-frequency polygon) of the category of the interval. The rightmost and leftmost points are zero. Table 1–7 gives the relative frequency of sales volume, in thousands of dollars per week, for pizza at a local establishment.

A relative-frequency polygon for these data is shown in Figure 1–10. Note that the frequency is located in the middle of the interval as a point with height equal to the relative frequency of the interval. Note also that the point zero is added at the left boundary and the right boundary of the data set: the polygon starts at zero and ends at zero even if zero is not part of the data.

FIGURE 1-8   Headquarters of the World's Largest Telecommunications Companies

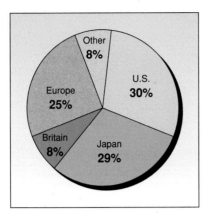

Reprinted by permission from *Business Week,* March 27, 1995, p. 177.

FIGURE 1-9   Airline Operating Expenses and Revenues

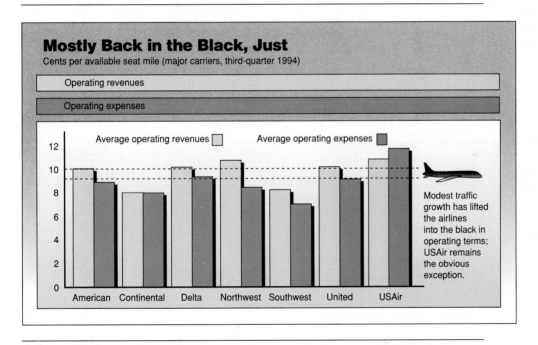

Reprinted from *Forbes,* March 27, 1995, p. 79, with data from Avitas Aviation, based on carrier Form 41 filings with the Department of Transportation.

An **ogive** is a cumulative-frequency (or cumulative relative-frequency) graph. An ogive starts at 0 and goes to 1.00 (for a relative-frequency ogive) or to the maximum cumulative frequency. The point with height corresponding to the cumulative frequency is located at the right end point of each interval. An ogive for the data in Table 1–7 is shown in Figure 1–11. While the ogive shown is for the cumulative *relative* frequency, an ogive can also be used for the cumulative absolute frequency.

TABLE 1-7   Pizza Sales

Sales ($000)	Relative Frequency	
6–14	0.20	0.20
15–22	0.30	0.50
23–30	0.25	0.75
31–38	0.15	0.90
39–46	0.07	0.97
47–54	0.03	1.0

FIGURE 1-10   Relative Frequency Polygon for Pizza Sales

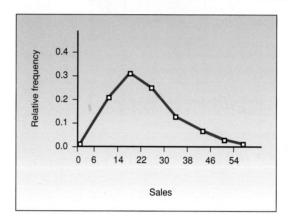

FIGURE 1-11   Ogive of Pizza Sales

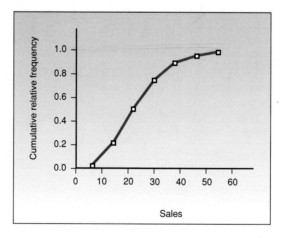

A Caution about Graphs

A picture is indeed worth a thousand words, but pictures can sometimes be deceiving. Often, this is where "lying with statistics" comes in: presenting data graphically on a stretched or compressed scale of numbers with the aim of making the data show whatever you want them to show. This is one important argument against a merely descriptive approach to data analysis and an argument for statistical *inference.* Statistical tests tend to be more objective than our eyes and are less prone to deception as long as our assumptions (random sampling and other assumptions) hold. As we will see, statistical inference gives us tools that allow us to objectively evaluate what we see in the data.

Pictures are sometimes deceptive even though there is no intention to deceive. When someone shows you a graph of a set of numbers, there may really be no particular scale of numbers that is "right" for the data.

Figure 1–12 is reprinted exactly as it appeared on the front page of *Investor's Business Daily,* February 14, 1995. Notice that there is *no scale* for this graph, and only one number, $36,959, is shown. What are the figures for the other years? For 1989, was the median income $50,000, or $36,970? This would make a big difference in how we interpret the graph.

Time Plots

Often we want to graph changes in a variable over time. An example is given in Figure 1–13.

PROBLEMS

1–39. The following data are estimated worldwide appliance sales (in millions of dollars). Use the data to construct a pie chart for the worldwide appliance sales of the listed manufacturers.

Electrolux	$5,100
General Electric	4,350
Matsushita Electric	4,180
Whirlpool	3,950
Bosch-Siemens	2,200
Philips	2,000
Maytag	1,580

1–40. Draw a bar graph for the data on the first five funds in problem 1–14. Is any one of the three kinds of plot more appropriate than the others for these data? If so, why?

1–41. Draw a bar graph for the endowments (stated in billions of dollars) of each of the universities specified in the following list.

Harvard	$3.4
Texas	2.5
Princeton	1.9
Yale	1.7
Stanford	1.4
Columbia	1.3
Texas A&M	1.1

FIGURE 1-12   Median Income for Families

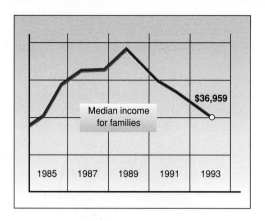

Reprinted from *Investor's Business Daily*, February 14, 1995, p. 1.

FIGURE 1-13   The Dow-Jones Average

Reprinted from *The Wall Street Journal,* March 22,1995, p. C1, with data from Tolerate-Teletranortal.

1–42.   The following are the amounts from the sales slips of a department store (in dollars): 3.45, 4.52, 5.41, 6.00, 5.97, 7.18, 1.12, 5.39, 7.03, 10.25, 11.45, 13.21, 12.00, 14.05, 2.99, 3.28, 17.10, 19.28, 21.09, 12.11, 5.88, 4.65, 3.99, 10.10, 23.00, 15.16, 20.16. Draw a frequency polygon for these data (start by defining intervals of the data and counting the data points in each interval). Also draw an ogive and a column graph.

1–43.   Interpret the following graph.

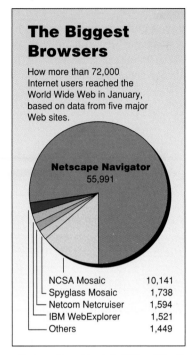

The Biggest Browsers

How more than 72,000 Internet users reached the World Wide Web in January, based on data from five major Web sites.

Netscape Navigator
55,991

NCSA Mosaic	10,141
Spyglass Mosaic	1,738
Netcom Netcruiser	1,594
IBM WebExplorer	1,521
Others	1,449

Reprinted from the *New York Times,* Business Day, March 1, 1995, p.D1, with data from *Interse*.

1–44.   Convert the graph in problem 1–43 into a bar graph.

1–45.   Interpret the following graph, from the front page of *The Wall Street Journal,* March 22, 1995.

Hourly Earnings (In dollars per hour)

Average hourly pay of factory workers rose in February to $12.25 from a revised $12.23 in January, the Labor Department reports.

1-9 Exploratory Data Analysis

Exploratory data analysis (EDA) is the name given to a large body of statistical and graphical techniques. These techniques provide ways of looking at data to determine relationships and trends, identify outliers and influential observations, and quickly describe or summarize data sets. Pioneering methods in this field, as well as the name *exploratory data analysis,* derive from the work of John W. Tukey. [John W. Tukey, *Exploratory Data Analysis* (Reading, Massachusetts: Addison-Wesley, 1977)].

Stem-and-Leaf Displays

A **stem-and-leaf display** is a quick way of looking at a data set. It contains some of the features of a histogram but avoids the loss of information in a histogram that results from aggregating the data into intervals. The stem-and-leaf display is based on the tallying principle, | || ||| |||| |||||, but also uses the decimal base of our number system. In a stem-and-leaf display, the *stem* is the number without its rightmost digit (the *leaf*). The stem is written to the left of a vertical line separating the stem from the leaf. For example, suppose we have the numbers 105, 106, 107, 107, 109. We would display them as

$$10 \mid 56779$$

With a more complete data set with different stem values, the last digit of each number is displayed at the appropriate place to the right of its stem digit(s). Stem-and-leaf displays help us identify, at a glance, numbers in our data set that have high frequency. Let's look at an example.

EXAMPLE 1-7

Virtual reality is the name given to a new system of simulating real situations on a computer in a way that gives people the feeling that what they see on the computer screen is a real situation. Flight simulators were the forerunners of virtual reality programs. A particular virtual reality program has been designed to give production engineers experience in real processes. Engineers are supposed to complete certain tasks as responses to what they see on the screen. The following data are the time, in seconds, it took a group of 42 engineers to perform a given task:

11, 12, 12, 13, 15, 15, 15, 16, 17, 20, 21, 21, 21, 22, 22, 22, 23, 24, 26, 27, 27, 27, 28, 29, 29, 30, 31, 32, 34, 35, 37, 41, 41, 42, 45, 47, 50, 52, 53, 56, 60, 62

SOLUTION

The data are already arranged in increasing order. We see that the data are in the 10s, 20s, 30s, 40s, 50s, and 60s. We will use the first digit as the stem and the second digit of each number as the leaf. The stem-and-leaf display of our data is shown in Figure 1–14.

As you can see, the stem-and-leaf display is a very quick way of arranging the data in a kind of a histogram (turned sideways) that allows us to see what the data look like. Here, we note that the data do not seem to be symmetrically distributed; rather, they are skewed to the right.

We may feel that this display does not convey very much information because there are too many values with first digit 2. To solve this problem, we may split the groups into two

FIGURE 1–14   Stem-and-Leaf Display of the Task Performance Times of Example 1–7

```
1 | 122355567
2 | 0111222346777899
3 | 012457
4 | 11257
5 | 0236
6 | 02
```

subgroups. We will denote the stem part as 1* for the possible numbers 10, 11, 12, 13, 14 and as 1. for the possible numbers 15, 16, 17, 18, 19. Similarly, the stem 2* will be used for the possible numbers 20, 21, 22, 23, and 24; stem 2. will be used for the numbers 25, 26, 27, 28, and 29; and so on for the other numbers. Our stem-and-leaf diagram for the data of Example 1–7 using this convention is shown in Figure 1–15. As you can see from the figure, we now have a more spread-out histogram of the data. The data still seem skewed to the right.

If desired, a further refinement of the display is possible by using the symbol * for a stem followed by the leaf values 0 and 1; the symbol t for leaf values 2 and 3; the symbol f for leaf values 4 and 5; s for 6 and 7; and . for 8 and 9. Also, the class containing the median observation is often denoted with its stem value in parentheses. We demonstrate this version of the display for the data of Example 1–7 in Figure 1–16. Note that the median is 27 (why?).

Note that for the data set of this example, the refinement offered in Figure 1–16 may be too much: we may have lost the general picture of the data. In cases where there are many observations with the same value (e.g., 22, 22, 22, 22, 22, 22, 22, . . .), it may be necessary to use a more stretched-out display in order to get a good picture of the way our data are clustered.

Box Plots

A *box plot* (also called a *box-and-whisker plot*) is another way of looking at a data set in an effort to determine its central tendency, spread, skewness, and the existence of outliers.

A **box plot** is a set of five summary measures of the distribution of the data:

1. The median of the data
2. The lower quartile
3. The upper quartile
4. The smallest observation
5. The largest observation

There are two qualifications to the preceding statements. We will assume that the *hinges* of the box plot are essentially the quartiles of the data set. (We will define hinges shortly.) The median is a line inside the box.

Second, the *whiskers* of the box plot are made by extending a line from the upper quartile to the largest observation and from the lower quartile to the smallest observation, only if the largest and smallest observations are within a distance of 1.5 times

FIGURE 1-15   Refined Stem-and-Leaf Display for Data of Example 1-7

```
1*  | 1223
1.  | 55567
2*  | 011122234
2.  | 6777899
3*  | 0124
3.  | 57
4*  | 112
4.  | 57
5*  | 023
5.  | 6
6*  | 02
```

FIGURE 1-16   Further Refined Stem-and-Leaf Display of Data of Example 1-7

```
                                      1*  | 1
                                      t   | 223
                                      f   | 555
                                      s   | 67
                                      .   |
                                      2*  | 0111
                                      t   | 2223
                                      f   | 4
(Median in this class)               (s)  | 6777
                                          | 899
                                      3*  | 01
                                      t   | 2
                                      f   | 45
                                      s   | 7
                                      .   |
                                      4*  | 11
                                      t   | 2
                                      f   | 5
                                      s   | 7
                                      .   |
                                      5*  | 0
                                      t   | 23
                                      f   |
                                      s   | 6
                                      .   |
                                      6*  | 0
                                      t   | 2
```

the interquartile range from the appropriate hinge (quartile). If one or more observations are farther away than that distance, they are marked as suspected outliers. If these observations are at a distance of over three times the interquartile range from the appropriate hinge, they are marked as outliers. The whisker then extends to the largest or smallest observation that is at a distance less than or equal to 1.5 times the interquartile range from the hinge.

Let us make these definitions clearer by using a picture. Figure 1–17 shows the parts of a box plot and how they are defined. The median is marked as a vertical line across the box. The **hinges** of the box are the upper and lower quartiles (the rightmost and leftmost sides of the box). The interquartile range (IQR) is the distance from the upper quartile to the lower quartile (the length of the box from hinge to hinge): $IQR = Q_U - Q_L$. We define the **inner fence** as a point at a distance of 1.5(IQR) above the upper quartile; similarly, the lower inner fence is $Q_L - 1.5(IQR)$. The **outer fences**

FIGURE 1–17   The Box Plot

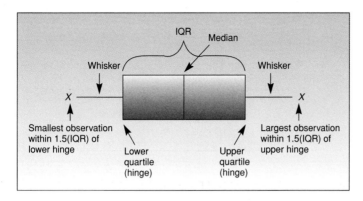

FIGURE 1–18   The Elements of a Box Plot

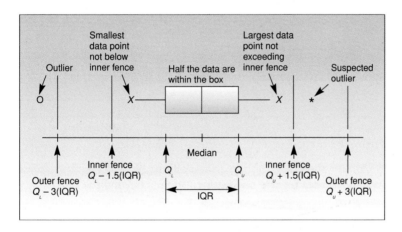

are defined similarly but are at a distance of 3(IQR) above or below the appropriate hinge. Figure 1–18 shows the fences (these are not shown on the actual box plot; they are only guidelines for defining the whiskers, suspected outliers, and outliers) and demonstrate how we mark outliers.

Box plots are very useful for the following purposes.

1. To identify the location of a data set based on the median.
2. To identify the spread of the data based on the length of the box, hinge to hinge (the interquartile range), and the length of the whiskers (the range of the data without extreme observations: outliers or suspected outliers).
3. To identify possible skewness of the distribution of the data set. If the portion of the box to the right of the median is longer than the portion to the left of the median, and/or the right whisker is longer than the left whisker, the data are right-skewed. Similarly, a longer left side of the box and/or left whisker implies a left-skewed data set. If the box and whiskers are symmetric, the data are symmetrically distributed with no skewness.

FIGURE 1–19   Box Plots and Their Uses

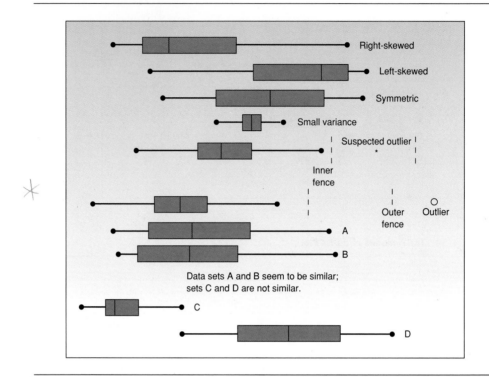

4. To identify suspected outliers (observations beyond the inner fences but within the outer fences) and outliers (points beyond the outer fences).

5. To compare two or more data sets. By drawing a box plot for each data set and displaying the box plots on the same scale, we can compare several data sets.

It has even been suggested that a special form of a box plot may be used for conducting a test of the equality of two population medians. The various uses of a box plot are demonstrated in Figure 1–19.

Let us now construct a box plot for the data of Example 1–7. For this data set, the median is 27, and we find that the lower quartile is 20.75 and the upper quartile is 41. The interquartile range is IQR = 41 − 20.75 = 20.25. One and one-half times this distance is 30.38; hence, the inner fences are −9.63 and 71.38. Since no observation lies beyond either point, there are no suspected outliers and no outliers, so the whiskers extend to the extreme values in the data: 11 on the left side and 62 on the right side. The box plot for the data of Example 1–7 is shown in Figure 1–20, along with the MINITAB program that produced it.

As you can see from the figure, there are no outliers or suspected outliers in this data set. The data set is skewed to the right. This confirms our observation of the skewness from consideration of the stem-and-leaf diagrams of the same data set, in Figures 1–14 to 1–16.

FIGURE 1-20   MINITAB-Produced Box Plot for the Data of Example 1-7

```
MTB > read 'ccc.dat' into c1
     42 ROWS READ

C1
    11    12    12    13

MTB > PRINT C1
C1
    11    12    12    13    15    15    15    16    17    20    21    21    21
    22    22    22    23    24    26    27    27    27    28    29    29    30
    31    32    34    35    37    41    41    42    45    47    50    52    53
    56    60    62

MTB > BOXPLOT FOR DATA IN C1
```

1–46.   The following data are monthly steel production figures, in millions of tons.

7.0, 6.9, 8.2, 7.8, 7.7, 7.3, 6.8, 6.7, 8.2, 8.4, 7.0, 6.7, 7.5, 7.2, 7.9, 7.6, 6.7,
6.6, 6.3, 5.6, 7.8, 5.5, 6.2, 5.8, 5.8, 6.1, 6.0, 7.3, 7.3, 7.5, 7.2, 7.2, 7.4, 7.6.

Draw a stem-and-leaf display of these data.

1–47.   Draw a box plot for the data in problem 1–46. Are there any outliers? Is the distribution of the data symmetric or skewed? If it is skewed, to what side?

1–48.   What are the uses of a stem-and-leaf display? What are the uses of a box plot?

1–49.   Worker participation in management is a new concept that involves employees in corporate decision making. The following data are the percentages of employees involved in worker participation programs in a sample of firms. Draw a stem-and-leaf display of the data.

5, 32, 33, 35, 42, 43, 42, 45, 46, 44, 47, 48, 48, 48, 49, 49, 50,
37, 38, 34, 51, 52, 52, 47, 53, 55, 56, 57, 58, 63, 78

1–50.   Draw a box plot of the data in problem 1–49, and draw conclusions about the data set based on the box plot.

1–51.   Consider the four box plots in the following output, and draw your conclusions about the data sets.

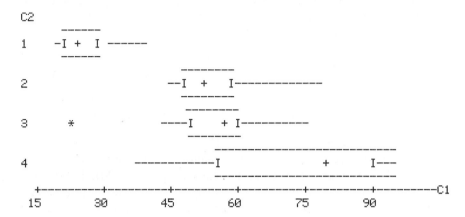

1–52.   Presented in the following list are data on government expenditures by Western Hemisphere countries, expressed as a percentage of a nation's gross domestic product.

Argentina: 12.7; Bahamas: 13.2; Belize: 14.0; Bolivia: 13.6; Brazil: 8.9; Canada: 19.4; Chile: 12.4; Colombia: 8.0; Costa Rica: 18.3; Cuba: 2.1; Dominican Republic: 7.8; Ecuador: 15.0; El Salvador: 15.1; Guadeloupe: 32.3; Guatemala: 7.7; Guyana: 28.9; Haiti: 87.4; Honduras: 14.6; Jamaica: 21.5; Martinique: 26.0; Mexico: 10.8; Netherlands Antilles: 21.3; Nicaragua: 11.6; Panama: 15.3; Paraguay: 7.3; Peru: 12.5; Puerto Rico: 17.1; Surinam: 16.4; Trinidad and Tobago: 16.8; Uruguay: 13.5; USA: 20.7; Venezuela: 13.1

Construct a box plot for the data on the listed countries. Are there any outliers (or suspected outliers)? Can you identify possible reasons for outliers in this case?

1–53.   The following data are the daily price quotations for a certain stock over a period of 45 days. Construct a stem-and-leaf display for these data. What can you conclude about the distribution of daily stock prices over the period under study?

10, 11, 10, 11, 11, 12, 12, 13, 14, 16, 15, 11, 18, 19, 20, 15, 14, 14, 22, 25, 27, 23, 22, 26, 27, 29, 28, 31, 32, 30, 32, 34, 33, 38, 41, 40, 42, 53, 52, 47, 37, 23, 11, 32, 23

1–54.   Discuss ways of dealing with outliers: their detection and what to do about them once they are detected. Can you always discard an outlier? Why or why not?

1–55.   Define the inner fences and the outer fences of a box plot; also define the whiskers and the hinges. What portion of the data is represented by the box? By the whiskers?

1–56.   The following data are the number of ounces of silver per ton of ore for two mines.

Mine A: 34, 32, 35, 37, 41, 42, 43, 45, 46, 45, 48, 49, 51, 52, 53, 60, 73, 76, 85

Mine B: 23, 24, 28, 29, 32, 34, 35, 37, 38, 40, 43, 44, 47, 48, 49, 50, 51, 52, 59

Construct a stem-and-leaf display for each data set, and a box plot for each data set. Compare the two displays and the two box plots. Draw conclusions about the data.

1–57.   Can you compare two *populations* by looking at box plots or stem-and-leaf displays of random samples from the two populations? Explain.

1–10 Using the Computer

Since statistics involves the processing of numerical data—often large sets of data—computers play a major role. The connection between statistics and computers is so strong, in fact, that most computer software packages with capabilities for handling numerical data have statistical analysis routines.

Among the best-known computer packages designed primarily for conducting statistical analysis are SAS (Statistical Analysis System, SAS Institute, Cary, NC), SPSS (Statistical Package for the Social Sciences, SPSS Inc., Chicago, IL), and MINITAB (a registered trademark of MINITAB, Inc., 3081 Enterprise Drive, State College, PA 16801); there are several others.

In this book we will use primarily the MINITAB package. MINITAB is not the most commonly used package in business and industry; there you are much more likely to use SPSS, SAS, or any of the other fine statistical packages. MINITAB, however, is possibly the easiest to use of all commonly available statistical packages. The data do not have to be specified in a rigid way. As long as blanks separate data, the data column format does not have to be strictly adhered to. This and other features make MINITAB a more "forgiving" package than most. It can be used with little preparation and, as a result, you will have more time to concentrate on learning the statistical concepts.

As always, a price is paid for simplicity: the MINITAB package is not quite as powerful as some of the others. Results are often rounded to few decimal places, and MINITAB does not have capabilities in one or two areas covered in this book. In such cases, we will use another package. However, familiarity with MINITAB will enable you to use any statistical package that you may later have access to or own.

MINITAB works with columns of data. When you enter a single data set into the computer, the data go into column 1, or C1. If you have two data sets, where one set represents one variable (say, personal income) and the other set a second variable (say, experience of the same person), one data set is entered into C1 and the second set into C2. This is basically the only "logic" of MINITAB you need to understand. It tells you how to enter and define your data.

We will demonstrate the use of MINITAB in producing descriptive statistics with the data of Example 1–2. The MINITAB command to enter the data into the first column, when done within the program, is

```
SET into C1
```

Later we will work with files of data that are defined separately. In such cases, we will tell the program to call the appropriate data set and analyze it. In this example, however, we will enter the data within the program itself, using the SET command. (The necessary commands will always be capitalized in our explanations; lowercase letters will be used for words needed only for our own documentation, which will be ignored by the computer.) When we finish entering the data, we give the command

```
END
```

Then we tell the computer what we want it to do with our data. The command

```
MEAN of C1
```

for example, will produce the mean of our data set. Similarly, the command

```
STDEV  of  C1
```

will give us the standard deviation of our data set. In our example, we will use a general command:

```
DESCRIBE  C1
```

This command will give us the mean and standard deviation of our data set, along with other statistics. We will also use the command

```
HISTOGRAM  of  C1
```

to produce a histogram of our data set. To get out of MINITAB, just type

```
STOP
```

Figures 1–21 and 1–22 show the commands, the data, and the output for the two operations DESCRIBE and HISTOGRAM, respectively. Compare the results with the ones we obtained without use of a computer.

The results include mean, median, and standard deviation, as well as the lower and upper quartiles, Q1 and Q3, respectively. In addition, the results provide the minimum and maximum values, which allow us to compute the range (their difference). Note that the computer chose the group boundaries for the histogram and gave us the midpoint of each interval.

Computer graphics is a fast-growing field. There are computer packages that allow you to plot any data set in two or three dimensions, and the graphs are continually improving. The computer language S is one example of a powerful graphical data analysis tool. Other packages for microcomputers include MacSpin for the Apple® Macintosh®. This program allows you to look at data in several dimensions (three at a time) and to rotate the data in space to detect relationships and outliers.

The MINITAB package has EDA capabilities. The command for a box plot is

```
BOXPLOT (name of data column)
```

and the command for a stem-and-leaf display is

```
STEM-AND-LEAF (name of data column)
```

The construction of a box plot was demonstrated in Figure 1–20. Now we will show how to use MINITAB to produce a stem-and-leaf display using the data of Example 1–7. The commands and the output are shown in Figure 1–23. Compare the stem-and-leaf display in the figure with the one we constructed by hand, in Figure 1–14.

FIGURE 1–21   MINITAB-Produced Descriptive Statistics, Example 1–2

```
MTB > SET into C1
DATA> 6 9 10 12 13 14 14 15 16 16 16 17 17 18 18 19 20 21 22 24
DATA> END
MTB > DESCRIBE C1

                N      MEAN    MEDIAN    TRMEAN     STDEV    SEMEAN
C1             20    15.850    16.000    15.944     4.464     0.998

              MIN       MAX        Q1        Q3
C1          6.000    24.000    13.250    18.750
```

FIGURE 1–22   MINITAB-Produced Histogram, Example 1–2

```
MTB > HISTOGRAM C1

Histogram of C1    N = 20

Midpoint    Count
        6      1    *
        8      0
       10      2    **
       12      1    *
       14      3    ***
       16      4    ****
       18      4    ****
       20      2    **
       22      2    **
       24      1    *
MTB > STOP
```

FIGURE 1–23   MINITAB Commands and Output for Stem-and-Leaf Display of Example 1–7

```
MTB > READ 'ccc.dat' into C1
      42 ROWS READ
MTB > STEM-AND-LEAF C1

Stem-and-leaf of C1        N = 42
Leaf Unit = 1.0
    4     1 1223
    9     1 55567
   18     2 011122234
  (7)     2 6777899
   17     3 0124
   13     3 57
   11     4 112
    8     4 57
    6     5 023
    3     5 6
    2     6 02
```

1-11   Summary and Review of Terms

In this chapter we introduced many terms and concepts. We defined a **population** as the set of all measurements in which we are interested. We defined a **sample** as a smaller group of measurements chosen from the larger population (the concept of random sampling will be discussed in detail in Chapter 4). We defined the process of using the sample for drawing conclusions about the population as **statistical inference.**

We discussed **descriptive statistics** as quantities computed from our data. We also defined the following statistics: **percentile,** a point below which lie a specified percentage of the data, and **quartile,** a percentile point in multiples of 25. The first quartile, the 25th percentile point, is also called the lower quartile. The 50th percentile point is the second quartile, also called the middle quartile, or the **median.** The 75th percentile is the third quartile, or the upper quartile. We defined the **interquartile range** as the difference between the upper and lower quartiles. We said that the median is a measure of central tendency, and we defined two other measures of central tendency: the **mode,** which is a *most frequent* value, and the **mean.** We called the mean the most important measure of central tendency, or location, of the data set. We said that the mean is the average of all the data points and is the point where the entire distribution of data points balances.

We defined measures of variability: the **range,** the **variance,** and the **standard deviation.** We defined the range as the difference between the largest and smallest data points. The variance was defined as the average squared deviation of the data points from their mean. For a sample (rather than a population), we saw that this averaging is done by dividing the sum of the squared deviations from the mean by $n - 1$ instead of by n. We defined the standard deviation as the square root of the variance.

We discussed grouped data and **frequencies** of occurrence of data points in **classes** defined by intervals of numbers. We defined **relative frequencies** as the absolute frequencies, or counts, divided by the total number of data points. We saw how to construct a **histogram** of a data set: a graph of the frequencies of the data. We mentioned **skewness,** a measure of the asymmetry of the histogram of the data set. We also mentioned **kurtosis,** a measure of the flatness of the distribution. We introduced **Chebyshev's theorem** and the **empirical rule** as ways of determining the proportions of data lying within several standard deviations of the mean.

We defined four scales of measurement of data: **nominal**—name only; **ordinal**—data that can be ordered as greater than or less than; **interval**—with meaningful distances as intervals of numbers; and **ratio**—a scale where ratios of distances are also meaningful.

The next topic we discussed was graphical techniques. These extended the idea of a histogram. We saw how a **frequency polygon** may be used instead of a histogram. We also saw how to construct an **ogive:** a cumulative frequency graph of a data set. We also talked about **bar graphs,** and **pie charts,** which are types of charts for displaying data, both categorical and numerical.

Then we discussed **exploratory data analysis,** a statistical area devoted to analyzing data using graphical techniques and other techniques that do not make restrictive assumptions about the structure of the data. Here we encountered two useful techniques for plotting data in a way that sheds light on their structure: **stem-and-leaf displays** and **box plots.** We saw that a stem-and-leaf display, which can be drawn quickly, is a type of histogram that makes use of the decimal structure of our number system. We saw how a box plot is made out of five quantities: the median, the two **hinges,** and the two **whiskers.** And we saw how the whiskers, as well as outliers and suspected outliers, are determined by the **inner fences** and **outer fences;** the first lies at a distance of 1.5 times the interquartile range from the hinges, and the second is found at 3 times the interquartile range from the hinges.

ADDITIONAL PROBLEMS

1–58. Choose a stock from among the ones listed in *The Wall Street Journal*, and follow its price for two weeks. Find the mean price and the variance. (Assume the data are a sample.)

1–59. Twenty randomly chosen people are shown a television commercial and asked to rank it as to overall appeal on a scale of 0 to 100. The results are given below.

      89, 75, 59, 96, 88, 71, 43, 62, 80, 92, 76, 72, 67, 60, 79, 85, 77, 83, 87, 53

Find the mean, variance, and standard deviation of the sample of ratings.

1–60. The following data are the number of tons shipped weekly across the Pacific by a shipping company.

      398, 412, 560, 476, 544, 690, 587, 600, 613, 457, 504, 477, 530, 641, 359, 566,

      452, 633, 474, 499, 580, 606, 344, 455, 505, 396, 347, 441, 390, 632, 400, 582

Assume these data represent an entire population. Find the population mean and the population standard deviation.

1–61. Group the data in problem 1–60 into classes, and draw a histogram of the frequency distribution.

1–62. Find the 90th percentile, the quartiles, and the range of the data in problem 1–60.

1–63. The following data are numbers of color television sets manufactured per day at a given plant: 15, 16, 18, 19, 14, 12, 22, 23, 25, 20, 32, 17, 34, 25, 40, 41. Draw a frequency polygon and an ogive for these data.

1–64. Construct a stem-and-leaf display for the data in problem 1–63.

1–65. Construct a box plot for the data in problem 1–63. What can you say about the data?

1–66. The following data are the number of cars passing a point on a highway per minute: 10, 12, 11, 19, 22, 21, 23, 22, 24, 25, 23, 21, 28, 26, 27, 27, 29, 26, 22, 28, 30, 32, 25, 37, 34, 35, 62. Construct a stem-and-leaf display of these data. What does the display tell you about the data?

1–67. For the data in Problem 1–66, construct a box plot. What does the box plot tell you about these data?

1–68. Following are data on U.S. market share for Japanese car makers:

Who's Hot and Who's Not

	1990 U.S. market share*	Percent change from previous year
Toyota	7.64%	17.5
Honda	6.12	14.3
Nissan	4.49	−1.5
Mazda	2.52	7.2
Mitsubishi	1.38	34.0
Subaru	0.80	−14.9
Isuzu	0.80	−2.4
Suzuki	0.15	−28.6
Daihatsu	0.11	—

*Vehicles sold under Japanese nameplates, including cars and light trucks.
From *Business Week,* January 21, 1991, p. 37.

Draw a bar graph of these data and a pie chart showing the total percentage of Japanese cars in the U.S. market for the period of this study.

Problems 1–69 through 1–72 refer to the following data on corporate profitability (five-year average return on equity).

Company	Percent	Company	Percent	Company	Percent
Apparel & shoes		**Gas distributors**		**Personal products**	
Jones Apparel Group	55.0	Nicor	16.2	Avon Products	60.2
Stride Rite	28.2	MCN	14.6	Tambrands	41.1
NIKE	27.2	Piedmont Natural Gas	13.3	Johnson & Johnson	30.6
Fruit of the Loom	25.2	Washington Gas Light	12.3	Kimberly-Clark	20.2
Liz Claiborne	23.9	Peoples Energy	12.0	First Brands	19.9
Reebok International	22.5	Laclede Gas	11.6	Church & Dwight	19.8
Phillips-Van Heusen	21.9	Brooklyn Union Gas	11.1	Stanhome	19.2
VF	18.7	Atlanta Gas Light	10.6	Clorox	18.8
Instrument Systems	18.2	UtiliCorp United	10.3	BIC	17.8
Justin Industries	17.4	Assoc Natural Gas	9.7	Colgate-Palmolive	16.9
Oxford Industries	13.0	Wicor	9.2	Procter & Gamble	16.8
Russell	13.0	UGI	8.9	Duracell Intl	15.8
Kellwood	10.7	Southwest Gas	3.9	Alberto-Culver	15.0
Tultex	7.3	Eastern Enterprises	3.6	Block Drug	12.9
Median	17.8	Median	10.9	Service Corp Intl	12.8
Home Furnishings		**Software**		Carter-Wallace	10.6
Mohawk Industries	34.8	Microsoft	39.7	Helene Curtis Inds	10.0
Newell Co	20.9	Oracle Systems	30.7	Gibson Greetings	9.8
Rubbermaid	20.9	Computer Associates	27.5	Median	16.9
Leggett & Platt	16.0	Novell	24.3	**International oils**	
Premark International	12.1	Lotus Development	16.2	Exxon	14.7
La-Z-Boy Chair	11.9	Legent	16.1	Texaco	12.8
Kimball International	11.4	Cadence Design	9.8	Royal Dutch Petroleum	10.8
Oneida	8.9	Policy Management Sys	5.5	Amoco	10.6
Bassett Furniture Inds	8.4	Medians	16.2	Chevron	10.4
Springs Industries	6.3			Mobil	10.3
Fieldcrest Cannon	4.4			British Petroleum	7.0
Armstrong World Inds	3.6			Median	10.6
Thomas Industries	3.4				
LADD Furniture	1.0				
Median	10.1				

Reproduced by permission from the Annual Report on American Industry, *Forbes,* January 2, 1995, pp. 123–168.

1–69.   For each of the six industry groups in the preceding data set, find the mean and the median. Compare your results with the medians reported in the table. Which of the two measures is more meaningful and why? Discuss.

1–70.   For each of the industry groups in the data set, find the range, the variance, and the standard deviation.

1–71.   Construct a box plot and a stem-and-leaf display for each industry group in the *Forbes* data set. Also construct a box plot for the entire data set, ignoring industry classification. Write a summary about outliers.

1–72. In the *Forbes* data set, ignore the industry groups and combine all the return data. Find the mean, median, mode, range, standard deviation, quartiles, and 10th and 90th percentiles. How do firms in the various industry groups compare in performance level with an average firm in the combined group?

The following table lists the leading fixed 30-year mortgage rates in the 24 largest metro areas, based on mortgages of $75,000.

Region	Institution	Rate as of Jan. 4	Percent Down	Points	Monthly payment
Atlanta	Citizens & Southern	9.00%	5	3.25	$603.47
Baltimore	Paine Webber Mortgage Finance	9.25	5	2.50	617.01
Boston	First New England Mortgage	9.13	5	2.00	610.23
Chicago	Sears Mortgage	9.25	5	3.00	617.01
Cleveland	Third Federal S&L	9.00	20	3.00	603.47
Dallas	Texas Commerce	9.13	10	3.00	610.23
Denver	WestAmerica Mortgage	8.75	20	4.00	590.03
Detroit	Detroit Savings	9.25	5	2.88	617.01
Houston	Liberty Savings	9.00	5	3.38	603.47
Los Angeles	Estate Mortgage	9.38	10	2.00	623.81
Miami	First Financial of Boston	9.00	5	3.50	603.47
Minneapolis	Metropolitan Financial Mortgage	9.13	5	3.25	610.23
New York City	Executive Mortgage	9.25	10	2.50	617.01
N. New Jersey	Maryland National Mortgage	9.13	5	2.75	610.23
Philadelphia	Huntington Mortgage	9.13	5	3.00	610.23
Phoenix	GMAC Mortgage	9.13	10	2.50	610.23
Pittsburgh	NVR Mortgage	9.00	5	2.75	603.47
San Diego	Weyerhaeuser Mortgage	9.25	5	2.75	617.01
San Francisco	Fleet Mortgage	9.50	10	2.00	630.64
Seattle	Olympic Savings	9.25	5	2.00	617.01
St. Louis	Magnum Mortgage	9.25	5	2.50	617.01
S.W. Connecticut	Shelter Mortgage	9.00	10	2.75	603.47
Tampa	American Home Funding	9.50	5	1.50	630.64
Washington, D.C.	TransCoastal Mortgage	9.00	5	3.00	603.47

National average: 9.66%, 9.96% a month ago, 9.92% a year ago.
Reproduced by permission from *Money*, February 1991, p. 26.)

1–73. In the table find the mean and the median rate (as of January 4). Compare the mean with the median. Also compare the mean with the national average reported at the bottom of the table. Discuss the reasons for the differences you may find.

1–74. Find the variance and the standard deviation of mortgage rates. Does Chebyshev's theorem apply to this data set? Does the empirical rule seem to apply?

1–75. Find the mode(s) of the distribution of rates and of the distribution of points from the leading mortgage rates table.

1–76. Again referring to the table, draw a box plot of monthly payments. Do you identify any outliers? Which cities, if any, are unusual with respect to any of the variables in the table?

1–77. Draw a stem-and-leaf display of monthly payments and of points using the data in the table above. Also draw histograms of these variables. What do you learn about the distributions of these variables?

1–78.   Interpret the following MINITAB computer output.

```
MTB > DESCRIBE C1

              N    MEAN   MEDIAN   TRMEAN   STDEV   SEMEAN
CI           12   39.08    34.00    33.90   19.31     5.57

             MIN     MAX      Q1      Q3
C1         30.00  100.00   32.00   35.75

MTB > HISTO C1

Histogram of C1   N = 12

Midpoint   Count
      30       8 ********
      40       3 ***
      50       0
      60       0
      70       0
      80       0
      90       0
     100       1 *
```

1–79.   Interpret the graph.

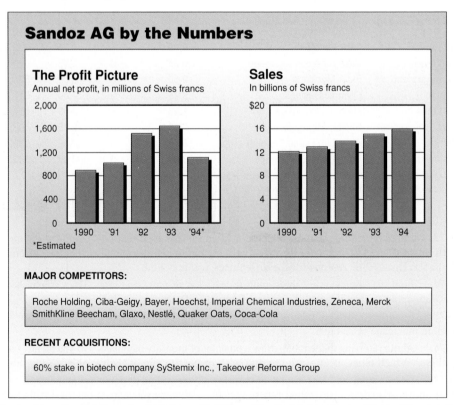

Reprinted from *The Wall Street Journal,* February 21, 1995, p. B4, with data from Sandoz AG, Merrill Lynch & Co.

1–80. Interpret this graph.

Reproduced from the *New York Times,* Business Day, March 21, 1995, p. D9

1–81. Examine the following two charts.

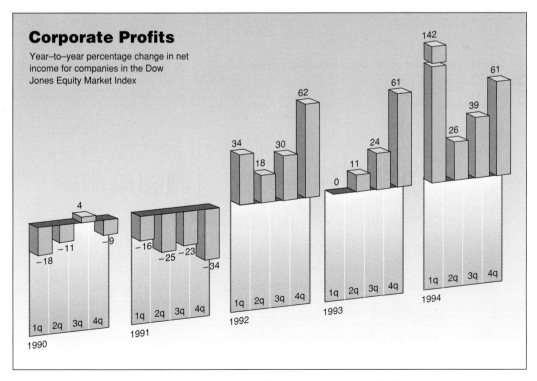

Reprinted from F. Bleakley, "Companies' Profits Surged on Higher Prices, Cost Cuts," *The Wall Street Journal,* February 21, 1995, p. A9.

Sector-by-Sector Performance

	Net Income in Billions 4th Qtr 1994	Percent Change
Basic Materials	$ 4.31	+ 442%
Energy	5.34	+ 69
Industrial	4.94	+ 102
Consumer, Cyclical	10.18	+ 42
Consumer, Noncyclical	10.03	+ 89
Technology	8.49	+ 61
Financial Services	11.08	− 2
Utilities	4.29	+5,035
Conglomerates	0.90	− 44
TOTAL	$59.55	+ 61%

Interpret the Corporate Profits chart.

1–82. Use the data in the chart of problem 1–81 to compute mean and standard deviation (population) of quarterly percentage change in net income for companies in the Dow Jones Equity Market Index.

1–83. Using the sector-by-sector performance chart data from problem 1–81, construct a pie chart of net income per sector for the fourth quarter of 1994.

1–84. Using the same chart, find the mean and median percentage change in sector net income. Identify outliers and comment on them. Also draw a box plot of these data.

1–85. In the information below, which sales were more variable in volume from bestseller to bestseller during the period in question (Feb. 1995), hardcovers or paperbacks? Why? Can you think of a logical explanation?

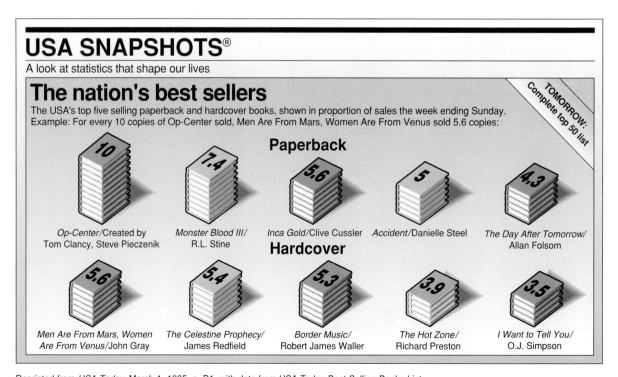

USA SNAPSHOTS®

A look at statistics that shape our lives

The nation's best sellers

The USA's top five selling paperback and hardcover books, shown in proportion of sales the week ending Sunday. Example: For every 10 copies of Op-Center sold, Men Are From Mars, Women Are From Venus sold 5.6 copies:

TOMORROW: Complete top 50 list

Paperback

10	7.4	5.6	5	4.3
Op-Center/Created by Tom Clancy, Steve Pieczenik	Monster Blood III/ R.L. Stine	Inca Gold/Clive Cussler	Accident/Danielle Steel	The Day After Tomorrow/ Allan Folsom

Hardcover

5.6	5.4	5.3	3.9	3.5
Men Are From Mars, Women Are From Venus/John Gray	The Celestine Prophecy/ James Redfield	Border Music/ Robert James Waller	The Hot Zone/ Richard Preston	I Want to Tell You/ O.J. Simpson

Reprinted from *USA Today*, March 1, 1995, p. D1, with data from USA Today Best-Selling Books List.

1–86. Comment on this graphic display. Are values proportional to height or area of icons?

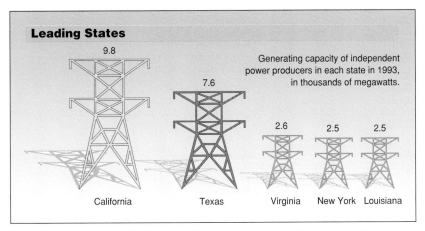

Reprinted from *The New York Times*, Business Day, March 17, 1995, p. D1, with data from National Independent Energy Producers.

Median U.S. Home Prices

Home resale prices rose 0.8% on average last year. Here are 1994 fourth-quarter prices in 133 metropolitan areas that saw the biggest gains and losses compared with fourth-quarter 1993:

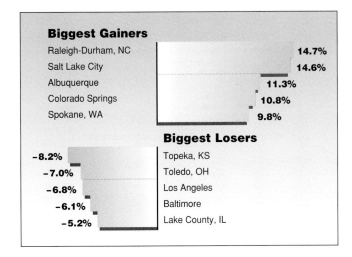

Metro Area	Median Price	Change from '93
Akron, Ohio	$83,300	−1.1%
Albany, N.Y.	$112,300	−2.7%
Albuquerque, N.M.	$114,500	11.3%
Amarillo, Texas	$63,800	−2.3%
Anaheim, Calif.	$215,000	0.1%
Appleton, Wis.	$80,200	3.0%
Atlanta	$93,400	1.1%
Atlantic City, N.J.	$107,300	−2.2%
Aurora, Ill.	$128,000	7.5%
Austin, Texas	$97,300	4.4%
Baltimore	$108,800	−6.1%
Baton Rouge	$77,100	−0.5%
Beaumont, Texas	$61,800	−4.8%

Metro Area	Median Price	Change from '93
Bergen, N.J.	$187,200	3.2%
Biloxi, Miss.	$72,900	2.2%
Birmingham, Ala.	$100,100	−0.1%
Boise, Idaho	$101,000	6.0%
Boston	$177,600	2.8%
Bradenton, Fla.	$90,300	3.3%
Buffalo	$83,700	0.1%
Canton, Ohio	$80,100	2.4%
Cedar Rapids, Iowa	$84,900	5.7%
Champaign, Ill.	$73,100	2.5%
Charleston, S.C.	$92,000	5.5%
Charleston, W.Va.	$78,100	6.3%
Charlotte, N.C.	$104,600	1.3%

(continued)

Metro Area	Median Price	Change from '93
Chattanooga, Tenn.	$77,700	5.1%
Chicago	$141,600	0.5%
Cincinnati	$96,400	4.4%
Cleveland	$98,100	2.4%
Colorado Springs	$105,500	10.8%
Columbia, S.C.	$84,900	−3.0%
Columbus, Ohio	$93,600	1.7%
Corpus Christi, Texas	$75,100	2.2%
Dallas	$92,300	−3.4%
Davenport, Iowa	$61,900	4.7%
Dayton, Ohio	$81,900	1.7%
Daytona Beach, Fla.	$69,900	0.4%
Denver	$119,000	9.2%
Des Moines	$82,000	−0.4%
Detroit	$85,800	2.3%
El Paso	$75,400	1.8%
Eugene, Ore.	$96,700	9.0%
Fargo, N.D.	$78,300	−1.3%
Fort Lauderdale, Fla.	$101,800	−1.6%
Fort Myers, Fla.	$76,900	0.8%
Fort Worth	$81,500	−3.4%
Gainesville, Fla.	$89,300	4.1%
Gary, Ind.	$88,000	4.5%
Grand Rapids, Mich.	$76,900	−1.4%
Green Bay, Wis.	$86,300	3.9%
Greensboro, N.C.	$98,900	0.8%
Greenville, S.C.	$88,500	2.8%
Hartford, Conn.	$130,800	−2.5%
Honolulu	$357,000	−0.8%
Houston	$77,600	−4.2%
Indianapolis	$89,200	2.1%
Jacksonville, Fla.	$82,300	3.0%
Kalamazoo, Mich.	$73,900	1.5%
Kansas City, Mo.	$87,700	4.9%
Knoxville, Tenn.	$90,100	3.7%
Lake County, Ill.	$124,500	−5.2%
Lansing, Mich.	$77,100	2.9%
Las Vegas	$111,000	1.0%
Lexington, Ky.	$88,600	5.2%
Lincoln, Neb.	$77,600	4.4%
Little Rock	$76,800	−3.4%
Los Angeles	$181,500	−6.8%
Louisville, Ky.	$80,900	8.4%
Madison, Wis.	$116,200	4.7%
Melbourne, Fla.	$77,600	2.2%
Memphis	$85,100	−1.8%
Miami	$103,300	4.1%
Middlesex, N.J.	$166,600	−1.3%
Milwaukee	$106,600	−1.2%
Minneapolis	$101,400	2.0%
Mobile, Ala.	$69,600	4.3%
Monmouth, N.J.	$133,800	−2.8%
Montgomery, Ala.	$81,700	−4.1%
Nashville	$99,500	7.1%

Metro Area	Median Price	Change from '93
Nassau, N.Y.	$154,600	−4.0%
Newark, N.J.	$181,800	−1.7%
New Haven, Conn.	$135,000	−2.1%
New Orleans	$77,800	1.4%
New York	$168,700	−2.5%
Norfolk, Va.	$101,600	−1.7%
Ocala, Fla.	$59,600	−4.5%
Oklahoma City	$65,700	−0.6%
Omaha	$75,800	3.6%
Orlando, Fla.	$89,200	−2.5%
Pensacola, Fla.	$74,600	−0.3%
Peoria, Ill.	$66,600	5.5%
Philadelphia	$115,400	−2.1%
Phoenix	$92,000	1.1%
Portland, Ore.	$120,000	9.5%
Providence, R.I.	$115,200	−1.1%
Raleigh/Durham, N.C.	$124,500	14.7%
Reno, Nev.	$133,500	1.7%
Richland, Wash.	$108,100	−0.6%
Richmond, Va.	$99,200	7.4%
Riverside, Calif.	$127,200	−3.6%
Rochester, N.Y.	$84,800	0.4%
Rockford, Ill.	$85,800	2.5%
Sacramento, Calif.	$121,500	−4.7%
Saginaw, Mich.	$57,000	0.4%
St. Louis	$82,900	−0.7%
Salt Lake City	$102,200	14.6%
San Antonio	$77,300	2.0%
San Diego	$170,400	−3.6%
San Francisco	$254,500	2.5%
Sarasota, Fla.	$97,900	1.1%
Seattle	$156,400	2.8%
Shreveport, La.	$70,900	6.9%
Sioux Falls, S.D.	$80,100	5.7%
South Bend, Ind.	$61,600	−3.0%
Spokane, Wash.	$97,300	9.8%
Springfield, Ill.	$74,400	1.9%
Springfield, Mo.	$75,500	7.9%
Syracuse, N.Y.	$81,400	−2.7%
Tacoma, Wash.	$119,400	4.8%
Tallahassee, Fla.	$98,700	2.0%
Tampa	$78,200	2.0%
Toledo, Ohio	$69,400	−7.0%
Topeka, Kan.	$61,300	−8.2%
Trenton, N.J.	$126,300	1.4%
Tucson, Ariz.	$91,400	4.5%
Tulsa	$73,300	1.8%
Washington	$155,800	−1.1%
Waterloo, Iowa	$55,000	4.8%
West Palm Beach, Fla.	$120,000	0.8%
Wichita, Kan.	$72,500	−0.1%
Worcester, Mass.	$130,000	0.1%
Youngstown, Ohio	$61,900	−0.5%
USA	$107,900	0.8%

Reprinted by permission from *USA Today*, February 10, 1995, with data from National Association of Realtors.

1–87. Use the table Median U.S. Home Prices. Find the *average* median U.S. home price and compare it with the USA median at the bottom of the table.

1–88. Using the same table, find the median of the data in the table. What is the difference between the median of the medians and the USA median? Explain.

1–89. In your opinion, why are medians reported in the table rather than means?

1–90. Draw a box plot of the data and identify outliers. Can you explain the reasons for the outliers?

Case 1   *POWER TO THE CREDITORS*

The traditional corporate bond is rigged against investors. When interest rates rise, it falls in value, just like a Treasury bond. But, unlike Treasury bonds, many corporate bonds don't rise much when interest rates fall. That's because corporate issuers of these bonds reserve the right to call them in early, at only a slight premium over the issue price. Heads you lose, tails you break even.

You can grab back some of this power by buying a bond with a built-in put option. This put gives you the right, but not the obligation, to sell the bond back to the issuer prior to maturity. The put exercise price is usually at par value. Puttable bonds are also generally noncallable—that is, the issuer does not have the right to force you to redeem early.

Nothing is free on Wall Street. You pay for this put feature in the form of reduced yield. Dennis Adler, a corporate bond strategist at Salomon Brothers, says the yield sacrifice on a noncallable 30-year A-rated corporate bond that can be put to the issuer at par five years out is perhaps 20 basis points (a fifth of a percentage point).

Giving up some yield makes sense for someone who is nervous about his principal. If worry about a coming spike in interest rates has kept you from buying long bonds at all, then puttables are definitely worth a look.

One important caveat here: Almost all bond puts are "European-style," meaning they can be exercised only for a very short time—perhaps on one specific day. Still, having only one day to redeem a bond is better than having none at all.

A few municipal bonds and about 900 corporate issues have some kind of put feature. But note that for many of the corporate issues, the put becomes exercisable only after a change in corporate control. These are called poison puts and are seldom of value to the investor. They are installed to protect the management.

The table lists 10 noncallable corporate bonds that can be put back to the issuer no matter who controls the company. In evaluating bonds like these, don't look at the maturity with your usual frame of reference. Often it's better to think of the put exercise date as the maturity.

To illustrate, look at the NBD Bank 8.25s of 2024. The Aa3-rated bond currently sells for 102 to yield 8.1% to maturity. But because the bond can be sold back to NBD at par on Nov. 1, 2004, it is easier to think of this as a 10-year bond yielding 7.9% to maturity. You'll redeem the bond in 2004 if interest rates have climbed or NBD's credit quality has deteriorated.

Alternatively, if rates have fallen and NBD still looks like a good bank, then you will hang on to the paper. At that point you will have, in effect, a new 20-year bond yielding 8.25% to maturity. In this light, your 30-year bond with a 10-year put becomes a 10-year bond with an attached call option on a 20-year bond. With bonds like this one the creditor is in the driver's seat.

Redeeming Virtue

Issuer	Coupon	Maturity	Moody's Rating	Amount Issued ($mil)	Recent Price	Yield to		Date of First Put	Yield Sacrifice*
						Put	Maturity		
Columbia/HCA Healthcare	8.360	4/15/24	A3	$150	$101.21	7.46%	8.25%	4/15/04	0.41%
Corning	7.625	8/1/24	A2	100	99.36	7.72	7.68	8/1/04	0.62
Eastman Chemical	7.625	6/15/24	Baa1	200	96.90	8.05	7.90	6/15/06	0.42
Eaton	8.000	8/15/06	A2	100	102.56	6.10	7.66	8/15/96	0.33
NBD Bank	8.250	11/1/24	Aa3	250	102.20	7.92	8.07	11/1/04	0.50
New England Telephone	7.875	11/15/29	Aa2	350	102.77	6.11	7.65	11/15/96	0.91
New Jersey Bell	7.850	11/15/29	Aaa	150	103.66	6.92	7.55	11/15/99	0.61
Pennsylvania Power & Light	7.700	10/1/09	A2	200	101.86	7.21	7.49	10/1/99	0.48
RJR Nabisco	6.800	9/1/01	Baa3	100	97.83	7.79	7.23	9/2/97	1.19
Torchmark	8.250	8/15/09	A3	100	101.27	7.28	8.10	8/15/96	0.34

*Yield forfeited by favoring puttable bond over nonputtable bond of comparable maturity and credit quality.
Sources: Bloomberg Financial Markets; Salomon Brothers Fixed Income Research.

What are the types of variables here? What are the scales of measurement? Explain the information in the article and table. Use the statistical methods described in this chapter to help you better understand the quantitative information in the table.

Reprinted from "Power to the Creditors," Eric S. Hardy, *Forbes,* March 27, 1995, p. 63.

2

PROBABILITY

2 - 1 INTRODUCTION

Probability is everywhere. It affects all aspects of our lives.

Giants Win Is No Surprise—They Had a 65.635738% Chance

BY STEVE RUBENSTEIN

The San Francisco Giants had a 65.6 percent chance of winning yesterday's game, said a statistics professor who worked it out.

"It wasn't that difficult a calculation," said statistics professor Bill Kaigh.

(Continued)

Today, statistics say, the Giants have a 100 percent chance of winning yesterday's game. Numbers don't lie.

"The estimates are derived from principal components and linear and logistic regression analyses of historical data," said Kaigh, a professor at the University of Texas-El Paso, shortly before Will Clark hit a triple to center field to give the Giants the lead.

Five thousand statisticians are in town this week for the meeting of the American Statistical Association. Kaigh, addressing a morning seminar on sports statistics, passed out a 24-page research paper showing exactly why the Giants would probably win yesterday's game, which they did, 10-7.

The formula involves multiplying the Giants' home-game record by the Cincinnati Reds' away-game record subtracted from one and dividing the whole thing by something else with four variables in it.

The answer is actually 65.635738 percent. That explains why Kurt Manwaring hit a two-run homer in the sixth inning.

Reprinted from the *San Francisco Chronicle,* August 10, 1993, p. A15.

probability is a quantitative measure of uncertainty—a number that conveys the strength of our belief in the occurrence of an uncertain event. Since life is full of uncertainty, people have always been interested in evaluating probabilities. The statistician I. J. Good suggests that "the theory of probability is much older than the human species," since the assessment of uncertainty incorporates the idea of learning from experience, which most creatures do.[1]

Among humans the history and lore of probability are often steeped in romantic legend about gambling. In the third book of the great epic of India, the *Mahabarata,* written before AD 400, King Rtuparna demonstrates a knowledge of statistics to Nala, a man possessed by the demigod of dicing. Rtuparna is described as able to estimate the number of leaves on a tree based on the number of leaves on a randomly chosen branch. This form of estimation is the essence of statistical inference. The story seems to prove that long ago Indians knew something about statistics. Rtuparna further says:

I of dice possess the science and in numbers thus am skilled.

Which seems to suggest a familiarity with the laws of probability.[2]

Further investigations will have to be conducted before we can determine to what extent probability and its relationship to statistical inference were known to the Indians of the fourth century. They certainly had some familiarity with the subject.

The rabbis of the early centuries following the destruction of the second Temple in Jerusalem also had some familiarity with the laws of probability. As evidenced in the Talmud (written about the same time as the *Mahábarata*), probability arguments were widely used for determining issues related to dietary laws, paternity, taxes, adultery, and other matters. There are some indications that these early scholars were familiar with the rules of addition and multiplication of probabilities and were able to compare probabilities and make judgments based on their relative magnitudes.[3]

---

[1] I. J. Good, "Kinds of Probability," *Science,* no. 129 (February 20, 1959), pp. 443–47.

[2] See Ian Hacking, *The Emergence of Probability* (New York: Cambridge University Press, 1975), p. 7.

[3] See Nachum L. Rabinovitch, "Probability in the Talmud," *Biometrika* 56, no. 2 (1969), pp. 437–41.

The theory of probability as we know it today, however, was largely developed by European mathematicians such as Galileo Galilei (1564–1642), Blaise Pascal (1623–1662), Pierre de Fermat (1601–1665), Abraham de Moivre (1667–1754), and others.

As in India, the development of probability theory in Europe is often associated with gamblers, who pursued their interests in the famous European casinos, such as the one at Monte Carlo. Many books on probability and statistics tell the story of the Chevalier de Mére, a French gambler who enlisted the help of Pascal in an effort to obtain the probabilities of winning at certain games of chance, leading to much of the European development of probability.

Today, the theory of probability is an indispensable tool in the analysis of situations involving uncertainty. It forms the basis for inferential statistics as well as for other fields that require quantitative assessments of chance occurrences, such as quality control, management decision analysis, and areas in physics, biology, engineering, and economics.

While most analyses using the theory of probability have nothing to do with games of chance, gambling models provide the clearest examples of probability and its assessment. The reason is that games of chance usually involve dice, cards, or roulette wheels—mechanical devices. If we assume there is no cheating, these mechanical devices tend to produce sets of outcomes that are *equally likely*, and this allows us to compute probabilities of winning at these games.

Suppose that a single die is rolled and that you win a dollar if the number 1 or 2 appears. What are your chances of winning a dollar? Since there are six equally likely numbers (assuming the die is fair) and you win as a result of either of two numbers appearing, the probability that you win is 2/6, or 1/3.

$$P(1 \text{ or } 2) = P(1) + P(2) - P(1 \cap 2)$$
$$= \frac{1}{6} + \frac{1}{6} - 0$$
$$= \frac{2}{6} = \frac{1}{3}$$

As another example, consider the following situation. An analyst follows the price movements of IBM stock for a period of time and wants to assess the probability that the stock will go up in price in the next week. This is a different type of situation. The analyst does not have the luxury of a known set of equally likely outcomes, where "IBM stock goes up next week" is one of a given number of these equally likely possibilities. Therefore, the analyst's assessment of the probability of the event will be a *subjective* one. The analyst will base his or her assessment of this probability on knowledge of the situation, guesses, or intuition. Different people may assign different probabilities to this event depending on their experience and knowledge; hence the name *subjective* probability.

Objective probability is probability based on symmetry of games of chance or similar situations. It is also called *classical probability*. This probability is based on the idea that certain occurrences are equally likely (the term *equally likely* is intuitively clear and will be used as a starting point for our definitions): the numbers 1, 2, 3, 4, 5, and 6 on a fair die are each equally likely to occur. Another type of objective probability is long-term *relative-frequency* probability. If, in the long run, 20 out of 1,000 consumers given a taste test for a new soup like the taste, then we say that the probability that a given consumer will like the soup is 20/1,000 = 0.02. If the probability that a head will apppear on any one toss of a coin is 1/2, then if the coin is tossed a large number of times, the proportion of heads will approach 1/2. Like the probability in games of chance and other symmetrical situations, relative-frequency probability is objective in the sense that no personal judgment is involved.

FIGURE 2–5   Sample Space for Drawing a Card

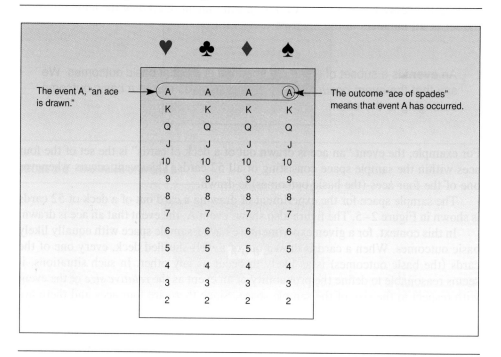

FIGURE 2–6   The Events A and ♥ and Their Union and Intersection

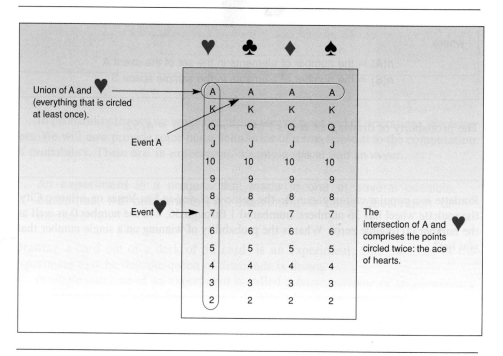

Let's now demonstrate the meaning of union and intersection with the example of drawing a card from a deck. Let A be the event that an ace is drawn, and ♥ the event that a heart is drawn. The sample space is shown in Figure 2–6. Note that the event A ∩ ♥ is the event that the card drawn is both an ace and a heart (i.e., the ace of hearts). The event A ∪ ♥ is the event that the card drawn is either an ace or a heart or both.

PROBLEMS

2–1. What are the two main types of probability?

2–2. What is an event? What is the union of two events? What is the intersection of two events?

2–3. Define a sample space.

2–4. Define the probability of an event.

2–5. Let G be the event that a girl is born. Let F be the event that a baby over 5 pounds is born. Characterize the union and the intersection of the two events.

2–6. Consider the event that a player scores a point in a game against team A and the event that the same player scores a point in a game against team B. What is the union of the two events? What is the intersection of the two events?

2–7. Let event A be acceptance to graduate school and event B be getting a job offer. What are the union and intersection of the two events?

2–8. The Ford Motor Company advertises its cars on radio and on television. The company is interested in assessing the probability that a randomly chosen person is exposed to at least one of these two modes of advertising. If we define event R as the event that a randomly chosen person was exposed to a radio advertisement and event T as the event that the person was exposed to a television commercial, define R ∪ T and R ∩ T in this context.

2–9. A brokerage firm deals in stocks and bonds. An analyst for the firm is interested in assessing the probability that a person who inquires about the firm will eventually purchase stock (event S) or bonds (event B). Define the union and the intersection of these two events.

2–10. Mathematician John Paulos makes the point that most people have no grasp of the probabilities of events that may affect them: They tend to have great fear of publicized events with small probability, while not worrying at all about events with much higher probability. As an example, Paulos gives the following data: In 1985, 28 million Americans traveled abroad, and 39 of them were killed by terrorists. Based on this information, what is the probability of being killed by terrorists while traveling abroad? Compare this with another statistic reported by Paulos: 1 in 5,300 Americans was killed in an automobile accident in 1985.

2–11. An airline passenger lost her luggage. When it finally arrived a few days later, she casually asked the ticket agent how often things like this happen. The ticket agent said that, in his experience, a piece of luggage in that particular airport was reported lost about once every two days. He also said that two flights arrive every day, each flight carrying approximately 200 passengers. The average passenger was reported to check in an average of two pieces of luggage. Given this information, what is the probability that you will not find your suitcase (or one of your suitcases, if you check more than one) upon arrival at this airport?

2–12. The European version of roulette is different from the American version in that the European roulette wheel doesn't have 00. How does this change the probability of winning when betting on a single number? European casinos charge a small admission fee, which is not the case in American casinos. Does this make sense to you, based on your answer to the earlier question?

2-3   Basic Rules for Probability

We have explored probability on a somewhat intuitive level and have seen rules that help us evaluate probabilities in special cases when we have a known sample space with equally likely basic outcomes. We will now look at some general probability rules that hold regardless of the particular situation or kind of probability (objective or subjective). First, let us give a general definition of probability.

> Probability is a measure of uncertainty. The **probability** of event A is a numerical measure of the likelihood of the event occurring.

The Range of Values

Probability obeys certain rules. The first rule sets the range of values that the probability measure may take.

> For any event, A, the probability $P(A)$ satisfies:
> $$0 \leq P(A) \leq 1 \tag{2-2}$$

When an event cannot occur, its probability is zero. The probability of the empty set is zero: $P(\emptyset) = 0$. In a deck where half the cards are red and half are black, the probability of drawing a green card is zero because the set corresponding to that event is the empty set: there are no green cards.

Events that are certain to occur have probability 1.00. The probability of the entire sample space S is equal to 1.00: $P(S) = 1.00$. If we draw a card out of a deck, 1 of the 52 cards in the deck will certainly be drawn, and so the probability of the sample space, the set of all 52 cards, is equal to 1.00.

Within the range of values 0 to 1, the greater the probability, the more confidence we have in the occurrence of the event in question. A probability of 0.95 implies a very high confidence in the occurrence of the event. A probability of 0.80 implies a high confidence. When the probability is 0.5, the event is as likely to occur as it is not to occur. When the probability is 0.2, the event is not very likely to occur. When we assign a probability of 0.05, we believe the event is unlikely to occur, and so on. Figure 2–7 is an informal aid in interpreting probability.

Note that probability is a measure that goes from 0 to 1. In everyday conversation we often describe probability in less formal terms. For example, people sometimes talk about **odds.** If the odds are 1 to 1, the probability is 1/2; if the odds are 1 to 2, the probability is 1/3; and so on. Also, people sometimes say, "The probability is 80 percent." Mathematically, this probability is 0.80.

The Rule of Complements

Our second rule for probability defines the probability of the complement of an event in terms of the probability of the original event. Recall that the complement of set A is denoted by $\overline{A}$.

FIGURE 2-7   Interpretation of a Probability

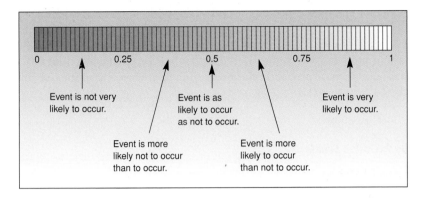

Probability of the complement:
$$P(\overline{A}) = 1 - P(A) \qquad\qquad (2\text{–}3)$$

As a simple example, if the probability of rain tomorrow is 0.3, then the probability of no rain tomorrow must be $1 - 0.3 = 0.7$. If the probability of drawing an ace is 4/52, then the probability of the drawn card not being an ace is $1 - 4/52 = 48/52$.

The Rule of Unions.   We now state a very important rule, the **rule of unions.** The rule of unions allows us to write the probability of the union of two events in terms of the probabilities of the two events and the probability of their intersection:[5]

The rule of unions:
$$P(A \cup B) = P(A) + P(B) - P(A \cap B) \qquad\qquad (2\text{–}4)$$

(The probability of the intersection of two events, $P(A \cap B)$, is called their **joint probability.**) The meaning of this rule is very simple and intuitive: When we add the probabilities of A and B, we are measuring, or counting, the probability of their intersection *twice*—once when measuring the relative size of A within the sample space, and once when doing this with B. Since the relative size, or probability, of the intersection of the two sets is counted twice, we subtract it once so that we are left with the true probability of the union of the two events (refer to Figure 2–6). Note that instead of finding the probability of A ∪ B by direct counting, we can use the rule of unions: We know that the probability of an ace is 4/52, the probability of a heart is 13/52, and the probability of their intersection—the drawn card being the ace

---

[5] The rule can be extended to more than two events. In the case of three events, we have $P(A \cup B \cup C) = P(A) + P(B) + P(C) - P(A \cap B) - P(A \cap C) - P(B \cap C) + P(A \cap B \cap C)$. With more events, this becomes even more complicated.

of hearts—is 1/52. Thus, $P(A \cup \heartsuit) = 4/52 + 13/52 - 1/52 = 16/52$, which is exactly what we find from direct counting.

The rule of unions is especially useful when we do not have the sample space for the union of events but do have the separate probabilities. For example, suppose your chance of being offered a certain job is 0.4, your probability of getting another job is 0.5, and your probability of being offered both jobs (i.e., the intersection) is 0.3. Using the rule of unions, your probability of being offered at least one of the two jobs (their union) is $0.4 + 0.5 - 0.3 = 0.6$.

Mutually Exclusive Events

When the sets corresponding to two events are disjoint (that is, have no intersection), the two events are called **mutually exclusive** (see Figure 2–4). For mutually exclusive events, the probability of the intersection of the events is zero. This is so because the intersection of the events is the empty set, and we know that the probability of the empty set, $\varnothing$, is zero.

For mutually exclusive events A and B:
$$P(A \cap B) = 0. \tag{2–5}$$

This fact gives us a special rule for unions of mutually exclusive events. Since the probability of the intersection of the two events is zero, there is no need to subtract $P(A \cap B)$ when computing the probability of the union of the two events. Therefore,

---

For mutually exclusive events A and B:
$$P(A \cup B) = P(A) + P(B) \tag{2–6}$$

This is not really a new rule since we can always use the rule of unions for the union of two events: If the events happen to be mutually exclusive, we subtract zero as the probability of the intersection.

Continuing our cards example, what is the probability of drawing either a heart or a club? We have: $P(\heartsuit \cup \clubsuit) = P(\heartsuit) + P(\clubsuit) = 13/52 + 13/52 = 26/52 = 1/2$. We need not subtract the probability of an intersection, since no card is a club and a heart.

PROBLEMS

2–13. Assign reasonable numerical probabilities to the three shaded region types in the chart on page 67.

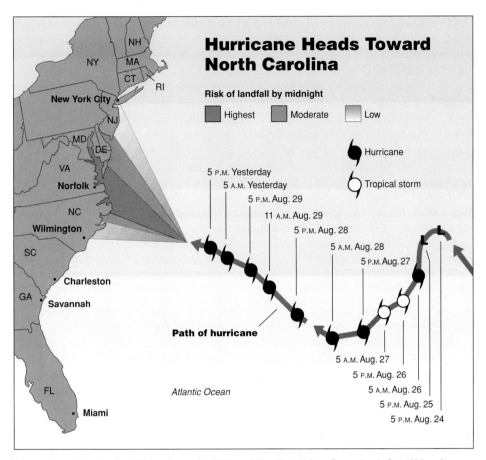

Hurricane Heads Toward North Carolina

Reprinted from *The New York Times,* August 31, 1993, p. A12, with data from Pennsylvania State University.

2–14. Compare the various risks of dying and their probabilities.

Radon Risk if You Have Never Smoked

Radon Level	If 1,000 people who never smoked were exposed to this level over a lifetime . . .	The risk of cancer from radon exposure compares to	What To Do
20 pCi/L	About 8 people could get lung cancer	The risk of being killed in a violent crime	Fix your home
10 pCi/L	About 4 people could get lung cancer		Fix your home
8 pCi/L	About 3 people could get lung cancer	10 times the risk of dying in an airplane crash	Fix your home
4 pCi/L	About 2 people could get lung cancer	The risk of drowning	Fix your home
			Consider fixing between 2 and 4 pCi/L
2 pCi/L	About 1 person could get lung cancer	The risk of dying in a home fire	
1.3 pCi/L	Less than 1 person could get lung cancer	(Average indoor radon level)	(Reducing randon levels below 2 pCi/L is difficult)
0.4 pCi/L	Less than 1 person could get lung cancer	(Average outdoor radon level)	

Note: If you are a former smoker, your risk may be higher.
Reprinted from U.S. Environmental Protection Agency, "A Citizen's Guide to Radon," March 1993.

2–15.   In the table in problem 2–14, are events mutually exclusive? Explain.

2–16.   According to a report on CNN Business News in April 1995, the probability of being murdered (in the United States) in one year is 9 in 100,000. How does this relate to the data in the table in problem 2–14?

2–17.   Assign a reasonable numerical probability to the statement: "Rain is very likely tonight."

2–18.   How likely is an event that has a 0.65 probability? Describe the probability in words.

2–19.   If a team has an 80% chance of winning a game, describe its chances in words.

2–20.   ShopperTrak is a hidden electric eye designed to count the number of shoppers entering a store. When two shoppers enter a store together, one walking in front of the other, the following probabilities apply: There is a 0.98 probability that the first shopper will be detected, a 0.94 probability that the second shopper will be detected, and a 0.93 probability that both of them will be detected by the device. What is the probability that the device will detect at least one of two shoppers entering together?

2–21.   A machine produces components for use in cellular phones. At any given time, the machine may be in one, and only one, of three states: operational, out of control, or down. From experience with this machine, a quality-control engineer knows that the probability that the machine is out of control at any moment is 0.02, and the probability that it is down is 0.015.

  a.   What is the relationship between the two events "machine is out of control" and "machine is down"?

  b.   When the machine is either out of control or down, a repairperson must be called. What is the probability that a repairperson must be called right now?

  c.   Unless the machine is down, it can be used to produce a single item. What is the probability that the machine can be used to produce a single component right now? What is the relationship between this event and the event "machine is down"?

2–22.   Following are age and sex data for 20 midlevel managers at a service company: 34 F, 49 M, 27 M, 63 F, 33 F, 29 F, 45 M, 46 M, 30 F, 39 M, 42 M, 30 F, 48 M, 35 F, 32 F, 37 F, 48 F, 50 M, 48 F, 61 F. A manager must be chosen at random to serve on a companywide committee that deals with personnel problems. What is the probability that the chosen manager will be either a woman or over 50 years old, or both? Solve both directly from the data, and by using the law of unions. What is the probability that the chosen manager will be under 30?

2–23.   Suppose that 25% of the population in a given area is exposed to a television commercial for Ford automobiles, and 34% is exposed to Ford's radio advertisements. Also, it is known that 10% of the population is exposed to both means of advertising. If a person is randomly chosen out of the entire population in this area, what is the probability that he or she was exposed to at least one of the two modes of advertising?

2–24.   Suppose it is known that 85% of the people who inquire about investment opportunities at a brokerage house end up purchasing stock, and 33% end up purchasing bonds. It is also known that 28% of the inquirers end up getting a portfolio with both stocks and bonds. If a person is just making an inquiry, what is the probability that he or she will get either stock or bonds, or both (that is, open any portfolio)?

2–25.   A firm has 550 employees; 380 of them have had at least some college education, and 412 of the employees underwent a vocational training program. Furthermore, 357 employees are both college-educated and have had the vocational training. If an employee is chosen at random, what is the probability that he or she is either college-educated or has had the training, or both?

2–26.   See the accompanying table of the performance of financial indexes. An investor chooses a financial index for her personal use in evaluating investments. Let us assume that the choice is made at random, with equal probability for each of the indexes in the table below, and without the investor knowing the information in this table.

- *a.* What is the probability that the index the investor has chosen lost money in the year ending January 1, 1991?
- *b.* What is the probability that the chosen index gained at least 200% in the 10 years preceding this date?
- *c.* What is the probability that the index had a yield of at least 5% in the last year, gained at least 35% in the preceding three years, or both?
- *d.* Are the event "index lost money in the preceding year" and the event "index had a yield of at least 4% in the preceding year" mutually exclusive? Explain.

	Percent Gain (or loss) to Jan. 1, 1991				
	1 Year	3 Years	5 Years	10 Years	Percent Yield
S&P 500 stock index	(3.1)	48.7	85.7	268.6	3.8
Dow Jones industrial average	(5.6)	38.3	65.8	216.5	3.9
Russell 2000 small-company stock index	(19.5)	16.9	12.7	125.3	2.3
Average equity fund	(5.3)	35.7	58.9	222.2	3.3
Salomon Bros. investment-grade bond index	9.1	34.8	59.6	240.8	8.5
Shearson Lehman Bros. long-term Treasury index	6.3	38.4	66.7	265.0	8.3
Shearson Lehman Bros. municipal bond index*	7.7	32.3	59.3	180.4	6.8

* All figures to Dec. 1, 1990.
Reproduced by permission from *Money* magazine (February 1991).

2–27. As part of a student project for the 1994 Science Fair in Orange, Massachusetts, 28 horses were made to listen to Mozart and heavy metal music. The results were as follows: 11 of the 28 horses exhibited some head movements when Mozart was played; 8 exhibited some head movements when the heavy metal was played; and 5 moved their heads when both were played. If a horse is chosen at random, what is the probability the horse exhibited head movements either to Mozart, or to heavy metal, or to both?

2–4 Conditional Probability

As a measure of uncertainty, probability depends on information. Thus, the probability you would give the event "Xerox stock price will go up tomorrow" depends on what you know about the company and its performance; the probability is *conditional* upon your information set. If you know much about the company, you may assign a different probability to the event than if you know little about the company. We may define the probability of event A *conditional* upon the occurrence of event B. In this example, event A may be the event that the stock will go up tomorrow, and event B may be a favorable quarterly report.

The **conditional probability** of event A given the occurrence of event B is

$$P(A \mid B) = \frac{P(A \cap B)}{P(B)} \tag{2–7}$$

assuming $P(B) \neq 0$.

The vertical line in $P(A|B)$ is read *given,* or *conditional upon.* The probability of event A given the occurrence of event B is defined as the probability of the intersection of A and B, divided by the probability of event B.

EXAMPLE 2-2

As part of a drive to modernize the economy, the government of an eastern European country is pushing for starting 100 new projects in computer development and telecommunications. Two American giants, IBM and AT&T, have signed contracts for these projects: 40 projects for IBM and 60 for AT&T. Of the IBM projects, 30 are in the computer area and 10 are in telecommunications; of the AT&T projects, 40 are in telecommunications and 20 are in computer areas. Given that a randomly chosen project is in telecommunications, what is the probability that it is undertaken by IBM?

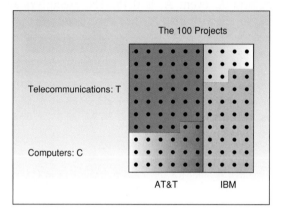

SOLUTION

$$P(\text{IBM} \,|\, \text{T}) = \frac{P(\text{IBM} \cap \text{T})}{P(\text{T})} = \frac{10/100}{50/100} = 0.2$$

But we see this directly from the fact that there are 50 telecommunications projects and 10 of them are by IBM. This confirms the definition of conditional probability in an intuitive sense.

When two events and their complements are of interest, it may be convenient to arrange the information in a **contingency table.** In Example 2–2 the table would be set up as follows:

	AT&T	IBM	Total
Telecommunication	40	10	50
Computers	20	30	50
Total	60	40	100

Contingency tables help us visualize information and solve problems. There are two other useful forms of the definition of conditional probability (Equation 2–7).

> Variation of the conditional probabililty formula:
>
> $$P(A \cap B) = P(A \mid B)P(B)$$
>
> and
>
> $$P(A \cap B) = P(B \mid A)P(A)$$
>
> (2–8)

These are illustrated in Example 2–3.

EXAMPLE 2-3

A consulting firm is bidding for two jobs, one with each of two large multinational corporations. The company executives estimate that the probability of obtaining the consulting job with firm A, event A, is 0.45. The executives also feel that if the company should get the job with firm A, then there is a 0.90 probability that firm B will also give the company the consulting job. What are the company's chances of getting *both* jobs?

SOLUTION

We are given $P(A) = 0.45$. We also know that $P(B \mid A) = 0.90$, and we are looking for $P(A \cap B)$, which is the probabillity that both A and B will occur. From the equation we have $P(A \cap B) = P(B \mid A)P(A) = 0.90 \times 0.45 = 0.405$.

EXAMPLE 2-4

Twenty-one percent of the executives in a large advertising firm are at the top salary level. It is further known that 40% of all the executives at the firm are women. Also, 6.4% of all executives are women *and* are at the top salary level. Recently, a question arose among executives at the firm as to whether there is any evidence of salary inequity. Assuming that some statistical considerations (explained in later chapters) are met, do the percentages reported above provide any evidence of salary inequity?

SOLUTION

To solve this problem, we pose it in terms of probabilities and ask whether the probability that a randomly chosen executive will be at the top salary level is approximately equal to the probability that the executive will be at the top salary level given the executive is a woman. To answer, we need to compute the probability that the executive will be at the top level given the executive is a woman. Defining T as the event of a top salary and W as the event that an executive is a woman, we get:

$$P(T \mid W) = \frac{P(T \cap W)}{P(W)} = \frac{0.064}{0.40} = 0.16$$

Since 0.16 is smaller than 0.21, we may conclude (subject to statistical considerations) that salary inequity does exist at the firm, because an executive is less likely to make a top salary if she is a woman.

Example 2–4 may incline us to think about the relations among different events. Are different events related, or are they independent of each other? In this example, we concluded that the two events, being a woman and being at the top salary level, are related in the sense that the event W made the event T less likely. Section 2–5 quantifies the relations among events and defines the concept of independence.

PROBLEMS

2–28. A financial analyst believes that if interest rates decrease in a given period, then the probability that the stock market will go up is 0.80. The analyst further believes that interest rates have a 0.40 chance of decreasing during the period in question. Given the above information, what is the probability that the market will go up and interest rates will go down during the period in question?

2–29. A bank loan officer knows that 12% of the bank's mortgage holders lose their jobs and default on the loan in the course of five years. She also knows that 20% of the bank's mortgage holders lose their jobs during this period. Given that one of her mortgage holders just lost his job, what is the probability that he will now default on the loan?

2–30. An express delivery service promises overnight delivery of all packages checked in before 5 P.M. The delivery service is not perfect, however, and sometimes delays do occur. Management knows that if delays occur in the evening flight to a major city from which distribution is made, then a package will not arrive on time with probability 0.25. It is also known that 10% of the evening flights to the major city are delayed. What percentage of the packages arrive late? (Assume that all packages are sent out on the evening flight to the major city and that all packages arrive on time if the evening flight is not delayed.)

2–31. The following table gives numbers of claims at a large insurance company by kind and by geographical region.

	East	South	Midwest	West
Hospitalization	75	128	29	52
Physician's visit	233	514	104	251
Outpatient treatment	100	326	65	99

Compute column totals and row totals. What do they mean?
- *a.* If a bill is chosen at random, what is the probability that it is from the Midwest?
- *b.* What is the probability that a randomly chosen bill is from the East?
- *c.* What is the probability that a randomly chosen bill is either from the Midwest or from the South? What is the relation between these two events?
- *d.* What is the probability that a randomly chosen bill is for hospitalization?
- *e.* Given that a bill is for hospitalization, what is the probability that it is from the South?
- *f.* Given that a bill is from the East, what is the probability that it is for physician's visit?
- *g.* Given that a bill is for outpatient treatment, what is the probability that it is from the West?
- *h.* What is the probability that a randomly chosen bill is either from the East or for outpatient treatment (or both)?
- *i.* What is the probability that a randomly selected bill is either for hospitalization or from the South (or both)?

2–32. One of the greatest problems in marketing research and other survey fields is the problem of nonresponse to surveys. In home interviews the problem arises when the respondent is not home at the time of the visit or, sometimes, simply refuses to answer questions. A market researcher believes that a respondent will answer all questions with probability 0.94 if found at home. He further believes that the probability that a given person will be found at home is 0.65. Given this information, what percentage of the interviews will be successfully completed?

2–33. An investment analyst collects data on stocks and notes whether or not dividends were paid and whether or not the stocks increased in price over a given period. Data are presented in the following table.

	Price Increase	No Price Increase	Total
Dividends paid	34	78	112
No dividends paid	85	49	134
Total	119	127	246

a. If a stock is selected at random out of the analyst's list of 246 stocks, what is the probability that it increased in price?

b. If a stock is selected at random, what is the probability that it paid dividends?

c. If a stock is randomly selected, what is the probability that it both increased in price and paid dividends?

d. What is the probability that a randomly selected stock neither paid dividends nor increased in price?

e. Given that a stock increased in price, what is the probability that it also paid dividends?

f. If a stock is known not to have paid dividends, what is the probability that it increased in price?

g. What is the probability that a randomly selected stock was worth holding during the period in question; that is, what is the probability that it either increased in price, or paid dividends, or both?

2–34. A recent cover article in *Business Week* dealt with the salaries of top executives at large corporations. The following table is compiled from data given in four tables in the article and lists the number of firms in the study where the top executive officer made over $1 million a year. The table also lists firms according to whether or not shareholder return was positive during the period in question.

	Top Executive Made More than $1 Million	Top Executive Made Less than $1 Million	Total
Shareholders made money	1	6	7
Shareholders lost money	2	1	3
Total	3	7	10

a. If a firm is randomly chosen from the list of 10 firms studied, what is the probability that its top executive made over $1 million a year?

b. If a firm is randomly chosen from the list, what is the probability that its shareholders lost money during the period studied?

c. Given that one of the firms in this group had negative shareholder return, what is the probability that its top executive made over $1 million?

d. Given that a firm's top executive made over $1 million, what is the probability that the firm's shareholder return was positive?

2–35. As part of pharmaceutical testing for drowsiness as a side effect of a drug, 100 patients were randomly assigned to one of two groups of 50: a group taking the drug, and a group taking a placebo. Then the number of people in each group who fell asleep in the next hour was recorded. The results were as follows:

	Drug	Placebo
Sleep	18	12
No sleep	32	38

a. If a patient is randomly chosen from the 100 patients in the study, what is the probability that he or she slept in the following hour?

b. Given that a randomly chosen patient was given the placebo, what is the probability that he or she slept in the following hour?

c. Given that a randomly chosen patient slept in the following hour, what is the probability that he or she was given the drug?

2-5   Independence of Events

In Example 2–4 we concluded that the probability that an executive made a top salary was lower when the executive was a woman, and we concluded that the two events T and W were *not* independent. We now give a formal definition of statistical independence of events.

Two events, A and B, are said to be *independent* of each other if and only if the following three conditions hold:

Conditions for the **independence of two events** A and B:

$$P(A \mid B) = P(A)$$
$$P(B \mid A) = P(B) \qquad (2\text{--}9)$$

and, most useful:

$$P(A \cap B) = P(A)P(B) \qquad (2\text{--}10)$$

The first two equations have a clear, intuitive appeal. The top equation says that when A and B are independent of each other then the probability of A stays the same even when we know that B has occurred—it is a simple way of saying that knowledge of B tells us nothing about A when the two events are independent. Similarly, when A and B are independent, then knowledge that A has occurred gives us absolutely no information about B and its likelihood of occurring.

The third equation, however, is the most useful in applications. It tells us that when A and B are independent (and only when they are independent), we can obtain the probability of the joint occurrence of A and B (i.e., the probability of their intersection) simply by multiplying the two separate probabilities. This rule is thus called the **product rule** for independent events. (The rule is easily derived from the first rule, using the definition of conditional probability.)

As an example of independent events, consider the following: Suppose I roll a single die. What is the probability of the number 6 turning up? The answer is 1/6. Now suppose that I told you that I just tossed a coin and it turned up heads. What is now the probability that the die will show the number 6? The answer is unchanged, 1/6, because events of the die and the coin are independent of each other. We see that $P(6 \mid H) = P(6)$, which is the first rule above.

In Example 2–2, we found that the probability that a project belongs to IBM given that it is in telecommunications is 0.2. We also knew that the probability that a project belongs to IBM was 0.4. Since these two numbers are not equal, the two events IBM and Telecommunication are not independent.

When two events are not independent, neither are their complements. Therefore, AT&T and computers are not independent events (and neither are the other two possibilities).

The probability that a consumer will be exposed to an advertisement for a certain product by seeing a commercial on television is 0.04. The probability that the consumer will be exposed to the product by seeing an advertisement on a billboard is 0.06. The two events, being exposed to the commercial and being exposed to the billboard ad, are assumed to be independent. (*a*) What is the probability that the consumer will be exposed to both advertisements? (*b*) What is the probability that he or she will be exposed to at least one of the ads?

EXAMPLE 2-5

(*a*) Since the two events are independent, the probability of the intersection of the two (i.e., being exposed to *both* ads) is $P(A \cap B) = P(A)P(B) = 0.04 \times 0.06 = 0.0024$. (*b*) We note that being exposed to at least one of the advertisements is, by definition, the union of the two events, and so the rule for union applies. The probability of the intersection was computed above, and we have $P(A \cup B) = P(A) + P(B) - P(A \cap B) = 0.04 + 0.06 - 0.0024 = 0.0976$. The computation of such probabilities is important in advertising research. Probabilities are meaningful also as proportions of the population exposed to different modes of advertising, and are thus important in the evaluation of advertising efforts.

SOLUTION

Product Rules for Independent Events

The rules for the union and the intersection of two independent events extend nicely to sequences of more than two events. These rules are very useful in **random sampling.**

Much of statistics involves random sampling from some population. When we sample randomly from a large population, or when we sample randomly with replacement from a population of any size, the elements are independent of one another. For example, suppose that we have an urn containing 10 balls, 3 of them red and the rest blue. We randomly sample one ball, note that it is red, and return it to the urn (this is sampling *with* replacment). What is the probability that a second ball we choose at random will be red? The answer is still 3/10 because the second drawing does not "remember" that the first ball was red. Sampling with replacement in this way ensures independence of the elements. The same holds for random sampling without replacement (i.e., without returning each element to the population before the next draw) *if* the population is relatively large in comparison with the size of the sample. Unless otherwise specfied, we will assume random sampling from a large population.

Random sampling from a large population implies independence.

Intersection Rule. The probability of the intersection of several independent events is just the product of the separate probabilities. The rate of defects in corks of wine bottles is very high, 75%. Assuming independence, if four bottles are opened, what is the probability that all four corks are defective? Using this rule: P(all 4 are defective) = P(first cork is defective) $\times$ P(second cork is defective) $\times$ P(third cork is defective) $\times$ P(fourth cork is defective) = $0.75 \times 0.75 \times 0.75 \times 0.75 = 0.316$.

If these four bottles were randomly selected, then we would not have to specify independence—a random sample always implies independence.

> **Union Rule.** The probability of the union of several independent events—A_1, $A_2, \ldots A_n$—is given by the following equation:
>
> $$P(A_1 \cup A_2 \cup \ldots \cdot \cdots \cup A_n) = 1 - P(\overline{A_1})P(\overline{A_2}) \cdots P(\overline{A_n}) \qquad (2\text{--}11)$$

The union of several events is the event that at least one of the events happens. In the example of the wine corks, suppose we want to find the probability that at least one of the four corks is defective. We compute this probability as follows: P (at least one is defective) $= 1 - P$(none are defective) $= 1 - 0.25 \times 0.25 \times 0.25 \times 0.25 = 0.99609.$

EXAMPLE 2-6

Read the accompanying article. Three women (assumed a random sample) in a developing country are pregnant. What is the probability that at least one will die?

Poor Nations' Mothers At Serious Health Risk

In the industrialized world, a woman's odds of dying from problems related to pregnancy are 1 in 1,687. But in the developing world the figure is 1 in 51. The World Bank also says that each year 7 million newborns die within a week of birth because of maternal health problems. The bank and the United Nations are in the midst of an initiative to cut maternal illnesses and deaths in half by the year 2000.

Reprinted from the *San Francisco Chronicle,* August 10, 1993, p. A10.

SOLUTION

P (at least one will die) $= 1 - P$(all 3 will survive) $= 1 - (50/51)^3 = 0.0577.$

EXAMPLE 2-7

A marketing research firm is interested in interviewing a consumer who fits certain qualifications, for example, use of a certain product. It is known that 10% of the public in a certain area use the product and would thus qualify to be interviewed. The company selects a random sample of 10 people from the population as a whole. What is the probability that at least 1 of these 10 people qualifies to be interviewed?

SOLUTION

First, we note that if a sample is drawn at random, then the event that any one of the items in the sample fits the qualifications is independent of the other items in the sample. This is an important property in statistics. Let Q_i, where $i = 1, 2, \ldots, 10$, be the event that person i qualifies. Then the probability that at least 1 of the 10 people will qualify is the probability of the union of the 10 events Q_i ($i = 1, \ldots, 10$). We are thus looking for $P(Q_1 \cup Q_2 \cup \cdots \cup Q_{10})$.

Now, since 10% of the people qualify, the probability that person i does not qualify, $P(\overline{Q}_i)$, is equal to 0.90 for each $i = 1, \ldots, 10$. Therefore, the required probability is equal to $1 - (0.9)(0.9) \cdots (0.9)$ (10 times), or $1 - (0.9)^{10}$. This is equal to 0.6513.

Be sure that you understand the difference between *independent* events and *mutually exclusive* events. Although these two concepts are very different, they often cause some confusion when introduced. When two events are mutually exclusive, they are *not* independent. In fact, they are dependent events in the sense that if one happens, the other one cannot happen. The probability of the intersection of two mutually exclusive events is equal to zero. The probability of the intersection of two independent events is *not* zero; it is equal to the product of the probabilities of the separate events.

PROBLEMS

2–36. According to a report in *Forbes* magazine, January 2, 1995, p. 120, based on a Forbes/Gallup poll of business executives nationwide, 50% of all executives believed at that time that by March 1995 overall U.S. business climate would improve. Assuming independence, if five executives were polled, what is the probability that at least one of them believed that by March overall U.S. business climate would improve? What is the probability that all five would believe the statement?

2–37. The Holly Sugar Company makes sugar cubes. Quality checks revealed that about 1 in 100 cubes is broken. If you reach for the sugar and randomly choose two cubes, what is the probability that at least one of them will be broken? (Assume independence—this assumption is inherent in random sampling.)

2–38. The chancellor of a state university is applying for a new position. At a certain point in his application process, he is being considered by seven universities. At three of the seven he is a finalist, which means that (at each of the three universities) he is in the final group of three applicants, one of which will be chosen for the position. At two of the seven universities he is a semifinalist, that is, one of six candidates (in each of the two universities). In two universities he is at an early stage of his application and believes there is a pool of about 20 candidates for each of the two positions. Assuming that there is no exchange of information, or influence, across universities as to their hiring decisions, and that the chancellor is as likely to be chosen as any other applicant, what is the chancellor's probability of getting at least one job offer?

2–39. A package of documents needs to be sent to a given destination, and it is important that it arrive within one day. To maximize the chances of on-time delivery, three copies of the documents are sent via three different delivery services. Service A is known to have a 90% on-time delivery record, service B has an 88% on-time delivery record, and service C has 91% on-time delivery record. What is the probability that at least one copy of the documents will arrive at its destination on time?

2–40. Using the data from the article "Have a Safe Flight," what is the danger of a crash in the next 20 (independent) flights in the next few years? 50 flights? 100 flights? How does this compare with information in the table in problem 2–14?

Have a Safe Flight

There is something reassuring about a silver-haired airline captain, with lashings of gold braid on his epaulettes. For most of the time, though, it will not be the captain or even his co-pilot who will actually fly your aircraft. It will be a computer. The crash of a Lauda Air Boeing 767 in Thailand on May 26th with the loss of 233 lives has again raised fears about the increasing automation of airliners. There will be more crashes to come, but that is no reason to take computers out of the cockpit. Pilots, maybe.

New technology is not making flying more dangerous—quite the opposite. If you traveled in an early 1960s Comet IV you had a one-in-100,000 chance of being killed. Board any jet built in the past ten years and, despite crowded skies and radar screens, your chances of being killed are just one in 500,000. Crashes are so rare that when they happen they are likely to be caused by unusual, even unique, combinations of events.

Reprinted from *The Economist,* June 29, 1991, p. 14.

2–41. Are the events "taking the drug" and "sleeping" independent of each other for the patients and the results given in problem 2–35?

2–42. In problem 2–31, are the events "hospitalization" and "the claim being from the Midwest" independent of each other?

2–43. In problem 2–33 are "dividends paid" and "price increase" independent events?

2–44. In problem 2–34, are the events "top executive made more than $1 million" and "shareholders lost money" independent of each other? If this is true for all firms, how would you interpret your finding?

2–45. The accompanying table shows the incidence of malaria and two other similar illnesses. If a person lives in an area affected by all three diseases, what is the probability that he or she will develop at least one of the three illnesses? (Assume that contracting one disease is an event independent from contracting any other disease.)

The Damage Done: Occurrence of Vector-Borne Disease

	Cases (m = million)	Number at Risk, m
Malaria	110m per year	2,100
Schistosomiasis	200m	600
Sleeping sickness	25,000 per year	50

Reprinted by permission from "The Deadly Hitch-Hikers," Science and Technology, *The Economist,* October 31, 1992, pp. 87–88, with data from UNDP, the World Bank, and the WHO.

2–46. An electronic device has four independent components with a reliability (probability of being functional) of 0.85 each. The device works only if all four components are functional. What is the probability that the device will work when needed?

2–47. A device similar to the one in problem 2–46 has three components, but the device works as long as at least one of the components is functional. The reliabilities of the components are 0.96, 0.91, and 0.80. What is the probability that the device will work when needed?

2–48. A market researcher needs to interview people who drive to work. In the area where the study is undertaken, 75% of the people drive to work. If three people agree to be interviewed, what is the probability that at least one satisfies the requirement? What is the necessary assumption, and how does it apply?

2–49. When randomly sampling four items from a population, what is the probability that all four elements will come from the top quartile of the population distribution? What is the probability that at least one of the four elements will come from the bottom quartile of the distribution?

2–6 Combinatorial Concepts

In this section we briefly discuss a few combinatorial concepts and give some formulas useful in the analysis. The interested reader may find more on combinatorial rules and their applications in the classic book by W. Feller or in other books on probability.[6]

> If there are n events and event i can occur in N_i possible ways, then the number of ways in which the sequence of n events may occur is $N_1 N_2 \cdots N_n$.

Suppose that a bank has two branches, each branch has two departments, and each department has three employees. Then there are $(2)(2)(3)$ choices of employees, and the probability that a particular one will be randomly selected is $1/(2)(2)(3) = 1/12$.

We may view the choice as done sequentially: first a branch is randomly chosen, then a department within the branch, and then the employee within the department. This is demonstrated in the tree diagram in Figure 2–8.

> For any positive integer n, we define **n factorial** as:
> $n(n − 1)(n − 2) \cdots (1)$. We denote n factorial by $n!$. The number $n!$ is the number of ways in which n objects can be ordered. By definition, $0! = 1$.

For example, 6! is the number of possible arrangements of six objects. We have $6! = (6)(5)(4)(3)(2)(1) = 720$. Suppose that six applications arrive at a center on the same day, all written at different times. What is the probability that they will be read in the order they were written? Since there are 720 ways to order six applications, the probability of a particular order (the order in which the applications were written) is $1/720$.

> **Permutations** are the possible ordered selections of r objects out of a total of n objects. The number of permutations of n objects taken r at a time is denoted $n\mathbf{P}r$.
>
> $$n\mathbf{P}r = \frac{n!}{(n − r)!} \qquad (2\text{–}12)$$

Suppose that 4 people are to be randomly chosen out of 10 people who agreed to be interviewed in a market survey. The four people are to be assigned to four interviewers. How many possibilities are there? The first interviewer has 10 choices, the second 9 choices, the third 8, and the fourth 7. Thus, there are $(10)(9)(8)(7) = 5,040$ selections. You can see that this is equal to $n(n − 1)(n − 2) \cdots (n − r + 1)$, which is

---

[6] William Feller, *An Introduction to Probability Theory and Its Applications,* vol. I, 3d ed. (New York: John Wiley & Sons, 1968).

FIGURE 2-8   Tree Diagram for Computing the Total Number of Employees by Multiplication

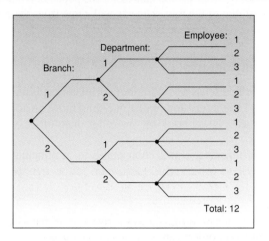

equal to $n!/(n - r)!$. If choices are made randomly, the probability of any predetermined assignment of 4 people out of a group of 10 is $1/5{,}040$.

> **Combinations** are the possible selections of r items from a group of n items regardless of the order of selection. The number of combinations is denoted by $\binom{n}{r}$ and is read *n choose r*. An alternative notation is $n\mathbf{C}r$. We define the number of combinations of r out of n elements as
>
> $$\binom{n}{r} = \frac{n!}{r!(n - r)!} \tag{2-13}$$

This is the most important of the combinatorial rules given in this chapter and is the only one we will use extensively. This rule is basic to the formula of the binomial distribution presented in the next chapter and will find use also in other chapters.

Suppose that 3 out of the 10 members of the board of directors of a large corporation are to be randomly selected to serve on a particular task committee. How many possible selections are there? Using equation 2–13, we find that the number of combinations is $\binom{10}{3} = 10!/3!7! = 120$. If the committee is chosen in a truly random fashion, what is the probability that the three committee members chosen will be the three senior board members? This is 1 combination out of a total of 120, so the answer is $1/120 = 0.00833$.

EXAMPLE 2-8   A certain university held a meeting of administrators and faculty members to discuss some important issues of concern to both groups. Out of eight members, two were faculty, and both were missing from the meeting. If two members are absent, what is the probability that they should be the two faculty members?

By definition, there are $\binom{8}{2}$ ways of selecting two people out of a total of eight people, disregarding the order of selection. Only one of these ways corresponds to the pair being the two faculty members. Hence, the probability is $1/\binom{8}{2} = 1/(8!/2!6!) = 1/28 = 0.0357$. This assumes randomness.

2–50. A company has four departments: manufacturing, distribution, marketing, and management. The number of people in each department is 55, 30, 21, and 13, respectively. Each department is expected to send one representative to a meeting with the company president. How many possible sets of representatives are there?

2–51. Nine sealed bids for oil drilling leases arrive at a regulatory agency in the morning mail. In how many different orders can the nine bids be opened?

2–52. Fifteen locations in a given area are believed likely to have oil. An oil company can only afford to drill at eight sites, sequentially chosen. How many possibilities are there, in order of selection?

2–53. A committee is evaluating six equally qualified candidates for a job. Only three of the six will be invited for an interview; among the chosen three, the order of invitation is of importance because the first candidate will have the best chance of being accepted, the second will be made an offer only if the committee rejects the first, and the third will be made an offer only if the committee should reject both the first and the second. How many possible ordered choices of three out of six candidates are there?

2–54. In the analysis of variance (discussed in Chapter 9) we compare several population means to see which is largest. After the primary analysis, pairwise comparisons are made. If we want to compare seven populations, each with all the others, how many pairs are there? (We are looking for the number of choices of seven items taken two at a time, regardless of order.)

2–55. In a shipment of 14 computer parts, 3 are faulty and the remaining 11 are in working order. Three elements are randomly chosen out of the shipment. What is the probability that all three faulty elements will be the ones chosen?

2–56. *Megabucks* is a lottery game played in Massachusetts with the following rules. A random drawing of 6 numbers out of all 36 numbers from 1 to 36 is made every Wednesday and every Saturday. The game costs $1 to play, and to win a person must have the correct six numbers drawn, regardless of their order. (The numbers are sequentially drawn from a bin and are arranged from smallest to largest. When a player buys a ticket prior to the drawing, the player must also arrange his or her chosen numbers in ascending order.) The jackpot depends on the number of players and is usually worth several million dollars. What is the probability of winning the jackpot?

2–57. In *Megabucks,* a player who correctly chooses five out of the six winning numbers gets $400. What is the probability of winning $400?

2–58. The display showing the Mazda RX-7 compares options offered in old and new models. Assume that all color, body type, hood, seat and other options are equally popular. If you drive an old-model Mazda RX-7 silver coupe that is turbocharged and has spoke wheels, what is the probability that the next Mazda of this model you meet on the road will be exactly like yours?

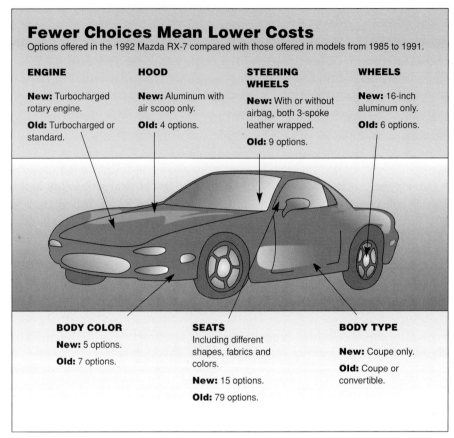

Fewer Choices Mean Lower Costs

Options offered in the 1992 Mazda RX-7 compared with those offered in models from 1985 to 1991.

ENGINE

New: Turbocharged rotary engine.

Old: Turbocharged or standard.

HOOD

New: Aluminum with air scoop only.

Old: 4 options.

STEERING WHEELS

New: With or without airbag, both 3-spoke leather wrapped.

Old: 9 options.

WHEELS

New: 16-inch aluminum only.

Old: 6 options.

BODY COLOR

New: 5 options.

Old: 7 options.

SEATS

Including different shapes, fabrics and colors.

New: 15 options.

Old: 79 options.

BODY TYPE

New: Coupe only.

Old: Coupe or convertible.

Reprinted by permission from A. Pollack "Japan Eases Varieties Marketing," *The New York Times,* October 15, 1992, p. D1, with data from Mazda.

2–7   The Law of Total Probability and Bayes' Theorem

In this section we present two useful results of probability theory. The first one, **the law of total probability,** allows us at times to evaluate probabilities of events that are difficult to obtain alone, but become easy to calculate once we *condition* on the occurrence of a related event. We first assume that the related event occurs, and then we assume it does not occur. The resulting conditional probabilities help us compute the total probability of occurrence of the event of interest.

The second rule, the famous **Bayes' theorem,** is easily derived from the law of total probability and the definition of conditional probability. The rule, discovered in 1761 by the English clergyman Thomas Bayes, has had a profound impact on the development of statistics and is responsible for the emergence of a new philosophy of science. Bayes himself is said to have been unsure of his extraordinary result, which was presented to the Royal Society by a friend in 1763—after Bayes' death.

The Law of Total Probability

Consider two events A and B. Whatever may be the relation between the two events, we can *always* say that the probability of A is equal to the probability of the intersection of A and B, plus the probability of the intersection of A and the complement of B (event $\bar{\text{B}}$).

The law of total probability:

$$P(A) = P(A \cap B) + P(A \cap \bar{B})$$ (2–14)

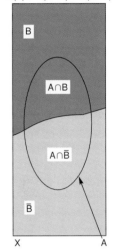

$P(A) = P(A \cap B) + P(A \cap \bar{B})$

The sets B and $\bar{B}$ form a **partition** of the sample space. A partition of a space is the division of the space into a set of events that are mutually exclusive (disjoint sets) and cover the whole space. Whatever event B may be, either B or $\bar{B}$ must occur, but not both. Figure 2–9 demonstrates this situation and the law of total probability.

The law of total probability may be extended to more complex situations, where the sample space X is partitioned into more than two events. Say we partition the space into a collection of n sets $B_1, B_2, \ldots, B_n$. The law of total probability in this situation is

$$P(A) = \sum_{i=1}^{n} P(A \cap B_i)$$ (2–15)

Figure 2–10 shows the partition of a sample space into the four events B_1, B_2, B_3, and B_4 and shows their intersections with set A.

We demonstrate the rule with a more specific example. Define A as the event that a picture card is drawn out of a deck of 52 cards (the picture cards are the aces, kings, queens, and jacks). Letting H, C, D, and S denote the events that the card drawn is a heart, club, diamond, or spade, respectively, we find that the probability of a picture card is $P(A) = P(A \cap H) + P(A \cap C) + P(A \cap D) + P(A \cap S) = 4/52 + 4/52 + 4/52 + 4/52 = 16/52$, which is what we know the probability of a picture card to be just by counting 16 picture cards out of a total of 52 cards in the deck. This demonstrates equation 2–15. The situation is shown in Figure 2–11. As can be seen from the figure, the event A is the set-addition of the intersections of A with each of the four sets H, D, C, and S. Note that in these examples we denote the sample space X.

The law of total probability can be extended by using the definition of conditional probability. Recall that $P(A \cap B) = P(A|B)P(B)$ (equation 2–8) and, similarly, $P(A \cap \bar{B}) = P(A|\bar{B})P(\bar{B})$. Substituting these relationships into equation 2–14 gives us another form of the law of total probability. This law and its extension to a partition consisting of more than two sets are given in equations 2–16 and 2–17.

The law of total probability using conditional probabilities:
Two-set case:

$$P(A) = P(A|B)P(B) + P(A|\bar{B})P(\bar{B})$$ (2–16)

More than two sets in the partition:

$$P(A) = \sum_{i=1}^{n} P(A|B_i)P(B_i)$$ (2–17)

where there are n sets in the partition: B_i, $i = 1, \ldots, n$.

EXAMPLE 2-9

An analyst believes the stock market has a 0.75 probability of going up in the next year if the economy should do well, and a 0.30 probability of going up if the economy should not do well during the year. The analyst further believes there is a 0.80 probability that

FIGURE 2-10   The Partition of Set A into Its Intersection with Four Partition Sets

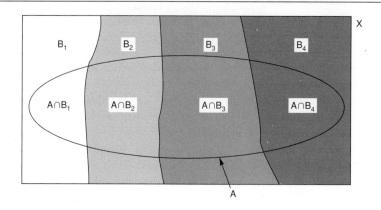

FIGURE 2-11   The Total Probabilty of Drawing a Picture Card as the Sum of the Probabilities of Drawing a Card in the Intersections of Picture and Suit

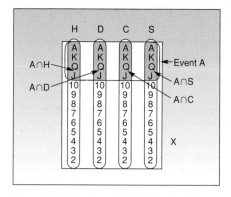

the economy will do well in the coming year. What is the probability that the stock market will go up next year (using the analyst's assessments)?

SOLUTION

We define U as the event that the market will go up and W as the event the economy will do well. Using equation 2–16, we find: $P(U) = P(U|W)P(W) + P(U|\overline{W})P(\overline{W}) = (0.75)(0.80) + (0.30)(0.20) = 0.66$.

Bayes' Theorem

We now develop the well-known Bayes' theorem. The theorem allows us to reverse the conditionality of events: we can obtain the probability of B given A from the probability of A *given* B (and other information).

By the definition of conditional probability, equation 2–7,

$$P(B|A) = \frac{P(A \cap B)}{P(A)} \qquad (2-18)$$

By another form of the same definition, equation 2–8,

$$P(A \cap B) = P(A|B)P(B) \qquad (2\text{--}19)$$

Substituting equation 2–19 into equation 2–18 gives us

$$P(B|A) = \frac{P(A|B)P(B)}{P(A)} \qquad (2\text{--}20)$$

From the law of total probability using conditional probabilities, equation 2–16, we have

$$P(A) = P(A|B)P(B) + P(A|\bar{B})P(\bar{B})$$

Substituting this expression for $P(A)$ in the denominator of equation 2–20 gives us Bayes' theorem.

Bayes' Theorem:

$$P(B|A) = \frac{P(A|B)P(B)}{P(A|B)P(B) + P(A|\bar{B})P(\bar{B})} \qquad (2\text{--}21)$$

As we see from the theorem, the probability of B given A is obtained from the probabilities of B and $\bar{B}$ and from the conditional probabilities of A given B and A given $\bar{B}$.

The probabilities $P(B)$ and $P(\bar{B})$ are called **prior probabilities** of the events B and $\bar{B}$; the probability $P(B \mid A)$ is called the **posterior probability** of B. It is possible to write Bayes' theorem in terms of $\bar{B}$ and A, thus giving the posterior probability of $\bar{B}$, $P(\bar{B} \mid A)$. Bayes' theorem may be viewed as a means of transforming our prior probability of an event, B, into a posterior probability of the event B—posterior to the known occurrence of event A.

The use of prior probabilities in conjunction with other information—often obtained from experimentation—has been questioned. The controversy arises in more involved statistical situations where Bayes' theorem is used in mixing the objective information obtained from sampling with prior information that could be subjective. We will explore this topic in more detail in Chapter 15. We now give some examples of the use of the theorem.

Consider a test for an illness. The test has a known reliability:

EXAMPLE 2-10

1. When administered to an ill person, the test will indicate so with probability 0.92.
2. When administered to a person who is not ill, the test will erroneously give a positive result with probability 0.04.

Suppose the illness is rare and is known to affect only 0.1% of the entire population. If a person is randomly selected from the entire population and is given the test and the result is positive, what is the posterior probability (posterior to the test result) that the person is ill?

SOLUTION

Let Z denote the event that the test result is positive and I the event that the person tested is ill. The preceding information gives us the following probabilities of events:

$$P(I) = 0.001, \qquad P(\bar{I}) = 0.999, \qquad P(Z|I) = 0.92, \qquad P(Z|\bar{I}) = 0.04$$

We are looking for the probability that the person is ill given a positive test result; that is, we need $P(I|Z)$. Since we have the probability with the reversed conditionality, $P(Z|I)$, we know that Bayes' theorem is the rule to be used here. Applying the rule, equation 2–21, to the events Z, I, and $\bar{I}$, we get

$$P(I|Z) = \frac{P(Z|I)P(I)}{P(Z|I)P(I) + P(Z|\bar{I})P(\bar{I})} = \frac{(0.92)(0.001)}{(0.92)(0.001) + (0.04)(0.999)}$$

$$= 0.0225$$

This result may surprise you. A test with a relatively high reliability (92% correct diagnosis when a person is ill and 96% correct identification of people who are not ill) is administered to a person, the result is positive, and yet the probability that the person is actually ill is only 0.0225!

The reason for the low probability is that we have used two sources of information here: the reliability of the test and the very small probability (0.001) that a randomly selected person is ill. The two pieces of information were mixed by Bayes' theorem, and the posterior probability reflects the mixing of the high reliability of the test with the fact that the illness is rare. The result is perfectly correct as long as the information we have used is accurate. Indeed, subject to the accuracy of our information, if the test should be administered to a large number of people selected randomly from the entire population, it would be found that about 2.25% of the people in the sample who test positive are indeed ill.

Problems with Bayes' theorem arise when we are not careful with the use of prior information. In this example, suppose the test is administered to people in a hospital. Since people in a hospital are more likely to be ill than people in the population as a whole, the overall-population probability that a person is ill, 0.001, no longer applies. If we should apply this low probability in the hospital, our results would not be correct. This caution extends to all situations where prior probabilities are used: we must always examine the appropriateness of the prior probabilities.

Bayes' theorem may be extended to a partition of more than two sets. This is done using equation 2–17, the law of total probability involving a partition of sets: B_1, B_2, ..., B_n. The resulting extended form of Bayes' theorem is given in equation 2–22. The theorem gives the probability of one of the sets in the partition, B_1, given the occurrence of event A. A similar expression holds for any of the events B_i.

Extended Bayes' theorem:

$$P(B_1|A) = \frac{P(A|B_1)P(B_1)}{\sum\limits_{i=1}^{n} P(A|B_i)P(B_i)} \tag{2-22}$$

We demonstrate the use of equation 2–22 with the following example. In the solution, we use a table format to facilitate computations. We also demonstrate the computations using a tree diagram.

An economist believes that during periods of high economic growth, the U.S. dollar appreciates with probability 0.70; in periods of moderate economic growth, the dollar appreciates with probability 0.40; and during periods of low economic growth, the dollar appreciates with probability 0.20. During any period of time, the probability of high economic growth is 0.30, the probability of moderate growth is 0.50, and the probability of low economic growth is 0.20. Suppose the dollar has been appreciating during the present period. What is the probability we are experiencing a period of high economic growth?

EXAMPLE 2–11

Our partition consists of three events: high economic growth (event H), moderate economic growth (event M), and low economic growth (event L). The prior probabilities of the three states are $P(H) = 0.30$, $P(M) = 0.50$, and $P(L) = 0.20$. Let A denote the event that the dollar appreciates. We have the following conditional probabilities: $P(A|H) = 0.70$, $P(A|M) = 0.40$, and $P(A|L) = 0.20$. Applying equation 2–22 using three sets ($n = 3$), we get

SOLUTION

$$P(H|A) = \frac{P(A|H)P(H)}{P(A|H)P(H) + P(A|M)P(M) + P(A|L)P(L)}$$

$$= \frac{(0.70)(0.30)}{(0.70)(0.30) + (0.40)(0.50) + (0.20)(0.20)} = 0.467$$

We can obtain this answer, along with the posterior probabilities of the other two states, M and L, by using a table. In the first column of the table we write the prior probabilities of the three states H, M, and L. In the second column we write the three conditional probabilities $P(A|H)$, $P(A|M)$, and $P(A|L)$. In the third column we write the joint probabilities $P(A \cap H)$, $P(A \cap M)$, and $P(A \cap L)$. The joint probabilities are obtained by multiplying across in each of the three rows (these operations make use of equation 2–8). The sum of the entries in the third column is the total probability of event A (by equation 2–15). Finally, the posterior probabilities $P(H|A)$, $P(M|A)$, and $P(L|A)$ are obtained by dividing the appropriate joint probability by the total probability of A at the bottom of the third column. For example, $P(H|A)$ is obtained by dividing $P(H \cap A)$ by the probability $P(A)$. The operations and the results are given in Table 2–1, and demonstrated in Figure 2–12.

Note that both the prior probabilities and the posterior probabilities of the three states add to 1.00, as required for probabilities of all the possibilities in a given situation. We conclude that, given that the dollar has been appreciating, the probability that our period is one of high economic growth is 0.467, the probability that it is one of moderate growth is 0.444, and the probability that our period is one of low economic growth is 0.089. The advantage of using a table is that we can obtain all posterior probabilities at once. If we use the formula directly, we need to apply it once for the posterior probability of each state.

PROBLEMS

2–59. In a takeover bid for a certain company, management of the raiding firm believes that the takeover has a 0.65 probability of success if a member of the board of the raided firm resigns, and a 0.30 chance of success if she does not resign. Management of the raiding firm further believes that the chances for a resignation of the member in question are 0.70. What is the probability of a successful takeover?

TABLE 2–1   Bayesian Revision of Probabilities, Example 2–11

Event	Prior Probability	Conditional Probability	Joint Probability	Posterior Probability
H	$P(H) = 0.30$	$P(A\mid H) = 0.70$	$P(A \cap H) = 0.21$	$P(H\mid A) = \dfrac{0.21}{0.45} = 0.467$
M	$P(M) = 0.50$	$P(A\mid M) = 0.40$	$P(A \cap M) = 0.20$	$P(M\mid A) = \dfrac{0.20}{0.45} = 0.444$
L	$P(L) = 0.20$	$P(A\mid L) = 0.20$	$P(A \cap L) = 0.04$	$P(L\mid A) = \dfrac{0.04}{0.45} = 0.089$
	Sum = 1.00		$P(A) = 0.45$	Sum = 1.000

FIGURE 2–12   Tree Diagram for Example 2–11

2–60. A drug manufacturer believes there is a 0.95 chance that the FDA will approve a new drug the company plans to distribute if the results of current testing show that the drug causes no side effects. The manufacturer further believes there is a 0.50 probability that the FDA will approve the drug if the test shows that the drug does cause side effects. A physician working for the drug manufacturer believes there is a 0.20 probability that tests will show that the drug causes side effects. What is the probability that the drug will be approved by the FDA?

2–61. An import-export firm has a 0.45 chance of concluding a deal to export agricultural equipment to a developing nation if a major competitor does not bid for the contract, and a 0.25 probability of concluding the deal if the competitor does bid for it. It is estimated that the competitor will submit a bid for the contract with probability 0.40. What is the probability of getting the deal?

2–62. A realtor is trying to sell a large piece of property. He believes there is a 0.90 probability that the property will be sold in the next six months if the local economy continues to improve throughout the period, and a 0.50 probability the property will be sold if the local economy does not continue its improvement during the period. A state economist consulted by the realtor believes there is a 0.70 chance the economy will continue its improvement during the next six months. What is the probability that the piece of property will be sold during the period?

2–63. Holland America Cruise Lines has three luxury cruise ships that sail to Alaska during the summer months. Since the business is very competitive, it is important that the ships run full during the summer if the company is to turn a profit on this line. A tourism expert hired by Holland America believes there is a 0.92 chance the ships will sail full during the coming summer if the dollar does not appreciate against European currencies, and a 0.75 chance they will sail full if the dollar does appreciate in Europe (appreciation of the dollar in Europe draws American tourists there, away from American destinations). Economists believe the dollar has a 0.23 chance of appreciating against European currencies soon. What is the probability the ships will sail full?

2–64. Saflok® is an electronic door lock system made in Troy, Michigan, and used in modern hotels and other establishments. To open a door you must insert the electronic card into the lock slip. Then a green light indicates that you can turn the handle and enter; or a yellow light indicates that the door is locked from inside, and you cannot enter. Suppose that 90% of the time when the card is inserted, the door should open because it is not locked from inside. When the door should open, a green light will appear with probability 0.98. When the door should not open, a green light may still appear (an electronic error) 5% of the time. Suppose that you just inserted the card and the light is green. What is the probability that the door will actually open?

2–65. A chemical plant has an emergency alarm system. When an emergency situation exists, the alarm sounds with probability 0.95. When an emergency situation does not exist, the alarm system sounds with probability 0.02. A real emergency situation is a rare event, with probability 0.004. Given that the alarm has just sounded, what is the probability that a real emergency situation exists?

2–66. When the economic situation is "high," a certain economic indicator rises with probability 0.6. When the economic situation is "medium," the economic indicator rises with probability 0.3. When the economic situation is "low," the indicator rises with probability 0.1. The economy is high 15% of the time, it is medium 70% of the time, and it is low 15% of the time. Given that the indicator has just gone up, what is the probability that the economic situation is high?

2–67. An oil explorer orders seismic tests to determine whether oil is likely to be found in a certain drilling area. The seismic tests have a known reliability: when oil does exist in the testing area, the test will indicate so 85% of the time; when oil does not exist in the test area, 10% of the time the test will erroneously indicate that it does exist. The explorer believes that the probability of existence of an oil deposit in the test area is 0.4. If a test is conducted and indicates the presence of oil, what is the probability that an oil deposit really exists?

2–68. Before marketing new products nationally, companies often test them on samples of potential customers. Such tests have a known reliability. For a particular product type, it is known that a test will indicate success of the product 75% of the time if the product is indeed successful and 15% of the time when the product is not successful. From past experience with similar products, a company knows that a new product has a 0.60 chance of success on the national market. If the test indicates that the product will be successful, what is the probability that it really will be successful?

2–69. A market research field worker needs to interview married couples about use of a certain product. The researcher arrives at a residential building with three apartments. From the names on the mailboxes downstairs, the interviewer infers that a married couple lives in one apartment, two men live in another, and two women live in the third apartment. The researcher goes upstairs and finds that there are no names or numbers on the three doors, so that it is impossible to tell in which of the three apartments the married couple lives. The researcher chooses a door at random and knocks. A woman answers the door. Having seen a woman at the door, what *now* is the probability of having reached the married couple? Make the (possibly unrealistic) assumptions that if the two men's apartment was reached, a woman cannot answer the door; if the two women's apartment was reached, then only a woman can answer; and that if the married couple was reached, then the probability of a woman at the door is 1/2. Also assume a 1/3 prior probability of reaching the married couple. Are you surprised by the numerical answer you obtained?

exactly 0.50. How can the coin still be used for making the choice? (Hint: Toss the coin *twice*, basing your decision on two possible outcomes.) Explain your answer.

2–100.   Is Marilyn right? (Hint: Create a sample space of 16 equally likely points. Each point is a quadruple of *ordered* symbols, e.g., BGGB; then count the number of points leading to each event: 1 girl, 3 boys; 2 girls, 2 boys; etc.)

Ask Marilyn℠

BY MARILYN VOS SAVANT

If you have four children, they may all be of one sex, there may be three of one sex and one of the other sex, or there may be two of each. Which is most likely?—Adrian R. Beck, Joplin, Mo.

I know it sounds strange, but more families with four children have three of one sex and one of the other sex than any other combination. The chance of having all girls or all boys is 1 in 8; the chances of having two of each are 3 in 8; and the chances of having three girls and one boy (or three boys and one girl) are 4 in 8.

Reprinted from *Parade* magazine, October 2, 1993. (I am indebted to Art O'Leary for bringing it to my attention.)

Case 2   THE PATRIOT ANTIMISSILE SYSTEM

Part of the great success of the war against Iraq was due to the incredibly high performance of Raytheon Corporation's Patriot Missile System. The Patriot missile was designed to intercept enemy missiles and destroy them in the air. The missile's rate of successful intercepts of Iraqi Scud missiles aimed at Israel and

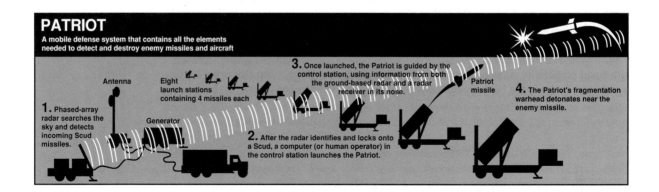

PATRIOT
A mobile defense system that contains all the elements needed to detect and destroy enemy missiles and aircraft

Antenna

Eight launch stations containing 4 missiles each

3. Once launched, the Patriot is guided by the control station, using information from both the ground-based radar and a radar receiver in its nose.

Patriot missile

4. The Patriot's fragmentation warhead detonates near the enemy missile.

1. Phased-array radar searches the sky and detects incoming Scud missiles.

Generator

2. After the radar identifies and locks onto a Scud, a computer (or human operator) in the control station launches the Patriot.

Saudi Arabia surprised even its makers. At a speech made at Raytheon's headquarters in Andover, Massachusetts, on February 15, 1991, President Bush praised the company and stated that (in a part of the campaign against Iraq) 41 out of 42 incoming Scud missiles were intercepted by the Patriot system. The exhibit, reproduced by permission from *Time* (February 14, 1991, p. 47) demonstrates how the missile system works.

From publicly available sources, we may infer the following about the Patriot system. There is a 99% chance that the system's radar will detect an incoming enemy missile such as the Scud. Once the missile is detected, a Patriot missile is immediately fired and has a 98.5% chance of exploding close enough to the incoming missile so that its fragments will damage the incoming missile. If this happens, there is a 65% chance that the enemy warhead will explode in the air and thus cause no damage. What is the probability that an incoming missile will be totally destroyed in the air? Interpret the president's statement. Based on the numbers, what event was President Bush likely referring to in his address?[12]

---

[12] Some news reports in March 1992 have questioned the early assessments of the Patriot's successes, and at this writing only 10% of missile firings during the war are confirmed as hits.

3

RANDOM VARIABLES

3-1 INTRODUCTION

arilyn Vos Savant (see problem 2–100) was interested in the matter of the probabilities of the number of babies of each sex in a given number of births. In solving problem 2–100 you constructed a sample space made up of the 16 equally likely points:

BBBB	BBBG	BGGB	GBGG
GBBB	GGBB	BGBG	GGBG
BGBB	GBGB	BBGG	GGGB
BBGB	GBBG	BGGG	GGGG

Continued

All of these 16 points are equally likely because when four children are born, the sex of each child is assumed to be independent of those of the other three. Hence the probability of each quadruple (e.g., GBBG) is equal to the product of the probabilities of the four separate, single outcomes—G, B, B, and G—and is thus equal to $(1/2)$ $(1/2)(1/2)(1/2) = 1/16$.

Now, let's look at the variable "the number of girls out of four births." This number *varies* among points in the sample space, and it is *random*—given to chance. That's why we call such a number a **random variable.**

> A **random variable** is an uncertain quantity whose value depends on chance.

A random variable has a probability law: A rule that assigns probabilities to the different values of the random variable. The probability law, the probability assignment, is called the **probability distribution** of the random variable. We usually denote the random variable by a capital letter, often X. The probability distribution will then be denoted by $P(X)$.

Look again at the sample space for the sexes of four babies, and remember that our variable is the number of girls out of four births. The first point in the sample space is BBBB; because the number of girls is zero here, $X = 0$. The next four points in the sample space all have one girl (and three boys). Hence, each one leads to the value $X = 1$. Similarly, the next six points in the sample space all lead to $X = 2$; the next four points to $X = 3$; and, finally, the last point in our sample space gives $X = 4$. The correspondence of points in the sample space with values of the random variable is as follows:

Sample Space	Random Variable
BBBB }	X = 0
GBBB	
BGBB	
BBGB	X = 1
BBBG	
GGBB	
GBGB	
GBBG	
BGGB	X = 2
BGBG	
BBGG	
BGGG	
GBGG	X = 3
GGBG	
GGGB	
GGGG }	X = 4

This correspondence, when a sample space clearly exists, allows us to define a random variable as follows.

> A **random variable** is a function of the sample space.

What is this function? The correspondence between points in the sample space and values of the random variable allows us to determine the probability distribution of X as follows: Notice that 1 of the 16 equally likely points of the sample space leads to $X = 0$. Hence, the probability that $X = 0$ is 1/16. Because 4 of the 16 equally likely points lead to a value $X = 1$, the probability that $X = 1$ is 4/16, and so forth. Thus, looking at the sample space and counting the number of points leading to each value of X, we find the following probabilities:

$$P(X = 0) = 1/16 = 0.0625$$
$$P(X = 1) = 4/16 = 0.2500$$
$$P(X = 2) = 6/16 = 0.3750$$
$$P(X = 3) = 4/16 = 0.2500$$
$$P(X = 4) = 1/16 = 0.0625$$

The probability statements above constitute the probability distribution of the random variable X = the number of girls in four births. Notice how this probability law was obtained simply by associating values of X with sets in the sample space. (For example, the set GBBB, BGBB, BBGB, BBBG leads to $X = 1$.) It is useful to write down the probability distribution of X in a table format, but first let's make a small, simplifying notational distinction so that we do not have to write complete probability statements such as $P(X = 1)$ and so on.

As stated earlier, we use a capital letter, such as X, to denote the random variable. But we use a lowercase letter to denote a particular value that the random variable can take. For example, $x = 3$ means that some particular set of four births resulted in three girls. Think of X as random and x as known. Before a coin is tossed, the number of heads (in one toss) is an unknown, X. Once the coin lands, we have $x = 0$ or $x = 1$.

Now let's return to the number of girls in four births. We can write the probability distribution of this random variable in a table format, as shown in Table 3–1.

Note an important fact: The sum of the probabilities of all the values of the random variable X must be 1.00. A picture of the probability distribution of the random variable X is given in Figure 3–1. Such a picture is a **probability histogram** for the random variable.

Marilyn is interested in the number of girls (or boys) in any fixed number of births, not necessarily four. Thus her discussion extends beyond this case. In fact, the random variable she describes, which in general counts the number of "successes" (here, a girl is a success) in a fixed number, n, of trials, is called a *binomial random variable*. We will study this particular important random variable in Section 3–3. ∎

EXAMPLE 3–1

Figure 3–2 shows the sample space for the experiment of rolling two dice. As can be seen from the sample space, the probability of every pair of outcomes is 1/36. This can be seen from the fact that, by the independence of the two dice, for example: P (6 on red die ∩ 5 on green die) = P (6 on red die) × P (5 on green die) = (1/6)(1/6) = 1/36, and that this holds for all 36 pairs of outcomes. Let X = the sum of the dots on the two dice. What is the distribution of x?

SOLUTION

Figure 3–3 shows the correspondence between sets in our sample space and the values of X. The probability distribution of X is given in Table 3–2. The probability distribution allows us to answer various questions about the random variable of interest. Draw a picture of this probability distribution. Such a graph need not be a histogram, used earlier, but can also be a bar graph or column chart of the probabilities of the different values of the random variable. Note from the graph you produced that the distribution of the random variable "the sum of two dice" is symmetric. The central value is $x = 7$, which has the highest probability, $P(7) = 6/36 = 1/6$. This is the *mode,* the most likely value. Thus, if you were to bet on one sum of two dice, the best bet is that the sum will be 7.

TABLE 3-1   Probability Distribution of the Number of Girls in Four Births

Number of Girls, x	Probability, $P(x)$
0	1/16
1	4/16
2	6/16
3	4/16
4	1/16
	16/16 = 1.00

FIGURE 3-1   Probability Distribution of the Number of Girls in Four Births

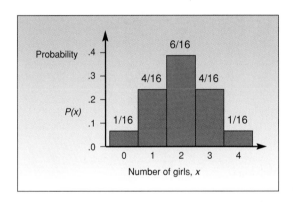

FIGURE 3-2   Sample Space for Two Dice

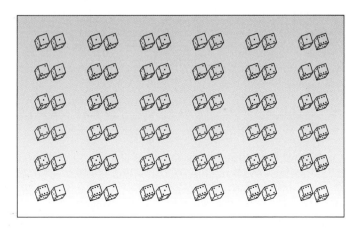

FIGURE 3-3   Correspondence between Sets and Values of X

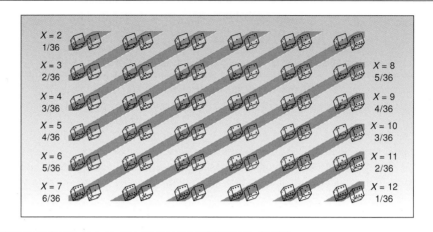

TABLE 3-2   Probability Distribution of the Sum of Two Dice

x	P(x)
2	1/36
3	2/36
4	3/36
5	4/36
6	5/36
7	6/36
8	5/36
9	4/36
10	3/36
11	2/36
12	1/36
	36/36 = 1.00

We can answer other probability questions, such as: What is the probability that the sum will be at most 5? This is $P(X \leq 5)$. Notice that to answer this question, we require the sum of all the probabilities of the values that are less than or equal to 5:

$$P(2) + P(3) + P(4) + P(5) = 1/36 + 2/36 + 3/36 + 4/36 = 10/36$$

Similarly, we may want to know what the probability is that the sum is greater than 9. This is calculated as follows:

$$P(X > 9) = P(10) + P(11) + P(12) = 3/36 + 2/36 + 1/36 = 6/36 = 1/6$$

Most often, unless we are dealing with games of chance, there is no evident sample space. In such situations the probability distribution is often obtained from lists or other data that give us the relative frequency in the recorded past of the various values of the random variable. This is demonstrated in Example 3–2.

EXAMPLE   3-2

800, 900, and Now: the 500 Telephone Numbers

The new code 500 is for busy, affluent people who travel a lot: it can work with a cellular phone, your home phone, office phone, second-home phone, up to five additional phones beside your regular one. The computer technology behind this service is astounding—the new phone service can find you wherever you may be on the planet at a given moment (assuming one of the phones you specify is cellular and you keep it with you when you are not near one of your stationary telephones). What the computer does is to first ring you up at the telephone number you specify as your primary one (your office phone, for example). If there is no answer, the computer switches to search for you at your second-specified phone number (say, home); if you do not answer there, it will switch to your third phone (maybe the phone at a close companion's home, or your car phone, or a portable cellular phone); and so on up to five allowable switches. The switches are the expensive part of this service (beside arrangements to have your cellular phone reachable overseas), and the service provider wants to get information on these switches. From data available on an experimental run of the 500 program, the following probability distribution is constructed for the number of dialing switches that are necessary before a person is reached. When $X = 0$, it means that the person was reached on his or her primary phone (no switching was necessary); when $X = 1$, it means that a dialing switch was necessary, and the person was found at his or her secondary phone; and so on up to five switches. Table 3–3 gives the probability distribution for this random variable.

A plot of the probability distribution of this random variable is given in Figure 3–4. When more than two switches occur on a given call, extra costs are incurred. What is the probability that for a given call there would be extra costs?

$$P(X > 2) = P(3) + P(4) + P(5) = 0.2 + 0.1 + 0.1 = 0.4$$

What is the probability that at least one switch will occur on a given call? $1 - P(0) = 0.9$, a high probability.

Discrete and Continuous Random Variables

Refer to Example 3–2. Notice that when switches occur, the number X jumps by one. It is impossible to have half a switch or 0.13278 of one. The same is true for the number of dots on two dice (you cannot see 2.3 dots or 5.87 dots, etc) and, of course, the number of girls in four births.

> A **discrete random variable** can assume at most a countable number of values.

The values of a discrete random variable do not have to be positive whole numbers; they just have to "jump" from one possible value to the next without being able to have any value in between. The price of a stock, for example, is a discrete random

TABLE 3–3   The Probability Distribution of the Number of Switches

x	P(x)
0	0.1
1	0.2
2	0.3
3	0.2
4	0.1
5	0.1
	1.00

FIGURE 3–4   The Probability Distribution of the Number of Switches

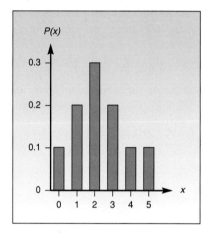

variable because it is reported to the nearest eighth of a dollar: 17 1/8, 17 2/8, 17 3/8, etc. As another example, the amount of money you make on an investment may be $500 or it may be a loss: −$200. At any rate, it can be measured at best to the nearest *cent,* so this variable is discrete.

What are continuous random variables, then?

> A **continuous random variable** may take on any value in an interval of numbers (i.e., its possible values are uncountably infinite).

The values of continuous random variables can be measured (at least in theory) to any degree of accuracy. They move continuously from one possible value to another, without having to jump. For example, temperature is a continuous random variable, since it can be measured as 72.00340981136 . . . °. Weight, height, and time are other examples of continuous random variables.

The difference between discrete and continuous random variables is illustrated in Figure 3–5. Is wind speed a discrete or a continuous random variable?

FIGURE 3–5   Discrete and Continuous Random Variables

The probability distribution of a discrete random variable X must satisfy the following two conditions.

$$1.\ \ P(x) \geq 0 \text{ for all values } x \qquad\qquad (3\text{–}1)$$

$$2.\ \ \sum_{\text{all } x} P(x) = 1 \qquad\qquad (3\text{–}2)$$

These conditions must hold because the $P(x)$ values are probabilities. Equation 3–1 states that all probabilities must be greater than or equal to zero, as we know from Chapter 2. For the second rule, equation 3–2, note the following. For each value x, $P(x) = P(X = x)$ is the probability of the event that the random variable equals x. Since by definition *all* x means all the values the random variable X may take, and since X may take on only one value at a time, the occurrences of these values are mutually exclusive events, and one of them must take place. Therefore, the sum of all the probabilities $P(x)$ must be 1.00.

Cumulative Distribution Function

The probability distribution of a discrete random variable lists the probabilities of occurrence of different values of the random variable. We may be interested in *cumulative* probabilities of the random variable. That is, we may be interested in the probability that the value of the random variable is *at most* some value x. This is the sum of all the probabilities of the values i of X that are less than or equal to x. We define the *cumulative distribution function* (also called *cumulative probability function*) as follows.

The **cumulative distribution function,** $F(x)$, of a discrete random variable X is

$$F(x) = P(X \leq x) = \sum_{\text{all } i \leq x} P(i) \qquad\qquad (3\text{–}3)$$

TABLE 3–4   Cumulative Distribution Function of the Number of Switches (Example 3–2)

x	P(x)	F(x)
0	0.1	0.1
1	0.2	0.3
2	0.3	0.6
3	0.2	0.8
4	0.1	0.9
5	0.1	1.00
	1.00	

FIGURE 3–6   Cumulative Distribution Function of Number of Switches

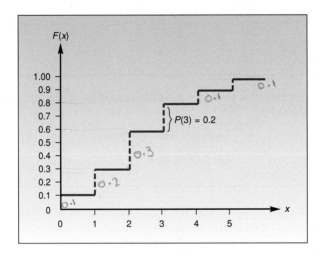

Table 3–4 gives the cumulative distribution function of the random variable of Example 3–2. Note that each entry of $F(x)$ is equal to the sum of the corresponding values of $P(i)$ for all values i less than or equal to x. For example, $F(3) = P(X \leq 3) = P(0) + P(1) + P(2) + P(3) = 0.1 + 0.2 + 0.3 + 0.2 = 0.8$. Of course, $F(5) = 1.00$ because $F(5)$ is the sum of the probabilities of all values that are less than or equal to 5, and 5 is the largest value of the random variable.

Figure 3–6 shows $F(x)$ for the number of switches on a given call. All cumulative distribution functions are nondecreasing and equal 1.00 at the largest possible value of the random variable.

Let us consider a few probabilities. The probability that the number of switches will be less than or equal to 3 is given by $F(3) = 0.8$. This is illustrated, using the probability distribution, in Figure 3–7.

The probability that *more than* one switch will occur, $P(X > 1)$, is equal to $1 - F(1) = 1 - 0.3 = 0.7$. This is so because $F(1) = P(X \leq 1)$, and $P(X \leq 1) + P(X > 1) = 1$ (the two events are complements of each other). This is demonstrated in Figure 3–8.

The probability that anywhere from one to three switches will occur is $P(1 \leq X \leq 3)$. From Figure 3–9 we see that this is equal to $F(3) - F(0 = 0.8 - 0.1 = 0.7$. (This is the probability that the number of switches that occur will be less than or equal to 3 and greater than zero.) This, and other probability

FIGURE 3-7   The Probability That at Most Three Switches Will Occur

FIGURE 3-8   Probability That More than One Switch Will Occur

FIGURE 3-9   Probability That Anywhere from One to Three Switches Will Occur

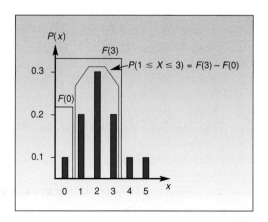

questions, could certainly be answered directly, without use of $F(x)$. We could just add the probabilities: $P(1) + P(2) + P(3) = 0.2 + 0.3 + 0.2 = 0.7$. The advantage of $F(x)$ is that probabilities may be computed by few operations (usually subtraction of two values of $F(x)$, as in this example), whereas use of $P(x)$ often requires lengthier computations.

If the probability distribution is available, use it directly. If, on the other hand, you have a cumulative distribution function for the random variable in question, you may use it as we have demonstrated. In either case, it is always helpful to draw a picture of the probability distribution. Then look at the signs in the probability statement, such as $P(X \leq x)$ versus $P(X < x)$, to see which values to include and which ones to leave out of the probability computation.

PROBLEMS   not done!

3–1.   The number of telephone calls arriving at an exchange during any given minute between noon and 1:00 PM on a weekday is a random variable with the following probability distribution.

x	P(x)
0	0.3
1	0.2
2	0.2
3	0.1
4	0.1
5	0.1

a.   Verify that $P(x)$ is a probability distribution.

b.   Find the cumulative distribution function of the random variable.

c.   Use the cumulative distribution function to find the probability that between 12:34 and 12:35 PM more than two calls will arrive at the exchange.

3–2.   Typing errors per page for a certain typing pool are known to follow the probability distribution:

x	P(x)
0	0.01
1	0.09
2	0.30
3	0.20
4	0.20
5	0.10
6	0.10

a.   Verify that $P(x)$ is a probability distribution.

b.   Find the cumulative distribution function.

c.   Find the probability that at most four errors will be made on a page.

d.   Find the probability that at least two errors will be made on a page.

3–3. The percentage of people (to the nearest ten) responding to an advertisement is a random variable with the following probability distribution.

x(%)	P(x)
0	0.10
10	0.20
20	0.35
30	0.20
40	0.10
50	0.05

a. Show that $P(x)$ is a probability distribution.

b. Find the cumulative distribution function.

c. Find the probability that more than 20% will respond to the ad.

3–4. An automobile dealership records the number of cars sold each day. The data are used in calculating the following probability distribution of daily sales.

x	P(x)
0	0.1
1	0.1
2	0.2
3	0.2
4	0.3
5	0.1

a. Find the probability that the number of cars sold tomorrow will be between 2 and 4 (both inclusive).

b. Find the cumulative distribution function of the number of cars sold per day.

c. Show that $P(x)$ is a probability distribution.

3–5. Consider the roll of a pair of dice, and let X denote the sum of the two numbers appearing on the dice. Find the probability distribution of X, and find the cumulative distribution function. What is the most likely sum?

3–6. The number of intercity shipment orders arriving daily at a transportation company is a random variable X with the following probability distribution.

x	P(x)
0	0.1
1	0.2
2	0.4
3	0.1
4	0.1
5	0.1

a. Verify that $P(x)$ is a probability distribution.

b. Find the cumulative probability function of X.

c. Use the cumulative probability function computed in *b* to find the probability that anywhere from one to four shipment orders will arrive on a given day.

d. When more than three orders arrive on a given day, the company incurs additional costs due to the need to hire extra drivers and loaders. What is the probability that extra costs will be incurred on a given day?

e. Assuming that the number of orders arriving on different days are independent of each other, what is the probability that no orders will be received over a period of five working days?

f. Again assuming independence of orders on different days, what is the probability that extra costs will be incurred two days in a row?

3–7. The number of wooden sailboats constructed per month in a small shipyard is a random variable with the following probability distribution.

x	P(x)
2	0.2
3	0.2
4	0.3
5	0.1
6	0.1
7	0.05
8	0.05

a. Find the probability that the number of boats constructed next month will be between 4 and 7 (both inclusive).

b. Find the cumulative distribution function of X.

c. Use $F(x)$ computed in b to evaluate the probability that the number of boats constructed in a month will be less than or equal to 6.

d. Find the probability that the number of boats made will be greater than 3 and less than or equal to 6.

3–8. The number of defects in a machine-made product is a random variable, X, with the following probability distribution.

x	P(x)
0	0.1
1	0.2
2	0.3
3	0.3
4	0.1

a. Show that $P(x)$ is a probability distribution.

b. Find the probability $P(1 < X \le 3)$.

c. Find the probability $P(1 \le X \le 4)$.

d. Find $F(x)$.

3–9. Returns on investments overseas, especially in Europe and the Pacific Rim, are expected to be higher than those of American markets in the 1990s, and analysts are now recommending investments in international portfolios.[1] An investment consultant believes that the probability distribution of returns (in percent per year) on one such portfolio is as follows.

---

[1] "Your Money," *Working Woman,* March, 1991, p. 58.

x (%)	P(x)
9	0.05
10	0.15
11	0.30
12	0.20
13	0.15
14	0.10
15	0.05

a. Verify that $P(x)$ is a probability distribution.

b. What is the probability that returns will be at least 12%?

c. Find the cumulative distribution of returns.

3–2 Expected Values of Discrete Random Variables

In Chapter 1, we discussed summary measures of data sets. The most important summary measures discussed were the mean and the variance (and also the square root of the variance, the standard deviation). We saw that the mean is a measure of *centrality,* or *location,* of the data or population, and that the variance and the standard deviation measure the *variability,* or *spread,* of our observations.

The mean of a probability distribution of a random variable is a measure of the centrality of the probability distribution. It is a measure that considers both the values of the random variable and their probabilities. The mean is a *weighted average* of the possible values of the random variable—the weights being the probabilities.

The mean of the probability distribution of a random variable is called the *expected value* of the random variable (sometimes called the *expectation* of the random variable). The reason for this name is that the mean is the (probability-weighted) average value of the random variable, and therefore it is the value we "expect" to occur. We denote the mean by two notations: μ for *mean* (as in Chapter 1 for a population) and $E(X)$ for *expected value of X*. In situations where no ambiguity is possible, we will often use μ. In cases where we want to stress the fact that we are talking about the expected value of a particular random variable (here, X), we will use the notation $E(X)$. The expected value of a discrete random variable is defined as follows.

The **expected value** of a discrete random variable X is equal to the sum of all values of the random variable, each value multiplied by its probability.

$$\mu = E(X) = \sum_{\text{all } x} xP(x) \tag{3–4}$$

Suppose a coin is tossed. If it lands heads you win a dollar, but if it lands tails you lose a dollar. What is the expected value of this game? Intuitively, you know you have an even chance of winning or losing the same amount, and so the average or expected value is zero. Your payoff from this game is a random variable, and we find its expected value from equation 3–4: $E(X) = (1)(1/2) + (-1)(1/2) = 0$. The definition of an expected value, or mean, of a random variable thus conforms with our intuition. Incidentally, games of chance with an expected value of zero are called *fair games.*

Let us now return to Example 3–2 and find the expected value of the random variable involved—the expected number of switches on a given call. It is convenient to compute the mean of a discrete random variable using a table. In the first column of the table we write the values of the random variable. In the second column we write the probabilities of the different values, and in the third column we write the products $xP(x)$ for each value x. We then add the entries in the third column, giving us $E(X) = \Sigma\, xP(x)$, as required by equation 3–4. This is shown for Example 3–2 in Table 3–5.

As indicated in the table, $\mu = E(X) = 2.3$. We can say that, on the average, 2.3 switches occur per call. As this example shows, the mean does not have to be one of the values of the random variable. There are no calls with 2.3 switches, but 2.3 is the average number of switches. It is the *expected* number of switches per call, although here the exact expectation will not be realized on any call.

As the weighted average of the values of the random variable, with probabilities as weights, the mean is the *center of mass* of the probability distribution. This is demonstrated for Example 3–2 in Figure 3–10.

The Expected Value of a Function of a Random Variable

It is possible to compute the expected value of a *function* of a random variable. Let $h(X)$ be a function of the discrete random variable X.

The expected value of $h(X)$, a function of the discrete random variable X, is

$$E[h(X)] = \sum_{\text{all } x} h(x)P(x) \qquad\qquad (3\text{–}5)$$

The function $h(X)$ could be X^2, $3X^4$, log X, or any function. As we will see shortly, equation 3–5 is most useful for computing the expected value of the special function $h(X) = X^2$. But let us first look at a simpler example, where $h(X)$ is a *linear* function of X. A linear function of X is a straight-line relation: $h(X) = a + bX$, where a and b are numbers.

EXAMPLE 3-3

Monthly sales of a certain product, recorded to the nearest thousand, are believed to follow the probability distribution given in Table 3–6. Suppose that the company has a fixed monthly production cost of $8,000 and that each item brings $2. Find the expected monthly profit from product sales.

SOLUTION

The company's profit function from sales of the product is $h(X) = 2X - 8,000$. Equation 3–5 tells us that the expected value of $h(X)$ is the sum of the values of $h(X)$, each value multiplied by the probability of the particular value of X. We thus add two columns to

TABLE 3-5 Computing the Expected Number of Switches [Example 3-2]

x	P(x)	xP(x)
0	0.1	0
1	0.2	0.2
2	0.3	0.6
3	0.2	0.6
4	0.1	0.4
5	0.1	0.5
	1.00	2.3 ⟵ Mean, $E(X)$

FIGURE 3-10 The Mean of a Discrete Random Variable as a Center of Mass [Example 3-2]

TABLE 3-6 Probability Distribution of Monthly Product Sales [Example 3-3]

Number of Items, x	P(x)
5,000	0.2
6,000	0.3
7,000	0.2
8,000	0.2
9,000	0.1
	1.00

Table 3–6: a column of values of $h(x)$ for all x and a column of the products $h(x)P(x)$. At the bottom of this column we find the required sum $E[h(X)] = \sum_{\text{all } x} h(x)P(x)$. This is done in Table 3–7. As shown in the table, expected monthly profit from sales of the product is $5,400.

In the case of a linear function of a random variable, as in Example 3–3, there is a possible simplification of our calculation of the mean of $h(X)$. The simplified formula of the expected value of a linear function of a random variable is as follows.

TABLE 3-7   Computing Expected Profit for Example 3-3

x	h(x)	P(x)	h(x)P(x)
5,000	2,000	0.2	400
6,000	4,000	0.3	1,200
7,000	6,000	0.2	1,200
8,000	8,000	0.2	1,600
9,000	10,000	0.1	1,000
			$E[h(X)] = $ 5,400

The expected value of a linear function of a random variable:

$$E(aX + b) = aE(X) + b \qquad (3\text{–}6)$$

where a and b are fixed numbers

Equation 3–6 holds for *any* random variable, discrete or continuous. Once you know the expected value of X, the expected value of $aX + b$ is just $aE(X) + b$. In Example 3–3 we could have obtained the expected profit by finding the mean of X first, and then multiplying the mean of X by 2 and subtracting from this the fixed cost of $8,000. The mean of X is 6,700 (prove this), and the expected profit is therefore $E[h(X)] = E(2X - 8,000) = 2E(X) - 8,000 = 2(6,700) - 8,000 = \$5,400$, as we obtained using Table 3–7.

As mentioned earlier, the most important expected value of a function of X is the expected value of $h(X) = X^2$. This is because this expected value helps us compute the *variance* of the random variable X and, through the variance, the standard deviation.

Variance and Standard Deviation of a Random Variable

The variance of a random variable is the expected squared deviation of the random variable from its mean. The idea is similar to that of the variance of a data set or a population, defined in Chapter 1. Probabilities of the values of the random variable are used as weights in the computation of the expected squared deviation from the mean of a discrete random variable. The definition of the variance follows. As with a population, we denote the variance of a random variable by σ^2. Another notation for the variance of X is $V(X)$.

The **variance** of a discrete random variable X is given by

$$\sigma^2 = V(X) = E[(X - \mu)^2] = \sum_{\text{all } x} (x - \mu)^2 P(x) \qquad (3\text{–}7)$$

Using equation 3–7, it is possible to compute the variance of a discrete random variable by subtracting the mean μ from each value x of the random variable, squaring the result, multiplying it by the probability $P(x)$, and finally adding the results for all *x*. Let us apply equation 3–7 and find the variance of the number of dialing switches in Example 3–2:

$$\sigma^2 = \sum (x - \mu)^2 P(x)$$

$$= (0 - 2.3)^2(0.1) + (1 - 2.3)^2(0.2) + (2 - 2.3)^2(0.3)$$
$$+ (3 - 2.3)^2(0.2) + (4 - 2.3)^2(0.1) + (5 - 2.3)^2(0.1)$$

$$= 2.01$$

There is, however, an easier way of computing the variance of a discrete random variable. It can be shown mathematically that equation 3–7 is equivalent to the following computational form of the variance.

Computational formula for the variance of a random variable:

$$\sigma^2 = V(X) = E(X^2) - [E(X)]^2 \qquad (3\text{–}8)$$

Equation 3–8 has the same relation to equation 3–7 as equation 1–7 has to equation 1–3 for the variance of a set of points.

Equation 3–8 states that the variance of *X* is equal to the expected value of X^2 minus the squared mean of *X*. In computing the variance using this equation, we use the definition of the expected value of a function of a discrete random variable, equation 3–5, in the special case $h(X) = X^2$. We compute x^2 for each *x*, multiply it by $P(x)$, and add for all *x*. This gives us $E(X^2)$. To get the variance, we subtract from $E(X^2)$ the mean of *X*, squared.

We now compute the variance of the random variable in Example 3–2 using this method. This is done in Table 3–8. The first column in the table gives the values of *X*, the second column gives the probabilities of these values, the third column gives the products of the values and their probabilities, and the fourth column is the product of the third column and the first (because we get $x^2P(x)$ by just multiplying each entry $xP(x)$ by *x* from column 1). At the bottom of the third column we find the mean of *X*, and at the bottom of the fourth column we find the mean of X^2. Finally, we perform the subtraction $E(X^2) - [E(X)]^2$ to get the variance of *X*:

$$V(X) = E(X^2) - [E(X)]^2 = 7.3 - (2.3)^2 = 2.01$$

TABLE 3–8 Computations Leading to the Variance of the Number of Switches in Example 3-2 Using the Shortcut Formula (equation 3–8)

x	P(x)	xP(x)	x²P(x)
0	0.1	0	0
1	0.2	0.2	0.2
2	0.3	0.6	1.2
3	0.2	0.6	1.8
4	0.1	0.4	1.6
5	0.1	0.5	2.5
	1.00	2.3 ⟵ Mean of X	7.3 ⟵ Mean of X²

This is the same value we found using the other formula for the variance, equation 3–7. Note that equation 3–8 holds for *all* random variables, discrete or otherwise. Once we obtain the expected value of X^2 and the expected value of X, we can compute the variance of the random variable using this equation.

For random variables, as for data sets or populations, the standard deviation is equal to the (positive) square root of the variance. We denote the standard deviation of a random variable X by σ or by SD(X).

The **standard deviation** of a random variable:

$$\sigma = SD(X) = \sqrt{V(X)} \qquad (3\text{--}9)$$

In Example 3–2, the standard deviation is $\sigma = \sqrt{2.01} = 1.418$.

What are the variance and the standard deviation, and how do we interpret their meaning? By definition, the variance is the average squared deviation of the values of the random variable from their mean. Thus, it is a measure of the *dispersion* of the possible values of the random variable about the mean. The variance gives us an idea of the variation or uncertainty associated with the random variable: the larger the variance, the further away from the mean are possible values of the random variable. Since the variance is a squared quantity, it is often more useful to consider its square root—the standard deviation of the random variable. When comparing two random variables, the one with the larger variance (standard deviation) is the more variable one. The risk associated with an investment is often measured by the standard deviation of investment returns. When comparing two investments with the same average (*expected*) return, the investment with the higher standard deviation is considered riskier (although a higher standard deviation implies that returns are expected to be more variable—both below and above the mean).

Variance of a Linear Function of a Random Variable

There is a formula, analogous to equation 3–6, that gives the variance of a linear function of a random variable. For a linear function of X given by $aX + b$, we have the following:

Variance of a linear function of a random variable:

$$V(aX + b) = a^2 V(X) = a^2 \sigma^2 \qquad (3\text{--}10)$$

where *a* and *b* are fixed numbers

Using equation 3–10, we will find the variance of the profit in Example 3–3. The profit is given by $2X - 8{,}000$. We need to find the variance of X in this example. We find

$$E(X^2) = (5{,}000)^2(0.2) + (6{,}000)^2(0.3) + (7{,}000)^2(0.2) + (8{,}000)^2(0.2)$$
$$+ (9{,}000)^2(0.1)$$
$$= 46{,}500{,}000.$$

The expected value of X is $E(X) = 6,700$. The variance of X is thus

$$V(X) = E(X^2) - [E(X)]^2 = 46,500,000 - (6,700)^2 = 1,610,000.$$

Finally, we find the variance of the profit, using equation 3–10, as $2^2(1,610,000) = 6,440,000$. The standard deviation of the profit is $\sqrt{6,440,000} = 2,537.72$.

Some Properties of Means and Variances

An investor has income from two sources. Investment A gives her a random amount, X, per month, with a certain probability distribution and mean $E(X) = \$350$. Investment B also gives her a random amount, Y, which has a different probability distribution, with mean $E(Y) = \$200$. What is the expected monthly income from both sources? The answer is very simple: $\$350 + \$200 = \$550$. The reason for this is a rule we have for means that says $E(X + Y) = E(X) + E(Y)$, which in this case is equal to $\$350 + \$200 = \$550$.

Our dice example demonstrates this property well. The expected value of the sum of the dots on two dice was 7. But let's look at each die separately. What is the expected number of a single die? Each of the six numbers 1 to 6 has probability 1/6. The mean, therefore, is found as follows:

$$(1)(1/6) + (2)(1/6) + (3)(1/6) + (4)(1/6) + (5)(1/6) + (6)(1/6) = 3.5$$

This should be intuitively clear since 3.5 is the center of the six equally likely points. Now, what is the mean of the sum of the two dice? By the rule above, it is just the sum of the two means: $3.5 + 3.5 = 7$.

The variance of the sum (or the difference) of two random variables is equal to the sum of the two variances if the two random variables are independent. If the variance of investment X is 84 and the variance of investment Y is 60, and the two investments are independent of each other, then the variance of the total income from both sources is $V(X) + V(Y) = 84 + 60 = 144$. This means that the standard deviation of the total income is the square root of this variance, which is \$12.

Chebyshev's Theorem

The standard deviation is useful in obtaining bounds on the possible values of the random variable with certain probability. The bounds are obtainable from a well-known theorem, *Chebyshev's theorem* (the name is sometimes spelled Tchebychev, Tchebysheff, or any of a number of variations). The theorem says that for any number k greater than 1.00, the probability that the value of a given random variable will be *within k standard deviations* of the mean is at least $1 - 1/k^2$. In Chapter 1, we listed some results for data sets that are derived from this theorem.

Chebyshev's Theorem

For a random variable X with mean μ and standard deviation σ, and for any number $k > 1$,

$$P(|X - \mu| < k\sigma) \geq 1 - 1/k^2 \qquad (3\text{–}11)$$

Let us see how the theorem is applied by selecting values of k. While k does not have to be an integer, we will use integers. When $k = 2$, we have $1 - 1/k^2 = 0.75$: the theorem says that there is at least a 0.75 probability that the value of the random variable will be within a distance of two standard deviations away from the mean. Letting $k = 3$, we find that there is at least a 0.89 probability that X will be within three standard deviations of its mean. We can similarly apply the rule for other values of k. The rule holds for data sets and populations in a similar way. When applied to a sample of observations, the rule says that at least 75% of the observations lie within two standard deviations of the sample mean, $\bar{x}$. It says that at least 89% of the observations lie within three standard deviations of the mean, and so on. Applying the theorem to the random variable of Example 3–2, which has mean 2.3 and standard deviation 1.418, we find that there is at least a 0.75 probability that X will be anywhere from $2.3 - 2(1.418)$ to $2.3 + 2(1.418) = -0.536$ to 5.136. From the actual probability distribution in this example, Table 3–3, we know that the probability that X will be between 0 and 5 is 1.00.

$\bar{x} \pm 2s$

Often, we will know the distribution of the random variable in question, in which case we will be able to use the distribution for obtaining actual probabilities rather than the bounds offered by Chebyshev's theorem. If the exact distribution of the random variable is not known, but we may assume an approximate distribution, the approximate probabilities may still be better than the general bounds offered by Chebyshev's theorem.

PROBLEMS

3–10. Find the expected value of the random variable in problem 3–1. Also find the variance of the random variable and its standard deviation.

3–11. Find the mean, variance, and standard deviation of the random variable in problem 3–2.

3–12. What is the expected percentage of people responding to an advertisement when the probability distribution is the one given in problem 3–3? What is the variance of the percentage of people who respond to the advertisement?

3–13. Find the mean, variance, and standard deviation of the number of cars sold per day using the probability distribution in problem 3–4.

3–14. What is the expected number of dots appearing on two dice? (Use the probability distribution you computed in your answer to problem 3–5.)

3–15. Use the probability distribution in problem 3–6 to find the expected number of shipment orders per day. What is the probability that on a given day there will be more orders than the average?

3–16. Find the mean, variance, and standard deviation of the number of wooden sailboats constructed in a month using the probability distribution in problem 3–7.

3–17. According to Chebyshev's theorem, what is the minimum probability that a random variable will be within four standard deviations of its mean?

3–18. At least 8/9 of a population lie within how many standard deviations of the population mean? Why?

3–19. The average annual return on a certain stock is 8.3%, and the variance of the returns on the stock is 2.3. Another stock has average return of 8.4% per year and variance of 6.4. Which stock is riskier? Why?

3–20.   Returns on a certain business venture, to the nearest $1,000, are known to follow the probability distribution:

x	P(x)
−2,000	0.1
−1,000	0.1
0	0.2
1,000	0.2
2,000	0.3
3,000	0.1

a.   What is the most likely monetary outcome of the business venture?

b.   Is the venture likely to be successful? Explain.

c.   What is the long-term average earning of business ventures of this kind? Explain.

d.   What is a good measure of the risk involved in a venture of this kind? Why? Compute this measure.

3–21.   Management of an airline knows that 0.5% of the airline's passengers lose their luggage on domestic flights. Management also knows that the average value claimed for a lost piece of luggage on domestic flights is $600. The company is considering increasing fares by an appropriate amount to cover expected compensation to passengers who lose their luggage. By how much should the airline increase fares? Why? Explain using the ideas of a random variable and its expectation.

3–22.   Refer to problem 3–7. Suppose that the sailboat builders have fixed monthly costs of $25,000 and an additional construction cost of $5,000 per boat. Find the expected monthly cost of the operation. What property of expected values are you using?

3–23.   Refer to problem 3–4. Suppose the car dealership's operation costs are well approximated by the square root of the number of cars sold, multiplied by $300. What is the expected daily cost of the operation? Explain.

3–24.   In problem 3–2, suppose that a penalty is imposed on the typing pool of an amount equal to the square of the number of errors per page. What is the expected penalty per page? Explain.

3–25.   What is the meaning of the expected value of a random variable, and what are its uses?

3–26.   Explain the meaning of the variance of a random variable. What are possible uses of the variance?

3–27.   Why is the standard deviation of a random variable more meaningful than its variance for interpretation purposes?

3–28.   Refer to problem 3–22. Find the variance and the standard deviation of the monthly production cost.

3-3   The Binomial Distribution

Consider the following examples.

1. A coin is tossed five times. Let H denote the number of heads that appear.
2. It is known that 30% of the people in a given city prefer to use public transportation. A random sample of 20 people is selected. Let T be the number of people in the sample found to prefer public transportation.
3. It is known that 15% of the items produced by a machine are defective. A random sample of 12 items is chosen from a very large lot. Let D be the number of defective items found in the sample.

What characterizes the random variables H, T, and D? They are just a few of the many examples of discrete random variables following a special probability distribution known as the *binomial distribution*. The binomial distribution is based on an experiment consisting of a sequence of *Bernoulli trials*. The trials are named after Jakob Bernoulli (1654–1705), who was the first to propose them.

Assumptions for the binomial probability distribution

Bernoulli trials are a sequence of *n* identical trials satisfying the following assumptions.

1. Each trial has two possible outcomes, called *success* and *failure*. The two outcomes are mutually exclusive and exhaustive.
2. The probability of success, denoted by *p*, remains constant from trial to trial. The probability of failure is denoted by *q*, where $q = 1 - p$.
3. The *n* trials are independent. That is, the outcome of any trial does not affect the outcomes of other trials.

The terms *success* and *failure* are statistical terms and do not necessarily have the everyday meaning attached to the two words. In fact, when dealing with defective items in a production process, we may define the outcome "item is defective" as a success. Success refers to the occurrence of a particular event (e.g., "item is defective"), and failure refers to the nonoccurrence of the event. We define the *binomial random variable* as a random variable that counts the number of successes in a sequence of *n* Bernoulli trials.

A random variable, *X*, that counts the number of successes in *n* Bernoulli trials, where *p* is the probability of success in any given trial, is said to follow the binomial distribution with parameters *n* and *p*. We call *X* a **binomial random variable.**

Note that the random variables in all three examples are binomial. The first, H, follows a binomial distribution with $n = 5$ and $p = 0.5$ (we assume a fair coin). Successive tosses of a coin are independent, the only outcomes are heads or tails (success versus failure), and the probability of either remains constant from toss to toss.

In the second example, our random variable T is binomial with $n = 20$ and $p = 0.3$. Recall from Chapter 2 that the assumption of random sampling implies the independence of outcomes. Note an important point: We are implicitly assuming that the number of people in the city is large so that the outcome of any trial does not affect the proportion of the remaining people in the city who prefer to use public transportation (i.e., the probability of the event "prefer public transportation" for any person in the sample is not seriously affected by the outcome for any other sampled person). If there were only 10 people in our population, 3 of whom preferred public transportation, the situation would be different. The probability that our first person (assume people are sampled in some order) prefers public transportation would indeed be 0.3.

The probability that the next sampled person prefers public transportation, however, is either $2/9 = 0.22$ or $3/9 = 0.33$, *depending* on whether the first person prefers public transportation or does not. In this case, assumptions 2 and 3 of the Bernoulli process would be violated, and T would *not* be binomial. The assumptions are not seriously violated as long as the size of the population, N, is large compared with the sample size n (a generally accepted rule of thumb is $N/n \geq 10$).

Finally, we see that D follows a binomial distribution with parameters $n = 12$ and $p = 0.15$. We assume that the machine produces a large number of items and that the sampling is done randomly from this large population. This reduces the chance that the sample is drawn from a batch of adjacent items that could be similar to each other (either more likely to be defective than the entire population, or less so).

Binomial Probabilities

Now that we have set the assumptions required for a binomial probability distribution, let us see how the probabilities are computed. In the coin-tossing example, the coin is tossed five times, and the random variable H is defined as the number of heads that appear. We want to find the probability distribution of H. The possible values of H are 0, 1, 2, 3, 4, and 5. Let us look, in particular, at the event $H = 2$. This is the event that the five tosses of the coin produce exactly two heads. We want to evaluate the probability of this event, $P(H = 2)$.

First, let us find the number of ways in which this event may occur. The sequences of five tosses of the coin that result in exactly two heads are TTTHH, TTHTH, THTTH, HTTTH, TTHHT, THTHT, HTTHT, THHTT, HTHTT, and HHTTT. There are 10 such sequences. Now we need to find the probability of each particular sequence. Owing to the independence of the five trials, the probability of a particular sequence, say, the sequence HHTTT, is the product of the probabilities of the events heads, heads, tails, tails, and tails, which is *ppqqq*. Since the order of appearance of heads or tails does not affect the probabilities, we see that this probability, p^2q^3, is the probability of any one of the 10 sequences. Since there are 10 possible sequences leading to the value $H = 2$, we multiply p^2q^3 by 10, giving us $P(H = 2) = 10p^2q^3$. Finally, for a fair coin $p = q = 0.5$; therefore, $P(H = 2) = 10(0.5)^5 = 0.3125$.

It is possible to compute the probabilities of the other events, $P(H = 0)$, $P(H = 1)$, $P(H = 3)$, $P(H = 4)$, and $P(H = 5)$ in a similar way. It would be more useful, however, if we could generalize the procedure by which we obtained the preceding probability and develop a formula for the binomial probabilities. We note the following:

1. The probability of any *given sequence* of x successes out of n trials with probability of success p and probability of failure q is equal to

$$p^x q^{n-x}$$

   Note that in our coin-tossing example, $p = q = 0.5$, $n = 5$, and $x = 2$, giving $(0.5)^2(0.5)^3 = (0.5)^5$.

2. The number of different sequences of n trials that result in exactly x successes is equal to the number of choices of x elements out of a total of n elements. This number is denoted $n\mathbf{C}x$, or $\binom{n}{x}$, and from equation 2–13 we know that it is equal to

$$\frac{n!}{x!(n-x)!}$$

[Handwritten margin note:]

$$\binom{5}{2} = \frac{5!}{3! \, 2!}$$

$$= \frac{5 \times 4 \times 3}{3! \times 2}$$

$$= 10$$

In our coin-tossing example,

$$\binom{n}{x} = \binom{5}{2} = \frac{5!}{2!(5-2)!} = \frac{(5)(4)(3)(2)(1)}{(2)(1)(3)(2)(1)} = 10$$

as we obtained earlier by direct counting.

Since there are $\binom{n}{x}$ sequences and each sequence has probability $p^x q^{n-x}$, the probability of x successes in n trials is the product of the two expressions. The resulting binomial probability law follows. We will use the simplified notation $P(x)$ for the probability: $P(X = x$ successes in n trials, where the probability of success is p).

The binomial probability distribution:

$$P(x) = \binom{n}{x}p^x q^{n-x} = \frac{n!}{x!(n-x)!}p^x q^{n-x} \qquad (3\text{–}12)$$

where:

p is the probability of success in a single trial,

$q = 1 - p$,

n is the number of trials,

and x is the number of successes

By substituting values of x, n, p, and q into equation 3–12, we are able to determine all the probabilities, that is, the probability *distribution,* of our binomial random variable of interest. Table 3–9 shows how the binomial probabilities for all values of a random variable are obtained using equation 3–12.

Table 3–10 gives the binomial probability distribution of the random variable H in our example. Use equation 3–12, or the equivalent, Table 3–9, to verify the probabilities in the table. Recall that 0! is defined as 1.00; and $p^0 = 1$ (for $p \neq 0$).

As the number of trials, n, increases, the computation of the probability distribution using equation 3–12 becomes more tedious. To facilitate use of the binomial probability model, the distribution has been tabulated for various values of n and p. Such a table of probabilities is Table 1 in Appendix C. The table lists the cumulative

TABLE 3-9   The Binomial Distribution

Number of Successes, x	Probability $P(x)$
0	$\binom{n}{0}p^0 q^n$
1	$\binom{n}{1}p^1 q^{n-1}$
2	$\binom{n}{2}p^2 q^{n-2}$
3	$\binom{n}{3}p^3 q^{n-3}$
$\vdots$	$\vdots$
n	$\binom{n}{n}p^n q^0$
	1.00

TABLE 3-10 **Binomial Probability Distribution of H, the Number of Heads Appearing in Five Tosses of a Fair Coin**

h	P(h)
0	$(5!/0!5!)(0.5)^0(0.5)^5 = 0.031$
1	$(5!/1!4!)(0.5)^1(0.5)^4 = 0.156$
2	$(5!/2!3!)(0.5)^2(0.5)^3 = 0.313$
3	$(5!/3!2!)(0.5)^3(0.5)^2 = 0.313$
4	$(5!/4!1!)(0.5)^4(0.5)^1 = 0.156$
5	$(5!/5!0!)(0.5)^5(0.5)^0 = 0.031$
	1.000

TABLE 3-11 **Reproduction of Part of the Table of the Cumulative Binomial Distribution (Table 1 in Appendix C)**

$n = 5$

x	0.01	0.05	0.10	0.20	0.30	0.40	0.50	0.60	0.70	0.80	0.90	0.95	0.99
0	.951	.774	.590	.328	.168	.078	.031	.010	.002	.000	.000	.000	.000
1	.999	.977	.919	.737	.528	.337	.187	.087	.031	.007	.000	.000	.000
2	1.000	.999	.991	.942	.837	.683	.500	.317	.163	.058	.009	.001	.000
3	1.000	1.000	1.000	.993	.969	.913	.813	.663	.472	.263	.081	.023	.001
4	1.000	1.000	1.000	1.000	.998	.990	.969	.922	.832	.672	.410	.226	.049

The column header *p* spans columns 0.01 through 0.99.

binomial probabilities, $F(x)$. Recall from equation 3–3 that the cumulative distribution function $F(x)$ is the sum of the probabilities of all values i less than or equal to x:

$$F(x) = P(X \leq x) = \sum_{\text{all } i \leq x} P(i)$$

Table 3–11 is a reproduction of the part of Table 1 corresponding to $n = 5$. In the column $p = 0.50$, we find the *cumulative* probabilities corresponding to the probability distribution given in Table 3–10. (Note: The cumulative probabilities for $x = 5$ are omitted because they are all equal to 1.00. Accuracy is to the third decimal only; the 1.000 in the last row of the column corresponding to $p = 0.05$ should be interpreted accordingly.) For $p = 0.50$, note, for example, that $P(X = 3) = \sum_{i=0}^{3} P(i) - \sum_{i=0}^{2} P(i) = F(3) - F(2) = 0.813 - 0.500 = 0.313$, which corresponds to what we find in Table 3–10. In general, $P(x) = F(x) - F(x - 1)$, as can be deduced from equation 3–3.

For random variable T, the number of people in a random sample of 20 who prefer to use public transportation, we find from Table 1 (using $p = 0.3$) that the probability that at most 5 in the sample will be found to prefer public transportation is $F(5) = 0.416$. Let us look at an example.

EXAMPLE 3-4

In her article "Now You See It, Now You Don't" (*Forbes,* April 24, 1995, p. 45), Riva Atlas reports that 60% of Brooke shares are owned by LeBow. Suppose that a random sample of 15 shares is selected. What is the probability that *at most three* of them will be found to be owned by LeBow?

SOLUTION

We need $P(X \leq 3)$ for a binomial random variable with $n = 15$ and $p = 0.60$. Looking at Table 1, we find $F(3) = 0.002$.

Mean, Variance, and Shape of the Binomial Distribution

The mean of a binomial distribution is equal to the number of trials, n, times the probability of success in a single trial, p. The variance is equal to the number of trials times p, times q. These formulas and the standard deviation are as follows.

Mean of a binomial distribution:

$$\mu = E(X) = np \tag{3-13}$$

Variance of a binomial distribution:

$$\sigma^2 = V(X) = npq \tag{3-14}$$

Standard deviation of a binomial distribution:

$$\sigma = SD(X) = \sqrt{npq} \tag{3-15}$$

Recall that the mean of the distribution is the expected value of the random variable. Using equations 3–13 and 3–14, we find that the expected value of H, the number of heads appearing in five tosses of a fair coin, is $E(X) = np = 5(0.5) = 2.00$. This conforms with our intuition: as a long-run average, we expect that 2.5 out of 5 tosses of a fair coin will result in heads. The variance of H is $npq = 5(0.5)(0.5) = 1.25$.

Find the mean and the standard deviation of the random variables T and D. In Example 3–4, assuming p is indeed 0.60, the expected number of shares owned by LeBow out of a sample of 15 is $E(X) = np = 15(0.60) = 9$. The variance of this random variable is $V(X) = npq = 15(0.60)(0.40) = 3.6$. The standard deviation is $SD(X) = \sqrt{3.6} = 1.897$.

It is possible to use Chebyshev's theorem to obtain probability bounds on the value of a random variable using its mean and standard deviation. In cases where the probability distribution is known, we may find probabilities of values directly. Suppose, however, that we are interested in probabilities for a binomial random variable that is not tabulated. For example, let $n = 100$ and $p = 0.25$. Using Chebyshev's theorem with $k = 2$, we know that there is at least a 0.75 probability $(1 - 1/k^2 = 1 - 1/4 = 0.75)$ that the number of successes will be within $\mu \pm 2\sigma$—that is, within the bounds: $np \pm 2(\sqrt{npq}) = 100(0.25) \pm 2\sqrt{(100)(0.25)(0.75)} = 25 \pm 2(4.33) = 16.34$ and 33.66. We used Chebyshev's theorem to demonstrate the significance of knowing the standard deviation of a distribution. In the next chapter we will see a much better approximation for probabilities associated with a binomial random variable with a large number of trials—an approximation based on the normal distribution.

The shape of the probability distribution of a binomial random variable is symmetrical when $p = 0.50$. The distribution is skewed to the right when $p < 0.5$ and skewed to the left when $p > 0.5$, both if the number of trials is small. As n increases, the distribution becomes more and more symmetric. Figure 3–11 shows the binomial distribution for various values of n and p.

FIGURE 3–11   Binomial Probability Distribution for Various Values of *n* and *p*

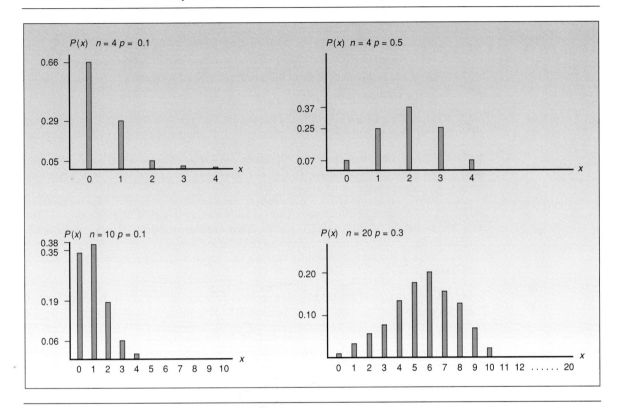

Sampling with or without Replacement

We noted earlier that the binomial distribution is appropriate when we are sampling from a population that is much larger than the sample. As a rule of thumb, we said that N/n should be at least 10. This is true for a sampling scheme *without replacement:* the sample is drawn and not returned into the population. If, on the other hand, we sample an item, note whether it is a success or a failure and *return* it to the population before the next item is selected for the sample, we are *sampling with replacement.* When sampling with replacement, the population need not be much larger than the sample for the binomial assumption to hold. The reason for this can be seen if we consider a simple case where the population consists of 10 items, 4 of which are successes and 6 are failures. For the item first selected, $p = 0.4$. Once the item is returned to the population and has an equal chance of being selected again, the probability of success for the second item is also $p = 0.4$, and the two drawings are independent. Sampling with replacement is not a frequently used procedure and will not be discussed further in this book.

PROBLEMS

3–29.   According to "Business Outlook," *Business Week,* April 24, 1995, p. 32, only 60% of the industries added workers during March 1995.

   a.   Let *A* be the total number of industries that added workers out of 5 that are of interest to an analyst. What assumptions must be satisfied for a binomial distribution of *A*?

b. What is the probability that 2 or more industries in a random sample of 5 added workers in March 1995?

c. Write the probability distribution of A in a table format.

d. What is the probability that at least one industry in the sample added workers?

e. What is the probability that exactly three industries in the sample added workers?

f. What is the expected number of industries that added workers?

h. Find the variance of A.

3–30.   Three of the 10 airplane tires at a hangar are faulty. Four tires are selected at random for a plane; let F be the number of faulty tires found. Is F a binomial random variable? Explain.

3–31.   A salesperson finds that, in the long run, two out of three sales calls are successful. Twelve sales calls are to be made; let X be the number of concluded sales. Is X a binomial random variable? Explain.

3–32.   A large shipment of computer chips is known to contain 10% defective chips. If 100 chips are randomly selected, what is the expected number of defective ones? What is the standard deviation of the number of defective chips? Use Chebyshev's theorem to give bounds such that there is at least a 0.75 chance that the number of defective chips will be within the two bounds.

3–33.   A new treatment for baldness is known to be effective in 70% of the cases treated. Four bald members of the same family are treated; let X be the number of successfully treated members of the family. Is X a binomial random variable? Explain.

3–34.   What are Bernoulli trials? What is the relationship between Bernoulli trials and the binomial random variable?

3–35.   In a given area, the probability that a person is exposed to an advertisement of a paper company is 0.20. If 10 people are randomly chosen from among the population in the area, what is the probability that at least 5 of them were exposed to the advertisement? What is the probability that at most 2 were exposed to the advertisement?

3–36.   Records of a health insurance company show that 30% of its policyholders over 50 years of age submit a claim during the year. Fifteen policyholders over 50 years of age are selected at random. What is the probability that at least 10 will submit a claim during the coming year? What are the mean and standard deviation of the distribution?

3–37.   In *acceptance sampling* in quality control, a lot is accepted only if the number of items that do not conform to production specifications out of a given total is no greater than some preset value. Suppose that out of a large collection of produced items, 20% are nonconforming. A random sample of 20 items is selected in an acceptance sampling scheme that requires that no more than 2 items out of 20 be nonconforming. What is the probability that the lot will be rejected?

3–38.   Samuel Adams beer, made by one of the nation's smallest breweries, Boston Brewing Co., is the only American beer exported to Germany. About 3,000 barrels are shipped to Germany each year.[2] Suppose that the beer is served on draft and randomly sent to establishments in an area of Germany where 27,000 barrels of German beer are also served annually. If five Americans arrive in this area and order draft beer, what is the probability that at least two of them will actually be served American beer? What assumptions are you making? If 10 Americans arrive, what is the expected number of drinkers to be served the Boston beer?

---

[2] "Wooing Jacques and Fritz Six-Pack," *Business Week,* February 4, 1991, p. 93.

3–39. Every week the Barbados Tourist Board interviews six randomly chosen vacationers on the island about their experience. In general, each vacationer's comments can be classified as mainly positive or mainly negative. The responses are then published in the *Visitor* newspaper. Suppose that only 5% of all visitors to Barbados are dissatisfied with their visit. What is the probability that at least two visitors out of the six interviewed will express negative comments?

3–40. A study found that 70% of all employees believed that employee involvement in a firm was important for improving quality.[3] If 15 employees are randomly chosen, what is the probability that at most 10 of them will be found to believe that employee involvement can improve quality?

3–4 Other Discrete Probability Distributions[4]

The binomial probability distribution is among the most commonly used discrete distributions in statistics. There are several other useful discrete distributions. In this section, we will give brief descriptions of some of these distributions. These are the *Poisson,* the *hypergeometric,* the *multinomial,* and the *geometric* probability distributions. These distributions are not in the main direction of statistical inference followed in this book but find use in areas of probability modeling, operations research, and other areas. All of these distributions are discussed in detail in advanced books on probability.

The Poisson Distribution

The Poisson distribution is useful in describing a random variable that counts the number of occurrences in a particular interval of time: the number of equipment failures per week, the number of traffic accidents per month, and so on. The Poisson distribution is a good approximation for the binomial when the number of trials, n, is large ($n \geq 20$) and the probability of success (the probability of an *occurrence* in this context) is small ($p \leq 0.05$).

Poisson distribution:

$$P(x) = \frac{\mu^x e^{-\mu}}{x!} \quad \text{for } x = 0, 1, 2, 3, \ldots \quad (3\text{–}16)$$

where μ is the mean of the distribution (and also happens to be the variance) and e is the base of the natural logarithms ($e = 2.71828 \ldots$)

When using the Poisson as an approximation to a binomial random variable, we set $\mu = np$ and use equation 3–16. We demonstrate the use of the Poisson distribution as an approximation for the binomial with the following example.

EXAMPLE 3-5

Today, people have more and more opportunities to get customized products rather than the usual uniform products of the past. Telephone manufacturers now offer 1,000 different choices for a telephone (as combinations of color, type, options, portability, etc.).[5] A company is opening a large regional office, and each of its 200 managers is allowed to

---

[3] "Is Industry Ready for Adult Relationships?" *Industry Week,* January 21, 1991, p. 18.

[4] This is an optional section, which may be skipped without loss of continuity.

[5] R. McKenna, "Marketing Is Everything," *Harvard Business Review,* January–February 1991, p. 72.

order his or her own choice of a telephone. Assuming independence of choices, and that each of the 1,000 different combinations of telephone are equally likely, what is the probability that a particular choice will be made by none, one, two, or three of the managers?

SOLUTION

Here we have a binomial random variable with large n (200) and small p (1/1,000 = 0.001), so the Poisson approximation should work well. The parameter value is $\mu = np = 200(0.001) = 0.2$. Using equation 3–16, we get

$$P(X = 0) = (0.2)^0 e^{-0.2}/0! = 0.8187$$
$$P(X = 1) = (0.2)^1 e^{-0.2}/1! = 0.1637$$
$$P(X = 2) = (0.2)^2 e^{-0.2}/2! = 0.0164$$
$$P(X = 3) = (0.2)^3 e^{-0.2}/3! = 0.0011$$

To avoid having to compute every probability using equation 3–16, a table is provided. This is Appendix C, Table 12. Use the table to verify the probabilities calculated directly in the solution of this example.

The Poisson distribution has other important applications in addition to its use as an approximation to the binomial. This distribution is useful in describing the number of occurrences over a fixed interval of time or space. The Poisson distribution requires the following assumptions.

Poisson assumptions:

1. The probability that an event will occur in a short interval of time (or space) is proportional to the size of the interval.
2. In a very small interval, the probability that two events will occur is close to zero.
3. The probability that any number of events will occur in a given interval is independent of where the interval begins.
4. The probability of any number of events occurring over a given interval is independent of the number of events that occurred prior to the interval.

In this general context, the parameter μ stands for the average number of occurrences in the period of time or space in question (e.g., 12 accidents per week, 2 typing errors per page, etc.). Figure 3–12 shows the Poisson distribution for various values of μ.

The Hypergeometric Distribution

In cases where we sample without replacement from a population that is relatively small compared with the sample size, we know that the binomial distribution is not appropriate. In such cases the random variable counting the number of successes in n trials follows the hypergeometric distribution. Denoting our random variable by X, the number of elements in the entire population by N, the number of successes in the entire population by S, and (as with the binomial) the number of trials by n, the probability distribution of X is given in equation 3–17.

FIGURE 3–12 Poisson Distribution for Different Values of μ

Hypergeometric distribution:

$$P(x) = \binom{S}{x}\binom{N-S}{n-x} \Big/ \binom{N}{n} \tag{3–17}$$

The mean of the hypergeometric distribution is $\mu = np$, where $p = S/N$. The variance is $\sigma^2 = (N - n/N - 1)npq$.

Since we usually sample from a large population, the hypergeometric distribution is somewhat less useful than the binomial. It is important to understand, however, that this is the correct distribution when sampling without replacement. We illustrate the use of this distribution in the following example.

EXAMPLE 3–6

Suppose that automobiles arrive at a dealership in lots of 10 and that for time and resource considerations, only 5 out of each 10 are inspected for safety. The 5 cars are randomly chosen from the 10 in the lot. If 2 out of the 10 cars in a lot are below standards for safety, what is the probability that at least 1 out of the 5 cars to be inspected will be found not meeting the safety standards?

SOLUTION

Here we have a hypergeometric random variable with $N = 10$, $S = 2$, $n = 5$, and $x = 1$ or 2. Using equation 3–17, we get

$$P(1) = \binom{2}{1}\binom{8}{4} \Big/ \binom{10}{5} = \frac{2!}{1!1!}\frac{8!}{4!4!} \Big/ \frac{10!}{5!5!} = 0.556$$

$$P(2) = \binom{2}{2}\binom{8}{3} \Big/ \binom{10}{5} = \frac{2!}{2!0!}\frac{8!}{3!5!} \Big/ \frac{10!}{5!5!} = 0.222$$

and the answer is $P(1) + P(2) = 0.556 + 0.222 = 0.778$.

The Multinomial Distribution

Recall that in the binomial experiment we classify outcomes as successes or failures, for example, user versus nonuser of a product. It is possible to generalize the experiment to situations where outcomes may be classified into more than two categories. Suppose there are k categories of outcomes. Instead of user versus nonuser of a product, suppose a member of the population may be classified as "user of product A," "user of product B," . . . , "user of product K." The probability distribution of (X_1 = number of users of product A, X_2 = number of users of product B, . . . , X_k = number of users of product K) in a sample of size n is the *multinomial distribution* with parameters n and $p_1, p_2, \ldots, p_k$ (where p_i is the probability of occurrence of category i). The p_i terms must add to 1.00, they are constant from trial to trial, and trials are independent. A formula for the multinomial distribution follows.

Multinomial distribution:

$$P(x_1, x_2, \ldots, x_k) = \frac{n!}{x_1! \, x_2! \cdots x_k!} \, p_1^{x_1} p_2^{x_2} \cdots p_k^{x_k} \qquad (3\text{–}18)$$

EXAMPLE 3-7

According to news reports in early 1995, among the first *Pentium* chips Intel made, some had a peculiar defect, which rendered some rarely carried-out arithmetic operations incorrect. Any chip could therefore be classified into one of three categories: Good, Broken (useless), or Defective (operable except for the peculiar defect described above). Suppose that 70% of the chips made were good, 25% had the peculiar defect, and 5% were broken. If a random sample of 20 chips was selected, what is the probability that 15 were good, 3 defective, and 2 broken?

SOLUTION

We use equation 3–18, where $p_G = 0.70$, $p_D = 0.25$, $p_B = 0.05$, $n = 20$, $x_G = 15$, $x_D = 3$, and $x_B = 2$. We get

$$P(15, 3, 2) = \frac{20!}{15! \, 3! \, 2!} \, (0.70)^{15}(0.25)^3(0.05)^2 = 0.0288$$

Similar computations (usually with a computer) can give us the entire probability distribution—for all values of x_G, x_D, x_B.

The Geometric Distribution

Consider the binomial experiment with its usual assumptions. Instead of counting the number of successes in n trials, let our random variable X count the *number of trials until the first success*. Our random variable has a *geometric probability distribution*:

> **Geometric distribution:**
>
> $$P(x) = pq^{x-1} \qquad\qquad (3\text{-}19)$$
>
> where $x = 1, 2, 3, \ldots$ and p and q are the binomial parameters. The mean and variance of the geometric distribution are $\mu = 1/p$ and $\sigma^2 = q/p^2$.

The number of items we need to sample until the first defective item is found is a geometric random variable. The expected value $\mu = 1/p$ conforms with our intuition: if the proportion of defective items is $p = 0.1$, then it seems logical that, *on the average*, we would have to sample 10 items until the first defective item is found. The geometric distribution is illustrated in the next example.

A recent study indicates that Pepsi-Cola has a market share of 33.2% (versus 40.9% for Coca-Cola).[6] A marketing research firm wants to conduct a new taste test for which it needs Pepsi drinkers. Potential participants for the test are selected by random screening of soft drink users to find Pepsi drinkers. What is the probability that the first randomly selected drinker qualifies? What is the probability that two soft drink users will have to be interviewed to find the first Pepsi drinker? three? four?

EXAMPLE 3-8

The first person qualifies if there is "success" in a single trial when the probability of success is 0.332. Using the geometric distribution with $x = 1$, we find from equation 3–19: $P(1) = (0.332)(0.668)^0 = 0.332$. Similarly, the first person will be a non-Pepsi drinker and the second will qualify with probability $P(2) = (0.332)(0.668)^1 = 0.2218$. Two non-Pepsi drinkers will be interviewed before the first Pepsi user with probability $P(3) = (0.332)(0.668)^2 = 0.1481$. And finally, $P(4) = (0.332)(0.668)^3 = 0.099$.

SOLUTION

PROBLEMS

3–41. In an effort to reach "zero defects" in its production process, a manufacturing firm managed to achieve 0.1% defective items produced. To check this rate, random samples are selected from time to time. Assuming this rate of defectives, what is the probability that out of a random sample of 100 items none will be found defective? one? two? three? (Use the Poisson approximation.)

3–42. The 3i company is the United Kingdom's largest venture capital provider, with a 35% share of the UK market.[7] Seven out of a total of exactly 20 firms under investigation are 3i-financed. If a random sample of 8 out of the 20 firms is to be selected for further scrutiny, what is the probability that at most 3 of them are 3i-financed?

3–43. As stated in the previous problem, 35% of all UK ventures are 3i-financed. If venture-capitalized firms are to be selected randomly until the first 3i-financed firm is found, what is the probability that three firms will be selected, with only the third being 3i-financed?

---

[6] "Pepsi Keeps on Going after No. 1," *Fortune,* March 11, 1991, pp. 62–70.

[7] "The Cautious Venture Capitalist," *Euromoney,* January 1991, pp. 41–46.

3–44.   The arrival of cars at a service station follows a Poisson distribution with parameter value of one car per minute. What is the probability that at least two cars will arrive in a given minute?

3–45.   Foreign banks now face extensive IRS reporting requirements.[8] Out of 15 banks with branches in Manhattan's Upper East Side, 6 are foreign-owned. The IRS plans to select a random sample of 10 out of the 15 banks for investigation. What is the probability that at least three of the selected banks will be foreign-owned?

3–46.   In 1995 the IRS announced its decision to audit 2 million taxpayers per year. If an additional 1 million taxpayers will be audited by mail (a somewhat less painful procedure), and assuming a total of 100 million taxpayers, find the probability that in a random sample of 50 taxpayers there will be one audit and one mail-audit.

3–47.   One in 5,000 salmon caught in Alaska's Bristol Bay has parasites that make it unfit for human consumption. Use the Poisson approximation to find the probability that out of a shipment of 1,800 fish, 2 at most will have to be destroyed due to parasites.

3–48.   An academic department has 11 faculty members, 4 of whom are tenured. Five faculty members are to be randomly selected from the entire department to serve on a committee. What is the probability that the tenured members in this committee will constitute a majority?

3–49.   I am stranded on a highway with a dead battery and no jumper cables. Every once in a while a car stops and the driver offers to help me. However, I have to let these drivers go if they have no jumper cables. If 10% of the cars carry jumper cables, then—on the average—how many cars will stop without being able to help before I find someone who can help me?

3-5   Continuous Random Variables

Instead of depicting probability distributions by simple graphs, where the height of the line above each value represents the probability of that value of the random variable, let us use a histogram. We will associate the *area* of each rectangle of the histogram with the probability of the particular value represented. Let us look at a simple example. Let X be the time, measured in minutes, it takes to complete a given task. A histogram of the probability distribution of X is shown in Figure 3–13.

   The probability of each value is the area of the rectangle over the value and is written on top of the rectangle. Since the rectangles all have the same base, the height of each rectangle is proportional to the probability. Note that the probabilities add to 1.00, as required. Now suppose that X can be measured more accurately. The distribution of X, with time now measured to the nearest half-minute, is shown in Figure 3–14.

   Let us continue the process. Time is a continuous random variable; it can take on any value measured on an interval of numbers. We may, therefore, refine our measurement to the nearest quarter minute, the nearest 5 seconds, or the nearest second, or we can use even more finely divided units. As we refine the measurement scale, the number of rectangles in the histogram increases and the width of each rectangle decreases. The probability of each value is still measured by the area of the rectangle

---

[8] "Foreign Banks Face IRS Scrutiny," *Bankers Monthly,* February 1991, p. 33.

FIGURE 3–13   Histogram of the Probability Distribution of the Time to Complete a Task, with Time Measured to the Nearest Minute

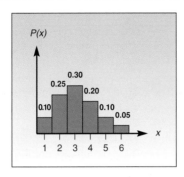

FIGURE 3–14   Histogram of the Probability Distribution of Time to Complete a Task, with Time Measured to the Nearest Half-Minute

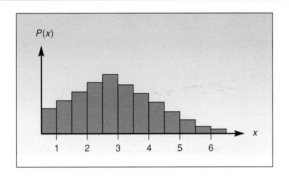

above it, and the total area of all rectangles remains 1.00, as required of all probability distributions. As we keep refining our measurement scale, the discrete distribution of X tends to a continuous probability distribution. The steplike surface formed by the tops of the rectangles in the histogram tends to a smooth function. This function is denoted by $f(x)$ and is called the *probability density function* of the continuous random variable X. Probabilities are still measured as areas under the curve. The probability that the task will be completed in 2 to 3 minutes is the area under $f(x)$ between the points $x = 2$ and $x = 3$. Histograms of the probability distribution of X with our measurement scale refined further and further are shown in Figure 3–15. Also shown is the density function, $f(x)$, of the limiting continuous random variable X. The density function is the limit of the histograms as the number of rectangles approaches infinity and the width of each rectangle approaches zero.

Now that we have developed an intuitive feel for continuous random variables, and for probabilities of intervals of values as areas under a density function, we make some formal definitions.

FIGURE 3–15   Histograms of the Distribution of Time to Complete a Task as Measurement Is Refined to Smaller and Smaller Intervals of Time, and the Limiting Density Function, $f(x)$

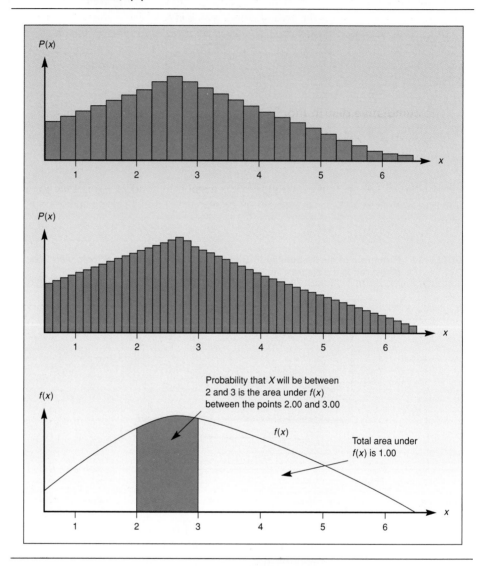

A **continuous random variable** is a random variable that can take on any value in an interval of numbers.

The probabilities associated with a continuous random variable X are determined by the **probability density function** of the random variable. The function, denoted $f(x)$, has the following properties.

1. $f(x) \geq 0$ for all x.
2. The probability that X will be between two numbers a and b is equal to the area under $f(x)$ between a and b.
3. The total area under the entire curve of $f(x)$ is equal to 1.00.

When the sample space is continuous, the probability of any single given value is zero. For a continuous random variable, therefore, the probability of occurrence of any given value is zero. We see this from property 2, noting that the area under a curve between a point and itself is the area of a line, which is zero. *For a continuous random variable, nonzero probabilities are associated only with intervals of numbers.*

We define the cumulative distribution function, $F(x)$, for a continuous random variable similarly to the way we defined it for a discrete random variable: $F(x)$ is the probability that X is less than (or equal to) x.

The **cumulative distribution function** of a continuous random variable:[9]

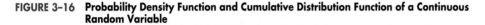

$F(x) = P(X \le x) =$ Area under $f(x)$ between the *smallest* possible value of X (often $-\infty$) and the point x.

The cumulative distribution function, $F(x)$, is a smooth, nondecreasing function that increases from 0 to 1.00. The connection between $f(x)$ and $F(x)$ is demonstrated in Figure 3–16.

FIGURE 3-16 **Probability Density Function and Cumulative Distribution Function of a Continuous Random Variable**

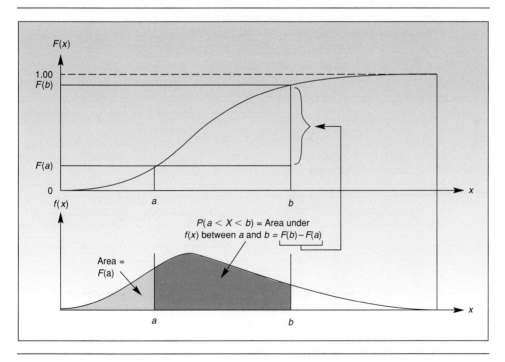

---

[9] If you are familiar with calculus, you know that the area under a curve of a function is given by the integral of the function. The probability that X will be between a and b is the definite integral of $f(x)$ between these two points: $P(a < X < b) = \int_a^b f(x)\,dx$. In calculus notation, we define the cumulative distribution function as $F(x) = \int_{-\infty}^x f(y)\,dy$.

We now give an example of a continuous random variable. The simplest continuous distribution is the uniform distribution over an interval. A continuous random variable has the uniform distribution over an interval I if it is equally likely to be in any subinterval of I as in any other subinterval of the same length. The density of a uniform random variable over the interval $I = [0,5]$ is as follows.

Uniform [0,5] density:

$$f(x) = \begin{cases} 1/5 & \text{for } 0 \le x \le 5 \\ 0 & \text{otherwise} \end{cases} \tag{3–20}$$

This density is shown in Figure 3–17. Note that the entire area under the curve is equal to the area of the rectangle with base 5 and height 1/5 and is therefore equal to 1.00, as required. Also, $f(x) \ge 0$ for all x. To find the probability that X will be between 1 and 3, $P(1 \le X \le 3)$, we need to compute the area under $f(x)$ between 1 and 3. This is the area of the rectangle with base $3 - 1 = 2$ and height 1/5. The probability is thus 2/5. This is also shown in the figure.

The expected value of a continuous random variable is the average value that would result from repeated drawing of values of the random variable. It is the center of the "mass" associated with the area under the graph of the density function if we assume this area were covered by some material, such as cardboard, of uniform thickness.[10] This is demonstrated in Figure 3–18. Using this intuitive principle, we find the mean of the uniform [0,5] distribution to be $E(X) = 2.5$.

Most continuous random variables with which we will work have density functions more complicated than the uniform density. Areas under the densities of these random variables, needed for probability calculations, are obtainable from tables such as the ones in Appendix C. The next chapter is devoted to the most important continuous distribution we will use: the normal distribution.

FIGURE 3–17   Uniform [0,5] Density

---

[10] Using calculus, we define the expected value of a continuous random variable X as $E(X) = \int_{-\infty}^{\infty} xf(x)\,dx$. A similar relation, $E(X^2) = \int_{-\infty}^{\infty} x^2f(x)\,dx$, allows us to compute the variance of X with the aid of equation 3–8. Calculus is not required for understanding the material in this book.

FIGURE 3-18 **Mean of a Continuous Distribution as the Center of the Mass under the Density Function**

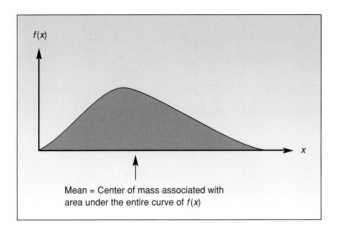

Mean = Center of mass associated with
area under the entire curve of $f(x)$

The Exponential Distribution[11]

We now present another example of a continuous random variable in common use in areas of applied probability. The random variable that measures the time between two occurrences that have a Poisson distribution is an *exponential* random variable. For example, if the number of cars that arrive at a service station per minute has a Poisson distribution, then the time between the arrivals of two consecutive cars (time being measured on a continuous scale) has an exponential distribution. The exponential distribution is the continuous limit of the discrete geometric distribution.

Exponential distribution:

The density function is

$$f(x) = \lambda e^{-\lambda x} \qquad \text{for } x \ge 0, \lambda > 0 \qquad (3\text{--}21)$$

The mean of the exponential distribution is $\mu = 1/\lambda$, and the standard deviation is also $1/\lambda$. The cumulative distribution is

$$F(x) = 1 - e^{-\lambda x} \qquad \text{for } x \ge 0 \qquad (3\text{--}22)$$

We demonstrate the use of the exponential distribution with the following example.

EXAMPLE 3-9

The time a particular machine operates before breaking down (time between breakdowns) is known to have an exponential distribution with parameter $\lambda = 2$. Time is measured in hours. What is the probability that the machine will work continuously for at least one hour? What is the average time between breakdowns?

---

[11] Optional subsection.

FIGURE 3-19   Exponential Density with $\lambda = 2$

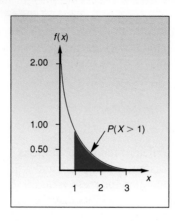

SOLUTION

Figure 3–19 shows the exponential density with parameter $\lambda = 2$. We require the area under the curve to the right of the point $x = 1$. Using equation 3–22, we get $P(X \geq 1) = 1 - F(1) = 1 - (1 - e^{-2(1)}) = 0.1353$. The average time between breakdowns is $\mu = 1/\lambda = 1/2$ hour.

PROBLEMS

3–50.   What is the main difference between a continuous random variable and a discrete one?

3–51.   How do we obtain probabilities of intervals of numbers for a continuous random variable?

3–52.   Let X be a continuous random variable. Explain why $P(X = a) = 0$ for any given number a.

3–53.   How is the cumulative probability function $F(x)$ defined for a continuous random variable?

3–54.   Let X have the probability density function:

$$f(x) = \begin{cases} (1/2)x & \text{for } 0 \leq x \leq 2 \\ 0 & \text{otherwise} \end{cases}$$

    a.   Sketch the probability density function.

    b.   Show that $f(x)$ is a probability density function.

    c.   Find the probability that X will be between 0 and 1.

3–55.   Write the density of a uniform [0,7] random variable. (Hint: The total area under $f(x)$ must equal 1.00.)

3–56.   Use the density of problem 3–55 to find the probability that X will be between 0 and 2.

3–57.   What is the expected value of the uniform [0,7] random variable of problem 3–55?

3–58.   For the random variable of problem 3–54, find the probability that X will be greater than 1.5.

3–59.   The time between customer arrivals at a bank has an exponential distribution with a mean time between arrivals of 3 minutes. If a customer just arrived, what is the probability that another customer will not arrive for at least 2 minutes?

3–60.   Light bulbs have an exponentially distributed life with mean 100 hours. What is the probability that the light bulb I am now putting in will last at least 65 hours?

3–61.   What is the standard deviation of the lifetime of a light bulb in the previous problem?

3-6   Using the Computer

Computers are often used for determining probabilities associated with random variables such as the binomial, Poisson, exponential, and others. We will now demonstrate how such probabilities are obtained for these random variables using the MINITAB package. Use the command PDF (probability distribution function) for the probability mass function of a discrete random variable or values of the density of a continuous random variable. The comand CDF is used for obtaining values of the cumulative distribution function. The particular distribution of interest is specified in a subcommand. Putting a semicolon at the end of the command PDF or CDF makes the computer ask for a subcommand. Then type BINOMIAL, POISSON, or EXPONEN-TIAL, followed by the parameter value(s). For the exponential, we also need to specify after the CDF command, the value x for which we require the cumulative probability. Note also that the parameter value for the exponential distribution in MINITAB is the mean rather than λ. Three examples are demonstrated in Figure 3–20.

3-7   Summary and Review of Terms

In this chapter we extended the ideas of probability presented in Chapter 2. We defined a **random variable** as a variable that takes on different numerical values determined by chance. We made a distinction between a **discrete** random variable—one that takes on discrete values—and a **continuous** random variable—one that may take on any value in an interval of numbers. We defined the **probability distribution** of a random variable as the rule that assigns probabilities to the different values of the random variable. In the discrete case, we saw that the probability distribution, $P(x)$, assigns probabilities to the numerical values the random variable may take. In the continuous case, we defined a **probability density function**, $f(x)$, and saw that probabilities are assigned only to intervals of numbers and are determined by areas under the density function. We defined the **cumulative distribution function** of a random variable, $F(x)$, as the function giving the probability that X is less than or equal to x. We also defined the **expected value** of a random variable as the mean of the probability distribution, and we defined the **variance** and the **standard deviation** for a discrete random variable. We saw how to compute the mean and variance of a function of a random variable; we also saw how to obtain probability bounds using **Chebyshev's theorem.** We discussed the **binomial distribution** as the discrete probability distribution of the number of successes in n independent trials with a fixed probability of success in all trials. We also discussed a few other probability distributions: the **Poisson, hypergeometric, geometric,** and **multinomial** discrete distributions, and the continuous **uniform** and **exponential** distributions.

3–80. Ten percent of the items produced at a plant are defective. A random sample of 20 items is selected. What is the probability that more than three items in the sample are defective? If items are selected randomly until the first defective item is encountered, how many items, on the average, will have to be sampled before the first defective item is found?

3–81. Lee Iacocca has volunteered to drive one of his Chryslers into a brick wall to demonstrate the effectiveness of airbags used in these cars.[16] Airbags are known to activate at random when the car decelerates anywhere from 9 to 14 miles per hour per second. The probability distribution for the deceleration speed at which bags activate is given below.

MPH/Second	Probability
9	0.12
10	0.23
11	0.34
12	0.21
13	0.06
14	0.04

    a. If the airbag activates at a deceleration of 12 MPH/second or more, Iacocca would get hurt. What is the probability of his being hurt in this demonstration?

    b. What is the mean deceleration at airbag activation moment?

    c. What is the standard deviation of deceleration at airbag activation time?

3–82. In the previous problem, the time that it takes the airbag to completely fill up from the moment of activation has an exponential distribution with mean 1 second. What is the probability that the airbag will fill up in less than 1/2 second?

3–83. The following is from *Business Week,* April 24, 1995, p. 6. If 20 consumers are randomly selected, what is the probability that at least 5 of them accept their date of birth being given out?

The List

A Private Affair

Like a bit of privacy? Good luck. Retailers happily sell data about you to direct mailers and others. And with the coming of "smart cards"—credit cards with info on you carried in a chip—worries intensify. But what data are consumers most leery about? A survey shows the closer a snoop comes to things you do every day—whom you call, what videos you watch—the more sensitive you get.

What Info Is OK to Give Out

Information	Percent Saying Acceptable
Your Name	73%
Your Date of Birth	70
Your Credit History	53
Your Medical History	28
Prescription Drugs You Buy	26
Videos You Rent	25
Credit Card Purchases	22
Phone Numbers You Call	15

Data: Mastercard International Inc., Yankelovich Partners Inc.

3–84. According to *The Economist,* 25% of all drugs sold in Japan are foreign, 20% are foreign drugs sold by Japanese companies, and the rest are Japanese made.[17] If 12 drugs are randomly chosen at a pharmacy, what is the probability that 4 are foreign, 4 are foreign sold by Japanese companies, and 4 are Japanese?

---

[16] "Surviving the Crash," *The Economist,* March 2, 1991, pp. 65–66.

[17] "Too Small to Compete?" *The Economist,* April 22, 1995, p. 65.

Case 3   DIRECT SHARE MARKETING AT WORK: "THE MILLIONAIRES' BANK"[18]

Pacific Bank raised its start-up capital in 1983 by subscriptions to units of $1 million each. As a result, a local San Francisco newspaper coined the name, "The Millionaires' Bank." There actually are only four investors who contributed a full million dollars. Most of the units are owned by groups of several individuals with a $20,000 minimum investment.

The unit arrangement is designed to ensure "management sufficient time and stability to achieve the bank's goals," according to the shareowners' Agreement and Proxy. During the bank's first five years, voting power was limited to the 22 "unit holders," who were all preapproved by the bank's board of directors. Any shareholder wishing to sell shares had to offer them first to others within the units before they could be sold to "outsiders."

When raising capital, organizers of the bank decided not to use a securities firm, either as an underwriter or as a commissioned agent. They also decided that they would pay no compensation—not even stock warrants or options—to the bank's officers or directors for their efforts in marketing shares.

Putting together an impressive and well-known team of managers and directors was the most important step for share marketing. Not only were the top executives experienced in running profitable and fast-growing banks, but they also had a history of ultimately merging those institutions into larger banks, returning a multiple of the shareowners' investment.

About 150 original shareowners were largely "locked in" to their investment during the five-year life of the units with no trading market for their shares. However, rapid growth required more equity, and existing shareholders invested another $5.7 million in a 1987 "rights offering" of one share for each share owned. The price was about 120% of book value, and the bank got a "fairness opinion" from a securities firm, declaring that the price was fair to shareowners whether or not they exercised their rights.

When the units expired in 1988, shares had been spread among over 300 holders. When these holders were offered another 1-for-5 subscription right the next year, the offering was 150% subscribed at a price very close to book value. Later in 1989, Pacific Bank made a direct offering to the general public at a price per share of about 130% of book value that was also oversubscribed.

Little marketing effort went into that public offering. The bank cleared the offering circular with the OCC and sent it to prospective investors along with a rather low-key letter from the bank's chairman. The key to success was the prospects who received that package—it included the bank's employees, a third of whom became shareowners.

Most of the new shareowners came from a file that bank management had been compiling in a computer for several years. It consisted of any customer who ever mentioned a desire to own shares in the bank. This list had gradually grown into the hundreds and was all the bank needed to find investors for another $24 million of equity capital.

Since January 1990, the shares of Pacific Bank have been quoted on the NASDAQ system. There are now 700 shareowners, and several securities firms act as market makers, providing continuous bid and asked prices.

1. If bank employees are randomly approached, what is the probability that in a random sample of 10, at least 3 shareholders will be found?

2. In a random sample of 100 shareholders, what is the probability of finding at most three million-dollar shareholders?

3. If shareholders attend meetings at random, what is the probability that of 15 attending shareholders, exactly 5 will be original shareholders locked in for 5 years?

---

[18] Adapted by permission from *The Bankers Magazine,* March/April 1991, p. 41.

4

THE NORMAL DISTRIBUTION

4-1 INTRODUCTION

igure 4–1 shows the binomial probability distribution with $p = 0.5$ and an increasing number of trials: $n = 6$, $n = 10$, and $n = 14$. Note the emerging pattern (the overlaid curve) as the number of trials increases. This smooth, bell-shaped curve is the **normal probability density function.** The normal random variable is a continuous random variable that appears here as the *limit* of the discrete binomial random variable as the number of trials, n, increases. The normal distribution appears not only as a limit of the binomial distribution, but also in a very wide variety of other situations. It is the

Continued

FIGURE 4–1   **Binomial Distributions with _p_ ≈ 0.5 and Increasing Number of Trials _n_**

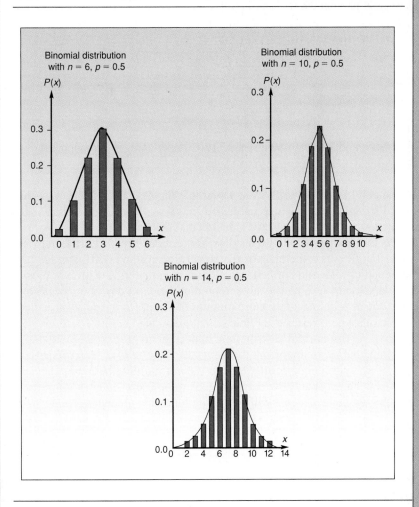

distribution of many random variables in situations where a large number of random effects from different sources come into play. The normal distribution was originally called the *law of errors*, the random effects of different magnitude and source considered "errors." The normal distribution is so prevalent, in fact, that Sir Francis Galton called it "the supreme law of unreason."

On November 12, 1733, a French-born mathematician who emigrated to England, Abraham De Moivre (1667–1754), privately published a small pamphlet and distributed it to his personal friends. The pamphlet was soon forgotten, and almost a century later the Marquis de Laplace (1749–1827) and Carl Friedrich Gauss (1777–1855) were jointly credited with the discovery of the normal distribution. To this day, the distribution is often called the *Gaussian* distribution. In 1924 the English statistician Karl Pearson happened upon a surviving copy of the forgotten pamphlet of 1733. Reading it, Pearson discovered to his great surprise that De Moivre had developed the formula for what we see in Figure 4–1—the tendency of the binomial distribution toward the normal distribution as *n* increases. The pamphlet contained the mathematical formula of the normal density. This formula, for a normal random variable with mean μ and standard deviation σ, is given as equation 4–1.

The probability density function of a normal random variable with mean μ and standard deviation σ:

$$f(x) = (1/\sqrt{2\pi}\,\sigma)e^{-(x-\mu)^2/2\sigma^2} \qquad \text{for } -\infty < x < \infty \qquad (4\text{–}1)$$

where e and π are the numbers 2.718 . . . and 3.141 . . . , respectively

---

Fortunately, Pearson had his own journal, *Biometrika,* and he was able to set the record straight. In an article published that year, Pearson recorded that De Moivre was actually the first to discover the normal distribution.[1]

As for De Moivre, what else do we know about him? Unfortunately, not much. We know that he was a member of the Royal Society and that he made his living as a mathematics tutor and coffeehouse advisor to gamblers. De Moivre died at the age of 87, and some believe he was able to predict the exact day of his death by noting that every day he required a few more minutes of sleep. He is said to have died the day his sleep requirement reached 24 hours.

Why is the normal distribution important in statistics? Statistics is based on sampling, and by an important theorem called the *central limit theorem,* the distributions of many sampling results tend to the normal distribution as the sample size, *n,* increases. The normal distribution is thus quite useful in evaluating the accuracy of sampling outcomes, as we will see in the following chapters. ∎

4-2   The Normal Probability Distribution

The normal random variable is continuous and has a density function given by equation 4–1. As with all continuous random variables, the probability that a normal random variable X will equal any particular value is zero. This holds for random variables that are *truly* continuous, such as time or size, measured on a continuous scale. The normal distribution is also used, however, as an excellent approximation for distributions of discrete random variables in a variety of situations. For example, profits of business ventures of a certain kind are approximately normally distributed. In this context, it does not necessarily mean that the probability of earning exactly $1,200 is equal to zero (although the probability may be small). Use of the normal distribution does mean that the probability that earnings will be in a given interval of numbers, say, $1,100 to $1,300, is approximated by the probability of this interval computed for a normal random variable with a given mean and standard deviation.

Equation 4–1 contains two parameters: the mean of the normal random variable, μ, and its standard deviation, σ. There are, therefore, infinitely many possible normal

---

[1] Karl Pearson, "Historical Note on the Origin of the Normal Curve of Errors," *Biometrika,* XVI (1924), pp. 402–4.

FIGURE 4–2   Normal Distributions with Different Means and Standard Deviations

random variables, depending on the value of the mean and the value of the standard deviation. The shape of all normal densities is the same: a symmetric bell shape. Knowing the mean of the normal random variable and its standard deviation (or equivalently, its variance) fixes a *particular* normal random variable out of the infinite collection of such variables. This gives us the exact density function and allows us to compute probabilities associated with intervals of values.

Figure 4–2 shows several normal distributions with different means and standard deviations. *The mean of the distribution is a measure of its location:* It tells us where on the number line the distribution is centered. Since the normal density is symmetrical with one peak in the center, the *mean,* μ, is also the *mode* and the *median* of the probability distribution; thus, μ is also the point where the density function is highest and the point that splits the area under the curve in half. The area to each side of μ is equal to 0.5. *The standard deviation of the distribution is a measure of the spread, or variability, of the distribution.* When the standard deviation is large, the density function is *wide* and, hence, also *low* (because the total area under the curve must equal 1.00). When the standard deviation is small, the curve is narrow and high. The normal distribution has an additional interesting property. The distance on the curve from the mean (the center line) to the inflection point of the density function (that point where the slope of the function starts to decrease) is equal to *one standard deviation.*

Notation

We now introduce some general notation for random variables and distributions that will prove to be especially useful in work with the normal probability model; however, it has uses also in the case of other random variables.

We will denote the distribution, mean, and variance of a random variable by a simple notational statement:

$$X \sim D(\mu, \sigma^2) \qquad (4-2)$$

This statement says in words: "The random variable X is distributed according to a probability distribution D, with mean equal to μ, and standard deviation equal to σ (equivalently, variance equal to σ^2)." This is the general notation for a random variable, with the distribution denoted by D. If we were talking about the binomial distribution, we would use the letter B to denote it. For a normally distributed random variable, we use the letter N. If we deal with a random variable with a normal distribution with mean $\mu = 5.7$ and standard deviation $\sigma = 2$, we say

$$X \sim N(5.7, 2^2)$$

Note that we wrote the variance σ^2 as 2^2, rather than its value, 4. We will always follow the convention of writing the variance as a squared quantity. This will prevent us from confusing the value of the variance with the value of the standard deviation. Here it is perfectly clear that the variance is $2^2 = 4$ and the standard deviation is 2.

4-3   The Standard Normal Distribution

Since, as noted earlier, there are infinitely many possible normal random variables, one of them is selected to serve as our *standard*. Probabilities associated with values of this standard normal random variable are tabulated. A special transformation then allows us to apply the tabulated probabilities to *any* normal random variable. The standard normal random variable has a special name, Z (rather than the general name X we use for other random variables).

> We define the **standard normal random variable**, Z, as the normal random variable with mean $\mu = 0$ and standard deviation $\sigma = 1$.

In the notation established in the previous section, we say

$$Z \sim N(0, 1^2) \qquad (4-3)$$

Since $1^2 = 1$, we may drop the superscript 2 as no confusion of the standard deviation and the variance is possible. A graph of the standard normal density function is given in Figure 4–3.

Finding Probabilities of the Standard Normal Distribution

Probabilities of intervals are areas under the density $f(z)$ over the intervals in question. From the range of values in equation 4–1, $-\infty < x < \infty$, we see that any normal random variable is defined over the entire real line. Thus, the intervals in which we will be interested are sometimes *semi-infinite* intervals, such as a to ∞ or $-\infty$ to b (where a and b are numbers). While such intervals have infinite length, the probabilities associated with them are finite; they are, in fact, no greater than 1.00, as required of all probabilities. The reason for this is that the area in either of the "tails" of the distribution (the two narrow ends of the distribution, extending toward $-\infty$ and $+\infty$) becomes very small very quickly as we move away from the center of the distribution.

Tabulated areas under the standard normal density are probabilities of intervals extending from the mean, $\mu = 0$, to points z to its right. Table 2 in Appendix C gives

FIGURE 4–3   The Standard Normal Density Function

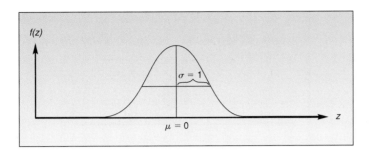

areas under the standard normal curve between 0 and points $z > 0$. The total area under the normal curve is equal to 1.00, and since the curve is symmetric, the area from 0 to $-\infty$ is equal to 0.5. The *table area* associated with a point z is thus equal to the value of the cumulative distribution function, $F(z)$, minus 0.5.

We define the **table area** as

$$TA = F(z) - 0.5 \qquad\qquad (4\text{–}4)$$

The table area, TA, is shown in Figure 4–4. Part of Table 2 is reproduced here as Table 4–1. Let us see how the table is used in obtaining probabilities for the standard normal random variable. In the following examples, refer to Figure 4–4 and Table 4–1.

1. Let us find the probability that the value of the standard normal random variable will be between 0 and 1.56. That is, we want $P(0 < Z < 1.56)$. In Figure 4–4, substitute 1.56 for the point z on the graph. We are looking for the table area in the row labeled 1.5 and the column labeled .06. In the table, we find the probability 0.4406.

2. Let us find the probability that Z will be less than -2.47. Figure 4–5 shows the required area for the probability $P(Z < -2.47)$. By the symmetry of the normal curve, the area to the left of -2.47 is exactly equal to the area to the right of 2.47. We find

$$P(Z < -2.47) = P(Z > 2.47) = 0.5000 - 0.4932 = 0.0068$$

3. Find $P(1 < Z < 2)$. The required probability is the area under the curve between the two points 1 and 2. This area is shown in Figure 4–6. The table gives us the area under the curve between 0 and 1, and the area under the curve between 0 and 2. Areas are additive; therefore, $P(1 < Z < 2) =$ TA(for 2.00) $-$ TA(for 1.00) $= 0.4772 - 0.3413 = 0.1359$.

In cases where we need probabilities based on values with greater than second-decimal accuracy, we may use a linear interpolation between two probabilities obtained from the table. For example, $P(0 \leq Z \leq 1.645)$ is found as the midpoint between the two probabilities $P(0 \leq Z \leq 1.64)$ and $P(0 \leq Z \leq 1.65)$. This is found, using the table, as the midpoint of 0.4495 and 0.4505, which is 0.45. If even more

FIGURE 4–4   The Table Area, TA, for a Point z of the Standard Normal Distribution

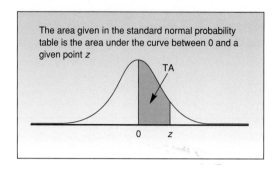

The area given in the standard normal probability table is the area under the curve between 0 and a given point z

TABLE 4–1   Standard Normal Probabilities

z	.00	.01	.02	.03	.04	.05	.06	.07	.08	.09
0.0	.0000	.0040	.0080	.0120	.0160	.0199	.0239	.0279	.0319	.0359
0.1	.0398	.0438	.0478	.0517	.0557	.0596	.0636	.0675	.0714	.0753
0.2	.0793	.0832	.0871	.0910	.0948	.0987	.1026	.1064	.1103	.1141
0.3	.1179	.1217	.1255	.1293	.1331	.1368	.1406	.1443	.1480	.1517
0.4	.1554	.1591	.1628	.1664	.1700	.1736	.1772	.1808	.1844	.1879
0.5	.1915	.1950	.1985	.2019	.2054	.2088	.2123	.2157	.2190	.2224
0.6	.2257	.2291	.2324	.2357	.2389	.2422	.2454	.2486	.2517	.2549
0.7	.2580	.2611	.2642	.2673	.2704	.2734	.2764	.2794	.2823	.2852
0.8	.2881	.2910	.2939	.2967	.2995	.3023	.3051	.3078	.3106	.3133
0.9	.3159	.3186	.3212	.3238	.3264	.3289	.3315	.3340	.3365	.3389
1.0	.3413	.3438	.3461	.3485	.3508	.3531	.3554	.3577	.3599	.3621
1.1	.3643	.3665	.3686	.3708	.3729	.3749	.3770	.3790	.3810	.3830
1.2	.3849	.3869	.3888	.3907	.3925	.3944	.3962	.3980	.3997	.4015
1.3	.4032	.4049	.4066	.4082	.4099	.4115	.4131	.4147	.4162	.4177
1.4	.4192	.4207	.4222	.4236	.4251	.4265	.4279	.4292	.4306	.4319
1.5	.4332	.4345	.4357	.4370	.4382	.4394	.4406	.4418	.4429	.4441
1.6	.4452	.4463	.4474	.4484	.4495	.4505	.4515	.4525	.4535	.4545
1.7	.4554	.4564	.4573	.4582	.4591	.4599	.4608	.4616	.4625	.4633
1.8	.4641	.4649	.4656	.4664	.4671	.4678	.4686	.4693	.4699	.4706
1.9	.4713	.4719	.4726	.4732	.4738	.4744	.4750	.4756	.4761	.4767
2.0	.4772	.4778	.4783	.4788	.4793	.4798	.4803	.4808	.4812	.4817
2.1	.4821	.4826	.4830	.4834	.4838	.4842	.4846	.4850	.4854	.4857
2.2	.4861	.4864	.4868	.4871	.4875	.4878	.4881	.4884	.4887	.4890
2.3	.4893	.4896	.4898	.4901	.4904	.4906	.4909	.4911	.4913	.4916
2.4	.4918	.4920	.4922	.4925	.4927	.4929	.4931	.4932	.4934	.4936
2.5	.4938	.4940	.4941	.4943	.4945	.4946	.4948	.4949	.4951	.4952
2.6	.4953	.4955	.4956	.4957	.4959	.4960	.4961	.4962	.4963	.4964
2.7	.4965	.4966	.4967	.4968	.4969	.4970	.4971	.4972	.4973	.4974
2.8	.4974	.4975	.4976	.4977	.4977	.4978	.4979	.4979	.4980	.4981
2.9	.4981	.4982	.4982	.4983	.4984	.4984	.4985	.4985	.4986	.4986
3.0	.4987	.4987	.4987	.4988	.4988	.4989	.4989	.4989	.4990	.4990

FIGURE 4–5   Finding the Probability That Z Is Less than –2.47

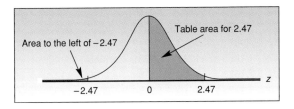

FIGURE 4–6   Finding the Probability That Z Is between 1 and 2

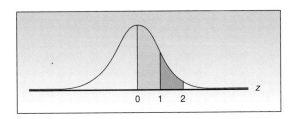

accuracy is required, we may use computer programs designed to produce standard normal probabilities.

Finding Values of Z Given a Probability

In many situations, instead of finding the probability that a standard normal random variable will be within a given interval, we may be interested in the reverse: finding an interval with a given probability. Consider the following examples.

1. Find a value z of the standard normal random variable such that the probability that the random variable will have a value between 0 and z is 0.40. We look *inside* the table for the value closest to 0.40; we do this by searching through the values inside the table, noting that they increase from 0 to numbers close to 0.5000 as we go down the columns and across rows. The closest value we find to 0.40 is the table area .3997. This value corresponds to 1.28 (row 1.2 and column .08). This is illustrated in Figure 4–7.

2. Find the value of the standard normal random variable that cuts off an area of 0.90 to its left. Here, we reason as follows. Since the area to the left of the given point, z, is greater than 0.50, z *must be on the right side of 0.* Furthermore, the area to the left of 0 all the way to $-\infty$ is equal to 0.5. Therefore, TA = 0.9 − 0.5 = 0.4. We need to find the point z such that TA = 0.4. We know the answer from the preceding example: $z = 1.28$. This is shown in Figure 4–8.

3. Find a 0.99 probability interval, symmetric about 0, for the standard normal random variable. The required area between the two z values that are equidistant from 0 on either side is 0.99. Therefore, the area under the curve between 0 and the positive z value is TA = 0.99/2 = 0.495. We now

FIGURE 4–7   Using the Normal Table to Find a Value, Given a Probability

z	.00	.01	.02	.03	.04	.05	.06	.07	.08	.09
0.0	.0000	.0040	.0080	.0120	.0160	.0199	.0239	.0279	.0319	.0359
0.1	.0398	.0438	.0478	.0517	.0557	.0596	.0636	.0675	.0714	.0753
0.2	.0793	.0832	.0871	.0910	.0948	.0987	.1026	.1064	.1103	.1141
0.3	.1179	.1217	.1255	.1293	.1331	.1368	.1406	.1443	.1480	.1517
0.4	.1554	.1591	.1628	.1664	.1700	.1736	.1772	.1808	.1844	.1879
0.5	.1915	.1950	.1985	.2019	.2054	.2088	.2123	.2157	.2190	.2224
0.6	.2257	.2291	.2324	.2357	.2389	.2422	.2454	.2486	.2517	.2549
0.7	.2580	.2611	.2642	.2673	.2704	.2734	.2764	.2794	.2823	.2852
0.8	.2881	.2910	.2939	.2967	.2995	.3023	.3051	.3078	.3106	.3133
0.9	.3159	.3186	.3212	.3238	.3264	.3289	.3315	.3340	.3365	.3389
1.0	.3413	.3438	.3461	.3485	.3508	.3531	.3554	.3577	.3599	.3621
1.1	.3643	.3665	.3686	.3708	.3729	.3749	.3770	.3790	.3810	.3830
1.2	.3849	.3869	.3888	.3907	.3925	.3944	.3962	.3980	.3997	.4015
1.3	.4032	.4049	.4066	.4082	.4099	.4115	.4131	.4147	.4162	.4177
1.4	.4192	.4207	.4222	.4236	.4251	.4265	.4279	.4292	.4306	.4319
1.5	.4332	.4345	.4357	.4370	.4382	.4394	.4406	.4418	.4429	.4441

FIGURE 4–8   Finding z Such That $P(Z \le z) = 0.9$

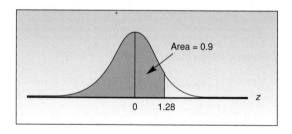

look in our normal probability table for the area closest to 0.495. The area 0.495 lies exactly between the two areas 0.4949 and 0.4951, corresponding to $z = 2.57$ and $z = 2.58$. Therefore, a simple linear interpolation between the two values gives us $z = 2.575$. This is correct to within the accuracy of the linear interpolation. The answer, therefore, is $z = \pm 2.575$. This is shown in Figure 4–9.

PROBLEMS

4–1. Find the following probabilities: $P(-1 < Z < 1)$, $P(-1.96 < Z < 1.96)$, $P(-2.33 < Z < 2.33)$, $P(Z < 2.58)$, $P(-3 < Z < 3)$.

4–2. What is the probability that a standard normal random variable will be between the values -2 and 1?

4–3. Find the probability that a standard normal random variable will have a value between -0.89 and -2.66.

4–4. Find the probability that a standard normal random variable will have a value greater than 3.02.

FIGURE 4–9 A Symmetric 0.99 Probability Interval about 0 for a Standard Normal Random Variable

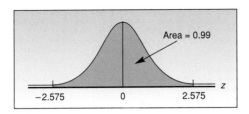

4–5. Find the probability that a standard normal random variable will be between 2 and 3.

4–6. Find the probability that a standard normal random variable will have a value less than or equal to -2.5.

4–7. Find the probability that a standard normal random variable will be greater in value than -2.33.

4–8. Find the probability that a standard normal random variable will have a value between -2 and 15.

4–9. Find the probability that a standard normal variable will have a value less than -45.

4–10. Find the probability that a standard normal random variable will be between -0.01 and 0.05.

4–11. A sensitive measuring device is calibrated so that errors in the measurements it provides are normally distributed with mean 0 and variance 1.00. Find the probability that a given error will be between -2 and 2.

4–12. Find two values defining tails of the normal distribution with an area of 0.05 each.

4–13. Is it likely that a standard normal random variable will have value less than -4? Explain.

4–14. Find a value such that the probability that the standard normal random variable will be above it is 0.85.

4–15. Find a value of the standard normal random variable cutting off an area of 0.575 to its left.

4–16. Find a value of the standard normal random variable cutting off an area of 0.50 to its right. (Do you need the table for this probability? Explain.)

4–17. Find z such that $P(Z > z) = 0.28$.

4–18. Find two values, equidistant from 0 on either side, such that the probability that a standard normal random variable will be between them is 0.40.

4–19. Find two values of the standard normal random variable, z and $-z$, such that $P(-z < Z < z) = 0.95$.

4–20. Find two values of the standard normal random variable, z and $-z$, such that the two corresponding "tail areas" of the distribution (the area to the right of z and the area to the left of $-z$) add up to 0.01.

4–21. The deviation of a magnetic needle away from the magnetic pole in a certain area in northern Canada is a normally distributed random variable with mean 0 and standard deviation 1.00. What is the probability that the absolute value of the deviation from the north pole at a given moment will be more than 2.4?

4–4 The Transformation of Normal Random Variables

The importance of the standard normal distribution derives from the fact that any normal random variable may be transformed to the standard normal random variable. We want to transform X, where $X \sim N(\mu, \sigma^2)$, into the standard normal random

FIGURE 4-10   Transforming a Normal Random Variable with Mean 50 and Standard Deviation 10 into the Standard Normal Random Variable

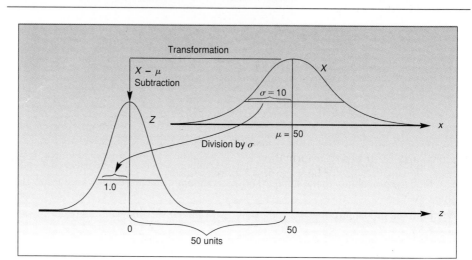

variable $Z \sim N(0,1^2)$. Look at Figure 4–10. Here we have a normal random variable, X, with mean $\mu = 50$ and standard deviation $\sigma = 10$. We want to transform this random variable to a normal random variable with $\mu = 0$ and $\sigma = 1$. How can we do this?

We move the distribution from its center of 50 to a center of 0. This is done by *subtracting* 50 from all the values of X. Thus, we shift the distribution 50 units back so that its new center is 0. The second thing we need to do is to make the width of the distribution, its standard deviation, equal to 1. This is done by squeezing the width down from 10 to 1. Because the total probability under the curve must remain 1.00, the distribution must grow upward to maintain the same area. This is shown in Figure 4–10. Mathematically, squeezing the curve to make the width 1 is equivalent to dividing the random variable by its standard deviation. The area under the curve adjusts so that the total remains the same. *All probabilities* (areas under the curve) *adjust accordingly*. The mathematical transformation from X to Z is thus achieved by first subtracting μ from X and then dividing the result by σ.

The transformation of X to Z:

$$Z = \frac{X - \mu}{\sigma} \tag{4–5}$$

The transformation of equation 4–5 takes us from a random variable X with mean μ and standard deviation σ to the standard normal random variable. We also have an opposite, or *inverse*, transformation, which takes us from the standard normal random variable Z to the random variable X with mean μ and standard deviation σ. The inverse transformation is given by equation 4–6.

> The inverse transformation of Z to X:
>
> $$X = \mu + Z\sigma \qquad\qquad (4\text{--}6)$$

You can verify mathematically that equation 4–6 does the opposite of equation 4–5. Note that multiplying the random variable Z by the number σ increases the width of the curve from 1 to σ, thus making σ the new standard deviation. Adding μ makes μ the new mean of the random variable. The actions of multiplying and then adding are the opposite of subtracting and then dividing. We note that the two transformations, one an inverse of the other, transform a *normal* random variable into a *normal* random variable. If this transformation is carried out on a random variable that is not normal, the result will not be a normal random variable.

Using the Normal Transformation

$\mu = 50$ $\qquad\qquad\qquad\qquad\qquad\qquad\qquad\qquad\qquad \sigma = 10$

Let us consider our random variable X with mean 50 and standard deviation 10, $X \sim N(50,10^2)$. Suppose we want the probability that X is greater than 60. That is, we want to find $P(X > 60)$. We cannot evaluate this probability directly, but if we can transform X to Z, we will be able to find the probability in the Z table, Table 2. Using equation 4–5, the required transformation is $Z = (X-\mu)/\sigma$. Let us carry out the transformation. In the probability statement, $P(X > 60)$, we will substitute Z for X. If, however, we carry out the transformation on one side of the probability inequality, we must also do it on the other side. In other words, transforming X into Z requires us also to transform the value 60 into the appropriate value of the standard normal distribution. We transform the value 60 into the value $(60-\mu)/\sigma$. The new probability statement is

$$P(X > 60) = P\left(\frac{X - \mu}{\sigma} > \frac{60 - \mu}{\sigma}\right) = P\left(Z > \frac{60 - \mu}{\sigma}\right)$$

$$= P\left(Z > \frac{60 - 50}{10}\right) = P(Z > 1)$$

Why does the inequality still hold? We subtracted a number from each side of an inequality; this does not change the inequality. In the next step we divide both sides of the inequality by the standard deviation, σ. The inequality does not change because we can divide both sides of an inequality by a positive number, and a standard deviation is always a positive number. (Recall that dividing by 0 is not permissible; and dividing, or multiplying, by a negative value would reverse the direction of the inequality.) From the transformation, we find that the probability that a normal random variable with mean 50 and standard deviation 10 will have a value greater than 60 is exactly the probability that the standard normal random variable Z will be greater than 1. The later probability can be found using Table 2. We find: $P(X > 60) = P(Z > 1) = 0.5000 - 0.3413 = 0.1587$. Let us now look at a few examples of the use of equation 4–5.

Suppose that the time it takes the electronic device in the car to respond to the signal from the toll plaza is normally distributed with mean 160 microseconds and standard deviation 30 microseconds. What is the probability that the device in the car will respond to a given signal within 100 to 180 microseconds?

EXAMPLE 4-1

Turnpike Fare to Go Electronic

How it works
Electronic equipment would let drivers pay tolls in designated lanes without stopping

1. Electronic tolls are prepaid by cash or credit card. Payment information is linked to a transponder in the car.

2. The toll plaza communicates with the transponder via radio link. Some systems alert the driver if prepaid funds are low.

3. The toll is deducted from the account. Cash tolls can be paid to attendants in other lanes.

4. If funds are insufficient or the toll is not paid, a video image of the car, including the license plate, is recorded.

Reprinted from *Boston Globe*, Tuesday, May 9, 1995, p. 1, with data from industry reports.

SOLUTION

Figure 4–11 shows the normal distribution for $X \sim N(160, 30^2)$ and the required area on the scale of the original problem and on the transformed z scale. We have the following (where the probability statement inequality has three sides and we carry out the transformation of equation 4–5 on all three sides).

$$P(100 < X < 180) = P\left(\frac{100 - \mu}{\sigma} < \frac{X - \mu}{\sigma} < \frac{180 - \mu}{\sigma}\right)$$

$$= P\left(\frac{100 - 160}{30} < Z < \frac{180 - 160}{30}\right)$$

$$= P(-2 < Z < 0.6666) = 0.4772 + 0.2475 = 0.7247$$

(Table area values were obtained by linear interpolation.) Thus, there is a 0.7247 chance that the device will respond within 100 to 180 microseconds.

EXAMPLE 4-2

The concentration of impurities in a semiconductor used in the production of microprocessors for computers is a normally distributed random variable with mean 127 parts per million and standard deviation 22. A semiconductor is acceptable only if its concentration of impurities is below 150 parts per million. What proportion of the semiconductors are acceptable for use?

SOLUTION

$X \sim N(127, 22^2)$, and we need $P(X < 150)$. Using equation 4–5, we have

$$P(X < 150) = P\left(\frac{X - \mu}{\sigma} < \frac{150 - \mu}{\sigma}\right) = P\left(Z < \frac{150 - 127}{22}\right)$$

$$= P(Z < 1.045) = 0.5 + 0.3520 = 0.8520$$

FIGURE 4–11   Probability Computation for Example 4–1

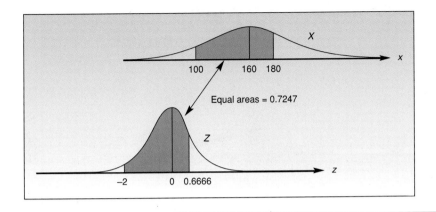

(The TA of 0.3520 was obtained by interpolation.) Thus, 85.2% of the semiconductors are acceptable for use. This also means that the probability that a randomly chosen semiconductor will be acceptable for use is 0.8520. The solution of this example is illustrated in Figure 4–12.

EXAMPLE 4-3

Fluctuations in the prices of precious metals such as gold have been empirically shown to be well approximated by a normal distribution when observed over short intervals of time. In May, 1995, the daily price of gold (1 troy oz.) was believed to have a mean of $383 and a standard deviation of $12. A broker, working under these assumptions, wanted to find the probability that the price of gold the next day will be between $394 and $399 per troy ounce. In this eventuality, the broker had an order from a client to sell the gold in the client's portfolio. What is the probability that the client's gold will be sold the next day?

SOLUTION

Figure 4–13 shows the setup for this problem and the transformation of X, where $X \sim N(383,12^2)$, into the standard normal random variable Z. Also shown are the required areas under the X curve and the transformed Z curve. We have

$$P(394 < X < 399) = P\left(\frac{394 - \mu}{\sigma} < \frac{X - \mu}{\sigma} < \frac{399 - \mu}{\sigma}\right)$$

$$= P\left(\frac{394 - 383}{12} < Z < \frac{399 - 383}{12}\right)$$

$$= P(0.9166 < Z < 1.3333) = 0.4088 - 0.3203 = 0.0885$$

(Both TA values were obtained by a linear interpolation, although this is not necessary if less accuracy is acceptable.)

Let us summarize the transformation procedure used in computing probabilities of events associated with a normal random variable $X \sim N(\mu,\sigma^2)$.

FIGURE 4–12   Probability Computation for Example 4–2

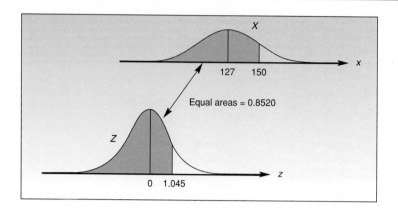

FIGURE 4–13   Probability Computation for Example 4–3

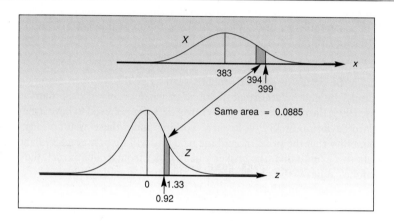

Transformation formulas of X to Z, where a and b are numbers:

$$P(X < a) = P\left(Z < \frac{a - \mu}{\sigma}\right)$$

$$P(X > b) = P\left(Z > \frac{b - \mu}{\sigma}\right)$$

$$P(a < X < b) = P\left(\frac{a - \mu}{\sigma} < Z < \frac{b - \mu}{\sigma}\right)$$

PROBLEMS

4–22.   For a normal random variable with mean 674 and standard deviation 55, find the probability that its value will be below 600.

4–23.   Let X be a normally distributed random variable with mean 410 and standard deviation 2. Find the probability that X will be between 407 and 415.

4–24. If X is normally distributed with mean 500 and standard deviation 20, find the probability that X will be above 555.

4–25. For a normally distributed random variable with mean -44 and standard deviation 16, find the probability that the value of the random variable will be above 0.

4–26. A normal random variable has mean 0 and standard deviation 4. Find the probability that the random variable will be above 2.5.

4–27. Let X be a normally distributed random variable with mean $\mu = 16$ and standard deviation $\sigma = 3$. Find $P(11 < X < 20)$. Also find $P(17 < X < 19)$ and $P(X > 15)$.

4–28. The time it takes an international telephone operator to place an overseas phone call is normally distributed with mean 45 seconds and standard deviation 10 seconds.

   a.   What is the probability that my call will go through in less than one minute?

   b.   What is the probability that I will get through in less than 40 seconds?

   c.   What is the probability that I will have to wait more than 70 seconds for my call to go through?

4–29. The number of votes cast in favor of a controversial proposition is believed to be approximately normally distributed with mean 8,000 and standard deviation 1,000. The proposition needs at least 9,322 votes in order to pass. What is the probability that the proposition will pass? (Assume numbers are on a continuous scale.)

4–30. Under the system of floating exchange rates, the rate of foreign money to U.S. dollar is affected by many random factors, and this leads to the assumption of a normal distribution of small daily fluctuations. The rate of German marks per U.S. dollar is believed in a certain period to have a mean of 2.06 and a standard deviation of 0.08. Find the following.

   a.   The probability that tomorrow's rate will be above 2.10.

   b.   The probability that tomorrow's rate will be below 1.90.

   c.   The probability that tomorrow's exchange rate will be between 2.00 and 2.20.

4-31.

Reprinted from the *New York Times*, May 18, 1995, p. D1, with data from Edison Electric Institute.

Assume that the rate charged in each region of the country is normally distributed with mean as shown on the map and standard deviation of 1.00.

  a. What is the probability that a randomly chosen customer in the Northeast will be charged over 8.00 cents per kilowatt-hour?

  b. What is the probability that a randomly chosen customer in the Mountain region will be charged less than 3.00 cents per kilowatt hour?

4–32. Electricity rates at different regions of the country are independent of each other. Use the map given with Problem 4–31 to find the following probabilities.

  a. What is the probability that a customer in New England and one in Alaska would both pay over 7.00 cents per kilowatt-hour?

  b. A company has one subsidiary in the Great Lakes, one in the Southeast, one in the Plains, and one in the Southwest. What is the probability that all of them pay less than 4.00 cents per kilowatt hour?

4-5 The Inverse Transformation

Let us look more closely at the relationship between X, a normal random variable with mean μ and standard deviation σ, and the standard normal random variable. The fact that the standard normal random variable has mean 0 and standard deviation 1 has some important implications. When we say that Z is greater than 2, we are also saying that Z is more than 2 *standard deviations above its mean*. This is so because the mean of Z is 0 and the standard deviation is 1; hence, $Z > 2$ is the same event as $Z > [0 + 2(1)]$.

Now consider a normal random variable X with mean 50 and standard deviation 10. Saying that X is greater than 70 is exactly the same as saying that X is 2 standard deviations above its mean. This is so because 70 is 20 units above the mean, 50, and 20 units $= 2(10)$ units, or 2 standard deviations of X. Thus, the event $X > 70$ is the same as the event $X > (2$ standard deviations above the mean$)$. This event is identical to the event $Z > 2$. Indeed, this is what results when we carry out the transformation of equation 4–5:

$$P(X > 70) = P\left(\frac{X - \mu}{\sigma} > \frac{70 - \mu}{\sigma}\right) = P\left(Z > \frac{70 - 50}{10}\right) = P(Z > 2)$$

Normal random variables are related to each other by the fact that the probability that a normal random variable will be above (or below) its mean a certain number of standard deviations is exactly equal to the probability that any other normal random variable will be above (or below) its mean the same number of (its) standard deviations. In particular, this property holds for the standard normal random variable. The probability that a normal random variable will be greater than (or less than) z standard-deviation units above its mean is the same as the probability that the standard normal random variable will be greater than (less than) z. The change from a *z value* of the random variable Z to z *standard deviations* above the mean for a given normal random variable X should suggest to us the inverse transformation, equation 4–6:

$$x = \mu + z\sigma$$

That is, the value of the random variable X may be written in terms of the number (z) of standard deviations (σ) it is above or below the mean (μ). Three examples are useful here. We know from the standard normal probability table that the probability that Z is greater than -1 and less than 1 is 0.6826 (show this). Similarly, we know that the probability that Z is greater that -2 and less than 2 is 0.9544. Also, the probability that Z is greater than -3 and less than 3 is 0.9974. These probabilities may be applied to *any* normal random variable as follows.[2]

1. The probability that a normal random variable will be within a distance of *1 standard deviation* from its mean (on either side) is 0.6826, or *approximately 0.68.*
2. The probability that a normal random variable will be within *2 standard deviations* of its mean is 0.9544, or *approximately 0.95.*
3. The probability that a normal random variable will be within 3 *standard deviations* of its mean is 0.9974.

We use the inverse transformation, equation 4–6, when we want to get from a given probability to the value or values of a normal random variable X. We illustrate the procedure with a few examples.

PALCO Industries, Inc. is a leading manufacturer of cutting and welding products. One of the company's products is an acetylene gas cylinder used in welding. The amount of nitrogen gas in a cylinder is a normally distributed random variable with mean 124 units of volume and standard deviation 12. We want to find the amount of nitrogen, x, such that 10% of the cylinders contain more nitrogen than this amount.

EXAMPLE 4–4

We have $X \sim N(124, 12^2)$. We are looking for the value of the random variable X such that $P(X > x) = 0.10$. In order to find it, we look for the value of the standard normal random variable Z such that $P(Z > z) = 0.10$. Figure 4–14 illustrates how we find the value z and transform it to x. If the area to the right of z is equal to 0.10, the area between 0 and z (the table area) is equal to $0.5 - 0.10 = 0.40$. We look inside the table for the z value corresponding to TA $= 0.40$ and find $z = 1.28$ (actually, TA $= 0.3997$, which is close enough to 0.4). We need to find the appropriate x value. Here we use equation 4–6:

SOLUTION

$$x = \mu + z\sigma = 124 + (1.28)(12) = 139.36$$

Thus, 10% of the acetylene cylinders contain more than 139.36 units of nitrogen.

The amount of fuel consumed by the engines of a jetliner on a flight between two cities is a normally distributed random variable, X, with mean $\mu = 5.7$ tons and standard deviation $\sigma = 0.5$. Carrying too much fuel is inefficient as it slows the plane. If, however, too little fuel is loaded on the plane, an emergency landing may be necessary. The airline would like to determine the amount of fuel to load so that there will be a 0.99 probability that the plane will arrive at its destination.

EXAMPLE 4–5

---

[2] This is the origin of the *empirical rule* (in Chapter 1) for mound-shaped data distributions. Mound-shaped data sets approximate the distribution of a normal random variable, and hence the proportions of observations within a given number of standard deviations away from the mean roughly equal those predicted by the normal distribution. Compare the empirical rule (section 1–7) with the numbers given here.

FIGURE 4–14   Solution of Example 4–4

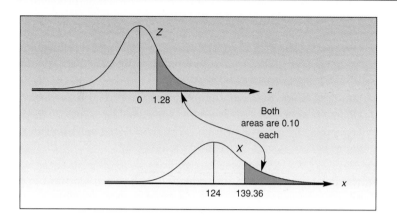

SOLUTION

We have $X \sim N(5.7, 0.5^2)$. First, we must find the value z such that $P(Z < z) = 0.99$. Following our methodology, we find that the required table area is TA = $0.99 - 0.5 = 0.49$, and the corresponding z value is 2.33. Transforming the z value to an x value, we get $x = \mu + z\sigma = 5.7 + (2.33)(0.5) = 6.865$. Thus, the plane should be loaded with 6.865 tons of fuel to give a 0.99 probability that the fuel will last throughout the flight. The transformation is shown in Figure 4–15.

EXAMPLE 4–6

Weekly sales of Campbell's soup cans at a grocery store are believed to be approximately normally distributed with mean 2,450 and standard deviation 400. The store management wants to find two values, symmetrically on either side of the mean, such that there will be a 0.95 probability that sales of soup cans during the week will be between the two values. Such information is useful in determining levels of orders and stock.

SOLUTION

Here $X \sim N(2,450, 400^2)$. From the section on the standard normal random variable, we know how to find two values of Z such that the area under the curve between them is 0.95 (or any other area). We find that $z = 1.96$ and $z = -1.96$ are the required values. We now need to use equation 4–6. Since there are *two* values, one the negative of the other, we may combine them in a single transformation:

$$x = \mu \pm z\sigma \qquad (4\text{–}7)$$

Applying this special formula we get: $x = 2,450 \pm (1.96)(400) = 1,666$ and $3,234$. Thus, management may be 95% sure that sales on any given week will be between 1,666 and 3,234 units.

FIGURE 4–15   Solution of Example 4–5

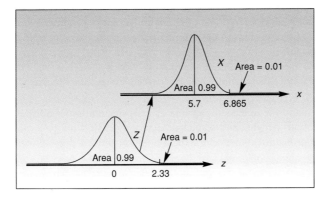

Summary of the procedure of obtaining values of a normal random variable, given a probability:

1. Draw a picture of the normal distribution in question and the standard normal distribution.
2. In the picture, shade in the area corresponding to the probability.
3. Use the table to find the z value (or values) that give the required probability.
4. Use the transformation from Z to X to get the appropriate value (or values) of the original normal random variable.

PROBLEMS

4–33. If X is a normally distributed random variable with mean 120 and standard deviation 44, find a value x such that the probability that X will be less than x is 0.56.

4–34. For a normal random variable with mean 16.5 and standard deviation 0.8, find a point of the distribution such that there is a 0.85 probability that the value of the random variable will be above it.

4–35. For a normal random variable with mean 19,500 and standard deviation 400, find a point of the distribution such that the probability that the random variable will exceed this value is 0.02.

4–36. Find two values of the normal random variable with mean 88 and standard deviation 5 lying symmetrically on either side of the mean and covering an area of 0.98 between them.

4–37. For $X \sim N(32,7^2)$, find two values, x_1 and x_2, symmetrically lying on each side of the mean, with $P(x_1 < X < x_2) = 0.99$.

4–38. If X is a normally distributed random variable with mean -61 and standard deviation 22, find the value such that the probability that the random variable will be above it is 0.25.

4–39. Let X be a normally distributed random variable with mean 97 and standard deviation 10. Find x such that $P(102 < X < x) = 0.05$.

4–40. Let X be a normally distributed random variable with mean 600 and variance 10,000. Find two values x_1 and x_2 such that $P(X > x_1) = 0.01$ and $P(X < x_2) = 0.05$.

4–41. Pierre operates a currency exchange office at Orly Airport in Paris. His office is open at night when the airport bank is closed, and he makes most of his business on returning

American tourists who need to change their remaining French francs back to U.S. dollars. From experience, Pierre knows that the demand for dollars on any given night during high season is approximately normally distributed with mean $25,000 and standard deviation $5,000. If Pierre carries too much cash in dollars overnight, he pays a penalty: interest on the cash. On the other hand, if he runs short of cash during the night, he needs to send a person downtown to an all-night financial agency to get the required cash. This, too, is costly to him. Therefore, Pierre would like to carry overnight an amount of money such that the demand on 85% of the nights will not exceed this amount. Can you help Pierre find the required amount of dollars to carry?

4–42.   The demand for unleaded gasoline at a service station is normally distributed with mean 27,009 gallons per day and standard deviation 4,530. Find two values that will give a symmetric 0.95 probability interval for the amount of unleaded gasoline demanded daily.

4–43.   The percentage of protein in a certain brand of dog food is a normally distributed random variable with mean 11.2% and standard deviation 0.6%. The manufacturer would like to state on the package that the product has a protein content of at least x_1% and no more than x_2%. They want their statement to be true for 99% of the packages sold. Determine the values x_1 and x_2.

4–44.   Debt as percent of equity (measured daily) for a firm tends to follow a normal distribution. A recent article reveals that for the Centex Corporation average debt as percent of equity in early 1995 was 113%.[3] If the standard deviation was 4%, find a value such that you can be 95% sure that debt as percent of equity was below that value on a given day.

4–45.   The following cartoon is from the *Harvard Business Review*. If scores on random tests for competence are normally distributed with mean 50 and standard deviation 5, find a score you may be 90% sure an executive would exceed on the random test.

Cartoon by S. Harris, *Harvard Business Review*, January–February 1995, p. 73.

4–6 More Complex Problems[4]

In this section, we show how more complicated problems related to normal random variables may be solved. The problems we solve are finding the mean, finding the standard deviation, and finding both the mean and standard deviation of a normal random variable, using information about probabilities of the random variable. The problems require the solution of one or two linear equations.

---

[3] Eric S. Hardy, "Statistical Spotlight," *Forbes*, January 2, 1995, p. 119.

[4] Optional section.

Suppose we know that the mean of a normal random variable is 120, and we know that the probability that the random variable will be above 125 is 0.05. We do not know the standard deviation of the random variable. How can we find the value of the standard deviation, σ? Let us set up the problem in probability statement notation and see what we get. We have

$$P(x > 125) = 0.05$$

We now transform to Z, so we can work with the probability. We know that $Z = (X - \mu)/\sigma$, and so

$$P\left(Z > \frac{125 - \mu}{\sigma}\right) = 0.05$$

Since $\mu = 120$, we have

$$P\left(Z > \frac{5}{\sigma}\right) = 0.05$$

Now we need to find z such that $P(Z > z) = 0.05$. From the table, we find $z = 1.645$. Finally, equating $z = 1.645$ with $z = 5/\sigma$, we get $\sigma = 5/1.645 = 3.04$. We illustrate the procedure of solving for an unknown mean with Example 4–7.

The net weight of a single cereal box is a normally distributed random variable. The variance of the net weights is known to be $\sigma^2 = 0.25$. Since the production process has changed, the mean is unknown (although the variance is believed not to have changed). A check of the weight of some boxes indicates that 20% of the boxes have net weight greater than 16.5 oz. Based on this information, find the mean net weight, μ, of the cereal boxes.

EXAMPLE 4-7

We have

SOLUTION

$$P(X > 16.5) = 0.20$$

Transforming X to Z we get

$$P\left(\frac{X - \mu}{\sigma} > \frac{16.5 - \mu}{\sigma}\right) = 0.20$$

Since $\sigma^2 = 0.25$, $\sigma = 0.5$ and

$$P\left(Z > \frac{16.5 - \mu}{0.5}\right) = 0.20$$

We now need to find that particular point of the standard normal distribution, $z = (16.5 - \mu)/0.5$, such that the area under the curve to its right is equal to 0.20. From the table, using TA $= 0.5 - 0.2 = 0.3$, we get $z = 0.84$. We now need to solve the equation for μ:

$$\frac{16.5 - \mu}{0.5} = 0.84$$

We get $\mu = 16.5 - (0.84)(0.5) = 16.08$. Thus, the mean net weight of a box of cereal is $\mu = 16.08$ oz.

We may also solve for both an unknown mean and an unknown variance (or standard deviation) of a normal distribution. From algebra, we know that to solve for two unknowns, we need two equations. Therefore, we will need to have two probability statements about the normal random variable in question. The two statements will lead to two equations with the unknowns μ and σ. Let us look at an example.

EXAMPLE 4–8

For a certain new automobile, gasoline consumption on the highway is normally distributed with an unknown mean and unknown standard deviation. The manufacturer does know, however, that 80% of the time the automobile gets more than 28 miles per gallon (mpg) on the highway, and 40% of the time it gets more than 32 mpg on the highway. Find the mean and the standard deviation of highway gasoline consumption.

SOLUTION

We have two probability statements:

$$P(X > 28) = 0.80 \qquad \text{and} \qquad P(X > 32) = 0.40$$

Let us transform these statements into statements about the random variable Z.

$$P\left(Z > \frac{28 - \mu}{\sigma}\right) = 0.80 \qquad \text{and} \qquad P\left(Z > \frac{32 - \mu}{\sigma}\right) = 0.40$$

We now look for the two z values, the first having an area to its right equal to 0.80 and the second having an area to its right equal to 0.40. From the table, we find that the first value is $z_1 = -0.84$, and the second value is $z_2 = 0.25$. Substituting these values into the expressions for μ and σ in the probability statements, we get two equations:

$$\frac{28 - \mu}{\sigma} = -0.84 \qquad \text{and} \qquad \frac{32 - \mu}{\sigma} = 0.25$$

Multiplying each equation by σ to get rid of denominators gives us the two equations:

$$28 - \mu = -0.84\sigma$$
$$32 - \mu = 0.25\sigma$$

We now solve the equations by substitution:

$$\mu = 28 + 0.84\sigma$$
$$\mu = 32 - 0.25\sigma$$

Equating the two expressions for μ gives $28 + 0.84\sigma = 32 - 0.25\sigma$. Solving the resulting equation for σ gives $\sigma = 4/1.09 = 3.67$. Finally, substituting this value for σ into any of the equations gives $\mu = 31.08$.

PROBLEMS

4–46. The time it takes a train to go from one station to another is a normally distributed random variable with mean 129 minutes and an unknown variance. Thirty percent of the time, the train makes the trip in more than 142 minutes. Find the variance of the length of a single trip.

4–47. The weight of a tropical fruit experimentally grown in the United States is normally distributed with known variance of 0.04 and an unknown mean. The growers do know that

65% of the fruits have weights less than 0.5 pound. Find the expected weight of a randomly chosen fruit.

4–48. Weekly earnings on a certain import venture are approximately normally distributed with a known mean of $3,250, and an unknown standard deviation. Ten percent of the time, earnings are over $4,000. Find the standard deviation of weekly earnings.

4–49. The number of orders received monthly by a mail order firm is approximately normally distributed with standard deviation 560 and an unknown mean. Ninety percent of the time, monthly orders exceed 12,439. Find the mean number of orders per month.

4–50. The construction time for certain buildings is a normally distributed random variable with an unknown mean and variance. We do know, however, that 75% of the time, construction takes less than 12 months, and 45% of the time, construction takes less than 10 months. Find the mean and the standard deviation of construction time.

4–51. The weight of goods shipped in containers of a certain size is a normally distributed random variable. It is known that 65% of the containers have net weight above 4.9 tons, and 25% of the containers have net weight less than 4.2 tons. Find the mean and the standard deviation of the net weight of a container.

4–52. Rates of return on bank assets are approximately normally distributed. For Bankers Trust NY Corp, the standard deviation is 1.75 (data are in annualized percentages). If the probability that the return will be above 7.4% is 0.55, find the mean annualized percentage return.

4–53. The average face value of total debt (in millions of dollars) for First Interstate Bancorp. is reported to be 36,405. If the face value of total debt is believed to be normally distributed and we know that 5% of the time it is over 45,000, what is the standard deviation of the face value of total debt for First Interstate Bancorp?

4–54. The standard deviation of the annual value of assets for First Pennsylvania Corp. is reported as 46.2. Assuming a normal distribution of the annual value of assets, and that the probability is 0.90 that assets value will be under $4,048 million, find the mean annual assets value.

4–55. Cover Story is a monthly ranking of celebrities' popularity as reflected in the number of appearances by the celebrities on the pages of hundreds of national publications. A celebrity's rating, computed in some way based on the number of such appearances, is a random variable. For Cher, the rating has an average of 5.2 points.[5] If ratings are normally distributed and 80% of the time Cher's rating is below 7.0, what is Cher's standard deviation of ratings?

4–56. The number of viewers of Cablevision systems is random and varies from day to day.[6] It may be assumed that 60% of the time there are more than 1.5 million viewers, and 90% of the time the number of viewers is below 2.1 million. Assuming a normal distribution, find the mean and the standard deviation of the daily number of Cablevision viewers.

4–7 The Normal Distribution as an Approximation to Other Probability Distributions

The normal distribution is, by its very nature, the limiting probability distribution in many situations. In fact, the majority of the probability distributions discussed in this book tend to the normal distribution as some quantity relevant to the distribution, such

---

[5] Cover Story, *Advertising Age,* February 4, 1991.
[6] F. Meeks, "Bell TV?" *Forbes,* March 4, 1991, p. 42.

as sample size, increases indefinitely. For example, the t distribution and the chi-square distribution—two important probability distributions used in statistics and introduced in the next chapters—tend to the normal distribution as the sample size from which they arise increases. As was noted in the beginning of this chapter, the normal distribution was originally discovered as the limit of the binomial distribution as n increases. We now return to this situation and show how the normal distribution serves as an approximation to the binomial.

As n, the number of trials in the binomial experiment, increases, the discrete binomial probability distribution tends to the continuous normal probability distribution. This means that, for large n, we may approximate a binomial probability with the probability obtained for a normal random variable with the same mean and the same standard deviation as the binomial. Let us look at an example.

EXAMPLE 4-9

Suppose that the proportion of people who use a certain product is $p = 0.50$. A random sample of seven people is chosen, and we want to evaluate the probability that at most four of them will be product users. We want to do this both directly and by way of a normal approximation. The situation is demonstrated in Figure 4–16, where the sum of the weights to the left of and including 4—that is, $F(4)$—is shown. Also shown is the normal approximation to the required probability: the area under the normal curve to the left of the point 4.5. (We use 4.5 because we want to include 4 but not 5, and the best way to do this—using a continuous approximation to a discrete distribution—is to draw the line centered between the two points 4 and 5.)[7]

The normal distribution we use is one with mean and standard deviation identical to those of the given binomial. We have $\mu = np = (0.5)(7) = 3.5$ and $\sigma = \sqrt{np(1 - p)} = \sqrt{(7)(0.5)(0.5)} = 1.323$. The normal approximation to the binomial probability $F(4)$ is

$$P(X < 4.5) = P\left(Z < \frac{4.5 - \mu}{\sigma}\right)$$

$$= P\left(Z < \frac{4.5 - 3.5}{1.323}\right) = P(Z < 0.756)$$

for which the value from the normal table, added to 0.5 as required, gives us 0.7749. The true probability, obtained from the binomial table (Table 1), is $F(4) = 0.7734$. Thus, the approximation, even with a small number of trials ($n = 7$), is quite good. Let us see what happens when the number of trials increases. Suppose that we now take a sample of 11 people, and we want to find the probability that at most 4 of them are users of the product of interest. Again, we evaluate the probability two ways. First, we refer directly to the binomial table: $F(4) = 0.2744$ (see Table 1 with $p = 0.5$ and $n = 11$). Then we use the approximating normal random variable with mean $\mu = np = 11(0.5) = 5.5$ and standard deviation $\sigma = \sqrt{np(1 - p)} = 1.6583$. We find

$$P(X < 4.5) = P\left(Z < \frac{4.5 - 5.5}{1.6583}\right) = P(Z < -0.603) = 0.2732$$

(from Table 2, with interpolation). Again, the approximation is excellent. The situation is shown in Figure 4–17.

As the number of trials, n, increased from 7 to 11, the normal approximation to the binomial improved by three units in the fourth decimal place. We showed how the normal distribution is used in approximating a binomial with $p = 0.5$. In this case, the

---

[7] This is sometimes called a *continuity correction*.

FIGURE 4-16   Approximating a Binomal Distribution with n = 7 and p = 0.5 by a Normal Distribution [Example 4-9]

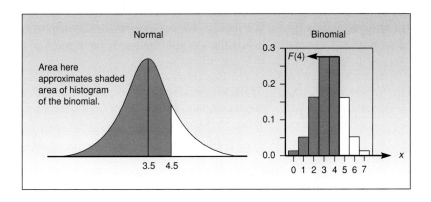

FIGURE 4-17   Approximating a Binomial Distribution with n = 11 and p = 0.5 by a Normal Distribution [Example 4-9]

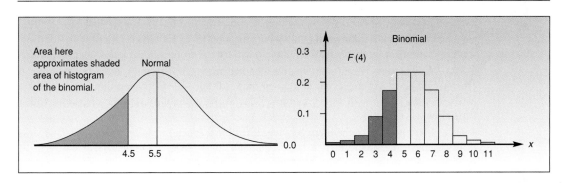

approximation is best and works well with relatively small *n* because the binomial distribution is *symmetric*. When $p \neq 0.5$, the binomial distribution is not symmetric, and the convergence to a normal distribution is slower. Approximations to the binomial with $p \neq 0.5$ improve more dramatically as *n* increases than was the case in our example. When can we safely use the normal distribution as an approximation to the binomial? A rule of thumb says that the normal approximation works well when both np and $n(1 - p)$ are greater than 5. Of course, the larger *n* is, the better the approximation. Also, the closer *p* is to 0.5, the better the approximation and the lower the minimum *n* required for good approximation accuracy.

Approximating a binomial probability using the normal distribution:

$$P(a \leq X \leq b) \doteq P\left(\frac{a - np}{\sqrt{np(1 - p)}} \leq Z \leq \frac{b - np}{\sqrt{np(1 - p)}}\right)$$

for *n* large ($n \geq 50$) and *p* not too close to 0 or 1.00.

Or:

$$P(a \le X \le b) \doteq P\left(\frac{a - 0.5 - np}{\sqrt{np(1-p)}} \le Z \le \frac{b + 0.5 - np}{\sqrt{np(1-p)}} \right)$$

for n only moderately large ($20 \le n < 50$). This is the continuity correction.

If p is either small (close to 0) or large (close to 1.00), use the Poisson approximation instead.

PROBLEMS

In the following problems, use a normal distribution to compute the required probabilities. Whenever you can, compare your answers with the true binomial probabilities obtained from the binomial table, Table 1 in Appendix C. In each problem, also state the assumptions necessary for a binomial distribution, and indicate whether the assumptions are reasonable.

4–57.   The manager of a restaurant knows from experience that 70% of the people who make reservations for the evening show up for dinner. The manager decides one evening to overbook and accept 20 reservations when only 15 tables are available. What is the probability that more than 15 parties will show up?

4–58.   An advertising research study indicates that 40% of the viewers exposed to an advertisement try the product during the following four months. If 100 people are exposed to the ad, what is the probability that at least 20 of them will try the product in the following four months?

4–59.   A computer system contains 45 identical microchips. The probability that any microchip will be in working order at a given time is 0.80. A certain operation requires that at least 30 of the chips be in working order. What is the probability that the operation will be carried out successfully?

4–60.   Sixty percent of the managers who enroll in a special training program will successfully complete the program. If a large company sends 28 of its managers to enroll in the program, what is the probability that at least half of them will pass?

4–61.   A large state university sends recruiters throughout the state in order to recruit graduating high school seniors to enroll in the university. From the university's records, it is known that 25% of the students who are interviewed by the recruiters actually enroll. If last spring the university recruiters interviewed 1,889 graduating seniors, what is the probability that at least 500 of them will enroll this fall?

4–62.

Formatting

Digital Esperanto

Electronic commerce is getting easier. Until now, corporations wanting to send documents to some courts and federal agencies had to convert them into a format called standard generalized markup language (SGML). This has required special editing software or tedious hand-coding. The conversion will be a breeze with an SGML version of WordPerfect coming from Novell Inc. Then, you can simply prepare documents in regular fashion; the program converts them when you save.

Reprinted from *Business Week*, April 24, 1995, p. 19.

If 75% of executives shown this new product were impressed by its performance and indicated an intention to purchase it, what is the probability that at least 20 executives in a group of 30 would be interested in this product once it is demonstrated to them?

4–63.   According to a survey conducted by *Money* magazine, 64% of middle-class earners say it would be difficult to find a new job if they were fired.[8] If a group of 50 randomly chosen middle-class breadwinners is selected, what is the probability that at most 30 of them feel this way?

4-8   Using the Computer

Computer packages, including MINITAB, can be used to evaluate probabilities for normal random variables. Again, we can use the command CDF followed by the value for which we need the cumulative normal probability. We end the command with a semicolon, after which the computer looks for a subcommand. Then we type NORMAL. If we put a period right after NORMAL, the computer assumes we mean the standard normal. Otherwise, we specify two numbers, one for the mean and one for the standard deviation before typing the final period and pressing "return." Two examples are demonstrated in Figure 4–18. Verify the simple answers using the normal table.

4-9   Summary and Review of Terms

In this chapter, we discussed the **normal probability distribution,** the most important probability distribution in statistics. We defined the **standard normal random variable** as the normal random variable with mean 0 and standard deviation 1. We saw how to use a table of probabilities for the standard normal random variable and how to transform a normal random variable with any mean and any standard deviation to the standard normal random variable using the **normal transformation.**

   We also saw how the standard normal random variable may, in turn, be transformed into any other normal random variable with a specified mean and standard deviation, and how this allows us to find values of a normal random variable that conform with some probability statement. We discussed a method of determining the mean and/or the standard deviation of a normal random variable from probability statements about the random variable. We saw how the normal distribution is used as a model in many real-world situations, both as the true distribution (a continuous one) and as an approximation to discrete distributions. In particular, we illustrated the use of the normal distribution as an approximation to the binomial distribution.

   In the following chapters, we will make much use of the material presented here. Most statistical theory relies on the normal distribution and on distributions that are derived from it.

ADDITIONAL PROBLEMS

4–64.   The time, in hours, a copying machine may work without breaking down is a normally distributed random variable with mean 549 and standard deviation 68. Find the probability that the machine will work for at least 500 hours without breaking down.

4–65.   The yield, in tons of ore per day, at a given coal mine is approximately normally distributed with mean 785 tons and standard deviation 60. Find the probability that at least

---

[8] J.S. Coyle, "How to Beat the Squeeze on the Middle Class," *Money,* May 1995, p. 108.

FIGURE 4–18   Examples of Using MINITAB to Find Normal Probabilities

```
MTB > CDF 1.00;
SUBC> NORMAL mean=0 stddev=1.
     1.0000     0.8413

MTB > CDF 20;
SUBC> NORMAL mean=10, stddev=5.
    20.0000     0.9772
```

800 tons of ore will be mined on a given day. Find the proportion of working days in which anywhere from 750 to 850 tons are mined. Find the probability that on a given day, the yield will be below 665 tons.

4–66.   Scores on a management aptitude examination are believed to be normally distributed with mean 650 (out of a total of 800 possible points) and standard deviation 50. What is the probability that a randomly chosen manager will achieve a score above 700? What is the probability that the score will be below 750?

4–67.   Assume that the price of a share of TWA stock is normally distributed with mean 48 and standard deviation 6. What is the probability that on a randomly chosen day in the period for which our assumptions are made, the price of the stock will be over $60 per share? below $60 per share? above $40 per share? between $40 and $50 per share? What are the limitations of your analysis?

4–68.   The amount of oil pumped daily at Standard Oil's facilities in Prudhoe Bay is normally distributed with mean 800,000 barrels and standard deviation 10,000. In determining the amount of oil the company must report as its lower limit of daily production, the company wants to choose an amount such that for 80% of the days, at least the reported amount, x, is produced. Determine the value of the lower limit x.

4–69.   Models of the pricing of stock options make the assumption of a normal distribution. An analyst believes that the price of an IBM stock option is a normally distributed random variable with mean $8.95 and variance 4. The analyst would like to determine a value such that there is a 0.90 probability that the price of the option will be above that value. Find the required value.

4–70.   Weekly rates of return (on an annualized basis) for certain securities over a given period of time are believed to be normally distributed with mean 8.00% and variance 0.25. Give two values, x_1 and x_2, such that you are 95% sure that annualized weekly returns will be between the two values.

4–71.   The impact of a television commercial, measured in terms of excess sales volume over a given time period, is believed to be approximately normally distributed with mean 50,000 and variance 9,000,000. Find 0.99 probability bounds on the volume of excess sales that would result from a given airing of the commercial.

4–72.   A travel agency believes that the number of people who sign up for tours to Hawaii during the Christmas–New Year holiday season is an approximately normally distributed random variable with mean 2,348 and standard deviation 762. For reservation purposes, the agency's management wants to find the number of people such that the probability is 0.85 that at least that many people will sign up. They also need 0.80 probability bounds on the number of people who will sign up for the trip.

4–73.   A loans manager at a large bank believes that the percentage of her customers who default on their loans during each quarter is an approximately normally distributed random variable with mean 12.1% and standard deviation 2.5%. Give a lower bound, x, with 0.75 probability that the percentage of people defaulting on their loans is at least x. Also give an upper bound, x', with 0.75 probability that the percentage of loan defaulters is below x'.

4–74.   The power generated by a solar electric generator is normally distributed with mean 15.6 kilowatts and standard deviation of 4.1 kilowatts. We may be 95% sure that the generator will deliver at least how many kilowatts?

4–75.   Short-term rates fluctuate daily. It may be assumed that the yield for 90-day Treasury bills in 1995 was approximately normally distributed with mean 5.9% and standard deviation 0.8%.[9] Find a value such that 95% of the time during that year the yield of 90-day T-bills was below this value.

4–76.   In quality-control projects, engineers use charts where item values are plotted and compared with 3-standard deviation bounds above and below the mean for the process. When items are found to fall outside the bounds, they are considered nonconforming, and the process is stopped when "too many" items are out of bounds. Assuming a normal distribution of item values, what percentage of values would you expect to be out of bounds when the process is in control? Accordingly, how would you define "too many"? What do you think is the rationale for this practice?

4–77.   Total annual textbook sales in a certain discipline are normally distributed. Forty-five percent of the time, sales are above 671,000 copies, and 10% of the time, sales are above 712,000 copies. Find the mean and the variance of annual sales.

4–78.   Typing speed on a new kind of keyboard for people at a certain stage in their training program is approximately normally distributed. The probability that the speed of a given trainee will be above 65 words per minute is 0.45. The probability that the speed will be better than 70 words per minute is 0.15. Find the mean and the standard deviation of typing speed.

4–79.   The number of people responding to a mailed information brochure on cruises of the Royal Viking Line through an agency in San Francisco is approximately normally distributed. The agency found that 10% of the time, over 1,000 people respond immediately after a mailing, and 50% of the time, at least 650 people respond right after the mailing. Find the mean and the standard deviation of the number of people who respond following a mailing.

4–80.   The Tourist Delivery Program was developed by several European automakers. In this program, a tourist from outside Europe—most are from the United States—may purchase an automobile in Europe and drive it in Europe for as long as six months, after which the manufacturer will ship the car to the tourist's home destination at no additional cost. In addition to the time limitations imposed, some countries impose mileage restrictions so that tourists will not misuse the privileges of the program. In setting the limitation, some countries use a normal distribution assumption. It is believed that the number of miles driven by a tourist in the program is normally distributed with mean 4,500 and standard deviation 1,800. If a country wants to set the mileage limit at a point such that 80% of the tourists in the program will want to drive fewer miles, what should the limit be?

4–81.   The number of newspapers demanded daily in a large metropolitan area is believed to be an approximately normally distributed random variable. If more newspapers are demanded than are printed, the paper suffers an opportunity loss, in that it could have sold more papers, and also a loss of public goodwill. On the other hand, if more papers are printed than will be demanded, the unsold papers are returned to the newspaper office at a loss. Suppose that management believes it is most important to guard against the first type of error, unmet demand, and would like to set the number of papers printed at a level such that 75% of the time, demand for newspapers will be below that point. How many papers should be printed daily if the average demand is 34,750 papers and the standard deviation of demand is 3,560?

4–82.   Arrival times of airplanes at their destination airports are normally distributed. Air traffic controllers must deal with these random arrivals in arranging for a free runway for a

---

[9] Investment Figures, *Business Week*, April 24, 1995, p. 145.

landing. The arrival time depends on many factors, such as weather conditions, flight duration, and flight altitude. Suppose that for a certain type of flight, arrival time is a normally distributed random variable with mean 42.0 minutes after the hour and standard deviation 2.4 minutes. If an air traffic controller wants to hold a runway for the plane until a time such that she can be 98% sure that the plane will not arrive any later, until what time should the controller wait?

4–83.   Pollution has caused the death of large numbers of trees in German forests. The proportion of dying trees in a certain region is as high as 0.30. Sometimes it happens that so many trees die, there are not enough trees to prevent erosion of the soil, and this causes the destruction of the entire forest. In a particular location, there are 238 trees. Scientists believe that if pollution should kill as many as 50 trees, all 238 trees in the location will eventually die. Assuming that the probability that any single tree will die from pollution is indeed 0.30, and that trees are affected independently of each other, what is the probability that out of 238 trees at least 50 will die, thus endangering the forest?

4–84.   The amount of electricity demanded in a midsized town is normally distributed. The utility serving the area needs estimates of electricity consumption in order to arrange for the purchase of electricity in excess of what they produce when demand exceeds production. They also want to be able to reduce their production when consumption is at lower levels and thus keep down the cost of electric power. Management knows that the standard deviation of demand in January is 5.1 megawatts. Management also knows that there is a 0.20 probability that electric demand in January will exceed 124.6 megawatts. What is the mean electric demand during the month of January? If the utility should decide to produce exactly the average electric demand for the month, what is the probability that demand will be less than production?

4–85.   In setting warranties on appliances, manufacturers want to set the time limit in such a way that few appliances will have to be repaired at the manufacturer's expense, yet they want the buyer to have some degree of protection against malfunctions over a period of time after the purchase. A manufacturer of a certain appliance would like to set the expiration time of the warranty at such a level that 90% of the appliances made will remain in working order throughout the period. What should the time period be if the life of the appliance (until first failure) is normally distributed with mean 38 months and standard deviation 11 months?

4–86.   Redo problem 3–69 using a normal approximation to the binomial distribution. Compare the two results.

4–87.   Emery Worldwide now specializes in transporting animals by air and making them feel comfortable while on board the aircraft. Recently, Emery flew six gorillas from Cincinnati to San Diego and treated them royally with large amounts of fresh fruit.[10] Such flights are very costly and average $40,000. The fare depends on the kind of animals and their particular requirements and is negotiated individually. Assuming the cost is normally distributed with standard deviation of $10,000, what is the probability that the next animal flight will cost between $25,000 and $35,000?

4–88.   Project costs are normally distributed with mean $1.5 million. What is the probability that the next project will cost at least $1.5 million?

4–89.   In the situation of the previous problem, 75% of the projects cost over $1 million. What is the standard deviation of project costs?

4–90.   *The round-numbers trap.* Supposedly, the IRS looks for "nice" numbers in taxpayers' returns for further investigation, which may lead to an audit. Thus for example, a return reporting an expense item of $3,000 would lead to initial scrutiny while numbers such as $3,137.12 would not.[11] A random sample of 10,000 returns is selected by the IRS out of a population of returns where 10% contain round numbers. What is the probability that at least 800 returns in the sample will contain round numbers?

---

[10] "Of Course, Sir, Sit Wherever You Like," *Business Week,* March 11, 1991, p. 41.

[11] *Tax Guide for College Teachers* (College Park, MD: Academic Information Service, 1995).

4–91.   According to an article in the *Harvard Business Review,* 80% of all joint ventures ultimately end in a sale by one of the partners.[12] If a random sample of 30 such alliances is chosen, what is the probability that at least 10 of them will end in a sale by one of the partners?

Case 4   OVERALL PERFORMANCE OF CASH EQUIVALENTS FOR STOCKS

A study was conducted on cash equivalents for stock. Annualized rates of return for these stocks were computed, and then the mean and the standard deviation were calculated for these percentages of return. The average for all stocks in the study was found to be 3.76%, and the standard deviation was found to be 3.48%.[13] A random sample of 105 of the returns is presented below.

4.2929	2.5078	0.0497	4.8775	4.7823	1.9127	5.6990
8.2220	5.1947	−0.0513	0.1797	7.7884	−0.3332	3.4602
−2.1203	2.1744	4.7451	4.2653	0.9926	7.5047	11.4342
1.4832	9.2090	4.5709	3.0776	0.5469	6.3069	−2.5981
3.6459	5.6322	4.0596	−1.8470	5.6297	5.5510	0.4241
2.3822	0.2255	0.5892	10.5601	3.4567	2.2958	9.1093
3.1829	7.6588	−2.1161	8.0557	5.9172	8.5991	3.4134
8.6449	3.8811	18.9001	2.9253	3.3914	4.8913	1.3166
10.9781	3.0342	1.5353	8.7480	3.1827	5.3145	4.8544
2.7868	5.6929	6.0649	0.4156	6.3927	2.6705	0.9061
0.4027	8.2145	7.3652	6.5483	−0.1128	−2.1665	6.5056
4.4936	0.0100	2.5397	3.3327	8.3862	2.2782	7.3212
1.9865	4.8451	1.7055	7.4952	0.0577	4.4249	8.6370
6.0416	3.9232	1.2513	4.0367	3.3105	5.8972	9.4582
5.6092	6.2703	5.4551	7.0799	−1.6761	1.2563	1.8623

a. Plot a histogram of the data. Compute the mean and the standard deviation of the data, and compare them with the numbers in the study. Now compute specific percentage points of the data distribution that may be compared with percentage points of a normal distribution with the same mean and standard deviation. Based on your results, can you conclude that the data distribution is approximately normal?

b. Assuming a normal distribution is appropriate, consider the following. The original investment in each case is $1,000. Once you sell the stock and realize your return, the brokerage house deducts an amount equal to 5% of your earnings as their commission. What can you say about the distribution of the net returns (after commissions are paid)? Explain.

---

[12] J. Bleeke and D. Ernst, "Is Your Strategic Alliance Really a Sale?" *Harvard Business Review,* January–February 1995, p. 97.

[13] G. Kester, "Market Timing," *Financial Analysts Journal,* September–October 1990, p. 64.

5

SAMPLING AND SAMPLING DISTRIBUTIONS

5 - 1   I N T R O D U C T I O N

S tatistics is a science of *inference*. It is the science of generalization from a *part* (the randomly chosen sample) to the *whole*
(the population).[1] Recall from Chapter 1 that the population
is the entire collection of measurements in which we are interested, and the sample is a smaller set of measurements selected from the
population. A random sample of *n* elements is a sample selected from
the population in such a way that every set of *n* elements is as likely to

Continued

---

[1] Not all of statistics concerns inferences about populations. One branch of statistics, called
descriptive statistics, deals with describing data sets — possibly with no interest in an underlying
population. The descriptive statistics of Chapter 1, when *not* used for inference, fall in this
category.

be selected as any other set of n elements.[2] It is important that the sample be drawn randomly from the entire population under study. This makes it likely that our sample will be truly representative of the population of interest and minimizes the chance of errors. As we will see in this chapter, random sampling also allows us to compute the probabilities of sampling errors, thus providing us with knowledge of the degree of accuracy of our sampling results. The need to sample correctly is best illustrated by the well-known story of the *Literary Digest*.

Digest Poll Gives Landon 32 States

Landon Leads 4–3 In Last Digest Poll

FINAL TABULATION GIVES HIM 370 ELECTORAL VOTES TO 161 FOR PRESIDENT ROOSEVELT

Governor Landon will win the election by an electoral vote of 370 to 161, will carry thirty-two of the forty-eight States, and will lead President Roosevelt about four to three in their share of the popular vote, if the final figures in The Literary Digest poll, made public yesterday, are verified by the count of the ballots next Tuesday.

The New York Times, Friday, October 30, 1936. Copyright © 1936 by The New York Times Company. Reprinted by permission.

Roosevelt's Plurality Is 11,000,000

History's Largest Poll

46 States Won By President, Maine And Vermont By Landon

Many Phases To Victory

Democratic Landslide Looked Upon as Striking Personal Triumph for Roosevelt

BY ARTHUR KROCK

As the count of ballots cast Tuesday in the 1936 Presidential election moved toward completion yesterday, these facts appeared:

Franklin Delano Roosevelt was reelected President, and John N. Garner Vice President, by the largest popular and electoral majority since the United States became a continental nation—a margin of approximately 11,000,000 plurality of all votes cast, and 523 votes in the electoral college to 8 won by the Republican Presidential candidate, Governor Alfred M. Landon of Kansas. The latter carried only Maine and Vermont of the forty-eight States of the Union . . . .

The New York Times, Thursday, November 5, 1936. Copyright © 1936 by The New York Times Company. Reprinted by permission.

---

[2] This is the definition of *simple random sampling*, and we will assume throughout that all our samples are simple random samples. Other methods of sampling are discussed in Chapter 17.

In 1936, the widely quoted *Literary Digest* embarked on the project of predicting the results of the presidential election to be held that year. The magazine boasted it would predict, to within a fraction of the percentage of the votes, the winner of the election—incumbent President Franklin Delano Roosevelt or the Republican governor of Kansas, Alfred M. Landon. The *Digest* tried to gather a sample of staggering proportion—10 million voters! One problem with the survey was that only a fraction of the people sampled, 2.3 million, actually provided the requested information. Should a link have existed between a person's inclination to answer the survey and his or her voting preference, the results of the survey would have been *biased*: slanted toward the voting preference of those who did answer. It is unknown whether such a link did exist in the case of the *Digest*. (This problem is known as *nonresponse bias* and is discussed in Chapter 17.) A very serious problem with the *Digest*'s poll, and one known to have affected the results, is the following.

The sample of voters chosen by the *Literary Digest* was obtained from lists of telephone numbers, automobile registrations, and names of *Digest* readers. Remember that this was 1936—not as many people owned phones or cars as today, and the ones who did tended to be wealthier and more likely to vote Republican (and the same goes for readers of the *Digest*). The selection procedure for the sample of voters was thus biased (slanted toward one kind of voter) because the sample was not randomly chosen from the entire population of voters. Figure 5–1 demonstrates a correct sampling procedure versus the sampling procedure used by the *Literary Digest*.

As a result of the *Digest* error, the magazine does not exist today; it went bankrupt soon after the 1936 election. Some say that hindsight is useful and that today we know more statistics, making it easy for us to deride mistakes made more than 50 years ago. Interestingly enough, however, the ideas of sampling bias were understood in 1936. A few weeks *before* the election, there appeared a small article in *The New York Times* criticizing the methodology of the *Digest* poll. Few paid it any attention.

Sampling is very useful in many situations besides political polling, including business and other areas where we need to obtain information about some population. Our information often leads to a *decision*. There are also situations, as demonstrated by the examples in the introduction to this book, where we are interested in a *process* rather than a single population. One such process is the relationship between advertising and sales. In these more involved situations, we still make the assumption of an underlying population—here, the population of *pairs* of possible advertising and sales values. Conclusions about the process are reached based on information in our data, which are assumed to constitute a random sample from the entire population. The ideas of a population and of a random sample drawn from the population are thus essential to all of inferential statistics.

In statistical inference we are concerned with populations; the samples are of no interest to us in their own right. We wish to use our *known* random sample in the extraction of information about the *unknown* population from which it is drawn. The information we extract is in the form of summary statistics: a sample mean, a sample standard deviation, or other measures computed from the sample. A statistic such as the sample mean is considered an *estimator* of a population *parameter*—the population mean. In the next section, we discuss and define sample estimators and population parameters. Then we explore the relationship between statistics and parameters via the *sampling distribution*. Finally, we discuss desirable properties of statistical estimators. ∎

FIGURE 5–1 A Good Sampling Procedure and the One Used by the *Literary Digest*

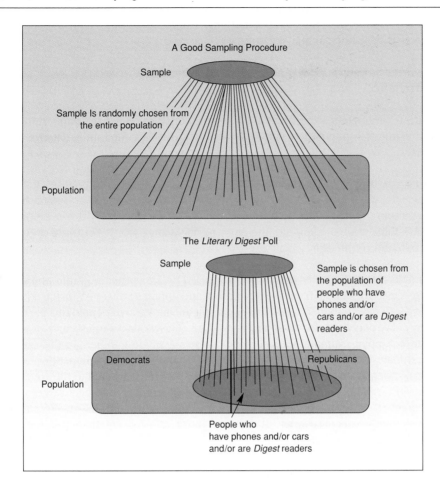

5-2   Sample Statistics as Estimators of Population Parameters

A population may be a large, sometimes infinite, collection of elements. The population has a *frequency distribution*—the distribution of the frequencies of occurrence of its elements. The population distribution, when stated in relative frequencies, is also the probability distribution of the population. This is so because the relative frequency of a value in the population is also the probability of obtaining the particular value when an element is randomly drawn from the entire population. As with random variables, we may associate with a population its mean and its standard deviation. In the case of populations, the mean and the standard deviation are called *parameters*. They are denoted by μ and σ, respectively.

A numerical measure of a population is called a **population parameter,** or simply a **parameter.**

Recall that in Chapter 4 we referred to the mean and the standard deviation of a normal probability distribution as the distribution parameters. Here we view parameters as descriptive measures of populations. Inference drawn about a population parameter is based on sample statistics.

> A numerical measure of the sample is called a **sample statistic,** or simply a **statistic.**

Population parameters are estimated by sample statistics. When a sample statistic is used to estimate a population parameter, the statistic is called an *estimator* of the parameter.

> An **estimator** of a population parameter is a sample statistic used to estimate the parameter. An **estimate** of the parameter is a *particular* numerical value of the estimator obtained by sampling. When a single value is used as an estimate, the estimate is called a **point estimate** of the population parameter.

The sample mean, $\bar{X}$, is the sample statistic used as an estimator of the population mean, μ. Once we sample from the population and obtain a value of $\bar{X}$ (using equation 1–1), we will have obtained a *particular* sample mean; we will denote this particular value by $\bar{x}$. We may have, for example, $\bar{x} = 12.53$. This value is our estimate of μ. The estimate is a point estimate because it constitutes a single number. In this chapter, every estimate will be a point estimate—a single number that, we hope, lies close to the population parameter it estimates. Chapter 6 is entirely devoted to the concept of an *interval estimate*—an estimate constituting an interval of numbers rather than a single number. An interval estimate is an interval believed likely to contain the unknown population parameter. It conveys more information than just the point estimate on which it is based.

In addition to the sample mean, which estimates the population mean, other statistics are useful. The sample standard deviation, S, is used as an estimator of the population standard deviation σ. A particular estimate obtained will be denoted by s. (This estimate is computed from the data using equation 1–5 or an equivalent formula.)

As demonstrated by the political polling example with which we opened this chapter, interest often centers not on a mean or standard deviation of a population, but rather on a population *proportion*. The population proportion parameter is also called a binomial proportion parameter.

> The **population proportion,** p, is equal to the number of elements in the population belonging to the category of interest, divided by the total number of elements in the population.

The population proportion of voters for Governor Landon in 1936, for example, was the number of people who intended to vote for the candidate, divided by the total number of voters. The estimator of the population proportion p is the *sample proportion* $\hat{P}$, defined as the number of *binomial successes* in the sample (i.e., the number of elements in the sample that belong to the category of interest) divided by the sample size, n. A particular estimate of the population proportion p is the sample proportion $\hat{p}$.

The **sample proportion:**

$$\hat{p} = \frac{x}{n} \qquad (5\text{--}1)$$

where x is the number of elements in the sample found to belong to the category of interest, and n is the sample size

Suppose that we want to estimate the proportion of consumers in a certain area that are users of a certain product. The (unknown) population proportion is p. We estimate p by the statistic $\hat{P}$, the sample proportion. Suppose a random sample of 100 consumers in the area reveals that 26 of them are users of the product. Our point estimate of p is then $\hat{p} = x/n = 26/100 = 0.26$.

In summary, we have the following estimation relationships.

Estimator (Sample Statistic)		Population Parameter
$\overline{X}$	estimates $\longrightarrow$	μ
S	estimates $\longrightarrow$	σ
$\hat{P}$	estimates $\longrightarrow$	p

Let us consider sampling to estimate the population mean, and let us try to visualize how this is done. Consider a population with a certain frequency distribution. The frequency distribution of the values of the population is the probability distribution of the value of an element in the population, drawn at random. Figure 5–2 shows a frequency distribution of some population, and the population mean, μ. If we knew the exact frequency distribution of the population, we would be able to determine μ directly in the same way we determine the mean of a random variable when we know its probability distribution. In reality, the frequency distribution of a population is not known; neither is the mean of the population. We try to estimate the population mean by the sample mean, computed from a random sample. Figure 5–2 shows the values of a random sample obtained from the population and the resulting sample mean, $\overline{x}$, computed from the data.

In this example, $\overline{x}$ happens to lie close to μ, the population parameter it estimates, although this does not always happen. The sample statistic $\overline{X}$ is a *random variable* whose actual value depends on the particular random sample obtained. The random variable $\overline{X}$ has a relatively high probability of being close to the population mean it estimates, and it has decreasing probabilities of falling further and further away from the population mean. Similarly, the sample statistic S is a random variable with a relatively high probability of being close to σ, the population parameter it estimates. Also, when sampling for a population proportion, p, the estimator $\hat{P}$ has a relatively high probability of being close to p. How high a probability, and how close to the parameter? The answer to this question is the main topic of this chapter, presented in the next section. Before discussing this important topic, we will say a few things about the mechanics of obtaining random samples.

Obtaining a Random Sample

All along we have been referring to random samples. We have stressed the importance of the fact that our sample should always be drawn randomly from the entire population about which we wish to draw an inference. How do we draw a random sample?

FIGURE 5-2   A Population Distribution, a Random Sample from the Population, and Their Respective Means

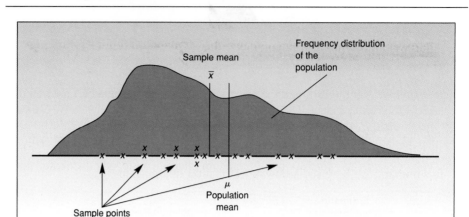

To obtain a random sample from the entire population, we need a list of all the elements in the population of interest. Such a list is called a *frame.* The frame allows us to draw elements from the population by randomly generating the numbers of the elements to be included in the sample. Suppose we need a simple random sample of 100 people from a population of 7,000. We make a list of all 7,000 people and assign each person an identification number. This gives us a list of 7,000 numbers—our frame for the experiment. Then we generate by computer or by other means a set of 100 random numbers in the range of values from 1 to 7,000. This procedure gives every set of 100 people in the population an equal chance of being included in the sample.

As mentioned, a computer (or an advanced calculator) may be used for generating random numbers. We will demonstrate an alternative method of choosing random numbers—a random numbers table. Table 5–1 is a part of such a table. A random number table is given in Appendix C as Table 14. To use the table, we start at any point, pick a number from the table, and continue in the same row or the same column (it does not matter which), systematically picking out numbers with the number of digits appropriate for our needs. If a number is outside our range of required numbers, we ignore it. We also ignore any number already obtained.

For example, suppose that we need a random sample of 10 data points from a population with a total of 600 elements. This means that we need 10 random drawings of elements from our frame of 1 through 600. To do this, we note that the number 600 has three digits; therefore, we draw random numbers with three digits. Since our population has only 600 units, however, we ignore any number greater than 600 and take the next number, assuming it falls in our range. Let us decide arbitrarily to choose the first three digits in each set of five digits in Table 5–1, and proceed by row, starting in the first row and moving to the second row, continuing until we have obtained our 10 required random numbers. We get the following random numbers: 104, 150, 15, 20, 816 (discard), 916 (discard), 691 (discard), 141, 223, 465, 255, 853 (discard), 309, 891 (discard), 279. Our random sample will, therefore, consist of the elements with serial numbers 104, 150, 15, 20, 141, 223, 465, 255, 309, and 279. A similar procedure would be used for obtaining the random sample of 100 people from the

TABLE 5–1   Random Numbers

10480	15011	01536	02011	81647	91646	69179	14194
22368	46573	25595	85393	30995	89198	27982	53402
24130	48360	22527	97265	76393	64809	15179	24830
42167	93093	06243	61680	07856	16376	93440	53537
37570	39975	81837	16656	06121	91782	60468	81305
77921	06907	11008	42751	27756	53498	18602	70659

population of 7,000 mentioned earlier. Random number tables are included in books of statistical tables. Random numbers can also be generated by computer. The output below demonstrates the generation of 12 random integers, uniformly distributed from 0 to 9, using MINITAB.

```
MTB > RANDOM 12 C1 ;
SUBC> INTEGER 0 9.
MTB > PRINT C1

C1
   3   6   9   7   2   5   4   1   5   7   6   6
```

In many situations it is not possible to obtain a frame of the elements in the population. In such situations we may still randomize some aspect of the experiment and thus obtain a random sample. For example, we may randomize the location and the time and date of the collection of our observations, as well as other factors involved. In estimating the average mpg rating of an automobile, for example, we may randomly choose the dates and times of our trial runs as well as the particular automobiles used, the drivers, the roads used, and so on. More will be said about sampling techniques in Chapter 17.

PROBLEMS

5–1. Discuss the concepts of a parameter, a sample statistic, an estimator, and an estimate. What are the relations among these entities?

5–2. An auditor selected a random sample of 12 accounts from all accounts receivable of a given firm. The amounts of the accounts, in dollars, are as follows: 87.50, 123.10, 45.30, 52.22, 213.00, 155.00, 39.00, 76.05, 49.80, 99.99, 132.00, 102.11. Compute an estimate of the mean amount of all accounts receivable. Give an estimate of the variance of all the amounts.

5–3. In problem 5–2, suppose the auditor wants to estimate the proportion of all the firm's accounts receivable with amounts over $100. Give a point estimate of this parameter.

5–4. Following is a random sample of personal incomes of industry workers in the state of New York, in thousands of dollars per year: 14.5, 13.2, 15.4, 12.8, 19.3, 13.4, 16.5, 17.2, 17.8, 11.5, 13.6, 18.8. Compute point estimates of the mean and the standard deviation of the population of incomes of industry workers in the state.

5–5. The following is a random sample of the total compensation, in thousands of dollars per year, received by corporate board directors in a category called well-paid:[3] 550, 275, 560, 400, 325, 300, 310, 415, 650, 340. Compute a point estimate of the proportion of all directors in

---

[3] D. Wechsler, R. Lenzner, and F. Wolfe, "The Cosseted Director," *Forbes,* May 22, 1995, pp. 168–173.

the nation's "well paid" category with compensation over \$500,000. Also compute a point estimate of the average annual pay of a director in this category.

5–6.   A market research worker interviewed a random sample of 18 people about their use of a certain product. The results, in terms of Y or N (for Yes, a user of the product, or No, not a user of the product), are as follows: Y N N Y Y Y N Y N Y Y Y N Y N Y Y N. Estimate the population proportion of users of the product.

5–7.   Use a random numbers table (you may use Table 5–1) to find identification numbers of elements to be used in a random sample of size $n = 25$ from a population of 950 elements.

5–8.   Find five random numbers from 0 to 5,600.

5–9.   Assume that you have a frame of 40 million voters (something the *Literary Digest* should have had for an unbiased polling). Randomly generate the numbers of five sampled voters.

5–10.   Suppose you need to sample the concentration of a chemical in a production process that goes on continuously 24 hours a day, seven days a week. You need to generate a random sample of six observations of the process over a period of one week. Use a computer, a calculator, or a random numbers table to generate the six observation times (to the nearest minute).

5–3   Sampling Distributions

> The **sampling distribution** of a statistic is the probability distribution of all possible values the statistic may take when computed from random samples of the same size, drawn from a specified population.

Let us first look at the sample mean, $\overline{X}$. The sample mean is a random variable. The possible values of this random variable depend on the possible values of the elements in the random sample from which $\overline{X}$ is to be computed. The random sample, in turn, depends on the distribution of the population from which it is drawn. As a random variable, $\overline{X}$ has a *probability distribution*. This probability distribution is the sampling distribution of $\overline{X}$.

> The **sampling distribution of $\overline{X}$** is the probability distribution of all possible values the random variable $\overline{X}$ may take when a sample of size n is taken from a specified population.

Let us derive the sampling distribution of $\overline{X}$ in the simple case of drawing a sample of size $n = 2$ items from a population uniformly distributed over the integers 1 through 8. That is, we have a large population consisting of equal proportions of the values 1 to 8. At each draw, there is a 1/8 probability of obtaining any of the values 1 through 8 (alternatively, we may assume there are only eight elements, 1 through 8, and that the sampling is done with replacement). The sample space of the values of the two sample points drawn from this population is given in Table 5–2. This is an example. In real situations, sample sizes are much larger.

Using the sample space from the table, we will now find all possible values of the sample mean $\overline{X}$ and their probabilities. We compute these probabilities using the fact that all 64 sample pairs shown are equally likely. This is so because the population is uniformly distributed and because in random sampling each drawing is independent of the other; therefore, the probability of a given pair of sample points is the product $(1/8)(1/8) = 1/64$. From Table 5–2, we compute the sample mean associated with each of the 64 pairs of numbers and find the probability of occurrence of each value of the sample mean. The values and their probabilities are given in Table 5–3. The

TABLE 5-2 **Possible Values of Two Sample Points from a Uniform Population of the Integers 1 through 8**

		First Sample Point							
		1	2	3	4	5	6	7	8
Second	1	1,1	2,1	3,1	4,1	5,1	6,1	7,1	8,1
Sample	2	1,2	2,2	3,2	4,2	5,2	6,2	7,2	8,2
Point	3	1,3	2,3	3,3	4,3	5,3	6,3	7,3	8,3
	4	1,4	2,4	3,4	4,4	5,4	6,4	7,4	8,4
	5	1,5	2,5	3,5	4,5	5,5	6,5	7,5	8,5
	6	1,6	2,6	3,6	4,6	5,6	6,6	7,6	8,6
	7	1,7	2,7	3,7	4,7	5,7	6,7	7,7	8,7
	8	1,8	2,8	3,8	4,8	5,8	6,8	7,8	8,8

TABLE 5-3 **The Sampling Distribution of $\bar{X}$ for a Sample of Size 2 from a Uniformly Distributed Population of the Integers 1 to 8**

Particular Value $\bar{x}$	Probability of $\bar{x}$	Particular Value $\bar{x}$	Probability of $\bar{x}$
1	1/64	5	7/64
1.5	2/64	5.5	6/64
2	3/64	6	5/64
2.5	4/64	6.5	4/64
3	5/64	7	3/64
3.5	6/64	7.5	2/64
4	7/64	8	1/64
4.5	8/64		1.00

table thus gives us the sampling distribution of $\bar{X}$ in this particular sampling situation. Verify the values in Table 5–3 using the sample space given in Table 5–2. Figure 5–3 shows the uniform distribution of the population and the sampling distribution of $\bar{X}$, as listed in Table 5–3.

Let us find the mean and the standard deviation of the *population.* We can do this by treating the population as a random variable (the random variable being the value of a single item randomly drawn from the population; each of the values 1 through 8 has a 1/8 probability of being drawn). Using the appropriate equations from Chapter 3, we find $\mu = 4.5$ and $\sigma = 2.29$ (verify these results).

Now let us find the expected value and the standard deviation of the random variable $\bar{X}$. Using the sampling distribution listed in Table 5–3, we find $E(\bar{X}) = 4.5$ and $\sigma_{\bar{x}} = 1.62$ (verify these values by computation). Note that the expected value of $\bar{X}$ is equal to the mean of the population: each is equal to 4.5. The standard deviation of $\bar{X}$, denoted $\sigma_{\bar{x}}$, is equal to 1.62, and the population standard deviation, σ, is 2.29. But observe an interesting fact: $2.29/\sqrt{2} = 1.62$. The facts we have discovered in this example are not an accident—they hold in all cases. The expected value of the sample mean, $\bar{X}$, is equal to the population mean, μ, and the standard deviation of $\bar{X}$ is equal to the population standard deviation divided by the square root of the sample size. Sometimes the estimated standard deviation of a statistic is called its *standard error.*

FIGURE 5-3   The Population Distribution and the Sampling Distribution of the Sample Mean

---

The expected value of the sample mean:[4]

$$E(\overline{X}) = \mu \qquad (5\text{--}2)$$

The standard deviation of the sample mean:[5]

$$SD(\overline{X}) = \sigma_{\bar{x}} = \sigma/\sqrt{n} \qquad (5\text{--}3)$$

We know the two parameters of the sampling distribution of $\overline{X}$: we know the mean of the distribution (the expected value of $\overline{X}$) and we know its standard deviation. What about the shape of the sampling distribution? If the population itself is *normally distributed,* the sampling distribution of $\overline{X}$ is also normal.

When sampling from a *normal* distribution with mean μ and standard deviation σ, the sample mean $\overline{X}$ has a **normal sampling distribution:**

$$\overline{X} \sim N(\mu,\, \sigma^2/n) \qquad (5\text{--}4)$$

Thus, when we sample from a normally distributed population with mean μ and standard deviation σ, the sample mean has a normal distribution with the same *center,* μ, as the population but with *width* (standard deviation) that is $1/\sqrt{n}$ the size

---

[4] The proof of equation 5–2 relies on the fact that the expected value of the sum of several random variables is equal to the sum of their expected values. Also, from equation 3–6 we know that the expected value of aX, where a is a number, is equal to a times the expected value of X. We also know that the expected value of each element X drawn from the population is equal to μ, the population mean. Using these facts, we find the following: $E(\overline{X}) = E(\Sigma X/n) = (1/n)E(\Sigma X) = (1/n)n\mu = \mu$.

[5] The proof of equation 5–3 relies on the fact that, when several random variables are *independent* (as happens in random sampling), the variance of the sum of the random variables is equal to the sum of their variances. Also, from equation 3–10, we know that the variance of aX is equal to $a^2V(X)$. The variance of each X drawn from the population is equal to σ^2. Using these facts, we find $V(\overline{X}) = V(\Sigma X/n) = (1/n)^2(\Sigma \sigma^2) = (1/n)^2(n\sigma^2) = \sigma^2/n$. Hence, $SD(\overline{X}) = \sigma/\sqrt{n}$.

FIGURE 5–4   **A Normally Distributed Population and the Sampling Distribution of the Sample Mean for Different Sample Sizes**

Density

Sampling distribution of $\overline{X}$ for $n = 16$

Sampling distribution of $\overline{X}$ for $n = 4$

Sampling distribution of $\overline{X}$ for $n = 2$

Normal population

Value

μ

of the width of the population distribution. This is demonstrated in Figure 5–4, which shows a normal population distribution and the sampling distribution of $\overline{X}$ for different sample sizes.

The fact that the sampling distribution of $\overline{X}$ has mean μ is very important. It means that, *on the average,* the sample mean is equal to the population mean. The distribution of the statistic is *centered* over the parameter to be estimated, and this makes the statistic $\overline{X}$ a good estimator of μ. This fact will become clearer in the next section, where we discuss estimators and their properties. The fact that the standard deviation of $\overline{X}$ is $\sigma/\sqrt{n}$ means that as the sample size *increases,* the standard deviation of $\overline{X}$ *decreases,* making $\overline{X}$ more likely to be close to μ. This is another desirable property of a good estimator, to be discussed later. Finally, when the sampling distribution of $\overline{X}$ is normal, this allows us to compute probabilities that $\overline{X}$ will be within specified distances of μ. What happens in cases where the population itself is *not* normally distributed?

In Figure 5–3, we saw the sampling distribution of $\overline{X}$ when sampling is done from a uniformly distributed population and with a sample of size $n = 2$. Let us now see what happens as we increase the sample size. Figure 5–5 shows results of a simulation giving the sampling distribution of $\overline{X}$ when the sample size is $n = 5$, when the sample size is $n = 20$, and the *limiting* distribution of $\overline{X}$—the distribution of $\overline{X}$ as the sample size increases indefinitely. As can be seen from the figure, the limiting distribution of $\overline{X}$ is, again, the *normal distribution.*

The Central Limit Theorem

The result we have just stated, that the distribution of the sample mean $\overline{X}$ tends to the normal distribution as the sample size increases, is one of the most important results in statistics. It is known as the *central limit theorem.*

FIGURE 5–5   The Sampling Distribution of $\overline{X}$ as the Sample Size Increases

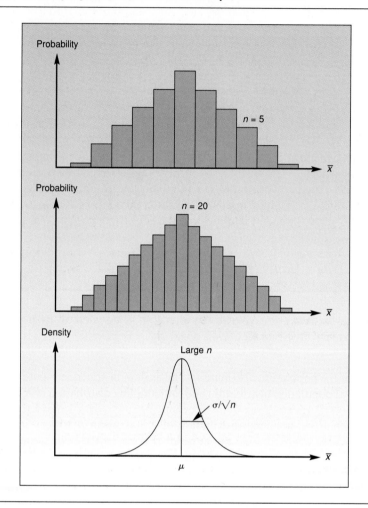

The Central Limit Theorem

When sampling from a population with mean μ and finite standard deviation σ, the sampling distribution of the sample mean, $\overline{X}$, will tend to a normal distribution with mean μ and standard deviation $\sigma/\sqrt{n}$ as the sample size n becomes large.

$$\text{For "large enough" } n, \quad \overline{X} \sim N(\mu, \sigma^2/n) \quad (5\text{--}5)$$

The central limit theorem is remarkable because it states that the distribution of the sample mean $\overline{X}$ tends to a normal distribution *regardless* of the distribution of the population from which the random sample is drawn. The theorem allows us to make probability statements about the possible range of values the sample mean may take. It allows us to compute probabilities of how far away $\overline{X}$ may be from the population mean it estimates. For example, using our rule of thumb for the normal distribution, we know that the probability that the distance between $\overline{X}$ and μ will be less than

$\sigma/\sqrt{n}$ is approximately 0.68. This is so because, as you remember, the probability that the value of a normal random variable will be within one standard deviation of its mean is 0.6826; here our normal random variable has mean μ and standard deviation $\sigma/\sqrt{n}$. Other probability statements can be made as well; we will see their use shortly. When is a sample size, n, "large enough" so that we may apply the theorem?

The central limit theorem says that, *in the limit*, as n goes to infinity $(n \to \infty)$, the distribution of $\overline{X}$ becomes a normal distribution (regardless of the distribution of the population). The *rate* at which the distribution approaches a normal distribution does depend, however, on the shape of the distribution of the parent population. If the population itself is normally distributed, the distribution of $\overline{X}$ is normal for *any* sample size n, as stated earlier. On the other hand, for population distributions that are very different from a normal distribution, a relatively large sample size is required to achieve a good normal approximation for the distribution of $\overline{X}$. Figure 5–6 shows several parent population distributions and the resulting sampling distributions of $\overline{X}$ for different sample sizes.

Since we often do not know the shape of the population distribution, it would be useful to have some general rule of thumb telling us when a sample is large enough so that we may apply the central limit theorem.

> In general, a sample of 30 or more elements is considered large enough for the central limit theorem to take effect.

We emphasize that this is a *general,* and somewhat arbitrary, rule. A larger minimum sample size may be required for a good normal approximation when the population distribution is very different from a normal distribution. By the same token, a smaller minimum sample size may suffice for a good normal approximation when the population distribution is close to a normal distribution.

Throughout this book, we will make reference to *small* samples versus *large* samples. By a small sample, we generally mean a sample of fewer than 30 elements. A large sample will generally mean a sample of 30 or more elements. The results we will discuss as applicable for large samples will be more meaningful, however, the larger the sample size. (By the central limit theorem, the larger the sample size, the better the approximation offered by the normal distribution.) The "30 rule" should, therefore, be applied with caution. Let us now look at an example of the use of the central limit theorem.

Mercury makes a 2.4-liter V-6 engine, the Laser XRi, used in speedboats. The company's engineers believe that the engine delivers an average power of 220 horsepower (HP) and that the standard deviation of power delivered is 15 HP. A potential buyer intends to sample 100 engines (each engine to be run a single time). What is the probability that the sample mean, $\overline{X}$, will be less than 217 HP?

EXAMPLE 5–1

In solving problems such as this one, we use the techniques of Chapter 4. There we used μ as the mean of the normal random variable and σ as its standard deviation. Here our random variable $\overline{X}$ is normal (at least approximately so, by the central limit theorem

SOLUTION

FIGURE 5–6 The Effects of the Central Limit Theorem: The Distribution of $\overline{X}$ for Different Populations and Different Sample Sizes

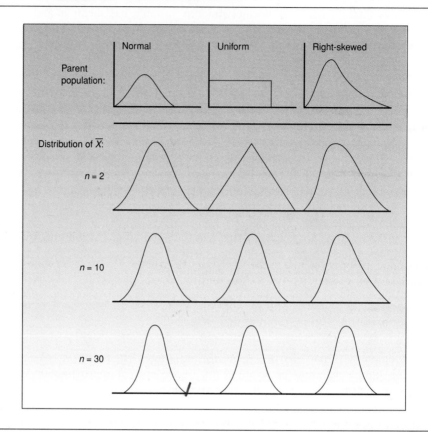

because our sample size is large) and has mean μ. Note, however, that the standard deviation of our random variable $\overline{X}$ is $\sigma/\sqrt{n}$ and not just σ. We proceed as follows:

$$P(\overline{X} < 217) = P\left(Z < \frac{217 - \mu}{\sigma/\sqrt{n}}\right)$$

$$= P\left(Z < \frac{217 - 220}{15/\sqrt{100}}\right) = P(Z < -2) = 0.0228$$

Thus, if the population mean is indeed $\mu = 220$ HP and the standard deviation is $\sigma = 15$ HP, there is a rather small probability that the potential buyer's tests will result in a sample mean lower than 217 HP.

Figure 5–7 should help clarify the distinction between the population distribution and the sampling distribution of $\overline{X}$. The figure emphasizes the three aspects of the central limit theorem:

1. When the sample size is large enough, the sampling distribution of $\overline{X}$ is normal.
2. The expected value of $\overline{X}$ is μ.
3. The standard deviation of $\overline{X}$ is $\sigma/\sqrt{n}$.

FIGURE 5-7   A (Nonnormal) Population Distribution and the Normal Sampling Distribution of the Sample Mean When a Large Sample Is Used

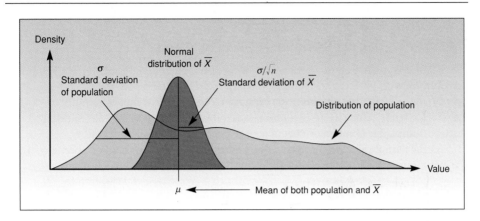

The last statement is the key to the important fact that as the sample size increases, the variation of $\overline{X}$ about its mean μ decreases. Stated another way, as we buy *more information* (take a larger sample), our *uncertainty* (measured by the standard deviation) about the parameter being estimated *decreases*.

The History of the Central Limit Theorem

What we call the central limit theorem actually comprises several theorems developed over the years. The first such theorem was discussed at the beginning of Chapter 4 as the discovery of the normal curve by Abraham De Moivre in 1733. Recall that De Moivre discovered the normal distribution as the *limit* of the binomial distribution. The fact that the normal distribution appears as a limit of the binomial distribution as n increases is a form of the central limit theorem. Around the turn of this century, Liapunov gave a more general form of the central limit theorem, and in 1922 the final form we use in applied statistics was given by Lindeberg. The proof of the necessary condition of the theorem was given in 1935 by W. Feller [see W. Feller, *An Introduction to Probability Theory and Its Applications* (New York: Wiley, 1971), vol. 2]. A proof of the central limit theorem is beyond the scope of this book, but the interested reader is encouraged to read more about it in the given reference or in other books.

The Standardized Sampling Distribution of the Sample Mean When σ Is Not Known

In order to use the central limit theorem, we need to know the population standard deviation, σ. When σ is not known, we use its estimator, the sample standard deviation, S, in its place. In such cases, the distribution of the standardized statistic

$$\frac{\overline{X} - \mu}{S/\sqrt{n}} \tag{5-6}$$

(where S is used in place of the unknown σ) is no longer the standard normal distribution. *If the population itself is normally distributed, the statistic in equation 5-6 has a t distribution with $n - 1$ degrees of freedom.* The t distribution has wider tails than the standard normal distribution. Values and probabilities of t distributions with different degrees of freedom are given in Table 3 in Appendix C. The t distribution and its uses will be discussed in detail in Chapter 6. The idea of degrees of freedom is explained in the last section of this chapter.

The Sampling Distribution of the Sample Proportion, $\hat{P}$

The sampling distribution of the sample proportion, $\hat{P}$, is based on the binomial distribution with parameters n and p, where n is the sample size and p is the population proportion. Recall that the binomial random variable, X, counts the number of successes in n trials. Since $\hat{P} = X/n$ and n is fixed (determined before the sampling), the distribution of the number of successes, X, leads to the distribution of $\hat{P}$.

As the sample size, n, increases, the central limit theorem applies here as well. In the beginning of Chapter 4, we saw how the binomial distribution approaches the normal distribution when $p = 0.5$—the case of a symmetric distribution for all n. The symmetry of the distribution makes the convergence to a normal distribution relatively fast. Figure 5–8 shows the effects of the central limit theorem in the case where the binomial distribution is *not* symmetric. We use a distribution with $p = 0.3$ (a distribution skewed to the right, when n is small).

We now state the central limit theorem when sampling for the population proportion, p.

As the sample size, n, increases, the sampling distribution of $\hat{P}$ approaches a *normal distribution* with mean p and standard deviation $\sqrt{p(1 - p)/n}$

(The estimated standard deviation of $\hat{P}$ is also called its *standard error*.) In order for us to use the normal approximation for the sampling distribution of $\hat{P}$, the sample size needs to be large. A commonly used rule of thumb says that the normal approximation to the distribution of $\hat{P}$ may be used only if *both np and $n(1 - p)$ are greater than* 5. We demonstrate the use of the theorem with Example 5–2.

EXAMPLE 5–2

In recent years, convertible sport coupes have become very popular in Japan. Toyota is currently shipping Celicas to Los Angeles, where a customizer does a roof lift and ships them back to Japan. Suppose that 25% of all Japanese in a given income and lifestyle category are interested in buying Celica convertibles. A random sample of 100 Japanese consumers in the category of interest is to be selected. What is the probability that at least 20% of those in the sample will express an interest in a Celica convertible?

SOLUTION

We need $P(\hat{P} \geq 0.20)$. Since $np = 100(0.25) = 25$ and $n(1 - p) = 100(0.75) = 75$, both numbers greater than 5, we may use the normal approximation to the distribution of $\hat{P}$. The mean of $\hat{P}$ is $p = 0.25$, and the standard deviation of $\hat{P}$ is $\sqrt{p(1 - p)/n} = 0.0433$. We have

$$P(\hat{P} \geq 0.20) = P\left(Z \geq \frac{0.20 - 0.25}{0.0433}\right) = P(Z \geq -1.15) = 0.8749$$

Sampling distributions are essential to statistics. In the following chapters, we will make much use of the distributions discussed in this section, as well as others that will

FIGURE 5-8   The Sampling Distribution of $\hat{P}$ When $p = 0.3$, as n Increases

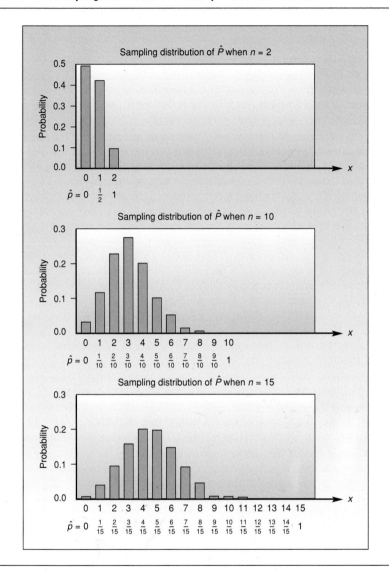

be introduced as we go along. In the next section, we discuss properties of good estimators.

PROBLEMS

5–11. What is a sampling distribution, and what are the uses of sampling distributions?

5–12. A sample of size $n = 5$ is selected from a population. Under what conditions is the sampling distribution of $\bar{X}$ normal?

5–13. In problem 5–12, suppose the population mean is $\mu = 125$ and the population standard deviation is 20. What are the expected value and the standard deviation of $\bar{X}$?

5–14. What is the most significant aspect of the central limit theorem?

5–15. Under what conditions is the central limit theorem most useful in sampling to estimate the population mean?

5–16.   What are the limitations of small samples?

5–17.   When sampling from a population with population proportion $p = 0.1$, using a sample size $n = 12$, what is the sampling distribution of $\hat{P}$? Is it reasonable to use a normal approximation for this sampling distribution? Explain.

5–18.   If the population mean is 1,247, the population variance is 10,000, and the sample size is 100, what is the probability that $\overline{X}$ will be less than 1,230?

5–19.   When sampling from a population with standard deviation $\sigma = 55$, using a sample of size $n = 150$, what is the probability that $\overline{X}$ will be at least eight units away from the population mean μ?

5–20.   The Colosseum, once the most popular monument in Rome, dates from about A.D. 70. Since then earthquakes have caused considerable damage to the huge structure, and engineers are currently trying to make sure the building will survive future shocks. The Colosseum can be divided into several thousand small sections. Suppose that the average section can withstand a quake measuring 3.4 on the Richter scale with a standard deviation of 1.5. A random sample of 100 sections is selected and tested for the maximum earthquake force they can withstand. What is the probability that the average section in the sample can withstand an earthquake measuring at least 3.6 on the Richter scale?

5–21.   Seventy percent of the art auctioned by Sotheby's in Japan is Japanese art since the demand for Western art in that country is declining.[6] If a random sample of 200 art pieces is selected from among the ones auctioned by Sotheby's, what is the probability that at least 80% of the art pieces in the sample will be Japanese?

5–22.   An economist wishes to estimate the average family income in a certain population. The population standard deviation is known to be $4,500, and the economist uses a random sample of size $n = 225$. What is the probability that the sample mean will fall within $800 of the population mean?

5–23.   When sampling for the proportion of defective items in a large shipment, where the population proportion is 0.18 and the sample size is 200, what is the probability that the sample proportion will be at least 0.20?

5–24.   A study of the investment industry claims that 58% of all mutual funds outperformed the stock market as a whole last year. An analyst wants to test this claim and obtains a random sample of 250 mutual funds. The analyst finds that only 123 of the funds outperformed the market during the year. Determine the probability that another random sample would lead to a sample proportion as low or lower than the one obtained by the analyst, assuming the proportion of all mutual funds that outperformed the market is indeed 0.58.

5–25.   According to *Fortune,* the average hotel occupancy rate in 1994 was 67.5%.[7] If a random sample of 100 hotels was selected in 1994 (with dates randomly chosen as well), what is the probability that the average occupancy rate in this sample was over 70%? Assume that the standard deviation of occupancy rates was 10%.

5–26.   It has been suggested that an investment portfolio selected randomly by throwing darts at the stock market page of *The Wall Street Journal* may be a sound (and certainly well-diversified) investment.[8] Suppose that you own such a portfolio of 16 stocks randomly selected from all stocks listed on the New York Stock Exchange (NYSE). On a certain day, you hear on the news that the average stock on the NYSE rose 1.5 points. Assuming that the standard deviation of stock price movements that day was 2 points and assuming stock price movements were normally distributed around their mean of 1.5, what is the probability that the average stock in your portfolio increased in price?

---

[6] "Japan Becomes the Land of the Falling Gavel," *Business Week,* February 25, 1991, p. 68.

[7] "Hotels and Cruise Lines—It's a Full House," *Fortune,* January 16, 1995, p. 76.

[8] See the very readable book by Burton G. Malkiel, *A Random Walk Down Wall Street,* (New York: W. W. Norton, 1995).

5–27. An advertisement for Citicorp Insurance Services, Inc., claims "one person in seven will be hospitalized this year." Suppose you keep track of a random sample of 180 people over an entire year. Assuming Citicorp's advertisement is correct, what is the probability that fewer than 10% of the people in your sample will be found to have been hospitalized (at least once) during the year? Explain.

5–28. Shimano mountain bikes are displayed in chic clothing boutiques in Milan, Italy, and the average price for the bike in the city is $700. Suppose that the standard deviation of the bike prices is $100. If a random sample of 60 boutiques is selected, what is the probability that the average price for a Shimano mountain bike in this sample will be between $680 and $720?

5–29. A quality-control analyst wants to estimate the proportion of imperfect jeans in a large warehouse. The analyst plans to select a random sample of 500 pairs of jeans and note the proportion of imperfect pairs. If the actual proportion in the entire warehouse is 0.35, what is the probability that the sample proportion will deviate from the population proportion by more than 0.05?

5–4 Estimators and Their Properties[9]

The sample statistics we discussed, $\overline{X}$, S, and $\hat{P}$, as well as other sample statistics to be introduced later, are used as estimators of population parameters. In this section, we discuss some important properties of good statistical estimators. These properties are *unbiasedness, efficiency, consistency,* and *sufficiency.*

> An estimator is said to be **unbiased** if its expected value is equal to the population parameter it estimates.

Consider the sample mean $\overline{X}$. From equation 5–2, we know $E(\overline{X}) = \mu$. *The sample mean, $\overline{X}$, is, therefore, an unbiased estimator of the population mean μ.* This means that if we were to sample repeatedly from the population and compute $\overline{X}$ for each of our samples, *in the long run,* the average value of $\overline{X}$ will be the parameter of interest, μ. This is an important property of the estimator because it means that there is no systematic *bias* away from the parameter of interest.

If we view the gathering of a random sample and the calculating of its mean as shooting at a target—the target being the population parameter, say, μ—then the fact that $\overline{X}$ is an unbiased estimator of μ means that the device producing the estimates is aiming at the *center* of the target (the parameter of interest), with no systematic deviation away from it.

> Any *systematic* deviation of the estimator away from the parameter of interest is called a **bias.**

The concept of unbiasedness is demonstrated for the sample mean $\overline{X}$ in Figure 5–9.

Figure 5–10 demonstrates the idea of a biased estimator of μ. The hypothetical estimator we denote by Y is centered on some point, M, that lies away from the parameter μ. The distance between the expected value of Y (the point M) and μ is the *bias.*

It should be noted that, in reality, we usually sample *once* and obtain our estimate. The multiple estimates shown in Figures 5–9 and 5–10 serve only as an illustration of the expected value of an estimator as the center of a large collection of the actual estimates that would be obtained in repeated sampling. (Note also that, in reality, the

---

[9] An optional, but recommended, section.

FIGURE 5-9   The Sample Mean, $\overline{X}$, as an Unbiased Estimator of the Population Mean, μ

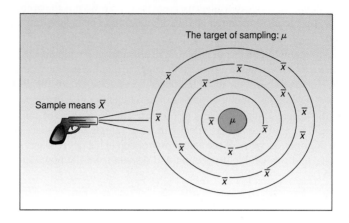

FIGURE 5-10   An Example of a Biased Estimator of the Population Mean, μ

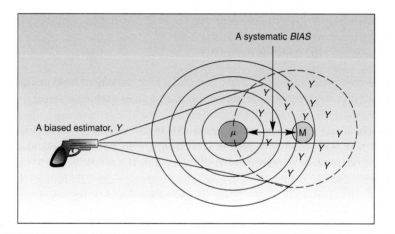

"target" at which we are "shooting" is one-dimensional—on a straight line rather than on a plane.)

The next property of good estimators we discuss is *efficiency*.

An estimator is **efficient** if it has a relatively small variance (and standard deviation).

Efficiency is a relative property. We say that one estimator is efficient *relative* to another. This means that the estimator has a smaller variance (also a smaller standard deviation) than the other. Figure 5–11 shows two hypothetical unbiased estimators of the population mean, μ. The two estimators, which we denote by X and Z, are unbiased: their distributions are centered at μ. The estimator X, however, is more efficient than the estimator Z because it has a smaller variance than that of Z. This is seen from the fact that repeated estimates produced by Z have a larger spread about their mean, μ, than repeated estimates produced by X.

FIGURE 5-11 Two Unbiased Estimators of μ, Where the Estimator X Is Efficient Relative to the Estimator Z

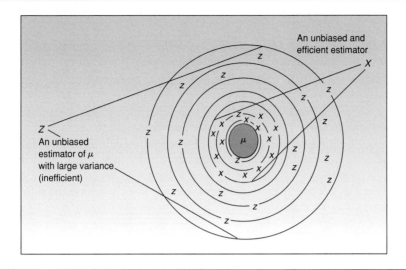

Another desirable property of estimators is *consistency.*

An estimator is said to be **consistent** if its probability of being close to the parameter it estimates increases as the sample size increases.

The sample mean $\overline{X}$ is a consistent estimator of μ. This is so because the standard deviation of $\overline{X}$ is $\sigma_{\overline{x}} = \sigma/\sqrt{n}$. As the sample size, n, increases, the standard deviation of $\overline{X}$ decreases and, hence, the probability that $\overline{X}$ will be close to its expected value μ increases.

We now define a fourth property of good estimators, *sufficiency.*

An estimator is said to be **sufficient** if it contains all the information in the data about the parameter it estimates.

Applying the Concepts of Unbiasedness, Efficiency, Consistency, and Sufficiency

We may evaluate possible estimators of population parameters based on whether or not they possess important properties of estimators and thus choose the best estimator to be used.

For a *normally distributed population,* for example, both the sample mean and the sample median are *unbiased* estimators of the population mean, μ. The sample mean, however, is more *efficient* than the sample median. This is so because the variance of the sample median happens to be 1.57 times as large as the variance of the sample mean. In addition, the sample mean is a *sufficient* estimator because in computing it we use the *entire* data set. The sample median is not sufficient; it is found as the point in the middle of the data set, regardless of the exact magnitudes of all other data elements. The sample mean, $\overline{X}$, is the *best* estimator of the population mean, μ, because it is unbiased and has the smallest variance of all unbiased estimators of μ. The sample mean is also *consistent.* (It should be noted that, while the sample mean is best, the sample median is sometimes used because it is more resistant to extreme observations.)

The sample proportion, $\hat{P}$, is the best estimator of the population proportion, p. Since $E(\hat{P}) = p$, the estimator $\hat{P}$ is unbiased. It also has the smallest variance of all unbiased estimators of p.

What about the sample variance, S^2? The sample variance, as defined in equation 1–3 is an unbiased estimator of the population variance, σ^2. Recall equation 1–3:

$$S^2 = \frac{\Sigma(x_i - \bar{x})^2}{n - 1}$$

It seems logical to divide the sum of squared deviations in the equation by n rather than by $n - 1$ because we are seeking the *average* squared deviation from the sample mean. There are n deviations from the mean, so why not divide by n? It turns out that if we were to divide by n rather than by $n - 1$, our estimator of σ^2 would be biased. Although the bias becomes small as n increases, we will always use the statistic given in equation 1–3 as an estimator of σ^2. The reason for dividing by $n - 1$ rather than n will become clearer in the next section, where we discuss the concept of degrees of freedom.

It should be noted that, while S^2 is an unbiased estimator of the population variance σ^2, the sample standard deviation S (the square root of S^2) is *not* an unbiased estimator of the population standard deviation σ. Still, we will use S as our estimator of the population standard deviation, ignoring the small bias that results and relying on the fact that S^2 is the unbiased estimator of σ^2.

PROBLEMS

5–30. Suppose that you have two statistics, A and B, as possible estimators of the same population parameter. Estimator A is unbiased, but has a large variance. Estimator B has a small bias, but has only one-tenth the variance of estimator A. Which estimator is better? Explain.

5–31. Suppose that you have an estimator with a relatively large bias. The estimator is consistent and efficient, however. If you have a generous budget for your sampling survey, would you use this estimator? Explain.

5–32. Suppose that in a sampling survey to estimate the population variance, the biased estimator (with n instead of $n - 1$ in the denominator of equation 1–3) was used instead of the unbiased one. The sample size used was $n = 100$, and the estimate obtained was 1,287. Can you find the value of the unbiased estimate of the population variance?

5–33. What are the advantages of a sufficient statistic? Can you think of a possible disadvantage of sufficiency?

5–34. Suppose that you have two biased estimators of the same population parameter. Estimator A has a bias equal to $1/n$ (that is, the mean of the estimator is $1/n$ units away from the parameter it estimates), where n is the sample size used. Estimator B has a bias equal to 0.01 (the mean of the estimator is 0.01 units away from the parameter of interest). Under what conditions is estimator A better than B?

5–35. Why is consistency an important property?

5–5   Degrees of Freedom

The concept of *degrees of freedom* is crucial for the understanding of many important statistical distributions. The concept also underlies the reason why our sample variance S^2 is the unbiased estimator of σ^2. Here lies the answer to our big question: Why divide by $n - 1$ and not by n?

Suppose we consider four data points, X_1, X_2, X_3, and X_4. The values of the data points are

$$x_1 = 10 \qquad x_2 = 12 \qquad x_3 = 16 \qquad x_4 = 18$$

Let's compute the sample mean of these data.

$$\bar{x} = \frac{\sum_{i=1}^{4} x_i}{n} = \frac{x_1 + x_2 + x_3 + x_4}{4}$$

$$= \frac{10 + 12 + 16 + 18}{4} = \frac{56}{4} = 14$$

Now, we ask the question: Given that we know that the mean of our set of four data points is $\bar{x} = 14$, how many of our data points X_1, X_2, X_3, and X_4 are "free to move"? In other words, of four data points with a known mean, how many points do not have predetermined values? Let's experiment with our data. First, assume that the value of our fourth data point, X_4, is not known to us. Would this data point be free to move, that is, free to take on any value? In this case, our data are

10, 12, 16, and X_4 (the unknown fourth point)

However, note the following. We know the mean of the four data points. The mean is 14, and so we have, by definition of the mean,

$$\frac{10 + 12 + 16 + X_4}{4} = 14$$

From this equation, we can solve for the unknown value of the fourth data point, X_4.

$$10 + 12 + 16 + X_4 = 56$$

or

$$X_4 = 56 - 10 - 12 - 16 = 18$$

So, if in a set of n data points we do not know *one* of the points but we do know the mean of all n data points, then the "unknown" point is actually known: it is predetermined. The point is fixed—not free to move. We can solve for the exact value the data point must have, using the known values of the remaining $n - 1$ data points and the sample mean.

What happens if we have *two* missing values? Suppose we do not know two of the data points, X_3 and X_4. Are these two missing values fixed or free to move? Again, using the definition of the mean, we have the following.

$$\frac{10 + 12 + X_3 + X_4}{4} = 14$$

or

$$10 + 12 + X_3 + X_4 = 56$$

We have one equation with two unknowns; thus, the equation cannot be solved for the two missing values. When two data points are unknown to us, there is a degree of freedom for these values; the values are free to move. Assign any value to one of the two missing points (this is the degree of freedom—the data point can be anything), and the last missing value will be *determined,* as we can solve for it using the now-known three points and the mean of all four. A similar thing happens if three points

FIGURE 5-12   The Four Deviations of the Data Points from Their Mean

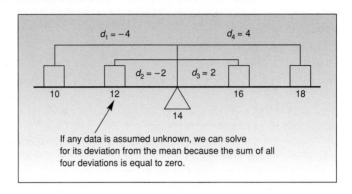

If any data is assumed unknown, we can solve for its deviation from the mean because the sum of all four deviations is equal to zero.

are unknown (now we have *two* degrees of freedom because we may freely choose any value for any two of the missing three points), and so on.

We may conclude that when we have n data points and we know their mean, the mean acts as a *restriction* on the data, leaving us with only $n - 1$ *degrees of freedom*. Let us now view the situation in terms of deviations from the mean. Figure 5–12 shows the four data points of our example, their mean, and the deviations from the mean. The mean is a restriction in the sense that deviations from the mean must sum to zero. In our particular example, the deviations from the mean are

$$d_1 = x_1 - \bar{x} = 10 - 14 = -4 \qquad d_2 = x_2 - \bar{x} = 12 - 14 = -2$$
$$d_3 = x_3 - \bar{x} = 16 - 14 = 2 \qquad d_4 = x_4 - \bar{x} = 18 - 14 = 4$$

We see that the sum of the four deviations of the data points from their mean is

$$d_1 + d_2 + d_3 + d_4 = (-4) + (-2) + 2 + 4 = 0$$

Any three of the four deviations from the known mean are free to move and will not violate the restriction $\bar{x} = 14$ as long as the fourth deviation is constrained to be the number required to make the sum of all four deviations from the mean zero. Again, we see that once the mean is known, $n - 1$ out of our n points are free to move. There are $n - 1$ degrees of freedom.

Now consider the sample variance, S^2. Equation 1–3 tells us that the sample variance is the sum of the squared deviations of the data points from their mean, $\Sigma(x_i - \bar{x})^2$, divided by $n - 1$. Since the computation involves the known quantity $\bar{x}$ and n data points (n deviations of data points from their mean in the sum of squares in the numerator of the equation), we know from the preceding discussion that only $n - 1$ of the data points (or, equivalently, $n - 1$ of the n deviations from the mean) are actually free to move. Therefore, if we want an average squared deviation from the mean as our measure of variation within the sample, *this average should be based on only $n - 1$ free points*. This is why we divide by $n - 1$ when we compute S^2, the unbiased estimator of the population variance, σ^2.

The concept of degrees of freedom will prove very important for us in other applications as well: in Chapter 8, on two-sample analysis, in Chapter 9, on analysis of variance, and in the chapters on regression analysis. In these applications, we will see degrees of freedom that are different from $n - 1$. It is important to develop an intuitive understanding of the concept of degrees of freedom.

The number of **degrees of freedom** is equal to the total number of measurements (these are not always raw data points), less the total number of restrictions on the measurements. A *restriction* is a quantity computed from the measurements.

For example, suppose we have two independent samples that are combined, and we know the mean of each sample. If the first sample has n_1 data points and the second sample has n_2 data points, then the degrees of freedom (df) associated with the combined deviations from the two sample means are the total number of data points minus the total number of restrictions: df $= n_1 + n_2 - 2$. $= n_1 - 1 + n_2 - 1 = n_1 + n_2 - 2$

This demonstrates that the degrees of freedom associated with independent samples are additive. The degrees of freedom associated with the first sample are $n_1 - 1$ and the degrees of freedom associated with the second sample are $n_2 - 1$. The degrees of freedom associated with the combined sample are df $= n_1 + n_2 - 2 = (n_1 - 1) + (n_2 - 1)$. As a final example illustrating the concept of degrees of freedom, we consider a business situation.

A company manager has a total budget of $150,000 to be completely allocated to four different projects. How many "degrees of freedom" does the manager have?

EXAMPLE 5-3

Fixing the total of several items is the same as fixing the mean of the items, because the total is just the mean multiplied by the number of items. In this case, saying that the total budget for the four projects is $150,000 is the same as fixing the mean allocation to $150,000/4 = $37,500. Now the manager is free to choose (within the total budget) whatever amount she desires for allocation to any three of the four projects. Once the first three allocations are made, however, the manager has no choice as to the fourth allocation: it is constrained to be exactly equal to the difference between the total budget of $150,000 and the sum of the allocations for the first three projects. The manager thus has three degrees of freedom.

SOLUTION

PROBLEMS

5–36.   Three random samples of sizes, 30, 48, and 32, respectively, are collected, and the three sample means are computed. What is the total number of degrees of freedom for deviations from the means?

5–37.   In simple linear regression analysis, which will be introduced in Chapter 10, we will use a data set with n observations, from which we will compute two estimates—a slope and an intercept. The data vary around the line with the computed slope and intercept. What are the degrees of freedom for the deviations of the data points about the line?

5–38.   Your bank sends you a summary statement, giving the average amount of all checks you wrote during the month. You have a record of the amounts of 17 out of the 19 checks you wrote during the month. Using this and the information provided by the bank, can you figure out the amounts of the two missing checks? Explain.

5–39.   In problem 5–38, suppose you know the amounts of 18 of the 19 checks you wrote and the average of all the checks. Can you figure out the amount of the missing check? Explain.

5–40.   Explain the relation between S^2 and the concept of degrees of freedom.

	Stock Price 12/9 1994			Stock Price 12/9 1994
25 **Georgia Gulf** (chemicals, polymers)	$36.50	38 **Manpower** (temporary-employment services)		$27.00
26 **Compaq Computer** (personal computers)	$39.88	39 **Eckerd** (retail drugstores)		$28.25
27 **Symbol Technologies** (bar-code data systems)	$29.25	40 **Revco D.S.** (retail drugstores)		$22.13
28 **Scott Paper** (paper products)	$65.25	41 **Fedders** (room air conditioners)		$6.75
29 **Input/Output** (seismic data systems)	$19.25	42 **Seitel** (seismic data)		$20.75
30 **First Mississippi** (chemicals, fertilizer, gold)	$20.63	43 **Lydall** (engineered materials)		$32.25
31 **Cypress Semiconductor** (computer chips)	$21.75	44 **Tandem Computers** (fault-tolerant computers)		$16.38
32 **Stone Container** (pulp, paper, packaging)	$15.25	45 **Oak Industries** (communications components)		$24.75
33 **Tektronix** (diversified technology)	$36.50	46 **Rite Aid** (retail drugstores)		$22.75
34 **Watkins-Johnson** (diversified technology)	$30.88	47 **Wellman** (polyester fibers and resins)		$26.88
35 **Mid Atlantic Medical Services** (managed care)	$19.88	48 **Nike** (athletic footwear and apparel)		$65.50
36 **International Rectifier** (power semiconductors)	$21.63	49 **Franklin Electronic Publishers** (electronic books)		$18.75
37 **Ann Taylor Stores** (specialty retailer)	$38.13	50 **CTS** (electronic components)		$27.50

A. Michels, "The Best and Worst Stocks of 1994," *Fortune,* January 16, 1995, pp. 100–102.

6

CONFIDENCE INTERVALS

6-1 INTRODUCTION

A nthropologists, armed with knowledge of molecular biology and statistics, announced in 1988 that they had discovered Eve. A long and involved research study resulted in the implication that all human beings are genetically descended from *one* woman.[1] The scientists did not claim to have found the *first* woman, but rather a common ancestor of all of humanity. The scientists' Eve

Continued

---

[1] See, for example, the cover article in *Newsweek*, January 11, 1988.

was the most genetically successful woman living in our distant past, a woman whose progeny are all people living in the world today, regardless of race, ethnic origin, or native continent. This finding brings with it far-reaching implications, which have stirred up heated debates. The most controversial implication is that humans did not slowly evolve in different parts of the world, as many anthropologists believed. The evolution to modern *Homo sapiens*, according to the new theory, occurred only in *one* place (scientists are still uncertain where, although it is believed to have been somewhere in Asia or Africa). Sometime between 90,000 and 180,000 years ago, Eve's descendents left their homeland and began their slow migration to all parts of the world, replacing local populations as they went along and eventually settling the entire planet. What we call racial characteristics or external differences of appearance all developed *after* these migrations. How did the scientists develop and demonstrate these incredible assertions?

Scientists asked a random sample of 147 pregnant women of all races, ethnic origins, and continents of birth to donate their babies' placentas. The genetic matter in the placentas, strings of the protein DNA, was then carefully scrutinized with interest centered on a particular type of mitochondrial DNA inherited only from one's mother. The scientists found that the genetic matter in the placentas of all the sampled babies contained segments of DNA traceable to a single source—a woman they called Eve. Statistical estimation was then used in analyzing the number of mutations inherent in the genetic material. Based on their random sample, the scientists estimated the average percentage of mutated mitochondrial DNA in the entire population of living people at 2–4%. This is an **interval estimate** of a population parameter. Such an interval has associated with it a measure of **confidence** (usually stated as a percentage, often 95% or 99%). Since the scientists also knew the approximate rate of mutation over time, they were able to use the interval estimate of the average percentage of mutated mitochondrial DNA in the present-day population and extrapolate back in time toward the beginning of these mutations. This led them to conclude, with a high degree of confidence, that Eve lived anywhere between 140,000 and 290,000 years ago. In this chapter, we discuss the computation and interpretation of interval estimates of population parameters. An interval estimate with its associated measure of confidence is usually called a *confidence interval*.

In the last chapter, we saw how sample statistics are used as estimators of population parameters. We defined a point estimate of a parameter as a single value obtained from the estimator. We saw that an estimator, a sample statistic, is a random variable with a certain probability distribution—its sampling distribution. A given point estimate is a single realization of the random variable. The actual estimate may or may not be close to the parameter of interest. Therefore, if we only provide a point estimate of the parameter of interest, we are not giving any information about the *accuracy* of the estimation procedure. For example, saying that the sample mean is 550 is giving a point estimate of the population mean. This estimate does not tell us how close μ may be to its estimate, 550. Suppose, on the other hand, that we also said: we are *99% confident* that μ is in the interval [449, 551]." This conveys much more information about the possible value of μ. Now compare this interval with another one: "We are *90% confident* that μ is in the interval [400, 700]." This interval conveys less information about the possible value of μ, both because it is wider and because the level of confidence is lower. (When based on the same information, however, an interval of lower confidence level is narrower.)

A **confidence interval** is a *range of numbers* believed to include an unknown population parameter. Associated with the interval is a measure of the *confidence* we have that the interval does indeed contain the parameter of interest.

The sampling distribution of the statistic gives a *probability* associated with a range of values the statistic may take. After the sampling has taken place and a *particular estimate* has been obtained, this probability is transformed into a *level of confidence* for a range of values that may contain the unknown parameter.

In the next section, we will see how to construct confidence intervals for the population mean, μ, when the population standard deviation, σ, is known. Then we will alter this situation and see how a confidence interval for μ may be constructed without knowledge of σ. Other sections present confidence intervals in other situations.

6–2 Confidence Interval for the Population Mean When the Population Standard Deviation Is Known

The central limit theorem tells us that when we select a large random sample from any population with mean μ and standard deviation σ, the sample mean, $\overline{X}$, is (at least approximately) normally distributed with mean μ and standard deviation $\sigma/\sqrt{n}$. If the population itself is normal, $\overline{X}$ is normally distributed for any sample size. Recall that the standard normal random variable Z has a 0.95 probability of being within the range of values -1.96 and 1.96 (you may check this using Table 2 in Appendix C). Transforming Z to the random variable $\overline{X}$ with mean μ and standard deviation $\sigma/\sqrt{n}$, we find that—*before the sampling*—there is a 0.95 probability that $\overline{X}$ will fall within the interval:

$$\mu \pm 1.96\frac{\sigma}{\sqrt{n}} \tag{6-1}$$

Once we have obtained our random sample, we have a particular value, $\overline{x}$. This particular $\overline{x}$ either lies within the range of values specified by equation 6–1 or does not lie within this range. Since we do not know the (fixed) value of the population parameter μ, we have no way of knowing whether $\overline{x}$ is indeed within the range given in equation 6–1. Since the random sampling has already taken place and a particular $\overline{x}$ has been computed, we no longer have a random variable and may no longer talk about probabilities. We do know, however, that since the presampling probability that $\overline{X}$ will fall in the interval in equation 6–1 is 0.95, about 95% of the values of $\overline{X}$ obtained in a large number of repeated samplings will fall within the interval. Since we have a single value $\overline{x}$ that was obtained by this process, we may say that we are *95% confident that $\overline{x}$ lies within the interval*. This idea is demonstrated in Figure 6–1.

Consider a particular $\overline{x}$ and note that the distance between $\overline{x}$ and μ is the same as the distance between μ and $\overline{x}$. Thus, $\overline{x}$ falls inside the interval $\mu \pm 1.96\sigma/\sqrt{n}$ *if and only if* μ happens to be inside the interval $\overline{x} \pm 1.96\sigma/\sqrt{n}$. In a large number of repeated trials, this would happen about 95% of the time. We therefore call the

FIGURE 6-1   Probability Distribution of $\overline{X}$ and Some Resulting Values of the Statistic in Repeated Samplings

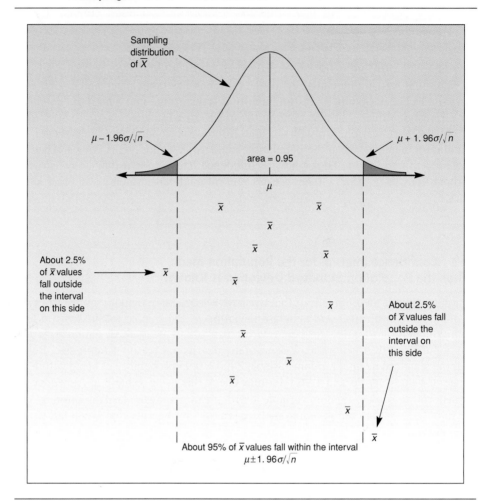

interval $\overline{x} \pm 1.96\sigma/\sqrt{n}$ *a 95% confidence interval for the unknown population mean* μ. This is demonstrated in Figure 6–2.

Instead of measuring a distance of $1.96\sigma/\sqrt{n}$ on either side of μ (an impossible task since μ is unknown), we measure the same distance of $1.96\sigma/\sqrt{n}$ on either side of our *known* sample mean, $\overline{x}$. Since, *before the sampling*, the random interval $\overline{X} \pm 1.96\sigma/\sqrt{n}$ had a 0.95 probability of capturing μ, *after the sampling* we may be 95% confident that our particular interval $\overline{x} \pm 1.96\sigma/\sqrt{n}$ indeed contains the population mean μ. We cannot say that there is a 0.95 *probability* that μ is inside the interval, because the interval $\overline{x} \pm 1.96\sigma/\sqrt{n}$ is not random, and neither is μ. The population mean μ is unknown to us but is a fixed quantity—not a random variable.[2] Either μ lies inside the confidence interval (in which case the probability of this event

---

[2] We are using what is called the *classical*, or *frequentist*, interpretation of confidence intervals. An alternative view, the Bayesian approach, will be discussed in Chapter 15. The Bayesian approach allows us to treat an unknown population parameter as a random variable. As such, the unknown population mean μ may be stated to have a 0.95 *probability* of being within an interval.

FIGURE 6-2　Construction of a 95% Confidence Interval for the Population Mean μ

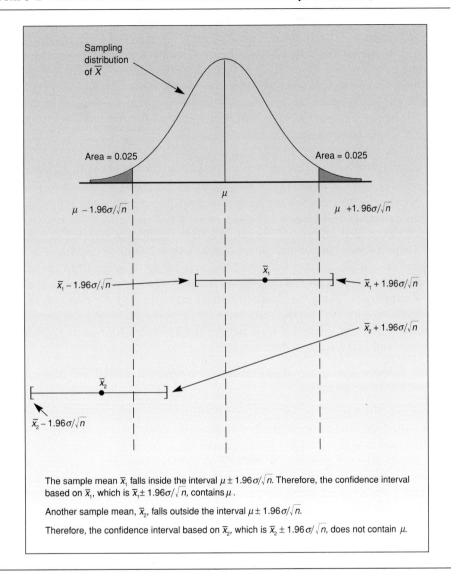

The sample mean $\bar{x}_1$ falls inside the interval $\mu \pm 1.96\sigma/\sqrt{n}$. Therefore, the confidence interval based on $\bar{x}_1$, which is $\bar{x}_1 \pm 1.96\sigma/\sqrt{n}$, contains μ.

Another sample mean, $\bar{x}_2$, falls outside the interval $\mu \pm 1.96\sigma/\sqrt{n}$.

Therefore, the confidence interval based on $\bar{x}_2$, which is $\bar{x}_2 \pm 1.96\sigma/\sqrt{n}$, does not contain μ.

is 1.00), or it does not (in which case the probability of the event is 0). We do know, however, that 95% of all possible intervals constructed in this manner will contain μ. Therefore, we may say that we are *95% confident* that μ lies in the particular interval we have obtained.

A 95% confidence interval for μ when σ is known and sampling is done from a normal population, or a large sample is used:

$$\bar{x} \pm 1.96 \frac{\sigma}{\sqrt{n}} \qquad (6\text{-}2)$$

The quantity $1.96 \dfrac{\sigma}{\sqrt{n}}$ is often called the *margin of error* or the *sampling error*. Its data-derived estimate (using s instead of the unknown σ) is commonly reported.

To compute a 95% confidence interval for μ, all we need to do is substitute the values of the required entities in equation 6–2. Suppose, for example, that we are sampling from a normal population, in which case the random variable $\bar{X}$ is normally distributed for any sample size. We use a sample of size $n = 25$, and we get a sample mean $\bar{x} = 122$. Suppose we also know that the population standard deviation is $\sigma = 20$. Let us compute a 95% confidence interval for the unknown population mean, μ. Using equation 6–2, we get

$$\bar{x} \pm 1.96\frac{\sigma}{\sqrt{n}} = 122 \pm 1.96\frac{20}{\sqrt{25}} = 122 \pm 7.84 = [114.16, 129.84]$$

Thus, we may be 95% confident that the unknown population mean μ lies anywhere between the values 114.16 and 129.84.

In business and other applications, the 95% confidence interval is commonly used. There are, however, many other possible levels of confidence. You may choose any level of confidence you wish, find the appropriate z value from the standard normal table, and use it instead of 1.96 in equation 6–2 to get an interval of the chosen level of confidence. Using the standard normal table, we find, for example, that for a 90% confidence interval we use the z value 1.645, and for a 99% confidence interval we use $z = 2.58$ (or, using an accurate interpolation, 2.576). Let us formalize the procedure and make some definitions.

We define $z_{\alpha/2}$ as the z value that cuts off a right-tail area of $\alpha/2$ under the standard normal curve.

For example, 1.96 is $z_{\alpha/2}$ for $\alpha/2 = 0.025$ because $z = 1.96$ cuts off an area of 0.025 to its right. (We find from Table 2 that, for $z = 1.96$, TA $= 0.475$; therefore, the right-tail area is $\alpha/2 = 0.025$.) Now consider the two points 1.96 and -1.96. Each of them cuts off a tail area of $\alpha/2 = 0.025$ in the respective direction of its tail. The area between the two values is therefore equal to $1 - \alpha = 1 - 2(0.025) = 0.95$. The area under the curve excluding the tails, $1 - \alpha$, is called the **confidence coefficient.** (And the combined area in both tails, α, is called the **error probability.** This probability will be important to us in the next chapter.) The confidence coefficient multiplied by 100, expressed as a percentage, is the **confidence level.**

A $(1 - \alpha)$ 100% confidence interval for μ when σ is known and sampling is done from a normal population, or with a large sample:

$$\bar{x} \pm z_{\alpha/2}\frac{\sigma}{\sqrt{n}} \qquad\qquad (6\text{–}3)$$

Thus, for a 95% confidence interval for μ we have

$$(1 - \alpha)100\% = 95\%$$
$$1 - \alpha = 0.95$$
$$\alpha = 0.05$$
$$\frac{\alpha}{2} = 0.025$$

From the normal table, we find $z_{\alpha/2} = 1.96$. This is the value we substitute for $z_{\alpha/2}$ in equation 6–3.

For example, suppose we want an 80% confidence interval for μ. We have $1 - \alpha = 0.80$ and $\alpha = 0.20$; therefore, $\alpha/2 = 0.10$. We now look in the standard normal table for the value of $z_{0.10}$, that is, the z value that cuts off an area of 0.10 to its right. We have TA $= 0.5 - 0.1 = 0.4$, and from the table we find $z_{0.10} = 1.28$. The confidence interval is therefore: $\bar{x} \pm 1.28\sigma/\sqrt{n}$. This is demonstrated in Figure 6–3.

Let us compute an 80% confidence interval for μ using the information presented earlier. We have: $n = 25$, and $\bar{x} = 122$. We also assume $\sigma = 20$. To compute an 80% confidence interval for the unknown population mean, μ, we use equation 6–3 and get:

$$\bar{x} \pm z_{\alpha/2}\frac{\sigma}{\sqrt{n}} = 122 \pm 1.28\frac{20}{\sqrt{25}} = 122 \pm 5.12 = [116.88, 127.12]$$

Comparing this interval with the 95% confidence interval for μ we computed earlier, we note that the present interval is *narrower*. This is an important property of confidence intervals.

When sampling from the same population, using a fixed sample size, *the higher the confidence level, the wider the interval.*

Intuitively, a wider interval has more of a presampling chance of "capturing" the unknown population parameter. If we want a 100% confidence interval for a parameter, the interval must be $[-\infty, \infty]$. The reason for this is that 100% confidence is derived from a presampling probability of 1.00 of capturing the parameter, and the only way to get such a probability using the standard normal distribution is by allowing

FIGURE 6–3 Construction of an 80% Confidence Interval for μ

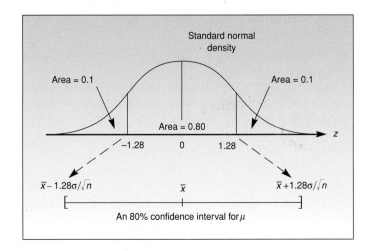

FIGURE 6-4   Width of a Confidence Interval as a Function of Sample Size

Z to be anywhere from $-\infty$ to ∞. If we are willing to be more realistic (nothing is *certain*) and accept, say, a 99% confidence interval, our interval would be finite and based on $z = 2.58$. The width of our interval would then be $2(2.58\sigma/\sqrt{n})$. If we further reduce our confidence requirement to 95%, the width of our interval would be $2(1.96\sigma/\sqrt{n})$. Since both σ and n are fixed, the 95% interval must be narrower. The more confidence you require, the more you need to sacrifice in terms of a wider interval.   *wide CI*

If you want both a narrow interval *and* a high degree of confidence, you need to acquire a large amount of information—take a large sample. This is so because the larger the sample size, n, the narrower the interval. This makes sense in that if you buy more information, you will have less uncertainty.

When sampling from the same population, using a fixed confidence level, the larger the sample size, n, the narrower the confidence interval.

Suppose that the 80% confidence interval developed earlier was based on a sample size $n = 2{,}500$ instead of $n = 25$. Assuming that $\bar{x}$ and σ are the same, the new confidence interval should be 10 times as narrow as the previous one (because $\sqrt{2{,}500} = 50$, which is 10 times as large as $\sqrt{25}$). Indeed, the new interval is

$$\bar{x} \pm z_{\alpha/2}\frac{\sigma}{\sqrt{n}} = 122 \pm 1.28\frac{20}{\sqrt{2{,}500}} = 122 \pm 0.512 = [121.49, 122.51]$$

This interval has width $2(0.512) = 1.024$, while the width of the interval based on a sample of size $n = 25$ is $2(5.12) = 10.24$. This demonstrates the value of information. The two confidence intervals are shown in Figure 6-4.

PROBLEMS

6-1. What is a confidence interval, and why is it useful? What is a confidence level?

6-2. Explain why in classical statistics it makes no sense to describe a confidence interval in terms of probability.

6–3. Explain how the postsampling confidence level is derived from a presampling probability.

6–4. Suppose that you computed a 95% confidence interval for a population mean. The user of the statistics claims your interval is too wide to have any meaning in the specific use for which it is intended. Discuss and compare two methods of solving this problem.

6–5. A real estate agent needs to estimate the average value of a residential property of a given size in a certain area. The real estate agent believes that the standard deviation of the property values is $\sigma = \$5,500.00$ and that property values are approximately normally distributed. A random sample of 16 units gives a sample mean of $89,673.12. Give a 95% confidence interval for the average value of all properties of this kind.

6–6. In problem 6–5, suppose that a 99% confidence interval is required. Compute the new interval, and compare it with the 95% confidence interval you computed in problem 6–5.

6–7. A car manufacturer wants to estimate the average mpg highway rating for a new model. From experience with similar models, the manufacturer believes the mpg standard deviation is 4.6. A random sample of 100 highway runs of the new model yields a sample mean of 32 mpg. Give a 95% confidence interval for the population average mpg highway rating.

6–8. In problem 6–7, do we need to assume that the population of mpg values is normally distributed? Explain.

6–9. A wine importer needs to report the average percentage of alcohol in bottles of French wine. From experience with previous kinds of wine, the importer believes the population standard deviation is 1.2%. The importer randomly samples 60 bottles of the new wine and obtains a sample mean $\bar{x} = 9.3\%$. Give a 90% confidence interval for the average percentage of alcohol in all bottles of the new wine.

6–10. A company is considering installing a fax machine at one of its offices. As part of the decision process as to whether or not to install the machine, the company's manager wants to estimate the average number of documents that would be transmitted daily if the machine were installed. From experience at other offices, the company manager believes the standard deviation of the number of documents sent daily is 32. The manager also believes the number of documents transmitted daily is a normally distributed random variable. The machine is tested over a random sample of 15 days, and the resulting sample mean is 267. Give a 99% confidence interval for the average number of documents that would be transmitted daily if the machine were installed.

6–11. In problem 6–10, suppose that the manager would be interested in installing the machine if she could be fairly confident that the average number of documents transmitted daily would be above 245. Do the findings in problem 6–10 justify installing the machine? Explain.

6–12. Beechcraft, Inc., wants to estimate the average time it takes their Beechjet corporate jet to climb from sea level to 41,000 feet. From previous experience, company engineers believe that the standard deviation of climbing times is 2 minutes. The model is tested in 100 random trials, and it is found that the sample mean is 22 minutes. Give a 95% confidence interval for the average climbing time from sea level to 41,000 feet.

6–13. A mining company needs to estimate the average amount of copper ore per ton mined. A random sample of 50 tons gives a sample mean of 146.75 pounds. The population standard deviation is assumed to be 35.2 pounds. Give a 95% confidence interval for the average amount of copper in the "population" of tons mined. Also give a 90% confidence interval and a 99% confidence interval for the average amount of copper per ton.

6–14. A survey reports that people with family incomes in the $75,000 to $100,000 range report an average of $8,562 in interest paid per year when filing their tax returns with the IRS.[3]

---

[3] "Take a Peek at Your Peers' Deductions," *Business Week*, March 11, 1991, p. 110.

Assuming that this result is based on a random sample of 2,000 taxpayers from all over the country and that the population standard deviation is $1,800, give a 95% confidence interval for the population average interest reported per year.

6–15.   An investment consultant reports that the average 12-month return on a random sample of 50 stocks was 20.74%.[4] If the standard deviation was 5.0% for the entire, large group of stocks from which the sample of 50 stocks was chosen, give a 95% confidence interval for the average 12-month return for all stocks in this group.

6–16.   Suppose you have a confidence interval based on a sample of size n. Using the same level of confidence, how large a sample is required to produce an interval of half the width?

6–17.   The width of a 95% confidence interval for μ is 10 units. If everything else stays the same, how wide would a 90% confidence interval be for μ?

6-3   Confidence Intervals for μ When σ Is Unknown—The t Distribution

In constructing confidence intervals for μ, we assume a normal population distribution or a large sample size (for normality via the central limit theorem). Until now, we have also assumed a known population standard deviation. This assumption was necessary for theoretical reasons so that we could use standard normal probabilities in constructing our intervals.

In real sampling situations, however, the population standard deviation, σ, is rarely known. The reason for this is that both μ and σ are population parameters. When we sample from a population with the aim of estimating its unknown mean, it is quite unlikely that the other parameter of the same population, the standard deviation, will be known.

The t Distribution

As we mentioned in Chapter 5, when the population standard deviation is not known, we may use the sample standard deviation, S, in its place. *If the population is normally distributed*, the standardized statistic

$$t = \frac{\bar{X} - \mu}{S/\sqrt{n}} \tag{6-4}$$

has a **t distribution** with $n - 1$ degrees of freedom. The degrees of freedom of the distribution are the degrees of freedom associated with the sample standard deviation, S (as explained in the last chapter). The t distribution is also called *Student's distribution*, or *Student's t distribution*. What is the origin of the name *Student*?

W. S. Gossett was a scientist at the Guinness brewery in Dublin, Ireland. In 1908, Gossett discovered the distribution of the quantity in equation 6–4. He called the new distribution the t distribution. The Guinness brewery, however, did not allow its workers to publish findings under their own names. Therefore, Gossett published his findings under the pen name Student. As a result, the distribution became known also as Student's distribution.

The t distribution is characterized by its degrees-of-freedom parameter, df. For any integer value, df = 1, 2, 3, . . . , there is a corresponding t distribution. The t distribution resembles the standard normal distribution, Z: it is symmetric and bell-shaped. The t distribution, however, has wider tails than the Z distribution.

---

[4] "Mind-Numbing Numbers," *Worth*, June, 1995, 14.

The mean of a t distribution is zero. For df > 2, the variance of the t distribution is equal to $df/(df - 2)$.

We see that the mean of t is the same as the mean of Z, but the variance of t is larger than the variance of Z. As df increases, the variance of t approaches 1.00, which is the variance of Z. Having wider tails and a larger variance than Z is a reflection of the fact that the t distribution applies to situations with a greater inherent *uncertainty*. The uncertainty comes from the fact that σ is unknown and is estimated by the *random variable S*. The t distribution thus reflects the uncertainty in *two* random variables, $\overline{X}$ and S, while Z reflects only an uncertainty due to $\overline{X}$. The greater uncertainty in t (which makes confidence intervals based on t wider than those based on Z) is the price we pay for not knowing σ and having to estimate it from our data. As df increases, the t distribution approaches the Z distribution. Figure 6–5 shows t distributions with different numbers of degrees of freedom, along with the standard normal distribution which is their limit as df goes to infinity.

Values of t distributions for selected tail probabilities are given in Table 3 in Appendix C (reproduced here as Table 6–1). Since there are infinitely many t distributions—one for every value of the degrees-of-freedom parameter—the table contains probabilities for only some of these distributions. For each distribution, the table gives values that cut off given areas under the curve to the *right*. The t table is thus a table of values corresponding to right-tail probabilities.

Let us consider an example. A random variable with a t distribution with 10 degrees of freedom has a 0.10 probability of exceeding the value 1.372. It has a 0.025 probability of exceeding the value 2.228, and so on for the other values listed in the table. Since the t distributions are symmetric about zero, we also know, for example, that the probability that a random variable with a t distribution with 10 degrees of freedom will be less than -1.372 is 0.10. These facts are demonstrated in Figure 6–6.

As we noted earlier, the t distribution approaches the standard normal distribution as the df parameter approaches infinity. The t distribution with "infinite" degrees of freedom is defined as the standard normal distribution. The last row in Appendix C, Table 3 (Table 6–1) corresponds to df $= \infty$, the standard normal distribution. Note that the value corresponding to a right-tail area of 0.025 in that row is 1.96, which we recognize as the appropriate z value. Similarly, the value corresponding to a right-tail area of 0.005 is 2.576, and the value corresponding to a right-tail area of 0.05 is 1.645. These, too, are values we recognize for the standard normal distribution. Look upward from the last row of the table to find cutoff values of the same right-tail probabilities for t distributions with different degrees of freedom. Suppose, for example, that we want to construct a 95% confidence interval for μ using the t distribution with 20 degrees of freedom. We may identify the value 1.96 in the last row (the appropriate z value for 95%) and then move up in the same column until we reach the row corresponding to df $= 20$. Here we find the required value $t_{\alpha/2} = t_{0.025} = 2.086$.

FIGURE 6–5
Several *t* Distributions Showing the Convergence to the Standard Normal Distribution as the Degrees of Freedom Increase

---

A $(1 - \alpha)$ 100% confidence interval for μ when σ is not known (assuming a normally distributed population):

$$\overline{x} \pm t_{\alpha/2} \frac{s}{\sqrt{n}} \tag{6–5}$$

where $t_{\alpha/2}$ is the value of the t distribution with $n - 1$ degrees of freedom that cuts off a tail area of $\alpha/2$ to its right

TABLE 6-1　Values and Probabilities of *t* Distributions

Degrees of Freedom	$t_{.100}$	$t_{.050}$	$t_{.025}$	$t_{.010}$	$t_{.005}$
1	3.078	6.314	12.706	31.821	63.657
2	1.886	2.920	4.303	6.965	9.925
3	1.638	2.353	3.182	4.541	5.841
4	1.533	2.132	2.776	3.747	4.604
5	1.476	2.015	2.571	3.365	4.032
6	1.440	1.943	2.447	3.143	3.707
7	1.415	1.895	2.365	2.998	3.499
8	1.397	1.860	2.306	2.896	3.355
9	1.383	1.833	2.262	2.821	3.250
10	1.372	1.812	2.228	2.764	3.169
11	1.363	1.796	2.201	2.718	3.106
12	1.356	1.782	2.179	2.681	3.055
13	1.350	1.771	2.160	2.650	3.012
14	1.345	1.761	2.145	2.624	2.977
15	1.341	1.753	2.131	2.602	2.947
16	1.337	1.746	2.120	2.583	2.921
17	1.333	1.740	2.110	2.567	2.898
18	1.330	1.734	2.101	2.552	2.878
19	1.328	1.729	2.093	2.539	2.861
20	1.325	1.725	2.086	2.528	2.845
21	1.323	1.721	2.080	2.518	2.831
22	1.321	1.717	2.074	2.508	2.819
23	1.319	1.714	2.069	2.500	2.807
24	1.318	1.711	2.064	2.492	2.797
25	1.316	1.708	2.060	2.485	2.787
26	1.315	1.706	2.056	2.479	2.779
27	1.314	1.703	2.052	2.473	2.771
28	1.313	1.701	2.048	2.467	2.763
29	1.311	1.699	2.045	2.462	2.756
30	1.310	1.697	2.042	2.457	2.750
40	1.303	1.684	2.021	2.423	2.704
60	1.296	1.671	2.000	2.390	2.660
120	1.289	1.658	1.980	2.358	2.617
∞	1.282	1.645	1.960	2.326	2.576

EXAMPLE 6-1

A stock market analyst wants to estimate the average return on a certain stock. A random sample of 15 days yields an average (annualized) return of $\bar{x} = 10.37\%$ and a standard deviation of $s = 3.5\%$. Assuming a normal population of returns, give a 95% confidence interval for the average return on this stock.

SOLUTION

Since the sample size is $n = 15$, we need to use the *t* distribution with $n - 1 = 14$ degrees of freedom. In Table 3, in the row corresponding to 14 degrees of freedom and the column corresponding to a right-tail area of 0.025 (this is $\alpha/2$), we find $t_{0.025} = 2.145$.

FIGURE 6-6   Table Probabilities for a Selected *t* Distribution (df = 10)

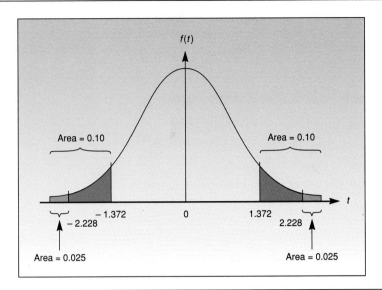

(We could also have found this value by moving upward from 1.96 in the last row.) Using this value, we construct the 95% confidence interval as follows:

$$\bar{x} \pm t_{\alpha/2} \frac{s}{\sqrt{n}} = 10.37 \pm 2.145 \frac{3.5}{\sqrt{15}} = [8.43, \ 12.31]$$

Thus, the analyst may be 95% sure that the average annualized return on the stock is anywhere from 8.43% to 12.31%.

Looking at the *t* table, we note the *convergence* of the *t* distributions to the *Z* distribution—the values in the rows preceding the last get closer and closer to the corresponding *z* values in the last row. Although the *t* distribution is the correct distribution to use whenever σ is not known (assuming the population is normal), when df is *large* we may use the standard normal distribution as an adequate approximation to the *t* distribution. Thus, instead of using 1.98 in a confidence interval based on a sample of size 121 (df = 120), we will just use the *z* value 1.96.

We divide estimation problems into two kinds: small-sample problems and large-sample problems. Example 6–1 demonstrated the solution of a small-sample problem. In general, *large sample* will mean a sample of 30 items or more, and *small sample* will mean a sample of size less than 30. For small samples, we will use the *t* distribution as demonstrated above. For large samples, we will use the *Z* distribution as an adequate approximation. We note that the larger the sample size, the better the normal approximation. Remember, however, that this division of large versus small samples is arbitrary.

Whenever σ is not known (and the population is assumed normal), the correct distribution to use is the *t* distribution with $n - 1$ degrees of freedom. Note, however, that for large degrees of freedom, the *t* distribution is approximated well by the *Z* distribution.

If you wish, you may always use the more accurate values obtained from the t table (when such values can be found in the table) rather than the standard normal approximation. In this chapter and elsewhere (with the exception of some examples in Chapter 14), we will assume that the population satisfies, at least approximately, a normal distribution assumption. For large samples, this assumption is less crucial.

> A large-sample $(1 - \alpha)100\%$ confidence interval for μ:
>
> $$\bar{x} \pm z_{\alpha/2} \frac{s}{\sqrt{n}} \qquad (6\text{--}6)$$

We demonstrate the use of equation 6–6 in Example 6–2.

EXAMPLE 6-2

An economist wants to estimate the average amount in checking accounts at banks in a given region. A random sample of 100 accounts gives $\bar{x} = \$357.60$ and $s = \$140.00$. Give a 95% confidence interval for μ, the average amount in any checking account at a bank in the given region.

SOLUTION

We find the 95% confidence interval for μ as follows.

$$\bar{x} \pm z_{\alpha/2} \frac{s}{\sqrt{n}} = 357.60 \pm 1.96 \frac{140}{\sqrt{100}} = [330.16, 385.04]$$

Thus, based on the data and the assumption of random sampling, the economist may be 95% confident that the average amount in checking accounts in the area is anywhere from \$330.16 to \$385.04.

PROBLEMS

6–18. A telephone company wants to estimate the average length of long-distance calls during weekends. A random sample of 50 calls gives a mean $\bar{x} = 14.5$ minutes and standard deviation $s = 5.6$ minutes. Give a 95% confidence interval and a 90% confidence interval for the average length of a long-distance phone call during weekends.

6–19. An insurance company handling malpractice cases is interested in estimating the average amount of claims against physicians of a certain specialty. The company obtains a random sample of 165 claims and finds $\bar{x} = \$16,530$ and $s = \$5,542$. Give a 95% confidence interval and a 99% confidence interval for the average amount of a claim.

6–20. The manufacturer of batteries used in small electrical appliances wants to estimate the average life of a battery. A random sample of 12 batteries yields $\bar{x} = 34.2$ hours and $s = 5.9$ hours. Give a 95% confidence interval for the average life of a battery.

6–21. A tire manufacturer wants to estimate the average number of miles that may be driven on a tire of a certain type before the tire wears out. A random sample of 32 tires is chosen; the tires are driven on until they wear out, and the number of miles driven on each tire is recorded. The data, in thousands of miles, are as follows.

32, 33, 28, 37, 29, 30, 25, 27, 39, 40, 26, 26, 27, 30, 25, 30, 31, 29, 24, 36,
25, 37, 37, 20, 22, 35, 23, 28, 30, 36, 40, 41

Give a 99% confidence interval for the average number of miles that may be driven on a tire of this kind.

6–22.   It is estimated that the average household charitable contribution to cultural institutions is $193.[5] Assume that this sample mean is based on a sample of size 500 and that the sample standard deviation is $78. Give a 95% confidence interval for the population mean contribution for all households.

6–23.   Pier 1 Imports is a nationwide retail outlet selling imported furniture and other home items. From time to time, the company surveys its regular customers by obtaining random samples based on customer zip codes. In one mailing, customers were asked to rate a new table from Thailand on a scale of 0 to 100. The ratings of 25 randomly selected customers are as follows: 78, 85, 80, 89, 77, 50, 75, 90, 88, 100, 70, 99, 98, 55, 80, 45, 80, 76, 96, 100, 95, 90, 60, 85, 90. Give a 99% confidence interval for the rating of the table that would be given by an average member of the population of regular customers. Assume normality.

6–24.   An executive placement service needs to estimate the average salary of executives placed in a given industry. A random sample of 40 executives gives $\bar{x} = \$42,539$ and $s = \$11,690$. Give a 90% confidence interval for the average salary of an executive placed in this industry.

6–25.   A bank is interested in extending its automated teller machine service to a new community. As part of the research prepared as an aid in making the decision, the bank's management undertakes an experiment to determine the average amount of a transaction, in dollars per person per day. A random sample of 10 experimental transactions on a trial run of the machine is collected. The following data (in dollars) are the result: 53, 40, 39, 10, 12, 60, 72, 65, 50, 45. Give a 95% confidence interval for the average amount of a transaction.

6–26.   For advertising purposes, the Beef Industry Council needs to estimate the average caloric content of 3 oz. top loin steak cuts. A random sample of 400 pieces gives a sample mean of 212 calories and a sample standard deviation of 38 calories. Give a 95% confidence interval for the average caloric content of a 3 oz. cut of top loin steak. Also give a 98% confidence interval for the average caloric content of a cut.

6–27.   A transportation company wants to estimate the average length of time goods are in transit across the country. A random sample of 20 shipments gives $\bar{x} = 2.6$ days and $s = 0.4$ days. Give a 99% confidence interval for the average transit time.

6–28.   To aid in planning the development of a tourist shopping area, a state agency wants to estimate the average dollar amount spent by a tourist in an existing shopping area. A random sample of 56 tourists gives $\bar{x} = \$258$ and $s = \$85$. Give a 95% confidence interval for the average amount spent by a tourist at the shopping area.

6–29.   A large drugstore wants to estimate average weekly sales for a brand of soap. A random sample of 13 weeks gives the following numbers: 123, 110, 95, 120, 87, 89, 100, 105, 98, 88, 75, 125, 101. Give a 90% confidence interval for average weekly sales.

6–30.   Citibank Visa gives its cardholders "bonus dollars," which may be spent in partial payment for gifts purchased with the Visa card. The company wants to estimate the average amount of bonus dollars that will be spent by a cardholder enrolled in the program during a year. A trial run of the program with a random sample of 225 cardholders is carried out. The results are $\bar{x} = \$259.60$ and $s = \$52.00$. Give a 95% confidence interval for the average amount of bonus dollars that will be spent by a cardholder during the year.

6–31.   An accountant wants to estimate the average amount of an account of a service company. A random sample of 46 accounts yields $\bar{x} = \$16.50$ and $s = \$2.20$. Give a 95% confidence interval for the average amount of an account.

6–32.   An art dealer wants to estimate the average value of works of art of a certain period and type. A random sample of 20 works of art is appraised. The sample mean is found to be $5,139 and the sample standard deviation $640. Give a 95% confidence interval for the average value of all works of art of this kind.

---

[5] *Working Woman*, March, 1991, p. 58.

6–33.   A management consulting agency needs to estimate the average number of years of experience of executives in a given branch of management. A random sample of 28 executives gives $\bar{x} = 6.7$ years and $s = 2.4$ years. Give a 99% confidence interval for the average number of years of experience for all executives in this branch.

6–34.   The Food and Drug Administration (FDA) needs to estimate the average content of an additive in a given food product. A random sample of 75 portions of the product gives $\bar{x} = 8.9$ units and $s = 0.5$ units. Give a 95% confidence interval for the average number of units of additive in any portion of this food product.

6–35.   The management of a supermarket needs to make estimates of the average daily demand for milk. The following data are available (number of half-gallon containers sold per day): 48, 59, 45, 62, 50, 68, 57, 80, 65, 58, 79, 69. Assuming that this is a random sample of daily demand, give a 90% confidence interval for average daily demand for milk.

6–36.   According to *Business Week,* average dealer stocks of U.S. made cars were 82-day supplies in the first quarter of 1995.[6]

a.   If this average is based on a random sample of 100 dealers and the sample standard deviation is 28 days, give a 90% confidence interval for the average number of days' supply for all dealers selling U.S. made cars

b.   According to the same article, 60-days' supply is desirable. Does your interval contain this number? Explain the meaning of your finding.

6–37.   Contact lenses can cause sore eyes due to protein buildup on the surface of the lens. A new technology promises a cure for this problem. A layer of polymer is deposited on the lens and prevents the tear proteins from building up on the lens. The polymer must have an average thickness of 10 atoms.[7] A random sample of 15 locations on a particular lens gives the following thickness readings (number of atoms): 9, 9, 8, 11, 12, 10, 9, 8, 13, 12, 10, 11, 10, 9, 7. Give a 90% confidence interval for the average polymer thickness on the entire lens. Does the population average value of 10 atoms lie inside the confidence interval? Explain the meaning of your answer.

6–38.   The following table, reproduced by permission from *American Banker,* shows total commercial and industrial loans, in millions of dollars for a random sample of 20 large regional banks in the United States (where "large" is defined as having total assets of at least $10 billion).[8] Use the information in the table to construct a 95% confidence interval for average total business loans of all large regional banks in the United States.

	Name of Bank, City	Business Loans (millions) 12/31/93
1	Citibank, NA, New York	$38,798
2	Bank of America NT&SA, San Francisco	27,628
3	Chemical Bank, New York	19,070
4	Chase Manhattan Bank NA, New York	17,700
5	First National Bank, Boston	13,766
6	Bank of New York	11,191
7	NationsBank of Texas, NA, Dallas	9,540
8	Mellon Bank, NA, Pittsburgh	8,905
9	Morgan Guaranty Trust Co., New York	8,730
10	PNC Bank, NA, Pittsburgh	8,117
11	Continental Bank NA, Chicago	7,886
12	Comerica Bank, Detroit	7,038
13	NationsBank of North Carolina NA, Charlotte	6,773
		Continued

[6] J. Cooper and K. Madigan, "*Business Outlook,*" *Business Week,* May 29, 1995, p. 23.

[7] "A Nonstick Lens to Cure Red-eye," *Business Week,* January 28, 1991, p. 95.

[8] "Ranking the Banks," *American Banker,* August 1994, p. 4A.

Name of Bank, City	Business Loans (millions) 12/31/93
14 NBD Bank, NA, Detroit	$6,479
15 Wells Fargo Bank NA, San Francisco	5,800
16 National Westminster Bank USA, New York	5,769
17 First National Bank, Chicago	5,460
18 CoreStates Bank NA, Philadelphia	5,108
19 NationsBank of Georgia, NA, Atlanta	4,547
20 Union Bank, San Francisco	4,170

6-4 Large-Sample Confidence Intervals for the Population Proportion, *p*

Sometimes interest centers on a qualitative, rather than a quantitative, variable. We may be interested in the relative frequency of occurrence of some characteristic in a population. For example, we may be interested in the proportion of people in a population who are users of some product or the proportion of defective items produced by a machine. In such cases, we want to estimate the population proportion, *p*.

The estimator of the population proportion, *p*, is the sample proportion, $\hat{P}$. In Chapter 5, we saw that when the sample size is large, $\hat{P}$ has an approximately normal sampling distribution. The mean of the sampling distribution of $\hat{P}$ is the population proportion, *p*, and the standard deviation of the distribution of $\hat{P}$ is $\sqrt{pq/n}$, where $q = 1 - p$. Since the standard deviation of the estimator depends on the unknown population parameter, its value is also unknown to us. It turns out, however, that for large samples we may use our actual estimate $\hat{p}$ instead of the unknown parameter *p* in the formula for the standard deviation. We will, therefore, use $\sqrt{\hat{p}\hat{q}/n}$ as our estimate of the standard deviation of $\hat{P}$. Recall our large-sample rule of thumb. For estimating *p*, a sample is considered large enough when both $n \cdot p$ and $n \cdot q$ are greater than 5. (We guess the value of *p* when determining whether the sample is large enough. As a check, we may also compute $n\hat{p}$ and $n\hat{q}$ once the sample is obtained.)

> A large-sample $(1 - \alpha)100\%$ confidence interval for the population proportion, *p*:
>
> $$\hat{p} \pm z_{\alpha/2}\sqrt{\frac{\hat{p}\hat{q}}{n}} \qquad (6\text{–}7)$$
>
> where the sample proportion, $\hat{p}$, is equal to the number of successes in the sample, *x*, divided by the number of trials (the sample size), *n*, and $\hat{q} = 1 - \hat{p}$

We demonstrate the use of equation 6–7 in Example 6–3.

A marketing research firm wants to estimate the share that foreign companies have in the American market for certain products. A random sample of 100 consumers is obtained, and it is found that 34 people in the sample are users of foreign-made products; the rest are users of domestic products. Give a 95% confidence interval for the share of foreign products in this market.

EXAMPLE 6-3

We have $x = 34$ and $n = 100$, so our sample estimate of the proportion is $\hat{p} = x/n = 34/100 = 0.34$. We now use equation 6–7 to obtain the confidence interval for the

SOLUTION

population proportion, p. A 95% confidence interval for p is

$$\hat{p} \pm z_{\alpha/2} \sqrt{\frac{\hat{p}\hat{q}}{n}} = 0.34 \pm 1.96 \sqrt{\frac{(0.34)(0.66)}{100}}$$

$$= 0.34 \pm 1.96(0.04737) = 0.34 \pm 0.0928$$

$$= [0.2472, 0.4328]$$

Thus, the firm may be 95% confident that foreign manufacturers control anywhere from 24.72% to 43.28% of the market.

Suppose the firm is not happy with such a wide confidence interval. What can be done about it? This is a problem of *value of information,* and it applies to all estimation situations. As we stated earlier, for a fixed sample size, the higher the confidence you require, the wider will be the confidence interval. The sample size is in the denominator of the standard error term, as we saw in the case of estimating μ. If we should increase n, the standard error of $\hat{P}$ will decrease, and there will be less uncertainty about the parameter being estimated. If the sample size cannot be increased but you still want a narrower confidence interval, you must reduce your confidence level. Thus, for example, if the firm agrees to reduce the confidence level to 90%, z will be reduced from 1.96 to 1.645, and the confidence interval will shrink to

$$0.34 \pm 1.645(0.04737) = 0.34 \pm 0.07792 = [0.2621, 0.4179]$$

The firm may be 90% confident that the market share of foreign products is anywhere from 26.21% to 41.79%. If the firm wanted a high confidence (say 95%) *and* a narrow confidence interval, it would have to take a larger sample. Suppose that a random sample of $n = 200$ customers gave us the same result; that is, $x = 68$, $n = 200$ and $\hat{p} = x/n = 0.34$. What would be a 95% confidence interval in this case? Using equation 6–7, we get

$$\hat{p} \pm z_{\alpha/2} \sqrt{\frac{\hat{p}\hat{q}}{n}} = 0.34 \pm 1.96 \sqrt{\frac{(0.34)(0.66)}{200}} = [0.2743, 0.4057]$$

This interval is considerably narrower than our first 95% confidence interval, which was based on a sample of 100.

When estimating proportions using small samples, the binomial distribution may be used in forming confidence intervals. Since the distribution is discrete, it may not be possible to construct an interval with an exact, prespecified confidence level such as 95% or 99%. We will not demonstrate the method here.

PROBLEMS

6–39. A maker of portable exercise equipment, designed for health-conscious people who travel too frequently to use a regular athletic club, wants to estimate the proportion of traveling businesspeople who may be interested in the product. A random sample of 120 traveling businesspeople indicates that 28 of them may be interested in purchasing the portable fitness equipment. Give a 95% confidence interval for the proportion of all traveling business people who may be interested in the product.

6–40. The makers of a medicated facial skin cream are interested in determining the percentage of people in a given age group who may benefit from the ointment. A random sample of 68 people results in 42 successful treatments. Give a 99% confidence interval for the proportion of people in the given age group who may be successfully treated with the facial cream.

6–41. An article on secretaries' salaries in the *The Wall Street Journal* reports: "Three-fourths of surveyed secretaries said they make less than $25,000 a year." Suppose that the *Journal* based its results on a random sample of 460 secretaries drawn from every category of business. Give a 95% confidence interval for the proportion of secretaries earning less than $25,000 per year.

6–42. A Pitney Bowes advertisement appearing in business magazines shows an irate manager kneeling on his desktop in a room full of playful seals, with his disgraced assistant looking at the floor. The caption reads: "SEALS? I said, bring in more DEALS!" Suppose the company wanted to test the comic effect of the ad and gathered a random sample of 80 viewers, 58 of whom thought the advertisement was funny. Give a 90% confidence interval for the proportion of people who consider this ad funny.

6–43. A study was undertaken to investigate the relative success of IBM "clones" in the microcomputer market. A random sample of 590 companies revealed that 88 were using computers made by either of two main competitors of IBM. Give a 95% confidence interval for the combined market share of the two "clone" companies.

6–44. A recent article describes the success of business schools in Europe and the demand on that continent for the MBA degree. The article reports that a survey of 280 European business positions resulted in the conclusion that only one-seventh of the positions for MBAs at European businesses are currently filled. Assuming that these numbers are exact and that the sample was randomly chosen from the entire population of interest, give a 90% confidence interval for the proportion of filled MBA positions in Europe.

6–45. The following is from *USA Today*. Suppose that after all audits for 1994 are done, an accountant finds that 81 of her 2,012 clients were audited. Construct a 95% confidence interval for the audit rate for the entire population of taxpayers. Why is this confidence interval not correct for this purpose? What does the confidence interval imply about the accountant?

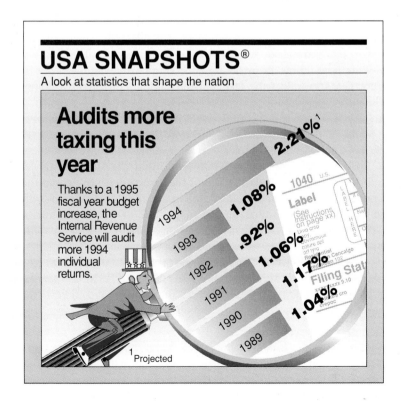

From *USA Today,* April 14, 1995, p. 1, with data from the Internal Revenue Service.

6–46.   A Gallup poll of 338 chief executives revealed that 79% support a flat tax with few deductions.[9] Construct a 99% confidence interval for the proportion of all chief executives in the nation who support a flat tax with few deductions.

6–47.   A machine produces safety devices for use in helicopters. A quality-control engineer regularly checks samples of the devices produced by the machine, and if too many of the devices are defective, the production process is stopped and the machine is readjusted. If a random sample of 52 devices yields 8 defectives, give a 98% confidence interval for the proportion of defective devices made by this machine.

6–48.   Before launching its Buyers' Assurance Program, American Express wanted to estimate the proportion of cardholders who would be interested in this automatic insurance coverage plan. A random sample of 250 American Express cardholders was selected and sent questionnaires. The results were that 121 people in the sample expressed interest in the plan. Give a 99% confidence interval for the proportion of all interested American Express cardholders.

6–49.   An airline wants to estimate the proportion of business passengers on a new route from New York to San Francisco. A random sample of 347 passengers on this route is selected, and 201 of them are found to be business travelers. Give a 90% confidence interval for the proportion of business travelers on the airline's new route.

6–50.   A survey of a random sample of 1,000 managers found that 81% of them had a high need for power. This led to a conclusion that power is a motivator for managers.[10] Construct a 90% confidence interval for the proportion of all managers in the population under study who are motivated by power.

6–51.   According to *Business Week*, color printers account for 9% of the desktop printer market.[11] If this estimate is based on a random sample of 5,000 printer users, give a 95% confidence interval for the population proportion of color printers.

6–5   The Finite-Population Correction Factor[12]

Until now, we have implicitly assumed an "infinite" population. That is, we have assumed that the population was much larger than the sample. This is often the case in practice. Still, there are cases where we sample (without replacement) a sizable fraction of a finite population. In such cases, the standard deviation of our estimator needs to be corrected to reflect the fact that the sample constitutes a nonnegligible fraction of the entire population.

      When the size of the sample, n, constitutes at least 5% of the size of the population, N, we have to use a finite-population correction factor and modify the standard deviation of our estimator. In Chapter 5, we gave the standard deviation of our estimator, $\overline{X}$, in equation 5–3: $\sigma_{\overline{X}} = \sigma/\sqrt{n}$. Note that the standard deviation, as stated, does *not* account for the relative size of the sample with respect to the size of the sampled population. The standard deviation in equation 5–3 depends only on the absolute size of the sample, n (and on the magnitude of the population standard deviation). When the sample constitutes a considerable fraction of the population, equation 5–3 does not correctly reflect the standard deviation of the sample mean. The reason is the following. If the sample size is *equal* to the population size, that is, $n = N$, the standard deviation of $\overline{X}$ is equal to *zero*. This is so because when we sample the *entire* population, we know the exact population mean, and there is no uncertainty—the standard deviation is zero. As the sample size, n, approaches the popula-

---

[9] "The Forbes/Gallup Poll of Chief Executives," *Forbes*, January 2, 1995, p. 120.

[10] "Power Is the Great Motivator," *Harvard Business Review*, January–February, 1995, p. 128.

[11] "Information Processing," *Business Week*, April 24, 1995, p. 134.

[12] This is an optional section.

565 - 9726
veronique.

tion size, N, the standard deviation of $\bar{X}$ should approach zero. This is not reflected in equation 5–3 because—according to that equation—the standard deviation of $\bar{X}$ is equal to zero only when the sample size is infinite. In cases where we sample a sizable fraction of the population, we thus need to account for the reduction in the *actual* standard error of $\bar{X}$ as n becomes close to N. This reduction in the standard error of the statistic is achieved by multiplying the standard deviation by a finite-population correction factor.

Finite-population correction factor:

$$\sqrt{\frac{N - n}{N - 1}} \qquad (6\text{–}8)$$

Note that the expression in equation 6–8 is close to 1.00 when the sample size is small relative to the population size. The expression approaches zero as the sample size approaches the population size, as required. When sampling for the population mean, we multiply the standard error of $\bar{X}$ by the correction factor. We thus have the following large-sample confidence interval for μ when the sample size is a sizable fraction of the population size.

A large-sample $(1 - \alpha)100\%$ confidence interval for μ using a finite-population correction:

$$\bar{x} \pm z_{\alpha/2} \frac{s}{\sqrt{n}} \sqrt{\frac{N - n}{N - 1}} \qquad (6\text{–}9)$$

The finite-population correction factor (equation 6–8) may also be used to modify the standard deviation of the sample proportion in estimating a population proportion, p.

A large-sample $(1 - \alpha)100\%$ confidence interval for p using a finite-population correction:

$$\hat{p} \pm z_{\alpha/2} \sqrt{\frac{\hat{p}\hat{q}}{n}} \sqrt{\frac{N - n}{N - 1}} \qquad (6\text{–}10)$$

A company has 1,000 accounts receivable. To estimate the average amount of these accounts, a random sample of 100 accounts is chosen. In the sample, the average amount is $\bar{x} = \$532.35$, and the standard deviation is $s = \$61.22$. Give a 95% confidence interval for the average of all 1,000 accounts.

EXAMPLE 6-4

Here we have $N = 1,000$ and $n = 100$, so the sampling fraction is $n/N = 100/1,000 = 0.10$. Since the fraction is greater than 0.05, we need to use a confidence interval with a finite-population correction factor. Using equation 6–9, we get

SOLUTION

$$\bar{x} \pm z_{\alpha/2} \frac{s}{\sqrt{n}} \sqrt{\frac{N-n}{N-1}} = 532.35 \pm 1.96\left(\frac{61.22}{10}\right)\left(\sqrt{\frac{900}{999}}\right)$$
$$= 532.35 \pm 1.96(6.122)(\sqrt{0.9009})$$
$$= 532.35 \pm 11.39 = [520.96, 543.74]$$

PROBLEMS

6–52.   A community branch of a large bank has 1,253 checking accounts. A random sample of 200 of these accounts was selected, and the average balance in the sample was found to be $648.32. The sample standard deviation was found to be $210.00. Give a 99% confidence interval for the average balance in a checking account at the branch.

6–53.   In problem 6–52, give a 90% confidence interval for the average amount in checking accounts at the branch.

6–54.   An article about nonalcoholic beer indicates that brands of the new beer contain an average of 50 calories per bottle, and the standard deviation is 5 calories. If these results are obtained from a random sample of 50 bottles drawn from a single shipment of 300 bottles, give a 95% confidence interval for the average caloric content of a bottle in this shipment of 300 bottles.

6–55.   A company wants to estimate the proportion of its employees who are satisfied with a new management decision. Out of a total of 1,242 employees, 160 were randomly selected and interviewed. Of the ones interviewed, 85 indicated that they were satisfied with the new decision. Give a 95% confidence interval for the proportion of all employees who are satisfied with the new decision.

6–56.   A marketer of candy products wants to estimate the average number of candy bars sold in a given month in all 538 candy stores in a given area. A random sample of 100 stores gives $\bar{x} = 1,220$ and $s = 550$. Give a 90% confidence interval for the average number of candy bars sold in all 538 stores.

6–57.   A large supermarket receives weekly shipments of 1,520 cartons of eggs. To estimate reimbursements for shipment damages, the supermarket opens a random sample of 100 cartons to determine whether eggs are damaged. If, in a regular weekly sampling, 12 cartons are found to contain damaged eggs, give a 95% confidence interval for the proportion of cartons that are damaged in the entire shipment of 1,520.

6–58.   A random sample of 65 stocks selected from among the stocks listed in the Standard & Poor's 500 Index are found to have gone up by an average of 2 points with a standard deviation of 0.5 points. Give a 99% confidence interval for the average price change of all 500 stocks in the index.

6–59.   A random sample of 20 stocks from London's FT-100 index of 100 stocks showed an average gain of 3.1% in early 1995. The standard deviation was 1.8%. Give a 90% confidence interval for the average gain in that period for all 100 stocks.

6–60.   A shipment of 1,000 items is sampled to determine the proportion of defective items. A random sample of 150 items reveals that 28 are defective. Give a 99% confidence interval for the proportion of defectives.

6–6   Confidence Intervals for the Population Variance[13]

In some situations, our interest centers on the population variance (or, equivalently, the population standard deviation). This happens in production processes, queuing (waiting line) processes, and other situations. As we know, the sample variance, S^2, is the (unbiased) estimator of the population variance, σ^2.

---

[13] This is an optional section, but the chi-square distribution presented in this section should be introduced before Chapter 14.

FIGURE 6-7   Several Chi-Square Distributions with Different Values of the df Parameter

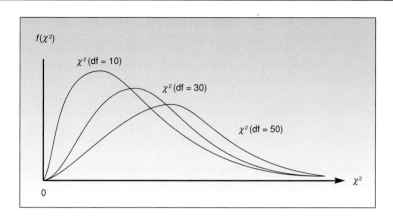

To compute confidence intervals for the population variance, we must learn to use a new probability distribution: the *chi-square distribution*. Chi (pronounced $k\bar{\imath}$) is one of two X letters in the Greek alphabet and is denoted by χ. Hence, we denote the chi-square distribution by χ^2.

The chi-square distribution, like the t distribution, has associated with it a degrees-of-freedom parameter, df. In the application of the chi-square distribution to estimation of the population variance, df $= n - 1$ (as with the t distribution in its application to sampling for the population mean). Unlike the t and the normal distributions, however, the chi-square distribution is *not* symmetric.

> The **chi-square distribution** is the probability distribution of the sum of several independent, squared standard normal random variables.

As a sum of squares, the chi-square random variable cannot be negative and is therefore bounded on the left by zero. The resulting distribution is skewed to the right. Figure 6–7 shows several chi-square distributions with different numbers of degrees of freedom.

> The mean of a chi-square distribution is equal to the degrees of freedom parameter, df. The variance of a chi-square distribution is equal to twice the number of degrees of freedom.

Note in Figure 6–7 that as df increases, the chi-square distribution looks more and more like a normal distribution. In fact, as df increases, the chi-square distribution approaches a normal distribution with mean df and variance 2(df).

Table 4 in Appendix C gives values of the chi-square distribution with different degrees of freedom, for given tail probabilities. An abbreviated version of part of the table is given on the next page as Table 6–2. We apply the chi-square distribution to problems of estimation of the population variance using the following property.

TABLE 6–2 Values and Probabilities of Chi-Square Distributions

	Area in Right Tail								
df	.995	.990	.975	.950	.900	.100	.050	.025	.010	.005
1	.0⁴393	.0³157	.0³982	.0²393	0.158	2.71	3.84	5.02	6.63	7.88
2	.0100	.0201	.0506	.103	.211	4.61	5.99	7.38	9.21	10.6
3	.0717	.115	.216	.352	.584	6.25	7.81	9.35	11.3	12.8
4	.207	.297	.484	.711	1.06	7.78	9.49	11.1	13.3	14.9
5	.412	.554	.831	1.15	1.61	9.24	11.1	12.8	15.1	16.7
6	.676	.872	1.24	1.64	2.20	10.6	12.6	14.4	16.8	18.5
7	.989	1.24	1.69	2.17	2.83	12.0	14.1	16.0	18.5	20.3
8	1.34	1.65	2.18	2.73	3.49	13.4	15.5	17.5	20.1	22.0
9	1.73	2.09	2.70	3.33	4.17	14.7	16.9	19.0	21.7	23.6
10	2.16	2.56	3.25	3.94	4.87	16.0	18.3	20.5	23.2	25.2
11	2.60	3.05	3.82	4.57	5.58	17.3	19.7	21.9	24.7	26.8
12	3.07	3.57	4.40	5.23	6.30	18.5	21.0	23.3	26.2	28.3
13	3.57	4.11	5.01	5.89	7.04	19.8	22.4	24.7	27.7	29.8
14	4.07	4.66	5.63	6.57	7.79	21.1	23.7	26.1	29.1	31.3
15	4.60	5.23	6.26	7.26	8.55	22.3	25.0	27.5	30.6	32.8
16	5.14	5.81	6.91	7.96	9.31	23.5	26.3	28.8	32.0	34.3
17	5.70	6.41	7.56	8.67	10.1	24.8	27.6	30.2	33.4	35.7
18	6.26	7.01	8.23	9.39	10.9	26.0	28.9	31.5	34.8	37.2
19	6.84	7.63	8.91	10.1	11.7	27.2	30.1	32.9	36.2	38.6
20	7.43	8.26	9.59	10.9	12.4	28.4	31.4	34.2	37.6	40.0
21	8.03	8.90	10.3	11.6	13.2	29.6	32.7	35.5	38.9	41.4
22	8.64	9.54	11.0	12.3	14.0	30.8	33.9	36.8	40.3	42.8
23	9.26	10.2	11.7	13.1	14.8	32.0	35.2	38.1	41.6	44.2
24	9.89	10.9	12.4	13.8	15.7	33.2	36.4	39.4	43.0	45.6
25	10.5	11.5	13.1	14.6	16.5	34.4	37.7	40.6	44.3	46.9
26	11.2	12.2	13.8	15.4	17.3	35.6	38.9	41.9	45.6	48.3
27	11.8	12.9	14.6	16.2	18.1	36.7	40.1	43.2	47.0	49.6
28	12.5	13.6	15.3	16.9	18.9	37.9	41.3	44.5	48.3	51.0
29	13.1	14.3	16.0	17.7	19.8	39.1	42.6	45.7	49.6	52.3
30	13.8	15.0	16.8	18.5	20.6	40.3	43.8	47.0	50.9	53.7

In sampling from a normal population, the random variable

$$\chi^2 = \frac{(n-1)S^2}{\sigma^2} \tag{6-11}$$

has a chi-square distribution with $n - 1$ degrees of freedom

The distribution of the quantity in equation 6–11 leads to a confidence interval for σ^2. Since the χ^2 distribution is not symmetric, we cannot use equal values with opposite signs (such as ±1.96 as we did with Z) and must construct the confidence interval using the two distinct tails of the distribution.

A $(1 - \alpha)100\%$ confidence interval for the population variance σ^2 (where the population is assumed normal):

$$\left[\frac{(n-1)s^2}{\chi^2_{\alpha/2}}, \frac{(n-1)s^2}{\chi^2_{1-\alpha/2}} \right] \qquad (6\text{--}12)$$

where $\chi^2_{\alpha/2}$ is the value of the chi-square distribution with $n - 1$ degrees of freedom that cuts off an area of $\alpha/2$ to its right and $\chi^2_{1-\alpha/2}$ is the value of the distribution that cuts off an area of $\alpha/2$ to its left (equivalently, an area of $1 - \alpha/2$ to its right)

We now demonstrate the use of equation 6–12 with an example.

EXAMPLE 6-5

In an automated process, a machine fills cans of coffee. If the average amount filled is different from what it should be, the machine may be adjusted to correct the mean. If the *variance* of the filling process is too high, however, the machine is out of control and needs to be repaired. Therefore, from time to time regular checks of the variance of the filling process are made. This is done by randomly sampling filled cans, measuring their amounts, and computing the sample variance. A random sample of 30 cans gives an estimate $s^2 = 18{,}540$. Give a 95% confidence interval for the population variance σ^2.

SOLUTION

Figure 6–8 shows the appropriate chi-square distribution with $n - 1 = 29$ degrees of freedom. From Table 6–2 we get, for df $= 29$, $\chi^2_{0.025} = 45.7$ and $\chi^2_{0.975} = 16.0$. Using these values, we compute the confidence interval as follows:

$$\left[\frac{29(18{,}540)}{45.7}, \frac{29(18{,}540)}{16.0} \right] = [11{,}765, 33{,}604]$$

We can be 95% sure that the population variance is between 11,765 and 33,604.

PROBLEMS

In the following problems, assume normal populations.

6–61. The service time in queues should not have a large variance; otherwise, the queue tends to build up. A bank regularly checks service time by its tellers to determine its variance. A random sample of 22 service times (in minutes) gives $s^2 = 8$. Give a 95% confidence interval for the variance of service time at the bank.

6–62. A sensitive measuring device should not have a large variance in the errors of measurements it makes. A random sample of 41 measurement errors gives $s^2 = 102$. Give a 99% confidence interval for the variance of measurement errors.

6–63. A random sample of 60 accounts gives a sample variance of 1,228. Give a 95% confidence interval for the variance of all accounts.

6–64. In problem 6–21, give a 99% confidence interval for the variance of the number of miles that may be driven on a tire.

6–65. In problem 6–25, give a 95% confidence interval for the variance of the population of transaction amounts.

6–66.   In problem 6–26, give a 95% confidence interval for the variance of the caloric content of all 3 oz. cuts of top loin steak. (Hint: Use a normal approximation to the chi-square distribution.)

6–67.   In problem 6–27, give a 95% confidence interval for the variance of the transit time for all goods.

6-7   Sample-Size Determination

One of the most common questions a statistician is asked before any actual sampling takes place is: "How large should my sample be?" From a *statistical* point of view, the best answer to this question is: "Get as large a sample as you can afford. If possible, 'sample' the entire population." If you need to know the mean or proportion of a population, and you can sample the entire population (i.e., carry out a census), you will have all the information and will know the parameter exactly. Clearly, this is better than any estimate. This, however, is unrealistic in most situations due to economic constraints, time constraints, and other limitations. "Get as large a sample as you can afford" is the best answer if we ignore all costs, because the larger the sample, the smaller the standard error of our statistic. The smaller the standard error, the less uncertainty with which we have to contend. This is demonstrated in Figure 6–9.

When the sampling budget is limited, the question often is how to find the *minimum* sample size that will satisfy some precision requirements. In such cases, you should explain to the designer of the study that he or she must first give you answers to the following three questions.

1. How close do you want your sample estimate to be to the unknown parameter? The answer to this question is denoted by B (for "bound").
2. What do you want the confidence level to be so that the distance between the estimate and the parameter is less than or equal to B?
3. The last, and often misunderstood, question that must be answered is: What is your estimate of the variance (or standard deviation) of the population in question?

Only after you have answers to all three questions can you give an answer as to the minimum required sample size. Often the statistician is told: "How can I give you an estimate of the variance? I don't know. You are the statistician." In such cases, try to

FIGURE 6-8   **Values and Tail Areas of a Chi-Square Distribution with 29 Degrees of Freedom**

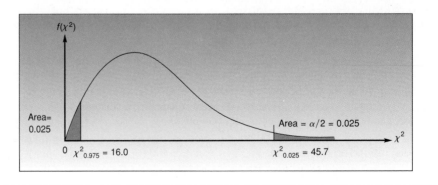

get from your client some idea about the variation in the population. If the population is approximately normal and you can get 95% bounds on the values in the *population*, *divide the difference between the upper and lower bounds by* 4; this will give you a rough guess of σ. Or you may take a small, inexpensive *pilot* survey and estimate σ by the sample standard deviation. Once you have obtained the three required pieces of information, all you need to do is substitute the answers into the appropriate formula that follows.

FIGURE 6-9
Standard Error of a Statistic as a Function of Sample Size

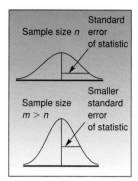

Minimum required sample size in estimating the population mean, μ:

$$n = \frac{z_{\alpha/2}^2 \sigma^2}{B^2} \qquad (6\text{-}13)$$

Minimum required sample size in estimating the population proportion, p:

$$n = \frac{z_{\alpha/2}^2 pq}{B^2} \qquad (6\text{-}14)$$

Equations 6–13 and 6–14 are derived from the formulas for the corresponding confidence intervals for these population parameters based on the normal distribution. In the case of the population mean, B is the half-width of a $(1 - \alpha)100\%$ confidence interval for μ, and therefore

$$B = z_{\alpha/2} \frac{\sigma}{\sqrt{n}} \qquad (6\text{-}15)$$

Equation 6–13 is the solution of equation 6–15 for the value of n. Note that B is the margin of error. We are solving for the minimum sample size for a given margin of error.

Equation 6–14, for the minimum required sample size in estimating the population proportion, is derived in a similar way. Note that the term pq in equation 6–14 acts as the population variance in equation 6–13. In order to use equation 6–14, we need a guess of p, the unknown population proportion. Any prior estimate of the parameter will do. When none is available, we may take a pilot sample, or—in the absence of any information—we use the value $p = 0.5$. This value maximizes pq and thus ensures us a minimum required sample size that will work for any value of p.

A marketing research firm wants to conduct a survey to estimate the average amount spent on entertainment by each person visiting a popular resort. The people who plan the survey would like to be able to determine the average amount spent by all people visiting the resort to within $120, with 95% confidence. From past operation of the resort, an estimate of the population standard deviation is $\sigma = \$400$. What is the minimum required sample size?

EXAMPLE 6-6

SOLUTION

Using equation 6–13, the minimum required sample size is

$$n = \frac{z_{\alpha/2}^2 \sigma^2}{B^2}$$

We know that $B = 120$, and σ^2 is estimated at $400^2 = 160{,}000$. Since we want a 95% confidence, $z_{\alpha/2} = 1.96$. Using the equation, we get

$$n = \frac{(1.96)^2 160{,}000}{120^2} = 42.684$$

Therefore, the minimum required sample size is 43 people (we cannot sample 42.684 people, so we go to the next higher integer).

EXAMPLE 6-7

The manufacturers of a sports car want to estimate the proportion of people in a given income bracket who are interested in the model. The company wants to know the population proportion, p, to within 0.10 with 99% confidence. Current company records indicate that the proportion p may be around 0.25. What is the minimum required sample size for this survey?

SOLUTION

Using equation 6–14, we get

$$n = \frac{z_{\alpha/2}^2 pq}{B^2} = \frac{(2.576)^2 (0.25)(0.75)}{0.10^2} = 124.42$$

The company should, therefore, obtain a random sample of at least 125 people. Note that a different guess of p would have resulted in a different sample size.

PROBLEMS

6–68. *The Economist* studied busines practices in Korea.[14] Its analysts wanted to estimate the proportion of Korean firms with high foreign investment to within 5% with 95% confidence. A guess is that the percentage of such firms is about 8%. What is the minimum size of a random sample of firms to investigate?

6–69. What is the required sample size for determining the proportion of defective items in a production process if the proportion is to be known to within 0.05 with 90% confidence? No guess as to the value of the population proportion is available.

6–70. How many test runs of an automobile are required for determining its average mpg rating on the highway to within 2 mpg with 95% confidence, if a guess is that the variance of the population of mpg is about 100?

6–71. A company that conducts surveys of current jobs for executives wants to estimate the average salary of an executive at a given level to within $2,000 with 95% confidence. From previous surveys it is known that the variance of executive salaries is about 40,000,000. What is the minimum required sample size?

---

[14] "The Frankenstein Economy," *The Economist*, June 3, 1995, p. 10.

6–72. Find the minimum required sample size for estimating the average return on investments of a certain kind to within 0.5% per year with 95% confidence. The standard deviation of returns is believed to be 2% per year.

6–73. A company believes its market share is about 14%. Find the minimum required sample size for estimating the actual market share to within 5% with 90% confidence.

6–74. Find the minimum required sample size for estimating the average number of designer shirts sold per day to within 10 units with 90% confidence if the standard deviation of the number of shirts sold per day is about 50.

6–75. Find the minimum required sample size of accounts if the proportion of accounts in error is to be estimated to within 0.02 with 95% confidence. A rough guess of the proportion of accounts in error is 0.10.

6-8 One-Sided Confidence Intervals[15]

In closing this chapter, we want to note that it is also possible to construct confidence intervals with only one side. When are such confidence intervals useful? We may be interested in finding an *upper bound* only, or a *lower bound* only, for a population parameter with a given level of confidence. For example, suppose we are interested in finding a bound such that we are 95% confident that the population mean is no greater than that bound. In such a case, we construct a right-hand confidence interval for the population mean. The left-hand bound is, then, defined as $-\infty$. Similarly, we may be interested in finding a bound such that we are 95% sure that the population mean is no smaller than the given bound. This is a left-hand confidence interval, and the right-hand bound of the interval is, then, defined as $+\infty$. Equations $6-16$ and $6-17$ give a right-hand and a left-hand confidence interval for μ, respectively.

A right-hand $(1 - \alpha)100\%$ confidence interval for μ:

$$\left[-\infty, \bar{x} + z_\alpha \frac{s}{\sqrt{n}} \right]$$

(6–16)

A left-hand $(1 - \alpha)100\%$ confidence interval for μ:

$$\left[\bar{x} - z_\alpha \frac{s}{\sqrt{n}}, +\infty \right]$$

(6–17)

Note that α replaces $\alpha/2$ because we have only *one* side where an error of probability α may take place in the estimation. This is illustrated in Figure $6-10$.

We now demonstrate the use of one-sided confidence intervals for the population mean with a right-hand interval. Formulas similar to equations $6-16$ and $6-17$ for the population proportion also apply.

A company wants to estimate a 95% upper bound for average daily production. A random sample of 36 days gives $\bar{x} = 1{,}150$ units and $s = 312$ units.

EXAMPLE 6-8

---

[15] This is an optional section.

FIGURE 6–10   Using One Tail of a Distribution Leads to a One-Sided Confidence Interval

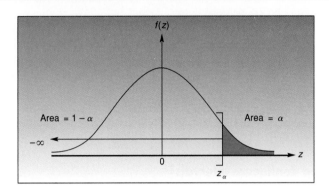

SOLUTION

Using equation 6–16, we get the following right-hand confidence interval.

$$\left[-\infty, \bar{x} + z_\alpha \frac{s}{\sqrt{n}}\right] = \left[-\infty, 1{,}150 + 1.645 \frac{312}{\sqrt{36}}\right]$$
$$= [-\infty, 1235.54]$$

Note that we used the z value 1.645 rather than 1.96. This is because 1.645 cuts off an area of 0.05 to its *right*, which is what we need here (1.96 and -1.96 would cut off a *combined* area of 0.05 on both sides).

PROBLEMS

6–76.   Give a 90% left-hand confidence interval for the population mean if $\bar{x} = 250$, $s = 28$, and $n = 100$.

6–77.   Give a 95% upper bound for the proportion of defective items produced by a machine if 15 items are found to be defective in a random sample of 100 items.

6–78.   Give a 99% lower bound for the average number of miles that can be driven on a tire of a given make if a random sample of 100 tires gives $\bar{x} = 42{,}000$ miles and $s = 10{,}000$ miles.

6–79.   Give a 99% lower bound for the proportion of salespeople in a given industry who make commissions of over \$10,000 a year if a random sample of 200 of these salespeople shows that 32 earn commissions of over \$10,000 a year.

6–80.   In problem 6–18, give a 95% upper bound for the average length of a long-distance phone call during weekends.

6–81.   In problem 6–19, give a 90% lower bound for the average amount of a claim.

6–82.   In problem 6–30, give a 99% lower bound for the average amount of bonus dollars spent per cardholder.

6–83.   In problem 6–39, give a 90% upper bound for the proportion of traveling business-people who may be interested in the product.

6-9   Using the Computer

In this chapter, we will again use the computer package MINITAB. The command for the construction of confidence intervals for the population mean is ZINTERVAL (followed by 90, for 90% confidence, for example, and then the column number) or

FIGURE 6-11   MINITAB-Produced Confidence Interval for Average Stock Price

```
MTB> SET C1
DATA> 17.125
DATA> 17
DATA> 17.375
DATA> 17.25
DATA> 16.625
DATA> 16.875
DATA> 17
DATA> 17
DATA> 17.25
DATA> 18
DATA> 18.125
DATA> 17.5
DATA> 17.375
DATA> 17.5
DATA> 17.25
DATA> END
MTB> TINTERVAL C1

            N    MEAN    STDEV  SE MEAN    95.0 PERCENT C.I.
C1         15   17.283   0.397   0.102   ( 17.064,  17.503)
```

FIGURE 6-12   MINITAB-Produced Confidence Interval for Average Stock Price Using the ZINTERVAL Command and an Assumed Known σ

```
MTB > ZINTERVAL 0.397 C1
THE ASSUMED SIGMA = 0.397

         N    MEAN    STDEV   SE MEAN    95.0 PERCENT C.I.
C1      15   17.283   0.397    0.103   ( 17.082, 17.485)
```

TINTERVAL (confidence, column), depending on whether the interval is to be based on the normal or the t distribution, respectively. ZINTERVAL assumes a known population standard deviation. You may specify the confidence level either as a percent or as a decimal value. In the case of ZINTERVAL, you may specify the population standard deviation after the confidence level. The default confidence level is 95%. Figure 6–11 shows a data set entered into the computer, the file of necessary commands for a 95% confidence interval for μ, and the resulting output using the TINTERVAL command. The data are a random sample of 15 daily price quotations of a certain stock. Figure 6–12 shows the output, using the same data, for the ZINTERVAL command inputting the sample standard deviation of 0.397 as a substitute for σ.

MINITAB can also be used to find cumulative probabilities to given values (CDF command) and to find values for a given cumulative probability (INVCDF command), for the t distribution and for the chi-square distribution. The distribution is specified in the subcommand along with the number of degrees of freedom. This is demonstrated in Figure 6–13. Compare the probabilities and values computed with table values of the t and chi-square distributions.

FIGURE 6-13   Using MINITAB for *t* Distribution and Chi-Square Distribution Probabilities

```
MTB > CDF 2.00;
SUBC> T df=24.
      2.0000    0.9715

MTB > INVCDF 0.95;
SUBC> T df=24.
      0.9500    1.7109

MTB > CDF 35;
SUBC> CHISQUARE 25.
     35.0000    0.9118

MTB > INVCDF 0.99;
SUBC> CHISQUARE 20.
      0.9900   37.5662
```

6-10   Summary and Review of Terms

In this chapter, we learned how to construct **confidence intervals** for population parameters. We saw how confidence intervals depend on the sampling distributions of the statistics used as estimators. We also encountered two new sampling distributions: the *t* **distribution,** used in estimating the population mean when the population standard deviation is unknown, and the **chi-square distribution,** used in estimating the population variance. The use of either distribution assumes a normal population. We saw how the new distributions, as well as the normal distribution, allow us to construct confidence intervals for population parameters. We saw how to determine the minimum required sample size for estimation. Finally, we saw how one may construct one-sided confidence intervals for population parameters.

ADDITIONAL PROBLEMS

6–84.   The following data are scores clients gave their banks for handling foreign exchange transactions.[16]

Citibank	72	UBS	27
Chemical	66	Deutche	43
NatWest	60	Indosuez	11
Chase	58	Bank of Tokyo	29
Dresdner	62	Barklays	30
BHF	57	AmEx	23
HSBC	85	WestPac	15
Sumitomo	17	Bank of America	43

[16] Reprinted by permission from "Treasurers Put Their Views on Banks," *Euromoney,* May, 1995, pp. 65–84.

Use these data to construct a 90% confidence interval for the average rating clients give their bank for foreign exchange services in the entire, large population from which these banks were randomly chosen.

6–85. An investment analyst needs to estimate the average investment amount in mutual fund portfolios by institutional investors. A random sample of 15 institutional investors gives a sample mean of $11.32 million and a sample standard deviation of $4.4 million. Give a 95% confidence interval for the mean investment by all institutional investors in this type of portfolio.

6–86. An insurance company needs to estimate the average amount claimed by 1,455 policyholders over one year. A random sample of 300 policyholders reveals that the sample mean claim is $739.98 and the sample standard deviation is $312.70. Give a 90% confidence interval for the average amount claimed by the 1,455 policyholders.

6–87. Radio Shack® markets many of its products by direct-mail advertising of reduced-price items. Before a large mailing, the company wants to estimate the proportion of people who will respond positively to an advertisement for a certain stereo component. The company needs to know the minimum sample size required for estimating the population proportion to within 0.10 with 95% confidence. From previous mailings, Radio Shack knows that the population proportion is around 0.45. Find the minimum required sample size.

6–88. In problem 6–87, suppose that a test mailing of 1,000 brochures resulted in 338 sales of the stereo component. Give a 95% confidence interval for the population proportion of sales that would result from a marketwide mailing.

6–89. Boeing, Inc., needs to estimate the variance of the number of possible failure-free landings on a brand of airplane tires being considered for use on the 767 jet made by Boeing. A random testing of 100 tires gives $s^2 = 870,432.76$. Give a 99% confidence interval for the variance of the number of landings before failure for all tires of this brand.

6–90. A new computer software package by Nestor, Inc., allows users to simulate pattern recognition on desktop computers. Fifteen trial runs of the new package are carried out. The time, in seconds, required to recognize a pattern in each run is 12, 13, 10, 17, 14, 16, 9, 15, 12, 18, 11, 14, 10, 9, 19. Give a 95% confidence interval for the average time required for performing this task.

6–91. An ice cream manufacturer wants to estimate the proportion of people who like the taste of emulsified protein in ice cream. A random sample of 200 people shows that 54 of them like the taste. Give a 99% confidence interval for the proportion of people who like the taste of emulsified protein in ice cream.

6–92. A battery manufacturer knows that the standard deviation of the life, in hours, of a certain type of battery is around 4.5. The manufacturer wants to estimate the average life of all batteries of this kind to within one hour with 95% confidence. What is the minimum required sample size?

6–93. In problem 6–90, give a 95% confidence interval for the variance of the simulation time.

6–94. In problem 6–91, give a 95% lower bound on the proportion of people who like the taste of emulsified protein.

6–95. A ski resort operator wants to estimate the average length of stay of skiers at the resort. A random sample of 67 skiers gives a sample mean stay of 2.5 days and a sample standard deviation of 1.1 days. Give a 90% confidence interval for the average length of stay of all skiers at this resort.

6–96. In problem 6–95, give a 90% confidence interval for the variance of length of stay.

6–97. In a random sample of 2,000 switches used in video display apparatus, 5 switches are found to be defective. Give a 99% confidence interval for the proportion of defective switches in the entire (large) population. How do you interpret this particular confidence interval?

6–98.   In problem 6–97, suppose the entire population of switches consists of a shipment of 4,520. Redo the problem to account for this information.

6–99.   A random sample of 128 condominiums in Minneapolis reveals a sample mean price of $356,080 and a sample standard deviation of $79,100. Give a 98% confidence interval for the average price of a condominium in Minneapolis.

6–100.   An express delivery service needs to estimate the average weight of a package sent overnight. A random sample of 20 packages is selected. The weights, in pounds, are as follows: 0.4, 1.2, 3.7, 1.1, 2.3, 5.0, 0.2, 4.1, 0.8, 6.8, 9.8, 7.5, 3.5, 4.7, 3.3, 2.8, 1.0, 5.9, 4.6, 0.1. Give a 95% confidence interval for the average weight of all packages sent overnight.

6–101.   In problem 6–100, give a 95% confidence interval for the variance of the weights of all packages sent overnight.

6–102.   In problem 6–99, assume that the 128 condominiums were selected from a population of 500 condominiums in a certain area of the city. How would you correct your confidence interval in that problem to account for this fact?

6–103.   What assumption must be made about the population if we are to use either the t distribution or the chi-square distribution? Make this assumption in all problems involving either distribution.

6–104.   A recent study reveals that the average after-tax income of an entry-level American executive is $24,500. Assuming that the result is based on a random sample of 100 executives and that the sample standard deviation is $2,500, give a 99% confidence interval for the average after-tax income of all American entry-level executives. Write your answer in the form of a memo.

6–105.   Use the Federal Reserve data set (Appendix D). Select a random sample, and construct a 95% confidence interval for the federal funds rate. Experiment with various sample sizes.

6–106.   Interpret the following computer output.

```
MTB > TINTERVAL 90 C1
            N     MEAN    STDEV    SE MEAN      90.0 PERCENT C.I.
C1         48   53.604    3.120     0.450   (   52.848,   54.360)
```

Compare the results with the ones you would get if you used the normal distribution instead of the t distribution.

6–107.   Recall that the median of a population is the point such that half the population values lie below it and half the population values lie above it.[17] Suppose that a random sample of two elements is selected from a population. We want to construct a confidence interval for the population *median* (if we assume the population distribution is symmetric, however, this is also a confidence interval for the population mean). We define the confidence interval as [the smaller of the two sample values, the larger of the two sample values]. What is the confidence level of such a confidence interval?

6–108.   Generalize the procedure of problem 6–107 as follows. We select a random sample of size n and define the confidence interval for the population median as [lowest sample value, highest sample value]. What is the confidence level of such an interval? What is one big limitation of this procedure?

---

[17] This problem and the next one are harder than the rest but instructive.

Case 6 THE ECONOMIST'S PORTFOLIO POLL

"Financial markets ended the first quarter of 1995 much chirpier than at the end of 1994, despite Mexico's troubles. Measured in dollars, the Morgan Stanley Capital International index of world stockmarkets rose 4.2% in the first three months of 1995, while Salomon Brothers' world government-bond index increased by almost 11%. Admittedly, this impressive performance was largely due to the plummeting dollar.

"According to our quarterly poll of fund managers, big institutional investors are still treading cautiously. They have, on average, trimmed their holdings of both equities (from an average of 50.8% of their portfolios to 49.6%) and bonds (from an average of 41.9% to 40.6%), and turned instead to a favourite refuge in uncertain times: cash, which now accounts, on average, for 9.8% of their ideal portfolios. (Both Lehman Brothers, an American investment bank, and Switzerland's Bank Julius Baer have also plumped for gold, another traditional safe haven, which now accounts for 5% and 3% of their assets respectively, but is counted as cash for the purposes of our table.)

"Of the big equity markets, Europe's are the only ones to be truly in vogue: portfolio managers have allocated an average of about 30% of their portfolios to them, compared with a neutral weighting of 28%. Fund managers are still uncomfortable about American and Japanese shares: holdings of both are, on average, below the neutral weighting suggested by the Morgan Stanley index (which shows each country's stockmarket capitalisation as a proportion of the global total).

"Our sample is, however, less contrarian than this might suggest: since the beginning of the year, managers have increased their exposure to American equities, which have performed well, and reduced their exposure to Japanese shares, which have performed horribly."

Assume *The Economist*'s sample of 10 financial institutions is a random one, selected from a large population of such institutions. Construct a 95% confidence interval for the population mean percentage of equity holdings.

The Perfect Portfolio?

- **Contributors:**

A	Merrill Lynch	F	Robeco Institutional Asset Management
B	Lehman Brothers	G	Bank Julius Baer (Zurich)
C	Nikko Securities	H	UBS International Investment
D	Daiwa Europe	I	Commerz International Capital Management
E	Crédit Agricole	J	Credit Suisse Asset Management

- **Holding by instrument, %**

	A	B	C	D	E	F	G	H	I	J
Equities	55	50	60	60	65	60	40	38	46	25
Bonds	35	30	35	35	35	40	45	56	47	48
Cash	10	20	5	5	0	0	15	6	7	27

From *The Economist*, April 22, 1995, p. 77.

7

HYPOTHESIS TESTING

7-1 INTRODUCTION

O n June 18, 1964, a woman was robbed while walking home along an alley in San Pedro, California. Some time later, police arrested Janet Collins and charged her with the robbery. The interesting thing about this case of petty crime is that the prosecution had *no* direct evidence against the defendant. Janet Collins was convicted of robbery on purely statistical grounds.

The case, *People* v. *Collins,* drew much attention because of its use of probability—or, rather, what was perceived as a probability—in determining guilt. An instructor of mathematics at a local college was brought in by the prosecution and testified as an expert witness in the trial. The instructor "calculated the probability" that the defendant was a person *other* than the one who committed the crime as 1 in 12,000,000. This led the jury to convict the defendant.

The Supreme Court of California later reversed the "guilty" verdict against Janet Collins when it was shown that the method of calculating the probability was incorrect. The mathematics instructor had made some very serious errors.[1]

Despite the erroneous procedure used in deriving the probability, and the justified reversal of the conviction by the Supreme Court of California, the *Collins* case serves as an excellent analogy for statistical hypothesis testing. Under the American legal system, the accused is assumed innocent until proven guilty "beyond a reasonable doubt." We will call this the *null hypothesis*—the hypothesis that the accused is *innocent*. We will hold the null hypothesis as true until a time when we can prove, beyond a reasonable doubt, that it is false and that the *alternative hypothesis*—the hypothesis that the accused is guilty—is true. We want to have a small probability (preferably *zero*) of convicting an innocent person, that is, of rejecting a null hypothesis when the null hypothesis is actually true.

In the *Collins* case, the prosecution claimed that the accused was guilty since, otherwise, an event with a very small probability had just been observed. The argument was that if Collins were *not* guilty, then another woman fitting her exact characteristics had committed the crime. According to the prosecution, the probability of this event was 1/12,000,000, and since the probability was so small, Collins was very likely the person who committed the robbery.

Continued

---

[1] The instructor *multiplied* the probabilities of the separate events comprising the reported description of the robber: the event that a woman has blond hair, the event that she drives a yellow car, the event that she is seen with a black man, the event that the man has a beard. Recall that the probability of the intersection of several events is equal to the product of the probabilities of the separate events *only* if the events are independent. In this case, there was no reason to believe that the events were independent. There were also some questions about how the separate "probabilities" were actually derived since they were presented by the instructor with no apparent justification. See W. Fairley and F. Mosteller, "A Conversation about Collins," *University of Chicago Law Review* 41, no. 2 (Winter 1974), pp. 242–53.

In statistical hypothesis testing, our null hypothesis will state something about one or more population parameters. For example, the null hypothesis may be that the population mean is equal to some number. The alternative hypothesis will be that the population mean is different from the number stated in the null hypothesis. We will assume that the null hypothesis is true and that the population mean is as stated. Then we will look at some evidence derived from a random sample. If our obtained sample mean should happen to fall so far away from the population mean as to constitute an event with a small presampling probability, then we will reject the null hypothesis in favor of the alternative hypothesis.

7–2   Statistical Hypothesis Testing

We will now define the concepts and sketch the framework of statistical tests of hypotheses. First, we define the null and alternative hypotheses.

> A **null hypothesis,** denoted by H_0, is an assertion about one or more population parameters. This is the assertion we hold as true until we have sufficient statistical evidence to conclude otherwise.

> The **alternative hypothesis,** denoted by H_1, is the assertion of all situations *not* covered by the null hypothesis.[2]

Together, the null and the alternative hypotheses constitute a set of hypotheses that covers all possible values of the parameter or parameters in question. An example of such a pair of hypotheses is the following.

$$H_0: \mu = 100$$
$$H_1: \mu \neq 100 \tag{7–1}$$

The null hypothesis in equation 7–1 is the assertion that the population mean is equal to 100. The alternative hypothesis is the assertion that the population mean is not equal to 100. Only one of the two competing hypotheses may be true, and one of them must be true: either the population mean is equal to 100, or it is equal to any of the infinitely many numbers other than 100.

Often, the null hypothesis represents a status quo situation or an existing belief. We wish to *test* the null hypothesis and see whether we can reject it in favor of the alternative hypothesis. The hypothesis test is carried out using information obtained by random sampling. In a test of the value of the population mean, such as the test in equation 7–1, the *test statistic* we employ is the sample mean, $\bar{X}$.

> A **test statistic** is a sample statistic computed from the data. The value of the test statistic is used in determining whether or not we may reject the null hypothesis.

We decide whether or not to reject the null hypothesis by following a rule called the *decision rule*.

> The **decision rule** of a statistical hypothesis test is a rule that specifies the conditions under which the null hypothesis may be rejected.

---

[2] Some authors use the notation H_a or H_A for the alternative hypothesis.

An example of a decision rule for the hypothesis test in equation 7–1 is: "Reject the null hypothesis if and only if $\overline{X}$ happens to be either greater than or equal to 105 or less than or equal to 95." We will now see how to determine a decision rule for a statistical hypothesis test.

Let us return to our courtroom analogy. The accused is either innocent (H_0 is true) or guilty (H_1 is true). The jury does not know the real *state of nature* (the actual innocence or guilt of the defendant). The jury must, however, make a *decision* as to whether or not they believe she is guilty (*reject* H_0) or innocent (*not reject* H_0).

Let us consider the consequences of the jury's decision. If the jury rejects the null hypothesis and declares the defendant guilty when in reality she is guilty (the state of nature is H_1), then the jury has made a correct decision. If, on the other hand, the defendant is actually innocent (the state of nature is H_0), then the jury has made an *error* and convicted an innocent person. We will call this error a **type I error.** Now consider the other possibility. Suppose the jury decides not to reject the null hypothesis. If the defendant is innocent, a correct decision has been made. If, on the other hand, she is guilty, then the jury has failed to convict a guilty person. We will call the error of failing to reject a false null hypothesis a **type II error.** This is shown in Table 7–1.

A moment's reflection will reveal that—within the American legal system—a type I error is considered more serious. "Innocent until proven guilty" means that we want to guard against the possibility of convicting an innocent person—*more so* than guarding against the other type of error, that of letting a guilty person go free. What are the probabilities of committing the two types of errors?

The probability of committing a type I error is denoted by α.

The probability of committing a type II error is denoted by β.

While we would like both error probabilities, α and β, to be *small,* the preceding discussion implies that it is more important for us to control the level of α. The probability of committing a type I error should be set to a predetermined small number. In criminal court cases, we would like α to be a very small number indeed—again, preferably zero. Let us now look at the statistical analogy.

We do not know the value of the population mean. If we decide to reject the null hypothesis in equation 7–1 when in actuality the population mean is 100, then we are committing a type I error. If we fail to reject the null hypothesis when in reality the population mean is different from 100, then we are committing a type II error. In either of the remaining two possibilities (rejecting the null hypothesis when the population mean is not 100, or *not* rejecting the null hypothesis when the population mean

TABLE 7–1   The State of Nature, the Decision, and the Two Possible Errors

		State of Nature	
		H_0	H_1
Decision	H_0	Correct decision	Type II error
	H_1	Type I error	Correct decision

is equal to 100), we are making a correct decision. Since, as stated earlier, the null hypothesis is usually a statement of an existing belief, we would like to control α, the probability of committing a type I error. Of course, we also hope not to commit a type II error, that is, we hope to reject H_0 when H_0 is false. But if we can control only one of the two error probabilities, then it is α, the probability of a type I error, that should be controlled.[3] In common statistical applications, α is usually set to less stringent standards than one would expect in the legal analogy ("beyond a reasonable doubt"). For us, type I error probabilities will often be $\alpha = 0.05$ or $\alpha = 0.01$.

Let us write α and β using the probability notation of Chapter 2. Both are *conditional probabilities:* α is the probability that, when we sample and obtain a value of the test statistic, we will end up rejecting the null hypothesis when the null hypothesis is actually true; similarly, β is the probability that we will end up not rejecting the null hypothesis when the null hypothesis is actually false. We thus have the following:

$$\alpha = P(\text{Reject } H_0 \mid H_0 \text{ is true}) \qquad (7-2)$$
$$\beta = P(\text{Not reject } H_0 \mid H_0 \text{ is false}) \qquad (7-3)$$

A word of explanation is in order here. Usually, we will be presented with a null hypothesis, a statistical assertion, which we will try to *reject*. Before carrying out the actual test, we know the probability that we will make a type I error. This probability, α, is preset to a small number, say 0.05. Knowing that we have a small probability of committing a type I error, that is, of rejecting a null hypothesis when it should not be rejected, makes our rejection of a null hypothesis a *strong conclusion*. Usually, the same cannot be said about *not rejecting* the null hypothesis. This is so because, unlike α, the probability β of failing to reject a null hypothesis when the null hypothesis *should* be rejected is usually not preset to a known small number. Thus, failing to reject the null hypothesis is usually a *weak conclusion* because we do not know the probability that we will fail to reject a null hypothesis when the null hypothesis should be rejected. When we reject the null hypothesis, we feel fairly confident that the hypothesis should indeed be rejected. When we fail to reject (i.e., we accept) the null hypothesis, we feel that *we did not have enough evidence to reject the hypothesis.* Either the null hypothesis is indeed true, or more evidence is needed for it to be rejected. For this reason, we prefer to use the terms:

reject   versus   *fail to reject* (or *do not reject*)

rather than the word *accept* when referring to the null hypothesis.

In statistical hypothesis testing, how do we decide whether or not to reject the null hypothesis? It turns out that our understanding of confidence intervals, developed in the last chapter, will allow us to conduct hypothesis tests. This is demonstrated in Example 7–1.

---

[3] As we will see, α is exactly the same error probability we used in Chapter 6 in the construction of confidence intervals.

EXAMPLE 7-1

A company that delivers packages within a large metropolitan area claims that it takes an average of 28 minutes for a package to be delivered from your door to the destination. Suppose that you want to carry out a hypothesis test of this claim.

Consistent with our desire to assume "innocent until proven guilty," we set the null and alternative hypotheses as follows:

$$H_0: \mu = 28$$
$$H_1: \mu \neq 28$$

To conduct the test, we select a random sample of $n = 100$ deliveries. We record the delivery times and compute the sample mean $\bar{x} = 31.5$ minutes and sample standard deviation $s = 5$. We will construct a 95% confidence interval for the mean of *all* delivery times of packages in the area (the population mean, μ). Since the sample is large, we can use the normal distribution. We compute the following confidence interval for μ.

$$\bar{x} \pm z_{\alpha/2}\frac{s}{\sqrt{n}} = 31.5 \pm 1.96\frac{5}{\sqrt{100}} = 31.5 \pm 0.98 = [30.52, 32.48]$$

Consistent with our interpretation of the meaning of confidence intervals, we can be 95% sure that the average time it takes a package to be delivered across town is anywhere from 30.52 to 32.48 minutes.

Let's take this one step further. If we are 95% confident that it takes, on average, anywhere from 30.52 to 32.48 minutes for a package to be delivered, then we are 95% confident that μ does not lie outside this range of values. Since μ under the null hypothesis is 28, a value outside the confidence interval, we may *reject* the null hypothesis. (If the null hypothesis is actually true, then—before the sampling takes place—there is only a 0.05 probability that the constructed interval would not include the population mean.) If we reject the null hypothesis whenever the population mean stated in the null hypothesis lies outside the 95% confidence interval for μ, then we have at most a 0.05 probability of committing a type I error. We are thus carrying out our test at the $\alpha = 0.05$ *level of significance.* Here we reject the null hypothesis in favor of the alternative hypothesis and conclude that we believe the average delivery time is *not* 28 minutes. Furthermore, since our confidence interval lies entirely *above* the hypothesized value of the population mean (*hypothesized* will mean "stated in the null hypothesis"), we may further conclude that, based on the information in our random sample, we believe that the average time it takes a package to be delivered in the metropolitan area is more than 28 minutes.

What have we learned from this example? We have learned that we may use a confidence interval for a population parameter as our decision rule for a statistical hypothesis test. If we use a confidence interval based on a $(1 - \alpha)$ probability (obtained through the sampling distribution of our statistic), then our probability of a type I error—rejecting a true null hypothesis—is at most α. This is demonstrated in Figure 7–1.

A confidence interval is useful when we are interested in giving a *range* of possible values that we believe the unknown parameter is likely to have. However, if we are only interested in testing a particular hypothesis about the value of a population

FIGURE 7–1   Confidence Interval for μ and the Null-Hypothesized Population Mean, μ_0, in Example 7–1

parameter, we can carry out the test in an easier way by using a test statistic calculated from our data.

Recall that in Chapter 6 we centered the sampling distribution of our statistic $\overline{X}$ over its obtained value because the value of the parameter μ was unknown to us. We used the sampling distribution to establish bounds on either side of the obtained $\overline{x}$ such that we may be, say, 95% sure that the unknown parameter μ lies within these bounds.

Let us now use the same idea in testing hypotheses about the population mean, μ. If someone asserts that the population mean is equal to 28, then let us *center* our sampling distribution of $\overline{X}$ over this hypothesized value of μ. We denote the null-hypothesized value of μ by μ_0. If the null hypothesis is correct, then $\mu_0 = 28$ *is* the mean of the sampling distribution of $\overline{X}$, and the distribution should be centered over that value. If μ_0 is indeed the population mean, then—when we sample from the population and obtain a value of the sample mean—this value, $\overline{x}$, should not fall too far away from μ_0. In fact, when H_0 is true, $\overline{X}$ will have a 0.95 probability (assuming a large sample) of falling within the bounds:

$$\mu_0 \pm 1.96 \frac{s}{\sqrt{n}} \qquad (7\text{–}4)$$

Thus, if we want to take only a 0.05 chance of making a type I error when we reject the null hypothesis, then we should only reject the null hypothesis if the sample mean $\overline{X}$ should fall outside the bounds given in equation 7–4. The range of values in equation 7–4 is called the nonrejection (or acceptance) *region* of the test, and the values outside this range are the *rejection region* of the test.

Our test statistic is $\overline{X}$. The obtained value of the test statistic, $\overline{x}$, is compared with the range of values in equation 7–4. If the test statistic falls outside the bounds, that is, in the rejection region, then we reject the null hypothesis at the $\alpha = 0.05$ level of significance. If $\overline{x}$ falls within the bounds, that is, in the nonrejection range, we do not reject the null hypothesis. In Example 7–1, the rejection region consists of all values outside the bounds: $\mu_0 \pm 1.96s/\sqrt{n} = 28 \pm 1.96(5/\sqrt{100}) = [27.02, \ 28.98]$. Since $\overline{x} = 31.5$, a value *outside* this range, we reject the null hypothesis at the $\alpha = 0.05$ level of significance.

It should be clear from these arguments that when the level of significance is α, *rejection* of the null hypothesis occurs if and only if a confidence interval with confidence coefficient $(1 - \alpha)$ based on the same sample results does *not* include the hypothesized value of the parameter. Similarly, nonrejection of the null hypothesis at the significance level α occurs if and only if a confidence interval with confidence

FIGURE 7-2   Equivalence of a 95% Confidence Interval for μ and a Hypothesis Test about μ at the 0.05 Level of Significance

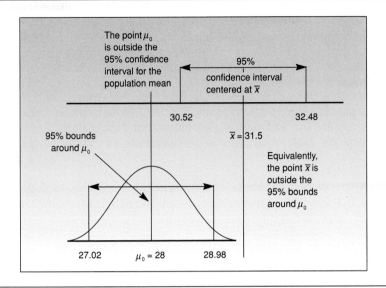

FIGURE 7-3   Rejection and Nonrejection Regions and the Actual Value of the Test Statistic, Falling in the Rejection Region [Example 7-1]

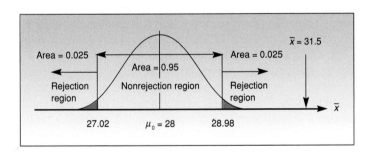

coefficient $(1 - \alpha)$ does contain the hypothesized value. This equivalence of hypothesis tests and confidence intervals is demonstrated in Figure 7–2.

Figure 7–3 shows the rejection and nonrejection regions for the test H_0: $\mu = 28$ versus H_1: $\mu \neq 28$. The figure shows the resulting rejection of the null hypothesis due to the fact that the value of the test statistic $\bar{x}$ falls in the rejection region. Let us now formalize our definitions.

> The **level of significance** of a statistical hypothesis test is α, the probability of committing a type I error.

The *decision rule* of a statistical hypothesis test consists of a comparison of the computed value of the test statistic with the values defining the rejection and nonrejection regions. We reject the null hypothesis at the level of significance α if and only if the test statistic falls in the rejection region.

The **rejection region** of a statistical hypothesis test is the range of numbers that will lead us to reject the null hypothesis in case the test statistic falls within this range. The rejection region, also called the **critical region,** is defined by the **critical points.** The rejection region is designed so that, before the sampling takes place, our test statistic will have a probability α of falling within the rejection region if the null hypothesis is true.

The **nonrejection region** is the range of values (also determined by the critical points) that will lead us not to reject the null hypothesis if the test statistic should fall within this region. The nonrejection region is designed so that, before the sampling takes place, our test statistic will have a probability $1 - \alpha$ of falling in the nonrejection region if the null hypothesis is true.

The *critical points* define the separation between the rejection and the nonrejection regions. In Example 7–1 these points were found to be 27.02 and 28.98, with the test statistic $\bar{x}$ in the rejection region (see Figure 7–3).

What about a type II error? What is the probability that such an error will be made? This depends on what value (covered by the *alternative* hypothesis) the parameter actually has. Consider our hypothesis test:

$$H_0: \mu = 28$$
$$H_1: \mu \neq 28$$

We commit a type I error if we reject the null hypothesis when the null hypothesis is actually true—in our example, when the population mean is really 28. On the other hand, we commit a type II error if we fail to reject the null hypothesis when the null hypothesis is false. As you can see, the null hypothesis can be false in many (infinitely many) ways. For example, if the population mean is 29.5, and we conclude that the null hypothesis $\mu = 28$ is true, then we are committing a type II error. The same happens if we fail to reject the null hypothesis when the population mean is 30.7, or 35.9, or 26.432, and so on. In all such situations, if we fail to reject the null hypothesis, we are committing a type II error: not rejecting a null hypothesis that is false. Thus, the probability of committing a type II error *depends* on the actual value of the parameter in question. The probability of a type II error should, therefore, be denoted by $\beta(\mu)$—a whole collection of values that depend on μ. The concept of β is more complicated than that of α, and we will return to it in a later section.

For now, we will concern ourselves only with α, the probability of type I error. Recall that, within our framework, a type I error is considered to be more serious than a type II error. We set the value of α before the test takes place (similar to the way we set the confidence level of a confidence interval), and this defines our critical points, which define our rejection and nonrejection regions for the statistical hypothesis test. For the population mean, the critical points were defined in equation 7–4. (In Example 7–1 these critical points were found to be 27.02 and 28.98.)

The test we have seen in this section is called a *two-tailed test*. A test as stated in equation 7–1 is a two-tailed test because rejection of the null hypothesis is allowed either when we believe the parameter is *greater than* the value stated in the null hypothesis or when we believe it is *less than* the value stated in the null hypothesis. Rejection is allowed when the test statistic falls in either of the *two tails* of the sampling distribution.

A **two-tailed test** is a test with a rejection region consisting of the values in *both* tails of the sampling distribution (under the null hypothesis) of the test statistic.

In the next section, we will see how to conduct a *standardized* two-tailed hypothesis test about a population mean. That is, instead of conducting the test using the actual values of μ_0 and $\bar{x}$, we will convert the test statistic, $\bar{x}$, to a standard normal value—a *z value*. This will be done the way we converted $\bar{X}$ to Z in Chapter 5. Using the new procedure, we will not have to compute the critical points from equation 7-4 as we have done here. The critical points will be values on the *z scale* of numbers (for example, ± 1.96 for a test using $\alpha = 0.05$). The standardized test procedure will be found to be simpler than the method we used in this section, and we will follow it throughout the book.

7-3   A Two-Tailed, Large-Sample Test for the Population Mean

In a two-tailed test, the null hypothesis is stated in terms of an equality. The format is H_0: $\mu = \mu_0$, where μ_0 is some stated number. The alternative hypothesis includes *all* other possible values of the population parameter μ. Logically, if the population parameter is not equal to μ_0, then the alternative hypothesis, H_1: $\mu \neq \mu_0$, is true. This is demonstrated in Figure 7-4.

You may raise some practical objections at this point. For example, if our null hypothesis is H_0: $\mu = 5.0$, you may ask what we should do if the true population mean is not exactly 5.0, but is equal to 4.99999. In such a case, strictly speaking, we should reject the null hypothesis, as it is not true that $\mu = 5.0$. This, however, is preposterous because 4.99999 is not very different from 5.0. Do we really want to detect such an infinitesimal deviation from the hypothesized value, 5.0? The answer is, of course, no. Usually, we will end up rejecting null hypotheses only when the deviation from the hypothesized value is more substantial than in this hypothetical example. You should know, however, that as the sample size increases, we are better able to detect smaller and smaller deviations from any hypothesized value of the parameter.

In all statistical hypothesis tests, not only in the two-tailed test, the equal sign ($=$) must be stated in the null hypothesis. In the one-tailed tests, which will follow, we will have an inequality in the null hypothesis. This inequality, however, will always be a nonstrict inequality and will include the equal sign. This is so because, as we will see, when we carry out a hypothesis test, we center the sampling distribution of the test statistic over the value stated in the null hypothesis. This is the assumption of "innocent until proven guilty"—we assume that the mean is as stated in the null hypothesis by centering the distribution of $\bar{X}$ over the hypothesized value, μ_0. The requirement of always having the equal sign in the null hypothesis is thus essential in all hypothesis tests. We now present a standardized form of the two-tailed test.

Standardized Form of the Statistical Hypothesis Test

Recall that if we subtract from a normally distributed random variable its mean and then divide the result by the standard deviation, we get the standard normal random variable, Z. Therefore, assuming that the null hypothesis is true ("innocent until proven guilty"), the mean of $\bar{X}$ is μ_0. We subtract this mean from the obtained $\bar{x}$ and then divide the result by the standard deviation of $\bar{X}$, which is $\sigma/\sqrt{n}$ (since σ is rarely known, we usually divide by $s/\sqrt{n}$). If the null hypothesis is true, the result (when the sample size is large) should be close to a value drawn from the standard normal distribution. If the null hypothesis is *not* true, the population mean, μ, is either larger than or smaller than μ_0. Hence, when H_0 is not true, the standardized test statistic will tend to be either too large or too small. The terms *too large* and *too small* will mean,

FIGURE 7-4
The Value of μ under H_0 and the Values of μ under H_1

All values except μ_0 are possible values of under H_1

μ_0

to us, above or below the $\alpha = 0.05$ probability bounds for the standard normal random variable (which are ± 1.96), or the $\alpha = 0.01$ probability bounds for the standard normal random variable (which are ± 2.576), or other bounds for some given significance level. Let us now define our terms in the context of a standardized, large-sample, two-tailed test for the population mean, μ.

The elements of a large-sample, two-tailed (standardized) test for the population mean, μ.

The null hypothesis:	$H_0: \mu = \mu_0$	(7–5)
The alternative hypothesis:	$H_1: \mu \neq \mu_0$	
The significance level of the test:	α (often, $\alpha = 0.05$ or 0.01)	

The test statistic:　　$z = \dfrac{\bar{x} - \mu_0}{s/\sqrt{n}}$　(assuming σ　(7–6) is unknown; otherwise, use $\sigma/\sqrt{n}$ in the denominator)

The critical points:　These depend on α. They are the bounds $\pm z_{\alpha/2}$ that capture between them an area of $1 - \alpha$. (When $\alpha = 0.05$, the critical points are ± 1.96; when $\alpha = 0.01$, the critical points are ± 2.576. For other values of α, the critical points may be obtained from the standard normal table.)

The decision rule:　Reject the null hypothesis if either $z > z_{\alpha/2}$ or $z < -z_{\alpha/2}$, where $z_{\alpha/2}$ and $-z_{\alpha/2}$ are the two critical points.

Figure 7–5 demonstrates the standardized test in the context of Example 7–1. The standardized test shown in the figure is equivalent to the test carried out in the preceding section. In that section, we compared the computed $\bar{x}$ with critical points corresponding to $\alpha = 0.05$ in the scale of the problem itself. Here, instead, we compare $\bar{x}$ converted to a z value with critical points of the Z distribution for $\alpha = 0.05$. These critical points are ± 1.96. The computed z value is (using equation 7–6):

$$z = \frac{\bar{x} - \mu_0}{s/\sqrt{n}} = \frac{31.5 - 28}{5/\sqrt{100}} = 7.0$$

As seen in the figure, the standardized test statistic $z = 7.0$ falls in the right-hand rejection region of the test, and the null hypothesis is rejected at the $\alpha = 0.05$ level of significance.

FIGURE 7–5   Test of Example 7–1 Carried Out on the z Scale, Where the Test Statistic Is Standardized

EXAMPLE 7-2

Recently the airlines and their regulating agencies have been locked in a battle over baggage. The Air Transport Association, the airlines' trade group, believes that most passengers try to carry on board with them as much of their baggage as they possibly can, to avoid long delays at the baggage-claim carousels upon arrival. Consequently, airlines have been spending millions of dollars redesigning storage space in aircraft cabins. Federal regulators, on the other hand, worry about safety when too much baggage is stored in aircraft cabins. As part of a survey to determine the extent of required in-cabin storage capacity, a researcher needs to test the null hypothesis that the average weight of carry-on baggage per person is $\mu_0 = 12$ pounds (traditionally considered the average weight), versus the alternative hypothesis that the average weight is not 12 pounds. The study is undertaken to determine whether the average weight of carry-on baggage is indeed still 12 pounds or whether trends have changed carry-on baggage weight in either direction— either increased it to more than the traditional average of 12 pounds or decreased it to below that average. In other words, the researcher does not take sides as to the direction of possible change in passenger behavior, allowing for the possibility that less baggage may now be carried on board, to avoid delays at X-ray checking machines, for example. The analyst wants to test the null hypothesis at $\alpha = 0.05$.

Suppose that the analyst collects a random sample of 144 passengers traveling on different airlines and different routes (both of which are randomly selected) and finds that the average weight of carry-on baggage per passenger is $\bar{x} = 14.6$ pounds and the sample standard deviation is $s = 7.8$. Carry out the statistical hypothesis test, and state your conclusion.

SOLUTION

The null and alternative hypotheses are

$$H_0: \mu = 12$$
$$H_1: \mu \neq 12$$

Using the standardized form of the test (which, certainly leads to the same results as does the other form of the test, which we discussed in the last section) makes things easier. For example, the fact that we want to carry out the test at the $\alpha = 0.05$ level of significance means that we already know the critical points before computing the test statistic. The critical points for Z are ± 1.96. These are shown in Figure 7–6.

We now have an objective decision rule, known even before the sample is collected. We

FIGURE 7-6   Determining the Rejection and Nonrejection Regions of the Test of Example 7-2

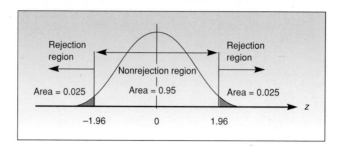

FIGURE 7-7   Conducting the Test of Example 7-2

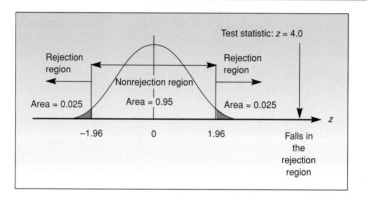

will reject the null hypothesis that the mean weight is 12 pounds if and only if our test statistic, Z, falls in the rejection region shown in Figure 7-6. Thus, if we should end up rejecting the null hypothesis, we will only be taking a 0.05 chance of committing a type I error. We now compute our test statistic using equation 7-6:

$$z = \frac{\bar{x} - \mu_0}{s/\sqrt{n}} = \frac{14.6 - 12}{7.8/\sqrt{144}} = 4.0$$

Since the computed value of the test statistic falls in the rejection region, our decision is to reject the null hypothesis. This is shown in Figure 7-7.

We reject the null hypothesis that the average weight of carry-on baggage per person is equal to 12 pounds in favor of the alternative that it is not equal to 12 pounds. Furthermore, since the rejection occurred in the right tail of the distribution, we may conclude that the average weight is probably higher than 12 pounds. (This conclusion should be made with some care. As we will see later, there is a very small probability that rejection on the right tail may occur when the value of the parameter is actually smaller than the value stated in the null hypothesis—in this example, if the mean is less than 12.)

EXAMPLE 7-3

An insurance company executive believes that, over the last few years, the average liability insurance per board seat in companies defined as "small companies" has been $2,000. A recent survey of small business by Growth Resources, Inc., reports that the average liability tab per board seat in their sample is $2,700. Assume that the sample used by Growth Resources contained 100 randomly chosen small firms (as defined by their total annual gross billing) and that the sample standard deviation was $947. Do these sampling results provide evidence to reject the executive's claim that the average liability per board seat is $2,000, using the $\alpha = 0.01$ level of significance?

SOLUTION

We are testing $H_0: \mu = 2,000$ versus the alternative $H_1: \mu \neq 2,000$. Since $\alpha = 0.01$ and our sample size is large, our test statistic is Z and has two critical points: 2.576 and -2.576. The rejection and nonrejection regions defined by these two points are shown in Figure 7–8. Now let us compute the test statistic.

$$z = \frac{\bar{x} - \mu_0}{s/\sqrt{n}} = \frac{2,700 - 2,000}{947/10} = \frac{700}{94.7} = 7.39$$

As seen from Figure 7–8, our test statistic falls in the rejection region, as 7.39 is much larger than the right-hand critical point 2.576. We therefore reject the null hypothesis that mean liability insurance per board member in small firms is $2,000 in favor of the alternative that it is not equal to $2,000.

In this example, the computed value of our test statistic turned out to be rather high. The value $z = 7.39$ lies far in the rejection region. In the previous example, the test statistic value was $z = 4$, which is smaller. Is there any information to be obtained from *where* in the rejection region the test statistic falls? The answer to this is yes, and we will discuss this topic in detail in a following section. You should already be intuitively aware that the further in the rejection region the test statistic falls, the *stronger* we feel about rejecting the null hypothesis.

This point is made clearer if we consider the following example. Suppose that you choose a level of significance $\alpha = 0.05$ and your test statistic value is $z = 2.1$. Can you reject the null hypothesis? Clearly you can, because 2.1 is greater than 1.96, which is the right-hand critical point for $\alpha = 0.05$. If you had chosen a significance level $\alpha = 0.01$, however, you would not be able to reject the null hypothesis because the right-hand critical point for $\alpha = 0.01$ is 2.576, and the test statistic value $z = 2.1$ is less than 2.576

FIGURE 7–8 Carrying Out the Hypothesis Test of Example 7–3

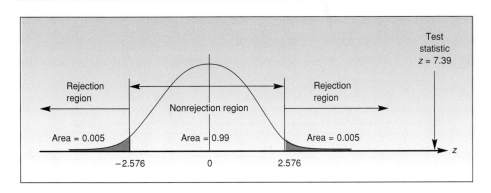

and, hence, inside the nonrejection region. This demonstrates that *the further out in the rejection region the test statistic falls, the smaller is the minimum significance level, α, we may use and still be able to reject the null hypothesis.*

EXAMPLE 7-4

The average time it takes a computer to perform a certain task is believed to be 3.24 seconds. In 1984, scientists at Bell Laboratories in New Jersey were testing several new algorithms, which they believed might change the speed of computation of the particular task. Scientists did not know whether a particular algorithm they developed would speed up, slow down, or bring no change at all to the average performance time. Therefore, it was decided to test the statistical hypothesis that the average performance time of the task using the new algorithm was the same as it was without the new procedure, versus the alternative hypothesis that the average performance time was no longer 3.24 seconds. A random test of 200 trial computations was carried out, and the result was $\bar{x} = 3.48$ seconds and $s = 2.8$ seconds. At the 0.05 level of significance, can we conclude that average time using the new algorithm is different?

SOLUTION

Here we test the null hypothesis $H_0: \mu = 3.24$ versus the alternative $H_1: \mu \neq 3.24$. Using $\alpha = 0.05$ means that our rejection region is marked by the critical points ± 1.96. We now compute our test statistic using equation 7–6 and get the following.

$$z = \frac{\bar{x} - \mu_0}{s/\sqrt{n}} = \frac{3.48 - 3.24}{2.8/\sqrt{200}} = 1.21$$

Our test statistic value is clearly inside the nonrejection region, and we therefore cannot reject the null hypothesis that the average performance time using the new algorithm is still 3.24 seconds. This is shown in Figure 7–9.

Recall that failing to reject a null hypothesis is not a strong or a definitive conclusion. It means that, using the level of significance we have chosen, we do not have enough evidence to reject the claim stated in the null hypothesis. In this partic-

FIGURE 7-9   Carrying Out the Hypothesis Test of Example 7-4

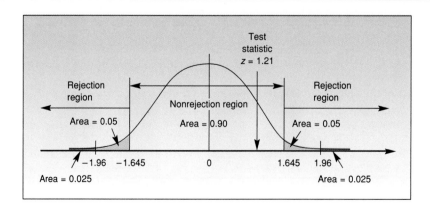

ular example, even if we had chosen to use $\alpha = 0.10$, we still would not have been able to reject the null hypothesis because the critical points for this level of significance are ± 1.645, and our test statistic would still be in the nonrejection region. This is also shown in Figure 7–9. The smallest probability of a type I error (the smallest level of significance, α) that will allow us to reject the null hypothesis in this example is greater than 0.10—a value of α considered risky and not often used. The null hypothesis cannot be rejected.

PROBLEMS

7–1. An automobile manufacturer substitutes a different engine in cars that were known to have an average mpg rating of 31.5 on the highway. The manufacturer wants to test whether the new engine changes the mpg rating of the automobile model. A random sample of 100 trial runs gives $\bar{x} = 29.8$ mpg and $s = 6.6$ mpg. Using the 0.05 level of significance, is the average mpg rating on the highway for cars using the new engine different from the rating for cars using the old engine?

7–2. A certain prescription medicine is supposed to contain an average of 247 parts per million (ppm) of a certain chemical. If the concentration is higher than 247 ppm, the drug may cause some side effects, and if the concentration is below 247 ppm, the drug may be ineffective. The manufacturer wants to check whether the average concentration in a large shipment is the required 247 ppm or not. A random sample of 60 portions is tested, and it is found that the sample mean is 250 ppm and the sample standard deviation is 12 ppm. Test the null hypothesis that the average concentration in the entire, large shipment is 247 ppm versus the alternative hypothesis that it is not 247 ppm using a level of significance $\alpha = 0.05$. Do the same using $\alpha = 0.01$. What is your conclusion? What is your decision about the shipment? If the shipment were guaranteed to contain an average concentration of 247 ppm, what would your decision be, based on the statistical hypothesis test? Explain.

7–3. A metropolitan transit authority wants to determine whether there is any need for changes in the frequency of service over certain bus routes. The transit authority needs to know whether the frequency of service should increase, decrease, or remain the same. It is determined that if the average number of miles traveled by bus over the routes in question by all residents of a given area is about 5 per day, then no change will be necessary. If the average number of miles traveled per person per day is either above 5 or below 5, then changes in service may be necessary. The authority wants, therefore, to test the null hypothesis that the average number of miles traveled per person per day is 5.0 versus the alternative hypothesis that the average is not 5.0 miles. The required level of significance for this test is $\alpha = 0.05$. A random sample of 120 residents of the area is taken, and it is found that the sample mean is 2.3 miles per resident per day and the sample standard deviation is 1.5 miles. Advise the authority on what should be done. Explain your recommendation. Could you state the same result at different levels of significance? Explain.

7–4. A study was undertaken to determine customer satisfaction in Canadian automobile markets following certain changes in customer service. Suppose that before the changes, average customer satisfaction rating, on a scale of 0 to 100, was 77. A survey questionnaire was sent to a random sample of 350 residents who bought new cars after the changes in customer service were instituted, and the average satisfaction rating for this sample was found to be $\bar{x} = 84$; the sample standard deviation was found to be $s = 28$. Use an α of your choice, and determine whether there is statistical evidence of a change in customer satisfaction. If you determine that a change did occur, state whether you believe customer satisfaction has improved or deteriorated.

7–5.   An investment services company claims that the average annual return on stocks within a certain industry is 11.5%. An investor wants to test whether this claim is true and collects a random sample of 50 stocks in the industry of interest. He finds that the sample average annual return is 10.8% and the sample standard deviation is 3.4%. Does the investor have enough evidence to reject the investment company's claim? (Use $\alpha = 0.05$.)

7–6.   Tara Pearl founded a multimillion-dollar furniture business that specializes in making futons. Retail prices for the futons vary from outlet to outlet, and it is believed that the average price is \$210 for a double futon.[4] To test this hypothesis, Tara's marketing director selects a random sample of 120 outlets and finds a mean price of \$225 and a standard deviation of \$82. Carry out the test using $\alpha = 0.05$ and also using $\alpha = 0.01$.

7–4   A Two-Tailed, Small-Sample Test for the Population Mean

Until now, we have assumed that the sample size, n, was large (or that the sampling was from a normally distributed population with a known standard deviation). In this section, we will extend our methodology to statistical hypothesis tests for the population mean when the sample size is small. This involves the t distribution. Recall that when we use the t distribution, we must assume that the population itself is normally distributed. Our standardized test statistic for testing hypotheses about the population mean using a small sample is given in equation 7–7.

Small-sample test statistic for the population mean, μ:

$$t = \frac{\bar{x} - \mu_0}{s/\sqrt{n}} \tag{7–7}$$

When the population is normally distributed and the null hypothesis is true, the test statistic has a t distribution with $n - 1$ degrees of freedom.

As you can see, the test statistic is identical to the one used earlier for large samples, equation 7–6. The difference is that the distribution of our test statistic is now the t distribution with $n - 1$ degrees of freedom instead of the standard normal distribution. Note, however, that *as long as the population standard deviation, σ, is unknown* (and the population is normal), the test statistic in equation 7–7 has a t distribution with $n - 1$ degrees of freedom. We use the z statistic, equation 7–6, only as a good approximation when the sample size is large. We now demonstrate the use of the t statistic with Example 7–5.

EXAMPLE 7–5

According to the Japanese National Land Agency, average land prices in central Tokyo soared 49% in the first six months of 1995. Suppose that an international real estate investment company wants to test this claim versus the alternative that the average land price did not increase by 49% (that is, the null hypothesis is H_0: $\mu = 49$, and it is to be tested against the two-sided alternative H_1: $\mu \neq 49$). The company manages to find a random sample of 18 properties in central Tokyo for which the prices in the second half

---

[4] "Sweet Dreams," *Entrepreneurial Woman,* March 1991, p. 54.

of 1995 as well as the prices in the first half of that year, are known. For each piece of property, the percentage of price increase is computed. Then the average percentage increase in price for the 18 pieces of property in the sample is computed, along with the standard deviation of the percentage price increases. The calculated sample statistics are $\bar{x} = 38\%$ and $s = 14\%$. Given this information, conduct the statistical hypothesis test using a level of significance $\alpha = 0.01$.

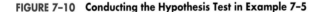

Since the sample size is small ($n = 18$) and the population standard deviation is not known, we will use the t distribution with $n - 1 = 17$ degrees of freedom. We will implicitly assume that percentage increases in all property values in central Tokyo are at least roughly approximated by a normal distribution. (This is a reasonable assumption in this case, as some properties may have increased very much, others very little, and most may have had an increase of around the average percentage.) Since we have chosen to use the $\alpha = 0.01$ level of significance, we need to find the two critical points of the t distribution with 17 degrees of freedom that cut off an area of $\alpha/2 = 0.005$ in each tail. From Table 3 in Appendix C we find that the two values are ± 2.898. Our objective decision rule is therefore to reject the null hypothesis if and only if our test statistic t given by equation 7–7 is either greater than 2.898 or less than -2.898. Computing the value of the t statistic, we find

$$t = \frac{\bar{x} - \mu_0}{s/\sqrt{n}} = \frac{38 - 49}{14/4.24} = -3.33$$

Since the test statistic falls in the rejection region, we reject the null hypothesis that the average percentage increase in price is 49% in favor of the alternative that the average price increase is not 49%. Furthermore, since the rejection took place on the left-hand tail of the t distribution, we are led to believe that the average percentage increase in property values in central Tokyo during the first half of 1995 was less than the 49% claimed by the Japanese National Land Agency. In rejecting their claim, we are taking less than a 0.01 chance of committing a type I error. Figure 7–10 shows the t distribution, the rejection

FIGURE 7-10   Conducting the Hypothesis Test in Example 7-5

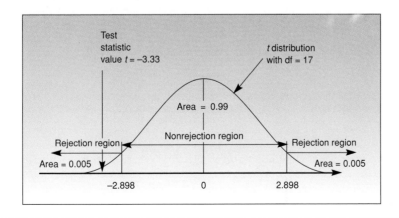

and nonrejection regions, and the computed value of the test statistic—located in the left-hand rejection region.

At this point, we will introduce a definition that is useful in all statistical hypothesis tests, whether small- or large-sample, two-tailed or one-tailed.

> We say that a statistical result is **significant** at the level of significance α if the result causes us to *reject our null hypothesis* when we carry out the test using level of significance α.

Thus, in the last example, the result $\bar{x} = 38\%$ was found to be significant at the 0.01 level. Of course, when a result is significant at a given level α, it is also significant at all levels higher than α. This can be seen from the fact that if we had used $\alpha = 0.05$ in the last example, we would have also rejected the null hypothesis; if our test statistic is in the rejection region for $\alpha = 0.01$, it must also be in the rejection region for $\alpha = 0.05$—a larger rejection region. This is demonstrated in the context of Example 7–5 in Figure 7–11.

EXAMPLE 7-6

Canon, Inc., introduced a copying machine that features two-color copying capability in a compact system copier. The average speed of the standard compact system copier is 27 copies per minute (as advertised in national business magazines and elsewhere). Suppose that the company wants to test whether the new two-color copier has the same average speed as its standard compact copier and it conducts a test of 24 runs of the new machines, giving a sample mean $\bar{x} = 24.6$ and sample standard deviation $s = 7.4$ (copies per minute). Using the significance level $\alpha = 0.05$, is there evidence to conclude that the average speed of the new machine is different from that of the standard model?

FIGURE 7-11   Rejection of the Null Hypothesis in Example 7–5 Using Levels $\alpha = 0.01$ and $\alpha = 0.05$

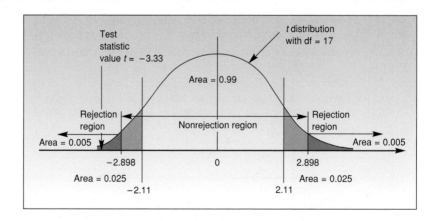

FIGURE 7–12   Carrying Out the Test of Example 7–6

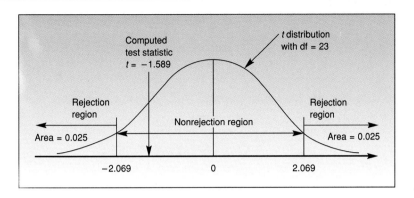

We want to test H_0: $\mu = 27$ versus H_1: $\mu \neq 27$. Since the sample size is $n = 24$, we use the t distribution, making the usual implicit assumption about the shape of the population. The critical points for $\alpha = 0.05$, found from Table 3 using df $= 23$, are ± 2.069. We now compute the value of our test statistic.

SOLUTION

$$t = \frac{\overline{x} - \mu_0}{s/\sqrt{n}} = \frac{24.6 - 27}{7.4/4.899} = -1.589$$

Is this result significant? No. Since the test statistic falls inside the nonrejection region for $\alpha = 0.05$, we cannot reject the null hypothesis. There is no evidence to conclude that the average speed of the new copier is different from the average speed of the standard compact copier. Our statistical hypothesis test is shown in Figure 7–12.

Usually, when we carry out statistical hypothesis tests, we want to disprove the null hypothesis in favor of the alternative hypothesis. This is so not because there is something intrinsically special about the alternative hypothesis, but rather because of our decision to give the type I error more importance by controlling its probability of occurrence (we set the level of this probability, α, to a given small number: 0.05, 0.01, or another preset value). Thus, as noted earlier, if we accept a null hypothesis, we have not made a strong conclusion (the null hypothesis may be true or may be false, but we cannot reject it without taking a chance greater than α of being wrong when we reject it.) In cases where we are able to reject the null hypothesis, we have some degree of confidence in our conclusion—we know that our chance of being wrong is small. This is why a result that leads to the rejection of a null hypothesis is called *significant*. Such a result implies a substantial finding—one with a small, known probability of being false.

PROBLEMS

7–7.   The following display is reprinted by permission from *The Wall Street Journal*. Reported numbers are averages. A broker wants to test the null hypothesis that the average time to break even for loans of this type is 3.75 years against the alternative that it is not. A random sample of 20 similar rates at banks leads to a sample mean of 4.15 years and a standard deviation of 2 years. Conduct the test and state your conclusion.

Time To Refinance?

How switching to a 30-year fixed-rate mortgage could mean significant savings for one hypothetical family with a one-year adjustable-rate mortgage with an outstanding balance of $140,000.

■ Current ARM rate	8.5%
■ Monthly payment	$1,134
■ New fixed rate	7.5%
■ New monthly payment	$979
■ Monthly Savings	$155
■ Refinancing costs (including 1.5 points)	$7,000
■ Time to break even:	3.75 years

K. Blumenthal, "More Homeowners Are Saying Farewell to ARMs," *The Wall Street Journal,* June 9, 1995, p. C1, with data from Countrywide Planning Corp., Certified Mortgage Planners, Inc.

7–8.   A certain commodity is known to have a price that is stable through time and does not change according to any known trend. Price, however, does change from day to day in a random fashion. If the price is at a certain level one day, it is as likely to be at any level the next day within some probability bounds approximately given by a normal distribution. The mean daily price is believed to be $14.25. To test the hypothesis that the average price is $14.25 versus the alternative hypothesis that it is not $14.25, a random sample of 16 daily prices is collected. The results are $\bar{x} = \$16.50$ and $s = \$5.8$. Using $\alpha = 0.05$, can you reject the null hypothesis?

7–9.   Average total daily sales at a small foodstore are known to be $452.80. The store's management recently implemented some changes in displays of goods, order within aisles, and other changes, and it now wants to know whether average sales volume has changed. A random sample of 12 days shows $\bar{x} = \$501.90$ and $s = \$65.00$. Using $\alpha = 0.05$, is the sampling result significant? Explain.

7–10. A study was undertaken to evaluate how stocks are affected by being listed in the Standard & Poor's 500 Index. The aim of the study was to assess average excess returns for these stocks, above returns on the market as a whole. The average excess return on *any* stock is zero because the "average" stock moves with the market as a whole. As part of the study, a random sample of 13 stocks newly included in the S&P 500 Index was selected. Before the sampling takes place, we allow that average "excess return" for stocks newly listed in the Standard & Poor's 500 Index may be either positive or negative; therefore, we want to test the null hypothesis that average excess return is equal to zero versus the alternative that it is not zero. If the excess return on the sample of 13 stocks averaged 3.1% and had a standard deviation of 1%, do you believe that inclusion in the Standard & Poor's 500 Index changes a stock's excess return on investment, and if so, in which direction? Explain.

7–11. A new chemical process is introduced in the production of nickel-cadmium batteries. For batteries produced by the old process, it is known that the average life of a battery is 102.5 hours. To determine whether the new process affects the average life of the batteries, the manufacturer collects a random sample of 25 batteries produced by the new process and uses them until they run out. The sample mean life is found to be 107 hours, and the sample standard deviation is found to be 10 hours. Are these results significant at the $\alpha = 0.05$ level? Are they significant at the $\alpha = 0.01$ level? Explain. Draw your conclusion.

7–12. Average soap consumption in a certain country is believed to be 2.5 bars per person per month. *The standard deviation of the population is known to be* $\sigma = 0.8$. While the standard deviation is not believed to have changed (and this may be substantiated by several studies), it is believed that the mean consumption may have changed either upward or downward. A survey is therefore undertaken to test the null hypothesis that average soap consumption is still 2.5 bars per person per month versus the alternative that it is not. A sample of size $n = 20$ is collected and gives $\bar{x} = 2.3$. The population is assumed to be normally distributed. What is the appropriate test statistic in this case? Conduct the test and state your conclusion. Use an α of your choice. Does the choice of level of significance change your conclusion? Explain.

7–13. What are the assumptions underlying the use of the t distribution in testing hypotheses about the population mean?

7–14. Average annualized return on common stock was 15.06% in early 1995.[5] A researcher wants to test whether or not this claim is true. The researcher collects a random sample of 38 stocks and finds $\bar{x} = 10.3\%$ and $s = 5.9\%$. Use $\alpha = 0.01$ to test the claim. State your conclusion.

7–15. It is known that the average stay of tourists in Hong Kong hotels has been 3.4 nights.[6] A tourism industry analyst wanted to test whether recent changes in the nature of tourism to Hong Kong have changed this average. The analyst obtained the following random sample of the number of nights spent by tourists in Hong Kong hotels: 5, 4, 3, 2, 1, 1, 5, 7, 8, 4, 3, 3, 2, 5, 7, 1, 3, 1, 1, 5, 3, 4, 2, 2, 2, 6, 1, 7. Conduct the test using the 0.05 level of significance.

7–5 A Two-Tailed, Large-Sample Test for the Population Proportion

As we know, when the sample size is large, the distribution of the sample proportion, $\hat{P}$, may be approximated by a normal distribution with mean p and standard deviation $\sqrt{pq/n}$. Therefore, for large samples (recall our rule of thumb: both $np > 5$ and $nq > 5$), we can test hypotheses about the population proportion p in a similar manner to the way we constructed confidence intervals for p in the last chapter. The

---

[5] "Are You Trading for Growth or Stability?" *Fidelity Focus,* Summer, 1995, p. 7.

[6] "Hong Kong's Tourism: Stay a While, Spend a Little," *The Economist*, March 16, 1991, p. 72.

test statistic we use is z, defined in equation 7–8. In computing the test statistic, we use p_0—the hypothesized value of p under the null hypothesis.

Large-sample test statistic for the population proportion, p:

$$z = \frac{\hat{p} - p_0}{\sqrt{p_0 q_0/n}} \qquad (7\text{–}8)$$

where $q_0 = 1 - p_0$.

We will demonstrate the use of this statistic in a two-tailed test for the population proportion in Example 7–7.

EXAMPLE 7–7

Recent changes, referred to as the "Big Bang," in regulation of the investment industry in Britain brought far-reaching consequences. For the first time, the London stock market was opened to foreign investors, and this gave many foreign investors direct access to British securities. The U.S. dollar, which had been declining during the period preceding and following the deregulation, was expected to bring massive American investments to the British Exchange. An investment analyst for Goldman Sachs and Company wanted to test the hypothesis made by British securities experts that 70% of all foreign investors in the British market were American. The analyst gathered a random sample of 210 accounts of foreign investors in London and found that 130 were owned by U.S. citizens. At the $\alpha = 0.05$ level of significance, is there evidence to reject the claim of the British securities experts?

SOLUTION

We want to test the null hypothesis H_0: $p = 0.70$ versus the alternative hypothesis H_1: $p \neq 0.70$. Our test statistic is z, and therefore, using $\alpha = 0.05$, our rejection region is defined by the two critical points ± 1.96. This is shown in Figure 7–13. We now compute the value of the test statistic using equation 7–8 and the calculated sample proportion $\hat{p} = x/n = 130/210 = 0.619$.

$$z = \frac{\hat{p} - p_0}{\sqrt{p_0 q_0/n}} = \frac{0.619 - 0.70}{\sqrt{(0.7)(0.3)/210}} = -2.5614$$

As can be seen from Figure 7–13, the computed value of the test statistic falls in the left-hand rejection region; hence, at $\alpha = 0.05$ our result is significant. We therefore may state that, based on our random sample of accounts, we believe that the percentage of American accounts in the London Exchange at the time of the study was lower than 70%.

Let us consider our rejection of the null hypothesis in this example a little more carefully. Since we decided, before the sampling took place, that we were willing to take a 0.05 probability of committing a type I error and rejecting a true null hypothesis, we were able to reject the null hypothesis. If, however, we had decided to take only a 0.01 probability of rejecting a true null hypothesis, we would not have been able to reject it because our test statistic value—although very close to the 0.01 critical point, -2.576—is still inside the nonrejection region for this level of significance (-2.5614 is to the *right* of -2.576).

FIGURE 7-13   Conducting the Hypothesis Test of Example 7-7

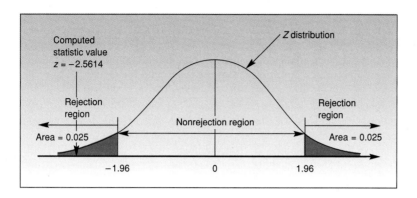

What can we say about the "real" level of significance of this test? What is the smallest probability of committing a type I error we could have chosen and still rejected the null hypothesis? Since our test statistic value falls close to the critical point for $\alpha = 0.01$, the "smallest possible α" we seek is very close to 0.01. To find the exact "smallest possible α" (the actual, or "real" level of significance of our finding), we look in the normal probability table and find the combined area in the two tails cut off by the two values ± 2.5614. We find that this value is around 0.0104. We use the combined area in both tails because our test is a two-tailed test; therefore, if the null hypothesis is true, then an error could occur either by rejecting on the left tail of the sampling distribution of the statistic Z or by rejecting on the right tail of the distribution. The value we found, 0.0104, is the smallest level of significance at which we may reject the null hypothesis. Such a value, called a *p-value*, will be discussed in detail in Section 7–7.

The elements of a large-sample, two-tailed test for the population proportion, p:

The null hypothesis:	$H_0: p = p_0$
The alternative hypothesis:	$H_1: p \neq p_0$
The significance level of the test:	α (often, $\alpha = 0.05$ or 0.01)
The test statistic:	$z = \dfrac{\hat{p} - p_0}{\sqrt{p_0 q_0/n}}$ where $q_0 = 1 - p_0$
The critical points:	These depend on α. They are the bounds $\pm z_{\alpha/2}$ that capture between them an area of $1 - \alpha$. (When $\alpha = 0.05$, the critical points are ± 1.96; when $\alpha = 0.01$, the critical points are ± 2.576. For other values of α, the critical points may be obtained from the standard normal table.)
The decision rule:	Reject the null hypothesis if either $z > z_{\alpha/2}$ or $z < -z_{\alpha/2}$, where $z_{\alpha/2}$ and $-z_{\alpha/2}$ are the two critical points.

PROBLEMS

7–16. A survey of schools of business indicates that 16% of the faculty positions in schools of business are currently vacant. A placement service working for a renowned university wants to test whether or not the claim is true and collects information on a random sample of 300 business faculty positions chosen from universities around the country. The results indicate that 51 out of the 300 positions surveyed are vacant. Use $\alpha = 0.05$ to conduct the test.

7–17. Suppose that the Goodyear Tire Company has historically held 42% of the market for automobile tires in the United States. Recent changes in company operations, especially its diversification to other areas of business, as well as changes in competing firms' operations, prompt the firm to test the validity of the assumption that it still controls 42% of the market. A random sample of 550 automobiles on the road shows that 219 of them have Goodyear tires. Conduct the test at $\alpha = 0.01$.

7–18. The manufacturer of electronic components needs to inform its buyers of the proportion of defective components in its shipments. The company has been stating that the percentage of defectives is 12%. The company wants to test whether or not the proportion of all components that are defective is as claimed. A random sample of 100 items indicates 17 defectives. Use $\alpha = 0.05$ to test the hypothesis that the percentage of defective components is 12%.

7–19. The percentage of farmers using fertilizers in an African country was known to be 35%. The drought and other events of the last few years are believed to have had a potential impact on the proportion of farmers using fertilizers. An international aid program wants to test whether or not the percentage is still around 35% and gathers a random sample of 150 farmers. The findings reveal that 68 of the farmers use fertilizers. Conduct the test at $\alpha = 0.05$ and $\alpha = 0.01$. State your conclusion.

7–20. A company's market share is very sensitive to both its level of advertising and the levels of its competitors' advertising. A firm known to have a 56% market share wants to test whether or not this value is still valid in view of recent advertising compaigns of its competitors and its own increased level of advertising. A random sample of 500 consumers reveals that 298 of them use the company's product. Is there evidence to conclude that the company's market share is no longer 56%, using the 0.01 level of significance?

7–21. According to *Money*, 31% of all households making between $50,000 and $100,000 annually own stocks.[7] An economist wants to test this claim using a random sample of 2,500 households with annual incomes in this range. The economist finds that 1,201 of the households in the sample own stocks. Conduct the test using $\alpha = 0.05$.

7–6   One-Tailed Tests

While reading the examples and problems of the previous sections, you may have wondered about situations where, instead of testing whether or not a population parameter is *equal* to some specified number, we may be interested in testing whether the parameter is greater than (or smaller than) some specified value. Such situations are generally more realistic and occur very often in practice. When we want to test whether a parameter is greater than or less than some value, our test is not a two-tailed test, but rather a **one-tailed test.** For example, in quality control, it is much more meaningful to test the null hypothesis that the proportion of defective items produced is equal to 0.10 versus the alternative hypothesis that the proportion of defective items

---

[7] J. Coyle, "Profile of the Middle Class," *Money,* May, 1995, p. 107.

is strictly greater than 0.10. In this case we would be conducting the right-tailed test given by

$$H_0: p \leq 0.10$$
$$H_1: p > 0.10$$

$$(7-9)$$

Here the assumption of "innocence" is the assumption that the proportion of defective items in a shipment is at most 0.10. We will conclude "guilty"—and reject the null hypothesis in favor of the alternative hypothesis—if we find statistical evidence indicating that the proportion of defective items is greater than 0.10. Note that, here too, the equal sign is included in the null hypothesis. This conforms with our requirement that the null hypothesis always include the equal sign. Our test is right-tailed because, as we will see, the rejection region is strictly in the right tail of the distribution.

In a given situation, how do we decide whether a test should be carried out as one-tailed or two-tailed? This is an important question, and to answer it we must consider the decision-making framework of hypothesis tests. Recall that our philosophy of hypothesis tests tells us that we will take action (decide "guilty") if we have enough evidence to believe that the situation presented to us in the null hypothesis is not true. *The action is, therefore, always associated with the alternative hypothesis.* Thus, we ask ourselves: In what situation do we want to take action? The answer to this question determines the alternative hypothesis. If the test is carried out by the manufacturer, and the manufacturer is interested in determining whether there is a deviation from the value $p = 0.10$ in either direction, that is, either up or down from 0.10, then the test is a two-tailed test. This is so because an action is to be taken if the proportion of defectives is below 0.10 (say, notify buyers that their shipment contains fewer defective items than stated by the manufacturer) as well as when the proportion of defective items is above 0.10 (again, the action is to notify buyers). On the other hand, suppose a supplier guarantees that its shipments contain at most 10% defectives, and there is no interest in taking action if fewer than 10% are defective. The buyer may now be the one conducting a hypothesis test to check whether the supplier's claim of no more than 10% defective items is correct. The buyer will only take action if it may be concluded that more than 10% are defective. Since the action is to be taken only in such a case, this means that the alternative hypothesis (the one that entails action) is $p > 0.10$, and the test is a right-tailed test. We summarize the distinction between one- and two-tailed tests as follows.

> The tails of a statistical hypothesis test are determined by the need for an action. If action is to be taken if a parameter is greater than some value *a*, then the alternative hypothesis is that the parameter is greater than *a*, and the test is a **right-tailed test.**

For example, if a population mean is claimed to be 50 and we are concerned about the possibility that the mean may be greater than 50 (but do not care if the mean is below 50), then the hypotheses are

$$H_0: \mu \leq 50$$
$$H_1: \mu > 50$$

which is a right-tailed test.

If action is to be taken only if the value of a parameter is believed to be less than a stated value *a*, then the alternative hypothesis is that the parameter is less than *a*, and the test is a **left-tailed test.**

For example, if the population mean is claimed to be 50 but action should only be taken if it is below 50, then the null and alternative hypotheses are

$$H_0: \mu \geq 50$$
$$H_1: \mu < 50$$

If action is to be taken if the value of a parameter is either greater than or less than *a*, then the test is a **two-tailed test.**

In our example, the test is

$$H_0: \mu = 50$$
$$H_1: \mu \neq 50$$

In a one-tailed test, the rejection region is either completely on the left (a left-tailed test) or completely on the right (a right-tailed test). Therefore, we have the following important property.

In a one-tailed test, the entire probability of a type I error, α, is placed in the tail of rejection.

This changes the critical points of the tests. For example, in a right-tailed test for the population mean, using a large sample size and $\alpha = 0.05$, there is only one critical point: $z = +1.645$. Why? The answer is shown in Figure 7–14.

The distribution of the statistic is normal, and the probability of a type I error is 0.05. We place this probability entirely on the right side of the distribution. We have to find that point *a* such that the area to its right is 0.05 (not 0.025, as in the case of a two-tailed test, where the sum of the areas in both tails is 0.05). From the standard normal table, we find that the point z_α that cuts off an area of 0.05 to its right is 1.645. (This is the same point we use together with its negative, -1.645, in a two-tailed test at $\alpha = 0.10$. Here it is used alone.)

FIGURE 7–14   Critical Point and Rejection and Nonrejection Regions for a Right-Tailed Test at
$\alpha = 0.05$

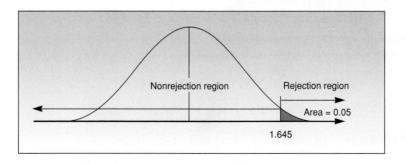

TABLE 7–2 Critical Points of Z for Selected Levels of Significance

	Level of Significance α		
	0.10	**0.05**	**0.01**
One-Tailed Test	+ or 1.28 −	+ or 1.645 −	+ or 2.326 −
Two-Tailed Test	+ and 1.645 −	+ and 1.96 −	+ and 2.576 −

Note: + or − means we use the positive value in the table for a right-tailed test and the negative value for a left-tailed test. In a two-tailed test, we use both the positive and the negative values.

The elements of a large-sample, right-tailed (standardized) test for the population mean, μ.

The null hypothesis:	$H_0: \mu \leq \mu_0$	(7–10)
The alternative hypothesis:	$H_1: \mu > \mu_0$	
The significance level of the test:	α (often, $\alpha = 0.05$ or 0.01)	
The test statistic:	$z = \dfrac{\bar{x} - \mu_0}{s/\sqrt{n}}$ (assuming σ is unknown; otherwise, use $\sigma/\sqrt{n}$ in the denominator)	(7–7)

The critical point: This depends on α. It is the bound z_α that captures an area of α to its right. (When $\alpha = 0.05$, the critical point is 1.645; when $\alpha = 0.01$, the critical point is 2.326. For other values of α, the critical point may be obtained from the standard normal table.)

The decision rule: Reject the null hypothesis if $z > z_\alpha$ where z_α is the critical point.

Table 7–2 gives the critical points for a test using the normal distribution in the cases of a one-tailed and a two-tailed test with commonly used values of α. When the distribution to be used is the t distribution, the critical point(s) may be determined by finding the value for appropriate degrees of freedom, where the infinite df value (the z value) is the value given in Table 7–2. Critical values for other levels of α are found in the standard normal table. Table 7–2 is only a quick-reference summary table provided for convenience. We demonstrate the use of one-tailed tests using the following examples.

The Environmental Protection Agency (EPA) sets limits on the concentrations of pollutants emitted by various industries. Suppose that the upper allowable limit on the emission

EXAMPLE 7-8

of vinyl chloride is set at an average of 55 parts per million (ppm) within a range of two miles around the plant emitting this chemical. To check compliance with this rule, the EPA collects a random sample of 100 readings at different times and dates within the two-mile range around the plant. The findings are that the sample average concentration is 60 ppm and the sample standard deviation is 20 ppm. Is there evidence to conclude that the plant in question is violating the law?

SOLUTION

The EPA is interested in determining whether or not the plant operators are violating the law. The EPA will be taking action against the plant operators only if there is enough evidence to conclude that the average concentration of vinyl chloride within the given range of 2 miles from the plant is *above* the allowed average of 55 ppm. Therefore, the test is right-tailed.

$$H_0: \mu \le 55$$
$$H_1: \mu > 55$$

Since the sample size is 100, we use the normal distribution. If a level of significance $\alpha = 0.01$ is desired, the critical point to be used is $+2.326$. The test statistic is the same as that used in the two-tailed test and is given by equation 7–6:

$$z = \frac{\bar{x} - \mu_0}{s/\sqrt{n}} = \frac{60 - 55}{20/10} = 2.5$$

As can be seen from Figure 7–15, the value of the test statistic falls in the rejection region for $\alpha = 0.01$, and the EPA may therefore reject the null hypothesis of "innocence" (nonviolation of the emission control rule) in favor of the alternative hypothesis that the plant operators are indeed violating the law. By using $\alpha = 0.01$, the EPA is willing to take at most a 0.01 chance of concluding that the plant operators are guilty when in reality they are innocent.

FIGURE 7–15   The One-Tailed Test in Example 7–8, Compared with a Two-Tailed Test

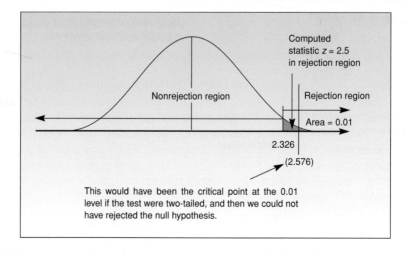

The elements of a large-sample, left-tailed (standardized) test for the population mean, μ.

The null hypothesis:	$H_0: \mu \geq \mu_0$ $\qquad$ (7–11)
The alternative hypothesis:	$H_1: \mu < \mu_0$
The significance level of the test:	α (often, $\alpha = 0.05$ or 0.01)
The test statistic:	$z = \dfrac{\bar{x} - \mu_0}{s/\sqrt{n}}$ (assuming σ $\qquad$ (7–7) is unknown; otherwise, use $\sigma/\sqrt{n}$ in the denominator)
The critical point:	This depends on α. It is the bound z_α that captures an area of α to its left. (When $\alpha = 0.05$, the critical point is -1.645; when $\alpha = 0.01$, the critical point is -2.326. For other values of α, the critical point may be obtained from the standard normal table.)
The decision rule:	Reject the null hypothesis if $z < z_\alpha$ where z_α is the critical point.

What are the advantages of a one-tailed test? From this example, we see that when we are interested in rejecting a null hypothesis only in one direction, setting up the test as a one-tailed test in the direction of interest (here a right-tailed test) is advantageous. Suppose the EPA had set up the test as a two-tailed test, with the understanding that action would only be taken if the rejection happened on the right-hand side. In such a case, the test would have had two critical points at the 0.01 level of significance, ± 2.576, and the obtained test statistic value, $z = 2.5$, would be found inside the nonrejection region for the test (although the null hypothesis would still be rejected if the EPA were willing to use an α of 0.05). Thus, we see that setting up the hypothesis test as a one-tailed test increases the *power* of the test (we will formally define power in a later section) in the sense that this allows us to reject null hypotheses in more cases than would be possible if we used two tails. It is very important, therefore, to first determine whether a test should be one-tailed or two-tailed.

EXAMPLE 7-9

A certain kind of packaged food bears the following statement on the package: "Average net weight 12 oz." Suppose that a consumer group has been receiving complaints from users of the product who believe that they are getting smaller quantities than the manufacturer states on the package. The consumer group wants, therefore, to test the hypothesis that the average net weight of the product in question is 12 oz. versus the alternative hypothesis that the packages are, on average, underfilled. A random sample of 144 packages of the food product is collected, and it is found that the average net weight in the sample is 11.8 oz. and the sample standard deviation is 6 oz. Given these findings, is there evidence that the manufacturer is underfilling the packages?

SOLUTION

As in every problem, we first need to determine whether the situation entails a one-tailed or a two-tailed test. In this particular example, the required test clearly is one-tailed and the tail of rejection is the left tail. This is seen by answering the question: Under what conditions do we want to take an action? The action always determines the alternative hypothesis, and the null hypothesis then covers all other possibilities (always including the equal sign). Here it is easy to see that since the consumer group is the one carrying out the test, they would be interested in taking action against the manufacturer (complaint, lawsuit, etc.) only if they end up believing, to within a small probability of being wrong, that the manufacturer is underfilling the packages it sells. If the packages are believed to be overfilled or filled with exactly 12 oz. of food on average, then no action whatsoever will be taken. Since action is to be taken only in the underfilled case, the test is a left-tailed test. You may want to think of "less than" implying a left-hand and "greater than" implying a right-hand test.

Now that we know what kind of test to perform, we can set up the distribution of the test statistic under the null hypothesis, noting that our sample size, $n = 144$, allows us to use the standard normal distribution. In the statement of the problem, we left out the required probability of a type I error, α. This was done purposely, because, in reality, the choice of α will often be left to the statistician performing the test. You may start, if you wish, by choosing a commonly used value, such as $\alpha = 0.05$. Figure 7–16 shows the distribution and the critical point $z_\alpha = -1.645$, which corresponds to $\alpha = 0.05$ and a left-tailed test using the normal distribution. The figure also shows the value of the test statistic, computed as

$$z = \frac{\bar{x} - \mu_0}{s/\sqrt{n}} = \frac{11.8 - 12}{6/12} = -0.4$$

As we see, the value of the test statistic falls in the nonrejection region. We cannot reject the null hypothesis $H_0: \mu \geq 12$. There is insufficient evidence to conclude that the manufacturer is underfilling the packages. The fact that we could not reject the null hypothesis does not mean that the manufacturer is *not* underfilling the packages; it merely means that, given our data, we cannot reject the null hypothesis without taking a large probability of being wrong. The probability of committing a type I error is large because the value of our test statistic falls far inside the nonrejection region, and we would have to accept the null hypothesis even if we were to choose a much larger value of α than 0.05.

FIGURE 7–16   Nonrejection of the Null Hypothesis in Example 7–9

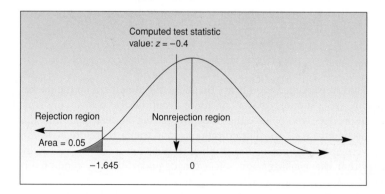

Recall that a two-tailed test at a given level α is equivalent to constructing a confidence interval for the parameter in question with confidence coefficient $1 - \alpha$ (a confidence interval of level 95%, for example, is equivalent to carrying out a two-tailed hypothesis test for the parameter at the 0.05 level of significance). What about a one-tailed test? *One-tailed tests are equivalent to one-sided confidence intervals.* This means that a one-sided confidence interval would contain the hypothesized value of a parameter if and only if a one-tailed test (in direction opposite to the confidence interval, using the corresponding level of significance, α) would lead to nonrejection of the null hypothesis. In the case of Example 7–9, we could have constructed a right-hand confidence interval for μ. If we do so, $\alpha = 0.05$ implies we need a 95% right-handed confidence interval. The interval is $[-\infty, \bar{x} + 1.645s/\sqrt{n}] = [-\infty, 12.6225]$. This confidence interval contains the hypothesized value $\mu_0 = 12$, as we would expect from the fact that the one-tailed test led us to nonrejection of the null hypothesis that μ is greater than or equal to 12.

As we saw in Chapter 6, the distance from $\bar{x}$ to μ is the same as the distance from μ to $\bar{x}$. Hence, we can measure this distance from our hypothesized value of the parameter to the test statistic as we do in the case of a hypothesis test, or we may measure the distance from our test statistic to the hypothesized value of the parameter, which is what we do in the case of a confidence interval. In either case the results are the same: A null hypothesis will not be rejected if and only if the confidence interval contains the hypothesized value of the parameter. The distance between the value of the test statistic and the hypothesized value of the parameter is measured in number of standard deviations of the test statistic. A distance greater than a few standard deviations (1.96 of them, 2.576 of them, etc.) leads to the rejection of the null hypothesis (or, equivalently, noninclusion of the hypothesized value of the parameter in the confidence interval).

The following two examples demonstrate one-tailed hypothesis tests for the mean when the sample size is small, and large-sample one-tailed tests for the population proportion, respectively.

A floodlight is stated to last an average of 65 hours. A competitor believes that the average life of the floodlight is less than that stated by the manufacturer and sets out to prove that the manufacturer's claim is false. A random sample of 21 floodlight elements is chosen and shows that the sample average is 62.5 hours and the sample standard deviation is 3. Using $\alpha = 0.01$, determine whether there is evidence to conclude that the manufacturer's claim is false.

EXAMPLE 7-10

We have the following hypotheses: $H_0: \mu \geq 65$ and $H_1: \mu < 65$. Since this is a left-tailed test at the 0.01 level of significance, we know that if the sample size were large enough for the normal distribution to be used, the critical point would be -2.326. Here the appropriate distribution is the t distribution with $n - 1 = 20$ degrees of freedom. Looking at the t table, Appendix C, Table 3, we find that the appropriate critical value (using the same column in which we have in the bottom row the value 2.326) is $t = -2.528$. This is shown in Figure 7–17, along with the computed value of the test statistic:

SOLUTION

$$t = \frac{\bar{x} - \mu_0}{s/\sqrt{n}} = \frac{62.5 - 65}{3/4.583} = -3.82$$

FIGURE 7-17   Carrying Out the Test of Example 7-10

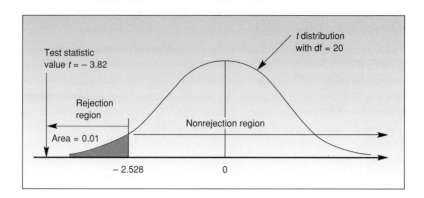

Since the test statistic falls in the rejection region, we reject the null hypothesis and conclude that there is statistical evidence that the manufacturer's claim is false. Our probability of a type I error in rejecting the claim is less than 0.01.

EXAMPLE 7-11

"After looking at 1,349 hotels nationwide, we've found 13 that meet our standards." This statement by the Small Luxury Hotels Association, which appeared in advertisements of the association in national magazines, implies that the proportion of all hotels in the United States that meet the association's standards is $13/1,349 = 0.0096$. The management of a hotel that was denied acceptance to the association on the grounds that it did not meet the association's standards wanted to prove that the standards set by the association are not quite as stringent as claimed and that, in fact, the proportion of hotels in the United States that would qualify under present standards is higher than 0.0096. The management hired an independent research agency, which visited a random sample of 600 hotels nationwide and found that 7 of them satisfied the exact standards set by the association. Is there evidence to conclude that the population proportion of all hotels in the country satisfying the standards set by the Small Luxury Hotels Association is greater than 0.0096?

SOLUTION

Note that in order to use the normal approximation for the sampling distribution of the sample proportion, $\hat{P}$, we must satisfy the rule that both np and nq be at least equal to 5. In this particular example, it is especially important to check this because under the null hypothesis, the population proportion, p, is very small ($p_0 = 0.0096$). This means that a relatively large sample size is needed. The condition is satisfied because $np_0 = 600(0.0096) = 5.76$. The other condition clearly holds.

Our test is a right-tailed test, as we are trying to prove that the proportion of hotels that satisfy the standards is greater than $p_0 = 0.0096$. The null and alternative hypotheses are $H_0: p \leq 0.0096$ and $H_1: p > 0.0096$. Again, no particular level of significance, α, is given, so let us first compute the value of the test statistic in this case. From equation 7–8, we find the required value of the test statistic as

$$z = \frac{\hat{p} - p_0}{\sqrt{p_0 q_0/n}} = \frac{7/600 - 0.0096}{\sqrt{(0.0096)(0.9904)/600}} = 0.519$$

FIGURE 7-18   Carrying Out the Test, Using $\alpha = 0.10$, in Example 7-11

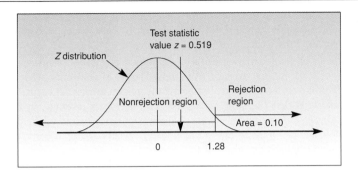

As can be seen, this result is not significant at any conventional level of significance because even if we were to take a 0.10 chance of a type I error, our right-hand critical point would be equal to $+1.28$, and the value of the test statistic would still lie in the nonrejection region. Clearly, for all smaller levels of α, we would also have to not reject the null hypothesis. We conclude that there is no statistical evidence to indicate that the association's claims are exaggerated. The test, carried out at the large level of significance $\alpha = 0.10$, is shown in Figure 7-18.

At this point, you may ask why we used a significance level of $\alpha = 0.10$ as the largest value for the probability of a type I error. Couldn't we have used larger values and shown that there really is no sufficient evidence that the null hypothesis is false? The computed test statistic value 0.519 lies inside the acceptance region for values of α even much larger than 0.10. How large would α have to be for us to *reject* the null hypothesis? That is, what is the "true" level of significance of this test—the *smallest* value of α for which we may reject the null hypothesis? This is the *p-value*, the topic of the next section.

PROBLEMS

In the following problems, first determine whether the required test is one-tailed or two-tailed, and then solve the problem. You will have to make your own decisions: what kind of test to use, whether it is one- or two-tailed, which is the appropriate distribution, and—in many cases— you will have to choose your own level of significance, α. As an aid in deciding whether a test is one-tailed or two-tailed, always ask yourself: Under what conditions do I want to take an action? The answer to this question will indicate to you the alternative hypothesis. (But remember that the equal sign must be in the null hypothesis.)

7-22.   An advertisement claims that three out of five doctors recommend a certain pharmaceutical product. The manufacturer of a competing brand of the medicine believes that this claim is exaggerated and sets out to prove so. A random sample of 100 doctors reveals that only 45 of them recommend the brand in question. Can you reject the manufacturer's claim?

7-23.   An advertisement for the Princess Hotel of Bermuda lists the price per person for weekend business meetings of more than 15 people as $194 (including airfare). The advertisement, which appeared in leading business journals, claims that $250 per person is the average price charged by hotels on the East Coast for business meetings of comparable length and attendance. The point of the advertisement was that it was cheaper to have a business meeting at the Princess in Bermuda than to have the meeting "at home" on the East Coast. A company planning a business meeting wanted to check whether the reported average price of $250 was correct or whether the Princess had exaggerated the East Coast average to make its own rate look good. A random sample of 19 hotels offering business meeting facilities gave a sample mean of $143 and a sample standard deviation of $52. Is there evidence to conclude that the advertisement for the Princess is false?

7–24. The theory of finance allows for the computation of "excess" returns, either above or below the current stock market average. An analyst wants to determine whether stocks in a certain industry group earn either above or below the market average at a certain time period. The null hypothesis is that there are no excess returns, on the average, in the industry in question. "No average excess returns" means that the population excess return for the industry is zero. A random sample of 24 stocks in the industry reveals a sample average excess return of 0.12 and sample standard deviation of 0.2. State the null and alternative hypotheses, and carry out the test at the $\alpha = 0.05$ level of significance.

7–25. The average weekly earnings for all full-time-equivalent employees are reported to be $344. Suppose that you want to check this claim since you believe it is too low. You want to prove that average weekly earnings of all employees are higher than the amount stated. You collect a random sample of 1,200 employees in all areas and find that the sample mean is $361 and the sample standard deviation is $110. Can you disprove the claim?

7–26. According to *Money,* the average amount of money that a typical American would need to make him or her feel rich is $1.5 million.[8] A researcher wants to test this claim. A random sample of 100 Americans reveals that their mean "amount to feel rich" is $2.3 million and the standard deviation is $0.5 million. Conduct the test.

7–27. The U.S. Department of Commerce estimates that 17% of all automobiles on the road in the United States at a certain time are made in Japan. An organization that wants to limit imports believes that the proportion of Japanese cars on the road during the period in question is higher than 17% and wants to prove this. A random sample of 2,000 cars is observed, 381 of which are made in Japan. Conduct the hypothesis test at $\alpha = 0.01$ and state whether you believe the reported figure.

7–28. Airplane tires are sensitive to the heat produced when the plane taxis along runways. A certain type of airplane tire used by Boeing is guaranteed to perform well at temperatures as high as 125°F. From time to time, Boeing performs quality control checks to determine whether the average maximum temperature for adequate performance is as stated, or whether the average maximum temperature is lower than 125°, in which case the company must replace all tires. Suppose that a random sample of 100 tires is checked. It is found that the average maximum temperature for adequate performance in the sample is 121° and the sample standard deviation is 2°. Conduct the hypothesis test, and conclude whether the company should take action to replace its tires.

7–29. A marine radar unit for use in small pleasure boats is guaranteed to detect objects as small as a 12-foot boat at an average maximum range of 8 nautical miles. A potential buyer conducts a test of 10 random trials of the radar unit. The results of the trials are that the average maximum distance at which a 12-foot boat was detected was 7.8 nautical miles and the sample standard deviation was 0.4 nautical miles. Use $\alpha = 0.05$ to determine whether the potential buyer should reject the radar manufacturer's claim.

7–30. A study of top executives' midlife crises indicates that 45% of all top executives suffer from some form of mental crisis in the years following corporate success. An executive who had undergone a midlife crisis opened a clinic providing counseling for top executives in the hope of reducing the number of executives who might suffer from this problem. A random sample of 125 executives who went through the program indicated that only 49 of them eventually showed signs of a midlife crisis. Do you believe that the program is beneficial and indeed reduces the proportion of executives who show signs of the crisis?

---

[8] G. Belsky, "Why Most of the Rich Will Get Richer," *Money,* May, 1995, p. 135.

7–31. The unemployment rate in Britain during a certain period was believed to have been 11%. At the end of the period in question, the government embarked on a series of projects to reduce unemployment. It was of interest to determine whether the average unemployment rate in the country had decreased as a result of these projects, or whether previously employed people were the ones hired for the project jobs, while the unemployed remained unemployed. A random sample of 3,500 people was chosen, and 421 of them were found to be unemployed. Do you believe that the government projects reduced the unemployment rate?

7–32. Certain eggs are stated to have reduced cholesterol content, with an average of only 2.5% cholesterol. A concerned health group wants to test whether the claim is true. The group believes that more cholesterol may be found, on the average, in the eggs. A random sample of 100 eggs reveals a sample average content of 5.2% cholesterol, and a sample standard deviation of 2.8%. Does the health group have cause for action?

7–33. The recent move toward internationalization in the financial markets has created an index called the World Market. Movements of stocks in this index reflect the average change in price, in U.S. dollars, of the "average" stock of all issues traded worldwide. For the week of November 24, the average percentage change in price in the World Market was reported to be −1.1%. An international investment firm regularly checks such reported price changes by collecting a random sample of 180 stocks, proportionally selected from all stock markets included in the World Market. Then a statistical hypothesis test is carried out to determine whether the average percentage change is as reported. The firm has no reason to believe that the actual average world price change is either above or below the reported value; it simply wants to check whether any deviation exists. For the week of November 24, the sample indicated $\bar{x} = -0.9\%$ and $s = 0.4\%$. Should the firm reject the stated average price change in the World Market as incorrect?

7–34. The following advertisement appeared in early 1991 in *Boston* magazine. An agency suspecting that *Boston* magazine was upwardly exaggerating its readers' average household income and frequency of dining out obtained the following data from a random sample of the magazine's readership:

Household income ($1,000/year): 45, 52, 30, 67, 90, 58, 35, 60, 44, 28, 50, 37, 69, 108, 46, 33, 48, 40, 65, 72, 39, 61, 56

Dining out (number of times/month): 3, 5, 1, 6, 5, 1, 2, 7, 4, 2, 4, 3, 5, 8, 0, 2, 5, 1, 5, 5, 2, 4, 3

Conduct the appropriate tests, and state your conclusions.

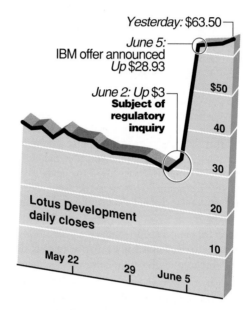

S. Antilla, "Regulatory Alarms Ring on Wall St.," the *New York Times,* Business Day Section, June 9, 1995, p. D1, with data from Datastream.

7–35.   This display is reprinted from the *New York Times.* The display refers to the jump in the price of Lotus common stock following the announcement by IBM that it made an offer to acquire Lotus. A trader wanted to test whether the new price, $63.50, reflected the average value computer industry executives would think reasonable for the firm's stock. The suspicion was that the price was overrated. The following is a random sample of computer industry executives' responses: 60, 60, 50, 50, 60, 55, 40, 35, 35, 40, 35, 35, 60, 30, 35, 40. Conduct the test.

7–36.   An article about transatlantic business claims that British Airways carried 11% of the 27 million people who fly across the Atlantic every year.[9] Suppose that you want to check this claim without any prior suspicion in mind. You get a random sample of passenger files from a random sample of travel agents, and you find that out of 2,000 people in your sample, 341 flew across the Atlantic with British Airways. Conduct the test, and state your conclusions.

---

[9] "Passing through Paris," *Forbes,* April 1, 1991, p. 90.

7-7   The *p*-Value

From all our examples, you already have an idea as to the nature of the *p*-value. Let us return to Example 7–11 of Section 7–6, where we tested the null hypothesis H_0: $p \leq 0.0096$ versus the alternative hypothesis H_1: $p > 0.0096$. Our sample size was large, and we used the approximate normal distribution of the sample proportion estimator. We computed the statistic $z = (\hat{p} - p_0)/\sqrt{p_0 q_0/n}$, and we found its value to be 0.519. We stated that this value of the test statistic leads us to nonrejection of the null hypothesis even at a significance level $\alpha = 0.10$ because the value 0.519 falls in the nonrejection region for $\alpha = 0.10$, defined by the critical point $z = +1.28$. We also noted that we used $\alpha = 0.10$ because it is the largest conventional level of significance employed, and if we can't reject the null hypothesis at this level, surely we have to not reject it at smaller values of α, which lead to greater values for the critical point (since 0.519 is smaller than 1.28, it is also smaller than 1.645, which corresponds to $\alpha = 0.05$). However, we know that 0.519 is much smaller than 1.28. Is it not true then, that the null hypothesis could also not be rejected at values of α larger than 0.10? The answer is yes, and we can—in the case of the normal distribution—actually compute the smallest possible α at which we may reject the null hypothesis.[10]

Let us ask ourselves: At what level, α, can we reject the null hypothesis, given that the value of our test statistic is $z = 0.519$, if we should insist on rejecting the null hypothesis? We know that the area to the right of 1.645 is 0.05, which is why we may reject the null hypothesis at the 0.05 level of significance if our test statistic value is as small as 1.645. Similarly, the area to the right of 1.28 is 0.10, which is why we could reject the null hypothesis at the 0.10 level if our test statistic is as small as 1.28. By this reasoning, let us find the area to the right of the actual computed value of our test statistic. That is, we seek the area to the right of $z = 0.519$. This area represents the smallest probability of a type I error, the smallest possible level α at which we may reject the null hypothesis. From Appendix C, Table 2, the table of probabilities of the standard normal distribution, we find that the area to the right of $z = 0.519$ is $0.5 - 0.1982$ (using an interpolation) $= 0.3018$. This number is called the *p-value*. The number 0.3018 means that, assuming that the null hypothesis is true, there is a 0.3018 probability of obtaining a test statistic value as extreme as we have (0.519) or more extreme (i.e., further to the right of $z = 0.519$ since this is a right-tailed test). Since this probability is rather high (much higher than the usually acceptable probability of a type I error: 0.01, 0.05, or even 0.10), we should not reject the null hypothesis.

Let us look at another example and then formally define the *p*-value and explore its ramifications. Returning to Example 7–8, Section 7–6, we see that the value of the test statistic in this example is $z = (\bar{x} - \mu_0)/(s/\sqrt{n}) = 2.5$. Clearly, this value of the test statistic leads us to reject the null hypothesis at values of α as small as 0.01 because the critical point for $\alpha = 0.01$ is 2.326, and $z = 2.5$ falls farther to the right—in the rejection region. However, 0.01 is not the smallest value of α at which we may reject the null hypothesis. To find the smallest level of significance at which

---

[10] This can be done also with the *t* distribution, as well as other distributions, although it is more difficult (due to the limitations of our tables) and usually requires a computer.

FIGURE 7–19   Computing the p-Value in Example 7–11

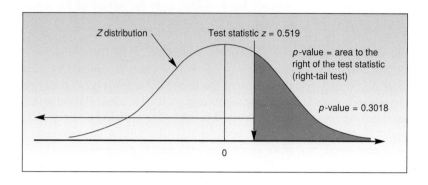

FIGURE 7–20   Computing the p-Value in Example 7–8

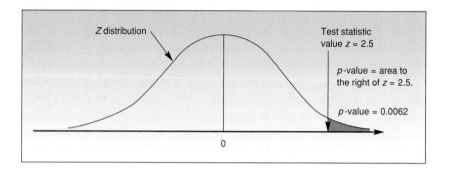

H_0 may be rejected, that is, the p-value, we need to find the area to the right of our computed value of the test statistic, $z = 2.5$. Looking in Table 2, we find the required probability as $0.5 - 0.4938 = 0.0062$. Thus, assuming that the null hypothesis is true, there is only a 0.0062 probability of observing a value of the test statistic as extreme as 2.5 or more extreme (larger than 2.5). If we were willing to take a 0.01 probability of committing a type I error, we could reject the null hypothesis. Even if we were willing to accept a probability of only 0.0062 of committing a type I error, we could still reject the null hypothesis. The p-value 0.0062 is the smallest value of α at which we may reject the null hypothesis. Suppose someone wants to take only a 0.001 probability of committing a type I error. Here that person could not reject the null hypothesis because the smallest probability of a type I error at which we may reject this particular hypothesis, given our value of z, is 0.0062.

In Example 7–9, Section 7–6, the obtained value of the test statistic is $z = -0.4$, and the test is a left-tailed test. Here the p-value is given as the area to the left of $z = -0.4$. Again, using the normal probability table, we find the p-value $= 0.5 - 0.1554 = 0.3446$. Here we may reject the null hypothesis only if we are willing to take a 0.3446 chance of committing a type I error. We therefore can't reject the null hypothesis if we use any conventional level of significance, α. Figures 7–19, 7–20, and 7–21 demonstrate the evaluation of the p-value in Examples 7–11, 7–8, and 7–9, respectively.

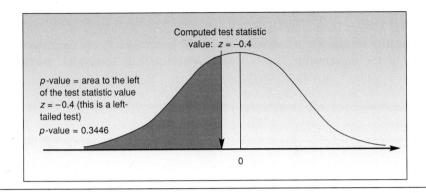

FIGURE 7–21 Computing the *p*-Value in Example 7–9

Computed test statistic
value: $z = -0.4$

p-value = area to the left
of the test statistic value
$z = -0.4$ (this is a left-
tailed test)
p-value = 0.3446

0

We now define the *p*-value:

The **p-value** is the smallest level of significance, α, at which a null hypothesis may be rejected using the obtained value of the test statistic.

Another way of looking at the *p*-value is as follows.

The *p*-value is the probability of obtaining a value of the test statistic as extreme as, or more extreme than, the actual value obtained, when the null hypothesis is true.

Logically, if our obtained value of the test statistic is not very likely (i.e., has a small *p*-value) assuming that the null hypothesis is true, then we should reject the null hypothesis. Similarly, if the obtained value of the test statistic is relatively likely (i.e., has a high *p*-value, say, above 0.05 or 0.10), then we should not reject the null hypothesis because there is no convincing evidence to reject it.

The *p*-value acts as a "personalized" level of significance that goes with our value of the test statistic. It is the *exact* α, or *attained* α, attached to the test statistic value we have and at which we may reject the null hypothesis. If this "exact α" is greater than, say, 0.05, then we can't reject the null hypothesis at $\alpha = 0.05$. If, on the other hand, the *p*-value is smaller than 0.05, we may reject the null hypothesis at $\alpha = 0.05$.

Reporting the *p*-value of a test is therefore a more general (less restrictive) way of reporting results of statistical hypothesis tests: it leaves the choice of α to the person using the results rather than the statistician performing the test. For example, suppose a test is carried out and we report that its *p*-value is 0.0002. This conveys much information to the reader. It tells him or her that the null hypothesis can be rejected at $\alpha = 0.01$ and that it can be rejected even at smaller values of α, such as 0.001. In fact, this *p*-value says that the null hypothesis can be rejected at values of α as small as $\alpha = 0.0002$. It also tells the receiver of the information that—assuming the null hypothesis is true—the probability of obtaining a test statistic value as extreme as the value obtained in the experiment, or more extreme than the obtained value, is 0.0002. Here, if one chooses to reject the null hypothesis given the obtained value of the test statistic, one is willing to take a chance of 2 in 10,000 of committing a type I error and thus "convicting an innocent person." Contrast the information content in the statement "*p*-value = 0.0002" with the very limited amount of information in the statement "we reject the null hypothesis at $\alpha = 0.05$," which could have been the reported result of the same test.

Suppose we have another case, where the p-value is 0.06. Reporting this value allows the reader to reject the null hypothesis if he or she is willing to use $\alpha = 0.06$. If the reader wants to use the $\alpha = 0.05$ level of significance, or anything smaller, then he or she will not be able to reject the null hypothesis. Reporting the p-value allows the reader to choose his or her own α and still know how to interpret the reported results of the experiment. The following are some rules of thumb developed by statisticians as aids in interpreting p-values.

When the *p*-value is *smaller than 0.01*, the result is called *very significant*.

When the *p*-value is *between 0.01 and 0.05*, the result is called *significant*.

When the *p*-value is *between 0.05 and 0.10*, the result is considered by some as *marginally significant* (and by most as not significant).

When the *p*-value is *greater than 0.10*, the result is considered *not significant*.

Reporting and using the p-value eliminates the necessity of making standard conclusions that may be too restrictive. Reporting a p-value of 0.000003 implies that the result is very unlikely if the null hypothesis is true; therefore, we feel strongly about rejecting the null hypothesis. The p-value gets smaller as the test statistic falls further away in the tail of the distribution. Therefore, even if we are unable to compute the p-value exactly, we may have an idea about its size. For example, suppose that we compute the value of a test statistic as $z = 120.97$. In a right-tailed test, this means that the p-value is equal to the area under the standard normal curve to the right of the point 120.97. Without a computer (which may not even give accurate results for a value as large as 120.97), we are unable to compute the exact p-value. We do know, however, that this probability is very, very small. We may then say that the p-value, although unknown, is an extremely small number; hence, we reject the null hypothesis with much conviction.

The further away in the tail of the distribution our test statistic falls, the smaller is the *p*-value and, hence, the more convinced we are that the null hypothesis is false and should be rejected.

Conversely, the closer our test statistic is to the center of the sampling distribution, the larger is the p-value; hence, we may be more convinced that we do not have enough evidence to reject the null hypothesis.

If you understand the idea of a p-value, and use it, your statistical conclusions will be more meaningful and more convincing. Try to report the p-value when you can compute it, or at least make a statement about its relative magnitude ("small p-value," "very small p-value," etc.) when you cannot compute it.

The t Distribution, the Chi-Square Distribution, and Others

In the case of statistical tests where the sampling distribution of the test statistic is the t distribution, we see from the t table (Appendix C, Table 3), that the exact p-values are not obtainable because the table contains values for only a few selected, "standard" values of α, such as 0.01 or 0.05. What do we do in such situations? As mentioned earlier, it is always possible to make some relative statements about the *p*-value. For example, suppose that in a left-tailed test we get a value of the test statistic $t = -2.4$, with df $= 15$. What is the *p*-value? From Appendix C, Table 3, we find that the value 2.4 for a *t* random variable with 15 degrees of freedom falls between the two values 2.131 and 2.602, corresponding to one-tail areas of 0.025 and 0.01, respectively. We may, therefore, conclude that the *p*-value is between 0.01 and 0.025. The use of a computer may allow us to give a more exact *p*-value. We know that the further in the tail the test statistic falls, the smaller the *p*-value. If we get a *t* statistic with 23 degrees of freedom equaling, say, 45.33, then we know that the *p*-value is very, very small (the area to the right of 2.807 is 0.005, from Table 3). The same holds for the chi-square distribution, as well as other distributions we will encounter that have few tabulated tail areas.

Two-Tailed Tests

> In a two-tailed test, we find the *p*-value by *doubling* the area in the tail of the distribution beyond the value of the test statistic.

In Example 7–4 the value of the test statistic was $z = (\bar{x} - \mu_0)/(s/\sqrt{n}) = 1.21$. What is the *p*-value? We must first find the area to the right of 1.21 (since 1.21 is a positive number, the area to its left would be over 0.5; if doubled, this would give the meaningless result of a number over 1.00). We find that the area to the right of $z = 1.21$ is equal to $0.5 - 0.3869$ (from Appendix C, Table 2) $= 0.1131$. Now, since the test is two-tailed, we must double the probability. The *p*-value is therefore equal to $2(0.1131) = 0.2262$. You may gain a feeling for the reason that the *p*-value must be twice the value it is for a one-tailed test from noting the following. The *z* value 1.645 corresponds to $\alpha = 0.05$ in a right-tailed test, but corresponds to $\alpha = 0.10$ in a two-tailed test. In a two-tailed test, there is another tail where possible rejection of the null hypothesis may occur. That tail contains an equal area beyond the negative of the obtained *z* value, on the other side of the distribution. The *p*-value for a one-tailed test and the *p*-value for a two-tailed test are shown in Figure 7–22.

FIGURE 7–22   The *p*-Value in a One-Tailed Test versus the *p*-Value in a Two-Tailed Test [Using the Statistic Value in Example 7–9]

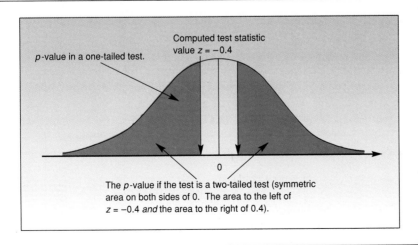

When we calculate the p-value, we are calculating the probability of obtaining a value of the test statistic as extreme as, or more extreme than, the value we have. If the null hypothesis in a two-tailed test is true, then we may obtain our value or more extreme values on *both* sides of the distribution, possibly leading us to commit a type I error in either of the two tails of the distribution. We must account for these possibilities and double the area in a single tail when calculating the p-value. In Example 7–4 we must account for values as extreme as, and more extreme than, 1.21 under the null hypothesis. We must account for values greater than or equal to 1.21, but we must also account for the possibility, under the null hypothesis, of obtaining the value -1.21 and all values to its left, which are as likely under the null hypothesis as the positive values 1.21 and beyond.

Since in a two-tailed test we may reject both on the left and on the right, and since under H_0 the positive and the negative values of the same absolute magnitude are equally likely, we must allow for this and include in the p-value both the area in the tail on which the test statistic falls and an equal area in the other tail of the distribution. This is demonstrated in Figure 7–23.

In a right-tailed test, the p-value is the area to the right of the test statistic if the test statistic is positive.

In a left-tailed test, the p-value is the area to the left of the test statistic if the test statistic is negative.

In a two-tailed test, the p-value is twice the area to the right of a positive test statistic or to the left of a negative test statistic.

For a quick interpretation of reported p-values you may want to use the following rule.

For a given level of significance, α:

Reject the null hypothesis if and only if $\alpha \geq p$-value.

FIGURE 7–23   The p-Value in a Two-Tailed Test

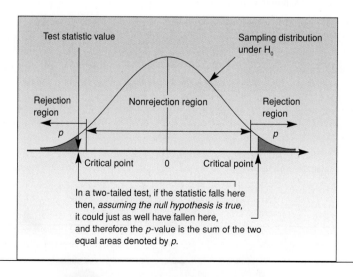

In other words, a result is *significant* at level α if the associated *p*-value is less than or equal to α. This rule is useful when looking at tables of reported results, such as computer-generated test results. It is easy to scan the results, comparing *p*-values (often reported as "significance") with, say, the value 0.05. Any result with a *p*-value less than or equal to 0.05 will then be noted as significant at the $\alpha = 0.05$ level. Remember, however, that a *p*-value contains much more information than just whether or not to reject the null hypothesis at a given level of significance, α. The *p*-value tells us how unusual our particular sample result is if we assume that the null hypothesis is true. This, in turn, gives us an indication as to how strongly we should feel about rejecting (or not rejecting) the null hypothesis in light of our evidence.

PROBLEMS

In the following problems, report the *p*-value if you can compute it exactly. If you cannot compute the *p*-value, give some bounds on its value or describe it as small, very small, large, etc., and state whether or not you reject the null hypothesis.

7–37. Several U.S. airlines carry passengers from the United States to countries in the Pacific region, and the competition in these flight routes is keen. One of the leverage factors for United Airlines in Pacific routes is that, whereas most other airlines fly to Pacific destinations two or three times weekly, United offers daily flights to Tokyo, Hong Kong, and Osaka. Before instituting daily flights, the airline needed to get an idea as to the proportion of frequent fliers in these routes who consider daily service an important aspect of business flights to the Pacific. From previous information, the management of United estimated that 60% of the frequent business travelers to the three destinations believed that daily service was an important aspect of airline service. Following changes in the airline industry, marked by reduced fares and other factors, the airline management wanted to check whether or not the proportion of frequent business travelers who believe that daily service is an important feature was still about 60%. A random sample of 250 frequent business fliers revealed that 130 of them thought daily service was important. Compute the *p*-value for this test (is this a one-tailed or a two-tailed test?) and state your conclusion.

7–38. An advertisement for the Toyota Supra model lists the following performance specifications: standing start, 0–50 mph in an average of 5.27 seconds; braking, 60 mph to 0 in 3.15 seconds on the average. An independent testing service hired by a competing manufacturer of high-performance automobiles wants to prove that Toyota's claims are exaggerated. A random sample of 100 trial runs gives the following results: standing start, 0–50 mph in an average of $\bar{x} = 5.8$ seconds and $s = 1.9$ seconds; braking, 60 mph to 0 in an average of $\bar{x} = 3.21$ seconds and $s = 0.6$ seconds. Carry out the two hypothesis tests, state the *p*-value of each test, and state your conclusions.

7–39. Borg-Warner manufactures hydroelectric miniturbines that generate low-cost, clean electric power from the energy in small rivers and streams. One of the models was known to produce an average of 25.2 kilowatts of electricity. Recently the model's design was improved, and the company wanted to test whether the model's average electric output had changed. There was no reason to suspect, a priori, a change in either direction. A random sample of 115 trial runs produced an average of 26.1 kilowatts and a standard deviation of 3.2 kilowatts. Carry out a statistical hypothesis test, give the *p*-value, and state your conclusion. Do you believe that the improved model has a different average output?

7–40. PepsiCo, Inc., tested a new orange-flavored soft drink, Mandarin Orange Slice. The company's research department determined that if more than 60% of the people who taste the drink like its taste, then the drink will be successful in terms of annual sales volume. Thus, they decided to test the null hypothesis that the proportion of people who respond positively to the new taste is at most 0.60 versus the alternative that the proportion is over 0.60. A random sample of 1,000 people turned out 845 positive responses. What can you say about the *p*-value of this test? How strongly do you feel about the potential success of Mandarin Orange Slice? Explain.

7–41. It is claimed that a two-bedroom apartment in Taiwan costs an average of $200,000.[11] This high price supposedly keeps many young Taiwanese couples from owning a home, and a government official in charge of the problem wanted to check whether the stated average is correct or is upwardly inflated. A random sample of 1,000 two-bedroom apartments throughout Taiwan gave a sample mean of $195,200 and a sample standard deviation of $49,750. Conduct the test, and find the p-value. Carefully explain what is happening here, both in statistical terms and in practical terms. Write your conclusions in the form of a memo.

7–42. The following results on abnormal trading volume of stocks before ex-dividend days are taken from an article in the *Journal of Financial Economics.*[12]

Yield Group	Trading Size Group	Abnormal Volume ($)	t-Value
1	1	−6,524	−5.16
1	2	−11,433	−5.43
1	3	−14,957	−2.97
1	4	60,856	2.51
2	1	−3,023	−5.90
2	2	−7,947	−5.41
2	3	−9,220	−1.91
2	4	116,189	3.17
3	1	−1,114	−2.50
3	2	−455	−0.35
3	3	3,677	0.78
3	4	265,023	7.95
4	1	811	1.52
4	2	6,560	3.77
4	3	32,288	4.28
4	4	397,997	4.34

The sample size in every case was well over 500; therefore, you may consider the reported t values as z values and use the normal distribution. The test implied in each yield group and trading size group is a test for the existence of average abnormal returns. Without getting into the technical details of these special tests, use the reported z values to determine the p-values. For each yield and trading size combination, state whether or not you believe that average abnormal returns are present in the entire population of stocks in the group. All tests are two-tailed.

7–43. Select a random sample of the problems in the preceding sections of this chapter, and determine the p-values of the hypothesis tests.

7–8   Tests Involving Finite Populations[13]

When we deal with a finite population containing N elements, and when the sample size, n, represents 5% or more of the population, we need to use a finite-population correction factor. Recall from our discussion in Chapter 6 that the finite-population correction factor is given by equation 6–8 as

$$\sqrt{\frac{N-n}{N-1}}$$

---

[11] "Rebuilding a Tiger: Who'll Get the Lion's Share?" *Business Week,* March 25, 1991, p. 46.

[12] J. Jakonishok and T. Vermaelen, "Tax-Induced Trading around Ex-dividend Days," *Journal of Financial Economics,* July, 1986.

[13] This is an optional section.

The finite-population correction factor multiplies the standard deviation of our estimator in hypothesis tests in the same way as in the construction of confidence intervals.

In the case of hypothesis tests of the population mean, μ, we incorporate a finite-population correction factor, by using the standard deviation given by equation 7–12. (When the population standard deviation, σ, is unknown, we substitute the sample standard deviation, s, for it.)

Standard deviation of $\overline{X}$ using a finite-population correction factor:

$$\sigma_{\overline{x}} = \frac{\sigma}{\sqrt{n}} \sqrt{\frac{N-n}{N-1}} \tag{7-12}$$

For testing hypotheses about the population proportion, p, the standard deviation of the sample proportion, $\hat{P}$, that incorporates a finite-population correction factor is given by equation 7–13.

Standard deviation of $\hat{P}$ using a finite-population correction factor:

$$\sigma_{\hat{P}} = \sqrt{\frac{pq}{n}} \sqrt{\frac{N-n}{N-1}} \tag{7-13}$$

We demonstrate the use of equations 7–12 and 7–13 in hypothesis tests with the following examples.

An accountant wants to test the hypothesis that the average balance of the 1,240 accounts at a sporting goods store is at most \$35.00 versus the alternative that the average account is over \$35.00. The sample size used is $n = 100$, and the sampling results are $\overline{x} = \$38.90$ and $s = \$15.00$.

EXAMPLE 7-12

Since the sample size is $n = 100$, the sampling fraction n/N is $100/1{,}240 = 0.0806$, which is over 5%. This makes it necessary to use the finite-population correction factor. The hypotheses are H_0: $\mu \le 35$ and H_1: $\mu > 35$. We now compute the test statistic, using equation 7–12 for the standard error of $\overline{X}$. We get

SOLUTION

$$z = \frac{\overline{x} - \mu_0}{(s/\sqrt{n})\sqrt{(N-n)/(N-1)}} = \frac{38.9 - 35}{(15/10)\sqrt{(1{,}140/1{,}239)}} = 2.71$$

Since this is a right-tailed test, we find that the p-value here is equal to 0.0034, and the null hypothesis can be rejected.

A company has 2,000 employees. Management wants to test the null hypothesis that no more than half the employees feel positively about the prospect of a takeover bid by a large multinational corporation, against the alternate hypothesis that more than half the employees feel positively about the impending takeover bid. A random sample of 200 employees is chosen, 180 of whom confess to having a positive feeling about the possible takeover bid. Carry out the hypothesis test.

EXAMPLE 7-13

SOLUTION

We want to test the hypotheses H_0: $p \leq 0.5$ and H_1: $p > 0.5$. The test statistic, using equation 7–13 for the standard error of $\hat{P}$, is

$$z = \frac{\hat{p} - p_0}{\sqrt{p_0 q_0 (N - n)/n(N - 1)}} = \frac{180/200 - 0.5}{\sqrt{(0.5)(0.5)/200}\ \sqrt{1800/1999}} = 11.92$$

The value of the test statistic is very large with a very small p-value (far outside the range of the normal table). We can therefore conclude that there is strong evidence to reject the null hypothesis and believe that over 50% of all employees feel positively about the takeover bid for their company.

PROBLEMS

7–44.   The Australian firm Elders IXL Ltd. became the first foreign concern to own a major British beermaker, Courage Brewing, Ltd., whose beers are sold in Britain's 5,000-odd pubs. Assume that before the takeover, Elders wanted to test the hypothesis that the percentage of pubs in England selling Courage beers is 90% versus the alternative hypothesis that it is over 90%. Elders gathered a random sample of 250 pubs, 229 of which were found to carry Courage beers. What conclusion can be made? (Assume there are exactly 5,000 pubs in England.)

7–45.   The Star Company recently signed a contract with Southland Corporation to supply videocassettes for rental in 1,400 7-Eleven stores throughout the country. Before signing the agreement, a test was carried out to determine whether average weekly revenues per store for the rental of videocassettes would be over $300, which was considered the break-even value. Thus, it was desired to test the null hypothesis H_0: $\mu \leq 300$ versus the alternative H_1: $\mu > 300$, and to go ahead with the deal only if the null hypothesis can be rejected at $\alpha = 0.01$. A random sample of 400 of the 1,400 7-Eleven stores was chosen. It was found that the sample mean was $521.05 and the sample standard deviation was $102.50. Conduct the test and state your conclusion. What effect did the finite-population correction have in this case?

7–46.   An analyst wants to test the null hypothesis that the average price change for all stocks listed in the Fortune 500 for a given week is zero, versus the alternative hypothesis that the average price change for the Fortune 500 stocks is not zero. A random sample of 45 stocks listed in the Fortune 500 gives $\bar{x} = +\$0.125$ and $s = \$0.275$. What is the p-value? What should the analyst conclude?

7–47.   There are 155 banks involved in certain international transactions. A federal agency claims that at least 35% of these banks have total assets of over $10 billion (in U.S. dollars). An independent agency wants to test this claim. It gets a random sample of 50 out of the 155 banks and finds that 15 of them have total assets of over $10 billion. Can the claim be rejected?

7–48.   An importer of jewelry from Italy has just received a shipment of 1,500 pieces of jewelry of the same kind. Usually, the shipment is acceptable if no more than 8% of the pieces are damaged. The importer gathers a random sample of 100 pieces and finds that 11 of them are damaged. Should the shipment be rejected on the grounds that over 8% of the total shipment is damaged?

7–9   Tests of Hypotheses about the Population Variance[14]

In Section 6–6 we noted that in some cases it is of interest to draw inferences about the population variance, σ^2. Examples of such situations involve production processes where the variance of the number of items produced by a machine must be controlled

---

[14] This is an optional section.

to within some upper bound, or the time spent in waiting lines, the variance of which must also be relatively small to prevent the queue from building up. While two-tailed tests *may* be carried out, it is usually of interest to test whether the population variance *exceeds* some level—in which case an action should be taken. Thus, a right-tailed test is most useful. The distribution used is the chi-square distribution with $n - 1$ degrees of freedom, and the test statistic is given by

---

Test statistic for the population variance:

$$\chi^2 = \frac{(n - 1)s^2}{\sigma_0^2} \qquad (7\text{--}14)$$

where σ_0^2 is the value of the variance stated in the null hypothesis

---

Tests using the chi-square distribution require the assumption of a *normally distributed population*. The rationale of a hypothesis test for the variance is the following: If the null hypothesis is true and the population variance is indeed σ_0^2, then the quantity in equation 7–14 possesses a chi-square distribution with $n - 1$ degrees of freedom. Hence, the probability that the statistic χ^2 will exceed any value is given by the area to the right of that value under the chi-square curve with $n - 1$ degrees of freedom. For example, suppose that some variable χ^2 has the chi-square distribution with 21 degrees of freedom. Then the probability that the variable will exceed 41.4 is 0.005. This is seen by consulting Appendix C, Table 4, and noting that the critical point for a right-hand tail area of 0.005 for a chi-square variable with 21 degrees of freedom is 41.4. This is shown in Figure 7–24.

Suppose that a null hypothesis about the variance is false and that the population variance is greater than the hypothesized value σ_0^2. Then the quantity in equation 7–14 will be greater than some critical point of the chi-square distribution, leading to the rejection of the null hypothesis. So, if we observe a value of the test statistic, χ^2, larger than, say, the critical point for $\alpha = 0.05$, we may reject the null hypothesis, taking a 0.05 chance of committing a type I error (if the null hypothesis is true, then only 5% of the time we would observe χ^2 values above that critical point). Let's look at an example.

FIGURE 7–24   A Critical Point of the Chi-Square Distribution with df = 21

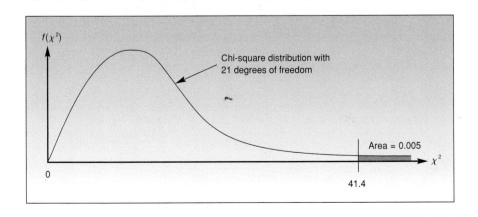

EXAMPLE 7-14   A machine makes small metal plates that are used in batteries for electronic games. The diameter of a plate is a random variable with mean 5 mm. As long as the variance of the diameter of the plates is at most 1.00 (mm²), the production process is under control and the plates are acceptable. If, however, the variance exceeds 1.00, the machine must be repaired. A quality-control engineer wants, therefore, to test the following hypotheses: H_0: $\sigma^2 \leq 1.00$ and H_1: $\sigma^2 > 1.00$. The engineer collects a random sample of 31 plates and finds that the sample variance is $s^2 = 1.62$. Is there evidence that the variance of the production process is above 1.00?

SOLUTION   We compute the test statistic χ^2 of equation 7–14:

$$\chi^2 = \frac{(n-1)s^2}{\sigma_0^2} = \frac{(30)(1.62)}{1.00} = 48.6$$

From Appendix C, Table 4, we find that, for a chi-square random variable with 30 degrees of freedom, the critical point for $\alpha = 0.05$ in a right-tailed test is 43.77. Therefore, the null hypothesis may be rejected at the 0.05 level of significance. For $\alpha = 0.025$, we find that the critical point is 46.98, so we may still reject the null hypothesis at this level. On the other hand, for $\alpha = 0.01$, the critical point is 50.89, and the null hypothesis cannot be rejected at this level of significance. These values allow us to establish bounds on the p-value for this test: the p-value is between 0.025 and 0.01. Reject the null hypothesis if you are willing to take a 0.025 chance of a type I error; do not reject the null hypothesis if you want to take no more than a 0.01 chance of a type I error. Since this is a production process, the engineer should probably decide to stop production and service the machine. The test is shown in Figure 7–25.

When we need to use a chi-square distribution that is not listed in Table 4, approximate values may be used. Also, recall that as the degrees of freedom increase, χ^2 approaches a normal distribution with mean df and variance 2 df (this is due to a form of the central limit theorem). This can be used in finding the critical points for a test. For example, if we have a chi-square random variable with 150 degrees of

FIGURE 7-25   Carrying out the Test of Example 7-14

freedom, we may use as an approximation a normal random variable with $\mu = 150$ and standard deviation $\sigma = \sqrt{300}$ (because the variance is twice 150). Find the right-hand critical point for this distribution using $\alpha = 0.05$. The solution is as follows. For the standard normal random variable Z, we know that the critical point would be 1.645. Here we need to find the point for a normal random variable with mean $\mu = 150$ and standard deviation $\sigma = \sqrt{300} = 17.32$. The critical point is $\mu + 1.645\sigma = 150 + (1.645)(17.32) = 178.49$. Let us find the two critical points for a two-tailed test at $\alpha = 0.05$ for a chi-square random variable with 100 degrees of freedom, using the normal approximation. They are $\mu \pm 1.96\sigma = 100 \pm 1.96(\sqrt{200}) = 100 \pm 1.96(14.1421) = 72.28$ and 127.72. These values are close to the corresponding table values for df $= 100$.[15]

PROBLEMS

7–49. An economist wants to test the null hypothesis that the variance of family incomes in the population in a certain region is less than or equal to 25,000,000 (dollars squared) versus the alternative that it is over 25,000,000. A random sample of 25 families gives a sample standard deviation of 7,000. Conduct the test at $\alpha = 0.01$, and state your conclusion.

7–50. An accountant wants to test the null hypothesis that the variance of the amounts in company accounts is equal to 10,000 (dollars squared) versus the alternative that the variance is not equal to 10,000. A random sample of 30 accounts gives a sample variance of 13,896. Conduct the two-tailed test at the $\alpha = 0.05$ level of significance.

7–51. Computer integrated manufacturing (CIM) is a method of integrating all manufacturing activities and controlling them by a central computer. The biggest problem faced by companies using CIM is system failure. The problem is that when the computer goes down, the entire manufacturing system shuts down. Stratus is one company that installs CIM systems for its clients. Once Stratus installs a system, it checks not only for the mean time until system failure occurs but also for the variance of times until failure. If the variance of failure times is believed to be above 530 (days squared), the system is reworked. System testing is carried out by computer, which allows running the system many times until failure without requiring the use of "real time." One such simulation was equivalent to a random sample of 300 time-until-failure trials and revealed a sample variance of 544. Is there evidence that the system needs reworking?

7–52. If the variance of waiting times at a certain bank is believed to be over 1.5 (minutes squared), the system needs adjustment. Such adjustments may include replacing tellers, adding tellers, or enrolling tellers in a training program. The bank regularly checks to see whether or not there is evidence that the variance of waiting times is above the allowed level. A random sample of 60 waiting times gives a sample variance of 1.8 minutes squared. Conduct the test, give an approximate p-value, and state your conclusion.

7–10   The Probability of a Type II Error and the Power of the Test[16]

You may have wondered why, until now, we have only concerned ourselves with the probability of a type I error, α—completely ignoring β, the probability of committing a type II error. Part of the reason for this is that we have determined—consistent with our analogy of the legal system—that a type I error is more serious than a type II error, and, therefore, we should try to control the type I error by setting its probability

---

[15] A better approximation is possible with the formula $\chi^2 = \frac{1}{2}(z + \sqrt{2 \text{ df} - 1})^2$. In this example, we get $\chi_1^2 = 73.77$ and $\chi_2^2 = 129.07$.

[16] In a short course, this section may be optional. However, some discussion of power should be provided from this section.

to a small level, α. From that point, we have carried out our tests at given levels of significance without knowing our probabilities of committing errors of type II.

Another reason we have ignored the type II error probability for so long is that it is complicated to compute, due to the fact that this probability depends on the particular value of the parameter, out of all values covered by the alternative hypothesis. Recall that, in the case of tests for μ, we said that β should actually be written $\beta(\mu)$ to indicate this dependence. We will now see why β depends on the value of the parameter. We will compute the probability β in certain situations, as well as the value $1 - \beta$, called the *power* of the test. As a simple example, let us consider the following hypothesis test:

$$\text{H}_0: \mu = 60$$
$$\text{H}_1: \mu = 65 \qquad\qquad (7-15)$$

These hypotheses are of a kind we have not seen before. The set consists of two simple hypotheses: either the mean is equal to 60, or it is equal to 65. Usually, our hypotheses are not simple but composite ones—covering a range of values.

Let us investigate the probability of a type II error in this simple case. Suppose that the sample size is $n = 100$ and that the population standard deviation is known and given as $\sigma = 20$. In our investigation of the probability of a type II error, we will find it convenient to consider the test in the scale of the problem itself, rather than in the standardized z scale. The particular simple test in equation $7-15$ is a right-tailed test. We have only two choices: either we conclude that the population mean is equal to 60 (not reject the null hypothesis), or we conclude that the population mean is equal to 65 (reject the null hypothesis). Clearly, such a situation rarely arises in a real application because it is too restrictive. This type of hypothesis testing is useful, however, in helping us understand the type II error and its probability.

Let us now determine the rejection region and the critical point for a given level of significance $\alpha = 0.05$. We know that the value of Z for a right-tailed test at $\alpha = 0.05$ is $z = 1.645$. Transforming this value to the scale of the problem in order to determine the critical point, C, we have: $C = \mu_0 + 1.645\sigma/\sqrt{n} = 60 + 1.645(20/10) = 63.29$. The critical point and the rejection region are shown in Figure $7-26$.

FIGURE 7-26 Determining the Rejection Region and the Probability of a Type II Error for the Test in Equation 7-15

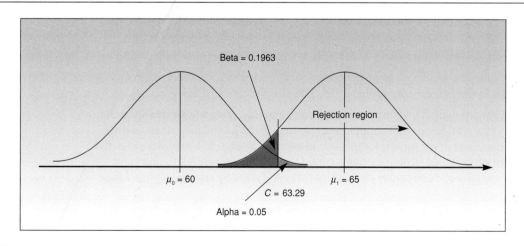

The figure shows two curves. One is the curve corresponding to the sampling distribution of $\overline{X}$ if the null hypothesis is true; this is the curve centered over the mean $\mu = 60$. The area under this curve to the right of the critical point $C = 63.29$ is equal to 0.05. This is the probability that the sample mean $\overline{X}$ will fall above the critical point when the population mean is indeed equal to 60; it is the probability of a type I error. Now, however, we are also interested in the probability of a type II error. The true state of nature could be only one of two possibilities: either the population mean is 60 (null hypothesis) or it is 65 (alternative hypothesis). Therefore, a type II error occurs if and only if we should decide that the true mean is 60 (i.e., not reject the null hypothesis) when in reality the alternative hypothesis is true and the population mean is 65. The question here is: When is a type II error committed? A type II error is committed if the test statistic $\overline{X}$ falls to the left of the critical point C when the population mean is equal to 65. This is so because if the mean is 65 and the test statistic falls to the left of C, then the test statistic is in the nonrejection region of the null hypothesis. We then fail to reject a false null hypothesis.

What is the probability, β, of committing such an error? *The probability that $\overline{X}$ will fall to the left of point C when the population mean is $\mu = 65$ is given by the area to the left of C under the normal curve centered over the mean 65.* We have the following conditional probabilities.

Probability of type I error:

$$\alpha = P(\overline{X} > C \mid \mu = \mu_0) \qquad (7\text{–}16)$$

Probability of type II error:

$$\beta = P(\overline{X} < C \mid \mu = \mu_1) \qquad (7\text{–}17)$$

The probability α was preset to 0.05 by construction. The probability of the type II error, β, is not determined by us; it is whatever the area to the left of C under the curve centered at 65 may be. Let us solve equation 7–17 to find the value of β.

$$\beta = P(\overline{X} < C \mid \mu = \mu_1) = P\!\left(\frac{\overline{X} - \mu_1}{\sigma/\sqrt{n}} < \frac{C - \mu_1}{\sigma/\sqrt{n}}\right)$$
$$= P\!\left(Z < \frac{63.29 - 65}{20/10}\right)$$
$$= P(Z < -0.855) = 0.1963$$

Thus, our probability of erroneously deciding to accept the null hypothesis that the population mean is 60, when in reality the population mean is equal to 65, is $\beta = 0.1963$.

We solved equation 7–17 for β by noting the following: If the alternative hypothesis is true, then the population mean is equal to μ_1, which is 65. Under this assumption, $\overline{X}$ is a normally distributed random variable (by the central limit theorem) with mean 65 and with the same standard deviation as in the case where H_0 is true: $\sigma/\sqrt{n}$. Therefore, in order to evaluate the probability β, we transform $\overline{X}$ into Z using the value μ_1 as the mean of $\overline{X}$.

The situation is shown in Figure 7–26 with both curves and both areas. We conclude that carrying out this hypothesis test allows us a 0.05 chance of rejecting the null hypothesis when the null hypothesis is true, and a 0.1963 chance of not rejecting the null hypothesis when the null hypothesis is false and the actual population mean is 65. We now define the *power* of a statistical hypothesis test.

> The **power** of a statistical hypothesis test is the probability of rejecting the null hypothesis when the null hypothesis is false.

Thus, the power of a test is the probability of rejecting a null hypothesis that should indeed be rejected. Clearly, the probability of rejecting H_0 when H_0 is false is equal to 1 minus the probability of not rejecting H_0 when H_0 is false. Thus, we have

$$\text{Power} = 1 - \beta \qquad (7-18)$$

The term *power* is quite appropriate. Considering the fact that we want to reject null hypotheses that are false, a test is *powerful* if it gives us a high probability of rejecting a false null hypothesis. Power is a measure of our ability to demonstrate that H_1, rather than H_0, is the correct hypothesis. In the preceding example, the power of the test is equal to $1 - \beta = 1 - 0.1963 = 0.8037$. We have a 0.8037 chance of rejecting the null hypothesis when the true mean is 65 rather than 60 as stated in the null hypothesis.

In most situations, the hypotheses to be tested are not simple hypotheses like the ones we have just considered. Most hypothesis tests are of the composite type; that is, they include a range of values to be tested. Whatever the form of our test, the null hypothesis always contains a single number to be used in carrying out the test (this is the value obtained from the equal sign in the null hypothesis). For example, the null hypothesis H_0: $\mu \leq 60$ is tested as if it were H_0: $\mu = 60$ because 60 is the maximum of all values of μ under the null hypothesis. The assumption of "innocence" means we allow the mean to be as large as 60, and test to see if it is greater than this maximum value. In two-tailed tests, the null hypothesis contains a single value only. However, the alternative hypothesis (except in simple cases such as the one just considered) always contains many—in fact, infinitely many—possible values. If the null hypothesis is H_0: $\mu \leq 60$, then the alternative hypothesis is H_1: $\mu > 60$. How can we define the power of the test in such situations?

Power is the probability of rejecting the null hypothesis when the null hypothesis is false. But in the example above, the null hypothesis can be false in an infinite number of ways: the population mean could be 61, or 67, or 72.8653, or 999.87, or *any* value above 60. What, then, is the probability of correctly rejecting the null hypothesis when the population mean is any number above 60? It should be easy to see that this probability depends on the actual value of the population mean. The larger the population mean, μ, the greater the probability that the sample mean, $\overline{X}$, will fall away from 60 and away from the critical point, C, determined by our level of significance, α. The power is demonstrated for the hypothesis test H_0: $\mu \leq 60$ versus H_1: $\mu > 60$ for various values of μ covered by the alternative hypothesis. We assume that the sample size is $n = 100$, the population standard deviation is $\sigma = 20$, and $\alpha = 0.05$. This is shown in Figure 7–27. The actual power, evaluated at each of several selected values of μ, is given in Table 7–3. Note that the figure also shows the power at $\mu = \mu_0 = 60$. This is the probability of rejecting the null hypothesis when $\mu = \mu_0$—the probability of a type I error, $\alpha = 0.05$.

Table 7–3 contains the value of β for each selected value of μ_1 and the corresponding power, $1 - \beta$. (The values selected for the table are integers, although the

FIGURE 7-27
Power at Different Values of μ

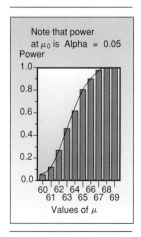

Note that power at μ_0 is Alpha = 0.05

Power

Values of μ

TABLE 7–3 The Power of the Test at Selected Values of μ under H_1

Value of μ	β	Power $= 1 - \beta$
61	0.8739	0.1261
62	0.7405	0.2595
63	0.5577	0.4423
64	0.3613	0.6387
65	0.1963	0.8037
66	0.0877	0.9123
67	0.0318	0.9682
68	0.0092	0.9908
69	0.0021	0.9979

power is defined for any value μ_1, integer or otherwise.) We see that the power of a test depends on the possible values of the population parameter under the alternative hypothesis. Thus, both the probability of a type II error, β, and its complement, the power, depend on the value of the mean. The dependence of the power on the value the parameter is called the **power function.** The power function, also called the *power curve*, is shown for our particular test in Figure 7–28.

Note that the values in Table 7–3, which were used in the construction of the function in Figure 7–28, were calculated in exactly the same way we computed the power in the simple hypothesis test described earlier, where the alternative value of the mean was $\mu_1 = 65$. Since our present, composite, one-tailed test has the same critical point, sample size, and assumed standard deviation, the same formula, equation 7–17, applies, and we obtain the values of β by substituting in the equation each appropriate value for the population mean for which we want to compute β and the power. Note that the power as shown for $\mu_1 = 65$ in Table 7–3 conforms with the value we computed earlier in the simple hypothesis test.

The power of a statistical hypothesis test depends on the following factors.

1. The power depends on the distance between the value of the parameter under the null hypothesis and the *true value* of the parameter in question: *the greater this distance, the greater the power.*
2. The power depends on the population standard deviation: *the smaller the population standard deviation, the greater the power.*
3. The power depends on the sample size used: *the larger the sample, the greater the power.*
4. The power depends on the level of significance of the test: *the smaller the level of significance, α, the smaller the power.*

Suppose that you look at the values of the power function shown in Table 7–3, and you decide that it is important to be able to reject the null hypothesis if the true population mean is $\mu = 62$. The value $\mu = 62$ falls under the alternative hypothesis; however, for this particular value, the test is rather weak—the power is only 0.2595. That is, if the true population mean is 62, we only have a 0.2595 chance of rejecting the null hypothesis. As we see from the table and from Figure 7–28, the power increases quickly, and if the true mean is equal to 69, we have a 0.9979 chance of rejecting the null hypothesis. That still doesn't solve the problem of what to do if we want to have a high power—a high probability of rejecting the null hypothesis—if the

**FIGURE 7–28
Power Function (for a One-Tailed Test)**

FIGURE 7-29
Power Curve for a
Two-Tailed Test and the
Power Curve for a One-
Tailed Test

Power curve for a
two-tailed test

Power curve for a
one-tailed test

true mean is $\mu = 62$. Looking at the four statements about power, we realize that we cannot control the first two factors. We can, however, use the next two properties. We can either reduce our demands on the level of significance, that is, increase α, or—the better solution—we can increase the sample size. Increasing the sample size is a way of increasing the power of a test without sacrificing the level of significance, α (our protection against a type I error).

Let us now use equation 7–17 to compute the power of the test at $\mu = 62$ if the sample size is increased to $n = 400$ (and the level of significance stays the same, $\alpha = 0.05$). Note that increasing the sample size changes the critical point as well. A larger sample size brings the critical point closer to the center of the distribution (the null-hypothesized value). First we solve for the new critical point. We have $C = \mu_0 + 1.645\sigma/\sqrt{n} = 60 + 1.645(20/20) = 61.645$. Now we compute the new power for $\mu = 62$. We have, using equation 7–17,

$$\beta = P\left(Z < \frac{C - \mu_1}{\sigma/\sqrt{n}}\right) = P\left(Z < \frac{61.645 - 62}{20/20}\right)$$

$$= P(Z < -0.355) = 0.3613$$

The power is $1 - \beta = 0.6387$. This is much higher than the power we had when the sample size was only 100.

What about two-tailed tests? The power curve for our test of the null hypothesis $H_0: \mu = \mu_0$ versus the two-tailed alternative $H_1: \mu \neq \mu_0$ is shown in Figure 7–29. Also shown, for comparison, is the power curve for a one-tailed test.

EXAMPLE 7-15

An advertisement for Saab states that *Car and Driver* magazine determined that the Saab 9000 goes from 0 to 60 mph in 7.7 seconds, while *Road & Track* magazine tested this car at 7.6 seconds in going from 0 to 60 mph. Makers of a competing automobile feel that if the true average number of seconds it takes the Saab 9000 to reach 60 mph from zero is *above* the 7.6 figure claimed by *Road & Track*, and in particular, if it takes an average of 7.7 seconds, as determined by *Car and Driver*, the competitor could advertise its own car as a better model with respect to this performance aspect. Thus, the makers of the competing automobile want to test the Saab 9000 and carry out the following hypothesis test: $H_0: \mu \leq 7.6$ and $H_1: \mu > 7.6$. Since the competitor wants to have a high probability of rejecting the null hypothesis if μ is equal to the value 7.7, covered under the alternative hypothesis, the firm is interested in finding the power of the test evaluated at $\mu_1 = 7.7$.

Suppose that the sample size available for this test is $n = 150$ trials and that the population standard deviation (from previous driving tests) is believed to be $\sigma = 0.4$ seconds. The required level of significance is $\alpha = 0.05$. What is the power? That is, if the true average time is 7.7 seconds, what is the probability of rejecting the null hypothesis that the average time is at most 7.6 seconds?

SOLUTION

First we find the critical point: $C = \mu_0 + 1.654\sigma/\sqrt{n} = 7.6 + 1.645(0.4/12.25) = 7.6537$. Now we find the power at $\mu = 7.7$.

$$\text{Power} = P(\bar{X} > C \mid \mu = 7.7) = P\left(Z > \frac{7.6537 - 7.7}{0.4/12.25}\right)$$

$$= P(Z > -1.42) = 0.9222$$

The competitor thus has a 0.9222 chance of rejecting the null hypothesis when the true average time it takes the Saab 9000 to go from 0 to 60 mph is 7.7 seconds. Note that in our calculation we used the probability definition of power directly, without first computing β.

7–53. Recent near misses in the air, as well as several fatal accidents, have brought air traffic controllers under close scrutiny. As a result of a high-level inquiry into the accuracy of speed and distance determinations through radar sightings of airplanes, a statistical test was proposed to check the air traffic controllers' claim that a commercial jet's position can be determined, on the average, to within 110 feet in the usual range around airports in the United States. The proposed test was given as: H_0: $\mu \leq 110$ versus the alternative H_1: $\mu > 110$. The test was to be carried out at the 0.05 level of significance using a random sample of 80 airplane sightings. The statistician designing the test wanted to determine the power of this test if the actual average distance at detection is 120 feet. An estimate of the standard deviation is 30 feet. Compute the power at $\mu_1 = 120$ feet.

7–54. McDonald's Corporation has been steadily moving into more countries around the world. Recent reports show that McDonald's has been interested in opening franchises in Poland. As part of its efforts to sell fast foods in Poland, McDonald's Corporation has been evaluating the potential of using Polish-grown potatoes not only in Poland, but also for distribution in other European countries. The feasibility of such an option depends on the demand for french-fried potatoes in all of McDonald's European franchises. Company analysts believe that if the average weekly demand for fries per franchise per week is above 500 package units, it may be feasible to use Polish-grown potatoes. Thus, the analysts want to test the null hypothesis H_0: $\mu \leq 500$ versus the alternative hypothesis H_1: $\mu > 500$. The company has data on 100 weekly sales randomly obtained from franchises throughout the continent. The test is to be carried out at the 0.05 level of significance, and an estimate of the population variance is 2,500 (units squared). What is the power of the test if the true mean is 520 units per franchise per week?

7–55. The Polaroid Spectra® camera has an electronic device that makes complex focusing and exposure decisions in 50 thousandths of a second. Before each device is installed in a camera, it is tested by quality control inspectors. The device is linked to a simulator that runs a random sample of 80 situations and measures the sample average reaction time of the device. The statistical test is H_0: $\mu \leq 50$ (thousandths of a second) versus the alternative H_1: $\mu > 50$ (thousandths of a second). If the null hypothesis is not rejected, the device is considered to have good quality and is installed in a camera; otherwise it is replaced. The test is carried out at the 0.01 level of significance, and the population standard deviation is $\sigma = 20$ (thousandths of a second). For quality control considerations, inspectors need to have a high power for this test, that is, a high probability of rejecting a faulty device, when the average speed of the device is 60 thousandths of a second. Find the power at this level of μ. Also compute the power at other levels, and sketch the power curve.

7–56. A large manufacturing firm believes that its market share is 45%. From time to time, a statistical hypothesis test is carried out to check whether the assertion is true. The test consists of gathering a random sample of 500 products sold nationally and finding what percentage of the sample constitutes brands made by the firm. Whenever the test is carried out, there is no suspicion as to the direction of a possible change in market share, i.e., increase or decrease; the company wants to detect any change at all. The tests are carried out at the $\alpha = 0.01$ level of significance. What is the probability of being able to statistically determine a true change in the market share of magnitude 5% in either direction? (That is, find the power at $p = 0.50$ or $p = 0.40$. Hint: Use the methods of this section in the case of sampling for proportions. You will have to derive the formulas needed for computing the power.)

7–100.

Cashless Society Becomes Reality

After 20 years of worthless hype, the cashless society will actually make its debut in July, in the English city of Swindon, 60 miles west of London's Heathrow Airport. There a joint venture of two big British banks, **National Westminster** and **Midland,** will begin test-marketing a plastic and silicon cash substitute called Mondex money.

Swindonians will get their hands on 40,000 or so Mondex cards, which look like familiar ATM cards but carry sophisticated computer chips inside. Tim Jones, chief of the NatWest unit that developed the system, says the chips will contain "real money as a form of data, money that was created by one of these chips and that can't live beyond one of these chips."

Customers with actual money in their bank accounts can get the data money into their cards by phone. **British Telecommunications** is equipping 2,000 households with new smart phones, augmented by 70 or 80 public pay phones. The phones can convey data from the Mondex cards to other such cards and to or from local banks. Bank customers can ring up a cash refill and go shopping in Swindon's stores.

A small wireless device Mondex calls a wallet can transfer money from one card to another, either from a shopper to a merchant or between individuals. Each customer also gets a small plastic reader that displays balances or a transaction log.

From *Fortune,* June 12, 1995, p. 24.

Suppose that out of the 2,000 household who used Mondex in the test period, 1,712 were considered successful users. If the banks require a 90% success rate in the entire population for the program to be implemented, test this hypothesis against a one-tailed alternative. Write a memorandum to the program manager explaining your statistical results.

Case 7   THE ALASKA MARINE HIGHWAY

The Alaska Marine Highway is the ferry system that serves southeast Alaska from the lower 48 states. Since much of southeast Alaska is inaccessible by land due to icefields that separate it from Canada, the Marine Highway is a very important means of transportation to and from the southeast Alaska region. Ferries leave from pier 48 in downtown Seattle every week and travel up the Inside Passage, a protected waterway between groups of forested islands and the mainland. This waterway remains calm even in winter. The ferries stop in the towns of Ketchikan, Wrangell, Petersburg, and Juneau and then continue on to Haines and Skagway. From there travelers may continue by land into interior Alaska. The map in Exhibit 1 shows the route of the Alaska Marine Highway from Seattle to the ports of southeast Alaska. The map also shows the port of Bellingham, Washington.

As early as 1977, rumors have surfaced from time to time about the intention of directors of the Marine Highway to move the base port of the system from Seattle to the town of Bellingham. Despite the lack of official confirmation of such intentions, newspaper articles about a proposed move prompted a group of Bellingham business leaders to form an association to lobby for the move. The association hired a professional legislative lobbyist, Mr. Howard Scaman of Juneau, Alaska. The group wanted Scaman to lobby the Alaska state legislature on their behalf. Since the state of Alaska owns the ferry system, the association believed it should concentrate its efforts on the state legislature. An important factor that favored the association's efforts was the prevailing economic conditions in the state of Alaska.

Until 1984, the Alaska economy boomed as high oil prices brought hefty revenues from royalties from the sale of oil found on state-owned land. With the decline in oil prices after 1984, the state's economy was uncertain. This situation had a profound contradictory effect on operating conditions of the Alaska Marine Highway: While oil had become cheaper—and with it marine fuel—the state of Alaska had less money for support of the Marine Highway and was therefore looking for ways to reduce fuel consumption. One way to reduce fuel consumption by Marine Highway vessels would be to place the base port closer to Alaska. Moving the base from Seattle to Bellingham would achieve that result. Since Bellingham is the Washington port town closest to the Canadian border, it would have been the perfect choice. Alaska state economists quickly calculated that fuel consumption would be reduced by more than $3 million a year if the ferry terminal was to move to Bellingham. Aware of these facts, Mr. Scaman approached the concerned bodies in Juneau. The lobbyist found strong opposition to his plan from a surprising source—Mr. Joe Kemp, director of the Alaska Marine Highway. Kemp agreed with the economists that fuel consumption would be

reduced by more than $3 million. He claimed, however, that moving the port to Bellingham would sharply reduce the number of passengers sailing on the ferries.

As negotiations continued, it was agreed that if less than 10% of the passengers would be lost, the move would be a viable solution. Scaman was thus left with the task of proving to the Alaska state legislature, the governor, and the director of the ferry system that moving the base port of the Marine Highway north to Bellingham would *not* result in a loss of passenger traffic of 10% or more. To prove this assertion, Scaman hired a statistician.

You are the statistician. You were hired to design a survey aboard Alaska Marine Highway ferries to determine what percentage of the passengers would not make the trip if the departure port was Bellingham instead of Seattle. Design the survey. Find the minimum required sample size, and give Scaman all the information he needs to start preparing the study. You have a $6,000 budget. A round-trip voyage aboard the ferry costs $400, and you may hire as many people as you need to make the trip and interview people. Other costs, for computing time, printing the questionnaire, and incidentals, are $420. The ferries make one trip every week from May through the end of September. The type of passengers throughout this period varies.

EXHIBIT 7-1   Alaska Marine Highway Route

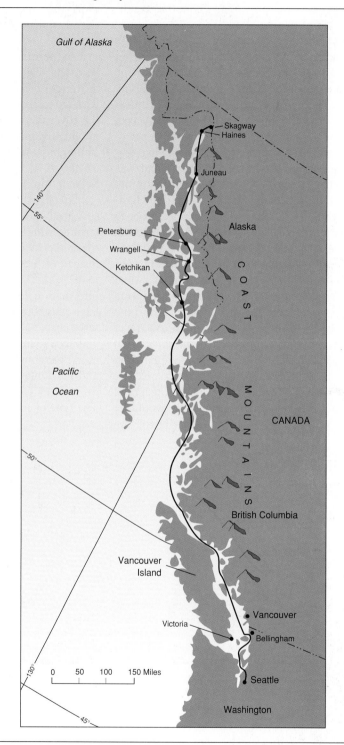

8 THE COMPARISON OF TWO POPULATIONS

8-1 INTRODUCTION

T he findings of the study had such potentially far-reaching implications that the Reuters agency, with advance knowledge of the findings, reported the information to its subscribing newspapers more than 24 hours before the article describing the study appeared in the January 28, 1988, issue of the *New England Journal of Medicine.*[1] The large-scale study was begun in 1982. Its subjects were a group of 22,071 male physicians 40 to 84 years of age

Continued

---

[1] The editors of the *New England Journal of Medicine* reacted by barring the London-based Reuters from all new information from the *Journal* for a period of six months.

living in the United States. Each physician was randomly assigned to take one of two kinds of pills: aspirin or beta carotene (as a placebo). Thus, 11,037 physicians were randomly assigned to take aspirin and 11,034 physicians were assigned to take the placebo. No physician knew which of the two kinds of pills he was taking. Each physician was to take his assigned pill every other day until the scheduled conclusion of the study in 1990. However, at a special meeting on December 18, 1987, the Data Monitoring Board of the Physicians' Health Study took the unusual step of recommending the early termination of the randomized aspirin experiment. At this point, the statistical results of the study had already exceeded everyone's expectations. It was shown, with a p-value of less than 0.00001, that a population (of male physicians, at least) taking a single aspirin pill once every two days would have a significantly lower proportion of heart attacks than a similar population not taking aspirin. The study confirmed what doctors have suspected for years—that the wonder drug aspirin can actually help prevent heart attacks.

The comparison of two populations with respect to some population parameter—the population mean, the population proportion, or the population variance—is the topic of this chapter. Testing hypotheses about population parameters in the single-population case, as was done in Chapter 7, is an important statistical undertaking. However, the true usefulness of statistics manifests itself in allowing us to make *comparisons*. Almost daily we compare products, services, investment opportunities, management styles, etc. In this chapter, we will learn how to conduct such comparisons in an objective and meaningful way. We will learn how to find statistically significant differences between two populations. If you understood the methodology of hypothesis testing presented in the last chapter and the idea of a confidence interval from Chapter 6, you will find the extension to two populations straightforward and easy to understand. We will learn how to conduct a test for the existence of a difference between the means of two populations. In the next section, we will see how such a comparison may be made in the special case where the observations may be paired in some way. Later we will learn how to conduct a test for the equality of the means of two populations using independent random samples. Then we will see how to compare two population proportions. Finally, we will encounter a test for the equality of the variances of two populations. In addition to statistical hypothesis tests, we will also learn how to construct confidence intervals for the difference between two population parameters. ■

8-2   Paired-Observations Comparisons

In this section, we describe a method for conducting a hypothesis test and constructing a confidence interval when our observations come from two populations and are *paired* in some way. What is the advantage of pairing our observations? Suppose that a taste test of two flavors is carried out. It seems intuitively plausible that if we let every person in our sample rate each one of the two flavors (with random choice of which flavor is tasted first), the resulting *paired* responses will convey more information about the taste difference than if we had used two different sets of people, each group rating only one flavor. Statistically, when we use the same people for rating the two products, we tend to remove much of the *extraneous variation* in taste ratings—the variation in people, experimental conditions, and other extraneous factors—and concentrate on the difference between the two flavors. When possible, it is often advisable to pair the observations, as this makes the experiment more precise. We will demonstrate the paired-observations test with an example.

Home Shopping Network, Inc., pioneered the idea of merchandising directly to customers through cable television. By watching what amounts to 24 hours of commercials, viewers can call a number to buy products. Before expanding their services, network managers wanted to test whether or not this method of direct marketing increased sales on the average. A random sample of 16 viewers was selected for an experiment. All viewers in the sample had recorded the amount of money they spent shopping during the holiday season of the previous year. The next year, these people were given access to the cable network and were asked to keep a record of their total purchases during the holiday season. The paired observations for each shopper are given in Table 8–1. Faced with these data, Home Shopping Network managers want to test the null hypothesis that their service does not increase shopping volume, versus the alternative hypothesis that it does. The following solution of this problem introduces the *paired-observations t test*.

EXAMPLE 8-1

The test involves two populations: the population of shoppers who have access to the Home Shopping Network and the population of shoppers who do not. We want to test the null hypothesis that the mean shopping expenditure in both populations is equal versus the alternative hypothesis that the mean for the home shoppers is greater. Using the same people for the test and pairing their observations in a before-and-after way makes the test more precise than it would be without pairing. The pairing removes the influence of factors other than home shopping. The shoppers are the same people; thus, we can concentrate on the effect of the new shopping opportunity, leaving out of the analysis other factors that may affect shopping volume. Of course, we must consider the fact that the first observations were taken a year before. Let us assume, however, that relative inflation between the two years has been accounted for and that people in the sample have not had significant changes in income or other variables since the previous year that might affect their buying behavior.

SOLUTION

TABLE 8-1   Total Purchases of 16 Viewers with and without Home Shopping

Shopper	Previous Year's Shopping ($)	Current Year's Shopping ($)	Difference ($)
1	334	405	71
2	150	125	−25
3	520	540	20
4	95	100	5
5	212	200	−12
6	30	30	0
7	1,055	1,200	145
8	300	265	−35
9	85	90	5
10	129	206	77
11	40	18	−22
12	440	489	49
13	610	590	−20
14	208	310	102
15	880	995	115
16	25	75	50

Under these circumstances, it is easy to see that the variable in which we are interested is the difference between the present year's per-person shopping expenditure and that of the previous year. The population parameter about which we want to draw an inference is the mean difference between the two populations. We denote this parameter by μ_D, the mean difference. This parameter is defined as $\mu_D = \mu_1 - \mu_2$, where μ_1 is the average holiday season shopping expenditure of people who use home shopping and μ_2 is the average holiday season shopping expenditure of people who do not. Our null and alternative hypotheses are, then,

$$H_0: \mu_D \leq 0$$
$$H_1: \mu_D > 0 \tag{8-1}$$

Looking at the null and alternative hypotheses and the data in the last column of Table 8–1, we note that the test is a simple t test with $n - 1$ degrees of freedom, where our variable is the *difference* between the two observations for each shopper. In a sense, our two-population comparison test has been reduced to a hypothesis test about one parameter—the difference between the means of two populations. The test, as given by equation 8–1, is a right-tailed test, but it need not be. In general, the paired-observations t test can be done as one-tailed or two-tailed. In addition, the hypothesized difference need not be zero. We can state any other value as the difference in the null hypothesis (although zero is most commonly used). The only assumption we make when we use this test is that *the population of differences is normally distributed.* Recall that this assumption was used whenever we carried out a test or constructed a confidence interval using the t distribution. Also note that, for large samples, the standard normal distribution may be used instead. This is also true for a normal population if you happen to know the population standard deviation of the differences, σ_D. The test statistic (assuming σ_D is not known and is estimated by s_D, the sample standard deviation of the differences) is given in equation 8–2.

Test statistic for the paired-observations t test:

$$t = \frac{\bar{D} - \mu_{D_0}}{s_D / \sqrt{n}} \tag{8-2}$$

where $\bar{D}$ is the sample average difference between each pair of observations, s_D is the sample standard deviation of these differences, and the sample size, n, is the number of pairs of observations (here, the number of people in the experiment). The symbol μ_{D_0} is the population mean difference under the null hypothesis. When the null hypothesis is true and the population mean difference is μ_{D_0}, the statistic has a t distribution with $n - 1$ degrees of freedom.

Let us now conduct the hypothesis test. From the differences reported in Table 8–1, we find that their mean is $\bar{D} = \$32.81$ and their standard deviation is $s_D = \$55.75$. Since the sample size is small, $n = 16$, we use the t distribution with $n - 1 = 15$ degrees of freedom. The null-hypothesized value of the population mean is $\mu_{D_0} = 0$. The value of our test statistic is obtained as

$$t = \frac{32.81 - 0}{55.75 / \sqrt{16}} = 2.354$$

FIGURE 8-1   Carrying Out the Test of Example 8-1

This computed value of the test statistic is greater than 1.753, which is the critical point for a right-tailed test at $\alpha = 0.05$ using a t distribution with 15 degrees of freedom (see Appendix C, Table 3). The test statistic value is smaller than 2.602, which is the critical point for a one-tailed test using $\alpha = 0.01$, but greater than 2.131, which is the critical point for a right-tailed area of 0.025. We may conclude that the p-value is between 0.025 and 0.01. This is shown in Figure 8–1. Home Shopping Network managers may conclude that the test gave moderate evidence for increased shopping volume by network viewers.

EXAMPLE 8-2

It has recently been asserted that returns on stocks may change once a story about a company appears in *The Wall Street Journal* column "Heard on the Street." An investment portfolio analyst wants to check the statistical significance of this claim. The analyst collects a random sample of 50 stocks that were recommended as winners by the editor of "Heard on the Street." The analyst proceeds to conduct a two-tailed test of whether or not the annualized return on stocks recommended in the column differs between the month before the recommendation and the month after the recommendation. The analyst decides to conduct a two-tailed rather than a one-tailed test because she wants to allow for the possibility that stocks may be recommended in the column after their price has appreciated (and thus returns may actually decrease in the following month), as well as allowing for an increased return. For each stock in the sample of 50, the analyst computes the return before and after the *event* (the appearance of the story in the column) and the difference in the two return figures. Then the sample average difference of returns is computed, as well as the sample standard deviation of return differences. The results are $\overline{D} = 0.1\%$, $s_D = 0.05\%$. What should the analyst conclude?

SOLUTION

The null and alternative hypotheses are $H_0: \mu_D = 0$ and $H_1: \mu_D \neq 0$. We now use the test statistic given in equation 8–2, noting that the distribution may be well approximated by the normal distribution because the sample size, $n = 50$, is large. We have

$$z = \frac{\overline{D} - \mu_{D_0}}{s_D/\sqrt{n}} = \frac{0.1 - 0}{0.05/7.07} = 14.14$$

The value of the test statistic falls very far in the right-hand rejection region, and the p-value, therefore, is very small. The analyst should conclude that there is strong evidence that the average returns on stocks increase (because the rejection occurred in the right-hand rejection region) for stocks recommended in "Heard on the Street," as asserted by financial experts. Incidentally, the assumption of normality of the population of return differences—while not crucial in this case because the sample size is large—is supported by research findings on stock returns.

Confidence Intervals

In addition to tests of hypotheses, it is also possible to construct confidence intervals for the average population difference, μ_D. Analogous to the case of a single-population parameter, we define a $(1 - \alpha)$ 100% confidence interval for the parameter μ_D as follows.

> A $(1 - \alpha)$ 100% confidence interval for the mean difference μ_D:
>
> $$\overline{D} \pm t_{\alpha/2} \frac{s_D}{\sqrt{n}} \tag{8-3}$$
>
> where $t_{\alpha/2}$ is the value of the t distribution with $n - 1$ degrees of freedom that cuts off an area of $\alpha/2$ to its right. When the sample size, n, is large, we may use $z_{\alpha/2}$ instead.

In Example 8–2, we may construct a 95% confidence interval for the average difference in annualized return on a stock before and after its being recommended in "Heard on the Street." The confidence interval is

$$\overline{D} \pm z_{\alpha/2} \frac{s_D}{\sqrt{n}} = 0.1 \pm 1.96 \frac{0.05}{7.07} = [0.086\%, 0.114\%]$$

Based on the data, the analyst may be 95% confident that the average difference in annualized return rate on a stock, measured the month before and the month following a positive recommendation in the column, is anywhere from 0.086% to 0.114%.

In this section, we compared population means for paired data. The following sections compare means of two populations where samples are drawn randomly and *independently* of each other from the two populations. When pairing can be done, our results tend to be more precise because the *experimental units* (for example, the people, each trying two different products) are different from each other, but each acts as an independent measuring device for the two products. This pairing of similar items is called *blocking,* and we will discuss it in detail in Chapter 9.

PROBLEMS

8–1. A market research study is undertaken to test which of two popular electric shavers, a model made by Norelco or a model made by Remington, is preferred by consumers. A random sample of 25 men who regularly use an electric shaver, but not one of the two models to be tested, is chosen. Each man is then asked to shave one morning with the Norelco and the next morning with the Remington, or vice versa. The order, which model is used on which day, is randomly chosen for each man. After every shave, each man is asked to complete a questionnaire rating his satisfaction with the shaver. From the questionnaire, a total satisfaction score on a scale of 0 to 100 is computed. Then, for each man, the difference between the satisfaction score for Norelco and that for Remington is computed. The score differences (Norelco score− Remington score) are 15, −8, 32, 57, 20, 10, −18, −12, 60, 72, 38, −5, 16, 22, 34, 41, 12, −38, 16, −40, 75, 11, 2, 55, 10. Which model, if any, is statistically preferred over the other? How confident are you of your finding? Explain.

8–2. The performance ratings of two sports cars, the Mazda RX7 and the Nissan 300ZX, are to be compared. A random sample of 40 drivers is selected to drive the two models. Each driver tries one car of each model, and the 40 cars of each model are chosen randomly. The time of each test drive is recorded for each driver and model. The difference in time (Mazda time— Nissan time) is computed, and from these differences a sample mean and a sample standard deviation are obtained. The results are $\bar{D} = 5.0$ seconds and $s_D = 2.3$ seconds. Based on these data, which model has higher performance? Explain. Also give a 95% confidence interval for the average time difference, in seconds, for the two models over the course driven.

8–3. Recent studies indicate that in order to be globally competitive, firms must form global strategic partnerships. An investment banker wants to test whether the return on investment for international ventures is different from return on investment for similar domestic ventures. A sample of 12 firms that recently entered into ventures with foreign companies is available. For each firm, the returns on investment for the international venture (I) and a similar domestic venture (D) are given:

$$D(\%): 10\ 12\ 14\ 12\ 12\quad 17\ \ 9\ 15\ \ 8.5\ 11\ 7\ 15$$
$$I(\%): 11\ 14\ 15\ 11\ 12.5\ 16\ 10\ 13\ 10.5\ 17\ 9\ 19$$

Assuming that these firms represent a random sample from the population of all firms involved in global strategic partnerships, can the investment banker conclude that there are differences between average returns on domestic ventures and average returns on international ventures? Explain.

8–4. A study is undertaken to determine how consumers react to energy conservation efforts. A random group of 60 families is chosen. Their consumption of electricity is monitored in a period before and a period after the families are offered certain discounts to reduce their energy consumption. Both periods are the same length. The difference in electric consumption between the period before and the period after the offer is recorded for each family. Then the average difference in consumption and the standard deviation of the difference are computed. The results are $\bar{D} = 0.2$ kW (kilowatts) and $s_D = 1.0$ kW. At $\alpha = 0.01$, is there evidence to conclude that conservation efforts reduce consumption?

8–5. A nationwide retailer wants to test whether new product shelf facings are effective in increasing sales volume. New shelf facings for the soft drink Country Time are tested at a random sample of 15 stores throughout the country. Data on total sales of Country Time for each store, for the week before and the week after the new facings are installed, are given below:

$$\text{Store:}\ \ 1\ \ 2\ \ 3\ \ 4\ \ 5\ \ 6\ \ 7\ \ 8\ \ 9\ 10\ 11\ 12\ 13\ 14\ 15$$
$$\text{Before:}\ 57\ 61\ 12\ 38\ 12\ 69\ \ 5\ 39\ 88\ \ 9\ 92\ 26\ 14\ 70\ 22$$
$$\text{After:}\ \ 60\ 54\ 20\ 35\ 21\ 70\ \ 1\ 65\ 79\ 10\ 90\ 32\ 19\ 77\ 29$$

Using the 0.05 level of significance, do you believe that the new shelf facings increase sales of Country Time?

8–6. Most international investors managing Asian portfolios invest in both Japan and Hong Kong. Favorable conditions are believed to have brought more of these investments to Hong Kong. A test is carried out during the month of October to determine whether investors have shifted the proportions of their portfolios in favor of Hong Kong investments versus the Japanese investments. A random sample of 25 international investors is collected. These investors voluntarily reveal the proportion of their Hong Kong investments before and after October 15. The difference in proportion (after–before) is computed for each of these investors, and from these differences an average and a standard deviation are obtained. The average difference is +4%, and the standard deviation of differences is 2%. Do you believe that the average international investor has shifted investments to Hong Kong during the period in question? Explain.

8–7.   In problem 8–4, suppose that the *population* standard deviation is 1.0 and that the true average reduction in consumption for the entire population in the area is $\mu_D = 0.1$. For a sample size of 60, and $\alpha = 0.01$, what is the power of the test?

8–8.   Consider the information in the following table.

Network	Program	Program Rating (scale: 0 to 100)	
		Men	Women
CBS	60 Minutes	99	96
ABC	ABC Monday Night Football	93	25
NBC	Cheers	88	97
ABC	America's Funniest Home Videos	90	35
ABC	America's Funniest People	81	33
NBC	Unsolved Mysteries	61	10
NBC	Matlock	54	50
CBS	Murder, She Wrote	60	48
ABC	Roseanne	73	73
NBC	The Heat of The Night	44	33
ABC	Davis Rules	30	11
CBS	Murphy Brown	25	58
CBS	Rescue 911	38	18
NBC	L.A. Law	52	12
ABC	ABC Sunday Night Movies	32	61
NBC	Empty Nest	16	96
CBS	Designing Women	8	94
NBC	The Cosby Show	18	80
NBC	A Different World	9	20
NBC	NBC Sunday Night Movies	10	6

Source: Adapted from *Variety*, February 25, 1991, p. 63.

Assume that the television programs were randomly selected from the population of all prime time TV programs. Also assume that ratings are normally distributed. Conduct a statistical test to determine whether there is a significant difference between average men's and women's ratings of prime time television programs.

8–3   A Test for the Difference between Two Population Means Using Independent Random Samples

It may not always be possible to pair our observations from two populations and carry out a test on the differences. In cases where the paired-observations test of the previous section does not apply, we may still compare the means of two populations by drawing two *independent* random samples from the two populations of interest.

The samples drawn from the populations do not have to be the same size. We denote the size of the sample from population 1 by n_1 and the size of the sample from population 2 by n_2.

We will first consider a large-sample test for the difference between two population means. *Large sample* will mean that both sample sizes are large enough to assure us of a good normal approximation for the distributions of the sample means $\bar{X}_1$ and $\bar{X}_2$ via the central limit theorem. Following our rule of thumb from Chapter 5, we will consider the sample sizes large if both $n_1 \geq 30$ and $n_2 \geq 30$ (the large-sample test may also apply to smaller samples if we can assume that both populations are normally distributed with known population variances σ_1^2 and σ_2^2). We assume that the random samples, the sample from population 1 and the sample from population 2, are drawn *independently* of each other. That is, there is no relationship between one sample and the other one.

There are several different hypotheses that may be tested. We may want to test whether the mean of one particular population, say, population 1, is greater than the mean of the other population (a one-tailed test), or we may want to test whether or not the two population means are equal (with no prior intention to prove that one mean is greater than the other—a two-tailed test). Or we may wish to test whether or not the difference between the two population means is greater than (or less than) some particular number, D. Let us look at some particular sets of hypotheses. We will show three hypothesis-testing situations, which we will call situation I, situation II, and situation III. These possible hypothesis tests are not exhaustive. There are other possible tests that may be carried out; these are simple extensions of the three situations discussed here. The test we show, for example, may be a right-tailed test; the analogous left-tailed test is also possible, and you should have no problem carrying it out as well.

Hypothesis-testing situation I:

$$H_0: \mu_1 - \mu_2 = 0$$
$$H_1: \mu_1 - \mu_2 \neq 0$$

This is the most common test for the difference between two population means, μ_1 and μ_2. The null hypothesis states that the two means are equal (their difference is 0), while the two-tailed alternative states that the two population means are not equal.

Hypothesis-testing situation II:

$$H_0: \mu_1 - \mu_2 \leq 0$$
$$H_1: \mu_1 - \mu_2 > 0$$

This is another common set of hypotheses. The null hypothesis says that the mean of population 1 is equal to that of population 2 or is smaller than the mean of population 2. The alternative hypothesis states that the mean of population 1 is greater than the mean of population 2. The alternative hypothesis is the one we try to prove. We want to prove that the mean of population 1 is greater; we choose the label 1 for the population we believe to have the higher mean. The test is a right-tailed test.

Hypothesis-testing situation III:

$$H_0: \mu_1 - \mu_2 \leq D$$
$$H_1: \mu_1 - \mu_2 > D$$

This situation is not very common. Here we have some special-purpose test that we want to carry out; namely, we want to prove that the mean of one population is greater than the mean of the other population by at least D units. (A two-tailed test of the hypothesis that the difference between μ_1 and μ_2 is equal to D is also possible.)

The test statistic in all three hypothesis-testing situations is the same. Due to our assumptions about sample size or normal populations with known population variances, the statistic is a z statistic.

Large-sample test statistic for the difference between two population means:

$$z = \frac{(\bar{x}_1 - \bar{x}_2) - (\mu_1 - \mu_2)_0}{\sqrt{\dfrac{s_1^2}{n_1} + \dfrac{s_2^2}{n_2}}} \qquad (8\text{--}4)$$

The term $(\mu_1 - \mu_2)_0$ is the difference between μ_1 and μ_2 under the null hypothesis. It is equal to zero in situations I and II and it is equal to the prespecified value D in situation III. The term in the denominator is the standard deviation of the difference between the two sample means (it relies on the assumption that the two samples are independent).

We demonstrate the test, in situation I, with the following example.

EXAMPLE 8-3   Until a few years ago, the market for consumer credit was considered to be segmented. Higher-income, higher-spending people tended to be American Express cardholders, and lower-income, lower-spending people were usually Visa cardholders. In the last few years, Visa has intensified its efforts to break into the higher-income segments of the market by using magazine and television advertising to create a high-class image. Recently, a consulting firm was hired by Visa to determine whether or not average monthly charges on the American Express Gold Card are approximately equal to the average monthly charges on Preferred Visa. A random sample of 1,200 Preferred Visa cardholders was selected, and it was found that the sample average monthly charge was $\bar{x}_1 = \$452$ and the sample standard deviation was $s_1 = \$212$. An independent random sample of 800 Gold Card members revealed a sample mean $\bar{x}_2 = \$523$ and $s_2 = \$185$. (Holders of both the Gold Card and Preferred Visa were excluded from the study.) Is there evidence to conclude that the average monthly charge in the entire population of American Express Gold Card members is different from the average monthly charge in the entire population of Preferred Visa cardholders?

FIGURE 8-2   Carrying Out the Test of Example 8-3

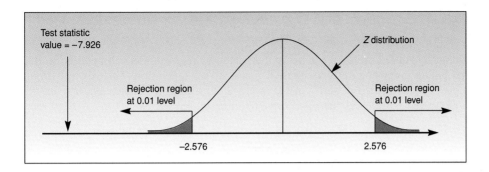

Test statistic
value = −7.926

Z distribution

Rejection region
at 0.01 level

Rejection region
at 0.01 level

−2.576

2.576

SOLUTION

Since we have no prior suspicion (before looking at the two sample means—remember our caution in Chapter 7 about data snooping!) that either of the two populations may have a higher mean, the test is two-tailed. The null and alternative hypotheses are therefore as stated in situation I:

$$H_0: \mu_1 - \mu_2 = 0$$
$$H_1: \mu_1 - \mu_2 \neq 0$$

The value of our test statistic (equation 8–4) is

$$z = \frac{(452 - 523) - 0}{\sqrt{\dfrac{212^2}{1,200} + \dfrac{185^2}{800}}} = -7.926$$

The computed value of the z statistic falls in the left-hand rejection region for any commonly used α, and the p-value is very small. We conclude that there is a statistically significant difference in average monthly charges between Gold Card and Preferred Visa cardholders. Note that this does not imply any *practical significance*. That is, while a difference in average spending in the two populations may exist, we cannot necessarily conclude that this difference is large. The test is shown in Figure 8–2.

The following example demonstrates the test in situation III.

EXAMPLE 8-4

Suppose that the makers of Duracell batteries want to prove that their size AA battery lasts an average of at least 45 minutes longer than Duracell's main competitor, the Energizer. Two independent random samples of 100 batteries of each kind are selected, and the batteries are run continuously until they are no longer operational. The sample average life for Duracell is found to be $\bar{x}_1 = 308$ minutes, and the sample standard deviation is $s_1 = 84$ minutes. The results for the Energizer batteries are $\bar{x}_2 = 254$ minutes and $s_2 = 67$ minutes. Is there evidence to substantiate Duracell's claim that their batteries last, on average, at least 45 minutes longer than Energizer batteries of the same size?

SOLUTION

Our null and alternative hypotheses are

$$H_0: \mu_1 - \mu_2 \leq 45$$

$$H_1: \mu_1 - \mu_2 > 45$$

The makers of Duracell hope to prove their claim by rejecting the null hypothesis. Recall that failing to reject a null hypothesis is not a strong conclusion. This is why—in order to prove that Duracell batteries last an average of at least 45 minutes longer—the claim to be proved is stated as the *alternative* hypothesis.

The value of the test statistic in this case is computed as follows:

$$z = \frac{(308 - 254) - 45}{\sqrt{\dfrac{84^2}{100} + \dfrac{67^2}{100}}} = 0.838$$

This value falls in the nonrejection region of our right-tailed test at any conventional level of significance, α. The p-value is equal to 0.2011. We must conclude that there is insufficient evidence to support Duracell's claim.

Confidence Intervals

Recall from Chapter 7 that there is a strong connection between hypothesis tests and confidence intervals. In the case of the difference between two population means, we have:

A large sample $(1 - \alpha)$ 100% confidence interval for the difference between two population means, $\mu_1 - \mu_2$, using independent random samples:

$$(\bar{x}_1 - \bar{x}_2) \pm z_{\alpha/2} \sqrt{\frac{s_1^2}{n_1} + \frac{s_2^2}{n_2}} \qquad (8\text{--}5)$$

Equation 8–5 should be intuitively clear. The bounds on the difference between the two population means are equal to the difference between the two sample means, plus or minus the z coefficient for $(1 - \alpha)$ 100% confidence times the standard deviation of the difference between the two sample means (which is the expression with the square root sign).

In the context of Example 8–3, a 95% confidence interval for the difference between the average monthly charge on the American Express Gold Card and the average monthly charge on the Preferred Visa Card is, by equation 8–5,

$$(523 - 452) \pm 1.96 \sqrt{\frac{212^2}{1,200} + \frac{185^2}{800}} = [53.44, 88.56]$$

The consulting firm may report to Visa that they are 95% confident that the average American Express Gold Card monthly bill is anywhere from $53.44 to $88.56 higher than the average Preferred Visa bill.

With one-tailed tests, the analogous interval is a one-sided confidence interval. We will not give examples of such intervals in this chapter. In general, we construct confidence intervals for population parameters when we have no *particular* values of the parameters we want to test and are interested in estimation only.

A Small-Sample Test for the Difference between Two Population Means

When the sample sizes are small ($n_1 < 30$, or $n_2 < 30$, or both) and we assume both populations are normally distributed, the test statistic in equation 8–4 has *approximately* a t distribution with degrees of freedom given by

$$\text{df} = \frac{(s_1^2/n_1 + s_2^2/n_2)^2}{\dfrac{(s_1^2/n_1)^2}{n_1 - 1} + \dfrac{(s_2^2/n_2)^2}{n_2 - 1}} \qquad (8\text{–}6)$$

When df as computed in equation 8–6 is not an integer, we round *downward* to the nearest integer for a conservative estimate of the degrees of freedom. We can also construct a confidence interval similar to equation 8–5 with $z_{\alpha/2}$ replaced by $t_{\alpha/2}$, with df given by equation 8–6. We will demonstrate the analysis with a short, hypothetical example.

Suppose that we want to test the null hypothesis that two population means are equal versus the alternative hypothesis that they are not equal. The two populations are assumed to be normally distributed. A random sample of size 15 from population 1 gives a sample mean of 100 and a sample standard deviation of 5. An independent random sample of size 10 from population 2 gives a sample mean of 110 and a sample standard deviation of 3. The test statistic value is

$$t = \frac{(100 - 110) - 0}{\sqrt{\dfrac{5^2}{15} + \dfrac{3^2}{10}}} = -6.242$$

This value is a realization of a random variable approximately following a t distribution with degrees of freedom given by

$$\text{df} = \frac{(s_1^2/n_1 + s_2^2/n_2)^2}{\dfrac{(s_1^2/n_1)^2}{n_1 - 1} + \dfrac{(s_2^2/n_2)^2}{n_2 - 1}}$$
$$= \frac{(25/15 + 9/10)^2}{\dfrac{(25/15)^2}{14} + \dfrac{(9/10)^2}{9}} = 22.84$$

We round downward from 22.84 and use the approximation df $= 22$. The critical points in a two-tailed test with $\alpha = 0.05$ for a t distribution with df $= 22$ are ± 2.074. Since the computed value of the test statistic, -6.242, is smaller than -2.074, we reject the null hypothesis. A confidence interval for $\mu_1 - \mu_2$ can be similarly constructed. In the next section, we will see an easier small-sample test.

PROBLEMS

8–9. LINC is a software tool developed by Burroughs Corporation. The program automatically writes some of the coding that programmers have to do manually. LINC supposedly saves programming time and allows programmers to operate more efficiently. In a test of the software package, 45 programmers (group 1) were asked to write a program without LINC and then run the program until it performed with no bugs. The times from start to finish for this group were recorded. Group 2 consisted of 32 programmers who were asked to prepare the same program with the aid of LINC. Before getting the data, it was decided to run the test as a one-tailed test to prove that the package reduces the average programming time. The results were $\bar{x}_1 = 26$ minutes, $\bar{x}_2 = 21$ minutes, $s_1 = 8$ minutes, and $s_2 = 6$ minutes. Conduct the test, and state your conclusion. Is LINC effective in reducing average programming time?

8–10.   The photography department of a glamour magazine needs to choose a camera. Of the two models the department is considering, one is made by Nikon and one by Minolta. The department contracts with an agency to determine if one of the two models gets a higher average performance rating by professional photographers, or whether the average performance ratings of these two cameras are not statistically different. The agency asks 60 different professional photographers to rate one of the cameras (30 photographers rate each model). The ratings are on a scale of 1 to 10. The average sample rating for Nikon is 8.5, and the sample standard deviation is 2.1. For the Minolta sample, the mean is 7.8, and the standard deviation is 1.8. Is there a difference between the average population ratings of the two cameras? If so, which one is rated higher?

8–11.   The Marcus Robert Real Estate Company wants to test whether the average sale price of residential properties in a certain size range in Bel Air, California, is approximately equal to the average sale price of residential properties of the same size range in Marin County, California. The company gathers data on a random sample of 32 properties in Bel Air and finds $\bar{x} = \$345,650$ and $s = \$48,500$. A random sample of 35 properties in Marin County gives $\bar{x} = \$289,440$ and $s = \$87,090$. Is the average sale price of all properties in both locations approximately equal or not? Explain.

8–12.   Global stock markets are fast becoming the best way to invest.[2] A random sample of 40 British stocks in early 1995 had a mean percentage annualized return of 12% (when measured in U.S. dollars) and a standard deviation of 6%. For 40 Swiss stocks the mean was 20% and the standard deviation was 7%. Is there statistical evidence that one stock market was better than the other, on average, during this period?

8–13.   Many companies that cater to teenagers have learned that young people respond to commercials that provide dance-beat music, adventure, and a fast pace rather than words. In one test, a group of 128 teenagers were shown commercials featuring rock music, and their purchasing frequency of the advertised products over the following month was recorded as a single score for each person in the group. Then a group of 212 teenagers were shown commercials for the same products, but with the music replaced by verbal persuasion. The purchase frequency scores of this group were computed as well. The results for the music group were $\bar{x} = 23.5$ and $s = 12.2$; and the results for the verbal group were $\bar{x} = 18.0$ and $s = 10.5$. Assume that the two groups were randomly selected from the entire teenage consumer population. Using the $\alpha = 0.01$ level of significance, test the null hypothesis that both methods of advertising are equally effective versus the alternative hypothesis that they are not equally effective. If you conclude that one method is better, state which one it is, and explain how you reached your conclusion.

8–14.   According to *Fortune*, the average annual pay for a biomedical engineer in 1995 was $72,500, and the average annual pay for a chemical engineer was $73,970.[3] If each statistic is based on two independent random samples of 120 engineers each, and the standard deviations were $5,000 for the biomedical engineers and $6,500 for the chemical engineers, test for the existence of a difference in the population average pay for the two professions.

8–15.   A fashion industry analyst wants to prove that models featuring Liz Claiborne clothing earn on average more than models featuring clothes designed by Calvin Klein. For a given period of time, a random sample of 32 Liz Claiborne models reveals average earnings of $4,238.00 and a standard deviation of $1,002.50. For the same period, an independent random

[2] "Global Stock Markets," *Business Week,* June 19, 1995, p. 94.

[3] "How Does Your Pay Really Stack Up?" Cover story, *Fortune,* June 26, 1995, pp. 79–88.

sample of 37 Calvin Klein models has mean earnings of \$3,888.72 and a sample standard deviation of \$876.05.

    a.   Is this a one-tailed or a two-tailed test? Explain.

    b.   Carry out the hypothesis test at the 0.05 level of significance.

    c.   State your conclusion.

    d.   What is the *p*-value? Explain its relevance.

    e.   Redo the problem assuming the results are based on a random sample of 10 Liz Claiborne models and 11 Calvin Klein models.

8–16.   An article on the growing trade gap in high-tech ideas between the United States and Japan claims that more royalties and licensing fees are paid to the United States by Japanese users of American ideas than the other way around. A random sample of 100 American patents used in Japan reveals an average royalty of \$1,838.69 and a standard deviation of \$461. A random sample of 80 Japanese patents used in the United States has an average royalty payment of \$1,050.22 and a standard deviation of \$560. Is there evidence to conclude that the Japanese pay, on the average, more to American patent holders than the other way around?

8–17.   A brokerage firm is said to provide both brokerage services and "research" if, in addition to buying and selling securities for its clients, the firm also furnishes clients with advice about the value of securities, information on economic factors and trends, and portfolio strategy. The Securities and Exchange Commission (SEC) has been studying brokerage commissions charged by both "research" and "nonresearch" brokerage houses. A random sample of 255 transactions at nonresearch firms is collected, as well as a random sample of 300 transactions at research firms. These samples reveal that the difference between the average sample percentage commission at research firms and the average percentage commission in the nonresearch sample is 2.54%. The standard deviation of the research firms' sample is 0.85%, and that of the nonresearch firms is 0.64%. Give a 95% confidence interval for the difference in the average percentage of commissions in research versus nonresearch brokerage houses.

8–4 A Test for the Difference between Two Population Means, Assuming Equal Population Variances

When the population variances σ_1^2 and σ_2^2 are assumed to be equal, there is another test that can be done for the difference between two population means. This test is especially useful in the case of small samples, as it allows us to conduct a test for the difference between two population means without having to use the complicated expression for the degrees of freedom of the approximate *t* statistic (equation 8–6). In addition to assuming equal (but usually unknown) population variances, we assume that the two populations of interest are *approximately normally distributed*.

    As before, there are many possible hypothesis tests. We will concentrate on the three situations we considered in the previous section:

$$\text{Situation I:}\quad \text{H}_0\!: \mu_1 - \mu_2 = 0$$
$$\text{H}_1\!: \mu_1 - \mu_2 \neq 0$$
$$\text{Situation II:}\quad \text{H}_0\!: \mu_1 - \mu_2 \leq 0$$
$$\text{H}_1\!: \mu_1 - \mu_2 > 0$$
$$\text{Situation III:}\quad \text{H}_0\!: \mu_1 - \mu_2 \leq D$$
$$\text{H}_1\!: \mu_1 - \mu_2 > D$$

We note again that other tests are possible as well. While the tests in situations II and III are right-tailed tests, it is possible in each of these situations to conduct a similar left-tailed test. It is also possible to conduct a two-tailed test, in situation I, using a specified value D as the null-hypothesized difference between μ_1 and μ_2,

FIGURE 8–3 Degrees of Freedom Associated with Deviations from the Sample Means of Two Independent Samples

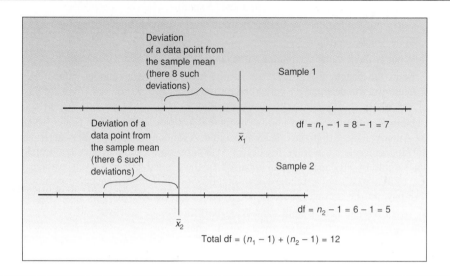

where D is not necessarily zero. Before we describe the test statistic and its distribution, let us analyze the situation giving rise to our statistic.

We select two independent random samples: a random sample from population 1 and a random sample from population 2. We denote the sample sizes by n_1 and n_2, respectively. Once we compute the mean for each sample, $\bar{x}_1$ and $\bar{x}_2$, we lose one degree of freedom in each sample with respect to the computation of the sample standard deviations, s_1 and s_2. (Refer to the explanation in Chapter 5 as to why this happens.) Figure 8–3 shows why, with two independent samples for which the two sample means are computed, the total number of degrees of freedom associated with deviations from the sample means is df $= (n_1 - 1) + (n_2 - 1) = n_1 + n_2 - 2$. This parameter, df, is associated with the *pooled estimate* of the common population variance, defined as follows.

We assume that the two population variances, σ_1^2 and σ_2^2, are equal. We denote this common variance of the two populations by σ^2. The two sample variances, s_1^2 and s_2^2, are then estimates of the same quantity, σ^2. What we are looking for is a *pooled* variance estimate, s_p^2. The variance estimator from sample 1 has $n_1 - 1$ degrees of freedom, and the variance estimator from sample 2 has $n_2 - 1$ degrees of freedom. We want to pool the two variance estimators S_1^2 and S_2^2 in such a way that the relative weights given to the two estimates produced will be proportional to the degrees of freedom of the estimators. (Obviously, an estimate based on a larger sample—larger df—should be given proportionally more weight in computing the pooled variance than an estimate based on smaller df.)

A **pooled estimate** of the common population variance, based on a sample variance s_1^2 from a sample of size n_1 and a sample variance s_2^2 from a sample of size n_2, is given by

$$s_p^2 = \frac{(n_1 - 1)s_1^2 + (n_2 - 1)s_2^2}{n_1 + n_2 - 2} \tag{8–7}$$

Equation 8–7 should make sense to you. The equation gives a weighted average of two sample variances, where the weights are the degrees of freedom upon which each estimate is based, and the total weight—the denominator in the formula—is the sum of the degrees of freedom associated with the two estimates: $df = (n_1 - 1) + (n_2 - 1) = n_1 + n_2 - 2$.

The estimate of the standard deviation of $(\bar{X}_1 - \bar{X}_2)$ is given by[4]

$$\sqrt{s_p^2\left(\frac{1}{n_1} + \frac{1}{n_2}\right)} \tag{8–8}$$

The expression in equation 8–8 has the same function as $s/\sqrt{n}$ in the case of a single-sample inference about a population mean. We are now ready to define our test statistic.

Test statistic for the difference between two population means, assuming equal population variances:

$$t = \frac{(\bar{X}_1 - \bar{X}_2) - (\mu_1 - \mu_2)_0}{\sqrt{s_p^2\left(\frac{1}{n_1} + \frac{1}{n_2}\right)}} \tag{8–9}$$

where $(\mu_1 - \mu_2)_0$ is the difference between the two population means under the null hypothesis (zero or some number, D). The degrees of freedom of the test statistic t are $n_1 + n_2 - 2$ (the degrees of freedom associated with s_p^2, the pooled estimate of the population variance).

For large samples, we may use the standard normal distribution instead of the t distribution with $n_1 + n_2 - 2$ degrees of freedom. Note that the test statistic in equation 8–9 follows the general form of a standardized test statistic given in Chapter 7: Test statistic = (Estimate − Hypothesized value of parameter)/(Standard deviation of estimator).

EXAMPLE 8–5

Changes in the price of oil have long been known to affect the economy of the United States. An economist wants to check whether the price of a barrel of crude oil affects the U.S. Consumer Price Index (CPI), a measure of price levels and inflation. The economist collects two sets of data: one set comprises 14 monthly observations on increases in the CPI, in percentage per month, when the price of crude oil is $27.50 per barrel; the other set consists of 9 monthly observations on percentage increase in the CPI when the price of crude oil is $20.00 per barrel. The economist assumes that her data are a random set of observations from a population of monthly CPI percentage increases when oil sells for

---

[4] Our assumption of independent random sampling from the two populations implies that $\bar{X}_1$ and $\bar{X}_2$ are *independent* random variables. Thus, the variance of $\bar{X}_1 - \bar{X}_2$ is equal to $V(\bar{X}_1 - \bar{X}_2) = V(\bar{X}_1) + V(\bar{X}_2) = \sigma^2/n_1 + \sigma^2/n_2 = \sigma^2[1/n_1 + 1/n_2]$, where σ^2 is the common population variance. This common variance is estimated by S_p^2.

$27.50 per barrel, and an independent set of random observations from a population of monthly CPI percentage increases when oil sells for $20.00 per barrel. She also assumes that the two populations of CPI percentage increases are normally distributed and that the variances of the two populations are equal. Considering the nature of the economic variables in question, these are reasonable assumptions. If we call the population of monthly CPI percentage increases when oil sells for $27.50 population 1, and that of oil at $20.00 per barrel population 2, then the economist's data are as follows:[5] $\bar{x}_1 = 0.317\%$, $s_1 = 0.12\%$, $n_1 = 14$; $\bar{x}_2 = 0.21\%$, $s_2 = 0.11\%$, $n_2 = 9$. Our economist is faced with the question: Do these data provide evidence to conclude that average percentage increase in the CPI differs when oil sells at these two different prices?

SOLUTION

Although the economist may have a suspicion about the possible direction of change in the CPI as oil prices decrease, she decides to approach the situation with an open mind and let the data speak for themselves. That is, she wants to carry out the two-tailed test, situation I. Her test is $H_0: \mu_1 - \mu_2 = 0$ versus $H_1: \mu_1 - \mu_2 \neq 0$. Using equation 8–9, the economist computes the value of the test statistic, which has a t distribution with $n_1 + n_2 - 2 = 21$ degrees of freedom:

$$t = \frac{(0.317 - 0.210) - 0}{\sqrt{\dfrac{(13)(0.12)^2 + (8)(0.11)^2}{21}\left(\dfrac{1}{14} + \dfrac{1}{9}\right)}} = 2.15$$

The computed value of the test statistic, $t = 2.15$, falls in the right-hand rejection region at $\alpha = 0.05$, but not very far from the critical point, 2.080. The p-value is therefore just under 0.05. The economist may thus conclude that, based on her data and the validity of the assumptions made, there is some evidence that the average monthly increase in the CPI is greater when oil sells for $27.50 per barrel than it is when oil sells for $20.00 per barrel.

EXAMPLE 8-6

The manufacturers of compact disk players want to test whether a small price reduction is enough to increase sales of their product. Randomly chosen data on 15 weekly sales totals at outlets in a given area before the price reduction show a sample mean of $6,598 and a sample standard deviation of $844. A random sample of 12 weekly sales totals after the small price reduction gives a sample mean of $6,870 and a sample standard deviation of $669. Is there evidence that the small price reduction is enough to increase sales of compact disk players?

SOLUTION

Our null and alternative hypotheses are those of situation II, a one-tailed test, except that we will reverse the notation 1 and 2 so we can conduct a right-tailed test to determine whether reducing the price increases sales (if sales increase, then μ_2 will be greater than μ_1, which is what we want the alternative hypothesis to be). We have $H_0: \mu_2 - \mu_1 \leq 0$ and $H_1: \mu_2 - \mu_1 > 0$. We assume an equal variance of the populations of sales at the two price levels. Our test statistic has a t distribution with

---

[5] The data are based on estimates reported by Data Resources, Inc.

FIGURE 8–4 Conducting the Test of Example 8–6

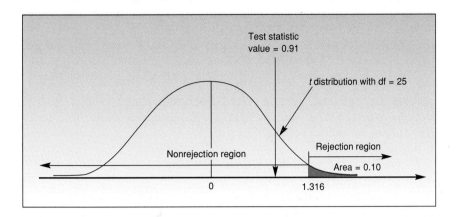

$n_1 + n_2 - 2 = 15 + 12 - 2 = 25$ degrees of freedom. The computed value of the statistic, by equation 8–9, is

$$t = \frac{(6,870 - 6,598) - 0}{\sqrt{\dfrac{(14)(844)^2 + (11)(669)^2}{25}\left(\dfrac{1}{15} + \dfrac{1}{12}\right)}} = 0.91$$

This value of the statistic falls inside the nonrejection region for any usual level of significance, as shown in Figure 8–4. The manufacturer may conclude that the data present no evidence that reducing the price by the small amount used in the experiment brings about increases in average sales.

Confidence Intervals

As usual, it is possible to construct confidence intervals for the parameter in question—here, the difference between the two population means. The confidence interval for this parameter is based on the t distribution with $n_1 + n_2 - 2$ degrees of freedom (or z when df is large).

A $(1 - \alpha)100\%$ confidence interval for $(\mu_1 - \mu_2)$, assuming equal population variance:

$$(\bar{x}_1 - \bar{x}_2) \pm t_{\alpha/2}\sqrt{s_p^2\left(\frac{1}{n_1} + \frac{1}{n_2}\right)} \qquad (8\text{–}10)$$

The confidence interval in equation 8–10 has the usual form: Estimate $\pm$ Distribution coefficient $\times$ Standard deviation of estimator.

In Example 8–6, forgetting that the test was carried out as a one-tailed test, let us compute a 95% confidence interval for the difference between the two means. Since the test resulted in nonrejection of the null hypothesis (and would have also resulted so had it been carried out as two-tailed), our confidence interval should contain the null-hypothesized difference between the two population means: zero. This is due to the connection between hypothesis tests and confidence intervals. Let us see if this really happens. The 95% confidence interval for $(\mu_1 - \mu_2)$ is

$$(\bar{x}_1 - \bar{x}_2) \pm t_{0.025} \sqrt{s_p^2 \left(\frac{1}{n_1} + \frac{1}{n_2}\right)} = (6{,}870 - 6{,}598) \pm 2.06\sqrt{(595{,}835)(0.15)}$$

$$= [-343.85,\ 887.85]$$

We see that the confidence interval indeed contains the null-hypothesized difference of zero, as expected from the fact that a two-tailed test would have resulted in nonrejection of the null hypothesis.

PROBLEMS

In each of the following problems assume that the two populations of interest are normally distributed with equal variance. Assume independent random sampling from the two populations.

8–18. The recent boom in sales of travel books has led to the marketing of other travel-related guides, such as video travel guides and audio walking-tour tapes. Waldenbooks has been studying the market for these travel guides. In one market test, a random sample of 25 potential travelers was asked to rate audiotapes of a certain destination, and another random sample of 20 potential travelers was asked to rate videotapes of the same destination. Both ratings were on a scale of 0 to 100 and measured the potential travelers' satisfaction with the travel guide they tested and the degree of possible purchase intent (with 100 the highest). The mean score for the audio group was 87, and their standard deviation was 12. The mean score for the video group was 64, and their standard deviation was 23. Do these data present evidence that one form of travel guide is better than the other? Advise Waldenbooks on a possible marketing decision to be made.

8–19. Business schools at certain prestigious universities offer nondegree management training programs for high-level executives. These programs supposedly develop executives' leadership abilities and help them advance to higher management positions within two years after program completion. A management consulting firm wants to test the effectiveness of these programs and sets out to conduct a one-tailed test, where the alternative hypothesis is that graduates of the programs under study do receive, on the average, salaries more than $4,000 per year higher than salaries of comparable executives without the special university training. To test the hypotheses, the firm traces a random sample of 28 top executives who earn, at the time the sample is selected, about the same salaries. Out of this group, 13 executives—randomly selected from the group of 28 executives—are enrolled in one of the university programs under study. Two years later, average salaries for the two groups and standard deviations of salaries are computed. The results are: $\bar{x} = 48$ and $s = 6$ for the nonprogram executives, and $\bar{x} = 55$ and $s = 8$ for the program executives. All numbers are in thousands of dollars per year. Conduct the test at $\alpha = 0.05$, and evaluate the effectiveness of the programs in terms of increased average salary levels.

8–20. According to *The Wall Street Journal*, the home office is fast becoming a way of life for millions of Americans, and the cost of maintaining a home office is dropping. In 1995, the average initial investment in setting up a home office (buying a computer, printer, fax machine) was $3,300, according to the *Journal*.[6] Assume that this is based on a random sample of 50 home offices set up in 1995 and that the standard deviation was $1,000. Corresponding figures for 50 home offices set up in 1990 were average cost $5,200 and standard deviation $1,000. Test for a reduction in cost from 1990 to 1995.

---

[6] J. Carlton, "The Home Office Is Quickly Becoming Less Expensive and More Sophisticated," *The Wall Street Journal,* June 19, 1995, p. R 32.

8–21. According to *The Economist*, the French cafe, once "the most solid of the institutions" of France, is disappearing. One reason is a reduction in alcohol consumption from 18 liters a year per person in 1960 to 11 liters per person a year in 1995.[7] Assuming this is based on two independent random samples of 100 people each, with equal standard deviation of 6 liters per year, test for significance. Is there proof of a decline in alcohol use in France?

8–22. Ikarus, the Hungarian bus maker, has lost its important Soviet market and is reported on the verge of collapse. The company is now trying a new engine in its buses and has gathered the following random samples of miles-per-gallon figures for the old engine versus the new:

Old engine: 8, 9, 7.5, 8.5, 6, 9, 9, 10, 7, 8.5, 6, 10, 9, 8, 9, 5, 9.5, 10, 8

New engine: 10, 9, 9, 6, 9, 11, 11, 8, 9, 6.5, 7, 9, 10, 8, 9, 10, 9, 12, 11.5, 10, 7, 10, 8.5

Is there evidence that the new engine is more economical than the old one?

8–23. *Air Transport World* recently named the Dutch airline KLM "Airline of the Year." One measure of the airline's excellent management is its research effort in developing new routes and improving service on existing routes. The airline wanted to test the profitability of a certain transatlantic flight route and offered daily flights from Europe to the United States over a period of six weeks on the new proposed route. Then, over a period of nine weeks, daily flights were offered from Europe to an alternative airport in the United States. Weekly profitability data for the two samples were collected, under the assumption that these may be viewed as independent random samples of weekly profits from the two populations (one population is flights to the proposed airport, and the other population is flights to an alternative airport). Data are as follows. For the proposed route, $\bar{x} = \$96,540$ per week and $s = \$12,522$. For the alternative route, $\bar{x} = \$85,991$ and $s = \$19,548$. Test the hypothesis that the proposed route is more profitable than the alternative route. Use a significance level of your choice.

8–24. Authors T. Peters and R. Waterman state in their book *In Search of Excellence* that the giant advertising firm of Ogilvy and Mather is more concerned with customer satisfaction than it is with company profits.[8] Suppose a test is carried out to determine whether or not new management decisions at Ogilvy and Mather increase average customer satisfaction. To test this claim, a random sample of company clients is polled before an important management decision, and customer satisfaction is measured for this sample on a scale of 1 to 10. Then, some time after the management decision has been made and a new company policy implemented, another sample of clients is polled, and their satisfaction scores are computed (on the same scale). Letting the subscript b denoted "before the new decision" and the subscript a denoted "after the new decision," the results of the surveys are: $n_b = 18$, $\bar{x}_b = 7.4$, $s_b = 1.3$; $n_a = 23$, $\bar{x}_a = 8.2$, $s_a = 2.4$. Using these data, do you believe that customer satisfaction is increased, on the average, after the new management decision and the resulting new company policy?

8–25. Mark Pollard, financial consultant for Merrill Lynch, Pierce, Fenner & Smith, Inc., is quoted in national advertisements for Merrill Lynch as saying: "I've made more money for clients by saying no than by saying yes." Suppose that Mr. Pollard allowed you access to his files so that you could conduct a statistical test of the correctness of his statement. Suppose further that you gathered a random sample of 25 clients to whom Mr. Pollard said yes when presented with their investment proposals, and you found that the clients' average gain on investments was 12% and the standard deviation was 2.5%. Suppose you gathered another sample of 25 clients to whom Mr. Pollard said no when asked about possible investments; the clients were then offered other investments, which they consequently made. For this sample, you found that the average return was 13.5% and the standard deviation was 1%. Test Mr. Pollard's claim at $\alpha = 0.05$. What assumptions are you making in this problem?

---

[7] "Mais Où Sont Les Cafés D'autan?" *The Economist,* June 10, 1995, p. 50.
[8] T. Peters and R. Waterman, *In Search of Excellence* (New York: Harper & Row, 1982).

8-26. An article reports the results of an analysis of stock market returns before and after antitrust trials that resulted in the breakup of AT&T. The study concentrated on two periods: the pre-antitrust period of 1966 to 1973, denoted period 1, and the antitrust trial period of 1974 to 1981, called period 2. An equation similar to equation 8–9 was used to test for the existence of a difference in mean stock return during the two periods. Conduct a two-tailed test of equality of mean stock return in the population of all stocks before and during the antitrust trials using the following data: $n_1 = 21$, $\bar{x}_1 = 0.105$, $s_1 = 0.09$; $n_2 = 28$, $\bar{x}_2 = 0.1331$, $s_2 = 0.122$. Use $\alpha = 0.05$.

8-27. A banker with Continental Illinois National Bank and Trust Company wants to test which method of raising cash for companies—borrowing from public sources or borrowing from private sources—results in higher average amounts raised by a company. The banker collects a random sample of 12 firms that borrowed only from public sources and finds that the average amount borrowed by a company per source is $12,500 and the standard deviation is $3,400. Another sample of 18 firms that borrowed only from private sources gives a sample average per source of $21,000 and a sample standard deviation of $5,000. Do you believe that either private or public sources lend, on the average, more than the other? Explain.

8-28. In problem 8–25, construct a 95% confidence interval for the difference between the average return to investors following a no recommendation and the average return to investors following a yes recommendation. Interpret your results.

8-5 A Large-Sample Test for the Difference between Two Population Proportions

When sample sizes are large enough that the distributions of the sample proportions $\hat{P}_1$ and $\hat{P}_2$ are both approximated well by a normal distribution, the difference between the two sample proportions is also approximately normally distributed, and this gives rise to a test for equality of two population proportions based on the standard normal distribution. It is also possible to construct confidence intervals for the difference between the two population proportions. Assuming the sample sizes are large and assuming independent random sampling from the two populations, the following are possible hypotheses (we consider situations similar to the ones discussed in the previous two sections; other tests are also possible).

$$\text{Situation I:} \quad H_0: p_1 - p_2 = 0$$
$$H_1: p_1 - p_2 \neq 0$$
$$\text{Situation II:} \quad H_0: p_1 - p_2 \leq 0$$
$$H_1: p_1 - p_2 > 0$$
$$\text{Situation III:} \quad H_0: p_1 - p_2 \leq D$$
$$H_1: p_1 - p_2 > D$$

where D is some number other than 0.

In the case of tests about the difference between two population proportions, there are two test statistics. One statistic is appropriate when the null hypothesis is that the difference between the two population proportions is equal to (or greater than or equal to, or less than or equal to) zero. This is the case, for example, in situations I and II. The other test statistic is appropriate when the null-hypothesized difference is some number, D, different from zero. This is the case, for example, in situation III (or in a two-tailed test, situation I, with D replacing 0).

Test statistic for the difference between two population proportions where the null-hypothesized difference is zero:

$$z = \frac{(\hat{p}_1 - \hat{p}_2) - 0}{\sqrt{\hat{p}(1 - \hat{p})\left(\frac{1}{n_1} + \frac{1}{n_2}\right)}} \qquad (8\text{--}11)$$

where $\hat{p}_1 = x_1/n_1$ is the sample proportion in sample 1 and $\hat{p}_2 = x_2/n_2$ is the sample proportion in sample 2. The symbol $\hat{p}$ stands for the *combined sample proportion in both samples*, considered as a single sample. That is,

$$\hat{p} = \frac{x_1 + x_2}{n_1 + n_2} \qquad (8\text{--}12)$$

Note that 0 in the numerator of equation 8–11 is the null-hypothesized difference between the two population proportions; we retain it only for conceptual reasons—to maintain the form of our test statistic: (Estimate − Hypothesized value of the parameter)/(Standard deviation of the estimator). When we carry out computations using equation 8–11, we will, of course, ignore subtracting zero. Under the null hypothesis that the difference between the two population proportions is zero, both sample proportions $\hat{p}_1$ and $\hat{p}_2$ are estimates of the same quantity, and therefore—assuming, as always, that the null hypothesis is true—we pool the two estimates when computing the estimated standard deviation of the difference between the two sample proportions: the denominator of equation 8–11.

When the null hypothesis is that the difference between the two population proportions is a number other than zero, we cannot assume that $\hat{p}_1$ and $\hat{p}_2$ are estimates of the same population proportion (because the null-hypothesized difference between the two population proportions is $D \neq 0$); in such cases we cannot pool the two estimates when computing the estimated standard deviation of the difference between the two sample proportions. In such cases, we use the following test statistic.

Test statistic for the difference between two population proportions when the null-hypothesized difference between the two proportions is some number, D, other than zero:

$$z = \frac{(\hat{p}_1 - \hat{p}_2) - D}{\sqrt{\frac{\hat{p}_1(1 - \hat{p}_1)}{n_1} + \frac{\hat{p}_2(1 - \hat{p}_2)}{n_2}}} \qquad (8\text{--}13)$$

We will now demonstrate the use of the test statistics presented in this section with the following examples.

EXAMPLE 8-7

A recent article describes how finance incentives by the major automakers are reducing banks' share of the market for automobile loans. The article reports that in 1980, banks wrote about 53% of all car loans, and in 1995, the banks' share was only 43%. Suppose that these data are based on a random sample of 100 car loans in 1980, where 53 of the loans were found to be bank loans; and the 1995 data are also based on a random sample of 100 loans, 43 of which were found to be bank loans. Carry out a two-tailed test of the equality of banks' share of the car loan market in 1980 and in 1995.

SOLUTION

Our hypotheses are those described as situation I, a two-tailed test of the equality of two population proportions. We have $H_0: p_1 - p_2 = 0$ and $H_1: p_1 - p_2 \neq 0$. Since the null-hypothesized difference between the two population proportions is zero, we can use the test statistic of equation 8–11. First we calculate $\hat{p}$, the combined sample proportion, using equation 8–12:

$$\hat{p} = \frac{x_1 + x_2}{n_1 + n_2} = \frac{53 + 43}{100 + 100} = 0.48$$

We also have $1 - \hat{p} = 0.52$.

We now compute the value of the test statistic, equation 8–11:

$$z = \frac{\hat{p}_1 - \hat{p}_2}{\sqrt{\hat{p}(1 - \hat{p})\left(\frac{1}{n_1} + \frac{1}{n_2}\right)}} = \frac{0.53 - 0.43}{\sqrt{(0.48)(0.52)(0.01 + 0.01)}} = 1.415$$

This value of the test statistic falls in the nonrejection region even if we use $\alpha = 0.10$. In fact, the p-value, found using the standard normal table, is equal to 0.157. We conclude that the data present insufficient evidence that the share of banks in the car loan market has changed from 1980 to 1995. The test is shown in Figure 8–5.

EXAMPLE 8-8

From time to time, BankAmerica Corporation comes out with its Free and Easy Travelers Cheques Sweepstakes, designed to increase the amounts of BankAmerica traveler's checks sold. Since the amount bought per customer determines the customer's chances of winning a prize, a manager hypothesizes that, during sweepstakes time, the proportion of BankAmerica traveler's checks buyers who buy more than $2,500 worth of checks will be at least 10% higher than the proportion of traveler's checks buyers who buy more than

FIGURE 8-5 Carrying Out the Test of Example 8-7

$2,500 worth of checks when there are no sweepstakes. A random sample of 300 traveler's checks buyers, taken when the sweepstakes are on, reveals that 120 of these people bought checks for more than $2,500. A random sample of 700 traveler's checks buyers, taken when no sweepstakes prizes are offered, reveals that 140 of these people bought checks for more than $2,500. Conduct the hypothesis test.

The manager wants to prove that the population proportion of traveler's checks buyers who buy at least $2,500 in checks when sweepstakes prizes are offered is at least 10% higher than the proportion of such buyers when no sweepstakes are on. Therefore, this should be the manager's alternative hypothesis. We have H_0: $p_1 - p_2 \leq 0.10$ and H_1: $p_1 - p_2 > 0.10$. The appropriate test statistic is the statistic given in equation 8–13:

$$z = \frac{(\hat{p}_1 - \hat{p}_2) - D}{\sqrt{\dfrac{\hat{p}_1(1 - \hat{p}_1)}{n_1} + \dfrac{\hat{p}_2(1 - \hat{p}_2)}{n_2}}}$$

$$= \frac{(120/300) - (140/700) - 0.10}{\sqrt{\dfrac{(120/300)(180/300)}{300} + \dfrac{(140/700)(560/700)}{700}}}$$

$$= \frac{(0.4 - 0.2) - 0.1}{\sqrt{[(0.4)(0.6)/300] + [(0.2)(0.8)/700]}} = 3.118$$

Ctect

This value of the test statistic falls in the rejection region for $\alpha = 0.001$ (corresponding to the critical point 3.09 from the normal table). The *p*-value is therefore smaller than 0.001, and the null hypothesis is rejected. The manager is probably right. Figure 8–6 shows the result of the test.

Confidence Intervals

When constructing confidence intervals for the difference between two population proportions, we do not use the pooled estimate because we do not assume that the two proportions are equal. The estimated standard deviation of the difference between the

FIGURE 8–6 Carrying Out the Test of Example 8-8

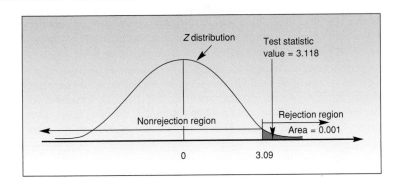

two sample proportions, to be used in the confidence interval, is the denominator in equation 8–13.

> A large-sample $(1 - \alpha)100\%$ confidence interval for the difference between two population proportions:
>
> $$(\hat{p}_1 - \hat{p}_2) \pm z_{\alpha/2} \sqrt{\frac{\hat{p}_1(1 - \hat{p}_1)}{n_1} + \frac{\hat{p}_2(1 - \hat{p}_2)}{n_2}} \qquad (8-14)$$

In the context of Example 8–8, let us now construct a 95% confidence interval for the difference between the proportion of BankAmerica traveler's checks buyers who buy more than $2,500 worth of checks during sweepstakes and the proportion of buyers of checks above this amount when no sweepstakes prizes are offered. Using equation 8–14, we get

$$(0.4 - 0.2) \pm 1.96 \sqrt{\frac{(0.4)(0.6)}{300} + \frac{(0.2)(0.8)}{700}} = 0.2 \pm 1.96(0.032)$$
$$= [0.137, 0.263]$$

The manager may be 95% confident that the difference between the two proportions of interest is anywhere from 0.137 to 0.263.

PROBLEMS

8–29. Airline mergers cause many problems for the airline industry. One variable often quoted as a measure of an airline's efficiency is the percentage of on-time departures. Following the merger of Republic Airlines with Northwest Airlines, the percentage of on-time departures for Northwest planes declined from approximately 85% to about 68%. Suppose that the percentages reported above are based on two random samples of flights: a sample of 100 flights over a period of two months before the merger, of which 85 are found to have departed on time; and a sample of 100 flights over a period of two months after the merger, 68 of which are found to have departed on time. Based on these data, do you believe that Northwest's on-time percentage has declined during the period following its merger with Republic?

8–30. A physicians' group is interested in testing to determine whether more people in small towns choose a physician by word of mouth in comparison with people in large metropolitan areas. A random sample of 1,000 people in small towns reveals that 850 have chosen their physicians by word of mouth; a random sample of 2,500 people living in large metropolitan areas reveals that 1,950 of them have chosen a physician by word of mouth. Conduct a one-tailed test aimed at proving that the percentage of popular recommendation of physicians is larger in small towns than in large metropolitan areas. Use $\alpha = 0.01$.

8–31. A corporate raider has been successful in 11 of 31 takeover attempts. Another corporate raider has been successful in 19 of 50 takeover bids. Assuming that the success rate of each raider at each trial is independent of all other attempts, and that the information presented can be regarded as based on two independent random samples of the two raiders' overall performance, can you say whether one of the raiders is more successful than the other? Explain.

8–32. A random sample of 2,060 consumers shows that 13% of them prefer California wines. Over the next three months, an advertising campaign is undertaken to show that California wines receive awards and win taste tests. The organizers of the campaign want to prove that the three-month campaign raised the proportion of people who prefer California wines by at least 5%. At the end of the campaign, a random sample of 5,000 consumers shows that 19% of them now prefer California wines. Conduct the test at $\alpha = 0.05$.

8–33.   In problem 8–32, give a 95% confidence interval for the increase in the population proportion of consumers preferring California wines following the campaign.

8–34.   Recent Federal Reserve Board regulations permit banks to offer their clients commercial paper. A random sample of 650 customers of Chase Manhattan Bank reveals that 48 of them own commercial paper as part of their investment portfolios with the bank. A random sample of customers of Manufacturers Hanover Bank reveals that out of 480 customers, only 20 own commercial paper as part of their investments with the bank. Can you conclude that Chase Manhattan has a greater share of the new market for commercial paper? Explain.

8–35.   Airbus Industrie, the European maker of the A320 medium-range jet capable of carrying 150 passengers, is currently trying to expand its market worldwide. At one point, Airbus managers wanted to test whether or not their potential market in the United States, measured by the proportion of airline industry executives who would prefer the A320, is greater than the company's potential market for the A320 in Europe (measured by the same indicator). A random sample of 120 top executives of U.S. airlines looking for new aircraft were given a demonstration of the plane, and 34 indicated that they would prefer the model to other new planes on the market. A random sample of 200 European airline executives were also given a demonstration of the plane, and 41 of them indicated that they would be interested in the A320. Test the hypothesis that more American airline executives prefer the A320 than their European counterparts.

8–36.   Data from the Bureau of Labor Statistics indicate that the 1994 unemployment rate in Cleveland was 7.5% and the unemployment rate in Chicago was 7.2%. Suppose that both figures are based on random samples of 1,000 people in each city. Test the null hypothesis that the unemployment rates in both cities are equal versus the alternative hypothesis that they are not equal. What is the p-value? State your conclusion.

8–37.   In problem 8–36, give a 99% confidence interval for the difference in unemployment rates between Cleveland and Chicago in 1994. Explain your results.

8–38.   Sales of laptop computers have been increasing rapidly and are expected to account for 35% of all personal computer sales in the United States.[9] The marketing manager for Toshiba wanted to test whether the company's laptop computer accounted for about the same share of the market in California as it did in New York. A random sample of 1,000 laptops sold in California revealed that 285 were made by Toshiba, while a random sample of 1,500 laptops sold in New York revealed that 452 were Toshiba's. Conduct the test, and state your conclusion in the form of a memo to the marketing director.

8–39.   Several companies have been developing electronic guidance systems for cars. Motorola and Germany's Blaupunkt are two firms in the forefront of such research. Out of 120 trials of the Motorola model, 101 were successful; and out of 200 tests of the Blaupunkt model, 110 were successful. Is there evidence to conclude that the Motorola electronic guidance system is superior to the German competitor?

8–6   The *F* Distribution and a Test for Equality of Two Population Variances

In this section, we encounter the last of the major probability distributions useful in statistics, the *F distribution*. The *F* distribution is named after the English statistician Sir Ronald A. Fisher.

> The **F distribution** is the distribution of the ratio of two chi-square random variables that are independent of each other, each of which is divided by its own degrees of freedom.

---

[9] "Laptops Take Off," *Business Week*, March 18, 1991, p. 118.

If we let χ_1^2 be a chi-square random variable with k_1 degrees of freedom, and χ_2^2 another chi-square random variable independent of χ_1^2 and having k_2 degrees of freedom, the ratio in equation 8–15 has the F distribution with k_1 and k_2 degrees of freedom.

> An F random variable with k_1 and k_2 degrees of freedom:
>
> $$F_{(k_1,\, k_2)} = \frac{\chi_1^2/k_1}{\chi_2^2/k_2}$$
>
> (8–15)

The F distribution thus has two kinds of degrees of freedom: k_1 is called the *degrees of freedom of the numerator* and is always listed as the first item in the parentheses; k_2 is called the *degrees of freedom of the denominator* and is always listed second inside the parentheses. The degrees of freedom of the numerator, k_1, are "inherited" from the chi-square random variable in the numerator; similarly, k_2 is "inherited" from the other, independent chi-square random variable in the denominator of equation 8–15.

Since there are so many possible degrees of freedom for the F random variable, tables of values of this variable for given probabilities are even more concise than the chi-square tables. Table 5 in Appendix C gives the critical points for F distributions with different degrees of freedom of the numerator and the denominator corresponding to right-tailed areas of 0.10, 0.05, 0.025 and 0.01. The second part of Table 5 gives critical points for $\alpha = 0.05$ and $\alpha = 0.01$ for a wider ranger of F random variables. For example, use Table 5 to verify that the point 3.01 cuts off an area of 0.05 to its right for an F random variable with 7 degrees of freedom for the numerator and 11 degrees of freedom for the denominator. This is demonstrated in Figure 8–7. Figure 8–8 shows various F distributions with different degrees of freedom. The F distributions are asymmetric (a quality inherited from their chi-square parents), and their shape resembles that of the chi-square distributions. Note that $F_{(7,11)} \neq F_{(11,7)}$. It is important to keep track of which degrees of freedom are for the numerator and which are for the denominator.

FIGURE 8–7   An F Distribution with 7 and 11 Degrees of Freedom

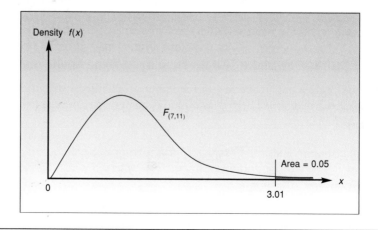

FIGURE 8-8   Several F Distributions

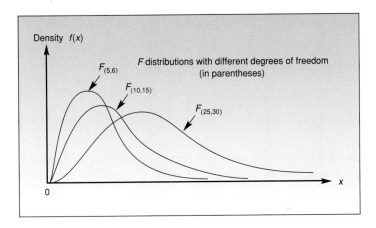

Table 8–2 is a reproduction of a part of Table 5, showing values of F distributions with different degrees of freedom cutting off a right-tailed area of 0.05.

The F distribution is useful in testing the equality of two population variances. Recall that in Chapter 7 we defined a chi-square random variable as

$$\chi^2 = \frac{(n-1)S^2}{\sigma^2} \tag{8–16}$$

where S^2 is the sample variance from a *normally distributed population*. This was the definition in the single-sample case, where $n-1$ was the appropriate number of degrees of freedom. Now suppose that we have two *independent* random samples from two *normally distributed populations*. The two samples will give rise to two sample variances, the random variables S_1^2 and S_2^2 with $n_1 - 1$ and $n_2 - 1$ degrees of freedom, respectively. The ratio of these two random variables is the random variable

$$\frac{S_1^2}{S_2^2} = \frac{\chi_1^2 \sigma_1^2/(n_1-1)}{\chi_2^2 \sigma_2^2/(n_2-1)} \tag{8–17}$$

When the two population variances, σ_1^2 and σ_2^2, are *equal*, the two terms σ_1^2 and σ_2^2 cancel out, and equation 8–17 is equal to equation 8–15, which is the ratio of two independent chi-square random variables, each divided by its own degrees of freedom (k_1 is $n_1 - 1$, and k_2 is $n_2 - 1$). This, therefore, is an F random variable with $n_1 - 1$ and $n_2 - 1$ degrees of freedom.

Test statistic for the equality of the variances of two normally distributed populations:

$$F_{(n_1-1, n_2-1)} = \frac{s_1^2}{s_2^2} \tag{8–18}$$

Now that we have encountered the important F distribution, we are ready to define the test for the equality of two population variances. Incidentally, the F distri-

TABLE 8-2   Critical Points Cutting off a Right-Tailed Area of 0.05 for Selected *F Distributions*

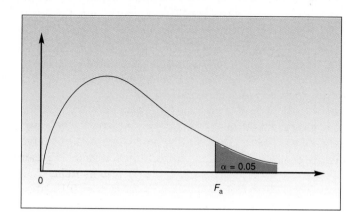

k_2 \ k_1	Degrees of Freedom of the Numerator								
	1	**2**	**3**	**4**	**5**	**6**	**7**	**8**	**9**
Degrees 1	161.4	199.5	215.7	224.6	230.2	234.0	236.8	238.9	240.5
of 2	18.51	19.00	19.16	19.25	19.30	19.33	19.35	19.37	19.38
Freedom 3	10.13	9.55	9.28	9.12	9.01	8.94	8.89	8.85	8.81
of the 4	7.71	6.94	6.59	6.39	6.26	6.16	6.09	6.04	6.00
Denomi- 5	6.61	5.79	5.41	5.19	5.05	4.95	4.88	4.82	4.77
nator 6	5.99	5.14	4.76	4.53	4.39	4.28	4.21	4.15	4.10
7	5.59	4.74	4.35	4.12	3.97	3.87	3.79	3.73	3.68
8	5.32	4.46	4.07	3.84	3.69	3.58	3.50	3.44	3.39
9	5.12	4.26	3.86	3.63	3.48	3.37	3.29	3.23	3.18
10	4.96	4.10	3.71	3.48	3.33	3.22	3.14	3.07	3.02
11	4.84	3.98	3.59	3.36	3.20	3.09	3.01	2.95	2.90
12	4.75	3.89	3.49	3.26	3.11	3.00	2.91	2.85	2.80
13	4.67	3.81	3.41	3.18	3.03	2.92	2.83	2.77	2.71
14	4.60	3.74	3.34	3.11	2.96	2.85	2.76	2.70	2.65
15	4.54	3.68	3.29	3.06	2.90	2.79	2.71	2.64	2.59

bution has many more uses than just testing for equality of two population variances. In chapters that follow, we will find this distribution extremely useful in a variety of involved statistical contexts.

A Statistical Test for Equality of Two Population Variances

We assume independent random sampling from the two populations in question. We also assume that the two populations are normally distributed. Let the two populations be labeled 1 and 2. The possible hypotheses to be tested are the following:

A two-tailed test: $H_0: \sigma_1^2 = \sigma_2^2$
                       $H_1: \sigma_1^2 \neq \sigma_2^2$

A one-tailed test: $H_0: \sigma_1^2 \leq \sigma_2^2$
                       $H_1: \sigma_1^2 > \sigma_2^2$

We will consider the one-tailed test first, because it is easier to handle. Suppose that we want to test whether σ_1^2 is greater than σ_2^2. We collect the two independent random samples from populations 1 and 2, and we compute the statistic in equation 8–18. We must be sure to put s_1^2 in the numerator, because in a one-tailed test, rejection may occur only on the right. If s_1^2 is actually smaller than s_2^2, we can immediately not reject the null hypothesis because the statistic value will be less than 1.00 and, hence, certainly within the nonrejection region for any level, α.

In a two-tailed test, we may do one of two things:

1. We may use the convention of always placing the *larger* sample variance in the *numerator*. That is, we label the population with the larger sample variance population 1. Then, if the test statistic value is greater than a critical point cutting off an area of, say, 0.05 to its right, we reject the null hypothesis that the two variances are equal at $\alpha = 0.10$ (that is, at *double* the level of significance from the table). This is so because, under the null hypothesis, either of the two sample variances could have been larger than the other, and we are carrying out a two-tailed test on one tail of the distribution. Similarly, if we can get a *p*-value on the one tail of rejection, we need to *double* it to get the actual *p*-value. Alternatively, we can conduct a two-tailed test as described next.

2. We may choose not to relabel the populations such that the larger sample variance is on top. Instead, we find the right-hand critical point for $\alpha = 0.01$ or 0.05 (or another level) from Appendix C, Table 5. We compute the left-hand critical point for the test (not given in the table) as follows.

The left-hand critical point to go along with $F_{(k_1, k_2)}$ is given by

$$\frac{1}{F_{(k_2, k_1)}} \qquad (8\text{–}19)$$

where $F_{(k_1, k_2)}$ is the right-hand critical point from the table and $F_{(k_2, k_1)}$ is the right-hand critical point from the table for an *F* random variable with the *reverse order of degrees of freedom*.

Thus, the left-hand critical point is the reciprocal of the right-hand critical point obtained from the table using the reverse order of degrees of freedom for numerator and denominator. Again, the level of significance, α, must be doubled. For example, from Table 8–2, we find that the right-hand critical point for $\alpha = 0.05$ with degrees of freedom for the numerator equal to 6 and degrees of freedom for the denominator equal to 9 is $C = 3.37$. So, for a two-tailed test at $\alpha = 0.10$ (double the significance level from the table), the critical points are 3.37 and the point obtained using equation 8–19, $1/F_{(9,6)}$, which, using the table, is found to be $1/4.10 = 0.2439$. This is shown in Figure 8–9.

We will now demonstrate the use of the test for equality of two population variances with examples.

FIGURE 8-9   The Critical Points for a Two-Tailed Test Using $F_{(6, 9)}$ and $\alpha = 0.10$

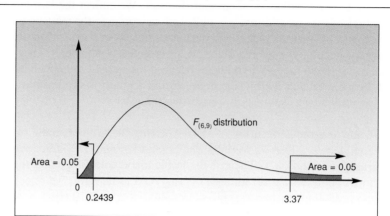

EXAMPLE 8-9

One of the problems that insider trading supposedly causes is unnaturally high stock price volatility. When insiders rush to buy a stock they believe will increase in price, the buying pressure causes the stock price to rise faster than under usual conditions. Then, when insiders dump their holdings to realize quick gains, the stock price dips fast. Price volatility can be measured as the variance of prices.

An economist wants to study the effect of the insider trading scandal and ensuing legislation on the volatility of the price of a certain stock. The economist collects price data for the stock during the period before the event (interception and prosecution of insider traders) and after the event. The economist makes the assumptions that prices are approximately normally distributed and that the two price data sets may be considered independent random samples from the populations of prices before and after the event. As we mentioned earlier, the theory of finance supports the normality assumption. (The assumption of random sampling may be somewhat problematic in this case, but later we will deal with time-dependent observations more effectively.) Suppose that the economist wants to test whether or not the event has decreased the variance of prices of the stock. The 25 daily stock prices before the event give $s_1^2 = 9.3$ (dollars squared) and the 24 stock prices after the event give $s_2^2 = 3.0$ (dollars squared). Conduct the test at $\alpha = 0.05$.

SOLUTION

Our test is a right-tailed test. We have H_0: $\sigma_1^2 \leq \sigma_2^2$ and H_1: $\sigma_1^2 > \sigma_2^2$. We compute the test statistic of equation 8–18:

$$F_{(n_1-1, n_2-1)} = F_{(24, 23)} = \frac{s_1^2}{s_2^2} = \frac{9.3}{3.0} = 3.1$$

As can be seen from Figure 8–10, this value of the test statistic falls in the rejection region for $\alpha = 0.05$ and for $\alpha = 0.01$. The critical point for $\alpha = 0.05$, from Table 5, is equal to 2.01 (see 24 degrees of freedom for the numerator and 23 degrees of freedom for the denominator). Referring to the F table for $\alpha = 0.01$ with 24 degrees of freedom for the numerator and 23 degrees of freedom for the denominator gives a critical point of 2.70. The computed value of the test statistic, 3.1, is greater than both of these values. The p-value is smaller than 0.01, and the economist may conclude that (subject to the validity

FIGURE 8-10   Carrying Out the Test of Example 8-9

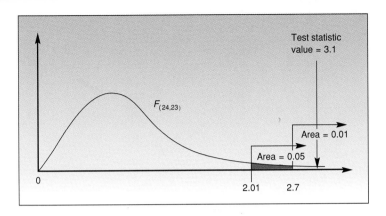

of the assumptions) the data present significant evidence that the event in question has reduced the variance of the stock's price.

EXAMPLE 8-10

Recall that in section 8–4 we made the special assumption that the variances of the two populations were equal. We can use the F test to determine whether or not our assumption of equal variance indeed holds. The test for equality for two population variances is, of course, a two-tailed test: $H_0: \sigma_1^2 = \sigma_2^2$ and $H_1: \sigma_1^2 \neq \sigma_2^2$. Let us use the data of Example 8–5, $n_1 = 14$, $s_1 = 0.12$; $n_2 = 9$, $s_2 = 0.11$, to test the assumption of equal population variances.

SOLUTION

The test statistic is the same as in the previous example, given by equation 8–18:

$$F_{(13,8)} = \frac{s_1^2}{s_2^2} = \frac{0.12^2}{0.11^2} = 1.19$$

Here we placed the larger variance in the numerator because it was already labeled 1 (we did not purposely label the larger variance as 1). We can carry this out as a one-tailed test, even though it is really two-tailed, remembering that we must double the level of significance. Choosing $\alpha = 0.05$ from the table makes this a test at true level of significance equal to $2(0.05) = 0.10$. The critical point, using 12 and 8 degrees of freedom for numerator and denominator, respectively, is 3.28. (This is the closest value, since our table does not list critical points for 13 and 8 degrees of freedom.) As can be seen, our test statistic falls inside the nonrejection region, and we may conclude that at the 0.10 level of significance, there is no evidence that the two population variances are different from each other.

Let us now see how this test may be carried out using the alternative method of solution: finding a left-hand critical point to go with the right-hand one. The right-hand critical point remains 3.28 (Let us assume that this is the exact value for 13 and 8 degrees of freedom). The left-hand critical point is found by equation 8–19 as $1/F_{(8,13)} = 1/2.77 = 0.36$ (recall that the left-hand critical point is the inverse of the critical point corresponding to reversed-order degrees of freedom). The two tails are shown in Figure 8–11. Again, the value of the test statistic falls inside the nonrejection region for this test at $\alpha = 2(0.05) = 0.10$.

FIGURE 8-11   Carrying Out the Two-Tailed Test of Example 8-10

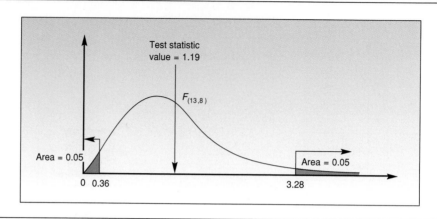

Confidence Intervals

Using the right-tailed value of an F distribution obtained from the table and the left-tailed value obtained using equation 8–19, we may construct a confidence interval for the ratio of two population variances. The confidence interval will have level $(1 - 2\alpha)100\%$, where α is the right-hand area from the table.

A $(1 - 2\alpha)100\%$ confidence interval for σ_1^2/σ_2^2:

$$\left[\frac{s_1^2/s_2^2}{F_\alpha}, \frac{s_1^2/s_2^2}{F_{1-\alpha}} \right] \qquad (8\text{--}20)$$

where F_α is the value obtained from the table and $F_{1-\alpha}$ is the left-tailed value of the distribution obtained through equation 8–19 as the reciprocal of the F value with reversed-order degrees of freedom.

Let us see how this confidence interval is constructed for the case of Example 8–10. Let us construct a 90% confidence interval for the ratio of the two population variances. Since we did not reject the null hypothesis that the two population variances are equal, a confidence interval (using the same level: $\alpha = 0.05, 2\alpha = 0.10$) for the *ratio* of the two variances should contain the point 1.00. This is so because if two quantities are approximately equal, their ratio should be approximately equal to 1.00. A 90% confidence interval for σ_1^2/σ_2^2 is given by

$$\left[\frac{(0.12)^2/(0.11)^2}{3.28}, \frac{(0.12)^2/(0.11)^2}{0.36} \right] = [0.363, 3.306]$$

The confidence interval does indeed contain the point 1.00 as a possible ratio of the two population variances.

In this section we encountered the F distribution. Like the t distribution and the chi-square distribution, the F distribution relies on the assumption that the population is normally distributed. The reason for this is that all these distributions are derived from the standard normal random variable: The chi-square distribution is defined as the distribution of the sum of k independent squared standard normal random vari-

FIGURE 8–12   **Relationships among Probability Distributions Useful in Statistics**

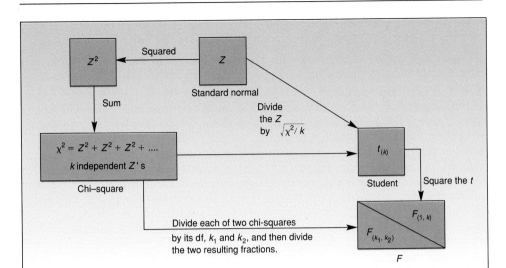

ables, Z (k is the number of degrees of freedom). The t distribution is defined as the ratio of Z to the square root of a chi-square random variable divided by its degrees of freedom (the t distribution has the same number of degrees of freedom, k, as its chi-square parent). The F distribution is the distribution of the ratio of two independent chi-square random variables, each divided by its degrees of freedom. Finally, the F distribution with degrees of freedom 1 and k (the special case with only *one* degree of freedom for the numerator) is also the distribution of the random variable obtained by squaring a t random variable with k degrees of freedom. The relationships among the distributions are shown in Figure 8–12.

PROBLEMS

In the following problems, assume that all populations are normally distributed.

8–40. Compaq Computer Corporation has an assembly plant in Houston, where the company's Deskpro computer is being built. Engineers at the plant are considering a new production facility and are interested in going on line with the new facility if and only if they can be fairly sure that the variance of the number of computers assembled per day using the new facility is lower than the production variance of the old system. A random sample of 40 production days using the old production method gives a sample variance of 1,288, and a random sample of 15 production days using the proposed new method gives a sample variance of 1,112. Conduct the appropriate test at $\alpha = 0.05$.

8–41. Test the validity of the equal-variance assumption in problem 8–27.

8–42. Test the validity of the equal-variance assumption for the data presented in problem 8–25. Also construct a 90% confidence interval for the ratio of the two population variances.

8–43. Test the validity of the equal-variance assumption for the data presented in problem 8–26. Also construct a 98% confidence interval for the ratio of the two population variances.

8–44. The following data are independent random samples of sales of the Nissan Pulsar model made in a joint venture of Nissan and Alfa Romeo. The data represent sales at dealerships before and after the announcement that the Pulsar model will no longer be made in Italy. Sales numbers are monthly.

Before: 329, 234, 423, 328, 400, 399, 326, 452, 541, 680, 456, 220
After: 212, 630, 276, 112, 872, 788, 345, 544, 110, 129, 776

Do you believe that the variance of the number of cars sold per month before the announcement is equal to the variance of the number of cars sold per month after the announcement?

8–45. A large department store wants to test whether or not the variance of waiting time in two checkout counters is approximately equal. Two independent random samples of 25 waiting times in each of the counters gives $s_1 = 2.5$ minutes and $s_2 = 3.1$ minutes. Carry out the test of equality of variances using $\alpha = 0.02$.

8–46. An important measure of the risk associated with a stock is the standard deviation, or variance, of the stock's price movements. A financial analyst wants to test the one-tailed hypothesis that stock A has a greater risk (larger variance of price) than stock B. A random sample of 25 daily prices of stock A gives $s_A^2 = 6.52$, and a random sample of 22 daily prices of stock B gives a sample variance of $s_B^2 = 3.47$. Carry out the test at $\alpha = 0.01$.

8–47. Discuss the assumptions made in the solution of the problems in this section.

8-7 Using the Computer

As we progress to more and more complicated statistical analyses, the computer becomes increasingly useful in solving problems. Many of the equations in this chapter can be very tedious to work out by hand. With a computer, however, the calculation of complicated expressions takes a fraction of a second. Let us see how the methods of this section are implementable on a computer. Again, we will use the package MINITAB, with which you now have some familiarity.

EXAMPLE 8-11

A potential buyer of a photocopying machine wants to test which of two models, one made by Savin and one made by Xerox, gives better average copy clarity. An optical device is available for measuring the clarity of copies produced from different originals. The device measures the resolution and the contrast of each copy and translates these characteristics into a single score per copy, measured on a scale of 0 to 100. Two random samples of originals are copied: one sample of 30 different copies done on a random sample of Savin copiers, and another sample of 30 originals copied on randomly chosen Xerox copiers. The results are

```
SAVIN: 95,98,83,97,72,89,86,91,98,98,76,91,85,87,86,92,87,89,86,
       93,95,99,86,96,98,90,98,86,85,79

XEROX: 86,87,89,79,91,92,89,90,84,83,82,99,98,78,98,81,87,82,83,
       88,85,95,80,93,99,98,81,80,90,92
```

SOLUTION

Figure 8–13 shows the MINITAB command and the computer output for the analysis of these data. In this case, we requested a two-tailed test of whether or not the two means are equal. Note that the reported statistic is labeled T. This is so because as long as the population standard deviations are not known, the distribution is a t distribution. However, as we noted, when the number of degrees of freedom is large, the t distribution is well approximated by the Z distribution, and this is the case here. Our computed test statistic value is equal to 1.00, and the reported p-value is 0.32. This can be verified from the

FIGURE 8-13   MINITAB Commands and Output Example 8-11

```
MTB > TWOSAMPLE ALTERNATIVE=0 for C1 C2

TWOSAMPLE T FOR C1 VS C2
        N      MEAN      STDEV     SE MEAN
C1    30      89.70      6.92        1.3
C2    30      87.97      6.50        1.2


95 PCT CI FOR MU C1 - MU C2:    (-1.7, 5.2)


TTEST MU C1 = MU C2 (VS NE):   T = 1.00   P=0.32
```

FIGURE 8-14   MINITAB Commands and Output Example 8-12

```
MTB > TWOSAMPLE ALTERNATIVE=0 for C1 C2;
SUBC> POOLED.

TWOSAMPLE T FOR C1 VS C2
        N      MEAN      STDEV     SE MEAN
C1    15      99.87      4.42        1.1
C2    14     103.57      4.75        1.3

95 PCT CI FOR MU C1 - MU C2: (-7.2, -0.2)

TTEST MU C1 = MU C2    (VS NE): T= -2.18 P=0.039 DF=  27

POOLED STDEV =         4.58
```

standard normal table (as an approximation). You may also remember that between $+1$ and -1 lies approximately 68% of the area under the normal curve; hence, the area in both tails, the *p*-value in a two-tailed test, is about 0.32.

EXAMPLE 8-12

An economist wants to test whether or not regular gasoline prices during a certain period of time were approximately equal, on average, on the East Coast and the West Coast. Two random samples, 15 gas stations in the East and 14 in the West, are collected and the prices per gallon recorded. Data are as follows.

```
EAST: 95,102,104,99,94,98,105,108,94,106,101,97,99,100,96
WEST: 101,104,99,105,98,107,108,109,98,99,110,97,106,109
```

SOLUTION

The program and the results of the two-tailed test are shown in Figure 8–14. We use the subcommand POOLED for pooled sample variances. The null hypothesis may be rejected at $\alpha = 0.05$ (consider the *p*-value), and we may conclude that, on the average, gasoline was more expensive in the West during the period in question.

FIGURE 8–15   Using MINITAB to Find Probabilities or Values of the *F* Distribution

```
MTB > CDF 3.29;
SUBC> F df numerator=7, df denominator= 9.
      3.2900    0.9499

MTB > CDF 1.35;
SUBC> F 120 120.
      1.3500    0.9492

MTB > INVCDF 0.95;
SUBC> F 40 4.
      0.9500    5.7170
```

Note that for small samples, and if the POOLED subcommand is not given, MINITAB defaults to the approximate degrees of freedom.

    MINITAB can also be used to find probabilities and values for the *F* distribution. The distribution and the degrees of freedom are specified in a subcommand that follows CDF or INVCDF. This is demonstrated in Figure 8–15. Compare the results with values in the *F* table.

8–8   Summary and Review of Terms

In this chapter, we extended the ideas of hypothesis tests and confidence intervals to the case of two populations. We discussed the comparisons of two population means, two population proportions, and two population variances. We developed a hypothesis test and confidence interval for the difference between two population means when the population variances were believed to be equal, and in the general case when they are not assumed equal. We introduced an important family of probability distributions: the **F distributions.** We saw that each *F* distribution has two kinds of degrees of freedom: one associated with the numerator and one associated with the denominator of the expression for *F*. We saw how the *F* distribution is used in testing hypotheses about two population variances. In the next chapter, we will make use of the *F* distribution in tests of the equality of *several* population means: the analysis of variance.

ADDITIONAL PROBLEMS

8–48.   Zim Container Service ships containers across both the Atlantic and the Pacific oceans. In 1994, the company had to decide whether to include Kingston, Jamaica, as a port of call instead of Savannah, Georgia, where the company's ships had been calling for some time. Zim's general manager of operations decided to use statistics to determine which of the two ports of call—Savannah or Kingston—would have a greater demand for shipped containers, or whether the average number of containers demanded by the two ports might be approximately equal (in which case the decision would be based on the cost of service). The manager had data on the last 17 calls at Savannah. The data, in number of containers unloaded per call, were 9, 6, 7, 7, 8, 7, 9, 4, 7, 6, 6, 5, 7, 5, 9, 8, 6. Then, as a test run, company ships unloaded containers at Kingston during 9 arrivals at that port. The data (number of containers unloaded at each trip) were 10, 5, 8, 8, 9, 10, 4, 9, 11. Use these data to conduct the test, and advise Zim's general manager of operations as to which port should be the regular port of call, or whether the ports will have approximately equal demand for containers.[10] Assume normal populations with equal variances.

8–49. In problem 8–48, construct a 99% confidence interval for the difference between the average number of containers per voyage demanded at Savannah and the average number of containers per voyage demanded at Kingston. Interpret your results.

8–50. According to the *Financial Times,* the Japanese are trying to stimulate creativity in the office by following the recent American trend of allowing casual wear in the office at least on Fridays.[11] A survey of 500 Japanese businesses reveals that 85 of them follow this new trend. A sample of 800 randomly chosen American businesses reveals that 312 of them allow casual dress at least on Friday. Test for equal proportions of casual wear in Japan and the United States.

8–51. For problem 8–50, construct a 95% confidence interval for the difference in proportion of casual-wear businesses between the two countries.

8–52. A study was undertaken by Montgomery Securities to assess average labor and materials costs incurred by Chrysler and General Motors in building a typical four-door, intermediate-sized car. The reported average cost for Chrysler was $9,500, and for GM it was $9,780. Suppose that these data are based on random samples of 25 cars for each company, and suppose that both standard deviations are equal to $1,500. Test the hypothesis that the average GM car of this type is more expensive to build than the average Chrysler car of the same type. Use $\alpha = 0.01$. Assume equal population variances.

8–53. For problem 8–52, give a 99% confidence interval for the difference between the average cost incurred by GM in building the car and the average cost incurred by Chrysler in building the same type of car. Interpret the results.

8–54. Suppose that the data in problem 8–52 are based on two random samples of 100 data points each. Discuss the advantages of using the method explained in section 8–3 instead of the method presented in section 8–4 in solving the problem. Discuss the various assumptions made when you use each of the two methods. Redo the problem using the results given in problem 8–52.

8–55. Two new movies are screen-tested at two different samples of theaters. *Pocahontas* is viewed at 80 theaters and is considered a success in terms of box office sales in 60 of these theaters. *The Bridges of Madison County* is viewed at a random sample of 100 theaters and is considered a success in 65 of them. Based on these data, do you believe that one of these movies will be a greater success than the other in the coming season? Explain.

8–56. For problem 8–55, give a 95% confidence interval for the difference in proportion of theaters nationwide where one movie will be preferred over the other. Is the point zero contained in the interval? Discuss.

8–57. Two 12-meter boats, the K boat and the L boat, are tested as possible contenders in the America's Cup races. The following data represent the time, in minutes, to complete a particular tack in independent random trials of the two boats.

> K boat: 12.0, 13.1, 11.8, 12.6, 14.0, 11.8, 12.7, 13.5, 12.4, 12.2, 11.6, 12.9
>
> L boat: 11.8, 12.1, 12.0, 11.6, 11.8, 12.0, 11.9, 12.6, 11.4, 12.0, 12.2, 11.7

Test the null hypothesis that the two boats perform equally well. Is one boat faster, on the average, than the other? Assume equal population variances.

8–58. In problem 8–57, assume that the data points are paired as listed and each pair represents performance of the two boats at a single trial. Conduct the test using this assumption. What is the advantage of testing using the paired data versus independent samples?

---

[10] Data provided courtesy of Zim Navigation Company, Ltd.

[11] E. Terazono, "Japan Tries on Fridaywear," *Financial Times,* May 26, 1995, p. 10.

8–59. The following table of test results for differences between means on a number of variables is from the *Journal of Marketing Research.* Interpret the results in the table. These variables are ratings of different variables that measure the effects of supplier fairness in the United States and in the Netherlands. The sample size in the United States was 1,640 car dealers. In the Netherlands, a sample of 1,600 car dealers was used.

Variable	United States	Netherlands	Difference
Relationship quality	4.77	4.93	n.s.
Procedural fairness	4.05	4.42	$p < .001$
Distributive fairness	4.72	4.62	n.s.
Outcomes given alternatives	3.79	4.06	$p < .001$
Age of relationship	28.12	19.01	$p < .001$
Environmental uncertainty	4.22	4.19	n.s.

Source: N. Kumar et al., "The Effects of Supplier Fairness," *Journal of Marketing Research* (February, 1995), pp. 54–65.

8–60. The IIT Technical Institute claims "94% of our graduates get jobs." Assume that the result is based on a random sample of 100 graduates of the program. Suppose that an independent random sample of 125 graduates of a competing technical institute reveals that 92% of these graduates got jobs. Is there evidence to conclude that one institute is more successful than the other in placing its graduates?

8–61. The power of supercomputers derives from the idea of parallel processing. Engineers at Cray Research are interested in determining whether one of two parallel processing designs produces faster average computing time, or whether the two designs are equally fast. The following are the results, in seconds, of independent random computation times using the two designs.

Design 1	Design 2
2.1, 2.2, 1.9, 2.0, 1.8, 2.4,	2.6, 2.5, 2.0, 2.1, 2.6, 3.0,
2.0, 1.7, 2.3, 2.8, 1.9, 3.0,	2.3, 2.0, 2.4, 2.8, 3.1, 2.7,
2.5, 1.8, 2.2	2.6

Assume that the two populations of computing time are normally distributed and that the two population variances are equal. Is there evidence that one parallel processing design allows for faster average computation than the other?

8–62. Test the validity of the equal-variance assumption in problem 8–61. If you reject the null hypothesis of equal population variance, redo the test of problem 8–61 using another method.

8–63. The senior vice president for marketing at Westin Hotels believes that the company's recent advertising of the Westin Plaza in New York has increased the average occupancy rate at that hotel by a least 5%. To test the hypothesis, a random sample of daily occupancy rates (in percentages) before the advertising is collected. A similar random sample of daily occupancy rates is collected after the advertising took place. The data are as follows.

Before Advertising (%)	After Advertising (%)
86, 92, 83, 88, 79, 81, 90	88, 94, 97, 99, 89, 93, 92
76, 80, 91, 85, 89, 77, 91	98, 89, 90, 97, 91, 87, 80
83	88, 96

Assume normally distributed populations of occupancy rates with equal population variances. Test the vice president's hypothesis.

8–64. For problem 8–63, test the validity of the equal-variance assumption.

8–65. Refer to problem 8–48. Test the null hypothesis that the variance of the number of containers demanded at Savannah is less than or equal to the variance of the number of containers demanded at Kingston, versus the alternative hypothesis that the variance of the number of containers demanded at Savannah is greater than that of Kingston.

8–66. Refer to problem 8–57. Do you believe that the variance of performance times for the K boat is about the same as the variance of performance times for the L boat? Explain. What are the implications of your result on the analysis of problem 8–57? If needed, redo the analysis in problem 8–57.

8–67. A company is interested in offering its employees one of two employee benefit packages. A random sample of the company's employees is collected, and each person in the sample is asked to rate each of the two packages on an overall preference scale of 0 to 100. The order of presentation of each of the two plans is randomly selected for each person in the sample. The paired data are:

Program A: 45 67 63 59 77 69 45 39 52 58 70 46 60 65 59 80

Program B: 56 70 60 45 85 79 50 46 50 60 82 40 65 55 81 68

Do you believe that the employees of this company prefer, on the average, one package over the other? Explain.

8–68. A company that makes electronic devices for use in hospitals needs to decide on one of two possible suppliers for a certain component to be used in the devices. The company gathers a random sample of 200 items made by supplier A and finds that 12 items are defective. An independent random sample of 250 items made by supplier B reveals that 38 are defective. Is one supplier more reliable than the other? Explain.

8–69. Refer to problem 8–68. Give a 95% confidence interval for the difference in the proportions of defective items made by suppliers A and B.

8–70. Refer to problem 8–63. Give a 90% confidence interval for the difference in average occupancy rates at the Westin Plaza hotel before and after the advertising.

8–71. Two machines are tested for the variance of the time they work before failure. A random sample of 25 trials of machine A gives a sample variance of 561 (hours squared), and an independent random sample of 18 trials of machine B gives a sample variance of 386 (hours squared). Assuming that the population of work times before failure for each machine is normally distributed, test for equality of population variances.

8–72. Explain the relationship between the F distribution and the chi-square distribution.

8–73. Refer to problem 8–61. Give a 99% confidence interval for the difference in mean time to complete a computation between each of the two designs.

8–74. An article on the global labor market reports that 39.5% of the work force in the United States is under age 34, while for Russia the figure is 42.9%.[12] Assuming that these percentages are based on a random sample of 1,000 workers in each country, test the significance of the observed difference.

8–75. Interpret the following computer output.

```
TWOSAMPLE T FOR C1 VS C2
       N       MEAN      STDEV     SE MEAN
C1   16       23.94      1.91       0.48
C2   17       24.82      2.88       0.70


95 PCT CI FOR MU C1 - MU C2:  (-2.62, 0.85)


TTEST MU C1 = MU C2 (VS GT):  T= -1.05  P=0.85  DF=  27
```

---

[12] W. B. Johnston, "Global Work Force 2000: The New World Labor Market," *Harvard Business Review,* March–April, 1991, p. 120.

8–76. Interpret the following computer output.

```
TWOSAMPLE T FOR C1 VS C2
        N      MEAN     STDEV    SE MEAN
C1 16      34.63      2.13      0.53
C2 17      24.82      2.88      0.70


95 PCT CI FOR MU C1 - MU C2: (8.00, 11.61)


TTEST MU C1 = MU C2 (VS NE): T= 11.07  P=0.0000  DF=  31


POOLED STDEV =      2.54
```

Case 8   PROGRAM TRADING

Program trading is the name given to stock market buy-and-sell schemes carried out on a computer. About a dozen major members of the New York Stock Exchange, and other companies, engage in this modern way of trading stocks. Usually, the computer programs are designed to follow a hedging strategy known as portfolio insurance or to follow strategies of stock index arbitrage. The computer keeps track of the quoted prices of single securities as well as traded portfolios. Whenever the computer finds that price differences exist, say, between the total quoted prices of a group of stocks and the price of a portfolio containing these stocks, the computer immediately issues an order to buy the cheaper form of the securities and to sell the equivalent, more expensive form of these securities. This is called *arbitrage*. The computer thus aids in determining the existence of price differences and in capitalizing on these differences.

Since the computer can act very quickly and handle large amounts of data, the result is trades of large quantities of stock in very short periods of time whenever a minute price difference is detected. It has recently been asserted that these sudden, large trades result in unnaturally high *volatility* of stock market prices. This volatility is believed to be the source of many recent problems with the operation of the market. On January 15, 1988, the New York Stock Exchange began an experiment lasting six days to determine whether or not program trading is indeed the culprit responsible for high stock price volatility. The Exchange asked its members that engage in program trading to refrain from doing so over the six working days from January 15, 1988, through January 22, 1988.

The following table lists the daily changes in the Dow Jones Industrial Average for the period of January 5, 1988, through January 25, 1988.

Date	Daily Change in Dow Jones Industrial Average	Date	Daily Change in Dow Jones Industrial Average
January 5, 1988	+ 76.42	January 15, 1988	− 8.62
January 6, 1988	+ 16.25	January 18, 1988	+ 39.96
January 7, 1988	+ 6.30	January 19, 1988	+ 7.79
January 8, 1988	+ 14.09	January 20, 1988	− 27.52
January 11, 1988	− 140.58	January 21, 1988	− 57.20
January 12, 1988	+ 33.82	January 22, 1988	+ 0.17
January 13, 1988	− 16.58	January 25, 1988	+ 24.20
January 14, 1988	− 3.82		

Separate the data into two groups. Make some necessary assumptions and state them. Analyze the data and, based on your findings, make a recommendation to the New York Stock Exchange.

ANALYSIS OF VARIANCE

9-1 INTRODUCTION

Bee it knowne unto all men by these presents
iune.17.1579.
By the grace of God and in the name of herr
maiesty Queen Elizabeth of England and herr
successors forever. I take possession of this
Kingdome whose King and people freely resigne
their right and title in the whole land unto herr
maiesties keeping. Now named by me an to bee
knowne unto all men as Nova Albion.
G

Francis Drake

n the summer of 1936, a young man named Beryle Shinn chanced upon a brass plate bearing the inscription above while hiking in a hilly area overlooking Point San Quentin and the San Francisco Bay. Mr. Shinn put the plate in the trunk of his car, where it remained for a few years. Later, by chance, the plate came to the attention of Professor Herbert E. Bolton at the Department of History at the University of California, Berkeley.

In a logbook kept during his circumnavigation of the earth, Sir Francis Drake wrote of entering a sheltered area in 1579 on what is now the northern California coast to refit his ship. He also mentioned leaving a brass plate attached to a post to record the event. Thus, upon being presented the Shinn plate, Professor Bolton declared: "One of the world's long-lost historical treasures apparently has been found!"

Although questions about the authenticity of the plate were immediately raised by many scholars—mainly because of the curious forms of many of the letters, and the writing style, which is different from known Elizabethan styles—the plate was nonetheless pronounced genuine and put on permanent display at the Bancroft Library of the University of California.

Contentions that the plate was the work of a modern forger continued to be expressed, and these led the Bancroft Library to order tests of the metallurgic structure of the brass. Finally, in 1976, several tiny holes were drilled in the plate, and a sample of brass particles was sent to the Research Laboratory of Archaeology at Oxford University for analysis. There the sample of brass particles from the plate was statistically compared with two random samples of brass: a sample of brasses made in the 20th century and a sample of English and Continental brasses created between 1540 and 1720. Analysis of the average zinc content of the sample from the discovered plate and that of the two other samples led to the conclusion that the average zinc content of the plate was equal to the average zinc content of modern brasses and very different from the average zinc content of brasses made in the 16th to 18th centuries.[1]

The results of the analysis led Dr. R. Hedges of Oxford University to conclude: "I would regard it as quite unreasonable to continue to believe in the authenticity of the plate." Thus, what was thought to be an ancient artifact was shown to be an ingenious modern forgery. The scientific studies left unanswered the questions of who made the plate, and why.

The statistical method of comparing the means of several populations, such as the mean zinc content of the three brasses relevant to the study of the plate, is the **analysis of variance.** The method is often referred to by its acronym, ANOVA. Analysis of variance is the first of several advanced statistical techniques to be discussed in this book. Along with regression analysis, described in the next two chapters, ANOVA is the most commonly quoted advanced research method in the professional business and economic literature. What is analysis of variance? The name of the technique may seem misleading.

> **ANOVA** is a statistical method for determining the existence of differences among several population means.

While the aim of ANOVA is to detect differences among several population *means,* the technique requires the analysis of different forms of *variance* associated with the random samples under study—hence the name *analysis of variance.*

---

[1] Several tests of the plate of brass were conducted. See "The Plate of Brass Reexamined," a report by the Bancroft Library (1979).

The original ideas of analysis of variance were developed by the English statistician Sir Ronald A. Fisher during the first part of this century. (Recall our mention of Fisher in Chapter 8 in reference to the F distribution.) Much of the early work in this area dealt with agricultural experiments where crops were given different "treatments," such as being grown using different kinds of fertilizers. The researchers wanted to determine whether all treatments under study were equally effective or whether some treatments were better than others. "Better" referred to those treatments that would produce crops of greater average weight. This question is answerable by the analysis of variance. Since the original work involved different *treatments*, the term remained, and we use it interchangeably with *populations* even when no actual treatment is administered. Thus, for example, if we compare the mean income in four different communities, we may refer to the four populations as four different *treatments*.

In the next section, we will develop the simplest form of analysis of variance, the one-factor, fixed-effects, completely randomized design model. We may ignore this long name for now. ■

9-2   The Hypothesis Test of Analysis of Variance

The hypothesis test of analysis of variance:

$$H_0: \mu_1 = \mu_2 = \mu_3 = \cdots = \mu_r$$
$$H_1: \text{Not all } \mu_i \ (i = 1, \ldots, r) \text{ are equal} \tag{9-1}$$

There are r populations, or treatments, under study. We draw an independent random sample from each of the r populations. The size of the sample from population i ($i = 1, \ldots, r$) is n_i, and the total sample size is

$$n = n_1 + n_2 + \cdots + n_r$$

From the r samples we compute several different quantities, and these lead to a computed value of a test statistic that follows a known F distribution when the null hypothesis is true. From the value of the statistic and the critical point for a given level of significance, we are able to make a determination of whether or not we believe that the r population means are equal.

Usually, the number of compared means, r, is greater than 2. Why greater than 2? If r is equal to 2, then the test in equation 9–1 is just a test for equality of two population means; although we could use ANOVA to conduct such a test, we have seen relatively simple tests of such hypotheses: the two-sample t tests discussed in Chapter 8. In this chapter, we are interested in investigating whether or not *several* population means may be considered equal. This is a test of a *joint hypothesis* about the equality of several population parameters. But why can we not use the two-sample t tests repeatedly? Suppose we are comparing $r = 5$ treatments. Why can we not conduct all possible pairwise comparisons of means using the two-sample t test? There are 10 such possible comparisons (10 choices of five items taken two at a time, found using a combinatorial formula presented in Chapter 2). It should be possible to make all 10 comparisons. However, if we use, say, $\alpha = 0.05$ for each test, then this means that the probability of committing a type I error in any particular test (deciding that the two population means are not equal when indeed they are equal) is 0.05. If each of the 10 tests has a 0.05 probability of a type I error, what is the probability of a type I error if we state "not all the means are equal" (i.e., rejecting H_0 in equation 9–1)? The answer to this question is not known![2]

If we need to compare more than two population means and we want to remain in control of the probability of committing a type I error, we need to conduct a *joint test*. Analysis of variance provides such a joint test of the hypotheses in equation 9–1. The reason for ANOVA's widespread applicability is that there are many situations where we need to compare more than two populations simultaneously. Even in cases where we need to compare only two treatments, say, test the relative effectiveness of two different prescription drugs, our actual test may require the use of a third treatment: a control treatment, or a placebo.

We now present the assumptions that must be satisfied so that we can use the analysis of variance procedure in testing our hypotheses of equation 9–1.

The required assumptions of ANOVA:

1. We assume *independent random sampling* from each of the r populations.
2. We assume that the r populations under study are *normally distributed*, with means μ_i that may or may not be equal, but with *equal variances, σ^2*.

Suppose, for example, that we are comparing three populations and want to determine whether or not the three population means μ_1, μ_2, and μ_3 are equal. We draw separate random samples from each of the three populations under study, and we assume that the three populations are distributed as shown in Figure 9–1.

These model assumptions are necessary for the test statistic used in analysis of variance to possess an F distribution when the null hypothesis is true. If the populations are not exactly normally distributed, but have distributions that are close to a

FIGURE 9–1   Three Normally Distributed Populations with Different Means but with Equal Variance

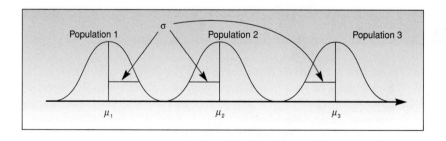

---

[2] The problem is complicated because we cannot assume independence of the 10 tests and, therefore, we cannot use a probability computation for independent events. The sample statistics used in the 10 tests are not independent since two such possible statistics are $(\bar{X}_1 - \bar{X}_2)$ and $(\bar{X}_2 - \bar{X}_3)$. Both statistics contain a common term $\bar{X}_2$, and thus are not independent of each other.

normal distribution, the method still yields good results. If, however, the distributions are highly skewed or otherwise different from normality, or if the population variances are not approximately equal, then ANOVA should not be used, and instead we must use a nonparametric technique called the Kruskal-Wallis test. This alternative technique is described in Chapter 14.

The Test Statistic

As mentioned earlier, when the null hypothesis is true, the test statistic of analysis of variance follows an F distribution. As you recall from Chapter 8, the F distribution has two kinds of degrees of freedom: degrees of freedom for the numerator and degrees of freedom for the denominator.

In the analysis of variance, the numerator degrees of freedom are $r - 1$, and the denominator degrees of freedom are $n - r$. In this section, we will not present the calculations leading to the computed value of the test statistic. Instead, we will assume that the value of the statistic is given. The computations are a topic in themselves and will be presented in the next section. Analysis of variance is an involved technique, and it is difficult and time-consuming to carry out the required computations by hand. Consequently, computers are indispensable in most situations involving analysis of variance, and we will make extensive use of the computer in this chapter. For now, let us assume that a computer is available to us, and that it provides us with the value of the test statistic.

$$\text{ANOVA test statistic} = F_{(r-1,\,n-r)} \qquad (9\text{--}2)$$

Figure 9–2 shows the F distribution with 3 and 50 degrees of freedom, which would be appropriate for a test of the equality of four population means using a total sample size of 54. Also shown is the critical point for $\alpha = 0.05$, found in Appendix C, Table 5. The critical point is 2.79. For reasons explained in the next section, the test is carried out as a right-tailed test.

We now have the basic elements of a statistical hypothesis test within the context of ANOVA: the null and alternative hypotheses, the required assumptions, and a

FIGURE 9–2 Distribution of the ANOVA Test Statistic for $r = 4$ Populations and a Total Sample Size $n = 54$

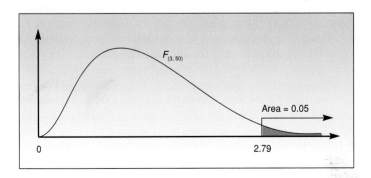

distribution of the test statistic when the null hypothesis is true. Let us look at an example.

EXAMPLE 9-1

Major roasters and distributors of coffee in the United States have long felt the great uncertainty in the price of coffee beans. Over the course of one year, for example, coffee futures prices went from a low of $1.40 per pound up to $2.50 and then down to $2.03. The main reason for such wild fluctuations in price, which strongly affect the performance of coffee distributors, is the constant danger of drought in Brazil. Since Brazil produces 30% of the world's coffee, the market for coffee beans is very sensitive to the annual rumors of impending drought.

Recently a domestic coffee distributor decided to avert the problem altogether by eliminating Brazilian coffee from all blends the company distributes. Before taking such action, the distributor wanted to minimize the chances of suffering losses in sales volume. Therefore, the distributor hired a marketing research firm to conduct a statistical test of consumers' taste preferences. The research firm made arrangements with several large restaurants to serve randomly chosen groups of their customers different kinds of after-dinner coffee. Three kinds of coffee were served: a group of 21 randomly chosen customers were served pure Brazilian coffee; another group of 20 randomly chosen customers were served pure Columbian coffee; and a third group of 22 randomly chosen customers were served pure African-grown coffee.

This is the *completely randomized design* part of the name of the ANOVA technique we mentioned at the end of the last section. In completely randomized design, the experimental units (in this case, the people involved in the experiment) are randomly assigned to the three treatments, the treatment being the kind of coffee they are served. Later in this chapter, we will encounter other designs useful in many situations. To prevent a response bias, the people in this experiment were not told the kind of coffee they were being served. The coffee was listed as a "house blend."

Suppose that data for the three groups were consumers' ratings of the coffee on a scale of 0 to 100 and that certain computations were carried out with these data (computations will be discussed in the next section), leading to the following value of the ANOVA test statistic: $F = 2.02$. Is there evidence to conclude that any of the three kinds of coffee leads to an average consumer rating different from the other two kinds?

SOLUTION

The null and alternative hypotheses here are, by equation 9–1,

$$H_0: \mu_1 = \mu_2 = \mu_3$$
$$H_1: \text{Not all three } \mu_i \text{ are equal}$$

Let us examine the meaning of the null and alternative hypotheses in this example. The null hypothesis states that average consumer responses to each of the three kinds of coffee are equal. The alternative hypothesis says that not all three population means are equal. What are the possibilities covered under the alternative hypothesis? The possible relationships among the relative magnitudes of any three real numbers μ_1, μ_2, and μ_3 are shown in Figure 9–3.

As you can see from Figure 9–3, the alternative hypothesis is composed of several different possibilities—it includes all the cases where *not all* three means are equal. Thus, if we reject the null hypothesis, all we know is that there is statistical evidence to conclude that not all three population means are equal. However, we do not know in what way the means are different. Therefore, once we reject the null hypothesis, we need to conduct

FIGURE 9-3 **Some of the Possible Relationships among the Relative Magnitudes of the Three Population Means μ_1, μ_2, and μ_3**

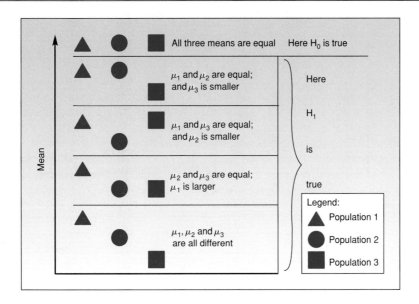

further analysis to determine which population means are different from one another. The further analysis following ANOVA will be discussed in a later section.

We have a null hypothesis and an alternative hypothesis. We also assume that the conditions required for ANOVA are met; that is, we assume that the three populations of consumer responses are (approximately) normally distributed with equal population variance. Now we need to conduct the test.

Since there are three populations, or treatments, under study, the degrees of freedom for the numerator are $r - 1 = 3 - 1 = 2$. Since the total sample size is $n = n_1 + n_2 + n_3 = 21 + 20 + 22 = 63$, we find that the degrees of freedom for the denominator are $n - r = 63 - 3 = 60$. Thus, when the null hypothesis is true, our test statistic has an F distribution with 2 and 60 degrees of freedom: $F_{(2,60)}$. From Appendix C, Table 5, we find that the right-tailed critical point at $\alpha = 0.05$ for an F distribution with 2 and 60 degrees of freedom is $C = 3.15$. Since the computed value of the test statistic is equal to 2.02, we may conclude that at the 0.05 level of significance there is insufficient evidence to conclude that the three means are different. The null hypothesis that all three population means are equal cannot be rejected. Since the critical point for $\alpha = 0.10$ is 2.39, we find that the p-value is greater than 0.10.

Based on our data, there is no evidence that consumers tend to prefer the Brazilian coffee to the other two brands. The distributor may substitute one of the other brands for the price-unstable Brazilian coffee. Note that we usually prefer to make conclusions based on the *rejection* of a null hypothesis because nonrejection is often considered a weak conclusion. The results of our test are shown in Figure 9–4.

In this section, we have seen the basic elements of the hypothesis test underlying analysis of variance: the null and alternative hypotheses, the required assumptions, the test statistic, and the decision rule. We have not, however, seen how the test statistic is computed from the data or the reasoning behind its computation. The theory and the computations of ANOVA are explained in the following sections.

FIGURE 9-4   Carrying Out the Test of Example 9-1

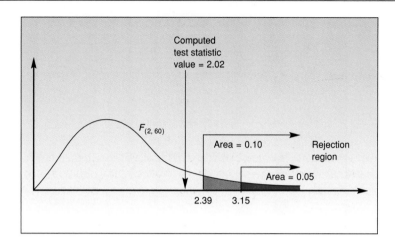

PROBLEMS

9–1.   Four populations are compared by analysis of variance. What are the possible relations among the four population means covered under the null and alternative hypotheses?

9–2.   What are the assumptions of ANOVA?

9–3.   Three methods of training managers are to be tested for relative effectiveness. The management training institution proposes to test the effectiveness of the three methods by comparing two methods at a time, using a paired t test. Explain why this is a poor procedure.

9–4.   In an analysis of variance comparing the output of five plants, data sets of 21 observations per plant are analyzed. The computed F statistic value is 3.6. Do you believe that there are differences in average output among the five plants? What is the approximate p-value? Explain.

9–5.   A real estate development firm wants to test whether there are differences in the average price of a lot of a given size in the center of each of four cities: Philadelphia, New York, Washington, and Baltimore. Random samples of 52 lots in Philadelphia, 38 lots in New York, 43 lots in Washington, and 47 lots in Baltimore lead to a computed test statistic value of 12.53. Do you believe that average lot prices in the four cities are equal? How confident are you of your conclusion? Explain.

9–3   The Theory and the Computations of ANOVA

Recall that the purpose of analysis of variance is to detect differences among several population means based on evidence provided by random samples from these populations. How can this be done? We want to compare r population means. We use r random samples, one from each population. Each random sample has its own mean. The mean of the sample from population i will be denoted by $\bar{x}_i$. We may also compute the mean of all data points in the study, regardless of which population they come from. The mean of all the data points (when all data points are considered a single set) is called the *grand mean* and is denoted by $\bar{\bar{x}}$. These means are given by the following equations.

The mean of sample i ($i = 1, \ldots, r$):

$$\bar{x}_i = \frac{\sum_{j=1}^{n_i} x_{ij}}{n_i} \qquad (9\text{--}3)$$

The **grand mean,** the mean of all the data points:

$$\bar{\bar{x}} = \frac{\sum_{i=1}^{r}\sum_{j=1}^{n_i} x_{ij}}{n} \qquad (9\text{--}4)$$

where x_{ij} is the particular data point in position j within the sample from population i. The subscript i denotes the population, or treatment, and runs from 1 to r. The subscript j denotes the data point within the sample from population i; thus, j runs from 1 to n_i.

In Example 9–1, $r = 3$, $n_1 = 21$, $n_2 = 20$, $n_3 = 22$, and $n = n_1 + n_2 + n_3 = 63$. The third data point (person) in the group of 21 people who consumed Brazilian coffee is denoted by x_{13} (that is, $i = 1$ denotes treatment 1 and $j = 3$ denotes the third point in that sample).

We will now define the main principle behind the analysis of variance.

If the r population means are different (that is, at least two of the population means are *not* equal), then it is likely that the variation of the data points about their respective sample means, $\bar{x}_i$, will be *small* when compared with the variation of the r sample means about the grand mean, $\bar{\bar{x}}$.

We will demonstrate the ANOVA principle using three hypothetical populations, which we will call the triangles, the squares, and the circles. Table 9–1 gives the values of the sample points from the three populations. For demonstration purposes, we use very small samples. In real situations, the sample sizes should be much larger. The data given in Table 9–1 are shown in Figure 9–5. The figure also shows the deviations of the data points from their sample means and the deviations of the sample means from the grand mean.

Look carefully at Figure 9–5. Note that the *average* distance (in absolute value) of data points from their respective group means (that is, the average distance, in absolute value, of a triangle from the mean of the triangles, $\bar{x}_1$, and similarly for the squares and the circles) is *relatively small* compared with the average distance (in absolute value) of the three sample means from the grand mean. If you are not convinced of this, note that there are only three distances of sample means to the grand mean (in the computation, each distance is weighted by the actual number of points in the group), and that only one of them, the smallest distance—that of $\bar{x}_1$ to $\bar{\bar{x}}$—is of the relative magnitude of the distances between the data points and their respective sample means. The two other distances are much greater; hence, the average distance of the sample means from the grand mean is greater than the average distance of all data points to their respective sample means.

The *average* deviation from a mean is zero. We talk about the average absolute deviation—actually, we will use the average *squared* deviation—to prevent the deviations from canceling out. This should remind you of the definition of the sample

TABLE 9-1   Data and the Various Sample Means for Triangles, Squares, and Circles

Treatment (i)	Sample Point (j)	Value (x_{ij})
i = 1 Triangle X_{11}	1	4
Triangle X_{12}	2	5
Triangle X_{13}	3	7
Triangle X_{14}	4	8
Mean of triangles		6
i = 2 Square X_{21}	1	10
Square X_{22}	2	11
Square X_{23}	3	12
Square X_{24}	4	13
Mean of squares		11.5
i = 3 Circle X_{31}	1	1
Circle X_{32}	2	2
Circle X_{33}	3	3
Mean of circles		2
Grand mean of all data points		6.909

FIGURE 9-5   Deviations of the Triangles, Squares, and Circles from Their Sample Means and the Deviations of the Sample Means from the Grand Mean

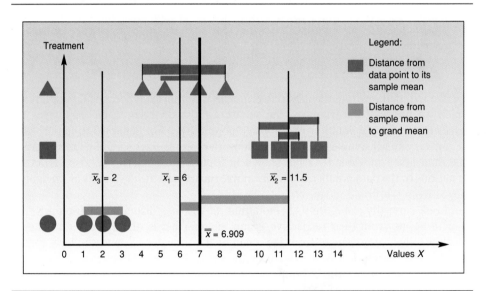

variance in Chapter 1. Now let us define some terms that will make our discussion simpler.

We define an **error deviation** as the difference between a data point and its sample mean. Errors are denoted by *e*, and we have

$$e_{ij} = x_{ij} - \overline{x}_i \qquad (9\text{--}5)$$

Thus, all the distances from the data points to their sample means in Figure 9–5 are errors (some are positive, and some are negative). The reason these distances are called errors is that they are unexplained by the fact that the corresponding data points belong to population *i*. The errors are assumed to be due to natural variation, or pure randomness, within the sample from treatment *i*.

On the other hand,

We define a **treatment deviation** as the deviation of a sample mean from the grand mean. Treatment deviations, t_i, are given by

$$t_i = \bar{x}_i - \bar{\bar{x}} \qquad (9\text{–}6)$$

The ANOVA principle thus says:

> When the population means are not equal, the "average" error is relatively small compared with the "average" treatment deviation.

Again, if we actually averaged all the deviations, we would get zero. Therefore, when we apply the principle computationally, we will square the error and treatment deviations before averaging them. This way, we will maintain the relative (squared) magnitudes of these quantities. The averaging process is further complicated because we have to average based on degrees of freedom (recall that degrees of freedom were used in the definition of a sample variance). For now, let the term *average* be used in a simplified, intuitive sense.

Since we noted that the average error deviation in our triangle-square-circle example looks small relative to the average treatment deviation, let us see what the populations that brought about our three samples look like. Figure 9–6 shows the

FIGURE 9–6   Samples of Triangles, Squares, and Circles and Their Respective Populations (the three populations are normal with equal variance but with different means)

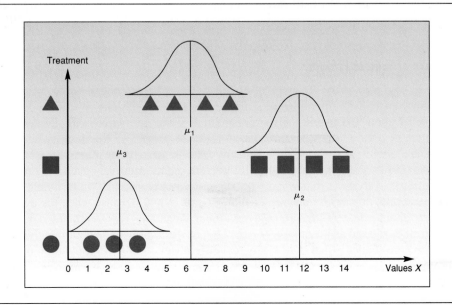

FIGURE 9–7   Samples of Triangles, Squares, and Circles Where the Average Error Deviation Is Not Smaller than the Average Treatment Deviation

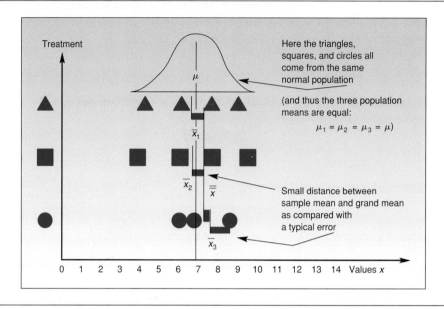

three populations, assumed normally distributed with equal variance. (This can be seen from the equal width of the three normal curves. Note also that the three samples seem to have equal dispersion about their sample means.) The figure also shows that the three population means are not equal.

Figure 9–7, in contrast, shows three samples of triangles, squares, and circles in which the average error deviation is of about the same magnitude (*not* smaller than) as the average treatment deviation. As can be seen from the superimposed normal populations from which the samples have arisen in this case, the three population means, μ_1, μ_2, and μ_3, are all equal. Compare the two figures to convince yourself of the ANOVA principle.

The Sum of Squares Principle

We have seen how, when the population means are different, the error deviations in the data are small when compared with the treatment deviations. We made general statements about the average error being small when compared with the average treatment deviation. The error deviations measure how close the data *within* each group are to their respective group means. The treatment deviations measure the distances *between* the various groups. It therefore seems intuitively plausible (as seen in Figures 9–5 to 9–7) that when these two kinds of deviations are of about equal magnitude, the population means are about equal. Why? Because when the average error is about equal to the average treatment deviation, the treatment deviation may itself be viewed as just another error. That is, the treatment deviation in this case is due to pure chance rather than to any real differences among the population means. In other words, when the average t is of the same magnitude as the average e, both are estimates of the internal variation within the data and carry no information about a difference between any two groups—about a difference in population means.

FIGURE 9-8 **Total Deviation as the Sum of the Treatment Deviation and the Error Deviation for a Particular Data Point**

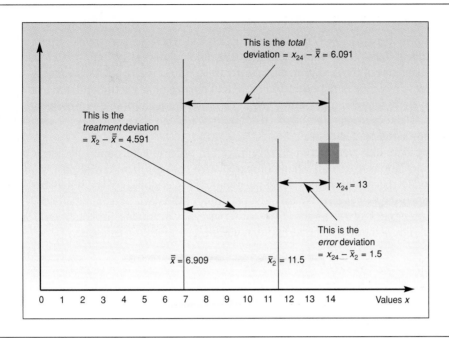

We will now make everything quantifiable, using the *sum of squares principle*. We start by returning to Figure 9–5, looking at a particular data point, and analyzing distances associated with the data point. We choose the fourth data point from the sample of squares (population 2). This data point is $x_{24} = 13$ (verify this from Table 9–1). We now magnify a section of Figure 9–5, the section surrounding this particular data point. This is shown in Figure 9–8.

We define the **total deviation** of a data point x_{ij} (denoted by Tot_{ij}) as the deviation of the data point from the grand mean:

$$\text{Tot}_{ij} = x_{ij} - \bar{\bar{x}} \qquad (9\text{--}7)$$

Figure 9–8 shows that the total deviation is equal to the treatment deviation plus the error deviation. This is true for *any* point in our data set (even when some of the numbers are negative).

For any data point, x_{ij},

$$\text{Tot} = t + e \qquad (9\text{--}8)$$

In words:

Total deviation = Treatment deviation + Error deviation

In the case of our chosen data point, x_{24}, we have

$$t_2 + e_{24} = 4.591 + 1.5 = 6.091 = \text{Tot}_{24}$$

Equation 9–8 works for every data point in our data set. Here is how it is derived algebraically:

$$t_i + e_{ij} = (\bar{x}_i - \bar{\bar{x}}) + (x_{ij} - \bar{x}_i) = x_{ij} - \bar{\bar{x}} = \text{Tot}_{ij} \qquad (9-9)$$

As seen in equation 9–9, the term $\bar{x}_i$ cancels out when the two terms in parentheses are added. This shows that for every data point, the total deviation is equal to the treatment part of the deviation plus the error part. This is also seen in Figure 9–8. The *total* deviation of a data point from the grand mean is thus partitioned into a deviation due to *treatment* and a deviation due to *error*. The deviation due to treatment differences is the *between-treatments* deviation, while the deviation due to error is the *within-treatment* deviation.

We have only considered one point, x_{24}. In order to determine whether or not the error deviations are small when compared with the treatment deviations, we need to aggregate the partition over all data points. This is done, as we noted earlier, by averaging the deviations. We take the partition of the deviations in equation 9–9 and we square each of the three terms (otherwise our averaging process would lead to zero).[3] The squaring of the terms in equation 9–9 gives, on one side,

$$t_i^2 + e_{ij}^2 = (\bar{x}_i - \bar{\bar{x}})^2 + (x_{ij} - \bar{x}_i)^2 \qquad (9-10)$$

and, on the other side,

$$\text{Tot}_{ij}^2 = (x_{ij} - \bar{\bar{x}})^2 \qquad (9-11)$$

Note an interesting thing: The two sides of equation 9–9 are equal, but when all three terms are squared, the two sides (now equations 9–10 and 9–11) are *not* equal. Try this with any of the data points. The surprising thing happens next.

We take the squared deviations of equations 9–10 and 9–11, and we *sum them over all our data points*. Interestingly, the sum of the squared error deviations and the sum of the squared treatment deviations do add up to the sum of the squared total deviations. Mathematically, cross-terms in the equation drop out, allowing this to happen. The result is the sum of squares principle.

We have the following:

$$\sum_{i=1}^{r}\sum_{j=1}^{n_i} \text{Tot}_{ij}^2 = \sum_{i=1}^{r} n_i t_i^2 + \sum_{i=1}^{r}\sum_{j=1}^{n_i} e_{ij}^2$$

This can be written in longer form as

$$\sum_{i=1}^{r}\sum_{j=1}^{n_i} (x_{ij} - \bar{\bar{x}})^2 = \sum_{i=1}^{r} n_i (\bar{x}_i - \bar{\bar{x}})^2 + \sum_{i=1}^{r}\sum_{j=1}^{n_i} (x_{ij} - \bar{x}_i)^2$$

The Sum of Squares Principle

The total sum of squares (SST) is the sum of the two terms: the sum of squares for treatment (SSTR) and the sum of squares for error (SSE).

$$\text{SST} = \text{SSTR} + \text{SSE} \qquad (9-12)$$

---

[3] This can be seen from the data in Table 9–1. Note that the sum of the deviations of the triangles from their mean of 6 is $(4 - 6) + (5 - 6) + (7 - 6) + (8 - 6) = 0$; hence, an average of these deviations, or those of the squares or circles, leads to zero.

The sum of squares principle partitions the total sum of squares within the data, SST, into a part due to treatment effect, SSTR, and a part due to errors, SSE. The squared deviations of the treatment means from the grand mean are *counted for every data point*—hence the term n_i in the first summation on the right side (SSTR) of equation 9–12. The second term on the right-hand side is the sum of the squared errors, i.e., the sum of the squared deviations of the data points from their respective sample means.

See Figure 9–8 for the different deviations associated with a single point. Imagine a similar relation among the three kinds of deviations for every one of the data points, as shown in Figure 9–5. Then imagine all these deviations squared and added together—errors to errors, treatments to treatments, and totals to totals. The result is equation 9–12, the sum of squares principle.

Sums of squares measure variation within the data. SST is the total amount of variation within the data set. SSTR is that part of the variation within the data that is due to differences among the groups, and SSE is that part of the variation within the data that is due to error—the part that cannot be explained by differences among the groups. Therefore, SSTR is sometimes called the sum of squares *between* (variation among the groups), and SSE is called the sum of squares *within* (within-group variation). SSTR is also called the *explained variation* (because it is the part of the total variation that can be explained by the fact that the data points belong to several different groups). SSE is, then, called the *unexplained variation*. The partition of the sum of squares in analysis of variance is shown in Figure 9–9.

Breaking down the sum of squares is not enough, however. If we want to determine whether or not the errors are small as compared with the treatment part, we need to find the *average* (squared) error and the *average* (squared) treatment deviation. Averaging, in the context of variances, is achieved by dividing by the appropriate number of degrees of freedom associated with each sum of squares.

The Degrees of Freedom

Recall our definition of degrees of freedom in Chapter 5. The degrees of freedom are the number of data points that are "free to move," that is, the number of elements in the data set, minus the number of restrictions. A restriction on a data set is a quantity already computed from the entire data set under consideration; thus, knowledge of this quantity makes one data point fixed and reduces by one the effective number of

FIGURE 9–9 Partition of the Total Sum of Squares into Treatment and Error Parts

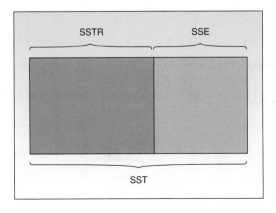

data points that are free to move. This is why, as was shown in Chapter 5, knowledge of the sample mean reduces the degrees of freedom of the sample variance to $n - 1$. What are the degrees of freedom in the context of analysis of variance?

Consider the total sum of squares, SST. In computing this sum of squares, we use the entire data set and information about *one* quantity computed from the data: the grand mean (because, by definition, SST is the sum of the squared deviations of all data points from the grand mean). Since we have a total of n data points and one restriction,

The number of degrees of freedom associated with SST is $n - 1$.

The sum of squares for treatment, SSTR, is computed from the deviations of r sample means from the grand mean. The r sample means are considered r independent data points, and the grand mean (which can be considered as having been computed from the r sample means) thus reduces the degrees of freedom by one.

The number of degrees of freedom associated with SSTR is $r - 1$.

The sum of squares for error, SSE, is computed from the deviations of a total of n data points $(n = n_1 + n_2 + \cdots + n_r)$ from r different sample means. Since each of the sample means acts as a restriction on the data set, the degrees of freedom for error are $n - r$. This can be seen another way: There are r groups with n_i data points in group i. Thus, each group, with its own sample mean acting as a restriction, has degrees of freedom equal to $n_i - 1$. The total number of degrees of freedom for error is the sum of the degrees of freedom in the r groups: df $= (n_1 - 1) + (n_2 - 1) + \cdots (n_r - 1) = n - r$.

The number of degrees of freedom associated with SSE is $n - r$.

An important principle in analysis of variance is that the degrees of freedom of the three components are *additive* in the same way that the sums of squares are additive.

$$df(\text{total}) = df(\text{treatment}) + df(\text{error}) \qquad (9\text{--}13)$$

This can easily be verified by noting the following: $n - 1 = (r - 1) + (n - r)$— the r drops out. We are now ready to compute the average squared deviation due to treatment and the average squared deviation due to error.

The Mean Squares

In finding the average squared deviations due to treatment and to error, we divide each sum of squares by its degrees of freedom. We call the two resulting averages **mean square treatment (MSTR)** and **mean square error (MSE),** respectively.

$$MSTR = \frac{SSTR}{r - 1} \qquad (9\text{--}14)$$

$$MSE = \frac{SSE}{n - r} \qquad (9\text{--}15)$$

The Expected Values of the Statistics MSTR and MSE under the Null Hypothesis

When the null hypothesis of ANOVA is true, all r population means are equal, and in this case there are *no treatment effects*. In such a case, the average squared deviation due to "treatment" is just another realization of an average squared error. In terms of the expected values of the two mean squares, we have

$$E(\text{MSE}) = \sigma^2 \tag{9–16}$$

and

$$E(\text{MSTR}) = \sigma^2 + \frac{\Sigma\, n_i(\mu_i - \mu)^2}{r - 1} \tag{9–17}$$

where μ_i is the mean of population i and μ is the combined mean of all r populations.

Equation 9–16 says that *MSE is an unbiased estimator of σ^2, the assumed common variance of the r populations.* The mean square error in ANOVA is therefore just like the sample variance in the one-population case of earlier chapters.

The mean square treatment, however, comprises two components, as seen from equation 9–17. The first component is σ^2, as in the case of MSE. The second component is a measure of the differences among the r population means, μ_i. If the null hypothesis is true, all r population means are equal—they are all equal to μ. In such a case, the second term in equation 9–17 is equal to *zero*. When this happens, the expected value of MSTR and the expected value of MSE are both equal to σ^2.

> When the null hypothesis of ANOVA is true and all r population means are equal, MSTR and MSE are two independent, unbiased estimators of the common population variance, σ^2.

If, on the other hand, the null hypothesis is not true and differences do exist among the r population means, then *MSTR will tend to be larger than MSE.* This happens because, when not all population means are equal, the second term in equation 9–17 is a positive number.

The F Statistic

The preceding discussion suggests that the ratio of MSTR to MSE is a good indicator of whether or not the r population means are equal. If the r population means are equal, then MSTR/MSE would tend to be close to 1.00. Remember that both MSTR and MSE are sample statistics derived from our data. As such, MSTR and MSE will have some randomness associated with them, and they are not likely to exactly equal their expected values. Thus, when the null hypothesis is true, MSTR/MSE will vary around the value 1.00. When the r population means are not all equal, the ratio MSTR/MSE will tend to be greater than 1.00 because the expected value of MSTR, from equation 9–17, will be larger than the expected value of MSE. How large is "large enough" for us to reject the null hypothesis?

This is where statistical inference comes in. We want to determine whether the difference between our observed value of MSTR/MSE and the number 1.00 is due just to chance variation, or whether MSTR/MSE is *significantly* greater than 1.00—implying that the population means are not all equal. We will make the determination with the aid of the *F* distribution.

> Under the assumptions of ANOVA, the ratio MSTR/MSE possesses an *F* distribution with $r - 1$ degrees of freedom for the numerator and $n - r$ degrees of freedom for the denominator when the null hypothesis is true.

In Chapter 8, we saw how the *F* distribution is used in determining differences between two population variances—noting that if the two variances are equal, then the ratio of the two independent, unbiased estimators of the assumed common variance follows an *F* distribution. There, too, the appropriate degrees of freedom for the numerator and the denominator of *F* came from the degrees of freedom of the sample variance in the numerator and the sample variance in the denominator of the ratio. In ANOVA, the numerator is MSTR and has $r - 1$ degrees of freedom; the denominator is MSE and has $n - r$ degrees of freedom. We thus have the following.

> The test statistic in analysis of variance: ANOVA
>
> $$F_{(r-1, n-r)} = \frac{\text{MSTR}}{\text{MSE}}$$ (9–18)

In this section, we have seen the theoretical rationale for the *F* statistic we used in section 9–2. We also saw the computations required for arriving at the value of the test statistic. In the next section, we will encounter a convenient tool for keeping track of computations and reporting our results: the ANOVA table.

PROBLEMS

9–6. Define *treatment* and *error*.

9–7. Explain why trying to compute a simple average of all error deviations and of all treatment deviations will not lead to any results.

9–8. Explain how the total deviation is partitioned into the treatment deviation and the error deviation.

9–9. Explain the sum of squares principle.

9–10. Where do errors come from, and what do you think are their sources?

9–11. If, in an analysis of variance, you find that MSTR is greater than MSE, why can you not immediately reject the null hypothesis without determining the *F* ratio and its distribution? Explain.

9–12. What is the main principle behind analysis of variance?

9–13. Explain how information about the variance components in a data set can lead to conclusions about population means.

9–14. Explain the meaning of the terms *within, between, unexplained, explained,* and the context in which these terms arise.

9–15. By the sum of squares principle, SSE and SSTR are additive, and their sum is SST. Does such a relation exist between MSE and MSTR? Explain.

9–16. Does the quantity MSTR/MSE follow an *F* distribution when the null hypothesis of ANOVA is false? Explain.

9–17. (A mathematically demanding problem) Prove the sum of squares principle, equation 9–12.

9-4 The ANOVA Table and Examples

Table 9–2 shows the data for our triangles, squares, and circles. In addition, the table shows the deviations from the group means, and their squares. From these quantities, we find the sum of squares and mean squares.

As we see in the last row of the table, the sum of all the deviations of the data points from their group means is zero, as expected. The sum of the *squared* deviations from the sample means (which, from equation 9–12, is SSE) is equal to 17.00.

$$\text{SSE} = \sum_{i=1}^{r} \sum_{j=1}^{n_i} (x_{ij} - \bar{x}_i)^2 = 17.00$$

Now we want to compute the sum of squares for treatment. Recall from Table 9–1 that $\bar{\bar{x}} = 6.909$. Again using the definitions in equation 9–12, we have

$$\text{SSTR} = \sum_{i=1}^{r} n_i(\bar{x}_i - \bar{\bar{x}})^2 = 4(6 - 6.909)^2 + 4(11.5 - 6.909)^2 + 3(2 - 6.909)^2$$
$$= 159.9$$

We now compute the mean squares. From equations 9–14 and 9–15, respectively, we get

$$\text{MSTR} = \frac{\text{SSTR}}{r-1} = \frac{159.9}{2} = 79.95$$

$$\text{MSE} = \frac{\text{SSE}}{n-r} = \frac{17}{8} = 2.125$$

Using equation 9–18, we get the computed value of the F statistic:

$$F_{(2,8)} = \frac{\text{MSTR}}{\text{MSE}} = \frac{79.95}{2.125} = 37.62$$

We are finally in a position to conduct the ANOVA hypothesis test to determine whether or not the means of the three populations are equal. From Appendix C, Table 5, we find that the critical point at $\alpha = 0.01$ (for a right-tailed test) for the F distribution with 2 degrees of freedom for the numerator and 8 degrees of freedom for the denominator is 8.65. We can therefore reject the null hypothesis. Since 37.62

TABLE 9-2 Computations for Triangles, Squares, and Circles

Treatment (*i*)	*j*	Value (*x_ij*)	$x_{ij} - \bar{x}_i$	$(x_{ij} - \bar{x}_i)^2$
Triangle	1	4	4 − 6 = −2	$(-2)^2 = 4$
Triangle	2	5	5 − 6 = −1	$(-1)^2 = 1$
Triangle	3	7	7 − 6 = 1	$(1)^2 = 1$
Triangle	4	8	8 − 6 = 2	$(2)^2 = 4$
Square	1	10	10 − 11.5 = −1.5	$(-1.5)^2 = 2.25$
Square	2	11	11 − 11.5 = −0.5	$(-0.5)^2 = 0.25$
Square	3	12	12 − 11.5 = 0.5	$(0.5)^2 = 0.25$
Square	4	13	13 − 11.5 = 1.5	$(1.5)^2 = 2.25$
Circle	1	1	1 − 2 = −1	$(-1)^2 = 1$
Circle	2	2	2 − 2 = 0	$(0)^2 = 0$
Circle	3	3	3 − 2 = 1	$(1)^2 = 1$
			Sum = 0	Sum = 17

is much greater than 8.65, the p-value is much smaller than 0.01. This is shown in Figure 9–10.

Note that, as usual, we must exercise caution in the interpretation of results based on such small samples. As we noted earlier, in real situations we use large data sets, and the computations are usually done by computer. In the rest of our examples, we will assume that sums of squares and other quantities are produced by a computer.[4] All statistical computer packages contain ANOVA routines, and in section 9–9, we will present examples of input and output.

An essential tool for reporting the results of an analysis of variance is the ANOVA table. An ANOVA table lists the sources of variation: treatment, error, and total. (In the two-factor ANOVA, which we will see in later sections, there will be more sources of variation.) The ANOVA table lists the sums of squares, the degrees of freedom, the mean squares, and the F ratio. The table format simplifies the analysis and the interpretation of the results. The structure of the ANOVA table is based on the fact that both the sums of squares and the degrees of freedom are additive. We will now present an ANOVA table for the triangles, squares, and circles example. Table 9–3 shows the results computed above.

FIGURE 9-10 Rejecting the Null Hypothesis in the Triangles, Squares, and Circles Example

TABLE 9-3 ANOVA Table

Source of Variation	Sum of Squares	Degrees of Freedom	Mean Square	F Ratio
Treatment	SSTR = 159.9	$r - 1 = 2$	$\text{MSTR} = \dfrac{\text{SSTR}}{r - 1}$ $= 79.95$	$F = \dfrac{\text{MSTR}}{\text{MSE}}$ $= 37.62$
Error	SSE = 17.0	$n - r = 8$	$\text{MSE} = \dfrac{\text{SSE}}{n - r}$	
Total	SST = 176.9	$n - 1 = 10$	$= 2.125$	

----

[4] If you must carry out ANOVA computations by hand, there are equivalent computational formulas for the sums of squares that may be easier to apply than equation 9–12. These are

$$\text{SST} = \Sigma_i \Sigma_j \, (x_{ij})^2 - (\Sigma_i \Sigma_j \, x_{ij})^2/n$$
$$\text{SSTR} = \Sigma_i \, ((\Sigma_j \, x_{ij})^2/n_i) - (\Sigma_i \Sigma_j \, x_{ij})^2/n$$

and we obtain SSE by subtraction: SSE = SST − SSTR.

TABLE 9-4 Club Med Survey Results

Resort (i)	Mean Response ($\bar{x}_i$)	
1. Guadeloupe	89	
2. Martinique	75	
3. Eleuthera		73
4. Paradise Island	91	
5. St. Lucia	85	
SST = 112,564 SSE = 98,356		

TABLE 9-5 Preliminary ANOVA Table for Club Med Example

Source of Variation	Sum of Squares	Degrees of Freedom	Mean Square	F Ratio
Treatment	SSTR =	$r - 1 =$ 4	MSTR =	$F =$
Error	SSE = 98,356	$n - r = 195$	MSE =	
Total	SST = 112,564	$n - 1 = 199$		

Note that the entries in the second and third columns, sum of squares and degrees of freedom, are both additive. The entries in the fourth column, mean square, are obtained by dividing the appropriate sums of squares by their degrees of freedom. We do not define a mean square total, which is why there is no entry in that particular position in the table. The last entry in the table is the main objective of our analysis: the F ratio, which is computed as the ratio of the two entries in the previous column. There are no other entries in the last column. Example 9–2 demonstrates the use of the ANOVA table.

EXAMPLE 9-2

Club Med has over 30 major resorts worldwide, from Tahiti to Switzerland. Many of the beach resorts are in the Caribbean, and at one point the club wanted to test whether or not the resorts on Guadeloupe, Martinique, Eleuthera, Paradise Island, and St. Lucia were all equally well liked by vacationing club members. The analysis was to be based on a survey questionnaire filled out by a random sample of 40 respondents in each of the resorts. From every returned questionnaire, a general satisfaction score, on a scale of 0 to 100, was computed. Analysis of the survey results yielded the statistics given in Table 9–4.

The results were computed from the responses using a computer program that calculated the sums of squared deviations from the sample means and from the grand mean. Given the values of SST and SSE, construct an ANOVA table and conduct the hypothesis test. (Note: the reported sample means in Table 9–4 will be used in the next section.)

SOLUTION

Let us first construct an ANOVA table and fill in the information we have: SST = 112,564; SSE = 98,356; $n = 200$; and $r = 5$. This has been done in Table 9–5. We now compute SSTR as the difference between SST and SSE and enter it in the appropriate place in the

TABLE 9-6   ANOVA Table for Club Med Example

Source of Variation	Sum of Squares	Degrees of Freedom	Mean Square	F Ratio
Treatment	SSTR = 14,208	$r - 1 =$ 4	MSTR = 3,552	F = 7.04
Error	SSE = 98,356	$n - r = 195$	MSE = 504.4	
Total	SST = 112,564	$n - 1 = 199$		

FIGURE 9-11   Club Med Test

table. We then divide SSTR and SSE by their respective degrees of freedom to give us MSTR and MSE. Finally, we divide MSTR by MSE to give us the F ratio. All these quantities are entered in the ANOVA table. The result is the complete ANOVA table for the study, Table 9–6.

Table 9–6 contains all the pertinent information for this study. We are now ready to conduct the hypothesis test.

H_0: $\mu_1 = \mu_2 = \mu_3 = \mu_4 = \mu_5$ (average vacationer satisfaction for each of the five resorts is equal)

H_1: Not all μ_i ($i = 1, \cdots, 5$) are equal (on the average, vacationer satisfaction is not equal among the five resorts)

As shown in Table 9–6, the test statistic value is $F_{(4, 195)} = 7.04$. As often happens, the exact number of degrees of freedom we need does not appear in Appendix C, Table 5. We use the nearest entry, which is the critical point for F with 4 degrees of freedom for the numerator and 200 degrees of freedom for the denominator. The critical point for $\alpha = 0.01$ is $C = 3.41$. The test is illustrated in Figure 9–11.

Since the computed test statistic value falls in the rejection region for $\alpha = 0.01$, we reject the null hypothesis and note that the p-value is smaller than 0.01. We may conclude that, based on the survey results and our assumptions, it is likely that the five resorts studied are not equal in terms of average vacationer satisfaction. Which resorts are more satisfying than others? This question will be answered when we return to this example in the next section.

TABLE 9-7   ANOVA Table for Job Involvement

Source of Variation	Sum of Squares	Degrees of Freedom	Mean Square	F Ratio
Treatment	SSTR = 879.3	$r - 1 = 3$	MSTR = 293.1	F = 8.52
Error	SSE = 18,541.6	$n - r = 539$	MSE = 34.4	
Total	SST = 19,420.9	$n - 1 = 542$		

EXAMPLE 9-3

Recent research studied job involvement of salespeople in the four major career stages: exploration, establishment, maintenance, and disengagement. Results of the study included an analysis of variance aimed at determining whether or not salespeople in each of the four career stages are, on the average, equally involved with their jobs. Involvement is measured on a special scale developed by psychologists. The analysis is based on questionnaires returned by a total of 543 respondents, and the reported F value is 8.52. The authors note the result is "significant at $p < .01$." Assuming that MSE = 34.4, construct an ANOVA table for this example. Also verify the authors' claim about the significance of their results.

SOLUTION

In this problem, another exercise in the construction of ANOVA tables, we are doing the opposite of what is usually done: we are going from the final result of an F ratio to the earlier stages of an analysis of variance. First, multiplying the F ratio by MSE gives us MSTR. Then, from the sample size $n = 543$ and from $r = 4$, we get the number of degrees of freedom for treatment, error, and total. Using our information, we construct the ANOVA table (Table 9–7).

From Appendix C, Table 5, we find that the critical point for a right-tailed test at $\alpha = 0.01$ for an F distribution with 3 and 400 degrees of freedom (the entry for degrees of freedom closest to the needed 3 and 539) is 3.83. Thus, we may conclude that differences do exist among the four career stages with respect to average job involvement. The authors' statement about the p-value is also true: the p-value is much smaller than 0.01.

PROBLEMS

9–18.   The Gulfstream Aerospace Company produced three different prototypes as candidates for mass production as the company's newest large-cabin business jet, the *Gulfstream* IV. Each of the three prototypes has slightly different features, which may bring about differences in performance. Therefore, as part of the decision-making process as to which model to produce, company engineers are interested in determining whether or not the three proposed models have about the same average flight range. Each of the models is assigned a random choice of 10 flight routes and departure times, and the flight range on a full standard fuel tank is measured (the planes carry additional fuel on the test flights, to allow them to land safely at certain destination points). Range data for the three prototypes, in nautical miles (measured to the nearest 10 miles), are as follows.[5]

---

[5] General information about the capabilities of the Gulfstream IV is provided courtesy of the Gulfstream Aerospace Company.

Prototype A	Prototype B	Prototype C
4,420	4,230	4,110
4,540	4,220	4,090
4,380	4,100	4,070
4,550	4,300	4,160
4,210	4,420	4,230
4,330	4,110	4,120
4,400	4,230	4,000
4,340	4,280	4,200
4,390	4,090	4,150
4,510	4,320	4,220

Do all three prototypes have the same average range? Construct an ANOVA table, and carry out the test. Explain your results.

9–19. In the theory of finance, a market for any asset or commodity is said to be *efficient* if items of identical quality and other attributes (such as risk, in the case of stocks) are sold at the same price. A Geneva-based oil industry analyst wants to test the hypothesis that the spot market for crude oil is efficient. The analyst chooses the Rotterdam oil market, and he selects Arabian Light as the type of oil to be studied. (Differences in location may cause price differences because of transportation costs, and differences in the type of oil—hence, in the quality of oil—also affect the price. Therefore, both the type and the location must be fixed.) A random sample of eight observations from each of four sources of the spot price of a barrel of oil during February is collected. Data, in U.S. dollars per barrel, are as follows.

U.K.	Mexico	U.A.E.	Oman
$17.80	$18.01	$18.10	$18.05
18.00	17.75	17.92	18.01
17.98	18.00	18.01	17.94
18.20	17.77	17.88	18.23
18.00	18.01	18.30	18.20
17.99	18.01	18.22	18.00
18.10	18.12	18.56	17.84
17.90	18.20	18.10	18.11

Based on these data, what should the analyst conclude about whether or not the market for crude oil is efficient? Are conclusions valid only for the Rotterdam market? Are conclusions valid for all types of crude oil? What assumptions are necessary for the analysis? Do you believe that all the assumptions are met in this case? What are the limitations, if any, of this study? Discuss.

9–20. The manager of a store wants to decide what kind of hand-knit sweaters to sell. The manager is considering three kinds of sweaters: Irish, Peruvian, and Shetland. The decision will depend on the results of an analysis of which kind of sweater, if any, lasts the longest before wearing out. The manager has some data collected from various customers who in the past bought different sweaters and reported how many years their sweaters lasted before wearing out. There are 20 observations on Irish sweaters, 18 on Peruvian sweaters, and 21 on Shetland sweaters. The data are assumed independent random samples from the three populations of sweaters. The manager hires a statistician, who carries out an ANOVA and finds SSE = 1,240 and SSTR = 740. Construct a complete ANOVA table, and determine whether there is evidence to conclude that the three kinds of sweaters do not have equal average durability.

9–21. An article in the *Journal of Marketing* describes a study of developing and managing a brand image. As part of the study, four social brand images were evaluated using a random sample of 193 firms. The reported *p*-value was $p = 0.117$. Interpret the meaning of this number in this context.[6]

9–22.   The Fidelity Overseas mutual fund consists of about equal proportions of Japanese and European stocks. The percentage of the fund invested in any individual country varies according to prevailing rates of return on stocks in different countries. At the end of October 1995, the fund manager was considering the possibility of shifting the proportions invested in French, Dutch, and Italian stocks. This change would be made if it could be statistically substantiated that differences in average annualized rates of return during the period ending in October existed among stocks from the three countries. Random samples of 50 French stocks, 32 Dutch stocks, and 28 Italian stocks were collected, and the annualized rate of return for each stock over the period under study was computed. Then an analysis of variance was carried out, which produced the following results: SSE = 22,399.8 and SST = 32,156.1. Based on these results, should the manager shift the proportions of the fund invested in the three countries? How confident are you of your answer? Construct a complete ANOVA table for this problem.

9–23.   A study is undertaken to determine whether differences exist in average consumer quality ratings of the following brands of color television sets: Magnavox, General Electric, Panasonic, Zenith, Sears, Philco, Sylvania, and RCA. For each brand, 100 randomly chosen consumer responses are available, and from these the following quantities are computed: SSTR = 45,210; SST = 92,340. Construct an ANOVA table for this study, and test the null hypothesis that all eight brands have equal average consumer quality ratings versus the alternative hypothesis that they do not.

9–5   Further Analysis

You have rejected the ANOVA null hypothesis. What next? This is an important question often overlooked in elementary introductions to analysis of variance. After all, what is the meaning of the statement "not all *r* population means are equal" if we cannot tell *in what way* the population means are not equal? We need to know which of our population means are large, which of them are small, and the magnitudes of the differences among them. These issues are addressed in this section.

ANOVA can be viewed as a machine or a box: in go the data, and out comes a conclusion—"all *r* population means are equal" or "not all *r* population means are equal." If the ANOVA null hypothesis, $H_0: \mu_1 = \mu_2 = \cdots = \mu_r$, is not rejected and we therefore state that there is no strong evidence to conclude that differences exist among the *r* population means, there is nothing more to say or do (unless, of course, you believe that differences do exist and you are able to gather more information to prove so). If the ANOVA null hypothesis is rejected, then we have evidence that the *r* population means are not all equal. This calls for *further analysis*—other hypothesis tests and/or the construction of confidence intervals to determine where the differences exist, their directions, and their magnitudes. The schematic diagram of the "ANOVA box" is shown in Figure 9–12.

Several methods have been developed for further analysis following the rejection of the null hypothesis in ANOVA. All the methods make use of the following two properties.

> The sample means, $\bar{X}_i$, are unbiased estimators of the corresponding population means, μ_i.
> The mean square error, MSE, is an unbiased estimator of the common population variance, σ^2.

---

[6] M. Roth, "The Effects of Culture and Socioeconomics on the Performance of Global Brand Image Strategies," *Journal of Marketing Research,* May 1995, pp. 163–75.

FIGURE 9-12   The ANOVA Diagram

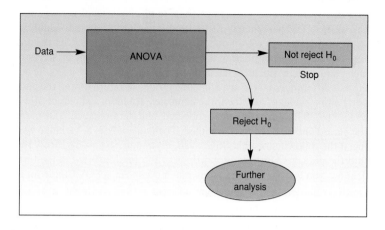

Since MSE can be read directly from the ANOVA table, we have another advantage of using an ANOVA table. This extends the usefulness of the table beyond the primary stages of analysis. The first and simplest post-ANOVA analysis is the estimation of separate population means, μ_i. It can be shown that, under the assumptions of analysis of variance, each sample mean, $\overline{X}_i$, has a normal distribution with mean μ_i and standard deviation $\sigma/\sqrt{n}$, where σ is the common standard deviation of the r populations. Since σ is not known, we estimate it by $\sqrt{MSE}$. We get the following relation:

$$\frac{\overline{X}_i - \mu_i}{\sqrt{MSE}/\sqrt{n_i}} \text{ has a } t \text{ distribution with } n - r \text{ degrees of freedom} \quad (9\text{–}19)$$

This property leads us to the possibility of constructing confidence intervals for individual population means.

A $(1 - \alpha)100\%$ confidence interval for μ_i, the mean of population i:

$$\overline{x}_i \pm t_{\alpha/2}\frac{\sqrt{MSE}}{\sqrt{n_i}} \qquad (9\text{–}20)$$

where $t_{\alpha/2}$ is the value of the t distribution with $n - r$ degrees of freedom that cuts off a right-tailed area equal to $\alpha/2$

Confidence intervals given by equation 9–20 are included in the standard output of ANOVA in many packages, such as MINITAB. This will be seen in Section 9–9.

We now demonstrate the use of equation 9–20 with the continuation of Example 9–2, the Club Med example. From Table 9–4, we get the sample means, $\overline{x}_i$:

$$\text{Guadeloupe: } \overline{x}_1 = 89$$
$$\text{Martinique: } \overline{x}_2 = 75$$
$$\text{Eleuthera: } \ \ \overline{x}_3 = 73$$
$$\text{Paradise Is.: } \overline{x}_4 = 91$$
$$\text{St. Lucia: } \ \ \ \overline{x}_5 = 85$$

From Table 9–6, the ANOVA table for this example, we get MSE = 504.4 and degrees of freedom for error $= n - r = 195$. We also know that the sample size in each group is $n_i = 40$ for all $i = 1, \ldots, 5$. Since a t distribution with 195 degrees of freedom is, for all practical purposes, a standard normal distribution, we use $z = 1.96$ in constructing 95% confidence intervals for the population mean responses of vacationers on the five islands. We will construct a 95% confidence interval for the mean response on Guadeloupe and leave the construction of the other four confidence intervals as an exercise. For Guadeloupe, we have the following 95% confidence interval for the population mean (μ_1):

$$\bar{x}_1 \pm t_{\alpha/2}\frac{\sqrt{MSE}}{\sqrt{n_1}} = 89 \pm 1.96\frac{\sqrt{504.4}}{\sqrt{40}} = [82.04, 95.96]$$

The real usefulness of ANOVA, however, does not lie in the construction of individual confidence intervals for population means (these are of limited use because the confidence coefficient does not apply to a *series* of estimates). The power of ANOVA lies in providing us with the ability to make *joint* conclusions about population parameters.

As mentioned earlier, several procedures have been developed for further analysis. The method we will discuss here is the *Tukey method* of pairwise comparisons of the population means. The method is also called the HSD (honestly significant differences) test. This method allows us to compare every possible pair of means using a *single level of significance,* say $\alpha = 0.05$ (or a single confidence coefficient, say, $1 - \alpha = 0.95$). The single level of significance applies to the *entire set* of pairwise comparisons.

The Tukey Pairwise Comparisons Test

We will use the *studentized range distribution.*

> The **studentized range distribution,** q, is a probability distribution with degrees of freedom r and $n - r$.

Note that the degrees of freedom of q are similar, but not identical, to the degrees of freedom of the F distribution in ANOVA. The F distribution has $r - 1$ and $n - r$ degrees of freedom. The q distribution has degrees of freedom r and $n - r$. Critical points for q with different numbers of degrees of freedom for $\alpha = 0.05$ and for $\alpha = 0.01$ are given in Appendix C, Table 6. Check, for example, that for $\alpha = 0.05$, $r = 3$, and $n - r = 20$, we have the critical point $q_\alpha = 3.58$. The table gives right-hand critical points, which is what we need since our test will be a right-tailed test. We now define the Tukey criterion, T.

The Tukey criterion

$$T = q_\alpha\frac{\sqrt{MSE}}{\sqrt{n_i}} \qquad (9\text{–}21)$$

Equation 9–21 gives us a critical point, at a given level α, with which we will compare the computed values of test statistics defined later. Now let us define the hypothesis tests. As mentioned, the usefulness of the Tukey test is that it allows us to perform *jointly* all possible pairwise comparisons of the population means using a single, "family" level of significance. What are all the possible pairwise comparisons associated with an ANOVA?

Suppose that we had $r = 3$. We compared the means of three populations using ANOVA and concluded that the means were not all equal. Now we would like to be able to compare every *pair* of means to determine where the differences among population means exist. How many pairwise comparisons are there? With three populations, there are

$$\binom{3}{2} = \frac{3!}{2!\ 1!} = 3 \text{ comparisons}$$

These comparisons are

$$1 \text{ with } 2$$
$$2 \text{ with } 3, \text{ and}$$
$$1 \text{ with } 3$$

As a general rule, the number of possible pairwise comparisons of r means is

$$\binom{r}{2} = \frac{r!}{2!\ (r - 2)!} \qquad (9\text{--}22)$$

You do not really need equation 9–22 for cases where it is relatively easy to list all the possible pairs. In the case of Example 9–2, there are, by equation 9–22, $5!/2!\ 3! = (5)(4)(3)(2)/(2)(3)(2) = 10$ possible pairwise comparisons. Let us list all the comparisons:

$$\text{Guadeloupe (1)–Martinique (2)}$$
$$\text{Guadeloupe (1)–Eleuthera (3)}$$
$$\text{Guadeloupe (1)–Paradise Island (4)}$$
$$\text{Guadeloupe (1)–St. Lucia (5)}$$
$$\text{Martinique (2)–Eleuthera (3)}$$
$$\text{Martinique (2)–Paradise Island (4)}$$
$$\text{Martinique (2)–St. Lucia (5)}$$
$$\text{Eleuthera (3)–Paradise Island (4)}$$
$$\text{Eleuthera (3)–St. Lucia (5)}$$
$$\text{Paradise Island (4)–St. Lucia (5)}$$

These pairings are apparent if you look at Table 9–4 and see that we need to compare the first island, Guadeloupe, with all four islands below it. Then we need to compare the second island, Martinique, with all three islands below it (we already have the comparison of Martinique with Guadeloupe). We do the same with Eleuthera and finally with Paradise Island, which has only St. Lucia listed below it; therefore, this is the last comparison. (In the preceding list, we wrote the number of each population in parentheses after the population name.)

The parameter μ_1 denotes the population mean of all vacationer responses for Guadeloupe. The parameters μ_2 to μ_5 have similar meanings. To compare the population mean vacationer responses for every pair of island resorts, we use the following *set of hypothesis tests.*

I. $H_0: \mu_1 = \mu_2$	VI. $H_0: \mu_2 = \mu_4$
$H_1: \mu_1 \neq \mu_2$	$H_1: \mu_2 \neq \mu_4$
II. $H_0: \mu_1 = \mu_3$	VII. $H_0: \mu_2 = \mu_5$
$H_1: \mu_1 \neq \mu_3$	$H_1: \mu_2 \neq \mu_5$
III. $H_0: \mu_1 = \mu_4$	VIII. $H_0: \mu_3 = \mu_4$
$H_1: \mu_1 \neq \mu_4$	$H_1: \mu_3 \neq \mu_4$
IV. $H_0: \mu_1 = \mu_5$	IX. $H_0: \mu_3 = \mu_5$
$H_1: \mu_1 \neq \mu_5$	$H_1: \mu_3 \neq \mu_5$
V. $H_0: \mu_2 = \mu_3$	X. $H_0: \mu_4 = \mu_5$
$H_1: \mu_2 \neq \mu_3$	$H_1: \mu_4 \neq \mu_5$

The Tukey method allows us to carry out simultaneously all 10 hypothesis tests at a single given level of significance, say, $\alpha = 0.05$. Thus, if we use the Tukey procedure for reaching conclusions as to which population means are equal and which are not, we know that the probability of reaching at least one erroneous conclusion, stating that two means are not equal when indeed they are equal, is at most 0.05.

The test statistic:

The test statistic for each test is the *absolute difference of the appropriate sample means.*

Thus, the test statistic for the first test (I) is

$$|\bar{x}_1 - \bar{x}_2| = |89 - 75| = 14$$

Conducting the Tests

We conduct the tests as follows. We compute each of the test statistics and compare them with the value of T that corresponds to the desired level of significance, α. *We reject a particular null hypothesis if the absolute difference between the corresponding pair of sample means exceeds the value of T.*

Using $\alpha = 0.05$, we now conduct the Tukey test for Example 9–2. All absolute differences of sample means corresponding to the pairwise tests I through X are computed and compared with the value of T. For $\alpha = 0.05$, $r = 5$, and $n - r = 195$ (we use ∞, the last row in the table), we get, from Appendix C, Table 6: $q = 3.86$. We also know that MSE = 504.4 and $n_i = 40$ for all i. (Later we will see what to do when not all r samples are of equal size.) Therefore, from equation 9–21,

$$T = q_\alpha \sqrt{\frac{\text{MSE}}{n_i}} = 3.86 \sqrt{\frac{504.4}{40}} = 13.7$$

We now compute all 10 pairwise absolute differences of sample means and compare them with $T = 13.7$ to determine which differences are statistically significant at $\alpha = 0.05$ (these are marked with an asterisk).

$$|\bar{x}_1 - \bar{x}_2| = |89 - 75| = 14 > 13.7*$$
$$|\bar{x}_1 - \bar{x}_3| = |89 - 73| = 16 > 13.7*$$
$$|\bar{x}_1 - \bar{x}_4| = |89 - 91| = 2 < 13.7$$

$$|\bar{x}_1 - \bar{x}_5| = |89 - 85| = 4 < 13.7$$
$$|\bar{x}_2 - \bar{x}_3| = |75 - 73| = 2 < 13.7$$
$$|\bar{x}_2 - \bar{x}_4| = |75 - 91| = 16 > 13.7*$$
$$|\bar{x}_2 - \bar{x}_5| = |75 - 85| = 10 < 13.7$$
$$|\bar{x}_3 - \bar{x}_4| = |73 - 91| = 18 > 13.7*$$
$$|\bar{x}_3 - \bar{x}_5| = |73 - 85| = 12 < 13.7$$
$$|\bar{x}_4 - \bar{x}_5| = |91 - 85| = 6 < 13.7$$

From these comparisons we determine that our data provide statistical evidence to conclude that μ_1 is different from μ_2; μ_1 is different from μ_3; μ_2 is different from μ_4; and μ_3 is different from μ_4. *There are no other statistically significant differences at* $\alpha = 0.05$.

For the purpose of interpretation, it will help to draw a diagram of the significant differences that we found. This has been done in Figure 9–13. Looking at the figure, you may be puzzled by the fact that we believe, for example, that μ_1 is different from μ_2, yet we believe that μ_1 is no different from μ_5 and μ_5 is no different from μ_2. You may say: If A is equal to B, and B is equal to C, then mathematically we must have A equal to C (the transitivity of equality). But remember that we are doing statistics, not discussing mathematical equality. In statistics, not rejecting the null hypothesis that two parameters are equal does not mean that they are necessarily equal. The nonrejection just means that we have no statistical evidence to conclude that they are different. Thus, in our present example, we conclude that there is statistical evidence to support the claim that, on the average, vacationers give higher ratings to Guadeloupe (1) than they give to Martinique (2) or Eleuthera (3); as well as the claim that Paradise Island (4) is, on the average, rated higher than Martinique or Eleuthera. There is no statistical evidence for any other claim of differences in average ratings among the five island resorts. Note also that we do not have to hypothesize any of the assertions of tests I through X *before* doing the analysis. The Tukey method allows us to make all the above conclusions at a single level of significance, $\alpha = 0.05$.

FIGURE 9–13   Differences Among the Population Means in Example 9–2 Suggested by the Tukey Procedure

Denotes that there is no statistical evidence that the covered population means are different

(The population means are placed approximately at the locations on the line where the sample means would be.)

The Case of Unequal Sample Sizes, and Alternative Procedures

What can we do if the sample sizes are not equal in all groups? We use the *smallest sample size* of all the n_i in computing the criterion T of equation 9–21. The Tukey procedure is the best follow-up to ANOVA when the sample sizes are all equal. The case of equal sample sizes is called the *balanced design.* For very unbalanced designs (i.e., when sample sizes are very different), there are other methods of further analysis to be used following ANOVA. Two of the better-known methods are the Bonferroni method and the Scheffé method. We will not discuss these methods.

PROBLEMS

9–24. Give 95% confidence intervals for the remaining four population mean responses to the Club Med resorts (the one for Guadeloupe having been given in the text).

9–25. Use the data of Table 9–1 and the Tukey procedure to determine where differences exist among the triangle, circle, and square population means. Use $\alpha = 0.01$.

9–26. For problem 9–18, find which, if any, of the three prototype planes has an average range different from the others. Use $\alpha = 0.05$.

9–27. For problem 9–19, use the Tukey method to determine which oil types, if any, have an average price different from the others. Use $\alpha = 0.05$.

9–28. For problem 9–20, suppose that the appropriate sample means are 6.4, 2.5, and 4.9 (in years and in order of type listed in problem 9–20). Find where differences, if any, exist among the three population means. Use $\alpha = 0.05$.

9–29. For problem 9–23, suppose the sample means, in the order listed in that problem, are: 77, 78, 82, 94, 88, 89, 90, 87. Use the Tukey procedure to determine where differences in average population ratings may exist. Use $\alpha = 0.01$.

9–30. An analysis of variance is carried out to determine differences among average annualized returns on four types of investments. The analysis leads to the rejection of the null hypothesis that no differences exist, using $\alpha = 0.05$. The mean square error is 49.5; the sample sizes are all $n_i = 31$. The sample means are 18, 11, 15, 14. Find the significant differences that exist among the four types of investment.

9–6   Models, Factors, and Designs

A **statistical model** is a set of equations and assumptions that capture the essential characteristics of a real-world situation.

The model discussed in this chapter is the one-factor ANOVA model. In this model, the populations are assumed to be represented by the following equation.

The one-factor ANOVA model:

$$x_{ij} = \mu_i + \epsilon_{ij} = \mu + \tau_i + \epsilon_{ij} \qquad (9\text{–}23)$$

where ϵ_{ij} is the error associated with the *j*th member of the *i*th population. The errors are assumed to be normally distributed with mean zero and variance σ^2.

The ANOVA model assumes that the r populations are normally distributed with means μ_i, which may be different, and with equal variance, σ^2. The right-hand side of equation 9–23 breaks the mean of population i into a common component, μ, and a unique component due to the particular population (or treatment) i. This component is written as τ_i. When we sample, the sample means $\bar{X}_i$ are unbiased estimators of the respective population means, μ_i. The grand mean, $\bar{X}$, is an unbiased estimator of the common component of the means, μ. The treatment deviations, t_i, are estimators of the differences among population means, τ_i. The data errors, e_{ij}, are estimates of the population errors, ϵ_{ij}.

Much more will be said about statistical models in the next chapter, dealing with regression analysis. The one-factor ANOVA null hypothesis, H_0: $\mu_1 = \mu_2 = \ldots = \mu_r$, may be written in an equivalent form, using equation 9–23, as H_0: $\tau_i = 0$ for all i. (This is so because if $\mu_i = \mu$ for all i, then the "extra" components, τ_i, are all zero.) This form of the hypothesis will be extended in the two-factor ANOVA model, also called the two-way ANOVA model, discussed in the following section.

We may want to check that the assumptions of the ANOVA model are indeed met. To check that the errors are approximately normally distributed, we may draw a histogram of the observed errors, e_{ij}, which are called *residuals*. If serious deviations from the normal-distribution assumption exist, the histogram will not resemble a normal curve. Plotting the residuals for each of the r samples under study will reveal whether or not the population variances are indeed (at least approximately) equal. If the *spread* of the data sets around their group means is not approximately equal for all r groups, then the population variances may not be equal. When model assumptions are violated, a nonparametric alternative to ANOVA must be used. An alternative method of analysis is the Kruskal-Wallis test, discussed in Chapter 14. Residual analysis will be discussed in detail in the next chapter.

One-Factor versus Multifactor Models

In each of the examples and problems you have seen so far, we were interested in determining whether or not differences existed among several populations, or treatments. These treatments may be considered as *levels* of a single *factor*.

A **factor** is a set of populations or treatments of a single kind.

Examples of factors are vacationer ratings of a *set of resorts,* the range of different *types of airplanes,* and the durability of different *kinds of sweaters.*

Sometimes, however, we may be interested in studying more than one factor. For example, an accounting researcher may be interested in testing whether there are differences in average error percentage rate among the Big Eight accounting firms, *and* among different geographical locations, such as the Eastern Seaboard, the South, the Midwest, and the West. In such an analysis, there are *two factors:* the different firms (factor A, with eight levels) and the geographical location (factor B, with four levels).

Another example is that of an advertising firm interested in studying how the public is influenced by color, shape, and size in an advertisement. The firm could carry out an ANOVA to test whether or not there are differences in average responses to three different colors, as well as to four different shapes of an ad, and to three different ad sizes. This would be a three-factor ANOVA. There are important statistical reasons for jointly studying the effects of several factors in a multifactor ANOVA. These will be explained in the next section, on two-factor ANOVA.

Fixed-Effects versus Random-Effects Models

Recall Example 9–2, where we wanted to determine whether differences existed among the five particular island resorts, Guadeloupe, Martinique, Eleuthera, Paradise Island, and St. Lucia. Once we reject or not reject the null hypothesis, *the inference is valid only for the five islands studied.* This is a *fixed-effects model.*

> A **fixed-effects model** is a model where the levels of the factor under study (the treatments) are *fixed* in advance. Inference is valid only for the levels under study.

Consider another possible context for the analysis. Suppose that Club Med had no particular interest in the 5 resorts listed, but instead wanted to determine whether differences existed among *any* of its more than 30 resorts. In such a case, we may consider all Club Med resorts as a *population of resorts,* and we may draw a random sample of five (or any other number) of the resorts and carry out an ANOVA to determine differences among population means. The ANOVA would be carried out in exactly the same way. However, since the resorts themselves were randomly selected for analysis from the population of all Club Med resorts, the inference would be valid for *all* Club Med resorts. This is called the *random-effects model.*

> The **random-effects model** is an ANOVA model in which the levels of the factor under study are *randomly chosen* from an entire population of levels (treatments). Inference is valid for the entire population of levels.

The idea should make sense to you if you recall the principle of inference using random sampling, discussed in Chapter 5, and the story of the *Literary Digest.* In order to make inferences that are valid for an entire population, we must randomly sample from the entire population. Here this principle is applied to a population of treatments.

Experimental Design

Analysis of variance often involves the ideas of **experimental design.** If we want to study the effects of different treatments, we are sometimes in a position to design the experiment by which we plan to study these effects. Designing the experiment involves the choice of elements from a population or populations and the assignment of elements to different treatments. The model we have been using involves a *completely randomized design.*

> A **completely randomized design** is a design in which elements are assigned to treatments *completely at random.* Thus, every element chosen for the study has an equal chance of being assigned to any treatment.

There are other types of design. Some designs, called **blocking designs,** are very useful in reducing experimental errors, that is, reducing variation due to factors other than the ones under study. In the *randomized complete block design,* for example, experimental units are assigned to treatments in blocks of similar elements, with randomized treatment order within each block. In the Club Med situation of Example 9–2, a randomized complete block design could involve sending each vacationer in the sample to all five resorts, the order of the resorts chosen randomly; each vacationer is then asked to rate all the resorts. A design such as this one, with *experimental units* (here, people) given all the treatments, is called a *repeated measures design*. More will be said about blocking designs later.

PROBLEMS

9–31. For problem 9–18, suppose that four more prototype planes are built after the study is completed. Could the inference from the ANOVA involving the first three proptotypes be extended to the new planes? Explain.

9–32. What is a blocking design?

9–33. For problem 9–18, can you think of a blocking design that would reduce experimental errors?

9–34. How can we determine whether there are violations of the ANOVA model assumptions? What should we do if such violations exist?

9–35. Explain why the factor levels must be randomly chosen in the random effects model to allow inference about an entire collection of treatments.

9–36. For problem 9–19, based on the given data, can you tell whether or not the world oil market is efficient?

9–7   Two-Way Analysis of Variance

In addition to being interested in possible differences in the general appeal of their five Caribbean resorts (Example 9–2), suppose that Club Med is also interested in the respective appeal of four vacation attributes: friendship, sports, culture, and excitement.[7] Club Med would like to have answers to the following two questions.

1. Are there differences in average vacationer satisfaction with the five Caribbean resorts?
2. Are there differences in average vacationer satisfaction in terms of the four vacation attributes?

In cases such as this one, where there is interest in *two* factors—resort and vacation attribute—we can answer the two questions *jointly*. In addition, we can answer a *third*, very important question, which may not be apparent to us.

3. Are there any *interactions* between some resorts and some attributes?

The three questions are statistically answerable by conducting a two-factor, or two-way, ANOVA. Why a two-way ANOVA? Why not conduct each of the two ANOVAs separately?

There are several reasons for conducting a two-way ANOVA. One reason is *efficiency*. When we conduct a two-way ANOVA, we may use a smaller total sample size for the analysis than would be required if we were to conduct each of the two tests separately. Basically, we use the same data resources to answer the two main questions. In the case of Club Med, the club may run a friendship program at each of the five resorts for one week; then the next week (with different vacationers) it may run

---

[7] Information on the attributes and the resorts was provided through the courtesy of Club Med.

a sports program in each of the five resorts; and so on. All vacationer responses could then be used for evaluating *both* the satisfaction from the resorts and the satisfaction from the attributes, rather than conducting two separate surveys, requiring twice the effort and number of respondents. A more important reason for conducting a two-way ANOVA is that there really are *three* questions to be answered.

Let us call the first factor of interest (here, resorts) factor A and the second factor (here, attributes) factor B. The effects of each factor alone are the factor's *main effects*. The combined effects of the two factors, beyond what we may expect from the consideration of each factor separately, is the *interaction* between the two factors.

Two factors are said to **interact** if the difference between levels (treatments) of one factor depends on the level of the other factor. Factors that do not interact are called *additive*.

An interaction is thus an *extra effect* that appears as a result of a particular combination of a treatment from one factor with a treatment from another factor. An interaction between two factors exists when, for at least one combination of treatments—say Eleuthera and sports—the effect of the combination is not additive: there is some special "chemistry" between the two treatments. Suppose that Eleuthera is rated lowest of all resorts and sports is rated lowest of all attributes. We then expect the Eleuthera-sports combination to be rated, on average, lowest of all combinations. If this does not happen, the two levels are said to interact.

The three questions answerable by two-way ANOVA:

1. Are there any factor A main effects?
2. Are there any factor B main effects?
3. Are there any interaction effects of factors A and B?

Let n_{ij} be the sample size in the "cell" corresponding to level i of factor A and level j of factor B. Assume there is a uniform sample size for each factor A–factor B combination, say, $n_{ij} = 4$. The layout of the data of a two-way ANOVA, using the Club Med example, is shown in Figure 9–14. Figure 9–15 shows the effects of an interaction. We arrange the levels of each factor in increasing order of sample mean responses. The general two-variable trend of increasing average response is the response plane shown in Figure 9–15. An exception to the plane is the Eleuthera-sports interaction, which leads to a higher-than-expected average response for this combination of levels.

The Two-Way ANOVA Model

There are a levels of factor A ($a = 5$ resorts in the Club Med example) and b levels of factor B ($b = 4$ attributes in the same example). Thus, there are $a \times b$ combinations of levels, or cells, as shown in Figure 9–14. Each one is considered a treatment. We must assume equal sample sizes in all the cells. If we do not have equal sample sizes, we must use an alternative to the method of this chapter and solve the ANOVA problem using multiple regression analysis (Chapter 11). Since we assume an equal

FIGURE 9–14   Two-Way ANOVA Data Layout

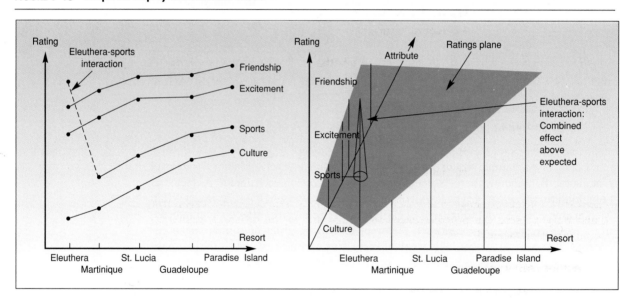

FIGURE 9–15   Graphical Display of Interaction Effects

sample size in each cell, we will simplify our notation and call the sample size in each cell n, omitting the subscripts i, j. We will denote the total sample size (formerly called n) by the symbol N. In the two-way ANOVA model, the assumptions of normal populations and equal variance for each two-factor combination treatment are still maintained.

> **The two-way ANOVA model:**
>
> $$x_{ijk} = \mu + \alpha_i + \beta_j + (\alpha\beta)_{ij} + \epsilon_{ijk} \qquad (9\text{--}24)$$
>
> where μ is the overall mean; α_i is the effect of level i ($i = 1, \ldots, a$) of factor A; β_j is the effect of level j ($j = 1, \ldots, b$) of factor B; $(\alpha\beta)_{ij}$ is the interaction effect of levels i and j; and ϵ_{ijk} is the error associated with the kth data point from level i of factor A and level j of factor B. As before, we assume that the error ϵ_{ijk} is normally distributed with mean zero and variance σ^2 for all i, j, and k.[8]

Our data, assumed to be random samples from populations modeled by equation 9–24, give us estimates of the model parameters. These estimates—as well as the different measures of variation, as in the one-way ANOVA case—are used in testing hypotheses. Since, in two-way ANOVA, three questions are to be answered rather than just one, there are three hypothesis tests relevant to any two-way ANOVA. The hypothesis tests that answer questions 1 to 3 are presented next.

The Hypothesis Tests in Two-Way ANOVA

Factor A main-effects test:

$$H_0: \alpha_i = 0 \text{ for all } i = 1, \ldots, a$$
$$H_1: \text{Not all } \alpha_i \text{ are } 0$$

This hypothesis test is designed to determine whether or not there are any factor A main effects. That is, the null hypothesis is true if and only if there are no differences in means due to the different treatments (populations) of factor A.

Factor B main-effects test:

$$H_0: \beta_j = 0 \text{ for all } j = 1, \ldots, b$$
$$H_1: \text{Not all } \beta_j \text{ are } 0$$

This test will detect evidence of any factor B main effects. The null hypothesis is true if and only if there are no differences in means due to the different treatments (populations) of factor B.

Test for (AB) interactions:

$$H_0: (\alpha\beta)_{ij} = 0 \text{ for all } i = 1, \ldots, a \text{ and } j = 1, \ldots, b$$
$$H_1: \text{Not all } (\alpha\beta)_{ij} \text{ are } 0$$

This is a test for the existence of interactions between levels of the two factors. The null hypothesis is true if and only if there are no two-way interactions between levels of factor A and levels of factor B, that is, if the factor effects are additive.

---

[8] Since the terms α_i, β_j, and $(\alpha\beta)_{ij}$ are deviations from the overall mean μ, in the fixed-effects model the sums of all these deviations are all zero: $\Sigma\alpha_i = 0$, $\Sigma\beta_j = 0$, and $\Sigma(\alpha\beta)_{ij} = 0$.

In carrying out a two-way ANOVA, we should test the third hypothesis first. We do so because it is important to first determine whether or not interactions exist. If interactions do exist, our interpretation of the ANOVA results will be different from the case where no interactions exist (that is, in the case where the effects of the two factors are additive).

Sums of Squares, Degrees of Freedom, and Mean Squares

We define the data, the various means, and the deviations from the means as follows.

x_{ijk} is the kth data point from level i of factor A and level j of factor B.
$\bar{\bar{x}}$ is the grand mean.
$\bar{x}_{ij}$ is the mean of cell ij.
$\bar{x}_i$ is the mean of all data points in level i of factor A.
$\bar{x}_j$ is the mean of all data points in level j of factor B.
Using these definitions, we have.

$$\sum_1^a \sum_1^b \sum_1^n (x_{ijk} - \bar{\bar{x}})^2 = \sum\sum\sum (\bar{x}_{ij} - \bar{\bar{x}})^2 + \sum\sum\sum (x_{ijk} - \bar{x}_{ij})^2 \quad (9\text{--}25)$$

$$SST = SSTR + SSE$$

(this can be further partitioned)

FIGURE 9–16
Partition of the Sum of Squares in Two-Way ANOVA

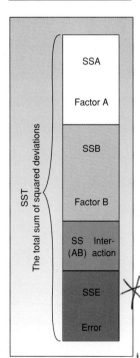

Equation 9–25 is the usual decomposition of the sum of squares, where each cell (a combination of a level of factor A and a level of factor B) is considered a separate treatment. Deviations of the data points from the cell means are squared and summed. Equation 9–25 is the same as equation 9–12 for the partition of the total sum of squares into sum of squares treatment and sum of squares error in one-way ANOVA. The only difference between the two equations is that here the summations extend over three subscripts: one subscript for levels of each of the two factors and one subscript for the data point number. The interesting thing is that SSTR can be further partitioned into a component due to factor A, a component due to factor B, and a component due to interactions of the two factors. The partition of the total sum of squares into its components is given in equation 9–26.

Do not worry about the mathematics of the summations. Two-way ANOVA is prohibitively tedious for hand computation, and we will always use a computer. The important thing to understand is that the total sum of squares is partitioned into a part due to factor A, a part due to factor B, a part due to interactions of the two factors, and a part due to error. This is shown in Figure 9–16.

What are the degrees of freedom? Since there are a levels of factor A, the degrees of freedom for factor A are $a - 1$. Similarly, there are $b - 1$ degrees of freedom for factor B, and there are $(a - 1)(b - 1)$ degrees of freedom for (AB) interactions. The degrees of freedom for error are $ab(n - 1)$. The total degrees of freedom is $abn - 1$. But we knew that! $[(a - 1) + (b - 1) + (a - 1)(b - 1) + ab(n - 1) = a + b - 2 + ab - a - b + 1 + abn - ab = abn - 1.]$ Note that since we assume an equal sample size, n, in each cell and since there are ab cells, we have $N = abn$, and the total number of degrees of freedom is $N - 1 = abn - 1$.

$$SST \quad = \quad SSTR \quad + \quad SSE$$

$$\sum\sum\sum(x - \bar{\bar{x}})^2 = \sum\sum\sum(\bar{x} - \bar{\bar{x}})^2 + \sum\sum\sum(x - \bar{x})^2$$

$$\sum\sum\sum(\bar{x}_i - \bar{\bar{x}})^2 + \sum\sum\sum(\bar{x}_j - \bar{\bar{x}})^2 + \sum\sum\sum(\bar{x}_{ij} - \bar{x}_i - \bar{x}_j + \bar{\bar{x}})^2$$

$$\quad SSA \quad + \quad SSB \quad + \quad SS(AB)$$

Thus,

$$SST = SSA + SSB + SS(AB) + SSE \qquad (9\text{--}26)$$

where SSA = sum of squares due to factor A, SSB = sum of squares due to factor B, and SS(AB) = sum of squares due to the interactions of factors A and B

Let us now construct an ANOVA table. The table includes the sums of squares, the degrees of freedom, and the mean squares. The mean squares are obtained by dividing each sum of squares by its degrees of freedom. The final products of the table are three F ratios. We define the F ratios as follows.

The F Ratios and the Two-Way ANOVA Table

The F ratio for each one of the hypothesis tests is the ratio of the appropriate mean square to the MSE. That is, for the test of factor A main effects, we use $F = $ MSA/MSE; for the test of factor B main effects, we use $F = $ MSB/MSE; and for the test of interactions of the two factors, we use $F = $ MS(AB)/MSE. We now construct the ANOVA table for two-way analysis, Table 9–8.

The degrees of freedom associated with each F ratio are the degrees of freedom of the respective numerator and denominator (the denominator is the same for all three tests). For the testing of factor A main effects, our test statistic is the first F ratio in the ANOVA table. When the null hypothesis is true (there are no factor A main effects), the ratio $F = $ MSA/MSE follows an F distribution with $a - 1$ degrees of freedom for the numerator and $ab(n - 1)$ degrees of freedom for the denominator. We denote this distribution by $F_{[a-1, ab(n-1)]}$. Similarly, for the test of factor B main effects, when the null hypothesis is true, the distribution of the test statistic is $F_{[b-1, ab(n-1)]}$. The test for the existence of (AB) interactions uses the distribution $F_{[(a-1)(b-1), ab(n-1)]}$.

TABLE 9–8 ANOVA Table for Two-Way Analysis

Source of Variation	Sum of Squares	Degrees of Freedom	Mean Square	F Ratio
Factor A	SSA	$a - 1$	$MSA = \dfrac{SSA}{a - 1}$	$F = \dfrac{MSA}{MSE}$
Factor B	SSB	$b - 1$	$MSB = \dfrac{SSB}{b - 1}$	$F = \dfrac{MSB}{MSE}$
Interaction	SS(AB)	$(a - 1)(b - 1)$	$MS(AB) = \dfrac{SS(AB)}{(a - 1)(b - 1)}$	$F = \dfrac{MS(AB)}{MSE}$
Error	SSE	$ab(n - 1)$	$MSE = \dfrac{SSE}{ab(n - 1)}$	
Total	SST	$abn - 1$		

We will demonstrate the use of the ANOVA table in two-way analysis, and the three tests, with a new example.

EXAMPLE 9-4

There are claims that the Japanese have now joined Americans and the English in paying top dollars for paintings at art auctions. Suppose that an art dealer is interested in testing two hypotheses. The first is that paintings sell for the same price, on the average, in London, New York, and Tokyo. The second hypothesis is that works of Picasso, Chagall, and Dali sell for the same average price. The dealer is also aware of a third question. This is the question of a possible interaction between the location (and thus the buyers: Americans, English, Japanese) and the artist. Data on auction prices of 10 works of art by each of the three painters at each of the three cities are collected, and a two-way ANOVA is run on a computer. The results include the following. The sums of squares associated with the location (factor A) is 1,824. The sum of squares associated with the artist (factor B) is 2,230. The sum of squares for interactions is 804. The sum of squares for error is 8,262. Construct the ANOVA table, carry out the hypothesis tests, and state your conclusions.

SOLUTION

We enter the sums of squares into the table. Since there are three levels in each of the two factors, and the sample size in each cell is 10, the degrees of freedom are $a - 1 = 2$, $b - 1 = 2$, $(a - 1)(b - 1) = 4$, and $ab(n - 1) = 81$. Also, $abn - 1 = 89$, which checks as the sum of all other degrees of freedom. These values are entered in the table as well. The mean squares are computed, and so are the appropriate F ratios. Check to see how each result in the ANOVA table, Table 9–9, is obtained.

Let us now conduct the three hypothesis tests relevant to this problem. We will state the hypothesis tests in words. The factor A test is

H_0: There is no difference in the average price of paintings of the kind studied across the three locations

H_1: There are differences in average price across locations

The test statistic is an F random variable with 2 and 81 degrees of freedom (see Table 9–9). The computed value of the test statistic is 8.94. From Appendix C, Table 5, we find that the critical point for $\alpha = 0.01$ is close to 4.88. Thus, the null hypothesis is rejected, and we know that the p-value is much smaller than 0.01. Computer printouts of ANOVA results often list p-values in the ANOVA table, in a column after the F ratios. Often, the

TABLE 9–9   ANOVA Table for Example 9-4

Source of Variation	Sum of Squares	Degrees of Freedom	Mean Square	F Ratio
Location	1,824	2	912	8.94
Artist	2,230	2	1,115	10.93
Interaction	804	4	201	1.97
Error	8,262	81	102	
Total	13,120	89		

FIGURE 9–17   Example 9–4: Location Hypothesis Test

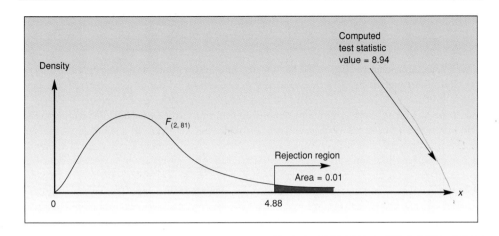

computer output will show $p = 0.0000$. This means that the p-value is smaller than 0.0001. The results of the hypothesis test are shown in Figure 9–17.

Now we perform the hypothesis test for factor B:

H_0: There are no differences in the average price of paintings by the three artists studied

H_1: There are differences in the average price of paintings by the three artists

Here again, the test statistic is an F random variable with 2 and 81 degrees of freedom, and the computed value of the statistic is 10.93. The null hypothesis is rejected, and the p-value is much smaller than 0.01. The test is shown in Figure 9–18.

The hypothesis test for interactions is

H_0: There are no interactions of the locations and the artists under study

H_1: There is at least one interaction of a location and an artist

The test statistic is an F random variable with 4 and 81 degrees of freedom. At a level of significance $\alpha = 0.05$, the critical point (see Appendix C, Table 5) is approximately equal to 2.48, and our computed value of the statistic is 1.97, leading us not to reject the null hypothesis of no interaction at levels of significance greater than 0.05. This is shown in Figure 9–19.

As mentioned earlier, we look at the test for interactions first. Since the null hypothesis of no interactions was not rejected, we have no statistical evidence of interactions of the two factors. This means, for example, that if a work by Picasso sells at a higher average price than works by the other two artists, then his paintings will fetch—on average—higher prices in all three cities. It also means that if paintings sell for a higher average price in London than in the other two cities, then this holds true—again, on average—for all three artists. Now we may interpret the results of the two main-effects tests.

We may conclude that there is statistical evidence that paintings (by these artists) do not fetch the same average price across the three cities. We may similarly conclude that paintings by the three artists under study do not sell, on average, for the same price. Where do the differences exist? This can be determined by a method for further analysis, such as the Tukey method.

FIGURE 9–18   Example 9–4: Artist Hypothesis Test

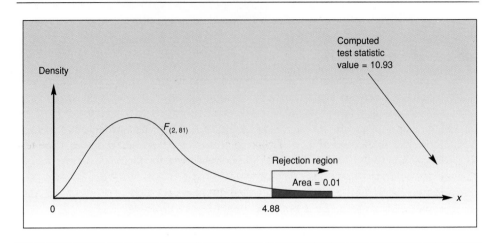

FIGURE 9–19   Example 9–4: Test for Interaction

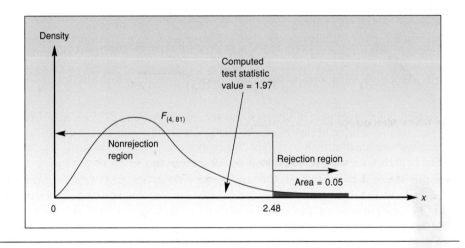

In cases where we *do* find evidence of an interaction effect, our results have a different interpretation. In such cases, we must qualify any statement about differences among levels of one factor (say, factor A) as follows: *There exist differences among levels of factor A, averaged over all levels of factor B.*

We demonstrate this with a brief example. An article in the *Accounting Review* reports the results of a two-way ANOVA on the factors "accounting" and "materiality." The exact nature of the study need not concern us here, as it is very technical. The results of the study include the following.

Source	df	Mean Square	F	Probability
Materiality	2	1.3499	4.5	0.0155
Accounting-materiality interaction	4	.8581	2.9	0.0298

From these partial results, we see that the *p*-values ("probability") are each less than 0.05. Therefore, at the 0.05 level of significance for each of the two tests (separately), we find that there is an interaction effect, and we find a main effect for materiality. We may now conclude that, at the 0.05 level of significance, there are differences among the levels of materiality, *averaged over all levels* of accounting.

The Overall Significance Level

Remember our discussion of the Tukey analysis and its importance in allowing us to conduct a family of tests at a single level of significance. In two-way ANOVA, as we have seen, there is a family of *three tests,* each carried out at a given level of significance. Here the question arises: What is the level of significance of the *set* of three tests? A bound on the probability of making at least one type I error in the three tests is given by *Kimball's inequality.* If the hypothesis test for factor A main effects is carried out at α_1, the hypothesis test for factor B main effects is carried out at α_2, and the hypothesis test for interactions is carried out at α_3, then the level of significance, α, of the three tests together is bounded from above as follows.

> **Kimball's inequality:**
>
> $$\alpha \leq 1 - (1 - \alpha_1)(1 - \alpha_2)(1 - \alpha_3) \tag{9-27}$$

In Example 9–4 we conducted the first two tests—the tests for main effects—at the 0.01 level of significance. We conducted the test for interactions at the 0.05 level. Using equation 9–27, we find that the level of significance of the family of three tests is *at most* $1 - (1 - 0.01)(1 - 0.01)(1 - 0.05) = 0.0689$.

The Tukey Method for Two-Way Analysis

Equation 9–21, the Tukey statistic for pairwise comparisons, is easily extended to two-way ANOVA. We are interested in comparing the levels of a factor once the ANOVA has led us to believe that differences do exist for that factor. The only difference in the Tukey formula is the number of degrees of freedom. In making pairwise comparisons of the levels of factor A, the test statistics are the pairwise differences between the sample means for all levels of factor A, regardless of factor B. For example, the pairwise comparisons of all the mean prices at the three locations in Example 9–4 will be done as follows. We compute the absolute differences of all the pairs of sample means:

$$|\bar{x}_{\text{London}} - \bar{x}_{\text{NY}}| \qquad = |15.1 - 19.6| = 4.5$$
$$|\bar{x}_{\text{Tokyo}} - \bar{x}_{\text{London}}| = |21.4 - 15.1| = 6.3$$
$$|\bar{x}_{\text{NY}} - \bar{x}_{\text{Tokyo}}| \qquad = |19.6 - 21.4| = 1.8$$

Now we compare these differences with the Tukey criterion:

> Tukey criterion for factor A:
>
> $$T = q_\alpha \sqrt{\frac{\text{MSE}}{bn}} \tag{9-28}$$
>
> where the degrees of freedom of the q distribution are now a and $ab(n - 1)$. Note also that MSE is divided by bn.

TABLE 9–10   Three-Way ANOVA Table

Source of Variation	Sum of Squares	Degrees of Freedom	Mean Square	F Ratio
Factor A	SSA	$a-1$	$MSA = \dfrac{SSA}{a-1}$	$F = \dfrac{MSA}{MSE}$
Factor B	SSB	$b-1$	$MSB = \dfrac{SSB}{b-1}$	$F = \dfrac{MSB}{MSE}$
Factor C	SSC	$c-1$	$MSC = \dfrac{SSC}{c-1}$	$F = \dfrac{MSC}{MSE}$
(AB)	SS(AB)	$(a-1)(b-1)$	$MS(AB) = \dfrac{SS(AB)}{(a-1)(b-1)}$	$F = \dfrac{MS(AB)}{MSE}$
(BC)	SS(BC)	$(b-1)(c-1)$	$MS(BC) = \dfrac{SS(BC)}{(b-1)(c-1)}$	$F = \dfrac{MS(BC)}{MSE}$
(AC)	SS(AC)	$(a-1)(c-1)$	$MS(AC) = \dfrac{SS(AC)}{(a-1)(c-1)}$	$F = \dfrac{MS(AC)}{MSE}$
(ABC)	SS(ABC)	$(a-1)(b-1)(c-1)$	$MS(ABC)$	$F = \dfrac{MS(ABC)}{MSE}$
Error	SSE	$abc(n-1)$	MSE	
Total	SST	$abcn-1$		

In Example 9–4 both a and b are 3. The sample size in each cell is $n = 10$. At $\alpha = 0.05$, the Tukey criterion is equal to $(3.4)(\sqrt{102}/\sqrt{30}) = 6.27$. Suppose that the sample mean in New York is 19.6 (hundred thousand dollars), in Tokyo it is 21.4, and in London it is 15.1. Comparing all absolute differences of the sample means leads us to the conclusion that the average prices in London and Tokyo are significantly different; but the average prices in Tokyo and New York are not different, and neither are the average prices in New York and London. The overall significance level of these joint conclusions is $\alpha = 0.05$.

Extension of ANOVA to Three Factors

It is possible to carry out a three-way ANOVA. In such cases, we assume that in addition to a levels of factor A and b levels of factor B, there are c levels of factor C. There are three possible pairwise interactions of factors and one possible triple interaction of factors. These are denoted (AB), (BC), (AC), and (ABC). Table 9–10 is the ANOVA table for three-way analysis.

It is beyond the scope of this book to give examples of three-way ANOVA. However, the extension of two-way analysis to this method is straightforward, and if you should need to carry out such an analysis, Table 9–10 will provide you with all the information you need. Three-factor interactions, (ABC), imply that at least some of the two-factor interactions, (AB), (BC), (AC), are dependent on the level of the third factor.

Two-Way ANOVA with One Observation per Cell

The case of one data point in every cell presents a problem in two-way ANOVA. Can you guess why? (*Hint:* degrees of freedom for error.) Look at Figure 9–20 which shows the layout of the data in a two-way ANOVA with five levels of factor A and four levels of factor B. Note that the sample size in each of the 20 cells is $n = 1$.

FIGURE 9–20   Data Layout in a Two-Way ANOVA with $n = 1$

$n = 1$ (one observation in each of
the $ab = (5)(4) = 20$ cells)

**TABLE 9–11   ANOVA Table for Two-Way Analysis with One Observation per Cell
Assuming No Interactions** between 2 factors

Source of Variation	Sum of Squares	Degrees of Freedom	Mean Square	F Ratio
Factor A	SSA	$a - 1$	$MSA = \dfrac{SSA}{a - 1}$	$F = \dfrac{MSA}{MS(AB)}$
Factor B	SSB	$b - 1$	$MSB = \dfrac{SSB}{b - 1}$	$F = \dfrac{MSB}{MS(AB)}$
"Error"	SS(AB)	$(a - 1)(b - 1)$	$MS(AB) = \dfrac{SS(AB)}{(a - 1)(b - 1)}$	
Total	SST	$ab - 1$		

$\dfrac{a-1}{(a-1)(b-1)}$

$\dfrac{b-1}{(a-1)(b-1)}$

As you may have guessed, there are no degrees of freedom for error! With one observation per cell, $n = 1$; the degrees of freedom for error are $ab(n - 1) = ab(1 - 1) = 0$. This can be seen from Table 9–11. What can we do? If we *believe* that there are no interactions (this assumption cannot be statistically tested when $n = 1$), then our sum of squares SS(AB) is due to error and contains no other information. In such a case, we can use SS(AB) and its associated degrees of freedom, $(a - 1)(b - 1)$, in place of SSE and its degrees of freedom. We can thus conduct the tests for the main effects by dividing MSA by MS(AB) when testing for factor A main effects. The resulting F statistic has $a - 1$ and $(a - 1)(b - 1)$ degrees of freedom. Similarly, when testing for factor B main effects, we divide MSB by MS(AB) and obtain an F statistic with $b - 1$ and $(a - 1)(b - 1)$ degrees of freedom.

Remember that this analysis assumes that there are no interactions between the two factors. Remember also that in statistics it is always desirable to have as much data as possible. Therefore, the two-way ANOVA with one observation per cell is, in itself, of limited use. The idea of two factors and one observation per cell is useful, however, as it brings us closer to the idea of blocking, presented in the next section.

PROBLEMS

9–37. Discuss the context in which Example 9–4 can be analyzed using a random-effects model.

9–38. What are the reasons for conducting a two-way analysis rather than two separate one-way ANOVAs? Explain.

9–39. What are the limitations of two-way ANOVA? What problems may be encountered?

9–40. (This is a hard problem.) Suppose that a limited data set is available. Explain why it is not desirable to increase the number of factors under study (say, four-way ANOVA, five-way ANOVA, and so on)? Give two reasons for this—one of the reasons a statistical one.

9–41. An article about process tracing and brand extension reports the results of a two-way ANOVA with the two factors "brand extension typicality" and "brand breadth." The article reports an F statistic for interaction of the two factors: $F_{(4,139)} = 4.27$.[9] Is there evidence that the two factors interact with each other, as believed by the authors of the article?

9–42. The following table reports salaries, in thousands of dollars per year, for executives in three job types and three locations. Conduct a two-way ANOVA on these data.

	Job		
Location	**Type I**	**Type II**	**Type III**
East	54, 61, 59, 56, 70, 62, 63, 57, 68	48, 50, 49, 60, 54, 52, 49, 55, 53	71, 76, 65, 70, 68, 62, 73, 60, 79
Central	52, 50, 58, 59, 62, 57, 58, 64, 61	44, 49, 54, 53, 51, 60, 55, 47, 50	61, 64, 69, 58, 57, 63, 65, 63, 50
West	63, 67, 68, 72, 68, 75, 62, 65, 70	65, 58, 62, 70, 57, 61, 68, 65, 73	82, 75, 79, 77, 80, 69, 84, 83, 76

9–43. The Neilsen Company, which issues television popularity rating reports, is interested in testing for differences in average viewer satisfaction with morning news, evening news, and late news. The company is also interested in determining whether or not differences exist in average viewer satisfaction with the three main networks, CBS, ABC, and NBC. Nine groups of 50 randomly chosen viewers are assigned to each combination cell, CBS-morning, CBS-evening, . . . , NBC-late. The viewers' satisfaction ratings are recorded. The results are analyzed via two-factor ANOVA, one factor being network and the other factor being news time. Complete the following ANOVA table for this study, and give a full interpretation of the results.

Source of Variation	Sum of Squares	Degrees of Freedom	Mean Square	*F* Ratio
Network	145			
News time	160			
Interaction	240			
Error	6,200			
Total				

---

[9] D. M. Boush and B. Loken, "A Process Tracing Study of Brand Extension Evaluation," *Journal of Marketing Research,* February 1991, p. 21.

9–44. An article reports the results of an analysis of salespersons' performance level as a function of two factors: task difficulty and effort. Included in the article is the following ANOVA table.

Variable	df	F Value	p
Task difficulty	1	0.39	0.5357
Effort	1	53.27	<0.0001
Interaction	1	1.95	0.1649

a. How many levels of task difficulty were studied?
b. How many levels of effort were studied?
c. Are there any significant task difficulty main effects?
d. Are there any significant effort main effects?
e. Are there any significant interactions of the two factors? Explain.

9–45. An article reports the results of a two-way ANOVA on the effects of the two factors—exercise price of an option and the time of expiration of an option—on implied interest rates (the measured variable). Included in the article is the following ANOVA table.

Source of Variance	Degrees of Freedom	Sum of Squares	Mean Square	F
Exercise prices	2	2.866	1.433	.420
Time of expiration	1	16.518	16.518	4.845
Interaction	2	1.315	.658	.193
Explained	5	20.699	4.140	1.214
Residuals (error)	144	490.964	3.409	

a. What is meant by *Explained* in the table, and what is the origin of the information listed under that source?
b. How many levels of exercise price were used?
c. How many levels of time of expiration were used?
d. How large was the total sample size?
e. Assuming an equal number of data points in each cell, how large was the sample in each cell?
f. Are there any exercise price main effects?
g. Are there any time of expiration main effects?
h. Are there any interactions of the two factors?
i. Interpret the findings of this study.
j. Give approximate *p*-values for the tests.
k. In this particular study, what other, equivalent distribution may be used for testing for time of expiration main effects? (*Hint:* df) Why?

9–46. An article in the *Accounting Review* reports analysis of variance results given in the following table.[10] Interpret the results.

---

[10] J. Kennedy, "Debiasing the Curse of Knowledge in Audit Judgement," *The Accounting Review* 70, no. 2 (April 1995), pp. 249–73.

Analysis of Variance—F statistics

Dependent Variable[a]		Estimates		Likelihood Judgments			
		X	Y	XH	XL	YH	YL
Source of Variance	**DF**						
Accountability[b]	1	0.47	1.28	0.00	0.00	3.59*	0.65
Outcome[c]	2	21.97***	8.21***	6.64***	5.50***	7.23***	1.31
Group	1	2.72*	23.98***	1.96	0.32	1.94	28.68***
Accountability × Outcome	2	0.30	0.31	0.20	0.11	0.23	2.41*
Accountability × Group	1	0.00	0.03	1.11	0.11	0.06	0.514
Outcome × Group	2	0.23	1.18	0.14	0.49	1.21	0.60
Account. × Outcome × Group	2	0.08	0.40	0.36	0.95	1.23	0.14
Error	396						
Total	407						

Planned Comparisons	DF			t-statistics			
High vs no outcome	1	2.08**	2.63***	1.54*	3.23***	3.24***	− 1.40
Low vs no outcome	1	4.51***	1.44*	2.15**	.90	.18	1.40*

[a] X and Y refer to the estimates for the 13th quarter's sales for graphs X and Y, respectively, XH, XL, YH, and YL refer to likelihood judgments that 13th quarter sales were at least as high as the high outcome (XH and YH) or as low as the low outcome (XL and YL) indicated by the asterisk on graphs X and Y. Predictions regarding outcome knowledge for X, XH, Y, and YH are high > none > low, while predictions for XL and YL are low > none > high.

[b] Accountable subjects were told before they saw the graphs that they might have to justify their responses.

[c] High and Low outcome conditions saw asterisks higher or lower than the 12th quarter's sales.

***, ** and * indicates statistically significant at $p < 0.01$, 0.05, and 0.10, respectively.

9-8   Blocking Designs

(In this section, we discuss alternatives to the completely randomized design.) We seek special designs for data analysis that will help us reduce the effects of extraneous factors (factors not under study) on the measured variable. That is, we seek to reduce the errors. These designs allow for *restricted randomization* by grouping the experimental units (people, items in our data) into homogeneous groups called **blocks** and then randomizing the treatments within each block.

The first, and most important, blocking design we will discuss is the *randomized complete block design*.

Randomized Complete Block Design

Recall the first part of the Club Med example, Example 9–2, where we were interested only in determining possible differences in average ratings among the five resorts (no attributes factor). Suppose that Club Med can get information about its vacationers' age, sex, marital status, socioeconomic level, etc., and then randomly assign vacationers to the different resorts. The club could form groups of five vacationers each such that the vacationers within each group are similar to one another in age, sex, marital status, etc. Each group of five vacationers is a *block*. Once the blocks are formed, one member from each block is *randomly assigned* to one of the five resorts (Guadeloupe, Martinique, Eleuthera, Paradise Island, or St. Lucia). Thus, the vacationers sent to each resort will comprise a mixture of ages, of males and females, of married and single people, of different socioeconomic levels, etc. The vacationers within each block, however, will be more or less homogeneous.

The vacationers' ratings of the resorts are then analyzed using an ANOVA that utilizes the blocking structure. Since the members of each block are similar to each other (and different from members of other blocks), we expect them to react to similar conditions in similar ways. This brings about a *reduction in the experimental errors.* Why? If we cannot block, it is possible, for example, that the sample of people we get for Eleuthera will happen to be wealthier (or predominantly married, predominantly male, or whatever) and will tend to react less favorably to a resort of this kind than a more balanced sample would react. In such a case, we will have greater experimental error. If, on the other hand, we can *block* and send one member of each homogeneous group of people to each of the resorts and then compare the responses of the block as a whole, we would be more likely to find real differences among the resorts rather than differences among the people. Thus, the errors (differences among people and not among the resorts) are reduced by the blocking design. When all members of every block are randomly assigned to all treatments, such as in this example, our design is called the **randomized complete block design.**

Figure 9–21 shows the formation of blocks in the case of Club Med. We assume that the club is able—for the purpose of a specific study—to randomly assign vacationers to resorts.

The analysis of the results in a randomized complete block design, with a single factor, is very similar to the analysis of two-factor ANOVA with one observation per

FIGURE 9–21   Blocking in the Club Med Example

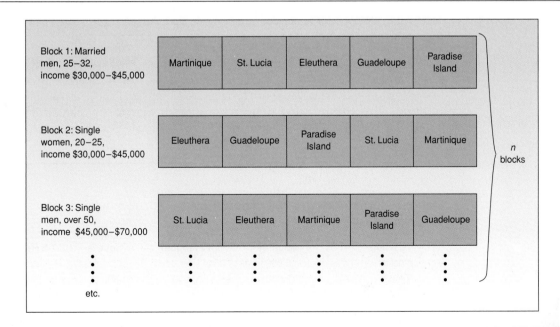

cell (see Table 9–11). Here, one "factor" is the blocks, and the other is the factor of interest (in our example, resorts). The ANOVA table for a randomized complete block design is illustrated in Table 9–12. Compare this table with Table 9–11. There are n blocks of r elements each. We assume that there are no interactions between blocks and treatments; thus, the degrees of freedom for error are $(n - 1)(r - 1)$. The F ratio reported in the table is for use in testing for treatment effects. It is possible to test for block effects with a similar F ratio, although, usually, such a test is of no interest.

As an example, suppose that Club Med did indeed use a blocking design with $n = 10$ blocks. Suppose the results are: SSTR = 3,200, SSBL = 2,800, and SSE = 1,250. Let us conduct the following test.

H_0: The average ratings of the five resorts are equal
H_1: The average ratings of the five resorts are not all equal

We enter the information into the ANOVA table and compute the remaining entries we need and the F statistic value, which has an F distribution with $r - 1$ and $(n - 1)(r - 1)$ degrees of freedom when H_0 is true. We have as a result Table 9–13.

We see that the value of the F statistic with 4 and 36 degrees of freedom is 23.04. This value exceeds, by far, the critical point of the F distribution with 4 and 36 degrees of freedom at $\alpha = 0.01$, which is 3.89. The p-value is, therefore, much smaller than 0.01. We thus reject the null hypothesis and conclude that there is evidence that not all resorts are rated equally, on the average. By blocking the respondents into homogeneous groups, Club Med was able to reduce the experimental errors.

You can probably find many examples where blocking can be useful. For example, recall the situation of problem 9–18. Three prototype airplanes were tested on different flight routes to determine whether differences existed in the average range of the planes. A design that would clearly reduce the experimental errors would be a blocking design where all planes are flown over the same routes, at the same time, under the same weather conditions, etc. That is, fly all three planes using each of the sample

TABLE 9–12   ANOVA Table for Randomized Complete Block Design

Source of Variation	Sum of Squares	Degrees of Freedom	Mean Square	F Ratio
Blocks	SSBL	$n - 1$	MSBL	
Treatments	SSTR	$r - 1$	MSTR	$F = \dfrac{\text{MSTR}}{\text{MSE}}$
Error	SSE	$(n - 1)(r - 1)$	MSE	
Total		$nr - 1$		

TABLE 9–13   Club Med Blocking Design ANOVA Table

Source of Variation	Sum of Squares	Degrees of Freedom	Mean Square	F Ratio
Blocks	2,800	9	311.11	
Resorts	3,200	4	800.00	23.04
Error	1,250	36	34.72	
Total	7,250			

route conditions. A block in this case is a route condition, and the three "treatments" are the three planes. A numerical example of this problem is given in section 9–9.

A special case of the randomized complete block design is the **repeated measures design.** In this design, each experimental unit (person or item) is assigned to *all* treatments in a randomly selected order. Suppose that a taste test is to be conducted, where four different flavors are to be rated by consumers. In a repeated measures design, each person in the random sample of consumers is assigned to taste all four flavors, in a randomly determined order, independent from all other consumers. A block in this design is one consumer. We demonstrate the repeated measures design with the following example.

Weintraub Entertainment is a new movie company backed by financial support from the Coca-Cola Company. For one of the company's first movies, the director wanted to find the best actress for the leading role. "Best" naturally means the actress who would get the highest average viewer rating. The director was considering three candidates for the role and had each candidate act in a particular test scene. A random group of 40 viewers was selected, and each member of the group watched the same scene enacted by each of the three actresses. The order of actresses was randomly and independently chosen for each viewer. Ratings were on a scale of 0 to 100. The results were analyzed using a block design ANOVA, where each viewer constituted a block of treatments. The results of the analysis are given in Table 9–14. Figure 9–22 shows the layout of the data in this example. Analyze the results. Are all three actresses equally rated, on the average?

EXAMPLE 9-5

The test statistic has an F distribution with 2 and 78 degrees of freedom when the following null hypothesis is true.

H_0: There are no differences among average population ratings of the three actresses

SOLUTION

TABLE 9-14 **The ANOVA Table for Example 9-5**

Source of Variation	Sum of Squares	Degrees of Freedom	Mean Square	F Ratio
Blocks	2,750	39 (40−1)	70.51	
Treatments	2,640	2 (3−1)	1,320.00	12.93
Error	7,960	78 40−1(3−1)	102.05	
Total	13,350	119 40(3)−1		

FIGURE 9-22 **Data Layout for Example 9-5**

	Randomized Viewing Order		
First sampled person	Actress B	Actress C	Actress A
Second sampled person	Actress C	Actress B	Actress A
Third sampled person	Actress A	Actress C	Actress B
Fourth sampled person etc.	Actress B	Actress A	Actress C

Check the appropriate critical point for $\alpha = 0.01$ in Appendix C, Table 5 to see that this null hypothesis is rejected in favor of the alternative that differences do exist and that not all three actresses are equally highly rated, on the average. Since the null hypothesis is rejected, there is place for further analysis to determine which actress rates best. Such analysis can be done using the Tukey method or another method of further analysis.

In cases where a repeated measures design is used on *rankings* of several treatments—here, if we had asked each viewer to rank the three actresses as 1, 2, or 3, rather than rate them on a 0 to 100 scale—there is another method of analysis. This method is the *Friedman test,* discussed in Chapter 14.

PROBLEMS

9–47. Explain the advantages of blocking designs.

9–48. An article on emerging markets reports the findings on returns on equity, bonds, and preferred stock.[11] Data are available on a random sample of firms that issue all three types of instruments. How would you use blocking in this study, aimed at finding which instrument gives the highest average return?

9–49. Suggest a blocking design for the situation in problem 9–19. Explain.

9–50. Suggest a blocking design for the situation in problem 9–21. Explain.

9–51. Is it feasible to design a study utilizing blocks for the situation in problem 9–20? Explain.

9–52. Suggest a blocking design for the situation in problem 9–23.

9–53. How would you design a block ANOVA for the two-way analysis of the situation described in problem 9–42? Which ANOVA method is appropriate for the analysis?

9–54. What important assumption about the relation between blocks and treatments is necessary for carrying out a block design ANOVA?

9–55. Public concern has recently focused on the fact that although Americans often try to lose weight, statistics show that the general population has gained weight, on the average, during the last 10 years. A researcher hired by a weight-loss organization is interested in determining whether three kinds of artificial sweetener currently on the market are approximately equally effective in reducing weight. As part of a study, a random sample of 300 people is chosen. Each person is given one of the three sweeteners to use for a week, and the number of pounds lost is recorded. To reduce experimental errors, the people in the sample are divided into 100 groups of three persons each. The three people in every group all weigh about the same at the beginning of the test week and are of the same sex and approximately the same age. The results are SSBL = 2,312, SSTR = 3,233, and SSE = 12,386. Are all three sweeteners equally effective in reducing weight? How confident are you of your conclusion? Discuss the merits of blocking in this case as compared with the completely randomized design.

9–56. IBM Corporation has been retraining many of its employees to assume marketing positions. As part of this effort, the company wanted to test four possible methods of training marketing personnel to determine if at least one of the methods was better than the others. Four groups of 70 employees each were assigned to the four training methods. The employees were pretested for marketing ability and grouped into groups of four, each group constituting a block with approximately equal prior ability. Then the four employees in each group were randomly assigned to the four training methods and retested after completion of the three-week training session. The differences between their initial scores and final scores were computed. The

---

[11] P. Misra, "Fund Watch," *Money,* May, 1995. p. 61.

results were analyzed using a block design ANOVA. The results of the analysis include: SSTR = 9,875, SSBL = 1,445, and SST = 22,364. Are all four training methods equally effective? Explain.

9-9   Using the Computer

Throughout this chapter, we have emphasized the important role that computers play in the implementation of analysis of variance. All advanced statistical software packages have ANOVA capabilities. The output of such programs includes the ANOVA table, and some packages provide more information. The MINITAB package is capable of carrying out one- and two-way ANOVA and gives individual confidence intervals for treatment means. Recent releases of MINITAB (8 or later) also provide Tukey pairwise comparisons. We demonstrate this in Example 9–6.

EXAMPLE 9-6

The following data set lists the sales resulting from the use of three different sales methods. We want to test the null hypothesis that all three sales methods lead to the same average sales volume, versus the alternative that they do not. The following data are entered into C1, and the levels (populations), coded as 1, 2, and 3, are entered in order into C2.

METHOD A	METHOD B	METHOD C	METHOD A	METHOD B	METHOD C
21	27	18	27	32	18
20	28	17	29	35	18
22	22	19	19	37	22
25	29	24	20	28	21
24	32	20	23	27	21
19	37	17	18	32	17
26	33	19	27	31	21
18	34	22	22	26	20
24	28	20	23	35	19
25	29	21	24	29	18
25	29	24	20	34	23

SOLUTION

Following are the MINITAB command and subcommand necessary for the analysis.

```
ONEWAY   C1, C2;
TUKEY    0.05.
```

The MINITAB output for this problem is shown in Figure 9–23. The output includes an ANOVA table for this problem, a table of the sample means and standard deviations, a picture of individual 95% confidence intervals for the three population means, and the Tukey comparisons. We note that the MINITAB command AOVONEWAY (data in columns C1, C2, etc.) will also carry out an ANOVA, but cannot be followed by the Tukey subcommand.

9-10   Summary and Review of Terms

In this chapter, we discussed a method of making statistical comparisons of more than two population means. The method is **analysis of variance,** often referred to as **ANOVA.** We defined **treatments** as the populations under study. A set of treatments is a **factor.** We defined **one-factor ANOVA,** also called one-way ANOVA, as the test for

FIGURE 9–23   MINITAB Output for Example 9–6

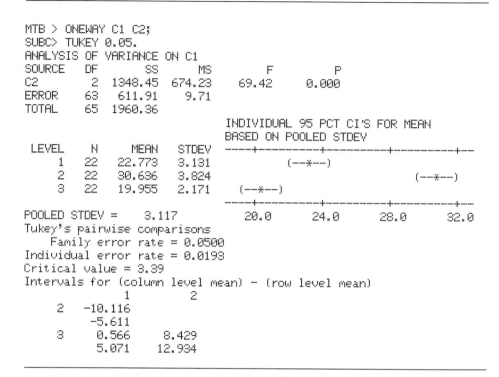

```
MTB > ONEWAY C1 C2;
SUBC> TUKEY 0.05.
ANALYSIS OF VARIANCE ON C1
SOURCE  DF      SS      MS       F       P
C2       2  1348.45  674.23   69.42   0.000
ERROR   63   611.91    9.71
TOTAL   65  1960.36
                            INDIVIDUAL 95 PCT CI'S FOR MEAN
                            BASED ON POOLED STDEV
 LEVEL    N    MEAN   STDEV  ----+---------+---------+---------+--
     1   22  22.773   3.131            (--*--)
     2   22  30.636   3.824                              (--*--)
     3   22  19.955   2.171    (--*--)
                            ----+---------+---------+---------+--
POOLED STDEV =    3.117       20.0      24.0      28.0      32.0
Tukey's pairwise comparisons
    Family error rate = 0.0500
Individual error rate = 0.0193
Critical value = 3.39
Intervals for (column level mean) - (row level mean)
                  1         2
     2   -10.116
          -5.611
     3     0.566     8.429
           5.071    12.934
```

equality of means of treatments belonging to one factor. We defined a **two-factor ANOVA**, also called two-way ANOVA, as a set of three hypothesis tests: (1) a test for main effects for one of the two factors, (2) a test for main effects for the second factor, and (3) a test for the **interaction** of the two factors. We defined the **fixed-effects** model and the **random effects** model. We discussed one method of further analysis to follow an ANOVA once the ANOVA leads to rejection of the null hypothesis of equal treatment means. The method is the **Tukey HSD procedure.** We also mentioned two other alternative methods of further analysis. We discussed experimental design in the ANOVA context. Among these designs, we mentioned **blocking** as a method of reducing experimental errors in ANOVA by grouping similar items. We also discussed the **repeated measures design.**

ADDITIONAL PROBLEMS

9–57.   An enterprising art historian recently started a new business: the production of walking-tour audiotapes for use by those visiting major cities. She originally produced tapes for eight cities: Paris, Rome, London, Florence, Jerusalem, Washington, New York, and New Haven. A test was carried out to determine whether or not all eight tapes (featuring different aspects of different cities) were equally appealing to potential users. A random sample of 160 prospective tourists was selected, 20 per city. Each person evaluated the tape he or she was given on a scale of 0 to 100. The results were analyzed using one-way ANOVA and included: SSTR = 7,102, SSE = 10,511. Are all eight tapes equally appealing, on the average? What can you say about the p-value?

9–58.   NAMELAB® is a San Francisco–based company that uses linguistic analysis and computers to invent catchy names for new products. The company is credited with the invention of Acura, Compaq, Sentra, and other names of successful products. Naturally, statistical analysis plays an important role in choosing the final name for a product. In choosing a name for a compact disc player, NAMELAB is considering four names and uses analysis of variance for determining whether or not all four names are equally liked, on the average, by the public. The results include: $n_1 = 32$, $n_2 = 30$, $n_3 = 28$, $n_4 = 41$, SSTR = 4,537, and MSE = 412. Are all four names approximately equally liked, on the average? What is the approximate p-value?

9–59. An article about gender differences in marketing reports the results of an analysis of variance aimed at assessing whether there was a taste cue positioning effect, a gender effect, and an interaction. The reported results were as follows.[12]

Taste cue positioning: $F_{(1,48)} = 4.79$

Gender: $F_{(1,48)} = 6.93$

Taste cue positioning by gender interaction: $F_{(1,48)} = 8.41$

Interpret the results fully and describe them in a memo to the research director.

9–60. As software for microcomputers becomes more and more sophisticated, the element of time becomes more crucial. Consequently, manufacturers of software packages need to work on reducing the time required for running application programs. Speed of execution also depends on the computer used. A two-way ANOVA is suggested for testing whether or not differences exist among three software packages, and among four microcomputers made by NEC, Toshiba, Kaypro, and Apple, with respect to the average time for performing a certain analysis. The results include SS(software) = 77,645, SS(computer) = 54,521, SS(interaction) = 88,699, and SSE = 434,557. The analysis used a sample of 60 runs of each software package/computer combination. Complete an ANOVA table for this analysis, carry out the tests, and state your conclusions.

9–61. Recently, the competition between Kodak and Fuji has been intensifying. Kodak has reportedly been analyzing films made by Fuji to determine the secrets of Fuji's bright colors. As part of an analysis, a random sample of five pieces of film by Kodak were developed by a process we will denote as process A, another random sample of five Kodak films were developed by process B, and a third sample by process C. The same was done with three sets of five pieces of film by Fuji. Also, as a third comparison for control, three sets of five pieces of film by Agfa were developed. All the developed films were photochemically tested for color brightness. The results were analyzed by two-way ANOVA aimed at determining whether color brightness differences existed among the three developing processes and among the three kinds of film. Kodak was also interested in finding out whether or not interactions existed—that is, whether one type of film, say, Agfa, resulted in lower-than-expected color brightness when developed by a particular process. The results are given in the following table (the higher the score, the brighter the colors). Use a computer to carry out the two-way ANOVA. State your conclusions.

	Process		
Film	**A**	**B**	**C**
Kodak	32, 34, 31, 30, 37	26, 29, 27, 30, 31	28, 28, 27, 30, 32
Fuji	43, 41, 44, 50, 47	32, 38, 38, 40, 36	32, 32, 36, 35, 34
Agfa	23, 24, 25, 21, 26	27, 30, 25, 25, 27	25, 27, 26, 22, 25

9–62. The following table summarizes results of ANOVAs of three separate "dependent variables." For each variable, a four-factor ANOVA is carried out. The table reports p-values. Interpret all the results in the table.

---

[12] J. Meyers-Levy and B. Sternthal, "Gender Differences in the Use of Message Cues and Judgments," *Journal of Marketing Research*, February, 1991, p. 91.

	Dependent Variable		
Effect Source	RDIFF	BIAS	BE
METH: factor scoring approach	.008	.009	.457
UNIQ: Factor uniqueness	.474	.510	.012
SE: assumed obliqueness relative to true obliqueness	.106	.086	.086
P: number of observed variances	.106	.091	.102
METH $\times$ UNIQ	.002	.006	.078
METH $\times$ SE	.010	.302	.110
METH $\times$ P	.150	.112	.125
UNIQ $\times$ SE	.206	.087	.210
UNIQ $\times$ P	.001	.176	.008
SE $\times$ P	.210	.011	.002

Source: Reproduced by permission from J. Lastovicka and K. Thamodaran, "Common Factor Score Estimates," *Journal of Marketing Research*, February, 1991, p. 109.

9–63. Among the young affluent professionals in America, there is a growing new demand for exotic pets. The most popular pets are the Shiba Inu dog breed, Rottweilers, Persian cats, and Maine coons. Prices for these pets vary and depend on supply and demand. A breeder of exotic pets wants to know whether these four pets fetch the same average prices, whether prices for these exotic pets are higher in some geographic areas than in others, and whether there are any interactions—one or more of the four pets being more favored in one location than in others. Prices for 10 of each of these pets at four randomly chosen locations around the country are recorded and analyzed. The results are SS(pet) = 22,245, SS(location) = 34,551, SS(interaction) = 31,778, and SSE = 554,398. Are there any pet main effects? Are there any location main effects? Are there any pet-location interactions? Explain your findings.

9–64. Analysis of variance has long been used in providing evidence of the effectiveness of pharmaceutical drugs. Such evidence is required before the FDA will allow a drug to be marketed. In a recent test of the effectiveness of a new sleeping pill, three groups of 25 patients each were given the following treatments. One group was given the drug, the second group was given a placebo, and the third group was given no treatment at all. The number of minutes it took each person to fall asleep was recorded. The results are as follows.

Drug group: 12, 17, 34, 11, 5, 42, 18, 27, 2, 37, 50, 32, 12, 27, 21, 10, 4, 33, 63, 22, 41,19, 28, 29, 8

Placebo group: 44, 32, 28, 30, 22, 12, 3, 12, 42, 13, 27, 54, 56, 32, 37, 28, 22, 22, 24, 9, 20, 4, 13, 42, 67

No-treatment group: 32, 33, 21, 12, 15, 14, 55, 67, 72, 1, 44, 60, 36, 38, 49, 66, 89, 63, 23, 6, 9, 56, 28, 39, 59

Use a computer (or hand calculations) to determine whether or not the drug is effective. What about the placebo? Give differences in average effectiveness, if any exist.

9–65. A more efficient experiment than the one described in problem 9–64 was carried out to determine whether or not a sleeping pill was effective. Each person in a random sample of 30 people was given the three treatments: drug, placebo, nothing. The order in which these treatments were administered was randomly chosen for each person in the sample.

a. Explain why this experiment is more efficient than the one described for the same investigation in problem 9–64. What is the name of the experimental design used here? Are there any limitations to the present method of analysis?

b. The results of the analysis include SSTR = 44,572, SSBL = 38,890, and SSE = 112,672. Carry out the analysis, and state your conclusions. Use $\alpha = 0.05$.

9–66. Three new enhanced-definition television models are compared.[13] The distances (in miles) over which a clear signal is received in random trials for each of the models are given below.

General Instrument: 111, 121, 134, 119, 125, 120, 122, 138, 115, 123, 130, 124, 132, 127, 130

Philips: 120, 121, 122, 123, 120, 132, 119, 116, 125, 123, 116, 118, 120, 131, 115

Zenith: 109, 100, 110, 102, 118, 117, 105, 104, 100, 108, 128, 117, 101, 102, 110

Carry out a complete analysis of variance, and report your results in the form of a memorandum. State your hypotheses and your conclusions. Do you believe there are differences among the three models? If so, where do they lie?

9–67. A professor of food chemistry at the University of Wisconsin has recently developed a new system for keeping frozen foods crisp and fresh: coating them with watertight, edible film. The Pillsbury Company wants to test whether the new product is tasty. The company collects a random sample of consumers who are given the following three treatments, in a randomly chosen order for each consumer: regular frozen pizza, frozen pizza packaged in a plastic bag, and the new edible-coating frozen pizza (all reheated, of course). Fifty people take part in the study, and the results include $SSTR = 128,899$, $SSBL = 538,217$, $SSE = 42,223,987$. (These are ANOVA results for taste scores on a 0–1000 scale.) Based on these results, are all three frozen pizzas perceived as equally tasty or not?

9–68. Give the statistical reason for the fact that a one-way ANOVA with only two treatments is equivalent to a two-sample t test discussed in Chapter 8.

9–69. Following is a computer output of an analysis of variance based on randomly chosen rents in four cities. Do you believe that the average rent is equal in the four cities studied? Explain.

```
MTB > AOVONEWAY C1, C2, C3, C4
ANALYSIS OF VARIANCE

SOURCE      DF       SS        MS          F
FACTOR       3     37402     12467       1.76
ERROR       44    311303      7075
TOTAL       47    348706
```

9–70. Write several paragraphs explaining the meaning of the following excerpt.[14]
Toy awareness level. A two-way ANOVA was conducted with two levels of language and two levels of income as independent factors and toy awareness level as the dependent measure. As hypothesized, English-speaking children were significantly more aware of the toys than were French-speaking children ($F = 400.47$, $p < 0.0001$). The latter were able to recognize an average of only 8.73 toys correctly, not significantly more than the one in three chance level (i.e., 6.67 toys). In comparison, English-speaking children were able to identify an average of 15.44 toys. A significant income effect is found ($F = 7.08$, $p < 0.01$). Upper-middle income children recognized more toys (mean = 11.94) than low-income children (mean = 9.94). Contrary to the hypothesis, no significant language by income interaction is found ($F < 1$). The likely reason is a ceiling effect, as all English-speaking children had very high scores. (Of the few mistakes made by English-speaking children, most consisted of boys misidentifying a few girls' toys, and vice versa.)

---

[13] A. Kupfer, "The U.S. Wins One in High-Tech TV," *Fortune*, April 8, 1991, p. 63.

[14] Reproduced by permission from M. Goldberg, "Assessing the Effectiveness of TV Advertising Directed at Children," *Journal of Marketing Research*, November, 1990, p. 450.

9–71. Interpret the following computer output.

```
ANALYSIS OF VARIANCE ON SALES
  SOURCE   DF      SS       MS        F        P
  STORE     2  1017.33   508.67    156.78    0.000
  ERROR    15    48.67     3.24
  TOTAL    17  1066.00
                                  INDIVIDUAL 95 PCT CI'S FOR MEAN
                                  BASED ON POOLED STDEV
  LEVEL     N     MEAN    STDEV   -+---------+---------+---------+-----
      1     6   53.667    1.862                 (-*--)
      2     6   67.000    1.673                                (--*-)
      3     6   49.333    1.862        (-*-)
                                  -+---------+---------+---------+-----
  POOLED STDEV = 1.801            48.0      54.0      60.0      66.0
```

Case 9   NEW COKE, OLD COKE, AND PEPSI

*I*n April 1985, the Coca-Cola Company announced that it would discontinue making its main brand of soft drink, a product the company had been making for 99 years. Instead, the company planned to market a drink based on a new formula. Thus, new Coke was born. Within three months, however, it became apparent that the switch to new Coke was one of the biggest marketing mistakes ever made. The Coca-Cola Company had no choice but to reintroduce the original formula of Coke, under the new name Coca-Cola Classic. In the process, the company's image was tarnished, and its distributors now had to deal with two Cokes.

In 1987, two years after the birth of new Coke and the new-old Coke Classic, a New York marketing research firm conducted a study to determine consumer preferences for the three brands: new Coke, Coke Classic, and Pepsi. The purpose of the study was to determine how well the two Cokes were selling vis-à-vis their competitor. Although Pepsi was known to sell more in supermarkets, Coke was believed to have a wide lead over Pepsi in vending machine sales. As part of the analysis, the researchers wanted to find out whether the three brands sold about equally well, on average, in public buildings that had both a Coke machine (selling both Cokes) and a Pepsi machine. A random sample of nine public buildings in Manhattan fitting the requirements was selected. The data (in number of cans sold over a given period of time) are as follows.

Building	1	2	3	4	5	6	7	8	9
New Coke	3	1	23	11	8	31	28	3	4
Coke Classic	8	9	27	27	29	44	16	8	7
Pepsi	9	6	18	20	10	26	21	0	9

Analyze the data. Discuss any assumptions you are making. Discuss your method of solution. Present the findings, and state your conclusions. What are the advantages of the method used? What are the limitations of the analysis, and how can the study be improved? How useful are the results? Explain. Note that by the mid-1990s New Coke has become extinct, and the Coca-Cola Company is back to making only its old product.

10

SIMPLE LINEAR REGRESSION AND CORRELATION

1 0 – 1 I N T R O D U C T I O N

n 1855, a 33-year-old Englishman settled down to a life of leisure in London after several years of travel throughout Europe and Africa. The boredom brought about by a comfortable life induced him to write, and his first book was, natu-

Continued

rally, *The Art of Travel*. As his intellectual curiosity grew, he shifted his interests to science and many years later published a paper on heredity, *Natural Inheritance* (1889). He reported his discovery that sizes of seeds of sweet pea plants appeared to "revert," or "regress," to the mean size in successive generations. He also reported results of a study of the relationship between heights of fathers and the heights of their sons. A straight line was fit to the data pairs: height of father versus height of son. Here, too, he found a "regression to mediocrity": the heights of the sons represented a movement away from their fathers, toward the average height. The man was Sir Francis Galton, a cousin of Charles Darwin. We credit him with the idea of statistical regression.

While most applications of regression analysis may have little to do with the "regression to the mean" discovered by Galton, the term **regression** remains. It now refers to the statistical technique of modeling the relationship between variables. In this chapter on **simple linear regression,** we model the relationship between two variables: a **dependent variable,** denoted by *Y*, and an **independent variable,** denoted by *X*. The model we use is a *straight-line relationship* between *X* and *Y*. When we model the relationship between the dependent variable *Y* and a set of several independent variables, or when the assumed relationship between *Y* and *X* is curved and requires the use of more terms in the model, we use a technique called *multiple regression*. This technique will be discussed in the next chapter.

Figure 10–1 is a general example of simple linear regression: fitting a straight line to describe the relationship between two variables, *X* and *Y*. The points on the graph are randomly chosen observations of the two variables, *X* and *Y*, and the straight line describes the general *movement* in the data—an increase in *Y* corresponding to an increase in *X*. An inverse straight-line relationship is also possible, consisting of a general decrease in *Y* as *X* increases (in such cases, the slope of the line is negative).

Regression analysis is one of the most important and widely used statistical techniques and has many applications in business and economics. A firm may be interested in estimating the relationship between advertising and sales (one of the most important topics of research in the field of marketing). Over a short range of values—when advertising is not yet overdone, giving diminishing returns—the relationship between advertising and sales may be well approximated by a straight line. The *X* variable in Figure 10–1 could denote advertising expenditure, and the *Y* variable could stand for the resulting sales for the same period. The data points in this case would be pairs of observations of the form $x_1 = \$75,570$, $y_1 = 134,679$ units; $x_2 = \$83,090$, $y_2 = 151,664$ units; etc. That is, the first month the firm spent $75,570 on advertising, and sales for the month were 134,679 units; the second month the company spent $83,090 on advertising, with resulting sales of 151,664 units for that month, and so on for the entire set of available data.

The data pairs, values of *X* paired with corresponding values of *Y*, are the points shown in a sketch of the data (such as Figure 10–1). A sketch of data on two variables is called a **scatter plot.** In addition to the scatter plot, Figure 10–1 shows the straight line believed to best show how the general trend of increasing sales corresponds, in this example, to increasing advertising expenditures. This chapter will teach you how to find the best line to fit a data set and how to use the line once you have found it.

Although, in reality, our sample may consist of all available information on the two variables under study, we always assume that our data set constitutes a random sample of observations from a population of possible pairs of values of *X* and *Y*. Incidentally, in our hypothetical advertising-sales example, we assume that there is no

FIGURE 10–1 Simple Linear Regression

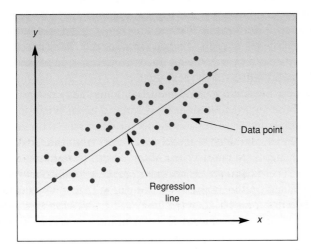

carryover effect of advertising from month to month; every month's sales depend only on that month's level of advertising. Other common examples of the use of simple linear regression in business and economics are the modeling of the relationship between job performance (the dependent variable Y) and extent of training (the independent variable X); the relationship between returns on a stock (Y) and the riskiness of the stock (X); and the relationship between company profits (Y) and the state of the economy (X).

Model Building

Like the analysis of variance, both simple linear regression and multiple regression are *statistical models*. Recall that a statistical model is a set of mathematical formulas and assumptions that describe a real-world situation. We would like our model to explain as much as possible about the process underlying our data. However, due to the uncertainty inherent in all real-world situations, our model will probably not explain everything, and we will always have some remaining errors. The errors are due to unknown outside factors that affect the process generating our data.

A good statistical model is *parsimonious,* which means that it uses as few mathematical terms as possible to describe the real situation. The model captures the systematic behavior of the data, leaving out the factors that are nonsystematic and cannot be foreseen or predicted—the errors. The idea of a good statistical model is illustrated in Figure 10–2. The errors, denoted by ϵ, constitute the random component in the model. In a sense, the statistical model breaks down the data into a nonrandom, systematic component, which can be described by a formula, and a purely random component.

How do we deal with the errors? This is where probability theory comes in. Since our model, we hope, captures everything systematic in the data, the remaining random errors are probably due to a large number of minor factors that we cannot trace. We assume that the random errors ϵ are *normally distributed.* If we have a properly

**FIGURE 10–2
A Statistical Model**

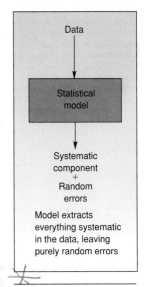

constructed model, the resulting observed errors will have an average of zero (although few, if any, will actually equal zero), and they should also be *independent* of each other. We note that the assumption of a normal distribution of the errors is not absolutely necessary in the regression model. The assumption is made so that we can carry out statistical hypothesis tests using the F and t distributions. The only necessary assumption is that the errors ϵ have mean zero and a constant variance σ^2 and that they be uncorrelated with each other. In the next section, we describe the simple linear regression model. We now present a general model-building methodology.

First, we propose a particular model to describe a given situation. For example, we may propose a simple linear regression model for describing the relationship between two variables. Then we estimate the model parameters from the random sample of data we have. The next step is to consider the observed errors resulting from the fit of the model to the data. These observed errors, called **residuals,** represent the information in the data not explained by the model. For example, in the ANOVA model discussed in Chapter 9, the within-group variation (leading to SSE and MSE) is due to the residuals. If the residuals are found to contain some nonrandom, *systematic* component, we reevaluate our proposed model and, if possible, adjust it to incorporate the systematic component found in the residuals; or we may have to discard the model and try another. When we believe that model residuals contain nothing more than pure randomness, we use the model for its intended purpose: *prediction* of a variable, *control* of a variable, or the *explanation* of the relationships among variables.

In the advertising-sales example, once the regression model has been estimated and found to be appropriate, the firm may be able to use the model for predicting sales for a given level of advertising within the range of values studied. Using the model, the firm may also be able to control its sales by setting the level of advertising expenditure. The model may also help explain the effect of advertising on sales within the range of values studied. Figure 10–3 shows the usual steps of building a statistical model. ∎

FIGURE 10-3   Steps in Building a Statistical Model

10-2 The Simple Linear Regression Model

Recall from algebra that the equation of a straight line is $Y = A + BX$, where A is the Y-intercept and B is the slope of the line. In simple linear regression, we model the relationship between two variables, X and Y, as a straight line. Therefore, our model must contain two parameters: an intercept parameter and a slope parameter. The usual notation for the **population intercept** is β_0, and the notation for the **population slope** is β_1. If we include the error term, ϵ, the population regression model is given in equation 10–1.

> The population simple linear regression model:
> $$Y = \beta_0 + \beta_1 X + \epsilon \qquad (10\text{--}1)$$
> where Y is the dependent variable, the variable we wish to explain or predict; X is the independent variable, also called the *predictor* variable; and ϵ is the error term, the only random component in the model and, thus, the only source of randomness in Y.

The model parameters are as follows.

β_0 is the Y-intercept of the straight line given by $Y = \beta_0 + \beta_1 X$ (the line does not contain the error term).

β_1 is the slope of the line $Y = \beta_0 + \beta_1 X$.

The simple linear regression model of equation 10–1 is composed of two components: a nonrandom component, which is the line itself, and a purely random component—the error term, ϵ. This is shown in Figure 10–4. The nonrandom part of the model, the straight line, is the equation for the *mean of Y, given X*. We denote the conditional mean of Y, given X, by $E(Y \mid X)$. Thus, if the model is correct, the *average* value of Y for a given value of X falls right *on* the regression line. The equation for the mean of Y, given X, is given as equation 10–2.

> The conditional mean of Y:
> $$E(Y \mid X) = \beta_0 + \beta_1 X \qquad (10\text{--}2)$$

FIGURE 10-4
Simple Linear Regression Model

$$Y = \underbrace{\beta_0 + \beta_1 X}_{} + \underbrace{\varepsilon}_{}$$

Nonrandom component: straight line   Random error

Comparing equations 10–1 and 10–2, we see that our model says that each value of Y comprises the average Y for the given value of X (this is the straight line), plus a random error. We will sometimes use the simplified notation $E(Y)$ for the line, remembering that this is the *conditional* mean of Y, for a given value of X. As X increases, the average population value of Y also increases, assuming a positive slope of the line (or decreases, if the slope is negative). The *actual* population value of Y is equal to the average Y conditional on X, plus a random error, ϵ. We thus have, for a given value of X,

actual
$$Y = \text{Average } Y \text{ for given } X + \text{Error} \quad \text{\Large ✳}$$

Figure 10–5 shows the population regression model.

FIGURE 10-5   Population Regression Line

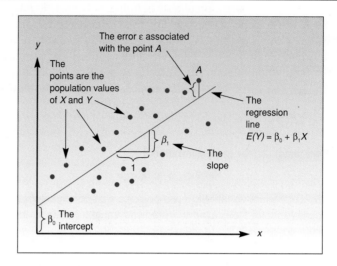

We now state the assumptions of the simple linear regression model.

Model assumptions:

1. The relationship between X and Y is a straight-line relationship.

2. The values of the independent variable X are assumed fixed (not random); the only randomness in the values of Y comes from the error term, ϵ.

3. The errors, ϵ, are normally distributed with mean 0 and a constant variance σ^2. The errors are uncorrelated (not related) with each other in successive observations.[1] *They should be independent of each other*

In symbols: $\epsilon \sim N(0, \sigma^2)$ (10–3)

FIGURE 10-6 Distributional Assumptions of the Linear Regression Model

Figure 10–6 shows the distributional assumptions of the errors of the simple linear regression model. The population regression errors are normally distributed about the population regression line, with mean zero and equal variance. (The errors are equally spread about the regression line; the error variance does not increase or decrease as X increases.)

The simple linear regression model applies only if the true relationship between the two variables X and Y is a straight-line relationship. If the relationship is curved (*curvilinear*), then we need to use the more involved methods of the next chapter. In Figure 10–7, we show various relationships between two variables. Some are straight-line relationships that can be modeled by simple linear regression, and others are not.

So far, we have described the population model, that is, the assumed true relationship between the two variables X and Y. Our interest is focused on this unknown

---

[1] The idea of statistical *correlation* will be discussed in detail in section 10–5. In the case of the regression errors, we assume that successive errors $\epsilon_1, \epsilon_2, \epsilon_3, \ldots$ are uncorrelated: they are not related with each other; there is no trend, no joint movement in successive errors. Incidentally, the assumption of zero correlation together with the assumption of a normal distribution of the errors implies the assumption that the errors are independent of each other. Independence implies noncorrelation, but noncorrelation does not imply independence, except in the case of a normal distribution (this is a technical point).

FIGURE 10–7 Some Possible Relationships between *X* and *Y*

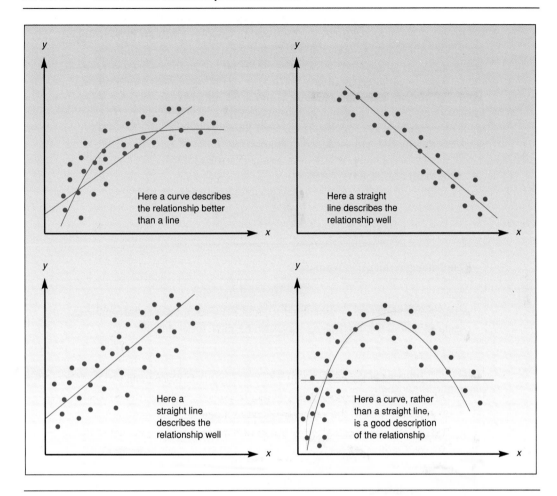

Here a curve describes the relationship better than a line

Here a straight line describes the relationship well

Here a straight line describes the relationship well

Here a curve, rather than a straight line, is a good description of the relationship

population relationship, and we want to *estimate* it using sample information. We obtain a random sample of observations on the two variables, and we estimate the regression model parameters, β_0 and β_1, from this sample. This is done by the *method of least squares,* which is discussed in the next section.

PROBLEMS

10–1. What is a statistical model?

10–2. What are the steps of statistical model building?

10–3. What are the assumptions of the simple linear regression model?

10–4. Define the parameters of the simple linear regression model.

10–5. What is the conditional mean of *Y*, given *X*?

10–6. What are the uses of a regression model?

10–7. What is the purpose and meaning of the error term in regression?

10–8. Give examples of business situations where you believe a straight-line relationship exists between two variables. What would be the uses of a regression model in each of these situations?

10-3   Estimation: The Method of Least Squares

We want to find good estimates of the regression parameters, β_0 and β_1. Remember the properties of good estimators, discussed in Chapter 5. Unbiasedness and efficiency are among these properties. A method that will give us good estimates of the regression coefficients is the **method of least squares.** The method of least squares gives us the *best linear unbiased estimators* (BLUE) of the regression parameters, β_0 and β_1. These estimators are both unbiased and have the lowest variance of all possible unbiased estimators of the regression parameters. These properties of the least-squares estimators are specified by a well-known theorem, the *Gauss-Markov theorem.* We denote the least-squares estimators by b_0 and b_1.

The least-squares estimators:

$$b_0 \xrightarrow{\text{estimates}} \beta_0$$
$$b_1 \xrightarrow{\text{estimates}} \beta_1$$

The estimated regression equation:

$$Y = b_0 + b_1 X + e \qquad (10\text{-}4)$$

where b_0 estimates β_0, b_1 estimates β_1, and e stands for the observed errors—the residuals from fitting the line $b_0 + b_1 X$ to the data set of n points

In terms of the data, equation 10–4 can be written with the subscript i to signify each particular data point:

$$y_i = b_0 + b_1 x_i + e_i \qquad (10\text{-}5)$$

where $i = 1, 2, \ldots, n$. Then, e_1 is the first residual, the distance from the first data point to the fitted regression line; e_2 is the distance from the second data point to the line; and so on to e_n, the nth error. The errors, e_i, are viewed as estimates of the true population errors, ϵ_i. The equation of the regression line itself is as follows.

The regression line:

$$\hat{Y} = b_0 + b_1 X \qquad (10\text{-}6)$$

where $\hat{Y}$ (pronounced "Y hat") is the Y value *lying on the fitted regression line* for a given X

Thus, $\hat{y}_1$ is the fitted value corresponding to x_1, that is, the value of y_1 without the error e_1, and so on for all $i = 1, 2, \ldots, n$. The fitted value $\hat{Y}$ is also called the *predicted value of Y* because, if we do not know the actual value of Y, it is the value we would predict for a given value of X using the estimated regression line.

Having defined the estimated regression equation, the errors, and the fitted values of Y, we will now demonstrate the principle of least squares, which gives us the BLUE regression parameter estimates. Consider the data set shown in Figure 10–8(a). In parts (b), (c), and (d) of the figure, we show different lines passing through the data set and the resulting errors, e_i.

FIGURE 10–8   A Data Set of X and Y Pairs, and Different Proposed Straight Lines to Describe the Data

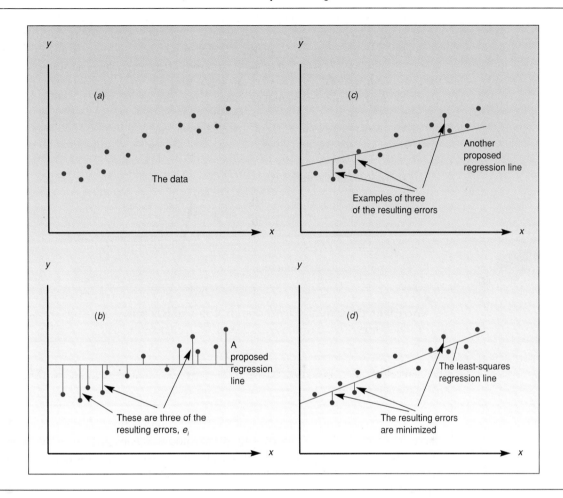

As can be seen from Figure 10–8, the regression line proposed in part (*b*) results in very large errors. The errors corresponding to the line of part (*c*) are smaller than the ones of part (*b*), but the errors resulting from using the line proposed in part (*d*) are by far the smallest. The line in part (*d*) seems to move with the data and *minimize* the resulting errors. This should convince you that the line that best describes the trend in the data is the line that lies "inside" the set of points; since some of the points lie above the fitted line and some below the line, some errors will be positive and others will be negative. If we want to minimize all the errors (both positive and negative ones), we should minimize the *sum of the squared errors* (SSE, as in ANOVA). Thus, we want to find the *least-squares* line—the line that minimizes SSE. We note that least squares is not the only method of fitting lines to data. There are other methods, such as minimizing the sum of the absolute errors. The method of least squares, however, is most commonly used method when estimating a regression relationship. Figure 10–9 shows how the errors lead to the calculation of SSE.

FIGURE 10–9   Regression Errors Leading to SSE

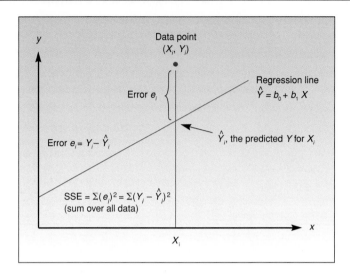

We define the sum of squares for error in regression as

$$SSE = \sum_{i=1}^{n} (e_i)^2 = \sum_{i=1}^{n} (y_i - \hat{y}_i)^2 \qquad (10\text{–}7)$$

Figure 10–10 shows different values of SSE corresponding to values of b_0 and b_1. The least-squares line is the particular line specified by values of b_0 and b_1 that minimize SSE, as shown in the figure.

Calculus is used in finding the expressions for b_0 and b_1 that minimize SSE. These expressions are called the *normal equations* and are given as equations 10–8.[2] This system of two equations with two unknowns is solved to give us the values of b_0 and b_1 that minimize SSE. The results are the least-squares estimators, b_0 and b_1, of the simple linear regression parameters, β_0 and β_1.

The **normal equations:**

$$\sum_{i=1}^{n} y_i = nb_0 + b_1 \sum_{i=1}^{n} x_i$$
$$\sum_{i=1}^{n} x_i y_i = b_0 \sum_{i=1}^{n} x_i + b_1 \sum_{i=1}^{n} x_i^2 \qquad (10\text{–}8)$$

Before we present the solutions to the normal equations, we define the sums of squares, SS_X and SS_Y, and the sum of the cross products, SS_{XY}. These will be very

---

[2] We leave it as an exercise to the reader with background in calculus to derive the normal equations by taking the partial derivatives of SSE with respect to b_0 and b_1 and setting them to zero.

FIGURE 10–10   The Particular Values b_0 and b_1 That Minimize SSE

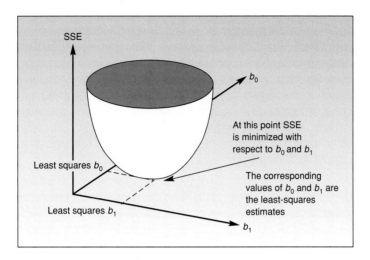

useful in defining the least-squares estimates of the regression parameters, as well as in other regression formulas we will see later. The definitions are given in equations 10–9.

Definitions of sums of squares and cross products useful in regression analysis:

$$SS_X = \sum (x - \bar{x})^2 = \sum x^2 - \frac{(\sum x)^2}{n}$$

$$SS_Y = \sum (y - \bar{y})^2 = \sum y^2 - \frac{(\sum y)^2}{n} \qquad (10-9)$$

$$SS_{XY} = \sum (x - \bar{x})(y - \bar{y}) = \sum xy - \frac{(\sum x)(\sum y)}{n}$$

The first definition in each case is the conceptual one using squared distances from the mean; the second part is a computational definition. Summations are over all data.

We now give the solutions of the normal equations, the least-squares estimators b_0 and b_1.

Least-squares regression estimators:
Slope:

$$b_1 = \frac{SS_{XY}}{SS_X} \qquad (10-10)$$

Intercept:

$$b_0 = \bar{y} - b_1\bar{x}$$

The formula for the estimate of the intercept makes use of the fact that the *least-squares line always passes through the point* $(\bar{x}, \bar{y})$, the intersection of the mean of X and the mean of Y.

It is important to remember that the obtained estimates b_0 and b_1 of the regression relationship are just realizations of *estimators* of the true regression parameters β_0 and β_1. As always, our estimators have standard deviations (and variances, which, by the Gauss-Markov theorem, are as small as possible). The estimates can be used, along with the assumption of normality, in the construction of confidence intervals for, and the conducting of hypothesis tests about, the true regression parameters β_0 and β_1. This will be done in the next section.

We demonstrate the process of estimating the parameters of a simple linear regression model in Example 10–1.

EXAMPLE 10-1

The American Express Company has long believed that its cardholders tend to travel more extensively than others—both on business and for pleasure. As part of a comprehensive research effort undertaken by a New York marketing research firm on behalf of American Express, a study was conducted to determine the relationship between travel and charges on the American Express card. The research firm selected a random sample of 25 cardholders from the American Express computer file and recorded their total charges over a specified period of time. For the selected cardholders, information was also obtained, through a mailed questionnaire, on the total number of miles traveled by each cardholder during the same period of time. The data for this study are given in Table 10–1. Figure 10–11 is a scatter plot of the data.

SOLUTION

As can be seen from the figure, it seems likely that a straight line will describe the trend of increase in dollar amount charged with increase in number of miles traveled. The least-squares line that fits these data is shown in Figure 10–12.

We will now show how the least squares regression line in Figure 10–12 is obtained. Table 10–2 shows the necessary computations. From equations 10–9, using sums at the bottom of Table 10–2, we get

$$\text{SS}_X = \sum x^2 - \frac{(\Sigma x)^2}{n} = 293,426,946 - \frac{79,448^2}{25} = 40,947,557.84$$

and

$$\text{SS}_{XY} = \sum xy - \frac{(\Sigma x)(\Sigma y)}{n} = 390,185,014 - \frac{(79,448)106,605}{25} = 51,402,852.4$$

Using equations 10–10 for the least-squares estimates of the slope and intercept parameters, we get

$$b_1 = \frac{\text{SS}_{XY}}{\text{SS}_X} = \frac{51,402,852.40}{40,947,557.84} = 1.255333776$$

and

$$b_0 = \bar{y} - b_1\bar{x} = \frac{106,605}{25} - (1.255333776)\frac{79,448}{25} = 274.8496866$$

TABLE 10-1   American Express Study Data

Miles X	Dollars Y
1,211	1,802
1,345	2,405
1,422	2,005
1,687	2,511
1,849	2,332
2,026	2,305
2,133	3,016
2,253	3,385
2,400	3,090
2,468	3,694
2,699	3,371
2,806	3,998
3,082	3,555
3,209	4,692
3,466	4,244
3,643	5,298
3,852	4,801
4,033	5,147
4,267	5,738
4,498	6,420
4,533	6,059
4,804	6,426
5,090	6,321
5,233	7,026
5,439	6,964

It is important to carry out as many significant digits as you can in these computations. Here we carried out the computations by hand, for demonstration purposes. Usually, all computations are done by computer or by calculator. There are many hand calculators with a built-in routine for simple linear regression. From now on, we will present only the computed results, the least-squares estimates. The estimated least-squares relationship for Example 10–1 is, reporting estimates to the second significant decimal,

$$Y = 274.85 + 1.26X + e \qquad (10-11)$$

The equation of the line itself, that is, the predicted value of Y for a given X, is

$$\hat{Y} = 274.85 + 1.26X \qquad (10-12)$$

In the next section, we will learn how to compute standard errors of the regression estimators using the sums of squares and cross products (equations 10–9). We will also see how these sums of squares are related to sums of squares used in ANOVA.

FIGURE 10–11   Data for the American Express Study

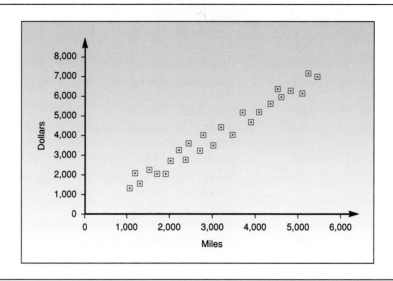

FIGURE 10–12   Least-Squares Line for the American Express Study

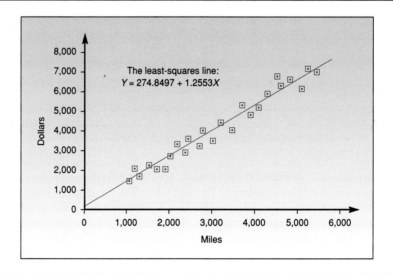

The least-squares line:
$Y = 274.8497 + 1.2553X$

PROBLEMS

10–9.   Explain the advantages of the least-squares procedure for fitting lines to data. Explain how the procedure works.

10–10.   (A conceptually advanced problem) Can you think of a possible limitation of the least-squares procedure?

TABLE 10-2 The Computations Required for the American Express Study

Miles (X)	Dollars (Y)	X^2	Y^2	XY
1,211	1,802	1,466,521	3,247,204	2,182,222
1,345	2,405	1,809,025	5,784,025	3,234,725
1,422	2,005	2,022,084	4,020,025	2,851,110
1,687	2,511	2,845,969	6,305,121	4,236,057
1,849	2,332	3,418,801	5,438,224	4,311,868
2,026	2,305	4,104,676	5,313,025	4,669,930
2,133	3,016	4,549,689	9,096,256	6,433,128
2,253	3,385	5,076,009	11,458,225	7,626,405
2,400	3,090	5,760,000	9,548,100	7,416,000
2,468	3,694	6,091,024	13,645,636	9,116,792
2,699	3,371	7,284,601	11,363,641	9,098,329
2,806	3,998	7,873,636	15,984,004	11,218,388
3,082	3,555	9,498,724	12,638,025	10,956,510
3,209	4,692	10,297,681	22,014,864	15,056,628
3,466	4,244	12,013,156	18,011,536	14,709,704
3,643	5,298	13,271,449	28,068,804	19,300,614
3,852	4,801	14,837,904	23,049,601	18,493,452
4,033	5,147	16,265,089	26,491,609	20,757,851
4,267	5,738	18,207,289	32,924,644	24,484,046
4,498	6,420	20,232,004	41,216,400	28,877,160
4,533	6,059	20,548,089	36,711,481	27,465,447
4,804	6,426	23,078,416	41,293,476	30,870,504
5,090	6,321	25,908,100	39,955,041	32,173,890
5,233	7,026	27,384,289	49,364,676	36,767,058
5,439	6,964	29,582,721	48,497,296	37,877,196
79,448	106,605	293,426,946	521,440,939	390,185,014

10–11. A banking analyst is interested in developing a prediction regression of the prime lending rate using the federal funds rate for the same week as the independent variable. A random sample of 15 weekly observations on both variables is obtained. Data are as follows.

Federal Funds Rate	Prime Lending Rate
6.23	7.75
6.87	8.50
5.54	6.85
5.90	6.78
6.45	8.00
6.55	7.80
5.75	7.05
6.00	7.35
6.20	7.30
6.70	8.00
7.00	8.69
7.23	8.86
5.30	6.25
6.35	7.90
7.15	8.96

Estimate the slope and intercept parameters of the simple linear regression model of the prime rate based on the federal funds rate.

10–12. For the data in problem 10–11, what are the values of SS_X, SS_Y, and SS_{XY}?

10–13. A financial analyst at Goldman Sachs ran a regression analysis of monthly returns on a certain investment (Y) versus returns for the same month on the Standard & Poor's Index (X). The regression results included $SS_X = 765.98$ and $SS_{XY} = 934.49$. Give the least-squares estimate of the regression slope parameter.

10–14. Recently, research efforts have focused on the problem of predicting a manufacturer's market share using information on the quality of its product. Suppose that the following data are available on market share, in percentage (Y), and product quality, on a scale of 0 to 100, determined by an objective evaluation procedure (X).

X:	27	39	73	66	33	43	47	55	60	68	70	75	82
Y:	2	3	10	9	4	6	5	8	7	9	10	13	12

Estimate the simple linear regression relationship between market share and product quality rating.

10–15. A pharmaceutical manufacturer wants to determine the concentration of a key component of cough medicine that may be used without the drug causing adverse side effects. As part of the analysis, a random sample of 45 patients is administered doses of varying concentration (X), and the severity of side effects (Y) is measured. The results include $\bar{x} = 88.9$, $\bar{y} = 165.3$, $SS_X = 2{,}133.9$, $SS_{XY} = 4{,}502.53$, $SS_Y = 12{,}500$. Find the least-squares estimates of the regression parameters.

10–16. An analyst for Blue Cross/Blue Shield wants to estimate the linear relationship between an examining physician's estimate of the number of days of hospitalization a patient would require and the total medical costs actually incurred. Results of the analysis are to be used for predicting medical costs based on a physician's preliminary report. The following data constitute a random sample of 11 accounts.

Estimated Number of Days	Total Cost (in dollars)
5	$2,845
6	3,030
2	2,568
7	3,288
1	2,327
4	2,966
8	3,760
3	2,580
2	2,772
5	3,199
9	3,520

Estimate the parameters of the simple linear regression model. Give the equation of the estimated regression line.

10–17. The following is reprinted by permission from *Business Week*.

1994 Salaries of Some Top CEOs.

	1994 Salary & Bonus*	Change 1993	1994 Stock Performance
Louis Gerstner—IBM	$12.40	+34%	+30.1%
Robert Allen—AT&T	$5.49	+38%	−4.3%
Jack Welch—General Electric	$4.35	+10%	−2.9%
George Fisher—Eastman Kodak	$5.96	NA**	+6.1%
Charles Sanford—Bankers Trust	$3.95	−57%	−29.9%
Deryck Maughan—Salomon	$1.00	−87%	−21.1%

"Executive Pay," *Business Week*, March 27, 1995, pp. 36–38, with data from company reports, Bloomberg Financial Markets.

* In millions of dollars

**Fisher started at Kodak in December, 1993.

Estimate the parameters of a simple linear regression model of CEO 1994 Salary & Bonus versus 1994 stock performance.

10–18. (A problem requiring knowledge of calculus) Derive the normal equations (10–8) by taking the partial derivatives of SSE with respect to b_0 and b_1 and setting them to zero. [*Hint:* set $SSE = \Sigma e^2 = \Sigma(y - \hat{y})^2 = \Sigma(y - b_0 - b_1 x)^2$, and take the derivatives of the last expression on the right.]

10–4 Error Variance and the Standard Errors of Regression Estimators

Recall that σ^2 is the variance of the population regression errors, ϵ, and that this variance is assumed to be constant for all values of X in the range under study. The error variance is an important parameter in the context of regression analysis because it is a measure of the spread of the population elements about the regression line. Generally, the smaller the error variance, the more closely the population elements follow the regression line. The error variance is the variance of the dependent variable Y as "seen" by an eye looking in the direction of the regression line (the error variance is not the variance of Y). These properties are demonstrated in Figure 10–13.

The figure shows two regression lines. The top regression line in the figure has a larger error variance than the bottom regression line. The error variance for each regression is the variation in the data points as seen by the eye located at the base of the line, looking *in the direction of the regression line*. The variance of Y, on the other hand, is the variation in the Y values regardless of the regression line. That is, the variance of Y for each of the two data sets in the figure is the variation in the data as seen by an eye looking in a direction parallel to the X-axis. Note also that the spread of the data is constant along the regression lines. This is in accordance with our assumption of equal error variance for all X.

Since σ^2 is usually unknown, we need to estimate it from our data. An unbiased estimator of σ^2, denoted by S^2, is the *mean square error* (MSE) of the regression. As you will soon see, sums of squares and mean squares in the context of regression analysis are very similar to those of ANOVA, presented in the preceding chapter. The degrees of freedom for error in the context of simple linear regression are $n - 2$ because we have n data points, from which two parameters, β_0 and β_1, are estimated (thus, two restrictions are imposed on the n points, leaving df $= n - 2$). The sum of

FIGURE 10–13   Two Examples of Regression Lines Showing the Error Variance

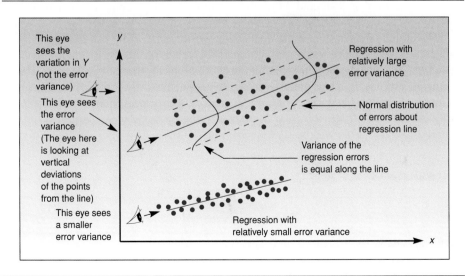

squares for error (SSE) in regression analysis is defined as the sum of squared deviations of the data values Y from the fitted values $\hat{Y}$. The sum of squares for error may also be defined in terms of a computational formula using SS_X, SS_Y, and SS_{XY} as defined in equations 10–9. We state these relationships in equations 10–13.

$$df\ (error) = n - 2$$

$$SSE = \sum (Y - \hat{Y})^2$$

$$= SS_Y - \frac{(SS_{XY})^2}{SS_X}$$

$$= SS_Y - b_1\, SS_{XY} \qquad (10\text{–}13)$$

An unbiased estimator of σ^2, denoted by S^2, is

$$MSE = \frac{SSE}{n - 2}$$

In Example 10–1, the sum of squares for error is

$$SSE = SS_Y - b_1\, SS_{XY} = 66{,}855{,}898 - (1.255333776)(51{,}402{,}852.4)$$
$$= 2{,}328{,}161.2$$

and

$$MSE = \frac{SSE}{n - 2} = \frac{2{,}328{,}161.2}{23} = 101{,}224.4$$

An estimate of the standard deviation of the regression errors, σ, is s, which is the square root of MSE. (The estimator S is not unbiased because the square root of an unbiased estimator, such as S^2, is not itself unbiased. The bias, however, is small, and the point is a technical one.) The estimate $s = \sqrt{MSE}$ of the standard deviation of the regression errors is sometimes referred to as *standard error of estimate*. In Example 10–1 we have

$$s = \sqrt{MSE} = \sqrt{101{,}224.4} = 318.1578225$$

The computation of SSE and MSE for Example 10–1 is demonstrated in Figure 10–14.

The standard deviation of the regression errors, σ, and its estimate, s, play an important role in the process of estimation of the values of the regression parameters, β_0 and β_1. This is so because σ is part of the expressions for the standard errors of both parameter estimators. The standard errors are defined next; they give us an idea of the accuracy of the least-squares estimates, b_0 and b_1. *The standard error of b_1 is especially important because it is used in a test for the existence of a linear relationship between X and Y.* This will be seen in Section 10–6.

The standard error of b_0 is

$$s(b_0) = \frac{s\sqrt{\sum x^2}}{\sqrt{n\, SS_X}} \qquad (10\text{–}14)$$

where $s = \sqrt{MSE}$.

FIGURE 10-14   Computing SSE and MSE in the American Express Study

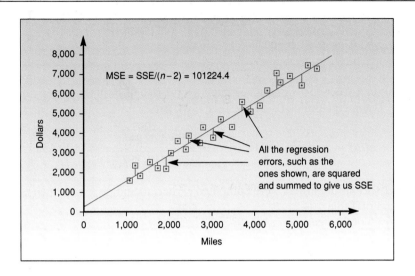

The standard error of b_1 is very important, for the reason just mentioned. The true standard deviation of b_1 is $\sigma/\sqrt{SS_X}$, but since σ is not known, we use the estimated standard deviation of the errors, s.

> The standard error of b_1 is
>
> $$s(b_1) = \frac{s}{\sqrt{SS_X}}$$ (10–15)

Formulas such as equation 10–15 are nice to know, but you should not worry too much about having to use them. Regression analysis is usually done by computer, and the computer output will include the standard errors of the regression estimates. We will now show how the regression parameter estimates and their standard errors can be used in the construction of confidence intervals for the true regression parameters, β_0 and β_1. In section 10–6, as mentioned, we will use the standard error of b_1 for conducting the very important hypothesis test about the existence of a linear relationship between X and Y.

Confidence Intervals for the Regression Parameters

Confidence intervals for the true regression parameters, β_0 and β_1, are easy to compute.

> A $(1 - \alpha)100\%$ confidence interval for β_0:
>
> $$b_0 \pm t_{(\alpha/2, n-2)} s(b_0)$$ (10–16)
>
> where $s(b_0)$ is as given in equation 10–14

> A $(1 - \alpha)100\%$ confidence interval for β_1:
>
> $$b_1 \pm t_{(\alpha/2, n-2)}s(b_1) \tag{10–17}$$
>
> where $s(b_1)$ is as given in equation 10–15

Let us construct 95% confidence intervals for β_0 and β_1 in the American Express example. Using equations 10–14 to 10–17, we get

$$s(b_0) = \frac{s\sqrt{\Sigma x^2}}{\sqrt{n\,SS_X}} = 318.16 \frac{\sqrt{293,426,946}}{\sqrt{(25)(40,947,557.84)}} = 170.338$$

where the various quantities were computed earlier, including Σx^2, which is found at the bottom of Table 10–2.

A 95% confidence interval for β_0 is

$$b_0 \pm t_{(\alpha/2, n-2)}s(b_0) = 274.85 \pm 2.069(170.338) = [-77.58, 627.28]$$

where the value 2.069 is obtained from Appendix C, Table 3 for $1 - \alpha = 0.95$ and 23 degrees of freedom. We may be 95% confident that the true regression intercept is anywhere from -77.58 to 627.28.

$$s(b_1) = \frac{s}{\sqrt{SS_X}} = \frac{318.16}{\sqrt{40,947,557.84}} = 0.04972 \tag{10–18}$$

A 95% confidence interval for β_1 is

$$b_1 \pm t_{(\alpha/2, n-2)}s(b_1) = 1.25533 \pm 2.069(0.04972)$$
$$= [1.15246, 1.35820] \tag{10–19}$$

From the confidence interval given in equation 10–19, we may be 95% confident that the *true* slope of the (*population*) regression line is anywhere from 1.15246 to 1.3582. This range of values is far from zero, and so we may be quite confident that the true regression slope is not zero. This conclusion is very important, as we will see in the following sections. Figure 10–15 demonstrates the meaning of the confidence interval given in equation 10–19.

In the next chapter, we will discuss *joint* confidence intervals for both regression parameters, β_0 and β_1, an advanced topic of secondary importance. (Since the two estimates are related, a joint interval will give us more accuracy and a more meaningful, single confidence coefficient, $1 - \alpha$. This topic is somewhat similar to the Tukey analysis of Chapter 9.) Again, we want to deemphasize the importance of inference about β_0, even though information about the standard error of the estimator of this parameter is reported in computer regression output. It is the inference about β_1 that is of interest to us. Inference about β_1 has implications about the existence of a linear relationship between X and Y; inference about β_0 has no such implications. In addition, there may be a temptation to use the results of the inference about β_0 to "force" this parameter to equal zero or another number. Such temptation should be resisted for reasons that will be explained in a later section; therefore, we deemphasize inference about β_0.

FIGURE 10-15 Interpretation of the Slope Estimation for Example 10-1

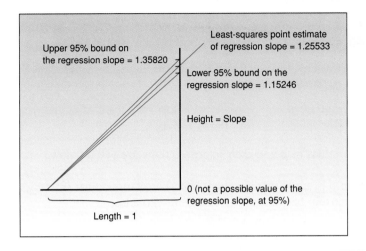

10–19. Give a 99% confidence interval for the slope parameter in Example 10–1. Is zero a credible value for the true regression slope?

10–20. Give an unbiased estimate for the error variance in the situation of problem 10–11. In this problem and others, you may either use a computer or do the computations by hand.

10–21. Find the standard errors of the regression parameter estimates for problem 10–11.

10–22. Give 95% confidence intervals for the regression slope and the regression intercept parameters for the situation of problem 10–11.

10–23. For the situation of problem 10–14, find the standard errors of the estimates of the regression parameters; give an estimate of the variance of the regression errors. Also give a 95% confidence interval for the true regression slope. Is zero a plausible value for the true regression slope at the 95% level of confidence?

10–24. Repeat problem 10–23 for the situation in problem 10–17. Comment on your results.

10–25. In addition to its role in the formulas of the standard errors of the regression estimates, what is the significance of s^2?

10-5 Correlation

We now digress from regression analysis to discuss an important related concept: statistical *correlation*. Recall that one of the assumptions of the regression model is that the independent variable, X, is fixed rather than random and that the only randomness in the values of Y comes from the error term, ϵ. Let us now relax this assumption and *assume that both X and Y are random variables*. In this new context, the study of the relationship between two variables is called *correlation analysis*.

In correlation analysis, we adopt a symmetric approach: we make no distinction between an independent variable and a dependent one. The correlation between two variables is a measure of the linear relationship between them. The correlation gives an indication of how well the two variables move together in a straight-line fashion.

The correlation between X and Y is the same as the correlation between Y and X. We now define correlation more formally.

> The **correlation** between two random variables, X and Y, is a measure of the *degree of linear association* between the two variables.

Two variables are highly correlated if they move well together. Correlation is indicated by the **correlation coefficient.**

> The population correlation coefficient is denoted by ρ. The coefficient ρ can take on any value from -1, through 0, to 1.

The possible values of ρ and their interpretations are given below.

1. When ρ is equal to zero, there is no correlation. That is, there is no linear relationship between the two random variables.
2. When $\rho = 1$, there is a perfect, positive, linear relationship between the two variables. That is, whenever one of the variables, X or Y, increases, the other variable also increases; and whenever one of the variables decreases, the other one must also decrease.
3. When $\rho = -1$, there is a perfect negative linear relationship between X and Y. When X or Y increases, the other variable decreases; and when one decreases, the other one must increase.
4. When the value of ρ is between 0 and 1 in absolute value, it reflects the relative strength of the linear relationship between the two variables. For example, a correlation of 0.90 implies a relatively strong positive relationship between the two variables. A correlation of -0.70 implies a weaker, negative (as indicated by the negative sign), linear relationship. A correlation $\rho = 0.30$ implies a relatively weak (positive) linear relationship between X and Y.

A few sets of data on two variables, and their corresponding population correlation coefficients, are shown in Figure 10–16.

How do we arrive at the concept of correlation? Consider the pair of random variables, X and Y. In correlation analysis, *we will assume that both X and Y are normally distributed random variables with means μ_X and μ_Y, and standard deviations σ_X and σ_Y, respectively.* We define the *covariance* of X and Y as follows.

> The **covariance** of two random variables X and Y:
> $$\text{Cov}(X,Y) = E[(X - \mu_X)(Y - \mu_Y)] \qquad (10\text{--}20)$$
> where μ_X is the (population) mean of X and μ_Y is the (population) mean of Y

The covariance of X and Y is thus the expected value of the product of the deviation of X from its mean and the deviation of Y from its mean. The covariance is positive when the two random variables move together in the same direction, it is negative when the two random variables move in opposite directions, and it is zero when the two variables are not linearly related. Other than this, the covariance does not convey much. Its magnitude cannot be interpreted as an indication of the *degree* of linear association between the two variables, because covariance magnitude depends on the

FIGURE 10-16 Several Possible Correlations between Two Variables

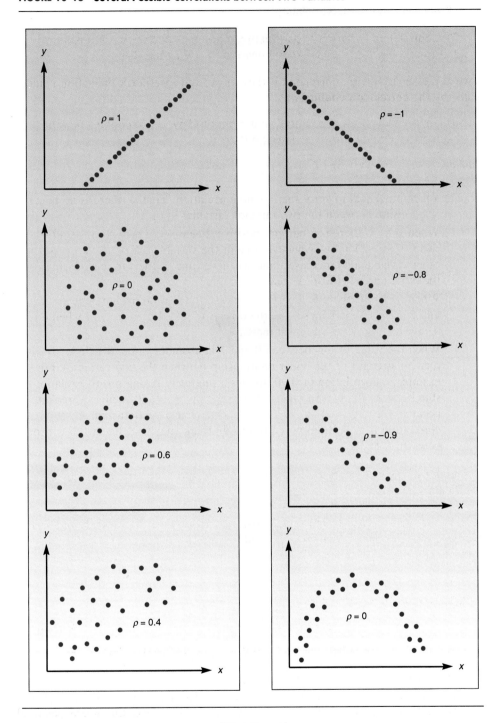

magnitudes of the standard deviations of X and Y. But if we divide the covariance by these standard deviations, we get a measure that is constrained to the range of values -1 to 1 and conveys information about the relative strength of the linear relationship between the two variables. This measure is the population correlation coefficient, ρ.

> ## The population correlation coefficient:
>
> $$\rho = \frac{\text{Cov}(X,Y)}{\sigma_X \sigma_Y}$$
>
> (10–21)

Figure 10–16 gives an idea as to what data from populations with different values of ρ may look like.

Like all population parameters, the value of ρ is not known to us, and we need to estimate it from our random sample of (X, Y) observation pairs. It turns out that a sample estimator of $\text{Cov}(X, Y)$ is $\text{SS}_{XY}/(n - 1)$; an estimator of σ_X is $\sqrt{\text{SS}_X/(n - 1)}$; and an estimator of σ_Y is $\sqrt{\text{SS}_Y/(n - 1)}$. Substituting these estimators for their population counterparts in equation 10–21, and noting that the term $n - 1$ cancels out, we get the *sample correlation coefficient,* denoted by r. This estimate of ρ, also referred to as the *Pearson product-moment correlation coefficient,* is given in equation 10–22.

> ## The sample correlation coefficient:
>
> $$r = \frac{\text{SS}_{XY}}{\sqrt{\text{SS}_X \text{SS}_Y}}$$
>
> (10–22)

In regression analysis, the square of the sample correlation coefficient, r^2, has a special meaning and importance. This will be seen in Section 10–7.

We often use the sample correlation coefficient for descriptive purposes as a point estimator of the population correlation coefficient, ρ. When r is large and positive (closer to $+1$), we say that the two variables are highly correlated in a positive way; when r is large and negative (toward -1), we say that the two variables are highly correlated in an inverse direction, and so on. That is, we view r as if it were the parameter ρ, which r estimates. It is possible, however, to use r as an estimator in testing hypotheses about the true correlation coefficient, ρ. When testing such hypotheses, the assumption of normal distributions of the two variables is required.

The most common test is a test of whether or not two random variables, X and Y, are correlated. The hypothesis test is

> $$H_0: \rho = 0$$
> $$H_1: \rho \neq 0$$
>
> (10–23)

The test statistic for this particular test is

> $$t_{(n-2)} = \frac{r}{\sqrt{\dfrac{1 - r^2}{n - 2}}}$$
>
> (10–24)

This test statistic may also be used for carrying out a one-tailed test for the existence of a positive only, or a negative only, correlation between X and Y. These would be one-tailed tests instead of the two-tailed test of equation 10–23, and the only difference is that the critical points for t would be the appropriate one-tailed values for a given α. The test statistic, however, is good *only* for tests where the null hypothesis assumes a zero correlation. When the true correlation between the two variables is anything but zero, the t distribution in equation 10–24 does not apply; in such cases the distribution is more complicated.[3] The test in equation 10–23 is the most common hypothesis test about the population correlation coefficient because it is a test for the existence of a linear relationship between two variables. We demonstrate this test with the following example.

An article in the *Journal of Marketing Research* reports the results of a study to determine whether there is a linear relationship between the time spent in negotiating a sale and the resulting profits.[4] A random sample of 27 market transactions was collected, and the time taken to conclude the sale as well as the resulting profit were recorded for each transaction. The sample correlation coefficient was computed: $r = 0.424$. Is there a linear relationship between the length of negotiations and transaction profits?

EXAMPLE 10-2

We want to conduct the hypothesis test $H_0: \rho = 0$ versus $H_1: \rho \neq 0$. Using the test statistic in equation 10–24, we get

SOLUTION

$$t_{(25)} = \frac{r}{\sqrt{(1 - r^2)/(n - 2)}} = \frac{0.424}{\sqrt{(1 - 0.424^2)/25}} = 2.34$$

From Appendix C, Table 3, we find that the critical points for a t distribution with 25 degrees of freedom and $\alpha = 0.05$ are ± 2.060. Therefore, we reject the null hypothesis of no correlation in favor of the alternative that the two variables are linearly related. Since the critical points for $\alpha = 0.01$ are ± 2.787, and $2.787 > 2.34$, we are unable to reject the null hypothesis of no correlation between the two variables if we want to use the 0.01 level of significance. If we wanted to test (before looking at our data) only for the existence of a positive correlation between the two variables, our test would have been $H_0: \rho \leq 0$ versus $H_1: \rho > 0$, and we would have used only the right tail of the t distribution. At $\alpha = 0.05$, the critical point of t with 25 degrees of freedom is 1.708, and at $\alpha = 0.01$ it is 2.485. The null hypothesis would, again, be rejected at the 0.05 level but not at the 0.01 level of significance.

---

[3] In cases where we want to test $H_0: \rho = a$ versus $H_1: \rho \neq a$, where a is some number other than zero, we may do so by using the Fisher transformation: $z' = (1/2)\log[(1 + r)/(1 - r)]$, where z' is approximately normally distributed with mean $\mu' = (1/2)\log[(1 + \rho)/(1 - \rho)]$ and standard deviation $\sigma' = 1/\sqrt{n - 3}$. (Here *log* is taken to mean *natural logarithm*.) Such tests are less common, and a more complete description may be found in advanced texts. As an exercise, the interested reader may try this test on some data. (You need to transform z' to an approximate standard normal: $z = (z' - \mu')/\sigma'$; use the null-hypothesized value of ρ in the formula for μ'.)

[4] L. McAlister, M. Bazerman, and P. Fader, "Power and Goal Setting in Channel Negotiations," *Journal of Marketing Research,* August, 1986.

In regression analysis, the test for the existence of a linear relationship between X and Y is a test of whether or not the regression slope, β_1, is equal to zero. The regression slope parameter is related to the correlation coefficient (as an exercise, compare the equations of the estimates r and b_1); when two random variables are uncorrelated, the population regression slope is zero.

We end this section with a word of caution. First, the existence of a correlation between two variables does not necessarily mean that one of the variables *causes* the other one. The determination of **causality** is a difficult question that cannot be directly answered in the context of correlation analysis or regression analysis. Also, the statistical determination that two variables are correlated may not always mean that they are correlated in any direct, meaningful way. For example, if we study any two population-related variables and find that both variables increase "together," this may merely be a reflection of the general increase in population rather than any direct correlation between the two variables. We should look for outside variables that may affect both variables under study.

PROBLEMS

10–26.   What is the main difference between correlation analysis and regression analysis?

10–27.   Compute the sample correlation coefficient for the data of problem 10–11.

10–28.   Compute the sample correlation coefficient for the data of problem 10–14.

10–29.   Using the data in problem 10–16, conduct the hypothesis test for the existence of a linear correlation between the two variables. Use $\alpha = 0.01$.

10–30.   Is it possible that a sample correlation of 0.51 between two variables will not indicate that the two variables are really correlated, while a sample correlation of 0.04 between another pair of variables will be statistically significant? Explain.

10–31.   The following data are indexed prices of gold and copper over a 10-year period. Assume that the indexed values constitute a random sample from the population of possible values, test for the existence of a linear correlation between the indexed prices of the two metals.

Gold: 76 62 70 59 52 53 53 56 57 56

Copper: 80 68 73 63 65 68 65 63 65 66

Also, state one limitation of the data set.

10–32.   Follow daily stock price quotations in *The Wall Street Journal* for a pair of stocks of your choice, and compute the sample correlation coefficient. Also, test for the existence of a nonzero linear correlation in the "population" of prices of the two stocks. For your sample, use as many daily prices as you can.

10–33.   Again using *The Wall Street Journal* as a source of data, determine whether there is a linear correlation between morning and afternoon price quotations in London for an ounce of gold (for the same day). Any ideas?

10–34.   A study was conducted to determine whether a correlation exists between consumers' perceptions of a television commercial (measured on a special scale) and their interest in purchasing the product (measured on a scale). The results are $n = 65$, $r = 0.37$. Is there statistical evidence of a linear correlation between the two variables?

10–35.   (Optional, advanced problem) Using the Fisher transformation (described in footnote 3), carry out a two-tailed test of the hypothesis that the population correlation coefficient for the situation of problem 10–34 is $\rho = 0.22$. Use $\alpha = 0.05$.

10-6 Hypothesis Tests about the Regression Relationship

When there is no linear relationship between X and Y, the population regression slope, β_1, is equal to zero. Why? The population regression slope is equal to zero in either one of two situations:

1. When Y is *constant* for all values of X. For example, $Y = 457.33$ for all X. This is shown in Figure 10–17(a). If Y is constant for all values of X, the slope of Y with respect to X, parameter β_1 is identically zero; there is no linear relationship between the two variables.

2. When the two variables are *uncorrelated*. When the correlation between X and Y is zero, as X increases Y may increase, or it may decrease, or it may remain constant. There is no *systematic* increase or decrease in the values of Y as X increases. This case is shown in Figure 10–17(b). As can be seen in the figure, data from this process are not "moving" in any pattern; thus, there is no direction for the line to follow. Since there is no direction, the slope of the line is, again, zero.

FIGURE 10-17   Two Possibilities Where the Population Regression Slope Is Zero

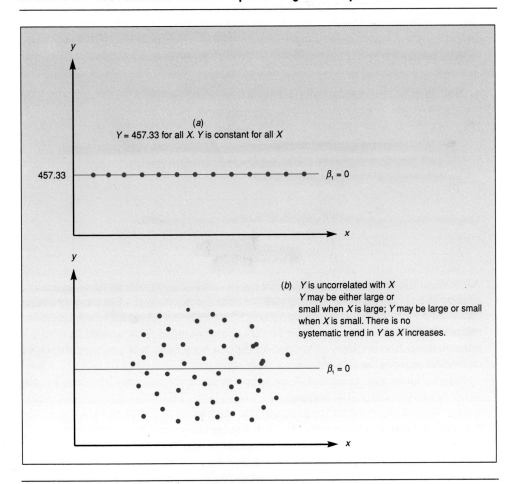

(a)
$Y = 457.33$ for all X. Y is constant for all X

457.33 — $\beta_1 = 0$

(b) Y is uncorrelated with X
Y may be either large or small when X is large; Y may be large or small when X is small. There is no systematic trend in Y as X increases.

$\beta_1 = 0$

Also, remember that the relationship may be curved, with no linear correlation, as was seen in the last part of Figure 10–16. In such cases, the slope may also be zero.

In all cases other than these, there is at least *some* linear relationship between the two variables X and Y; the slope of the line in all such cases would be either positive or negative, but not zero. Therefore, *the most important statistical test in simple linear-regression is the test of whether or not the slope parameter, β_1, is equal to zero.* If we conclude in any particular case that the true regression slope is equal to zero, this means that there is no linear relationship between the two variables: either the dependent variable is constant, or—more commonly—the two variables are not linearly related. We thus have the following test for determining the existence of a linear relationship between two variables, X and Y.

A hypothesis test for the existence of a linear relationship between X and Y:

$$H_0: \beta_1 = 0$$

$$H_1: \beta_1 \neq 0 \qquad \qquad (10\text{–}25)$$

This test is, of course, a two-tailed test. Either the true regression slope is equal to zero, or it is not. If it is equal to zero, there is no linear relationship between the two variables; if the slope is not equal to zero, then it is either positive or negative (the two tails of rejection), in which case there is a linear relationship between the two variables. The test statistic for determining the rejection or nonrejection of the null hypothesis is given in equation 10–26. Given the assumption of normality of the regression errors, the test statistic possesses the t distribution with $n - 2$ degrees of freedom.

Test statistic for the existence of a linear relationship between X and Y:

$$t_{(n-2)} = \frac{b_1}{s(b_1)} \qquad \qquad (10\text{–}26)$$

where b_1 is the least-squares estimate of the regression slope and $s(b_1)$ is the standard error of b_1. When the null hypothesis is true, the statistic has a t distribution with $n - 2$ degrees of freedom.

This test statistic is a special version of a general test statistic:

$$t_{(n-2)} = \frac{b_1 - \beta_{10}}{s(b_1)} \qquad \qquad (10\text{–}27)$$

where β_{10} is the value of β_1 under the null hypothesis. This statistic follows the format: (Estimate − Hypothesized parameter value)/(Standard error of estimator). Since, in the test of equation 10–25, the hypothesized value of β_1 is zero, we have the simplified version of the test statistic, equation 10–26. One advantage of the simple form of our test statistic is that it allows us to conduct the test very quickly. Computer output for regression analysis usually contains a table similar to Table 10–3.

The estimate associated with X (or whatever name the user may have given to the independent variable in the computer program) is b_1. The standard error associated with X is $s(b_1)$. To conduct the test, all you need to do is divide b_1 by $s(b_1)$. In the example of Table 10–3, $4.88/0.1 = 48.8$. The answer is reported in the table as the t ratio. The t ratio can now be compared with critical points of the t distribution with $n - 2$ degrees of freedom. Suppose that the sample size used was 100. Then the critical points for $\alpha = 0.05$ are ± 1.96, and since $48.8 > 1.96$, we conclude that there

TABLE 10-3   An Example of a Part of the Computer Output for Regression

Variable	Estimate	Standard Error	t Ratio
Constant	5.22	0.5	10.44
X	4.88 b_1	0.1 $s(b_1)$	48.80

is evidence of a linear relationship between X and Y in this hypothetical example. (Actually, the p-value is very small. Some computer programs will also report the p-value in an extra column on the right.) What about the first row in the table? The test suggested here is a test of whether or not the intercept β_0 (this is the "constant") is equal to zero. The test statistic is the same as equation 10–26, but with subscripts 0 instead of 1. As we mentioned earlier, this test, although suggested by the output of computer routines, is usually not meaningful and should generally be avoided.

We now conduct the hypothesis test for the existence of a linear relationship between miles traveled and amount charged on the American Express card in Example 10–1. Our hypotheses are H_0: $\beta_1 = 0$ and H_1: $\beta_1 \neq 0$. Recall that for the American Express study, $b_1 = 1.25533$ and $s(b_1) = 0.04972$ (from equations 10–11 and 10–18). We now compute the test statistic, using equation 10–26:

$$t = \frac{b_1}{s(b_1)} = \frac{1.25533}{0.04972} = 25.25$$

From the magnitude of the computed value of the statistic, we know that there is statistical evidence of a linear relationship between the variables, because 25.25 is certainly greater than any critical point of a t distribution with 23 degrees of freedom. We show the test in Figure 10–18. The critical points of t with 23 degrees of freedom and $\alpha = 0.01$ are obtained from Appendix C, Table 3. We conclude that there is evidence of a linear relationship between the two variables "miles traveled" and "dollars charged" in Example 10–10.

Other Tests[5]

Although the test of whether or not the slope parameter is equal to zero is a very important test, because it is a test for the existence of a linear relationship between the two variables, there are other possible tests in the context of regression. These tests serve secondary purposes. In financial analysis, for example, it is often important to determine from past performance data of a particular stock whether or not the stock generally moves with the market as a whole. If the stock does move with the stock market as a whole, the slope parameter of the regression of the stock's returns (Y) versus returns on the market as a whole (X) would be equal to 1.00. That is, $\beta_1 = 1$. We demonstrate this test with Example 10–3.

The *Market Sensitivity Report,* issued by Merrill Lynch, Inc., lists estimated beta coefficients of common stocks as well as their standard errors. *Beta* is the term used in the finance literature for the estimate b_1 of the regression of returns on a stock versus

EXAMPLE 10-3

---

[5] This subsection may be skipped without loss of continuity.

FIGURE 10-18   Test for a Linear Relationship for Example 10-1

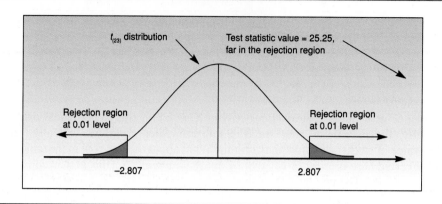

returns on the stock market as a whole. Returns on the stock market as a whole are taken by Merrill Lynch as returns on the Standard & Poor's 500 Index. The November 1995 issue of the report lists the following findings for common stock of Time, Inc.: beta = 1.24, standard error of beta = 0.21, $n = 60$. Is there statistical evidence to reject the claim that the Time stock moves, in general, with the market as a whole?

SOLUTION

We want to carry out the special-purpose test $H_0: \beta_1 = 1$ versus $H_1: \beta_1 \neq 1$. We use the general test statistic of equation 10–27:

$$t_{(n-2)} = \frac{b_1 - \beta_{10}}{s(b_1)} = \frac{1.24 - 1}{0.21} = 1.14$$

Since $n - 2 = 58$, we use the standard normal distribution. The test statistic value is in the nonrejection region for any usual level α, and we conclude that there is no statistical evidence against the claim that Time moves with the market as a whole.

PROBLEMS

10–36.   A regression analysis of fuel efficiency (X) versus sales (Y) of different types of corporate aircraft includes the following results: $b_1 = 2.435$, $s(b_1) = 1.567$, $n = 12$. Do you believe there is a linear relationship between sales of corporate aircraft and the aircraft's fuel efficiency?

10–37.   An article in the *Financial Analysts Journal* reports the results of a regression analysis of returns on stocks (Y) versus the ratio of book to market value (X).[6] The resulting prediction equation is

$$\text{Return} = 1.21 + 3.1 \text{ BMV}$$
$$(2.89)$$

where the number in parentheses is the standard error of the slope estimate. The sample size used is $n = 18$. Is there evidence of a linear relationship between returns and book to market value?

---

[6] R. Harris and F. Marston, "Value versus Growth," *Financial Analysts Journal*, September–October, 1994, p. 18.

10–38. In the situation of problem 10–11, test for the existence of a linear relationship between the two variables.

10–39. In the situation of problem 10–14, test for the existence of a linear relationship between the two variables.

10–40. In the situation of problem 10–16, test for the existence of a linear relationship between the two variables.

10–41. For Example 10–3, test for the existence of a linear relationship between returns on the stock and returns on the market as a whole.

10–42. An advertising research firm conducts a study to determine the relationship between the length of a commercial and the resulting product recall scores of people viewing the commercial. Results of the analysis include $b_1 = 3.467$, $s(b_1) = 0.775$, and $n = 23$. Is there evidence of a linear relationship between commercial length and viewer recall score?

10–43. An article in the *Financial Analysts Journal* discusses results of a regression analysis of average price per share (P) on the independent variable X/k, where X/k is the contemporaneous earnings per share divided by firm-specific discount rate. The regression was run using a random sample of 213 firms listed in the *Value Line Investment Survey*. The reported results are

$$P = 16.67 + 0.68X/k$$
$$(12.03)$$

where the number in parentheses is the standard error. Is there a linear relationship between the two variables?

10–44. A management recruiter wants to estimate a linear regression relationship between an executive's experience and the salary the executive may expect to earn after placement with an employer. From data on 28 executives, which are assumed a random sample from the population of executives that the recruiter places, the following regression results are obtained: $b_1 = 5.49$, $s(b_1) = 1.21$. Is there a linear relationship between the experience and the salary of executives placed by the recruiter?

10-7 How Good Is the Regression?

Once we have determined that a linear relationship exists between the two variables, the question is: How strong is the relationship? If the relationship is a strong one, prediction of the dependent variable can be relatively accurate, and other conclusions drawn from the analysis may be given a high degree of confidence.

We have already seen one measure of the regression fit: the mean square error. The MSE is an estimate of the variance of the true regression errors and is a measure of the variation of the data about the regression line. The MSE, however, depends on the nature of the data, and what may be a large error variation in one situation may not be considered large in another. What we need, therefore, is a *relative* measure of the degree of variation of the data about the regression line. Such a measure allows us to compare the fits of different models.

The relative measure we are looking for is a measure that compares the variation of Y about the regression line with the variation of Y without a regression line. This should remind you of analysis of variance, and we will soon see the relation of ANOVA to regression analysis. It turns out that the relative measure of regression fit we are looking for is the square of the estimated correlation coefficient, r. It is called the *coefficient of determination*.

> The **coefficient of determination,** r^2**,** is a descriptive measure of the strength of the regression relationship, a measure of how well the regression line fits the data.

The coefficient of determination, r^2, is an estimator of the corresponding population parameter, ρ^2, which is the square of the population coefficient of correlation between two variables X and Y. Usually, however, we use r^2 as a descriptive statistic: a relative measure of how well the regression line fits the data. Ordinarily, we do not use r^2 for inference about ρ^2.

We will now see how the coefficient of determination is obtained directly from a decomposition of the variation in Y into a component due to error and a component due to the regression. Figure 10–19 shows the least-squares line that was fitted to a data set. One of the data points, (x, y), is highlighted. For this data point, the figure shows three kinds of deviations: the deviation of y from its mean $(y - \bar{y})$, the deviation of y from its predicted value using the regression $(y - \hat{y})$, and the deviation of the regression-predicted value of y from the mean of y, which is $(\hat{y} - \bar{y})$. Note that the least-squares line passes through the point $(\bar{x}, \bar{y})$.

We will now follow exactly the same mathematical derivation we used in Chapter 9 when we derived the ANOVA relationships. There we looked at the deviation of a data point from its respective group mean—the error; here the error is the deviation of a data point from its regression-predicted value. In ANOVA, we also looked at the total deviation, the deviation of a data point from the grand mean; here we have the deviation of the data point from the mean of Y. Finally, in ANOVA we also considered the treatment deviation, the deviation of the group mean from the grand mean; here we have the *regression deviation:* the deviation of the predicted value from the mean of Y.

The error is also called the *unexplained deviation* because it is a deviation that cannot be explained by the regression relationship; the regression deviation is also called the *explained deviation* because it is that part of the deviation of a data point from the mean that can be explained by the regression relationship between X and Y. We *explain* why the Y value of a particular data point is above the mean of Y by the fact that its X component happens to be above the mean of X and by the fact that X and

FIGURE 10–19   The Three Deviations Associated with a Data Point

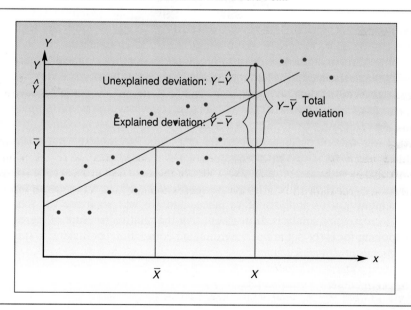

Y are linearly (and positively) related. As can be seen from Figure 10–19, and by simple arithmetic, we have

$$(y - \bar{y}) \quad = \quad (y - \hat{y}) \quad + \quad (\hat{y} - \bar{y})$$

Total	=	Unexplained	+	Explained	
deviation		deviation (Error)		deviation (Regression)	(10–28)

As in the analysis of variance, we square all three deviations for each one of our data points, and sum over all *n* points. Here, again, cross terms drop out, and we are left with the following important relationship for the sums of squares:[7]

$$\sum_{i=1}^{n} (y_i - \bar{y})^2 = \sum_{i=1}^{n} (y_i - \hat{y}_i)^2 + \sum_{i=1}^{n} (\hat{y}_i - \bar{y})^2$$

SST	=	SSE	+	SSR	
(Total sum	=	(Sum of	+	(Sum of	
of squares)		squares for error)		squares for regression)	(10–29)

The term SSR is also called the *explained variation:* it is the part of the variation in *Y* that is explained by the relationship of *Y* with the explanatory variable *X*. Similarly, SSE is the *unexplained variation,* due to error; the sum of the two is the *total variation* in *Y*.

We define the coefficient of determination as the sum of squares due to the regression divided by the total sum of squares. Since by equation 10–29 SSE and SSR add up to SST, the coefficient of determination is equal to 1 minus SSE/SST. We have

$$r^2 = \frac{SSR}{SST} = 1 - \frac{SSE}{SST} \qquad (10\text{--}30)$$

The coefficient of determination can be interpreted as *the proportion of the variation in Y that is explained by the regression relationship of Y with X.*

Recall that the correlation coefficient *r* can be between -1 and 1. Its square, r^2, can therefore be anywhere from 0 to 1. This is in accordance with the interpretation of r^2 as the *percentage of the variation in Y explained by the regression.* The coefficient is a measure of how closely the regression line fits the data; it is a measure of how much the variation in the values of *Y* is reduced once we regress *Y* on the variable *X*. When $r^2 = 1$, we know that 100% of the variation in *Y* is explained by *X*. This means that the data all lie right on the regression line, and there are no resulting errors (because, from equation 10–30, SSE must be equal to zero). Since r^2 cannot be negative, we do not know whether the line slopes upward or downward (the direction can be found from b_1 or *r*), but we know that the line gives a *perfect fit* to the data. Such cases do not occur in business or economics. In fact, when there are no errors, no natural variation, there is no need for statistics.

---

[7] The proof of the relation is left as an exercise for the mathematically interested reader.

At the other extreme is the case where the regression line explains nothing. Here the errors account for everything, and SSR is zero. In this case, we see from equation 10–30 that $r^2 = 0$. In such cases, there is no linear relationship between X and Y, and the true regression slope is probably zero (we say "probably" because r^2 is only an estimator, given to chance variation; it could possibly be estimating a nonzero ρ^2). Between the two cases, $r^2 = 0$ and $r^2 = 1$, are values of r^2 that give an indication of the *relative fit* of the regression model to the data. *The higher r^2 is, the better the fit and the higher our confidence in the regression.* Be wary, however, of situations where the reported r^2 is exceptionally high, such as 0.99 or 0.999. In such cases, something may be wrong. We will see an example of this in the next chapter. Incidentally, in the context of multiple regression, discussed in the next chapter, we will use the notation R^2 for the coefficient of determination to indicate that the relationship is based on several explanatory X variables.

How high should the coefficient of determination be before we can conclude that a regression model fits the data well enough to use the regression with confidence? There is no clear-cut answer to this question. The answer depends on the intended use of the regression model. If we intend to use the regression for *prediction,* the higher the r^2, the more accurate will be our predictions.

An r^2 value of 0.9 or above is very good, a value above 0.8 is good, and a value of 0.6 or above may be satisfactory in some applications, although we must be aware of the fact that, in such cases, errors in prediction may be relatively high. When the r^2 value is 0.5 or below, the regression explains only 50% or less of the variation in the data; therefore, predictions may be poor. If we are interested only in understanding the relationship between the variables, lower values of r^2 may be acceptable, as long as we realize that the model does not explain much.

Figure 10–20 shows several regressions and their corresponding r^2 values. If you think of the total sum of squared deviations as being in a box, then the r^2 is the proportion of the box that is filled with the explained sum of squares, the remaining part being the squared errors. This is shown for each regression in the figure.

It is easy to compute r^2 if we express SSR, SSE, and SST in terms of the computational sums of squares and cross products (equations 10–9):

$$\text{SST} = \text{SS}_Y \qquad \text{SSR} = b_1\,\text{SS}_{XY} \qquad \text{SSE} = \text{SS}_Y - b_1\,\text{SS}_{XY} \qquad (10\text{–}31)$$

We will now use equation 10–31 in computing the coefficient of determination for Example 10–1. For this example, we have

$$\text{SST} = \text{SS}_Y = 66{,}855{,}898$$
$$\text{SSR} = b_1\,\text{SS}_{XY} = (1.255333776)(51{,}402{,}852.4) = 64{,}527{,}736.8$$

and

$$\text{SSE} = \text{SST} - \text{SSR} = 2{,}328{,}161.2$$

(These were computed when we found the MSE for this example.) We now compute r^2 as

$$r^2 = \frac{\text{SSR}}{\text{SST}} = \frac{64{,}527{,}736.8}{66{,}855{,}898} = 0.96518$$

The r^2 in this example is very high. The interpretation is that over 96.5% of the variation in charges on the American Express card can be explained by the relation-

FIGURE 10–20   Value of the Coefficient of Determination in Different Regressions

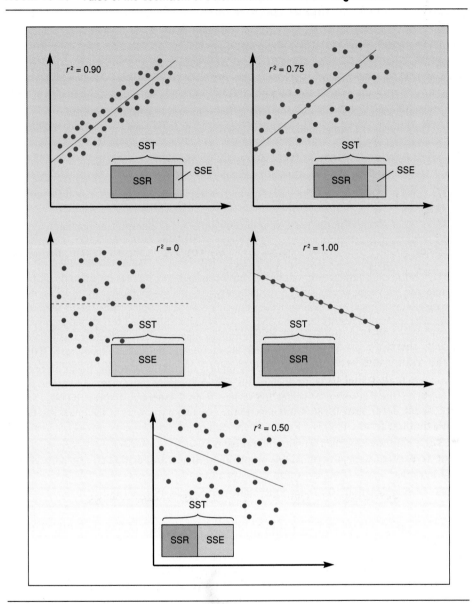

ship between charges on the card and extent of travel (miles). Again we note that while the computational formulas are easy to use, r^2 is always reported in a prominent place in regression computer output. We will see this in Section 10–11.

In the next section, we will see how the sums of squares, along with the corresponding degrees of freedom, lead to mean squares—and to an analysis of variance in the context of regression. In closing this section, we note that in Chapter 11, we will introduce an adjusted coefficient of determination that accounts for degrees of freedom.

PROBLEMS

10–45. In the regression analysis of problem 10–37, the reported coefficient of determination is $r^2 = 0.067$. Does this surprise you? Explain.

10–46. Results of a study reported in the *Financial Analysts Journal* include a simple linear regression analysis of firms' pension funding (Y) versus profitability (X). The regression coefficient of determination is reported to be $r^2 = 0.02$. (The sample size used is 515.)

    a. Would you use the regression model to predict a firm's pension funding?

    b. Does the model explain much of the variation in firms' pension funding on the basis of profitability?

    c. Do you believe these regression results are worth reporting? Explain.

10–47. What percentage of the variation in Y is explained by the regression in problem 10–11?

10–48. What is the r^2 in the regression of problem 10–14? Interpret its meaning.

10–49. What is the r^2 in the regression of problem 10–16?

10–50. What is the r^2 for the regression in problem 10–17? Explain its meaning.

10–51. Mita, the manufacturer of copiers, has been spending increasing amounts of money on radio and television advertising in recent years. An analyst employed by Mita wanted to estimate a simple linear regression of the company's annual copier sales versus advertising dollars. The regression results included SSE = 12,745 and SSR = 87,691. What is the coefficient of determination for this regression? Interpret its meaning. Do you believe this regression model would prove a useful tool for predicting sales based on advertising expenditure? Explain.

10–52. An article in the *Journal of Finance* reports the results of simple linear regressions of New York Stock Exchange share price versus after-hours price movements for various firms. Following are the regression r^2 values for various firms:[8] American Express 0.068, DuPont 0.091, Kodak 0.049, IBM 0.188. Comment on the explanatory powers of the linear regression models for these firms.

10–53. Find the r^2 for the regression in problem 10–15.

10–54. (A mathematically demanding problem) Starting with equation 10–28, derive equation 10–29.

10–55. Using equation 10–31 for SSR, show that SSR $= (SS_{XY})^2/SS_X$.

10–8   Analysis of Variance Table and an *F* Test of the Regression Model

We know from our discussion of the *t* test for the existence of a linear relationship that the degrees of freedom for *error* in simple linear regression are $n - 2$. For the *regression,* we have 1 degree of freedom because there is one independent X variable in the regression. The *total* degrees of freedom are $n - 1$ because here we only consider the mean of Y, to which one degree of freedom is lost. These are similar to the degrees of freedom for ANOVA in the last chapter. Mean squares are obtained, as usual, by dividing the sums of squares by their corresponding degrees of freedom. This gives us the mean square regression, MSR, and mean square error (which we encountered earlier), MSE. Further dividing MSR by MSE gives us an *F* ratio with degrees of freedom 1 and $n - 2$. All these can be put in an ANOVA table for regression. This has been done in Table 10–4.

---

[8] D. Neumark, P. A. Tinsley, and S. Tosini, "After-Hours Stock Prices and Post-Crash Hangovers," *Journal of Finance* (March 1991), p. 165.

TABLE 10-4 ANOVA Table for Regression

Source of Variation	Sum of Squares	Degrees of Freedom	Mean Square	F Ratio
Regression	SSR	1	$MSR = \dfrac{SSR}{1}$	$F_{(1, n-2)} = \dfrac{MSR}{MSE}$
Error	SSE	$n - 2$	$MSE = \dfrac{SSE}{n - 2}$	
Total	SST	$n - 1$		

TABLE 10-5 ANOVA Table for American Express Example

Source of Variation	Sum of Squares	Degrees of Freedom	Mean Square	F Ratio	p
Regression	64,527,736.8	1	64,527,736.8	637.47	0.000
Error	2,328,161.2	23	101,224.4		
Total	66,855,898.0	24			

In regression, there are three sources of variation (see Figure 10–19). These are: *regression*—the explained variation; *error*—the unexplained variation; and their sum, the *total* variation. We know how to obtain the sums of squares and the degrees of freedom, and from them the mean squares. Dividing the mean square regression by the mean square error should give us another measure of the accuracy of our regression because MSR is the average squared explained deviation and MSE is the average squared error (where averaging is done using the appropriate degrees of freedom). The ratio of the two has an F distribution with 1 and $n - 2$ degrees of freedom *when there is no regression relationship between X and Y*. This suggests an F test for the existence of a linear relationship between X and Y. *In simple linear regression, this test is equivalent to the t test*. In multiple regression, as we will see in the next chapter, the F test serves a general role, and separate t tests are used to evaluate the significance of different variables. In simple linear regression, we may conduct either an F test or a t test; the results of the two tests will be the same. The hypothesis test is as given in equation 10–25; the test is carried on the right tail of the F distribution with 1 and $n - 2$ degrees of freedom. We illustrate the analysis with data from Example 10–1. The ANOVA results are given in Table 10–5.

To carry out the test for the existence of a linear relationship between miles traveled and dollars charged on the card, we compare the computed F ratio of 637.47 with a critical point of the F distribution with 1 degree of freedom for the numerator and 23 degrees of freedom for the denominator. Using $\alpha = 0.01$, the critical point from Appendix C, Table 5 is found to be 7.88. Clearly, the computed value is far in the rejection region, and the p-value is very small. We conclude, again, that there is evidence of a linear relationship between the two variables.

Recall from Chapter 8 that an F distribution with 1 degree of freedom for the numerator and k degrees of freedom for the denominator is the *square* of a t distribution with k degrees of freedom. In Example 10–1 our computed F statistic value is 637.47, which is the square of our obtained t statistic, 25.25 (to within rounding error). The same relationship holds for the critical points: for $\alpha = 0.01$, we have a critical point for $F_{(1,23)}$ equal to 7.88, and the (right-hand) critical point of a two-tailed test at $\alpha = 0.01$ for t with 23 degrees of freedom is $2.807 = \sqrt{7.88}$.

PROBLEMS

10–56.   Conduct the F test for the existence of a linear relationship between the two variables in problem 10–11.

10–57.   Carry out an F test for a linear relationship in problem 10–14. Compare your results with those of the t test.

10–58.   Repeat problem 10–57 for the data of problem 10–17.

10–59.   Conduct an F test for the existence of a linear relationship in the case of problem 10–15.

10–60.   For problem 10–51, assume the sample size used was $n = 104$, and conduct an F test for the existence of a linear relationship between the two variables.

10–61.   In a simple linear regression analysis, it is found that $b_1 = 2.556$ and $s(b_1) = 4.122$. The sample size is $n = 22$. Conduct an F test for the existence of a linear relationship between the two variables.

10–62.   (A mathematically demanding problem) Using the definition of the t statistic in terms of sums of squares, prove (in the context of simple linear regression) that $t^2 = F$.

10-9   Residual Analysis and Checking for Model Inadequacies

Recall our discussion of statistical models in section 10–1. We said that a good statistical model accounts for the systematic movement in the process, leaving out a series of uncorrelated, purely random errors, ϵ, which are assumed to be normally distributed with mean zero and a constant variance, σ^2. In Figure 10–3, we saw a general methodology for statistical model building, consisting of model identification, estimation, tests of validity, and, finally, use of the model. We are now at the third stage of the analysis of a simple linear regression model: examining the residuals and testing the validity of the model.

Analysis of the residuals could reveal whether or not the assumption of normally distributed errors holds. In addition, the analysis could reveal whether the variance of the errors is indeed constant, that is, whether the spread of the data around the regression line is uniform. The analysis could also indicate whether or not there are any missing variables that should have been included in our model (leading to a multiple regression equation). The analysis may reveal whether the order of data collection (for example, time of observation) has any effect on the data and whether the order should have been incorporated as a variable in the model. Finally, analysis of the residuals may determine whether or not the assumption that the errors are uncorrelated is satisfied. A test of this assumption, the Durbin-Watson test, entails more than a mere examination of the model residuals, and discussion of this test is postponed until the next chapter. We now describe some graphical methods for the examination of the model residuals that may lead to discovery of model inadequacies.

A Check for the Equality of Variance of the Errors

A graph of the regression errors, the residuals, versus the independent variable X, or versus the predicted values $\hat{Y}$, will reveal whether or not the variance of the errors is constant. The variance of the residuals is indicated by the width of the scatter plot of the residuals as X increases. If the width of the scatter plot of the residuals either

FIGURE 10–21   A Residual Plot Indicating Heteroscedasticity

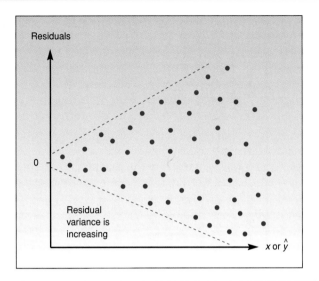

increases or decreases as X increases, then the assumption of constant variance is not met. This problem is called **heteroscedasticity.** When heteroscedasticity exists, we cannot use the ordinary least-squares method for estimating the regression and should use a more complex method called *generalized least squares.* Figure 10–21 shows how a plot of the residuals versus X or $\hat{Y}$ looks in the case of heteroscedasticity. Figure 10–22 shows a residual plot in a good regression, with no heteroscedasticity.

Testing for Missing Variables

Figure 10–22 also shows how the residuals should look when plotted against time (or the order in which data are collected). There should be no trend in the residuals when plotted versus time. A linear trend in the residuals as plotted versus time is shown in Figure 10–23.

If the residuals exhibit a pattern when plotted versus time, then time should be incorporated as an explanatory variable in the model in addition to X. The same is true for any other variable against which we may plot the residuals: if there is any trend in the plot, the variable should be included in our model along with X. Incorporating additional variables leads to a multiple regression model.

Detecting a Curvilinear Relationship between Y and X

If the relationship between X and Y is curved, "forcing" a straight line to fit the data will result in a poor fit. This is shown in Figure 10–24. In this case, the residuals are at first large and negative, then decrease, become positive, and then again become negative. The residuals are not random and independent; they show curvature. This pattern appears in a plot of the residuals versus X, shown in Figure 10–25.

The situation can be corrected by adding the variable X^2 to the model. This also entails the techniques of multiple regression analysis. We note that, in cases where we have repeated Y observations at some levels of X, there is a statistical test for model

FIGURE 10-22   A Residual Plot Indicating No Heteroscedasticity

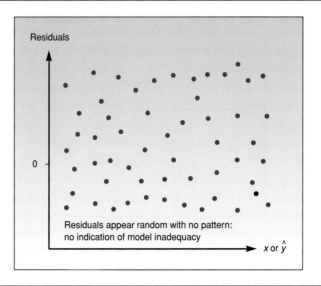

FIGURE 10-23   A Residual Plot Indicating a Trend with Time

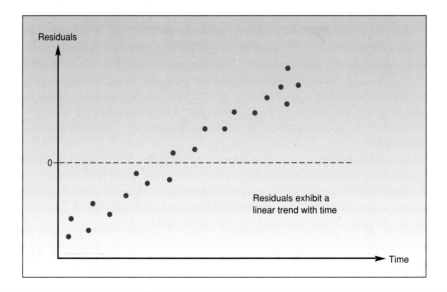

lack of fit such as that shown in Figure 10–24. The test entails decomposing the sum of squares for error into a component due to lack of fit and a component due to pure error. This gives rise to an F test for lack of fit. This test is described in advanced texts. We point out, however, that examination of the residuals is an excellent tool for detecting such model deficiencies, and this simple technique does not require the special data format needed for the formal test.

FIGURE 10–24   Results of Forcing a Straight Line to Fit a Curved Data Set

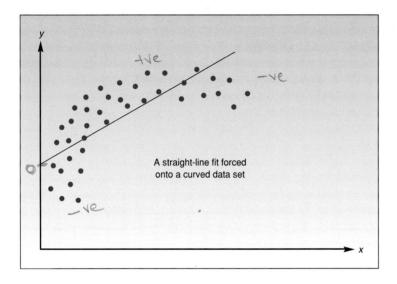

FIGURE 10–25   Resulting Pattern of the Residuals When a Straight Line Is Forced to Fit a Curved Data Set

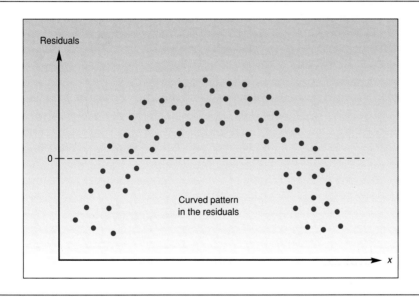

Detecting Deviations from the Normal Distribution Assumption

When trying to detect deviations from the normal distribution assumption by use of residual plots, we need to plot the regression residuals on a special "probability paper" scale. Such paper is available in stationery stores. However, if we run the regression on a computer, we may include a command that will produce a residual plot on the required scale. When plotted on a probability-paper scale, *the residuals should form*

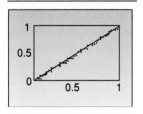

a straight diagonal line. Serious deviations from the line indicate that the residuals are not approximately normally distributed. An example of approximately normally distributed residuals is shown in Figure 10–26.

It may also be useful to plot *standardized* residuals, that is, the residuals divided by their (sample) standard deviation. (The mean of the residuals should be zero, so we need not subtract it when forming the standardized residuals.) The computer will standardize the residuals upon request. A histogram of the residuals should look similar to a normal curve. In Section 10–11, we will see residual plots for the American Express example.

PROBLEMS

10–63. For each of the following plots of regression residuals versus X, state whether there is any indication of model inadequacy; if so, identify the inadequacy.

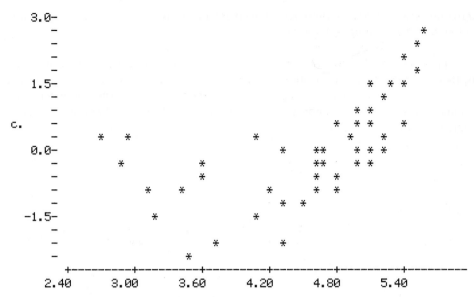

10–64.   In the following plots of the residuals versus time of observation, state whether there is evidence of model inadequacy. How would you correct any inadequacy?

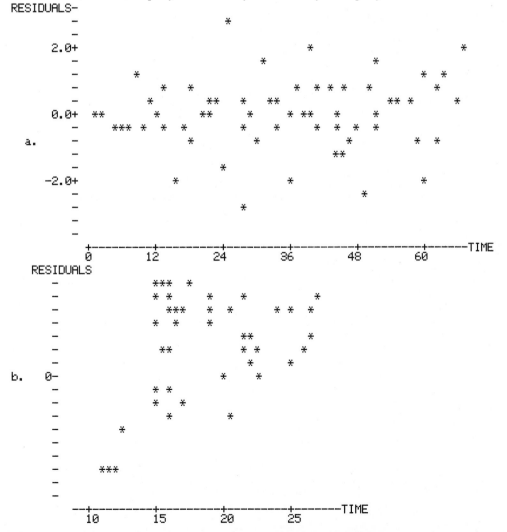

10–65.   Is there any indication of model inadequacy in the following plots of residuals on a normal probability scale?

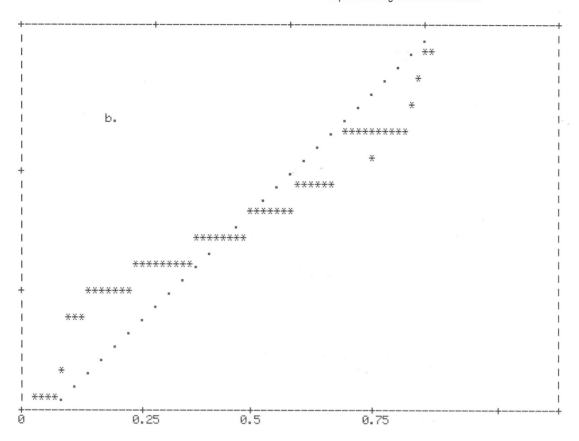

10–66. Produce residual plots for the regression of problem 10–11. Is there any apparent model inadequacy?

10–67. Repeat problem 10–66 for the regression of problem 10–14.

10–68. Repeat problem 10–66 for the regression of problem 10–16.

10–10 Use of the Regression Model for Prediction

As mentioned in the introduction of this chapter, there are several possible uses of a regression model. One is to understand the relationship between the two variables. As with correlation analysis, understanding a relationship between two variables in regression does not imply that one variable causes the other. Causality is a much more complicated issue and cannot be determined by a simple regression analysis.

A more common use of a regression analysis is *prediction*: providing estimates of values of the dependent variable by using the prediction equation $\hat{Y} = b_0 + b_1 X$. It is important that prediction be done in the region of the data used in the estimation process. *You should be aware that using a regression for extrapolating outside the estimation range is risky, as the estimated relationship may not be appropriate outside this range*. This is demonstrated in Figure 10–27.

Point Predictions

It is very easy to produce point predictions using the estimated regression equation. All we need to do is substitute the value of X for which we want to predict Y into the prediction equation. In Example 10–1 suppose that American Express wants to

FIGURE 10–27   The Danger of Extrapolation

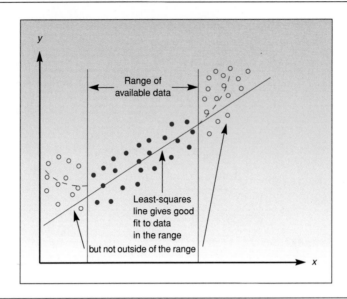

predict charges on the card for a member who traveled 4,000 miles during a period equal to the one studied (note that $x = 4,000$ is in the range of X values used in the estimation). We use the prediction equation, equation 10–12, but with higher accuracy for b_1:

$$\hat{y} = 274.85 + 1.2553x = 274.85 + 1.2553(4,000) = 5,296.05 \text{ (dollars)}$$

The process of prediction in this example is demonstrated in Figure 10–28.

Prediction Intervals

Point predictions are not perfect and are subject to error. The error is due to the uncertainty in estimation as well as the natural variation of points about the regression line. A $(1 - \alpha)100\%$ prediction interval for Y is given in equation 10–32.

A $(1 - \alpha)100\%$ prediction interval for Y:

$$\hat{y} \pm t_{\alpha/2} s \sqrt{1 + \frac{1}{n} + \frac{(x - \bar{x})^2}{SS_x}} \qquad (10\text{–}32)$$

As can be seen from the formula, the width of the interval depends on the distance of our value x (for which we wish to predict Y) from the mean, $\bar{x}$. This is shown in Figure 10–29.

    We will now use equation 10–32 to compute a 95% prediction interval for the amount charged on the American Express card by a member who traveled 4,000 miles. We know that in this example $\bar{x} = \Sigma\, x/n = 79,448/25 = 3,177.92$. We also know

FIGURE 10-28   Prediction in American Express Study

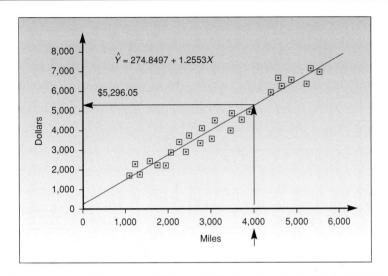

that $SS_x = 40,947,557.84$ and $s = 318.16$. From Appendix C, Table 3 we get the critical point for t with 23 degrees of freedom: 2.069. Applying equation 10–32, we get

$$5,296.05 \pm (2.069)(318.16)\sqrt{1 + 1/25 + (4,000 - 3,177.92)^2/40,947,557.84}$$
$$= 5,296.05 \pm 676.62 = [4,619.43,\ 5,972.67]$$

Based on the validity of the study, we are 95% confident that a cardholder who traveled 4,000 miles during a period of the given length will have charges on his or her card totaling anywhere from $4,619.43 to $5,972.67. What about the *average* total charge of all cardholders who traveled 4,000 miles? This is $E(Y \mid x = 4,000)$. The point estimate of $E(Y \mid x = 4,000)$ is also equal to $\hat{Y}$, but the confidence interval for this quantity is different.

A Confidence Interval for the Average Y, Given a Particular Value of X

We may compute a confidence interval for $E(Y \mid X)$, the expected value of Y for a given X. Here the variation is smaller because we are dealing with the average Y for a given X, rather than a particular Y. Thus, the confidence interval is narrower than a prediction interval of the same confidence level. The confidence interval for $E(Y \mid X)$ is given in equation 10–33.

A $(1 - \alpha)100\%$ confidence interval for $E(Y \mid X)$:

$$\hat{y} \pm t_{\alpha/2}\, s \sqrt{\frac{1}{n} + \frac{(x - \bar{x})^2}{SS_X}} \qquad (10\text{–}33)$$

FIGURE 10–29   Prediction Band and Its Width

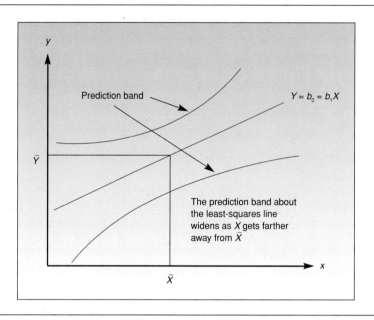

The confidence band for $E(Y \mid X)$ around the regression line looks like Figure 10–29 except that the band is narrower. The standard error of the estimator of the conditional mean, $E(Y \mid X)$, is smaller than the standard error of the predicted Y. Therefore, the 1 is missing from the square root quantity in equation 10–33 as compared with equation 10–32.

For the American Express example, let us now compute a 95% confidence interval for $E(Y \mid x = 4,000)$. Applying equation 10–33, we have

$$5{,}296.05 \pm (2.069)(318.16)\sqrt{1/25 + (4{,}000 - 3{,}177.92)^2/40{,}947{,}557.84}$$
$$= 5{,}296.05 \pm 156.48 = [5{,}139.57,\ 5{,}452.53]$$

Being a confidence interval for a conditional mean, the interval is much narrower than the prediction interval, which has the same confidence level for covering *any given* observation at the level of X.

PROBLEMS

10–69.   For the American Express example, give a 95% prediction interval for the amount charged by a member who traveled 5,000 miles. Compare the result with the one for $x = 4,000$ miles.

10–70.   Give a 95% confidence interval for $E(Y \mid x = 5,000)$ in the American Express example. Compare with your answer to problem 10–69.

10–71.   For problem 10–69, give a 99% prediction interval.

10–72.   For problem 10–11, give a point prediction and a 99% prediction interval for the prime lending rate when the federal funds rate is 6.5%.

10–73. For problem 10–72, give a 99% confidence interval for the average prime lending rate when the federal funds rate is 6.5%.

10–74. For problem 10–16, give a 95% confidence interval for the average cost incurred by patients who stay in the hospital for five days.

10–75. For problem 10–16, give a 95% prediction interval for the cost incurred by a patient who will stay in the hospital for five days.

10–76. For problem 10–17 predict CEO pay for a firm, in this category of firms that made a 20% return. Give a 90% confidence interval for the average pay at this return level.

10-11 Using the Computer

All commonly used statistical packages have regression capabilities. In fact, most advanced calculators can do simple linear regression. In this section, we present a complete computer solution to Example 10–1 using the MINITAB package.

We enter the data in two columns: miles in column C1 and dollars in column C2. We then name the variables accordingly.

The regression command in MINITAB is very simple:

```
REGRESS (name of dependent variable, or column) on 1 predictor (name
of independent variable, or column)
```

If we add a number of another column, such as C3, the computer will put the standardized residuals in that column. If we add the name of another column, such as C4, the computer will put the fitted values (the predicted values of Y for all data points) in that column.

There are also possible subcommands, separated from the main command and from each other by semicolons. The last subcommand must end with a period. One subcommand we use here is RESIDUALS, followed by a column number—here, C5. This will allow us to plot the residuals versus X and versus the fitted values ($\hat{Y}$). Another subcommand we use is PREDICT, followed by the value of X for which we want a prediction of Y. (We predict Y for $x = \$4,000$.) The prediction gives us a 95% confidence interval for $E(Y \mid X)$ and a 95% prediction interval, along with the point prediction. The command PLOT (variable name or column number) versus (variable name or column number) produces the required plot.

The MINITAB commands and the output are given in Figure 10–30. Note that in the residual plots, there is no evidence of any model inadequacy. Look at all the results: parameter estimates, r^2 (the "adjusted r^2" will be explained in the next chapter), ANOVA table, and the predicted value with its intervals. Compare the results with what we obtained throughout the chapter.

We end this section with a cautionary note. Computer programs allow you to run a regression with no intercept, no "constant." This is a dangerous thing to do. Even if the situation tends to imply that Y should be zero when X is zero (no profit for zero investment, for example), it still is not a good practice to follow. This is so because our data set may not extend to the range of values containing zero, and the relationship may be different in that region (not a continuation of the straight line). If we do force the regression to go through zero, our least-squares estimates may be poor. This is demonstrated in Figure 10–31.

FIGURE 10–30   MINITAB Analysis of the American Express Example

```
MTB> REGRESS 'DOLLARS' on 1 predictor 'MILES' tres in C3 fits in C4;
SUBC>    PREDICT 4000:
SUBC>    PRESIDUALS in C5.

The regression equation is
dollars = 275 + 1.26 miles

Predictor       Coef        Stdev      t-ratio         p
Constant       274.8        170.3         1.61      0.120
miles        1.25533      0.04972        25.25      0.000

s = 318.2      R-sq = 96.5%     R-sq(adj) = 96.4%

Analysis of Variance

SOURCE       DF            SS           MS         F         p
Regression    1      65427736     64527736    634.60     0.000
Error        23       2328161       101224
Total        24      66855896

    Fit   Stdev.Fit        95% C.I.            95% P.I.
 5296.2        75.6     (5139.7, 5452.7)    (4619.5, 5972.8)

    MTB > NAME c3 'stres', c4 'fits', c5 'resids'
    MTB > PLOT 'resids' vs 'fits'
```

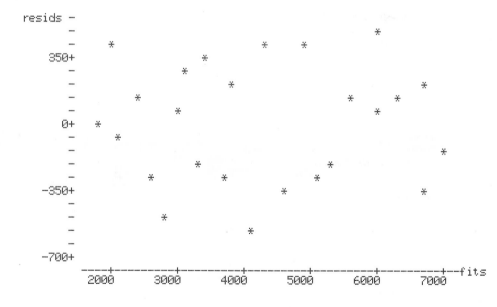

FIGURE 10–30 *(concluded)*

```
MTB > PLOT 'resids' vs 'miles'
```

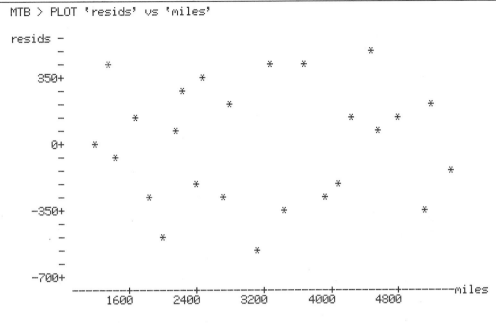

```
MTB > HISTOGRAM of 'stres'

Histogram of stres   N = 25

Midpoint    Count
   -2.0       1   *
   -1.5       1   *
   -1.0       5   *****
   -0.5       3   ***
    0.0       3   ***
    0.0       6   ******
    1.0       3   ***
    1.5       3   ***

MTB > PLOT 'dollars' vs 'miles'
```

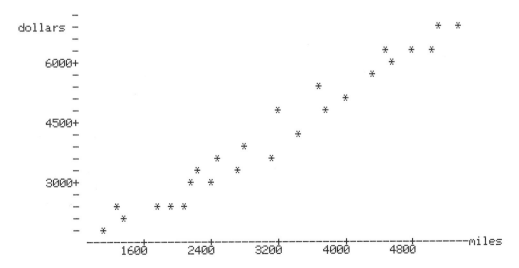

FIGURE 10–31   The Danger in Forcing the Regression to Go through the Origin

10-12   Summary and Review of Terms

In this chapter, we introduced simple linear regression, a technique for estimating the straight-line relationship between two variables. We defined the **dependent variable** as the variable we wish to predict by, or understand the relation with, the **independent variable** (also called the **explanatory** or **predictor** variable). We described the **least-squares** estimation procedure as the procedure that produces the **best linear unbiased estimators (BLUE)** of the regression coefficients, the **slope** and **intercept** parameters. We learned how to conduct two statistical tests for the existence of a linear relationship between the two variables: the t test and the F test. We noted that in the case of simple linear regression, the two tests are equivalent. We saw how to evaluate the fit of the regression model by considering the **coefficient of determination,** r^2. We learned how to check the validity of the assumptions of the simple linear regression model by examining the **residuals.** Finally, we saw how the regression model can be used for prediction. In addition, we discussed a linear **correlation** model. We saw that the correlation model is appropriate when the two variables are viewed in a symmetric role: both being normally distributed random variables, rather than one of them (X) being considered nonrandom, as in regression analysis.

ADDITIONAL PROBLEMS

10–77. The computer output for a simple linear regression of sales of one product versus sales of another product includes the following: $n = 128$, SSE $= 3,343$, SSR $= 45,678$. Compute the remaining sums of squares, the mean squares, the F ratio, and the coefficient of determination. Write an ANOVA table for this regression. What can you say about the relationship between sales of the two products?

10–78. A real estate agent is looking for a single independent variable to explain the variation in property values in a certain metropolitan area as much as possible. The analyst runs two separate simple linear regression models: model 1—property value (Y) versus distance from the center of town (X); model 2—property values (Y) versus area affluence (X). The first regression analysis gives SSE = 546, SSR = 1,756. The second regression includes the results SSR = 1,178 and SST = 2,345. Which single variable explains more of the variation in property values?

10–79. Recently, interest has centered on the relationship between foreign economic growth and the decline in U.S. exports.[9] A regression of these two variables using a sample of 23 months gave the following results: SSE = 5,432.87, SST = 87,695.98. Conduct the F test for the existence of a linear relationship between the two variables.

10–80. An economist conducts a regression analysis of a country's foreign exchange rate versus the country's current money supply. The results of the simple linear regression of 60 monthly observations (five years of data) are $\Sigma x = 0.0046$, $\Sigma y = 0.5108$, $\Sigma xy = -0.0082$, $\Sigma x^2 = 0.0102$, $\Sigma y^2 = 0.076$. Carry out the required regression calculations. Would you use this regression for predicting the exchange rate? Would you use these results for understanding the effect of the money supply on local exchange rates? Explain.

10–81. The amount of money a manufacturer is willing to pay for shipping its goods is believed to be inversely related to the length of time the goods are in transit. A shipping company analyst carries out a simple linear regression analysis of the time in transit (X) versus shipping costs (Y) and obtains $b_1 = -3.453$, $s(b_1) = 0.987$. Conduct the t test for the existence of a linear relationship between shipping costs and length of transit time. From this information, can you also give the F statistic value? (The sample size is $n = 16$ transatlantic crossings.)

10–82. A retail outlet selling yarn and fabric in California is interested in the relationship between sales of the two product lines. A data set of 16 weekly observations on sales of the two product lines is collected, and the sample correlation coefficient is computed: $r = 0.16$. Conduct a statistical test of whether or not sales of the two product lines are correlated.

10–83. A computer software manufacturer wants to study the relationship between the number of microcomputers in use in different areas and the number of software packages the company sells in the areas. A simple linear regression analysis of 21 geographical regions reveals the following: $b_0 = 12.43$, $b_1 = 1.076$, $s(b_0) = 13.65$, $s(b_1) = 0.083$, SSE = 1,076.11, $SS_X = 72.641$, $\bar{x} = 12,453$ computers. Using this information, construct 95% confidence intervals for the regression parameters β_0 and β_1, a 95% confidence interval for the *average* number of software packages sold in an area where 10,000 computers are in use, and a 95% prediction interval for the number of packages sold in that area.

10–84. The management of an international hotel chain is in the process of evaluating the possible sites for a new unit on a beach resort. As part of the analysis, the management is interested in evaluating the relationship between the distance of a hotel from the beach (X) and the hotel's average occupancy rate for the season (Y). A sample of 14 existing hotels in the area is chosen, and each hotel reports its average occupancy rate. The management records the hotel's distance (in miles) from the beach. The following table presents the obtained data. Carry out a complete regression analysis of these data. If building the new hotel is feasible only if the average occupancy rate will be at least 75% during a season, what is the farthest distance from the beach for a possible site of the new hotel?

Distance (miles): 0.1 0.1 0.2 0.3 0.4 0.4 0.5 0.6 0.7 0.7 0.8 0.8 0.9 0.9

Occupancy(%): 92 95 96 90 89 86 90 83 85 80 78 76 72 75

10–85. A car rental agency is interested in studying the relationship between the mileage of their subcompact cars (X) and the monthly maintenance cost for the cars (Y). Following are data on 15 randomly chosen cars. Carry out a simple linear regression analysis of the relationship between the two variables. What is the expected monthly maintenance cost for a car with 13,000 miles?

Miles (in thousands): 6 7 8 9 10 11 12 13 14 15 16 17 18 19 20

Cost (dollars): 13 16 15 20 19 21 26 24 30 32 30 35 34 40 39

---

[9] Economic Trends, *Business Week,* February 4, 1991, p. 20.

10–86. (This is a difficult problem.) A financial analyst carried out a regression analysis of the relationship between returns on a stock and a certain characteristic of the stockholders. A sample of 6,154 stockholders was obtained, and the regression results revealed $r^2 = 0.008$, F ratio = 12.56. Explain.

10–87. The following data, reprinted by permission from *Variety,* report weekly values (October 5, 1990, to March 22, 1991) of the Entertainment Stock Index versus values of Standard & Poor's 500 Index. Run a complete regression analysis on these data, and report your results in the form of a memorandum to the director of a mutual fund specializing in entertainment stocks.

Entertainment Stocks	S&P 500	Entertainment Stocks	S&P 500
179.4	367.5	160.6	331.8
180.8	373.6	157.8	326.8
190.1	375.0	156.4	327.8
185.1	370.5	153.6	322.2
181.5	365.7	146.9	315.1
182.6	369.0	145.4	317.1
176.5	359.4	140.1	313.7
171.5	343.1	132.7	311.9
161.2	336.1	134.5	304.7
159.5	332.2	135.2	312.5
150.8	315.2	132.3	300.0
156.1	321.0	144.5	311.5
158.5	328.7		

Source: "Variety Entertainment, Composite," *Variety,* March 25, 1991, p. 1.

10–88. The following data, reprinted by permission from *The Economist,* report annual industrial production and gross national product figures for 13 industrial countries. Run a regression analysis of these data aimed at constructing a prediction equation of GNP on industrial production for industrialized nations.

	Industrial Production	GNP
Australia	−1.5	+0.6
Belgium	+5.0	+4.0
Canada	−6.6	−1.0
France	+0.7	+1.8
Germany	+5.2	+4.5
Holland	+3.9	+3.4
Italy	−5.3	+1.8
Japan	+7.3	+4.7
Spain	−0.7	+3.7
Sweden	−3.4	−0.5
Switzerland	+3.6	+1.7
UK	−3.8	−1.3
USA	−2.6	+0.4

Source: Economic and Financial Indicators, *The Economist,* March 30, 1991, p. 93.

Case 10   THE JANUARY INDICATOR

It has been suggested that January is a good indicator of the behavior of the stock market during the entire year. The following data set consists of the changes in stocks in the Standard & Poor's 500 Index during January and the corresponding changes in the same index for the entire year. Data are for the years 1950 to 1987. (Data were obtained from the Hirsch Organization, Inc.)

	January Change	Yearly Change		January Change	Yearly Change
1950	1.7%	21.8%	1969	− 0.8%	−11.4%
1951	6.1%	16.5%	1970	− 7.6%	0.1%
1952	1.6%	11.8%	1971	4.0%	10.8%
1953	− 0.7%	− 6.6%	1972	1.8%	15.6%
1954	5.1%	45.0%	1973	−1.7%	−17.4%
1955	1.8%	26.4%	1974	− 1.0%	−29.7%
1956	−3.6%	2.6%	1975	12.3%	31.5%
1957	−4.2%	−14.3%	1976	11.8%	19.1%
1958	4.3%	38.1%	1977	− 5.1%	−11.5%
1959	0.4%	8.5%	1978	− 6.2%	1.1%
1960	−7.1%	− 3.0%	1979	4.0%	12.3%
1961	6.3%	23.1%	1980	5.8%	25.8%
1962	−3.8%	−11.8%	1981	− 4.6%	− 9.7%
1963	4.9%	18.9%	1982	− 1.8%	14.8%
1964	2.7%	13.0%	1983	3.3%	17.3%
1965	3.3%	9.1%	1984	− 0.9%	1.4%
1966	0.5%	−13.1%	1985	7.4%	26.0%
1967	7.8%	20.1%	1986	0.5%	14.9%
1968	−4.4%	7.7%	1987	13.2%	2.0%

Conduct an analysis of the reported data, and answer the following questions.

1. Do you believe that January can serve as a predictor of the stock market's performance? Explain.
2. How confident are you of your answer to question 1?
3. In January 1988, the Standard & Poor's 500 Index increased by 4%. Predict the performance of the index for the entire year. Also give a 95% prediction interval.
4. What percentage of the variation in the yearly performance of the Standard & Poor's 500 Index can be explained by the performance of this index in January? Explain the relevance of this percentage (note that January and the year use the same baseline in computing the index).

11 MULTIPLE REGRESSION

1 1 – 1   I N T R O D U C T I O N

n regression analysis, it often happens that the variable of interest depends on more than just one other variable. There may be several independent variables that contain information about the variable we are trying to predict or understand.

Continued

In such cases, it may be worthwhile to formulate a model that allows us to consider the relation of our variable of interest with a set of independent variables. In the American Express example of Chapter 10, the company may be able to predict more accurately the amount charged on the American Express card from knowledge of cardholders' incomes, in addition to miles traveled. When several independent variables are included in a regression equation, our model is called a **multiple regression** model.

How many independent variables should we include in our regression equation? It seems logical that if our equation incorporates information about as many variables as possible, we will have maximum prediction power of the variable of interest. There are, however, some serious limitations to this assertion.

In the summer of 1983, a student of economics had an idea about predicting the nation's economic future. The student decided to collect data on as many economic variables as possible and to formulate a multiple regression equation linking these variables with the gross national product (GNP). The student thought that if the number of variables used was large enough, he would be able to predict the GNP with great accuracy. The student collected 12 years' worth of quarterly data, 48 observations in total, and information on 47 economic variables: national income, prime lending rate, unemployment rate, etc., corresponding to the 48 quarters for which GNP values were known. He formulated the regression relation: $Y = \beta_0 + \beta_1 X_1 + \beta_2 X_2 + \beta_3 X_3 + \cdots + \beta_{47} X_{47} + \epsilon$.

In the next section, we will see that this equation is a generalization to k variables (in this case, $k = 47$) of the population regression equation with one variable, introduced in Chapter 10. The student went on to carry out an estimation of the model parameters β_0 to β_{47} using a computer and to compute the multiple coefficient of determination, denoted R^2. (The coefficient R^2 is an extension to multiple regression of the coefficient of determination, r^2, in simple linear regression. This coefficient is a measure of how well the regression equation fits the data.) To his great delight, the student noted that the value of R^2 for his regression was 0.9999. The regression equation apparently had a perfect fit with the data! The student was sure, therefore, that he would be able to predict the GNP from knowledge of the 47 variables with great accuracy. As it turned out, not only were model predictions very poor—the forecasts produced from the model were worse than pure guesses of the GNP[1]—but the model was deemed erroneous, misleading, and in violation of statistical methodology. Why?

Recall that in Chapter 10, we said that a good statistical model fits the data well but is also parsimonious, that is, it has as few parameters as possible. At the time, you may have wondered why a model should be parsimonious; you may have reasoned that the more parameters in your model, the better the model. Examine Figure 11–1, which demonstrates

---

[1] There are statistical methods for evaluating how good a prediction is, once the actual values become known. These methods consist of looking at the difference between forecast and actually. Methods of evaluating forecast accuracy will be discussed in the next chapter.

FIGURE 11-1   The Dimensionality of Surfaces Fitting Two, Three, and Four Points

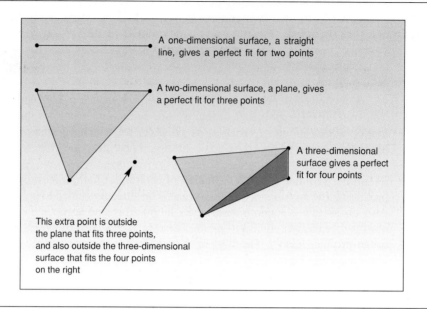

A one-dimensional surface, a straight line, gives a perfect fit for two points

A two-dimensional surface, a plane, gives a perfect fit for three points

A three-dimensional surface gives a perfect fit for four points

This extra point is outside the plane that fits three points, and also outside the three-dimensional surface that fits the four points on the right

an important mathematical fact. Given any two points, it is possible to find a one-dimensional surface, a straight line, that will pass through the two points and fit the two points perfectly. Once a third point is obtained, it may not lie on the straight line connecting the original twopoints. Thus, the line—though providing a perfect fit for two points—may be a poor *predictor* of future observations. With three points, however, we can always find a two-dimensional surface, a plane, that will pass through the three points and thus provide a perfect fit. When a fourth point is added, the point may not lie on the original plane. With four points, we can find a three-dimensional surface (a surface of more than two dimensions is called a *hyperplane*) that will provide a perfect fit. Add a fifth point, and a three-dimensional surface is not enough, but a four-dimensional surface will provide a perfect fit. Thus, given n points, we can find an $(n - 1)$-dimensional surface that will provide a perfect fit for the data. When we do this, however, we are not doing statistics. We are overfitting our data. This procedure leaves no degrees of freedom for error.

Remember that in simple linear regression, there are $n - 2$ degrees of freedom for error. This is so because there are two parameters to be estimated from the data—an intercept and a slope. In a multiple regression model with k variables, there are $k + 1$ parameters to be estimated from the data set—one slope parameter for each of the k variables, and an intercept. Hence, the degrees of freedom for error in a multiple regression model with k independent variables are $n - (k + 1)$. Our student, fitting a regression model with $k = 47$ variables to a data set of $n = 48$ points, is left with $n - (k + 1) = 48 - (47 + 1) = 0$ degrees of freedom for error! This means that there is no allowance for error whatsoever. The model tracks the data, adding a dimension to the regression surface for each data point. The model does not allow for any chance variation. Since real-world data always have some chance variation, future observations do not follow such an overfitted model. Recall that a statistical model should capture as much as possible of the *systematic* movement within the data set, leaving out pure errors—variation due to chance. An overfitted model forces the regression surface to go through every point. This is why the R^2 coefficient is high: the error part of the regression is forced to zero. (The R^2 in the student's model was actually 1.00; the computer-reported value 0.9999 is due to rounding in the computations.)

The idea of overfitting can be seen another way. Multiple regression includes a technique called *polynomial regression*. In polynomial regression, we regress a dependent variable Y on powers of the independent variables. Each power of a variable, say, X_1^2, is considered an independent variable in its own right. For example, a fourth-degree polynomial regression in X is modeled as $Y = \beta_0 + \beta_1 X + \beta_2 X^2 + \beta_3 X^3 + \beta_4 X^4 + \epsilon$. This is treated as a four-variable regression equation. Overfitting in this context is shown in Figure 11–2.

As shown in the figure, a 15-degree polynomial provides a perfect fit to a set of 16 data points (here again, df for error $= 16 - (15 + 1) = 0$). The prediction of a new data point using this model is worse than the prediction provided by a one degree model—a least-squares line. The line captures the systematic trend in the data, leaving the rest of the movements within the data to error. In this case, the straight line is a good statistical model, while the 15-degree polynomial—analogous to the model proposed by the student—is not. In the next section, we will formally develop the multiple regression model with k independent variables. ∎

11-2   The *k*-Variable Multiple Regression Model

The population regression model of a dependent variable, Y, on a set of k independent variables, $X_1, X_2, \ldots, X_k$, is given by

$$Y = \beta_0 + \beta_1 X_1 + \beta_2 X_2 + \cdots + \beta_k X_k + \epsilon \qquad (11–1)$$

where β_0 is the Y-intercept of the regression surface and each β_i, $i = 1, \ldots, k$, is the slope of the regression surface—sometimes called the **response surface**—with respect to variable X_i

As with the simple linear regression model, we have some assumptions.

Model assumptions:
1. For each observation, the error term, ϵ, is normally distributed with mean zero and standard deviation σ and is independent of the error terms associated with all other observations. That is,

$$\epsilon_j \sim N(0, \sigma^2) \qquad \text{for all } j = 1, 2, \ldots, n \qquad (11–2)$$

   independent of other errors.[2]
2. In the context of regression analysis, the variables X_i are considered *fixed quantities,* although in the context of correlational analysis, they are random variables. In any case, X_i *are independent of the error term,* ϵ. When we assume that X_i are fixed quantities, we are assuming that we have realizations of k variables X_i and that the only randomness in Y comes from the error term, ϵ.

---

[2] The multiple regression model is valid under less restrictive assumptions than these. The assumption of normality of the errors allows us to perform t tests and F tests of model validity. Also, all we need is that the errors are *uncorrelated* with each other. However, normal distribution + noncorrelation = independence.

FIGURE 11-2   Overfitting a Data Set with a 15-Degree Polynomial

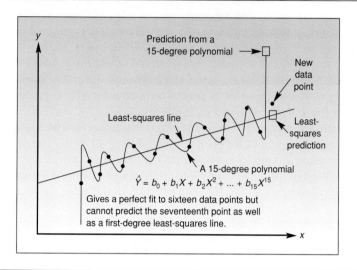

For a case with $k = 2$ variables, the response surface is a plane in three dimensions (the dimensions are Y, X_1, and X_2). The plane is the surface of average response $E(Y)$ for any combination of the two variables X_1 and X_2. The response surface is given by the equation for $E(Y)$, which is the expected value of equation 11–1 with two independent variables. Taking the expected value of Y gives the value 0 to the error term, ϵ. The equations for Y and $E(Y)$ in the case of regression with two independent variables are as follows.

$$Y = \beta_0 + \beta_1 X_1 + \beta_2 X_2 + \epsilon \qquad (11-3)$$

$$E(Y) = \beta_0 + \beta_1 X_1 + \beta_2 X_2 \qquad (11-4)$$

These are equations analogous to the case of simple linear regression. Here, instead of a regression line, we have a regression plane. Some values of Y (that is, combinations of the X_i variables times their coefficients, β_i, and the errors, ϵ) are shown in Figure 11–3. The figure also shows the response surface, the plane corresponding to equation 11–4.

We estimate the regression parameters of equation 11–3 by the method of least squares. This is an extension of the procedure used in simple linear regression. In the case of two independent variables where the population model is equation 11–3, we need to estimate an equation of a plane that will minimize the sum of the squared errors, $(Y - \hat{Y})^2$, over the entire data set of n points. The method is extendable to any k independent variables. In the case of $k = 2$, there are three normal equations, and their solutions are the least-squares estimates b_0, b_1, and b_2. These are estimates of the Y-intercept, the slope of the plane with respect to X_1, and the slope of the plane with respect to X_2. The normal equations for $k = 2$ are as follows.

When the various sums, Σy, Σx_1, and the other sums and products, are entered into these equations, it is possible to solve the three equations for the three unknowns b_0, b_1, and b_2. These computations are always done by computer. We will, however, demonstrate the solution of equations 11–5 with a simple example.

FIGURE 11-3   A Two-Dimensional Response Surface $E(Y) = \beta_0 + \beta_1 X_1 + \beta_1 X_2$ and Some Points

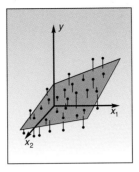

The normal equations for the case of two independent variables:

$$\sum y = nb_0 + b_1 \sum x_1 + b_2 \sum x_2$$

$$\sum x_1 y = b_0 \sum x_1 + b_1 \sum x_1^2 + b_2 \sum x_1 x_2$$

$$\sum x_2 y = b_0 \sum x_2 + b_1 \sum x_1 x_2 + b_2 \sum x_2^2 \qquad (11\text{--}5)$$

EXAMPLE 11-1

Alka-Seltzer recently embarked on an in-store promotional campaign, with displays of its antacid featured prominently in supermarkets. The company also ran its usual radio and television commercials. Over a period of 10 weeks, the company kept track of its expenditure on radio and television advertising, variable X_1, as well as its spending on in-store displays, variable X_2. The resulting sales for each week in the area studied were recorded as the dependent variable, Y. The company analyst conducting the study hypothesized a linear regression model of the form

$$Y = \beta_0 + \beta_1 X_1 + \beta_2 X_2 + \epsilon$$

linking sales volume with the two independent variables, advertising and in-store promotions. The analyst wanted to use the available data, considered a random sample of 10 weekly observations, to estimate the parameters of the regression relationship.

SOLUTION

Table 11–1 gives the data for this study in terms of Y, X_1, and X_2, all in thousands of dollars. The table also gives additional columns of products and squares of data values needed for the solution of the normal equations. These columns are $X_1 X_2$, X_1^2, X_2^2, $X_1 Y$, and $X_2 Y$. The sums of these columns are then substituted into equations 11–5, which are solved for the estimates b_0, b_1, and b_2 of the regression parameters.

From Table 11–1, the sums needed for the solution of the normal equations are $\Sigma y = 743$, $\Sigma x_1 = 123$, $\Sigma x_2 = 65$, $\Sigma x_1 y = 9{,}382$, $\Sigma x_2 y = 5{,}040$, $\Sigma x_1 x_2 = 869$,

TABLE 11-1   Various Quantities Needed for the Solution of the Normal Equations for Example 11-1 (numbers are in thousands of dollars)

Y	X_1	X_2	$X_1 X_2$	X_1^2	X_2^2	$X_1 Y$	$X_2 Y$
72	12	5	60	144	25	864	360
76	11	8	88	121	64	836	608
78	15	6	90	225	36	1,170	468
70	10	5	50	100	25	700	350
68	11	3	33	121	9	748	204
80	16	9	144	256	81	1,280	720
82	14	12	168	196	144	1,148	984
65	8	4	32	64	16	520	260
62	8	3	24	64	9	496	186
90	18	10	180	324	100	1,620	900
743	123	65	869	1,615	509	9,382	5,040

$\Sigma x_1^2 = 1{,}615$, $\Sigma x_2^2 = 509$. When these sums are substituted into equations 11–5, we get the resulting normal equations:

$$743 = 10b_0 + 123b_1 + 65b_2$$
$$9{,}382 = 123b_0 + 1{,}615b_1 + 869b_2$$
$$5{,}040 = 65b_0 + 869b_1 + 509b_2$$

Solution of this system of equations by substitution, or by any other method of solution, gives

$$b_0 = 47.164942, \qquad b_1 = 1.5990404, \qquad b_2 = 1.1487479$$

These are the *least-squares estimates* of the true regression parameters β_0, β_1, and β_2. Recall that the normal equations (equations 11–5) are originally obtained by calculus methods. (They are the results of differentiating the sum of squared errors with respect to the regression coefficients and setting the results to zero.)

The meaning of the estimates b_0, b_1, and b_2 as the Y-intercept, the slope with respect to X_1, and the slope with respect to X_2, respectively, of the estimated regression surface is illustrated in Figure 11–4.

The general multiple regression model, equation 11–1, has one Y-intercept parameter and k slope parameters. Each slope parameter β_i, $i = 1, \ldots, k$, represents the amount of increase (or decrease, in case it is negative) in $E(Y)$ for an increase of one unit in variable X_i when all other variables are kept constant. The regression coefficients β_i are therefore sometimes referred to as *net regression coefficients* because they represent the net change in $E(Y)$ for a change of one unit in the variable they represent, all else remaining constant.[3] The X_i variables should be independent of each other, as we want each coefficient β_i to reflect change in $E(Y)$ for a unit change in X_i, *with all other independent variables left constant*. This is often difficult to achieve in multiple regression analysis since the explanatory variables are often interrelated in some way.

---

[3] For the reader with knowledge of calculus, we note that the coefficient β_i is the partial derivative of $E(Y)$ with respect to X_i: $\beta_i = \partial E(Y)/\partial X_i$.

FIGURE 11-4   The Least-Squares Regression Surface for Example 11-1

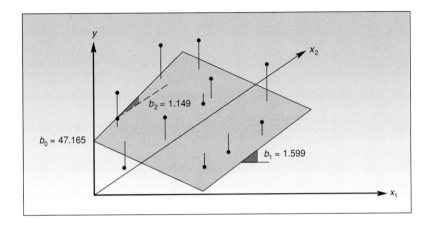

The Estimated Regression Relationship

The **estimated regression relationship:**

$$\hat{Y} = b_0 + b_1 X_1 + b_2 X_2 + \cdots + b_k X_k \qquad (11\text{-}6)$$

where $\hat{Y}$ is the predicted value of Y, the value lying *on* the estimated regression surface. The terms b_i, $i = 0, \ldots, k$, are the least-squares estimates of the population regression parameters β_i.

The least-squares estimators giving us the b_i are BLUE (best linear unbiased estimators).

It is also possible to write the estimated regression relationship in a way that shows how each value of Y is expressed as a linear combination of the values of X_i plus an error term. This is given in equation 11–7.

$$y_j = b_0 + b_1 x_{1j} + b_2 x_{2j} + \cdots + b_k x_{kj} + e_j \qquad (11\text{-}7)$$

where $j = 1, \ldots, n.$

In Example 11–1 the estimated regression relationship of sales volume (Y) on advertising (X_1) and in-store promotions (X_2) is given by

$$\hat{Y} = 47.164942 + 1.5990404 X_1 + 1.1487479 X_2$$

PROBLEMS

11–1.   What are the assumptions underlying the multiple regression model? What is the purpose of the assumption of normality of the errors?

11–2.   In a regression analysis of job performance (Y) versus the explanatory variables age (X_1) and experience (X_2), the estimated coefficient b_2 is equal to 1.34. Explain the meaning of this estimate in terms of the impact of experience on performance.

11–3. In terms of model assumptions, what is the difference between a multiple regression model with k independent variables and a correlational analysis involving these variables?

11–4. What is a response surface? For a regression model with seven independent variables, what is the dimensionality of the response surface?

11–5. Again, for a multiple regression model with $k = 7$ independent variables, how many normal equations are there leading to the values of the estimates of the regression parameters?

11–6. What are the BLUE estimators of the regression parameters?

11–7. For a multiple regression model with two independent variables, results of the analysis include $\Sigma y = 852$, $\Sigma x_1 = 155$, $\Sigma x_2 = 88$, $\Sigma x_1 y = 11{,}423$, $\Sigma x_2 y = 8{,}320$, $\Sigma x_1 x_2 = 1{,}055$, $\Sigma x_1^2 = 2{,}125$, $\Sigma x_2^2 = 768$, $n = 100$. Solve the normal equations for this regression model, and give the estimates of the parameters.

11–8. A realtor is interested in assessing the impact of size (in square feet) and distance from the center of town (in miles) on the value of homes (in thousands of dollars) in a certain area. Nine randomly chosen houses are selected; data are as follows.

Y (value):	345,	238,	452,	422,	328,	375,	660,	466,	290
X_1 (size):	1,650,	1,870,	2,230,	1,740,	1,900,	2,000,	3,200,	1,860,	1,230
X_2 (distance):	3.5,	0.5,	1.5,	4.5,	1.8,	0.1,	3.4,	3.0,	1.0

Compute the estimated regression coefficients and explain their meaning.

11–9. The estimated regression coefficients in Example 11–1 are $b_0 = 47.165$, $b_1 = 1.599$, and $b_2 = 1.149$ (rounded to three decimal places). Explain the meaning of each of the three numbers in terms of the situation presented in the example.

11–3 The F Test of a Multiple Regression Model

The first statistical test we need to conduct in our evaluation of a multiple regression model is a test that will answer the basic question: Is there a linear regression relationship between the dependent variable Y and *any* of the explanatory, independent variables X_i suggested by the regression equation under consideration? If the proposed regression relationship is as given in equation 11–1, a statistical test that can answer this important question is as follows.

A statistical hypothesis test for the existence of a linear relationship between Y and any of the X_i:

$$H_0: \quad \beta_1 = \beta_2 = \beta_3 = \cdots = \beta_k = 0$$
$$H_1: \quad \text{Not all the } \beta_i (i = 1, \ldots, k) \text{ are zero} \qquad (11\text{–}8)$$

If the null hypothesis is true, there is no linear relationship between Y and any of the independent variables in the proposed regression equation. In such a case, there is nothing more to do. There is no regression. If, on the other hand, we reject the null hypothesis, there is statistical evidence to conclude that there is a regression relationship between Y and at least one of the independent variables proposed in the regression model.

In order to carry out the important test in equation 11–8, we will perform an analysis of variance. The ANOVA is the same as the one given in Chapter 10 for simple linear regression, except that here we have k independent variables instead of just one. Therefore, the F test of the analysis of variance is not equivalent to the t test for the significance of the slope parameter, as was the case in Chapter 10. Since in

FIGURE 11-5   Decomposition of the Total Deviation in Multiple Regression Analysis

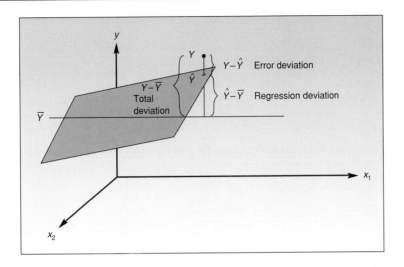

multiple regression there are k slope parameters, we have k different t tests to follow the ANOVA.

Figure 11–5 is an extension of Figure 10–19 to the case of $k = 2$ independent variables—to a regression plane instead of a regression line. The figure shows a particular data point, y, the predicted point, $\hat{y}$, which lies on the estimated regression surface, and the mean of the dependent variable, $\bar{y}$. The figure shows the three deviations associated with the data point: the error deviation $y - \hat{y}$, the regression deviation $\hat{y} - \bar{y}$, and the total deviation $y - \bar{y}$. As seen from the figure, the three deviations satisfy the relation: Total deviation = Regression deviation + Error deviation. As in the case of simple linear regression, when we square the deviations and sum them over all n data points, we get the following relation for the sums of squares. The sums of squares are denoted by SST for the total sum of squares, SSR for the regression sum of squares, and SSE for the error sum of squares.

$$SST = SSR + SSE \qquad (11-9)$$

This is the same as equation 10–29. The difference is in the degrees of freedom. In simple linear regression, the degrees of freedom for error were $n - 2$ because two parameters, an intercept and a slope, were estimated from a data set of n points. In multiple regression, we estimate k slope parameters and an intercept from a data set of n points. Therefore, the degrees of freedom for error are $n - (k + 1)$. The degrees of freedom for the regression are k, and the total degrees of freedom are $n - 1$. Again, the degrees of freedom are additive. Table 11–2 is the ANOVA table for a multiple regression model with k independent variables.

For Example 11–1, we present the ANOVA table computed using the MINITAB computer package. The results are shown in Table 11–3. Since the p-value is small, we reject the null hypothesis that both slope parameters β_1 and β_2 are zero (equation 11–8), in favor of the alternative that the slope parameters are not both zero. We conclude that there is evidence of a linear regression relationship between sales and at least one of the two variables, advertising or in-store promotions (or both). The F test is shown in Figure 11–6.

TABLE 11–2   ANOVA Table for Multiple Regression

Source of Variation	Sum of Squares	Degrees of Freedom	Mean Square	F Ratio
Regression	SSR	k	$MSR = \dfrac{SSR}{k}$	$F = \dfrac{MSR}{MSE}$
Error	SSE	$n - (k + 1)$	$MSE = \dfrac{SSE}{n - (k + 1)}$	
Total	SST	$n - 1$		

TABLE 11–3   MINITAB-Produced ANOVA Table for the Regression Data of Example 11–1

```
Analysis of Variance
    SOURCE      DF        SS         MS         F         P
 Regression      2     630.54     315.27     86.34     0.000
 Error           7      25.56       3.65
 Total           9     656.10
```

FIGURE 11–6   Regression F Test for Example 11–1

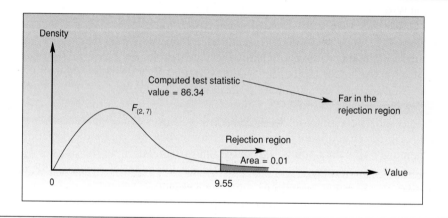

Note that since there are two independent variables in Example 11–1, we do not yet know whether there is a regression relationship between sales and both advertising and in-store promotions, or whether the relationship exists between sales and one of the two variables only, and if so, which one. All we know is that our data present statistical evidence to conclude that a relationship exists between sales and at least one of the two independent variables. This is, of course, true for all cases where there are two or more independent variables. The F test only tells us that there is evidence of a relationship between the dependent variable and at least one of the independent variables in the full regression equation under consideration. Once we conclude that a relationship exists, we need to conduct separate tests to determine which of the slope parameters β_i, where $i = 1, \ldots, k$, are different from zero. There are, therefore, k further tests.

Compare the use of ANOVA tables in multiple regression with the analysis of variance discussed in Chapter 9. Once we rejected the null hypothesis that all r

population means are equal, we required further analysis (the Tukey procedure or an alternative technique) to determine where the differences existed. In multiple regression, the further tests necessary for determining which variables are important are *t* tests. These tests tell us which variables help explain the variation in the values of the dependent variable and which variables have no explanatory power and should be eliminated from the regression model. Before we get to the separate tests of multiple regression parameters, we want to be able to evaluate how good the regression relationship is as a whole.

PROBLEMS

11–10. Explain what is tested by the hypothesis test in equation 11–8. What conclusion should be reached if the null hypothesis is not rejected? What conclusion should be reached if the null hypothesis is rejected?

11–11. In a multiple regression model with 12 independent variables, what are the degrees of freedom for error? Explain.

11–12. An article about banks' profitability lists four independent variables that may affect profitability.[4] A regression analysis with four independent variables is carried out. The data are a random sample of 120 observations. The results of the analysis include SSE = 4,560, and SSR = 562. Is there a regression relationship between the dependent variable and any of the four proposed explanatory variables? Explain.

11–13. Avis is interested in estimating weekly costs of maintenance of its rental cars of a certain size based on the variables: number of miles driven during the week, number of renters during the week, the car's total mileage, and the car's age. A regression analysis is carried out, and the results include $n = 45$ cars (each car selected randomly, during a randomly selected week of operation), SSR = 7,768, and SST = 15,673. Construct a complete ANOVA table for this problem, and test for the existence of a linear regression relationship between weekly maintenance costs and any of the four independent variables considered.

11–14. The Nissan Motor Company wanted to find leverage factors for marketing the Maxima model in the United States. The company hired a marketing research firm in New York City to carry out an analysis of the factors that make people favor the model in question. As part of the analysis, the marketing research firm selected a random sample of 17 people and asked them to fill out a questionnaire about the importance of three automobile characteristics: prestige, comfort, and economy. Each respondent reported the importance he or she gave to each of the three attributes on a 0 to 100 scale. Each respondent then spent some time becoming acquainted with the car's features and drove it on a test run. Finally, each of the respondents gave an overall appeal score for the model on a 0 to 100 scale. The appeal score was considered the dependent variable, and the three attribute scores were considered independent variables. A multiple regression analysis was carried out, and the results included the following ANOVA table. Complete the table. Based on the results, is there a regression relationship between appeal score and at least one of the attribute variables? Explain.

```
Analysis of Variance

  SOURCE      DF      SS        MS
Regression          7474.0
Error
Total               8146.5
```

---

[4] "Regional, but Less Power," *The Economist,* March 30, 1991, p. 74.

11-4   How Good Is the Regression?

The mean square error, MSE, is an unbiased estimator of the variance of the population errors, ϵ, which we denote by σ^2. The mean square error is defined in equation 11–10.

The mean square error:

$$\text{MSE} = \frac{\text{SSE}}{n - (k + 1)} = \frac{\sum\limits_{j=1}^{n} (y_j - \hat{y}_j)^2}{n - (k + 1)} \qquad (11\text{–}10)$$

The errors resulting from the fit of a regression surface to our set of n data points are shown in Figure 11–7. The smaller the errors, the better the fit of the regression model. Since the mean square error is the average squared error, where averaging is done by dividing by the degrees of freedom, MSE is a measure of how well the regression fits the data. The square root of MSE is an estimator of the standard deviation of the population regression errors, σ. (Note that a square root of an unbiased estimator is not unbiased; therefore, $\sqrt{\text{MSE}}$ is not an unbiased estimator of σ, but it is still a good estimator.) The square root of MSE is usually denoted by s and is referred to as the *standard error of estimate*.

Standard error of estimate:

$$s = \sqrt{\text{MSE}} \qquad (11\text{–}11)$$

This statistic is usually reported in computer output of multiple regression analysis. The mean square error and its square root are measures of the size of the errors in regression and do not give an indication about the *explained* component of the regression fit (see Figure 11–5, showing the breakdown of the total deviation of any data point to the error and regression components). A measure of regression fit that does incorporate the explained as well as the unexplained components is the *multiple coefficient of determination,* denoted by R^2. This measure is an extension to multiple regression of the coefficient of determination in simple linear regression, denoted by r^2.

The **multiple coefficient of determination, R^2**, measures the proportion of the variation in the dependent variable that is explained by the combination of the independent variables in the multiple regression model.

$$R^2 = \frac{\text{SSR}}{\text{SST}} = 1 - \frac{\text{SSE}}{\text{SST}} \qquad (11\text{–}12)$$

Note that R^2 is also equal to SSR/SST because SST = SSR + SSE. We prefer the definition in equation 11–12 for consistency with another measure of how well the regression model fits our data, the *adjusted* multiple coefficient of determination, which will be introduced shortly.

The measures SSE, SSR, and SST are reported in the ANOVA table for multiple regression. Because of the importance of R^2, however, it is reported separately in

FIGURE 11-7 Errors in a Multiple Regression Model (shown for *k* = 2)

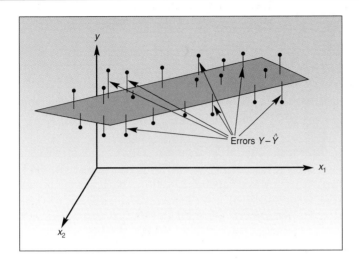

computer output of multiple regression analysis. The square root of the multiple coefficient of determination, $R = \sqrt{R^2}$, is the **multiple correlation coefficient.** In the context of multiple regression analysis (rather than correlation analysis), the multiple coefficient of determination, R^2, is the important measure, not R. The coefficient of determination measures the percentage of variation in Y explained by the X variables; thus, it is an important measure of how well the regression model fits the data. In correlation analysis, where the X_i variables as well as Y are assumed to be random variables, the multiple correlation coefficient R measures the strength of the linear relationship between Y and the k variables X_i.

Figure 11–8 shows the breakdown of the total sum of squares (the sum of squared deviations of all n data points from the mean of Y; see Figure 11–5) into the sum of squares due to the regression (the explained variation) and the sum of squares due to error (the unexplained variation). The interpretation of R^2 is the same as that of r^2 in simple linear regression. The difference is that here the regression errors are measured as deviations from a regression surface that has higher dimensionality than a regression line. The multiple coefficient of determination, R^2, is a very useful measure of performance of a multiple regression model. It does, however, have some limitations.

Recall the story at the beginning of this chapter about the student who wanted to predict the nation's economic future with a multiple regression model that had many variables. It turns out that, for any given data set of n points, as the number of variables in the regression model increases, so does R^2. You have already seen how this happens: The greater the number of variables in the regression equation, the more the regression surface "chases" the data until it overfits them. Since the fit of the regression model increases as we increase the number of variables, R^2 cannot decrease and approaches 1.00, or 100% explained variation in Y. This can be very deceptive, as the model— while appearing to fit the data very well—would produce poor predictions.

Therefore, a new measure of fit of a multiple regression model must be introduced: the *adjusted* (or corrected) *multiple coefficient of determination.* The adjusted multiple coefficient of determination, denoted $\bar{R}^2$, is the multiple coefficient of determination corrected for degrees of freedom. It accounts, therefore, not only for SSE and SST, but also for their appropriate degrees of freedom. This measure does not always increase as new variables are entered into our regression equation. When $\bar{R}^2$

FIGURE 11-8   Decomposition of the Sum of Squares in Multiple Regression, and the Definition of R^2

does increase as a new variable is entered into the regression equation, it may be worthwhile to include the variable in the equation. The adjusted measure is defined as follows.

> **The adjusted multiple coefficient of determination:**
>
> $$\overline{R}^2 = 1 - \frac{\text{SSE}/(n - (k + 1))}{\text{SST}/(n - 1)} \qquad (11\text{–}13)$$

The adjusted R^2 is the R^2 (defined in equation 11–12) where both SSE and SST are divided by their respective degrees of freedom. Since $\text{SSE}/(n - (k + 1))$ is the MSE, we can say that, in a sense, $\overline{R}^2$ is a mixture of the two measures of the performance of a regression model: MSE and R^2. The denominator on the right-hand side of equation 11–13 would be *mean square total,* were we to define such a measure.

Computer output for multiple regression analysis usually includes the adjusted R^2. If it is not reported, we can get $\overline{R}^2$ from R^2 by a simple formula:

$$\overline{R}^2 = 1 - (1 - R^2)\left(\frac{n - 1}{n - (k + 1)}\right) \qquad (11\text{–}14)$$

It is instructional to prove this relation between R^2 and $\overline{R}^2$, and the proof is left as an exercise. *Note:* Unless the number of variables is relatively large compared to the number of data points (as in the economic student's problem), R^2 and $\overline{R}^2$ are close to each other in value. Thus, in many situations, it suffices to consider the uncorrected measure, R^2. We evaluate the fit of a multiple regression model based on this measure. When considering whether to include an independent variable in a regression model that already contains other independent variables, the increase in R^2 when the new variable is added must be weighed against the loss of one degree of freedom for error resulting from the addition of the variable (a new parameter would be added to the equation). With a relatively small data set and several independent variables in the

FIGURE 11-9 Measures of Performance of a Regression Model and the ANOVA Table

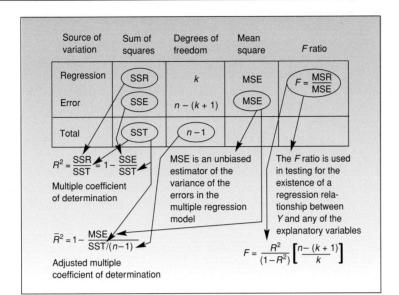

model, it may not be worthwhile to add a new variable if R^2 increases, say, from 0.85 to 0.86. As mentioned earlier, in such cases, the adjusted measure $\bar{R}^2$ may be a good indicator of whether or not to include the new variable. We may decide to include the variable if $\bar{R}^2$ increases when the variable is added.

Of several possible multiple regression models with different independent variables, the model that minimizes MSE will also maximize $\bar{R}^2$. This should not surprise you, since MSE is related to the adjusted measure, $\bar{R}^2$. The use of the two criteria, MSE and $\bar{R}^2$, in selecting variables to be included in a regression model will be discussed in a later section.

We now present another part of the MINITAB output of the analysis of Example 11–1, reporting the standard error of estimate, s, as well as R^2 and the adjusted measure, $\bar{R}^2$, for this regression analysis:

```
s = 1.911              R-sq = 96.1%              R-sq(adj) = 95.0%
```

Note that $R^2 = 0.961$, which means that 96.1% of the variation in sales volume is explained by the combination of the two independent variables, advertising and in-store promotions. Note also that the adjusted R^2 is 0.95, which is very close to the unadjusted measure. We conclude that the regression model fits the data very well since a high percentage of the variation in Y is explained by X_1 and/or X_2 (we do not yet know which of the two variables, if not both, is important). The standard error of estimate, s, is an estimate of σ, the standard deviation of the population regression errors. Note that R^2 is also a *statistic*, like s or MSE. It is a sample estimate of the population multiple coefficient of determination, ρ^2, a measure of the proportion of the explained variation in Y in the entire population of Y and X_i values.

All three measures of the performance of a regression model, MSE (and its square root, s), the coefficient of determination R^2, and the adjusted measure $\bar{R}^2$, are obtainable from quantities reported in the ANOVA table. This is shown in Figure 11–9, which demonstrates the relations among the different measures.

PROBLEMS

11–15. Under what conditions is it important to consider the adjusted multiple coefficient of determination?

11–16. Explain why the multiple coefficient of determination never decreases as variables are added to the multiple regression model.

11–17. Would it be useful to consider an adjusted coefficient of determination in a simple linear regression situation? Explain.

11–18. Prove equation 11–14.

11–19. Can you judge how well a regression model fits the data by considering the mean square error only? Explain.

11–20. A multiple regression analysis is carried out with three independent variables and a data set of 44 points. The results include SSE = 6,980 and SSR = 11,778. Construct an ANOVA table, and find MSE, s, R^2, $\overline{R}^2$, and the F ratio. Analyze the results. Is this a good regression model? Why or why not?

11–21. A portion of the MINITAB regression output for the Nissan Motor Company study of problem 11–14 follows. Interpret the findings, and show how these results are obtainable from the ANOVA table results presented in problem 11–14. How good is the regression relationship between the overall appeal score for the automobile and the attribute-importance scores? Also, obtain the adjusted R^2 from the multiple coefficient of determination.

```
s = 7.192          R-sq = 91.7%          R-sq(adj) = 89.8%
```

11–22. An article in the *Journal of Marketing Research* reports the results of a regression analysis of brand attitude on the independent variables: "ad reactions" and "brand reactions."[5] The reported results are $n = 103$, $R^2 = 0.67$, $F = 2.53$. Find the adjusted R^2. Also, conduct the F test for the existence of a linear relationship between the dependent variable and at least one of the independent variables. How good is the relationship?

11–23. In the Nissan Motor Company situation in problem 11–21, suppose that a new variable is considered for inclusion in the equation and a new regression relationship is analyzed with the new variable included. Suppose that the resulting multiple coefficient of determination is $R^2 = 91.8\%$. Find the adjusted multiple coefficient of determination. Should the new variable be included in the final regression equation? Give your reasons for including or excluding the variable.

11–24. In the situation of problem 11–22, suppose that a new regression is run with the variable "brand reactions" removed from the equation. The resulting new coefficient of determination is $R^2 = 0.61$. Should the new equation, with the variable omitted, be used for prediction of the dependent variable?

11–25. The following excerpt reports the results of a regression of excess stock returns on firm size and stock price, both variables being ranked on some scale. Explain, critique, and evaluate the reported results.

---

[5] K. Keller, "Cue Compatibility and Framing in Advertising," *Journal of Marketing Research,* February, 1991, p. 51.

Estimated Coefficient Value (*t*-Statistic)

INTCPT	SIZRNK	PRCRNK	ADJUSTED-R^2

Ordinary Least Squares Regression Results

0.484	−0.030	−0.017	0.093
(5.71)***	(−2.91)***	(−1.66)*	

*Denotes significance at the 10% level.
**Denotes significance at the 5% level.
***Denotes significance at the 1% level.

Source: M. Bajaj and A. Vijh, "Trading Behavior and Market Reaction," *Journal of Finance* 50, no. 1 (March 1995), p. 265.

11–26. A study of Dutch tourism behavior included a regression analysis using a sample of 713 respondents. The dependent variable, number of miles traveled on vacation, was regressed on the independent variables, family size and family income, and the multiple coefficient of determination was $R^2 = 0.72$. Find the adjusted multiple coefficient of determination, $\overline{R}^2$. Is this a good regression model? Explain.

11–27. In a regression analysis with six independent variables and a data set of 250 points, it is found that SSE = 5,445 and SST = 22,679. Construct an ANOVA table, conduct the *F* test, find R^2 and $\overline{R}^2$, and find MSE.

11–5   Tests of the Significance of Individual Regression Parameters

Until now, we have discussed the multiple regression model in general. We saw how to test for the existence of a regression relationship between *Y* and at least one of a set of independent X_i variables using an *F* test. We also saw how to evaluate the fit of the general regression model using the multiple coefficient of determination and the adjusted multiple coefficient of determination. We have not yet seen, however, how to evaluate the significance of individual regression parameters, β_i. A test for the significance of an individual parameter is important because it tells us whether or not the variable in question, X_h, has explanatory power with respect to the dependent variable. Such a test tells us whether or not the variable in question should be included in the regression equation.

In the last section, we saw that some indication about the benefit from inclusion of a particular variable in the regression equation is given by comparing the adjusted coefficient of determination of a regression that includes the variable of interest with the value of this measure when the variable is not included. In this section, we will perform individual *t* tests for the significance of each slope parameter, β_i. As we will see, however, we must use caution in interpreting the results of the individual *t* tests.

In Chapter 10 we saw that the hypothesis test

$$H_0: \beta_1 = 0$$
$$H_1: \beta_1 \neq 0$$

can be carried out using either a *t* statistic, $t = b_1/s(b_1)$, or an *F* statistic. Both tests were shown to be equivalent because *F* with one degree of freedom for the numerator is a squared *t* random variable with the same number of degrees of freedom as the denominator of F. In simple linear regression, there is only one slope, β_1, and if that slope is zero, there is no linear regression relationship. In multiple regression, where $k > 1$, the two tests are not equivalent. The F test tells us whether or not a relationship exists between Y and at least one of the X_i, and the k ensuing t tests tell us which of the X_i variables are important and should be included in the regression equation. From the similarity of this situation with the situation of analysis of variance discussed in Chapter 9, you probably have guessed at least one of the potential problems: The individual t tests are each carried out at a single level of significance, α, and we cannot determine the level of significance of the family of all k tests of the regression slopes jointly. The problem is further complicated by the fact that the tests are not independent of each other because the regression estimates come from the same data set.

Recall that hypothesis tests and confidence intervals are related. We may test hypotheses about regression slope parameters (in particular, the hypothesis that a slope parameter is equal to zero), or we may construct confidence intervals for the values of the slope parameters. If a 95% confidence interval for a slope parameter, β_h, contains the point zero, then the hypothesis test H_0: $\beta_h = 0$ carried out using $\alpha = 0.05$ would lead to nonrejection of the null hypothesis and thus to the conclusion that there is no evidence that the variable X_h has a linear relationship with Y.

We will demonstrate the interdependence of the separate tests of significance of the slope parameters with the use of confidence intervals for these parameters. When $k = 2$, there are two regression slope parameters: β_1 and β_2. (As in simple linear regression, usually there is no interest in testing hypotheses about the intercept parameter.) The sample estimators of the two regression parameters are b_1 and b_2. These estimators (and their standard errors) are correlated with each other (and assumed to be normally distributed). Therefore, the joint confidence region for the pair of parameters (β_1, β_2) is an *ellipse*. If we consider the estimators b_1 and b_2 separately from each other, the joint confidence region would be a rectangle, with each side a separate confidence interval for a single parameter. This is demonstrated in Figure 11–10. A point inside the rectangle formed by the two separate confidence intervals for the parameters, such as point A in the figure, seems like a plausible value for the pair of regression slopes (β_1, β_2) but is not *jointly* plausible for the parameters. Only points inside the ellipse in the figure are jointly plausible for the pair of parameters.

Another problem that may arise in making inferences about individual regression slope coefficients is due to **multicollinearity**—the problem of correlations among the independent variables themselves. In multiple regression, we hope to have a strong correlation between each independent variable and the dependent variable, Y. Such correlations give the independent X_i variables predictive power with respect to Y. However, we do not want the independent variables to be correlated with each other. When the independent variables are correlated with each other, we have multicollinearity. When this happens, the independent variables rob each other of explanatory power. Many problems may then arise. One problem is that the standard errors of the individual slope estimators become unusually high, making the slope coefficients seem statistically not significant (not different from zero). For example, if we run a regression of job performance (Y) versus the variables age (X_1) and experience (X_2), we may encounter multicollinearity. Since, in general, as age increases so does experience, the two independent variables are not independent of each other; the two variables rob each other of explanatory power with respect to Y. If we run this regression, it is likely that—even though experience affects job performance—the individual test for significance of the slope parameter β_2 would lead to

FIGURE 11-10   Joint Confidence Region and Individual Confidence Intervals for the Slope Parameters β_1 and β_2

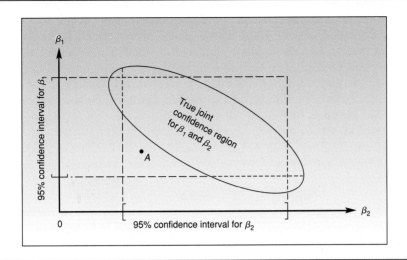

nonrejection of the null hypothesis that this slope parameter is equal to zero. Much will be said later about the problem of multicollinearity. It is important to remember that in the presence of multicollinearity, the significance of any regression parameter depends on the other variables included in the regression equation. Multicollinearity may also cause the signs of some estimated regression parameters to be opposite of what we expect.

Another problem that may affect the individual tests of significance of model parameters occurs when one of the model assumptions is violated. Recall from Section 11-2 that one of the assumptions of the regression model is that the error terms, ϵ_j, are uncorrelated with each other. When this condition does not hold, as may happen when our data are time series observations (observations ordered by time: yearly data, monthly data, etc.), we encounter the problem of autocorrelation of the errors. This causes the standard errors of the slope estimators to be unusually small, making some parameters seem more significant than they really are. This problem, too, should be considered, and we will discuss it in detail later.

Forewarned of problems that may arise, let us now consider the tests of the individual regression parameters. In a regression model of Y versus k independent variables $X_1, X_2, \ldots, X_k$, there are k tests of significance of the slope parameters $\beta_1, \beta_2, \ldots, \beta_k$:

Hypothesis tests about individual regression slope parameters:

$$
\begin{aligned}
(1) \quad & H_0 : \beta_1 = 0 \\
& H_1 : \beta_1 \neq 0 \\
(2) \quad & H_0 : \beta_2 = 0 \\
& H_1 : \beta_2 \neq 0 \\
& \quad \vdots \qquad \vdots \\
(k) \quad & H_0 : \beta_k = 0 \\
& H_1 : \beta_k \neq 0
\end{aligned}
$$

(11-15)

These tests are carried out by comparing each test statistic with a critical point of the distribution of the test statistic. The distribution of each test statistic, when the appropriate null hypothesis is true, is the t distribution with $n - (k + 1)$ degrees of freedom. The distribution depends on our assumption that the regression errors are normally distributed. The test statistic for each hypothesis test, (i), in equation $11-15$ (where $i = 1, 2, \ldots, k$) is the slope estimate b_i divided by the standard error of the estimator, $s(b_i)$. The estimates and the standard errors are reported in the computer output. Each $s(b_i)$ is an estimate of the population standard deviation of the estimator, $\sigma(b_i)$, which is unknown to us.[6] The test statistics for the hypothesis tests $(1)-(k)$ in equation $11-15$ are as follows.

Test statistics for tests about individual regression slope parameters:

$$\text{For test } i \ (i = 1, \ldots, k): \quad t_{(n-(k+1))} = \frac{b_i - 0}{s(b_i)} \qquad (11\text{–}16)$$

We write each test statistic as the estimate minus zero (the null-hypothesized value of β_i) to stress the fact that we may test the null hypothesis that β_i is equal to any number, not necessarily zero. Testing for equality to zero is most important because it tells us whether there is evidence that variable X_i has a linear relationship with Y. It tells us whether there is statistical evidence that variable X_i has explanatory power with respect to the dependent variable.

Let us look at a quick example. Suppose that a multiple regression analysis is carried out relating the dependent variable Y to five independent variables: $X_1, X_2, X_3, X_4,$ and X_5. In addition, suppose that the F test resulted in rejection of the null hypothesis that none of the predictor variables has any explanatory power with respect to Y; suppose also that the R^2 of the regression is respectably high. As a result, we believe that the regression equation gives a good fit to the data and potentially may be used for prediction purposes. Our task now is to test the importance of each of the X_i variables separately. Suppose that the sample size used in this regression analysis is $n = 150$. The results of the regression estimation procedure are given in Table $11-4$.

From the information in Table $11-4$, which variables are important, and which are not? Note that the first variable listed is "Constant." This is the Y-intercept. As we noted earlier, testing whether the intercept is zero is less important than testing whether the coefficient parameter of any of the k variables is zero. Still, we may do so by dividing the reported coefficient estimate, 53.12, by its standard error, 5.43. The result is the value of the test statistic that has a t distribution with $n - (k + 1) = 150 - 6 = 144$ degrees of freedom when the null hypothesis that the intercept is zero is true. For all practical purposes, this t random variable is a standard normal variable, Z. The test statistic value is $z = 53.12/5.43 = 9.78$. This value is greater than 1.96, and we may reject the null hypothesis that β_0 is equal to zero at the $\alpha = 0.05$ level of significance. Actually, the p-value is very small. The regression hyperplane, therefore, most probably does not pass through the origin.

---

[6] Each $s(b_i)$ is the product of $s = \sqrt{\text{MSE}}$ and a term denoted by c_i, which is a diagonal element in a matrix obtained in the regression computations. You need not worry about matrices. However, the matrix approach to multiple regression is discussed in a section at the end of this chapter for the benefit of students familiar with matrix theory.

TABLE 11-4 Regression Results for Individual Parameters

Variable	Coefficient Estimate	Standard Error
Constant	53.12	5.43
X_1	2.03	0.22
X_2	5.60	1.30
X_3	10.35	6.88
X_4	3.45	2.70
X_5	-4.25	0.38

Let us now turn to the tests of significance of the slope parameters of the variables in the regression equation. We start with the test for the significance of variable X_1 as a predictor variable. The hypothesis test is H_0: $\beta_1 = 0$ versus H_1: $\beta_1 \neq 0$. We now compute our test statistic (again, we will use Z for $t_{(144)}$):

$$z = \frac{b_1 - 0}{s(b_1)} = \frac{2.03}{0.22} = 9.227$$

The value of the test statistic, 9.227, lies far in the right-hand rejection region of Z for any conventional level of significance; the p-value is very small. We therefore conclude that there is statistical evidence that the slope of Y with respect to X_1, the population parameter β_1, is not zero. X_1 is shown to have some explanatory power with respect to the dependent variable.

If it is not zero, what is the value of β_1? The parameter, as in the case of all population parameters, is not known to us. An unbiased estimate of the parameter's value is $b_1 = 2.03$. We can also compute a confidence interval for β_1. A 95% confidence interval for β_1 is $b_1 \pm 1.96s(b_1) = 2.03 \pm 1.96(0.22) = [1.599, 2.461]$. Based on our data and the validity of our assumptions, we can be 95% confident that the true slope of Y with respect to X_1 is anywhere from 1.599 to 2.461. Figure 11–11 shows the hypothesis test for the significance of variable X_1.

For the other variables, X_2 through X_5, we show the hypothesis tests without figures. The tests are carried out in the same way, with the same distribution. We also do not show the computation of confidence intervals for the slope parameters. These are done exactly as shown for β_1. Note that when the hypothesis test for the significance of a slope parameter leads to nonrejection of the null hypothesis that the slope parameter is zero, the point zero will be included in a confidence interval with the same confidence level as the level of significance of the test.

The hypothesis test for β_2 is H_0: $\beta_2 = 0$ versus H_1: $\beta_2 \neq 0$. The test statistic value is $z = 5.60/1.30 = 4.308$. This value, too, is in the right-hand rejection region for usual levels of significance; the p-value is small. We conclude that X_2 is also an important variable in the regression equation.

The hypothesis test for β_3 is H_0: $\beta_3 = 0$ versus H_1: $\beta_3 \neq 0$. Here the test statistic value is $z = 10.35/6.88 = 1.504$. This value lies in the nonrejection region for levels of α even larger than 0.10. The p-value is over 0.133, as you can verify from a normal table. We conclude that variable X_3 is probably not important. Remember our cautionary comments that preceded this discussion—there is a possibility that X_3 is actually an important variable. The variable may *appear* to have a slope that is not different from zero because its standard error, $s(b_3) = 6.88$, may be unduly inflated; the variable may be correlated with another explanatory variable (the problem of multi-

FIGURE 11–11   Testing Whether or Not $\beta_1 = 0$

collinearity). A way out of this problem is to drop another variable, one that we suspect to be correlated with X_3, and see if X_3 becomes significant in the new regression model. We will come back to this problem in the section on multicollinearity and in the section on selection of variables to be included in a regression model.

The hypothesis test about β_4 is $H_0: \beta_4 = 0$ versus $H_1: \beta_4 \neq 0$. The value of the test statistic for this test is $z = 3.45/2.70 = 1.278$. Again, we cannot reject the null hypothesis that the slope parameter of X_4 is zero and that the variable has no explanatory power. Note, however, the caution in our discussion of the test of β_3. It is possible, for example, that X_3 and X_4 are collinear and that this is the reason for their respective tests resulting in nonsignificance. It would be wise to drop one of these two variables and check whether the other variable then becomes significant. If it does, the reason for our test result is multicollinearity and not the absence of explanatory power of the variable in question. Another point worth mentioning is the idea of joint inference, discussed earlier. Although the separate tests of β_3 and β_4 both may lead to the nonrejection of the hypothesis that the parameters are zero, it may be that the two parameters are not jointly equal to zero. This would be the situation if, in Figure 11–10, the rectangle contained the point zero while the ellipse—the true joint confidence region for both parameters—did not contain that point. It is important to note that the *t* tests are *conditional*. The significance or nonsignificance of a variable in the equation is conditional on the fact that the regression equation contains the other variables.

Finally, the test for the parameter β_5 is $H_0: \beta_5 = 0$ versus $H_1: \beta_5 \neq 0$. The computed value of the test statistic is $z = -4.25/0.38 = -11.184$. This value falls far in the left-hand rejection region, and we conclude that variable X_5 has explanatory power with respect to the dependent variable and therefore should be included in the regression equation. The slope parameter is negative, which means that, everything else staying constant, the dependent variable Y decreases on the average as X_5 increases. We note that these tests can be carried out very quickly by just considering the p-values.

We now return to Example 11–1 and give the rest of the MINITAB output of the analysis of the relationship between sales and the independent variables, advertising and in-store promotions. Table 11–5 gives the values of the estimates, the standard errors of the estimators, the value of every test statistic, denoted "t-ratio," and the p-values. The output also includes the estimated regression equation. We see that both independent variables are significant.

TABLE 11-5 MINITAB Output for Example 11-1

```
MTB > REGRESS 'sales' on 2 predictors, 'advert', 'prom'

The regression equation is
sales = 47.2 + 1.60 advert + 1.15 prom

Predictor      Coef        Stdev       t-ratio        P
Constant      47.165       2.470        19.09       0.000
advert        1.5990       0.2810        5.69       0.000
prom          1.1487       0.3052        3.76       0.007
```

EXAMPLE 11-2

In recent years, many American firms have intensified their efforts to market their products in the Pacific Rim. Among the major economic powers in that area are Japan, Hong Kong, and Singapore. A consortium of U.S. firms that produce raw materials used in Singapore is interested in predicting the level of exports from the United States to Singapore, as well as understanding the relationship between U.S. exports to Singapore and certain variables affecting the economy of that country. Understanding this relationship would allow the consortium members to time their marketing efforts to coincide with favorable conditions in the Singapore economy. Understanding the relationship would also allow the exporters to determine whether or not there is room for expansion of exports to Singapore. The economist hired to do the analysis obtained from the Monetary Authority of Singapore (MAS) monthly data on five economic variables for the period January 1989 to August 1995. The variables were: U.S. exports to Singapore in billions of Singapore dollars (the dependent variable, Exports), money supply figures in billions of Singapore dollars (variable M1), minimum Singapore bank lending rate in percentages (variable Lend), an index of local prices where the base year is 1974 (variable Price), and the exchange rate of Singapore dollars per U.S. dollar (variable Exchange). The monthly data and the MINITAB program that reads them into the computer and names the variables are given in Table 11–6.

SOLUTION

The economist used the MINITAB package to perform a multiple regression analysis with exports as the dependent variable and the four economic variables M1, Lend, Price, and Exchange as the predictor variables. The MINITAB command for this regression and the resulting output are given in Table 11–7.

Let us analyze the regression results. We start with the ANOVA table and the F test for the existence of a linear relationships between the independent variables and exports from the United States to Singapore. We have $F_{(4, 62)} = 73.08$ with a p-value of "0.000". We conclude that there is strong evidence of a linear regression relationship here. This is further confirmed by noting that the coefficient of determination is high: $R^2 = 0.825$. Thus, the combination of the four economic variables explains 82.5% of the variation in exports to Singapore. The adjusted coefficient of determination, $\bar{R}^2$, is a little smaller: 0.814. Now the question is which of the four variables are important as predictors of export volume to Singapore and which are not. Looking at the reported p-values, we see that the Singapore money supply, M1, is an important variable; the level of prices in Singapore is also an important variable. The remaining two variables, minimum lending rate and exchange rate, have very large p-values. It is surprising that the lending rate and the exchange rate of Singapore dollars to U.S. dollars seem to have no effect on the volume of Singapore's imports from the United States. Remember, however, that we may have a

TABLE 11-6   Example 11-2 Data as Read into MINITAB

```
MTB > NAME C1 'M1', C2 'LEND', C3 'PRICE', C4 'EXCHANGE', C5 'EXPORTS'
MTB > READ 'REGRESS.DAT' INTO 'M1', 'LEND','PRICE', 'EXCHANGE', 'EXPORTS'
67 ROWS READ
MTB > PRINT 'EXPORTS', 'M1', 'LEND', 'PRICE', 'EXCHANGE'
```

| | C5 | C1 | C2 | C3 | C4 |
ROW	EXPORTS	M1	LEND	PRICE	EXCHANGE
1	2.6	5.1	7.8	114	2.16
2	2.6	4.9	8.0	116	2.17
3	2.7	5.1	8.1	117	2.18
4	3.0	5.1	8.1	122	2.20
5	2.9	5.1	8.1	124	2.21
6	3.1	5.2	8.1	128	2.17
7	3.2	5.1	8.3	132	2.14
8	3.7	5.2	8.8	133	2.16
9	3.6	5.3	8.9	133	2.15
10	3.4	5.4	9.1	134	2.16
11	3.7	5.7	9.2	135	2.18
12	3.6	5.7	9.5	136	2.17
13	4.1	5.9	10.3	140	2.15
14	3.5	5.8	10.6	147	2.16
15	4.2	5.7	11.3	150	2.21
16	4.3	5.8	12.1	151	2.24
17	4.2	6.0	12.0	151	2.16
18	4.1	6.0	11.4	151	2.12
19	4.6	6.0	11.1	153	2.11
20	4.4	6.0	11.0	154	2.13
21	4.5	6.1	11.3	154	2.11
22	4.6	6.0	12.6	154	2.09
23	4.6	6.1	13.6	155	2.09
24	4.2	6.7	13.6	155	2.10
25	5.5	6.2	14.3	156	2.08
26	3.7	6.3	14.3	156	2.09
27	4.9	7.0	13.7	159	2.10
28	5.2	7.0	12.7	161	2.11
29	4.9	6.6	12.6	161	2.15
30	4.6	6.4	13.4	161	2.14
31	5.4	6.3	14.3	162	2.16
32	5.0	6.5	13.9	160	2.17
33	4.8	6.6	14.5	159	2.15
34	5.1	6.8	15.0	159	2.10
35	4.4	7.2	13.2	158	2.06
36	5.0	7.6	11.8	155	2.05
37	5.1	7.2	11.2	155	2.06
38	4.8	7.1	10.1	154	2.11
39	5.4	7.0	10.0	154	2.12
40	5.0	7.5	10.2	154	2.13
41	5.2	7.4	11.0	153	2.04
42	4.7	7.4	11.0	152	2.14
43	5.1	7.3	10.7	152	2.15
44	4.9	7.6	10.2	152	2.16
45	4.9	7.8	10.0	151	2.17
46	5.3	7.8	9.8	152	2.20
47	4.8	8.2	9.3	152	2.21
48	4.9	8.2	9.3	152	2.15
49	5.1	8.3	9.5	152	2.08
50	4.3	8.3	9.2	150	2.08
51	4.9	8.0	9.1	147	2.09
52	5.3	8.2	9.0	147	2.10

ROW	EXPORTS	M1	LEND	PRICE	EXCHANGE
53	4.8	8.2	9.0	146	2.09
54	5.3	8.0	8.9	145	2.12
55	5.0	8.1	9.0	145	2.13
56	5.1	8.1	9.0	146	2.14
57	4.8	8.1	9.0	147	2.14
58	4.8	8.1	8.9	147	2.13
59	5.2	8.6	8.9	147	2.13
60	4.9	8.8	9.0	146	2.13
61	5.5	8.4	9.1	147	2.13
62	4.3	8.2	9.0	146	2.13
63	5.2	8.3	9.2	146	2.09
64	4.7	8.3	9.6	146	2.09
65	5.4	8.4	10.0	146	2.10
66	5.2	8.3	10.0	147	2.11
67	5.6	8.2	10.1	146	2.15

TABLE 11-7   Exports to Singapore Regression Analysis Results

```
MTB > REGRESS 'EXPORTS' on 4 predictors, 'M1', 'LEND', 'PRICE', 'EXCHANGE'

    The regression equation is
    EXPORTS = - 4.02 + 0.368 M1 + 0.0047 LEND + 0.0365 PRICE + 0.27 EXCHANGE

    Predictor      Coef        Stdev      t-ratio      p
    Constant      -4.015       2.766       -1.45     0.152
    M1             0.36846     0.06385      5.77     0.000
    LEND           0.00470     0.04922      0.10     0.924
    PRICE          0.036511    0.009326     3.91     0.000
    EXCHANGE       0.268       1.175        0.23     0.820

    s = 0.3358       R-sq = 82.5%     R-sq(adj) = 81.4%

    Analysis of Variance

    SOURCE        DF       SS         MS        F         p
    Regression     4     32.9463    8.2366    73.06     0.000
    Error         62      6.9898    0.1127
    Total         66     39.9361
```

problem of multicollinearity. This is especially true when dealing with economic variables, which tend to be correlated with each other.[7]

When M1 is dropped from the equation and the new regression analysis considers the independent variables Lend, Price, and Exchange, we see that the lending rate, which was not significant in the full regression equation, now becomes significant! This is seen in Table 11–8. Note that R^2 has dropped greatly with the removal of M1. The fact that the lending rate is significant in the new equation is an indication of *multicollinearity;* the variables M1 and Lend are correlated with each other. Therefore, Lend is not significant when M1 is in the equation, but in the absence of M1, Lend does have explanatory power.

---

[7] The analysis of economic variables presents special problems. Economists have developed methods that account for the intricate interrelations among economic variables. These methods, based on multiple regression and time series analysis, are usually referred to as *econometric methods.*

TABLE 11-8   Exports to Singapore without the Variable M1 in the Equation

```
MTB > REGRESS 'EXPORTS' on 3 predictors, 'LEND', 'PRICE', 'EXCHANGE'

    The regression equation is
    EXPORTS = - 0.29 - 0.211 LEND + 0.0781 PRICE - 2.10 EXCHANGE
    Predictor      Coef        Stdev       t-ratio      p
    Constant      -0.289       3.308        -0.09      0.931
    LEND          -0.21140     0.03929      -5.38      0.000
    PRICE          0.078148    0.007268     10.75      0.000
    EXCHANGE      -2.095        1.355        -1.55      0.127

    s = 0.4130      R-sq = 73.1%      R-sq(adj) = 71.8%

    Analysis of Variance

       SOURCE      DF       SS          MS          F          p
    Regression      3     29.1919     9.7306      57.06      0.000
    Error          63     10.7442     0.1705
    Total          66     39.9361
```

TABLE 11-9   Exports to Singapore versus the Variables M1 and Price

```
    MTB > REGRESS 'EXPORTS' on 2 predictors, 'M1', 'PRICE',

    The regression equation is
    EXPORTS = - 3.42 + 0.361 M1 + 0.0370 PRICE

    Predictor      Coef        Stdev       t-ratio      p
    Constant      -3.4230      0.5409       -6.33      0.000
    M1             0.36142     0.03925       9.21      0.000
    PRICE          0.037033    0.004094      9.05      0.000

    s = 0.3306      R-sq = 82.5%      R-sq(adj) = 81.9%

    Analysis of Variance

       SOURCE      DF       SS          MS          F          p
    Regression      2     32.940      16.470     150.67      0.000
    Error          64      6.996       0.109
    Total          66     39.936
```

Note that the exchange rate is still not significant. Since R^2 and the adjusted R^2 both decrease significantly when the money supply, M1, is dropped, let us put that variable back into the equation and run U.S. exports to Singapore versus the independent variables M1 and Price only. The results are shown in Table 11–9. In this regression equation, both independent variables are significant. Note that R^2 in this regression is the same as R^2 with all four variables in the equation (see Table 11–7); both are 0.825. However, the adjusted coefficient of determination, $\bar{R}^2$, is different. The adjusted R^2 actually *increases* as we drop the variables Lend and Exchange. In the full model with the four variables (Table 11–7), $\bar{R}^2 = 0.814$, while in the reduced model, with variables M1 and Price only (Table 11–9), $\bar{R}^2 = 0.819$. This demonstrates the usefulness of the adjusted R^2. When unimportant variables are added into the equation (unimportant in the presence of other variables), $\bar{R}^2$ decreases even if R^2 increases (here R^2 is reported to first-decimal accuracy, so we do not see an increase). The best model, in terms of explanatory power gauged against the loss of degrees of freedom, is the reduced model in Table 11–9, which relates exports to Singapore with only the money supply and price level. This is also seen by the fact that the other two variables are not significant once M1 and Price are in the equation. Later, when we discuss stepwise regression—a method of letting the computer choose the best variables to be included in the model—we will see that this automatic procedure also chooses the variables M1 and Price as the best combination for predicting U.S. exports to Singapore.

11–28. A regression analysis is carried out, and a confidence interval for β_1 is computed to be [1.25, 1.55]; a confidence interval for β_2 is [2.01, 2.12]. Both confidence intervals are of 95%. Explain the possibility that the point (1.26, 2.02) may not lie inside a joint confidence region for (β_1, β_2) at a confidence level of 95%.

11–29. A regression analysis of total bank deposits versus the independent variable area affluence is carried out. The estimated slope coefficient is 1.27, and its standard error is 0.11. A second independent variable, average value of a single-family home in the area, is added to the model. The estimated slope coefficient of area affluence in the new regression equation is 1.02, and its standard deviation is 0.87. Explain what happened and why.

11–30. Give three reasons why caution must be exercised in interpreting the significance of single regression slope parameters.

11–31. Give 95% confidence intervals for the slope parameters β_2 through β_5 using the information in Table 11–4. Which confidence intervals contain the point zero? Explain the interpretation of such outcomes.

11–32. Suppose that in a regression equation, two slope parameters are significant and two are not. One of the two insignificant variables is dropped, and the other one remains insignificant in the new equation. Give two possible reasons for this finding, and suggest a way of determining the correct reason.

11–33. A computer program for regression analysis produces a joint confidence region for the two slope parameters considered in the regression equation, β_1 and β_2. The elliptical region of confidence level 95% does not contain the point (0, 0). Not knowing the value of the F statistic, or R^2, do you believe there is a linear regression relationship between Y and at least one of the two explanatory variables? Explain.

11–34. In the Nissan Motor Company situation of problems 11–14 and 11–21, part of the information produced by the MINITAB program relevant to tests of separate regression parameters is as follows. Give a complete interpretation of these results.

```
MTB > REGRESS 'RATING' on 3 predictors, 'PRESTIGE', 'COMFORT', 'ECONOMY'

The regression equation is
RATING = 24.1 - 0.166 PRESTIGE + 0.324 COMFORT + 0.514 ECONOMY

Predictor      Coef        Stdev
Constant       24.14       18.22
PRESTIGE       -0.1658      0.1215
COMFORT        0.3236       0.1228
ECONOMY        0.5139       0.1143
```

11–35. Refer to Example 11–2, where exports to Singapore were regressed on several economic variables. Interpret the results of the following analysis, and compare them with the results reported in the text. How does the present model fit with the rest of the analysis? Explain.

```
MTB > REGRESS 'EXPORTS' on 3 predictors, 'M1', 'LEND', 'PRICE'

The regression equation is
EXPORTS = - 3.40 + 0.363 M1 + 0.0021 LEND + 0.0367 PRICE
```

```
Predictor        Coef          Stdev       t-ratio        p
Constant       -3.4047        0.6821        -4.99       0.000
M1              0.36339       0.05940        6.12       0.000
LEND            0.00211       0.04753        0.04       0.965
PRICE           0.036666      0.009231       3.97       0.000

s = 0.3332      R-sq = 82.5%      R-sq(adj) = 81.6%
```

11–36. After the model of problem 11–35, the next model was run:

```
MTB > REGRESS 'EXPORTS' on 2 predictors, 'M1', 'LEND'

The regression equation is
EXPORTS = - 1.09 + 0.552 M1 + 0.171 LEND

Predictor        Coef          Stdev       t-ratio        p
Constant       -1.0859        0.3914        -2.77       0.007
M1              0.55222       0.03950       13.98       0.000
LEND            0.17100       0.02357        7.25       0.000

s = 0.3697      R-sq = 78.1%      R-sq(adj) = 77.4%

Analysis of Variance

  SOURCE       DF        SS          MS          F          p
Regression      2      31.189      15.594      114.09     0.000
Error          64       8.748       0.137
Total          66      39.936
```

    a. What happened when Price was dropped from the regression equation? Why?

    b. Compare this model with all previous models of exports versus the economic variables, and draw conclusions.

    c. Which model is best overall? Why?

    d. Conduct the F test for this particular model.

    e. Compare the reported value of s in this model with the reported s value in the model of problem 11–35. Why is s higher in this model?

    f. For the model in problem 11–35, what is the mean square error?

11–37. A regression analysis of monthly sales versus four independent variables is carried out. One of the variables is known not to have any effect on sales, yet its slope parameter in the regression is significant. In your opinion, what may have caused this to happen?

11–38. An article in the *Journal of Finance* reports the results of a regression analysis of stock returns for firms that are targeted for takeover versus two financial ratios: the Q ratio of the target firm and the Q ratio of the bidder. The results are given in the table below. Give a complete interpretation of the regression results.

	Target Returns
Intercept	0.3270 (0.00)
Target Q is large	−0.1323 (0.00)
Bidder Q is large	−0.0163 (0.70)
F value	5.47 (0.00)
R^2	0.03
N	384

p-values in parentheses.

Source: H. Servaes, "Tobin's Q and the Gains from Takeovers," *Journal of Finance* 46, no.1 (March 1991), p. 416.

11–39.   The following results are of a multiple regression analysis of consideration scores on the independent variables price, store feature, television advertising, and brand loyalty. Interpret these results.

Consideration Function

Constant	$-89*$
Price	$-.52*$
Store feature	$10.47**$
Television advertising	$1.14*$
Brand loyalty	$19.84*$

$*p < .05$

$**p < .10$

Source: R. Andrews and T. Srinivasan, "Studying Consideration Effects," *Journal of Marketing Research 32* (February 1995), pp. 30–41.

11–6   Testing the Validity of the Regression Model

In Chapter 10, we stressed the importance of the three stages of statistical model building: model specification, estimation of parameters, and testing the validity of the model assumptions. We will now discuss the third and very important stage of checking the validity of the model assumptions in multiple regression analysis.

Residual Plots

As with simple linear regression, the analysis of regression residuals is an important tool for determining whether the assumptions of the multiple regression model are met. Residual plots are easy to use, and they convey much information quickly. The saying "A picture is worth a thousand words" is a good description of the technique of examining plots of regression residuals. As with simple linear regression, we may plot the residuals against the predicted values of the dependent variable, against each independent variable, against time (or the order of selection of the data points), and on a probability scale, to check the normality assumption. Since we have already discussed the use of residual plots in Chapter 10, we will demonstrate only some of the residual plots using Example 11–2. Figure 11–12 is a plot of the residuals produced from the model with the two independent variables, M1 and Price (Table 11–9), against the variable M1. It appears that the residuals are randomly distributed with no pattern and with equal variance as M1 increases.

Figure 11–13 is a plot of the regression residuals against the variable Price. Here the picture is quite different. As we examine this figure carefully, we see that the spread of the residuals increases as Price increases. Thus, the variance of the residuals is not constant. We have the situation called *heteroscedasticity*—a violation of the assumption of equal error variance. In such cases, the ordinary least squares (OLS) estimation method is not efficient, and an alternative method called *weighted least squares* (WLS) should be used instead. The WLS procedure is discussed in advanced texts on regression analysis.

Figure 11–14 is a plot of the regression residuals against the variable Time, that is, the order of the observations. (The observations are a time sequence of monthly data.) This variable was not included in the model, and the plot could reveal whether time should have been included as a variable in our regression model. The plot of the

FIGURE 11–12   Residuals against MI (Example 11–2)

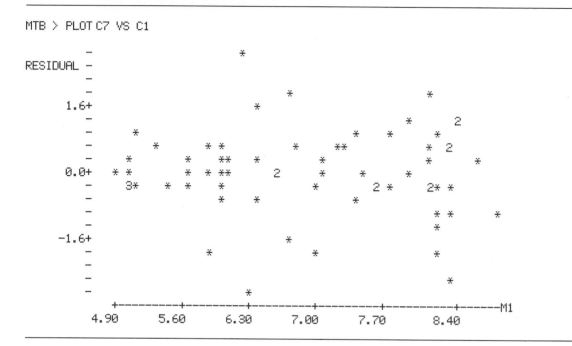

FIGURE 11–13   Residuals against Price (Example (11–2)

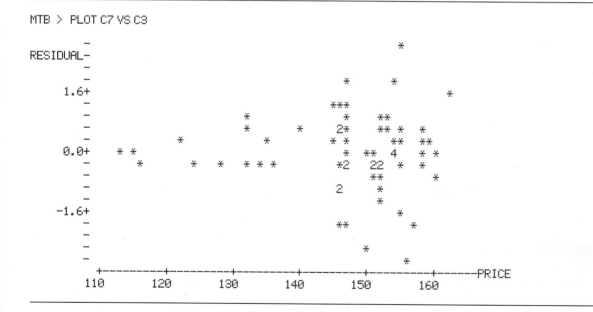

residuals against time reveals no pattern in the residuals as time increases. The residuals seem to be more or less randomly distributed about their mean of zero.

Figure 11–15 is a plot of the regression residuals against the predicted export values, $\hat{Y}$. We leave it as an exercise to the reader to interpret the information in this plot.

FIGURE 11-14   Residuals against Time Example (11-2)

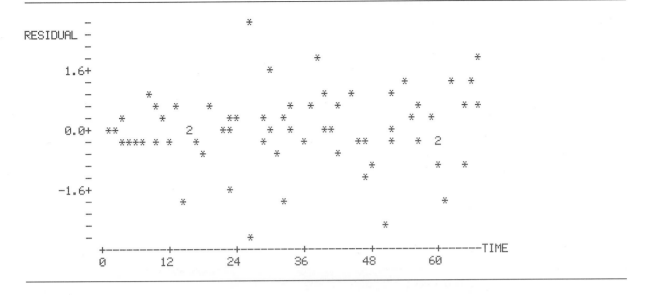

FIGURE 11-15   Residuals against Predicted Y Values Example (11-2)

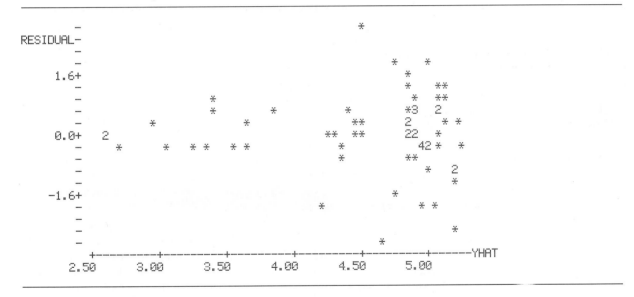

Standardized Residuals

Remember that under the assumptions of the regression model, the population errors, ϵ_j, are normally distributed with mean zero and standard deviation σ. As a result, the errors divided by their standard deviation should follow the standard normal distribution:

$$\frac{\epsilon_j}{\sigma} \sim N(0, 1) \qquad \text{for all } j$$

FIGURE 11-16   Histogram of the Standardized Residuals (Example 11-2)

```
Histogram of   C7      N = 67
   Midpoint    Count
     -3.0        1     *
     -2.5        1     *
     -2.0        3     ***
     -1.5        1     *
     -1.0        5     *****
     -0.5       13     *************
      0.0       19     *******************
      0.5       12     ************
      1.0        6     ******
      1.5        3     ***
      2.0        2     **
      2.5        0
      3.0        1     *
```

Therefore, dividing the observed regression errors, e_j, by their estimated standard deviation, s, will give us standardized residuals. Examination of a histogram of these residuals may give us an idea as to whether or not the normal assumption is valid.[8]

The MINITAB program produces, on request, the standardized residuals, which may be plotted as a histogram. We give this plot for the data of Example 11–2, shown in Figure 11–16. These standardized residuals are computed by the more accurate method referred to in the footnote, which accounts for differences in the variance of different error terms. Looking at the plot in Figure 11–16, it seems that the normality assumption is reasonable. There are three observations with standard residuals over 2 in absolute value. Since there are $n = 76$ observations, we expect an average of $76(0.05) = 3.8$ residuals to be above 2 in absolute value purely by chance. Thus, three residuals are within the range we expect under the model assumptions.

Outliers and Influential Observations

An **outlier** is an extreme observation. It is a point that lies away from the rest of the data set. Because of this, outliers may exert greater influence on the least-squares estimates of the regression parameters than do other observations. To see why, consider the data in Figure 11–17. The graph shows the estimated least-squares regression line without the outlier and the line obtained when the outlier is considered.

As can be seen from Figure 11–17, the outlier has a strong effect on the estimation of model parameters. (We used a line showing Y versus variable X_1. The same is true for a regression plane or hyperplane: the outlier "tilts" the regression surface away from the other points.) The reason for this effect is the nature of least squares: the procedure minimizes the squared deviations of the data points from the regression surface. A point with an unusually large deviation "attracts" the surface toward itself so as to make its squared deviation smaller.

We must, therefore, give special attention to outliers. If an outlier can be traced to an error in recording the data or to another type of error, it should, of course, be removed. On the other hand, if an outlier is not due to error, it may have been caused

---

[8] Actually, the residuals are not independent and do not have equal variance; therefore, we really should divide the residuals, e_j, by something a little more complicated than s. However, the simpler procedure outlined here and implemented in some computer packages is usually sufficiently accurate.

FIGURE 11-17   A Least-Squares Regression Line Estimated with and without the Outlier

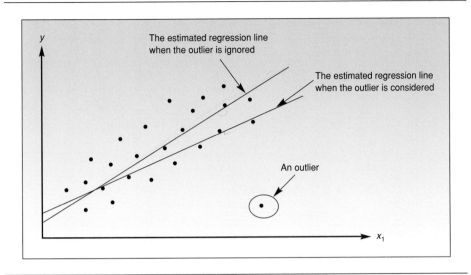

by special circumstances, and the information it provides may be important. For example, an outlier may be an indication of a missing variable in the regression equation. The data shown in Figure 11–17 may be maximum speed for an automobile as a function of engine displacement. The outlier may be an automobile with four cylinders, while all others are six-cylinder cars. Thus, the fact that the point lies away from the rest may be explained. Because of the possible information content in outliers, they should be carefully scrutinized before one decides to discard them. There are some alternative regression methods that do not use a squared-distance approach and are therefore more robust—less sensitive to the influence of outliers.

Sometimes an outlier is actually a point that is distant from the rest because the value of one of its independent variables is larger than the rest of the data. For example, suppose we measure chemical yield (Y) as a function of temperature (X_1). There may be other variables, but we will consider only these two. Suppose that most of our data are obtained at low temperatures within a certain range, but one observation is taken at a high temperature. This outlying point, far in the X_1 direction, exerts strong influence on the estimation of the model parameters. This is shown in Figure 11–18. Without the point at high temperature, the regression line may have slope zero, and no relationship may be detected, as can be seen from the figure. We must also be careful in such cases to guard against estimating a straight-line relation where a curvilinear one may be more appropriate. This could become evident if we had more data points in the region between the far point and the rest of the data. This is shown in Figure 11–19.

Figure 11–19 serves as a good reminder that regression analysis should not be used for extrapolation. We do not know what happens in the region in which we have no data. This region may be between two regions where we have data, or it may lie beyond the last observation in a given direction. The relationship may be quite different from what we estimate from the data. This is also a reason why it is not a good idea to force the regression surface to go through the origin (that is, carry out a regression with no constant term: $\beta_0 = 0$), as is done in some applications. The reasoning in such cases follows the idea expressed in the statement "In this particular case, when there is zero input, there must be zero output," which may very well be

FIGURE 11-18   Influence of an Observation Far in the X_1 Direction

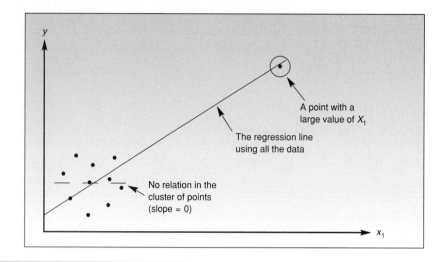

FIGURE 11-19   Possible Relation in the Region between the Available Cluster of Data and the Far Point

true. Forcing the regression to go through the origin, however, may make the estimation procedure biased. This is because in the region where the data points are located—assuming they are not near the origin—the best straight line to describe the data may not have an intercept of zero. This happens when the relationship is not a straight-line relationship. We mentioned this problem in Chapter 10.

A data point far from the other points in some X_i direction is called an *influential observation* if it strongly affects the regression fit. There are statistical techniques of testing whether or not the regression fit is strongly affected by a given observation. Computer routines such as MINITAB automatically search for outliers and influential observations, reporting in the regression output so that the user is alerted to the possible effects of these observations. Table 11-10 shows part of the MINITAB output for the analysis of Example 11.2. The table reports "unusual observations": large residuals and influential observations that affect the estimation of the regression relationship.

TABLE 11-10   Part of the MINITAB Output for Example 11-2

```
Unusual Observations
Obs.    M1      EXPORTS     Fit     Stdev.Fit   Residual    St.Resid
  1    5.10     2.6000    2.6420    0.1288     -0.0420     -0.14  X
  2    4.90     2.6000    2.6438    0.1234     -0.0438     -0.14  X
 25    6.20     5.5000    4.5949    0.0676      0.9051      2.80R
 26    6.30     3.7000    4.6311    0.0651     -0.9311     -2.87R
 50    8.30     4.3000    5.1317    0.0648     -0.8317     -2.57R
 67    8.20     5.6000    4.9474    0.0668      0.6526      2.02R

R   denotes an obs. with a large st. resid.
X   denotes an obs. whose X value gives it large influence.
```

Lack of Fit and Other Problems

Model lack of fit occurs if, for example, we try to fit a straight line to curved data. There is a statistical method of determining the existence of lack of fit. The method consists of breaking down the sum of squares for error to a sum of squares due to pure error and a sum of squares due to lack of fit. The method requires that we have observations at equal values of the independent variables or near-neighbor points. This method is described in advanced texts on regression.

A statistical method for determining whether the errors in a regression model are correlated through time (thus violating the regression model assumptions) is the Durbin-Watson test. This test is discussed in a later section of this chapter. Once we determine that our regression model is valid and that there are no serious violations of assumptions, we can use the model for its intended purpose.

PROBLEMS

11-40. Analyze the following plot showing the residuals against $\hat{Y}$.

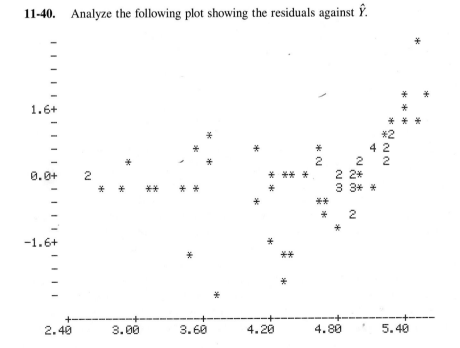

11–41.   What is indicated by the following plot of the standardized residuals from a multiple regression analysis?

```
MTB > histogram of C3

Histogram of C3   N = 20

Midpoint    Count
   -1.5      2      **
   -1.0      5      *****
   -0.5      2      **
    0.0      3      ***
    0.5      2      **
    1.0      3      ***
    1.5      2      **
    2.0      1      *
```

11–42.   Explain what an outlier is.

11–43.   How can you detect outliers? Discuss two ways of doing so.

11–44.   Why should outliers not be discarded and the regression run without them?

11–45.   Discuss the possible effects of an outlier on the regression analysis.

11–46.   What is an influential observation? Give a few examples.

11–47.   What are the limitations of forcing the regression surface to go through the origin?

11–48.   Analyze the residual plot of Figure 11–15.

11-7   Using the Multiple Regression Model for Prediction

The use of the multiple regression model for prediction follows the same lines as in the case of simple linear regression, discussed in Chapter 10. We obtain a regression model prediction of a value of the dependent variable, Y, based on given values of the independent variables, by substituting the values of the independent variables into the prediction equation. That is, we substitute the values of the X_i variables into the equation for $\hat{Y}$. We demonstrate this in Example 11–1.

The predicted value of Y is given by substituting the given values of advertising (X_1) and in-store promotions (X_2) for which we want to predict sales (Y) into equation 11–6 using the parameter estimates obtained in section 11–2. Let us predict sales when advertising is at a level of $10,000 and in-store promotions are at a level of $5,000.

$$\hat{Y} = 47.165 + 1.599X_1 + 1.149X_2$$
$$= 47.165 + (1.599)(10) + (1.149)(5) = 68.9 \text{ (thousand dollars)}$$

This prediction is not bad, since the value of Y actually occurring for these values of X_1 and X_2 is known from Table 11–1 to be $Y = 70$ (thousand dollars). Our point estimate of the expected value of Y, $E(Y)$, given these values of X_1 and X_2 is also 68.9 (thousand dollars). Note that our predictions lie *on* the estimated regression surface. The estimated regression surface for Example 11–1 is the plane shown in Figure 11–20.

We may also compute prediction intervals as well as confidence intervals for $E(Y)$, given values of the independent variables. As you recall, while the predicted value and the estimate of the mean value of Y are equal, the prediction interval is wider than a confidence interval for $E(Y)$ using the same confidence level. There is more uncertainty about the predicted value than there is about the average value of Y given

FIGURE 11-20 Estimated Regression Plane for Example 11-1

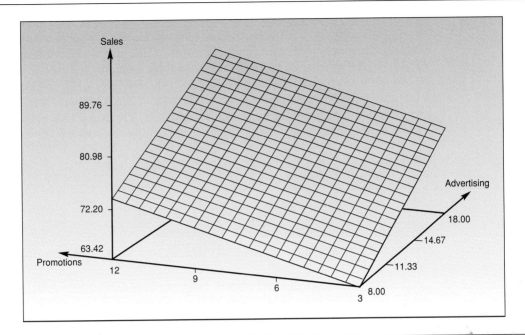

the values X_i. The equation for a $(1 - \alpha)100\%$ prediction interval is an extension of equation 10–32 for simple linear regression. The only difference is that the degrees of freedom of the t distribution are $n - (k + 1)$ rather than just $n - 2$, as is the case for $k = 1$. The standard error, when there are several explanatory variables, is a complicated expression, and we will not give it here; we will denote it by $s(\hat{Y})$. The prediction interval is given in equation 11–17.

> A $(1 - \alpha)100\%$ prediction interval for a value of Y given values of X_i:
>
> $$\hat{y} \pm t_{[\alpha/2, n - (k + 1)]} \sqrt{s^2(\hat{Y}) + \text{MSE}} \qquad (11\text{--}17)$$

While the expression in the square root is complex, it is computed by most computer packages for regression. The prediction intervals for any values of the independent variables and a given level of confidence are produced as output.

Similarly, the equation for a $(1 - \alpha)100\%$ confidence interval for the conditional mean of Y is an extension of equation 10–33 for the simple linear regression. It is given as equation 11–18. Again, the degrees of freedom are $n - (k + 1)$. The formula for the standard error is complex and will not be given here. We will call the standard error $s[\hat{E}(Y)]$. The confidence interval for the conditional mean of Y is computable and may be reported, upon request, in the output of most computer packages that include regression analysis.

> A $(1 - \alpha)100\%$ confidence interval for the conditional mean of Y:
>
> $$\hat{y} \pm t_{[\alpha/2, n - (k + 1)]} s[\hat{E}(Y)] \qquad (11\text{--}18)$$

We demonstrate the use of equations 11–17 and 11–18 by computer analysis with Example 11–2. We use the MINITAB program to produce predictions of the level of U.S. exports to Singapore for given levels of local prices and money supply. We will also obtain a 95% prediction interval for each prediction and a 95% confidence interval for the mean level of exports for the given values of Price and M1. The MINITAB subcommand PREDICT is used for obtaining the output.

We want to predict exports to Singapore at three levels of M1 and Price. These levels are 6 billion Singapore dollars and 160 (index value), 5 billion Singapore dollars and 150, and 4 billion Singapore dollars and 130. The MINITAB subcommands asking for the predictions and the prediction and confidence intervals (both 95%) are:

```
MTB > regress 'exports' on 2 'M1', 'PRICE';
SUBC>    predict 6 160;
SUBC>    predict 5 150;
SUBC>    predict 4 130.
```

The computer-produced predictions, standard errors, confidence intervals for the conditional means, and prediction intervals are given for the three selected points in Table 11–11.

The predictions are not very reliable because of the heteroscedasticity we discovered in the last section, but they are useful as a demonstration of the procedure. Remember that it is never a good idea to try to predict values outside the region of the data used in the estimation of the regression parameters because the regression relationship may be different outside that range. In this example, all predictions use values of the independent variables within the range of the estimation data.

When using regression models, it is important to know that a regression relationship between the dependent variable and some independent variables does not imply causality. Thus, if we find a linear relationship between Y and X, it does not necessarily mean that X causes Y. Causality is very difficult to determine and to prove. There is also the issue of spurious correlations between variables—correlations that are not real. Montgomery and Peck give an example of a regression analysis of the number of mentally disturbed people in the United Kingdom versus the number of radio receiver licenses issued in that country.[9] The regression relationship is close to a perfect straight line, with $r^2 = 0.9842$. Can the conclusion be drawn that there is a relationship between the number of radio receiver licenses and the incidence of mental illness? Probably not. Both variables—the number of licenses and the incidence of mental illness—are related to a third variable: population size. The increase in both of these variables reflects the growth of the population in general, and there is probably no *direct* connection between the two variables. We must be very careful in our interpretation of regression results.

PROBLEMS

11-49.   Explain why it is not a good idea to use the regression equation for predicting values outside the range of the estimation data set.

11–50.   Use equation 11–6 to predict sales in Example 11–1 when the level of advertising is $8,000 and in-store promotions are at a level of $12,000.

---

[9] D. Montgomery and E. Peck, *Introduction to Linear Regression Analysis* (New York: Wiley, 1982).

TABLE 11-11   Predictions, Confidence Intervals, and Prediction Intervals for Example 11-2

Fit	Stdev.Fit	95% C. I.	95% P. I.
4.6708	0.0853	(4.5003, 4.8412)	(3.9885, 5.3530)
3.9390	0.0901	(3.7590, 4.1190)	(3.2543, 4.6237)
2.8370	0.1116	(2.6140, 3.0599)	(2.1397, 3.5342)

11–51.   Using the regression relationship you estimated in problem 11–8, predict the value of a home of 1,800 square feet located 2.0 miles from the center of the town.

11–52.   Using the regression equation from problem 11–25, predict excess stock return when SIZRNK = 5 and PRCRNK = 6.

11–53.   Using the information in Table 11–11, what is the standard error of $\hat{Y}$? What is the standard error of $\hat{E}(Y)$?

11–54.   Use a computer to produce a prediction interval and a confidence interval for the conditional mean of Y for the prediction in problem 11–50. Use the data in Table 11–1.

11–55.   What is the difference between a predicted value of the dependent variable and the conditional mean of the dependent variable?

11–56.   Why is the prediction interval of 95% wider than the 95% confidence interval for the conditional mean using the same values of the independent variables?

11-8   Qualitative Independent Variables

The variables we have encountered so far in this chapter have all been *quantitative* variables: variables that can take on values on a scale. Sales volume, advertising expenditure, exports, the money supply, and people's ratings of an automobile are all examples of quantitative variables. In this section, we will discuss the use of *qualitative* variables as explanatory variables in a regression model. Qualitative variables are variables that describe a quality rather than a quantity. This should remind you of analysis of variance in Chapter 9. There we had qualitative variables such as the kind of resort in the Club Med example, type of airplane, type of coffee, etc.

In some cases, it is very useful to include information on one or more qualitative variables in our multiple regression model. For example, a hotel chain may be interested in predicting the number of occupied rooms as a function of the economy of the area in which the hotel is located, as well as advertising level and some other quantitative variables. The hotel may also want to know whether or not the peak season is in progress—a qualitative variable that may have a lot to do with the level of occupancy at the hotel. A property appraiser may be interested in predicting the value of different residential units on the basis of several quantitative variables, such as age of the unit and area in square feet, as well as the qualitative variable of whether the unit is owned or rented.

Each of these qualitative variables has only two *levels:* peak season versus nonpeak season, rental unit versus nonrental unit. An easy way to quantify such a qualitative variable is by way of a single **indicator variable,** also called a **dummy variable.** An indicator variable is a variable that indicates whether or not some condition holds. It has the value 1 when the condition holds and the value 0 when the condition does not hold. If you are familiar with computer science, you probably know the indicator variable by another name: *binary variable,* because it takes on only two possible values, 0 and 1.

When included in the model of hotel occupancy, the indicator variable will equal 0 if it is not peak season and 1 if it is (or vice versa; it makes no difference). Similarly, in the property value analysis, the dummy variable will have the value 0 when the unit is rented and 1 when the unit is owned, or vice versa. We define the general form of an indicator variable in equation (11–19).

An indicator variable of qualitative level A:

$$X_h = \begin{cases} 1 & \text{if level A is obtained} \\ 0 & \text{if level A is not obtained} \end{cases} \qquad (11\text{–}19)$$

The use of indicator variables in regression analysis is very simple. No special computational routines are required. All we do is code the indicator variable as 1 whenever the quality of interest is obtained for a particular data point and as 0 when it is not obtained. The rest of the variables in the regression equation are left the same. We demonstrate the use of an indicator variable in modeling a qualitative variable with two levels in the following example.

EXAMPLE 11-3   A motion picture industry analyst wants to estimate the gross earnings generated by a movie. The estimate will be based on different variables involved in the film's production. The independent variables considered are $X_1 =$ production cost of the movie and $X_2 =$ total cost of all promotional activities. A third variable that the analyst wants to consider is the qualitative variable of whether or not the movie is based on a book published before the release of the movie. This third, qualitative variable is handled by the use of an indicator variable: $X_3 = 0$ if the movie is not based on a book, and $X_3 = 1$ if it is. The analyst obtains information on a random sample of 20 Hollywood movies made within the last five years (the inference is to be made only about the population of movies in this particular category). The data are given in Table 11–12. The variable Y is gross earnings, in millions of dollars. The two quantitative independent variables are also in millions of dollars.

SOLUTION   The data are entered into the regression program of the MINITAB package. The resulting output is presented in Table 11–13. The coefficient of determination of this regression is very high; the F statistic value is very significant, and we have a good regression relationship. From the individual t ratios and their p-values, we find that all three independent variables are important in the equation.

From the intercept of 7.84, we could (erroneously, of course) deduce that a movie costing nothing to produce or promote, and that is not based on a book, would still gross $7.84 million! The point 0 ($X_1 = 0$, $X_2 = 0$, $X_3 = 0$) is outside the estimation region, and the regression relationship may not hold for that region. In our case, it evidently does not. The intercept is merely a reference point used to move the regression surface upward to where it should be in the estimation region.

The estimated slope for the cost variable, 2.85, means that—within the estimation region—an increase of $1 million in a movie's production cost (the other variables held constant) increases the movie's gross earnings by an average of $2.85 million. Similarly, the estimated slope coefficient for the promotion variable means that, in the estimation region of the variables, an increase of $1 million in promotional activities (with the other variables constant) increases the movie's gross earnings by an average of $2.28 million.

TABLE 11-12 Data for Example 11-3

Movie	Gross Earnings, Million $ (Y)	Production Cost, Million $ (X_1)	Promotion Cost, Million $ (X_2)	Book (X_3)
1	28	4.2	1	0
2	35	6.0	3	1
3	50	5.5	6	1
4	20	3.3	1	0
5	75	12.5	11	1
6	60	9.6	8	1
7	15	2.5	0.5	0
8	45	10.8	5	0
9	50	8.4	3	1
10	34	6.6	2	0
11	48	10.7	1	1
12	82	11.0	15	1
13	24	3.5	4	0
14	50	6.9	10	0
15	58	7.8	9	1
16	63	10.1	10	0
17	30	5.0	1	1
18	37	7.5	5	0
19	45	6.4	8	1
20	72	10.0	12	1

TABLE 11-13 MINITAB Regression Output for Example 11-3

```
MTB > REGRESS 'EARN' on 3 predictors 'COST', 'PROM', 'BOOK'

The regression equation is
EARN = 7.84 + 2.85 COST + 2.28 PROM + 7.17 BOOK

Predictor      Coef       Stdev      t-ratio        P
Constant       7.836      2.333       3.36       0.004
Cost           2.8477     0.3923      7.26       0.000
Prom           2.2782     0.2534      8.99       0.000
Book           7.166      1.818       3.94       0.001

s = 3.690      R-Sq = 96.7%     R-Sq(adj) = 96.0%

Analysis of Variance

  SOURCE      DF        SS         MS         F          P
Regression     3      6325.2     2108.4    154.89     0.000
Error         16       217.8       13.6
Total         19      6543.0
```

How do we interpret the estimated coefficient of variable X_3? The estimated coefficient of 7.17 means that having the movie based on a published book ($X_3 = 1$) increases the movie's gross earnings by an average of \$7.17 million. Again, the inference is valid only for the region of the data used in the estimation. When $X_3 = 0$, that is, when the movie is not based on a book, the last term in the estimated equation for $\hat{Y}$ in Table 11–13 drops out—there is no added \$7.17 million.

What do we learn from this example about the function of the indicator variable? Note that the predicted value of Y, given the values of the quantitative independent variables, shifts upward (or downward, depending on the sign of the estimated coefficient) by an amount equal to the coefficient of the indicator variable whenever the variable is equal to 1. In this particular case, the surface of the regression—the plane formed by the variables Y, X_1, and X_2—is split into two surfaces: one corresponding to movies based on books and the other corresponding to movies not based on books. The appropriate surface depends on whether $X_3 = 0$ or $X_3 = 1$; the two estimated surfaces are separated by a distance equal to $b_3 = 7.17$. This is demonstrated in Figure 11–21. The regression surface in this example is a plane, so we can draw its image (for a higher-dimensional surface, the same idea holds).

We will now look at the simpler case, with one independent quantitative variable and one indicator variable. Here we assume an estimated regression relationship of the form: $\hat{Y} = b_0 + b_1 X_1 + b_2 X_2$, where X_1 is a quantitative variable and X_2 is an indicator variable. The regression relationship is a straight line, and the indicator variable splits the line into two parallel straight lines, one for each level (0 or 1) of the qualitative variable. The points belonging to one level (a level could be Book, as in Example 11–3) are shown as triangles, and the points belonging to the other level are shown as squares. The distance between the two parallel lines (measured as the difference between the two intercepts) is equal to the estimated coefficient of the dummy variable, X_2. The situation is demonstrated in Figure 11–22.

We have been dealing with qualitative variables that have only two levels. Therefore, it has sufficed to use an indicator variable with two possible values, 0 or 1. What about situations where we have a qualitative variable with more than two levels? Should we use an "indicator" variable with more than two values? The answer to this is no. Were we to do this and give our variable values such as 0, 1, 2, 3, . . . to indicate qualitative levels, we would be using a quantitative variable that has several discrete values but no values in between. Also, the assignment of the qualities to the values would be arbitrary. Since there may be no justification for using the values 1, 2, 3, etc., we would be imposing a very special measuring scale on the regression problem—a scale that may not be appropriate. Instead, we will use several indicator variables.

> We account for a qualitative variable with r levels by the use of $r - 1$ indicator (0/1) variables.

We will now demonstrate the use of this rule by changing Example 11–3 somewhat. Suppose that the analyst is not interested in whether or not a movie is based on a book, but rather in using an explanatory variable that represents the category to which each movie belongs: adventure, drama, or romance. Since this qualitative variable has $r = 3$ levels, the rule tells us that we need to model this variable by using $r - 1 = 2$ indicator variables. Each of the two indicator variables will have one of two possible values, as before: 0 or 1. The setup of the two dummy variables indicating the level of the qualitative variable, movie category, is shown in the following table. For simplicity, let us also assume that the only quantitative variable in the equation is production cost (we leave out the promotion variable). This will allow us to have lines rather than planes. We let $X_1 =$ production cost, as before. We now define the two dummy variables, X_2 and X_3.

FIGURE 11–21   Two Regression Planes of Example 11–3

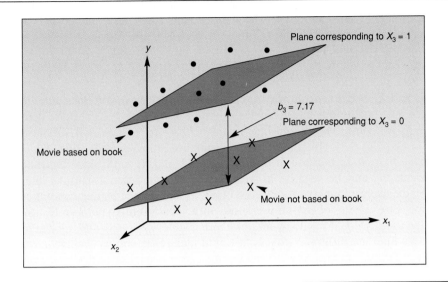

FIGURE 11–22   A Regression with One Quantitative Variable and One Dummy Variable

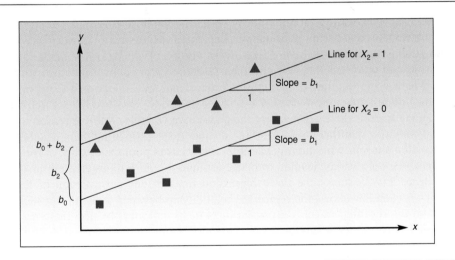

Category	X_2	X_3
Adventure	0	0
Drama	0	1
Romance	1	0

The definition of the values of X_2 and X_3 for representing the different categories is arbitrary: we could just as well have assigned the values ($X_2 = 0$, $X_3 = 0$) to drama or to romance rather than to adventure. The important thing to remember is that the number of dummy variables is one less than the number of categories they represent. Otherwise our model will be overspecified, and problems will occur. In this example, the variable X_2 is the indicator variable for romance; when a movie is in the romance category, the variable has the value 1. Similarly, X_3 is the indicator for drama and has the value 1 in cases where a movie is in the drama category. There are only three categories under consideration, so when both X_2 and X_3 are zero, the movie is neither a drama nor a romance; therefore, it must be an adventure movie.

If we use the model

$$Y = \beta_0 + \beta_1 X_1 + \beta_2 X_2 + \beta_3 X_3 + \epsilon \qquad (11-20)$$

with X_2 and X_3 as defined, we will be estimating three regression lines, one line per category. The line for adventure movies would be $\hat{Y} = b_0 + b_1 X_1$ because here both X_2 and X_3 are zero. The drama line would be $\hat{Y} = b_0 + b_3 + b_1 X_1$ because here $X_3 = 1$ and $X_2 = 0$. In the case of romance movies, our line would be $\hat{Y} = b_0 + b_2 + b_1 X_1$ because in this case $X_2 = 1$ and $X_3 = 0$. Since the estimated coefficients, b_i, may be negative as well as positive, the different parallel lines may position themselves above or below each other, as determined by the data. Of course, the b_i may be estimates of zero. If we should not reject the null hypothesis $H_0: \beta_3 = 0$, using the usual t test, it would mean that there is no evidence that the adventure and the drama lines are different. That is, it would mean that, on the average, adventure movies and drama movies have the same gross earnings as determined by the production costs. If we determine that β_2 is not different from zero, the adventure and romance lines will be the same and the drama line may be different. In case the adventure line is different from drama and romance, these two being the same, we would determine statistically that both β_2 and β_3 are different from zero, but not different from each other.

If we have three regression lines, why bother with indicator variables at all? Why not just run three separate regressions, each for a different movie category? One answer to this question has already been given: The use of indicator variables and their estimated regression coefficients with their standard errors allows us to *test statistically* whether the qualitative variable of interest has any effect on the dependent variable. We are able to test whether we have one distinct line, two lines, three lines, or as many lines as there are levels of the qualitative variable. Another reason is that even if we know that there are, say, three distinct lines, estimating them together via a regression analysis with dummy variables allows us to pool the degrees of freedom for the three regressions, leading to better estimation and a more efficient analysis.

Figure 11–23 shows the three regression lines of our new version of Example 11–3; each line shows the regression relationship between a movie's production cost and the resulting movie's gross earnings in its category. In case there are two independent quantitative variables, say, if we add promotions as a second quantitative variable, we would have three regression *planes* like the two planes shown in Figure 11–21. In Figure 11–23, we show adventure movies as triangles, romance movies as squares, and drama movies as circles. Assuming that adventure movies have the highest average gross earnings, followed by romance and drama, the estimated coefficients b_2 and b_3 would have to be negative, as can be seen from the figure.

Can we run a regression on a qualitative variable (by use of dummy variables) only? Yes. You have already seen this model, essentially. Running a regression on a qualitative variable only means modeling some quantitative response by levels of a qualitative factor: it is the *analysis of variance,* discussed in Chapter 9. Doing the analysis by regression means using a different computational procedure than was done in Chapter 9, but it is still the analysis of variance. Two qualitative variables make the analysis a two-way ANOVA, and interaction terms are cross products of the appropriate dummy variables, such as $X_2 X_3$. We will say more about cross products

FIGURE 11-23   The Three Possible Regression Lines, Depending on Movie Category (modified Example 11-3)

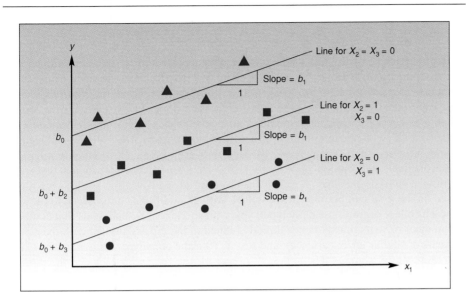

a little later. For now, we note that the regression approach to ANOVA allows us more freedom. Remember that a two-way ANOVA, using the method in Chapter 9, required a balanced design (equal sample size in each cell). If we use the regression approach, we are no longer restricted to the balanced design and may use any sample size.

Let us go back to regressions using quantitative independent variables with some qualitative variables. In some situations, we are not interested in using a regression equation for prediction or for any of the other common uses of regression analysis. Instead, we are intrinsically interested in a qualitative variable used in the regression. Let us be more specific. Recall our original Example 11–30. Suppose we are not interested in predicting a movie's gross earnings based on the production cost, promotions, and whether or not the movie is based on a book. Suppose instead that we are interested in answering the question: Is there a difference in average gross earnings between movies based on books and movies not based on books?

To answer this question, we use the estimated regression relationship. We use the estimate b_3 and its standard error in testing the null hypothesis $H_0: \beta_3 = 0$ versus the alternative $H_1: \beta_3 \neq 0$. The question is really an ANOVA question. We want to know whether a difference exists in the population means of the two groups movies based on books and movies not based on books. However, we have some quantitative variables that affect the variable we are measuring (gross earnings). We therefore incorporate information on these variables (production cost and promotions) in a regression model aimed at answering our ANOVA question. When we do this, that is, when we attempt to answer the question of whether differences in population means exist, using a regression equation to account for other sources of variation in our data (the quantitative independent variables), we are conducting an **analysis of covariance.** The independent variables used in the analysis of covariance are called **concomitant variables,** and their purpose in the analysis is not to explain or predict the independent variable, but rather to reduce the errors in the test of significance of the indicator variable or variables.

One of the interesting applications of analysis of covariance is in providing statistical evidence in cases of sex or race descrimination. We demonstrate this particular use in the following example.

EXAMPLE 11-4

A large service company was sued by its female employees in a class action suit alleging sex discrimination in salary levels. The claim was that, on the average, a man and a woman of the same education and experience received different salaries: the man's salary was believed higher than the woman's salary. The attorney representing the women employees hired a statistician to provide statistical evidence supporting the women's side of the case. The statistician was allowed access to the company's payroll files and obtained a random sample of 100 employees, 40 of whom were women. In addition to salary, the files contained information on education and experience. The statistician then ran a regression analysis of salary, Y, versus the three variables: education level, X_1 (on a scale based on the total number of years in school, with an additional value added to the score for each college degree earned, by type); years of experience, X_2 (on a scale that combined the number of years of experience directly related to the job assignment with the number of years of similar job experience); and sex, X_3 (0 if the employee was a man and 1 if the employee was a woman). The computer output for the regression included the results F ratio = 1,237.56 and R^2 = 0.67, as well as the coefficient estimates and standard errors given in Table 11–14. Based on this information, does the attorney for the women employees have a case against the company?

SOLUTION

Let us analyze the regression results. Remember that we are using a regression with a dummy variable to perform an analysis of covariance. There is certainly a regression relationship between salary and at least some of the variables, as evidenced by the very large F value, which is beyond any critical point we can find in a table. The p-value is very small. The coefficient of determination is not extremely high, but then we are using very few variables to explain variation in salary levels. This being the case, 67% explained variation, based on these variables only, is quite respectable. Now we consider the information in Table 11–14.

Dividing the four coefficient estimates by their standard errors, we find that all three variables are important, and the intercept is different from zero. However, we are particularly interested in the hypothesis test:

$$H_0: \beta_3 = 0$$
$$H_1: \beta_3 \neq 0$$

Our test statistic is $t_{(96)} = b_3/s(b_3) = -3,256/212.4 = -15.33$. Since t with 96 degrees of freedom [df $= n - (k + 1) = 100 - 4 = 96$] is virtually a standard normal random variable, we conduct this as a Z test. The computed test statistic value of -15.33 lies very far in the left-hand rejection region. This means that there are two regressions: one for men and one for women. Since we coded X_3 as 0 for a man and 1 for a woman, the women's estimated regression plane lies \$3,256 below the regression plane for men. Since the parameter of the sex variable is significantly different from zero (with an extremely small p-value) and is negative, there is statistical evidence of sex discrimination in this case. The situation here is as seen in Figure 11–21 for the previous example: we have two regression planes, one below the other. The only difference is that in this example, we were not interested in using the regression for prediction, but rather for an ANOVA-type statistical test.

TABLE 11-14 Regression Results for Example 11-4

Variable	Coefficient Estimate	Standard Error
Constant	8,547	32.6
Education	949	45.1
Experience	1,258	78.5
Sex	−3,256	212.4

Interactions between Qualitative and Quantitative Variables

Do the different regression lines or higher-dimensional surfaces have to be parallel? The answer is no. Sometimes, there are *interactions* between a qualitative variable and one or more quantitative variables. The idea of an interaction in regression analysis is the same as the idea of interaction between factors in a two-way ANOVA model (as well as higher-order ANOVAs). In regression analysis with qualitative variables, the interaction between a qualitative variable and a quantitative variable makes the regression lines or planes at different levels of the dummy variables have *different slopes*. Let us look at the simple case where we have one independent quantitative variable, X_1, and one qualitative variable with two levels, modeled by the dummy variable X_2. When an interaction exists between the qualitative and the quantitative variables, the slope of the regression line for $X_2 = 0$ is different from the slope of the regression line for $X_2 = 1$. This is shown in Figure 11–24.

We model the interactions between variables by the cross product of the variables. The interaction of X_1 with X_2 in this case is modeled by adding the term $X_1 X_2$ to the regression equation. We are thus interested in the model

$$Y = \beta_0 + \beta_1 X_1 + \beta_2 X_2 + \beta_3 X_1 X_2 + \epsilon \qquad (11\text{–}21)$$

We can use the results of the estimation procedure to test for the existence of an interaction. We do so by testing the significance of the parameter β_3.

When the regression parameters β_1, β_2, and β_3 are all nonzero, we have two distinct lines with different intercepts and different slopes. When β_2 is zero, we have two lines with the same intercept and different slopes (this is unlikely to happen, except when both intercepts are zero). When β_3 is zero, we have two parallel lines, as in the case of equation 11–20. If β_1 is zero, of course, we have no regression—just an ANOVA model; we then assume that β_3 is also zero. Assuming the full model of equation 11–21, representing two distinct lines with different slopes and different intercepts, the intercept and the slope of each line will be as shown in Figure 11–24. By substituting $X_2 = 0$ or $X_2 = 1$ into equation 11–21, verify the definition of each slope and each intercept.

Again, there are advantages to estimating a single model for the different levels of the indicator variable. These are the pooling of degrees of freedom (we assume that the spread of the data about the two or more lines is equal) and an understanding of the joint process generating the data. More important, we may use the model to statistically test for the equality of intercepts and slopes. Note that when several indicator variables are used in modeling one or more qualitative variables, there are several possible interaction terms in the model. We will learn more about interactions in general in the next section.

FIGURE 11-24   Effects of an Interaction between a Qualitative Variable and a Quantitative Variable

PROBLEMS

11-57. Echlin, Inc., makes parts for automobiles. The company is engaged in strong competition with Japanese, Taiwanese, and Korean manufacturers of the same auto parts. Recently, the company hired a statistician to study the relationship between monthly sales and the independent variable, number of cars on the road. Data on the explanatory variable are published in national statistical reports. Because of the keen competition with firms in the Orient, an indicator variable was also used. This variable was given the value 1 during months when restrictions on imports from the Orient were in effect, and 0 when such restrictions were not in effect. Denoting sales by Y, total number of cars on the road by X_1, and the import restriction dummy variable by X_2, the following regression equation was estimated:

$$\hat{Y} = -567.3 + 0.006X_1 + 26,540X_2$$

The standard error of the intercept estimate was 38.5, that of the coefficient of X_1 was 0.0002, and the standard error of the coefficient of X_2 was 1,534.67. The multiple coefficient of determination was $R^2 = 0.783$. The sample size used was $n = 60$ months (five years of data). Analyze the results presented. What kind of regression model was used? Comment on the significance of the model parameters and the value of R^2. How many distinct regression lines are there? What likely happens during times of restricted trade with the Orient?

11-58. A chemical company has three plants. Due to a shortage of labor and the intense heat involved in production, only one plant is operated at a time, and operations are shifted every few days to another plant. The company wants to estimate the relationship between daily production (Y) and the independent variable, labor force present (X_1). Since it is known that differences may exist among the different plants, it is proposed that a qualitative variable, X_2, also be used. This variable is defined as $X_2 = 1$ if plant A is used, 2 if plant B is used, and 3 if plant C is used during the day. Comment on the proposed regression model.

11–59. If we have a regression model with no quantitative variables and only two qualitative variables, represented by some indicator variables and cross products, what kind of analysis is carried out?

11–60. Recall our Club Med example of Chapter 9. Suppose that vacationers at the Club Med resorts do not all stay an equal length of time at the resort—different people stay different numbers of days. The club's research director knows that people's ratings of the resorts tend to differ depending on the number of days spent at the resort. Design a new method for studying whether or not there are differences among the average population ratings of the five Caribbean resorts. What is the name of your method of analysis, and how is the analysis carried out? Explain.

11–61. A financial institution specializing in venture capital is interested in predicting the success of business operations the institution helps to finance. Success is defined by the institution as return on its investment, as a percentage, after three years of operation. The explanatory variables used are Investment (in thousands of dollars), Early investment (in thousands of dollars), and two dummy variables denoting the category of business. The values of these variables are (0, 0) for high-tech industry, (0, 1) for biotechnology companies, and (1, 0) for aerospace firms. Following is part of the computer output for this analysis, generated by MINITAB. Interpret the output, and give a complete analysis of the results of this study based on the provided information.

```
The regression equation is
Return = 6.16 + 0.617 INVEST + 0.151 EARLY + 11.1 DUM1 + 4.15 DUM2
Predictor       Coef         Stdev
 Constant       6.162        1.642
 INVEST         0.6168       0.1581
 EARLY          0.1509       0.1465
 DUM1          11.051        1.355
 DUM2           4.150        1.315

s = 2.148        R-sq = 91.6%       R-sq (adj) = 89.4%

Analysis of Variance

  SOURCE        DF           SS
Regression      4         755.99
Error          15          69.21
Total          19         825.20
```

11-9 Polynomial Regression

Often, the relationship between the dependent variable, Y, and one or more of the independent X variables is not a straight-line relationship but, rather, has some curvature to it. Several such situations are shown in Figure 11–25 (we show the curved relationship between Y and a *single* explanatory variable, X). In each of the situations shown, a straight line provides a poor fit to the data. Instead, polynomials of order higher than 1, that is, functions of higher powers of X, such as X^2 and X^3, provide much better fit to our data. Such polynomials in the X variable or in several X_i variables are still considered linear regression models. Only models where the parameters, β_i, are not all of the first power are called nonlinear models. The multiple linear regression model thus covers situations of fitting data to polynomial functions. The general form of a polynomial regression model in one variable, X, is given in equation 11–22.

FIGURE 11-25   Situations Where the Relationship between X and Y is Curved

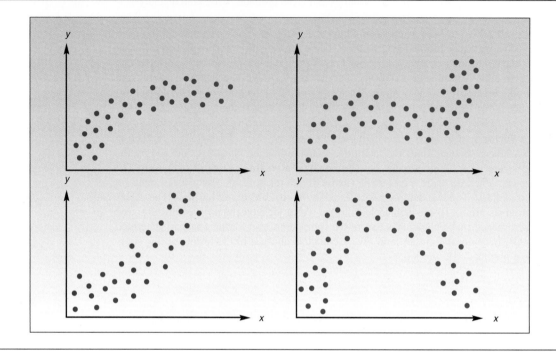

One-variable polynomial regression model:

$$Y = \beta_0 + \beta_1 X + \beta_2 X^2 + \beta_3 X^3 + \cdots + \beta_m X^m + \epsilon \qquad (11\text{--}22)$$

where *m* is the *degree* of the polynomial—the highest power of *X* appearing in the equation. The degree of the polynomial is the *order* of the model.

Figure 11–26 shows how second- and third-degree polynomial models provide good fits for the data sets in Figure 11–25. A straight line is also shown in each case, for comparison. Compare the fit provided in each case by a polynomial with the poor fit provided by a straight line. Also compare the use of low-order polynomials in these examples with the polynomial fit shown in Figure 11–2 in the introduction of this chapter. There the polynomial of a high order was matching the variation in the data and thus modeling the random variation rather than the general trend, unlike the examples shown in Figure 11–26. Some authors, for example, Weisberg, recommend using polynomials of order no greater than 2 (the third-order example in Figure 11–26 would be an exception) because of the overfitting problem.[10] At any rate, models should never be of order 6 or higher (unless the powers of *X* have been transformed in a special way). Seber shows that when a polynomial of degree 6 or greater is fit to a data set, a matrix involved in regression computations becomes *ill-conditioned,* which means that very small errors in the data cause relatively large

---

[10] Sanford Weisberg, *Applied Linear Regression*, 2nd ed. (New York: Wiley, 1985).

FIGURE 11-26   The Fits Provided for the Data Sets in Figure 11-25 by Polynomial Models

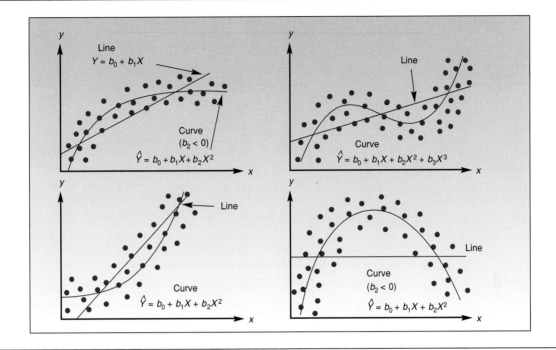

errors in the estimated model parameters.[11] In short, we must be very careful with polynomial regression models and try to obtain the most parsimonious polynomial model that will fit our data. In the next section, we will discuss *transformations* of data that often can change curved data sets into a straight-line form. If we can find such a transformation for a data set, it is always better to use a first-order model on the transformed data set than to use a higher-order polynomial model on the original data. It should be intuitively clear that problems may arise in polynomial regression. The variables X and X^2, for example, are clearly not independent of each other. This may cause the problem of multicollinearity in cases where the data are confined to a narrow range of values.

Having seen what to beware of in using polynomial regression, let us see how these models are used. Since powers of X can be obtained directly from the value of the variable X, it is relatively easy to run polynomial models. We enter the data into the computer and add a command that uses X to form a new variable. In a second-order model, using the MINITAB package, we add a command to multiply the data column corresponding to X by itself, thus forming the variable X^2. Then we run a multiple regression model with two "independent" variables: X and X^2. We demonstrate this with a new example.

EXAMPLE 11-5

It is well known that sales response to advertising usually follows a curve reflecting the diminishing returns to advertising expenditure. As a firm increases its advertising expenditure, sales increase, but the rate of increase drops continually after a certain point. If

---

[11] G. A. F. Seber, *Linear Regression Analysis* (New York: Wiley, 1977).

FIGURE 11–27   A Quadratic Response Function of Sales Profits to Advertising Expenditure

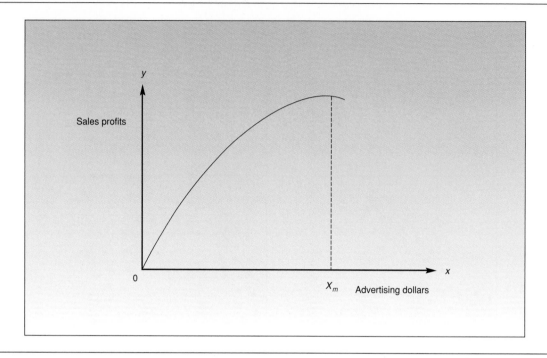

we consider company sales profits as a function of advertising expenditure, we find that the response function can be very well approximated by a second-order (quadratic) model of the form

$$Y = \beta_0 + \beta_1 X + \beta_2 X^2 + \epsilon$$

A quadratic response function such as this one is shown in Figure 11–27.

It is very important for a firm to identify its own point X_m shown in the figure. At this point, a maximum benefit is achieved from advertising in terms of the resulting sales profits. Figure 11–27 shows a general form of the sales response to advertising. In order to find its own maximum point, X_m, a firm needs to estimate its response-to-advertising function from its own operation data, obtained by using different levels of advertising at different time periods and observing the resulting sales profits. For a particular firm, the data on monthly sales (Y) and monthly advertising expenditure (X), both in hundred thousand dollars, are given in Table 11–15. The table shows the data as entered into the MINITAB program. The table also shows the values of X^2 used in the regression analysis.

SOLUTION

Figure 11–28 shows the computer-generated plot of the data, sales versus advertising. Above the plot, the figure also shows the MINITAB command that multiplies column C2 (the advertising expenditure column) by itself to form X^2. The next command names the variables, Sales and Advert, and the newly formed variable Advsqr. From the plot, we see that the increases in sales diminish as advertising expenditure increases, and a saturation point will be reached at some level. From the plot, it seems that a quadratic regression model may fit the data well.

Table 11–16 gives the regression command and the output of the regression analysis of sales versus advertising expenditure and squared advertising expenditure, a quadratic

TABLE 11-15 Data for Example 11-5

ROW	SALES	ADVERT	ADVSQR
1	5.0	1.0	1.00
2	6.0	1.8	3.24
3	6.5	1.6	2.56
4	7.0	1.7	2.89
5	7.5	2.0	4.00
6	8.0	2.0	4.00
7	10.0	2.3	5.29
8	10.8	2.8	7.84
9	12.0	3.5	12.25
10	13.0	3.3	10.89
11	15.5	4.8	23.04
12	15.0	5.0	25.00
13	16.0	7.0	49.00
14	17.0	8.1	65.61
15	18.0	8.0	64.00
16	18.0	10.0	100.00
17	18.5	8.0	64.00
18	21.0	12.7	161.29
19	20.0	12.0	144.00
20	22.0	15.0	225.00
21	23.0	14.4	207.36

FIGURE 11-28 MINITAB Commands for Forming an X^2 Variable and a Plot of the Data for Example 11-5

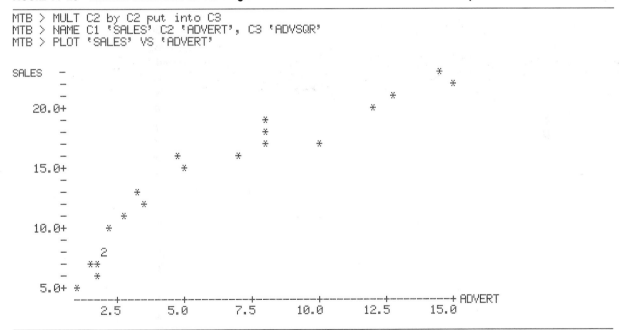

```
MTB > MULT C2 by C2 put into C3
MTB > NAME C1 'SALES' C2 'ADVERT', C3 'ADVSQR'
MTB > PLOT 'SALES' VS 'ADVERT'
```

regression model. From the results, we see that a second-order regression model, a quadratic model in the advertising variable, fits the data very well. The coefficient of determination is $R^2 = 0.959$, the F ratio is significant, and both Advert and Advsqr are very significant. The negative sign of the squared variable, Advsqr, is logical because a quadratic function with a maximum point has a negative leading coefficient (the

TABLE 11-16   Regression Results for Example 11-5

```
MTB > REGRESS 'SALES' on 2 predictors, 'ADVERT', 'ADVSQR'

The regression equation is
SALES = 3.52 + 2.51 ADVERT - 0.0875 ADVSQR

Predictor      Coef          Stdev         t-ratio        P
Constant       3.5150        0.7385         4.76        0.000
ADVERT         2.5148        0.2580         9.75        0.000
ADVSQR        -0.08745       0.01658       -5.28        0.000

s = 1.228       R-sq = 95.9%        R-sq (adj) = 95.4%

Analysis of Variance

   SOURCE       DF       SS            MS          F          p
Regression       2     630.26        315.13      208.99     0.000
Error           18      27.14          1.51
Total           20     657.40
```

coefficient of X^2). We may write the estimated quadratic regression model of Y in terms of X and X^2 as follows:

$$Y = 3.52 + 2.51X - 0.0875X^2 + e \qquad (11-23)$$

The equation of the estimated regression curve itself is given by dropping the error term, e, giving an equation for the predicted values, $\hat{Y}$, that lie on the quadratic curve

$$\hat{Y} = 3.52 + 2.51X - 0.0875X^2 \qquad (11-24)$$

In our particular example, the equation of the curve (equation 11–24) is of importance, as it can be differentiated with respect to X, with the derivative then set to zero and the result solved for the maximizing value X_m shown in Figure 11–27. (If you have not studied calculus, you may ignore the preceding statement.) The result here is $x_m = 14.34$ (hundred thousand dollars). This value maximizes sales profits with respect to advertising (within estimation error of the regression). Thus, the firm should set its advertising level at \$1.434 million. The fact that polynomials can always be differentiated gives these models an advantage over alternative models. Remember, however, to keep the order of the model low.

Other Variables and Cross-Product Terms

The polynomial regression model in one variable, X, given in equation 11–22, can easily be extended to include more than one independent explanatory variable. The new model, which includes several variables at different powers, is a mixture of the usual multiple regression model in k variables (equation 11–1) and the polynomial regression model (equation 11–22). When several variables are in a regression equation, we may also consider interactions among variables. We have already encountered interactions in the previous section, where we discussed interactions between an indicator variable and a quantitative variable. We saw that an interaction term is just the cross product of the two variables involved. In this section, we discuss the general concept of interactions between variables, quantitative or not.

The interaction term, $X_i X_j$, is a second-order term (the product of two variables is classified the same way as an X^2 term). Similarly, $X_i X_j^2$, for example, is a third order term. Thus, models that incorporate interaction terms find their natural place within

FIGURE 11–29   An Example of the Regression Surface of a Second-Order Model in Two Variables

the class of polynomial models. Equation 11–25 is a second-order regression model in two variables, X_1 and X_2. This model includes both first and second powers of both variables and an interaction term.

$$Y = \beta_0 + \beta_1 X_1 + \beta_2 X_2 + \beta_3 X_1^2 + \beta_4 X_2^2 + \beta_5 X_1 X_2 + \epsilon \qquad (11{-}25)$$

A regression surface of a model like that of equation 11–25 is shown in Figure 11–29. There are, of course, many possible surfaces depending on the values of the coefficients of all terms in the equation. Equation 11–25 may be generalized to more than two explanatory variables, to higher powers of each variable, and to more interaction terms.

When considering polynomial regression models in several variables, it is very important not to get carried away by the number of possible terms one can include in the model. The number of variables, as well as the powers of these variables and the number of interaction terms, should be kept to a minimum.

How do we choose the terms to include in a model? This question will be answered in section 11–13, where we discuss methods of variable selection. You already know several criteria for the inclusion of variables, powers of variables, and interaction terms in a model. One thing to consider is the adjusted coefficient of determination. If this measure decreases when a term is included in the model, then the term should be dropped. Also, the significance of any particular term in a model depends on which other variables, powers, or interaction terms are in the model. We must consider the significance of each term by its t statistic, and we must consider what happens to the significance of regression terms once other terms are added to the model or removed from it. For example, let us consider the regression output in Table 11–17.

From the results in the table, it is clear that only X_1, X_2, and X_1^2 are significant. The apparent nonsignificance of X_2^2 and $X_1 X_2$ may be due to multicollinearity. At any rate, a regression without these last two variables should be carried out. We must also look

TABLE 11–17   Example of Regression Output for a Second-Order Model in Two Variables

Variable	Estimate	Standard Error	t-Ratio
X_1	2.34	0.92	2.54
X_2	3.11	1.05	2.96
X_1^2	4.22	1.00	4.22
X_2^2	3.57	2.12	1.68
$X_1 X_2$	2.77	2.30	1.20

at the R^2 and the adjusted R^2 of the different regressions, and find the most parsimonious model with statistically significant parameters that explain as much as possible of the variation in the values of the dependent variable. Incidentally, the surface in Figure 11–29 was generated by computer using all the coefficient estimates given in Table 11–17 (regardless of their significance) and an intercept of zero.

PROBLEMS

11–62. The following results pertain to a regression analysis of the difference between the mortgage rate and the treasury bill rate (SPREAD) on the shape of the yield curve (SHAPE) and the corporate bond yields spread (RISK).[12] What kind of regression model is used? Explain.

$$\text{SPREAD}_t = b_0 + b_1\,\text{STD}_t + b_2\,\text{SHAPE}_t + b_3\,\text{RISK}_t + b_4\,\text{STD}_t^2$$
$$- b_5\,\text{SHAPE}_t^2 - b_6\,\text{STD}_t^*\,\text{SHAPE}_t$$

11–63. Use the data in Table 11–6 to run a polynomial regression model of exports to Singapore versus M1 and M1 squared, as well as Price and Price squared, and an interaction term. Also try to add a squared exchange rate variable into the model. Find the best, most parsimonious regression model for the data.

11–64. Use the data of Example 11–3, presented in Table 11–12, to try to fit a polynomial regression model of movie gross earnings on production cost and production cost squared. Also try promotion and promotion squared. What is the best, most parsimonious model?

11–65. Give at least two reasons why a polynomial regression model in one or more independent variables should be kept as parsimonious as possible.

11–66. A regression model of sales (Y) versus advertising (X_1), advertising squared (X_1^2), competitors' advertising (X_2), competitors' advertising squared (X_2^2), and the interaction of X_1 and X_2 is run. The results are as follows.

Variable	Parameter Estimate	Standard Error
X_1	5.324	2.478
X_2	3.229	1.006
X_1^2	4.544	3.080
X_2^2	1.347	0.188
$X_1 X_2$	2.692	1.517

$$R^2 = 0.657 \qquad \text{Adjusted } R^2 = 0.611 \qquad n = 197$$

Interpret the regression results. Which regression equation should be tried next? Explain.

---

[12] M. Bradley et al., "Mortgage Credit Intermediation," *Journal of Money, Credit, and Banking* 27, no. 2 (May 1995), p. 484.

11–67. What regression model would you try for the following data? Give your reasons why.

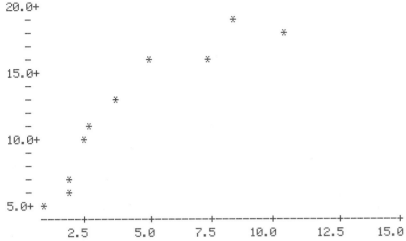

11–68. The regression model $Y = \beta_0 + \beta_1 X + \beta_2 X^2 + \beta_3 X^3 + \beta_4 X^4 + \epsilon$ was fit to the following data set. Can you suggest a better model? If so, which?

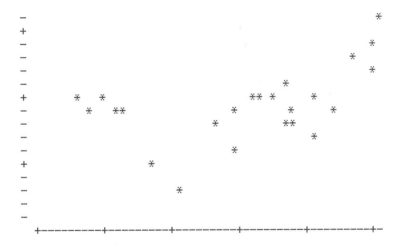

11-10   Nonlinear Models and Transformations

Sometimes the relationship between Y and one or more of the independent X_i variables is nonlinear. Remember that powers of the X_i variables in the regression model still keep the model linear, but that powers of the coefficients, β_i, make the model nonlinear. We may have prior knowledge about the process generating the data that indicates that a nonlinear model is appropriate; or we may observe that the data follow one of the general nonlinear curves shown in the figures in this section.

In many cases, a nonlinear model may be changed to a linear model by use of an appropriate **transformation.** Models that can be transformed into linear models are called **intrinsically linear** models. These models are the subject of this section. The "hard-core" nonlinear models, those that cannot be transformed into linear models, are difficult to analyze and therefore are outside the scope of this book.

The first model we will encounter is the *multiplicative model,* given by equation 11–26.

The multiplicative model:

$$Y = \beta_0 X_1^{\beta_1} X_2^{\beta_2} X_3^{\beta_3} \epsilon \qquad (11-26)$$

This is a multiplicative model in three variables: X_1, X_2, and X_3. The generalization to k variables is clear. The β_i are unknown parameters, and ϵ is a multiplicative random error.

The multiplicative model of equation 11–26 can be transformed into a linear regression model by the use of a **logarithmic transformation.** A logarithmic transformation is the most common transformation of data in statistical analysis. We will use natural logarithms, logs to base e; although any log transformation would do (we may use logs to any base, as long as we are consistent throughout the equation). Taking natural logs (sometimes denoted by ln) of both sides of equation 11–26 gives us the following linear model:

$$\log Y = \log \beta_0 + \beta_1 \log X_1 + \beta_2 \log X_2 + \beta_3 \log X_3 + \log \epsilon \quad (11-27)$$

Equation 11–27 is now in the form of equation 11–1: it is a linear regression equation of $\log Y$ in terms of $\log X_1$, $\log X_2$, and $\log X_3$ as independent variables. The error term in the linearized model is $\log \epsilon$. In order to conform with the assumptions of the multiple regression model and to allow us to perform tests of significance of model parameters, we must assume that the linearized errors, $\log \epsilon$, are normally distributed with mean 0 and equal variance σ^2 for successive observations and that these errors are independent of each other.

When we consider only one independent variable, the model of equation 11–26 is a power curve in X, of the form

$$Y = \beta_0 X^{\beta_1} \epsilon \qquad (11-28)$$

Depending on the values of the parameters, β_0 and β_1, equation 11–28 gives rise to a wide-range family of power curves. Several members of this family of curves, showing the relationship between X and Y, leaving out the errors, ϵ, are shown in Figure 11–30. When more than one independent variable is used, as in equation 11–26, the graph of the relationship between the X_i variables and Y is a multidimensional extension of Figure 11–30.

As you can see from the figure, many possible data relationships may be well modeled by a power curve in one variable or its extension to several independent variables. The resemblance of the curves in Figure 11–30 to at least two curves shown in Figure 11–26 is also evident. As you look at Figure 11–30, we repeat our suggestion from the last section that, when possible, a transformed model with few parameters is better than a polynomial model with more parameters.

When dealing with a multiplicative, or power, model, we take logs of both sides of the equation and run a linear regression model on the logs of the variables. Again, it is important to understand that the errors must be multiplicative. This makes sense in situations where the magnitude of an error is proportional to the magnitude of the response variable. We assume that the logs of the errors are normally distributed and satisfy all the assumptions of the linear regression model. Models where the error term is additive rather than multiplicative, such as $Y = \beta_0 X_1^{\beta_1} X_2^{\beta_2} X_3^{\beta_3} + \epsilon$ are *not* intrinsically linear because there is no expression for logs of *sums*.

When using a model such as equation 11–26 or equation 11–28, we enter the data into the computer, form new variables by having the computer take logs of the Y and X_i variables, and run a regression on the transformed variables. In addition to making

FIGURE 11–30   A Family of Power Curves of the Form $Y = \beta_0 X^{\beta_1}$

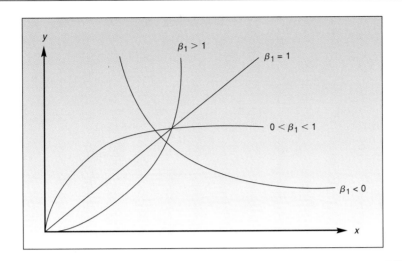

sure that the model assumptions seem to hold, we must also remember that computer-generated predictions and confidence intervals will be in terms of the transformed variables unless the computer algorithm is designed to convert information back to the original variables. The conversion back to the original variables is done by taking antilogs.

In many situations, it is possible to determine the need for a log transformation by inspecting a scatter plot of the data. We demonstrate the analysis using the data of Example 11–5. We will assume that a model of the form of equation 11–28 fits the relationship between sales profits (Y) and advertising dollars (X). We assume a power curve with multiplicative errors. Thus, we assume that the relationship between X and Y is given by

$$Y = \beta_0 X^{\beta_1} \epsilon$$

Taking logs of both sides of the equation, we get the linearized model:

$$\log Y = \log \beta_0 + \beta_1 \log X + \log \epsilon \qquad (11\text{–}29)$$

Our choice of a power curve and a transformation using logarithms is prompted by the fact that our data in this example exhibit curvature that may resemble a member of the family of curves in Figure 11–30, and by the fact that a quadratic regression model, which is similar to a power curve, was found to fit the data well. (Data for this example are shown in Figure 11–28.)

We use the MINITAB program for this analysis. Data are given in column C1 (sales) and C2 (advertising expenditure). The first thing we ask the computer to do is take logs to base e (natural logarithms) of both variables X and Y. The MINITAB command LOGE takes natural logs of the data in the prescribed column and places these logs in a given column. In this case, we put the logs of the Y values and the logs of the X values into columns C3 and C4, respectively. Then we ask the computer to carry out a regression analysis of the logarithms of the two variables. Results of the analysis are given in Table 11–18. The table also shows the MINITAB commands needed for carrying out the analysis. Comparing the results in Table 11–18 with those

TABLE 11-18   MINITAB Analysis Using a Logarithmic Transformation, Example 11-5

```
MTB > LOGE C1, into C3
MTB > LOGE C2, into C4
MTB > NAME C3 'LOGSALE', C4 'LOGADV'
MTB > REGRESS 'LOGSALE' on 1 predictor 'LOGADV'

The regression equation is
LOGSALE = 1.70 + 0.553 LOGADV

Predictor      Coef        Stdev       t-ratio       P
Constant      1.70082      0.05123      33.20      0.000
LOGADV        0.55314      0.03011      18.37      0.000

s = 0.1125      R-sq = 94.7%      R-sq(adj) = 94.4%
Analysis of Variance

  SOURCE       DF        SS         MS          F          P
Regression      1      4.2722      4.2722      336.39      0.000
Error          19      0.2405      0.0127
Total          20      4.5126
```

of the quadratic regression, given in Table 11−16, we find that, in terms of R^2 and the adjusted R^2, the quadratic regression is slightly better than the log Y versus log X regression.

Do we have to take logs of both X and Y, or can we take the log of one of the variables only? That depends on the kind of nonlinear model we wish to linearize. It turns out that there is indeed a nonlinear model that may be linearized by taking the log of one of the variables. Equation 11−30 is a nonlinear regression model of Y versus the independent variable X that may be linearized by taking logs of both sides of the equation. To use the resulting linear model, given in equation 11−31, we run a regression of log Y versus X (not log X). The nonlinear relationship of equation 11−30, an exponential model, is shown in Figure 11−31.

The **exponential model:**

$$Y = \beta_0 \, e^{\beta_1 X} \epsilon \qquad\qquad (11\text{--}30)$$

The linearized model of the exponential relationship, obtained by taking logs of both sides of equation 11−30, is given by

$$\log Y = \log \beta_0 + \beta_1 X + \log \epsilon \qquad\qquad (11\text{--}31)$$

As can be seen from the plots in Figure 11−31, when the relationship between Y and X is of the exponential form, the relationship is mildly curved upward or downward. Thus, taking log of Y only and running a regression of log Y versus X may be useful when our data display curvature similar to what is seen in Figure 11−31.

The exponential model of equation 11−30 is extendable to several independent X_i variables. The model is given in equation 11−32.

An exponential model in two independent variables:

$$Y = e^{\beta_0 + \beta_1 X_1 + \beta_2 X_2} \epsilon \qquad (11-32)$$

FIGURE 11-31
Exponential Curves

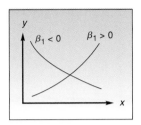

The letter e in equation 11–32, as in equation 11–30, denotes the natural number $e = 2.7182 \ldots$, the base of the natural logarithm. Taking the natural logs of both sides of equation 11–32 gives us the following linear regression model:

$$\log Y = \beta_0 + \beta_1 X_1 + \beta_2 X_2 + \log \epsilon \qquad (11-33)$$

This relationship is extendable to any number of independent variables. The transformation of $\log Y$, leaving the X_i variables in their natural form, allows us to perform linear regression analysis. The data of Example 11–5, shown in Figure 11–28, do not display a curvature of the type shown in Figure 11–31. The next model we discuss, however, may be more promising.

Figure 11–32 shows curves corresponding to the logarithmic model given in equation 11–34.

FIGURE 11-32
**Curves Corresponding to
a Logarithmic Model**

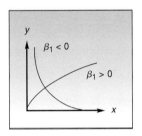

The **logarithmic model:**

$$Y = \beta_0 + \beta_1 \log X + \epsilon \qquad (11-34)$$

This nonlinear model can be linearized by substituting the variable $X' = \log X$ into the equation. This gives us the linear model in X':

$$Y = \beta_0 + \beta_1 X' + \epsilon \qquad (11-35)$$

From Figure 11–32, it seems that the logarithmic model with $\beta_1 > 0$ may fit the data of Example 11–5. We will therefore try to fit this model. The required transformation to obtain the linearized model in equation 11–35 is to take the log of X only, leaving Y as is. We will tell the computer program to run Y versus $\log X$. By doing so, we assume that our data follow the logarithmic model of equation 11–34. The results of the regression analysis of sales profits versus the natural logarithm of advertising expenditure are given in Table 11–19.

As seen from the regression results, the model of equation 11–35 is probably the best model to describe the data of Example 11–5. The coefficient of determination is $R^2 = 0.978$, which is higher than those of both the quadratic model and the power curve model we tried earlier. Figure 11–33 is a plot of the sales variable versus the log of advertising (the regression model of equation 11–35). As can be seen from the figure, we have a straight-line relationship between log advertising and sales. Compare this figure with Figure 11–34, which is the relationship of log sales versus log advertising, the model of equation 11–31 we tried earlier. In the latter graph, there is some extra curvature, and a straight line does not quite fit the transformed variable. We conclude that the model given by equation 11–34 fits the sales profits versus advertising expenditure relationship best. The estimated regression relationship is as given in Table 11–19: Sales $= 3.67 + 6.78$ Logadv.

Remember that when we transform our data, the least-squares method minimizes the sum of the squared errors for the *transformed* variables. It is, therefore, very important for us to check for any violations of model assumptions that may occur as a result of the transformations. We must be especially careful with the assumptions

TABLE 11-19   Results of a Regression Analysis Fitting a Logarithmic Model to the Data of Example 11-5

```
The regression equation is
SALES = 3.67 + 6.78 LOGADV

Predictor          Coef        Stdev        t-ratio         P
Constant         3.6683       0.4016          9.13       0.000
LOGADV           6.7840       0.2360         28.74       0.000

s = 0.8819       R-sq = 97.8%      R-sq(adj) = 97.6%

Analysis of Variance

   SOURCE        DF          SS          MS          F         P
Regression        1       642.62      642.62     823.87     0.000
Error            19        14.78        0.78
Total            20       657.40
```

FIGURE 11-33   Plot of Sales versus the Natural Log of Advertising Expenditure (Example 11-5)

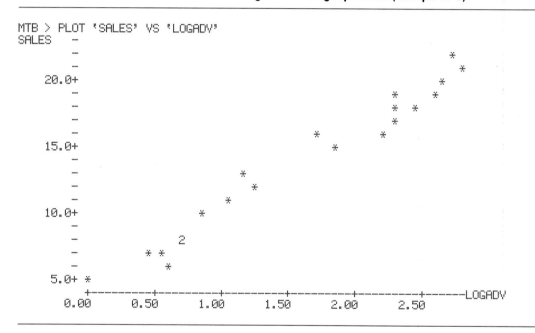

```
MTB > PLOT 'SALES' VS 'LOGADV'
SALES   -
        -                                                    *
        -                                                      *
 20.0+  -                                              *
        -                                   *       *
        -                                   *   *
        -                                   *
        -                          *      *
 15.0+  -                        *
        -
        -              *
        -                *
        -              *
 10.0+  -          *
        -
        -      2
        -    * *
        -        *
  5.0+  *
        +---------+---------+---------+---------+---------+-------LOGADV
      0.00      0.50      1.00      1.50      2.00      2.50
```

about the regression errors and their distribution. This is why residual plots are very important when transformations of variables are used. In our present model for the data of Example 11–5, a plot of the residuals versus the predicted sales values, $\hat{Y}$, is given in Figure 11–35. The plot of the residuals does not indicate any violation of assumptions, and we therefore conclude that the model is adequate. We note also that confidence intervals for transformed models do not always correspond to correct intervals for the original model.

Another nonlinear model that may be linearized by an appropriate transformation is the *reciprocal model*. A reciprocal model in several variables is given in equation 11–36.

FIGURE 11-34   Plot of Log Sales versus Log Advertising Expenditure (Example 11-5)

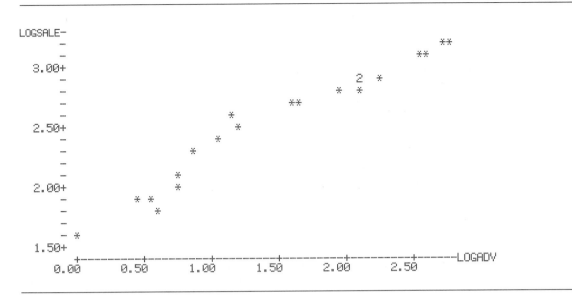

FIGURE 11-35   Residual Plot for the Estimated Model, Sales = 3.67 + 6.78 Logadv (Example 11-5)

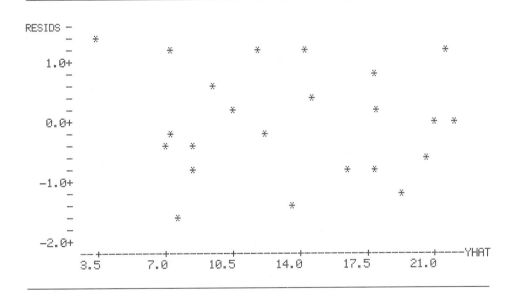

The **reciprocal model:**

$$Y = \frac{1}{\beta_0 + \beta_1 X_1 + \beta_2 X_2 + \beta_3 X_3 + \epsilon} \tag{11–36}$$

FIGURE 11–36
Two Examples of a
Relationship Where a
Regression of 1/Y versus
1/X Is Appropriate

This model becomes a linear model upon taking the reciprocals of both sides of the equation. In practical terms, we run a regression of $1/Y$ versus the X_i variables unchanged. A particular reciprocal model with one independent variable has a complicated form, which will not be explicitly stated here. This model calls for linearization by taking the reciprocals of both X and Y. Two curves corresponding to this particular reciprocal model are shown in Figure 11–36. When our data display the acute curvature of one of the curves in the figure, running a regression of $1/Y$ versus $1/X$ may be fruitful.

Next we will discuss transformations of the dependent variable, Y, only. These are transformations designed to stabilize the variance of the regression errors.

Variance-Stabilizing Transformations

Remember that one of the assumptions of the regression model is that the regression errors, ϵ, have equal variance. If the variance of the errors increases or decreases as one or more of the independent variables change, we have the problem of heteroscedasticity. When heteroscedasticity is present, our regression coefficient estimators are not efficient. This violation of the regression assumptions may sometimes be corrected by the use of a transformation. We will consider three major transformations of the dependent variable, Y, to correct for heteroscedasticity.

> Transformations of Y that may help correct the problem of heteroscedasticity:
>
> 1. The square root transformation: $Y' = \sqrt{Y}$
>   This is the least "severe" transformation. It is useful when the variance of the regression errors is approximately proportional to the mean of Y, conditional on the values of the independent variables X_i.
> 2. The logarithmic transformation: $Y' = \log Y$ (to any base)
>   This is a transformation of a stronger nature and is useful when the variance of the errors is approximately proportional to the square of the conditional mean of Y.
> 3. The reciprocal transformation: $Y' = 1/Y$
>   This is the most severe of the three transformations and is required when the violation of equal variance is serious. This transformation is useful when the variance of the errors is approximately proportional to the conditional mean of Y to the fourth power.

There are transformations other than these, although the preceding transformations are most commonly used. In a given situation, we want to find the transformation that makes the errors have approximately equal variance as evidenced by the residual plots. An alternative to using transformations to stabilize the variance is use of the weighted least-squares procedure mentioned in our earlier discussion of the heteroscedasticity problem. We note that a test for heteroscedasticity exists. The test is the Goldfeld-Quandt test, discussed in econometrics books.

It is important to note that transformations may also correct problems of nonnormality of the errors. A variance-stabilizing transformation may thus make the distribution of the new errors closer to a normal distribution. In using transformations—

whether to stabilize the variance, to make the errors approximate a normal distribution, or to make a nonlinear model linear—it is important to remember that all results should be converted back to the original variables. As a final example of a nonlinear model that can be linearized by using a transformation, we present the *logistic regression model.*

FIGURE 11-37
The Logistic Function

Regression with Dependent Indicator Variable

In section 11–8, we discussed models with indicator variables as independent X_i variables. In this subsection, we discuss regression analysis where the dependent variable, Y, is an indicator variable and may obtain only the value 0 or the value 1. This is the case when the response to a set of independent variables is in the binary form: success or failure. An example of such a situation is the following.

A bank is interested in predicting whether or not a given loan applicant would be a good risk, i.e., pay back his or her loan. The bank may have data on past loan applicants, such as applicant's income, years of employment with the same employer, and value of home. All these independent variables may be used in a regression analysis where the dependent variable is binary: $Y = 0$ if the applicant did not repay the loan, and $Y = 1$ if he or she did pay back the loan. When only one explanatory variable, X, is used, the model is the *logistic function,* given in equation 11–37.

The **logistic function:**

$$E(Y \mid X) = \frac{e^{(\beta_0 + \beta_1 X)}}{1 + e^{(\beta_0 + \beta_1 X)}} \qquad (11\text{–}37)$$

The expected value of Y given X, that is, $E(Y \mid X)$, has a special meaning: It is the probability that Y will equal 1 (the probability of success), given the value of X. Thus, we write $E(Y \mid X) = p$. The transformation given below linearizes equation 11–37.

Transformation to linearize the logistic function:

$$p' = \log\left(\frac{p}{1 - p}\right) \qquad (11\text{–}38)$$

We leave it to the reader to show that the resulting regression equation is linear. In practical terms, the transformed model is difficult to employ because resulting errors are intrinsically heteroscedastic. A better approach is to use the more involved methods of nonlinear regression analysis. We present the example to show that, in many cases, the dependent variable may be an indicator variable as well. Much research is being done today on the logistic regression model, which reflects the model's growing importance. Fitting data to the curve of the logistic function is called *logit analysis.* A graph of the logistic function of equation 11–37 is shown in Figure 11–37. Note the typical elongated S shape of the graph. This function is useful as a "threshold model," where the probability that the dependent variable, Y, will be equal to 1 (a success in the experiment) increases as X increases. This increase becomes very dramatic as X reaches a certain threshold value (the point T in the figure).

PROBLEMS

11–69. What are the two main reasons for using transformations?

11–70. Explain why a transformed model may be better than a polynomial model. Under what conditions is this true?

11–71. Refer to the residual plot in Figure 11–13. What transformation would you recommend be tried to correct the situation?

11–72. For the Singapore data of Example 11–2, presented in Table 11–6, use several different data transformations of the variables Exports, M1, and Price, and find a better model to describe the data. Comment on the properties of your new model.

11–73. Which transformation would you try for modeling the following data set?

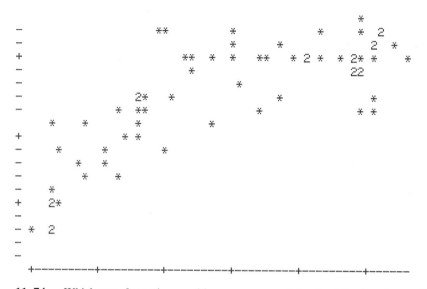

11–74. Which transformation would you recommend for the following data set?

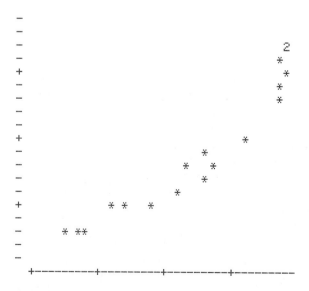

11–75. An analysis of the effect of advertising on consumer price sensitivity is carried out. The log of the quantity purchased (ln q), the dependent variable, is run against the log of an advertising-related variable called *RP* (the log is variable ln *RP*). There is an additive error term, ϵ, in the transformed regression. What assumptions about the model relating q and *RP* are implied by the transformation?

11–76. The following regression model is run.

$$\log Y = 3.79 + 1.66\, X_1 + 2.91\, X_2 + \log e$$

Give the equation of the original, nonlinear model linking the explanatory variables with Y.

11–77. Consider the following nonlinear model.

$$Y = e^{\beta_1 X_1} + e^{\beta_2 X_2} + \epsilon$$

Is this model intrinsically linear? Explain.

11–78. The following model is used in economics to describe production.

$$Q = \beta_0\, C^{\beta_1} K^{\beta_2} L^{\beta_3} \epsilon$$

where the dependent variable, Q, is the quantity produced; C is the capacity of a production unit; K is the capital invested in the project; and L is labor input, in days. Transform the model to linear regression form.

11–79. Consider the nonlinear model:

$$Y = \frac{1}{\beta_0 + \beta_1 X_1 + \beta_2 X_2 + \epsilon}$$

What transformation linearizes this model?

11–80. If the residuals from fitting a linear regression model display mild heteroscedasticity, what data transformation may correct the problem?

11–81. The model in problem 11–78 is transformed to a linear regression model and analyzed using a computer. Do the estimated regression coefficients minimize the sum of the squared deviations of the data from the original curve? Explain.

11–82. An article reports the results of a regression of a firm's restructuring level on the log of total assets in the previous year.[13] The equation is

$$Y = -2.039 + 0.034 \log X$$
$$(0.001)\quad (0.71)$$

Explain this regression.

11-11 Multicollinearity

The idea of multicollinearity permeates every aspect of multiple regression, and we have encountered this idea in earlier sections of this chapter. The reason multicollinearity (or simply *collinearity*) has such a pervasive effect on multiple regression is that whenever we study the relationship between Y and several X_i variables, we are bound to encounter some relationships among the X_i variables themselves. Ideally, the X_i variables in a regression equation are uncorrelated with each other; each variable contains a unique piece of information about Y—information that is not contained in any of the other X_i. When the ideal occurs in practice, we have no multicollinearity. On the other extreme, we encounter the case of perfect collinearity. Suppose that we run a regression of Y on two explanatory variables, X_1 and X_2. Perfect collinearity occurs when one X variable can be expressed precisely in terms of the other X variable for all elements in our data set.

---

[13] E. Hotchkiss, "Postbankruptcy Performance and Management Turnover," *Journal of Finance* 50, no. 1 (March 1995), p. 17.

Variables X_1 and X_2 are perfectly collinear if

$$X_1 = a + bX_2 \qquad\qquad (11\text{–}39)$$

for some real numbers a and b.

In the case of equation 11–39, the two variables are on a straight line and one of them perfectly determines the other. Here there is no new information about Y to be gained by adding X_2 to a regression equation that already contains X_1 (or vice versa).

In practice, most situations fall between the two extremes. Often, there is some degree of collinearity among several of the independent variables in a regression equation. A measure of the collinearity between two X_i variables is the *correlation* between the two. Recall that in regression analysis we assume that the X_i are constants and not random variables. Here we relax this assumption and measure the correlation between the independent variables (this assumes they are random variables in their own right). When two independent X_i variables are found to be highly correlated with each other, we may expect the adverse effects of multicollinearity on the regression estimation procedure.

In the case of perfect collinearity, the regression algorithm breaks down completely. Even if we were able to get regression coefficient estimates in such a case, their variance would be infinite. When the degree of collinearity is less severe, we may expect the variance of the regression estimators (and the standard errors) to be large. There are other problems that may occur, and we will discuss them shortly. Multicollinearity is a problem of degree. When the correlations among the independent regression variables are minor, the effects of multicollinearity may not be serious. In cases of strong correlations, the problem may affect the regression more adversely, and we may need to take some corrective action. Note that in a multiple regression analysis with several independent variables, *several* of the X_i may be correlated. A set of independent variables that are correlated with each other is called a *multicollinearity set*.

Let us imagine a variable and its information content as a direction in space. Two uncorrelated variables can be viewed as *orthogonal* directions in space: directions that are at $90°$ to each other. Perfectly correlated variables represent directions that have an angle of $0°$ or $180°$ between them, depending on whether the correlation is $+1$ or -1. Variables that are partly correlated are directions that form an angle greater than $0°$ but less than $90°$ (or between $90°$ and $180°$ if the correlation is negative). The closer the angle between the directions is to $0°$ or $180°$, the greater the collinearity. This is illustrated in Figure 11–38.

Causes of Multicollinearity

There are several different causes of multicollinearity. A data collection method may produce multicollinearity if, without intention, we tend to gather data with related values on several variables. For example, we may be interested in running a regression of size of home (Y) versus family income (X_1) and family size (X_2). If, unwittingly, we always sample families with high income and large size (rather than also obtaining sample families with low income and large size or high income and small size), then we have multicollinearity. In such cases, improving the sampling method would solve the problem. In other cases, the variables may by nature be related with each other, and sampling adjustments may not work. In such cases, one of the correlated variables should probably be excluded from the model to avoid the collinearity problem.

FIGURE 11–38   Collinearity Viewed as the Relationship between Two Directions in Space

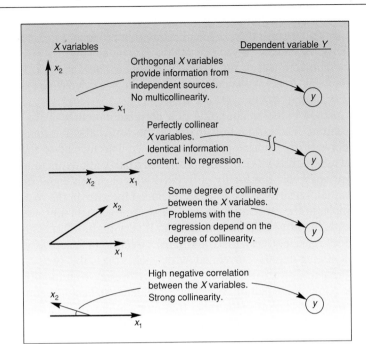

In industrial processes, sometimes there are physical constraints on the data. For example, if we run a regression of chemical yield (Y) versus the concentration of two elements (X_1 and X_2), and the total amount of material in the process is constant, then as one chemical increases in concentration, we must reduce the concentration of the other. In this case, X_1 and X_2 are (negatively) correlated, and multicollinearity is present.

Yet another source of collinearity is the inclusion of higher powers of the X_i. Including X^2 in a model that contains the variable X may cause collinearity if our data are restricted to a narrow range of values. This was seen in one of the problems in an earlier section.

Whatever the source of the multicollinearity, it is important to be aware of its existence so that we may guard against its adverse effects on the estimation procedure and the ensuing use of the regression equation in prediction, control, or understanding the underlying process. We now present several methods of detecting multicollinearity and a description of its major symptoms.

Detecting the Existence of Multicollinearity

Many statistical computer packages have built-in warnings about severe cases of multicollinearity. When multicollinearity is extreme (that is, when we have near-perfect correlation between some of the explanatory variables), the program may automatically drop collinear variables so that computations may be possible. In such cases, the MINITAB program, for example, will print the following message.

```
[variable name] is highly correlated with other X variables.
[variable name] has been omitted from the equation.
```

In less serious cases, the program prints the first line of the warning above but does not drop the variable.

In cases where multicollinearity is not serious enough to cause computational problems, it may still disturb the statistical estimation procedure and make our estimators have large variances. In such cases, the computer may not print a message telling us about multicollinearity, but we will still want to know about it. There are two methods available in most statistical packages to help us determine the extent of multicollinearity present in our regression.

The first method is the computation of a **correlation matrix** of the independent regression variables. The correlation matrix is an array of all estimated pairwise correlations between the independent variables, X_i. The format of the correlation matrix is shown in Figure 11–39. The correlation matrix allows us to identify those explanatory variables that are highly correlated with each other and thus cause the problem of multicollinearity when they are included together in the regression equation. For example, in the correlation matrix shown in Figure 11–39, we see that the correlation between variable X_1 and variable X_2 is very high (0.92). This means that the two variables represent very much the same direction in space, as was shown in Figure 11–38. Being highly correlated with each other, the two variables contain much of the same information about Y and therefore cause multicollinearity when both are in the regression equation. A similar statement can be made about X_3 and X_6, which have a 0.89 correlation. Remember that multicollinearity is a matter of extent or degree. It is hard to give a rule of thumb as to how high a correlation may be before multicollinearity has adverse effects on the regression analysis. Correlations as high as the ones just mentioned are certainly large enough to cause multicollinearity problems.

We will demonstrate the use of the correlation matrix with the data of Example 11–2. The MINITAB package features the command CORRELATION, which is followed by the names of specified variables (or columns). This command produces the desired matrix. (The MINITAB output does not include the diagonal of 1s, as do some other packages.) Table 11–20 is the MINITAB-produced correlation matrix showing all pairwise correlations between the independent variables of the Singapore exports example. The table also shows the MINITAB command that produces the output.

The highest pairwise correlation exists between Lend and Price. This correlation of 0.745 is the source of the multicollinearity detected in problem 11–36. Recall that the model we chose as best in our solution of Example 11–2 did not include the lending rate. In our solution of Example 11–2, we discussed other collinear variables as well. The multicollinearity may have been caused by the smaller pairwise correlations in Table 11–20, or it may have been caused by more complex correlations in the data than just the pairwise correlations. This brings us to the second statistical method of detecting multicollinearity: variance inflation factors.

The degree of multicollinearity introduced to the regression by variable X_h, once variables $X_1, \ldots, X_k$ are in the regression equation, is a function of the multiple correlation between X_h and the other variables $X_1, \ldots, X_k$. Thus, suppose we run a multiple regression—not of Y, but of X_h on all the other X variables. From this multiple regression, we get an R^2 value. This R^2 is a measure of the multicollinearity "exerted" by the variable X_h. Recall that a major problem caused by multicollinearity is the inflation of the variance of the regression coefficient estimators. To measure this ill effect of multicollinearity, we use the *variance inflation factor* (VIF) associated with variable X_h.

FIGURE 11–39   A Correlation Matrix

TABLE 11–20   MINITAB-Produced Correlation Matrix for Example 11–2

```
MTB > CORRELATION 'm1', 'lend', 'price', 'exch'

            m1          lend            price
lend     -0.112
price     0.447         0.745
exch     -0.410        -0.279          -0.420
```

The **variance inflation factor** associated with X_h:

$$\text{VIF}(X_h) = \frac{1}{1 - R_h^2} \qquad (11\text{–}40)$$

where R_h^2 is the R^2 value obtained for the regression of X_h, as dependent variable, on the other X variables in the original equation aimed at predicting Y

It can be shown that the VIF of variable X_h is equal to the ratio of the variance of the coefficient estimator, b_h, in the original regression (with Y as dependent variable) and the variance of the estimator, b_h, in a regression where X_h is orthogonal to the other X variables.[14] The VIF is the inflation factor of the variance of the estimator as compared with what that variance would have been if X_h were not collinear with any of the other X variables in the regression. A graph of the relationship between R_h^2 and the VIF is shown in Figure 11–40.

As can be seen from the figure, when the R^2 of X_h versus the other X variables increases from 0.9 to 1, the VIF rises very dramatically. In fact, for $R_h^2 = 1.00$, the VIF is infinite. The graph, however, should not deceive you. Even for values of R_h^2 less than 0.9, the VIF is still large. A VIF of 6, for example, means that the variance of

---

[14] J. Johnston, *Econometric Methods* (New York: McGraw-Hill, 1984).

FIGURE 11-40   Relationship between R_h^2 and VIF

the regression coefficient estimator, b_h, is six times what it should be (when no collinearity exists). Most computer packages will report, on request, the VIFs for all the independent variables in a regression model.

Table 11–21 is the MINITAB output for the full regression model of Example 11–2, which includes all the variables we considered. Using the regression subcommand VIF, we produce an extra column in the coefficient estimates output that reports the variance inflation factors for all the independent variables. The table also shows the regression command and the VIF subcommand. As we may have expected, multicollinearity is present, as evidenced by the variance inflation factors. Two of these factors are as high as 5 and 6.

What symptoms and effects of multicollinearity would we find without looking at a variable correlation matrix or the VIFs? There are several noticeable effects of multicollinearity. The major ones are presented in the following list.

The effects of multicollinearity:

1. The variances (and standard errors) of regression coefficient estimators are inflated.
2. The magnitudes of the regression coefficient estimates may be different from what we expect them to be.
3. The signs of the regression coefficient estimates may be opposite of what we expect them to be.
4. Adding or removing variables produces large changes in the coefficient estimates or their signs.
5. Removing a data point causes large changes in the coefficient estimates or their signs.
6. In some cases, the F ratio is significant, but the t ratios are not.

When any or all of these effects are present, multicollinearity is likely to be present. How bad is the problem? What are the adverse consequences of multicollinearity? The problem is not always as bad as it may seem. Actually, if we wish to use the

TABLE 11-21   MINITAB Analysis of the Full Model in Example 11-2, Including VIFs

```
MTB > REGRESS 'export' on 4 predictors 'm1', 'lend', 'price', 'exch';
SUBC > VIF.

The regression equation is
export = - 4.02 + 0.368 m1 + 0.0047 lend + 0.0365 price + 0.27 exch

Predictor     Coef        Stdev       t-ratio       p        VIF
Constant     -4.015       2.766       -1.45       0.152
  m1          0.36846     0.06385      5.77       0.000       3.2
  lend        0.00470     0.04922      0.10       0.924       5.4
  price       0.036511    0.009326     3.91       0.000       6.3
  exch        0.268       1.175        0.23       0.820       1.4

s = 0.3358     R-sq = 82.5%     R-sq(adj) = 81.4%
```

regression model for prediction purposes, multicollinearity may not be a serious problem.

From the effects of multicollinearity just listed (some of them were mentioned in earlier sections), we know that the regression coefficient estimates are not reliable when multicollinearity is present. The most serious effect is the variance inflation, which makes some variables seem not significant. Then there is the problem of the magnitudes of the estimates, which may not be accurate, and the problem of the signs of the estimates. We see that in the presence of multicollinearity, it may not be possible for us to assess the impact of a particular variable on the dependent variable Y because we do not have a reliable estimate of the variable's coefficient. If we are interested in prediction only and do not care about understanding the net effect of each independent variable on Y, the regression model may be adequate even in the presence of multi-collinearity. Even though individual regression parameters may be poorly estimated when collinearity exists, the combination of all regression coefficients in the regression may, in some cases, be estimated with sufficient accuracy so that satisfactory predictions are possible. In such cases, however, we must be very careful to predict values of Y only within the range of the X variables where the multicollinearity is the same as in the region of estimation. If we try to predict in regions of the X variables where the multicollinearity is not present or is different from that present in the estimation region, large errors may result. We will now explore some of the solutions commonly used to remedy the problem of multicollinearity.

Solutions to the Multicollinearity Problem

1. One of the best solutions to the problem of multicollinearity is to *drop collinear variables from the regression equation.* Suppose that we have a regression of Y on $X_1, X_2, X_3,$ and X_4 and we find that X_1 is highly correlated with X_4. In this case, much of the information about Y in X_1 is also contained in X_4. If we drop one of the two variables from the regression model, we would solve the multicollinearity problem and lose little information about Y. By comparing the R^2 and the adjusted R^2 of different regressions with and without one of the variables, we can decide which of the two independent variables we should drop from the regression. We want to maintain a high R^2 and therefore should drop a variable if the R^2 is not reduced much when the variable is removed from the equation. When the adjusted R^2 increases when a variable is deleted, we certainly want to drop the variable. For example, suppose that

the R^2 of the regression with all four independent variables is 0.94, the R^2 when X_1 is removed is 0.87, and the R^2 of the regression of X_1, X_2, and X_3 on Y (X_4 removed) is 0.92. In this case, we clearly want to drop X_4 and not X_1. The variable selection methods to be discussed in Section 11–13 will help us determine which variables to include in a regression model.

We note a limitation of this remedy to multicollinearity. In some areas, such as economics, theoretical considerations may require that certain variables must be in the equation. In such cases, the bias resulting from deletion of a collinear variable must be weighed against the increase in the variance of the coefficient estimators when the variable is included in the model. The method of weighing the consequences and choosing the best model is presented in advanced books.

2. When the multicollinearity is caused by sampling schemes that, by their nature, tend to favor elements with similar values of some of the independent variables, a change in the sampling plan to include elements outside the multicollinearity range may reduce the extent of this problem.

3. Another method that sometimes helps in reducing the extent of the multicollinearity, or even eliminating it, is changing the form of some of the variables. This can be done in several ways. The best way is to form new combinations of the X variables that are uncorrelated with each other and then run the regression on the new combinations instead of the original variables. (See section 16–4.) This way the information content in the original variables is maintained, but the multicollinearity is removed. There are other ways of changing the form of the variables, such as centering the data: a technique of subtracting the means from the variables and running a regression on the resulting new variables.

4. The problem of multicollinearity may be remedied by using an alternative to the least-squares procedure called *ridge regression*. The coefficient estimators produced by ridge regression are biased, but in some cases, it may be worthwhile to tolerate some bias in the regression estimators in exchange for a reduction in the high variance of the estimators that results from multicollinearity.

In summary, the problem of multicollinearity is an important one. We need to be aware of the problem when it exists and to try to solve it when we can. Removing collinear variables from the equation, when possible, is the simplest method of solving the multicollinearity problem.

PROBLEMS

11–83. For the data of Example 11–3 presented in Table 11–12, find the sample correlations between every pair of variables (the correlation matrix), and determine whether or not you believe that multicollinearity exists in the regression.

11–84. For the data of Example 11–3, find the variance inflation factors, and comment on their relative magnitudes.

11–85. Find the correlation between X_1 and X_2 for the data of Example 11–1 presented in Table 11–1. Is multicollinearity a problem here? Also find the variance inflation factors, and comment on their magnitudes.

11–86. Give an intuitive explanation of the problem of multicollinearity.

11–87. How does multicollinearity manifest itself in a regression situation?

11–88. Explain what is meant by perfect collinearity. What happens when perfect collinearity is present?

11–89. Is it true that the regression equation can never be used adequately for prediction purposes if multicollinearity exists? Explain.

11–90. In a regression of Y on the two explanatory variables X_1 and X_2, the F ratio was found not to be significant. Neither t ratios were found to be significant, and the R^2 was found to be 0.12. Do you believe that multicollinearity is a problem here? Explain.

11–91. In a regression of Y on X_1, X_2, and X_3, the F ratio is very significant, and the R^2 is 0.88, but none of the t ratios are significant. Then X_1 is dropped from the equation, and a new regression is run of Y on X_2 and X_3 only. The R^2 remains approximately the same, and the F is still very significant, but the two t ratios are still not significant. What do you think is happening here?

11–92. A regression is run of Y versus X_1, X_2, X_3, and X_4. The R^2 is high, and the F is significant, but only the t ratio corresponding to X_1 is significant. What do you propose to do next? Why?

11–93. In a regression analysis with several X variables, the sign of the coefficient estimate of one of the variables is opposite of what you believe it should be. How would you test to determine whether multicollinearity is the cause of this?

11–12 Residual Autocorrelation and the Durbin-Watson Test

Remember that one of the assumptions of the regression model is that the errors, ϵ, are independent from observation to observation. This means that successive errors are not correlated with each other at any lag; that is, the error at position i is not correlated with the error at position $i - 1, i - 2, i - 3$, etc. The idea of correlation of the values of a variable (in this case we consider the errors as a variable) with values of the same variable lagged one, two, three, or more time periods back is called *autocorrelation*.

> An **autocorrelation** is a correlation of the values of a variable with values of the same variable lagged one or more time periods back.

Here we demonstrate autocorrelation in the case of regression errors. Suppose that we have 10 observed regression errors: $e_{10} = 1$, $e_9 = 0$, $e_8 = -1$, $e_7 = 2$, $e_6 = 3$, $e_5 = -2$, $e_4 = 1$, $e_3 = 1.5$, $e_2 = 1$, and $e_1 = -2.5$. We arrange the errors in descending order of occurrence, i. Then we form the lag 1 errors, the regression errors lagged one period back in time. The first error is now $e_{10-1} = e_9 = 0$, the second error is now $e_{9-1} = e_8 = -1$, and so on. We demonstrate the formation of the variable e_{i-1} from the variable e_i (that is, the formation of the lag 1 errors from the original errors), as well as the variables e_{i-2}, e_{i-3}, etc., in Table 11–22.

We now define the autocorrelations. The error autocorrelation of lag 1 is the correlation between the *population* errors ϵ_i and ϵ_{i-1}. We denote this correlation by ρ_1. This autocorrelation is estimated by the *sample* error autocorrelation of lag 1, denoted r_1, which is the computed correlation between the variables e_i and e_{i-1}. Similarly ρ_2 is the lag 2 error autocorrelation. This autocorrelation is estimated by r_2, computed from the data for e_i and e_{i-2} in the table. Note that lagging the data makes us lose data points; one data point is lost for each lag. When computing the estimated error autocorrelations, r_j, we use as many points as we have for e_{i-j} and shorten e_i appropriately. We will not do any of these computations.

The assumption that the regression errors are uncorrelated means that they are uncorrelated at *any* lag. That is, we assume $\rho_1 = \rho_2 = \rho_3 = \rho_4 = \cdots = 0$. A statistical test was developed in 1951 by Durbin and Watson for the purpose of detecting when the assumption is violated. The test, called the *Durbin-Watson test*, checks for evidence of the existence of a first-order autocorrelation.

TABLE 11–22 Formation of the Lagged Errors

i	e_i	e_{i-1}	e_{i-2}	e_{i-3}	$e_{i-4}\cdots$
10	1	0	−1	2	3
9	0	−1	2	3	−2
8	−1	2	3	−2	1
7	2	3	−2	1	1.5
6	3	−2	1	1.5	1
5	−2	1	1.5	1	−2.5
4	1	1.5	1	−2.5	—
3	1.5	1	−2.5	—	—
2	1	−2.5	—	—	—
1	−2.5	—	—	—	—

The **Durbin-Watson test:**

$$H_0: \rho_1 = 0$$
$$H_1: \rho_1 \neq 0 \qquad\qquad (11\text{–}41)$$

In testing for the existence of a first-order error autocorrelation, we use the Durbin-Watson test statistic. Critical points for this test statistic are given in Appendix C, Table 7. Part of the table is reproduced here as Table 11–23: The formula of the Durbin-Watson test statistic is equation 11–42.

The Durbin-Watson test statistic:

$$d = \frac{\sum_{i=2}^{n} (e_i - e_{i-1})^2}{\sum_{i=1}^{n} e_i^2} \qquad\qquad (11\text{–}42)$$

Note that the test statistic, d, is not the sample autocorrelation, r_1.[15] The statistic d has a known, tabulated distribution. Also note that the summation in the numerator extends from 2 to n rather than from 1 to n as in the denominator. An inspection of the first two columns in Table 11–22, corresponding to e_i and e_{i-1}, and our comment on the "lost" data points (here, one point) reveal the reason for this.

Using a given level α from the table (0.05 or 0.01), we may conduct either a test for $\rho_1 < 0$ or a test for $\rho_1 > 0$. The test has two critical points for testing for a positive autocorrelation (the one-tailed half of H_1 in equation 11–41). When the test statistic,

---

[15] Actually, d is approximately equal to $2(1 - r_1)$.

TABLE 11–23 **Critical Points of the Durbin-Watson Statistic *d* at α = 0.05 (*n* = sample size, *k* = number of independent variables in the regression) (partial table)**

	k = 1		*k* = 2		*k* = 3		*k* = 4		*k* = 5	
n	d_L	d_U	d_L	d_U	d_L	d_U	d_L	d_U	d_L	d_U
15	1.08	1.36	0.95	1.54	0.82	1.75	0.69	1.97	0.56	2.21
16	1.10	1.37	0.98	1.54	0.86	1.73	0.74	1.93	0.62	2.15
17	1.13	1.38	1.02	1.54	0.90	1.71	0.78	1.90	0.67	2.10
18	1.16	1.39	1.05	1.53	0.93	1.69	0.82	1.87	0.71	2.06
⋮	⋮	⋮	⋮	⋮	⋮	⋮	⋮	⋮	⋮	⋮
65	1.57	1.63	1.54	1.66	1.50	1.70	1.47	1.73	1.44	1.77
70	1.58	1.64	1.55	1.67	1.52	1.70	1.49	1.74	1.46	1.77
75	1.60	1.65	1.57	1.68	1.54	1.71	1.51	1.74	1.49	1.77
80	1.61	1.66	1.59	1.69	1.56	1.72	1.53	1.74	1.51	1.77
85	1.62	1.67	1.60	1.70	1.57	1.72	1.55	1.75	1.52	1.77
90	1.63	1.68	1.61	1.70	1.59	1.73	1.57	1.75	1.54	1.78
95	1.64	1.69	1.62	1.71	1.60	1.73	1.58	1.75	1.56	1.78
100	1.65	1.69	1.63	1.72	1.61	1.74	1.59	1.76	1.57	1.78

d, falls to the left of the lower critical point, d_L, we conclude that there is evidence of a positive error autocorrelation of order 1. When *d* falls between d_L and the upper critical point, d_U, the test is inconclusive. When *d* falls above d_U, we conclude that there is no evidence of a positive first-order autocorrelation (conclusions are at the appropriate level, α). Similarly, when testing for negative autocorrelation, if *d* is greater than $4 - d_L$, we conclude that there is evidence of negative first-order error autocorrelation. When *d* is between $4 - d_U$ and $4 - d_L$, the test is inconclusive; and when *d* is below $4 - d_U$, there is no evidence of negative first-order autocorrelation of the errors. When we test the two-tailed hypothesis in equation 11–41, the actual level of significance, α, is double what is shown in the table. In cases where we have no prior suspicion of one type of autocorrelation (positive or negative), we carry out the two-tailed test and double the α. The critical points for the two-tailed test are shown in Figure 11–41.

For example, suppose we run a regression using *n* = 18 data points and *k* = 3 independent variables, and the computed value of the Durbin-Watson statistic is *d* = 3.1. Suppose that we want to conduct the two-tailed test. From Table 11–23 (or Appendix C, Table 7), we find that at α = 0.10 (twice the level of the table) we have: d_L = 0.93 and d_U = 1.69. We compute $4 - d_L$ = 3.07 and $4 - d_U$ = 2.31. Since the computed value *d* = 3.1 is greater than $4 - d_L$, we conclude that there is evidence of a negative first-order autocorrelation in the errors. As another example, suppose *n* = 80, *k* = 2, and *d* = 1.6. In this case, the statistic value falls between d_L and d_U, and the test is inconclusive.

The Durbin-Watson statistic helps us test for first-order autocorrelation in the errors. In most cases, when autocorrelation exists, there is a first-order autocorrelation. There are cases, however, when second- or higher-order autocorrelation exists without there being a first-order autocorrelation. In such cases, the test does not help us. Fortunately, such cases are not common.

The nice thing about the Durbin-Watson statistic is that it is computed by most statistical computer packages. In MINITAB, the regression subcommand DW pro-

FIGURE 11–41   Critical Regions of the Durbin-Watson Test

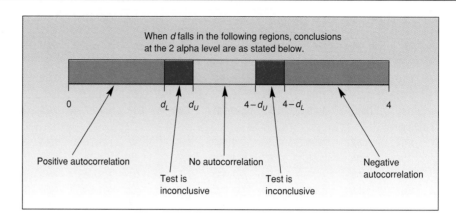

duces the value of the Durbin-Watson statistic. We demonstrate the computer output for the Durbin-Watson test with the data of Example 11–2. The regression command and the DW subcommand are shown, as well as the computed value of the statistic in this example.

```
MTB > REGRESS 'export' on 4 predictors 'm1', 'lend', 'price', 'exch';
SUBC>    DW.
Durbin-Watson statistic = 2.58
```

Recall that for this example, $n = 67$ and $k = 4$ (in this version of the equation). At $\alpha = 0.10$, for a two-tailed test, we have $d_U = 1.73$, $d_L = 1.47$, $4 - d_L = 2.53$, $4 - d_U = 2.27$. We conclude that there is evidence that our regression errors are negatively correlated at lag 1. This, of course, sheds doubt on the regression results; an alternative to least-squares estimation should be used. One alternative procedure that is useful in cases where the ordinary least-squares routine produces autocorrelated errors is a procedure called *generalized least squares* (GLS). This method is described in advanced books.

PROBLEMS

11–94.   What is the purpose of the Durbin-Watson test?

11–95.   Discuss the meaning of autocorrelation. What is a third-order autocorrelation?

11–96.   What is a first-order autocorrelation? If a fifth-order autocorrelation exists, is it necessarily true that a first-order autocorrelation exists as well? Explain.

11–97.   State three limitations of the Durbin-Watson test.

11–98.   Find the value of the Durbin-Watson statistic for the data of Example 11–5, and conduct the Durbin-Watson test. State your conclusion.

11–99.   Find the value of the Durbin-Watson statistic for the model of Example 11–3, and conduct the Durbin-Watson test. Is the assumption of no first-order error autocorrelation satisfied? Explain.

11–100.   Do problem 11–99 for the data of Example 11–1.

11–101. State the conditions under which a one-sided Durbin-Watson test is appropriate (that is, a test for positive autocorrelation only, or a test for a negative autocorrelation only).

11–102. The following table, reprinted by permission from the *Journal of Finance,* reports the results of several regressions of percentage change in the Tokyo and London stock markets on several variables relating to the time following the October 1987 stock market crash. Interpret the results of all the implied Durbin-Watson tests.

Trading Days Following October 20, 1987

Regressors	Intercept	Days 1–30	Days 30+	Days 1–10	Days 11–20	Days 20+	N	R^2	DW
Tokyo Index									
(1)	.000	1.058	.868	—	—	—	104	.93	1.17
	(.001)	(0.045)	(.032)						
(2)	.000	—	—	1.065	1.033	.882	104	.92	1.13
	(.001)			(.057)	(.135)	(.031)			
London Index									
(3)	.000	1.001	.805	—	—	—	129	.89	2.45
	(.001)	(.044)	(.035)						
(4)	.000	—	—	.994	1.038	821	129	.89	2.40
	(.001)			(.056)	(.103)	(.034)			

Source: D. Neumark, P. Tinsley, and S. Tosini, "After-Hours Stock Prices and Post-Crash Hangovers," *Journal of Finance,* March, 1991, p. 167.

11–13   Partial F Tests and Variable Selection Methods

Our method of deciding which variables to include in a given multiple regression model has been through trial and error. We started by asserting that several variables may have an effect on our variable of interest, Y, and we tried to run a multiple linear regression model of Y versus these variables. The "independent" variables have included dummy variables, powers of a variable, transformed variables, and a combination of all the above. Then we scrutinized the regression model and tested the significance of any individual variable (while being cautious about multicollinearity). We also tested the predictive power of the regression equation as a whole. If we found that an independent variable seemed insignificant due to a low t ratio, we dropped the variable and reran the regression without it, observing what happened to the remaining independent variables. By a process of adding and deleting variables, powers, or transformations, we hoped to end up with the best model: the most parsimonious model with the highest relative predictive power.

In this section, we present a statistical test, based on the F distribution and, in simple cases, the t distribution, for evaluating the relative significance of parts of a regression model. The test is sometimes called a *partial F test* because it is an F test (or a t test, in simple cases) of a part of our regression model.

Suppose that a regression model of Y versus k independent variables is postulated, and the analysis is carried out (the k variables may include dummy variables, powers, etc.). Suppose that the equation of the regression model is as given in Equation 11–1:

$$Y = \beta_0 + \beta_1 X_1 + \beta_2 X_2 + \beta_3 X_3 + \cdots + \beta_k X_k + \epsilon$$

We will call this model the *full model.* It is the full model in the sense that it includes the maximal set of independent variables, X_i, that we consider as predictors of Y. Now suppose that we want to test the relative significance of a subset of r out of the k independent variables in the full model. (By relative significance we mean the significance of the r variables given that the remaining $k - r$ variables are in the model.) We will do this by comparing the *reduced model,* consisting of Y and the $k - r$ independent variables that remain once the r variables have been removed, with the full model, equation 11–1. The statistical comparison of the reduced model with the full model is done by the **partial *F* test.**

We will present the partial F test using a more specific example. Suppose that we are considering the following two models.

Full model:

$$Y = \beta_0 + \beta_1 X_1 + \beta_2 X_2 + \beta_3 X_3 + \beta_4 X_4 + \epsilon \qquad (11\text{–}43)$$

Reduced model:

$$Y = \beta_0 + \beta_1 X_1 + \beta_2 X_2 + \epsilon \qquad (11\text{–}44)$$

By comparing the two models, we are asking the question: Given that variables X_1 and X_2 are already in the regression model, would we be gaining anything by adding X_3 and X_4 into the model? Will the reduced model be improved in terms of its predictive power by the addition of the two variables X_3 and X_4?

The statistical way of posing and answering this question is, of course, by way of a test of a hypothesis. The null hypothesis that the two variables X_3 and X_4 have no additional value once X_1 and X_2 are in the regression model is the hypothesis that both β_3 and β_4 are zero (given that X_1 and X_2 are in the model). The alternative hypothesis is that the two slope coefficients are not both zero. The hypothesis test is stated in equation 11–45.

Partial *F* test:

$$H_0: \beta_3 = \beta_4 = 0 \text{ (given that } X_1 \text{ and } X_2 \text{ are in the model)}$$
$$H_1: \beta_3 \text{ and } \beta_4 \text{ are not both zero} \qquad (11\text{–}45)$$

The test statistic for this hypothesis test is the partial F statistic.

The partial *F* statistic:

$$F_{(r,\, n-(k+1))} = \frac{(SSE_R - SSE_F)/r}{MSE_F} \qquad (11\text{–}46)$$

where SSE_R is the sum of squares for error of the reduced model; SSE_F is the sum of squares for error of the full model; MSE_F is the mean square error of the full model: $MSE_F = SSE_F/(n - (k + 1))$; k is the number of independent variables in the full model ($k = 4$ in the present example); and r is the number of variables dropped from the full model in creating the reduced model (in the present example, $r = 2$)

The difference $SSE_R - SSE_F$ is called the *extra sum of squares* associated with the reduced model. Since this additional sum of squares for error is due to r variables, it has r degrees of freedom. [Like the sums of squares, degrees of freedom are additive. Thus, the extra sum of squares for error has degrees of freedom: $(n - (k + 1)) - (n - (k - r + 1)) = r$.]

Suppose that the sum of squares for error of the full model, equation 11–43, is 37,653 and that the sum of squares for error of the reduced model, equation 11–44, is 42,900. Suppose also that the regression analysis is based on a data set of $n = 45$ points. Is there a statistical justification for including X_3 and X_4 in a model already including X_1 and X_2?

To answer this question, we conduct the hypothesis test, equation 11–45. To do so, we compute the F statistic of equation 11–46:

$$F_{(2,40)} = \frac{(\text{SSE}_R - \text{SSE}_F)/2}{\text{SSE}_F/40} = \frac{(42{,}900 - 37{,}653)/2}{37{,}653/40} = 2.79$$

This value of the statistic falls in the nonrejection region for $\alpha = 0.05$, and so we do not reject the null hypothesis and conclude that the decrease in the sum of squares for error when we go from the reduced model to the full model, adding X_3 and X_4 to the model that already has X_1 and X_2, is not statistically significant. It is not worthwhile to add the two variables.

In this example, we conducted a partial F test for the conditional significance of a set of $r = 2$ independent variables. This test can be carried out for the significance of any number of independent variables, powers of variables, or transformed variables, considered *jointly* as a set of variables to be added to a model. Frequently, however, we are interested in considering the relative merit of a single variable at a time. We may be interested in sequentially testing the conditional significance of a single independent variable, once other variables are already in the model (when no other variables are in the model, the F test is just a test of the significance of a single-variable regression). The F statistic for this test is still given by equation 11–46, but since the degrees of freedom are 1 and $n - (k + 1)$, this statistic is equal to the square of a t statistic with $n - (k + 1)$ degrees of freedom. Thus, the partial F test for the significance of a *single* variable may be carried out as a t test.

It may have occurred to you that a computer may be programmed to sequentially test the significance of each variable as it is added to a potential regression model, starting with one variable and building up until a whole set of variables has been tested and the best subset of variables chosen for the final regression model. We may also start with a full model, consisting of the entire set of potential variables, and delete variables from the model, one by one, whenever these variables are found not to be significant. Indeed, computers have been programmed to carry out both kinds of sequential single-variable tests and even a combination of the two methods. We will now discuss these three methods of variable selection called, respectively, *forward selection, backward elimination,* and their combination, *stepwise regression.* We will also discuss a fourth method called *all possible regressions.*

Variable Selection Methods

1. **All possible regressions:** This method consists of running all possible regressions when k independent variables are considered and choosing the best model. If we assume that every one of the models we consider has an intercept term, then there are 2^k possible models. This is so because each of the k variables may be either included in the model or not included, which means that there are two possibilities for each variable—2^k possibilities for

a model consisting of k potential variables. When four potential variables are considered, such as in Example 11–2, there are $2^4 = 16$ possible models: four models with a single variable, six models with a pair of variables, four models with three variables, one model with all four variables, and one model with no variables (an intercept term only). As you can see, the number of possible regression models increases very quickly as the number of variables considered increases.

The different models are evaluated according to some criterion of model performance. There are several possible criteria: We may choose to select the model with the highest adjusted R^2 or the model with the lowest MSE (an equivalent condition). We may also choose to find the model with the highest R^2 for a given number of variables and then assess the increase in R^2 as we go to the best model with one more variable, to see if the increase in R^2 is worth the addition of a parameter to the model. There are other criteria, such as Mallows's C_p statistic described in advanced books. The SAS computer package has a routine called RSQUARE that runs all possible regressions and identifies the model with the highest R^2 for each number of variables included in the model. The all-possible-regressions procedure is thorough but tedious to carry out. The next three methods we describe are all stepwise procedures for building the best model. While the procedure called stepwise regression is indeed stepwise, the other two methods, forward selection and backward elimination, are also stepwise methods. These procedures are usually listed in computer manuals as variations of the stepwise method.

2. **Forward selection:** Forward selection starts with a model with no variables. The method then considers all k models with one independent variable and chooses the model with the highest significant F statistic, assuming that at least one such model has an F statistic with a p-value smaller than some predetermined value (this may be set by the user; otherwise a default value is used). Then the procedure looks at the variables remaining outside the model, considers all partial F statistics (that is, keeping the added variables in the model, the statistic is equation 11–46), and adds the variable with the highest F value to the equation, again assuming at least one variable is found to meet the required level of significance. The procedure is then continued until no variable left outside the model has a partial F statistic that satisfies the level of significance required to enter the model.

3. **Backward elimination:** This procedure works in a manner opposite to forward selection. We start with a model containing all k variables. Then the partial F statistic, equation 11–46, is computed for each variable, treated as if it were the last variable to enter the regression (that is, we evaluate each variable in terms of its contribution to a model that already contains all other variables). When the significance level of a variable's partial F statistic is found not to meet a preset standard (that is, when the p-value is above the preset p-value), the variable is removed from the equation. All statistics are then computed for the new, reduced model, and the remaining variables are screened to see if they meet the significance standard. When a variable is found to have a higher p-value than required, the variable is dropped from the equation. The process continues until all variables left in the equation are significant in terms of their partial F statistic.

4. **Stepwise regression:** This is probably the most commonly used, wholly computerized method of variable selection. The procedure is an interesting mixture of the backward-elimination and the forward-selection methods. In forward selection, once a variable enters the equation, it remains there. This method does not allow for a reevaluation of a variable's significance once it is in the model. Recall that multicollinearity may cause a variable to become redundant in a model once other variables with much of the same information are included. This is a weakness of the forward-selection technique. Similarly, in the backward-elimination method, once a variable is out of the model, it stays out. Since it is possible that a variable that was not significant due to multicollinearity and was dropped may have predictive power once other variables are removed from the model, there are limitations to backward elimination as well.

Stepwise regression is a combination of forward selection and backward elimination that reevaluates the significance of every variable at every stage. This minimizes the chance of leaving out important variables or keeping unimportant ones. The procedure works as follows. The algorithm starts, as with the forward-selection method, by finding the most significant single-variable regression model. Then the variables left out of the model are checked via a partial F test, and the most significant variable, assuming it meets the entry significance requirement, is added to the model. At this point, the procedure diverges from the forward-selection scheme, and the logic of backward elimination is applied. The original variable in the model is reevaluated to see if it meets preset significance standards for staying in the model once the new variable has been added. If not, the variable is dropped. Then variables still outside the model are screened for entry requirement, and the most significant one, if found, is added. All variables in the model are then checked again for staying-significance once the new variable has been added. The procedure continues until there are no variables outside that should be added to the model and no variables inside the model that should be out.

The minimum significance requirements to enter the model and to stay in the model are often called P_{IN} and P_{OUT}, respectively. These are significance levels of the partial F statistic. For example, suppose that P_{IN} is 0.05 and P_{OUT} is also 0.05. This means that a variable will enter the equation if the p-value associated with its partial F statistic is less than 0.05, and it will stay in the model as long as the p-value of its partial F statistic is less than 0.05 after the addition of other variables. The two significance levels, P_{IN} and P_{OUT}, do not have to be equal, but we must be careful when setting them (or leave their values as programmed) because if P_{IN} is less strict than P_{OUT} (that is $P_{IN} > P_{OUT}$), then we may end up with a circular routine where a variable enters the model, then leaves it, then reenters, etc., in an infinite loop. We demonstrate the stepwise regression procedure as a flowchart in Figure 11–42. Note that since we test the significance of one variable at a time, our partial F test may be carried out as a t test. This is done in some computer packages.

It is important to note that computerized variable selection algorithms may not find the best model. When a model is found, it may not be a unique best model: there may be several possibilities. The best model based on one evaluation criterion may not be best using other criteria. Also, since there is order dependence in the selection process, we may not always arrive at the same "best" model. We must remember that

FIGURE 11–42   The Stepwise Regression Algorithm

computers only do what we tell them to do, and so, if we have not considered some good variables to include in the model, including cross products of variables, powers, and transformations, our model may not be as good as it could be. We must always use judgment in model selection and not rely blindly on the computer to dind the best model. The computer should be used as an aid.

Table 11–24 shows output from a MINITAB stepwise regression for the Singapore exports example, Example 11–2. Note that the peocedure chose the same "best" model (out of the 16 possible regression models) as we did in our analysis. The table also shows the needed commands for the stepwise regression analysis. Note that MINITAB uses t tests rather than the equivalent F tests.

PROBLEMS

11–103.   Use equation 11–46 and the information in Table 11–7 and 11–9 to conduct a partial F test for the significance of the lending rate and the exchange rate in the model of Example 11–2.

11–104.   Use a stepwise regression program to find the best set of variables for Example 11–1.

11–105.   Do problem 11–104 using the data of Example 11–3.

11–106.   Discuss the relative merits and limitations of the four variable selection methods described in this section.

11–107.   In the stepwise regression method, why do we need to test the significance of a variable that is already determined to be included in the model, assuming $P_{IN} = P_{OUT}$?

11–108.   Discuss the commonly used criteria for determining the "best" model.

11–109.   Is there always a single "best" model in a given situation? Explain.

TABLE 11-24   Stepwise Regression Using MINITAB for Example 11-2

```
MTB > STEPWISE regression of 'EXPORTS', PREDICTORS 'M1', 'LEND', 'PRICE', ' EXCHANGE'
 STEPWISE REGRESSION OF EXPORTS ON 4 PREDICTORS, WITH N = 67

      STEP       1       2
    CONSTANT   0.9348  -3.4230

    M1         0.520    0.361
    T-RATIO    9.89     9.21

    PRICE               0.0370
    T-RATIO             9.05

    S          0.495    0.331

    R-SQ       60.08    82.48
```

11-14   Using the Computer

In this chapter, we have made extensive use of the MINITAB package, and by now you should be very familiar with its use in regression analysis. We will review the main commands for regression analysis using this package. Then we will give examples of the use of three other packages; SPSS, SAS, and SYSTAT.

MINITAB

The main regression command in MINITAB is the REGRESS command, which has the following format.

```
REGRESS [name or column of dependent variable] on [number of
independent variables] predictors [names of independent variables,
separated by commas]
```

For example,

```
REGRESS C1 on 3 predictors C2, C3, C4
```

or

```
REGRESS 'Exports' on 2 predictors 'Price', 'M1'
```

Within the REGRESS command, if we mention the name of another column, the standardized residuals will be put into that column. If we then mention another column name, the fitted values ($\hat{Y}$) will be placed in that column. For example,

```
REGRESS C1 on 4 predictors C2, C3, C4, C5 put standardized
residuals into C6
REGRESS C1 on 2 predictors C2, C3 put standardized residuals
into C4, fitted values into C5
```

Other options of the regression program are offered as subcommands. Subcommands are separated from the regression command and from each other by a semicolon (;), and the last subcommand is followed by a period (.). Some of the subcommands we have used in this chapter are RESIDUALS, PREDICT, VIF, and DW. Other useful subcommands are described in the MINITAB manual. An example of the use of subcommands is

```
REGRESS C1 on 2 predictors C2, C3;
  VIF;
  DW.
```

The MINITAB command for carrying out a stepwise regression is of the form

```
STEPWISE regression of C1, predictors in C2, C3, C4, C5
```

Subcommands that allow us to set the value of the F statistic to enter or leave the equation are FENTER = [number, as critical point] and FREMOVE = [number, as critical point of F]. The default is $F = 4.00$.

SAS

The SAS computer package has several different routines that carry out multiple regression analysis. The simplest one is the REG procedure. This procedure performs general-purpose regression and provides many useful statistics as output. A more comprehensive procedure is the GLM (general linear model) procedure. This procedure is designed to handle complex models, including analysis of variance and analysis of covariance. The procedure automatically generates dummy variables for modeling qualitative variables and is well suited for handling polynomial terms. The RSQUARE procedure is an all-possible-regressions method. The STEPWISE procedure allows the performance of forward selection, backward elimination, and the stepwise regression procedure. The SAS package has other regression routines as well. We will demonstrate the use of the REG procedure using the movie example, Example 11–3. We use the data in Table 11–12. The program is as follows.

```
DATA MOVIE;
        INPUT EARN 1-3 COST 5-8 PROM 10-12 BOOK 14;
PROC REG DATA=MOVIE;
        MODEL EARN=COST PROM BOOK;
```

In SAS, every command ends with a semicolon (;). Data have been entered separately into the columns indicated (earnings in columns 1–3, etc.). The results of the analysis are given in Table 11–25.

SPSS

In SPSS, the regression methods are all contained in the REGRESSION procedure, which includes a wide variety of options. We demonstrate the use of this package with an example of stepwise regression. We use Example 11–2 again, and our results parallel the ones obtained using MINITAB in the last section. The output produced by SPSS is more extensive, however, and is given for comparison in Table 11–26. The SPSS commands for carrying out the stepwise regression are

TABLE 11-25 SAS Output for the Analysis of Example 11-3

```
                ANALYSIS OF VARIANCE

              SUM OF        MEAN
 SOURCE   DF  SQUARES       SQUARE      F VALUE  PROB>F

 MODEL    3   6325.151      2108.384    154.887  0.0001
 ERROR    16  217.7987      13.61242
 C TOTAL  19  6542.95

     ROOT MSE    3.689501    R-SQUARE   0.9667
     DEP MEAN    46.05       ADJ R-SQ   0.9607
     C.V.        8.011946

              PARAMETER ESTIMATES

              PARAMETER   STANDARD    T FOR H0:
 VARIABLE  DF ESTIMATE    ERROR       PARAMETER=0  PROB > |T|
 INTERCEP  1  7.83619     2.33338     3.358        0.0040
 COST      1  2.847692    0.3923395   7.258        0.0001
 PROM      1  2.278237    0.2534369   8.989        0.0001
 BOOK      1  7.166093    1.817964    3.942        0.0012
```

```
REGRESSION VARIABLES=M1 TO EXPORTS/
        DEPENDENT=EXPORTS/STEPWISE
```

(Data are entered separately.)

SYSTAT

In SYSTAT, we first call the module that carries out regression; this is done by the command MGLH. Then we specify the regression as MODEL (variable name) = CONSTANT + (variable names, separated by + signs). Finally, we write the command ESTIMATE. These commands, and the resulting output, are demonstrated for Example 11–5 in Table 11–27. Note that SYSTAT is now part of the SPSS company.

11-15 The Matrix Approach to Multiple Regression Analysis[16]

Computers carry out regression calculations by working with arrays of numbers. An array of numbers is called a *matrix* (the plural is *matrices*). The use of matrices vastly simplifies the operations of the computer because rules of matrix algebra make it possible to program the computer to perform operations on matrices that are similar to operations on individual numbers. The use of matrices and their underlying theory also allows the statistician to define properties of regression statistics in clear and concise terms.

　　If you are familiar with matrix algebra, the following brief description of the matrix approach to regression analysis will enhance your understanding of regression theory. You will also see definitions of various statistics, such as standard errors of

---

[16] This section is optional and requires familiarity with linear algebra.

TABLE 11-26 SPSS Output for Example 11-2

```
                                   * * * *  M U L T I P L E   R E G R E S S I O N  * * * *

Listwise Deletion of Missing Data
Equation Number 1   Dependent Variable..   EXPORT   EXPORTS TO SIGAPORE (THOU)
Beginning Block Number  1.  Method: Stepwise

Variable(s) Entered on Step Number 1..     M1        MONEY SUPPLY (BILLION S$)

Multiple R            .77514        Analysis of Variance
R. Square             .60084                            DF      Sum of Squares    Mean Square
Adjusted R Square     .59470        Regression           1        23.99528         23.99528
Standard Error        .49522        Residual            65        15.94084           .24524

                                    F =   97.84259       Signif F =  .0000

------------ Variables in the Equation ------------            ------------ Variables not in the Equation ------------

Variable      B         SE B      Beta         T      Sig T      Variable    Beta In   Partial   Min Toler     T      Sig T

M1          .520133   .052584   .775140     9.892    .0000       LEND        .427090   .671750    .987465    7.255   .0000
(Constant)  .934784   .368301               2.538    .0136       PRICE       .529083   .749090    .800141    9.046   .0000
                                                                 EXCHANGE   -.138520  -.200002    .832123   -1.633   .1074

                         * * * * * * * * * * * * * * * * * * * * * * * * * * * * * * * *

Variable(s) Entered on Step Number 2..     PRICE     PRICE LEVEL (1975 = 100)

Multiple R            .90820        Analysis of Variance
R Square              .82482                            DF      Sum of Squares    Mean Square
Adjusted R Square     .81935        Regression           2        32.94026         16.47013
Standard Error        .33062        Residual            64         6.99586           .10931

                                    F =  150.67317       Signif F =  .0000

------------ Variables in the Equation ------------            ------------ Variables not in the Equation ------------

Variable      B         SE B      Beta         T      Sig T      Variable    Beta In   Partial   Min Toler     T      Sig T

M1           .361417   .039246   .538610     9.209    .0000      LEND        .005276   .005600    .159866    .044    .9647
PRICE        .037033   .004094   .529083     9.046    .0000      EXCHANGE    .012875   .026858    .732976    .213    .8318
(Constant)  -3.427957  .540853              -6.329    .0000

                         * * * *  M U L T I P L E   R E G R E S S I O N  * * * *     EXPORTS   EXPORTS TO SINGAPORE (THOU)

Equation Number 1   Dependent Variable..   EXPORT    EXPORTS TO SINGAPORE (THOU)

End Block Number    1    PIN =    .050 Limits reached.
```

558

TABLE 11-27   SYSTAT Commands and Output for Example 11-5

```
>MGLH
>MODEL SALES = CONSTANT + ADVERT + ADVERT2
>ESTIMATE

DEP VAR:    SALES        N:        21   MULTIPLE R: 0.979   SQUARED MULTIPLE R: 0.959
ADJUSTED SQUARED MULTIPLE R: 0.954        STANDARD ERROR OF ESTIMATE:        1.228

VARIABLE       COEFFICIENT      STD ERROR      STD COEF   TOLERANCE      T      P(2 TAIL)

CONSTANT          3.515          0.73847        0.000        .        4.760      0.000
   ADVERT         2.515          0.258          1.996      0.055      9.749      0.000
   ADVERT2       -0.087          0.017         -1.080      0.055     -5.275      0.000

                             ANALYSIS OF VARIANCE

   SOURCE       SUM-OF-SQUARES        DF     MEAN-SQUARE       F-RATIO        P

REGRESSION         630.258            2        315.129        208.987      0.000
  RESIDUAL          27.142           18          1.508
```

estimators, that are not easily defined without the use of matrices and therefore were not given earlier. If you have not yet studied matrix algebra but will do so sometime in the future, you may always go back to this section and gain a deeper understanding of regression analysis.

Suppose we have a data set of n observations on the dependent variable, Y, and k independent variables, X_1, X_2, X_3, ..., X_k. We may write the multiple regression equation, equation $11-1$, in a format that includes all our data points. We do so in terms of arrays of numbers as follows:

$$\begin{bmatrix} y_1 \\ y_2 \\ y_3 \\ \cdot \\ \cdot \\ \cdot \\ y_n \end{bmatrix} = \begin{bmatrix} 1 & x_{11} & x_{12} & x_{13} & \cdots & x_{1k} \\ 1 & x_{21} & x_{22} & x_{23} & \cdots & x_{2k} \\ 1 & x_{31} & x_{32} & x_{33} & \cdots & x_{3k} \\ \cdot & \cdot & \cdot & \cdot & \cdots & \cdot \\ \cdot & \cdot & \cdot & \cdot & \cdots & \cdot \\ \cdot & \cdot & \cdot & \cdot & \cdots & \cdot \\ 1 & x_{n1} & x_{n2} & x_{n3} & \cdots & x_{nk} \end{bmatrix} \cdot \begin{bmatrix} \beta_0 \\ \beta_1 \\ \beta_2 \\ \cdot \\ \cdot \\ \cdot \\ \beta_k \end{bmatrix} + \begin{bmatrix} \epsilon_1 \\ \epsilon_2 \\ \epsilon_3 \\ \cdot \\ \cdot \\ \cdot \\ \epsilon_n \end{bmatrix} \qquad (11-47)$$

Compare equation $11-47$ with equation $11-1$ and note that here, for each data point, the value of Y is written as the sum of the products of the unknown β parameters and the point's X_i values, plus the error term associated with the data point. The operations are matrix operations.

As an example of the application of equation $11-47$, we write the data of Example $11-1$, presented in Table $11-1$, in this format. These data are shown in equation $11-48$.

$$\begin{bmatrix} 72 \\ 76 \\ 78 \\ 70 \\ 68 \\ 80 \\ 82 \\ 65 \\ 62 \\ 90 \end{bmatrix} = \begin{bmatrix} 1 & 12 & 5 \\ 1 & 11 & 8 \\ 1 & 15 & 6 \\ 1 & 10 & 5 \\ 1 & 11 & 3 \\ 1 & 16 & 9 \\ 1 & 14 & 12 \\ 1 & 8 & 4 \\ 1 & 8 & 3 \\ 1 & 18 & 10 \end{bmatrix} \cdot \begin{bmatrix} \beta_0 \\ \beta_1 \\ \beta_2 \end{bmatrix} + \begin{bmatrix} \epsilon_1 \\ \epsilon_2 \\ \epsilon_3 \\ \epsilon_4 \\ \epsilon_5 \\ \epsilon_6 \\ \epsilon_7 \\ \epsilon_8 \\ \epsilon_9 \\ \epsilon_{10} \end{bmatrix} \qquad (11-48)$$

As an exercise, multiply the matrices as shown, and add the error vector. You will get a set of n equations, one for each data point. Note that the **X** matrix contains a column of 1s. This is necessary for picking up the intercept term, β_0, which has no X value multiplying it.

We now name the matrices in equation 11–47. We use boldface letters to denote matrices and vectors. The $n \times 1$ matrix (n-dimensional vector) of Y values is called **Y**; the $n \times (k + 1)$ matrix of X values is called **X**; the $(k + 1)$-dimensional vector of β coefficients is called **β**; and the n-dimensional vector of errors is called **ε**. We now may write the regression equation, equation 11–47, in terms of matrices as follows:

$$\mathbf{Y} = \mathbf{X}\boldsymbol{\beta} + \boldsymbol{\epsilon} \qquad (11\text{–}49)$$

The estimated regression model, with the b estimates replacing the unknown βs, and the observed errors e replacing the unobserved ϵs, can be written in matrix notation as

$$\mathbf{Y} = \mathbf{Xb} + \mathbf{e} \qquad (11\text{–}50)$$

As you can see, matrix notation greatly simplifies our regression formulas. Using the definitions of matrix multiplication and addition, the relations between possibly large arrays of numbers can be written with very few symbols. Adding the concept of a transposed matrix, $\mathbf{A}' = $ transpose of matrix **A**, we can present more results.

The *normal equations* (for a regression with any number of variables and data points) are written in matrix format as follows:

$$\mathbf{X}'\mathbf{Xb} = \mathbf{X}'\mathbf{Y} \qquad (11\text{–}51)$$

Adding the concept of an inverse of a matrix, $\mathbf{A}^{-1} = $ inverse of matrix **A**, we can solve the normal equations by premultiplying each side of equation 11–51 by the matrix $(\mathbf{X}'\mathbf{X})^{-1}$:

$$(\mathbf{X}'\mathbf{X})^{-1}(\mathbf{X}'\mathbf{X})\mathbf{b} = (\mathbf{X}'\mathbf{X})^{-1}\mathbf{X}'\mathbf{Y}$$
$$\mathbf{Ib} = (\mathbf{X}'\mathbf{X})^{-1}\mathbf{X}'\mathbf{Y}$$

where **I** is the *identity matrix,* resulting from the multiplication of a matrix by its inverse. Since $\mathbf{Ib} = \mathbf{b}$, we arrive at the solution of the normal equations in terms of the least-squares estimate vector **b**:

$$\mathbf{b} = (\mathbf{X}'\mathbf{X})^{-1}\mathbf{X}'\mathbf{Y} \qquad (11\text{–}52)$$

Thus, for any number of variables and data points, we obtain the vector of parameter estimates, the transpose of which is $(b_0, b_1, b_2, \ldots, b_k)$, as the result of the matrix operation in equation 11–52. We now present more results.

The predicted values of Y, denoted $\hat{Y}$, corresponding to the observed data (these are called the *fitted values* of Y) are given by

$$\hat{\mathbf{Y}} = \mathbf{Xb} \qquad (11\text{–}53)$$

Since $\mathbf{b} = (\mathbf{X}'\mathbf{X})^{-1}\mathbf{X}'\mathbf{Y}$, we can write the fitted values in terms of a transformation of the observed values:

$$\hat{\mathbf{Y}} = \mathbf{X}(\mathbf{X}'\mathbf{X})^{-1}\mathbf{X}'\mathbf{Y} \qquad (11\text{–}54)$$

The matrix $\mathbf{H} = \mathbf{X}(\mathbf{X}'\mathbf{X})^{-1}\mathbf{X}'$ is called the *hat matrix.* Using it, we may write

$$\hat{\mathbf{Y}} = \mathbf{HY}$$

The hat matrix, as well as other matrices, such as **X** and $(\mathbf{X}'\mathbf{X})^{-1}$, can be obtained from many regression computer programs.

The variance-covariance matrix of the coefficient estimates vector **b** is given by

$$\mathbf{V}(\mathbf{b}) = \sigma^2 (\mathbf{X}'\mathbf{X})^{-1} \qquad (11\text{--}55)$$

Since σ^2 is unknown and estimated by MSE, we have an estimated variance-covariance matrix of **b** given by

$$\mathbf{s}^2(\mathbf{b}) = \text{MSE}(\mathbf{X}'\mathbf{X})^{-1} \qquad (11\text{--}56)$$

If we define the matrix **C** as $\mathbf{C} = (\mathbf{X}'\mathbf{X})^{-1}$, the standard error of each b_i is given using the diagonal of **C**, C_{ii}, as

$$s(b_i) = \sqrt{\text{MSE } C_{ii}} \qquad (11\text{--}57)$$

Another formula that has not been given until now is the definition of the elliptical joint confidence region for p regression parameters (shown in Figure 11–10). The region is defined by the equation

$$\frac{(\boldsymbol{\beta} - \mathbf{b})'\mathbf{X}'\mathbf{X}(\boldsymbol{\beta} - \boldsymbol{b})}{p \text{ MSE}} \leq F_{(\alpha;\, p,\, n-p)} \qquad (11\text{--}58)$$

A computer may generate values using Equation 11–58 that will give us a joint confidence region for several regression parameters.

What about Multicollinearity?

Earlier we said that in cases of severe multicollinearity, regression calculations cannot be carried out. Stated in terms of matrices, there is a very simple explanation for this.

When perfect multicollinearity exists, the columns of the **X** matrix are *linearly dependent*. Perfect multicollinearity means that at least two of the X_i variables are dependent on each other. From equation 11–47, you can see that this means that the columns of the **X** matrix are dependent. This dependency carries through to the matrix **X'X**, and this matrix, therefore, *cannot be inverted* (its determinant is zero). Thus, we cannot compute $(\mathbf{X}'\mathbf{X})^{-1}$ and cannot obtain the vector of parameter estimates, **b**. In cases where multicollinearity exists but is not perfect, the matrix is invertible but has much instability in it (the matrix is ill-conditioned). It is the matrix $(\mathbf{X}'\mathbf{X})^{-1}$ that causes the variance inflation in cases of multicollinearity.

The purpose of this section is just to give you an idea about regression results that are obtained via the matrix approach. Other results are given in advanced books.

11-16 Summary and Review of Terms

In this chapter, we extended the simple linear regression method of Chapter 10 to include several independent variables. We saw how the F test and the t test are adapted to the extension: The F test is aimed at determining the existence of a linear relationship between Y and any of the explanatory variables, and the separate t tests are each aimed at checking the significance of a single variable. We saw how the geometry of least-squares estimation is extended to planes and to higher-dimensional surfaces as more independent variables are included in a model. We extended the coefficient of determination to multiple regression situations, as well as the correlation coefficient. We discussed the problem of **multicollinearity** and its effects on estimation and prediction. We extended our discussion of the use of residual plots and mentioned the problem of **outliers** and the problem of **autocorrelation** of the errors and its detection. We discussed **qualitative variables** and their modeling using **indicator (dummy) variables.** We also talked about higher-order models: **polynomials** and **cross-product**

terms. We emphasized the need for parsimony. We showed the relationship between regression and ANOVA and between regression and **analysis of covariance.** We also talked about **nonlinear** models and about **transformations.** Finally, we discussed methods for selecting variables to find the "best" multiple regression model: **forward selection, backward elimination, stepwise regression,** and **all possible regressions.**

ADDITIONAL PROBLEMS

11–110. The following data, on the market value of firms, their total sales volume, profits, and total assets, all in millions of dollars for the year 1994, are obtained from *Business Week*'s list of the top 1,000 U.S. companies. Assume the data constitute a random sample. Use a computer package of your choice to carry out a stepwise regression analysis of a firm's market value versus the other variables as independent variables. Also, try to add powers of variables, cross-product terms, and transformations. Find the best prediction model; make sure your model is parsimonious.

12 Months—1994 ($ Mil.)

Value ($ Mil.)	Sales	Profits	Assets
93402	60108	5915.4	194484
81000	75094	4710.0	79262
79298	101092	5100.0	87790
70176	16172	2554.0	13873
54202	82494	2681.0	34493
52877	14970	2997.0	21857
52317	53776	4725.0	52649
45619	31572	2430.0	27337
44261	64052	3021.0	81091
38211	39333	2727.0	37914
36603	5266	1307.0	5961
36490	15734	2006.0	14833
34452	67111	1759.0	41760
33810	22245	1560.0	17536
33048	11521	2288.0	13272
32792	22442	2175.5	114559
32210	19944	2451.0	42500
32124	154951	5658.6	193871
18486	10052	821.9	8787
15046	14062	1079.6	14850
31388	11984	1842.4	12910
31036	35844	1595.0	34994

Source: "The Top 1000 U.S. Companies Ranked by Stock Market Valuation," *Business Week*, March 27, 1995, pp. 96–165.

11–111. An article reports the following results of a regression analysis aimed at predicting performance. The sample size used in section *A* was $n = 86$, and the sample size used in section B was $n = 74$. Interpret all the findings in the table.

Variable Entered	Step	R^2	ΔR^2	T
Section A				
Feedback condition	1	0.39	0.39	12.01**
Power distance				1.96*
Collectivism				2.17**
Trust in supervisor	2	0.52	0.13	3.45**
Importance of praise				2.11**
Importance of criticism				1.95*
Feedback $\times$ power distance	3	0.54	0.02	−1.99*
Feedback $\times$ collectivism				−2.01*
Section B				
Importance of praise	1	0.41	0.41	3.42**
Importance of criticism				2.35**
Trust in supervisor				6.71**
Feedback condition	2	0.52	0.11	3.14**
Power distance				0.84
Collectivism				1.07
Feedback $\times$ power distance	3	0.54	0.02	−1.99*
Feedback $\times$ collectivism				−2.01*

*$p < 0.05$. **$p < 0.01$

11–112. A regression analysis of share price was conducted on standardized dividends per share and standardized retained earnings. The results are given in the following equation. The author also reports that the R^2 is 0.56. What can you say about this regression?

$$P = 22.59 + 5.26D + 5.38R$$
$$(20.87) \quad (21.37)$$

11–113. An article in *Fortune* expounds upon a problem that has become serious in recent years: near collisions of airplanes and airline safety. Data on the total number of flights and the total number of near collisions for the years 1988 through 1994 are given in the article and are reproduced here (by permission of Dow Jones & Company):

Year	Flights (in Millions)	Near Collisions (per 100,000 flight hours)
1988	4.95	2.0
1989	4.65	1.5
1990	4.55	1.0
1991	4.90	0.9
1992	5.56	0.7
1993	5.75	0.6
1994	6.25	0.9

Source: Adapted from "Airline Safety," *Fortune*, June 26, 1995, p. 20.

Find the best regression model to fit the relationship between the total number of flights and the total number of near collisions in the sky. What are the implications of your model?

11–114. The following data are on the asking price and other variables for condominiums in Brookline, Massachusetts, in early 1990.[17] Try to construct a prediction equation for the asking price based on any or all of the other reported variables.

---

[17] I am indebted to Lisa Glucksman of Prudential Edna Kranz Real Estate for the data on condominiums in Brookline in 1990.

Price ($)	Number of Rooms	Number of Bedrooms	Number of Baths	Age	Assessed Value ($)	Area (square feet)
145,000	4	1	1	69	116,500	790
144,900	4	2	1	70	127,200	915
145,900	3	1	1	78	127,600	721
146,500	4	1	1	75	121,700	800
146,900	4	2	1	40	94,800	718
147,900	4	1	1	12	169,700	915
148,000	3	1	1	20	151,800	870
148,900	3	1	1	20	147,800	875
149,000	4	2	1	70	140,500	1,078
149,000	4	2	1	60	120,400	705
149,900	4	2	1	65	160,800	834
149,900	3	1	1	20	135,900	725
149,900	4	2	1	65	125,400	900
152,900	5	2	1	37	134,500	792
153,000	3	1	1	100	132,100	820
154,000	3	1	1	18	140,800	782
158,000	5	2	1	89	158,000	955
158,000	4	2	1	69	127,600	920
159,000	4	2	1	60	152,800	1,050
159,000	5	2	2	49	157,000	1,092
179,900	5	2	2	90	165,800	1,180
179,900	6	3	1	89	158,300	1,328
179,500	5	2	1	60	148,100	1,175
179,000	6	3	1	87	158,500	1,253
175,000	4	2	1	80	156,900	650

11–115. The following table reports the results of a multiple regression of the logarithm of annual earnings in Australia in 1984–85 versus three independent variables and a product of two of them. The sample size was $n = 44$. Discuss the results.

Variable	Coefficient	p-Value	Adj R^2
Injury rate	0.00063	0.8467	
Fatality rate	10.6851	0.3373	
WC benefit	0.000016	0.0031	
Fatality rate ˙WC benefit	−0.00018	0.4194	0.73

Source: Reproduced from T. J. Kniesner and J. D. Leeth, "Compensating Wage Differentials for Fatal Injury Risk in Australia, Japan, and the United States," *Journal of Risk and Uncertainty,* 1991, pp. 75–90.

Case 11 DIAMOND STATE TELEPHONE COMPANY

The Diamond State Telephone Company is interested in assessing the relationship between the total number of telephone lines that would be demanded by 1,317 new businesses in Delaware and various costs associated with telephone lines. Results of the study would help the company determine the level of monthly service charges per line, the level of installation charges, and the call-waiting charge that would maximize revenue.

A random sample of 62 new businesses is selected from the population of 1,317 businesses that submitted requests for telephone service. Each company in the sample is sent a questionnaire listing various possible cost schedules for the installation of new lines and monthly charges, as well as the call-waiting service charge. For each proposed cost schedule, the respondent is asked to specify how many telephone lines would be requested.

The idea is to use regression analysis to determine the price-elasticity of the demand for telephone lines. When the monthly charges and installation charges are low, businesses will presumably demand a greater number of telephone lines. As the costs involved increase, a business may decide to use fewer telephone lines.

The following data are the total number of lines that would be demanded by the entire sample of 62 busi-

nesses at each corresponding combination of costs. You have been assigned to carry out an analysis of the data. Discuss your suggested methodology. Discuss all the required assumptions. Carry out an analysis and state your conclusions. Remember that interest centers on the population of 1,317 new businesses. Can the results of the study be applied to other populations? Predict the total demand for lines by the 1,317 new businesses if line installation, monthly, and call-waiting charges are all set at the highest level used in the study. Predict total population demand for lines using other cost schedules within the range of the estimation data.

Number of Lines	Line Installation Charge	Monthly Charge per Line	Call-Waiting Charge	Number of Lines	Line Installation Charge	Monthly Charge per Line	Call-Waiting Charge
201	$12.50	$10.32	$2.55	147	25.12	20.92	4.50
199	12.50	10.32	3.05	140	37.10	20.92	4.50
195	12.50	10.32	4.50	121	37.10	27.18	2.55
196	18.60	10.32	2.55	120	37.10	27.18	3.05
187	18.60	15.65	2.55	125	25.12	27.18	4.50
190	12.50	15.65	3.05	145	18.60	27.18	2.55
181	18.60	15.65	4.50	114	18.60	34.00	2.55
167	18.60	20.92	2.55	113	18.60	34.00	4.50
165	18.60	20.92	3.05	108	25.12	34.00	4.50
166	25.12	15.65	3.05	105	37.10	34.00	3.05
150	25.12	20.92	2.55				

12

TIME SERIES, FORECASTING, AND INDEX NUMBERS

12-1   INTRODUCTION

he desire to forecast the future is as old as the human race—older if you allow that animals also form anticipations of what the future may bring. A predator may try to predict where the prey will run, and there are other such examples. In ancient times, people relied on prophets, soothsayers, and crystal balls. Today we have computers and with them an impressive, ever-expanding array of quantitative capabilities. Are these powerful quantitative tools useful in predicting the future?

It is important to understand that many economic and business-related variables (as well as others) cannot be forecast well. The future values of these variables cannot be predicted from their past history. This is especially true of the prices of assets traded in efficient markets,

Continued

such as stocks. The *efficient markets hypothesis* states that the future price of a stock cannot be predicted from its past. This hypothesis is widely held by academics. Stock market analysts who do not believe this hypothesis are known as *chartists,* people who chart stock price movements in an effort to extrapolate them into the future. The rationale behind the efficient markets hypothesis is that the demand for a given stock at any point in time reflects people's expectations of the future value of the stock. If the future value of the stock is expected to increase, people exert buying pressure, and the price increases immediately in fulfillment of this expectation. Mathematically, the theory states that movements of a stock are a *random walk:* the stock moves up or down like a drunk who takes each step randomly and moves with no apparent pattern.

> A **time series** is a set of measurements of a variable that are ordered through time.

A time series variable is often denoted by Z_t to distinguish it from the X and Y variables used in regression analysis and other areas. The particular value of the variable at time t is denoted by z_t. We denote the *error* occurring at time t by a_t. The error a_t in a time series model serves the same purpose as the regression error, ϵ. The random error at time t, a_t, is assumed to have mean zero and constant variance σ^2, and successive errors are assumed to be uncorrelated with each other.

Using our new time series notation, a random walk is modeled by equation 12–1.

A **random walk:**

$$Z_t - Z_{t-1} = a_t \qquad (12\text{--}1)$$

or equivalently:

$$Z_t = Z_{t-1} + a_t$$

Equation 12–1 says that the difference between the value of variable Z at time t and its value at time $t - 1$ is a random error. The time series Z_t is a random walk if each step, as we go from time $t - 1$ to t, is just a random error, a_t. An example of a random walk is shown in Figure 12–1. As can be seen from the figure, there is no persistent pattern or trend in the movement of the variable Z_t through time. The difference between the stock price today and the stock price tomorrow is a purely random "error." Since the error a_t cannot be forecast, because it is purely random, we cannot forecast Z_t. Our best forecast within this framework assumes that a_t will equal its mean of zero, and, therefore, that the price tomorrow will be equal to the price today. This is called the naive approach to forecasting.

FIGURE 12-1   A Random Walk

Many variables, however, such as sales and other business variables, can be forecast, and the use of statistics plays an important role in forecasting these variables. While there are many different methods of forecasting—subjective, naive, and others—this is a book on statistics, and we will therefore concentrate our discussion on the statistical methods of forecasting.

On January 15, 1884, a physicist, Professor J. H. Poynting of Trinity College, Cambridge, delivered a paper at a meeting of the Royal Statistical Society in London. The paper was entitled "A Comparison of the Fluctuations in the Price of Wheat and in the Cotton and Silk Imports into Great Britain." The paper contained an analysis of these variables and of sunspots. On page 43 of the paper, Poynting described his statistical method. He wrote as follows.

> Suppose that while a full band is playing, we could draw a curve to represent the pressure of the air at a given moment along a line drawn in the direction in which the sound is travelling. Such a curve would appear to fluctuate irregularly. But we know that it is really made up by the superposition of the perfectly regular waves of pressure corresponding to the separate notes sent out by all the various instruments, and a well-trained ear stationed in the line which can pick out the notes practically analyses this irregular pressure curve, that is, breaks it up into its simple harmonics. What is true of this pressure curve is true of all curves however irregularly they fluctuate, and the ear performs for the pressure curve what the mathematician seeks to perform for any other curve by Fourier's theorem.[1]

One of the aims of time series analysis is to forecast future values of time series variables. Incidentally, in this book we make a distinction between the terms *forecasting* and *prediction*. We use the word *prediction* in the context of regression analysis; the word *forecasting* is reserved for time series analysis, where *forecasting is an extrapolation of the series values beyond the region of the estimation data.* Remember the warning we gave about extrapolation in Chapter 10; we will return to that problem later in this chapter.

---

[1] J. H. Poynting, "A Comparison of the Fluctuations in the Price of Wheat and in the Cotton and Silk Imports into Great Britain," *Statistical Journal* XLVII (March 1884), pp. 34–48.

FIGURE 12–2 A Time Series as a Superposition of two Regular Wave Functions and a Random Error Component (not shown)

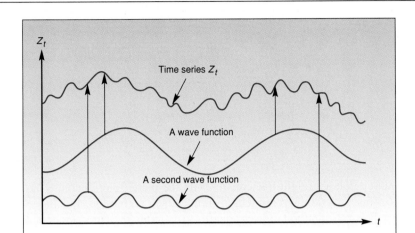

Now let us return to Professor Poynting. His statements suggest that a time series may look very irregular, but we should be able to break it down into its harmonics. These are regular wavelike functions (sines and cosines) of different frequencies, and they are superimposed on one another. Poynting suggests that we break down a time series into its different wave components. Then we can forecast the time series by forecasting where each wave component is moving. In his paper, Poynting does just that with the different time series: English cotton imports, Italian silk imports, Bengal silk imports, Brutia silk imports, English bank rate, sunspots, and other time series occurring between 1780 and 1880. The decomposition of a time series into wave components is demonstrated in Figure 12–2.

Much of time series analysis makes use of the idea of breaking down a time series into functions like the two shown in Figure 12–2, plus a random error term. The regular (wavelike) functions in the figure have a cycle, and they can be forecast. This reduces the forecasting errors to the magnitude of the nonforecastable residual error once the regularity has been accounted for. Another regularity in a time series may be an increasing or decreasing *trend,* that is, a general movement of increase or decrease. The trend, too, may be accounted for, thus helping us get better forecasts. Remember the idea of a statistical model presented in Chapter 10. Here we see an application of that important idea in the context of time series modeling. A good time series model is one that accounts for as much as possible of the *regular movement* in the time series, leaving out only a random error, which cannot be forecast. By comparison, the random walk series, given in equation 12–1, has *no regular components,* only random errors as the series moves through time. Since there is no regularity, the series cannot be forecast.

12–2 Trend Analysis

Sometimes a time series displays a steady tendency of increase or decrease through time. Such a tendency is called a **trend.** When we plot the observations against time,

TABLE 12-1   Annual Total Net Loans by Commercial Banks

Year	Loans ($ billions)
1988	833
1989	936
1990	1,006
1991	1,120
1992	1,212
1993	1,301
1994	1,490
1995	1,608

we may notice that a straight line can describe the increase or decrease in the series as time goes on. This should remind us of simple linear regression, and, indeed, in such cases we will use the method of least squares to estimate the parameters of a straight-line model.

At this point, we make an important remark. *When dealing with time series data, the errors of the regression model may not be independent of each other: time series observations tend to be sequentially correlated.* Therefore, we cannot give much credence to regression results. Our estimation and hypothesis tests may not be accurate. We must be aware of such possible problems and realize that fitting lines to time series data is less an accurate statistical method than a simple, *descriptive* method that may work in some cases. We will now demonstrate the procedure of trend analysis with an example.

EXAMPLE 12-1

An economist is researching banking activity and wants to find a model that would help her forecast total net loans by commercial banks. The economist gets the data presented in Table 12–1. A plot of the data is shown in Figure 12–3.

SOLUTION

As can be seen from the figure, the observations may be described by a straight line. A simple linear regression equation is fit to the data by least squares. A straight-line model to account for a trend is of the form

$$Z_t = \beta_0 + \beta_1 t + a_t \qquad (12\text{–}2)$$

where t is time and a_t is the error term. The coefficients β_0 and β_1 are the regression intercept and slope, respectively.

To carry out the trend analysis, we first *recode* the data to simplify the analysis. Instead of using the years, 1988, 1989, and so on, we renumber the observations so that their mean will be zero. This simplifies computations done by hand, and it makes sense because there is nothing quantitatively meaningful about the numerical value of the year. In order to have a mean of zero and keep the relative scaling correct, we renumber the eight years consecutively as $-7, -5, -3, -1, 1, 3, 5, 7$. (If we had an odd number of years, the middle one would be 0 and the others $1, 2, 3, \ldots$, and $-1, -2, -3, \ldots$, symmetrically on both sides of zero.) We do not show the simple linear regression computations; we have done quite a few in Chapter 10. We show the line, its equation, and the r^2 value in Figure 12–4.

FIGURE 12–3   Annual Total Net Loans by Commercial Banks

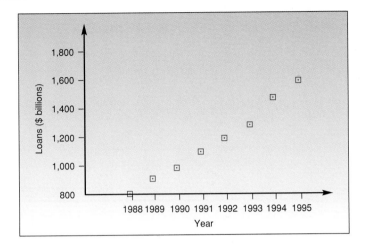

FIGURE 12–4   A Least-Squares Line for the Data of Example 12–1

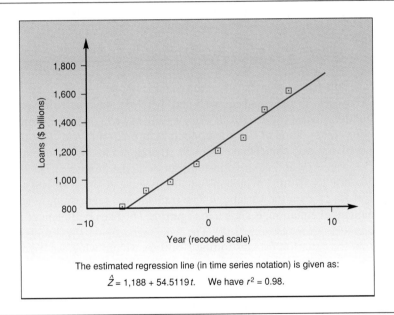

The estimated regression line (in time series notation) is given as:

$$\hat{Z} = 1,188 + 54.5119t. \quad \text{We have } r^2 = 0.98.$$

We note that, *in the context of time series, the coefficient of determination, r^2, is not a reliable measure.* Also, in this example, we have only eight observations, and the inference drawn from few observations is of limited use. Having pointed out the limitations of our analysis, we note that the line seems to fit our data very well. We may want to use our estimated trend line in forecasting. To forecast total loans in 1996, we note that in the recoded scale, 1996 is 9. We substitute $t = 9$ into the estimated regression equation and get

$$\hat{z} = 1,188 + 54.5119t = 1,188 + 54.5119(9) = 1,678.6 \text{ (billion dollars)}$$

Remember that forecasting is an extrapolation outside the region of the estimation data. This, in addition to the fact that the regression assumptions are not met in trend

FIGURE 12–5   Least-Squares Line and 1996 Forecast of Total Net Loans by Commercial Banks

analysis, causes our forecast to have an unknown accuracy. We will, therefore, not construct any prediction interval. Figure 12–5 shows our trend line and the forecast total loans for 1996.

Trend analysis includes cases where the trend is not necessarily a straight line. It is possible to model *curved* trends as well, and here we may use either polynomials or transformations, as we have seen in Chapter 11. In fact, a careful examination of the data in Figure 12–3 and of the fitted line in Figure 12–4 reveals that the data are actually curved upward somewhat. We will, therefore, fit an exponential model: $Z = \beta_0 e^{\beta_1 t} a_t$, where β_0 and β_1 are constants and e is the number $2.71828 \ldots$, the base of the natural logarithm. We assume a multiplicative error a_t. We run a regression of the natural log of Z on the variable t. The transformed regression, in terms of the original exponential equation, is shown in Figure 12–6. The coefficient of determination of this model is very close to 1.00. The figure also shows the forecast for 1996, obtained from the equation by substituting $t = 9$, as we did when we tried fitting the straight line.

A polynomial regression with t and t^2 leads to a fit very similar to the one shown in Figure 12–6, and the forecast is very close to the one obtained by the exponential equation. We do not elaborate the details of the analysis here because much was explained about regression models in Chapters 10 and 11. Remember that trend analysis does not enjoy the theoretical strengths that regression analysis does in non-time-series contexts; therefore, your forecasts are of questionable accuracy. In the case of Example 12–1 we conclude that an exponential or quadratic fit is probably better than a straight line, but there is no way to objectively evaluate our forecast. The main advantage of trend analysis is that when the model is appropriate and the data exhibit a clear trend, we may carry out a simple analysis.

PROBLEMS

12–1.   What are the advantages and disadvantages of trend analysis? When would you use this method of forecasting?

FIGURE 12-6   Fitting an Exponential Model to the Data of Example 12-1

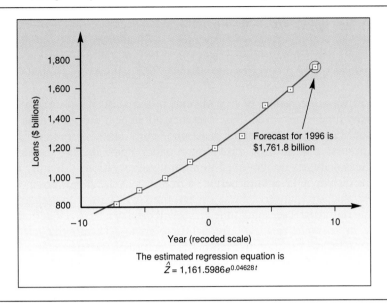

The estimated regression equation is
$$\hat{Z} = 1,161.5986e^{0.04628t}$$

12-2. An economist wants to construct a forecasting model for U.S. Gross Domestic Product. From the 1994 *Statistical Abstract of the United States* [Washington D.C.: U.S. Department of Commerce, 1994, p. 451], the economist gets the following data.

Year:	1986	1987	1988	1989	1990	1991	1992	1993
GDP ($ trillions):	17.7	18.7	19.9	21.2	22.2	22.6	23.6	24.7

Estimate a trend line for these data, and predict GDP for 1994. Compare your forecast with the actual value for 1994, which you may find in the current *Statistical Abstract*.

12-3. The following data are a local newspaper's readership figures, in thousands.

Year:	1984	1985	1986	1987	1988	1989	1990	1991	1992	1993	1994	1995
Readers:	53	65	74	85	92	105	120	128	144	158	179	195

Carry out a trend analysis of these data, and forecast the total number of readers for 1996 and for 1997.

12-4. The following data are annual corporate revenues for a midwestern manufacturing firm, in thousands of dollars. Carry out a trend analysis, and forecast revenues for the next year of operation.

Year:	1985	1986	1987	1988	1989	1990	1991	1992	1993	1994	1995
Revenue:	126	122	125	119	121	120	117	119	115	116	113

12-5. Would trend analysis, by itself, be a useful forecasting tool for monthly sales of swimming suits? Explain.

12-6. A firm's profits are known to vary with a business cycle of several years. Would trend analysis, by itself, be a good forecasting tool for the firm's profits? Why?

12-3   Seasonality and Cyclical Behavior

Monthly time series observations very often display seasonal variation. The seasonal variation follows a complete cycle throughout a whole year, with the same general pattern repeating itself year after year. The obvious examples of such variation are sales of seasonal items—for example, suntan oil. We expect that sales of suntan oil will be very high during the summer months. We expect sales to taper off during the onset of fall and decline drastically in winter—with another peak during the winter holiday season, when many people travel to sunny places on vacation—and then increase again as spring progresses into summer. The pattern repeats itself the following year.

Seasonal variation, which is very obvious in a case such as suntan oil, actually exists in many time series, even those that may not appear at first to have a seasonal characteristic. Electricity consumption, gasoline consumption, credit card spending, corporate profits, and sales of most discretionary items display distinct seasonal variation. Seasonality is not confined to monthly observations. Monthly time series observations display a 12-month period: a one-year cycle. If our observations of a seasonal variable are quarterly, these observations will have a four-quarter period. Weekly observations of a seasonal time series will display a 52-week period. The term *seasonality,* or *seasonal variation,* frequently refers to a 12-month cycle.

The second wave function in Figure 12–2 describes the seasonality in the time series, and the first wave function—with a longer period—reflects *cyclical variation.* In addition to a linear or curvilinear trend and seasonality, a time series may exhibit cyclical variation (where the period is not one year). In the context of business and economics, cyclical behavior is often referred to as the *business cycle.* The business cycle is marked by troughs and peaks of business activity in a cycle that lasts several years. The cycle is often of irregular, unpredictable pattern, and the period may be anything from 2 to 15 years and may change within the same time series. We repeat the distinction between the terms *seasonal variation* and *cyclical variation:*

> When a cyclical pattern in our data has a period of one year, we usually call the pattern **seasonal variation.** When a cyclical pattern has a period other than a year, we refer to it as **cyclical variation.**

FIGURE 12–7   Monthly Sales of Suntan Oil

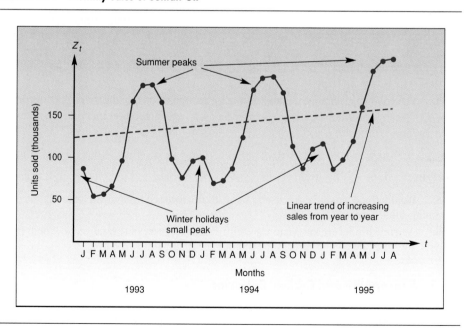

We now give an example of a time series with a linear trend and with seasonal variation and no cyclical variation. Figure 12–7 shows sales data for suntan oil. Note that the data display both a trend (increasing sales as one compares succeeding years), and a seasonal variation.

Figure 12–8 shows a time series of annual corporate gross earnings for a given company. Since the data are annual, there is no seasonal variation. As seen in the figure, the data exhibit both a trend and a cyclical pattern. The business cycle here has a period of approximately four years (the period does change during the time span under study). Figure 12–9 shows monthly total numbers of airline passengers traveling between two cities. See what components you can visually detect in the plot of the time series.

How do we incorporate seasonal behavior in a time series model? There are several different approaches to the problem. Having studied regression analysis, and having used it (somewhat informally) in trend analysis, let us now extend regression

FIGURE 12-8 Annual Corporate Gross Earnings

FIGURE 12-9 Monthly Total Numbers of Airline Passengers Traveling between Two Cities

analysis to account for seasonal behavior. If you think about it for a while and recall the methods described in Chapter 11, you probably realize that one of the tools of multiple regression—the dummy variable—is applicable here. We can formulate a regression model for the trend, whether linear or curvilinear, and add 11 dummy variables to the model to account for seasonality if our data are monthly. (Why 11? Reread the appropriate section of Chapter 11 if you don't know.) If data are quarterly, we use three dummy variables to denote the particular quarter. You have probably spotted a limitation to this analysis, in addition to the fact that the assumptions of the regression model are not met in the context of time series. The new limitation is lack of parsimony. If you have two years' worth of monthly data and you use the dummy variable technique along with linear trend, then you have a regression analysis of 24 observations using a model with 12 variables. If, on the other hand, your data are quarterly and you have many years of data, then the problem of the proliferation of variables does not arise. Since the regression assumptions are not met anyway, we will not worry about this problem.

Using the dummy variable regression approach to seasonal time series assumes that the effect of the seasonal component of the series is additive. The seasonality is added to the trend and random error, as well as to the cycle (nonseasonal periodicity)—if one exists. We are thus assuming a model of the following form.

An additive model:

$$Z_t = T_t + S_t + C_t + I_t \tag{12-3}$$

where T is the trend component of the series, S is the seasonal component, C is the cyclical component, and I is the irregular component

(The irregular component is the error, a_t; we use I_t because it is the usual notation in decomposition models.) Equation 12–3 states the philosophy inherent in the use of dummy variable regression to account for seasonality: the time series is viewed as comprising four components that are added to each other to give the observed values of the series.

The particular regression model, assuming our data are quarterly, is given by the following equation.

A regression model with dummy variables for seasonality:

$$Z_t = \beta_0 + \beta_1 t + \beta_2 Q_1 + \beta_3 Q_2 + \beta_4 Q_3 + a_t \tag{12-4}$$

where $Q_1 = 1$ if the observation is in the first quarter of the year and 0 otherwise; $Q_2 = 1$ if the observation is in the second quarter of the year and 0 otherwise; $Q_3 = 1$ if the observation is in the third quarter of the year and 0 otherwise; and all three Q_i are 0 if the observation is in the fourth quarter of the year

Since the procedure is a straightforward application of the dummy variable regression technique of Chapter 11, we will not give an example.

A second way of modeling seasonality assumes a *multiplicative* model for the components of the time series. This is more commonly used than the additive model, equation 12–3, and is found to describe appropriately time series in a wide range of applications. The overall model is of the following form.

A multiplicative model:

$$Z_t = (T_t)(S_t)(C_t)(I_t) \qquad (12\text{–}5)$$

Here the observed time series values are viewed as the *product* of the four components, when all of them exist. If there is no cyclicity, for example, then $C_t = 1$. When equation 12–5 is the assumed overall model for the time series, we deal with the seasonality using a method called *ratio to moving average*. Once we account for the seasonality, we may also model the cyclical variation and the trend. We describe the procedure in the next section.

PROBLEMS

12–7. Explain the difference between the terms *seasonal variation* and *cyclical variation*.

12–8. What particular problem would you encounter in fitting a dummy variable regression to 70 weekly observations of a seasonal time series?

12–9. In your opinion, what could be the reasons why the seasonal component is not constant? Give examples where you believe the seasonality may change.

12–10. Cyclical variation may also refer to cycles less than a year. Give examples of time series where you believe there may be a week-long cycle.

12–4   The Ratio-to-Moving-Average Method

A **moving average** of a time series is an average of a fixed number of observations (say, five observations) that moves as we progress down the series.[2]

A moving average based on five observations is demonstrated in Table 12–2. Figure 12–10 shows how the moving average in Table 12–2 is obtained and how this average *moves* as the series progresses. Note that the first moving average is obtained from the first five observations, so we must wait until $t = 5$ to produce the first moving average. Therefore, there are fewer observations in the moving-average series than there are in the original series, Z_t. *A moving average smooths the data of its variations.* The original data of Table 12–2 along with the smoothed moving-average series are displayed in Figure 12–11.

TABLE 12–2   Demonstration of a Five-Observation Moving Average

Time, t:	1	2	3	4	5	6	7	8	9	10	11	12	13	14
Series values, Z_t:	15	12	11	18	21	16	14	17	20	18	21	16	14	19
Corresponding series of five-observation moving average:			15.4	15.6	16	17.2	17.6	17	18	18.4	17.8	17.6		

----

[2] The term *moving average* has another meaning within the Box-Jenkins methodology (an advanced forecasting technique not discussed in this book).

The idea may have already occurred to you that if we have a seasonal time series and we compute a moving-average series for the data, then we will smooth out the seasonality. This is indeed the case. Assume a multiplicative time series model of the form given in equation 12–5:

$$Z = TSCI$$

(here we drop the subscript t). If we smooth out the series by using a 12-month moving average when data are monthly, or four-quarter moving average when data are quarterly, then the resulting smoothed series will contain trend and cycle but not

FIGURE 12-10   Computing the Five-Observation Moving Averages for the Data in Table 12–2

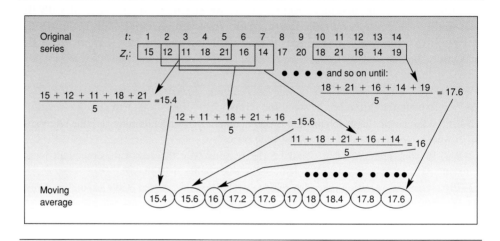

FIGURE 12-11   Original Series and Smoothed Moving-Average Series

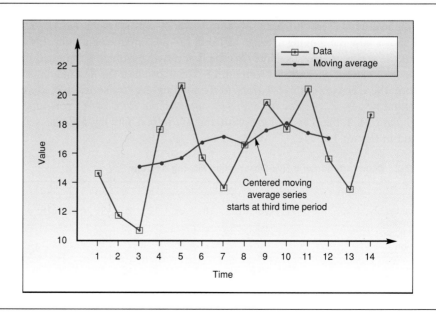

seasonality or the irregular component; the last two will have been smoothed out by the moving average. If we then divide each observation by the corresponding value of the moving-average series (MA), we will have isolated the seasonal and irregular components. Notationally,

$$\frac{Z_t}{MA} = \frac{TSCI}{TC} = SI \qquad (12\text{--}6)$$

This is the **ratio to moving average.** If we average each seasonal value with all values of Z_t/MA for the same season (that is, for quarterly data, we average all values corresponding to the first quarter, all values of the second quarter, and so on), then we cancel out *most* of the irregular component I_t and isolate the seasonal component of the series. There are two more steps to be followed in the general procedure just described: (1) we compute the seasonal components as percentages by multiplying Z_t/MA by 100; and (2) we *center* the dates of the moving averages by averaging them. In the case of quarterly data, we average every two consecutive moving averages and center them midway between quarters. Centering is required because the number of terms in the moving average is even (4 quarters or 12 months).

> Summary of the ratio-to-moving-average procedure for quarterly data (a similar procedure is carried out when data are monthly):
>
> 1. Compute a four-quarter moving-average series.
> 2. Center the moving averages by averaging every consecutive pair and placing the average between quarters.
> 3. For each data point, divide the original series value by the corresponding moving average. Then multiply by 100.
> 4. For each quarter, average all data points corresponding to the quarter. The averaging can be done in one of several ways: find the simple average; find a modified average, which is the average after dropping the highest and lowest points; or find the median. Once we average the ratio-to-moving-average figures for each quarter, we will have four *quarterly indexes.* Finally, we adjust the indexes so that their mean will be 100. This is done by multiplying each by 400 and dividing by their sum.

We demonstrate the procedure with Example 12–2.

The distribution manager of the Northern Natural Gas Company needs to analyze the time series of quarterly sales of natural gas in a midwestern region served by the company. Quarterly data for 1992 through 1995 are given in Table 12–3. The table also shows the four-quarter moving averages, the centered moving averages, and the ratio to moving average (multiplied by 100 to give percentages). Figure 12–12 shows both the original series and the centered four-quarter moving-average series. Note how the seasonal variation is smoothed out.

The ratio-to-moving-average column in Table 12–3 gives us the contribution of the seasonal component and the irregular component within the multiplicative model, as seen from equation 12–6. We now come to step 4 of the procedure: averaging each seasonal term so as to average out the irregular effects and isolate the purely seasonal component as much as possible. We will use the simple average in obtaining the four seasonal indexes. This is done in Table 12–4, with the ratio-to-moving-average figures from Table 12–3.

EXAMPLE 12-2

TABLE 12–3 Data and Four-Quarter Moving Averages for Example 12–2

Quarter	Sales (Btu in billions)	Four-Quarter Moving Average	Centered Moving Average	Ratio to Moving Average (percent)
1992 W	170			
S	148		(141/151.125)100	
S	141	152.25	151.125	93.3
F	150	150	148.625	100.9
1993 W	161	147.25	146.125	110.2
S	137	145	146	93.8
S	132	147	146.5	90.1
F	158	146	147	107.5
1994 W	157	148	147.5	106.4
S	145	147	144	100.7
S	128	141	141.375	90.5
F	134	141.75	141	95.0
1995 W	160	140.25	140.5	113.9
S	139	140.75	142	97.9
S	130	143.25	(139/142)100	
F	144			

FIGURE 12–12 Nothern Natural Gas Sales: Original Series and Moving Average

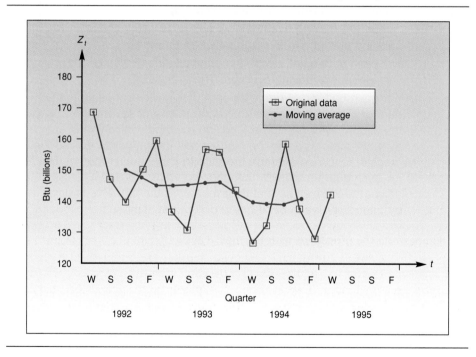

Due to rounding, the indexes do not add to exactly 400, but their sum is very close to 400. The seasonal indexes quantify the seasonal effects in the time series of natural gas sales. We will see shortly how these indexes and other quantities are used in forecasting future values of the time series.

TABLE 12-4 Obtaining the Seasonal Indexes for Example 12-2

	Quarter			
	Winter	**Spring**	**Summer**	**Fall**
1992			93.3	100.9
1993	110.2	93.8	90.1	107.5
1994	106.4	100.7	90.5	95.0
1995	113.9	97.9		
Sum	330.5	292.4	273.9	303.4
Average	110.17	97.47	91.3	101.13
	Sum of averages = 400.07			
	Seasonal index = (Average)(400)/(400.07):			
	110.15	97.45	91.28	101.11

TABLE 12-5 Deseasonalizing the Series for Example 12-2

Quarter	Sales (Z) (Btu, in billions)	Seasonal Indexes (S)	Deseasonalized Series (Z/S)(100)
1992 W	170	110.15	154.34
S	148	97.45	151.87
S	141	91.28	154.47
F	150	101.11	148.35
1993 W	161	110.15	146.16
S	137	97.45	140.58
S	132	91.28	144.61
F	158	101.11	156.27
1994 W	157	110.15	142.53
S	145	97.45	148.79
S	128	91.28	140.23
F	134	101.11	132.53
1995 W	160	110.15	145.26
S	139	97.45	142.64
S	130	91.28	142.42
F	144	101.11	142.42

The ratio-to-moving-average procedure, which gives us the seasonal indexes, may also be used for **deseasonalizing** the data. Deseasonalizing a time series is a procedure that is often used to display the general movement of a series without regard to the seasonal effects. Many government economic statistics are reported in the form of deseasonalized time series. To deseasonalize the data, we divide every data point by its appropriate seasonal index. If we assume a multiplicative time series model (equation 12–5), then dividing by the seasonal index gives us a series containing the other components only:

$$\frac{Z}{S} = \frac{TSCI}{S} = CTI \qquad (12\text{--}7)$$

Table 12–5 shows how the series of Example 12–2 is deseasonalized. The deseasonalized natural gas time series, along with the original time series, is shown in Figure 12–13. Note that we have to multiply our results Z/S by 100 to cancel out the fact that our seasonal indexes were originally multiplied by 100 by convention.

The deseasonalized series in Figure 12–13 does have some variation in it. Comparing this series with the moving-average series in Figure 12–12, containing only the

FIGURE 12-13   Original and Deseasonalized Series for the Northern Natural Gas Example

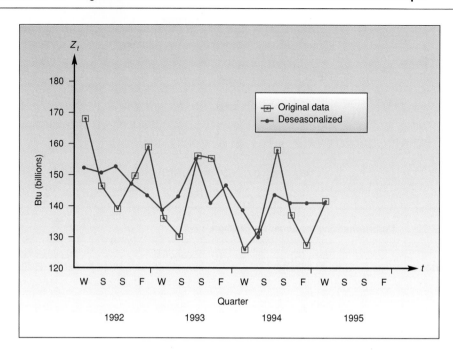

trend and cyclical components TC, we conclude that the relatively high residual variation in the deseasonalized series is due to the irregular component, I (because the deseasonalized series is TCI and the moving average series is TC). The large irregular component is likely due to variation in the weather throughout the period under study.

The Cyclical Component of the Series

Since the moving-average series is TC, we could isolate the cyclical component of the series by dividing the moving-average series by the trend, T. We must, therefore, first estimate the trend. By visually inspecting the moving-average series in Figure 12–12, we notice a slightly decreasing linear trend and what looks like two cycles. We should therefore try to fit a straight line to the data. The line, fitted by simple linear regression using the original data, is shown in Figure 12–14. The figure also shows the moving average series. The estimated trend line is

$$\hat{Z} = 155.275 - 1.1059t \tag{12–8}$$

From Figure 12–14, it seems that the cyclical component is relatively small in comparison with the other components of this particular series.

If we want to isolate the cyclical component, we divide the moving-average series (the product TC) by the corresponding trend value for the period. Multiplying the answer by 100 gives us a kind of cyclical index for each data point. There are problems, however, in dealing with the cycle. Unlike the seasonal component, which is fairly regular (with a one-year cycle), the cyclical component of the time series may not have a dependable cycle at all. Both the amplitude and the cycle (peak-to-peak distance) of the cyclical component may be erratic, and it may be very difficult, if not impossible, to predict. This makes it difficult to forecast future series observations.

FIGURE 12–14   Trend Line and Moving Average for the Northern Natural Gas Example

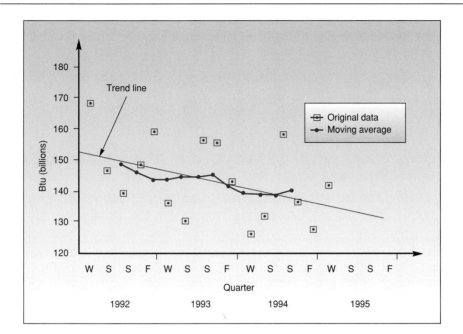

Forecasting a Multiplicative Series

Forecasting a series of the form $Z = TSCI$ entails trying to forecast the three "regular" components C, T, and S. We try to forecast each component separately and then multiply them to get a series forecast:

The forecast of a multiplicative series:
$$\hat{Z} = TSC \qquad\qquad (12\text{–}9)$$

As we noted, it is very difficult to obtain reliable forecasts of the cyclical component. The trend is forecast simply by substituting the appropriate value of t in the least-squares line, as was done in section 12–2. Then we multiply the value by the seasonal index (expressed as a decimal—divided by 100) to give us TS. Finally, we follow the cyclical component and try to guess what it may be at the point we need to forecast; then we multiply by this component to get TSC. In our example, since the cyclical component seems small, we may avoid the nebulous task of guessing the future value of the cyclical component. We will therefore forecast using only S and T.

Let us forecast natural gas sales for winter 1996. Equation 12–8 for the trend was estimated with each quarter sequentially numbered from 1 to 16 (we did not renumber so that the mean would be zero, as suggested in section 12–2). Therefore, winter 1996 is $t = 17$. Substituting this value into equation 12–8, we get

$$\hat{z} = 155.275 - 1.1059(17) = 136.475 \text{ (billion Btu)}$$

The next stage is to multiply this result by the seasonal index (divided by 100). Since the point is a winter quarter, we use the winter index. From the bottom of Table 12–4 (or the second column of Table 12–5), we get the seasonal index for winter: 110.15. Ignoring the (virtually unforecastable) cyclical component by letting it equal 1, we find, using the forecast equation, equation 12–9:

$$\hat{z} = TSC = (1)(136.475)(1.1015) = 150.327 \text{ (billion Btu)}$$

This is our forecast of sales for winter 1996.

PROBLEMS

12–11.   The following data represent average factory worker weekly pay, in dollars, for the months June 1992 to May 1995.

375, 370, 374, 378, 376, 380, 384, 380, 378, 380, 382, 383, 382, 381, 385, 387, 390, 392, 403, 398, 393, 389, 394, 392, 393, 391, 392, 396, 395, 400, 409, 404, 404, 405, 399, 402.

Decompose this time series into trend and seasonal components, as well as a cyclical component (if it exists) and the irregular component. Describe each component. Develop the seasonal (monthly) indexes. Use the ratio-to-moving-average method. Also, deseasonalize the series. Forecast average weekly pay for factory workers for June 1995.

12–12.   The following data are monthly figures of U.S. steel production, in millions of tons, from July 1992 through April 1995.

7.4, 6.8, 6.4, 6.6, 6.5, 6.0, 7.0, 6.7, 8.2, 7.8, 7.7, 7.3, 7.0, 7.1, 6.9, 7.3, 7.0,
6.7, 7.6, 7.2, 7.9, 7.7, 7.6, 6.7, 6.3, 5.7, 5.6, 6.1, 5.8, 5.9, 6.2, 6.0, 7.3, 7.4.

Decompose the series into its components using the methods of this section, and forecast steel production for May 1995.

12–13.   A company importing Italian cameos needs to forecast the exchange rate of Italian lire to U.S. dollars. Quarterly data from the third quarter of 1985 through the first quarter of 1991 are obtained from *International Financial Statistics* and are as follows (in Italian lire per U.S. dollar):[3]

1,654, 1,695, 1,697, 1,659, 1,708, 1,772, 1,807, 1,757, 1,794, 1,761, 1,747, 1,670,
1,625, 1,624, 1,630, 1,608, 1,594, 1,607, 1,630, 1,629, 1,612, 1,608, 1,604.

Try to forecast the exchange rate for the second quarter of 1991.

12–14.   The following are monthly electrical consumption data, in megawatts, for a town in Arizona from January 1989 through December 1992:

21, 23, 20, 24, 33, 41, 45, 50, 42, 28, 25, 26, 25, 27, 24, 30, 48, 53, 58, 62, 55, 32, 30, 32,
29, 32, 28, 35, 37, 50, 58, 66, 60, 45, 39, 40, 40, 43, 39, 45, 61, 68, 70, 72, 65, 54, 40, 39.

Decompose the series to its components, and forecast consumption for January 1993.

12–15.   The following are quarterly data of spot prices for a barrel of oil (in U.S. dollars) on the Gulf Coast of the United States, from 1991 through 1995: 21.6, 23.0, 22.9, 24.0, 23.1, 21.7, 21.1, 20.6, 21.2, 19.8, 20.6, 22.0, 21.1, 19.6, 18.4, 21.1, 20.0, 19.0, 18.8, 19.9. Decompose the series and forecast the price of a barrel of oil for the first quarter of 1996.

12–5   Exponential Smoothing Methods

One method that is often useful in forecasting time series is *exponential smoothing*. There are exponential smoothing methods of varying complexity, but we will discuss

---

[3] From *International Financial Statistics*, March 1991, p. 136.

only the simplest model, called *simple exponential smoothing*. Simple exponential smoothing is a useful method for forecasting time series that have no pronounced trend or seasonality. The concept is an extension of the idea of a moving average, introduced in the last section. Look at Figures 12–11 and 12–12, and notice how the moving average *smooths* the original series of its sharp variations. The idea of exponential smoothing is to smooth the original series the way the moving average does and to use the smoothed series in forecasting future values of the variable of interest. In exponential smoothing, however, we want to allow the more recent values of the series to have greater influence on the forecasts of future values than the more distant observations.

> **Exponential smoothing** is a forecasting method where the forecast is based on a *weighted average* of current and past series values. The largest weight is given to the present observation, less weight to the immediately preceding observation, even less weight to the observation before that, and so on. *The weights decline geometrically as we go back in time.*

We define a **weighting factor,** w, as a selected number between zero and one:

$$0 < w < 1 \qquad (12\text{–}10)$$

Once we select w—for example, $w = 0.4$—we define the forecast equation. The forecast equation is

$$\hat{Z}_{t+1} = w(Z_t) + w(1 - w)(Z_{t-1}) + w(1 - w)^2(Z_{t-2})$$
$$+ w(1 - w)^3(Z_{t-3}) + \cdots \qquad (12\text{–}11)$$

where $\hat{Z}_{t+1}$ is the *forecast* value of the variable Z at time $t + 1$ from knowledge of the *actual* series values Z_t, Z_{t-1}, Z_{t-2}, and so on back in time to the first known value of the time series, Z_1.

The series of weights used in producing the forecast $\hat{Z}_{t+1}$ is w, $w(1 - w)$, $w(1 - w)^2$, ... These weights decline toward zero in an *exponential* fashion; thus, as we go back in the series, each value has a smaller weight in terms of its effect on the forecast. If $w = 0.4$, then the rest of the weights are $w(1 - w) = 0.24$, $w(1 - w)^2 = 0.144$, $w(1 - w)^3 = 0.0864$, $w(1 - w)^4 = 0.0518$, $w(1 - w)^5 = 0.0311$, $w(1 - w)^6 = 0.0187$, and so on. The exponential decline of the weights toward zero is evident. This is shown in Figure 12–15.

Before we go on to show how the exponential smoothing model is used, we will rewrite the model in a recursive form that uses both previous observations and previous forecasts. Let us look at the forecast of the series value at time $t + 1$, denoted $\hat{Z}_{t+1}$. It can be shown that the exponential smoothing model of equation 12–11 is equivalent to the following model.

The exponential smoothing model:

$$\hat{Z}_{t+1} = w(Z_t) + (1 - w)(\hat{Z}_t) \qquad (12\text{–}12)$$

where Z_t is the actual, known series value at time t and $\hat{Z}_t$ is the forecast value for time t

---

The recursive equation, equation 12–12, can be restated in words as

Next forecast $= w$ (Present actual value) $+ (1 - w)$ (Present forecast)

The forecast value for time period $t + 1$ is thus seen as a weighted average of the actual value of the series at time t and the forecast value of the series at time t (the

FIGURE 12-15   Exponentially Declining Weights

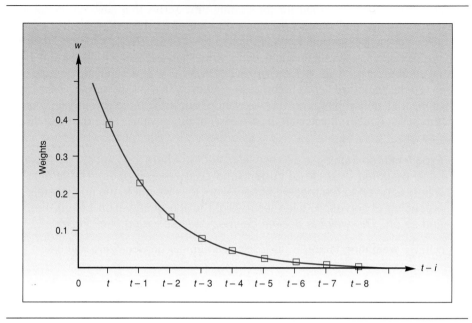

forecast having been made at time $t - 1$). There is yet a third way of writing the formula for the simple exponential smoothing model.

An equivalent form of the exponential smoothing model:

$$\hat{Z}_{t+1} = Z_t + (1 - w)(\hat{Z}_t - Z_t) \qquad (12\text{–}13)$$

The proofs of the equivalence of equations 12–11, 12–12, and 12–13 are left as exercises at the end of this section. The importance of equation 12–13 is that it describes the forecast of the value of the variable at time $t + 1$ as the actual value of the variable at the previous time period, t, plus a fraction of the previous *forecast error*. The forecast error is the difference between the forecast, $\hat{Z}_t$, and the actual series value, Z_t. We will formally define the forecast error soon.

The recursive equation (equation 12–12) allows us to compute the forecast value of the series for each time period in a sequential manner. This is done by substituting values for t ($t = 1, 2, 3, 4, \ldots$) and using equation 12–12 for each t to produce the forecast at the next period, $t + 1$. Then the forecast and actual values at the last known time period, $\hat{Z}_t$ and Z_t, are used in producing a forecast of the series into the future. The recursive computation is done by applying equation 12–12 as follows.

$$\hat{Z}_2 = w(Z_1) + (1 - w)(\hat{Z}_1)$$
$$\hat{Z}_3 = w(Z_2) + (1 - w)(\hat{Z}_2)$$
$$\hat{Z}_4 = w(Z_3) + (1 - w)(\hat{Z}_3)$$
$$\hat{Z}_5 = w(Z_4) + (1 - w)(\hat{Z}_4)$$
$$\vdots$$

$$(12\text{–}14)$$

The problem is how to determine the first forecast, $\hat{Z}_1$. Customarily, we use $\hat{Z}_1 = Z_1$. Since the effect of the first forecast in a series of values diminishes as the series progresses toward the future, the choice of the first forecast is of little importance (it is an *initial value* of the series of forecasts, and its influence diminishes exponentially).

The choice of w, which is up to the person carrying out the analysis, is of much importance, however. *The larger the value of w, the faster the forecast series responds to change in the original series.* Conversely, the smaller the value of w, the less sensitive is the forecast to changes in the variable Z_t. If we want our forecasts not to respond quickly to changes in the variable, we set w to be a relatively small number. Conversely, if we want the forecast to quickly follow abrupt changes in the variable Z_t, we set w to be relatively large (closer to 1.00 than to 0). We demonstrate this, as well as the computation of the exponentially smoothed series and the forecasts, in Example 12–3.

EXAMPLE 12-3

A sales analyst is interested in forecasting weekly firm sales in thousands of units. The analyst collects 15 weekly observations in 1995, and recursively computes the exponentially smoothed series of forecasts using $w = 0.4$ and the exponentially smoothed forecast series for $w = 0.8$. The original data and both exponentially smoothed series are given in Table 12–6.

SOLUTION

The original series and the two exponentially smoothed forecast series, corresponding to $w = 0.4$ and $w = 0.8$, are shown in Figure 12–16. The figure also shows the forecasts of the unknown value of the series at the 16th week produced by the two exponential smoothing procedures ($w = 0.4$ and $w = 0.8$). As was noted earlier, the smoothing coefficient, w, is set at the discretion of the person carrying out the analysis. Since w has a strong effect on the magnitude of the forecast values, the forecast accuracy depends on

TABLE 12-6   Exponential Smoothing Sales Forecasts Using $w = 0.4$ and $w = 0.8$

Day	Z_t Original Series	$\hat{Z}_t$ Forecast Using $w = 0.4$	$\hat{Z}_t$ Forecast Using $w = 0.8$
1	925	925	925
2	940	$0.4(925) + 0.6(925) = 925$	925
3	924	$0.4(940) + 0.6(925) = 931$	937
4	925	928.2	926.6
5	912	926.9	925.3
6	908	920.9	914.7
7	910	915.7	909.3
8	912	913.4	909.9
9	915	912.8	911.6
10	924	913.7	914.3
11	943	917.8	922.1
12	962	927.9	938.8
13	960	941.5	957.4
14	958	948.9	959.5
15	955	952.5	958.3
16 (Forecasts)		953.5	955.7

FIGURE 12-16   The Sales Data: Original Series and Two Exponentially Smoothed Series

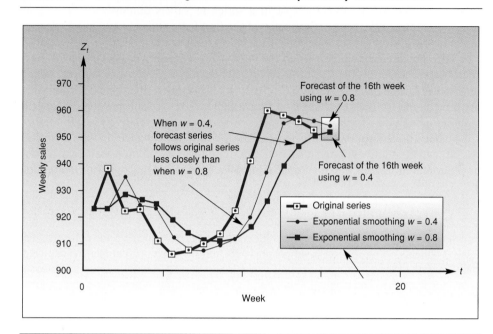

guessing a "correct" value for the smoothing coefficient. We have presented a simple exponential smoothing method. When the data exhibit a trend or a seasonal variation, or both, more complicated exponential smoothing methods apply.

PROBLEMS

12–16.   The following are monthly Dow Jones Commodity Price Index values from June 1994 through June, 1995:[4]

> 142, 137, 143, 142, 149, 143, 151, 150, 151, 146, 144, 145, 147.

Construct an exponential smoothing model for these data using $w = 0.6$ and forecast the Commodity Index Value for July 1995. Experiment with other values of w. See if you can improve forecasts of the data points that you have.

12–17.   The following are weekly sales data, in thousands of units, for microcomputer disks: 57, 58, 60, 54, 56, 53, 55, 59, 62, 57, 50, 48, 52, 55, 58, 61. Use $w = 0.3$ and also $w = 0.8$ to produce an exponential smoothing model for these data. Which value of w produces better forecasts? Explain.

12–18.   Construct an exponential smoothing forecasting model, using $w = 0.7$, for new orders reported by manufacturers. Monthly data (in billions of dollars) to April 1995 are

> 195, 193, 190, 185, 180, 190, 185, 186, 184, 185, 198, 199, 200, 201,
> 199, 187, 186, 191, 195, 200, 200, 190, 186, 196, 198, 200, 200

12–19.   The following data are average monthly prices, in U.S. dollars, for a barrel of Urals crude oil from May 1994 through April 1995: 16.4, 17.1, 16.9, 17.3, 17.5, 17.2, 17.3, 17.1,

---

[4] From *The Wall Street Journal,* June 19, 1995, p. C14.

16.9, 17.0, 17.1, 17.2. Construct an exponential smoothing model for these data, and use it to forecast the price of a barrel of Urals crude oil for May 1995.

12–20. Use *The Wall Street Journal* or another source to gather information on the daily price of gold. Collect a series of prices, and construct an exponential smoothing model. Choose the weighting factor, w, that seems to fit the data best. Forecast the next day's price of gold, and compare the forecast with the actual price once it is known.

12–21. Prove that equation 12–11 is equivalent to equation 12–12.

12–22. Prove the equivalence of equations 12–12 and 12–13.

12–6 Index Numbers

It was dubbed the "Crash of '87." Measured as a percentage, the decline was worse than the one that occurred during the same month in 1929 and ushered in the Great Depression. Within a few hours on Monday, October 19, 1987, the Dow Jones Industrial Average plunged 508.32 points, a drop of 22.6%—the greatest percentage drop ever recorded in one day.

What is the Dow Jones Industrial Average, and why is it useful? The Dow Jones average is an example of an **index.** It is one of several quantitative measures of price movements of stocks through time. Another commonly used index is the New York Stock Exchange (NYSE) Index, and there are others. The Dow Jones captures in one number (the 508.32 points just mentioned, for example) the movements of 30 industrial stocks considered by some to be representative of the entire market. Other indexes are based on a wider proportion of the market than just 30 big firms.

Indexes are useful in many other areas of business and economics. Another commonly quoted index is the **consumer price index** (CPI), which measures price fluctuations. The CPI is a single number representing the general level of prices that affect consumers.

> An **index number** is a number that measures the relative change in a set of measurements over time.

When the measurements are of a *single variable,* for example, the price of a certain commodity, the index is called a *simple index number*. A simple index number is the ratio of two values of a variable, expressed as a percentage. First, a *base period* is chosen. The value of the index at any time period is equal to the ratio of the current value of the variable divided by the base period value, times 100.

The following data are annual cost figures for residential natural gas for the years 1982 to 1995 (in dollars per thousand cubic feet).

EXAMPLE 12–4

121, 121, 133, 146, 162, 164, 172, 187, 197, 224, 255, 247, 238, 222

If we want to describe the relative change in price of residential natural gas, we construct a simple index of these prices. Suppose that we are interested in comparing prices of residential natural gas of any time period to the price in 1982 (the first year in our series). In this case, 1982 is our base year, and the index for that year is defined as 100. The index for any year is defined by equation 12–15.

$$\text{Index number for period } i = 100 \frac{\text{Value in period } i}{\text{Value in base period}} \qquad (12\text{–}15)$$

Thus, the index number for 1984 (using the third data point in the series) is computed as

$$\text{Index number for 1984} = 100 \frac{\text{Price in 1984}}{\text{Price in 1982}}$$

$$= 100 \frac{133}{121} = 109.9$$

This means that the price of residential natural gas increased by 9.9% from 1982 to 1984. Incidentally, the index for 1983 is also 100 since the price did not change from 1982 to 1983. Let us now compute the index for 1985.

$$\text{Index number for 1985} = 100 \frac{146}{121} = 120.66$$

Thus, compared with the price in 1982, the price in 1985 was 20.66% higher. It is very important to understand that changes in the index from year to year *may not be interpreted as percentages* except when one of the two years is the base year. The fact that the index for 1985 is 120.66 and for 1984 is 109.9 does not imply that the price in 1985 was $20.66 - 9.9 = 10.76\%$ higher than in 1984. Comparisons in terms of percentages may only be made with the base year. We can only say that the price in 1984 was 9.9% higher than 1982, and the price in 1985 was 20.66% higher than in 1982. Table 12–7 shows the year, the price, and the price index for residential natural gas from 1982 to 1995, inclusive.

From the table, we see, for example, that the price in 1992 was over 210% of what it was in 1982 and that by 1995 the price declined to only 183.5% of what it was in 1982. Figure 12–17 shows both the raw price and the index with base year 1982. (The units of the two plots are different, and no comparison between them is suggested.)

As time goes on, the relevance of any base period in the past decreases in terms of comparison with values in the present. Therefore, it is sometimes useful to change the base period and move it closer to the present. Many indexed economic variables, for example, use the base year 1967. As we move into more recent years, the base year for

TABLE 12–7   Price Index for Residential Natural Gas, Base Year 1982

Year	Price	Index
1982	121	100
1983	121	100
1984	133	109.9
1985	146	120.7
1986	162	133.9
1987	164	135.5
1988	172	142.1
1989	187	154.5
1990	197	162.8
1991	224	185.1
1992	255	210.7
1993	247	204.1
1994	238	196.7
1995	222	183.5

these variables is changed to 1980 or later. There is a simple way of changing the base period of an index. All we need to do is change the index number of the new base period so that it will equal 100 and change all other numbers using the *same operation*. Thus, we divide all numbers in the index by the index value of the proposed new base period and multiply them by 100. This is shown in equation 12–16.

Changing the base period of an index:

$$\text{New index value} = \frac{\text{Old index value}}{\text{Index value of new base}} \cdot 100 \qquad (12\text{–}16)$$

Suppose that we want to change the base period of the residential natural gas index (Table 12–7) from 1982 to 1989. We want the index for 1989 to equal 100, so we will divide all index values in the table by the current value for 1989, which is 154.5, and multiply these values by 100. For 1990, the new index value is $(162.8/154.5)100 = 105.4$. The new index, using 1989 as base, is shown in Table 12–8.

Figure 12–18 shows the two indexes of the price of residential natural gas using the two different base years. Note that the changes in the index numbers that use 1982 as the base year are more pronounced. This is so because 1989, when used as the base year, is close to the middle of the series, and percentage changes with respect to that year are smaller.

An important use of index numbers is as *deflators*. This allows us to compare prices or quantities through time in a meaningful way. Using information on the relative price of natural gas at different years, as measured by the price index for this commodity, we can better assess the effect of changes in consumption by consumers. The most important use of index numbers as deflators, however, is in the case of *composite index numbers*. In particular, the consumer price index is an overall mea-

FIGURE 12-17 Price and Index (Base Year 1982) of Residential Natural Gas

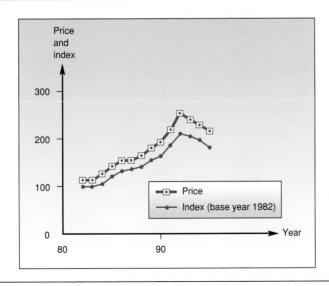

TABLE 12-8   Residential Natural Gas Price Index

Year	Index Using 1982 Base	Index Using 1989 Base
1982	100	64.7
1983	100	64.7
1984	109.9	71.1
1985	120.7	78.1
1986	133.9	86.7
1987	135.5	87.7
1988	142.1	92.0
1989	154.5	100
1990	162.8	105.4
1991	185.1	119.8
1992	210.7	136.4
1993	204.1	132.1
1994	196.7	127.3
1995	183.5	118.7

Note: All entries in the right-hand column are obtained from the entries in the middle column by multiplication by 100/154.5.

FIGURE 12-18   Comparison of the Two Price Indexes for Residential Natural Gas

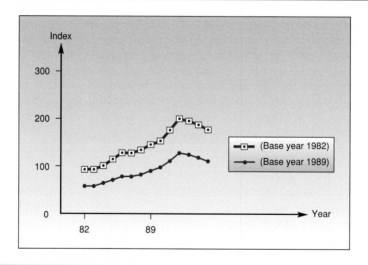

sure of relative changes in the prices of many goods and thus reflects changes in the value of the dollar. We all know that a dollar today is not worth the same as a dollar 20 years ago. Using the consumer price index, or another composite index, allows us to compare prices through time in "constant" dollars.

The Consumer Price Index

The CPI is probably the best-known price index. It is published by the U.S. Bureau of Labor Statistics and is based on the prices of several hundred items. The base year is 1967. For obtaining the base year quantities used as weights, the Bureau of Labor

TABLE 12-9   The Consumer Price Index [1967 = 100]

Year	CPI	Year	CPI
1950	72.1	1973	133.1
1951	77.8	1974	147.7
1952	79.5	1975	161.2
1953	80.1	1976	170.5
1954	80.5	1977	181.5
1955	80.2	1978	195.4
1956	81.4	1979	217.4
1957	84.3	1980	246.8
1958	86.6	1981	272.4
1959	87.3	1982	289.1
1960	88.7	1983	298.4
1961	89.6	1984	311.1
1962	90.6	1985	322.2
1963	91.7	1986	328.4
1964	92.9	1987	340.4
1965	94.5	1988	354.3
1966	97.2	1989	371.3
1967	100.0	1990	391.4
1968	104.2	1991	408.0
1969	109.8	1992	420.3
1970	116.3	1993	432.7
1971	121.3	1994	444.0
1972	125.3		

Statistics interviewed thousands of families to determine their consumption patterns. Since the CPI reflects the general price level in the country, it is used, among other purposes, in converting nominal amounts of money to what are called *real* amounts of money: amounts that can be compared through time without requiring us to consider changes in the value of money due to inflation. This use of the CPI is what we referred to earlier as using an index as a *deflator*. By simply dividing X dollars in year i by the CPI value for year i and multiplying by 100, we convert our X *nominal* (year i) dollars to *constant* (base year) dollars. This allows us to compare amounts of money across time periods. Let us look at an example.

EXAMPLE 12-5

Table 12–9 gives the CPI values for the years 1950 to 1994. The base year is 1967. This is commonly denoted by [1967 = 100]. The data in Table 12–9 are from the U.S. Bureau of Labor Statistics publication *Monthly Labor Review* (March 1995).

We see, for example, that the general level of prices in the United States in 1994 was almost four and a half times what it was in 1967 (the base year). Thus, a dollar in 1994 could buy, on average, only what $1/4.44 = \$0.225$, or 22.5 cents, could buy in 1967. By dividing any amount of money in a given year by the CPI value for that year and multiplying by 100, we convert the amount to constant (1967) dollars. The term *constant* means dollars of a constant point in time—the base year.

Let us illustrate the use of the CPI as a price deflator. Suppose that during the years 1980 to 1985, an analyst was making the following annual salaries.

1980	$29,500	1983	$35,000
1981	$31,000	1984	$36,700
1982	$33,600	1985	$38,000

Looking at the raw numbers, we may get the impression that this analyst has done rather well. His or her salary has increased from $29,500 to $38,000 in just five years. Actually the analyst's salary has not even kept up with inflation! That is, in *real* terms, or in terms of *actual buying power*, this analyst's 1985 salary is smaller than what it was in 1980. To see why this is true, we use the CPI.

SOLUTION

If we divide the 1980 salary of $29,500 by the CPI value for that year and multiply by 100, we will get the equivalent salary in 1967 dollars: $(29,500/246.8)(100) = \$11,953$. We now take the 1985 salary of $38,000 and divide it by the CPI value for 1985 and multiply by 100. This gives us $(38,000/322.2)(100) = \$11,794$—*decrease* of $159 (1967)!

If you perform a similar calculation for the salaries of all the other years, you will find that none of them have kept up with inflation. If we transform all salaries to 1967 dollars (or for that matter, to dollars of any single year), the figures can be compared with each other. Often, time series data such as these are converted to constant dollars of a single time period and then analyzed using methods of time series analysis such as the ones presented earlier in this chapter. To convert to dollars of another year (not the base year), you need to divide the salary by the CPI for the current year and multiply by the CPI value for the constant year in which you are interested. For example, let us convert the 1985 salary to 1980 (rather than 1967) dollars. We do this as follows: $(38,000/322.2)(246.8) = \$29,107$. Thus, in terms of 1980 dollars, the analyst was making only $29,107 in 1985, whereas in 1980 he or she was making $29,500 (1980)! Figure 12–19 shows the CPI for the years 1950 to 1994.

PROBLEMS

12–23. In 1987, the base year was changed to [1982 = 100]. Change the base for all the figures in Table 12–9.

12–24. *Business Week*, along with several other business publications, has its own indexes of economic activity. The *BW* production index is based on several national production activities and uses base year 1992 [1992 = 100]. For the week of July 3, 1995, the magazine reported the following figures for the *BW* production index: June 1995: 250; February 1994: 124; October 1994: 117.[5] Compare national production in the time periods reported by *Business Week* as reflected by the *BW* index.

12–25. What is a simple price index?

12–26. What are the uses of index numbers?

---

[5] "The Business Week Index," *Business Week*, July 3, 1995, p. 95.

FIGURE 12-19   The Consumer Price Index, 1950–1994 (Base Year = 1967)

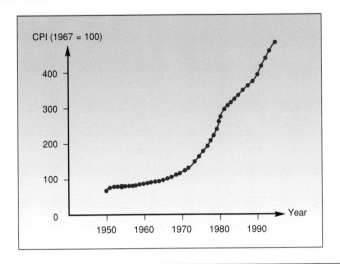

12–27.   The following is Nigeria's Industrial Output Index for the years 1981 to 1994.

Year	Index of Output
1981	175
1982	190
1983	132
1984	96
1985	100
1986	78
1987	131
1988	135
1989	154
1990	163
1991	178
1992	170
1993	145
1994	133

Source: "Nigeria's Industry," *The Financial Times*, May 26, 1995, p. VII.

   a.   What is the base year used here?

   b.   Change the base year to 1990.

   c.   What happened to Nigeria's industrial output from 1993 to 1994?

   d.   Describe the trends in industrial output throughout the years 1981 to 1994.

12–28.   The following data are Nigerian private consumption per head for the years 1981 through 1993. Construct a simple index of private consumption per head using 1990 as base year.

**Private Consumption per Head
Naira (1984 prices)**

1981	795
1982	765
1983	690
1984	660
1985	705
1986	708
1987	665
1988	720
1989	705
1990	730
1991	790
1992	820
1993	830

Source: "Commodities," *The Wall Street Journal,* June 19, 1995, p. C14. With data from the *Federal Office of Statistics.*

12–29.   The following data are June 1994 to June 1995 commodity prices as described by the Dow Jones Commodity Index:[6] 142, 137, 143, 142, 145, 151, 147, 144, 149, 154, 148, 153, 154. Form a new index, using January 1995 as the base month.

12-7   Using the Computer

MINITAB is very useful in analyzing time series and producing forecasts. Version 10 for WINDOWS makes it especially easy to perform time series analysis in MINITAB. The commands TREND, DECOMP, and SES will perform a trend analysis, a decomposition (either additive or multiplicative), and an exponential-smoothing analysis, respectively. There are extensive menus and dialogue boxes that allow the user to carry out these analyses. Try these with any of the data sets in this chapter.

12-8   Summary and Review of Terms

In this chapter, we discussed forecasting methods. We saw how simple **Cycle ×
Trend × Seasonality × Irregular components models** are created and used. We then talked about **exponential smoothing models.** We also discussed **index numbers.**

ADDITIONAL PROBLEMS

12–30.   The following data are monthly existing-home sales, in millions of dwelling units, for January 1994 through June 1995.[7] Construct a forecasting model for these data and use it in forecasting sales for July 1995.

4.4, 4.2, 3.8, 4.1, 4.1, 4.0, 4.0, 3.9, 3.9, 3.8, 3.7, 3.7, 3.8, 3.9, 3.8, 3.7, 3.5, 3.4

---

[6] "Commodities," *The Wall Street Journal,* June 19, 1995, p. C14.

[7] "Existing-Home Sales," *The Wall Street Journal,* June 27, 1995, p. 1.

12–31. Discuss and compare all the forecasting methods presented in this chapter. What are the relative strengths and weaknesses of each method? Under what conditions would you use any of the methods?

12–32. Discuss the main principle of the exponential smoothing method of forecasting. What effect does the smoothing constant, w, have on the forecasts?

12–33. The following data show the average number of days a single family housing unit has been on the market until sold, recorded for the month in which the unit was sold, in a Western city.

1993 Month	Average Number of Days	1994 Month	Average Number of Days
January	56	January	69
February	53	February	66
March	57	March	63
April	47	April	60
May	48	May	62
June	46	June	64
July	50	July	66
August	58	August	69
September	55	September	70
October	57	October	71
November	63	November	74
December	72	December	90

a. Is this time series seasonal? Explain.

b. Decompose the series into components, and forecast the average number of days a single family unit was on the market for January 1995.

c. Try another forecasting model. Test both models' performance using available data points. Which model is better?

12–34. The following data are the annual gross earnings, in millions of dollars, for a firm in its first seven years of operation: 1.2, 1.6, 2.2, 2.9, 3.1, 4.3, 6.0. What is the best forecasting model for these data? Now forecast the company's gross earnings for its eighth year of operation. What are the limitations of your forecasting scheme? Discuss.

12–35. The following data are weekly values of the Bel-20, the Belgian Stock Exchange Index, in U.S. dollar terms, for January through May 1995.[8]

$$100, 98, 97, 99, 100, 104, 105, 107, 105, 104,$$

$$108, 110, 113, 117, 118, 120, 118, 118, 117, 119.$$

a. Plot the data.

b. Why was the first data point set to equal 100?

c. Change base so that the value for the 10th week is 100.

d. Forecast the next week's index value using a method of your choice.

12–36. Use your library to research the Standard & Poor's 500 Index. Write a short report explaining this index, its construction, and its use.

---

[8] "Bel-20 Index Sails," *The Financial Times,* May 26, 1995, p. 32.

Case 12   FORECASTING THE DEMAND FOR SHIPS

Shipbuilding is a risky business. The industry is labor- and capital-intensive, and the required investments are very high. Thus, the profitability of a shipyard depends strongly on management's ability to obtain relatively accurate forecasts of the demand for ships up to several years in the future. This need was accentuated during the 1970s when many shipyards worldwide suffered serious losses due to the sudden drop in demand for supertankers following the oil glut that resulted from the 1973 embargo.

A medium-sized shipyard in Taipei, Taiwan, embarked on a research study aimed at forecasting future demand for ships of a given size (8 to 21 thousand tons displacement). The following data are annual demand figures for ships received by the shipyard from 1931 to 1995.

2, 4, 3, 1, 2, 4, 0, 1, 2, 0, 2, 3, 5, 6, 10, 12, 12, 15, 18, 15, 16, 20, 15, 14, 17, 18, 18, 19, 14, 10, 12, 11, 15, 12, 10, 10, 9, 12, 8, 9, 7, 5, 7, 10, 11, 12, 13, 16, 19, 17, 4, 7, 8, 10, 14, 10, 12, 13, 15, 13, 14, 15, 14, 16, 17

Try several different forecasting methods for these data. Test your models' validity, and produce forecasts. Using your best model, can you forecast the demand for ships with some accuracy? Explain and discuss.

13

QUALITY CONTROL AND IMPROVEMENT

1 3 – 1 I N T R O D U C T I O N

N ot long after the Norman Conquest of England, the Royal Mint was established in London. The Mint has been in constant operation from its founding to this very day, producing gold and silver coins for the Crown (and in later periods, coins from cheaper metals). Some time during the reign of Henry II (1154–1189), a mysterious ceremony called the "Trial of the Pyx" was initiated.

The word *pyx* is Old English for "box," and the ceremony was an actual trial by jury of the contents of a box. The ancient trial had

Continued

religious overtones, and the jurors were all members of the Worshipful Company of Goldsmiths. The box was thrice locked and held under guard in a special room, the Chapel of the Pyx, in Westminster Abbey. It was ceremoniously opened at the trial, which was held once every three or four years.

What did the Pyx box contain, and what was the trial? Every day, a single coin of gold (or silver, depending on what was being minted) was randomly selected by the minters and sent to Westminster Abbey to be put in the Pyx. In three or four years, the Pyx contained a large number of coins. For a given type of coin, say a gold sovereign, the box also contained a royal standard, which was the exact desired weight of a sovereign. At the trial, the contents of the box were carefully inspected, counted, and later some coins were assayed. The total weight of all gold sovereigns was recorded. Then the weight of the royal standard was multiplied by the number of sovereigns in the box and compared with the actual total weight of the sovereigns. A given tolerance was allowed in the total weight, and the trial was declared a success if the total weight was within the tolerance levels established above and below the computed standard.

The trial was designed so that the King or Queen could maintain control of the use of the gold and silver ingots furnished to the Mint for coinage. If, for example, coins were too heavy, then the monarch's gold was being wasted. A shrewd merchant could then melt down such coins and sell them back to the Mint at a profit. This actually happened often enough that such coins were given the name "come again guineas" as they would return to the Mint in melted-down form, much to the minters' embarrassment. On the other hand, if coins contained too little gold, then the currency was being debased and would lose its value. In addition, somebody at the Mint could then be illegally profiting from the leftover gold.

When the trial was successful, a large banquet would be held in celebration. We may surmise that when the trial was not successful . . . the Tower of London was not too far away. The Trial of the Pyx is practiced (with modifications) to this very day. Interestingly, the famous scientist and mathematician Isaac Newton was at one time (1699 to 1727) Master of the Mint. In fact, one of the trials during Newton's tenure was not successful, but he survived.[1]

The Trial of the Pyx is a classic example, and probably the earliest on record, of a two-tailed statistical test for the population mean. The Crown wants to test the null hypothesis that, on the average, the weight of the coins is as specified. The Crown wants to test this hypothesis against the two-tailed alternative that the average coin is either too heavy or too light—both having negative consequences for the Crown. The test statistic used is the sum of the weights of n coins, and the critical points are obtained as: n times the standard weight, plus or minus the allowed tolerance.[2] The Trial of the Pyx is also a wonderful example of *quality control*. We have a production process, the minting of coins, and we want to ensure that high quality is maintained throughout the operation. We sample from the production process, and we take corrective action whenever we believe that the process is *out of control*—producing items that, on average, lie outside our specified target limits. ■

---

[1] Adapted from S. Stigler, "Eight Centuries of Sampling Inspection: The Trial of the Pyx," *Journal of the American Statistical Association,* September 1977, pp. 493–500.

[2] According to Professor Stigler, the tolerance was computed in a manner incongruent with statistical theory, but he feels we may forgive this error as the trial seems to have served its purpose well through the centuries.

13-2   W. Edwards Deming Instructs

We now jump 800 years, to the middle of our present century and to the birth of modern quality-control theory. In 1950 Japan was trying to revive from the devastation of World War II. Japanese industry was all but destroyed, and its leaders knew that industry must be rebuilt well if their nation was to survive. But how? By an ironic twist of fate, Japanese industrialists decided to hire an American statistician as their consultant. The man they chose was the late W. Edwards Deming, at the time a virtually unknown government statistician. No one in America paid much attention to Deming's theories on how statistics could be used to improve industrial quality. The Japanese wanted to listen. They brought Deming to Japan in 1950, and in July of that year he met with the top management of Japan's leading companies. He then gave the first of many series of lectures to Japanese management. The title of the course was "Elementary Principles of the Statistical Control of Quality," and it was attended by 230 Japanese managers of industrial firms, engineers, and scientists.

The Japanese listened closely to Deming's message. In fact, they listened so well that in a few short decades, Japan became one of the most successful industrial nations on earth. Whereas "Made in Japan" once meant low quality, the phrase has now come to denote the highest quality. In 1960, Emperor Hirohito awarded Dr. Deming the Medal of the Sacred Treasure. The citation with the medal stated that the Japanese people attribute the rebirth of Japanese industry to W. Edwards Deming. In addition, the Deming Award was instituted in Japan to recognize outstanding developments and innovations in the field of quality improvement. On the walls of the main lobby of Toyota's headquarters in Tokyo hang three portraits. One portrait is of the company's founder, another is of the current chairman, and the largest portrait is of Ed Deming.

Ironically, Dr. Deming's ideas did get recognized back in the United States—alas, when he was 80 years old. For years, American manufacturing firms have been feeling the pressure to improve quality, but not much was actually being done while the Japanese were conquering the world markets. In June 1980, Dr. Deming appeared in a network television documentary entitled "If Japan Can, Why Can't We?" Starting the next morning, Dr. Deming's mail quadrupled, and the phone was constantly ringing. Offers came from Ford, General Motors, Xerox, and many others.

While well into his 90s, Dr. Ed Deming was one of the most sought-after consultants to American industry. His appointment book was filled years in advance, and companies were willing to pay very high fees for an hour of his time. He traveled around the country lecturing on quality and how to achieve it. The first American company to adopt the Deming philosophy and to institute a program of quality improvement at all levels of production was the Nashua Corporation. The company kindly agreed to provide us with actual data of a production process and its quality improvement. This is presented as Case 13 at the end of this chapter. How did Deming do it? How did he apply statistical quality-control schemes so powerful that they could catapult a nation to the forefront of the industrialized world and are now helping American firms improve as well? This chapter should give you an idea.

13-3   Statistics and Quality

In all fairness, Dr. Deming did not invent the idea of using statistics to control and improve quality; that honor goes to a colleague of his. What Deming did was to expand the theory and demonstrate how it could be used very successfully in industry. Since then, Deming's theories have gone beyond statistics and quality control, and they now encompass the entire firm. His tenets to management are the well-known "14 Points" he advocated, which deal with the desired corporate approach to costs, prices, profits, labor, and other factors. Deming even liked to expound about antitrust laws and capitalism, and to have fun with his audience. At a lecture attended by the author around Deming's 90th birthday, Dr. Deming opened by writing on a transparency: "Deming's Second Theorem: 'Nobody gives a hoot about profits.'" He then stopped and addressed the audience, "Ask me what is Deming's First Theorem." He looked expectantly at his listeners and answered, "I haven't thought of it yet!" The philosophical approach to quality and the whole firm, and how it relates to profits and costs is described in the ever-growing literature on this subject. It is sometimes referred to as *total quality management* (TQM). Dr. Deming's vision of what a firm can do using the total quality management approach to continual improvement is summarized in his famous 14 points. The Deming approach centers on creating an environment where the 14 points can be implemented toward the achievement of quality.

Deming's 14 Points

1. Create constancy of purpose for continual improvement of products and service to society, allocating resources to provide for long-range needs rather than only short-term profitability, with a plan to become competitive, to stay in business, and to provide jobs.

2. Adopt the new philosophy. We are in a new economic age, created in Japan. We can no longer live with commonly accepted levels of delays, mistakes, defective materials, and defective workmanship. Transformation of Western management style is necessary to halt the continued decline of industry.

3. Eliminate the need for mass inspection as the way of life to achieve quality by building quality into the product in the first place. Require statistical evidence of built-in quality in both manufacturing and purchasing functions.

4. End the practice of awarding business solely on the basis of price tag. Instead, require meaningful measures of quality along with the price. Reduce the number of suppliers for the same item by eliminating those that do not qualify with statistical and other evidence of quality. The aim is to minimize *total* cost, not merely initial cost, by minimizing variation. This may be achievable by moving toward a single supplier for any one item, on a long-term relationship of loyalty and trust. Purchasing managers have a new job and must learn it.

5. Improve constantly and forever every process for planning, production, and service. Search continually for problems in order to improve every activity in the company, to improve quality and productivity, and thus to constantly decrease costs. Institute innovation and constant improvement of product, service, and process. It is the management's job to work continually on the system (design, incoming materials, maintenance, improvement of machines, supervision, training, and retraining).

6. Institute modern methods of training on the job for all, including management, to make better use of every employee. New skills are required to keep up with changes in materials, methods, product design, machinery, techniques, and service.

7. Adopt and institute leadership aimed at helping people to do a better job. The responsibility of managers and supervisors must be changed from

sheer numbers to quality. Improvement of quality will automatically improve productivity. Management must ensure that immediate action is taken on reports of inherited defects, maintenance requirements, poor tools, fuzzy operational definitions, and all conditions detrimental to quality.

8. Encourage effective two-way communication and other means to drive out fear throughout the organization so that everybody may work effectively and more productively for the company.

9. Break down barriers between departments and staff areas. People in different areas, such as research, design, sales, administration, and production, must work in teams to tackle problems that may be encountered with products or service.

10. Eliminate the use of slogans, posters, and exhortations for the workforce, demanding zero defects and new levels of productivity, without providing methods. Such exhortations only create adversarial relationships; the bulk of the causes of low quality and low productivity belong to the system, and thus lie beyond the power of the workforce.

11. Eliminate work standards that prescribe quotas for the workforce and numerical goals for people in management. Substitute aids and helpful leadership in order to achieve continual improvement of quality and productivity.

12. Remove the barriers that rob hourly workers, and people in management, of their right to pride of workmanship. This implies, *inter alia,* abolition of the annual merit rating (appraisal of performance) and of management by objective. Again, the responsibility of managers, supervisors, foremen must be changed from sheer numbers to quality.

13. Institute a vigorous program of education, and encourage self-improvement for everyone. What an organization needs is not just good people; it needs people that are improving with education. Advances in competitive position will have their roots in knowledge.

14. Clearly define top management's permanent commitment to ever-improving quality and productivity, and their obligation to implement all of these principles. Indeed, it is not enough that top management commit themselves for life to quality and productivity. They must know what it is that they are commited to—that is, what they must do. Create a structure in top management that will push every day on the preceding 13 points, and take action in order to accomplish the transformation. Support is not enough: action is required.

Process Capability

Process capability is the best in-control performance that an existing process can achieve without major expenditures. The capability of any process is the natural behavior of the particular process after disturbances are eliminated. In an effort to improve quality and productivity in the firm, it is important to first try to establish the capability of the process. An investigation is undertaken to actually achieve a state of statistical control in a process based on current data. This gives a live image of the process. For example, in trying to improve the quality of car production, we first try to find how the process operates in the best way, then make improvements. Control charts are a useful tool in this analysis.

Control Charts

The first modern ideas on how statistics could be used in quality control came in the mid-1920s from a colleague of Deming's, Walter Shewhart of Bell Laboratories. Shewhart invented the **control chart** for industrial processes. A control chart is a graphical display of measurements (usually aggregated in the form of means or other statistics) of an industrial process through time. By carefully scrutinizing the chart, a quality-control engineer can identify any potential problems with the production process. The idea is that when a process is in control, the variable being measured— the mean of every four observations, for example—should remain stable through time. The mean should stay somewhere around the middle line (the grand mean for the process) and not wander off "too much." By now you understand what "too much" means in statistics: more than several standard deviations of the process. The required number of standard deviations is chosen so that there will be a small probability of exceeding them when the process is in control. Addition and subtraction of the required number of standard deviations (generally 3) gives us the **upper control limit** (UCL) and the **lower control limit** (LCL) of the control chart. The UCL and LCL are similar to the "tolerance" limits in the story of the Pyx. When the bounds are breached, the process is deemed **out of control** and must be corrected. A control chart is illustrated in Figure 13–1. We assume throughout that the variable being charted is at least approximately normally distributed.

In addition to looking for the process exceeding the bounds, quality-control workers also look for patterns and trends in the charted variable. For example, if the mean of four observations at a time keeps increasing or decreasing, or it stays too long above or below the center line (even if the UCL and LCL are not breached), the process may be out of control.

> A **control chart** is a time plot of a statistic, such as a sample mean, range, standard deviation, or proportion, with a center line and *upper and lower control limits.* The limits give the desired range of values for the statistic. When the statistic is outside the bounds, or when its time plot reveals certain patterns, the process may be out of control.

FIGURE 13–1   A Control Chart

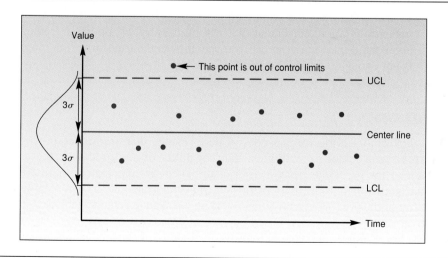

Central to the idea of a control chart—and, in general, to the use of statistics in quality control—is the concept of **variance**. If we were to summarize the entire field of statistical quality control (also called *statistical process control*, or SPC) in one word, that word would have to be *variance*. Shewhart, Deming, and others wanted to bring the statistical concept of variance down to the shop floor. If foremen and production line workers could understand the existence of variance in the production process, then this awareness by itself could be used to help minimize the variance. Furthermore, the variance in the production process could be partitioned into two kinds: the natural, random variation of the process, and variation due to assignable causes. Examples of assignable causes are fatigue of workers and breakdown of components. Variation due to assignable causes is especially undesirable because it is due to something being wrong with the production process, and may result in low quality of the produced items. Looking at the chart helps us detect an assignable cause, by asking what has happened at a particular point in time on the chart where the process looks unusual.

A process is considered in **statistical control** when it has no assignable causes, only natural variation.

Figure 13–2 shows how a process could be in control or out of control. Recall the assumption of a normal distribution—this is what is meant by the normal curves shown on the graphs. These curves stand for the hypothetical populations from which our data are assumed to have been randomly drawn.

Actually, any kind of variance is undesirable in a production process. Even the natural variance of a process due to purely random causes rather than to assignable causes can be detrimental. The control chart, however, will detect only assignable causes. As the following story shows, one could do very well by removing all variance.

An American car manufacturer was having problems with transmissions made at one of its domestic plants, and warranty costs were enormous. The identical type of transmission made in Japan was not causing any problems at all. Engineers carefully examined 12 transmissions made at the company's American plant. They found that variations existed among the 12 transmissions, but there were no assignable causes and a control chart revealed nothing unusual. All transmissions were well within specifications. Then they looked at 12 transmissions made at the Japanese plant. The engineer who made the measurements reported that the measuring equipment was broken: in testing one transmission after the other, the needle did not move at all. A closer investigation revealed that the measuring equipment was perfectly fine: the transmissions simply had *no variation*. They did not just satisfy specifications; for all practical purposes, the 12 transmissions were identical![3]

Such perfection may be difficult to achieve, but the use of control charts can go a long way toward improving quality. Control charts are the main topic in this chapter, and we will discuss them in later sections. We devote the remainder of this section to brief descriptions of other quality-control tools.

---

[3] From L. Dobyns, "Ed Deming Wants Big Changes and He Wants Them Fast," *Smithsonian,* August, 1990, p. 80.

FIGURE 13-2   A Production Process In, and Out of, Statistical Control

a.
Process in
control.

b.
Process
mean
is not stable.
Process out
of control.

c.
Process
variance
is not stable.
Process out
of control.

d.
Here both the
process mean
and the
process
variance are
unstable.
Process out
of control.

Pareto Diagrams

In instituting a quality-control and improvement program, one important question to answer is: What are the exact causes of lowered quality in the production process? A ceramics manufacturer may be plagued by several problems: scratches, chips, cracks, surface roughness, uneven surfaces, and so on. It would be very desirable to find out which of these problems are serious and which are not. A good and simple tool for such analysis is the **Pareto diagram**. Although the diagram is named after an Italian economist, its use in quality control is due to J. M. Juran.

A **Pareto diagram** is a bar chart of the various problems in production and their percentages, which must add to 100%.

FIGURE 13-3   Pareto Diagram for Ceramics Example

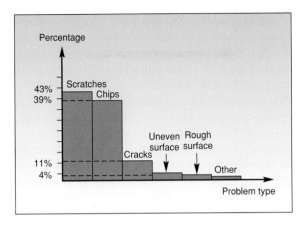

A Pareto diagram for the ceramics example above is given in Figure 13–3. As can be seen from the figure, scratches and chips are serious problems, accounting for most of the nonconforming items produced. Cracks occur less frequently, and the other problems are relatively rare. A Pareto diagram thus helps management to identify the most significant problems and concentrate on their solution rather than wasting time and resources on unimportant causes.

Acceptance Sampling

Finished products are grouped in lots before being shipped to customers. The lots are numbered, and random samples from these lots are inspected for quality. Such checks are made before lots are shipped out and when lots arrive at their destination. The random samples are measured to find out which and how many items do not meet specifications.

A lot is rejected whenever the sample mean exceeds or falls below some pre-specified limit. For attribute data, the lot is rejected when the number of defective or nonconforming items in the sample exceeds a prespecified limit. Acceptance sampling does not, by itself, improve quality; it simply removes bad lots. To improve quality, it is necessary to control the production process itself, removing any assignable causes and striving to reduce the variation in the process.

Analysis of Variance and Experimental Design

As statistics in general is an important collection of tools to improve quality, so in particular is experimental design. Industrial experiments are performed to find production methods that can bring about high quality. Experiments are designed to identify the factors that affect the variable of interest, for example, the diameter of a rod. We may find that method B produces rods with diameters that conform to specifications more often than those produced by method A or C. Analysis of variance (as well as regression and other techniques) is used in making such a determination. These tools are more "active" in the quest for improved quality than the control charts, which are merely diagnostic and look at a process already in place. However, both types of tools should be used in a comprehensive quality improvement plan.

Taguchi Methods

The Japanese engineer Genichi Taguchi developed new notions about quality engineering. Taguchi's ideas transcend the customary wisdom of tolerance limits, where we implicitly assume that any value for a parameter within the specified range is as good as any other value. Taguchi aims at the ideal *optimal* value for a parameter in question. For example, if we look at a complete manufactured product, such as a car, the car's quality may not be good even if all of its components are within desired levels when considered alone. The idea is that the quality of a large system deteriorates as we add up the small variations in quality for all of its separate components.

To try to solve this problem, Taguchi developed the idea of a total loss to society due to the lowered quality of any given item. That loss to society is to be minimized. That is, we want to *minimize* the variations in product quality, not simply keep them within limits. This is done by introducing a *loss function* associated with the parameter in question (e.g., rod diameter) and by trying to create production systems that minimize this loss both for components and for finished products.

In the following sections we describe Shewhart's control charts in detail, since they are the main tool currently used for maintaining and improving quality. Information on the other methods we mentioned in this section can be found in the ever-increasing literature on quality improvement. (For example, see the appropriate references in Appendix A at the end of this book.) Our discussion of control charts will roughly follow the order of their frequency of use in industry today. The charts we will discuss are the $\bar{x}$ chart, the R chart, the s chart, the p chart, the c chart, and the x chart.

PROBLEMS

13–1. Discuss what is meant by *quality control* and *quality improvement*.

13–2. What is the main statistical idea behind current methods of quality control?

13–3. Describe the two forms of variation in production systems and how they affect quality.

13–4. What is a quality-control chart, and how is it used?

13–5. What are the components of a quality-control chart?

13–6. What are the limitations of quality-control charts?

13–7. What is acceptance sampling?

13–8. Describe how one would use experimental design in an effort to improve industrial quality.

13–9. What is the main contribution of Genichi Taguchi to the theory of quality improvement?

13–10. Out of 1,000 automobile engines tested for quality, 62 had cracked blocks, 17 had leaky radiators, 106 had oil leaks, 29 had faulty cylinders, and 10 had ignition problems. Draw a Pareto diagram for these data, and identify the key problems in this particular production process.

13–11. In an effort to improve quality, AT&T has been trying to control pollution problems.[4] Problem causes and their relative seriousness, as a percentage of the total, are as follows: chlorofluorocarbons, 61%; air toxins, 30%; manufacturing wastes, 8%; other, 1%. Draw a Pareto diagram of these causes.

13–12. Discuss the quality implications of the data displayed in the following figure.

---

[4] "AT&T's Clean Goals," *Business Week* Quality Issue, 1991, p. 49.

A Long, Hard Battle to Squash the Bugs

A study of 80 software projects of NASA's Goddard Space Center shows that reliability of the software used for ground-based tracking of space missions is slowly improving. And the gap between best and worst is narrowing, making software performance more predictable as well as more reliable.

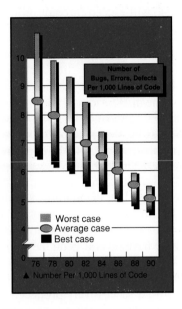

Source: "Turning Software from a Black Art into a Science," *Business Week,* Quality Issue 1991, pp. 80–81, with data from Univ. of Maryland Software Engineering Lab. Reprinted by permission.

13–4   The x̄ Chart

We want to compute the center line and the upper and lower control limits for a process believed to be in control. Then future observations can be checked against these bounds to make sure the process remains in control. To do this, we first conduct an *initial run.* We determine trial control limits to test for control of past data and then we remove out-of-control observations and recompute the control limits. We then apply these improved control limits to future data. This is the philosophy behind all control charts discussed in this chapter. Although we present the x̄ chart first, in an actual quality-control program we would first want to test that the process variation is under control. This is done using the R (range) or the s (standard deviation) chart. Unless the process variability is under statistical control, there is no stable distribution of values with a fixed mean.

An **x̄ chart** can help us to detect shifts in the process mean. One reason for a control chart for the process mean (rather than for a single observation) has to do with the central limit theorem. We want to be able to use the known properties of the normal curve in designing the control limits. By the central limit theorem, the distribution of the sample mean tends toward a normal distribution as the sample size increases. Thus, when we aggregate data from a process, the aggregated statistic, sample mean, becomes closer to a normal random variable than the original, unaggregated quantity. Typically, a set number of observations will be aggregated and averaged. For example, a set of four measurements of rod diameter will be made every hour of production. The four rods will be chosen randomly from all rods made during that hour. If the distribution of rod diameters is roughly mound-shaped, then the sample means of the groups of four diameters will have a distribution closer to normal.

The mean of the random variable $\overline{X}$ is the population mean μ, and the standard deviation of $\overline{X}$ is $\sigma/\sqrt{4}$, where σ is the population standard deviation. We know all this from the theory in Chapter 5. We also know from the theory that the probability that a normal random variable will exceed three of its standard deviations on either side of the mean is 0.0026 (check this using the normal table). Thus, the interval

$$\mu \pm 3\sigma/\sqrt{n} \qquad\qquad (13\text{--}1)$$

should contain about 99.74% of the sample means. This is, in fact, the logic of the control chart for the process mean. The idea is the same as that of a hypothesis test (conducted in a form similar to a confidence interval). We try to select the bounds so that they will be as close as possible to equation 13–1. We then chart the bounds, an estimate of μ in the center (the center line), and the upper and lower bounds (UCL and LCL) as close as possible to the bounds of the interval specified by equation (13–1). Out of 1,000 $\overline{x}$s, fewer than 3 are expected to be out of bounds. Therefore, with a limited number of $\overline{x}$s on the control chart, observing even one of them out of bounds is cause to reject the null hypothesis that the process is in control, in favor of the alternative that it is out of control. (One could also compute a p-value here, although it is more complicated since we have several $\overline{x}$s on the chart, and in general this is not done.)

We note that the assumption of random sampling is important here as well. If somehow the process is such that successively produced items have values that are correlated—thus violating the independence assumption of random sampling—the interpretation of the chart may be misleading. Various new techniques have been devised to solve this problem.

To construct the control chart for the sample mean, we need estimates of the parameters in equation 13–1. The grand mean of the process, that is, the mean of all the sample means (the mean of all the observations of the process), is our estimate of μ. This is our center line. To estimate σ, we use s, the standard deviation of all the process observations. However, this estimate is only good for large samples, $n > 10$. For smaller sample sizes we use an alternative procedure. When sample sizes are small, we use the *range* of the values in each sample used to compute an $\overline{x}$. Then we average these ranges, giving us a mean range, $\overline{R}$. When the mean range, $\overline{R}$, is multiplied by a constant, which we call A_2, the result is a good estimate for 3σ. Values of A_2 for all sample sizes up to 25 are found in Appendix C, Table 13, at the end of the book. The table also contains the values for all other constants required for the quality-control charts discussed in this chapter.

The box on page 611 shows how we compute the center line and the upper and lower control limits when constructing a control chart for the process mean.

In addition to a sample mean being outside the bounds given by the UCL and LCL, other occurrences on the chart may lead us to conclude that there is evidence that the process is out of control. Several such sets of rules have been developed, and the idea behind them is that they represent occurrences that have a very low probability when the process is indeed in control. The set of rules we use is given in Table 13–1.[5]

---

[5] This particular set of rules was provided courtesy of Dr. Lloyd S. Nelson of the Nashua Corporation, one of the pioneers in the area of quality control. See L. S. Nelson "The Shewhart Control Chart—Tests for Special Causes," *Journal of Quality Technology* 16 (1984), pp. 237–39. The MINITAB package tests for special causes using Nelson's criteria.

Elements of a control chart for the process mean:

Center line: $\bar{\bar{x}} = \dfrac{\sum_{i=1}^{k} \bar{x}_i}{k}$

UCL: $\bar{\bar{x}} + A_2 \bar{R}$ LCL: $\bar{\bar{x}} - A_2 \bar{R}$

where: k = Number of samples, each of size n
$\bar{x}_i$ = Sample mean for the ith sample $\bar{R} = \dfrac{\sum_{i=1}^{k} R_i}{k}$
R_i = *Range of the* ith sample

If the sample size in each group is over 10, then

$$UCL = \bar{\bar{x}} + 3\,\frac{\bar{s}/c_4}{\sqrt{n}} \qquad\qquad LCL = \bar{\bar{x}} - 3\,\frac{\bar{s}/c_4}{\sqrt{n}}$$

where $\bar{s}$ is the average of the standard deviations of all groups, and c_4 is a constant found in Appendix C, Table 13

TABLE 13-1   Tests for Assignable Causes

Test 1: One point beyond 3σ ($3s$)

Test 2: Nine points in a row on one side of the center line

Test 3: Six points in a row steadily increasing or decreasing

Test 4: Fourteen points in a row alternating up and down

Test 5: Two out of three points in a row beyond 2σ ($2s$)

Test 6: Four out of five points in a row beyond 1σ ($1s$)

Test 7: Fifteen points in a row within 1σ ($1s$) of the center line

Test 8: Eight points in a row on both sides of the center line, all beyond 1σ ($1s$)

EXAMPLE 13-1

A pharmaceutical manufacturer needs to control the concentration of the active ingredient in a formula used to restore hair to bald people. The concentration should be around 10%, and a control chart is desired to check the sample means of 30 observations, aggregated in groups of three. The data and the MINITAB program, as well as the control chart it produced, are given in Figure 13–4. As can be seen from the control chart, there is no evidence here that the process is out of control.

The grand mean is $\bar{\bar{x}} = 10.253$. The ranges of the groups of three observations each are 0.15, 0.53, 0.69, 0.45, 0.55, 0.71, 0.90, 0.68, 0.11, and 0.24. Thus, $\bar{R} = 0.501$. From Table 13 we find for $n = 3$, $A_2 = 1.023$. Thus, UCL = $10.253 + 1.023(0.501) = 10.766$, and LCL = $10.253 - 1.023(0.501) = 9.74$. The MINITAB program estimates using the sample standard deviation instead of $\bar{R}$ (the use of $\bar{R}$ is a special option), hence the slight differences. Note that the $\bar{x}$ chart cannot be interpreted unless the R or s chart has been examined and is in control. These two charts are presented in the next section.

PROBLEMS

13–13. What is the logic behind the control chart for the sample mean, and how is the chart constructed?

13–14. Legal Seafoods in Boston prides itself on having instituted an advanced quality control system that includes the control of both the food quality and the service quality. The following are successive service times at one of the chain's restaurants on a Saturday night in May (time is stated in minutes from customer entry to appearance of waitperson):

5, 6, 5, 5.5, 7, 4, 12, 4.5, 2, 5, 5.5, 6, 6, 13, 2, 5, 4, 4.5, 6.5, 4, 1,

2, 3, 5.5, 4, 4, 8, 12, 3, 4.5, 6.5, 6, 7, 10, 6, 6.5, 5, 3, 6.5, 7

FIGURE 13-4   MINITAB-Produced Output for Example 13-1

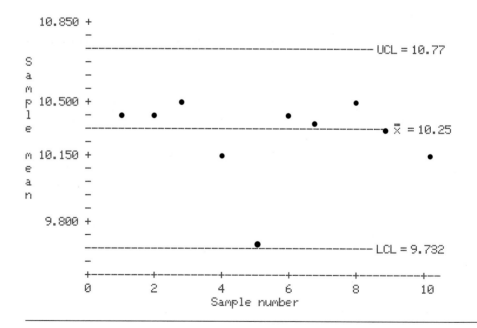

Aggregate the data into groups of four, and construct a control chart for the process mean. Is the waiting time at the restaurant under control?

13–15. What assumptions are necessary for constructing an $\bar{x}$ chart?

13–16. The manufacturer of jet engines needs to control the maximum power delivered by engines. The following are readings related to power for successive engines produced:

121, 122, 121, 125, 123, 121, 129, 123, 122, 122, 120, 121, 119, 118, 121,

125, 139, 150, 121, 122, 120, 123, 127, 123, 128, 129, 122, 120, 128, 120

Aggregate the data in groups of three, and create a control chart for the process mean. Use the chart to test the assumption that the production process is under control.

13–17. The following data are tensile strengths, in pounds, for a sample of string for industrial use made at a plant. Construct a control chart for the mean, using groups of five observations each. Test for statistical control of the process mean.

5, 6, 4, 6, 5, 7, 7, 7, 6, 5, 3, 5, 5, 5, 6, 5, 5, 6, 7, 7, 7, 7, 6, 7, 5,
5, 5, 6, 7, 7, 7, 7, 7, 5, 5, 6, 4, 6, 6, 6, 7, 6, 6, 6, 6, 6, 7, 5, 7, 6

13–5 The *R* Chart and the *s* Chart

In addition to the process mean, we want to control the process variance as well. When the variation in the production process is high, it means that produced items will have a wider range of values, and this jeopardizes the product's quality. Recall also that in general we want as small a variance as possible. As noted earlier, it is advisable to check the process variance first and then check its mean. Two charts are commonly used to achieve this aim. The more common of the two is a control chart for the process range, called **the *R* chart**. The other is a control chart for the process standard deviation, **the *s* chart**. A third chart is a chart for the actual variance, called the s^2 chart, but we will not discuss it since it is the least commonly used of the three.

The R Chart

Like the $\bar{x}$ chart, the *R* chart also contains a center line and upper and lower control limits. The lower limit is bounded by zero, and sometimes turns out to be zero. Similar to what was done in the previous section for the process mean, we want to specify the upper and lower control limits in the form

$$\bar{R} \pm 3\sigma_{\bar{R}} \qquad (13-2)$$

Although the distribution of the sample range is not normal, it is still common in practice to use symmetric bounds such as the ones given above. These bounds still assure us that the probability of breaching them (we are mostly interested in the eventuality of exceeding the upper control limit) is small.

Quality-control experts have calculated that appropriate bounds for small samples (as used in practice) in accordance with the bounds of equation 13–2 are given using constants D_3 and D_4 multiplied by $\bar{R}$. The first gives us the LCL; the second gives us the UCL. The constants D_3 and D_4 are given in Appendix C, Table 13. The center line, UCL, and LCL for the control chart for the process range are given in the following box.

The elements of an *R* chart:

Center Line: $\bar{R}$

LCL: $D_3\bar{R}$

UCL: $D_4\bar{R}$

where $\bar{R}$ = Sum of group ranges / Number of groups

Returning to Example 13–1, we find that $\bar{R} = 0.501$, and from Table 13, $D_3 = 0$ and $D_4 = 2.574$. Thus, the center line is 0.501, the lower control limit is 0, and the

FIGURE 13-5   MINITAB-Produced R Chart for Example 13-1

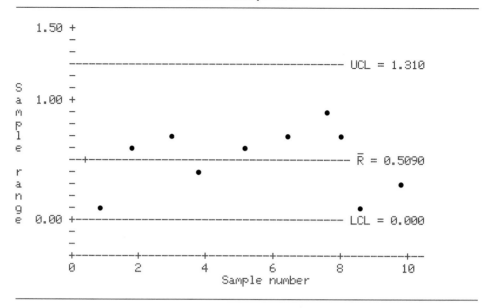

upper control limit is $(0.501)(2.574) = 1.29$. Figure 13–5 gives the MINITAB-produced control chart for the process range for this example.

There is a small difference in the UCL because of the way MINITAB computes it. The test for control in the case of the process range is just to look for at least one observation outside the bounds. Based on the R chart for Example 13–1, we conclude that the process range seems to be in control.

The s Chart

The R chart is in common use because it is easier (by hand) to compute ranges rather than to compute standard deviations. Today (as compared with the 1920s, when these charts were invented), computers are usually used to create control charts, and an s chart should be at least as good as an R chart. We note, however, that the standard deviation suffers from the same nonnormality (skewness) as does the range. Again, symmetric bounds as suggested by equation 13–2, with s replacing R, are still used. The control chart for the process standard deviation is similar to that for the range. Here we use constants B_3 and B_4, also found in Appendix C, Table 13. The bounds and the center line are given in the following box.

Elements of the s chart:

Center line: $\bar{s}$

LCL: $B_3\bar{s}$

UCL: $B_4\bar{s}$

where $\bar{s}$ is the sum of group standard deviations divided by the number of groups.

The s chart for Example 13–1 is given in Figure 13–6.

FIGURE 13-6   An *s* Chart for the Process of Example 13-1

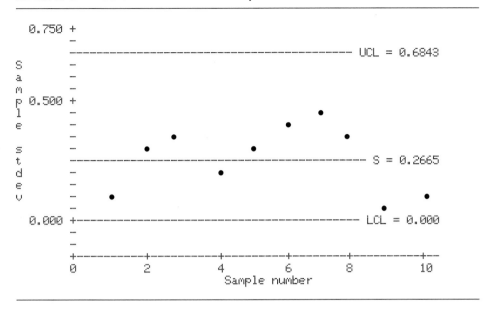

Again, we note that the process standard deviation seems to be in control. Since *s* charts are done by computer, we will not carry out the computations of the standard deviations of all the groups.

PROBLEMS

13–18.   Why do we need a control chart for the process range?

13–19.   Compare and contrast the control charts for the process range and the process standard deviation.

13–20.   What are the limitations of symmetric LCL and UCL? Under what conditions are symmetric bounds impossible in practice?

13–21.   Create an *R* chart for the process in problem 13–14.

13–22.   Create an *R* chart for the process in problem 13–16.

13–23.   Create an *R* chart for the process in problem 13–17.

13–24.   Create an *s* chart for the process in problem 13–14.

13–25.   Create an *s* chart for the data in problem 13–16.

13–26.   Is the standard deviation of the process in problem 13–17 under control?

13-6   The *p* Chart

The most common example of a quality-control problem used throughout the book has been that of controlling the proportion of defective items in a production process. This, indeed, is the topic of this section. Here we approach the problem using a control chart.

The number of defective items in a random sample chosen from a population has a binomial distribution: the number of successes, x, out of a number of trials, n, with a constant probability of success, p, in each trial. The parameter p is the proportion of defective items in the population. If the sample size, n, is fixed in repeated samplings, then the sample proportion, $\hat{P}$, derives its distribution from a binomial distribution. Recall that the binomial distribution is symmetric when $p = 0.5$, and it is skewed for other values of p. By the central limit theorem, as n increases, the distribution of $\hat{P}$ approaches a normal distribution. Thus, a normal approximation to the binomial should work well with large sample sizes; a relatively small sample size would suffice if $p = 0.5$ because of the symmetry of the binomial in this case.

The central limit theorem is the rationale for the control chart for p, called the **p chart**. Using the normal approximation, we want bounds of the form

$$\hat{p} \pm 3\sigma_{\hat{p}} \tag{13-3}$$

The idea is, again, that the probability of a sample proportion falling outside the bounds is small when the process is under control. When the process is not under control, the proportion of defective or nonconforming items will tend to exceed the upper bound of the control chart. The lower bound is sometimes zero, which happens when $\hat{p}$ is sufficiently small. Being at the lower bound of zero defectives is, of course, a very good occurrence.

Recall that the sample proportion, $\hat{p}$, is given by the number of defectives, x, divided by the sample size, n. We estimate the population proportion, p, by the total number of defectives in all the samples of size n we have obtained, divided by the entire sample size (all the items in all our samples). This is denoted by $\bar{p}$, and serves as the center line of the chart. Also recall that the standard deviation of this statistic is given by

$$\sqrt{\frac{\bar{p}(1 - \bar{p})}{n}}$$

Thus, the control chart for the proportion of defective items is given in the following box. The process is believed to be out of control when at least one sample proportion falls outside the bounds.

The elements of a control chart for the process proportion:

Center line: $\qquad\qquad\qquad\qquad \bar{p}$

LCL: $\qquad\qquad\qquad\qquad \bar{p} - 3\sqrt{\dfrac{\bar{p}(1 - \bar{p})}{n}}$

UCL: $\qquad\qquad\qquad\qquad \bar{p} + 3\sqrt{\dfrac{\bar{p}(1 - \bar{p})}{n}}$

where n is the number of items in each sample; and $\bar{p}$ is the proportion of defectives in the combined, overall sample.

EXAMPLE 13-2   A tire manufacturer randomly samples 40 tires at the end of each shift to test for tires that are defective. The number of defectives in 12 shifts are as follows: 4, 2, 0, 5, 2, 3, 14, 2, 3, 4, 12, 3. Construct a control chart for this process. Is the production process under control?

SOLUTION   We use MINITAB. We enter the number of defective items for all shifts into column c1 and then state the constant sample size (40 for each shift). The results are shown in Figure 13–7. Our estimate of p, the center line, is the sum of all the defective tires divided by

FIGURE 13–7   MINITAB-Produced *p* Chart for Example 13–2

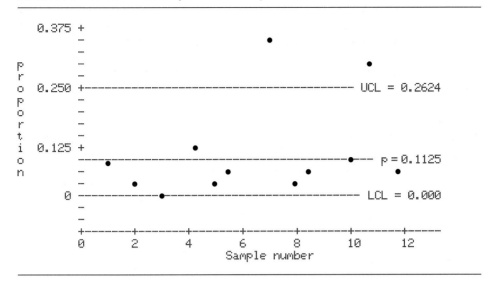

40 × 12. It is $\bar{p} = 0.1125$. Our standard error of $\bar{p}$ is $\sqrt{\bar{p}(1 - \bar{p})/n} = 0.05$; thus, LCL = $0.1125 - 3(0.05) = -0.0375$, which means that the LCL should be zero. Similarly, UCL = $0.1125 + 3(0.05) = 0.2625$.

As we can see from the figure, two sample proportions are outside the UCL. These correspond to the samples with 14 and 12 defective tires respectively. There is ample evidence that the production process is out of control.

PROBLEMS

13–27.   The manufacturer of steel rods looks at random samples of 20 items from each production shift and notes the number of nonconforming rods in these samples. The results of 10 shifts are 8, 7, 8, 9, 6, 7, 8, 6, 6, 8. Is there evidence that the process is out of control? Explain.

13–28.   A battery manufacturer looks at samples of 30 batteries at the end of every day of production and notes the number of defective batteries. Results (numbers of defectives in samples of 10) are 1, 1, 0, 0, 1, 2, 0, 1, 0, 0, 2, 5, 0, 1. Is the production process under control?

13–29.   BASF Inc. makes 3.5-inch two-sided double-density disks for use in microcomputers. A quality-control engineer at the plant tests batches of 50 disks at a time and plots the proportions of defective disks on a control chart. The first 10 batches used to create the chart had the following numbers of defective disks: 8, 7, 6, 7, 8, 4, 3, 5, 5, 8. Construct the chart and interpret the results.

13–30.   If the proportion of defective items in a production process is very small, and few items are tested in each batch, what problems do you foresee? Explain.

13–7   The c Chart

It often happens in production activities that we want to control the *number of defects or imperfections per item.* When fabric is woven, for example, it is of interest to keep a record of the number of blemishes per yard and take corrective action when this number is out of control.

Recall from Chapter 3 that the random variable representing the count of the number of errors occurring in a fixed period of time or space is often modeled using the *Poisson distribution*. This is the model we use here. For the Poisson distribution, we know that the mean and the variance are both equal to the same parameter. Here we call that parameter c, and our chart for the number of defects per item (or yard, etc.) is **the c chart**. In this chart we plot a random variable, the number of defects per item. We estimate c by $\bar{c}$, which is the average number of defects per item, the total number averaged over all the items we have. The standard deviation of the random variable is thus the square root of c. Now, the Poisson distribution can be approximated by the normal distribution for large sample sizes, and this again suggests the form

$$\bar{c} \pm 3\sqrt{\bar{c}} \tag{13–4}$$

Equation 13–4 leads to the control bounds and center line given in the box that follows.

Elements of the c chart:

Center line: $\bar{c}$

LCL: $\bar{c} - 3\sqrt{\bar{c}}$

UCL: $\bar{c} + 3\sqrt{\bar{c}}$

where $\bar{c}$ is the average number of defects or imperfections per item (or area, volume, etc.).

EXAMPLE 13-3

The following data are the numbers of nonconformities in bolts for use in cars made by the Ford Motor Company:[6] 9, 15, 11, 8, 17, 11, 5, 11, 13, 7, 10, 12, 4, 3, 7, 2, 3, 3, 6, 2, 7, 9, 1, 5, 8. Is there evidence that the process is out of control?

SOLUTION

We need to find the mean number of nonconformities per item. This is the sum of the numbers divided by 25, or 7.56. The standard deviation of the statistic is the square root of this number, or 2.75, and the control limits are obtained as shown in the box. Figure 13–8 gives the MINITAB solution.

From the figure we see that one observation is outside the upper control limit, indicating that the production process may be out of control. We also note a general downward trend, which should be investigated (maybe the process is improving).

PROBLEMS

13–31. The following are the numbers of imperfections per yard of yarn: 5, 3, 4, 8, 2, 3, 1, 2, 5, 9, 2, 2, 2, 3, 4, 2, 1. Is there evidence that the process is out of control?

---

[6] From T. P. Ryan, *Statistical Methods for Quality Improvement* (New York: Wiley, 1989), p. 198.

FIGURE 13-8   MINITAB-Produced Control Chart for Example 13-3

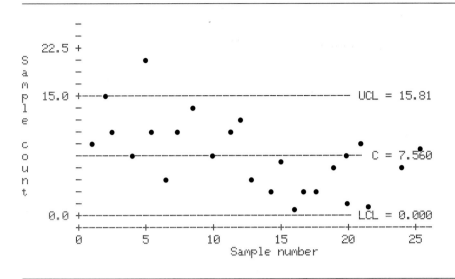

13–32. The following are the numbers of blemishes in the coat of paint of new automobiles: 12, 25, 13, 20, 5, 22, 8, 17, 31, 40, 9, 62, 14, 16, 9, 28. Is there evidence that the painting process is out of control?

13–33. The following are the numbers of imperfections in rolls of wallpaper: 5, 6, 3, 4, 5, 2, 7, 4, 5, 3, 5, 5, 3, 2, 0, 5, 5, 6, 7, 6, 9, 3, 3, 4, 2, 6. Construct a c chart for the process, and determine whether there is evidence that the process is out of control.

13–34. What are the assumptions underlying the use of the c chart?

13-8   The x Chart

Sometimes we are interested in controlling the process mean, but our observations come so slowly from the production process that we cannot aggregate them into groups. In such a case, and in other situations as well, we may consider an **x chart.** An x chart is a chart for the raw values of the variable in question.

As you may guess, the chart is effective if the variable in question has a distribution that is close to normal. We want to have the bounds as mean of the process ± 3 standard deviations of the process. The mean is estimated by $\bar{x}$, and the standard deviation is estimated by s/c_4.

The tests for special causes in Table 13–1 can be used in conjunction with an x chart as well. Case 13 at the end of this chapter will give you an opportunity to study an actual x chart using all of these tests.

13-9   Using the Computer

MINITAB is an excellent package for quality-control work. The commands are simply: XBARCHART (followed by the column number where data are found and then the number of elements in each group); RCHART (again followed by column number and group number); PCHART (column number where numbers of defects are given and then sample size for all groups); CCHART (followed by a column number). There are numerous subcommands, allowing many different options. There are also many other control charts that the package can produce. These are listed in the MINITAB manual. Other packages also produce control charts.

13-10   Summary and Review of Terms

Quality control and improvement is a fast-growing, important area of application of statistics in both production and services. We discussed **Pareto diagrams**, which are relatively simple graphical ways of looking at problems in production. We discussed quality control in general and how it relates to statistical theory and hypothesis testing. We mentioned **process capability** and **Deming's 14-Points**. Then we described **control charts**, graphical methods of determining when there is evidence that a process is out of statistical control. The control chart has a **center line**, an **upper control limit**, and a **lower control limit**. The process is believed to be out of control when one of the limits is breached at least once. The control charts we discussed were the $\bar{x}$ **chart**, for the mean; the **R chart**, for the range; the **s chart**, for the standard deviation; the **p chart**, for the proportion; the **c chart**, for the number of defects per item; and the **x chart**, a chart of individual observations for controlling the process mean.

ADDITIONAL PROBLEMS

13-35.   Discuss and compare the various control charts discussed in this chapter.

13-36.   The number of blemishes in rolls of tape coming out of a production process are as follows: 17, 12, 13, 18, 12, 13, 14, 11, 18, 29, 13, 13, 15, 16. Is there evidence that the production process is out of control?

13-37.   The number of defective items out of random samples of 100 windshield wipers selected at the end of each production shift at a factory are as follows: 4, 4, 5, 4, 4, 6, 6, 3, 3, 3, 3, 2, 2, 4, 5, 3, 4, 6, 4, 12, 2, 2, 0, 1, 1, 1, 2, 3, 1. Is there evidence that the production process is out of control?

13-38.   Weights of pieces of tile (in ounces) are as follows: 2.5, 2.66, 2.8, 2.3, 2.5, 2.33, 2.41, 2.88, 2.54, 2.11, 2.26, 2.3, 2.41, 2.44, 2.17, 2.52, 2.55, 2.38, 2.89, 2.9, 2.11, 2.12, 2.13, 2.16. Create an R chart for these data, using subgroups of size 4. Is the process variation under control?

13-39.   Use the data in problem 13-38 to create an $\bar{x}$ chart to test whether the process mean is under control.

13-40.   Create an s chart for the data in problem 13-38.

Case 13   *QUALITY CONTROL AND IMPROVEMENT AT THE NASHUA CORPORATION** *

In 1979, the Nashua Corporation, with an increasing awareness of the importance of always maintaining and improving quality, invited Dr. W. Edwards Deming for a visit and a consultation. Dr. Deming, then almost 80 years old, was the most sought-after quality guru in America.

Following many suggestions by Deming, Nashua hired Dr. Lloyd S. Nelson the following year as director of statistical methods. The idea was to teach everyone at the company about quality and how it can be maintained and improved using statistics.

Dr. Nelson instituted various courses and workshops lasting 4 to 10 weeks for all the employees. Workers on the shop floor are now familiar with statistical process control (SPC) charts and their use in maintaining and improving quality. Nashua uses individual (x) charts as well as $\bar{x}$, R, and p charts. These are among the most commonly used SPC charts today. Here we will consider the x chart. This chart is used when values come slowly, as in the following example, and it is not practical to take the time to form the subgroups necessary for an $\bar{x}$ or R chart.

Among the many products Nashua makes is thermally responsive paper, which is used in printers and recording instruments. The paper is coated with a

*I am indebted to Dr. Lloyd S. Nelson of the Nashua Corporation for providing me with this interesting and instructive case.

chemical mixture that is sensitive to heat, thus producing marks in a printer or instrument when heat is applied by a print head or stylus. The variable of interest is the amount of material coated on the paper (the "weight coat"). Large rolls, some as long as 35,000 feet, are coated, and samples are taken from the ends of the rolls. A template 12×18 inches is used in cutting through four layers of the paper—first from an area that was coated and second from an uncoated area. A gravimetric comparison of the coated and uncoated samples gives four measurements of the weight coat. The average of these is the individual x value for that roll.

Assume that 12 rolls are coated per shift and that each roll is tested as described above. For two shifts, the 24 values of weight coat, in pounds per 3,000 square feet, were:

3.46, 3.56, 3.58, 3.49, 3.45, 3.51, 3.54, 3.48, 3.54, 3.49, 3.55, 3.60, 3.62, 3.60, 3.53, 3.60, 3.51, 3.54, 3.60, 3.61, 3.49, 3.60, 3.60, 3.49.

Exhibit 1 shows the individual control chart for this process, using all 24 values to calculate the limits. Is the production process in statistical control? Explain. Discuss any possible actions or solutions.

EXHIBIT 1 Standardized x Chart

```
              x - bar equals  3.54333
s (est sigma) = 5.12725e - 2

SAMPLE              STANDARDIZED VALUE           TEST
 NO.    - 3s   - 2s   - 1s    0    1s    2s    3s   NO.
                                                        SAMPLE      WEIGHT
                                                          NO.        COAT
                                                        --------------------
  1                                                        1.        3.46
  2                                                        2.        3.56
  3                                                        3.        3.58
  4                                                        4.        3.49
  5                                                        5.        3.45
  6                                                        6.        3.51
  7                                                        7.        3.54
  8                                                        8.        3.48
  9                                                        9.        3.54
 10                                                       10.        3.49
 11                                                       11.        3.55
 12                                                       12.        3.60
 13                                                       13.        3.62
 14                                                       14.        3.60
 15                                                       15.        3.53
 16                                                   (b) 16.        3.60
 17                                                       17.        3.51
 18                                                       18.        3.54
 19                                                       19.        3.60
 20                                                       20.        3.61
 21                                                       21.        3.49
 22                                                       22.        3.60
 23                                                   (b) 23.        3.60
 24                                                       24.        3.49
```

14 NONPARAMETRIC METHODS AND CHI-SQUARE TESTS

1 4 – 1   I N T R O D U C T I O N

n 1710, Dr. John Arbuthnott, Physician in Ordinary to Her Majesty, published an article in the *Philosophical Transactions of the Royal Society of London.* The article was aimed at proving the existence of God and was titled "An Argument for

Continued

Divine Providence, taken from the constant Regularity observ'd in the Births of both Sexes." Here is an excerpt from his paper.

> Among innumerable Footsteps of Divine Providence to be found in the Works of Nature, there is a very remarkable one to be observed in the exact Ballance that is maintained, between the Numbers of Men and Women, for by this means it is provided, that the Species may never fail, nor perish, since every Male may have its Female, and of a proportionable Age. This Equality of Males and Females is not the Effect of Chance but Divine Providence, working for a good End, which I thus demonstrate.[1]

The distribution of the number of "successes" (girls, or boys) in a fixed number of independent trials with the same probability of success is binomial. Arbuthnott tried in his article to use the binomial distribution to show that the roughly equal number of boys and girls born could not be by chance, hence an argument for Divine Providence. While Dr. Arbuthnott may not have proved the existence of God, the scientific method presented in his paper is believed to constitute the oldest known statistical test, the *sign test*. The sign test is a *nonparametric test*.

So far, the statistical procedures we have discussed have dealt with particular population parameters and made use of specific assumptions about the probability distributions of sample estimators, or assumptions about the nature of the population. In particular, we have usually assumed a *normal distribution*. The statistical procedures described in this chapter do not require stringent assumptions. Many of the tests do not deal with particular *parameters* of the population and, thus, are nonparametric. Some tests do not require assumptions about the distributions of the populations of interest. Therefore, nonparametric methods are often called *distribution-free methods*.

The chi-square methods we will discuss do make an assumption of a probability distribution: a limiting normal distribution of sampling outcomes. This assumption leads to a chi-square test statistic. These methods, however, are more general, and our analysis often does not deal with population parameters. In this sense, the chi-square analysis of enumerative data is a nonparametric one.

Typically, nonparametric methods require less stringent assumptions than do their parametric counterparts; on the other hand, they also use less information from the data. This makes the nonparametric tests somewhat less powerful than the corresponding parametric tests for the same situations, when the assumptions of the parametric tests are met. When the assumptions of the parametric tests are *not* met, the nonparametric tests are the ones we should use. Remember, for example, that in the analysis of variance, we assume that the populations of interest are normally distributed with equal variance. If these assumptions are met, then the F test of ANOVA is a powerful method for determining whether several population means are equal. If these assumptions are seriously violated, we must use an alternative method. Here,

---

[1] From J. Arbuthnott, "An Argument for Divine Providence, Taken from the Constant Regularity Observed in the Births of Both Sexes," *Philosophical Transactions* 27 (1710), pp. 186–90.

nonparametric statistics offers a good solution. There is a nonparametric ANOVA procedure called the Kruskal-Wallis test. This test requires no assumptions about the populations involved and uses less of the information in the data: the procedure uses only the *ranks* of the observations.

Many other hypothesis-testing situations have nonparametric alternatives to be used when the usual assumptions we make are not met. In other situations, nonparametric methods offer *unique* solutions to problems at hand. Because a nonparametric test usually requires fewer assumptions and uses less information in the data, it is often said that *a parametric procedure is an exact solution to an approximate problem*, whereas *a nonparametric procedure is an approximate solution to an exact problem*.

In short, we define a **nonparametric method** as one that satisfies at least one of the following criteria.

1. The method deals with *enumerative data* (data that are frequency counts).
2. The method *does not deal with specific population parameters* such as μ or σ.
3. The method *does not require assumptions about specific population distributions* (in particular, the assumption of normality).

Since nonparametric methods require fewer assumptions than do parametric ones, the methods are useful when the scale of measurement is weaker than required for parametric methods. As we will refer to different measurement scales, you may want to review section 1-7 at this point.

14-2   The Sign Test

In Chapter 8, we discussed statistical methods of comparing the means of two populations. There we used the *t* test, which required the assumption that the populations were normally distributed with equal variance. In many situations, one or both of these assumptions are not satisfied. In some situations, it may not even be possible to make exact measurements except for determining the relative magnitudes of the observations. In such cases, the **sign test** is a good alternative. The sign test is also useful in testing for a trend in a series of ordinal values and in testing for a correlation, as we will see soon.

As a test for comparing two populations, the sign test is stated in terms of the probability that values of one population are greater than values of a second population that are paired with the first in some way. For example, we may be interested in testing whether or not consumer responses to one advertisement are about the same as responses to a second advertisement. We would take a random sample of consumers, show them both ads, and ask them to rank the ads on some scale. For each person in our sample, we would then have two responses: one response for each advertisement. The null hypothesis is that the probability that a consumer's response to one ad will be greater than his or her response to the other ad is equal to 0.50. The alternative hypothesis is that the probability is not 0.50. Note that these null and alternative hypotheses are more general than those of the analogous parametric test—the paired *t* test—which is stated in terms of the means of the two populations. When the two populations under study are symmetric, the test is equivalent to a test of the equality of two means, like the parametric t test. As stated, however, the sign test is more general and requires fewer assumptions.

We define p as the probability that X will be greater than Y, where X is the value from population 1 and Y is the value from population 2. Thus,

$$p = P(X > Y) \qquad (14-1)$$

The test could be a two-tailed test, or a one-tailed test in either direction. Under the null hypothesis, it is as likely that X will exceed Y as it is likely that Y will exceed X: the probability of either occurrence is 0.50. We leave out the possibility of a tie, that is, the possibility that $X = Y$. When we gather our random sample of observations, we denote every pair X, Y where X is greater than Y by a plus sign ($+$), and we denote every pair where Y is greater than X by a minus sign ($-$) (hence the name *sign test*). In terms of signs, the null hypothesis is that the probability of a $+$ sign [that is, $P(X > Y)$] is equal to the probability of a $-$ sign [that is, $P(X < Y)$], and both are equal to 0.50. These are the possible hypothesis tests:

Possible hypotheses for the sign test:
Two-tailed test

$$H_0: p = 0.50$$
$$H_1: p \neq 0.50 \qquad (14-2)$$

Right-tailed test

$$H_0: p \leq 0.50$$
$$H_1: p > 0.50 \qquad (14-3)$$

Left-tailed test

$$H_0: p \geq 0.50$$
$$H_1: p < 0.50 \qquad (14-4)$$

The test assumes that the pairs of (X, Y) values are independent and that the measurement scale within each pair is at least *ordinal*. After discarding any ties, we are left with the number of $+$ signs and the number of $-$ signs. These are used in defining the test statistic.

The test statistic:

$$T = \text{Number of } + \text{ signs} \qquad (14-5)$$

We define n as the number of paired data points, once tied values have been discarded. The test is a *binomial* test with parameter $p = 0.50$: that is, when the null hypothesis $p = 0.50$ is true, the distribution of the number of $+$ signs is the binomial distribution with parameter $p = 0.50$ and n trials. We look at values in the binomial table, Appendix C, Table 1, and determine the appropriate cutoff value(s) that corresponds as closely as possible to the desired level of significance, α. Then we compare T with the cutoff point(s).

The decision rule:

For a two-tailed test (equation 14–2), we find a critical point corresponding as closely as possible to $\alpha/2$ and call it C_1, and we define C_2 as $n - C_1$. We reject the null hypothesis at a level of (approximately) α if T is either less than or equal to C_1 or is greater than or equal to C_2.

For a right-tailed test (equation 14–3), we reject H_0 if T is greater than or equal to $n - C$, where C is that value of the binomial distribution with parameters n and $p = 0.5$ such that the sum of the probabilities of all values less than or equal to C is as close as possible to our chosen level of significance, α.

For a left-tailed test (equation 14–4), we reject H_0 at an approximate level of significance α if T is less than or equal to C, where C is defined as above.

Note that instead of $n - C$, we could use C if we define the test statistic T in equation 14–5 as the number of $-$ signs instead of the number of $+$ signs.

When the sample size is large enough to use the normal approximation to the binomial distribution, we may do so. In such cases, the test becomes the Z test for proportions, discussed in Chapter 7. Our test statistic (in a simplified form) is as follows.

A large-sample test statistic for the sign test:

$$z = \frac{2T - n}{\sqrt{n}} \qquad (14\text{–}6)$$

The decision rule is to compare z with critical point(s) of the standard normal distribution for the appropriate level of α (and according to whether or not the test is one or two-tailed). For example, in a left-tailed test at $\alpha = 0.05$, we reject the null hypothesis if and only if z is less than -1.645.

We now demonstrate the use of the sign test with Example 14–1.

EXAMPLE 14-1

According to a recent survey of 220 chief executive officers of *Fortune 1000* companies, 18.3% of the CEOs in these firms hold MBA degrees. A management consultant wants to test whether there are differences in attitude toward CEOs who hold MBA degrees. In order to control for extraneous factors affecting attitudes toward different CEOs, the consultant designed a study that recorded the attitudes toward the same group of 19 CEOs before and after these people completed an MBA program. The consultant had no prior intention of proving one kind of attitudinal change; she believed it was possible that the attitude toward a CEO could change for the better, change for the worse, or not change at all following the completion of an MBA program. Therefore, the consultant decided to use the following two-tailed test.

H_0: There is no change in attitude toward a CEO following his/her being awarded an MBA degree

versus

H_1: There is a change in attitude toward a CEO following the award of an MBA degree

TABLE 14-1 Data for Example 14-1

CEO:	1	2	3	4	5	6	7	8	9	10	11	12	13	14	15	16	17
Attitude Before:	3	5	2	2	4	2	1	5	4	5	3	2	2	2	1	3	4
Attitude After:	4	5	3	4	4	3	2	4	5	4	4	5	5	3	2	2	5

The consultant defined variable X_i as the attitude toward CEO i before receipt of the MBA degree, as rated by his or her professional associates on a scale of 1 to 5 (5 being highest). Similarly, she defined Y_i as the attitude toward CEO i following receipt of the MBA degree, as rated by his or her professional associates on the same scale.

SOLUTION

In this framework, the null and alternative hypotheses may be stated in terms of the probability that the attitude score *after* (Y) is greater than the attitude *before* (X). The null hypothesis is that the probability that the attitude after receipt of the degree is higher than the attitude before is 0.50 (i.e., the attitude is as likely to improve as it is to become worse, where *worse* means a lower numerical score). The alternative hypothesis is that the probability is not 0.50 (i.e., the attitude is likely to change in one or the other direction). The null and alternative hypotheses can now be stated in the form of equation 14–2:

$$H_0: p = 0.50$$

versus

$$H_1: p \neq 0.50$$

The consultant looked at her data of general attitude scores toward the 17 randomly chosen CEOs both before and after these CEOs received their MBAs. Data are given in Table 14–1. The first thing to note is that there are two ties: for CEOs number 2 and 5. We thus remove these two from our data set and reduce the sample size to $n = 15$. We now (arbitrarily) define a $+$ sign to be any data point where the after-attitude score is greater than the before score. In terms of $+$ and $-$ symbols, the data in Table 14–1 are as follows:

$$+ \ + \ + \ + \ + \ - \ + \ - \ + \ + \ + \ + \ + \ - \ +$$

According to our definition of the test statistic, equation 14–5, we have

$$T = \text{Number of } +\text{s} = 12$$

We now carry out the statistical hypothesis test. From Appendix C, Table 1, the binomial table, we find for $p = 0.5$ and $n = 15$ that the point $C_1 = 3$ corresponds to a "tail" probability of 0.018. That is, $F(3) = 0.018$. This is as close as we can get to an $\alpha/2 = 0.025$ level, which would be needed for a two-tailed test at the level of significance $\alpha = 0.05$. Using our rule for defining the rejection region in a two-tailed test, we find the second critical point: $C_2 = n - C_1 = 15 - 3 = 12$. Our rejection region is thus defined as all points of the statistic that are greater than or equal to 12, or less than or equal to 3. The significance level of this test is $2(0.018) = 0.036$, which is as close as we can get to $\alpha = 0.05$ with a discrete distribution such as the binomial. The distribution and the decision rule for this particular test are illustrated in Figure 14–1.

Since our computed test statistic value is $T = 12$, we reject the null hypothesis. The p-value is 0.036. Since the rejection happened in the right-hand rejection region, the consultant may conclude that there is evidence that attitudes toward CEOs who recently received their MBA degrees have become more positive (as defined by the attitude test).

Let us now look at the normal approximation to the binomial. Since here $np = 15(0.5) = 7.5$ and $n(1 - p) = 7.5$, both of which are over 5, we may use the

FIGURE 14-1   Carrying Out the Test for Example 14-1

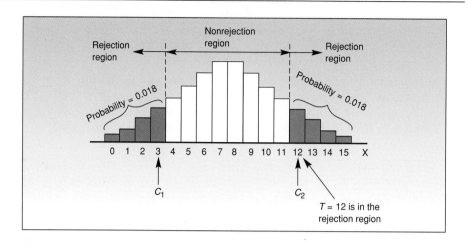

normal approximation to the binomial and carry out the test as a Z test. We use the test statistic of equation 14-6:

$$z = \frac{2T - n}{\sqrt{n}} = \frac{2(12) - 15}{\sqrt{15}} = 2.32$$

This value of the test statistic falls in the right-hand rejection region for a two-tailed Z test at $\alpha = 0.05$. In fact, the p-value is found from the standard normal table to be 0.0204 for a two-tailed test. For a right-tailed test, the p-value would be half that number.

The sign test can be viewed as a test of the hypothesis that the *median* difference between two populations is zero. As such, the test may be adapted for testing whether the median of a single population is equal to any prespecified number. The null and alternative hypotheses here are

$$H_0: \text{Population median} = a$$

$$H_1: \text{Population median} \neq a$$

where a is some number. One-tailed tests of this hypothesis are also possible, and the extension is straightforward.

To conduct the test, we pair our data observations with the null-hypothesized value of the median and perform the sign test. If the null hypothesis is true, then we expect that about half the signs will be +s and half −s because, by the definition of the median, half the population values are above it and half are below it.

Suppose that we wish to test the null hypothesis that median income in a certain region is $24,000 per family per year. The following random sample of family incomes is available (in thousands of dollars): 22, 30, 28, 22, 34, 19, 42, 18, 16, 26, 30, 25, 29, 20, 17, 33, 32, 24, 15, 21. In terms of + signs, − signs, and ties (t), the data are as follows when paired with the hypothesized median of 24: − + + − + − + − − + + + + − − − + + t − −. (The choice of how to define a + versus a − is, again, arbitrary.) Discarding the single tie, we see that the number of + signs is 10, and the sample size is $n = 19$.

If we use the normal approximation to the binomial distribution, we find from equation 14-6 that the value of the test statistic is as follows:

TABLE 14–2   Contingency Table for the McNemar Test

	$Y = 0$	$Y = 1$
$X = 0$	a	b
$X = 1$	c	d

$$z = \frac{2T - n}{\sqrt{n}} = \frac{20 - 19}{4.36} = 0.23$$

This value is, of course, well inside the nonrejection region for any commonly used level of significance, α. The p-value is 0.82. We could have used the binomial distribution. Note that obtaining 10 or more successes with 19 trials where $p = 0.5$ (that is, assuming H_0 is true) is very probable.

We now discuss two variations of the sign test.

The McNemar Test

The McNemar test is designed for determining the existence of differences in pairs of *qualitative* variables (X, Y). Suppose that X may equal either 0 or 1 and that the same is true for Y. We define a $+$ as the event that $X = 0$ and $Y = 1$; similarly, we define a $-$ as the event that $X = 1$ and $Y = 0$. Applying the sign test to these possibilities allows us to test whether or not the probability that $X = 0$ and $Y = 1$ is the same as the probability that $X = 1$ and $Y = 0$.

This test is useful in testing whether changes occur as a result of an experiment. In this context, X may be a consumer's response (yes or no) before he or she is exposed to an advertisement, and Y is the response (yes or no) after exposure to the ad. There are four possibilities: $X = 0$, $Y = 0$; $X = 0$, $Y = 1$; $X = 1$, $Y = 0$; and $X = 1$, $Y = 1$. The cases $(X = 0, Y = 0)$ and $(X = 1, Y = 1)$ are considered ties; as in the simple sign test, ties are discarded from the analysis. The two other possibilities— $X = 0, Y = 1$ and $X = 1, Y = 0$—contain information about possible change in the population from yes to no or vice versa. We denote the first case by a $+$ and the second one by a $-$. The sample size is $n = $ (total number of $+$s and $-$s). We conduct the usual sign test for determining whether or not we can reject the null hypothesis that no change from yes to no or vice versa is evident in the population.

When the sample size (without the ties) is large, we may use the chi-square distribution, and we use a different test statistic. For such cases, we define a *contingency table*—a table of all possibilities. Table 14–2 is the contingency table for this situation. We see that a and d are the numbers of ties ($X = 0$, $Y = 0$ and $X = 1$, $Y = 1$, respectively), b is the number of $+$ signs ($X = 0, Y = 1$), and c is the number of $-$ signs ($X = 1, Y = 0$). The test statistic is simply $b = $ number of $+$ signs. When the sample size $n = b + c$ is large, we use the following test statistic.

Large-sample test statistic for the McNemar test:

$$T = \frac{(b - c)^2}{b + c} \qquad (14\text{--}7)$$

We assume that the distribution of differences between the two populations is symmetric, that the differences are mutually independent, and that the measurement scale is at least interval. By the assumption of symmetry, hypotheses may be stated in terms of means. The alternative hypothesis may also be a directed one: that the mean (or median) of one population is greater than the mean (or median) of the other population.

First, we list the pairs of observations we have on the two variables (the two populations). The data are assumed to be a random sample of paired observations. For each pair, we compute the difference:

$$D = x_1 - x_2 \qquad (14-21)$$

Then we rank the absolute values of the differences, D.

In the next step, we form sums of the ranks of the positive and of the negative differences.

The Wilcoxon T statistic is defined as the smaller of the two sums of ranks—the sum of the negative or the positive ones.

$$T = \min\left(\sum(+), \sum(-) \right) \qquad (14-22)$$

where $\sum(+)$ is the sum of the ranks of the positive differences and $\sum(-)$ is the sum of the ranks of the negative differences

---

The decision rule: Critical points of the distribution of the test statistic T (when the null hypothesis is true) are given in Appendix C, Table 10. We carry out the test on the left tail, that is, we reject the null hypothesis if the computed value of the statistic is less than a critical point from the table, for a given level of significance.

For a one-tailed test, suppose that the alternative hypothesis is that the mean (median) of population 1 is greater than that of population 2; that is,

$$\begin{aligned} H_0&: \mu_1 \leq \mu_2 \\ H_1&: \mu_1 > \mu_2 \end{aligned} \qquad (14-23)$$

Here we use the sum of the ranks of the negative differences. If the alternative hypothesis is reversed (populations 1 and 2 switched), then we use the sum of the ranks of the positive differences as the statistic. In either case, the test is carried out on the left "tail" of the distribution. Appendix C, Table 10 gives critical points for both one-tailed and two-tailed tests.

Large-Sample Version of the Test

As in other situations, when the sample size increases, the distribution of the Wilcoxon statistic, T, approaches the normal probability distribution. In the Wilcoxon test, n is defined as the number of *pairs* of observations from populations 1 and 2. As the number of pairs, n, gets large (as a rule of thumb, $n > 25$ or so), T may be approximated by a normal random variable as follows.

The mean of T:

$$E(T) = \frac{n(n + 1)}{4} \qquad (14\text{–}24)$$

The standard deviation of T:

$$\sigma_T = \sqrt{\frac{n(n + 1)(2n + 1)}{24}} \qquad (14\text{–}25)$$

The standardized z statistic:

$$z = \frac{T - E(T)}{\sigma_T} \qquad (14\text{–}26)$$

We now demonstrate the Wilcoxon signed-rank test with Example 14–9.

EXAMPLE 14-9

The Sunglass Hut of America, Inc., operates kiosks occupying previously unused space in the well-traveled aisles of shopping malls. Sunglass Hut owner, Sanford Ziff, hopes to expand within a few years to every major shopping mall in America. He is using the present $4.5 million business as a test of the marketability of different types of sunglasses. Two types of sunglasses are sold: violet and pink. Ziff wants to know whether there is a difference in the quantities sold of each type. The numbers of sunglasses sold of each kind are paired by store; these data for each of 16 stores during the first month of operation are given in Table 14–4. The table also shows how the differences and their absolute values are computed and ranked, and how the signed ranks are summed, leading to the computed value of T.

TABLE 14-4 Data and Computations for Example 14-9

Store	Number Violet Sold (X_1)	Number Pink Sold (X_2)	Difference ($D = X_1 - X_2$)	Rank of Absolute Difference $|D|$	Rank of Positive D	Rank of Negative D
1	56	40	16	9	9	
2	48	70	−22	12		12
3	100	60	40	15	15	
4	85	70	15	8	8	
5	22	8	14	7	7	
6	44	40	4	2	2	
7	35	45	−10	6		6
8	28	7	21	11	11	
9	52	60	−8	5		5
10	77	70	7	3.5	3.5	
11	89	90	−1	1		1
12	10	10	0			
13	65	85	20	10	10	
14	90	61	29	13	13	
15	70	40	30	14	14	
16	33	26	7	3.5	3.5	
					$\Sigma(+) = 96$	$\Sigma(-) = 24$

SOLUTION

Note that a difference of zero is discarded, and the sample size is reduced by one. The effective sample size for this experiment is now $n = 15$. Note also that ties are handled as before: We assign the average rank to tied differences. Since the smaller sum is the one associated with the negative ranks, we define T as that sum. We therefore have the following value of the Wilcoxon test statistic.

$$T = \sum(-) = 24$$

We now conduct the test of the hypotheses in equation 14–20. We compare the computed value of the statistic, $T = 24$, with critical points of T from Table 10. For a two-tailed test, we find that for $\alpha = 0.05$ ($P = 0.05$ in the table) and $n = 15$, the critical point is 25. Since the test is carried out on the "left tail"—that is, we reject the null hypothesis if the computed value of T is *less than or equal* to the table value—we reject the null hypothesis that the distribution of sales of the violet sunglasses is identical to the distribution of sales of the pink sunglasses. Furthermore, since the sum of the ranks of the negative differences is smaller, and since we defined violet as 1 and pink as 2, we further believe that the violet glasses sell better than the pink ones. If we allow the assumption that if differences occur, they are differences in the mean of the distributions, we may conclude that there is statistical evidence that the *average* sales of violet sunglasses in the *population* of stores will be higher than those of the pink sunglasses.

A Test for the Mean or Median of a Single Population

As stated earlier, the Wilcoxon signed-rank test may be adapted for testing whether or not the mean (or median) of a single population is equal to any given number. There are three possible tests. The first is a left-tailed test where the alternative hypothesis is that the mean (or median—both are equal if we assume a *symmetric* population distribution) is smaller than some value specified in the null hypothesis. The second is a right-tailed test where the alternative hypothesis is that the mean (or median) is greater than some value. The third is a two-tailed test where the alternative hypothesis is that the mean (or median) is not equal to the value specified in the null hypothesis.

The computational procedure is as follows. Using our n data points, $x_1, x_2, \ldots, x_n$, we form pairs: (x_1, m), (x_2, m), $\ldots$, (x_n, m) where m is the value of the mean (or median) specified in the null hypothesis. Then we perform the usual Wilcoxon signed-rank test on these pairs.

In a right-tailed test, if the negative ranks have a larger sum than the positive ranks, we do not reject the null hypothesis. If the negative ranks have a smaller sum than the positive ones, we conduct the test (on the "left tail" of the distribution, as usual) and use the critical points in the table corresponding to the one-tailed test. We use the same procedure in the left-tailed test. For a two-tailed test, we use the two-tailed critical points. In any case, we always reject the null hypothesis if the computed value of T is less than or equal to the appropriate critical point from Appendix C, Table 10.

We will now demonstrate the single-sample Wilcoxon test for a mean using the large-sample normal approximation.

The average hourly number of messages transmitted by a private communications satellite is believed to be 149. The satellite's owners have recently been worried about the possibility that demand for this service may be declining. They therefore want to test the null hypothesis that the average number of messages is 149 (or more) versus the alternative hypothesis that the average hourly number of relayed messages is less than 149. A random sample of 25 operation hours is selected. The data (numbers of messages relayed per hour) are

EXAMPLE 14–10

$n = 25$

$H_0: \mu \geq 149$

$H_1: \mu < 149$

151, 144, 123, 178, 105, 112, 140, 167, 177, 185, 129, 160, 110, 170, 198, 165, 109, 118, 155, 102, 164, 180, 139, 166, 182

Is there evidence of declining use of the satellite?

SOLUTION

We form 25 pairs, each pair consisting of a data point and the null-hypothesized mean of 149. Then we subtract the second number from the first number in each pair (that is, we subtract 149 from every data point). This gives us the differences, D.

2, −5, −26, 29, −44, −37, −9, 18, 28, 36, −20, 11, −39, 21, 49, 16, −40, −31, 6, −47, 15, 31, −10, 17, 33

The next step is to rank the absolute value of the differences from smallest to largest. We have the following ranks, in the order of the data

1, 2, 13, 15, 23, 20, 4, 10, 14, 19, 11, 6, 21, 12, 25, 8, 22, 16.5, 3, 24, 7, 16.5, 5, 9, 18

Note that the differences 31 and −31 are tied and, since they would occupy positions 16 and 17, each is assigned the average of these two ranks, 16.5.

The next step is to compute the sum of the ranks of the positive differences and the sum of the ranks of the negative differences. The ranks associated with the positive differences are 1, 15, 10, 14, 19, 6, 12, 25, 8, 3, 7, 16.5, 9, and 18. (Check this.) The sum of these ranks is $\Sigma(+) = 163.5$. When using the normal approximation, we may use either sum of ranks. Since this is a left-tailed test, we want to reject the null hypothesis that the mean is 149 only if there is evidence that the mean is less than 149, that is, when the sum of the positive ranks is too small. We will therefore carry out the test on the left tail of the normal distribution.

Using equations 14–24 to 14–26, we compute the value of the test statistic, Z, as

$$z = \frac{T - E(T)}{\sigma_T} = \frac{T - n(n+1)/4}{\sqrt{n(n+1)(2n+1)/24}} = \frac{163.5 - (25)(26)/4}{\sqrt{(25)(26)(51)/24}} = 0.027$$

This value of the statistic lies inside the nonrejection region, far from the critical point for any conventional level of significance. (If we had decided to carry out the test at $\alpha = 0.05$, our critical point would have been $C = -1.645$.) We do not reject the null hypothesis and conclude that there is no evidence that use of the satellite is declining.

In closing this section, we note that the Wilcoxon signed-rank test assumes that the distribution of the population is symmetric in the case of the single-sample test, and that the distribution of differences between the two populations in the paired, two-sample case is symmetric. This assumption allows us to make inferences about population means or medians. Another assumption inherent in our analysis is that the random variables in question are continuous. The measurement scale of the data is at least ordinal.

PROBLEMS

14–32. Explain the purpose of the Wilcoxon signed-rank test. When is this test useful? Why?

14–33. For problem 14–30, suppose that the returns for the Chicago and Dallas investments are paired by month: the first observation for each investment is for the first month (say, January), the second is for the next month, and so on. Conduct the analysis again, using the Wilcoxon signed-rank test. Is there a difference in your conclusion? Explain.

14–34. An article discusses differences in management style between North American and European corporations. The following are paired management achievement scores for a European subsidiary and a North American subsidiary of the same firm for a random sample of 10 firms. Test the hypothesis of no difference in management style.

(25, 41), (28, 18), (37, 35), (10, 56), (14, 15), (51, 72), (30, 43),(28, 66), (33, 31), (20, 29).

14–35. The average life of a 100-watt light bulb is stated on the package to be 750 hours. The quality-control director at the plant making the light bulbs needs to check whether the statement is correct. The director is only concerned about a possible reduction in quality and will stop the production process only if statistical evidence exists to conclude that the average life of a light bulb is less than 750 hours. A random sample of 20 bulbs is collected and left on until they burn out. The lifetime of each bulb is recorded. The data are (in hours of continuous use) 738, 752, 710, 701, 689, 779, 650, 541, 902, 700, 488, 555, 870, 609, 745, 712, 881, 599, 659, 793. Should the process be stopped and corrected? Explain why or why not.

14–36. A retailer of tapes and compact discs wants to test whether people can differentiate by the quality of sound only—between the two products. A random sample of consumers who agreed to participate in the test and who have no particular experience with high-quality audio equipment is selected. The same musical performance is played for each person, once on a disc and once on a tape. The listeners do not know which is playing, and the order has been determined randomly. Each person is asked to state which of the two performances he or she prefers. What statistical test is most appropriate here? Why?

14–37. From experience, a manager knows that the commissions earned by her salespeople are very well approximated by a normal distribution. The manager wants to test whether the average commission is $439 per month. A random sample of 100 observations is available. What statistical test is best in this situation? Why?

14–38. Returns on stock of small firms have been shown to be symmetrically distributed, but the distributions are believed to be "long-tailed"—not well approximated by the normal distribution. If it is desired to test whether or not the average return on a stock of a small firm is equal to 12% per year, what test would you recommend? Why?

14–39. Sky Pies® is a recently opened shop at O'Hare International Airport in Chicago that sells frozen, packaged-to-go pizzas. "You can bring sourdough bread from San Francisco, then why not pizza from Chicago?" says founder Bill Gramas. Bill calculated that his business will turn a profit if he can sell at least 120 pizzas per day. Sales data, in number sold per day for the first 15 days, are as follows (assume these data are a random sample of daily sales): 145, 190, 206, 167, 120, 178, 110, 102, 119, 201, 100, 118, 127, 148, 155. Test the null hypothesis that average sales are less than or equal to 120 per day versus the alternative that the average is over 120. What is the main, serious limitation of this analysis?

14–40. Air New Zealand offers two package tours from the United States to New Zealand. One, which includes airfare and five nights' hotel accommodation in Auckland, is advertised at $1,799. The other includes only two nights' accommodation and is advertised at $1,710. For a random sample of 12 days, the airline records the number of bookings for each package. The paired observations are as follows. Do you believe that one package is more popular than the other? Explain.

$1,799 package: 56, 79, 85, 77, 32, 48, 88, 95, 57, 70, 52, 90
$1,710 package: 60, 85, 70, 82, 41, 60, 89, 80, 77, 86, 66, 75

14–41.   A stock market analyst wants to test whether there are higher-than-usual returns on stocks following a two-for-one split. A random sample of 10 stocks that recently split is available. For each stock, the analyst records the percentage return during the month preceding the split and the percentage return for the month following the split. The data are

Before split (%): 0.5, −0.2, 0.9, 1.1, −0.7, 1.5, 2.0, 1.3, 1.6, 2.1
After split (%): 1.1,   0.3, 1.2, 1.9, −0.2, 1.4, 1.8, 1.8, 2.4, 2.2

Is there evidence that a stock split causes excess returns for the month following the split? Redo the problem using the sign test. Compare the results of the sign test with those of the Wilcoxon test.

14–42.   Much has been said about airline deregulation and the effects it has had on the airline industry and its performance. Following a deluge of complaints from passengers, the public relations officer of one of the major airlines asked the company's operations manager to look into the problem. The operations manager obtained average takeoff delay figures for a random sample of the company's routes over time periods of equal length before and after the deregulation. The data, in minutes of average delay per route, are as follows.

Before: 3, 2, 4, 5, 1, 0, 1,   5, 6, 3, 10,   4, 11,   7
After: 6, 8, 2, 9, 8, 2, 6, 12, 5, 9,   8, 12, 11, 10

Is there evidence in these data that the airline's delays have increased after deregulation?

14–43.   The average score on a vocational training test has been known to be 64. Recently, several changes have been instituted in the program; the effect of these changes on performance on the test is unknown. It is therefore desirable to test the null hypothesis that the average score for all people who will complete the program will be 64 versus the alternative that it will not be 64. The following random sample of scores is available.

87, 91, 65, 31, 8, 53, 99, 44, 42, 60, 77, 73, 42, 50, 79, 90, 54, 39, 77, 60,

33, 41, 42, 85, 71, 50, 63, 58, 89, 5, 66, 99, 57, 12, 47, 72, 80, 84

Conduct the test.

14-6   The Kruskal-Wallis Test—A Nonparametric Alternative to One-Way ANOVA

Remember that the ANOVA procedure discussed in Chapter 9 requires the assumption that the populations being compared are all normally distributed with equal variance. When there is reason to believe that the populations under study are not normally distributed, we cannot use the ANOVA procedure. There is, however, a nonparametric test designed to detect differences among populations that does not require any assumptions about the shape of the population distributions. This test is the **Kruskal-Wallis test.** The test is the nonparametric alternative to the (completely randomized design) one-way analysis of variance. In the next section, we will see a nonparametric alternative to the randomized block design analysis of variance, the *Friedman test*. Both of these tests use ranks.

The Kruskal-Wallis test is an analysis of variance that uses the ranks of the observations rather than the data themselves. This assumes, of course, that the observations are on an interval scale. If our data are in the form of ranks, we use them as they are. The Kruskal-Wallis test is identical to the Mann-Whitney test when only two populations are involved. We thus use the Kruskal-Wallis test for comparing k populations, where k is greater than 2. The null hypothesis is that the k populations under study have the same distribution, and the alternative hypothesis is that at least two of the population distributions are different from each other.

The Kruskal-Wallis hypothesis test:

H_0: All k populations have the same distribution
H_1: Not all k populations have the same distribution   (14–27)

Although the hypothesis test is stated in terms of the distributions of the populations of interest, the test is most sensitive to differences in the locations of the populations. Therefore, the procedure is actually used to test the ANOVA hypothesis of equality of k population means. The only assumptions required for the Kruskal-Wallis test are that the k samples are random and are independently drawn from the respective populations. The random variables under study are continuous, and the measurement scale used is at least ordinal.

We rank all data points in the entire set from smallest to largest, without regard to which sample they come from. Then we sum all the ranks from each separate sample. Let n_1 be the sample size from population 1, n_2 the sample size from population 2, and so on up to n_k, which is the sample size from population k. Define n as the total sample size: $n = n_1 + n_2 + \cdots n_k$. We define R_1 as the sum of the ranks from sample 1, R_2 as the sum of the ranks from sample 2, and so on to R_k, the sum of the ranks from sample k. We now define the Kruskal-Wallis test statistic, H.

The Kruskal-Wallis test statistic

$$H = \frac{12}{n(n+1)}\left(\sum_{j=1}^{k} \frac{R_j^2}{n_j}\right) - 3(n+1)   (14–28)$$

For very small samples ($n_j < 5$), there are tables for the exact distribution of H under the null hypothesis; these are found in books devoted to nonparametric statistics. Usually, however, we have samples that are greater than 5 for each group (remember the serious limitations of inference based on very small samples). For larger samples, as long as each n_j is at least 5, the distribution of the test statistic H under the null hypothesis is well approximated by the chi-square distribution with $k - 1$ degrees of freedom.

We reject the null hypothesis on the right-hand tail of the chi-square distribution. That is, we reject the null hypothesis if the computed value of H is too large, exceeding a critical point of $\chi^2_{(k-1)}$ for a given level of significance, α. We demonstrate the Kruskal-Wallis test with an example.

EXAMPLE 14-11   A company is planning to buy a word processing software package to be used by its office staff. Three available packages, made by different companies, are considered: Multimate™, WordPerfect™, and Microsoft Word™. Demonstration packages of the three alternatives are available, and the company selects a random sample of 18 staff members, 6 members assigned to each package. Every person in the sample learns how to use the particular package to which he or she is assigned. The time it takes every member to learn how to use the word processing package is recorded. The question is: Does it take approximately the same amount of time to learn how to use each package proficiently?

None of the office staff has used any of these packages before, and, because of similarity in use, each person is assigned to learn only one package. The staff, however, have varying degrees of experience. In particular, some are very experienced typists, and others are beginners. Therefore, it is believed that the three populations of time it takes to learn how to use a package are not normally distributed. If a conclusion is reached that one package takes longer to learn than the others, then learning time will be a consideration in the purchase decision. Otherwise, the decision will be based only on package capabilities and price. Table 14–5 gives the data, in minutes, for every person in the three samples. It also shows the ranks and the sum of the ranks for each group.

SOLUTION

Using the obtained sums of ranks for the three groups, we compute the Kruskal-Wallis statistic, H. From equation 14–28 we get

$$H = \frac{12}{n(n+1)}\left(\sum \frac{R_j^2}{n_j}\right) - 3(n+1) = \frac{12}{(18)(19)}\left(\frac{90^2}{6} + \frac{56^2}{6} + \frac{25^2}{6}\right) - 3(19)$$
$$= 12.3625$$

We now perform the test of the hypothesis that the populations of the learning times of the three software packages are identical. We compare the computed value of H with critical points of the chi-square distribution with $k - 1 = 3 - 1 = 2$ degrees of freedom. Using Appendix C, Table 4, we find that $H = 12.36$ exceeds the critical point for $\alpha = 0.01$, which is given as 9.21. We therefore reject the null hypothesis and conclude that there is evidence that the time it takes to learn how to use the word processing packages is not the same for all three; at least one package takes longer to learn. Our p-value is smaller than 0.01. The test is demonstrated in Figure 14–6.

We note that even though our example had a balanced design (equal sample sizes in all groups), the Kruskal-Wallis test can also be performed if sample sizes are

TABLE 14-5   The Data (in minutes) and the Ranks for Example 14-11

Multimate		WordPerfect		Microsoft Word	
Time	**Rank**	**Time**	**Rank**	**Time**	**Rank**
45	14	30	8	22	4
38	10	40	11	19	3
56	16	28	7	15	1
60	17	44	13	31	9
47	15	25	5	27	6
65	18	42	12	17	2
	$R_1 = 90$		$R_2 = 56$		$R_3 = 25$

FIGURE 14–6   Carrying Out the Test for Example 14–11

different. We also note that we had no ties in this example. If ties do exist, we assign them the average rank, as we have done in previous tests based on ranks. It is possible to correct for the effect of ties by using a correction formula, which may be found in advanced books.

Further Analysis

As in the case of the usual ANOVA, once we reject the null hypothesis of no difference among populations, the question arises: Where are the differences? That is, which populations are different from which? Here we use a procedure that is similar to the Tukey method of further analysis following ANOVA. For every pair of populations we wish to compare (populations i and j, for example), we compute the average rank of the sample.

$$\bar{R}_i = \frac{R_i}{n_i} \quad \text{and} \quad \bar{R}_j = \frac{R_j}{n_j} \tag{14–29}$$

where R_i and R_j are the sums of the ranks from samples i and j, respectively, computed as part of the original Kruskal-Wallis test. We now define the test statistic D as the absolute difference between $\bar{R}_i$ and $\bar{R}_j$.

> The test statistic for determining whether there is evidence to reject the null hypothesis that populations i and j are identical:
> $$D = |\bar{R}_i - \bar{R}_j| \tag{14–30}$$

We carry out the test by comparing the test statistic D with a quantity that we compute from the critical point of the chi-square distribution at the same level, α, at which we carried out the Kruskal-Wallis test. The quantity is computed as follows.

The critical point for the paired comparisons:

$$C_{\text{KW}} = \sqrt{(\chi^2_{\alpha, k-1})\left[\frac{n(n+1)}{12}\right]\left(\frac{1}{n_i} + \frac{1}{n_j}\right)} \qquad (14\text{–}31)$$

where $\chi^2_{\alpha, k-1}$ is the critical point of the chi-square distribution used in the original, overall test

By comparing the value of the statistic D with C_{KW} for every pair of populations, we can perform all pairwise comparisons *jointly* at the level of significance, α, at which we performed the overall test. We reject the null hypothesis if and only if $D > C_{\text{KW}}$. We demonstrate the procedure by performing all three pairwise comparisons of the populations in Example 14–11.

Since we have a balanced design, $n_i = n_j = 6$ for all three samples, the critical point, C_{KW}, will be the same for all pairwise comparisons. Using equation 14–31, and 9.21 as the value of chi-square for the overall test at $\alpha = 0.01$, we get

$$C_{\text{KW}} = \sqrt{(9.21)\left[\frac{(18)(19)}{12}\right]\left(\frac{1}{6} + \frac{1}{6}\right)} = 9.35$$

Comparing populations 1 and 2: From the bottom of Table 14–5, we find that $R_1 = 90$ and $R_2 = 56$. Since the sample sizes are each 6, we find that the average rank for sample 1 is $90/6 = 15$, and the average rank for sample 2 is $56/6 = 9.33$. Hence, the test statistic for comparing these two populations is the absolute value of the difference between 15 and 9.33, which is 5.67. This value is less than C_{KW}, and we must conclude that there is no evidence, at $\alpha = 0.01$, of a difference between populations 1 and 2.

Comparing populations 1 and 3: Here the absolute value of the difference between the average ranks is $|(90/6) - (25/6)| = 10.83$. Since 10.83 is greater than $C_{\text{KW}} = 9.35$, we conclude that there is evidence, at $\alpha = 0.01$, that population 1 is different from population 3.

Comparing populations 2 and 3: Here we have $D = |(56/6) - (25/6)| = 5.17$, which is less than 9.35. Therefore we conclude that there is no evidence, at $\alpha = 0.01$, that populations 2 and 3 are different.

Our interpretation of the data is that at $\alpha = 0.01$, there are significant differences only between the time it takes to learn Multimate and the time it takes to learn Microsoft Word. Since the values for Multimate are larger, we conclude that the study provides evidence that Multimate takes longer to learn.

PROBLEMS

14–44. Electronic Data Interchange (EDI) is an electronic pipeline linking suppliers with their customers. The system cuts the delivery time of goods by as much as 50% compared with other means of communication. The system allows specially formatted documents, such as purchase orders, to be sent from one company's computer to that of another. Currently, the system is used mainly by three industries: grocery, transportation, and pharmaceutical. EDI's management plans great expansion in the next few years and wants to know whether the three industry groups make about equal use of the system, or whether one group uses it more frequently than another group. A random sample of 10 grocery retailers using the system is gathered, as well as a random sample of 8 transportation users and 7 pharmaceutical users. For each company, the number of times EDI was used in the last month is recorded. The data are as follows. Is the frequency of use of EDI's services about the same for all three industry groups?

Groceries:	12, 14, 30, 5, 9, 18, 52, 19, 65, 25
Transportation:	48, 72, 99, 30, 62, 79, 120, 88
Pharmaceuticals:	40, 48, 67, 112, 31, 141, 69

14–45.   An analyst in the publishing industry wants to find out whether the cost of a newspaper advertisement of a given size is about the same in four large newspaper groups. Random samples of seven newspapers from each group are selected, and the cost of an ad is recorded. The data follow (in dollars). Do you believe that there are differences in the price of an ad across the four groups?

Group A:	57, 65, 50, 45, 70, 62, 48
Group B:	72, 81, 64, 55, 90, 38, 75
Group C:	35, 42, 58, 59, 46, 60, 61
Group D:	73, 85, 92, 68, 82, 94, 66

14–46.   Lawyers representing the Beatles filed a $15 million suit in New York against Nike, Inc., over Nike's Air Max shoe commercial set to the Beatles' 1968 hit song "Revolution." As part of all such lawsuits, the plaintiff must prove a financial damage—in this case, that Nike improperly gained from the unlicensed use of the Beatles' song. In proving their case, lawyers for the Beatles had to show that "Revolution," or any Beatles' song, is not just a tune played with the commercial and that, in fact, the use of the song made the Nike commercial more appealing than it would have been if it had featured another song or melody. A statistician was hired to aid in proving this point. The statistician designed a study in which the Air Max commercial was recast using two other randomly chosen songs that were in the public domain and did not require permission, and that were not sung by the Beatles. Then three groups of 12 people each were randomly selected. Each group was shown one of the commercials, and every person's appeal score for the commercial was recorded. Using the following appeal scores, determine whether there is statistical evidence that not all three songs would be equally effective in the commercial. If you do reject the null hypothesis of equal appeal, go the required extra step to prove that the Beatles' "Revolution" does indeed have greater appeal over other songs, and that Nike should pay the Beatles for using it.

"Revolution":	95, 98, 96, 99, 91, 90, 97, 100, 96, 92, 88, 93
Random alternative A:	65, 67, 66, 69, 60, 58, 70, 64, 64, 68, 61, 62
Random alternative B:	59, 57, 55, 63, 59, 44, 49, 48, 46, 60, 47, 45

14–47.   A researcher at an accounting firm wants to find out whether the current ratio for three industries is about the same. Random samples of eight firms in Industry A, six firms in Industry B, and six firms in Industry C are available. The current ratios are

Industry A:	1.38, 1.55, 1.90, 2.00, 1.22, 2.11, 1.98, 1.61
Industry B:	2.33, 2.50, 2.79, 3.01, 1.99, 2.45
Industry C:	1.06, 1.37, 1.09, 1.65, 1.44, 1.11

Conduct the test at $\alpha = 0.05$, and state your conclusion.

14–48.   Recently, Japan's asset-rich life insurance companies have been venturing overseas and becoming a force in world financial markets. The insurance companies invest in real estate in New York, Canada, and the U.S. Sun Belt. A real estate investment broker hired by one Japanese insurance company wanted to find out whether or not the return on investment in comparable real estate in each of these three areas is approximately the same. Random sample data for investments in the three areas follow (figures represent annualized percentage return).

New York: 15, 18, 17, 19, 18, 10, 12, 16
Canada: 10, 9, 8, 11, 7, 13
Sun Belt: 21, 20, 22, 14, 23, 16, 24

Conduct the test. Are returns approximately equal in the three areas?

14–49. The following data are small random samples of rents (in dollars) in five American cities. The New York data are for Manhattan only.

New York (Manhattan):   900, 1,200, 850, 1,320, 1,400, 1,150, 975
Chicago: 625, 640, 775, 1,000, 690, 550, 840, 750
Detroit: 415, 400, 420, 560, 780, 620, 800, 390
Tampa: 410, 310, 320, 280, 500, 385, 440
Orlando: 340, 425, 275, 210, 575, 360

Conduct the Kruskal-Wallis test to determine whether evidence exists that there are differences in the rents in these cities. If differences exist, where are they?

14–50. What assumptions have you used when solving problems 14–44 through 14–49? What assumptions did you not make about the populations in question? Explain.

14–7   The Friedman Test for a Randomized Block Design

Recall the randomized block design, which was discussed in Chapter 9. In this design, each block of units is assigned all k treatments, and our aim is to determine possible differences among treatments or treatment means (in the context of ANOVA). A *block* may be one person who is given all k treatments (asked to try k different products, to rate k different items, etc.). The Kruskal-Wallis test discussed in the previous section is a nonparametric version of the one-way ANOVA with completely randomized design. Similarly, the **Friedman test,** the subject of this section, is a nonparametric version of the randomized block design ANOVA. Sometimes this design is referred to as a two-way ANOVA with one item per cell because it is possible to view the blocks as one factor and the treatment levels as the other. In the randomized block design, however, we are interested in the treatments as a factor and not in the blocks themselves. Like the methods we discussed in preceding sections, the Friedman test is based on ranks. The test may be viewed as an extension of the Wilcoxon signed-rank test or an extension of the sign test to more than two treatments per block. Recall that in each of these tests, there are two treatments assigned to each element in the sample—the observations are paired. In the Friedman test, the observations are more than paired: each block, or person, is assigned to all $k > 2$ treatments.

   Since the Friedman test is based on the use of ranks, it is especially useful for testing treatment effects when the observations are in the form of ranks. In fact, in such situations, we cannot use the randomized block design ANOVA because the assumption of a normal distribution cannot hold for very discrete data such as ranks. The Friedman test is a unique test for a situation where data are in the form of ranks within each block. Our example will demonstrate the use of the test in this particular situation. When our data are on an interval scale and not in the form of ranks, but we believe that the assumption of normality may not hold, we use the Friedman test instead of the parametric ANOVA and transform our data to ranks.

The null and alternative hypotheses of the Friedman test:

H_0: The distributions of the k treatment populations are identical

H_1: Not all k distributions are identical   (14–32)

The data for the Friedman test are arranged in a table in which the rows are blocks (or units, if each unit is a block). There are n blocks. The columns are the treatments, and there are k of them. Let us assume that each block is one person who is assigned to all treatments. The data in this case are arranged as in Table 14–6.

If the data are not already in the form of ranks within each block, we rank the observations within each block from 1 to k. That is, the smallest observation in the block is given rank 1, the second smallest gets rank 2, and the largest gets rank k. Then we sum all the ranks for every treatment. The sum of all the ranks for treatment 1 is R_1, the sum of the ranks for treatment 2 is R_2, and so on to R_k, the sum of all the ranks given to treatment k.

If the distributions of the k populations are indeed identical, as stated in the null hypothesis, then we expect that the sum of the ranks for each treatment would not differ much from the sum of the ranks of any other treatment. The differences among the sums of the ranks are measured by the Friedman test statistic, denoted by X^2. When this statistic is too large, we reject the null hypothesis and conclude that at least two treatments do not have the same distribution.

The Friedman test statistic:

$$X^2 = \frac{12}{nk(k+1)} \sum_{j=1}^{k} R_j^2 - 3n(k+1) \qquad (14\text{–}33)$$

When the null hypothesis is true, the distribution of X^2 approaches the chi-square distribution with $k - 1$ degrees of freedom as n increases. For small values of k and n, tables of the exact distribution of X^2 under the null hypothesis may be found in nonparametric statistics books. Here we will use the chi-square distribution as our decision rule. We note that for small n, the chi-square approximation is *conservative;* that is, we may not be able to reject the null hypothesis as easily as we would if we use the exact distribution table. Our decision rule is to reject H_0 at a given level, α, if X^2 exceeds the critical point of the chi-square distribution with $k - 1$ degrees of freedom and right-tail area α. We now demonstrate the use of the Friedman test with an example.

EXAMPLE 14–12   There is a segment of the population, mostly retired people, who frequently go on low-budget cruises. Many travel agents specialize in this market and maintain mailing lists of people who take frequent cruises. One such travel agent in Fort Lauderdale wanted to find out whether "frequent cruisers" prefer some of the cruise lines in the low-budget range over others. If so, the agent would concentrate on selling tickets on the preferred line(s) rather than on a wider variety of lines. From a mailing list of people who have taken at least one cruise on each of the three cruise lines Carnival, Costa, and Sitmar, the agent selected a random sample of 15 people and asked them to rank their overall experiences

TABLE 14–6 Data Layout for the Friedman Test

	Treatment 1	Treatment 2	Treatment 3	. . .	Treatment k
Person 1					
Person 2					
Person 3					
⋮	⋮	⋮	⋮	. . .	⋮
Person n					
Sum of ranks:	R_1	R_2	R_3	. . .	R_k

TABLE 14–7 Sample Results of Example 14–12

Respondent	Carnival	Costa	Sitmar
1	1	2	3
2	2	1	3
3	1	3	2
4	2	1	3
5	3	1	2
6	3	1	2
7	1	2	3
8	3	1	2
9	2	1	3
10	1	2	3
11	2	1	3
12	3	1	2
13	1	2	3
14	3	1	2
15	3	1	2
	$R_1 = 31$	$R_2 = 21$	$R_3 = 38$

with the three lines. The ranks were 1 (best), 2 (second best), and 3 (worst). The results are given in Table 14–7. Are the three cruise lines equally preferred by people in the target population?

Using the sums of the ranks of the three treatments (the three cruise lines), we compute the Friedman test statistic. From equation 14–33, we get

$$X^2 = \frac{12}{nk(k + 1)}(R_1^2 + R_2^2 + R_3^2) - 3n(k + 1)$$

$$= \frac{12}{(15)(3)(4)}(31^2 + 21^2 + 38^2) - 3(15)(4) = 9.73$$

We now compare the computed value of the statistic with values of the right tail of the chi-square distribution with $k - 1 = 2$ degrees of freedom. The critical point for

SOLUTION

> The **Spearman rank correlation coefficient** (assuming no ties):
>
> $$r_s = 1 - \frac{6 \sum_{i=1}^{n} d_i^2}{n(n^2 - 1)} \tag{14–34}$$
>
> where d_i, $i = 1, \ldots, n$, are the differences in the ranks of x_i and y_i:
> $$d_i = R(x_i) - R(y_i)$$

If we do have ties within the X values or the Y values, but the number of ties is small compared with n, equation 14–34 is still useful.

The Spearman correlation coefficient satisfies the usual requirements of correlation measures. It is equal to 1 when the variables X and Y are perfectly positively related, that is, when Y increases whenever X does, and vice versa. It is equal to -1 in the opposite situation, where X increases whenever Y decreases. It is equal to 0 when there is no relation between X and Y. Values between these extremes give a relative indication of the degree of association between X and Y.

As with the parametric Pearson correlation coefficient, there are two possible uses for the Spearman statistic. It may be used as a descriptive statistic giving us an indication of the association between X and Y. We may also use it for *statistical inference*. In the context of inference, we assume that there is a certain correlation in the ranks of the values of the bivariate population of X and Y. This population rank correlation is denoted by ρ_s. We want to test whether $\rho_s = 0$, that is, whether or not there is an association between the two variables X and Y.

> Hypothesis test for association between two variables:
>
> $$H_0: \rho_s = 0$$
> $$H_1: \rho_s \neq 0 \tag{14–35}$$

This is a two-tailed test for the existence of a relation between X and Y. One-tailed versions of the test are also possible. If we want to test for a positive association between the variables, then the alternative hypothesis is that the parameter ρ_s is strictly greater than zero. If we want to test for a negative association only, then the alternative hypothesis is that ρ_s is strictly less than zero. The test statistic is simply r_s, as defined in equation 14–34.

When the sample size is less than or equal to 30, we use Appendix C, Table 11. The table gives critical points for various levels of significance, α. For a two-tailed test, we double the α level given in the table and reject the null hypothesis if r_s is either greater than or equal to the table value, C, or less than or equal to $-C$. In a right-tailed test, we reject only if r_s is greater than or equal to C; and in a left-tailed test, we reject only if r_s is less than or equal to $-C$. In either one-tailed case, we use the α given in one of the columns in the table (we do not double it).

For larger sample sizes, we use the normal approximation to the distribution of r_s under the null hypothesis. The Z statistic for such a case is as follows.

> A large-sample test statistic for association:
>
> $$z = r_s \sqrt{n - 1} \tag{14–36}$$

We demonstrate the computation of Spearman's statistic, and a test of whether the population rank correlation is zero, with Example 14–13.

EXAMPLE 14-13

The S&P100 Index is an index of 100 stock options traded on the Chicago Board of Options Exchange. The MMI is an index of 20 stocks with options traded on the American Stock Exchange. Since options are volatile, the assumption of a normal distribution may not be appropriate, and the Spearman rank correlation coefficient may provide us with information about the association between the two indexes.[5] Using the reported data on the two indexes, given in Table 14–8, compute the r_s statistic, and test the null hypothesis that the MMI and the S&P100 are not related against the alternative that they are positively correlated.

SOLUTION

We rank the MMI values and the S&P100 values and compute the 10 differences: $d_i =$ Rank $(MMI_i) - $ Rank$(S\&P100_i)$. This is shown in Table 14–9. The order of the values in the table corresponds to their order in Table 14–8.

We now use equation 14–34 and compute r_s.

$$r_s = 1 - \frac{6(d_1^2 + d_2^2 + \cdots + d_{10}^2)}{10(10^2 - 1)} = 1 - \frac{24}{990} = 0.9758$$

The sample correlation is very high.

We now use the r_s statistic in testing the hypotheses:

$$H_0: \rho_s \leq 0$$
$$H_1: \rho_s > 0 \qquad\qquad (14–37)$$

We want to test for the existence of a positive rank correlation between MMI and S&P100 in the *population* of values of the two indexes. We want to test whether the high sample rank correlation we found is statistically significant. Since this is a right-tailed test, we reject the null hypothesis if r_s is greater than or equal to a point C found in Table 11 at a level of α given in the table. We find from the table that for $\alpha = 0.005$

TABLE 14-8   Data on the MMI and S&P100 Indexes (Example 14-13)

MMI	S&P100
220	151
218	150
216	148
217	149
215	147
213	146
219	152
236	165
237	162
235	161

[5] *Volatility* means that there are jumps to very small and very large values. This gives the distribution long tails and makes it different from the normal distribution. For *stock returns,* however, the normal assumption is a good one, as mentioned in previous chapters.

TABLE 14-9   Ranks and Rank Differences for Example 14-13

Rank(MMI)	Rank(S&P100)	Difference
7	6	1
5	5	0
3	3	0
4	4	0
2	2	0
1	1	0
6	7	−1
9	10	−1
10	9	1
8	8	0

and $n = 10$, the critical point is 0.794. Since $r_s = 0.9758 > 0.794$, we reject the null hypothesis and conclude that the MMI and the S&P100 are positively correlated. The p-value is less than 0.005.

In closing this section, we note that Spearman's rank correlation coefficient is sometimes referred to as *Spearman's rho* (the Greek letter p). There is another commonly used nonparametric measure of correlation. This one was developed by Kendall and is called *Kendall's tau* (the Greek letter τ). Since Kendall's measure is not as simple to compute as the Spearman coefficient of rank correlation, we leave it to texts on nonparametric statistics.

PROBLEMS

14–55. The director of a management training program wants to test whether there is a positive association between an applicant's score on a test prior to his or her being admitted to the program and the same person's success in the program. The director ranks 15 participants according to their performance on the pretest and separately ranks them according to their performance in the program:

Participant:	1	2	3	4	5	6	7	8	9	10	11	12	13	14	15
Pretest rank:	8	9	4	2	3	10	1	5	6	15	13	14	12	7	11
Performance rank:	7	5	9	6	1	8	2	10	15	14	4	3	11	12	13

Using these data, carry out the test for a positive rank correlation between pretest scores and success in the program.

14–56. The following data are a random sample of consumers' income and expenditure on certain luxury items. Compute the Spearman rank correlation coefficient, and test for the existence of a population correlation.

Income ($1000's/year):   23, 17, 34, 56, 49, 31, 28, 80, 65, 40, 26
Luxury Item Spending ($/Month):   10, 50, 120, 225, 90, 60, 55, 340, 170, 25, 80

14–57. The following table is a listing from the Fortune 500 and gives profits as percent of sales and assets for 10 firms.[6] Is there a rank correlation between the two variables?

---

[6] "The Fortune 500 Largest U.S. Industrial Corporations," *Fortune,* April 22, 1991, p. 286.

	Profits as Percent of	
	Sales	Assets
International Business Machines, Armonk, N.Y.	8.7	6.9
Mobil, Fairfax, Va.	3.3	4.6
General Electric, Fairfield, Conn.	7.4	2.8
Philip Morris, New York	8.0	7.6
Texaco, White Plains, N.Y.	3.5	5.6
E. I. Du Pont De Nemours, Wilmington, Del.	5.8	6.1
Chevron, San Francisco	5.5	6.1
Chrysler, Highland Park, Mich.	0.2	0.1
Amoco, Chicago	6.8	5.9
Boeing, Seattle	5.0	9.5

14–58. Recently the European Community (EC) decided to lower its subsidies to makers of pasta. In deciding by what amount to reduce total subsidies, experiments were carried out for determining the possible reduction in exports, mainly to the United States, that would result from the subsidy reduction. Over a small range of values, economists wanted to test whether there is a positive correlation between level of subsidy and level of exports. A computer simulation of the economic variables involved in the pasta exports market was carried out. The results are as follows. Assuming that the simulation is an accurate description of reality and that the values obtained may be viewed as a random sample of the populations of possible outcomes, state whether you believe that a positive rank correlation exists between subsidy level and exports level over the short range of values studied.

Subsidy (millions of dollars/year): 5.1 5.3 5.2 4.9 4.8 4.7 4.5 5.0 4.6 4.4 5.4
Exports (millions of dollars/year): 22 30 35 29 27 36 40 39 42 45 21

14–59. An advertising research analyst wanted to test whether there is any relationship between a magazine advertisement's color intensity and the ad's appeal. Ten ads of varying degrees of color intensity, but identical in other ways, were shown to randomly selected groups of respondents. The respondents rated each ad for its general appeal. The respondents were segmented in such a way that each group viewed a different ad, and every group's responses were aggregated. The results were ranked as follows.

Color intensity: 8 7 2 1 3 4 10 6 5 9
Appeal score: 1 3 4 2 5 8 7 6 9 10

Is there a rank correlation between color intensity and appeal?

14–9 A Chi-Square Test for Goodness of Fit

In this section and the next two, we describe tests that make use of the chi-square distribution. The data used in these tests are *enumerative:* the data are counts, or ✳ frequencies. Our actual observations may be on a nominal (or higher) scale of measurement. Because many real-world situations in business and other areas allow for the collection of count data (for example, the number of people in a sample who fall into different categories of age, sex, income, and job classification), chi-square analysis is very common and very useful. The tests are easy to carry out and are versatile: we can employ them in a wide variety of situations. The tests presented in this and the next two sections are among the most useful statistical techniques of analyzing data. Quite often, in fact, a computer program designed merely to count the number of items falling in some categories automatically prints out a chi-square value. The user then has to consider the question: What statistical test is implied by the chi-square statistic in this particular situation? Among their other purposes, these sections should help you answer this question.

There is a common principle in all the chi-square tests we will discuss. The principle is summarized in the following steps:

Steps in a chi-square analysis:

1. We hypothesize about a population by stating the null and alternative hypotheses.
2. We compute frequencies of occurrence of certain events that we expect under the null hypothesis. These give us the *expected* counts of data points in different cells.
3. We note the *observed* counts of data points falling in the different cells.
4. We consider the difference between the observed and the expected. This difference leads us to a computed value of the chi-square statistic. The formula of the statistic is given as equation 14–38.
5. We compare the value of the statistic with critical points of the chi-square distribution and make a decision.

The analysis in this section and the next two involves tables of data counts. The chi-square statistic has the same form in the applications in all three sections. The statistic is equal to the *squared difference between the observed count and the expected count in each cell, divided by the expected count, summed over all cells.* If our data table has k cells, let the observed count in cell i be O_i and the expected count (expected under H_0) be E_i. The definition is for all cells $i = 1, 2, \ldots, k$.

The chi-square statistic:

$$X^2 = \sum_{i=1}^{k} \frac{(O_i - E_i)^2}{E_i} \qquad (14\text{–}38)$$

As the total sample size increases, for a given number of cells, k, the distribution of the statistic X^2 in equation 14–38 approaches the chi-square distribution. The degrees of freedom of the chi-square distribution are determined separately in each situation.

The reason for the chi-square limiting distribution is the central limit theorem. Remember the binomial experiment, where the number of *successes* (items falling in a particular category) is a random variable. The probability of a success is a fixed number, p. Recall from the beginning of Chapter 4 that as the number of trials, n, increases, the distribution of the number of binomial successes approaches a normal distribution. In the situations in this and the next two sections, the number of items falling in any of *several* categories is a random variable, and as the number of trials increases, the observed number in any cell, O_i, approaches a normal random variable. Remember also that the sum of several squared standard normal random variables has a chi-square distribution. The terms summed in equation 14–38 are standardized random variables that are squared. Each one of these variables approaches a normal random variable. The sum, therefore, approaches a chi-square distribution as the sample size, n, gets large.

A **goodness-of-fit test** is a statistical test of how well our data support an assumption about the distribution of a population or random variable of interest. The test determines how well an assumed distribution fits the data.

For example, we often make an assumption of a normal population. It may be of interest to test how well a normal distribution fits a given data set. Shortly we will see how to carry out a test of the normal distribution assumption.

We start our discussion of goodness-of-fit tests with a simpler test, and a very useful one—a test of goodness of fit in the case of a **multinomial distribution.** The multinomial distribution is a generalization of the binomial distribution to more than two possibilities (success vs. failure). In the multinomial situation, we have $k > 2$ possible categories for the data. A data point can fall into only one of the k categories, and the probability that the point will fall in category i (where $i = 1, 2, \ldots, k$) is constant and equal to p_i. The sum of all k probabilities p_i is 1.

Given five categories, for example, such as five age groups, a respondent can fall into only one of the (nonoverlapping) groups. If the probabilities that the respondent will fall into any of the k groups are given by the five parameters $p_1, p_2, p_3, p_4,$ and p_5, then the multinomial distribution with these parameters and n, the number of people in a random sample, specifies the probability of any combination of cell counts. For example, if $n = 100$ people, the multinomial distribution gives us the probability that 10 people will fall in category 1, 15 in category 2, 12 in category 3, 50 in category 4, and the remaining 13 in category 5. The distribution gives us the probabilities of *all possible counts* of 100 people (or items) distributed into five cells.

When we have a situation such as this, we may use the multinomial distribution to test how well our data fit the assumption of k fixed probabilities $p_1, \ldots, p_k$ of falling into k cells. However, working with the multinomial distribution is difficult, and the chi-square distribution is a very good alternative when sample size considerations allow its use.

A Goodness-of-Fit Test for the Multinomial Distribution

The null and the alternative hypotheses for the multinomial distribution:

> H_0: The probabilities of occurrence of events
> $\quad E_1, \ldots E_k$ are given by the specified probabilities
> $\quad p_1, p_2, \ldots, p_k$
> H_1: The probabilities of the k events are not the
> $\quad p_i$ stated in the null hypothesis   (14–39)

The test statistic is as given in equation 14–38. For large enough n (a rule for how large is "enough" will be given shortly), the distribution of the statistic may be approximated by a chi-square distribution with $k - 1$ degrees of freedom. We demonstrate the test with Example 14–14.

Raymond Weil is about to come out with a new watch and wants to find out whether people have special preferences for the color of the watchband, or whether all four colors under consideration are equally preferred. A random sample of 80 prospective watch

EXAMPLE 14-14

TABLE 14–10   Watchband Color Preferences

	Tan	Brown	Maroon	Black	Total
	12	40	8	20	80

buyers is selected. Each person is shown the watch with four different band colors and asked to state his or her preference. The results—the *observed counts*—are given in Table 14–10.

SOLUTION

The null and alternative hypotheses, equation 14–39, take the following specific form:

H₀: The four band colors are equally preferred;
   that is, the probabilities of choosing any of
   the four colors are equal: $p_1 = p_2 = p_3 = p_4 = 0.25$

H₁: Not all four colors are equally preferred
   (the probabilities of choosing the four colors
   are not all equal)

To compute the value of our test statistic (equation 14–38), we need to find the *expected* counts in all four cells (in this example, each cell corresponds to a color).

 Recall that for a binomial random variable, the mean—the *expected value*—is equal to the number of trials, n, times the probability of success in a single trial, p. Here, in the multinomial experiment, we have k cells, each with probability p_i, where $i = 1, 2, \ldots, k$. For each cell, we have a binomial experiment with probability p_i and number of trials n. The expected number in each cell is therefore equal to n times p_i.

The expected count in cell i:

$$E_i = np_i \tag{14–40}$$

In this example, the number of trials is the number of people in the random sample: $n = 80$. Under the null hypothesis, the expected number of people who will choose color i is equal to $E_i = np_i$. Furthermore, since all the probabilities in this case are equal to 0.25, we have the following:

$$E_1 = E_2 = E_3 = E_4 = (80)(0.25) = 20$$

When the null hypothesis is true, and the probability that any person will choose any one of the four colors is equal to 0.25, we may not observe 20 people in every cell. In fact, observing *exactly* 20 people in each of the four cells is an event with a small probability. However, the number of people we observe in each cell should not be too far from the expected number, 20. Just how far is "too far" is determined by the chi-square distribution. We use the expected counts and the observed counts in computing the value of the chi-square test statistic. From equation 14–38, we get the following:

$$X^2 = \sum_{i=1}^{k} \frac{(O_i - E_i)^2}{E_i} = \frac{(12 - 20)^2}{20} + \frac{(40 - 20)^2}{20} + \frac{(8 - 20)^2}{20} + \frac{(20 - 20)^2}{20}$$

$$= \frac{64}{20} + \frac{400}{20} + \frac{144}{20} + 0 = 3.2 + 20 + 7.2 + 0 = 30.4$$

We now conduct the test by comparing the computed value of our statistic, $X^2 = 30.4$, with critical points of the chi-square distribution with $k - 1 = 4 - 1 = 3$ degrees of freedom. From Appendix C, Table 4, we find that the critical point for a chi-square random variable with 3 degrees of freedom and right-hand-tail area $\alpha = 0.01$ is 11.3. (*Note that all the chi-square tests in this chapter are carried out only on the right-hand tail of the distribution.*) Since the computed value is much greater than the critical point at $\alpha = 0.01$, we conclude that there is evidence to reject the null hypothesis that all four colors are equally likely to be chosen. Some colors are probably preferable to others. Our p-value is very small.

The test for multinomial probabilities does not always entail equal probabilities, as was the case in our example. The probabilities may very well be different. All we need to do is specify the probabilities in the null hypothesis and then use the hypothesized probabilities in computing the expected cell counts (using equation 14–40). Then we use the expected counts along with the observed counts in computing the value of the chi-square statistic.

Under what conditions can we assume that, under the null hypothesis, the distribution of the test statistic in equation 14–38 is well-approximated by a chi-square distribution? This important question has no exact answer. As the sample size, n, increases, the approximation gets better and better. On the other hand, there is also a dependence on the cell, k. If the expected number of counts in some cells is too small, the approximation may not be valid. We will give a good rule of thumb that specifies the minimum expected count in each cell needed for the chi-square approximation to be valid. The rule is conservative in the sense that other rules have been given that allow smaller expected counts under certain conditions. If we follow the rule given here, we will usually be safe using the chi-square distribution.

> The chi-square distribution may be used as long as the expected count in every cell is at least 5.0.

Suppose that while conducting an analysis, we find that for one or more cells, the expected number of items is less than 5. We may still continue our analysis if we can *combine cells* so that the expected number has a total of at least 5. For example, suppose that our null hypothesis is that the distribution of ages in a certain population is as follows: 20% are between the ages of 0 to 15, 10% are in the age group of 16 to 25, 10% are in the age group of 26 to 35, 20% are in the age group of 36 to 45, 30% are in the age group of 45 to 60, and 10% are 61 or over. If we number the age group cells consecutively from 1 to 6, then the null hypothesis is H_0: $p_1 = 0.20$, $p_2 = 0.10$, $p_3 = 0.10$, $p_4 = 0.20$, $p_5 = 0.30$, $p_6 = 0.10$.

Now suppose that we gather a random sample of $n = 40$ people from this population and use this group to test for goodness of fit of the multinomial assumption in the null hypothesis. What are our expected cell counts? In the $0-15$ cell, the expected number of people is $np_1 = (40)(0.20) = 8$, which is fine. But for the next age group, $16-25$, we find that the expected number is $np_2 = (40)(0.10) = 4$, which is less than 5. If we want to continue the analysis, we may combine age groups that have small expected counts with other age groups. We may combine the $16-25$ age group with the $26-35$ age group, which also has a low expected count. Or we may combine the $16-25$ group with the $0-15$ group, and the $26-35$ group with the $36-45$ group— whichever makes more sense in terms of the interpretation of the analysis. We also need to combine the 61-and-over group with the $45-60$ age group. Once we make

FIGURE 14–7   Demonstration of a Loss of 1 Degree of Freedom

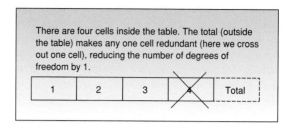

There are four cells inside the table. The total (outside the table) makes any one cell redundant (here we cross out one cell), reducing the number of degrees of freedom by 1.

| 1 | 2 | 3 | 4 | Total |

sure that all expected counts are at least 5, we may use the chi-square distribution. Instead of combining groups, we may choose to increase the sample size.

We will now discuss the determination of the number of degrees of freedom. Figure 14–7 shows the table of counts for Example (14–14). Note that there are four cells, corresponding to the four colors in the analysis, *and* there is a fifth outside cell, which we have so far ignored. This is the cell containing the *total count* of the four cells—the total sample size, $n = 80$. The total count acts similarly to the way $\bar{x}$ does when we use it in computing the sample standard deviation. *The total count reduces the number of degrees of freedom by 1.* Why? Because knowing the total allows us not to know directly *any one* of the cell counts. If we knew, for example, the counts in the cells corresponding to tan, black, and maroon but did not know the count in the brown cell, we could still figure out the count for this cell by subtracting the sum of the three cell counts we do know from the total of 80. Thus, when we know the total, one degree of freedom is lost from the category cells. Out of four cells in this example, any three are free to move. Out of k cells, since we know their total, only $k - 1$ are free to move: df $= k - 1$.

As a general rule, we know that the number of degrees of freedom is equal to the number of items (here items are cells inside the table) less the number of restrictions. The total count acts as a restriction on the cell counts and so one cell is lost. Any time you have such a table, cross out any one column (as shown in Figure 14–7) and count the remaining number of cells. This will give you the number of degrees of freedom. Later, when we show tables with several rows and several columns, this principle will still hold. We will cross out any one row (due to our knowledge of the column totals) and any one column (due to our knowledge of row totals) and the remaining number of cells inside the table will give us the number of degrees of freedom of the chi-square statistic.

We now note another fact that will be important in our next example.

> If we have to use the data for estimating the parameters of the probability distribution stated in the null hypothesis, then for every parameter we estimate from the data, we lose an additional degree of freedom.

The chi-square goodness-of-fit test may be applied to testing any hypothesis about the distribution of a population or a random variable. As mentioned earlier, the test may be applied in particular to testing how well an assumption of a normal distribution is supported by a given data set. The standard normal distribution table, Appendix C, Table 2, gives us the probability that a standard normal random variable will be between any two given values. Through the transformation $X = \mu + \sigma Z$, we may then find boundaries in terms of the original variable, X, for any given probabilities of occurrence. These boundaries can be used in forming cells with known probabilities and, hence, known expected counts for a given sample size. This analysis, however, assumes that we know μ and σ, the mean and the standard deviation of the population or variable in question.

When μ and σ are *not* known, and the null and alternative hypotheses are stated as

   H_0: The population (or random variable) has a normal distribution
   H_1: The population (or random variable) is not normally distributed   (14–41)

there is no mention in the statement of the hypotheses of what the mean or standard deviation may be, and we need to estimate them directly from our data. When this happens, we lose a degree of freedom for each parameter estimated from the data (unless we use another data set for the estimation). We estimate μ by $\overline{X}$ and σ by S, as usual. The degrees of freedom of the chi-square statistic are df $= k - 2 - 1 = k - 3$ (instead of $k - 1$, as before). We will now demonstrate the test for a normal distribution with Example 14–15.

An analyst working for a department store chain wants to test the assumption that the amount of money spent by a customer in any store is approximately normally distributed. It is important to test this assumption because the analyst plans to conduct an analysis of variance to determine whether average sales per customer are equal at several stores in the same chain (as we recall, the normal-distribution assumption is required for ANOVA). A random sample of 100 shoppers at one of the department stores reveals that the average spending is $\overline{x} = \$125$ and the standard deviation is $s = \$40$. These are sample estimates of the *population* mean and standard deviation. (The breakdown of the data into cells is included in the solution.)

EXAMPLE 14-15

We begin by defining boundaries with known probabilities for the standard normal random variable, Z. We know that the probability that the value of Z will be between -1 and $+1$ is about 0.68. We also know that the probability that Z will be between -2 and $+2$ is about 0.95, and we know other such probabilities. We may use Appendix C, Table 2 to find more exact probabilities. Let us use the table and define several nonoverlapping intervals for Z with known probabilities. We will form intervals of about the same probability. Figure 14–8 shows one possible partition of the standard normal distribution to intervals and their probabilities, obtained from Table 2. You may use any partition you desire.

The partition was obtained as follows. We know that the area under the curve between 0 and 1 is 0.3413 (from Table 2). Looking for an area of about half that size, 0.1700, we find that the appropriate point is $z = 0.44$. A similar relationship exists on the negative side of the number line. Thus, using just the values 0.44 and 1 and their negatives, we get a complete partition of the Z scale into the six intervals: $-\infty$ to -1, with associated probability of 0.1587; -1 to -0.44, with probability 0.1713; -0.44 to 0, with probability 0.1700; 0 to 0.44, with probability 0.1700; 0.44 to 1, with probability 0.1713; and, finally, 1 to ∞, with probability 0.1587. Breakdowns into other intervals may also be used.

Now we transform the Z scale values into interval boundaries for the original problem. Taking $\overline{x}$ and s as if they were the mean and the standard deviation of the *population*, we use the transformation $X = \mu + \sigma Z$, with $\overline{x} = 125$ and $s = 40$ substituted for the

SOLUTION

FIGURE 14-8   Intervals and Their Standard Normal Probabilities

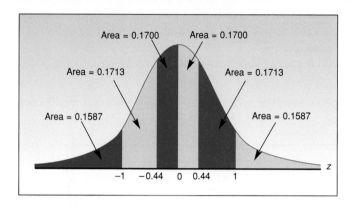

unknown parameters. The Z value boundaries we just obtained are substituted into the transformation, giving us the following cell boundaries:

$$x_1 = 125 + (-1)(40) = 85$$
$$x_2 = 125 + (-0.44)(40) = 107.4$$
$$x_3 = 125 + (0)(40) = 125$$
$$x_4 = 125 + (0.44)(40) = 142.6$$
$$x_5 = 125 + (1)(40) = 165$$

The cells and their expected counts are given in Table 14–11. Cell boundaries are broken at the nearest cent. Recall that the expected count in each cell is equal to the cell probability times the sample size: $E_i = np_i$. In this example, the p_i are obtained from the normal table and are, in order, 0.1587, 0.1713, 0.1700, 0.1700, 0.1713, and 0.1587. Multiplying these probabilities by $n = 100$ gives us the expected counts. (Note that the theoretical boundaries of $-\infty$ and $+\infty$ have no practical meaning; therefore, the lowest bound is replaced by 0 and the highest bound by *and above*.) Note that all expected cell counts are above 5, and, therefore, the chi-square distribution is an adequate approximation to the distribution of the test statistic X^2 in equation 14–38 under the null hypothesis.

Table 14–12 gives the observed counts of the sales amounts falling in each of the cells. The table was obtained by the analyst by looking at each data point in the sample and classifying the amount into one of the chosen categories.

To facilitate the computation of the chi-square statistic, we arrange the observed and expected cell counts in a single table and show the computations necessary for obtaining the value of the test statistic. This has been done in Table 14–13. The sum of all the entries in the last column in the table is the value of the chi-square statistic. The appropriate distribution has $k - 3 = 6 - 3 = 3$ degrees of freedom. We now consult the chi-square table, Appendix C, Table 4, and we find that the computed statistic value $X^2 = 1.12$ falls in the nonrejection region for any level of α in the table. There is therefore no statistical evidence that the population is not normally distributed.

The chi-square goodness-of-fit test may be applied to testing the fit of any hypothesized distribution. In general, we use an appropriate probability table for obtaining probabilities of intervals of values. The intervals define our data cells. Using the sample size, we then find the expected count in each cell. We compare the expected counts with the observed counts and compute the value of the chi-square test statistic.

TABLE 14-11 Cells and Their Expected Counts

0–$84.99	$85.00–$107.39	$107.4–$124.99	$125–$142.59	$142.6–$164.99	$165 and above	
15.87	17.13	17.00	17.00	17.13	15.87	Total = 100

TABLE 14-12 Observed Cell Counts

0–$84.99	$85.00–$107.39	$107.4–$124.99	$125–$142.59	$142.6–$164.99	$165 and above	
14	20	16	19	16	15	Total = 100

TABLE 14-13 Computing the Value of the Chi-Square Statistic for Example 14-15

Cell	i	O_i	E_i	$O_i - E_i$	$(O_i - E_i)^2$	$(O_i - E_i)^2/E_i$
0–$84.99	1	14	15.87	−1.87	3.50	0.22
$85.00–$107.39	2	20	17.13	2.87	8.24	0.48
$107.40–$124.99	3	16	17.00	−1.00	1.00	0.06
$125.00–$142.59	4	19	17.00	2.00	4.00	0.24
$142.60–$164.99	5	16	17.13	−1.13	1.28	0.07
$165.00 and above	6	15	15.87	−0.87	0.76	0.05
						1.12

The chi-square statistic is useful in other areas as well. In the next section, we will describe the use of the chi-square statistic in the analysis of contingency tables—an analysis of whether two principles of classification are contingent on one another or independent of each other. The following section extends the contingency table analysis to a test of homogeneity of several populations.

PROBLEMS

14-60.   An article in the *Columbia Journal of World Business* reports on foreign ownership of U.S. assets.[7] A table in the article suggests that the national breakdown (in percentages) of European firms owning U.S. investments is as follows: United Kingdom, 40.2%; Germany, 9.1%; Netherlands, 19.5%; and other nations, 31.2%. A random sample of 212 European firms that bought American assets in 1995 revealed the following breakdown (in number of firms): 91 firms from the United Kingdom, 22 from the Netherlands, 10 from Germany, and 89 from other countries. Do you believe that the percentages of all European firms who invested in the United States in 1995 are the same as reported in the journal? Explain.

14-61.   A company is considering five possible names for its new product. Before choosing a name, the firm decides to test whether all five names are equally appealing. A random sample of 100 people is chosen, and each person is asked to state his or her choice of the best name

[7] B. Majumdar, "Foreign Ownership of America: A Matter of Concern," *Columbia Journal of World Business,* Fall, 1990, p. 17.

among the five possibilities. The numbers of people who chose each one of the names are as follows.

Name:	A	B	C	D	E
Number of choices:	4	12	34	40	10

Conduct the test.

14–62.   A study reports an analysis of 35 key product categories. At the time of the study, 72.9% of the products sold were of a national brand, 23% were private-label, and 4.1% were generic. Suppose that you want to test whether these percentages are still valid for the market today. You collect a random sample of 1,000 products in the 35 product categories studied, and you find the following: 610 products are of a national brand, 290 are private-label, and 100 are generic. Conduct the test, and state your conclusions.

14–63.   An industry analyst wants to test the null hypothesis that the market share figures for firms in the industry are as follows.

Firm:	A	B	C	D	E	Other
Share:	1%	9%	14%	26%	0.5%	49.5%

The analysis is to be based on a classification of 100 randomly chosen products.

a.   Can you use the chi-square statistic to conduct this test?

b.   If you cannot use the chi-square statistic, can you make changes that will allow you to use it?

c.   Suppose that the 100 products in the sample are classified as follows: firm A, 0; firm B, 0; firm C, 26; firm D, 15; firm E, 2; other, 57. Conduct the analysis (if you can), and state your conclusion.

14–64.   Returns on an investment have been known to be normally distributed with mean 11% (annualized rate) and standard deviation 2%. A brokerage firm wants to test the null hypothesis that this statement is true and collects the following returns data (assumed a random sample): 8%, 9%, 9.5%, 9.5%, 8.6%, 13%, 14.5%, 12%, 12.4%, 19%, 9%, 10%, 10%, 11.7%, 15%, 10.1%, 12.7%, 17%, 8%, 9.9%, 11%, 12.5%, 12.8%, 10.6%, 8.8%, 9.4%, 10%, 12.3%, 12.9%, 7%. Conduct the analysis and state your conclusion.

14–65.   Using the data provided in problem 14–64, test the null hypothesis that returns on the investment are normally distributed, but with *unknown* mean and standard deviation. That is, test only for the validity of the normal-distribution assumption. How is this test different from the one in problem 14–64?

14–10   Contingency Table Analysis—A Chi-Square Test for Independence

Recall the important concept of *independence* of events, which we discussed in Chapter 2. Two events, A and B, are independent if the probability of their joint occurrence is equal to the product of their marginal (i.e., separate) probabilities. This was given as:

A and B are independent if $P(A \cap B) = P(A)P(B)$

In this chapter, we will develop a statistical test that will help us determine whether or not two classification criteria, such as sex and job performance, are independent of each other. The technique will make use of **contingency tables:** tables with cells corresponding to cross-classifications of attributes or events. In marketing research studies, such tables are referred to as *cross-tabs.* The basis for our analysis will be the property of independent events just stated.

FIGURE 14–9 Layout of a Contingency Table

Second Classification Category	First Classification Category						Total
	1	2	3	4	5	6	
1	O_{11}	O_{12}	O_{13}	O_{14}	O_{15}	O_{16}	R_1
2	O_{21}	O_{22}	O_{23}	O_{24}	O_{25}	O_{26}	R_2
3	O_{31}	O_{32}	O_{33}	O_{34}	O_{35}	O_{36}	R_3
4	O_{41}	O_{42}	O_{43}	O_{44}	O_{45}	O_{46}	R_4
5	O_{51}	O_{52}	O_{53}	O_{54}	O_{55}	O_{56}	R_5
Total	C_1	C_2	C_3	C_4	C_5	C_6	n

The contingency tables may have several rows and several columns. The rows correspond to levels of one classification category, and the columns correspond to another. We will denote the number of rows by r, and the number of columns by c. The total sample size is n, as before. The count of the elements in cell (i, j), that is, the cell in row i and column j (where $i = 1, 2, \ldots, r$ and $j = 1, 2, \ldots, c$) is denoted by O_{ij}. The total count for row i is R_i, and the total count for column j is C_j. The general form of a contingency table is shown in Figure 14–9. The table is demonstrated for $r = 5$ and $c = 6$. Note that n is also the sum of all r row totals and the sum of all c column totals.

Let us now state the null and alternative hypotheses.

Hypothesis test for independence:

H_0: The two classification variables are independent of each other

H_1: The two classification variables are not independent   (14–42)

The principle of our analysis is the same as that used in the previous section. The chi-square test statistic for this set of hypotheses is the one we used before, given in equation 14–38. The only difference is that the summation extends over all cells in the table: the c columns and the r rows (in the previous application, goodness-of-fit tests, we only had one row). We will rewrite the statistic to make it clearer:

Chi-square test statistic for independence:

$$X^2 = \sum_{i=1}^{r}\sum_{j=1}^{c} \frac{(O_{ij} - E_{ij})^2}{E_{ij}}   (14\text{–}43)$$

The double summation in equation 14–43 means summation over all rows and all columns.

The degrees of freedom of the chi-square statistic are

$$df = (r - 1)(c - 1)$$

Now all we need to do is find the expected cell counts, E_{ij}. Here is where we use the assumption that the two classification variables are independent. Remember that the philosophy of hypothesis testing is to assume that H_0 is true and to use this assumption in determining the distribution of the test statistic. Then we try to show that the result is unlikely under H_0 and thus reject the null hypothesis.

Assuming that the two classification variables are independent, let us derive the expected counts in all cells. Look at a particular cell in row i and column j. Recall from equation 14–40 that the expected number of items in a cell is equal to the sample size times the probability of the occurrence of the event signified by the particular cell. In the context of an $r \times c$ contingency table, the probability associated with cell (i, j) is the probability of occurrence of event i and event j. Thus, the expected count in cell (i, j) is $E_{ij} = nP(i \cap j)$. If we assume independence of the two classification variables, then event i and event j are independent events, and, by the law of independence of events, $P(i \cap j) = P(i)P(j)$.

From the row totals, we can estimate the probability of event i as R_i/n. Similarly, we estimate the probability of event j by C_j/n. Substituting these estimates of the marginal probabilities, we get the following expression for the expected count in cell (i, j): $E_{ij} = n(R_i/n)(C_j/n) = R_i C_j/n$.

The expected count in cell (i, j):

$$E_{ij} = \frac{R_i C_j}{n} \qquad (14\text{–}44)$$

Equation 14–44 allows us to compute the expected cell counts. These, along with the observed cell counts, are used in computing the value of the chi-square statistic, which leads us to a decision about the null hypothesis of independence.

We will now illustrate the analysis with two examples. The first example is an illustration of an analysis of the simplest contingency table: a 2×2 table. In such tables, the two rows correspond to the occurrence versus nonoccurrence of one event, and the two columns correspond to the occurrence or nonoccurrence of another event.

EXAMPLE 14–16

An article in *Business Week* reports profits and losses of firms by industry.[8] A random sample of 100 firms is selected, and for each firm in the sample, we record whether the company made money or lost money, and whether or not the firm is a service company. The data are summarized in the 2×2 contingency table, Table 14–14. Using the information in the table, determine whether or not you believe that the two events "the company made a profit this year" and "the company is in the service industry" are independent.

SOLUTION

Table 14–14 is the table of observed counts. We now use its marginal totals, R_1, R_2, C_1, and C_2, as well as the sample size, n, in creating a table of expected counts. Using equation 14–44,

---

[8] "The Business Week 1000," *Business Week*, March 27, 1995, pp. 102–65.

TABLE 14-14   Contingency Table of Profit/Loss versus Industry Type

| | Industry Type | | |
	Service	Nonservice	Total
Profit	42	18	60
Loss	6	34	40
Total	48	52	100

$$E_{11} = R_1 C_1/n = (60)(48)/100 = 28.8$$
$$E_{12} = R_1 C_2/n = (60)(52)/100 = 31.2$$
$$E_{21} = R_2 C_1/n = (40)(48)/100 = 19.2$$
$$E_{22} = R_2 C_2/n = (40)(52)/100 = 20.8$$

We now arrange these values in a table of expected counts, Table 14–15. Using the values shown in the table, we now compute the chi-square test statistic of equation 14–43:

$$X^2 = \frac{(42 - 28.8)^2}{28.8} + \frac{(18 - 31.2)^2}{31.2} + \frac{(6 - 19.2)^2}{19.2} + \frac{(34 - 20.8)^2}{20.8} = 29.09$$

To conduct the test, we compare the computed value of the statistic with critical points of the chi-square distribution with $(r - 1)(c - 1) = (2 - 1)(2 - 1) = 1$ degree of freedom. From Appendix C, Table 4, we find that the critical point for $\alpha = 0.01$ is 6.63, and, since our computed value of the X^2 statistic is much greater than the critical point, we reject the null hypothesis and conclude that the two qualities, profit/loss and industry type, are probably not independent.

In the analysis of 2×2 contingency tables, our chi-square statistic has *1 degree of freedom.* In such cases, it is often recommended that the value of the statistic be "corrected" so that its discrete distribution will be better approximated by the *continuous* chi-square distribution. The correction is called the **Yates correction** and entails subtracting the number $1/2$ from the absolute value of the difference between the observed and the expected counts before squaring them as required by equation 14–43. The Yates-corrected form of the statistic is as follows.

$$\text{Yates-corrected } X^2 = \sum_{\text{all cells}}\sum \frac{(|O_{ij} - E_{ij}| - 0.5)^2}{E_{ij}} \qquad (14\text{–}45)$$

For our example, the corrected value of the chi-square statistic is found as

Yates-corrected X^2

$$= \frac{(13.2 - 0.5)^2}{28.8} + \frac{(13.2 - 0.5)^2}{31.2} + \frac{(13.2 - 0.5)^2}{19.2} + \frac{(13.2 - 0.5)^2}{20.8}$$

$$= 26.92$$

As we see, the correction yields a smaller computed value. This value still leads to a strong rejection of the null hypothesis of independence. In many cases, the correction will not significantly change the results of the analysis. We will not emphasize the correction in the applications in this book.

TABLE 14–15 Expected Counts (with the observed counts shown in paretheses) for Example 14–16

	Service	Nonservice
Profit	28.8	31.2
	(42)	(18)
Loss	19.2	20.8
	(6)	(34)

As the number of cells in the contingency table becomes large, the use of a computer in the analysis becomes indispensable. As mentioned earlier, many computer programs automatically give a computed value of the chi-square statistic with any cross-tabulation of data. In section 14–12, we give a description of the use of the MINITAB package in chi-square analysis (as well as in many nonparametric tests). The following example is analyzed using the MINITAB program for chi-square analysis.

EXAMPLE 14–17

To better identify its target market, Alfa Romeo conducted a market research study. A random sample of 669 respondents was chosen, each of whom was asked to select one of four qualities that he or she believed described him or her best as a driver. The four possible self-descriptive qualities were *defensive, aggressive, enjoying,* and *prestigious.* Each respondent was then asked to choose one of three Alfa Romeo models as his or her choice of the most suitable car. The three models were Alfasud, Giulia, and Spider. The purpose of the study was to determine whether a relationship existed between a driver's self-image and his or her choice of an Alfa Romeo model. The response data are given in Table 14–16.

SOLUTION

For each cell, we need to multiply the row total by the column total and divide by the sample size, $n = 669$, to get the expected cell count. Then we use the expected counts and the observed counts in computing the value of the chi-square statistic given by equation 14–43. These operations are performed by the MINITAB program. The computer output is shown in Figure 14–10.

Follow the computations indicated in the figure, and make sure that you understand how each number is obtained. The degrees of freedom are $(r - 1)(c - 1) = (3 - 1)(4 - 1) = 6$. The computed value of the statistic is $X^2 = 20.87$. Comparing this value with critical points of the chi-square distribution with 6 degrees of freedom, we reject the null hypothesis with a p-value less than 0.01. We conclude that there is evidence of a dependence between a driver's self-image and his or her preference for one of the Alfa Romeo models.

Degrees of Freedom

Why are the degrees of freedom for the test statistic based on a contingency table with r rows and c columns equal to $(r - 1)(c - 1)$? Recall from our earlier discussion that the degrees of freedom are obtained by subtracting the number of restrictions from the number of cells under consideration. In the goodness-of-fit tests, we had k cells and

TABLE 14-16   The Observed Counts: Alfa Romeo Study

Alfa Romeo Model	Self-Image				Total
	Defensive	Aggressive	Enjoying	Prestigious	
Alfasud	22	21	34	56	133
Giulia	39	45	42	68	194
Spider	77	89	96	80	342
Total	138	155	172	204	669

FIGURE 14-10   MINITAB Output for Example 14-17

```
MTB > CHISQUARE ANALYSIS on C1, C2, C3, C4

Expected counts are printed below observed counts

            C1       C2       C3       C4     Total
    1       22       21       34       56       133
          27.4     30.8     34.2     40.6

    2       39       45       42       68       194
          40.0     44.9     49.9     59.2

    3       77       89       96       80       342
          70.5     79.2     87.9    104.3

  Total    138      155      172      204       669

ChiSq =   1.08 +   3.13 +   0.00 +   5.88 +
          0.03 +   0.00 +   1.24 +   1.32 +
          0.59 +   1.20 +   0.74 +   5.66 = 20.87
df = 6
```

one restriction—the total count. In the context of a two-dimensional contingency table, we have *one row restriction for each row* (the row total, R_i) *and one column restriction for each column* (the column total, C_j). This leaves us with $(r - 1)(c - 1)$ cells that are "free to move."

This idea is demonstrated in Figure 14–11. The example in the figure parallels the setup in Figure 14–9, demonstrating a situation with $r = 5$ rows and $c = 6$ columns. Since many people prefer a visual explanation (and aid to memory) rather than an algebraic one, you may find the idea shown in Figure 14–11 useful in determining the number of degrees of freedom in the analysis of any contingency table. The idea is to cross out any one row and any one column in the table, then count the remaining cells. The number of cells left intact is the number of degrees of freedom of the statistic.

PROBLEMS

14–66. An article reports that smaller firms seem to be hiring more than large ones as the economy picks up its pace. The table below gives numbers of employees hired and those laid

FIGURE 14-11   Degrees of Freedom = Number of Cells Left in the Table after One Row and One Column Have Been Crossed Out

$r = 5; c = 6$

df = number of uncrossed cells = 20

off, out of a random sample of 1,032, broken down by firm size. Is there evidence that hiring practices are dependent on firm size?

	Small Firm	Medium-Sized Firm	Large Firm	Total
Number hired	210	290	325	825
Number laid off	32	95	80	207
Total	242	385	405	1,032

14–67.   An analyst in the soft drink industry wants to conduct a statistical test to determine whether there is a relationship between a person's preference for one of the four brands: Coke, Pepsi, 7Up, and Dr Pepper; and whether the person drinks regular or diet drinks. A random sample of 330 people is selected, and their responses are as follows.

	Soft Drink Preference				
	Coke	Pepsi	7Up	Dr Pepper	Total
Diet	55	32	47	21	155
Regular	60	43	35	37	175
Total	115	75	82	58	330

Conduct the test, and state your conclusion.

14–68.   *Fortune* reports on the competition among car rental companies. The table below gives the number of cars, out of a random sample of 100 rental cars, belonging to each of the listed firms in 1979 and in 1990. Is there evidence of a change in the market shares of the car rental firms?

	Hertz	Avis	National	Budget	Other	Total
1979	39	26	18	14	3	100
1990	29	25	16	19	11	100

Source: "Rental Firms for Market Share," *Fortune*, April 22, 1991, p. 17.

14–69. An article on the stock market describes stock-buying behavior by institutions and individuals, as well as foreign and domestic buyers.[9] The following table describes recent purchases of U.S. stocks by individual or institution as well as domestic or foreign. Is there evidence of a dependence of institutional buying on whether the buyer is foreign or domestic?

	Domestic	Foreign
Individual	25	32
Institution	30	13

14–70. A study was conducted to determine whether a relationship existed between certain shareholder characteristics and the level of risk associated with the shareholders' investment portfolios. As part of the analysis, portfolio risk (measured by the portfolio beta) was divided into three categories: low risk, medium risk, and high risk; and the portfolios were cross-tabulated according to the three risk levels and seven family-income levels. The results of the analysis, conducted using a random sample of 180 investors, are shown in the following contingency table. Test for the existence of a relationship between income and investment risk taking. [Be careful here! (Why?)]

	Portfolio Risk Level			
Income Level ($)	Low	Medium	High	Total
0 to 19,999	5	4	1	10
20,000 to 24,999	6	3	0	9
25,000 to 29,999	22	30	11	63
30,000 to 34,999	11	20	20	51
35,000 to 39,999	8	10	4	22
40,000 to 44,999	2	0	10	12
45,000 and above	1	1	11	13
Total	55	68	57	180

14–71. When new paperback novels are promoted at bookstores, a display is often arranged with copies of the same book with differently colored covers. A publishing house wanted to find out whether there is a dependence between the place where the book is sold and the color of its cover. For one of its latest novels, the publisher sent displays and a supply of copies of the novel to large bookstores in five major cities. The resulting sales of the novel for each city-color combination are as follows. Numbers are in thousands of copies sold over a three-month period.

	Color				
City	Red	Blue	Green	Yellow	Total
New York	21	27	40	15	103
Washington	14	18	28	8	68
Boston	11	13	21	7	52
Chicago	3	33	30	9	75
Los Angeles	30	11	34	10	85
Total	79	102	153	49	383

a. Assume that the data are random samples for each particular color-city combination and that the inference may apply to all novels. Conduct the overall test for independence of color and location.

---

[9] S. Kuhn, "What's Driving the Dow?" *Fortune,* June 12, 1995, pp. 54–56.

b. Before the analysis, the publisher stated a special interest in the issue of whether there is any dependence between the red versus blue preference and the two cities Chicago versus Los Angeles. Conduct the test. Explain.

14–11   A Chi-Square Test for Equality of Proportions

Contingency tables and the chi-square statistic are also useful in another kind of analysis. Sometimes we are interested in whether the proportion of some characteristic is equal in several populations. An insurance company, for example, may be interested in finding out whether the proportion of people who submit claims for automobile accidents is about the same for the three age groups: 25 and under, over 25 and under 50, and 50 and over. In a sense, the question of whether the proportions are equal is a question of whether the three age populations are *homogeneous* with respect to accident claims. Therefore, tests of equality of proportions across several populations are also called tests of *homogeneity*.

The analysis is carried out in exactly the same way as in the previous application. We arrange the data in cells corresponding to population-characteristic combinations, and for each cell, we compute the expected count based on its row and column totals. The chi-square statistic is computed exactly as before. Two things are different in this analysis. First, we identify our populations of interest before the analysis and sample directly from these populations. Contrast this with the previous application, where we sampled from one population and then cross-classified according to two criteria. Second, because we identify populations and sample from them directly, the sizes of the samples from the different populations of interest are fixed. This is called *a chi-square analysis with fixed marginal totals*. This fact, however, does not affect the analysis.

We will demonstrate the analysis with the insurance company example just mentioned. The null and alternative hypotheses are

H_0: The proportion of claims is the same
for all three age groups (i.e., the
age groups are homogeneous with respect
to claim proportions)

H_1: The proportion of claims is not the
same across age groups (the age groups
are not homogeneous)   (14–46)

Suppose that random samples, selected from company records for the three age categories, are classified according to *claim* versus *no claim* and counted. The data are presented in Table 14–17.

To carry out the test, we first calculate the expected counts in all the cells. The expected cell counts are obtained, as before, by using equation 14–44. The expected count in each cell is equal to the row total times the column total, divided by the total sample size (the pooled sample size from all populations). The reason for the formula in this new context is that if the proportion of items in the class of interest (here, the proportion of people who submit a claim) is equal across all populations, as stated in the null hypothesis, then *pooling* this proportion across populations gives us the expected proportion in the cells for the class. Thus, the expected proportion in the claim class is estimated by the total in the claim class divided by the grand total, or $R_1/n = 135/300 = 0.45$. If we multiply this pooled proportion by the total number in the sample from the population of interest (say, the sample of people 25 and under), this should give us the *expected* count in the cell *claim—25 and under*. We get:

TABLE 14–17   Data for the Insurance Company Example

	Age Group			
	25 and under	Over 25 and under 50	50 and over	Total
Claim	40	35	60	135
No Claim	60	65	40	165
Total	100	100	100	300

There are fixed sample sizes for all three populations.

TABLE 14–18   Expected Counts for the Insurance Company Example

	25 and under	Over 25 and under 50	50 and over	Total
Claim	45	45	45	135
No Claim	55	55	55	165
Total	100	100	100	300

$E_{11} = C_1(R_1/n) = (C_1 R_1)/n$. This is exactly as prescribed by equation 14–44 in the test for independence. Here we get $E_{11} = (100)(0.45) = 45$. This is the expected count under the null hypothesis. We compute the expected counts for all other cells in the table in a similar manner. Table 14–18 is the table of expected counts in this example.

Note that since we have used equal sample sizes (100 from each age population), the expected count is equal in all cells corresponding to the same class. The proportions are expected to be equal under the null hypothesis. Since these proportions are multiplied by the same sample size, the counts are also equal.

We are now ready to compute the value of the chi-square test statistic. From equation 14–43, we get

$$X^2 = \sum_{\text{all cells}} \frac{(O - E)^2}{E} = \frac{(40 - 45)^2}{45} + \frac{(35 - 45)^2}{45} + \frac{(60 - 45)^2}{45}$$
$$+ \frac{(60 - 55)^2}{55} + \frac{(65 - 55)^2}{55} + \frac{(40 - 55)^2}{55} = 14.14$$

The degrees of freedom are obtained as usual. We have three rows and two columns, so the degrees of freedom are $(3 - 1)(2 - 1) = 2$. Alternatively, cross out any one row and any one column in Table 14–17 or 14–18 (ignoring the *Total* row and column). This leaves you with two cells, giving df $= 2$.

Comparing the computed value of the statistic with critical points of the chi-square distribution with 2 degrees of freedom, we find that the null hypothesis may be rejected and that the *p*-value is less than 0.01. (Check this, using Appendix C, Table 4.) We conclude that the proportions of people who submit claims to the insurance company are not the same across the age groups studied.

In general, when we compare c populations (or r populations, if they are arranged as the rows of the table rather than the columns), the hypotheses in equation 14–46 may be written as

$$H_0: p_1 = p_2 = \cdots = p_c$$
$$H_1: \text{Not all } p_i, i = 1, \ldots, c, \text{ are equal} \qquad (14\text{–}47)$$

where $p_i(i = 1, \ldots c)$, is the proportion in population i of the characteristic of interest. The test of equation 14–47 is a generalization to c populations of the test of equality of two population proportions discussed in Chapter 8. In fact, when $c = 2$, the test is identical to the simple test for equality of two population proportions. In our present context, the two-population test for proportion may be carried out using a 2×2 contingency table. The results of such a test would be identical to the results of a test using the method of Chapter 8 (a Z test).

The test presented in this section may also be applied to several proportions within each population. That is, instead of just testing for the proportion of *claim* versus *no claim,* we could be testing a more general hypothesis about the proportions of *several* different types of claims: no claim, claim under $1,000, claim of $1,000 to $5,000, and claim over $5,000. Here the null hypothesis would be that the proportion of each type of claim is equal across all populations. (This does not mean that the proportions of all types of claims are equal within a population.) The alternative hypothesis would be that not all proportions are equal across all populations under study. The analysis is done using an $r \times c$ contingency table (instead of the $2 \times c$ table we used in the preceding example). The test statistic is the same, and the degrees of freedom are as before: $(r - 1)(c - 1)$. We will now discuss another extension of the test presented in this section.

The Median Test

> The hypotheses for the median test:
>
> H_0: The c populations have the same median
> H_1: Not all c populations have the same median   (14–48)

Using the c random samples from the populations of interest, we determine the grand median, that is, the median of all our data points regardless of which population they are from. Then we divide each sample into two sets. One set contains all points that are greater than the grand median, and the second set contains all points in the sample that are less than or equal to the grand median. We construct a $2 \times c$ contingency table in which the cells in the top row contain the counts of all points above the median for all c samples. The second row contains cells with the counts of the data points in each sample that are less than or equal to the grand median. Then we conduct the usual chi-square analysis of the contingency table. If we reject H_0, then we may conclude that there is evidence that not all c population medians are equal. We now demonstrate the median test with Example 14–18.

EXAMPLE 14-18   An economist wants to test the null hypothesis that median family incomes in three rural areas are approximately equal. Random samples of family incomes in the three regions (in thousands of dollars per year) are given in Table 14–19.

TABLE 14-19   Family Incomes ($1,000s per year)

Region A	Region B	Region C
22	31	28
29	37	42
36	26	21
40	25	47
35	20	18
50	43	23
38	27	51
25	41	16
62	57	30
16	32	48

TABLE 14-20   Observed and Expected Counts for Example 14-18

	Region A	Region B	Region C	Total
Above grand median	4	5	6	15
	(5)	(5)	(5)	
Less than or equal to grand median	6	5	4	15
	(5)	(5)	(5)	
Total	10	10	10	30

SOLUTION

For simplicity, we chose an equal sample size of 10 in each population. This is not necessary; the sample sizes may be different. There is a total of 30 observations, and the median is therefore the average of the 15th and the 16th observations. Since the 15th observation (counting from smallest to largest) is 31, and the 16th is 32, the grand median is 31.5. Table 14–20 shows the counts of the sample points in each sample that are above the grand median and those that are less than or equal to the grand median. The table also shows the expected cell counts (in parentheses). Note that all expected counts are 5—the minimum required for the chi-square test. We now compute the value of the chi-square statistic.

$$X^2 = \frac{1}{5}[(4 - 5)^2 + (5 - 5)^2 + (6 - 5)^2 + (6 - 5)^2 + (5 - 5)^2 + (4 - 5)^2]$$

$$= \frac{4}{5} = 0.8$$

Comparing this value with critical points of the chi-square distribution with 2 degrees of freedom, we conclude that there is no evidence to reject the null hypothesis. The p-value is greater than 0.20.

Note that the median test is a weak test. Other tests could have resulted in the rejection of the null hypothesis (try them). We presented the test as an illustration of the wide variety of possible uses of the chi-square statistic. Other uses may be found in advanced books. We note that if the test had led to rejection, then other tests would probably have done so, too. Sometimes this test is easier to carry out and may lead to a quick answer (when we reject the null hypothesis).

PROBLEMS

14–72. An advertiser runs a commercial on national television and wants to determine whether the proportion of people exposed to the commercial is equal throughout the country. A random sample of 100 people is selected at each of five locations, and the number of people in each location who have seen the commercial at least once during the week is recorded. The numbers are as follows: location A, 32 people; location B, 59 people; location C, 78 people; location D, 40 people; and location E, 10 people. Do you believe that the proportion of people exposed to the commercial is equal across the five locations?

14–73. An accountant wants to test the hypothesis that the proportion of incorrect transactions at four client accounts is about the same. A random sample of 80 transactions of one client reveals that 21 are incorrect; for the second client, the sample proportion is 25 out of 100; for the third client, the proportion is 30 out of 90 sampled; and for the fourth, 40 are incorrect out of a sample of 110. Conduct the test at $\alpha = 0.05$.

14–74. An article in *The Wall Street Journal* raises the question of whether experienced fund managers are performing about the same as less experienced ones in the new bull market.[10] A sample of 128 fund managers with at least eight years of experience revealed that 54 of them beat the market, 43 of them did about as well as the market, and 31 did worse than the market. In a sample of 95 less experienced fund managers, 65 were found to beat the market, 21 did about the same as the market, and 9 did poorer than the market. Test the null hypothesis that experienced fund managers do as well as inexperienced ones versus the alternative that differences in performance exist between the two groups.

14–75. A quality-control engineer wants to test the null hypothesis that the proportion of defective components in three large shipments is approximately equal. A random sample of 100 components is selected from each shipment. The first sample reveals 25 defective items, the second has 15, and the third has 8. Conduct the test at $\alpha = 0.05$.

14–76. As markets become more and more international, many firms invest in research aimed at determining the maximum possible extent of sales in foreign markets. An American manufacturer of coffee makers wants to find out whether the company's market share and the market shares of two main competitors are about the same in three European countries to which all three companies export their products. The results of a market survey are summarized in the following table. The data are random samples of 150 consumers in each country. Conduct the test of equality of population proportions across the three countries.

	Country			
	France	England	Spain	Total
Company	55	38	24	117
First competitor	28	30	21	79
Second competitor	20	18	31	69
Other	47	64	74	185
Total	150	150	150	450

14–77. New production methods stressing teamwork have recently been instituted at car manufacturing plants in Detroit. Three teamwork production methods are to be compared to see if they are equally effective. Since large deviations often occur in the numbers produced daily, it is desired to test for equality of medians (rather than means). Samples of daily production volume for the three methods are as follows. Assume that these are random samples

---

[10] R. McGough, "Finding Thrills in Boring Index Funds," *The Wall Street Journal*, June 27, 1995, p.c1.

from the populations of daily production volume. Use the median test to help determine whether the three methods are equally effective.

Method A: 5, 7, 19, 8, 10, 16, 14, 9, 22, 4, 7, 8, 15, 18, 7

Method B: 8, 12, 15, 28, 5, 14, 19, 16, 23, 19, 25, 17, 20

Method C: 14, 28, 13, 10, 8, 29, 30, 26, 17, 13, 10, 31, 27, 20

14-12   Using the Computer

While many nonparametric tests are easy to carry out by hand, other tests, such as the chi-square tests, are more tedious, and a computer is very useful in carrying out the computations. Companies involved with research often use their own in-house computer programs for chi-square analysis (cross-tabs). The computer programs produce high-quality reports with values of the chi-square statistic and its associated *p*-value for every possible comparison of data attributes.

All commonly used computer packages have nonparametric capabilities. In this section, we will present examples of the use of MINITAB in nonparametric analysis. The MINITAB commands are very simple. Usually, all that is needed is to enter the data and specify the name of the nonparametric test required. We start with the runs test.

Figure 14–12 shows the results of a runs test carried out on a data set where the aim is to find whether runs of numbers above and below 30 indicate that the series of numbers is a random one. As seen in the output, the *p*-value is 0.0128. We may conclude (at levels of α greater than 0.0128) that the sequence probably does not represent a random process.

We now demonstrate the use of the Mann-Whitney test. Two sales techniques are tested, and the null hypothesis is that both techniques are equally effective. The alternative hypothesis is that the first method is more effective than the second (a right-tailed test). The MINITAB command is

```
MANN-WHITNEY (ALTERNATIVE=1) C1, C2
```

The data are in C1 and C2. The specification ALTERNATIVE=1 tells the program that the test is a right-tailed test for the location parameter (mean, median) of the population from which the C1 data came, minus that of the population from which the

FIGURE 14-12   A MINITAB-Computed Runs Test

```
C1
    21    13    14    53    44    37    49    11     3     6    16    36    55
    44    33    21    18    19    17    61    18    22    21    23    24    38
    34    35    31    28    26    44    16    33    32    27    21    12    34
    21    22    14    16    33    38    45    66    71    29    28    37    45

MTB > RUNS ABOVE AND BELOW 30, C1

    C1

    K =     30.0000

THE OBSERVED NO. OF RUNS =   18
THE EXPECTED NO. OF RUNS =   26.8462
24 OBSERVATIONS ABOVE K    28 BELOW
        THE TEST IS SIGNIFICANT AT   0.0128
```

FIGURE 14–13   MINITAB-Computed Mann-Whitney Test

```
MTB > PRINT C1, C2
 ROW   C1    C2
   1   35    26
   2   38    29
   3   44    18
   4   59    30
   5   27    28
   6   36    22
   7   37    21
   8   40    29
   9   38    19
  10   28    31
MTB > MANN-WHITNEY (ALTERNATIVE=1) C1, C2
Mann-Whitney Confidence Interval and Test

C1            N =  10      MEDIAN =      37.500
C2            N =  10      MEDIAN =      27.000
POINT ESTIMATE FOR ETA1-ETA2 IS      10.9992
95.5  PCT C.I. FOR ETA1-ETA2 IS (     7.0,      18.0)
W =     145.5
TEST OF ETA1 = ETA2 VS. ETA1 G.T. ETA2 IS SIGNIFICANT AT 0.0012
```

data in C2 came. ALTERNATIVE$=-1$ would indicate a left-tailed test, and the default (that is, no ALTERNATIVE statement) indicates a two-tailed test.

A list of the data, 10 points from each method (the data are *not* paired), as well as the output, are given in Figure 14–13. The words ETA1 and ETA2 are the MINITAB terms for the population parameters (mean or median) of populations 1 and 2, respectively. Note that a confidence interval for the difference between the parameters of the two populations is also provided. Throughout this chapter we have discussed only tests and not confidence intervals. We have done so because the most common applications of nonparametric methods are in the area of hypothesis testing. The computation of confidence intervals is also possible (recall the relationship between hypothesis tests and confidence intervals). The construction of confidence intervals, however, is often more difficult than in the parametric case and we have not emphasized them here.

We see that the test leads to rejection of the null hypothesis and the p-value is very small (0.0012). We conclude that there is statistical evidence that method 1 is more effective than method 2.

We now demonstrate the MINITAB solution to a problem using the Wilcoxon signed-rank test. Paired data are available constituting a random sample of ratings of two managers by 10 randomly chosen employees. Figure 14–14 shows the listing of the data entered into columns C1 and C2 and the output of the analysis. We need to ask the computer to subtract one column from the other; we are testing the null hypothesis that the median difference is zero versus the two-tailed alternative that it is not zero. As in the case of the Mann-Whitney test, an ALTERNATIVE= statement tells the computer to conduct a one-tailed test. For a two-tailed test, we leave out this command. The main command to perform the Wilcoxon signed-rank test is WTEST data in C3. (We put the difference between the columns C1 and C2 into C3 prior to this command.) The results of the test indicate that the p-value is 0.075, so we do not reject the null hypothesis that the median difference is zero (assuming we want to reject at levels of α less than or equal to 0.05).

FIGURE 14–14   MINITAB-Computed Wilcoxon Signed-Rank Test

```
ROW     C1     C2

  1     143    165
  2     124    170
  3     179    231
  4     166    154
  5     133    200
  6     167    169
  7     134    149
  8     104    111
  9     190    202
 10     121     98
 11     144    152

MTB > SUBTRACT C1 FROM C2, PUT IN C3
MTB > WTEST C3

TEST OF MEDIAN = 0.000000000 VERSUS MEDIAN N.E.   0.000000000

                   N FOR    WILCOXON              ESTIMATED
              N    TEST    STATISTIC   P-VALUE     MEDIAN
C3           11     11        53.5      0.075       14.75
```

For the Kruskal-Wallis test, data are entered into two columns, C1 and C2. In C1 we put the data elements; in C2 we put indicators: 1, 2, 3, and so on, denoting the population to which any given data point belongs. In the example shown in Figure 14–15, there are three samples to be analyzed, as evidenced by the indicators 1, 2, and 3 in column C2. The data have presumably been entered into the two columns prior to the analysis. The data represent random samples of mpg ratings for three types of high-performance V-8 engines. The null hypothesis is that the three engines have about the same mpg rating, and the alternative is that they do not.

The computed value of the Kruskal-Wallis statistic is $H = 14.52$ (14.72 when adjusted for ties). We compare this value with critical points of the chi-square distribution with $k - 1 = 3 - 1 = 2$ degrees of freedom. We conclude that there is evidence that the three engines do not have equal mpg ratings. The p-value is 0.001.

Computing rank correlation is simple in MINITAB. First, we replace values by their ranks. This is done by the commands:

```
RANK C1, put into C3
RANK C2, put into C4
```

(The RANK command may also be used in conjunction with other nonparametric methods requiring analysis of ranks rather than raw data.) Afterwards, we simply write the command

```
CORRELATION between C3 and C4
```

Recall that the Spearman coefficient is the correlation between the ranks of the observations. The result of the analysis is therefore the Spearman statistic, r_s.

An analysis of the rank correlation between two variables is shown in Figure 14–16. The result is $r_s = -0.236$. With $n = 10$ observations, we find from Appendix C, Table 11 that the critical points for r_s at $\alpha = 0.05$ are ± 0.564. Since

FIGURE 14–15   MINITAB-Computed Kruskal-Wallis Test

```
MTB > PRINT C1, C2
 ROW    C1   C2

   1    12    1
   2    14    1
   3    15    1
   4    12    1
   5    15    1
   6    17    1
   7    15    1
   8    17    1
   9    16    1
  10    18    2
  11    16    2
  12    17    2
  13    19    2
  14    18    2
  15    21    2
  16    20    2
  17    11    3
  18    12    3
  19    10    3
  20    12    3
  21    14    3

MTB > KRUSKAL WALLIS FOR DATA IN C1 SUBSCRIPTS IN C2

LEVEL      NOBS      MEDIAN   AVE. RANK     Z VALUE
    1         9       15.00        9.9       -0.71
    2         7       18.00       17.5        3.39
    3         5       12.00        3.9       -2.93
OVERALL      21                   11.0

H = 14.52           df = 2           p = 0.001
H = 14.72           df = 2           p = 0.001   (ADJ. FOR TIES)
```

FIGURE 14–16   MINITAB-Computed Rank Correlation

```
MTB > PRINT C1, C2
 ROW     C1   C2
   1     86   54
   2     89   59
   3     97   66
   4     54   20
   5     66   70
   6     49   57
   7     40   81
   8     69   90
   9     22   60
  10     39   95
MTB > RANK C1, PUT IN C3
MTB > RANK C2, PUT IN C4
MTB > CORRELATION BETWEEN C3 AND C4
Correlation of C3 and C4 = -0.236
```

FIGURE 14–17   MINITAB-Produced Contingency Table Analysis

```
MTB > CONTINGENCY TABLE ANALYSIS ON C1, C2

Expected counts are printed below observed counts

Rows C1   Columns C2
                1         2         3       Total
       3        4         0         0         4
              1.6       1.2       1.1

       4       10         2         9        21
              8.6       6.4       6.0

       5        6        13         5        24
              9.8       7.3       6.9
Total          20        15        14        49
ChiSq =     3.43 +    1.22 +    1.14 +
            0.24 +    3.05 +    1.50 +
            1.47 +    4.35 +    0.50 = 16.91

df = 4
3 cells with expected counts less than 5.0
```

$-0.236 > -0.564$, we accept the null hypothesis. The data do not present evidence of a nonzero rank correlation.

The use of MINITAB in chi-square analysis was demonstrated in section 14–10 (the output was shown in Figure 14–10). There we used the MINITAB command CHISQUARE analysis on C1, C2, . . . , Ck. The ith entry in column C_j was the *count* in cell (i, j). The same analysis could be done using the command TABLE and the subcommand CHISQUARE.

The MINITAB package automatically checks for the validity of the chi-square distribution assumption. The package will warn us every time it finds a cell with expected count less than 5.0; the output will list all such occurrences. The program uses a less stringent rule for the validity of the chi-square approximation—a rule due to Cochran that states that the approximation may be valid as long as none of the expected cell counts are less than 1.0 and no more than 20% of the expected counts are less than 5.0. This is demonstrated in Figure 14–17. The program will also list all cells with expected counts less than 1.0, and, if it finds such cells, will state that the chi-square approximation is probably not valid.

14–13   Summary and Review of Terms

This chapter was devoted to **nonparametric tests** (summarized in Table 14–21). Interpreted loosely, the term refers to statistical tests in situations where stringent assumptions about the populations of interest may not be warranted. Most notably, the very common assumption of a normal distribution—required for the parametric t and F tests—is not necessary for the application of nonparametric methods. The methods often use less of the information in the data and thus tend to be less powerful than parametric methods, when the assumptions of the parametric methods are met. The nonparametric methods include methods for handling categorical data, and here the analysis entails use of a limiting chi-square distribution for our test statistic. **Chi-square analysis** is often discussed separately from nonparametric methods, although the analysis is indeed "nonparametric," as it usually involves no specific reference to

TABLE 14–21   Summary of Nonparametric Tests

Situation	Nonparametric Test(s)	Corresponding Parametric Test
Single-sample test for location	Sign test Wilcoxon test (more powerful)	Single-sample t test
Goodness of fit	Chi-square test	
Randomness	Runs test	
Paired test for changes	McNemar test	
Paired-differences test	Sign test Wilcoxon test (more powerful)	Paired-data t test
Test for difference of two independent samples	Wald-Wolfowitz (weaker) Mann-Whitney (more powerful) Median test (weaker)	Two-sample t test
Test for difference of more than two independent samples	Kruskal-Wallis test Median test (weaker)	ANOVA
Test for difference of more than two samples, blocked	Friedman test	Randomized block-design ANOVA
Test for trend in single series	Cox and Stuart test	Time series tests
Correlation	Cox and Stuart test Spearman's statistic and test Chi-square test for independence	Pearson's product-moment
Equality of several population proportions	Chi-square test	

population *parameters* such as μ and σ. The other nonparametric methods (ones that require no assumptions about the distribution of the population) are often called *distribution-free* methods.

Besides chi-square analyses of **goodness of fit, independence,** and tests for **equality of proportions,** the methods we discussed included many based on **ranks.** These included a **rank correlation coefficient** due to Spearman; a test analogous to the parametric paired-sample t test—the **Wilcoxon signed-rank test;** a ranks-based ANOVA—the **Kruskal-Wallis test;** and a method for investigating two independent samples analogous to the parametric two-sample t test, called the **Mann-Whitney test.** We also discussed a test for randomness—the **runs test;** a paired-difference test called the **sign test,** which uses less information than the Wilcoxon signed-rank test; and several other methods.

ADDITIONAL PROBLEMS

14–78.   At the conclusion of the first episode of "Infiltrator," a message flashed onto the screen asking viewers to call one of two "800" phone numbers if they liked the program and to call the other number if they did not. The program's sponsor wanted to know if the program was likely to be equally popular in several regions of the country. Since at different regions different "800" numbers were used, counting the yes and no votes for the separate regions was relatively easy. Assume that the following results were presented to the sponsor, producer, and network executives the next day. What would be your recommendation as a hired statistician?

| | Region | | | | |
	Northeast	Midwest	Southwest	South	West
Yes	13,278	7,091	2,310	3,106	15,442
No	871	308	119	565	101

14–79. An article in *Business Week* discusses recent buyouts of companies and how some analysts are able to predict them.[11] If an analyst has been able to predict six successive buyouts, miss the next one, predict the next six, miss the next five, and predict the next three, is this analyst's performance random?

14–80. There are reports of increasing success of Hollywood movies in Europe. In Germany, 12 out of 70 theaters selected at random showed American-made movies; in France the number was 10 out of 65; and in Italy, 15 out of 100 movie theaters showed Hollywood movies. Test for equality of the proportion of theaters showing American-made movies in these three countries.

14–81. Jordan Furniture Store advertises on the radio. Before hiring the announcer for its ad, the store tested four different announcers. A random sample of 10 people was asked to rank the voice quality of the four announcers from best (1) to worst (4). The data are as follows.

Announcer			
A	**B**	**C**	**D**
1	3	2	4
3	4	2	1
4	2	1	3
3	1	2	4
1	2	4	3
3	1	2	4
3	2	4	1
2	3	4	1
3	4	1	2
4	2	3	1

   a. What is the appropriate test in this situation?

   b. Conduct the test. Are the voices of all four announcers equally well liked?

14–82. Follow the daily movements of a stock for three weeks and test for a trend up or down.

14–83. A random sample of 12 consumers ranked four brands of hair conditioner, labeled A, B, C, and D. The results follow.

A	**B**	**C**	**D**
2	1	3	4
1	4	3	2
2	1	4	3
1	3	4	2
1	2	4	3
1	3	2	4
1	3	4	2
2	1	4	3
3	1	4	2
1	3	2	4
2	3	1	4
1	2	4	3

Are there differences in the appeal of the four brands? Explain.

---

[11] G. Marcial, "Buyout Bait," *Business Week,* June 19, 1995, p. 116.

14–84.   Discuss the different measures of correlation, their use, the required assumptions, and their limitations.

14–85.   The following data are annual corporate revenues for the years 1983 to 1995 (data are in millions of dollars): 4.5, 4.1, 5.0, 4.4, 4.3, 3.9, 5.6, 5.8, 4.9, 6.0, 5.4, 4.8, 5.5. Is there evidence of a trend in the series of annual revenues? Explain.

14–86.   The following data are daily price quotations of two stocks.

Stock A: 12.50,   12.75,   12.50,   13.00,   13.25,   13.00,   13.50,   14.25,   14.00
Stock B: 35.25,   36.00,   37.25,   37.25,   36.50,   36.50,   36.00,   36.00,   36.25

Is there a correlation between the two stocks? Explain.

14–87.   The Hyatt Gold Passport® is a card designed to allow frequent guests at Hyatt hotels to enjoy privileges similar to the ones enjoyed by frequent air travelers. When the program was initiated, a random sample of 15 Hyatt Gold Passport members was asked to rate the program on a scale of 0 to 100 and also to rate (on the same scale) an airline frequent-flier card that all of them had. The results are as follows.

Hyatt card: 98, 99, 87, 56, 79, 89, 86, 90, 95, 99, 76, 88, 90, 95
Airline card: 84, 62, 90, 77, 80, 98, 65, 97, 58, 74, 80, 90, 85, 70

Is the Hyatt Gold Passport better liked than the airline frequent-flier card by holders of both cards? Explain.

14–88.   Two telecommunication systems are to be compared. A random sample of 14 users of one system independently rate the system on a scale of 0 to 100. An independent random sample of 12 users of the other system rate their system on the same scale. The data are as follows. System A: 65, 67, 83, 39, 45, 20, 95, 64, 99, 98, 76, 78, 82, 90. System B: 45, 57, 76, 54, 60, 72, 34, 50, 63, 39, 44, 70. Based on these data, are the two telecommunication systems equally liked? Explain.

14–89.   Refer to problem 14–88. Suppose that a third telecommunication system is to be compared with the two systems of problem 14–88. Ratings by a random sample of 13 users of the third system, on the same scale of 0 to 100, are as follows: 56, 58, 64, 59, 48, 49, 60, 75, 33, 72, 48, 51, 37. Are all three systems equally liked? Explain.

14–90.   Explain why you used the statistical methods you chose in problems 14–88 and 14–89. Compare your methods with the corresponding parametric methods, and discuss the relative advantages and disadvantages of the different methods.

14–91.   What is the distinction between *distribution-free* methods and *nonparametric* methods?

14–92.   The following data are salaries, in thousands of dollars per year, of a random sample of employees in a certain industry.

28.5,   29,   29.7,   31,   28,   32.5,   32.6,   33,   31.8,   37.4,   24.6,
38.1,   28.8,   30.1,   32.5,   34.4,   26.7,   28.1,   39.2,   40.3,   33.5,   33.8,
38.2,   23.0,   22.9,   29.9,   31.2,   33.0,   31.7,   37,   35,   32.1,   37,
29.9,   22,   23.8,   27,   35,   37.5,   40.1,   22.1,   26.3,   30.0,   40.1

Do you believe that salaries in this industry are normally distributed? Explain.

14–93.   In a chi-square analysis, the expected count in one of the cells is 2.1. Can you conduct the analysis? If not, what can be done?

EXHIBIT 1   The Nine Nations

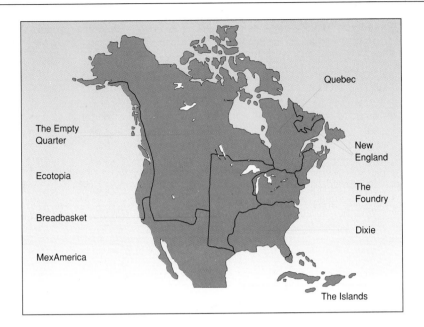

Case 14   THE NINE NATIONS OF NORTH AMERICA

In a fascinating article in the *Journal of Marketing* (April 1986), "The Nine Nations of North America and the Value Basis of Geographic Segmentation," Professor Lynn Kahle explores the possible marketing implications of Joel Garreau's idea of the nine nations.

Garreau traveled extensively throughout North America, studying people, customs, traditions, and ways of life. This research led Garreau to the conclusion that state boundaries or the census bureau's division of the United States into regions are not very indicative of the cultural and social boundaries that really exist on the continent. Instead, Garreau suggested in his best-selling book *The Nine Nations of North America* (New York: Avon, 1981) that the real boundaries divide the entire North American continent into nine separate, homogeneous regions, which he called "nations." Each nation, according to Garreau, is inhabited by people who share the same traditions, values, hopes, and world outlook and are different from the people of the other nations. The nine nations cross national boundaries of the United States, Canada, and the Caribbean. Garreau named his nations very descriptively, as follows: New England, Quebec, The Foundry, Dixie, The Islands, Empty Quarter, Breadbasket, MexAmerica, and Eco-

topia. Exhibit 1 shows the boundaries of these nations.

Geographic segmentation is a very important concept in marketing. Thus, Garreau's novel idea promised potential gains in marketing. Professor Kahle suggested a statistical test of whether or not Garreau's division of the country (without the nation of Quebec, which lies entirely outside the United States) could be found valid with respect to marketing-related values. Such a division could then replace currently used geographic segmentation methods.

Two currently used segmentation schemes studied by Kahle were the quadrants and the census bureau regions. Kahle used a random sample of 2,235 people across the country and collected responses pertaining to eight self-assessed personal attributes: self-respect, security, warm relationships with others, sense of accomplishment, self-fulfillment, being well respected, sense of belonging, and fun-enjoyment-excitement. Kahle showed that these self-assessment attributes were directly related to marketing variables. The attributes determine, for example, the magazines a person is likely to read and the television programs he or she is likely to watch.

Kahle's results, using the nine nations division (without Quebec), the quadrants division, and the

EXHIBIT 2   Distribution of Values across the Nine Nations

Values	New England	The Foundry	Dixie	The Islands	Bread-basket	Mex-America	Empty Quarter	Eco-topia	N
Self-respect	22.5%	20.5%	22.5%	25.0%	17.9%	22.7%	35.3%	18.0%	471
Security	21.7	19.6	23.3	15.6	20.2	17.3	17.6	19.6	461
Warm relationships with others	14.2	16.7	13.8	9.4	20.5	18.0	5.9	18.5	362
Sense of accomplishment	14.2	11.7	10.0	9.4	12.4	11.3	8.8	12.2	254
Self-fulfillment	9.2	9.9	8.4	3.1	7.5	16.0	5.9	12.7	214
Being well respected	8.3	8.7	11.0	15.6	10.1	2.7	2.9	4.2	196
Sense of belonging	5.0	8.4	7.5	12.5	7.8	6.7	17.6	7.9	177
Fun—enjoyment—excitement	5.0	4.5	3.5	9.4	3.6	5.3	5.9	6.9	100
Total	100.0	100.0	100.0	100.0	100.0	100.0	100.0	100.0	2.235
N	120	750	653	32	307	150	34	189	

EXHIBIT 3   Distribution of Values across Quadrants of the United States

Value	East	Midwest	South	West	N
Self-respect	19.7%	19.1%	23.4%	21.6%	471
Security	18.9	21.6	22.0	18.4	461
Warm relationships with others	16.0	17.8	14.5	17.1	362
Sense of accomplishment	13.2	12.5	9.2	11.4	254
Self-fulfillment	9.5	9.0	8.1	13.5	214
Being well respected	8.0	9.1	11.6	3.6	196
Sense of belonging	8.4	7.3	8.0	8.3	117
Fun—enjoyment—excitement	6.3	3.3	3.4	6.2	100
Total	100.0	100.0	100.0	100.0	2,235
N	476	634	740	385	

census division of the country, are presented in Exhibits 2 through 4. These tables are reprinted by permission from Kahle (1986). (Values reported in the exhibits are percentages.)

Carefully analyze the results presented in the exhibits. Is the nine nations segmentation a useful alternative to the quadrants or the census bureau divisions of the country? Explain.

EXHIBIT 4   **Distribution of Values Across Census Regions of the United States**

Values	New England	Middle Atlantic	South Atlantic	East South Central	East North Central	West North Central	West South Central	Mountain	Pacific	N
Self-respect	22.6%	18.6%	23.1%	23.4%	20.2%	16.7%	23.8%	29.2%	19.8%	471
Security	21.2	18.0	18.3	26.9	22.1	20.6	23.8	18.1	18.5	461
Warm relationships with others	13.9	16.8	15.7	11.4	16.0	21.6	14.9	15.3	17.6	362
Sense of accomplishment	13.9	13.0	10.7	9.6	11.4	14.7	6.8	8.3	12.1	254
Self-fulfillment	8.0	10.0	10.1	7.8	9.3	8.3	5.5	6.9	15.0	214
Being well respected	8.8	7.7	9.8	12.0	10.0	7.4	14.0	4.2	3.5	196
Sense of belonging	7.3	8.8	9.2	7.8	7.4	6.9	6.4	13.9	7.0	177
Fun—enjoyment—excitement	4.4	7.1	3.3	1.2	3.5	3.9	4.7	4.2	6.4	100
Total	100.0	100.0	100.0	100.0	100.0	100.0	100.0	100.0	100.0	2.235
N	137	339	338	167	430	204	235	72	313	

15

BAYESIAN STATISTICS AND DECISION ANALYSIS

1 5 – 1   I N T R O D U C T I O N

nly two hours after the polls closed in the Spanish general election on October 28, 1982, the statistician José M. Bernardo made a stunning prediction about the outcome of the election. Bernardo accurately forecast that the Spanish Socialist party would win a landslide victory and be returned to power for the first time since the Spanish Civil War in the late 1930s. Furthermore, Bernardo predicted (to within a fraction of 1%) the number of votes that each

Continued

political party would receive. He also estimated the number of seats (to within a single seat) that each party would hold in the new parliament. Bernardo made these amazing predictions hours before any other attempt was made to forecast the outcome of the election.

How did Bernardo do it? Instead of using the usual statistical approach to inference, an approach based solely on random sampling and usually referred to as the *classical* or *frequentist* approach, Bernardo chose to follow a different statistical philosophy. He chose to use the **Bayesian** approach.[1]

The Bayesian approach allows the statistician to use *prior information* about a particular problem, in addition to the information obtained from sampling. This approach is called *Bayesian* because the mathematical link between the probabilities associated with data results and the probabilities associated with the prior information is Bayes' theorem, which was introduced in Chapter 2. The theorem allows us to combine the prior information with the results of our sampling, giving us *posterior* (postsampling) information. A schematic comparison of the classical and the Bayesian approaches is shown in Figure 15–1.

In the case of the Spanish election, Bernardo used the results of the 1979 general election as his prior information. He used the 1979 results in identifying polling stations that seemed to be representative of the political behavior of Spanish voters as a whole and sampled from these stations. The undecided votes were distributed using information about proportions obtained in the 1979 election. The use of prior information led to more precise statistical conclusions than would have been obtained by pure random sampling. It is the *mixing* (using Bayes' theorem) of the prior information with sampling information from the 1982 election that gave Bernardo his stunningly precise conclusions.

The Bayesian philosophy does not necessarily lead to conclusions that are more accurate than those obtained by using the frequentist approach. If the prior information we have is accurate, then using it in conjunction with sample information leads to more accurate results than would be obtained without prior information. If, on the other hand, the prior information is inaccurate, then using it in conjunction with our sampling results leads to a worse outcome than would be obtained by using frequentist statistical inference. It is the very use of prior knowledge in a statistical analysis that often brings the entire Bayesian methodology under attack.

When prior information is a direct result of previous statistical surveys, or when prior information reflects no knowledge about the problem at hand (in which case the prior probabilities are called *noninformative*), the Bayesian analysis is purely objective, and few people would argue with its validity. Sometimes, however, the prior information reflects the personal opinions of the individual doing the analysis—or possibly those of an expert who has knowledge of the particular problem

---

[1] A description of Professor Bernardo's study may be found in his article: J. M. Bernardo, "Monitoring the 1982 Spanish Socialist Victory: A Bayesian Analysis," *Journal of the American Statistical Association* 79 (September 1984), pp. 510–15.

FIGURE 15-1   A Comparison of Bayesian and Classical Approaches

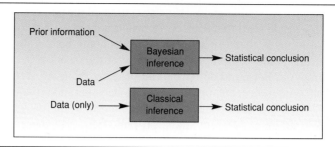

at hand. In such cases, where the prior information is of a subjective nature, one may criticize the results of the analysis.

One way to classify statisticians is according to whether they are Bayesian or non-Bayesian (i.e., frequentist). The Bayesian group used to be a minority, but in recent years its numbers have grown. Even though differences between the two groups exist, it can be shown that when noninformative prior probabilities are used, the Bayesian results parallel the frequentist statistical results. This fact lends credibility to the Bayesian approach. If we are careful with the use of any prior information, we may avoid criticism and produce good results via the Bayesian methodology. Bernardo, for example, used no subjective elements in his analysis of the Spanish election: his prior knowledge—his prior probabilities—all came from the known results of the 1979 election. There is, of course, the question: Why would one believe that any results obtained in 1979 should have any relevance to the 1982 election? We may assume that Bernardo's answer to this question was subjective. If indeed it were, he certainly made a good bet.

In the next two sections, we give some basic elements of *Bayesian statistics*. These sections extend the idea of Bayes' theorem, first to discrete random variables and then to continuous ones. Section 15–4 discusses some aspects of subjective probabilities and how they can be elicited from a person who has knowledge of the situation at hand.

There is another important area, not entirely in the realm of statistics, that makes use of Bayes' theorem as well as subjective probabilities. This is the area of **decision analysis.** Decision analysis is a methodology developed in the 1960s, and it quantifies the elements of a decision-making process in an effort to determine the optimal decision.

15–2   Bayes' Theorem and Discrete Probability Models

In section 2–7, we introduced Bayes' theorem. The theorem was presented in terms of *events*. The theorem was shown to transform *prior probabilities* of the occurrence of certain events into *posterior probabilities* of occurrence of the same events. Recall Example 2–10. In that example, we started with a prior probability that a randomly chosen person has a certain disease, given by $P(I) = 0.001$. Through the information that the person tested positive for the disease, and the reliability of the test, known to be $P(Z \mid I) = 0.92$ and $P(Z \mid \bar{I}) = 0.04$, we obtained through Bayes' theorem (equation 2–11) the posterior probability that the person was sick:

$$P(\text{I} \mid \text{Z}) = \frac{P(\text{Z} \mid \text{I})P(\text{I})}{P(\text{Z} \mid \text{I})P(\text{I}) + P(\text{Z} \mid \bar{\text{I}})P(\bar{\text{I}})} = 0.0225$$

The fact that the person had a positive reaction to the test may be considered our data. The conditional probabilities $P(\text{Z} \mid \text{I})$ and $P(\text{Z} \mid \bar{\text{I}})$ help incorporate the data information in the computation. We will now extend these probabilities to include more than just an event and its complement, as was done in this example, or one of three events, as was the case in Example 2–10. Our extension will cover a whole set of values and their prior probabilities. The *conditional* probabilities, when extended over the entire set of values of a random variable, are called the *likelihood function*.

> The **likelihood function** is the set of conditional probabilities $P(x \mid \theta)$ for given data x, considered a function of an unknown population parameter, θ.

Using the likelihood function and the prior probabilities $P(\theta)$ of the values of the parameter in question, we define Bayes' theorem for discrete random variables in the following form:

Bayes' theorem for a discrete random variable:

$$P(\theta \mid x) = \frac{P(x \mid \theta)P(\theta)}{\Sigma_i\, P(x \mid \theta_i)P(\theta_i)} \qquad (15\text{–}1)$$

where θ is an unknown population parameter to be estimated from the data. The summation in the denominator is over all possible values of the parameter of interest, θ_i, and x stands for our particular data set.

> In Bayesian statistics, we assume that population parameters such as the mean, the variance, or the population proportion are *random variables* rather than fixed (but unknown) quantities, as in the classical approach.

We assume that the parameter of interest is a random variable; thus, we may specify our prior information about the parameter as a **prior probability distribution** of the parameter. Then we obtain our data, and from them we get the likelihood function, that is, a measure of how likely we are to obtain our particular data, given different values of the parameter specified in the parameter's prior probability distribution. This information is transformed via Bayes' theorem, equation 15–1, to a **posterior probability distribution** of the value of the parameter in question. The posterior distribution includes the prior information as well as the data results. The posterior distribution can then be used in statistical inference. Such inference may include computing confidence intervals. Bayesian confidence intervals are often called **credible sets** of given posterior probability.

The following example illustrates the use of Bayes' theorem when the population parameter of interest is the population proportion, p.

EXAMPLE 15-1

TABLE 15-1
Prior Probabilities of Market Share, S

S	P(S)
0.1	0.05
0.2	0.15
0.3	0.20
0.4	0.30
0.5	0.20
0.6	0.10
	1.00

A market research analyst is interested in estimating the proportion of people in a certain area who use a product made by her client. That is, the analyst is interested in estimating her client's market share. The analyst denotes the parameter in question—the true (population) market share of her client—by S. From previous studies of a similar nature, and from other sources of information about the industry, the analyst constructs the following table of prior probabilities of the possible values of the market share, S. This is the analyst's prior probability distribution of S. It contains different values of the parameter in question and the analyst's degree of belief that the parameter is equal to any of the values, given as a probability. The prior probability distribution is presented in Table 15-1.

As seen from the prior probabilities table, the analyst does not believe that her client's market share could be above 0.6 (60% of the market). For example, she may know that a competitor controls 40% of the market, so values above 60% are impossible as her client's share. Similarly, she may know for certain that her client's market share is at least 10%. The assumption that S may equal one of six discrete values is a restrictive approximation. In the next section, we will explore a continuous space of values.

The analyst now gathers a random sample of 20 people and finds out that 4 out of the 20 in the sample do use her client's product. The analyst wishes to use Bayes' theorem to combine her prior distribution of market share with the data results to obtain a posterior distribution of market share. Recall that in the classical approach, all that can be used is the sample estimate of the market share, which is $\hat{p} = x/n = 4/20 = 0.2$ and may be used in the construction of a confidence interval or a hypothesis test.

SOLUTION

Using Bayes' theorem for discrete random variables (equation 15-1), the analyst updates her prior information to incorporate the data results. This is done in a tabular format and is shown in Table 15-2. As required by equation 15-1, the conditional probabilities $P(x \mid S)$ are evaluated. These conditional probabilities are our likelihood function. To evaluate these probabilities, we ask the following questions:

1. How likely are we to obtain the data results we have, that is, 4 successes out of 20 trials, if the probability of success in a single trial (the true *population proportion*) is equal to 0.1?

2. How likely are we to obtain the results we have if the population proportion is 0.2?

3. How likely are we to obtain these results when the population proportion is 0.3?

4. How likely are we to obtain these results when the population proportion is 0.4?

5. How likely are we to obtain these results when the population proportion is 0.5?

6. How likely are we to obtain these results when the population proportion is 0.6?

The answers to these six questions are obtained from a table of the binomial distribution (Appendix C, Table 1) and written in the appropriate places in the third column of Table 15-2. The fourth column is the product, for each value of S, of the prior probability of S and its likelihood. The sum of the entries in the fourth column is equal to the denominator in equation 15-1. When each entry in column 4 is divided by the sum of that

TABLE 15–2   **Prior Distribution, Likelihood, and Posterior Distribution of Market Share (Example 15–1)**

S	P(S)	P(x | S)	P(S)P(x | S)	P(S | x)
0.1	0.05	0.0898	0.00449	0.06007
0.2	0.15	0.2182	0.03273	0.43786
0.3	0.20	0.1304	0.02608	0.34890
0.4	0.30	0.0350	0.01050	0.14047
0.5	0.20	0.0046	0.00092	0.01230
0.6	0.10	0.0003	0.00003	0.00040
	1.00		0.07475	1.00000

FIGURE 15–2
Prior Distribution of Market Share (Example 15–1)

column, we get the posterior probabilities, which are written in column 5. This procedure corresponds to an application of equation 15–1 for each one of the possible values of the population proportion, S.

By comparing the values in column 2 of Table 15–2 with the values in column 5, we see how the prior probabilities of different possible market share values changed by the incorporation, via Bayes' theorem, of the information in the data (i.e., the fact that 4 people in a sample of 20 were found to be product users). The influence of the prior beliefs about the actual market share is evident in the posterior distribution. This is illustrated in Figure 15–2, which shows the prior probability distribution of S, and Figure 15–3, which shows the posterior probability distribution of S.

As the two figures show, starting with a prior distribution that is spread in a somewhat symmetric fashion over the six possible values of S, we end up, after the incorporation of data results, with a posterior distribution that is concentrated over the three values 0.2, 0.3, and 0.4, with the remaining values having small probabilities. The total posterior probability of the three values 0.2, 0.3, and 0.4 is equal to 0.92723 (from summing Table 15–2 entries). The three adjacent values are thus a set of highest posterior probability and can be taken as a credible set of values for S with posterior probability close to the standard 95% confidence level. Recall that with discrete random variables, it is hard to get values corresponding to exact, prespecified levels such as 95%, and we are fortunate in this case to be close to 95%. We may state as our conclusion that we are about 93% confident that the market share is anywhere between 0.2 and 0.4. Our result is a Bayesian conclusion, which may be stated in terms of a probability; it includes both the data results and our prior information. (As a comparison, compute an approximate classical confidence interval based on the sampling result.)

FIGURE 15–3
Posterior Distribution of Market Share (Example 15–1)

One of the great advantages of the Bayesian approach is the possibility of carrying out the analysis in a sequential fashion. Information obtained from one sampling study can be used as the prior information set when new information becomes available. The second survey results are considered the data set, and the two sources are combined by use of Bayes' theorem. The resulting posterior distribution may then be used as the prior distribution when new data become available, and so on.

We now illustrate the sequential property by continuing Example 15–1. Suppose that the analyst is able to obtain a *second* sample after her analysis of the first sample is completed. She obtains a sample of 16 people and finds that there are 3 users of the product of interest in this sample. The analyst now wants to combine this new sampling information with what she already knows about the market share. To do this, the analyst considers her last posterior distribution, from column 5 of Table 15–2, as her new prior distribution when the new data come in. Note that the last posterior distribution contains *all* of the analyst's information about market share before the incorporation of the new data, because it includes both her prior information and the results of the first sampling. Table 15–3 shows how this information is transformed into a new posterior probability distribution by incorporating the new sample results. The likelihood function is again obtained by consulting Appendix C, Table 1. We look for the binomial probabilities of obtaining 3 successes of 16 trials, using the given values of $S(0.1, 0.2, \ldots, 0.6)$, each in turn taken as the binomial parameter, p.

The new posterior distribution of S is shown in Figure 15–4. Note that the highest posterior probability after the second sampling is given to the value $S = 0.2$, the posterior probability being 0.6191. With every additional sampling, the posterior distribution will get more peaked at values indicated by the data. The posterior distribution keeps moving toward data-derived results, and the effects of the prior distribution become less and less important. This fact becomes clear as we compare the distributions shown in Figures 15–2, 15–3, and 15–4. This property of Bayesian analysis is reassuring. It allows the data to speak for themselves, thus moving away from prior beliefs if these beliefs are away from reality. In the presence of limited data, Bayesian analysis allows us to compensate for the small data set by allowing us to use previous information—obtained either by prior sampling or by other means.

Incidentally, what would have happened if our analyst had decided to combine the results of the two surveys before considering them in conjunction with her prior information? That is, what would have happened if the analyst had decided to consider the two samples as one, where the total number of trials is $20 + 16 = 36$ and the total number of successes is $4 + 3 = 7$ users? Surprisingly, the posterior probability distribution for the combined sample incorporated with the prior distribution would have been exactly the same as the posterior distribution presented in Table 15–3. This fact demonstrates how well the Bayesian approach handles successive pieces of information. It does not matter when or how information is incorporated in the model—the posterior distribution will contain *all* information available at any given time.

In the next section, we discuss Bayesian statistics in the context of continuous probability distributions. In particular, we develop the normal probability model for Bayesian analysis. As will be seen in the next section, the normal distribution is particularly amenable to Bayesian analysis. If our prior distribution is normal and the likelihood function is normal, then the posterior distribution is also normal. We will

FIGURE 15–4
Second Posterior Distribution of Market Share

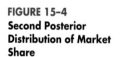

TABLE 15–3   Prior Distribution, Likelihood, and Posterior Distribution of Market Share for Second Sampling

S	$P(S)$	$P(x \mid S)$	$P(S)P(x \mid S)$	$P(S \mid x)$
0.1	0.06007	0.1423	0.0085480	0.049074
0.2	0.43786	0.2463	0.1078449	0.619138
0.3	0.34890	0.1465	0.0511138	0.293444
0.4	0.14047	0.0468	0.0065740	0.037741
0.5	0.01230	0.0085	0.0001046	0.000601
0.6	0.00040	0.0008	0.0000003	0.000002
	1.00000		0.1741856	1.000000

develop two simple formulas: one for the posterior mean and one for the posterior variance (and standard deviation) in terms of the prior distribution parameters and the likelihood function.

PROBLEMS

15–1. In 1995, the Wells Fargo Bank of San Francisco launched a special credit card. The card was designed to reward people who pay their bills on time by allowing them to pay a lower-than-usual interest rate. Some research went into designing the new program. The director of the bank's regular credit card systems was consulted, and she gave her prior probability distribution of the proportion of cardholders who would qualify for the new program. Then a random sample of 20 cardholders was selected and traced over several months. It was found that 6 of them paid all their credit card bills on time. Using this information and the information in the following table—the director's prior distribution of the proportion of all cardholders who pay their bills on time—construct the posterior probability distribution for this parameter. Also give a credible set of highest posterior probability close to 95% for the parameter in question. Plot both the prior and the posterior distributions of the parameter.

Proportion	Probability
0.1	0.2
0.2	0.3
0.3	0.1
0.4	0.1
0.5	0.1
0.6	0.1
0.7	0.1

15–2. In the situation of problem 15–1, suppose that a second random sample of cardholders was selected, and it was found that 7 out of the 17 people in the sample paid their bills on time. Construct the new posterior distribution containing information from the prior distribution and both samplings. Again, give a credible set of highest posterior probability close to 95%, and plot the posterior distribution.

15–3. For Example 15.1 suppose that a third sample is obtained. Three out of 10 people in the sample are product users. Update the probabilities of market share after the third sampling, and produce the new posterior distribution.

15–4. The company that markets the Yugoslav car Yugo in the United States needed to estimate the proportion of the market that the car would capture once it was introduced. Based on experience with Korean, French, and other foreign cars marketed in the country, one of the company's executives gave his prior probability distribution of the proportion of the foreign-car market that would go to Yugo. The prior probability distribution of this proportion (M = market share) is as follows.

M	$P(M)$
0.05	0.3
0.15	0.5
0.20	0.1
0.25	0.1

A random sample of 18 potential buyers of new foreign cars revealed that one of them would buy a Yugo. Compute the posterior probability distribution of M.

15–5.   Recent years have seen a sharp decline in the Alaska king crab fishery. One problem identified as a potential cause of the decline has been the prevalence of a deadly parasite believed to infect a large proportion of the adult king crab population. A fisheries management agency monitoring crab catches needed to estimate the proportion of the adult crab population infected by the parasite. The agency's biologists constructed the following prior probability distribution for the proportion of infected adult crabs (denoted by R).

R	$P(R)$
0.25	0.1
0.30	0.2
0.35	0.2
0.40	0.3
0.45	0.1
0.50	0.1

A random sample of 10 adult king crabs was collected, and it was found that 3 of them were infected with the parasite. Construct the posterior probability distribution of the proportion of infected adult crabs, and plot it.

15–6.   Continuing problem 15–5, a second random sample of 12 adult crabs was collected, and it revealed that 4 individual crabs had been infected. Revise your probability distribution, and plot it. Give a credible set of highest posterior probability close to 95%.

15–7.   For problem 15–5, suppose the biologists believed the proportion of infected crabs in the population was equally likely to be anywhere from 10% to 90%. Using the discrete points 0.1, 0.2, etc., construct a uniform prior distribution for the proportion of infected crabs, and compute the posterior distribution after the results of the sampling in problem 15–5.

15–8.   An airline is interested in the proportion of flights that are full during a given season. The airline uses data from past experience and constructs the following prior distribution of the proportion of flights that are full to capacity.

S	$P(S)$
0.70	0.1
0.75	0.2
0.80	0.3
0.85	0.2
0.90	0.1
0.95	0.1
	1.0

A sample of 20 flights shows that 17 of these flights are full. Update the probability distribution to obtain a posterior distribution for the proportion of full flights.

15–9.   In the situation of problem 15–8, another sample of 20 flights reveals that 18 of them are full. Obtain the second posterior distribution of the proportion of full flights. Graph the prior distribution of problem 15–8, as well as the first posterior and the second posterior distributions. How did the distribution of the proportion in question change as more information became available?

15–10.   A quality-control engineer has the following prior probability distribution for the proportion of defective items in a production process.

x	$P(x)$
0.05	0.1
0.10	0.2
0.15	0.4
0.20	0.2
0.25	0.1
	1.0

The engineer collects a random sample of 15 items and finds that 2 are defective. Compute the posterior distribution for the proportion of defective items, and give a credible set for the population proportion of defective items with posterior probability close to 95%.

15-3 Bayes' Theorem and Continuous Probability Distributions

We will now extend the results of the preceding section to the case of continuous probability models. Recall that a continuous random variable has a probability density function, denoted by $f(x)$. The function $f(x)$ is nonnegative, and the total area under the curve of $f(x)$ must equal 1.00. Recall that the probability of an event is defined as the area under the curve of $f(x)$ over the interval or intervals corresponding to the event.

> We define $f(\theta)$ as the **prior probability density** of the parameter θ. We define $f(x \mid \theta)$ as the conditional density of the data x, given the value of θ. This is the likelihood function.

The **joint density** of θ and x is obtained as the product:

$$f(\theta, x) = f(x \mid \theta) f(\theta) \qquad (15\text{-}2)$$

Using these functions, we may now write Bayes' theorem for continuous probability distributions. The theorem gives us the **posterior density** of the parameter θ, *given* the data x.

Bayes' theorem for continuous distributions:[2]

$$f(\theta \mid x) = \frac{f(x \mid \theta) f(\theta)}{\text{Total area under } f(\theta, x)} \qquad (15\text{-}3)$$

Equation 15–3 is the analog for continuous random variables of equation 15–1. We may use the equation for updating a prior probability density function of a parameter θ once data, x, are available. In general, computing the posterior density is a complicated operation. However, in the case of a normal prior distribution and a normal data-generating process (or large samples, leading to central-limit conditions), the posterior distribution is also a normal distribution. The parameters of the posterior distribution are easy to calculate, as will be shown next.

The Normal Probability Model

Suppose that you want to estimate the population mean, μ, of a normal population that has a *known* standard deviation, σ. Also suppose that you have some prior beliefs about the populaton in question. Namely, you view the population mean as a random variable with a normal (prior) distribution with mean M' and standard deviation σ'.

If you draw a random sample of size n from the normal population in question and obtain a sample mean M, then the posterior distribution for the population mean, μ,

---

[2] For the reader with knowledge of calculus, we note that Bayes' theorem is written as $f(\theta \mid x) = f(x \mid \theta) f(\theta)/[\int_{-\infty}^{\infty} f(x \mid \theta) f(\theta) d\theta]$.

is a *normal distribution with mean M″ and standard deviation σ″* obtained, respectively, from equations 15–4 and 15–5.

The posterior mean and variance of the normal distribution of the population mean, μ:

$$M'' = \frac{(1/\sigma'^2)M' + (n/\sigma^2)M}{(1/\sigma'^2) + (n/\sigma^2)} \qquad (15–4)$$

$$\sigma''^2 = \frac{1}{(1/\sigma'^2) + (n/\sigma^2)} \qquad (15–5)$$

The two equations are very useful in many applications. We are fortunate that the normal distribution family is *closed*, that is, when the prior distribution of a parameter is normal and the population (or process) is normal, the posterior distribution of the parameter in question is also normal. Be sure that you understand the distinction among the various quantities involved in the computations—especially the distinction between σ^2 and σ'^2. The quantity σ^2 is the variance of the population, and σ'^2 is the prior variance of the population mean, μ. We demonstrate the methodology with Example 15–2.

EXAMPLE 15-2

A stockbroker is interested in the return on investment for a particular stock. Since Bayesian analysis is especially suited for the incorporation of opinion or prior knowledge with data, the stockbroker wishes to use a Bayesian model. The stockbroker quantifies his beliefs about the *average return* on the stock by a normal probability distribution with mean 15 (percent return per year) and a standard deviation of 8. Since it is relatively large, as compared with the mean, the stockbroker's prior standard deviation of μ reflects a state of relatively little prior knowledge about the stock in question. However, the prior distribution allows the broker to incorporate in the analysis some of his limited knowledge about the stock. The broker collects a sample of 10 monthly observations on the stock and computes the annualized average percentage return. He gets a mean $M = 11.54$ (percent) and a standard deviation $s = 6.8$. Assuming that the population standard deviation is equal to 6.8 and that returns are normally distributed, what is the posterior distribution of average stock returns?

SOLUTION

We know that the posterior distribution is normal, with mean and variance given by equations 15–4 and 15–5, respectively. We have

$$M'' = \frac{(1/64)15 + (10/46.24)11.54}{(1/64) + (10/46.24)} = 11.77$$

$$\sigma'' = \sqrt{\frac{1}{(1/64) + (10/46.24)}} = 2.077$$

Note how simple it is to update probabilities when one starts with a normal prior distribution, and a normal population. Incidentally, the assumption of a normal population is very appropriate in our case, as the theory of finance demonstrates that stock returns are well approximated by the normal curve. If the population standard deviation is unknown, the sample standard deviation provides a reasonable estimate.

FIGURE 15–5   **Prior Distribution, Likelihood Function, and Posterior Distribution of Average Return, μ (Example 15–2)**

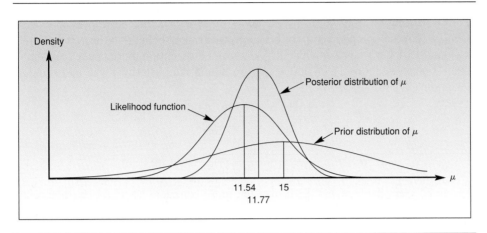

Figure 15–5 shows the stockbroker's prior distribution, the normal likelihood function (normalized to have a unit area), and the posterior density of the average return on the stock of interest. Note that the prior distribution is relatively flat—this is due to the relatively large standard deviation. The standard deviation is a measure of uncertainty, and here it reflects the fact that the broker does not know much about the stock. Prior distributions such as the one used here are called **diffuse priors.** They convey little a priori knowledge about the process in question. A relatively flat prior normal distribution conveys some information but lets the data tell us more.

Credible Sets

Unlike the discrete case, it is possible in the continuous case to construct credible sets for parameters with an exact, prespecified probability level. These are easy to construct. In Example 15–2, the stockbroker may construct a 95% highest-posterior-density (HPD) credible set for the average return on the stock directly from the posterior density. The posterior distribution is normal, with mean 11.77 and standard deviation 2.077. Therefore, the 95% HPD credible set for μ is simply

$$M'' \pm 1.96 \; \sigma'' = 11.77 \pm 1.96(2.077)$$
$$= [7.699, 15.841]$$

Thus, the stockbroker may conclude there is a 0.95 probability that the average return on the stock is anywhere from 7.699% to 15.841% per year.

Recall that in the classical approach, we would have to rely only on the data and not be able to use prior knowledge. As a conclusion, we would have to say: "Ninety-five percent of the intervals constructed in this manner will contain the parameter of interest." In the Bayesian approach, we are free to make *probability* statements as conclusions. Incidentally, the idea of attaching a probability to a result extends to the Bayesian way of testing hypotheses. A Bayesian statistician can give a posterior probability to the null hypothesis. Contrast this with the classical *p*-value, as defined in Chapter 7.

Suppose the stockbroker believed differently. Suppose that he believed that returns on the stock had a mean of 15 and a standard deviation of 4. In this case, the broker admits less uncertainty in his knowledge about average stock returns. The sampling results are the same, so the likelihood is unchanged. However, the posterior distribution does change as it now incorporates the data (through the likelihood) with a prior distribution that is not diffuse, as in the last case, but more peaked over its mean of 15. In our present case, the broker has a stronger belief that the average return is around 15% per year, as indicated by a normal distribution more peaked around its mean. Using equations 15–4 and 15–5, we obtain the posterior mean and standard deviation:

$$M'' = \frac{(1/16)15 + (10/46.24)11.54}{(1/16) + (10/46.24)} = 12.32$$

$$\sigma'' = \sqrt{\frac{1}{(1/16) + (10/46.24)}} = 1.89$$

As can be seen, the fact that the broker felt more confident about the average return being around 15% (as manifested by the smaller standard deviation of his prior probability distribution) caused the posterior mean to be closer to 15% than it was when the same data were used with a more diffuse prior (the new mean is 12.32, compared with 11.77, obtained earlier). The prior distribution, the likelihood function, and the posterior distribution of the mean return on the stock are shown in Figure 15–6. Compare this figure with Figure 15–5, which corresponds to the earlier case with a more diffuse prior.

PROBLEMS

15–11.   The partner-manager of a franchise of Au Bon Pain, Inc., the French bakery-restaurant chain, believes that the *average* daily revenue of her business may be viewed as a random variable (she adheres to the Bayesian philosophy) with mean $8,500 and standard deviation $1,000. Her prior probability distribution of average daily revenue is normal. A random sample of 35 days reveals a mean daily revenue of $9,210 and a standard deviation of $365. Construct the posterior distribution of average daily revenue. Assume a normal distribution of daily revenues.

15–12.   Video Dog™ is an ingenious invention. It allows you to enjoy the pleasures of owning a pet without having to feed it, take it for walks, or worry about fleas and ticks. Before marketing the idea, the manufacturer wanted to estimate average monthly sales that would

FIGURE 15–6   Prior Distribution, Likelihood Function, and Posterior Distribution of Average Return Using a More Peaked Prior Distribution

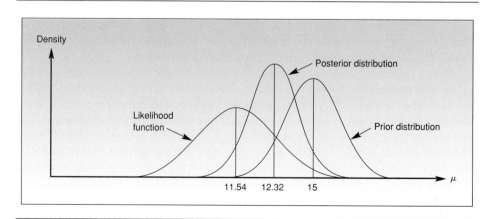

result in an area with a given population. From experience with similar products (probably the Pet Rock), the manufacturer assessed a normal prior probability distribution for average monthly sales in the area, with mean 15,000 and standard deviation 4,000. A random sample of 12 monthly sales in an area of about the same population and in the same geographical region gave a mean of 9,867 and a standard deviation of 1,055. Give a 95% highest-posterior-density credible set for the average monthly sales the manufacturer may expect in a region of the given size. Assume sales are normally distributed.

15–13.   Mr. Claude Vrinat, owner of Taillevent—one of Europe's most highly acclaimed restaurants—is reported to regularly sample the tastes of his patrons.[3] From experience, Vrinat believes that the average rating (on a scale of 0 to 100) that his clients give his *foie gras de canard* may be viewed as normally distributed with mean 94 and standard deviation 2. A random sample of 10 diners gives an average rating of 96 and standard deviation of 1. What should be Vrinat's posterior distribution of average rating of *foie gras de canard*, assuming ratings are normally distributed?

15–14.   In the context of problem 15–13, a second random sample of 15 diners is asked to rate the *foie gras*, giving a mean rating of 95 and standard deviation of 1. Incorporate the new information to give a posterior distribution that accounts for both samplings and the prior distribution. Give a 95% HPD credible set for mean rating.

15–15.   The operator of a film developing business believes that the average time it takes to develop a roll of film of a particular type is uncertain and may be described by a normal distribution with mean 22 minutes and standard deviation 2 minutes. Using this information as the prior distribution, and the fact that a random sample of 14 rolls had an average development time of 24 minutes per roll and a standard deviation of 3 minutes, construct the posterior distribution of average development time. Assume normality.

15–16.   Continuing problem 15–15, a second random sample of 20 rolls of film gave a mean development time of 25 minutes and a standard deviation of 2 minutes. Construct the second posterior distribution, and use it in constructing a 99% HPD credible set for average development time.

15–17.   In an effort to predict Alaska's oil-related state revenues, a delphi session is regularly held where experts in the field give their expectations of the average future price of crude oil over the next year. The views of five prominent experts who participated in the last delphi session may be stated as normal prior distributions with means and standard deviations given in the following table. To protect their identities (the delphi sessions are closed to the public), we will denote them by the letters A through E. Data are in dollars per barrel.

Expert	Mean	Standard Deviation
A	23	4
B	19	7
C	25	1
D	20	9
E	27	3

Compare the views of the five experts using this information. What can you say about the different experts' degrees of belief in their own respective knowledge? One of the experts is the governor of Alaska, who, due to the nature of his post, devotes little time to following oil prices. All other experts have varying degrees of experience with price analysis; one of them is the ARCO expert who assesses oil prices on a daily basis. Looking only at the reported prior standard deviations, who is likely to be the governor, and who is likely to be the ARCO expert? Now suppose that at the end of the year it was found that the average daily price of crude oil was $18 per barrel. Who should be most surprised (and embarrassed), and why?

---

[3] Patricia Wells, "Three-Star Galaxy," in *Beloved Cities: Europe*, ed. A. Rosenthal and A. Gelb (New York: Viking Penguin, 1985), pp. 240–55.

15-4   The Evaluation of Subjective Probabilities

Since Bayesian analysis makes extensive use of people's subjective beliefs in the form of prior probabilities, it is only natural that the field should include methods for the elicitation of personal probabilities. We begin by presenting some simple ideas on how to identify a normal prior probability distribution and give a rough estimate of its mean and standard deviation. Then we present the de Finetti game, which is a useful tool for calibrating one's personal probability of occurrence of an event. We also give an interactive computer program that can be used for this purpose.

Assessing a Normal Prior Distribution

As you well know by now, the normal probability model is useful in a wide variety of applications. Furthermore, since we know probabilities associated with the normal distribution, results can easily be obtained if we do make the assumption of normality. How can we estimate a decision maker's subjective normal probability distribution? For example, how did the stockbroker of Example 15–2 decide that his prior distribution of average returns was normal with mean 15 and standard deviation 8?

The normal distribution appears naturally and as an approximation in many situations due to the central limit theorem. Therefore, in many instances, it makes sense to assume a normal distribution. In other cases, it frequently happens that we have a distribution that is not normal but still is *symmetric* with a *single mode*. In such cases, it may still make sense to assume a normal distribution as an approximation because this distribution is easily estimated as a subjective distribution, and the resulting inaccuracies will not be great. In cases where the distribution is *skewed*, however, the normal approximation will not be adequate.

Once we determine that the normal distribution is appropriate for describing our personal beliefs about the situation at hand, we need to estimate the mean and the standard deviation of the distribution. For a symmetric distribution with one mode, the mean is equal to the median and to the mode. Therefore, we may ask the decision maker whose subjective probability we are trying to assess what he or she believes to be the center of the distribution. We may also ask for the most likely value. We may ask for the average, or we may ask for the point that splits the distribution into two equal parts. All of these questions would lead us to the central value, which we take to be the mean of the subjective distribution. It is useful to ask the person whose probabilities we are trying to elicit several of these questions, so that we have a few checks on the answer. Any discrepancies in the answers may lead to possible violations of our assumption of the symmetry of the distribution or its unimodality (having only one mode), which would obviate the normal approximation. Presumably, questions such as these lead the stockbroker of Example 15–2 to determine that the mean of his prior distribution for average returns is 15%.

How do we estimate the standard deviation of a subjective distribution? Recall the simple rules of thumb for the normal probability model:

> Approximately 68% of the distribution lies within one standard deviation of the mean.

> Approximately 95% of the distribution lies within two standard deviations of the mean.

These rules lead us to the following questions for the decision maker whose probabilities we are trying to assess: "Give me two values of the distribution in question such that you are 95% sure that the variable in question is between the two values," or equivalently, "give me two values such that 95% of the distribution lies between them." We may also ask for two values such that 68% of the distribution is between these values.

For 95% sureness, assuming symmetry, we know that the two values we obtain as answers are each two standard deviations away from the mean. In the case of the stockbroker, he must have felt there was a 0.95 chance that the average return on the stock was anywhere from -1% to 31%. The two points, -1 and 31, are 2×8 units on either side of the mean, 15. Hence, the standard deviation is 8. The stockbroker could also have said that he was 68% sure that the average return was anywhere from 7% to 23% (each of these two values is one standard deviation away from the mean, 15). Using 95% bounds is more useful than 68% limits because people are more likely to think in terms of 95% sureness. Be sure you understand the difference between this method of obtaining bounds on values of a population (or random variable) and the construction of confidence intervals (or credible sets) for population *parameters*.

The de Finetti Game

One of the most active statisticians in the area of subjective probability was the late Italian statistician Bruno de Finetti. De Finetti embarked on a thorough investigation of the way people perceive probability and obtained some profound results in this area as early as 1937. In later years he developed a game that he played with his students at the University of Rome. In this game, each student stated his or her estimated probability that a given soccer team would win the game to be played on the coming weekend. Each student was then asked a series of questions designed to gauge the probability that the team in question would win, against a certain lottery with known probabilities. This game led to a more precise assessment of the probability of the event in question. Most people playing this game find that the probabilities they state initially for an event are changed by the end of the game. This gives the player a better feel for what his or her true beliefs are with regard to the event in question. The game proceeds as follows.

As an example, let us take the event that a particular presidential candidate will win the election; you must state what you think are the candidate's chances. Suppose you say that the chances are 0.40. We then present you with the following choices. (1) "There is a bag that contains 50 red balls and 50 black balls. If you choose to do so, you may reach inside the bag and pick a ball at random. If the ball turns out to be red, then we will give you one million dollars! (2) On the other hand, you may choose not to draw a ball out of the bag. Instead we will wait until after the presidential election in November, and if your candidate wins you will get one million dollars. You must state now if you choose to draw a ball or await the outcome of the election (you cannot do both)."

Suppose your answer is that you will wait until the election and collect your million dollars if the candidate wins. We would then present you with the following choice. "The bag now contains 60 red balls and 40 black ones. If you draw a red ball, you will win one million dollars as before. You must choose whether to draw a ball now or wait until the election results are known." Suppose that you think about this and decide to draw a ball out of the bag. The next question will be: "There are now 55 red balls in the bag and 45 black ones. Will you draw now or wait until November?" Suppose you now say that you will wait until the election; the next question will then be: "There are 57 red balls and 43 black ones. Will you draw or wait?" Suppose that you say that you will draw. If you draw when there are 57 red balls in the bag and wait when there are 55 red balls, then the last question is: "What will you do if there are 56 red balls in the bag?" Suppose you say that you are indifferent at this point. This means that you actually believe that the probability that the candidate will win the election is 0.56. Here the weighing of the probability of a win against an objective lottery with an exact, known probability of success revealed that you really feel that the probability of success of the candidate in question is 0.56, which is a change from your originally stated probability of 0.40. As mentioned earlier, most people do change their stated probabilities during the course of the game. The game allows you to gauge your probability against a precisely measured analog: the hypothetical lottery.

Figure 15–7 shows sample output of a run of an interactive program written in the BASIC language for playing the de Finetti game of eliciting personal probabilities. It should be noted that our version of the game is not the most sophisticated or accurate one possible. Our program does not check for *consistency* by checking probabilities of the complement of the event in question. Additional checks would

FIGURE 15-7   Sample Computer Output of the de Finetti Game

```
HELLO!
LET US ASSESS THE PROBABILITY OF AN EVENT OF INTEREST TO YOU. IMAGINE
THAT I HAVE AN URN CONTAINING 100 BALLS. THERE ARE AS MANY RED BALLS
AS INDICATED BELOW, AND THE REST OF THEM ARE BLACK. NOW, IF YOU DRAW A
RED BALL FROM THE URN, I WILL GIVE YOU ONE MILLION DOLLARS!!! ON THE
OTHER HAND, IF YOU WAIT FOR THE EVENT OF INTEREST TO OCCUR, THEN I
WILL GIVE YOU ONE MILLION DOLLARS IF IT DOES INDEED OCCUR. HOWEVER,
YOU MUST MAKE THE DECISION NOW AS TO WHETHER TO DRAW A BALL, OR TO
WAIT TO SEE IF THE EVENT WILL OCCUR AND COLLECT THE MONEY IF IT DOES.
YOU CANNOT DO BOTH, DEPENDING ON THE COMPOSITION OF THE URN AT EACH
STAGE, TYPE A 'D' FOR DRAW, OR A 'W' FOR WAIT OR AN 'I' IF YOU ARE
INDIFFERENT AT THAT PARTICULAR POINT
THERE ARE      50
RED BALLS IN THE URN
WAIT, DRAW, OR INDIFFERENT? W
THERE ARE      75
RED BALLS IN THE URN
WAIT, DRAW, OR INDIFFERENT? W
THERE ARE      87
RED BALLS IN THE URN
WAIT, DRAW, OR INDIFFERENT? D
THERE ARE      81
RED BALLS IN THE URN
WAIT, DRAW, OR INDIFFERENT? D
THERE ARE      78
RED BALLS IN THE URN
WAIT, DRAW, OR INDIFFERENT? D
THERE ARE      76
RED BALLS IN THE URN
WAIT, DRAW, OR INDIFFERENT? W
THERE ARE      77
RED BALLS IN THE URN
WAIT, DRAW, OR INDIFFERENT? W
THERE ARE      77
RED BALLS IN THE URN
THE PROBABILITY OF YOUR EVENT IS
 77        PERCENT
PLAY ANOTHER ONE?
```

complicate our game somewhat. The interested reader is referred to Bruno de Finetti's book *Probability, Induction, and Statistics* (New York: John Wiley & Sons, Inc, 1972).

PROBLEMS

15–18. Choose an event of interest to you, and play the de Finetti game to quantify your degree of belief in the occurrence of the event.

15–19. In answering your questions as you try to elicit a personal probability distribution, an executive tells you that she believes that profits are approximately normally distributed and that she is 95% sure that profits will be anywhere from $1.5 million to $3.5 million. What are the mean and the standard deviation of the distribution of profits?

15-5   Decision Analysis: An Overview

Some years ago, the state of Massachusetts had to solve a serious problem: There were an alarming number of road fatalities due to icy roads in the winter. The state department of transportation wanted to solve the problem by salting the roads to reduce ice buildup. The introduction of large amounts of salt into the environment, however, would eventually cause an increase in the sodium content of drinking water, thus increasing the risk of heart problems in the general population.

This is the kind of problem that can be solved by *decision analysis*. There is a decision to be made: to salt or not to salt. With each of the two possible actions, we may associate a final outcome, and each outcome has a probability of occurrence. An additional number of deaths from heart disease would result if roads are salted. The number of deaths is uncertain, but its probability may be assessed. On the other hand, a number of highway deaths could be prevented if salt were used. Here again, the number is uncertain and governed by some probability law. In decision analysis we seek the best decision in a given situation. Although it is unpleasant to think of deaths, the best (optimal) decision here is the decision that would minimize the expected total number of deaths. *Expected* means averaged using the different probabilities as weights.

The area of decision analysis is independent of most of the material in this book. To be able to perform decision analysis, you need to have a rudimentary understanding of probability and of expected values. Some problems make use of additional information, obtained either by sampling or by other means. In such cases, we may have an idea about the *reliability* of our information—which may be stated as a probability—and the information is incorporated in the analysis by use of Bayes' theorem.

When a company is interested in introducing a new product, decision analysis offers an excellent aid in coming to a final decision. When one company considers a merger with another, decision analysis may be used as a way of evaluating all possible outcomes of the move and deciding whether or not to go ahead based on the best expected outcome. Decision analysis can help you decide which investment or combination of investments to choose. It could help you choose a job or career. It could help you decide whether or not to pursue an MBA degree.

We emphasize the use of decision analysis as an aid in corporate decision making. Since it is often difficult to quantify the aspects of human decision making, it is important to understand that decision analysis should not be the only criterion for making a decision. A stockbroker's hunch, for example, may be a much better indication of the best investment decision than a formal mathematical analysis, which may very well miss some important variables.

Decision analysis, as described in this book, has several elements.

The elements of a decision analysis:

1. Actions
2. Chance occurrences
3. Probabilities
4. Final outcomes
5. Additional information
6. Decision

Actions

By an action, we mean anything that the decision maker can do. An action is something you, the decision maker, can control. You may choose to take an action, or you may choose not to take it. Often, there are several choices for action: you may buy one of several different products, travel one of several possible routes, etc. Many decision problems are sequential in nature: you choose one action from among several possibilities; later, you are again in a position to take an action. You may keep taking actions until a final outcome is reached; you keep playing the game until the game is over. Finally, you have reached some final outcome—you have gained a certain amount or lost an amount, achieved a goal or failed.

Chance Occurrences

Even if the decision problem is essentially nonsequential in nature (you take an action, something happens, and that's it), we may gain a better understanding of the problem if we view the problem as sequential. We assume that the decision maker takes an action, and afterwards "chance takes an action." The action of chance is the chance occurrence. When you decide to buy ABC stock, you have taken an action. When the stock falls three points the next day, chance has taken an action.

Probabilities

All actions of chance are governed by probabilities, or at least we view them that way because we cannot predict chance occurrences. The probabilities are obtained by some method. Often, the probabilities of chance occurrences are the decision maker's (or consulted expert's) subjective probabilities. Thus, the chief executive officer of a firm bidding for another firm will assign certain probabilities to the various outcomes that may result from the attempted merger.

In other cases, the probabilities of chance occurrences are more objective in nature. If we use sampling results as an aid in the analysis (see the section on additional information, which follows), then statistical theory gives us measures of the reliability of results and, hence, probabilities of relevant chance occurrences.

Final Outcomes

We assume that the decision problem is of finite duration. After you, the decision maker, have taken an action or a sequence of actions, and after chance has taken action or a sequence of actions, there is a final outcome. An outcome may be viewed as a *payoff* or *reward*, or it may be viewed as a *loss*. We will look at outcomes as rewards (positive or negative). A payoff is an amount of money (or other measure of benefit, called a *utility*) that you receive at the end of the game—at the end of the decision problem.

Additional Information

Each time chance takes over, a random occurrence takes place. We may have some prior information that allows us to assess the probability of any chance occurrence. Often, however, we may be able to purchase additional information. We may consult an expert, at a cost, or we may sample from the population of interest (assuming there is such a population), for a price. The costs of obtaining additional information are subtracted from our final payoff. Therefore, buying new information is, in itself, an action that we may choose to take or not to take. Deciding whether or not to obtain such information is part of the entire decision process. We must weigh the benefit of the additional information against its cost.

Decision

The action, or sequential set of actions, we decide to take is called our *decision*. The decision obtained through a useful analysis is that set of actions that maximizes our expected final-outcome payoff. The decision will often give us a set of *alternative actions* in addition to the optimal set of actions. In a decision to introduce a new product, suppose that the result of the decision analysis indicates that we should proceed with the introduction of the product without any market testing—that is, without any sampling. Suppose, however, that a higher official in the company requires us to test the product even though we may not want to do so. A comprehensive solution to the decision problem would provide us not only with the optimal action (market the product), but also with information on how to proceed in the best possible way when we are forced to take some suboptimal actions along the way. The complete solution to the decision problem would thus include information on how to treat the results of the market test. If the results are unfavorable, the optimal action at this point may be not to go ahead with introducing the product. The solution to the decision problem—the *decision*—gives us all information on how to proceed at any given stage or circumstance.

As you see, we have stressed a sequential approach to decision making. At the very least, a decision analysis consists of two stages: the decision maker takes an action out of several possible ones, and then chance takes an action. This sequential approach to decision making is very well modeled and visualized by what is called a **decision tree.**

A decision tree is a set of nodes and branches. At a *decision node*, the decision maker takes an action; the action is the choice of a branch to be followed. The branch leads to a *chance node*, where chance determines the outcome; that is, chance chooses the branch to be followed. Then either the final outcome is reached (the branch ends) or the decision maker gets to take another action, and so on. We mark a decision node by a square and a chance node by a circle. These are connected by the branches of the decision tree. An example of a decision tree is shown in Figure 15–8. The decision tree shown in the figure is a simple one: it consists of only four branches, one decision node, and one chance node. In addition, there is no product-testing option. As we go on, we will see more complicated decision trees, and we will explore related topics.

FIGURE 15-8   An Example of a Decision Tree for New-Product Introduction

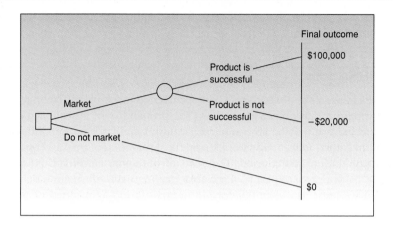

PROBLEMS

15–20.   What are the uses of decision analysis?

15–21.   What are the limitations of decision analysis?

15–22.   List the elements of a decision problem, and explain how they interrelate.

15–23.   What is the role of probabilities in a decision problem, and how do these probabilities arise?

15–24.   What is a decision tree?

15–6   Decision Trees

As mentioned in the last section, a decision tree is a useful aid in carrying out a decision analysis because it allows us to visualize the decision problem. If nothing else, the tree gives us a good perspective on our decision problem: it lets us see when we, as decision makers, are in control and when we are not. To handle the instances when we are not in control, we use probabilities. These probabilities—assuming they are assessed in some accurate, logical, and consistent way—are our educated guesses as to what will happen when we are not in control.

The aforementioned use of decision trees in clarifying our perspective on a decision problem may not seem terribly important, say, compared with a quantitatively rigorous solution to a problem involving exact numbers. However, this use of decision trees is actually more important than it seems. After you have seen how to use a decision tree in computing the expected payoff at each chance node and the choice of the optimal action at each decision node, and after you have tried several decision problems, you will find that the trees have an added advantage. You will find that just drawing the decision tree helps you better understand the decision problem you need to solve. Then, even if the probabilities and payoffs are not accurately assessed, making you doubt the exact optimality of the solution you have obtained, you will still have gained a better understanding of your decision problem. This in itself should help you find a good solution to the problem.

In a sense, a decision tree is a good psychological tool. People are often confused about decisions. They are not always perfectly aware of what they can do and what they cannot do, and they often lack an understanding of uncertainty and how it affects the outcomes of their decisions. This is especially true of large-scale decision problems, where there are several possible actions at several different points, each followed by chance outcomes, leading to a distant final outcome. In such cases, drawing a decision tree is an indispensable way of gaining familiarity with all aspects of the decision problem. The tree shows us which actions affect which, and how the actions interrelate with chance outcomes. The tree shows us how combinations of actions and chance outcomes lead to possible final outcomes and payoffs.

Having said all this, let us see how decision problems are transformed into visual decision trees and how these trees are analyzed. Let us see how decision trees can lead us to optimal solutions to decision problems. We will start with the simple new-product introduction example shown in the decision tree in Figure 15-8. Going step-by-step, we will show how that simple tree was constructed. The same technique is used in constructing more complicated trees, with many branches and nodes.

The Payoff Table

The first step in the solution of any decision problem is to prepare the *payoff table* (also called the *payoff matrix*). The payoff table is a table of the possible payoffs we would receive if we took certain actions, and certain chance occurrences followed. Generally, what takes place will be called *state of nature* and what we do will be called the *decision*. This leads us to a table that is very similar to Table 7–2. There we dealt with hypothesis testing, and the state of nature was whether or not the null hypothesis was true; our decision was either to reject or not reject the null hypothesis. In that context, we could have associated the result "not reject H_0 when H_0 is true" with some payoff (because a correct decision was made); the outcome "not reject H_0 when H_0 is false" could have been associated with another (negative) payoff, and similarly for the other two possible outcomes. In the context of decision analysis, we might view the hypothesis testing as a sequential process. We make a decision (to reject or not to reject H_0), and then "chance" takes over and either makes H_0 true or makes it false.

Let us now write the payoff table for the new-product introduction problem. Here we assume that if we do not introduce the product, there is nothing gained and nothing lost. This assumes we have not invested anything in developing the product, and it assumes no opportunity loss. If we do not introduce the new product, our payoff is zero.

If our action is to introduce the product, two things may happen: the product may be successful, or it may not. If the product is successful, our payoff will be $100,000, and if it is not successful, we will lose $20,000 so our payoff will be −$20,000. The payoff table for this simple problem is Table 15–4. In real-world situations, we may assess more possible outcomes: finely divided *degrees* of success. For example, the product may be extremely successful—with payoff $150,000; very successful—payoff $120,000; successful—payoff $100,000; somewhat successful—payoff $80,000; barely successful—payoff $40,000; breakeven—payoff $0; unsuccessful—payoff −$20,000; or disastrous—payoff −$50,000. Table 15–4 can be easily extended to cover these expanded states of nature. Instead of two columns, we would have eight, and we would still have two rows corresponding to the two possible actions.

The values in Table 15–4 give rise to the decision tree that was shown in Figure 15–8. We take an action: If we do not market the product, the payoff is zero, as shown by the arc from the decision node to the final outcome of zero. If we choose to market the product, chance will either take us to success and a payoff of $100,000, or it will

TABLE 15–4   Payoff Table: New-Product Introduction

	Product Is	
Action	**Successful**	**Not Successful**
Market the product	+$100,000	−$20,000
Do not market the product	0	0

lead us to failure and a loss of $20,000. We now need to deal with chance. We do so by assigning probabilities to the two possible states of nature, that is, to the two possible actions of chance. Here, some elicitation of personal probabilities is done. Suppose that our marketing manager plays the de Finetti game and concludes that the probability of success of the new product is 0.75. The probability of failure then must be $1 - 0.75 = 0.25$. Let us write these probabilities on the appropriate branches of our decision tree. The tree, with payoffs and probabilities, is shown in Figure 15–9.

We now have all the elements of the decision tree, and we are ready to solve the decision problem.

> The solution of decision tree problems is achieved by working backward from the final outcomes.

The method we use is called **averaging out and folding back.** Working backward from the final outcomes, we *average out all chance occurrences.* This means that we find the *expected value* at each chance node. At each chance node (each circle in the tree), we write the expected monetary value of all branches leading out of the node; we *fold back* the tree. At each decision node (each square in the tree), we *choose the action that maximizes our (expected) payoff.* That is, we look at all branches emanating from the decision node, and we choose the branch leading to the highest monetary value. Other branches may be *clipped*; they are not optimal. The problem is solved once we reach the beginning: the first decision node.

Let us solve the decision problem of the new-product introduction. We start at the final outcomes. There are three such outcomes, as seen in Figure 15–9. The outcome with payoff zero emanates directly from the decision node; we leave it for now. The other two payoffs, $100,000 and −$20,000, both emanate from a chance node. We therefore average them out—using their respective probabilities—and fold back to the chance node. To do this, we find the expected monetary value at the chance node (the circle in Figure 15–9). Recall the definition of the expected value of a random variable, given as equation 3–4.

The expected value of X, denoted $E(X)$:

$$E(X) = \sum_{\text{all } x} xP(x)$$

The outcome as you leave the chance node is a random variable with two possible values: 100,000 and −20,000. The probability of the outcome 100,000 is 0.75, and the probability of the outcome −20,000 is 0.25. To find the expected value at the chance node, we apply equation 3–4:

$$E(\text{outcome at chance node}) = (100,000)(0.75) + (-20,000)(0.25)$$
$$= 70,000$$

FIGURE 15–9   Decision Tree for New-Product Introduction

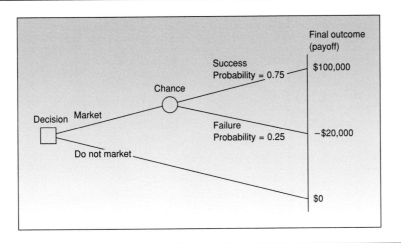

Thus, the expected value associated with the chance node is +$70,000; we will write this value next to the circle in our decision tree. We can now look at the decision node (the square), since we have folded back and reached the first node in the tree. We know the (expected) monetary values associated with the two branches emanating from this node. Recall that at decision nodes we do not average. Rather, we choose the best branch to be followed and clip the other branches, as they are not optimal. Thus, at the decision node, we compare the two values +$70,000 and $0. Since 70,000 is greater than 0, the expected monetary outcome of the decision to market the new product is greater than the monetary outcome of the decision not to market the new product. We follow the rule of choosing the decision that maximizes the expected payoff, so we choose to market the product. (We clip the branch corresponding to "not market" and put a little arrow by the branch corresponding to "market.") In Section 15–8, where we discuss *utility*, we will see an alternative to the "maximum expected monetary value" rule, which takes into account our attitudes toward risk rather than simply aiming for highest *average* payoff, as we have done here. The solution of the decision tree is shown in Figure 15–10.

We follow the arrow and make the decision to market the new product. Then chance takes over, and the product either becomes successful (an event which, a priori, we believe to have a 0.75 probability of occurring), or does not become successful. On the average—that is, if we make decisions such as this one very many times—we should expect to make $70,000.

Let us now consider the extended market possibilities mentioned earlier. Suppose that the outcomes and their probabilities in the case of extended possibilities are as given in Table 15–5. In this new example, the payoff is more realistic: it has many possible states. Our payoff is a random variable. The expected value of this random variable is computed, as usual, by multiplying the values by their probabilities and adding (equation 3–4). This can easily be done by adding a column for Payoff $\times$ Probability to Table 15–5 and adding all entries in the column. This gives us: $E(\text{payoff}) = \$77,500$ (verify this). The decision tree for this example—with many branches emanating from the chance node—is shown in Figure 15–11. The optimal decision in this case is, again, to market the product.

FIGURE 15–10   Solution of the New-Product Introduction Decision Tree

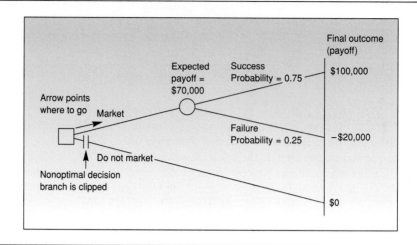

TABLE 15–5   Possible Outcomes and Their Probabilities

Outcome	Payoff	Probability
Extremely successful	$150,000	0.1
Very successful	120,000	0.2
Successful	100,000	0.3
Somewhat successful	80,000	0.1
Barely successful	40,000	0.1
Breakeven	0	0.1
Unsuccessful	−20,000	0.05
Disastrous	−50,000	0.05

FIGURE 15–11   Extended-Possibilities Decision Tree for New-Product Introduction

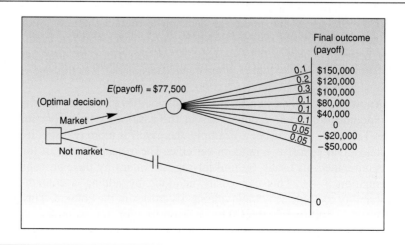

We have seen how to analyze a decision problem by using a decision tree. Let us now look at an example. In Example 15–3 chance takes over after either action we take, and the problem involves more than one action. We will take an action; then a chance occurrence will take place. Then we will again decide on an action, after which chance will again take over, leading us to a final outcome.

EXAMPLE 15-3

In 1995, Digital Equipment Corporation arranged to get the Cunard Lines ship *Queen Elizabeth 2* (QE2) for use as a floating hotel for the company's annual convention. The meeting took place in September and lasted nine days. In agreeing to lease the QE2, Cunard had to make a decision. If the cruise ship were leased to Digital, Cunard would get a flat fee and an additional percentage of profits from the gala convention, which could attract as many as 50,000 people. Cunard analysts therefore estimated that if the ship were leased, there would be a 0.50 probability that the company would make $700,000 for the nine days; a 0.30 probability that profits from the venture would be about $800,000; a 0.15 probability that profits would be about $900,000; and a 0.05 probability that profits would be as high as $1 million. If the ship were not leased to Digital, the vessel would be used for its usual Atlantic crossing voyage, also lasting nine days. If this happened, there would be a 0.90 probability that profits would be $750,000 and a 0.10 probability that profits would be about $780,000. The tighter distribution of profits on the voyage was due to the fact that Cunard analysts knew much about the company's usual business of Atlantic crossings but knew relatively little about the proposed venture.

Cunard had one additional option. If the ship were leased to Digital, and it became clear within the first few days of the convention that Cunard's profits from the venture were going to be in the range of only $700,000, the steamship company could choose to promote the convention on its own by offering participants discounts on QE2 cruises. The company's analysts believed that if this action were chosen, there would be a 0.60 probability that profits would increase to about $740,000 and a 0.40 probability that the promotion would fail, lowering profits to $680,000 due to the cost of the promotional campaign and the discounts offered. What should Cunard have done?

SOLUTION

Let us analyze all the components of this decision problem. There are two possible actions, one of which must be chosen: to lease or not to lease. We can start constructing our tree by drawing the square denoting this decision node and showing the two appropriate branches leading out of it.

Once we make our choice, chance takes over. If we choose to lease, chance will lead us to one of four possible outcomes. We show these possibilities by attaching a circle node at the end of the Lease action branch, with four branches emanating from it. If we choose not to lease, chance again takes over, leading us to two possible outcomes. This is shown by a chance node attached at the end of the Not lease action branch, with two branches leading out of it and into the possible final outcome payoffs of $750,000 and $780,000.

We now go back to the chance occurrences following the Lease decision. At the end of the branch corresponding to an outcome of $700,000, we attach another decision node corresponding to the promotion option. This decision node has two branches leaving it: one goes to the final outcome of $700,000, corresponding to nonpromotion of the convention; and the other, the one corresponding to promotion, leads to a chance node, which in turn leads to two possible final outcomes: a profit of $740,000 and a profit of $680,000. All other chance outcomes following the Lease decision lead directly to final outcomes. These outcomes are profits of $800,000, $900,000, and $1 million. At each chance

FIGURE 15–12 Decision Tree for the Cunard Lease Example

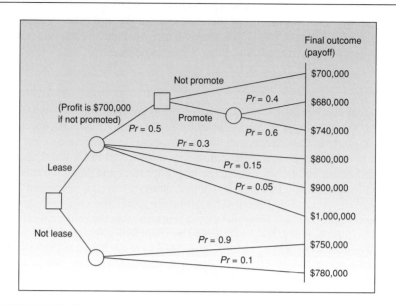

branch, we note its probability. The chance outcomes of the Lease action have probabilities 0.5, 0.3, 0.15, and 0.05 (in order of increasing monetary outcome). The probabilities of the outcomes following the Not lease action are 0.9 and 0.1, respectively. Finally, the probabilities corresponding to the chance outcomes following the Promote action are 0.4 and 0.6, again in order of increasing profit.

Our decision tree for the problem is shown in Figure 15–12. Having read the preceding description of the details of the tree, you will surely agree that "a picture is worth a thousand words."

We now solve the decision tree. Our method of solution, as you recall, is averaging out and folding back. We start at the end; that is, we look at the final-outcome payoffs and work backward from these values. At every chance node, we average the payoffs using their respective probabilities. This gives us the expected monetary value associated with the chance node. At every decision node, we choose the action with the highest expected payoff and clip the branches corresponding to all other, nonoptimal actions. Once we reach the first decision node in the tree, we are done and will have obtained a complete solution to the decision problem.

Let us start with the closest chance node to the final outcomes—the one corresponding to the possible outcomes of the Promote action. The expected payoff at this chance node is obtained as

$$E(\text{payoff}) = (680,000)(0.4) + (740,000)(0.6) = \$716,000$$

We now move back to the Promote/Not promote decision node. Here we must choose the action that maximizes the expected payoff. This is done by comparing the two payoffs: the payoff of $700,000 associated with the Not promote action and the expected payoff of $716,000 associated with the Promote action. Since the *expected* value of $716,000 is greater, we choose to promote. We show this with an arrow, and we clip the nonoptimal action not to promote. The expected value of $716,000 now becomes associated with the decision node, and we write it next to the node.

We now fold back to the chance node following the Lease action. There are four branches leading out of that node. One of them leads to the Promote decision node, which,

FIGURE 15–13   Solution of the Cunard Leasing Problem

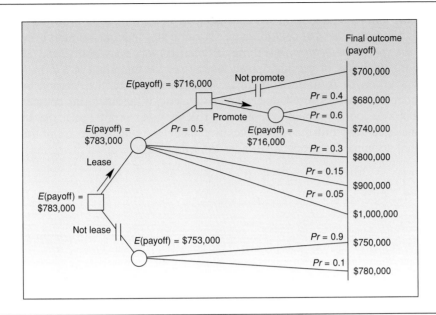

as we just decided, is associated with an (expected) outcome of $716,000. The probability of reaching the decision node is 0.5. The next branch leads to an outcome of $800,000 and has a probability of 0.3; and the next two outcomes are $900,000 and $1 million, with probabilities 0.15 and 0.05, respectively. We now average out the payoffs at this chance node as follows.

$$E(\text{payoff}) = (716,000)(0.5) + (800,000)(0.3) + (900,000)(0.15)$$
$$+ (1,000,000)(0.05)$$

$$= \$783,000$$

This expected monetary value is now written next to the chance node.

Let us now look at the last chance node, the one corresponding to outcomes associated with the Not lease action. Here, we have two possible outcomes: a payoff of $750,000, with probability 0.9; and a payoff of $780,000, with probability 0.1. We now find the expected monetary value of the chance node:

$$E(\text{payoff}) = (750,000)(0.9) + (780,000)(0.1) = \$753,000$$

We are now finally at the first decision node of the entire tree. Here we must choose the action that maximizes the expected payoff. The choice is done by comparing the expected payoff associated with the Lease action, $783,000, and the expected payoff associated with not leasing, $753,000. Since the higher expected payoff is that associated with leasing, the decision is to lease. This is shown by an arrow on the tree and by clipping the Not lease action as nonoptimal. The stages of the solution are shown in Figure 15–13.

We now have a final solution to the decision problem: We choose to *lease* our ship to Digital Equipment Corporation. Then, if we should find out that our profit from the lease would be in the range of only $700,000, our action would be to *promote* the con- vention. Note that in this decision problem, the decision consists of a pair of actions. The decision tells us what to do in any eventuality.

If the tree had more than just two decision nodes, the final solution to the problem would have consisted of a set of optimal actions at all decision nodes. The solution would have told us what to do at any decision node to maximize our expected payoff, given that we arrive at that decision node. Note, again, that our solution is optimal only in an *expected monetary value* sense. If Cunard is very conservative and does not want to take any risk of getting a profit lower than the minimum of $750,000 it is assured of receiving from an Atlantic crossing, then, clearly, the decision to lease would not be optimal because it does admit such a risk. If the steamship company has some risk aversion but would accept some risk of lower profits, then the analysis should be done using utilities rather than pure monetary values. The use of utility in a way that accounts for people's attitudes toward risk is discussed in section 15–8.

PROBLEMS

15–25. Spuds MacKenzie, the stocky, bow-ledged, white English bull terrier featured in Bud Light beer commercials, was probably one of the greatest advertising discoveries of all time. Few people know, however, that Spuds began appearing for Anheuser-Busch, the makers of Bud Light, in 1983 but played only a minor role in Bud Light advertising. Spuds's career really started four years (almost thirty dog-years!) later, at the Super Bowl in January 1987, when Anheuser-Busch paid CBS *$20,000 a second* to put Spuds on the air.

What went into that fateful decision? Let us say that Anheuser-Busch's marketing director felt that there would be a 0.35 probability that a series of three 60-second commercials during the Super Bowl could boost sales volume of Bud Light beer by $8 million during the following three months. The director also believed that there was a 0.65 probability that the resulting excess sales would be about $4 million. Considering also the cost of airing the company's commercials, carry out the decision analysis of whether or not to advertise on television featuring the then-unknown Spuds MacKenzie. Construct a complete decision tree and solve it.

15–26. Boeing has drawn up plans for a new fuel-saving jet, the 7J7, that is designed to compete with the European-built Airbus 320. Boeing is currently conducting research to assess the feasibility of building the 7J7. Company experts believe there is a 0.20 chance that sales of the new plane would bring in gross revenues of $400 million over a period of two years; a 0.30 chance that sales of the plane during this period would bring $300 million; and a 0.50 chance that sales would bring in only $200 million. Were Boeing not to manufacture the plane and instead use its resources to make other planes that are currently being used by airlines all over the world, there is a 0.75 chance that sales of these other planes during the period in question will bring in gross revenues of $250 million, and a 0.25 chance that sales will bring in $300 million. Draw a decision tree for this problem, and solve it. What should Boeing do?

15–27. Atari Corporation is facing a decision about whether or not to acquire all the outstanding stock of Federated Stores, Inc., a stereo and electronic equipment retailer. Atari's financial analysts believe that there is a 0.40 probability that ownership of Federated Stores would bring Atari profits of $55 million over the next three years, a 0.45 probability of $70 million in profits over the period in question, and a 0.15 probability of $80 million in profits. Atari is considering two alternative plans. One plan is to start its own chain of retail outlets. Analysts believe that this plan has a 0.10 probability of failing, producing a loss of $10 million over the next three years; it has a 0.30 probability of bringing in profits of $30 million; a 0.40 probability of producing profits of $75 million over the same period; and a 0.20 probability of bringing in $100 million in profits. The second plan is to divert the efforts to manufacturing a new computer. This plan is believed to have a 0.5 probability of bringing in profits of $150 million over the next three years, a 0.3 probability of bringing in only $50 million, and a 0.2 probability of causing a loss of $20 million over the period in question. Construct and solve the decision tree. Advise Atari about what to do and why.

15–28.   Predicting the styles that will prevail in a coming year is one of the most important and difficult problems in the fashion industry. A fashion designer must work on designs for the coming fall long before he or she can find out for certain what styles are going to be "in." A well-known designer believes that there is a 0.20 chance that short dresses and skirts will be popular in the coming fall; a 0.35 chance that popular styles will be of medium length; and a 0.45 chance that long dresses and skirts will dominate fall fashions. The designer must now choose the styles on which to concentrate. If she chooses one style and another turns out to be more popular, profits will be lower than if the new style were guessed correctly. The following table shows what the designer believes she would make, in hundreds of thousands of dollars, for any given combination of her choice of style and the one that prevails in the new season.

	Prevailing Style		
Designer's Choice	Short	Medium	Long
Short	8	3	1
Medium	1	9	2
Long	4	3	10

Construct a decision tree, and determine what style the designer should choose to maximize her expected profits.

15–29.   For problem 15–28, suppose that if the designer starts working on long designs, she can change them to medium designs after the prevailing style for the season becomes known — although she must then pay a price for this change because of delays in delivery to manufacturers. In particular, if the designer chooses long and the prevailing style is medium, and she then chooses to change to medium, there is a 0.30 chance that her profits will be $200,000 and a 0.70 chance that her profits will be $600,000. No other change from one style to another is possible. Incorporate this information in your decision tree of problem 15–28, and solve the new tree. Give a complete solution in the form of a pair of decisions under given circumstances that maximize the designer's expected profits.

15–30.   Commodity futures provide an opportunity for buyers and suppliers of commodities such as wheat to arrange in advance sales of a commodity, with delivery and payment taking place at a prespecified time in the future. The price is decided at the time the order is placed, and the buyer is asked to deposit an amount less than the value of the order, but enough to protect the seller from loss in case the buyer should decide not to meet his or her obligation.

An investor is considering investing $15,000 in wheat futures and believes that there is a 0.10 probability that he will lose $5,000 by the expiration of the contract, a 0.20 probability that he will make $2,000, a 0.25 probability that he will make $3,000, a 0.15 probability he will make $4,000, a 0.15 probability he will make $5,000, a 0.10 probability he will make $6,000, and a 0.05 probability that he will make $7,000. If the investor should find out that he is going to lose $5,000, he can pull out of his contract, losing $3,500 for certain and an additional $3,000 with probability 0.20 (the latter amount deposited with a brokerage firm as a guarantee). Draw the decision tree for this problem, and solve it. What should the investor do?

15–31.   For problem 15–30, suppose that the investor is considering another investment as an alternative to wheat. He is considering investing his $15,000 in a limited partnership for the same duration of time as the futures contract. This alternative has a 0.50 chance of earning $5,000 and a 0.50 chance of earning nothing. Add this information to your decision tree of problem 15–30, and solve it.

15–7   Handling Additional Information Using Bayes' Theorem

In any kind of decision problem, it is very natural to ask: Can I gain additional information about the situation? Any additional information will help in making a decision under uncertainty. The more we know, the better able we are to make decisions that are likely to maximize our payoffs. If our information is perfect, that is, if we can find out exactly what chance will do, then there really is no randomness, and the situation is perfectly determined. In such cases, there is no need for decision analysis because we can determine the exact action that will maximize the actual (rather than the expected) payoff. Here we are concerned with making decisions under uncertainty, and we assume that when additional information is available, such information is probabilistic in nature. Our information has a certain degree of reliability. The reliability is stated as a set of conditional probabilities.

If we are considering the introduction of a new product into the market, it would be wise to try and gain information about the prospects for success of the new product by sampling potential consumers and soliciting their views about the product. (Isn't this what statistics is all about?) Results obtained from random sampling are always probabilistic in nature; the probabilities originate in the sampling distributions of our statistics. The reliability of survey results may be stated as a set of *conditional probabilities* in the following way. Given that the market is ripe for our product and that it is in fact going to be successful, there is a certain probability that the sampling results will tell us so. Conversely, given that the market will not accept the new product, there is a certain probability that the random sample of people we select will be representative enough of the population in question to tell us so.

To show the use of the conditional probabilities, let S denote the event that the product will be a success and $F = \bar{S}$ (the complement of S) be the event that the product will fail. Let IS be the event that the sample indicates that the product will be a success, and IF the event that the sample indicates that the product will fail. The reliability of the sampling results may be stated by the conditional probabilities: $P(\text{IS}|\text{S})$, $P(\text{IS}|\text{F})$, $P(\text{IF}|\text{S})$, and $P(\text{IF}|\text{F})$. (Each pair of conditional probabilities with the same condition has a sum of 1.00. Thus, $P(\text{IS}|\text{S}) + P(\text{IF}|\text{S}) = 1$, and $P(\text{IS}|\text{F}) + P(\text{IF}|\text{F}) = 1$. So we only need to be given two of the four conditional probabilities.)

Once we have sampled, we know the sample outcome: either the event IS (the sample telling us that the product will be successful) or the event IF (the sample telling us that our product will not be a success). What we need is the probability that the product will be successful given that the sample told us so or the probability that the product will fail, if that is what the sample told us. In symbols, what we need is $P(\text{S}|\text{IS})$ and $P(\text{F}|\text{IS})$ (its complement), or the pair of probabilities $P(\text{S}|\text{IF})$ and $P(\text{F}|\text{IF})$. We have $P(\text{IS}|\text{S})$, and we need $P(\text{S}|\text{IS})$. The conditions in the two probabilities are reversed. Remember that Bayes' theorem reverses the conditionality of events. This is why decision analysis is usually associated with Bayesian theory. In order to transform information about the reliability of additional information in a decision problem to usable information about the likelihood of states of nature, we need to use Bayes' theorem.

Restating the theorem in this context, suppose that the sample told us that the product will be a success. The (posterior) probability that the product will indeed be a success is given by

$$P(\text{S}|\text{IS}) = \frac{P(\text{IS}|\text{S})P(\text{S})}{P(\text{IS}|\text{S})P(\text{S}) + P(\text{IS}|\text{F})P(\text{F})} \qquad (15-6)$$

The probabilities $P(\text{S})$ and $P(\text{F})$ are our *prior* probabilities of the two possible outcomes: successful product versus unsuccessful product. Knowing these prior probabilities and knowing the reliability of survey results, here in the form of $P(\text{IS}|\text{S})$ and $P(\text{IS}|\text{F})$, allows us to compute the posterior, updated probability that the product will be successful given that the sample told us that it will be successful.

FIGURE 15-14   New-Product Decision Tree with Testing

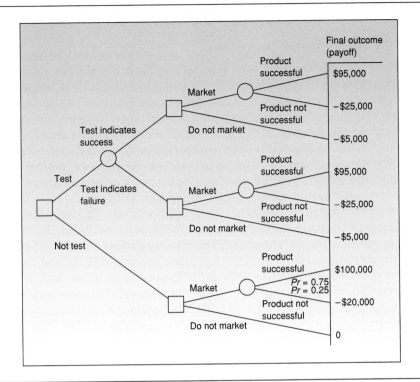

How is all this used in a decision tree? We extend our decision problem to include two possible actions: to test or not to test, that is, to obtain additional information or not to obtain such information. The decision of whether or not to test must be made before we make any other decision. In the case of a new-product introduction decision problem, our decision tree must be augmented to include the possibility of testing or not testing before deciding on whether or not to market our new product. We will assume that the test costs $5,000. Our new decision tree is shown in Figure 15–14.

As shown in Figure 15–14, we first decide whether or not to test. If we test, we get a test result. The result is a *chance outcome*—the test indicates success, or the test indicates failure (event IS or event IF). If the test indicates success, we may choose to market, or we may choose not to market. The same happens if the test indicates failure: we may still choose to market, or we may choose not to market. If the test is worthwhile, it is not logical to market once the test tells us the product will fail. But the point of the decision analysis is that we do not know whether the test is worthwhile; this is one of the things on which we need to decide. Therefore, we allow for the possibility of marketing even if the test tells us not to market, as well as allowing for all other possible combinations of decisions.

Determining the Payoffs

Recall that if the product is successful, we make $100,000, and if it is not successful, we lose $20,000. The test is assumed to cost $5,000. Thus, we must subtract $5,000 from all final-outcome payoffs that are reached via testing. If we test, we spend $5,000. If we then market and the product is successful, we make $100,000, but we must deduct the $5,000 we had to pay for the test, leaving us a net profit of $95,000.

Similarly, we must add the $5,000 cost of the market test to the possible loss of $20,000. This brings the payoff that corresponds to product failure to −$25,000.

Determining the Probabilities

We have now reached the crucial step of determining the probabilities associated with the different branches of our decision tree. As shown in Figure 15–14, we only know two probabilities: the probability of a successful product without any testing and the probability of an unsuccessful product without any testing. (These are our old probabilities from the decision tree of Figure 15–9.) These probabilities are $P(S) = 0.75$ and $P(F) = 0.25$. The two probabilities are also our *prior* probabilities—the probabilities before any sampling or testing is undertaken. As such, we will use them in conjunction with Bayes' theorem for determining the posterior probabilities of success and of failure, and the probabilities of the two possible test results: $P(IS)$ and $P(IF)$. The latter are the total probabilities of IS and IF, respectively, and are obtained from the *denominator* in equation 15–6 and its analog using the event IF. These are sometimes called *predictive probabilities* because they predict the test results.

For the decision tree in Figure 15–14, we have *two* probabilities, and we need to fill in the other six. First, let us look at the particular branches and define our probabilities. The probabilities of the two upper branches of the chance node immediately preceding the payoffs correspond to the two sequences:

Test → Test indicates success → Market → Product is successful

and

Test → Test indicates success → Market → Product is not successful

These are the two sequences of events leading to the payoffs $95,000 and −$25,000, respectively. The probabilities we seek for the two final branches are

P(Product is successful | Test has indicated success)

and

P(Product is not successful | Test has indicated success)

These are the required probabilities because we have reached the branches Success and No success via the route: Test → Test indicates success. In symbols, the two probabilities we seek are: $P(S \mid IS)$ and $P(F \mid IS)$. The first probability will be obtained from Bayes' theorem, equation 15–6, and the second will be obtained as $P(F \mid IS) = 1 - P(S \mid IS)$. What we need for Bayes' theorem—in addition to the prior probabilities—are the conditional probabilities that contain the information about the reliability of the market test. Let us suppose that these probabilities are

$$P(IS \mid S) = 0.9; P(IF \mid S) = 0.1; P(IF \mid F) = 0.85; P(IS \mid F) = 0.15$$

Thus, when the product is indeed going to be successful, the test has a 0.90 chance of telling us so. Ten percent of the time, however, when the product is going to be successful, the test erroneously indicates failure. When the product is not going to be successful, the test so indicates with probability 0.85 and fails to do so with probability 0.15. This information is assumed to be known to us at the time we consider whether or not to test.

Applying Bayes' theorem, equation 15–6, we get

$$P(S \mid IS) = \frac{P(IS \mid S)\, P(S)}{P(IS \mid S)\, P(S) + P(IS \mid F)\, P(F)} = \frac{(0.9)(0.75)}{(0.9)(0.75) + (0.15)(0.25)}$$

$$= \frac{0.675}{0.7125} = 0.9474$$

The denominator in the equation, 0.7125, is an important number. Recall from section 2–7 that this is the *total probability* of the conditioning event; it is the probability of IS. We therefore have

$$P(S \mid IS) = 0.9474 \quad \text{and} \quad P(IS) = 0.7125$$

These two probabilities give rise to two more probabilities (namely, those of their complements): $P(F \mid IS) = 1 - 0.9474 = 0.0526$ and $P(IF) = 1 - P(IS) = 1 - 0.7125 = 0.2875$.

Using Bayes' theorem and its denominator, we have found that the probability that the test will indicate success is 0.7125, and the probability that it will indicate failure is 0.2875. Once the test indicates success, there is a probability of 0.9474 that the product will indeed be successful and a probability of 0.0526 that it will not be successful. This gives us four more probabilities to attach to branches of the decision tree. Now all we need are the last two probabilities: $P(S \mid IF)$ and $P(F \mid IF)$. These are obtained via an analog of equation 15–6 for when the test indicates failure. It is given as equation 15–7.

$$P(S \mid IF) = \frac{P(IF \mid S)\, P(S)}{P(IF \mid S)P(S) + P(IF \mid F)\, P(F)} \tag{15–7}$$

The denominator of equation 15–7 is, by the law of total probability, simply the probability of the event IF, and we have just solved for it: $P(IF) = 0.2875$. The numerator is equal to $(0.1)(0.75) = 0.075$. We thus get $P(S \mid IF) = 0.075/0.2875 = 0.2609$. The last probability we need is $P(F \mid IF) = 1 - P(S \mid IF) = 1 - 0.2609 = 0.7391$.

We will now enter all these probabilities into our decision tree. The complete tree with all probabilities and payoffs is shown in Figure 15–15. (To save space in the figure, events are denoted by their symbols: S, F, IS, etc.)

We are finally in a position to solve the decision problem by averaging out and folding back our tree. Let us start by averaging out the three chance nodes closest to the final outcomes:

$$E(\text{payoff}) = (0.9474)(95{,}000) + (0.0526)(-25{,}000)$$
$$= \$88{,}688 \quad \text{(Top chance node)}$$
$$E(\text{payoff}) = (0.2609)(95{,}000) + (0.7391)(-25{,}000)$$
$$= \$6{,}308 \quad \text{(Middle chance node)}$$
$$E(\text{payoff}) = (0.75)(100{,}000) + (0.25)(-20{,}000)$$
$$= \$70{,}000 \quad \text{(Bottom chance node)}$$

We can now fold back and look for the optimal actions at each of the three preceding decision nodes. Again, starting from top to bottom, we first compare $88,688 with −$5,000 and conclude that—once the test indicates success— we should market the product. Then, comparing $6,308 with −$5,000, we conclude that even if the test says that the product will fail, we are still better off if we go ahead

FIGURE 15–15   New-Product Decision Tree with Probabilities

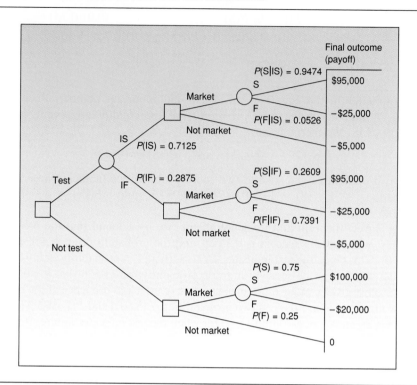

and market the product (remember, all our conclusions are based on the expected monetary value and have no allowance for risk aversion). The third comparison again tells us to market the product, because $70,000 is greater than zero.

We are now at the chance node corresponding to the outcome of the test. At this point, we need to average out $88,688 and $6,308, with probabilities 0.7125 and 0.2875, respectively. This gives us

$$E(\text{payoff}) = (0.7125)(88,688) + (0.2875)(6,308) = \$65,003.75$$

Finally, we are at the very first decision node, and here we need to compare $65,003.75 with $70,000. Since $70,000 is greater, our optimal decision is not to test and to go right ahead and market the new product. If we must, for some reason, test the product, then we should go ahead and market it regardless of the outcome of the test if we want to maximize our expected monetary payoff. Note that our solution is, of course, strongly dependent on the numbers we have used. If these numbers were different—for example, if the prior probability of success were not as high as it is—the optimal solution could very well have been to test first and then follow the result of the test. Our solution to this problem is shown in Figure 15–16.

We now demonstrate the entire procedure of decision analysis with additional information by Example 15–4. To simplify the calculations, which were explained earlier on a conceptual level using equations, we will use tables.

EXAMPLE 15–4   Insurance companies need to invest large amounts of money in opportunities that provide high yields and are long-term in nature. One type of investment that has recently attracted some insurance companies is real estate.

FIGURE 15–16   New-Product Introduction: Expected Values and Optimal Decision

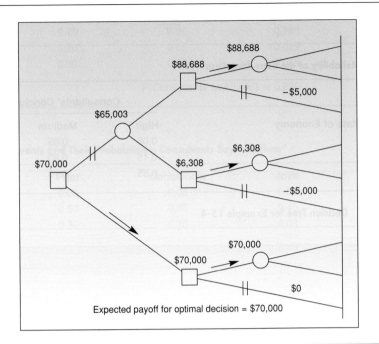

Expected payoff for optimal decision = $70,000

The Aetna life and casualty company is considering an investment in real estate in central Florida. The investment is for a period of 10 years, and company analysts believe that the investment will lead to returns that depend on future levels of economic activity in the area. In particular, the analysts believe that the invested amount would bring the profits listed in Table 15–6, depending on the listed levels of economic activity and their given (prior) probabilities. The alternative to this investment plan—one that the company has used in the past—is a particular investment that has a 0.5 probability of yielding a profit of $4 million and a 0.5 probability of yielding $7 million over the period in question.

The company may also seek some expert advice on economic conditions in central Florida. For an amount that would be equivalent to $1 million 10 years from now (when invested at a risk-free rate), the company could hire an economic consulting firm to study the future economic prospects in central Florida. From past dealings with the consulting firm, Aetna analysts believe that the reliability of the consulting firm's conclusions is as listed in Table 15–7. The table lists as columns the three conclusions the consultants may reach about the future of the area's economy. The rows of the table correspond to the true level of the economy 10 years in the future, and the table entries are conditional probabilities. For example, if the future level of the economy is going to be high, then the consultants' statement will be "high" with probability 0.85. What should Aetna do?

SOLUTION

First, we construct the decision tree, including all the known information. The decision tree is shown in Figure 15–17. Now we need to use the prior probabilities in Table 15–6 and the conditional probabilities in Table 15–7 in computing both the posterior probabilities of the different payoffs from the investment given the three possible consultants' conclusions, and the predictive probabilities of the three consultants' conclusions. This is done in Tables 15–8, 15–9, and 15–10. Note that the probabilities of the outcomes of the alternative investment do not change with the consultants' conclusions (the consul-

D for information that is less reliable. Since sample information is imperfect (in fact, it is probabilistic in nature, as we well know from our discussion of sampling), the value of sample information is less than the value of perfect information. It will only equal the value of perfect information if the entire population is sampled.

Let us see how the upper bound on the value of information is obtained. Since we do not know what the perfect information is, we can only compute the *expected value of perfect information* in a given decision-making situation. The expected value is a *mean* computed using the prior probabilities of the various states of nature. It assumes, however, that at any given point when we actually take an action, we know its exact outcome. Before we (hypothetically) buy the perfect information, we do not know what the state of nature will be, and therefore we must average payoffs using our prior probabilities.

The expected value of perfect information (EVPI):

EVPI = The expected monetary value of the decision situation when perfect information is available minus the expected value of the decision situation when no additional information is available

This definition of the expected value of perfect information is logical: it says that the (expected) maximum amount we should be willing to pay for perfect information is equal to the difference between our expected payoff from the decision situation when we have the information and our expected payoff from the decision situation without the information. The expected value of information is equal to what we stand to gain from this information. We will demonstrate the computation of the expected value of perfect information with an example.

EXAMPLE 15-6

An article in the *Journal of Marketing Research* gives an example of decision making in the airline industry. The situation involves a price war that ensues when one airline determines the fare it will set for a particular route. Profits depend on the fare that will be set by a competing airline for the same route. Competitive situations such as this one are modeled using game theory. In this example, however, we will look at the competitor's action as a chance occurrence and consider the problem within the realm of decision analysis.

Table 15–11 shows the payoffs (in millions of dollars) to the airline over a given period of time, for a given fare set by the airline and by its competitor. We assume that there is a certain probability that the competitor will choose the low ($200) price and a certain probability that the competitor will choose the high price. Suppose that the probability of the low price is 0.6 and that the probability of the high price is 0.4.

TABLE 15-11   Airline Payoffs (in millions of dollars)

Airline's Fare (Action)	Competitor's Fare (State of Nature)	
	$200	$300
$200	8	9
$300	4	10

The decision tree for this situation is given in Figure 15–26. Solving the tree, we find that if we set our price at $200, the expected payoff is equal to $E(\text{payoff}) = (0.6)(8) + (0.4)(9) = \$8.4$ million. If we set our price at $300, then our expected payoff is $E(\text{payoff}) = (0.6)(4) + (0.4)(10) = \$6.4$ million. The optimal action is, therefore, to set our price at $200. This is shown with an arrow in Figure 15–26.

Now we may ask the question of whether or not it may be worthwhile to obtain more information. Obtaining new information in this case may entail hiring a consultant who is knowledgeable about the operating philosophy of the competing airline. We may seek other ways of obtaining information; we may, for example, make an analysis of the competitor's past pricing behavior. The important question is: What do we stand to gain from the new information? Suppose that we know exactly what our competitor plans to do. If we know that the competitor plans to set the price at $200, then our optimal action is to set ours at $200 as well; this is seen by comparing the two amounts in the first payoff column of Table 15–11, the column corresponding to the competitor's setting the price at $200. We see that our maximum payoff is then $8 million, obtained by choosing $200 as our own price as well. If the competitor chooses to set its price at $300, then our optimal action is to set our price at $300 as well and obtain a payoff of $9 million.

We know that without any additional information, the optimal decision is to set the price at $200, obtaining an *expected* payoff of $8.4 million (the expected value of the decision situation without any information). What is the expected payoff with *perfect* information? We do not know what the perfect information may be, but we assume that the prior probabilities we have are a true reflection of the long-run proportion of the time our competitor sets either price. Therefore, 60% of the time our competitor sets the low price, and 40% of the time the competitor sets the high price. If we had perfect information, we would know—at the time—how high to set the price. If we knew that the competitor planned to set the price at $200, we would do the same because this would give us the maximum payoff, $8 million. Conversely, when our perfect information tells us that the competitor is setting the price at $300, we would again follow suit and gain a maximum payoff, $10 million. Analyzing the situation now, we do not know what the competitor will do (we do not have the perfect information), but we do know the probabilities. We therefore average the maximum payoff in each case, that is, the payoff that would be obtained under perfect information, using our probabilities. This gives us the

FIGURE 15–26   Decision Tree for Example 15–6

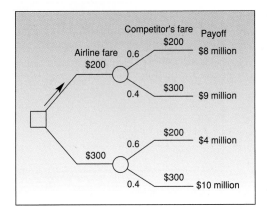

expected payoff under perfect information. We get E(payoff under perfect information) = (Maximum payoff if the competitor chooses \$200) × (Probability that the competitor will choose \$200) + (Maximum payoff if the competitor chooses \$300) × (Probability that the competitor will choose \$300) = (8)(0.6) + (10)(0.4) = \$8.8 million. If we could get perfect information, we could expect (on the average) to make a profit of \$8.8 million. Without perfect information, we expect to make \$8.4 million (the optimal decision without any additional information).

We now use the definition of the expected value of perfect information:

$$EVPI = E(\text{payoff under perfect information}) - E(\text{payoff without information})$$

Applying the rule in this case, we get: EVPI = 8.8 − 8.4 = \$0.4 million, or simply \$400,000. Therefore, \$400,000 is the maximum amount of money we should be willing to pay for additional information about our competitor's price intentions. This is the amount of money we should be willing to pay to know for certain what our competitor plans to do. We should pay less than this amount for all information that is not as reliable.

What about sampling, when sampling is possible? (In the airlines example, it probably is not possible to sample.) The expected value of sample information is equal to the expected value of perfect information, minus the expected cost of sampling errors. The expected cost of sampling errors is obtained from the probabilities of errors—known from sampling theory—and the resulting loss of payoff due to making less-than-optimal decisions. The *expected net gain* from sampling is equal to the expected value of sampling information, minus the cost of sampling. As the sample size increases, the expected net gain from sampling first increases, as our new information is valuable and improves our decision-making ability. Then the expected net gain decreases because we are paying for the information at a constant rate, while the information content in each additional data point becomes less and less important as we get more and more data. (A sample of 1,100 does not contain much more information than a sample of 1,000. However, the same 100 data points may be very valuable if they are all we have.)

At some particular sample size, n, we maximize our expected net gain from sampling. Determining the optimal sample size to be used in a decision situation is a difficult

FIGURE 15-27   Expected Net Gain from Sampling (in Dollars) as a Function of the Sample Size

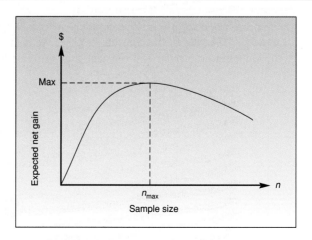

problem, and we will not say more about it here. We will, however, show the relationship between sample size and the expected net gain from sampling in Figure 15–27. The interested reader is referred to advanced works on the subject.[4]

PROBLEMS

15–46. Explain the value of additional information within the context of decision making.

15–47. Explain how we compute the expected value of perfect information, and why it is computed that way.

15–48. Compute the expected value of perfect information for the situation in problem 15–28.

15–49. For the situation in problem 15–28, suppose the designer is offered expert opinion about the new fall styles for a price of $300,000. Should she buy the advice? Explain why or why not.

15–50. What is the expected value of perfect information in the situation of problem 15–25? Explain.

15-10   Using the Computer

Most statistical computer packages do not have extensive Bayesian statistics or decision analysis capabilities. There are, however, some computer programs for microcomputers that do decision analysis. One such program is *Arborist*.™[5] It is also possible to write your own computer program for solving a decision tree.

15-11   Summary and Review of Terms

In this chapter, we presented two related topics: **Bayesian statistics** and **decision analysis.** We saw that the Bayesian statistical methods are extensions of Bayes' theorem to discrete and continuous random variables. We saw how the Bayesian approach allows the statistician to use, along with the data, **prior information** about the situation at hand. The prior information is stated in terms of a **prior probability distribution** of population parameters. We saw that the Bayesian approach is less restrictive in that it allows us to consider an unknown parameter as a random variable. In this context, as more sampling information about a parameter becomes available to us, we can update our prior probability distribution of the parameter, thus creating a **posterior probability distribution.** The posterior distribution may then serve as a prior distribution when more data become available. We also may use the posterior distribution in computing a **credible set** for a population parameter, in the discrete case, and a **highest posterior density (HPD) set** in the continuous case. We discussed the possible dangers in using the Bayesian approach and the fact that we must be careful in our choice of prior distributions.

We saw how decision analysis may be used to find the decision that maximizes our **expected payoff** from an uncertain situation. We discussed personal, or **subjective probabilities** and saw how these can be assessed and used in a Bayesian statistics

---

[4] See C. Barenghi, A. Aczel, and R. Best, "Determining the Optimal Sample Size for Decision Making," *Journal of Statistical Computation and Simulation,* Spring 1986, pp. 135–45. Figure 15–27 is reprinted, by permission, from that article.

[5] Arborist™ is a trademark of Texas Instruments Incorporated.

problem or in a decision problem. We saw that a **decision tree** is a good method of solving problems of decision making under uncertainty. We learned how to use the method of **averaging out and folding back,** which leads to the determination of the **optimal decision**—the decision that maximizes the expected monetary payoff. We saw how to assess the usefulness of obtaining additional information within the context of the decision problem, using a decision tree and Bayes' theorem. Finally, we saw how to incorporate people's attitudes toward risk in our analysis and how these attitudes lead to a **utility function.** We saw that this leads to solutions to decision problems that maximize the **expected utility** rather than the expected monetary payoff. We also discussed the **expected value of perfect information** and saw how this value serves as an upper bound for the amount of money we are willing to pay for additional information about a decision-making situation.

ADDITIONAL PROBLEMS

15–51. A quality-control engineer believes that the proportion of defective items in a production process is a random variable with a probability distribution that is approximated as follows.

x	P(x)
0.1	0.1
0.2	0.3
0.3	0.2
0.4	0.2
0.5	0.1
0.6	0.1

The engineer collects a random sample of items and finds that 5 out of the 16 items in the sample are defective. Find the engineer's posterior probability distribution of the proportion of defective items.

15–52. Continuing problem 15–51, determine a credible set for the proportion of defective items with probability close to 0.95. Interpret the meaning of the credible set.

15–53. For problem 15–51, suppose that the engineer collects a second sample of 20 items and finds that 5 items are defective. Update the probability distribution of the population proportion you computed in problem 15–51 to incorporate the new information.

15–54. What are the main differences between the Bayesian approach to statistics and the classical (frequentist) approach? Discuss these differences.

15–55. What is the added advantage of the normal probability distribution in the context of Bayesian statistics?

15–56. The average life of a battery is believed to be normally distributed with an unknown mean, μ. The mean is viewed as a random variable with expected value of 45 hours and standard deviation of 5 hours. The population standard deviation is believed to be 10 hours. A random sample of 100 batteries gives a sample mean of 102 hours. Find the posterior probability distribution of the population mean, μ.

15–57. For problem 15–56, give a highest-posterior-density credible set of probability 0.95 for the population mean.

15–58. For problem 15–56, a second sample of 60 batteries gives a sample mean of 101.5 hours. Update the distribution of the population mean, and give a new HPD credible set of probability 0.95 for μ.

15–59. What is a payoff table? What is a decision tree? Can a payoff table be used in decision making without a decision tree?

15–60. What is a subjective probability, and what are its limitations?

15–61. Discuss the advantages and the limitations of the de Finetti game. What is the main principle behind the game?

15–62. Why is Bayesian statistics controversial? Try to argue for, and then against, the Bayesian methodology.

15–63. Suppose that I am indifferent about the following two choices: a sure $3,000 payoff, and a payoff of $5,000 with probability 0.2 and $500 with probability 0.8. Am I a risk taker or a risk-averse individual (within the range $500 to $5,000)? Explain.

15–64. An investment is believed to earn $2,000 with probability 0.2, $2,500 with probability 0.3, and $3,000 with probability 0.5. An alternative investment may earn zero with probability 0.1, $3,000 with probability 0.2, $4,000 with probability 0.5, and $7,000 with probability 0.2. Construct a decision tree for this problem, and determine the investment with the highest expected monetary outcome. What are the limitations of the analysis?

15–65. Assess your own utility in the range of values of problem 15–64, and redo that problem using utilities instead of dollars. Has the optimal decision changed? Explain.

15–66. A company is considering merging with a smaller firm in a related industry. The company's chief executive officer believes that the merger has a 0.55 probability of success. If the merger is successful, the company stands to gain in the next two years $5 million with probability 0.2; $6 million with probability 0.3; $7 million with probability 0.3; and $8 million with probability 0.2. If the attempted merger should fail, the company stands to lose $2 million (due to loss of public goodwill) over the next two years with probability 0.5 and to lose $3 million over this period with probability 0.5. Should the merger be attempted? Explain.

15–67. For problem 15–66, suppose that the chief executive may hire a consulting firm for a fee of $725,000. The consulting firm will advise the CEO about the possibility of success of the merger. This consulting firm is known to have correctly predicted the outcomes of 89% of all successful mergers and the outcomes of 97% of all unsuccessful ones. What is the optimal decision?

15–68. What is the expected value of perfect information about the success or failure of the merger in problem 15–66?

15–69. A company is interested in hiring a new manager. There are two candidates for the position. Candidate A successfully managed two out of three firms that he headed and improved profits by an average of 10%. In his third previous job, the candidate caused a profit loss of 4%. Candidate B successfully managed four out of five firms she previously headed. This candidate increased profits by an average of 6% at the firms she successfully managed, and caused a profit loss of 5% at the firm she managed unsuccessfully. Which candidate should be hired, and why?

15–70. For problem 15–69, add the option of not hiring a new manager, and assume no change in profits. Redo the problem.

15–71. For a cost of 1% of profits, the firm may allow one of the two candidates in problem 15–69 to manage the company for a trial period to determine whether the candidate will be successful. Such a test has a reliability of 90%. What is the optimal decision?

Forbes Informer[6]

EDITED BY KATE BOHNER LEWIS

O.J. Futures

Wall Streeters will bet on anything. Twenty or so young traders at New York–based Ziff Brothers Investments have created a futures exchange based on the outcome of the O.J. Simpson trial.

A contract that pays $100 if O.J. gets nailed goes for around $65. An acquittal contract goes for just $25. Those odds haven't changed much since the trial began—suggesting that the trial has produced few surprises and suggesting that maybe O.J. needs a new lawyer. Wouldn't a hedge, costing $90, be a sure thing? No. There could be a hung jury and no payout. Sorry. The market is open only to the folks at Ziff Brothers.

15–72.   Discuss the preceding article in the context of the concepts described in this chapter (and in light of the outcome of the trial).

Case 15   GETTING BUMPED

The overbooking of airplane seats is not a new phenomenon. However, as airlines become more and more competitive, their profit margins narrow, and they find it increasingly necessary to fill every possible seat. Virtually the only way of achieving a flight that is as full as possible is to overbook the seats on the plane, counting on the fact that some people will fail to show up for the flight. If the number of no-shows is smaller than the number of overbooked seats, the plane will be full and some ticketed passengers will have to get "bumped" —for a suitable compensation. Often, the compensation is in the form of a free round-trip flight ticket between any two domestic airports served by the airline.

The operations managers of airlines have ready access to all information on flight capacities, peak and off-peak demand, and any other relevant information directly from computers. This has enabled some of these managers to make surprisingly accurate calculations of the probabilities of the number of no-shows for any given flight. The operations manager of Western Airlines (before the company was taken over by Delta) used such probability calculations. The manager was able to predict to within a few people the number of passengers expected to show up for some flights. This allowed the airline to determine the extent of overbooking that would maximize the number of filled seats and minimize the number of free tickets offered.

Instead of looking at airline seat overbooking from the airlines' point of view, let us look at it from the point of view of an individual traveler. Let us see how an airline passenger can (in fact, at least one did) use decision analysis to beat the airline in this game, maximizing the *passenger's* expected payoff. Let us suppose that you are the passenger and that this is your decision problem.

You are staying at the Hilton Hawaiian Village on Waikiki beach. You have been attending a professional conference at the hotel, paid for by your organization. It is the day before Thanksgiving, and this is your last night at the hotel. The front desk has just informed you that the hotel is full and that if you decide that you want to stay an extra night, you will have to call in the morning and ask if there is a vacancy. The desk attendant tells you that the chances of a vacancy tomorrow morning are about 0.30. You also know that most hotel rooms in Hawaii are full for the Thanksgiving holiday,

---

[6] K. Lewis, "Forbes Informer," *Forbes,* April 24, 1995, p. 18.

and you believe that the chances of finding a hotel room tomorrow, assuming the Hilton will not be able to accommodate you, are about 0.50.

If you find a room at the Hilton, then—since your conference is over—you will have to pay for the room. Your room costs $110 per day. The pleasure you will derive from staying an extra day in Hawaii is worth $500 to you. This is your utility for staying a day: the amount someone would have to pay you to forgo your one-day vacation at the Hilton, assuming you can stay there. This amount is inclusive of the cost of your stay. If you cannot stay at the Hilton, you will have to spend much of the next day searching for a room, thus reducing your pleasure from staying. In addition, since you are likely to find a less comfortable hotel than the Hilton (if you find one at all), these factors reduce your utility from staying an extra day to about $150. A room at another hotel will cost you $50.

What about flying home? You can either fly home tonight, the day before Thanksgiving, or you can fly back tomorrow, Thanksgiving Day. You can also fly home the day after Thanksgiving. Your flight ticket is good for any of the three flights, but you cannot leave any later than the day after tomorrow.

Reading a newspaper, you find that about 250,000 people were bumped from their flights in the last four months. Using this information in conjunction with what you know about the total number of flights and other information, you estimate that the overall probability of being bumped from a flight is about 0.04. The newspaper article further tells you that the worst time for the airlines—and the best time for you if you want to get bumped and earn a free ticket—is today: the day before Thanksgiving, when everyone is rushing home.

The worst day to fly, from your point of view, is tomorrow. Then everyone will be home; few people will fly, and you are not very likely to be bumped. You therefore estimate that the chances of being bumped from your flight today, if you try to return home right now and not stay the night, which has already been paid for, is about 0.16 (four times the "usual" probability). You believe that the chances of being bumped tomorrow are only 0.01, and the probability of being bumped if you try to fly the next day is 0.06. If you get bumped that third day, you will stay at the airport until the late-night flight. You believe that you will surely find a place on that flight.

Getting bumped from a flight is worth $1,100 to you. You are planning a long-distance trip, which will cost this much, and if you get bumped and earn a free ticket, you will use it for the trip.

You allow yourself one more possibility: If you decide to go to the airport tonight in the hope of getting bumped, and you see that your plane is not going to be full, you can return to your hotel. In this case, you will only lose the taxi fare to the airport and back—$40—and you will miss a hula show worth $50 in utility to you but costing nothing. You will not allow yourself such an option tomorrow or the next day. Then, if you are bumped, you will collect your free ticket and fly home on the late-night flight; if you are not bumped, you will take the regular flight. What should you do to maximize your expected payoff from this unusual situation?

16

MULTIVARIATE ANALYSIS

1 6 – 1   I N T R O D U C T I O N

A couple living in a suburb of Chicago, earning a modest living on salaries and claiming only small and reasonable deductions on their taxes, nonetheless gets audited by the IRS every year. The reason: the couple has 21 children. A formula residing deep inside the big IRS computer in West Virginia plucks taxpayers for audit based on the information on their tax returns. The formula is a statistical one and constitutes one of the advanced methods described in this chapter. The technique is called *discriminant analysis.* This example shows how not to use statistics, since the IRS has never been able to collect additional tax from this couple. And the IRS's discriminant analysis makes a variety of other errors with thousands of taxpayers.[1] Used correctly, however, discriminant analysis can lead to a

Continued

---

[1] More on the IRS's use of statistics can be found in A. Aczel, *How to Beat the IRS at Its Own Game,* Second edition (New York: Four Walls, 1995).

reasonable breakdown of a population into two categories (in this example: the category of people who owe more tax and the category of people who do not owe more tax). This multivariate technique will be introduced in this chapter, along with a few others.

Multivariate statistical methods, or simply **multivariate methods,** are statistical methods for the simultaneous analysis of data on several variables. Suppose that a company markets two related products, say, toothbrushes and toothpaste. The company's marketing director may be interested in analyzing consumers' preferences for the two products. The exact type of analysis may vary depending on what the company needs to know. What distinguishes the analysis—whatever form it may take—is that it should consider people's perceptions of both products *jointly*. Why? If the two products are related, it is likely that consumers' perceptions of the two products will be correlated. Incorporating knowledge of such correlations in our analysis makes the analysis more accurate and more meaningful.

Recall that regression analysis and correlation analysis are methods involving several variables. In a sense, they are multivariate methods even though, strictly speaking, in regression analysis we make the assumption that the independent variable or variables are not random but are fixed quantities. In this chapter, we discuss statistical methods that are usually referred to as *multivariate*. These are more advanced than regression analysis or simple correlational analysis. In a multivariate analysis, we usually consider data on several variables as a single element—for example, an ordered set of values such as (x_1, x_2, x_3, x_4) is considered a single element in an analysis that concerns four variables. In the case of the analysis of consumers' preference scores for two products, we will have a consumer's response as the *pair* of scores (x_1, x_2), where x_1 is the consumer's preference for the toothbrush, measured on some scale, and x_2 is his or her preference for the toothpaste, measured on some scale. In the analysis, we consider the pair of scores (x_1, x_2) as one sample point. When k variables are involved in the analysis, we will consider the *k-tuple* of numbers $(x_1, x_2, \ldots, x_k)$ as one element—one data point. Such an ordered set of numbers is called a **vector.** Vectors form the basic elements of our analysis in this chapter.

As you recall, the normal distribution plays a crucial role in most areas of statistical analysis. You should therefore not be surprised that the normal distribution plays an equally important role in multivariate analysis. Interestingly, the normal distribution is easily extendable to several variables. As such, it is the distribution of *vector random variables* of the form $\mathbf{X} = (X_1, X_2, X_3, \ldots, X_k)$. The distribution is called the **multivariate normal distribution.** When $k = 2$, the *bivariate* case, we have a two-dimensional normal distribution. Instead of a bell-shaped curve, we have a (three-dimensional) bell-shaped *mound* as our density function. When k is greater than 2, the probability function is a surface of higher dimensionality than 3, and we cannot graph it. The mulitvariate normal distribution will be discussed in the next section. It forms the basis for multivariate methods. ∎

16–2   The Multivariate Normal Distribution

In the introduction, we mentioned that in multivariate analysis our elements are vectors rather than single observations. We did not define a vector, counting on the intuitive interpretation that a vector is an ordered set of numbers. For our purposes, a vector is just that: an ordered set of numbers, with each number representing a value of one of the k variables in our analysis.

A k-dimensional random variable **X**:

$$\mathbf{X} = (X_1, X_2, \ldots, X_k) \tag{16–1}$$

where k is some integer

A realization of the random variable **X** is a drawing from the populations of values of the k variables and will be denoted, as usual, by lowercase letters.

A realization of a k-dimensional random variable **X**:

$$\mathbf{x} = (x_1, x_2, \ldots, x_k) \tag{16–2}$$

Thus, in our simple example of consumer preferences for two products, we will be interested in the bivariate (two-component) random variable $\mathbf{X} = (X_1, X_2)$, where X_1 denotes a consumer's preference for the toothbrush and X_2 is the same consumer's preference for the toothpaste. A particular realization of the bivariate random variable may be (89, 78). If this is a result of random sampling from a population, it means that the particular sampled individual rates the toothbrush an 89 (on a scale of 0 to 100) and the toothpaste a 78.

For the k-dimensional random variable $\mathbf{X} = (X_1, X_2, X_3, \ldots, X_k)$, we may define a cumulative probability distribution function $F(x_1, x_2, x_3, \ldots, x_k)$. This is a joint probability function for all k random variables X_i, where $i = 1, 2, 3, \ldots, k$.

A joint cumulative probability distribution function of a k-dimensional random variable **X**:

$$F(x_1, x_2, \ldots, x_k) = P(X_1 \le x_1, X_2 \le x_2, \ldots, X_k \le x_k) \tag{16–3}$$

Equation 16–3 is a statement of the probability that X_1 is less than or equal to some value x_1, *and X_2* is less than or equal to some value x_2, *and* . . . , *and X_k* is less than or equal to some value x_k. In our simple example, $F(55, 60)$ is the *joint* probability that a consumer's preference score for the toothbrush is less than or equal to 55 and that his or her preference score for the toothpaste is less than or equal to 60.

The multivariate normal distribution is an extension of the normal curve to several variables—it is the distribution of a k-dimensional vector random variable.

FIGURE 16–1   The Bivariate Normal Probability Density Function

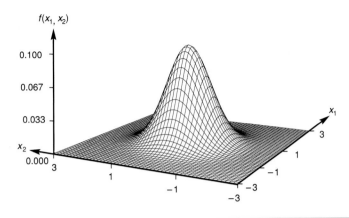

A multivariate normal random variable has the following probability density function

$$f(x_1, x_2, \ldots, x_k) = \frac{1}{(2\pi)^{k/2} |\, \Sigma \,|^{1/2}} e^{-(1/2)(X - \mu)' \Sigma^{-1}(X - \mu)} \qquad (16\text{–}4)$$

where **X** is the vector random variable defined in equation 16–1; the term $\mu = (\mu_1, \mu_2, \ldots, \mu_k)$ is the *vector of means* of the component variables X_i; and Σ is the *variance-covariance matrix*. The operations $'$ and $^{-1}$ are transposition and inversion of matrices, respectively, and $|\ \ |$ denotes the determinant of a matrix.

The multivariate normal distribution is an essential element in multivariate statistical techniques. Most such techniques assume that the data (on several variables), and the underlying multivariate random variable, are distributed according to a multivariate normal distribution. Figure 16–1 shows a bivariate (two-dimensional) normal probability density function.

16–3   Discriminant Analysis

A bank is faced with the following problem: Due to economic conditions in the area the bank serves, a large percentage of the bank's mortgage holders are defaulting on their loans. It therefore is very important for the bank to develop some criteria for making a statistical determination about whether or not any particular loan applicant is likely to be able to repay his or her loan. Is such a determination possible?

There is a very useful multivariate technique aimed at answering such a question. The idea is very similar to that of multiple regression analysis. In multiple regression, we try to predict values of a continuous-scale variable—the dependent variable—based on the values of a set of independent variables. The independent variables may be continuous or they may be qualitative (in which case we use dummy variables to model them, as you recall from Chapter 11). In **discriminant analysis,** the situation is similar. We try to develop an equation that will help us predict the value of a dependent variable based on values of a set of independent variables. The difference is that the dependent variable is *qualitative*. In the bank loan example, the qualitative dependent variable is a classification: repay or default. The independent variables that help us make a classification of the loan outcome category may be: family income, family assets, job stability (number of years with present employer), and any other variables we think may have an effect on whether or not the loan will be repaid. There is also an option where the algorithm itself chooses which variables should be included in the prediction equation. This is similar to a stepwise regression procedure.

If we let our dependent, qualitative variable be D and we consider k independent variables, then our prediction equation has the following form.

The form of an estimated prediction equation:

$$D = b_0 + b_1 X_1 + b_2 X_2 + \cdots + b_k X_k \qquad (16\text{-}5)$$

where the b_i, $i = 1, \ldots, k$, are the *discriminant weights*—they are like the estimated regression coefficients in multiple regression; b_0 is a constant

---

Developing a Discriminant Function

In discriminant analysis, we aim at deriving the linear combination of the independent variables that *discriminates best* between the two or more a priori defined groups (the repay group versus the default group in the bank loan example). This is done by finding coefficient estimates b_i in equation 16–5 that maximize the among-groups variation relative to the within-groups variation.

FIGURE 16–2   Maximizing the Separation between Two Groups

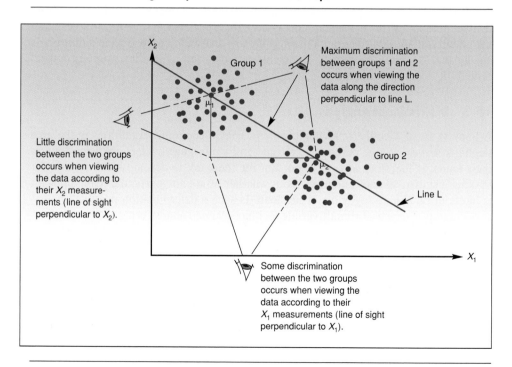

Figure 16–2 shows how we develop a **discriminant function.** We look for a *direction in space,* a combination of variables (here, two variables, X_1 and X_2) that *maximizes the separation* between the two groups. As seen in the figure, if we consider only the X_2 component of every point in the two groups, we do not have much separation between the two groups. Look at the data in Figure 16–2 from the direction specified by having the eye located by the X_2 axis. As you see from your vantage point, the two groups overlap, and some of the upper points in group 2 look like they belong in group 1. Now look at the data with the eye located below the X_1 axis. Here you have better separation between the two groups. From this vantage point, however, the points blend together into one big group, and you will still not be able to easily classify a point as belonging to a single group based solely on its location. Now look at the data with the eye above and perpendicular to line L. Here you have perfect separation of the two groups, and if you were given the coordinate along line L of a new point, you would probably be able to logically classify that point as belonging to one group or the other. (Such classification will never be perfect with real data because there will always be the chance that a point belonging to population 1 will somehow happen to have a low X_2 component and/or a large X_1 component that would throw it into the region we classify as belonging to population 2.) In discriminant analysis, we find the combination of variables (i.e., the direction in space) that maximizes the discrimination between groups. Then we classify new observations as belonging to one group or the other based on their score on the weighted combination of variables chosen as the discriminant function.

Since in multivariate analysis we assume that the points in each group have a multivariate normal distribution (with possibly different means), the marginal distribution of each of the two populations, when viewed along the direction that maximizes the differentiation between groups, is univariate *normal.* This is shown in Figure 16–3.

The point C on the discriminant scale is the *cutting score.* When a data point gets a score smaller than C, we classify that point as belonging to population 1, and when

FIGURE 16–3   The Discriminant Function

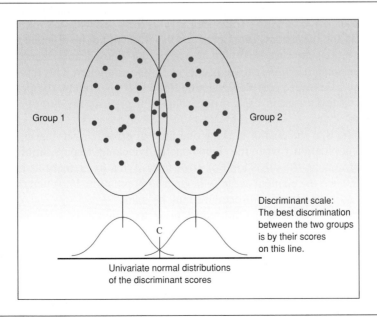

Group 1

Group 2

Discriminant scale:
The best discrimination between the two groups is by their scores on this line.

C

Univariate normal distributions of the discriminant scores

a data point receives a score greater than *C*, we classify that point as belonging to population 2. This assumes, of course, that we do not know which population the point really belongs to and we use the discriminant function to classify the point based on the values the point has with respect to the independent variables. In our bank loan example, we use the variables family income, assets, job stability, and other variables to estimate a discriminant function that will maximize the differences (i.e., the multivariate distance) between the two groups: the repay group and the default group. Then, when new applicants arrive, we find their score on our discriminant scale and classify the applicants as to whether we believe they are going to repay or default. Errors will, of course, occur. Someone we classify as a defaulter may (if given the loan) actually repay it, and someone we classify in the repay group may not.

Look at Figure 16–3. There is an area under the univariate normal projection of group 1 to the right of *C*. This is the probability of erroneously classifying an observation in population 1 as belonging to population 2. Similarly, the area under the right-hand normal curve to the left of the cutting score *C* is the probability of misclassifying a point that belongs to population 2 as being from population 1.

When the population means of the two groups are equal, there would be *no discrimination* between the groups based on the values of the independent variables considered in the analysis. In such a case, the univariate normal distributions of the discriminant scores will be identical (the two curves will overlap). The reason the curves overlap is due to the model assumptions. In discriminant analysis, we assume that the populations under study have multivariate normal distributions with equal variance-covariance matrices and possibly different means.

Evaluating the Performance of the Model

We test the accuracy of our discriminant function by evaluating its success rate when the function is applied to cases with known group memberships. It is best to withhold some of our data when we carry out the estimation phase of the analysis, and then use the withheld observations in testing the accuracy of the predictions based on our estimated discriminant function. If we try to evaluate the success rate of our discriminant function based only on observations used in the estimation phase, then we run the risk of overestimating the success rate. Still, we will use our estimation data in estimating the success rate because it usually will not be efficient to withhold many observations for use solely in assessing our classification success rate. A *classification summary table* will be produced by the computer. This table will show us how many cases were correctly classified and will also report the percentage of correctly classified cases in each group. This will give us the *hit rate* or *hitting probabilities.*

We assume that the cost of making one kind of error (classifying an element as belonging to population 1 when the element actually belongs to population 2) is equal to the cost of making the other kind of error (classifying an element as belonging to population 2 when the element actually belongs to population 1). When the costs are unequal, an adjustment to the procedure may be made.

The procedure may also be adjusted for prior probabilities of group membership. That is, when assigning an element to one of the two groups, we may account not only for its discriminant score, but also for its prior probability of belonging to the particular population, based on the relative size of the population as compared with the other populations under study. In the bank loan example, suppose that defaulting on the loan is a very rare event, with a priori probability 0.001. We may wish to adjust our discriminant criterion to account for this fact, appropriately reducing our rate of classifying people as belonging to the default category. Such adjustments are based on the use of Bayes' theorem. We demonstrate discriminant analysis with the example we used at the beginning of this section—the bank loan example—which we will call Example 16–1.

EXAMPLE 16–1

The bank we have been discussing has data on 32 loan applicants. Data are available on each applicant's total family assets, total family income, total debt outstanding, family size, number of years with present employer for household head, and a qualitative variable that equals 1 if the applicant has repaid the loan and 0 if he or she has not repaid the loan. Data are presented in Table 16–1. The bank will use the data to estimate a discriminant function. The bank intends to use this function in classifying future loan applicants.

TABLE 16–1 **Data of Example 16–1 (assets, income, and debt, in thousands of dollars)**

Assets	Income	Debt	Family Size	Number of Years with Present Employer	Repay/Default
98	35	12	4	4	1
65	44	5	3	1	1
22	50	0	2	7	1
78	60	34	5	5	1
50	31	4	2	2	1
21	30	5	3	7	1
42	32	21	4	11	1
20	41	10	2	3	1
33	25	0	3	6	1
57	32	8	2	5	1
8	23	12	2	1	0
0	15	10	4	2	0
12	18	7	3	4	0
7	21	19	4	2	0
15	14	28	2	1	0
30	27	50	4	4	0
29	18	30	3	6	0
9	22	10	4	5	0
12	25	39	5	3	0
23	30	65	3	1	0
34	45	21	2	5	0
21	12	28	3	2	1
10	17	0	2	3	1
57	39	13	5	8	0
60	40	10	3	2	1
78	60	8	3	5	1
45	33	9	4	7	0
9	18	9	3	5	1
12	23	10	4	4	1
55	36	12	2	5	1
67	33	35	2	4	1
42	45	12	3	8	0

SOLUTION

The data, a random sample of 32 cases, are analyzed using the SPSS program DISCRIMINANT. The output of the analysis is given in the following figures. We use a stepwise procedure similar to stepwise multiple regression. At each stage, the computer chooses a variable to enter the discriminant function. The criterion for entering the equation may be specified by the user. Here we choose the Wilks lambda criterion. The variable to enter is the variable that best fits the entry requirements in terms of the associated Wilks' lambda value. Variables may enter and leave the equation at each step in the same way that they are processed in stepwise regression. The reason for this is that multicollinearity may exist. Therefore, we need to allow variables to leave the equation once other variables are in the equation. Figure 16–4 shows the variables that enter and leave the equation at each stage of the discriminant analysis.

We see that the procedure chose total family assets, total debt, and family size as the three most discriminating variables between the repay and the default groups. The summary table in Figure 16–4 shows that all three variables are significant, the largest p-value being 0.0153. The three variables have some discriminating power. Figure 16–5 shows the estimated discriminant function coefficients. The results in the figure give us the following estimated discriminant function:

$$D = -0.995 - 0.0352 \text{ ASSETS} + 0.0429 \text{ DEBT} + 0.483 \text{ FAMILY SIZE}$$

$$(16-6)$$

The cutting score is zero. Discriminant scores greater than zero (i.e., positive scores) indicate a predicted membership in the default group (population 0), while negative scores imply predicted membership in the repay group (population 1). This can be seen by looking at the predicted group membership chart, Figure 16–6. The figure shows all cases used in the analysis. Since we have no holdout sample for testing the effectiveness of prediction of group membership, the results are for the estimation sample only. For each case, the table gives the *actual group* to which the data point (person, in our example) belongs. A double asterisk (**) next to the actual group indicates that the point was incorrectly classified. The next column, under the heading "Highest Probability: Group," gives the predicted group membership (0 or 1) for every element in our sample.

The next column, "Highest Probability: $P(D \mid G)$," gives the likelihood—the probability of obtaining the discriminant score received, given that the point belongs to the group to which it is predicted to belong. The following column, "Highest Probability: $P(G \mid D)$," is the posterior probability of membership in the predicted group, given the obtained discriminant score. Posterior probabilities are obtained using Bayes' theorem. We did not specify prior probabilities here, and the assumption is that the *sample* proportions reflect the true *population* proportions of the two groups.

The next set of two columns labeled "Second highest," gives the other possibility: group membership in the opposite group and its probability. Since there are only two possible groups, this probability is $1 - P(G \mid D)$, where G is the predicted group. The last column in the table gives the discriminant score. For example, the first case belongs to group 1; it is predicted by the discriminant function to belong to group 1; its likelihood, $P(D \mid G)$ is 0.1798; its posterior probability of belonging to group 1 is $P(G \mid D) = 0.9587$. This point has the second highest probability of belonging to group 0 (there are only two groups, so the other group must, of course, be second). This probability is $0.0413(= 1 - 0.9587)$. Finally, the discriminant score for this point is -1.999. Figure 16–7 gives the summary results of the classification of the data in the estimation set (we have no holdout data set) using the discriminant function.

The classification results table shown in Figure 16–7 gives us a summary of the results in Figure 16–6, as well as the resulting percentages. The table in Figure 16–7 is often called the *hit ratio table*. Let us analyze the results presented in the table. In our data,

FIGURE 16-4   SPSS-Produced Stepwise Discriminant Analysis for Example 16-1

```
---------------------------- D I S C R I M I N A N T   A N A L Y S I S

ON GROUPS DEFINED BY REPAY

ANALYSIS NUMBER        1

STEPWISE VARIABLE SELECTION

SELECTION RULE:  MINIMIZE WILKS' LAMBDA

        MAXIMUM NUMBER OF STEPS. . . . . . . . .      10
        MINIMUM TOLERANCE LEVEL. . . . . . . . . 0.00100
        MINIMUM F TO ENTER . . . . . . . . . . .  1.0000
        MAXIMUM F TO REMOVE. . . . . . . . . . .  1.0000

CANONICAL DISCRIMINANT FUNCTIONS

        MAXIMUM NUMBER OF FUNCTIONS. . . . . . .       1
        MINIMUM CUMULATIVE PERCENT OF VARIANCE . . 100.00
        MAXIMUM SIGNIFICANCE OF WILKS' LAMBDA. . . 1.0000

PRIOR PROBABILITY FOR EACH GROUP IS 0.50000

----------------- VARIABLES NOT IN THE ANALYSIS AFTER STEP    0 ----------------

                        MINIMUM
VARIABLE   TOLERANCE   TOLERANCE   F TO ENTER    WILKS' LAMBDA

ASSETS     1.0000000   1.0000000    6.6152         0.81933
INCOME     1.0000000   1.0000000    3.0672         0.90724
DEBT       1.0000000   1.0000000    5.2263         0.85164
FAMSIZE    1.0000000   1.0000000    2.5292         0.92225
JOB        1.0000000   1.0000000    0.24457        0.99191

* * * * * * * * * * * * * * * * * * * * * * * * * * * * * * * * * * * * * *

AT STEP   1, ASSETS    WAS INCLUDED IN THE ANALYSIS.

                          DEGREES OF FREEDOM   SIGNIF.   BETWEEN GROUPS

WILKS' LAMBDA      0.81933    1     1    30.0
EQUIVALENT F       6.61516          1    30.0    0.0153

----------------- VARIABLES NOT IN THE ANALYSIS AFTER STEP    1 ----------------

VARIABLE   TOLERANCE   F TO REMOVE    WILKS' LAMBDA

ASSETS     1.0000000      6.6152
```

FIGURE 16–4 *(Continued)*

```
--------------- VARIABLES NOT IN THE ANALYSIS AFTER STEP    1 ----------------


                          MINIMUM
VARIABLE   TOLERANCE   TOLERANCE   F TO ENTER    WILKS' LAMBDA


INCOME     0.5784563   0.5784563   0.90821E-02      0.81908
DEBT       0.9706667   0.9706667   6.0662           0.67759
FAMSIZE    0.9492947   0.9492947   3.9269           0.72162
JOB        0.9631433   0.9631433   0.47688E-06      0.81933


F STATISTICS AND SIGNIFICANCES BETWEEN PAIRS OF GROUPS AFTER STEP    1
EACH F STATISTIC HAS    1 AND        30.0 DEGREES OF FREEDOM.


                    GROUP          0


     GROUP
        1                        6.6152
                                 0.0153


* * * * * * * * * * * * * * * * * * * * * * * * * * * * * * * * * * * * * *

AT STEP    2, DEBT      WAS INCLUDED IN THE ANALYSIS.
                             DEGREES OF FREEDOM   SIGNIF.  BETWEEN GROUPS
WILKS' LAMBDA     0.67759        2   1      30.0
EQUIVALENT F      6.89923            2      29.0    0.0035

----------------- VARIABLES IN THE ANALYSIS AFTER STEP    2 ------------------

VARIABLE   TOLERANCE   F TO REMOVE    WILKS' LAMBDA

ASSETS     0.9706667    7.4487          0.85164
DEBT       0.9706667    6.0662          0.81933

--------------- VARIABLES NOT IN THE ANALYSIS AFTER STEP    2 ----------------


                          MINIMUM
VARIABLE    TOLERANCE   TOLERANCE   F TO ENTER    WILKS' LAMBDA


INCOME      0.5728383   0.5568120   0.17524E-01      0.67717
FAMSIZE     0.9323959   0.9308959   2.2214           0.62779
JOB         0.9105435   0.9105435   0.27914          0.67091


F STATISTICS AND SIGNIFICANCES BETWEEN PAIRS OF GROUPS AFTER STEP    2
EACH F STATISTIC HAS    2 AND        29.0 DEGREES OF FREEDOM.


                    GROUP          0


     GROUP
        1                        6.8992
                                 0.0035

* * * * * * * * * * * * * * * * * * * * * * * * * * * * * * * * * * * * * *
```

FIGURE 16–4   *(Concluded)*

```
* * * * * * * * * * * * * * * * * * * * * * * * * * * * * * * * * * *

AT STEP   3, FAMSIZE  WAS INCLUDED IN THE ANALYSIS.


                              DEGREES OF FREEDOM   SIGNIF.  BETWEEN GROUPS
WILKS' LAMBDA      0.62779        3      1    30.0
EQUIVALENT F       5.53369               3    28.0    0.0041


----------------- VARIABLES IN THE ANALYSIS AFTER STEP    3 ----------------


VARIABLE   TOLERANCE   F TO REMOVE   WILKS' LAMBDA


ASSETS     0.9308959    8.4282           0.81676
DEBT       0.9533874    4.1849           0.72162
FAMSIZE    0.9323959    2.2214           0.67759


----------------- VARIABLES NOT IN THE ANALYSIS AFTER STEP   3 ------------------


                       MINIMUM
VARIABLE   TOLERANCE   TOLERANCE  F TO ENTER    WILKS' LAMBDA


INCOME     0.5725772  0.5410775  0.24098E-01      0.62723
JOB        0.8333526  0.8333526  0.86952E-02      0.62759


F STATISTICS AND SIGNIFICANCES BETWEEN PAIRS OF GROUPS AFTER STEP    3
EACH F STATISTIC HAS   3 AND        28.0 DEGREES OF FREEDOM.


                  GROUP        0


     GROUP
       1                    5.5337
                            0.0041


F LEVEL OR TOLERANCE OR VIN INSUFFICIENT FOR FURTHER COMPUTATION

                         SUMMARY TABLE


            ACTION     VARS  WILKS'
STEP ENTERED REMOVED    IN   LAMBDA    SIG.     LABEL


  1  ASSETS            1    .81933    .0153
  2  DEBT              2    .67759    .0035
  3  FAMSIZE           3    .62779    .0041
```

FIGURE 16–5   SPSS-Produced Estimates of the Discriminant Function Coefficients for Example 16–1

```
UNSTANDARDIZED CANONICAL DISCRIMINANT FUNCTION COEFFICIENTS


                    FUNC   1


ASSETS          -0.3522450E-01
DEBT             0.4291033E-01
FAMSIZE          0.4832695
(CONSTANT)      -0.9950070
```

FIGURE 16–6   Predicted Group Membership Chart for Example 16–1

CASE SEGNUM	MIS VAL	SEL	ACTUAL GROUP		HIGHEST GROUP	PROBABILITY P(D/G)	P(G/D)	2ND HIGHEST GROUP	P (G/D)	DISCRIMINANT SCORES...
1			1		1	0.1798	0.9587	0	0.0413	-1.9990
2			1		1	0.3357	0.9293	0	0.0707	-1.6202
3			1		1	0.8840	0.7939	0	0.2061	-0.8034
4			1	**	0	0.4761	0.5146	1	0.4854	0.1328
5			1		1	0.3368	0.9291	0	0.0709	-1.6181
6			1		1	0.5571	0.5614	0	0.4386	-0.0704
7			1	**	0	0.6272	0.5986	1	0.4014	0.3598
8			1		1	0.7236	0.6452	0	0.3548	-0.3039
9			1		1	0.9600	0.7693	0	0.2307	-0.7076
10			1		1	0.3004	0.9362	0	0.0638	-1.6930
11			0		0	0.5217	0.5415	1	0.4585	0.2047
12			0		0	0.6018	0.8714	1	0.1286	1.3672
13			0		0	0.6080	0.5887	1	0.4113	0.3325
14			0		0	0.5083	0.8932	1	0.1068	1.5068
15			0		0	0.8409	0.6959	1	0.3041	0.6447
16			0		0	0.2374	0.9481	1	0.0519	2.0269
17			0		0	0.9007	0.7195	1	0.2805	0.7206
18			0		0	0.8377	0.8080	1	0.1920	1.0502
19			0		0	0.0677	0.9797	1	0.0203	2.6721
20			0		0	0.1122	0.9712	1	0.0288	2.4338
21			0	**	1	0.7395	0.6524	0	0.3476	-0.3250
22			1	**	0	0.9432	0.7749	1	0.2251	0.9166
23			1		1	0.7819	0.6711	0	0.3289	-0.3807
24			0	**	1	0.5294	0.5459	0	0.4541	-0.0286
25			1		1	0.5673	0.8796	0	0.1204	-1.2296
26			1		1	0.1964	0.9557	0	0.0443	-1.9494
27			0	**	1	0.6916	0.6302	0	0.3698	-0.2608
28			1	**	0	0.7479	0.6562	1	0.3438	0.5240
29			1	**	0	0.9211	0.7822	1	0.2178	0.9445
30			1		1	0.4276	0.9107	0	0.0893	-1.4509
31			1		1	0.8188	0.8136	0	0.1864	-0.8866
32			0	**	1	0.8825	0.7124	0	0.2876	-0.5097

FIGURE 16–7 Summary Table of Classification Results for Example 16–1

```
CLASSIFICATION RESULTS -

                      NO. OF    PREDICTED GROUP MEMBERSHIP
      ACTUAL GROUP     CASES           0            1
-----------------------  --------    --------    --------


   GROUP      0           14           10           4
                                     71.4%        28.6%


   GROUP      1           18            5          13
                                     27.8%        72.2%


   PERCENT OF 'GROUPED' CASES CORRECTLY CLASSIFIED:  71.88%
```

there were 14 cases belonging to group 0 and 18 cases belonging to group 1. The next column shows us that 10 of the group 0 cases were correctly classified by the discriminant function and that these 10 observations constitute 71.4% of the group 0 cases. Four cases belonging to category 0 were incorrectly classified as belonging to category 1. Similarly, the table shows that 72.2% of the group 1 cases were correctly classified by the discriminant function, while 27.8% (five cases) were not. The diagonal elements in the table, here 71.4% and 72.2%, are the important figures. They give us the prediction accuracy of the discriminant function. The percentage of the total number of cases that were correctly classified is given at the bottom of the table. Here the table shows "Percent of 'grouped' cases correctly classified: 71.88%." This is the overall success rate, or hit ratio, of the discriminant function. This value is obtained by dividing the number of correctly classified cases by the total number of cases and multiplying by 100 to get a percentage: $[(10 + 13)/32]100 = 71.88\%$.

In a sense, the hit ratio, the overall percentage of cases that were correctly classified by the discriminant function, is similar to the R^2 statistic in multiple regression. The hit ratio is a measure of how well the discriminant function discriminates between groups. When this measure is 100%, the discrimination is very good; when it is small, the discrimination is poor. How small is "small"? Let us consider this problem logically. Suppose that our data set contains 100 observations: 50 in each of the two groups. Now, if we arbitrarily assign all 100 observations to one of the groups, we would have a 50% prediction accuracy! We should expect the discriminant function to give us better than 50% correct classification ratio; otherwise we can do as well without it. Similarly, suppose that one group has 75 observations and the other 25. In this case, we would get 75% correct classification if we assigned all our observations to the large group. Here the discriminant function should give us better than 75% correct classification if it is to be useful.

Another criterion for evaluating the success of the discriminant function is the *proportional chance criterion.*

The **proportional chance criterion:**

$$C = p^2 + (1 - p)^2 \qquad (16\text{–}7)$$

where p is the proportion of observations in one of the two groups (given as a decimal quantity)

In our example, the discriminant function passes both of these tests. The proportions of people in each of the two groups are $14/32 = 0.4375$, and $18/32 = 0.5625$. From Figure 16–7, we know that the hit ratio of the discriminant function is 0.7188 (71.88%). This figure is much higher than that we could obtain by arbitrary assignment (56.25%). The proportional chance criterion, equation 16–7, gives us $C = (0.4375)^2 + (0.5625)^2 = 0.5078$. The hit ratio is clearly larger than this criterion as well. While the hit ratio is better than expected under arbitrary classification, it is not great. We would probably like to have a greater hit ratio if we are to classify loan applicants in a meaningful way. In this case, over 28% may be expected to be incorrectly classified. We must also keep in mind two facts: (1) Our sample size was relatively small, and therefore our inference may be subject to large errors; and (2) our hit ratio is overestimated because it is based on the estimation data. To get a better idea, we would need to use the discriminant function in classifying cases not used in the estimation and see how well the function performs with this data set.

Figure 16–8 shows the locations of the data points in the two groups in relation to their discriminant scores. It is a *map* of the locations of the two groups along the direction of greatest differentiation between the groups (the direction of the discriminant function). Note the overlap of the two groups in the middle of the graph and the separation on the two sides. (Group 0 is denoted by 1s and group 1 by 2s.)

Discriminant Analysis with More than Two Groups

Discriminant analysis is extendable to more than two groups. When we carry out an analysis with more than two groups, however, we have more than one discriminant function. The first discrimination function is the function that discriminates best among the r groups. The second discriminant function is a function that has zero correlation with the first and has second-best discriminating power among the r groups, and so on. With r groups, there are $r - 1$ discriminant functions. Thus, with three groups, for example, there are two discriminant functions.

For Example 16–1, suppose that the bank distinguishes three categories: people who repay the loan (group 1), people who default (group 0), and people who have some difficulties and are several months late with payments, but do not default (group 2). The bank has data on a random sample of 46 people, each person falling into one of the three categories. Figure 16–9 shows the classification probabilities and the predicted groups for the new analysis. The classification is based on scores on both discriminant functions. The discriminant scores of each person on each of the two discriminant functions are also shown. Again, double asterisks denote a misclassified case. Figure 16–10 gives the estimated coefficients of the two discriminant functions.

Figure 16–11 gives the classification summary. We see that 86.7% of the group 0 cases were correctly classified by the two discriminant functions, 78.6% of group 1 were correctly classified, and 82.4% of group 2 were correctly classified. The overall percentage of correctly classified cases is 82.61%, which is fairly high.

Figure 16–12 is a scatter plot of the data in the three groups. The figure also shows the three group means. The following figure, Figure 16–13, is especially useful. This is a *territorial map* of the three groups as determined by the pair of estimated discriminant functions. The map shows the boundaries of the plane formed by looking at the pair of scores: (discriminant function 1 score, discriminant function 2 score). Any new point may be classified as belonging to one of the groups depending on where its pair of computed scores make it fall on the map. For example, a point with the

FIGURE 16-8   A Map of the Location of the Two Groups for Example 16-1

```
SYMBOLS USED IN PLOTS
SYMBOL GROUP LABEL
------ ----- -----

   1       0
   2       1
```

ALL-GROUPS STACKED HISTOGRAM

CANONICAL DISCRIMINANT FUNCTION 1

scores: 2 on function 1 and −4 on function 2 falls in the territory of group 0 (this group is denoted by 1 in the plot, as indicated). A group territory is marked by its symbol on the inside of its boundaries with other groups. Group means are also shown, denoted by asterisks.

Many more statistics relevant to discriminant analysis may be computed and reported by computer packages. These are beyond the scope of our discussion, but explanations of these statistics may be found in books on multivariate analysis. This section should give you the basic ideas of discriminant analysis so that you may build on the knowledge acquired here.

PROBLEMS

16-1. What are the purposes of discriminant analysis?

16-2. Suppose that a discriminant analysis is carried out on a data set consisting of two groups. The larger group constitutes 125 observations and the smaller one 89. It is believed that the relative sizes of the two groups reflect their relative sizes within the population. If the classification summary table indicates that the overall percentage of correct classification is 57%, would you use the results of this analysis? Why or why not?

FIGURE 16-9 Predicted Group Membership Chart for Three Groups (extended Example 16-1)

CASE SEGNUM	MIS VAL	SEL	ACTUAL GROUP		HIGHEST GROUP	PROBABILITY P(D/G)	P(G/D)	2ND HIGHEST GROUP	P(G/D)	DISCRIMINANT SCORES...	
1			1		1	0.6966	0.9781	2	0.0198	-2.3023	-0.4206
2			1		1	0.3304	0.9854	2	0.0142	-2.8760	-0.1267
3			1		1	0.9252	0.8584	2	0.1060	-1.2282	-0.3592
4			1		1	0.5982	0.9936	2	0.0040	-2.3031	-1.2574
5			1	**	0	0.6971	0.8513	1	0.1098	0.6072	-1.3190
6			1		1	0.8917	0.8293	2	0.1226	-1.1074	-0.3643
7			1	**	0	0.2512	0.5769	1	0.4032	-0.0298	-1.8240
8			1		1	0.7886	0.9855	2	0.0083	-1.9517	-1.1657
9			0		0	0.3132	0.4869	1	0.4675	-0.1210	-1.3934
10			0		0	0.4604	0.9951	2	0.0032	2.1534	-1.7015
11			0		0	0.5333	0.9572	1	0.0348	1.0323	-1.9002
12			0		0	0.8044	0.9762	2	0.0204	1.9347	-0.9280
13			0		0	0.6697	0.8395	1	0.1217	0.5641	-1.3381
14			0		0	0.2209	0.7170	2	0.2815	2.2185	0.6586
15			0		0	0.6520	0.9900	2	0.0075	2.0176	-1.3735
16			0		0	0.0848	0.9458	2	0.0541	3.2112	0.3004
17			0	**	2	0.2951	0.7983	0	0.1995	1.6393	1.4480
18			1	**	0	0.1217	0.6092	1	0.3843	-0.0234	-2.3885
19			0		0	0.6545	0.6144	2	0.3130	0.7054	-0.0932
20			1		1	0.7386	0.9606	2	0.0362	-2.1369	-0.2312
21			1		1	0.0613	0.9498	2	0.0501	-3.2772	0.8831
22			0		0	0.6667	0.6961	1	0.1797	0.3857	-0.7874
23			1		1	0.7659	0.8561	2	0.1320	-1.6001	0.0635
24			0	**	1	0.5040	0.4938	2	0.3454	-0.4694	-0.0770
25			2	**	1	0.9715	0.8941	2	0.0731	-1.2811	-0.5314
26			2		2	0.6241	0.5767	0	0.2936	0.2503	0.2971
27			2		2	0.9608	0.9420	0	0.0353	0.1808	1.5221
28			2		2	0.9594	0.9183	0	0.0589	0.3557	1.3629
29			2	**	0	0.2982	0.5458	2	0.4492	1.6705	0.6994
30			2	**	1	0.9627	0.9160	2	0.0462	-1.2538	-0.8067
31			2		2	0.0400	0.9923	0	0.0076	1.7304	3.1894
32			2		2	0.9426	0.9077	1	0.0620	-0.2467	1.3298
33			2		2	0.7863	0.7575	0	0.2075	0.6256	0.8154
34			2		2	0.3220	0.9927	0	0.0060	0.6198	2.6635
35			2		2	0.9093	0.8322	1	0.1113	-0.2519	0.9826
36			2		2	0.5387	0.5528	0	0.4147	0.8843	0.4770
37			2		2	0.7285	0.9752	1	0.0160	-0.1655	2.0088
38			2		2	0.7446	0.9662	1	0.0248	-0.3220	1.9034
39			0		0	0.6216	0.9039	1	0.0770	0.7409	-1.6165
40			2		2	0.9461	0.8737	1	0.0823	-0.2246	1.1434
41			1		1	0.7824	0.9250	2	0.0690	-1.8845	-0.0819
42			0		0	0.3184	0.9647	1	0.0319	1.0456	-2.3016
43			1		1	0.7266	0.7304	0	0.1409	-0.6875	-0.6183
44			2		2	0.8738	0.9561	1	0.0278	-0.1642	1.7082
45			0		0	0.6271	0.9864	2	0.0121	2.2294	-1.0154
46			2		2	0.2616	0.9813	1	0.0175	-0.8946	2.5641

16-3. Refer to the results in Figure 16-5 and to equation 16-6. Suppose that a loan applicant has assets of $23,000, debt of $12,000, and a family with three members. How should you classify this person, if you are to use the results of the discriminant analysis? (Remember that debt and assets values are listed without the "000" digits in the program.)

FIGURE 16-10   Estimated Coefficients of the Two Discriminant Functions (extended Example 16-1)

```
UNSTANDARDIZED CANONICAL DISCRIMINANT FUNCTION COEFFICIENTS


                  FUNC  1           FUNC  2

ASSETS       -0.4103059E-01  -0.5688170E-03
INCOME       -0.4325325E-01   0.6726829E-01
DEBT          0.3644035E-01   0.4154356E-01
FAMSIZE       0.7471749       0.1772388
JOB           0.1787231      -0.4592559E-01
(CONSTANT)   -0.9083139      -3.743060
```

FIGURE 16-11   Summary Table of Classification Results (extended Example 16-1)

```
CLASSIFICATION RESULTS -

                            NO. OF    PREDICTED GROUP MEMBERSHIP
       ACTUAL GROUP          CASES       0          1          2
       ------------------   -------   --------   --------   --------

GROUP            0            15         13          1          1
                                       86.7%       6.7%       6.7%

GROUP            1            14          3         11          0
                                       21.4%      78.6%       0.0%

GROUP            2            17          1          2         14
                                        5.9%      11.8%      82.4%

PERCENT OF 'GROUPED' CASES CORRECTLY CLASSIFIED:   82.61%
```

16-4.   For problem 16-3, suppose an applicant has $54,000 in assets, $10,000 of debt, and a family of four. How would you classify this applicant? In this problem and the preceding one, be careful to interpret the *sign* of the score correctly.

16-5.   Why should you use a holdout data set and try to use the discriminant function for classifying its members? How would you go about doing this?

16-6.   A mail-order firm wants to be able to classify people as prospective buyers versus nonbuyers based on some of the people's demographics provided on mailing lists. From prior experience, it is known that only 8% of those who receive a brochure end up buying from the company. Use two criteria to determine the minimum overall prediction success rate you would expect from a discriminant function in this case.

16-7.   In the situation of problem 16-6, how would you account for the prior knowledge that 8% of the population of those who receive a brochure actually buy?

16-8.   Use the territorial map shown in Figure 16-13 to predict group membership for a point with a score of -3 on discriminant function 1 and a score of 0 on discriminant function 2. What about a point with a score of 2 on function 1 and 4 on function 2?

FIGURE 16-12   Scatter Plot of the Data (extended Example 16-1)

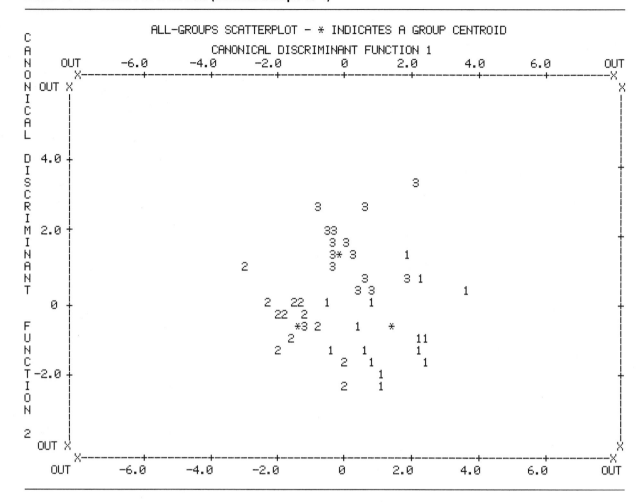

16–9. Use the information in Figure 16–10 and the territorial map in Figure 16–13 to classify a person with assets of $50,000, income of $37,500, debt of $23,000, family size of 2, and three years' employment at the current job.

16–10. What are the advantages of a stepwise routine for selection of variables to be included in the discriminant function(s)?

16–11. A discriminant function is estimated, and the p-value based on Wilks' lambda is found to be 0.239. Would you use this function? Explain.

16–12. What is the meaning of $P(G \mid D)$, and how is it computed when prior information is specified?

16–13. In trying to classify members of a population into one of six groups, how many discriminant functions are possible? Will all of these functions necessarily be found significant? Explain.

FIGURE 16-13 Territorial Map (extended Example 16-1)

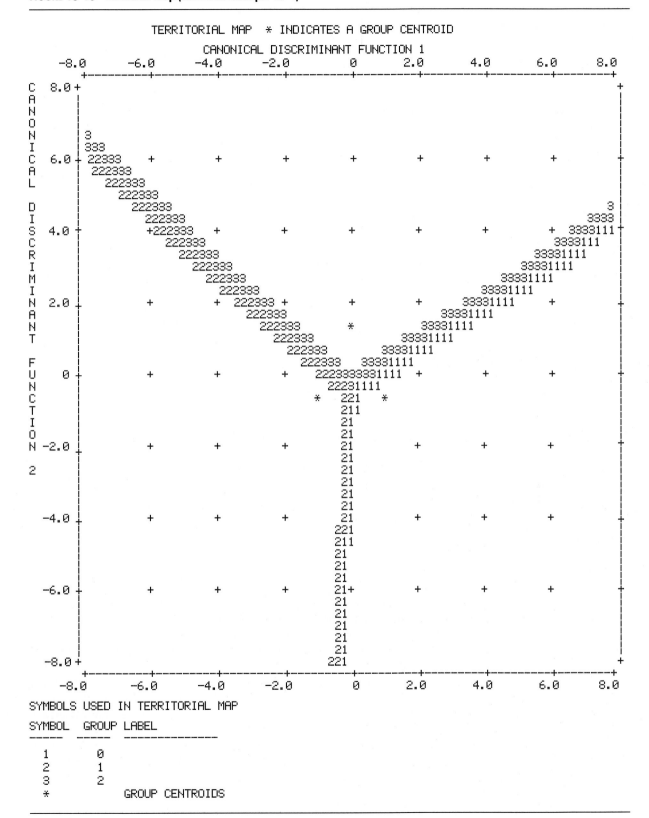

16–14.   A discriminant analysis was carried out to determine whether a firm belongs to one of three classes: build, hold, or pull back. The results, reported in an article in the *Journal of Marketing Research*, include the following territorial map. How would you classify a firm that received a score of 0 on both discriminant functions?

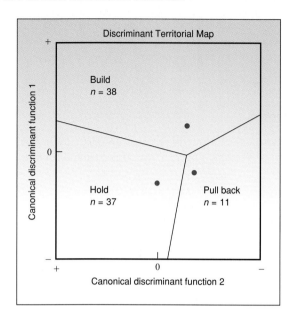

16–4   Principal Components and Factor Analysis

In this section, we discuss two related methods for decomposing the information content in a set of variables into information about an inherent set of latent components. The first method is called **principal component analysis.** Our aim with this method is to decompose the variation in a multivariate data set into a set of components such that the first component accounts for as much of the variation in the data as possible, the second component accounts for the second largest portion of the variation, and so on. In addition, each component in this method of analysis is *orthogonal* to the others; that is, each component is uncorrelated with the others: as a direction in space, each component is at right angles to the others.

In **factor analysis,** which is the second method for decomposing the information in a set of variables, our approach to the decomposition is different. We are not always interested in the orthogonality of the components (in this context, called *factors*); neither do we care whether the proportion of the variance accounted for by the factors decreases as each factor is extracted. Instead, we look for meaningful factors in terms of the particular application at hand. The factors we seek are the underlying, latent dimensions of the problem. The factors summarize the larger set of original variables.

For example, consider the results of a test consisting of answers to many questions administered to a sample of students. If we apply principal components analysis, we will decompose the answers to the questions into scores on a (usually smaller) set of components that account for successively smaller portions of the variation in the student answers and that are independent of each other. If we apply factor analysis, on the other hand, we seek to group the question variables into a smaller set of meaningful factors. One factor, consisting of responses to several questions, may be a measure of raw intelligence; another factor may be a measure of verbal ability and will consist of another set of questions; and so on.

We will start by discussing principal components and then present a detailed description of the techniques of factor analysis. There are two kinds of factor analysis. One is called *R*-factor analysis, and this is the method we will describe. Another is called *Q*-factor analysis. *Q*-factor analysis is a technique where we group the respondents, people or data elements, into sets with certain meanings rather than grouping the variables.

Principal Components

Figure 16–14 shows a data set in two dimensions. Each point in the ellipsoid-shaped cluster has two components: X and Y. If we look at the direction of the data cluster, however, we see that it is not oriented along either of the two axes X and Y. In fact, the data are oriented in space at a certain angle to the X axis. Look at the two principal axes of the ellipse of data, and you will notice that one contains much variation along its direction. The other axis, at 90° to the first, represents less variation of the data along its direction. We choose that direction in space about which the data are most variable (the principal axis of the ellipse) and call it the *first principal component*. The *second principal component* is at 90° to the first (it is **orthogonal** to the first). These axes are shown in Figure 16–14. Note that all we really have to do is rotate the original X and Y axes until we find a direction in space where the principal axis of the elliptical cluster of data lies along this direction. Since this is the larger axis, it represents the largest variation in the data, the data vary most along the direction we labeled *first component*. The second component captures the second largest variation in the data.

With three variables, there are three directions in space. We find that rotation of the axes of the three variables X, Y, and Z such that the first component is the direction in which the ellipsoid of data is widest. The second component is the direction with the second largest proportion of variance, and the third component is the direction with the third largest variation. All three components are at 90° to each other. Such rotations, which preserve the orthogonality (90° angle) of the axes, are called *rigid rotations*. With more variables, the procedure is the same (except that we can no longer graph it). The successive reduction in the variation in the data with the extraction of each component is shown schematically in Figure 16–15.

The Extraction of the Components

There is a remarkable mathematical theorem, the fundamental theorem of principal components, that allows us to find the components. The theorem says that if we have any set of k variables $X_1, X_2, \ldots, X_k$, where the variance-covariance matrix of these variables, denoted Σ, *is invertible* (an algebraic condition you need not worry about), we can always transform the original variables to a set of k uncorrelated variables $Y_1, Y_2, \ldots, Y_k$ by an appropriate rotation. Note that we do not require a normal distribution assumption.

Can you think of one very good use of principal component analysis as a preliminary stage for an important statistical technique? Remember the ever-present problem of *multicollinearity* in multiple regression analysis? There the fact that k "independent" variables turned out to be dependent on each other caused many

FIGURE 16–14   Principal Components of a Bivariate Data Set

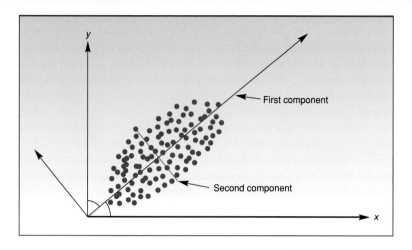

FIGURE 16–15   Reduction in the Variance in a Data Set with Successive Extraction of Components

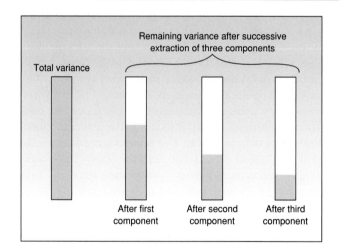

problems. One solution to the problem of multicollinearity is to transform the original k variables, which are correlated with each other, into a new set of k uncorrelated variables. These uncorrelated variables are the principal components of the data set. Then we can run the regression on the new set, the principal components, and avoid the multicollinearity altogether. We still have to consider, however, the contribution of each original variable to the dependent variable in the regression.

Equation 16–8 is the equation of the first principal component, which is a linear combination of the original k variables $X_1, X_2, \ldots, X_k$.

$$Y_1 = a_{11}X_1 + a_{12}X_2 + \cdots + a_{1k}X_k \qquad (16\text{–}8)$$

Similarly, the second principal component is given by

$$Y_2 = a_{21}X_1 + a_{22}X_2 + \cdots + a_{2k}X_k \qquad (16\text{–}9)$$

and so on. The a_{ij} are constants, like regression coefficients. The linear combinations are formed by the rotation of the axes.

If we use k new independent variables $Y_1, Y_2, \ldots, Y_k$, then we have accounted for all the variance in the observations. In that case, all we have done is to transform the original variables into linear combinations that are uncorrelated with each other (orthogonal) and that account for all the variance in the observations, the first component accounting for the largest portion, the second for less, and so on. When we use k new variables, however, there is no *economy* in the number of new variables. If, on the other hand, we want to reduce the number of original variables to a smaller set where each new variable has some meaning—each new variable represents a hidden *factor*—we need to use factor analysis. Factor analysis (the *R*-factor kind), also called *common factor analysis,* is one of the most commonly used multivariate methods, and we devote the rest of this section to a description of this important method. In factor analysis, we assume a multivariate normal distribution.

Factor Analysis

In factor analysis, we assume that each of the variables we have is made up of a linear combination of common factors (hidden factors that affect the variable and possibly affect other variables) and a specific component unique to the variable.

The k original X_i variables written as linear combinations of a smaller set of m common factors and a unique component for each variable:

$$X_1 = b_{11} F_1 + b_{12} F_2 + \cdots + b_{1m} F_m + U_1$$
$$X_2 = b_{21} F_1 + b_{22} F_2 + \cdots + b_{2m} F_m + U_2$$
$$\vdots$$
$$X_k = b_{k1} F_1 + b_{k2} F_2 + \cdots + b_{km} F_m + U_k \qquad (16\text{--}10)$$

The F_j, $j = 1, \ldots, m$, are the common factors. Each U_i, $i = 1, \ldots, k$, is the unique component of variable X_i. The coefficients b_{ij} are called *factor loadings*.

The total variance in the data in factor analysis is composed of the common-factor component, called the *communality,* and the *specific* part, due to each variable alone.

The Extraction of Factors

The factors are extracted according to the communality. We determine the number of factors in an analysis based on the percentage of the variation explained by each factor. Sometimes prior considerations lead to the determination of the number of factors. One rule of thumb in determining the number of factors to be extracted considers the total variance explained by the factor. In computer output, the total variance explained by a factor is listed as the *eigenvalue*. (Eigenvalues are roots of determinantal equations and are fundamental to much of multivariate analysis. Since understanding them requires some familiarity with linear algebra, we will not say much about eigenvalues, except that they are used as measures of the variance explained by factors.) The rule just mentioned says that a factor with an eigenvalue less than 1.00 should not be used because it accounts for less than the variation explained by a single variable. This rule is conservative in the sense that we probably want to summarize the variables with a set of factors smaller than indicated by this rule. Another, less conservative, rule says that the factors should account for a relatively large portion of the variation in the variables: 80%, 70%, 65%, or any relatively high percentage of the variance. The consideration in setting the percentage is similar to our evaluation of R^2 in regression. There really is no absolute rule.

We start the factor analysis by computing a correlation matrix of all the variables. This diagonal matrix has 1s on the diagonal because the correlation of each variable with itself is equal to 1.00. The correlation in row i and column j of this matrix is the correlation between variables X_i and X_j. The correlation matrix is then used by the computer in extracting the factors and producing the factor matrix. The factor matrix is a matrix showing the factor loadings—the sample correlations between each factor and each variable. These are the coefficients b_{ij} in equation 16–10. Principal component analysis is often used in the preliminary factor extraction procedure, although other methods are useful as well.

The Rotation of Factors

Once the factors are extracted, the next stage of the analysis begins. In this stage, the factors are *rotated*. The purpose of the rotation is to find the best distribution of the factor loadings in terms of the meaning of the factors. If you think of our hypothetical example of scores of students on an examination, it could be that the initial factors derived (these could be just the principal components) explain proportions of the variation in scores, but not in any meaningful way. The rotation may then lead us to find a factor that accounts for intelligence, a factor that accounts for verbal ability, a third factor that accounts for artistic talent, and so on. The rotation is an integral part of factor analysis and helps us derive factors that are as meaningful as possible. Usually, each of the initially derived factors will tend to be correlated with *many* of the variables. The purpose of the rotation is to identify each factor with only *some* of the variables—different variables with each factor—so that each factor may be interpreted in a meaningful way. Each factor will then be associated with *one* hidden attribute: intelligence, verbal ability, or artistic talent.

There are two classes of rotation methods. One is **orthogonal,** or **rigid, rotation.** Here the axes maintain their orthogonality; that is, they maintain an angle of 90° between every two of them. This means that the factors, once they are rotated, will maintain the quality of being uncorrelated with each other. This may be useful if we believe that the inherent, hidden dimensions in our problem are independent of each other (here this would mean that we believe intelligence is independent of verbal ability and that both are independent of artistic talent). The rigid rotation is also simpler to carry out than nonrigid rotation. A nonrigid rotation is called an **oblique rotation.** In an oblique rotation, we allow the factors to have some correlations among them. We break the initial 90° angles between pairs of axes (pairs of factors), and we seek the *best association* between factors and variables that are included in them, regardless of whether the factors are orthogonal to each other (i.e., at 90° to each other).

Figure 16–16 shows the two possible kinds of rotation. The dots on the graph in each part of the figure correspond to variables, and the axes correspond to factors. In the first example, orthogonal rotation, look at the projections of the seven points (seven variables) along the two axes. These are the factor loadings. When we rotate the axes (the factors), maintaining their 90° angle, we find a better fit of the variables with the factors. The top four variables load highly on the shifted vertical axis, while the

FIGURE 16-16 **An Orthogonal Factor Rotation and an Oblique Factor Rotation**

bottom three variables load highly on the shifted horizontal axis. In the lower figure, we see that an oblique rotation provides a better association of the factors with the variables in this different situation.

There are several algorithms for orthogonal rotation. The most commonly used algorithm is call VARIMAX. The VARIMAX rotation aims at finding a solution where a variable loads highly on one particular factor and loads as low as possible on other factors. The algorithm maximizes the sum of the variances of the loadings in the factor matrix; hence the name VARIMAX. When we use this method, our final solution will have factors with loadings that are high on some variables and low on others. This simplifies the interpretation of the factors. Two other methods are QUARTIMAX and EQUIMAX. Since they are less commonly used, we will not discuss them. Let us look at an example.

An analysis of the responses of 1,076 randomly sampled people to a survey about job satisfaction was carried out. The questionnaire contained 14 questions related to satisfac-

EXAMPLE 16-2

TABLE 16–2 Factor Analysis of Satisfaction Items

	Factor Loadings[a]			
	1	**2**	**3**	**4**
Satisfaction with Information				
1. I am satisfied with the information I receive from my superior about my job performance	0.87	0.19	0.13	0.22
2. I receive enough information from my supervisor about my job performance	0.88	0.14	0.15	0.13
3. I receive enough feedback from my supervisor on how well I'm doing	0.92	0.09	0.11	0.12
4. There is enough opportunity in my job to find out how I am doing	0.65	0.29	0.31	0.15
Satisfaction with Variety				
5. I am satisfied with the variety of activities my job offers	0.13	0.82	0.07	0.17
6. I am satisfied with the freedom I have to do what I want on my job	0.17	0.59	0.45	0.14
7. I am satisfied with the opportunities my job provides me to interact with others	0.18	0.48	0.32	0.22
8. There is enough variety in my job	0.11	0.75	0.02	0.12
9. I have enough freedom to do what I want in my job	0.17	0.62	0.46	0.12
10. My job has enough opportunity for independent thought and action	0.20	0.62	0.47	0.06
Satisfaction with Closure				
11. I am satisfied with the opportunities my job gives me to complete tasks from beginning to end	0.17	0.21	0.76	0.11
12. My job has enough opportunity to complete the work I start	0.12	0.10	0.71	0.12
Satisfaction with Pay				
13. I am satisfied with the pay I receive for my job	0.17	0.14	0.05	0.51
14. I am satisfied with the security my job provides me	0.10	0.11	0.15	0.66

[a]Varimax rotation. R^2 for each of the four factors is 41.0, 13.5, 8.5, and 7.8, respectively.

tion on the job. The responses to the questions were analyzed using factor analysis with VARIMAX rotation of factors. The results, the 4 factors extracted and their loadings with respect to each of the original 14 variables, are shown in Table 16–2.

SOLUTION

The highest loading variables are chosen for each factor. Thus, the first factor has loadings of 0.87, 0.88, 0.92, and 0.65 on the questions relabeled as 1, 2, 3, and 4, respectively. After looking at the questions, the analysts named this factor *satisfaction with information*. After looking at the highest-loading variables on the next factor, factor 2, the analysts named this factor *satisfaction with variety*. The two remaining factors were named in a similar way. The key to identifying and interpreting the factors is to look for the variables with highest loadings on each factor and to find a common meaning: a summary name for all the variables loading high on that factor. The VARIMAX rotation is especially useful for such interpretations because it will make each factor have some variables with high loadings and the rest of the variables with low loadings. The factor is then identified with the high-loading variables.

The factor loadings are the standardized regression coefficients in a multiple regression equation of each original variable as dependent, and with the factors as independent variables. When the factors are uncorrelated, as is the case when we use an orthogonal rotation, the total proportion of the variance explained for each variable is equal to the sum of the proportions of the variance explained by all the factors. The proportion of the variance of each variable that is explained by the common factors is the communality. For each variable we therefore have

$$\text{Communality} = \% \text{ variance explained} = \sum_i (b_{ij})^2 \qquad (16\text{–}11)$$

where b_{ij} are the coefficients from the appropriate equation for the variable in question from equation 16–11. In this example, we have for the variable "I am satisfied with the information I receive from my superior about my job performance" (variable 1):

$$\text{Communality} = (0.87)^2 + (0.19)^2 + (0.13)^2 + (0.22)^2 = 0.8583, \text{ or } 85.83\%$$

(See the loadings of this variable on the four factors in Table 16–2.) This means that 85.83% of the variation in values of variable 1 is explained by the four factors. We may similarly compute the communality of all other variables. Variable 1 is assigned to factor 1, as indicated in the table. That factor accounts for $(0.87)^2 = 0.7569$, or 75.69% of the variation in this variable. Variable 5, for example, is assigned to factor 2, and factor 2 accounts for $(0.82)^2 = 0.6724$, or 67.24% of the variation in variable 5.

Finally, we mention a use of factor analysis as a preliminary stage for other forms of analysis. We can assign factor scores to each of the respondents (each member of our data set) and then conduct whatever analysis we are interested in, using the factor scores instead of scores on the original variables. This is meaningful when the factors summarize the information in a way that can be interpreted easily.

PROBLEMS

16–15. What is the main purpose of factor analysis?

16–16. What are the differences between factor analysis and principal components analysis?

16–17. What are the two kinds of factor analysis, and why is one of them more commonly used than the other?

16–18. What are the two kinds of factor rotation? What is the aim of rotating the factors? What is achieved by each of the two kinds of rotation?

16–19. What is achieved by the VARIMAX rotation, and what are two other rotation methods?

In the following problems, we present tables of results of factor analyses in different contexts reported in the marketing research literature. Give a brief interpretation of the findings in each problem.

16–20.

	Rotated Factor Loadings		
	Factor 1 (Scale 3)	Factor 2 (Scale 2)	Factor 3 (Scale 1)
1. Argument evaluation			
a. Supplier's argument	0.31	0.38	0.76
b. User's argument	0.15	0.35	0.85
2. Who-must-yield			
a. Who must give in	0.15	0.85	0.29
b. Who has best case	0.18	0.78	0.37
3. Overall supplier evaluation			
a. Overall impression	0.90	0.18	0.26
b. Buy from in future	0.94	0.14	0.12

16–21.

	Pattern Matrix			
	Factor 1 **Price**	**Factor 2** **Retailing/Selling**	**Factor 3** **Advertising**	**Factor 4** **Product**
Price item 1	0.37964	−0.11218	0.21009	−0.16767
Price item 2	0.34560	−0.11200	0.18910	−0.09073
Price item 3	0.60497	0.07133	−0.04858	0.03024
Price item 6	0.81856	0.03963	−0.01044	0.01738
Price item 7	0.74661	0.03967	0.00884	−0.06703
Retailing/selling item 1	0.07910	0.74098	−0.02888	0.07095
Retailing/selling item 2	−0.13690	0.58813	0.15950	−0.14141
Retailing/selling item 3	0.01484	0.74749	−0.02151	0.02269
Retailing/selling item 6	−0.05868	0.56753	0.10925	−0.13337
Retailing/selling item 7	0.07788	0.69284	−0.02320	−0.00457
Advertising item 2	−0.03460	−0.03414	0.65854	−0.01691
Advertising item 3	−0.06838	0.01973	0.71499	−0.06951
Advertising item 4	0.01481	−0.00748	0.57196	−0.03100
Advertising item 5	0.20779	0.13434	0.38402	0.12561
Advertising item 7	0.00921	0.11200	0.64330	−0.02534
Product item 2	0.24372	0.16809	−0.05254	−0.33600
Product item 3	−0.00370	0.02951	−0.00013	−0.61145
Product item 5	−0.03193	0.00631	0.04031	−0.78286
Product item 6	0.02346	0.01814	0.09122	−0.73298
Product item 7	0.03854	0.08088	−0.05244	−0.33921

16–22.   Name the factors; consider the signs of the loadings.

	Factor 1	**Factor 2**	**Factor 3**	**Factor 4**
Importance 1	0.59			
Importance 2	0.56			
Importance 3	0.62			
Importance 4	0.74			
Pleasure 1		−0.73		
Pleasure 2		−0.68		
Pleasure 3		−0.82		
Pleasure 4		−0.67		
Pleasure 5		−0.58		
Sign 1			0.78	
Sign 2			0.94	
Sign 3			0.73	
Sign 4			0.77	
Risk importance 1	0.62			
Risk importance 2	0.74			
Risk importance 3	0.74			
Risk probability 1				0.76
Risk probability 2				0.64
Risk probability 3				0.50

Omitted loadings are inferior to 0.25.

16–23. Identify each of the variables with one factor only. Also find the communality of each variable.

Business Policy	Factor 1 Market Penetration Issues	Factor 2 Project Quality Issues
Pricing policies	0.331	0.626
Record and reporting procedures	0.136	0.242
Advertising copy and expenditures	0.468	0.101
Selection of sources of operating supplies	0.214	0.126
Customer service and complaints	−0.152	0.792
Market forecasting and performance standards	0.459	0.669
Warranty decisions	0.438	0.528
Personnel staffing and training	0.162	0.193
Product delivery scheduling	0.020	0.782
Construction/installation procedures	0.237	0.724
Subcontracting agreements	−0.015	0.112
Number of dealerships	0.899	0.138
Location of dealerships	0.926	0.122
Trade areas	0.885	0.033
Size of building projects	0.206	0.436
Building design capabilities	−0.047	0.076
Sales promotion materials	0.286	0.096
Financial resources	0.029	0.427
Builder reputation	0.076	0.166
Offering competitors' lines	0.213	0.111
Variance explained	3.528	3.479
Percentage of total variance	17.64	17.39
Reliability (coefficient alpha)	.94	.83

16–24. Name the factors.

	Factor 1	Factor 2
Developing end-user preferences	−.04	.88
Product quality and technical leadership	.19	.65
Sales promotion programs and promotional aids	−.11	.86
Pricing policy	.78	−.03
Return goods policy	.79	−.04
Product availability (delivery and reliability)	.63	.26
Cooperativeness and technical competence of its personnel	.59	.45

16–25. Try to carry out a factor analysis on random samples of rows of data in the Federal Reserve data set at the end of the book (Appendix D).

16–5 Using the Computer

In MINITAB, the command PCA, followed by column numbers C1, C2, and so on, will result in a principal components analysis on data in the specified columns. Similarly, the command DISCRIMINANT will produce a discriminant analysis. In SPSS, the commands for factor analysis and discriminant analysis are simply FACTOR and DISCRIMINANT, respectively. In addition to the SPSS User's

FIGURE 16-17   Examples of SPSS Program Commands for Discriminant Analysis and Factor Analysis

```
DATA LIST FILE=QUALA
        /1 LEMON 1-2 ORANGE 4-5 REGION 7 STORE 9
DISCRIMINANT GROUPS=REGION(1,3)
        /VARIABLES=LEMON TO ORANGE
        /METHOD=WILKS
STATISTICS ALL
UNNUMBERED
INPUT PROGRAM
N OF CASES 100
NUMERIC A B C D E F G H I J K
INPUT MATRIX FREE
END INPUT PROGRAM
FACTOR READ=CORRELATION TRIANGLE
        /VARIABLES=A TO K
```

Guide, there is a book called *SPSS Advanced Statistics User's Guide* by Marija J. Norusis (Chicago: SPSS Inc., 1995). This guide is highly recommended. The background you have acquired in this chapter should allow you to conduct multivariate analysis using the guidebook.

To show the commands necessary for multivariate analysis, we present Figure 16–17, which illustrates the program commands for running the analyses just mentioned.

16-6   Summary and Review of Terms

There is a large body of statistical techniques called **multivariate methods.** These methods are useful in analyzing data in situations that involve several variables. The data and parameters are **vectors.** In this chapter, we discussed some of these methods. We began by describing the **multivariate normal distribution.** We then discussed **discriminant analysis,** a method of classifying members of a population into one of two (or more) groups. The analysis entailed the postulation and estimation of one or more **discriminant functions.** We then discussed **factor analysis,** a statistical technique for reducing the dimensionality of a problem by summarizing a set of variables as a smaller set of inherent, latent common factors. We also discussed a related technique often used as a first stage in factor analysis: **principal components analysis.** We discussed the concept of independence in several dimensions: the concept of **orthogonality** of factors or variables. We discussed rotations used in factor analysis: **orthogonal rotations,** which maintain the noncorrelation of the factors, and **oblique rotations,** which do not.

ADDITIONAL PROBLEMS

16–26.   What are the uses of the multivariate normal distribution? Why is it needed?

16–27.   How many discriminant functions may be found significant in classifying an observation into one of four groups?

16–28.   Is it possible that only one discriminant function will be found significant in discriminating among three groups? Explain.

16–29.   What is a hit ratio? Would a hit ratio of 67% be sufficient when one group has 100 observations, another group has 200 observations, and the ratio of these groups is believed to reflect their ratio in the population? Explain.

16–30.   What is achieved by principal components analysis? How can it be used as a preliminary stage in factor analysis? What important stages must follow it, and why?

16–31.   In a factor analysis of 17 variables, a solution is found consisting of 17 factors. Comment on the analysis.

16–32.   When is an oblique rotation superior to an orthogonal one, and why?

16–33.   What is a communality, and what does it indicate?

16–34.   What is the communality of variable 9 listed in Table 16–2?

16–35.   Name a statistical method of analysis for which principal components may be a first stage. Explain.

16–36.   What are factor loadings, and what do they measure?

16–37.   A television producer wants to predict the success of new television programs. A program is considered successful if it survives its first season. Data on production costs, number of sponsors, and the total amount spent on promoting the program are available. A random sample of programs is selected, and the data are presented in the following table. Production costs are in millions of dollars, and promotions in hundreds of thousands of dollars: S denotes success and F failure.

Success/Failure	Production Cost	Number of Sponsors	Promotions
S	2.5	1	2.1
F	1.1	1	3.7
S	2.0	1	2.8
F	2.5	1	1.8
F	2.5	1	1.0
S	3.7	2	5.5
S	3.6	3	5.0
S	2.7	1	4.1
S	1.9	1	6.9
F	1.3	1	1.5
S	2.6	2	2.0
S	3.5	3	3.8
F	1.9	1	1.0
S	6.8	1	2.1
S	5.0	1	1.9
S	4.6	3	4.1
S	3.0	2	3.9
S	2.5	3	7.0
S	1.8	2	6.6
F	2.0	2	1.1
S	3.5	3	3.8
S	1.8	3	8.1
S	5.6	1	4.2
F	1.5	2	3.0
S	4.4	4	5.0

Conduct a discriminant analysis, and state your conclusions.

16–38.   A factor analysis was conducted with 24 variables. The VARIMAX rotation was used, and the results were 2 factors. Comment on the analysis.

Case 16   PREDICTING COMPANY FAILURE

The following article is reprinted in its entirety by permission from *Forbes* (April 1, 1991). Discuss the statistical method alluded to in this article. Could you reproduce (or improve upon) Professor Platt's results? Explain.

Is a former $40 stock now trading at $2.50 a bargain? Or an invitation to get wiped out? Depends.

How Cheap?

BY STEVE KICHEN

HARLAN PLATT, an associate professor of finance at Northeastern University, has written *Why Companies Fail*, a study that should be of considerable interest to bargain-hunting investors. Platt's study can be useful in helping determine whether a stock that has fallen sharply in price is a bargain or a prospective piece of wallpaper. Platt developed a mathematical model that predicts the probability of bankruptcy from certain ratios on a company's balance sheet.

Here's the thesis: Some companies trading very cheaply still have large sales, considerable brand recognition and a chance at recovery, or at least takeover at a premium. Their stocks could double or triple despite losses and weak balance sheets. Other borderline companies will land in bankruptcy court and leave common shareholders with nothing.

Even though it more than tripled from its October low, Unisys, with $10 billion in sales, is not a Wall Street favorite: At a recent 5 1/2, its market capitalization is only $890 million. Will Unysis fail? Almost certainly not within the next 12 months, according to Platt.

For the list below, we found cheap stocks with low price-to-sales ratios. Then we eliminated all but the ones Platt says are highly unlikely to fail within a year. Platt put cheap stocks such as Gaylord Container, Masco Industries and Kinder-Care Learning Centers in the danger zone.

Among low-priced stocks, Unisys and Navistar, however, make the safety grade. So does Wang Laboratories. Says Platt, "They are still selling over $2 billion worth of computers and their $575 million in bank debt is now down to almost nothing."

Platt, who furnishes his probabilities to Prospect Street Investment Management Co., a Boston fund manager, refuses to disclose his proprietary formula. But among the ratios he considers are total debt to total assets, cash flow to sales, short-term debt to total debt, and fixed assets to total assets.

"Companies with large fixed assets are more likely to have trouble because these assets are less liquid," Platt says. But norms for a company's industry are also important. An unusually high level of such current assets as inventory and receivables may itself be a sign of weakness.

The low-priced stocks on the list may or may not rise sharply in the near future, but they are not likely to disappear into insolvency.

Big Companies with Little Prices

These 10 companies are in poor financial shape, but not so poor, according to calculations by finance professor Harlan Platt, that they are likely to go bankrupt within the next year. Thus, these stocks are plausible bets for rebounds.

Company/Industry	Recent Price	Earnings per Share Latest 12 Months	1991 Estimated	Total Assets ($mil)	Total Debt/Total Assets	Sales ($mil)	Cash Flow/ Sales	Price/ Sales
Highland Superstores/ consumer electronics stores	2 1/8	$−0.89	NA	$320	57%	$892	−1.6%	0.04
Businessland/computer stores	2 1/2	−1.65	$−1.02	616	72	1,306	−2.0	0.06
Jamesway/discount stores	3 1/2	−0.06	0.18	435	61	909	1.6	0.06
Merisel/computer equipment wholesaler	3 1/8	0.03	0.33	432	73	1,192	0.4	0.06
Unisys/computers	5 1/2	−3.45	−0.56	10,484	65	10,111	3.1	0.09
National Convenience Stores/convenience stores	5 1/8	−0.43	0.21	406	65	1,067	2.0	0.11
TW Holdings/restaurants	4 7/16	−0.61	−0.43	3,531	79	3,682	3.9	0.13
Varity/farm and construction equipment	2 3/4	0.35	0.32	3,177	61	3,472	6.4	0.20
Wang Laboratories Cl B/minicomputers	3 3/8	4.04	−0.29	1,750	72	2,369	−20.1	0.24
Navistar International/trucks	4 1/8	−0.24	−0.08	3,795	60	3,810	−0.6	0.27

NA: Not available.

Sources: Harlan Platt, Northeastern University; Institutional Brokers Estimate System (a service of Lynch, Jones & Ryan), via Lotus One Source; *Forbes.*

SAMPLING METHODS

17-1 INTRODUCTION

T hroughout this book, we have always assumed that information is obtained through random sampling. The method we have used until now is called simple random sampling. In simple random sampling, we assume that our sample is randomly chosen from the entire population of interest, and that every set of n elements in the population has an equal chance of being selected as our sample.

We assume that a randomization device is always available to the experimenter. We also assume that the entire population of interest is known, in the sense that it is possible to draw a random sample from the entire population where every element has an equal chance of being included in our sample. Randomly choosing our sample from the entire population in question is our insurance against sampling bias. This was demonstrated in Chapter 5 with the story of the *Literary Digest*.

Continued

But do these conditions always hold in real sampling situations? Also, are there any easier ways—more efficient, more economical ways—of drawing random samples? Are there any situations where, instead of randomly drawing every single sample point, we may randomize less frequently and still obtain an adequately random sample for use in statistical inference? Consider the situation where our population is made up of several groups and the elements within each group are similar to each other, but different from the elements in other groups (for example, sampling an economic variable in a city where some people live in rich neighborhoods and thus form one group, while others live in poorer neighborhoods, forming other groups). Is there a way of using the homogeneity within the groups to make our sampling more efficient? The answers to these questions, as well as many other questions related to sampling methodology, are the subject of this chapter.

In the next section, we will thoroughly explore the idea of random sampling and discuss its practical limitations. We will see that biases may occur if samples are chosen without randomization. We will also discuss criteria for the prevention of such selection biases. In the following sections, we will present more efficient and involved methods of drawing random samples that are appropriate in different situations.

17-2   Nonprobability Sampling and Bias

The advantage of random sampling is that the probabilities that the sample estimator will be within a given number of units from the population parameter it estimates are known. Sampling methods that do not use samples with known probabilities of selection are known as *nonprobability sampling methods*. In such sampling methods, we have no objective way of evaluating how far away from the population parameter our estimate may be. In addition, when we do not select our sample randomly out of the entire population of interest, our sampling results may be biased. That is, the average value of the estimate in repeated sampling is not equal to the parameter of interest. Put simply, our sample may not be a true representative of the population of interest.

EXAMPLE 17-1

A marketing research firm wants to estimate the proportion of consumers who might be interested in purchasing the Spanish sherry Jerez if this product were available at liquor stores in this country. How should information for this study be obtained?

SOLUTION

The population relevant to our case is not a clear-cut one. Before embarking on our study, we need to define our population more precisely. Do we mean all consumers in the United States? Do we mean all families of consumers? Do we mean only people of drinking age? Perhaps we should consider our population to be only those people who, at least occasionally, consume similar drinks. These are important questions to answer before we begin the sampling survey. The population must be defined in accordance with the purpose of the study. In the case of a proposed new product like Jerez, we are interested in the product's potential market share. We are interested in estimating the proportion of the market for alcoholic beverages that will go to Jerez once it is introduced. Therefore, we define our population as all people who, at least occasionally, consume alcoholic beverages.

Now we need to know how to obtain a random sample from this population. To obtain a random sample out of the whole population of people who drink alcoholic beverages at least occasionally, we must have a *frame*. That is, we need a list of all such people, from which we can randomly choose as many people as we need for our sample. In reality, of course, no such list is available. Therefore, we must obtain our sample in some other way. Market researchers send field workers to places where consumers may be found, usually shopping malls. There shoppers are randomly selected and prescreened to ascertain that they are in the population of interest—in this case, whether they are people who at least occasionally consume alcoholic beverages. Then the selected people are given a taste test of the new product and asked to fill out a questionnaire about their response to the product and their future purchase intent. This method of obtaining a random sample works as long as the interviewers do not choose people in a nonrandom fashion, for example, choosing certain types of people because of their appearance. If this should happen, a bias may be introduced if the variable favoring selection is somehow related to interest in the product.

Another point we must consider is the requirement that people selected at the shopping mall should constitute a representative sample from the entire population in which we are interested. We must consider the possibility that potential buyers of Jerez may not be found in shopping malls, and if their proportion outside the malls is different from what it is in the malls where surveys take place, a bias will be introduced. We must consider the location of shopping malls and ascertain that we are not favoring some segments of the population over others. Preferably, several shopping malls, located in different areas, should be chosen.

We should randomize the selection of people or elements in our sample. However, if our sample is not chosen in a purely random way, it may still suffice for our purposes as long as it behaves as a purely random sample and no biases are introduced. In designing the study, we should collect a few random samples at different locations, chosen at different times and handled by different field workers, to minimize the chances of a bias. The results of different samples validate the assumption that we are indeed getting a representative sample.

17–3   Stratified Random Sampling

In some cases, a population may be viewed as comprising different groups where elements in each group are similar to each other in some way. In such cases, we may gain sampling precision (that is, reduce the variance of our estimators) as well as reduce the costs of the survey by treating the different groups separately. If we consider these groups, or *strata,* as separate subpopulations and draw a separate random sample from each stratum and combine the results, our sampling method is called *stratified random sampling.*

> In **stratified random sampling,** we assume that the population of N units may be divided into m groups with N_i units in group i, $i = 1, \ldots, m$. The m strata are nonoverlapping and together they make up the total population: $N_1 + N_2 + \cdots + N_m = N$.

We define the true *weight* of stratum i as $W_i = N_i/N$. That is, the weight of stratum i is equal to the proportion of the size of stratum i in the whole population. Our total sample, of size n, is divided into subsamples from each of the strata. We sample n_i items in stratum i, and $n_1 + n_2 + \cdots + n_m = n$. We define the sampling fraction in stratum i as $f_i = n_i/N_i$.

The true mean of the entire population is μ, and the true mean in stratum i is μ_i. The variance of stratum i is σ_i^2, and the variance of the entire population is σ^2. The sample mean in stratum i is $\bar{X}_i$, and the combined estimator, the sample mean in stratified random sampling, $\bar{X}_{st}$, is defined as follows.

The **estimator of the population mean** in stratified random sampling:

$$\bar{X}_{st} = \sum_{i=1}^{m} W_i \bar{X}_i \qquad (17\text{--}1)$$

In simple random sampling with no stratification, the stratified estimator in equation 17–1 is, in general, *not equal* to the simple estimator of the population mean. The reason is that the estimator in equation 17–1 uses the true weights of the strata, W_i. The simple random sampling estimator of the population mean is $\bar{X} = (\sum_{\text{all data}} X)/n = (\sum_{i=1}^{m} n_i \bar{X}_i)/n$. This is equal to $\bar{X}_{st}$ only if we have $n_i/n = N_i/N$ for each stratum, that is, if the proportion of the sample taken from each stratum is equal to the proportion of each stratum in the entire population. Such a stratification is called stratification with *proportional allocation*.

Following are some important properties of the stratified estimator of the population mean.

1. If the estimator of the mean in each stratum, $\bar{X}_i$, is *unbiased,* then the stratified estimator of the mean, $\bar{X}_{st}$, is an unbiased estimator of the population mean, μ.

2. If the samples in the different strata are drawn *independently* of each other, then the variance of the stratified estimator of the population mean, $\bar{X}_{st}$, is given by

$$V(\bar{X}_{st}) = \sum_{i=1}^{m} W_i^2 V(\bar{X}_i) \qquad (17\text{--}2)$$

where $V(\bar{X}_i)$ is the variance of the sample mean in stratum i.

3. If sampling in all strata is *random,* then the variance of the estimator, given in equation 17–2, is further equal to

$$V(\bar{X}_{st}) = \sum_{i=1}^{m} W_i^2 \left(\frac{\sigma_i^2}{n_i} \right) (1 - f_i) \qquad (17\text{--}3)$$

When the sampling fractions, f_i, are small and may be ignored, we get

$$V(\bar{X}_{st}) = \sum_{i=1}^{m} W_i^2 \frac{\sigma_i^2}{n_i} \qquad (17\text{--}4)$$

4. If the sample allocation is proportional $[n_i = n(N_i/N)$ for all $i]$, then

$$V(\bar{X}_{st}) = \left(\frac{1 - f}{n} \right) \sum_{i=1}^{m} W_i \sigma_i^2 \qquad (17\text{--}5)$$

which reduces to $(1/n)\Sigma_{i=1}^{m} W_i \sigma_i^2$ when the sampling fraction is small. Note that f is the sampling fraction—that is, the size of the sample divided by the population size.

In addition, if the population variances in all the strata are equal, then

$$V(\bar{X}_{\text{st}}) = \frac{\sigma^2}{n} \qquad (17\text{-}6)$$

when the sampling fraction is small.

Practical Applications

In practice, the true population variances in the different strata are usually not known. When the variances are not known, we estimate them from our data. An unbiased estimator of σ_i^2, the population variance in stratum i, is given by

$$S_i^2 = \sum_{\text{data in stratum } i} \frac{(X - \bar{X}_i)^2}{n_i - 1} \qquad (17\text{-}7)$$

The estimator in equation 17–7 is the usual unbiased sample estimator of the population variance in each stratum as a separate population. A particular estimate of the variance in stratum i will be denoted by s_i^2. If sampling in each stratum is random, then an unbiased estimator of the variance of the sample estimator of the population mean is

$$S^2(\bar{X}_{\text{st}}) = \sum_{i=1}^{m} \left(\frac{W_i^2 S_i^2}{n_i} \right)(1 - f_i) \qquad (17\text{-}8)$$

Any of the preceding formulas apply in the special situations where they can be used with the estimated variances substituted for the population variances.

Confidence Intervals

We now give a confidence interval for the population mean, μ, obtained from stratified random sampling.

A $(1 - \alpha)100\%$ confidence interval for the population mean, μ, using stratified sampling:

$$\bar{X}_{\text{st}} \pm z_{\alpha/2} s(\bar{X}_{\text{st}}) \qquad (17\text{-}9)$$

where $s(\bar{X}_{\text{st}})$ is the square root of the estimate of the variance of $\bar{X}_{\text{st}}$ given in equation 17–8.

When the sample sizes in some of the strata are small and the population variances are unknown, but the populations are at least approximately normal, we use the t distribution instead of Z. We denote the degrees of freedom of the t distribution by df. The exact value of df is difficult to determine, but it lies somewhere between the smallest $n_i - 1$ (the degrees of freedom associated with the sample from stratum i) and the sum of the degrees of freedom associated with the samples from all strata, $\Sigma_{i=1}^{m} (n_i - 1)$. An approximation for the effective number of degrees of freedom is given by

$$\text{Effective df} = \frac{\left[\sum_{i=1}^{m} N_i(N_i - n_i)s_i^2/n_i \right]^2}{\sum_{i=1}^{m} [N_i(N_i - n_i)/n_i]^2 s_i^4/(n_i - 1)} \qquad (17\text{-}10)$$

TABLE 17-1　The Fortune Service 500

Group	Number of Firms
1.　Diversified service companies	100
2.　Commercial banking companies	100
3.　Financial service companies (including savings and insurance)	150
4.　Retailing companies	50
5.　Transportation companies	50
6.　Utilities	50
	500

We demonstrate the application of the theory of stratified random sampling presented so far by the following example.

EXAMPLE 17-2

Once a year, *Fortune* magazine publishes the Fortune Service 500: a list of the largest service companies in America. The 500 firms belong to six major industry groups. The industry groups and the number of firms in each group are listed in Table 17–1.

The 500 firms are considered a complete population: the population of the top 500 service companies in the United States. An economist who is interested in this population wants to estimate the mean net income of all firms in the index. However, obtaining the data for all 500 firms in the index is either difficult, time-consuming, or costly. Therefore, the economist wants to gather a random sample of the firms, compute a quick average of the net income for the firms in the sample, and use it to estimate the mean net income for the entire population of 500 firms.

SOLUTION

The economist believes that firms in the same industry group share common characteristics related to net income. Therefore, the six groups are treated as different strata, and a random sample is drawn from each stratum. The weights of each of the strata are known exactly as computed from the strata sizes in Table 17–1. Using the definition of the population weights, $W_i = N_i/N$, we get the following weights.

$$W_1 = N_1/N = 100/500 = 0.2$$
$$W_2 = N_2/N = 100/500 = 0.2$$
$$W_3 = N_3/N = 150/500 = 0.3$$
$$W_4 = N_4/N = 50/500 = 0.1$$
$$W_5 = N_5/N = 50/500 = 0.1$$
$$W_6 = N_6/N = 50/500 = 0.1$$

The economist decides to select a random sample of 100 of the 500 firms listed in *Fortune*. The economist chooses to use a proportional allocation of the total sample to the six strata (another method of allocation will be presented shortly). With proportional allocation, the total sample of 100 must be allocated to the different strata in proportion to the computed strata weights. Thus, for each i, $i = 1, \ldots, 6$, we compute n_i as $n_i = nW_i$. This gives the following sample sizes.

$$n_1 = 20, \quad n_2 = 20, \quad n_3 = 30, \quad n_4 = 10, \quad n_5 = 10, \quad n_6 = 10$$

TABLE 17-2 Sampling Results for Example 17-2

Stratum	Mean	Variance	n_i	W_i
1	52.7	97,650	20	0.2
2	112.6	64,300	20	0.2
3	85.6	76,990	30	0.3
4	12.6	18,320	10	0.1
5	8.9	9,037	10	0.1
6	52.3	83,500	10	0.1

We will assume that the net income values in the different strata are approximately normally distributed and that the estimated strata variances (to be estimated from the data) are the true strata variances, σ_i^2, so that the normal distribution may be used.

The economist draws the random samples and computes the sample means and variances. The results, in millions of dollars (for the means) and in millions of dollars squared (for the variances), are given in Table 17–2, along with the sample sizes in the different strata and the strata weights. From the table, and with the aid of equation 17–1 for the mean and equation 17–5 for the variance of the sample mean (with the estimated sample variances substituted for the population variances in the different strata), we will now compute the stratified sample mean and the estimated variance of the stratified sample mean.

$$\bar{x}_{st} = \sum_{i=1}^{6} W_i \bar{x}_i = (0.2)(52.7) + (0.2)(112.6) + (0.3)(85.6) + (0.1)(12.6)$$
$$+ (0.1)(8.9) + (0.1)(52.3)$$
$$= \$66.12 \text{ million}$$

and

$$s(\bar{X}_{st}) = \sqrt{\frac{1 - f}{n} \sum_{i=1}^{6} W_i s_i^2}$$
$$= \sqrt{\frac{0.8}{100}[(0.2)(97,650) + (0.2)(64,300) + (0.3)(76,990) + (0.1)(18,320) + (0.1)(9,037) + (0.1)(83,500)]}$$
$$= 23.08$$

(Our sampling fraction is $f = 100/500 = 0.2$.) Our unbiased point estimate of the average net income of all firms in the Fortune Service 500 is \$66.12 million.

Using equation 17–9, we now compute a 95% confidence interval for μ, the mean net income of all firms in the index. We have the following:

$$\bar{x}_{st} \pm z_{\alpha/2} s(\bar{X}_{st}) = 66.12 \pm (1.96)(23.08) = [20.88, 111.36]$$

Thus, the economist may be 95% confident that the average net income for all firms in the Fortune Service 500 is anywhere from 20.88 to 111.36 million dollars. Incidentally, the true population mean net income for all 500 firms in the index is $\mu = \$61.496$ million.

Stratified Sampling for the Population Proportion

The theory of stratified sampling extends in a natural way to sampling for the population proportion, p. Let the sample proportion in stratum i be $\hat{P}_i = X_i/n_i$, where X_i is the number of successes in a sample of size n_i. Then the stratified estimator of the population proportion p is the following.

Stratified estimator of the population proportion, p:

$$\hat{P}_{st} = \sum_{i=1}^{m} W_i \hat{P}_i \qquad (17\text{--}11)$$

where the weights, W_i, are defined as in the case of sampling for the population mean: $W_i = N_i/N$

The following is an approximate expression for the variance of the estimator of the population proportion $\hat{P}_{st}$, for use with large samples.

The approximate variance of $\hat{P}_{st}$:

$$V(\hat{P}_{st}) = \sum_{i=1}^{m} W_i^2 \frac{\hat{P}_i \hat{Q}_i}{n_i} \qquad (17\text{--}12)$$

where $\hat{Q}_i = 1 - \hat{P}_i$

When finite-population correction factors, f_i, must be considered, the following expression is appropriate for the variance of $\hat{P}_{st}$:

$$V(\hat{P}_{st}) = \frac{1}{N^2} \sum_{i=1}^{m} N_i^2 (N_i - n_i) \frac{\hat{P}_i \hat{Q}_i}{(N_i - 1)n_i} \qquad (17\text{--}13)$$

When proportional allocation is used, an approximate expression is

$$V(\hat{P}_{st}) = \frac{1 - f}{n} \sum_{i=1}^{m} W_i \hat{P}_i \hat{Q}_i \qquad (17\text{--}14)$$

Let us now return to Example 17–1, sampling for the proportion of people who might be interested in purchasing the Spanish sherry Jerez. Suppose that the marketing researchers believe that preferences for imported wines differ between consumers in metropolitan areas and those in other areas. The area of interest for the survey covers a few states in the Northeast, where it is known that 65% of the people live in metropolitan areas and 35% live in nonmetropolitan areas. A sample of 130 people randomly chosen at shopping malls in metropolitan areas shows that 28 of them are interested in Jerez, while a random sample of 70 people selected at malls outside the metropolitan areas shows that 18 of them are interested in the sherry.

Let us use these results in constructing a 90% confidence interval for the proportion of people in the entire population who are interested in the product. From equation 17–11, using two strata with weights 0.65 and 0.35, we get

$$\hat{p}_{st} = \sum_{i=1}^{2} W_i \hat{p}_i = (0.65)\frac{28}{130} + (0.35)\frac{18}{70} = 0.23$$

Our allocation is proportional because $n_1 = 130$, $n_2 = 70$, and $n = 130 + 70 = 200$, so that $n_1/n = 0.65 = W_1$ and $n_2/n = 0.35 = W_2$. In addition, the sample sizes of 130 and 70 represent tiny fractions of the two strata; hence, no finite-population correction factor is required. The equation for the estimated variance of the sample estimator of the proportion is therefore equation 17–14 without the finite-population correction:

$$V(\hat{P}_{st}) = \frac{1}{n} \sum_{i=1}^{2} W_i \hat{p}_i \hat{q}_i = \frac{1}{200}[(0.65)(0.215)(0.785) + (0.35)(0.257)(0.743)]$$

$$= 0.0008825$$

The standard error of $\hat{P}_{st}$ is therefore $\sqrt{V(\hat{P}_{st})} = \sqrt{0.0008825} = 0.0297$. Thus, our 90% confidence interval for the population proportion of people interested in Jerez is

$$\hat{p}_{st} \pm z_{\alpha/2} s(\hat{P}_{st}) = 0.23 \pm (1.645)(0.0297) = [0.181, 0.279]$$

The stratified point estimate of the percentage of people in the proposed market area for Jerez who may be interested in the product, if it is introduced, is 23%. A 90% confidence interval for the population percentage is 18.1% to 27.9%. In the next subsections, we will explore some optional, advanced aspects of stratified sampling.

What Do We Do When the Population Strata Weights Are Unknown?

When the true strata weights, $W_i = N_i/N$, are unknown—that is, when we do not know what percentage of the whole population belongs to each stratum—we may still use stratified random sampling. In such cases, we use estimates of the true weights, denoted by w_i. The consequence of using estimated weights instead of the true weights is the introduction of a bias into our sampling results. The interesting thing about this kind of bias is that it is not eliminated as the sample size increases. When errors in the strata weights exist, our results are always biased; the greater the errors, the greater the bias. These errors also cause the standard error of the sample mean, $s(\overline{X}_{st})$, to underestimate the true standard deviation. Consequently, confidence intervals for the population parameter of interest tend to be narrower than they should be.

How Many Strata Should We Use?

The number of strata to be used is an important question to consider when designing any survey that uses stratified sampling. In many cases, there is a natural breakdown of the population into a given number of strata. In other cases, there may be no clear, unique way of separating the population into groups. For example, if age is to be used as a stratifying variable, there are many ways of breaking the variable and forming strata. There are two guidance rules for constructing strata. The rules are presented below.

Rules for Constructing Strata

1. The number of strata should preferably be less than or equal to 6.
2. Choose the strata so that Cum $\sqrt{f(x)}$ is approximately constant for all strata (where Cum $\sqrt{f(x)}$ is the cumulative square root of the frequency of X, the variable of interest).

TABLE 17–3   Constructing Strata by Age

Age	Frequency (f)	$\sqrt{f}$	Cum$\sqrt{f}$
20–25	1	1	
26–30	16	4	5
31–35	25	5	5
36–40	4	2	
41–45	9	3	5

The first rule is clear. The second rule says that in the absence of other guidelines for breaking down a population into strata, we partition the variable used for stratification into categories so that the cumulative square root of the frequency function of the variable is approximately equal for all strata. We illustrate this rule in the hypothetical case of Table 17–3. As can be seen in this simplified example, the combined age groups 20–30, 31–35, and 36–45 all have a sum of $\sqrt{f}$ equal to 5; hence, these groups make good strata with respect to age as a stratifying variable according to rule 2.

Post-Sampling Stratification

At times, we conduct a survey using simple random sampling with no stratification, and, after obtaining our results, we note that the data may be broken into categories of similar elements. Can we now use the techniques of stratified random sampling and enjoy its benefits in terms of reduced variances of the estimators? Surprisingly, the answer is yes. In fact, if the subsamples in each of our strata contain at least 20 elements, and if our estimated weights of the different strata, w_i (computed from the data as n_i/n, or from more accurate information), are close to the true population strata weights, W_i, then our stratified estimator will be almost as good as that of stratified random sampling with proportional allocation. This procedure is called *post-stratification*. We close this section with a discussion of an alternative to proportional allocation of the sample in stratified random sampling, called *optimum allocation*.

Optimum Allocation

With optimum allocation, we select the sample sizes to be allocated to each of the strata so as to minimize one of two criteria. We either minimize the cost of the survey for a given value of the variance of our estimator, or we minimize the variance of our estimator for a given cost of taking the survey.

We assume a cost function of the form

$$C = C_0 + \sum_{i=1}^{m} C_i n_i \qquad (17\text{--}15)$$

where C is the total cost of the survey, C_0 is the fixed cost of setting up the survey, and C_i is the cost per item sampled in stratum i. Clearly, the total cost of the survey is the sum of the fixed cost and the costs of sampling in all the strata (where the cost of sampling in stratum i is equal to the sample size, n_i, times the cost per item sampled, C_i).

Under the assumption of a cost function given in equation 17–15, the optimum allocation that will minimize our total cost for a fixed variance of the estimator, or minimize the variance of the estimator for a fixed total cost, is as follows.

Optimum allocation:

$$\frac{n_i}{n} = \frac{W_i\sigma_i/\sqrt{C_i}}{\sum\limits_{i=1}^{m} W_i\sigma_i/\sqrt{C_i}} \tag{17–16}$$

Equation 17–16 has an intuitive appeal. It says that for a given stratum, we should take a larger sample if the stratum is *more variable internally* (greater σ_i), if the relative *size of the stratum is larger* (greater W_i), or if *sampling in the stratum is cheaper* (smaller C_i).

If the cost per unit sampled is the same in all the strata (that is, if $C_i = c$ for all i), then the optimum allocation for a fixed total cost is the same as the optimum allocation for fixed sample size, and we have what is called the *Neyman allocation* (after J. Neyman, although this allocation was actually discovered earlier by A. A. Tschuprow in 1923).

The Neyman allocation:

$$\frac{n_i}{n} = \frac{W_i\sigma_i}{\sum\limits_{i=1}^{m} W_i\sigma_i} \tag{17–17}$$

Suppose that we want to allocate a total sample of size 1,000 to three strata, where stratum 1 has weight 0.4, standard deviation 1, and cost per sampled item 4 cents; stratum 2 has weight 0.5, standard deviation 2, and cost per item 9 cents; and stratum 3 has weight 0.1, standard deviation 3, and cost per item 16 cents. How should we allocate this sample if optimum allocation is to be used? We have

$$\sum_{i=1}^{3} \frac{W_i\sigma_i}{\sqrt{C_i}} = \frac{(0.4)(1)}{\sqrt{4}} + \frac{(0.5)(2)}{\sqrt{9}} + \frac{(0.1)(3)}{\sqrt{16}} = 0.608$$

From equation 17–16, we get

$$\frac{n_1}{n} = \frac{W_1\sigma_1/\sqrt{C_1}}{\sum\limits_{i=1}^{3}(W_i\sigma_i/\sqrt{C_i})} = \frac{(0.4)(1)/\sqrt{4}}{0.608} = 0.329$$

$$\frac{n_2}{n} = \frac{W_2\sigma_2/\sqrt{C_2}}{\sum\limits_{i=1}^{3}(W_i\sigma_i/\sqrt{C_i})} = \frac{(0.5)(2)/\sqrt{9}}{0.608} = 0.548$$

$$\frac{n_3}{n} = \frac{W_3\sigma_3/\sqrt{C_3}}{\sum\limits_{i=1}^{3}(W_i\sigma_i/\sqrt{C_i})} = \frac{(0.1)(3)/\sqrt{16}}{0.608} = 0.123$$

The optimum allocation in this case is 329 items from stratum 1, 548 items from stratum 2, and 123 items from stratum 3 (making a total of 1,000 sample items, as specified).

Let us now compare this allocation with proportional allocation. With a sample of size 1,000 and a proportional allocation, we would allocate our sample only by the strata weights, which are 0.4, 0.5, and 0.1, respectively. Therefore, our allocation will be 400 from stratum 1, 500 from stratum 2, and 100 from stratum 3. The optimum allocation is different, as it incorporates the cost and variance considerations. Here, the difference between the two sets of sample sizes is not large.

Suppose, in this example, that the costs of sampling from the three strata are the same. In this case, we can use the Neyman allocation and get, from equation 17–17

$$\frac{n_1}{n} = \frac{W_1 \sigma_1}{\sum\limits_{i=1}^{3} W_i \sigma_i} = \frac{(0.4)(1)}{1.7} = 0.235$$

$$\frac{n_2}{n} = \frac{W_2 \sigma_2}{\sum\limits_{i=1}^{3} W_i \sigma_i} = \frac{(0.5)(2)}{1.7} = 0.588$$

$$\frac{n_3}{n} = \frac{W_3 \sigma_3}{\sum\limits_{i=1}^{3} W_i \sigma_i} = \frac{(0.1)(3)}{1.7} = 0.176$$

Thus, the Neyman allocation gives a sample of size 235 to stratum 1, 588 to stratum 2, and 176 to stratum 3. Note that these subsamples add only to 999, due to rounding error. The last sample point may be allocated to any of the strata.

In general, stratified random sampling gives more precise results than those obtained from simple random sampling: the standard errors of our estimators from stratified random sampling are usually smaller than those of simple random sampling. Furthermore, in stratified random sampling, an optimum allocation will produce more precise results than a proportional allocation if some strata are more expensive to sample than others or if the variances within strata are different from each other.

PROBLEMS

17–1. A securities analyst wants to estimate the average percentage of institutional holding of all publicly traded stocks in the United States. The analyst believes that stocks traded on the three major exchanges have different characteristics and therefore decides to use stratified random sampling. The three strata are the New York Stock Exchange (NYSE), the American Exchange (AMEX), and the Over the Counter (OTC) exchange. The weights of the three strata, as measured by the number of stocks listed in each exchange divided by the total number of stocks, are: NYSE, 0.44; AMEX, 0.15; OTC, 0.41. A total random sample of 200 stocks is selected, with proportional allocation. It is found that the average percentage of institutional holdings of the subsample selected from the issues of the NYSE is 46% and the standard deviation is 8%. The corresponding results for the AMEX are 9% average institutional holdings and a standard deviation of 4%, and the corresponding results for the OTC stocks are 29% average institutional holdings and a standard deviation of 16%.

   a. Give a stratified estimate of the mean percentage of institutional holdings per stock.

   b. Give the standard error of the estimate in *a.*

   c. Give a 95% confidence interval for the mean percentage of institutional holdings.

   d. Explain the advantages of using stratified random sampling in this case. Compare with simple random sampling.

17–2. A company has 2,100 employees belonging to the following groups: production, 1,200; marketing, 600; management, 100; other, 200. The company president wants to obtain an estimate of the views of all employees about a certain impending executive decision. The president knows that the management employees' views are most variable, along with employees in the "other" category, while the marketing and production people have rather uniform views within their groups. The production people are the most costly to sample, because of the time required to find them at their different jobs, and the management people are easiest to sample.

- *a.* Suppose that a total sample of 100 employees is required. What are the sample sizes in the different strata under proportional allocation?
- *b.* Discuss how you would design an optimum allocation in this case.

17–3. Last year, consumers increasingly bought fleece (industry jargon for hot-selling jogging suits, which now rival jeans as the uniform for casual attire). A New York designer of jogging suits is interested in the new trend and wants to estimate the amount spent per person on jogging suits during the year. The designer knows that people who belong to health-and-fitness clubs will have different buying behavior than people who do not. Furthermore, the designer finds that, within the proposed study area, 18% of the population are members of health-and-fitness clubs. A random sample of 300 people is selected, and the sample is proportionally allocated to the two strata: members of health clubs and nonmembers of health clubs. It is found that among members, the average amount spent is $152.43 and the standard deviation is $25.77, while among the nonmembers, the average amount spent is $15.33 and the standard deviation is $5.11.

- *a.* What is the stratified estimate of the mean?
- *b.* What is the standard error of the estimator?
- *c.* Give a 90% confidence interval for the population mean, μ.
- *d.* Discuss one possible problem with the data. (*Hint:* Can the data be considered normally distributed? Why?)

17–4. A financial analyst is interested in estimating the average amount of a foreign loan by American banks. The analyst believes that the amount of a loan may be different depending on the bank, or, more precisely, on the extent of the bank's involvement in foreign loans. The analyst obtains the following data on the percentage of profits of U.S. banks from loans to Mexico and proposes to use these data in the construction of strata weights. The strata are the different banks: First Chicago: 33%; Manufacturers Hanover: 27%; Bankers Trust: 21%; Chemical Bank: 19%; Wells Fargo Bank: 19%; Citicorp: 16%; Mellon Bank: 16%; Chase Manhattan: 15%; Morgan Guarantee Trust: 9%.

- *a.* Construct the strata weights for proportional allocation.
- *b.* Discuss two possible problems with this study.

17–4   Cluster Sampling

Let us consider the case where we have no frame (i.e., no list of all the elements in the population) and the elements are *clustered* in larger units. Each unit, or cluster, contains several elements of the population. In this case, we may choose to use the method of **cluster sampling.** This may also be the case when the population is large and spread over a geographical area in which smaller subregions are easily sampled and where a simple random sample or a stratified random sample may not be carried out as easily.

Suppose that the population is composed of M clusters and there is a list of all M clusters from which a random sample of m clusters is selected. There are two possibilities. First, we may sample *every element* in every one of the m selected clusters. In this case, our sampling method is called *single-stage cluster sampling.* Second, we may select a random sample of m clusters and then select a random sample of n elements from each of the selected clusters. In this case, our sampling method is called *two-stage cluster sampling.*

The Relation with Stratified Sampling

In stratified sampling, we sample elements from every one of our strata, and this assures us of full representation of all segments of the population in the sample. In cluster sampling, we sample only some of the clusters, and although elements within any cluster may tend to be homogeneous, as is the case with strata, not all of the clusters are represented in the sample; this leads to lowered precision of the cluster sampling method. In stratified random sampling, we use the fact that the population may be broken into subgroups. This usually leads to a smaller variance of our estimators. In cluster sampling, however, the method is used mainly because of ease of implementation or reduction in sampling costs, and the estimates do not usually lead to more precise results.

Single-Stage Cluster Sampling for the Population Mean

Let $n_1, n_2, \ldots, n_m$ be the number of elements in each of the m sampled clusters. Let $\bar{X}_1, \bar{X}_2, \ldots, \bar{X}_m$ be the means of the sampled clusters. The cluster sampling unbiased estimator of the population mean, μ, is given as follows.

Cluster sampling estimator of μ:

$$\bar{X}_{cl} = \frac{\sum\limits_{i=1}^{m} n_i \bar{X}_i}{\sum\limits_{i=1}^{m} n_i} \tag{17–18}$$

An estimator of the variance of the estimator of μ in equation 17–18 is

$$s^2(\bar{X}_{cl}) = \left(\frac{M - m}{Mm\bar{n}^2}\right) \frac{\sum\limits_{i=1}^{m} n_i^2(\bar{X}_i - \bar{X}_{cl})^2}{m - 1} \tag{17–19}$$

where $\bar{n} = (\sum_{i=1}^{m} n_i)/m$ is the average number of units in the sampled clusters.

Single-Stage Cluster Sampling for the Population Proportion

The cluster sampling estimator of the population proportion, p:

$$\hat{P}_{cl} = \frac{\sum\limits_{i=1}^{m} n_i \hat{P}_i}{\sum\limits_{i=1}^{m} n_i} \tag{17–20}$$

where the $\hat{P}_i$ are the proportions of interest within the sampled clusters

The estimated variance of the estimator in equation 17–20 is given by

$$s^2(\hat{P}_{cl}) = \frac{M - m}{Mm\bar{n}^2} \frac{\sum\limits_{i=1}^{m} n_i^2(\hat{P}_i - \hat{P}_{cl})^2}{m - 1} \tag{17–21}$$

We now demonstrate the use of cluster sampling for the population mean with the following example.

EXAMPLE 17-3   The J. B. Hunt Transport Company is especially interested in lowering fuel costs in order to survive in the tough world of deregulated trucking. Recently, the company introduced new measures to reduce fuel costs for all its trucks. Suppose that company trucks are based in 110 centers throughout the country and that the company's management wants to estimate the average amount of fuel saved per truck for the week following the institution of the new measures. For reasons of lower cost and administrative ease, management decides to use single-stage cluster sampling and to select a random sample of 20 trucking centers and measure the weekly fuel saving for each of the trucks in the selected centers (each center is a cluster). The average fuel savings per truck, in gallons, for each of the 20 selected centers are as follows (the number of trucks in each center is given in parentheses): 21 (8), 22 (8), 11 (9), 34 (10), 28 (7), 25 (8), 18 (10), 24 (12), 19 (11), 20 (6), 30 (8), 26 (9), 12 (9), 17 (8), 13 (10), 29 (8), 24 (8), 26 (10), 18 (10), 22 (11). From these data, compute an estimate of the average amount of fuel saved per truck for all of Hunt's trucks over the week in question. Also give a 95% confidence interval for this parameter.

SOLUTION   From equation 17–18, we get

$$\bar{x}_{cl} \frac{\sum\limits_{i=1}^{m} n_i \bar{x}_i}{\sum\limits_{i=1}^{m} n_i} = [21(8) + 22(8) + 11(9) + 34(10) + 28(7) + 25(8) + 18(10) +$$
$$24(12) + 19(11) + 20(6) + 30(8) + 26(9) + 12(9) + 17(8) +$$
$$13(10) + 29(8) + 24(8) + 26(10) + 18(10) + 22(11)]/(8 +$$
$$8 + 9 + 10 + 7 + 8 + 10 + 12 + 11 + 6 + 8 + 9 + 9 +$$
$$8 + 10 + 8 + 8 + 10 + 10 + 11)$$
$$= 21.83$$

From equation 17–19, we find that the estimated variance of our sample estimator of the mean is

$$s^2(\bar{X}_{cl}) = \left(\frac{M - m}{Mm\bar{n}^2}\right) \frac{\sum\limits_{i=1}^{20} n_i^2(\bar{x}_i - \bar{x}_{cl})^2}{m - 1}$$
$$= \frac{110 - 20}{(110)(20)(9)^2}[8^2(21 - 21.83)^2 + 8^2(22 - 21.83)^2 +$$
$$9^2(11 - 21.83)^2 + \cdots + 11^2(22 - 21.83)^2]/19$$
$$= 1.587$$

Using the preceding information, we construct a 95% confidence interval for μ as follows:

$$\bar{x}_{cl} \pm 1.96s(\bar{X}_{cl}) = 21.83 \pm 1.96\sqrt{1.587} = [19.36, 24.30]$$

Thus, based on the sampling results, Hunt's management may be 95% confident that average fuel savings per truck for all of their trucks over the week in question is anywhere from 19.36 to 24.30 gallons.

Two-Stage Cluster Sampling

When clusters are very large or when elements within each cluster tend to be similar, we may gain little information by sampling every element within the selected clusters. In such cases, it may be more economical to select more clusters and to sample only some of the elements within the chosen clusters. The formulas for the estimators and their variances in the case of two-stage cluster sampling are more complicated and may be found in advanced books on sampling methodology.

PROBLEMS

17–5. There are 602 aerobics-and-fitness centers in Japan (up from 170 five years ago). Adidas, the European maker of sports shoes and apparel, is very interested in this fast-growing potential market for its products. As part of a marketing survey, Adidas wants to estimate the average income of all members of Japanese fitness centers. (Members of one such club pay $62 to join and another $62 per month. Adidas believes that the average income of all fitness club members in Japan may be higher than that of the general population, for which census data exist.) Since travel and administrative costs for conducting a simple random sample of all members of fitness clubs throughout Japan would be prohibitively high, Adidas decided to conduct a cluster sampling survey. Five clubs were chosen at random out of the entire collection of 602 clubs, and all members of the 5 clubs were interviewed. The following are the average incomes (in U.S. dollars) for the members of each of the 5 clubs (the number of members in each club is given in parentheses): $37,237 (560), $41,338 (435), $28,800 (890), $35,498 (711), $47,446 (230). Give the cluster sampling estimate of the population mean income for all fitness club members in Japan. Also give a 90% confidence interval for the population mean. Are there any limitations to the methodology in this case?

17–6. Israel's kibbutzim are by now well diversified beyond their agrarian roots, producing everything from lollipops to plastic pipe. These 282 widely scattered communes of several hundred members maintain hundreds of factories and other production facilities. An economist wants to estimate the average annual revenues of all kibbutz production facilities. Since each kibbutz has several production units, and since travel and other costs are high, the economist wants to consider a sample of 15 randomly chosen kibbutzim and find the annual revenues of all production units in the selected kibbutzim. From these data, the economist hopes to estimate the average annual revenue per production unit in all 282 kibbutzim. The sample results are as follows.

Kibbutz	Number of Production Units	Total Kibbutz Annual Revenues (in millions of dollars)
1	4	4.5
2	2	2.8
3	6	8.9
4	2	1.2
5	5	7.0
6	3	2.2
7	2	2.3
8	1	0.8
9	8	12.5
10	4	6.2
11	3	5.5
12	3	6.2
13	2	3.8
14	5	9.0
15	2	1.4

From these data, compute the cluster sampling estimate of the mean annual revenue of all kibbutzim production units, and give a 95% confidence interval for the mean.

17–7.   Under what conditions would you use cluster sampling? Explain the differences among cluster sampling, simple random sampling, and stratified random sampling. Under what conditions would you use two-stage cluster sampling? Explain the difference between single-stage and two-stage cluster sampling. What are the limitations of cluster sampling?

17–8.   Recently a survey was conducted to assess the quality of investment brokers. A random sample of 6 brokerage houses was selected from a total of 27 brokerage houses. Each of the brokers in the selected brokerage houses was evaluated by an independent panel of industry experts as "highly qualified" or was given an evaluation below this rating. The designers of the survey wanted to estimate the proportion of all brokers in the entire industry who would be considered highly qualified. The survey results are in the following table.

Brokerage House	Total Number of Brokers	Number of HQ Brokers
1	120	80
2	150	75
3	200	100
4	100	65
5	88	45
6	260	200

Use the cluster sampling estimator of the population proportion to estimate the proportion of all highly qualified brokers in the investment industry. Also give a 99% confidence interval for the population proportion you estimated.

17–9.   Forty-two cruise ships come to Alaska's Glacier Bay every year. The state tourist board wants to estimate the average cruise passenger's satisfaction from this experience, rated on a scale of 0 to 100. Since the ships' arrivals are evenly spread throughout the season, simple random sampling is costly and time-consuming. Therefore, the agency decides to send its volunteers to board the first five ships of the season, consider them as clusters, and randomly choose 50 passengers in each ship for interviewing.

  a.   Is the method employed single-stage cluster sampling? Explain.

  b.   Is the method employed two-stage cluster sampling? Explain.

  c.   Suppose that each of the ships has exactly 50 passengers. Is the proposed method single-stage cluster sampling?

  d.   The 42 ships belong to 12 cruise ship companies. Each company has its own characteristics in terms of price, luxury, services, and type of passengers. Suggest an alternative sampling method, and explain its benefits.

17–5   Systematic Sampling

Sometimes a population is arranged in some order: files in a cabinet, crops in a field, goods in a warehouse, etc. In such cases it may be easier to draw our random sample in a *systematic* way rather than generate a simple random sample that would entail looking for particular items within the population. To select a **systematic sample** of n elements from a population of N elements, we divide the N elements in the population into n groups of k elements and then use the following rule.

> We randomly select the first element out of the first k elements in the population, and then we select every kth unit afterwards until we have a sample of n elements.

For example, suppose $k = 20$, and we need a sample of $n = 30$ items. We randomly select the first item from among the integers 1 to 20. If the random number selected is 11, then our systematic sample will contain the elements: 11, 11 + 20 = 31, 31 + 20 = 51, . . . , and so on until we have 30 elements in our sample.

A variant of this rule, which solves the problems that may be encountered when k is not an integer multiple of the sample size, n (their product being N), is to let k be the nearest integer to N/n. We now regard the N elements as being arranged in a circle (with the last element preceding the first element). We randomly select the first element from all N population members and then select every kth item until we have n items in our sample.

The Advantages of Systematic Sampling

In addition to the ease of drawing samples in a systematic way—for example, by simply measuring distances with a ruler in a file cabinet and sampling every fixed number of inches—the method has some statistical advantages as well. First, when $k = N/n$, the sample estimator of the population mean is unbiased. Second, systematic sampling is usually more precise than simple random sampling because it actually stratifies the population into n strata, each stratum containing k elements. Therefore, systematic sampling is approximately as precise as stratified random sampling with one unit per stratum. The difference between the two methods is that the systematic sample is spread more evenly over the entire population than a stratified sample, because in stratified sampling the samples in the strata are drawn separately. This adds precision in some cases. Systematic sampling is also related to cluster sampling in that it amounts to selecting one cluster out of a population of k clusters.

Estimation of the Population Mean in Systematic Sampling

> The systematic sampling estimator of the population mean, μ:
>
> $$\overline{X}_{sy} = \frac{\sum_{i=1}^{n} X_i}{n} \qquad (17\text{--}22)$$

The estimator is, of course, the same as the simple random sampling estimator of the population mean based on a sample of size n. The variance of the estimator in equation 17–22 is difficult to estimate from the results of a single sample. The estimation requires some assumptions about the order of the population. The estimated variances of $\overline{X}_{sy}$ in different situations are given below.

1. When the population values are assumed to be in no particular order with respect to the variable of interest, the estimated variance of the estimator of the mean is the same as in the case of simple random sampling:

$$s^2(\overline{X}_{sy}) = \left(\frac{N - n}{Nn}\right) S^2 \qquad (17\text{--}23)$$

   where S^2 is the usual sample variance, and the first term accounts for finite-population correction as well as division by n.

2. When the mean is constant within each stratum of k elements but different from stratum to stratum, the estimated variance of the sample mean is

$$s^2(\bar{X}_{sy}) = \frac{N - n}{Nn} \frac{\sum_{i=1}^{n} (X_i - X_{i+k})^2}{2(n - 1)} \tag{17-24}$$

3. When the population is assumed to be either increasing or decreasing linearly in the variable of interest, and when the sample size is large, the appropriate estimator of the variance of our estimator of the mean is

$$s^2(\bar{X}_{sy}) = \left(\frac{N - n}{Nn}\right) \frac{\sum_{i=1}^{n} (X_i - 2X_{i+k} + X_{i+2k})^2}{6(n - 2)} \tag{17-25}$$

for $1 \leq i \leq n - 2$.

There are formulas that apply in more complicated situations as well.
We demonstrate the use of systematic sampling with the following example.

EXAMPLE 17-4

An investor obtains a copy of *The Wall Street Journal* and wants to get a quick estimate of how the New York Stock Exchange has performed since the previous day. The investor knows that there are about 2,100 stocks listed on the NYSE and wants to look at a quick sample of 100 stocks and determine the average price change for the sample. The investor thus decides on an "every 21st" systematic sampling scheme. The investor uses a ruler and finds that this means that a stock should be selected about every 1.5 inches along the listings columns in the *Journal*. The first stock is randomly selected from among the first 21 stocks listed on the NYSE by using a random-number generator in a calculator. The selected stock is the seventh from the top, which happens to be ANR. For the day in question, the price change for ANR is $-1/4$. The next stock to be included in the sample is the one in position $7 + 21 = 28$th from the top. The stock is Aflpb, which on this date had a price change of 0 from the previous day. As mentioned, the selection is not done by counting the stocks, but by the faster method of successively measuring 1.5 inches down the column from each selected stock. The resulting sample of 100 stocks gives a sample mean of $\bar{x}_{sy} = +0.5$ and $s^2 = 0.36$. Give a 95% confidence interval for the average price change of all stocks listed on the NYSE.

SOLUTION

We have absolutely no reason to believe that the order in which the NYSE stocks are listed in *The Wall Street Journal* (i.e., alphabetically) has any relationship to the stocks' price changes. Therefore, the appropriate equation for the estimated variance of $\bar{X}_{sy}$ is equation 17–23. Using this equation, we get

$$s^2(\bar{X}_{sy}) = \left(\frac{N - n}{Nn}\right)s^2 = \left(\frac{2,100 - 100}{210,000}\right)0.36 = 0.0034$$

A 95% confidence interval for μ, the average price change on this day for all stocks on the NYSE, is therefore:

$$\bar{x}_{sy} \pm 1.96s(\bar{X}_{sy}) = 0.5 \pm (1.96)(\sqrt{0.0034}) = [0.386, 0.614]$$

The investor may be 95% sure that the average stock on the NYSE gained anywhere from $0.386 to $0.614.

When sampling for the population proportion, use the same equations as the ones used for simple random sampling if it may be assumed that no inherent order exists in the population. Otherwise use variance estimators given in advanced texts.

17–10. The Bridgestone Corporation maintains strict quality control of its tire production. This entails frequent sampling of tires from large stocks shipped to retailers. Samples of tires are selected and run continuously until they are worn out, and the average number of miles "driven" in the laboratory is noted. Suppose a warehouse contains 11,000 tires arranged in a certain order. The company wants to select a systematic sample of 50 tires to be tested in the laboratory. Use randomization to determine the first item to be sampled, and give the rule for obtaining the rest of the sample in this case.

17–11. A large discount store gives its sales personnel bonuses based on their average sale amount. Since each salesperson makes hundreds of sales each month, the store management decided to base average sale amount for each salesperson on a random sample of the person's sales. Since records of sales are kept in books, it is convenient to use systematic sampling. Suppose a salesperson has made 855 sales over the month, and management wants to choose a sample of 30 sales for estimation of the average amount of all sales. Suggest a way of doing this in such a way that no problems would result due to the fact that 855 is not an integer multiple of 30. Give the first element you choose to select, and explain how the rest of the sample is obtained.

17–12. An accountant always audits the second account and every fourth account thereafter when sampling a client's accounts.

    a. Does the accountant use systematic sampling? Explain.

    b. Explain the problems that may be encountered when this sampling scheme is used.

17–13. Beer sales in a tavern are cyclical over the week, with large volume during weekend nights, lower volume during the beginning of the week, and somewhat higher volume at midweek. Explain the possible problems that could arise, and the conditions under which they might arise, if systematic sampling were used to estimate beer sales volume per night.

17–14. A population is composed of 100 items arranged in some order. It is known that every stratum of 10 items in the order of arrangement tends to be similar in its values. An "every 10th" systematic sample is selected. The first item, randomly chosen, is the 6th item, and its value is 20. The following items in the sample are, of course, the 16th, the 26th, etc. The values of all items in the systematic sample are as follows: 20, 25, 27, 34, 28, 22, 28, 21, 37, 31. Give a 90% confidence interval for the population mean.

17–15. Explain the relationship between the method employed in problem 17–14 and the method of stratified random sampling. Explain the differences between the two methods.

17–6 Nonresponse

Nonresponse to sample surveys is one of the most serious problems that occur in practical applications of sampling methodology. The problem is one of loss of information. For example, suppose that a survey questionnaire dealing with some issue is mailed to a randomly chosen sample of 500 people and that only 300 people respond to the survey. The question is: What can you say about the 200 people who did not respond? This is a very important question, and there is no immediate answer to it precisely because the people did not respond; we know nothing about them. Suppose that the questionnaire asks for a yes or no answer to a particular public issue over which people have differing views, and we want to estimate the proportion of people who would respond yes. People may have such strong views about the issue that those who would respond no may refuse to respond altogether. In this case, the 200 nonre-spondents to our survey will contain a higher proportion of "no" answers than the 300 responses we have. But, again, we would not know about this. The result will be a bias. How can we compensate for such a possible bias?

We may want to consider the population as made up of two *strata:* the respon-dents' stratum and the nonrespondents' stratum. In the original survey, we managed to sample only the respondents' stratum, and this caused the bias. What we need to do is to obtain a random sample from the nonrespondents' stratum. This is easier said than done. Still, there are ways we can at least reduce the bias and get some idea about the proportion of "yes" answers in the nonresponse stratum. This entails *callbacks:* returning to the nonrespondents and asking them again. In some mail questionnaires, it is common to send several requests for response, and these reduce the uncertainty. There may, however, be hard-core refusers who just do not want to answer the questionnaire. It is likely that these people have very distinct views about the issue in question, and if you leave them out, there will be a significant bias in your conclusions. In such a situation, it may be useful to gather a small random sample of the hard-core refusers and offer them some monetary reward for their answers. In cases where people may find the question embarrassing or may worry about revealing their per-sonal views, there is the possibility of using a random-response mechanism whereby the respondent randomly answers one of two questions: one is the sensitive question, and the other is an innocuous question of no relevance. The interviewer does not know which question any particular respondent answered but does know the probability of answering the sensitive question. This still allows for computation of the aggregated response to the sensitive question while protecting any given respondent's privacy.

17-7   Summary and Review of Terms

In this chapter, we considered some advanced sampling methods that allow for better precision than simple random sampling, or for lowered costs and easier survey imple-mentation. We concentrated on **stratified random sampling,** the most important and useful of the advanced methods and one that offers statistical advantages of improved precision. We then discussed **cluster sampling** and **systematic sampling,** two methods that are used primarily for their ease of implementation and reduced sampling costs. We mentioned a few other advanced methods, which are described in books devoted to sampling methodology. We discussed the problem of **nonresponse.**

ADDITIONAL PROBLEMS

17–16.   Bloomingdale's in New York has the following departments on its mezzanine level: Stendahl, Ralph Lauren, The Beauty Spot, and Lauder Prescriptives. The mezzanine level is managed separately from the other levels, and during the store's post-holiday sale, the level manager wanted to estimate the average sales amount per customer throughout the sale. The following table gives the relative weights of the different departments (known from previous operation of the store), as well as the sample means and variances of the different strata for a total sample of 1,000 customers, proportionally allocated to the four strata. Give a 95% confidence interval for the average sale (in dollars) per customer for the entire level over the period of the post-holiday sale.

Stratum	Weight	Sample Mean	Sample Variance
Stendahl	0.25	65.00	123.00
Ralph Lauren	0.35	87.00	211.80
Beauty Spot	0.15	52.00	88.85
Lauder Prescriptives	0.25	38.50	100.40

Note: We assume that shoppers visit the mezzanine level to purchase from only one of its departments. Since the brands and designers are competitors, and since shoppers are known to have a strong brand loyalty in this market, the assumption seems reasonable.

17–17.   A state department of transportation is interested in sampling commuters to determine certain of their characteristics. The department arranges for its field workers to board buses at random, as well as stop private vehicles at intersections and ask the commuters to fill out a short questionnaire. Is this method cluster sampling? Explain.

17–18.   Use systematic sampling to estimate the average performance of all stocks in one of the listed stock exchanges on a given day. Compare your results with those reported in the media for the day in question.

17–19.   An economist wants to estimate average annual profits for all businesses in a given community and proposes to draw a systematic sample of all businesses listed in the local Yellow Pages. Comment on the proposed methodology. What potential problem do you foresee?

17–20.   In an "every 23rd" systematic sampling scheme, the first item was randomly chosen to be the 17th element. Give the numbers of 6 sample items out of a population of 120.

17–21.   A quality-control sampling scheme was carried out by Sony for estimating the percentage of defective radios in a large shipment of 1,000 containers with 100 radios in each container. Twelve containers were chosen at random, and every radio in them was checked. The numbers of defective radios in each of the containers are: 8, 10, 4, 3, 11, 6, 9, 10, 2, 7, 6, 12. Give a 95% confidence interval for the proportion of defective radios in the entire shipment.

17–22.   Suppose that the radios in the 1,000 containers of problem 17–21 were produced in five different factories, each factory known to have different internal production controls. Each container is marked with a number denoting the factory where the radios were made. Suggest an appropriate sampling method in this case, and discuss its advantages.

17–23.   The makers of Taster's Choice® instant coffee want to estimate the proportion of underfilled jars of a given size. The jars are in 14 warehouses around the country, and each warehouse contains crates of cases of jars of coffee. Suggest a sampling method, and discuss it.

17–24.   Cadbury, Inc., is interested in estimating people's responses to a new chocolate. The company believes that people in different age groups differ in their preferences for chocolate. The company believes that in the region of interest, 25% of the population are children, 55% are young adults, and 20% are older people. A proportional allocation of a total random sample of size 1,000 is undertaken, and people's responses on a scale of 0 to 100 are solicited. The results are as follows. For the children, $\bar{x} = 90$ and $s = 5$; for the young adults, $\bar{x} = 82$ and $s = 11$; and for the older people, $\bar{x} = 88$ and $s = 6$. Give a 95% confidence interval for the population average rating for the new chocolate.

17–25.   For problem 17–24, suppose that it costs twice as much money to sample a child compared with the younger and older adults, where costs are the same per sampled person. Use the information in problem 17–24 (the weights and standard deviations) to determine an optimal allocation of the total sample.

17–26.   Refer to the situation in problem 17–24. Suppose that the following relative age frequencies in the population are known.

Age Group	Frequency	Age Group	Frequency
under 10	0.10	31 to 35	0.10
10 to 15	0.10	36 to 40	0.10
16 to 18	0.05	41 to 45	0.05
19 to 22	0.05	46 to 50	0.05
23 to 25	0.15	51 to 55	0.05
26 to 30	0.15	56 and over	0.05

Define strata to be used in the survey.

17–27. Name two sampling methods that are useful when there is information about a variable related to the variable of interest.

17–28. Suppose that a study was undertaken using a simple random sample from a particular population. When the results of the study became available, it was apparent that the population could be viewed as consisting of several strata. What can be done now?

17–29. For problem 17–28, suppose that the population is viewed as comprising 18 strata. Is using this number of strata advantageous? Are there any alternative solutions?

17–30. Discuss and compare the three sampling methods: cluster sampling, stratified sampling, and systematic sampling.

17–31. The following table reports return on capital for insurance companies. Consider the data a population of U.S. insurance companies, and select a random sample of firms to estimate mean return on capital. Do the sampling two ways: first, as a systematic sample considering the entire list as a uniform, ordered population; and second, use stratified random sampling, the strata being the types of insurance company. Compare your results.

Company Diversified	Return on Capital Latest 12 Mos. %	Company Life & health	Return on Capital Latest 12 Mos. %	Company Property & casualty	Return on Capital Latest 12 Mos. %
Marsh & McLennan Cos	25.4	Conseco	13.7	20th Century Inds	25.1
Loews	13.8	First Capital Holding	10.7	Geico	20.4
American Intl Group	14.6	Torchmark	18.4	Argonaut Group	17.1
General Re	17.4	Capital Holding	9.9	Hartford Steam Boiler	19.1
Safeco	11.6	American Family	8.5	Progressive	10.1
Leucadia National	27.0	Kentucky Central Life	6.3	WR Berkley	11.5
CNA Financial	8.6	Provident Life & Acc	13.1	Mercury General	28.3
Aon	12.8	NWNL	8.4	Selective Insurance	13.6
Kemper	1.4	UNUM	13.2	Hanover Insurance	6.3
Cincinnati Financial	10.7	Liberty Corp	10.1	St Paul Cos	16.9
Reliance Group	23.1	Jefferson-Pilot	9.5	Chubb	14.3
Alexander & Alexander	9.9	USLife	6.7	Ohio Casualty	9.3
Zenith National Ins	9.8	American Natl Ins	5.2	First American Finl	4.8
Old Republic Intl	13.4	Monarch Capital	0	Berkshire Hathaway	7.3
Transamerica	7.5	Washington National	1.2	ITT	10.2
Uslico	7.7	Broad	8.0	USF&G	6.6
Aetna Life & Cas	8.0	First Executive	0	Xerox	5.3
American General	8.2	ICH	0	Orion Capital	10.8
Lincoln National	9.2			Fremont General	12.6
Sears, Roebuck	7.2			Foremost Corp of Amer	0
Independent Insurance	7.8			Continental Corp	6.6
Cigna	7.0			Alleghany	9.0
Travelers	0				
American Bankers	8.3				
Unitrin	6.1				

Reproduced by permission from "Annual Report on American Industry," *Forbes*, January 7, 1991, p. 176.

The Boston Redevelopment Authority is mandated the task of improving and developing urban areas in Boston. One of the Authority's main concerns is with the development of the community of Roxbury. This community has undergone many changes in recent years, and much interest is given to its future development.

Currently, only 2% of the total land in this community is used in industry, and 9% is used commercially. As part of its efforts to develop the community, the Boston Redevelopment Authority is interested in determining the attitudes of the residents of Roxbury toward the development of more business and industry in their region. The authority therefore plans to sample residents of the community to determine their views and use the sample or samples to infer about the views of all residents of the community. Roxbury is divided into 11 planning subdistricts. The population density is believed to be uniform across all 11 subdistricts, and the population of each subdistrict is approximately proportional to the subdistrict's size. There is no known list of all the people in Roxbury. A map of the community is shown in Exhibit 1. Advise the Boston Redevelopment Authority on designing their survey.

EXHIBIT 1 Roxbury Planning Subdistricts

REFERENCES

Books on Data Analysis (Chapter 1):

Chambers, J. M.; W. S. Cleveland; B. Kleiner; and P. A. Tukey. *Graphical Methods for Data Analysis.* Boston: Duxbury Press, 1983. An interesting approach to graphical techniques and EDA using computer-intensive methods. The book requires no mathematical training.

Tukey, J. W. *Exploratory Data Analysis.* Reading, Mass.: Addison-Wesley Publishing, 1977. This is the original EDA book. Some material in our Chapter 1 is based on this text.

Books Primarily about Probability and Random Variables (Chapters 2, 3, 4):

Chung, K. L. *Probability Theory with Stochastic Processes.* New York: Springer-Verlag, 1979. This is a lucidly written book. The approach to the theory of probability is similar to the one used in our text.

Feller, William. *An Introduction to Probability Theory and Its Applications.* Vol. 1, 3rd ed.; vol. 2, 2nd ed. New York: John Wiley & Sons, 1968, 1971. This is a classic textbook in probability theory. Volume 1 should be understandable to a reader of our text. Volume 2, which deals with continuous probability models, is more difficult and requires considerable mathematical ability.

Loève, Michel. *Probability Theory.* 4th ed. New York: Springer-Verlag, 1977. This is a mathemat-

ically demanding classic text in probability (an understanding of mathematical analysis is required).

Ross, Sheldon M. *A First Course in Probability.* 3rd ed. New York: Macmillan, 1988. An intuitive introduction to probability that requires a knowledge of calculus.

Ross, Sheldon M. *Introduction to Probability Models.* 4th ed. New York: Academic Press, 1989. A very intuitive introduction to probability theory that is consistent with the development in our text.

Statistical Theory and Sampling (Chapters 5, 6, 7, 8, and 17):

Cochran, William G. *Sampling Techniques.* 3rd ed. New York: John Wiley & Sons, 1977. This is a classic text on sampling methodology. Much of the material in our Chapter 17 draws on the results in this book.

Cox, D. R., and D. V. Hinkley. *Theoretical Statistics.* London: Chapman and Hall, 1974. A thorough discussion of the theory of statistics.

Fisher, Sir Ronald A. *The Design of Experiments.* 7th ed. Edinburgh: Oliver and Boyd, 1960. A classic treatise on statistical inference.

Fisher, Sir Ronald A. *Statistical Methods for Research Workers.* Edinburgh: Oliver and Boyd, 1941.

Hogg, R. V., and A. T. Craig. *Introduction to Mathematical*

Statistics. 4th ed. New York: Macmillan, 1978. A good introduction to mathematical statistics that requires an understanding of calculus.

Kendall, M. G., and A. Stuart. *The Advanced Theory of Statistics.* Vol. 1, 2nd ed.; vols. 2, 3. London: Charles W. Griffin, 1963, 1961, 1966.

Mood, A. M.; F. A. Graybill; and D. C. Boes. *Introduction to the Theory of Statistics.* 3rd ed. New York: McGraw-Hill, 1974.

Rao, C. R. *Linear Statistical Inference and Its Applications.* 2nd ed. New York: John Wiley & Sons, 1973. This is a classic book on statistical inference that provides in-depth coverage of topics ranging from probability to analysis of variance, regression analysis, and multivariate methods. This book contains theoretical results that are the basis of statistical inference. The book requires advanced mathematical ability.

Books Primarily about Experimental Design, Analysis of Variance, Regression Analysis, and Econometrics (Chapters 9, 10, and 11):

Chatterjee, S., and B. Price. *Regression Analysis by Example.* 2nd ed. New York: John Wiley & Sons, 1991.

Cochran, W. G., and G. M. Cox. *Experimental Designs.* 2nd ed. New York: John Wiley & Sons, 1957

Draper, N. R., and H. Smith. *Applied Regression Analysis.* 2nd ed. New York: John Wiley & Sons, 1981. A thorough text on regression analysis that requires an understanding of matrix algebra.

Johnston, J. *Econometric Methods.* 3rd ed. New York: McGraw-Hill, 1984. A good, comprehensive introduction to econometric models and regression analysis at a somewhat higher level than that of our text.

Judge, G. R.; C. Hill; W. Griffiths; H. Lutkepohl; and T. Lee. *Introduction to the Theory and Practice of Econometrics.* New York: John Wiley & Sons, 1982.

Montgomery, D. C., and E. A. Peck. *Introduction to Linear Regression Analysis.* 2nd ed. New York: John Wiley & Sons, 1992. A very readable book on regression analysis that is recommended for further reading after our Chapter 11.

Neter, J.; W. Wasserman; and M. H. Kutner. *Applied Linear Regression Models.* 2nd ed. Homewood, Ill.: Richard D. Irwin, 1989. A good introduction to regression analysis.

Neter, J.; W. Wasserman; and M. H. Kutner. *Applied Linear Statistical Models.* 3rd ed. Homewood, Ill.: Richard D. Irwin, 1990. A good introduction to regression and analysis of variance that requires no advanced mathematics.

Scheffé, H. *The Analysis of Variance.* New York: John Wiley & Sons, 1959. This is a classic text on analysis of variance that requires advanced mathematical ability.

Seber, G. A. F. *Linear Regression Analysis.* New York: John Wiley and Sons, 1977. An advanced book on regression analysis. Some of the results in this book are used in our Chapter 11.

Snedecor, George W., and William G. Cochran. *Statistical Methods.* 7th ed. Ames: Iowa State University Press, 1980. This well-known book is an excellent introduction to analysis of variance and experimental design, as well as regression analysis. The book is very readable and requires no advanced mathematics.

Weisberg, S. *Applied Linear Regression.* 2nd ed. New York: John Wiley & Sons, 1985. A good introduction to regression analysis.

Books on Forecasting (Chapter 12):

Abraham, B., and J. Ledolter. *Statistical Methods for Forecasting.* New York: John Wiley & Sons, 1983. This is an excellent book on forecasting methods.

Armstrong, S. *Long-Range Forecasting.* 2nd ed. New York: John Wiley & Sons, 1985.

Granger, C. W. J., and P. Newbold. *Forecasting Economic Time Series.* 2nd ed. New York: Academic Press, 1986. A good introduction to forecasting models.

Books on Quality Control (Chapter 13):

Duncan, A. J. *Quality Control and Industrial Statistics.* 5th ed. Homewood, Ill.: Richard D. Irwin, 1986.

Gitlow, H.; S. Gitlow; A. Oppenheim; and R. Oppenheim. *Tools and Methods for the Improvement of Quality.* Homewood, Ill.: Richard D. Irwin, 1989.

Ott, E. R., and E. G. Schilling. *Process Quality Control.* 2nd ed. New York: McGraw-Hill, 1990.

Ryan, T. P. *Statistical Methods for Quality Improvement.* New York: John Wiley & Sons, 1989. Much of the material in our Chapter 13 is inspired by the approach in this book.

Books on Nonparametric Methods (Chapter 14):

Conover, W. J. *Practical Nonparametric Statistics.* 2nd ed. New York: John Wiley & Sons, 1980. This is an excellent, readable textbook covering a wide range of nonparametric methods. Much of the material in our Chapter 14 is based on results in this book.

Hollander, M., and D. A. Wolfe. *Nonparametric Statistical Methods.* New York: John Wiley & Sons, 1973.

Siegel, S. *Nonparametric Statistics for the Behavioral Sciences.* 2nd ed. New York: McGraw-Hill, 1988.

Books on Subjective Probability, Bayesian Statistics, and Decision Analysis (Chapter 15 and Chapter 2):

Berger, James O. *Statistical Decision Theory and Bayesian Analysis.* 2nd ed. New York: Springer-Verlag, 1985. A comprehensive book on Bayesian methods at an advanced level.

de Finetti, Bruno. *Probability, Induction, and Statistics.* New York: John Wiley & Sons, 1972. This excellent book on subjective probability and the Bayesian philosophy is the source of the de Finetti game in our Chapter 15. The book is readable at about the level of our text.

de Finetti, Bruno. *Theory of Probability.* Vols. 1 and 2. New York: John Wiley & Sons, 1974, 1975. An excellent introduction to subjective probability and the Bayesian approach by one of its pioneers.

DeGroot, M. H. *Optimal Statistical Decisions.* New York: McGraw-Hill, 1970.

Good, I. J. *Good Thinking: The Foundations of Probability and Its Applications.* Minneapolis: University of Minnesota Press, 1983.

Jeffreys, Sir Harold. *Theory of Probability.* 3rd rev. ed. London: Oxford University Press, 1983. First published in 1939, this book truly came before its time. The book explains the Bayesian philosophy of science and its application in probability and statistics. It is readable and thought-provoking and is highly recommended for anyone with an interest in the ideas underlying Bayesian inference.

Books on Multivariate Analysis (Chapter 16):

Anderson, T. W. *An Introduction to Multivariate Statistical Analysis.* 2nd ed. New York: John Wiley & Sons, 1984. First published in 1958, this advanced book contains much of the theory underlying the more commonly used multivariate methods.

Morrison, Donald F. *Multivariate Statistical Methods.* 3rd ed. New York: McGraw-Hill, 1990. This is an applied text explaining some of the more important multivariate techniques and illustrating their use with many examples.

Norusis, M. *Advanced Statistics Guide SPSS.* Chicago, Ill.: SPSS, 1995. This is an excellent introduction to the use of multivariate statistics and other advanced statistical techniques from a computer-user point of view. The book contains detailed examples of how to carry out a multivariate analysis using the SPSS package.

Sharma, S. *Applied Multivariate Techniques.* New York: John Wiley & Sons, 1996.

Tatsuoka, M. M. *Multivariate Analysis.* 2nd ed. New York: Macmillan, 1987. This is an excellent book on the theory of multivariate analysis that requires a knowledge of matrix algebra. Much of the material in our Chapter 16 is based on results in this book.

ANSWERS TO MOST ODD-NUMBERED PROBLEMS

Chapter 1

1–1.
1. quantitative/ratio
2. qualitative/nominal
3. quantitative/ratio
4. qualitative/nominal
5. quantitative/ratio
6. quantitative/interval
7. quantitative/ratio
8. quantitative/ratio
9. quantitative/ratio
10. quantitative/ratio
11. quantitative/ordinal

1–3. Weakest to strongest: Nominal, Ordinal, Interval, Ratio

1–5. Ordinal

1–7. Non-random sample; frame is random sample

1–11. Ordinal

1–13. LQ = 121, MQ = 128, UQ = 133.5, 10th percentile = 114.8, 15th percentile = 118.1, 65th percentile = 131.1, IQR = 12.5

1–15. Median = 70, 20th percentile = 45, 30th percentile = 53.8, 60th percentile = 76.8, 90th percentile = 89.4

1–17. Median = 51, LQ = 30.5, UQ = 194.25, IQR = 163.75, 45th percentile = 42.2

1–19. Mean = 126.63, median = 128, modes = 128, 134, 136

1–21. Mean = 66.954, median = 70, mode = 45

1–23. Mean = 199.875, median = 51, mode: none

1–25. Mean = 13.001, median = 11.94

1–27. Variance, standard deviation

1–29. Range = 27, variance = 57.74, standard deviation = 7.5986

1–31. Range = 60, variance = 321.38, standard deviation = 17.927

1–33. Range = 1,186, variance = 110,287.45, standard deviation = 332.096

1–35. Chebyshev holds; data not mound-shaped, empirical rule does not apply.

1–37. Chebyshev holds; data not mound-shaped, empirical rule does not apply.

1–47. No outliers; left-skewed distribution

1–53. Right-skewed distribution

1–57. No; statistical inference needed.

1–59. $\bar{x} = 74.7$ $s = 13.944$ $s^2 = 194.43$

1–65. The data set is skewed to the right.

1–67. Four outliers

1–69.

Industry group	Mean	Median
Apparel & shoes	21.59	20.30
Home furnishings	11.71	10.15
Gas distributors	10.52	10.85
Software	21.23	20.25
Personal products	20.46	17.35
International oils	10.94	10.60

1–73. Mortgage rates tend to be lower in large cities than elsewhere.

1–75. Rates have two modes: 9.00 and 9.25. Points have the single mode 3.00.

1–77. Monthly payment is symmetrically distributed with two modes; points is a somewhat left-skewed distribution.

1–85. Paperbacks are much more variable.

1–87. $\mu = 101,141.4$, a little smaller than the listed USA median.

1–89. Medians are used to minimize the influence of outliers.

Chapter 2

2–1. Objective and subjective

2–3. The sample space is the set of all possible outcomes of an experiment.

2–5. $G \cup F$: the baby is either a girl, or is over 5 pounds (of either sex). $G \cap F$: the baby is a girl over 5 pounds.

2–7. $A \cup B$: getting the grad school acceptance or the job offer or both. $A \cap B$: receiving both.

2–9. $S \cup B$: purchase stock or bonds, or both. $S \cap B$: purchase stock and bonds.

2–11. 0.000625

2–13. Roughly: Highest = 0.80, Moderate = 0.50, Low = 0.10

2–15. Yes

2–17. 0.85 is a typical "very likely" probability.

2–19. The team is very likely to win.

2–21. *a.* Mutually exclusive
b. 0.035
c. 0.985

2–23. 0.49

2–25. 0.7909

2–27. 0.500

2–29. 0.60

2–31. *a.* 0.1002
b. 0.2065
c. 0.59
d. 0.144
e. 0.451
f. 0.571
g. 0.168

h. 0.454
i. 0.569

2–33.   a. 0.484
b. 0.455
c. 0.138
d. 0.199
e. 0.285
f. 0.634
g. 0.801

2–35.   a. $3/10 = 0.30$
b. $6/25 = 0.24$
c. $3/5 = 0.60$

2–37.   0.0199
2–39.   0.99892
2–41.   Not independent
2–43.   Not independent
2–45.   0.3686
2–47.   0.99928
2–49. $175/256 = 0.684$
2–51. $9! = 362,880$
2–53.   120
2–55.   0.00275
2–57. $180/1,947,792 = 0.0000924$
2–59.   0.545
2–61.   0.37
2–63.   0.8809
2–65.   0.1602
2–67.   0.85
2–69.   1/3
2–71.   0.0248
2–73.   0.6
2–75. $2/3 = 0.667$
2–77.   0.18
2–79.   0.7254
2–81.   0.51
2–83.   0.524
2–85.   0.41
2–87.   0.0715
2–89.   0.8113
2–91.   0.2034
2–93.   0.5508
2–95.   Yes, $0.7695 > 0.70$
2–97. $1 - (1/2)^{n-1}$
2–99.   Caller preselects either *H-T* or *T-H* for the two ordered outcomes. Flip the coin twice; if two different outcomes, the caller attends if her choice was correct. If the two flips were the same, then flip twice again and repeat as needed.

Chapter 3

3–1.   a. $\Sigma P(x) = 1.0$

b.
x	F(x)
0	0.3
1	0.5
2	0.7
3	0.8
4	0.9
5	1.0

c. 0.3

3–3.   a. $\Sigma P(x) = 1.0$

b.
x	F(x)
0	0.10
10	0.30
20	0.65
30	0.85
40	0.95
50	1.00

c. 0.35

3–5.
x	P(x)	F(x)
2	1/36	1/36
3	2/36	3/36
4	3/36	6/36
5	4/36	10/36
6	5/36	15/36
7	6/36	21/36
8	5/36	26/36
9	4/36	30/36
10	3/36	33/36
11	2/36	35/36
12	1/36	1.0

3–7.   a. 0.55

b.
x	F(x)
2	0.20
3	0.40
4	0.70
5	0.80
6	0.90
7	0.95
8	1.00

c. 0.9
d. 0.5

3–9.   a. $\Sigma P(x) = 1.0$
b. 0.50

c.
x	F(x)
9	0.05
10	0.20
11	0.50
12	0.70
13	0.85
14	0.95
15	1.00

3–11. $E(X) = 3.19$
$E(X^2) = 12.39$
$V(X) = 2.2139$
$SD(X) = 1.4879$

3–13. $E(X) = 2.8$
$E(X^2) = 10$
$V(X) = 2.16$
$SD(X) = 1.47$

3–15. $E(X) = 2.2$
$P(X > E(X)) = 0.3$

3–17.   0.9375
3–19. $E(X) = 8.3$ $V(X) = 2.3$
$E(Y) = 8.4$ $V(Y) = 6.4$
Y is riskier because $V(Y) > V(X)$ while $E(X)$ is close to $E(Y)$.

3–21. $3
3–23. $E(cost) = 465.85$
3–25.   Long–term average value of the random variable. Used as a typical value of the random variable, a central value.

3–29.   b. 0.913

c.
s	F(s)	P(s)
0	0.010	0.010
1	0.087	0.077
2	0.317	0.230
3	0.663	0.346
4	0.922	0.259
5	1.000	0.078

d. 0.98976
e. 0.346
f. 3.0
g. 1.2

3–31.   *X* is binomial if sales calls are independent.
3–33.   *X* is not binomial because members of the same family are related and not independent of each other.
3–35. $P(X \geq 5) = 0.0328$
$P(X \leq 2) = 0.6778$
3–37.   0.794
3–39.   0.033
3–41. $P(0) = 0.905$,
$P(1) = 0.0905$,
$P(2) = 0.00452$,
$P(3) = 0.000151$
3–43.   0.148
3–45.   0.953
3–47.   0.9940
3–49.   10
3–51.   Probabilities are obtained as areas under the density function $f(x)$ graphed over the intervals in question.
3–53. $F(x)$ = area under $f(y)$ from $-\infty$ (smallest *y*) to *x*.
3–55. $f(x) = \begin{cases} 1/7 & \text{if } 0 \leq x \leq 7 \\ 0 & \text{otherwise} \end{cases}$
3–59. $e^{-2/3} = 0.5134$
3–61.   10
3–63.   0.984

3–65. *a.* Y is binomial: the number of "successes" (no orders) in 52 trials.
b. 5.2

3–67. E(Profit) = $1,130, V(Profit) = 3,513,600, SD(Profit) = 1,874.46

3–69. *a.* 0.0031
b. 0.0036
c. Do not believe the advertisement.
d. 8

3–71. X is geometric.

3–73. *a.* $f(x) =$
$$\begin{cases} 1/4 & \text{for } 5 \le x \le 9 \\ 0 & \text{otherwise} \end{cases}$$
b. 0.75
c. 7

3–75. 0.9979

3–77. 0.59185

3–79. *a.* 0.222
b. 23.889

3–81. *a.* 0.31
b. 10.980
c. 1.233

3–83. 0.9999945 (extremely close to 1.0)

Chapter 4

4–1. 0.6826, 0.95, 0.9802, 0.9951, 0.9974

4–3. 0.1828

4–5. 0.0215

4–7. 0.9901

4–9. A very small number, close to 0.

4–11. 0.9544

4–13. Not likely. P = 0.00003

4–15. $z = 0.19$

4–17. $z = 0.583$ (approximately)

4–19. $z = \pm 1.96$

4–21. 0.0164

4–23. 0.927

4–25. 0.003

4–27. 0.8609, 0.2107, 0.6306

4–29. 0.0931

4–31. *a.* 0.1357
b. 0.0951

4–33. 126.6

4–35. 20,321.6

4–37. 13.97 and 50.03

4–39. 103.5

4–41. $30,185

4–43. 9.654, 12.746

4–45. 43.59

4–47. 0.423

4–49. 13,155.8

4–51. Mean = 5.829; standard deviation = 2.414

4–53. 5,224.92

4–55. 2.138

4–57. Using binomial: 0.2375; using a normal approximation: 0.2321

4–59. 0.9922

4–61. 0.0738

4–63. 0.278

4–65. 0.4013, 0.5808, 0.0228

4–67. 0.0228, 0.9772, 0.9088, 0.5394. Limitation: stock prices are very discrete.

4–69. $6.39

4–71. [42,272, 57,728]

4–73. 10.4125%, 13.7875%

4–75. 7.22

4–77. Standard deviation = 35,528.596, mean = 666,523.4

4–79. Mean = 650, standard deviation = 273.44

4–81. 37,153 papers.

4–83. 0.999

4–85. 23.92, so set warranty for 24 months

4–87. 0.242

4–89. $741,000

4–91. Very close to 1.00

Chapter 5

5–1. Parameters are numerical measures of populations. Sample statistics are numerical measures of samples. An estimator is a sample statistic used for estimating a population parameter.

5–3. $5/12 = 0.41667$

5–5. $586,687

5–11. The probability distribution of a sample statistic; useful in determining the accuracy of estimation results.

5–13. $E(\bar{X}) = 125$
$SE(\bar{X}) = 8.944$

5–15. When the population distribution is unknown.

5–17. Binomial. Cannot use normal approximation since $np = 1.2$.

5–19. 0.075

5–21. 0.001

5–23. 0.2308

5–25. 0.0062

5–27. 0.0502

5–29. 0.0190

5–31. A consistent estimator means as $n \to \infty$ the probability of getting close to the parameter increases. A generous budget affords a large sample size, making this probability high.

5–33. Advantage: uses all information in the data. Disadvantage: may be too sensitive to the influence of outliers.

5–37. $df = n - 2$, because there are 2 restrictions: an intercept and a slope.

5–39. Yes, we can solve the equation for the one unknown amount.

5–41. $E(\bar{X}) = 1,065$
$V(\bar{X}) = 2,500$

5–43. $E(\bar{X}) = 53 \quad SE(\bar{X}) = 0.5$

5–45. $E(\hat{P}) = 0.2$
$SE(\hat{P}) = 0.04216$

5–47. 0.0384

5–49. 0.9544

5–51. 0.0023

5–55. The sample median is unbiased. The sample mean is more efficient and is sufficient. Must assume normality for using the sample median to estimate μ; it is more resistant to outliers.

5–57. 0.1727

5–59. 0.0499

5–61. 0.9503

5–63. No minimum ($n = 1$ is enough for normality).

5–65. This estimator is consistent, and is more efficient than $\bar{X}$, because $\sigma^2/n^2 < \sigma^2/n$.

5–67. Relative minimum sample sizes:
$n_a < n_b < n_d < n_e < n_c$

5–69. Use a computer simulation, draw repeated samples, determine the empirical distribution.

5–71. $P(Z < -5) = 0.0000003$
Not probable

5–73. 0.923

Chapter 6

6–5. [86,978.12, 92,368.12] dollars

6–7. [31.098, 32.902] m.p.g

6–9. [9.045, 9.555] percent

6–11. Yes; all values in the 99% confidence interval are above 245.

6–13. 95% C.I.: [136.99, 156.51]
90% C.I.: [138.56, 154.94]
99% C.I.: [133.93, 159.57]

6–15. [19.35, 22.13]

6–17. 8.393

6–19. 95% C.I.: [15,684.37, 17,375.63]
99% C.I.: [15,418.6, 17,641.4]

6–21. [27.93, 33.19] thousand miles

6–23. [72.599, 89.881]

6–25. [29.87, 59.33] dollars

6–27. [2.344, 2.856] days

6–29. [93.75, 108.71] sales

6–31. [15.86, 17.14] dollars

6–33. [5.44, 7.96] years

6–35. [55.85, 67.48] containers

6–37. [9.101, 10.633]

6–39. [0.1577, 0.3090]

6–41. [0.7104, 0.7896]

6–43. [0.1204, 0.1779]

6–45. [0.0317, 0.0488]

6–47. [0.0375, 0.2702]

6–49. [0.5357, 0.6228]

6–51. [0.0821, 0.0979]

6–53. [625.92, 670.72]

6–55. [0.4590, 0.60345]

6–57. [0.0584, 0.1816]

6–59. [2.505, 3.695]

6–61. [4.74, 16.34]

6–63. [869.8, 1,789.7]

6–65. [200.58, 1,412.95]

6–67. [0.0925, 0.3413]

6–69. 271 items

6–71. 39 executives

6–73. 131

6–75. 865

6–77. 0.2087

6–79. 0.0997

6–81. $15,477.75

6–83. 0.2828

6–85. [8.883, 13.757] million dollars

6–87. 96 people

6–89. [615,081.0, 1,280,428.6]

6–91. [0.1891, 0.3509]

6–93. [5.625, 26.102]

6–95. [2.279, 2.721] days

6–97. [−0.000376, 0.00538]
Lower bound is really 0

6–99. [339,817.73, 372,342.27]

6–101. [4.145, 15.291]

6–103. Need to assume a normal population distribution.

6–107. 50%

Chapter 7

7–1. $z = -2.575$
Reject H_0 almost at $\alpha = .01$

7–3. $z = -19.72$
Reject H_0 very strongly (p-value is very small)

7–5. $z = -1.456$
Do not reject H_0 (p-value = 0.1454)

7–7. $t_{(19)} = 0.8944$
Cannot reject H_0

7–9. $t_{(11)} = 2.617$
Reject H_0 at $\alpha = .05$

7–11. $t_{(24)} = 2.25$
Reject H_0 at $\alpha = .05$, but not at $\alpha = .01$

7–13. Assume random sampling from a normal population.

7–15. $t_{(27)} = 0.248$
Do not reject H_0

7–17. $z = -1.037$
Do not reject H_0 (p-value = 0.2998)

7–19. $z = 2.653$
Reject H_0 (p-value = 0.008)

7–21. $z = 18.422$
Strongly reject H_0 (p-value is very small)

7–23. $t_{(18)} = -8.97$
Reject H_0 (p-value is very small)

7–25. $z = 5.354$
Reject H_0 (p-value is very small)

7–27. $z = 2.44$
Reject H_0 (p-value = .0073)

7–29. $t_{(9)} = -1.581$
Cannot reject H_0 (.05 < p-value < .10)

7–31. Since $\hat{p} = .1203 > .11 = p$, do not reject H_0 that unemployment has been reduced.

7–33. $z = 6.708$
Reject H_0 (p-value is very small)

7–35. $t_{(15)} = -6.663$
Reject H_0 (p-value extremely small)

7–37. $z = -2.582$
Reject H_0 (p-value = 0.0098)

7–39. $z = 3.016$
Reject H_0 (p-value = 0.0026)

7–41. $z = -3.05$
Reject H_0 (p-value = 0.0011)

7–45. $z = 51.02$
Reject H_0 (p-value is extremely small). Without finite population correction, $z = 43.13$ (so still reject)

7–47. $z = -0.898$
Do not reject H_0 (p-value = .1846)

7–49. $\chi^2_{(24)} = 47.04$
Reject H_0 (p-value < .005)

7–51. $\chi^2_{(299)} = 306.9$
Do not reject H_0

7–53. 0.9092

7–55. Power at $\mu_1 = 60$ is 0.984; Power at 55: 0.4641

7–57. 1,241 eleventh-graders

7–59. 737 shareholders

7–61. 591 transactions

7–65. $z = 8.0$
Reject H_0 (p-value is very small)

7–71. α is the probability of rejecting H_0 when H_0 is true; β is the probability of not rejecting H_0 when H_0 is false.

7–75. The power is determined by the distance of the true parameter value in H_1 from the null-hypothesized value of the parameter; α; σ; n.

7–77. $z = -5.0$
Reject H_0 (p-value is very small)

7–79. *a.* 14
b. Reject H_0 (p-value is very small)

7–81. Two-tailed test: $z = 2.07$
Reject H_0 (p-value = 0.0384)

7–83. $z = 4.249$
Reject H_0
(p-value < .00003)

7–87. $z = -4.86$
Reject H_0; very small p-value. Power for $p_1 = 4\%$ is 0.5214

7–89. $\chi^2_{(24)} = 26.923$
Cannot reject H_0
(p-value > 0.10)

7–91. $z = -5.33$
Reject H_0 (p-value very small)

7–93. $z = 1.705$
Reject H_0
(p-value = 0.0441)

7–95. $t_{(13)} = -3.987$
Reject (p-value < 0.005)

7–97. $z = 2.53$
Reject H_0
(p-value = 0.0057)

7–99. $t_{(17)} = 2.828$
Reject H_0
($0.005 < p$-value < 0.01)

Chapter 8

8–1. $t_{(24)} = 3.11$
Reject H_0 (p-value < 0.01)

8–3. $t_{(11)} = 2.034$
Cannot reject H_0

8–5. $t_{(14)} = 1.469$
Cannot reject H_0

8–7. Power = $P(Z > 1.55)$
= 0.0606

8–9. $z = -3.13$
Reject H_0

8–11. $z = 3.3$
Reject H_0

8–13. $z = 4.24$
Reject H_0

8–15. *a.* One-tailed: H_0:
$\mu_1 - \mu_2 \leq 0$
b. $z = 1.53$
c. At $\alpha = .05$, do not re-ject H_0
d. 0.063
e. $t_{(19)} = 0.846$; do not re-ject H_0

8–17. [2.416, 2.664] percent

8–19. $t_{(26)} = 1.132$
Do not reject H_0
(p-value > 0.10)

8–21. $z = -8.2496$
Strongly reject H_0 (p-value very small)

8–23. $t_{(13)} = 1.164$
Strongly reject H_0
(p-value > 0.10)

8–25. $z = 2.785$
Reject H_0 (p-value = 0.0026)

8–27. $t_{(28)} = 5.136$
Strongly reject H_0

8–29. $z = 2.835$
Reject H_0 (p-value = 0.0023)

8–31. $z = -0.228$
Do not reject H_0

8–33. [0.0419, 0.0781]

8–35. $z = 1.601$
Do not reject H_0 at $\alpha = .05$
(p-value= 0.0547)

8–37. [−0.027, 0.033]

8–39. $z = 5.33$
Strongly reject H_0 (p-value is very small)

8–41. $F_{(17,11)} = 2.16$
Do not reject H_0 at $\alpha = 0.10$

8–43. $F_{(27,20)} = 1.838$
At $\alpha = .10$, cannot reject H_0.
[0.652, 4.837]

8–45. $F_{(24,24)} = 1.538$
Do not reject H_0

8–47. Independent random sam-pling from the populations and normal population dis-tributions.

8–49. [−3.4777, 0.6803]

8–51. [−0.267, −0.173]

8–53. [−812.9, 1,372.9]

8–55. $z = 1.447$
Do not reject H_0
(p-value = 0.1478)

8–57. $t_{(22)} = 2.719$
Reject H_0 (.01 < p-value < .02)

8–59. Relationship quality, dis-tributive fairness, and envi-ronmental uncertainty all show nonsignificant differ-ences; remaining variables

all show very significant differences with quite low p-values.

8–61. $t_{(26)} = 2.479$
Reject H_0 (p-value= .02)

8–63. $t_{(29)} = 1.08$
Do not reject H_0

8–65. Since $s_1^2 < s_2^2$, do not reject H_0

8–67. $t_{(15)} = -0.9751$
Do not reject H_0

8–69. [0.0366, 0.1474]

8–71. $F_{(24,17)} = 1.453$
Do not reject H_0 at $\alpha = 0.10$

8–73. [−0.0413, 0.7254]

8–75. t-test for H_0: $\mu_1 \leq \mu_2$ of two independent samples of sizes 16, 17. p-value = 0.85, no rejection.

Chapter 9

9–1. H_0: All 4 means are equal
H_1: All 4 are different; or 2 equal, 2 different; or 3 equal, 1 different; or 2 equal, other 2 equal but dif-ferent from first 2.

9–3. Series of paired t-tests are *dependent* on each other. No control over the proba-bility of a Type I error.

9–5. $F_{(3,176)} = 12.53$
Reject H_0

9–7. The sum of all the devia-tions from a mean is equal to 0.

9–11. Both MSTR and MSE are *sample statistics* given to natural variation about their own means.

9–19. (From Minitab):

Source	df	SS
Treatment	3	0.1152
Error	28	0.7315
Total	31	0.8467

MS	F
0.0384	1.47
0.0261	

Critical point $F_{(3,28)}$ for $\alpha = 0.01$ is 2.29; cannot reject H_0.

9–21. H_0 that all 4 means of brand effectiveness are

9–23. $F_{(7, 792)} = 108.53$
Reject H_0

9–25. $T = 4.738$. The mean for squares is significantly greater than those for circles and for triangles; circles and triangles show no significant difference.

9–27. $T = 0.22$
No differences are significant—as expected.

9–29. $T = 3.85$
Mean for Zenith is significantly greater than all others; Sylvania, Philco, Sears, and RCA are next, not significantly different from one another; then Panasonic, different from the preceding; and then GE and Magnavox, not significantly different from each other.

9–31. No; the 3 prototypes were not randomly chosen from a population of levels.

9–33. Fly all 3 planes on the same route every time.

9–35. Otherwise not a random sample from a population of treatments, and inference is thus not valid for the entire "population."

9–37. If the locations and the artists are chosen randomly, we have a random effects model.

9–41. Nearest is $F_{(4,150)} = 3.44$
Reject H_0 of no interaction (p-value < 0.01)

9–43.

Source	SS	df
Network	145	2
Newstime	160	2
Interaction	240	4
Error	6200	441
Total	6745	449

MS	F
72.5	5.16
80	5.69
60	4.27
14.06	

equal could not be rejected because the F-ratio was well within a normal range given the data.

All are significant at $\alpha = 0.01$. There are interactions. There are Network main effects averaged over Newstime levels. There are Newstime main effects averaged over Network levels.

9–45. a. Explained is treat = Factor A + Factor B + (AB)
b. a = 3
c. b = 2
d. N = 150
e. n = 25
f. There are no exercise-price main effects.
g. There are time-of-expiration main effects at $\alpha = 0.05$ but not at $\alpha = 0.01$.
h. There are no interactions.
i. Some evidence for time-of-expiration main effects; no evidence for exercise-price main effects or interaction effects.
j. For time-of-expiration main effects, $.01 < p$-value $< .05$. For the other two tests, the p-values are very high.
k. Could use a t-test for time-of-expiration effects: $t_{(144)}^2 = F_{(1, 144)}$

9–47. Advantages: reduced experimental errors and great economy of sample size. Disadvantages: restrictive, because it requires that number of treatments = number of rows = number of columns.

9–49. Could have a Latin square: 4 observations, UK, Mexico, UAE, Oman at 4 locations and 4 different dates.

9–51. Yes; have people of the same occupation/age/demographics use sweaters of the 3 kinds under study. Each group of 3 people is a block.

9–53. Group the executives into blocks according to some choice of common characteristics such as age, sex, or years employed at current firm; these blocks would then form a third variable beyond Location and Type to use in a 3-way ANOVA.

9–55. $F_{(2,198)} = 25.84$
Reject H_0 (p-value very small)

9–57. $F_{(7, 152)} = 14.67$
Reject H_0 (p-value very small)

9–59. Nearest is $F_{(1, 40)} = 4.08$
There is evidence of a taste cue positioning effect, a gender effect, and an interaction.

9–61.

Source	SS	df
Process	165.644	2
Film	1,363.378	2
Interaction	247.022	4
Error	209.200	36

MS	F
82.822	14.252
681.689	117.308
61.756	10.627
5.811	

Film and process effects are highly significant and so are the interactions.

9–63.

Source	SS	df
Pet	22,245	3
Location	34,551	3
Interaction	31,778	9
Error	554,398	144
Total	642,972	159

MS	F
7,415	1.93
11,517	2.99
3,530.89	0.92
3,849.99	

No interactions; no pet main effects. There are location main effects at $\alpha = 0.05$

9–65. b. $F_{(2,58)} = 11.47$; reject H_0

9–67. $F_{(2,98)} = 0.14958$
Do not reject H_0

9–69. Rents are equal on average; no evidence of differences among the four cities.

9–71. A one-way ANOVA strongly rejecting H_0. For the three levels of store, 95% confidence intervals are calculated for the means, as shown, which don't overlap at all.

Chapter 10

10–11. $b_1 = 1.35$ $b_0 = -0.847$

10–13. $b_1 = 1.22$

10–15. $b_1 = 2.11$ $b_0 = -22.279$

10–17. $b_1 = 0.160$ $b_0 = 6.11$

10–19. [1.1158, 1.3949]

10–21. $s(b_0) = 0.538$ $s(b_1) = 0.084$

10–23. $s(b_0) = 0.971$ $s(b_1) = 0.016$
Estimate of error variance is
MSE = 0.991
95% C.I.: [0.1518, 0.2222]

10–25. s^2 gives information about the variation of the data points about the computed regression line.

10–27. $r = 0.976$

10–29. $t_{(9)} = 7.53$
Reject H_0 (p-value is very small)

10–31. $t_{(8)} = 5.11$
Reject H_0

10–35. $z = 1.297$
Cannot reject H_0

10–37. $t_{(16)} = 1.0727$
Do not reject H_0

10–39. $t_{(11)} = 11.69$
Strongly reject H_0

10–41. $t_{(58)} = 5.90$
Reject H_0

10–43. $t_{(211)} = z = 0.0565$
Do not reject H_0

10–47. 95.2% of the variation in the dependent variable is explained by the regression relationship.

10–49. $r^2 = 0.864$

10–51. $r^2 = 0.873$

10–53. $r^2 = 0.76$

10–57. $F_{(1,11)} = 129.525$ $t_{(11)} = 11.381$ $t^2 = 11.381^2 = 129.525$

10–59. $F_{(1,n-2)} = 136.19$
Strongly reject H_0

10–61. $F_{(1,20)} = 0.3845$
Do not reject H_0

10–63. *a.* Heteroscedasticity.
b. No apparent inadequacy.
c. Data display curvature, not a straight-line relationship.

10–65. *a.* No serious inadequacy.
b. Yes. A deviation from the normal-distribution assumption is apparent.

10–69. 6,551.35
P.I.: [5,854.4, 7,248.3]

10–71. [5,605.75, 7,496.95]

10–73. [7.793, 8.089]

10–75. 3,028.7
P.I.: [2,631.5, 3,425.9]

10–77. $F = 1,721.64$
Strongly reject H_0
($r^2 = 0.93$)

10–79. $F = 317.98$
Strongly reject H_0

10–81. $t_{(14)} = -3.498$, significant at $\alpha = 0.01$
$F_{(1,14)} = 12.24$, also significant at $\alpha = 0.01$

10–83. 95% C.I. for β_0:
[−16.14, 41.00]
95% C.I. for β_1:
[0.90228, 1.250]
95% C.I. for the average Y when $x = 10,000$:
[6,238.86, 15,306.00]
95% P.I.:
[6,238.83, 15,306.03]

10–85. $b_0 = 1.1952$ $b_1 = 1.9286$ $t_{(13)} = 18.512$
Evidence of a linear relationship. $r^2 = 0.963$
$\hat{y}$ (for $x = 13$) = 1.1952 + 1.9286(13) = \$26.27

10–87. Entertainment
$= -81.04 + 0.7183(S\&P)$
$R^2 = 0.942$ $F = 374.6$
(p-value very close to 0)

Chapter 11

11–5. 8 equations

11–7. $b_0 = -1.145$
$b_1 = 0.0487$ $b_2 = 10.898$

11–11. $n - 13$

11–13. $F_{(4,40)} = 9.827$
Evidence of a linear regression relationship

11–21. $R^2 = 0.9174$, a good regression. $\bar{R}^2 = 0.8983$
$s = 7.192$

11–23. $\bar{R}^2 = 0.8907$
Do not include the new variable

11–25. *b.* $R^2 = 0.130$

13% of the variation is due to the two independent variables.
c. Adjusted R^2 is quite low; try regressing on size alone.

11–27. $F_{(6,243)} = 128.19$
Reject H_0.
$R^2 = 0.7599$ $\bar{R}^2 = 0.754$

11–31. β_2: [3.052, 8.148]
β_3: [−3.135, 23.835]
β_4: [−1.842, 8.742]
β_5: [−4.995, −3.505]

11–33. Yes

11–35. Lend seems insignificant because of collinearity with M_1 or price.

11–37. Autocorrelation of the regression errors.

11–39. All variables except "Store feature" have significant t-ratios for a linear relationship with consideration function, but no R^2 result is reported.

11–41. The residuals do not appear to be normally distributed.

11–47. Creates a bias. There is no reason to force the regression surface to go through the origin.

11–51. 363.78

11–53. 0.341, 0.085

11–55. The estimators are the same although their standard errors are different.

11–59. Two-way ANOVA

11–61. Early investment is not statistically significant (or may be collinear with another variable). Rerun the regression without it. The dummy variables are both significant.

11–63. The STEPWISE routine chooses Price and M_1*Price as the best set of explanatory variables. Exports $= -1.39 + 0.0229$Price $+ 0.00248 M_1$*Price t-statistics: −2.36, 4.57, 9.08, respectively. $R^2 = 0.822$

11–67. Quadratic regression (should get a negative estimated x^2 coefficient)

11–69. Linearizing a model; finding a more parsimonious model than is possible without a transformation; stabilizing the variance.

11–71. The transformation log Y

11–73. A logarithmic model

11–77. No

11–79. Taking reciprocals of both sides of the equation.

11–81. No. They minimize the sum of the squared deviations relevant to the estimated, transformed model.

11–83.

	Earn	Prod	Prom
Prod	.867		
Prom	.882	.638	
Book	.547	.402	.319

Multicollinearity does not seem to be serious.

11–85. Sample correlation is 0.740

11–89. Not true. Predictions may be good when carried out within the same region of the multicollinearity as used in the estimation procedure.

11–91. X_2 and X_3 are probably collinear.

11–93. Drop some of the other variables one at a time and see what happens to the suspected sign of the estimate.

11–97. 1) The test checks only for first-order autocorrelation. 2) The test may not be conclusive. 3) The usual limitations of a statistical test owing to the two possible types of errors.

11–99. DW = 2.13 At the 0.10 level, no evidence of a first-order autocorrelation.

11–103. $F_{(r, n-(k+1))} = 0.0275$ Cannot reject H_0

11–105. The STEPWISE procedure selects all three variables. $R^2 = 0.9667$

11–107. Because a variable may lose explanatory power and become insignificant once other variables are added to the model.

11–109. No. There may be several different "best" models.

11–111. All variables except power distance and collectivism in section B are significant.

11–113. After removing the 1991 data as an outlier, a plot of the six remaining near collisions numbers versus flights looks like a cubic curve. $NC = 3.32F^3 - 54.12F^2 + 291.73F - 518.52$

11–115. Only for WC Benefit is there any evidence of a linear relationship.

Chapter 12

12–3. $\hat{y}(1996) = 226,399$ $\hat{y}(1997) = 253,660$

12–5. No, because of the seasonality.

12–11. Forecast using trend and seasonal index = 403.82

12–13. Forecast using trend and seasonal index = 1,582.61

12–15. Forecast using trend and seasonal index = 19.24

12–17. The $w = .8$ forecasts follow the raw data much more closely.

12–19. Forecast = 17.14

12–23.

Year	Old CPI	New CPI
1950	72.1	24.9
1951	77.8	26.9
1952	79.5	27.5
1953	80.1	27.7
⋮	⋮	⋮

12–25. A simple price index reflects changes in a single price variable of time, relative to a single base time.

12–27. *a.* 1985
b. Divide each index number by $\dfrac{163}{100}$
c. It fell, from 145% of the 1985 output down to 133% of that output.

12–29. Divide each data point by 1.44: Jun.'94: 98.6 Jul.'94: 95.14 . . .

12–33. *a.* The series is seasonal.
b. 85

12–35. *d.* 122.5, using simple linear regression.

Chapter 13

13–3. 1) Natural, random variation; 2) variation due to assignable causes.

13–15. Random sampling, so that the observations are independent.

13–17. Process in is control.

13–27. All points are well within the p-chart limits; process is in control.

13–29. All points are well within the p-chart limits; process is in control.

13–31. The tenth sample barely exceeds the UCL = 8.953; otherwise in control.

13–33. All points within c-chart limits; process is in control.

13–37. The 20th observation far exceeds the UCL = 8.92/100; the last nine observations are all on one side of the center line $\bar{P} = 3.45/100$

13–39. Last group's mean is below the LCL = 2.136

Chapter 14

14–1. $\Sigma+ = 10$ Cannot reject H_0 (p-value = 0.18)

14–3. $z = 3$ Reject H_0

14–5. $z = 1.85$ At $\alpha = .05$, cannot reject H_0

14–7. $T = 14.29$ Reject H_0 (p-value < .005)

14–9. $T = 25.33$ Reject H_0

14–11. Yes, upward trend; p-value = 0.0039

14–13. The t test requires the assumption of a normal distribution.

14–15. $z = 1.46$ We cannot reject H_0

14–17. $T = 113.8$ Reject H_0

14–19. $z = -4.82$
Reject H_0. Not random.

14–21. $z = -4.42$
Reject H_0. Not random.

14–23. $z = -3.13$
Reject H_0

14–25. $R = 6$
Cannot reject H_0
(p-value = 0.298)

14–27. $z = 3.00$
Reject H_0

14–29. $z = -0.984$
Do not reject H_0.

14–31. $z = 2.14$
Reject H_0

14–33. $T = 6$.
We cannot reject H_0
(p-value = 0.10)

14–35. $T = 56$.
Reject H_0 at $\alpha = 0.05$

14–37. Use the parametric t test (actually use z since the sample is large).

14–39. $T = 18 \quad n = 14$
Reject H_0 at $\alpha = 0.025$

14–41. $T = 4.5 < 5$.
Reject H_0 at $\alpha = 0.01$

14–43. Using SYSTAT: p-value = 0.468, so we do not reject H_0.

14–45. $H = 13.716$
Reject H_0 (p-value < .005)

14–47. $H = 13.54$
Reject H_0
(p-value = 0.001)

14–49. $H = 26.49$
Reject H_0

14–51. $X^2 = 20.4$
Reject H_0 (p-value < 0.001)

14–53. $X^2 = 6.22$
Reject H_0 (p-value < .05)

14–55. $r_s = 0.275$
Do not reject H_0 if no positive correlation.

14–57. $r_s = 0.486$
Reject H_0 (p-value just under 0.05)

14–59. $r_s = 0.297$
Do not reject H_0

14–61. $X^2_{(4)} = 50.8$
Reject H_0 (p-value < .005)

14–63. *a.* No. E(count) in cells A and E are < 5

b. Combine cells A and B, and cell E with other.

c. $X^2_{(3)} = 26.56$
Reject H_0 (p-value < 0.005)

14–65. $X^2_{(1)} = 2.88$
Do not reject H_0 at $\alpha = 0.05$

14–67. $X^2 = 6.81$
Do not reject H_0.

14–69. $X^2 = 6.65$
Reject H_0 at $\alpha = 0.01$.

14–71. *a.* $X^2 = 33.958$
Reject H_0
b. $X^2 = 32.90$
Reject H_0

14–73. $X^2 = 4.23$
Do not reject H_0

14–75. $X^2 = 10.86$
Reject H_0 (p-value < .005)

14–77. $X^2 = 4.159$
Do not reject H_0

14–79. MINITAB runs test rejects H_0, p-value = 0.0113

14–81. *a.* The Friedman test
b. $X^2 = 0.36$
Do not reject H_0

14–83. $X^2 = 13.5$
Reject H_0 (p-value <.005)

14–85. Using SYSTAT:
p-value = 0.031
Reject H_0

14–87. Use the Wilcoxon signed-rank test. Using SYSTAT, the reported 2-tailed p-value is 0.209. Do not reject H_0.

14–89. We use the Kruskal-Wallis test. $H = 7.43$, p-value = 0.024. Not all three systems are equally well liked.

14–93. You should combine this cell with another so that the expected count will be at least 5.

Chapter 15

15–1. .02531, .46544, .27247, .17691, .05262, .00697, .00028. Credible set is [0.2, 0.4].

15–3. .0126, .5829, .3658, .0384, .0003

15–5. .1129, .2407, .2275, .2909, .0751, .0529

15–7. .0633, .2216, .2928, .2364, .1286, .0465, .0099, .0009

15–9. .0071, .0638, .3001, .3962, .1929, .0399

15–11. Normal with mean 9,207.3 and standard deviation 61.58

15–13. Normal with mean 95.95 and standard deviation 0.312

15–15. Normal with mean 23.72 and standard deviation 0.7442

15–17. Governor: D (largest s.d.)
ARCO expert: C (smallest s.d.)
Most embarrassed: C

15–19. Mean = 2.5, S.D. = 0.5

15–25. Expected profit = $1.8 million

15–27. Expected profit is $86 million

15–29. Optimal decision is *long*—change if possible. Expected profit is $698,000

15–31. Optimal decision is invest in wheat futures. Expected value is $3,040

15–35. Don't test; E(payoff) = $1.8 million. If you must test, advertise anyway.

15–37. Don't test. E(payoff) = $16,000. If you must test, sell watches anyway.

15–39. Test and follow the test's recommendation. E(payoff) = $587,000

15–41. A utility function is a value-of-money function of an individual.

15–49. EVPI = $290,000. Buy information if it is perfect.

15–51. .01142, .30043, .35004, .27066, .05561, .01184

15–53. .0026, .3844, .4589, .1480, .0060, .0001

15–57. 95% HPD region = [97.888, 101.732]

15–63. 1,400 < 3,000: a risk taker

15–67. Merge; do not consult. E(payoff) = $2.45 million

15–69. Choose candidate A

15–71. Test candidate A

Chapter 16

16–1. Statistically classifying elements into one of several groups.

16–3. Classify as default.

16–7. Used the information in a Bayesian formulation of a discriminant function, using $P(G)$, $P(D \mid G)$, leading to $P(G \mid D)$

16–9. Group 3

16–11. The discriminant function is not statistically significant and should not be used.

16–13. 5 functions; some may not be significant

16–19. VARIMAX maximizes the sum of the variances of the loadings in the factor matrix. Other rotation methods are QUARTIMAX and EQUIMAX.

16–21. Factor 1 is price items, factor 2 is retailing/selling, factor 3 is advertising, and factor 4 is negative (or opposite) of product ratings.

16–23. Pricing policies: associate with factor 2; communality = 0.501. Record and reporting procedures: associate with factor 2; communality = 0.077

16–27. 3 functions

16–31. Not a worthwhile result since the dimensionality has not been reduced.

16–33. Communality of a variable is the sum of its squared factor loadings.

16–37. Wilks' $\lambda = .412$
$F_{(3,21)} = 9.987$ (p-value = .000)
Production cost p-value = .009. Number of sponsors p-value = .066 (n.s.). Promotions p-value = .004
Discriminant function coefficients: production cost = 0.945, promotions = 0.996
84% correct prediction.

Chapter 17

17–1. *a.* $\bar{x}_{st} = 33.48\%$
b. S.D. = 0.823%
c. [31.87, 35.09]

17–3. *a.* $\bar{x}_{st} = \$40.01$
b. S.D. = 0.6854
c. [38.88,41.14]
d. Data has many zero values

17–5. $35,604.5   [26,333.8, 44,875.2]

17–9. a–c) All no. Clusters need to be randomly chosen.

d) Consider the companies as strata, ships as clusters. Randomly draw clusters from the strata.

17–11. Arrange elements in a circle, randomly choose a number from 1 to 28, and then add 28 to element number until you have a sample of 30 sales.

17–13. If k is a multiple of 7, we would sample on the same day for different weeks and bias the results due to weekly sales cycles.

17–17. Yes, with each vehicle a cluster.

17–19. OK unless a non-negligible fraction of the businesses in the community are unlisted in the Yellow Pages.

17–21. [0.055, 0.091]

17–25. Sample about 109 children, 744 young adults, 147 older people

17–27. Regression and ratio estimators

17–29. No; benefits are not substantial when the number of strata is much greater than 6. Combine some.

STATISTICAL TABLES

TABLE 1 Cumulative Binomial Distribution

$$F(x) = P(X \le x) = \sum_{i=0}^{x} \binom{n}{i} p^i (1-p)^{n-i}$$

Example: if $p = 0.10$, $n = 5$, and $x = 2$, then $F(x) = 0.991$

							p							
n	x	.01	.05	.10	.20	.30	.40	.50	.60	.70	.80	.90	.95	.99
5	0	.951	.774	.590	.328	.168	.078	.031	.010	.002	.000	.000	.000	.000
	1	.999	.977	.919	.737	.528	.337	.187	.087	.031	.007	.000	.000	.000
	2	1.000	.999	.991	.942	.837	.683	.500	.317	.163	.058	.009	.001	.000
	3	1.000	1.000	1.000	.993	.969	.913	.813	.663	.472	.263	.081	.023	.001
	4	1.000	1.000	1.000	1.000	.998	.990	.969	.922	.832	.672	.410	.226	.049
6	0	.941	.735	.531	.262	.118	.047	.016	.004	.001	.000	.000	.000	.000
	1	.999	.967	.886	.655	.420	.233	.109	.041	.011	.002	.000	.000	.000
	2	1.000	.998	.984	.901	.744	.544	.344	.179	.070	.017	.001	.000	.000
	3	1.000	1.000	.999	.983	.930	.821	.656	.456	.256	.099	.016	.002	.000
	4	1.000	1.000	1.000	.998	.989	.959	.891	.767	.580	.345	.114	.033	.001
	5	1.000	1.000	1.000	1.000	.999	.996	.984	.953	.882	.738	.469	.265	.059
7	0	.932	.698	.478	.210	.082	.028	.008	.002	.000	.000	.000	.000	.000
	1	.998	.956	.850	.577	.329	.159	.063	.019	.004	.000	.000	.000	.000
	2	1.000	.996	.974	.852	.647	.420	.227	.096	.029	.005	.000	.000	.000
	3	1.000	1.000	.997	.967	.874	.710	.500	.290	.126	.033	.003	.000	.000
	4	1.000	1.000	1.000	.995	.971	.904	.773	.580	.353	.148	.026	.004	.000
	5	1.000	1.000	1.000	1.000	.996	.981	.937	.841	.671	.423	.150	.044	.002
	6	1.000	1.000	1.000	1.000	1.000	.998	.992	.972	.918	.790	.522	.302	.068
8	0	.923	.663	.430	.168	.058	.017	.004	.001	.000	.000	.000	.000	.000
	1	.997	.943	.813	.503	.255	.106	.035	.009	.001	.000	.000	.000	.000
	2	1.000	.994	.962	.797	.552	.315	.145	.050	.011	.001	.000	.000	.000
	3	1.000	1.000	.995	.944	.806	.594	.363	.174	.058	.010	.000	.000	.000
	4	1.000	1.000	1.000	.990	.942	.826	.637	.406	.194	.056	.005	.000	.000
	5	1.000	1.000	1.000	.999	.989	.950	.855	.685	.448	.203	.038	.006	.000
	6	1.000	1.000	1.000	1.000	.999	.991	.965	.894	.745	.497	.187	.057	.003
	7	1.000	1.000	1.000	1.000	1.000	.999	.996	.983	.942	.832	.570	.337	.077
9	0	.914	.630	.387	.134	.040	.010	.002	.000	.000	.000	.000	.000	.000
	1	.997	.929	.775	.436	.196	.071	.020	.004	.000	.000	.000	.000	.000
	2	1.000	.992	.947	.738	.463	.232	.090	.025	.004	.000	.000	.000	.000
	3	1.000	.999	.992	.914	.730	.483	.254	.099	.025	.003	.000	.000	.000
	4	1.000	1.000	.999	.980	.901	.733	.500	.267	.099	.020	.001	.000	.000
	5	1.000	1.000	1.000	.997	.975	.901	.746	.517	.270	.086	.008	.001	.000
	6	1.000	1.000	1.000	1.000	.996	.975	.910	.768	.537	.262	.053	.008	.000
	7	1.000	1.000	1.000	1.000	1.000	.996	.980	.929	.804	.564	.225	.071	.003
	8	1.000	1.000	1.000	1.000	1.000	1.000	.998	.990	.960	.866	.613	.370	.086
10	0	.904	.599	.349	.107	.028	.006	.001	.000	.000	.000	.000	.000	.000
	1	.996	.914	.736	.376	.149	.046	.011	.002	.000	.000	.000	.000	.000
	2	1.000	.988	.930	.678	.383	.167	.055	.012	.002	.000	.000	.000	.000
	3	1.000	.999	.987	.879	.650	.382	.172	.055	.011	.001	.000	.000	.000
	4	1.000	1.000	.998	.967	.850	.633	.377	.166	.047	.006	.000	.000	.000
	5	1.000	1.000	1.000	.994	.953	.834	.623	.367	.150	.033	.002	.000	.000
	6	1.000	1.000	1.000	.999	.989	.945	.828	.618	.350	.121	.013	.001	.000
	7	1.000	1.000	1.000	1.000	.998	.988	.945	.833	.617	.322	.070	.012	.000
	8	1.000	1.000	1.000	1.000	1.000	.998	.989	.954	.851	.624	.264	.086	.004
	9	1.000	1.000	1.000	1.000	1.000	1.000	.999	.994	.972	.893	.651	.401	.096

TABLE 1 *(concluded)*　**Cumulative Binomial Distribution**

n	x	.01	.05	.10	.20	.30	.40	.50	.60	.70	.80	.90	.95	.99
15	0	.860	.463	.206	.035	.005	.000	.000	.000	.000	.000	.000	.000	.000
	1	.990	.829	.549	.167	.035	.005	.000	.000	.000	.000	.000	.000	.000
	2	1.000	.964	.816	.398	.127	.027	.004	.000	.000	.000	.000	.000	.000
	3	1.000	.995	.944	.648	.297	.091	.018	.002	.000	.000	.000	.000	.000
	4	1.000	.999	.987	.836	.515	.217	.059	.009	.001	.000	.000	.000	.000
	5	1.000	1.000	.998	.939	.722	.403	.151	.034	.004	.000	.000	.000	.000
	6	1.000	1.000	1.000	.982	.869	.610	.304	.095	.015	.001	.000	.000	.000
	7	1.000	1.000	1.000	.996	.950	.787	.500	.213	.050	.004	.000	.000	.000
	8	1.000	1.000	1.000	.999	.985	.905	.696	.390	.131	.018	.000	.000	.000
	9	1.000	1.000	1.000	1.000	.996	.966	.849	.597	.278	.061	.002	.000	.000
	10	1.000	1.000	1.000	1.000	.999	.991	.941	.783	.485	.164	.013	.001	.000
	11	1.000	1.000	1.000	1.000	1.000	.998	.982	.909	.703	.352	.056	.005	.000
	12	1.000	1.000	1.000	1.000	1.000	1.000	.996	.973	.873	.602	.184	.036	.000
	13	1.000	1.000	1.000	1.000	1.000	1.000	1.000	.995	.965	.833	.451	.171	.010
	14	1.000	1.000	1.000	1.000	1.000	1.000	1.000	1.000	.995	.965	.794	.537	.140
20	0	.818	.358	.122	.012	.001	.000	.000	.000	.000	.000	.000	.000	.000
	1	983	.736	.392	.069	.008	.001	.000	.000	.000	.000	.000	.000	.000
	2	.999	.925	.677	.206	.035	.004	.000	.000	.000	.000	.000	.000	.000
	3	1.000	.984	.867	.411	.107	.016	.001	.000	.000	.000	.000	.000	.000
	4	1.000	.997	.957	.630	.238	.051	.006	.000	.000	.000	.000	.000	.000
	5	1.000	1.000	.989	.804	.416	.126	.021	.002	.000	.000	.000	.000	.000
	6	1.000	1.000	.998	.913	.608	.250	.058	.006	.000	.000	.000	.000	.000
	7	1.000	1.000	1.000	.968	.772	.416	.132	.021	.001	.000	.000	.000	.000
	8	1.000	1.000	1.000	.990	.887	.596	.252	.057	.005	.000	.000	.000	.000
	9	1.000	1.000	1.000	.997	.952	.755	.412	.128	.017	.001	.000	.000	.000
	10	1.000	1.000	1.000	.999	.983	.872	.588	.245	.048	.003	.000	.000	.000
	11	1.000	1.000	1.000	1.000	.995	.943	.748	.404	.113	.010	.000	.000	.000
	12	1.000	1.000	1.000	1.000	.999	.979	.868	.584	.228	.032	.000	.000	.000
	13	1.000	1.000	1.000	1.000	1.000	.994	.942	.750	.392	.087	.002	.000	.000
	14	1.000	1.000	1.000	1.000	1.000	.998	.979	.874	.584	.196	.011	.000	.000
	15	1.000	1.000	1.000	1.000	1.000	1.000	.994	.949	.762	.370	.043	.003	.000
	16	1.000	1.000	1.000	1.000	1.000	1.000	.999	.984	.893	.589	.133	.016	.000
	17	1.000	1.000	1.000	1.000	1.000	1.000	1.000	.996	.965	.794	.323	.075	.001
	18	1.000	1.000	1.000	1.000	1.000	1.000	1.000	.999	.992	.931	.608	.264	.017
	19	1.000	1.000	1.000	1.000	1.000	1.000	1.000	1.000	.999	.988	.878	.642	.182
25	0	.778	.277	.072	.004	.000	.000	.000	.000	.000	.000	.000	.000	.000
	1	.974	.642	.271	.027	.002	.000	.000	.000	.000	.000	.000	.000	.000
	2	.998	.873	.537	.098	.009	.000	.000	.000	.000	.000	.000	.000	.000
	3	1.000	.966	.764	.234	.033	.002	.000	.000	.000	.000	.000	.000	.000
	4	1.000	.993	.902	.421	.090	.009	.000	.000	.000	.000	.000	.000	.000
	5	1.000	.999	.967	.617	.193	.029	.002	.000	.000	.000	.000	.000	.000
	6	1.000	1.000	.991	.780	.341	.074	.007	.000	.000	.000	.000	.000	.000
	7	1.000	1.000	.998	.891	.512	.154	.022	.001	.000	.000	.000	.000	.000
	8	1.000	1.000	1.000	.953	.677	.274	.054	.004	.000	.000	.000	.000	.000
	9	1.000	1.000	1.000	.983	.811	.425	.115	.013	.000	.000	.000	.000	.000
	10	1.000	1.000	1.000	.994	.902	.586	.212	.034	.002	.000	.000	.000	.000
	11	1.000	1.000	1.000	.998	.956	.732	.345	.078	.006	.000	.000	.000	.000
	12	1.000	1.000	1.000	1.000	.983	.846	.500	.154	.017	.000	.000	.000	.000
	13	1.000	1.000	1.000	1.000	.994	.922	.655	.268	.044	.002	.000	.000	.000
	14	1.000	1.000	1.000	1.000	.998	.966	.788	.414	.098	.006	.000	.000	.000
	15	1.000	1.000	1.000	1.000	1.000	.987	.885	.575	.189	.017	.000	.000	.000
	16	1.000	1.000	1.000	1.000	1.000	.996	.946	.726	.323	.047	.000	.000	.000
	17	1.000	1.000	1.000	1.000	1.000	.999	.978	.846	.488	.109	.002	.000	.000
	18	1.000	1.000	1.000	1.000	1.000	1.000	993	.926	.659	.220	.009	.000	.000
	19	1.000	1.000	1.000	1.000	1.000	1.000	.998	.971	.807	.383	.033	.001	.000
	20	1.000	1.000	1.000	1.000	1.000	1.000	1.000	.991	.910	.579	.098	.007	.000
	21	1.000	1.000	1.000	1.000	1.000	1.000	1.000	.998	.967	.766	.236	.034	.000
	22	1.000	1.000	1.000	1.000	1.000	1.000	1.000	1.000	.991	.902	.463	.127	.002
	23	1.000	1.000	1.000	1.000	1.000	1.000	1.000	1.000	.998	.973	.729	.358	.026
	24	1.000	1.000	1.000	1.000	1.000	1.000	1.000	1.000	1.000	.996	.928	.723	.222

TABLE 2 Areas of the Standard Normal Distribution

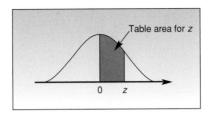

Table area for *z*

0 z

The table areas are probabilities that the standard normal random variable is between 0 and *z*.

Second Decimal Place in z

z	0.00	0.01	0.02	0.03	0.04	0.05	0.06	0.07	0.08	0.09
0.0	0.0000	0.0040	0.0080	0.0120	0.0160	0.0199	0.0239	0.0279	0.0319	0.0359
0.1	0.0398	0.0438	0.0478	0.0517	0.0557	0.0596	0.0636	0.0675	0.0714	0.0753
0.2	0.0793	0.0832	0.0871	0.0910	0.0948	0.0987	0.1026	0.1064	0.1103	0.1141
0.3	0.1179	0.1217	0.1255	0.1293	0.1331	0.1368	0.1406	0.1443	0.1480	0.1517
0.4	0.1554	0.1591	0.1628	0.1664	0.1700	0.1736	0.1772	0.1808	0.1844	0.1879
0.5	0.1915	0.1950	0.1985	0.2019	0.2054	0.2088	0.2123	0.2157	0.2190	0.2224
0.6	0.2257	0.2291	0.2324	0.2357	0.2389	0.2422	0.2454	0.2486	0.2517	0.2549
0.7	0.2580	0.2611	0.2642	0.2673	0.2704	0.2734	0.2764	0.2794	0.2823	0.2852
0.8	0.2881	0.2910	0.2939	0.2967	0.2995	0.3023	0.3051	0.3078	0.3106	0.3133
0.9	0.3159	0.3186	0.3212	0.3238	0.3264	0.3289	0.3315	0.3340	0.3365	0.3389
1.0	0.3413	0.3438	0.3461	0.3485	0.3508	0.3531	0.3554	0.3577	0.3599	0.3621
1.1	0.3643	0.3665	0.3686	0.3708	0.3729	0.3749	0.3770	0.3790	0.3810	0.3830
1.2	0.3849	0.3869	0.3888	0.3907	0.3925	0.3944	0.3962	0.3980	0.3997	0.4015
1.3	0.4032	0.4049	0.4066	0.4082	0.4099	0.4115	0.4131	0.4147	0.4162	0.4177
1.4	0.4192	0.4207	0.4222	0.4236	0.4251	0.4265	0.4279	0.4292	0.4306	0.4319
1.5	0.4332	0.4345	0.4357	0.4370	0.4382	0.4394	0.4406	0.4418	0.4429	0.4441
1.6	0.4452	0.4463	0.4474	0.4484	0.4495	0.4505	0.4515	0.4525	0.4535	0.4545
1.7	0.4554	0.4564	0.4573	0.4582	0.4591	0.4599	0.4608	0.4616	0.4625	0.4633
1.8	0.4641	0.4649	0.4656	0.4664	0.4671	0.4678	0.4686	0.4693	0.4699	0.4706
1.9	0.4713	0.4719	0.4726	0.4732	0.4738	0.4744	0.4750	0.4756	0.4761	0.4767
2.0	0.4772	0.4778	0.4783	0.4788	0.4793	0.4798	0.4803	0.4808	0.4812	0.4817
2.1	0.4821	0.4826	0.4830	0.4834	0.4838	0.4842	0.4846	0.4850	0.4854	0.4857
2.2	0.4861	0.4864	0.4868	0.4871	0.4875	0.4878	0.4881	0.4884	0.4887	0.4890
2.3	0.4893	0.4896	0.4898	0.4901	0.4904	0.4906	0.4909	0.4911	0.4913	0.4916
2.4	0.4918	0.4920	0.4922	0.4925	0.4927	0.4929	0.4931	0.4932	0.4934	0.4936
2.5	0.4938	0.4940	0.4941	0.4943	0.4945	0.4946	0.4948	0.4949	0.4951	0.4952
2.6	0.4953	0.4955	0.4956	0.4957	0.4959	0.4960	0.4961	0.4962	0.4963	0.4964
2.7	0.4965	0.4966	0.4967	0.4968	0.4969	0.4970	0.4971	0.4972	0.4973	0.4974
2.8	0.4974	0.4975	0.4976	0.4977	0.4977	0.4978	0.4979	0.4979	0.4980	0.4981
2.9	0.4981	0.4982	0.4982	0.4983	0.4984	0.4984	0.4985	0.4985	0.4986	0.4986
3.0	0.4987	0.4987	0.4987	0.4988	0.4988	0.4989	0.4989	0.4989	0.4990	0.4990
3.1	0.4990	0.4991	0.4991	0.4991	0.4992	0.4992	0.4992	0.4992	0.4993	0.4993
3.2	0.4993	0.4993	0.4994	0.4994	0.4994	0.4994	0.4994	0.4995	0.4995	0.4995
3.3	0.4995	0.4995	0.4995	0.4996	0.4996	0.4996	0.4996	0.4996	0.4996	0.4997
3.4	0.4997	0.4997	0.4997	0.4997	0.4997	0.4997	0.4997	0.4997	0.4997	0.4998
3.5	0.4998									
4.0	0.49997									
4.5	0.499997									
5.0	0.4999997									
6.0	0.499999999									

TABLE 3   Critical Values of the *t* Distribution

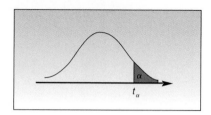

Degrees of Freedom	$t_{.100}$	$t_{.050}$	$t_{.025}$	$t_{.010}$	$t_{.005}$
1	3.078	6.314	12.706	31.821	63.657
2	1.886	2.920	4.303	6.965	9.925
3	1.638	2.353	3.182	4.541	5.841
4	1.533	2.132	2.776	3.747	4.604
5	1.476	2.015	2.571	3.365	4.032
6	1.440	1.943	2.447	3.143	3.707
7	1.415	1.895	2.365	2.998	3.499
8	1.397	1.860	2.306	2.896	3.355
9	1.383	1.833	2.262	2.821	3.250
10	1.372	1.812	2.228	2.764	3.169
11	1.363	1.796	2.201	2.718	3.106
12	1.356	1.782	2.179	2.681	3.055
13	1.350	1.771	2.160	2.650	3.012
14	1.345	1.761	2.145	2.624	2.977
15	1.341	1.753	2.131	2.602	2.947
16	1.337	1.746	2.120	2.583	2.921
17	1.333	1.740	2.110	2.567	2.898
18	1.330	1.734	2.101	2.552	2.878
19	1.328	1.729	2.093	2.539	2.861
20	1.325	1.725	2.086	2.528	2.845
21	1.323	1.721	2.080	2.518	2.831
22	1.321	1.717	2.074	2.508	2.819
23	1.319	1.714	2.069	2.500	2.807
24	1.318	1.711	2.064	2.492	2.797
25	1.316	1.708	2.060	2.485	2.787
26	1.315	1.706	2.056	2.479	2.779
27	1.314	1.703	2.052	2.473	2.771
28	1.313	1.701	2.048	2.467	2.763
29	1.311	1.699	2.045	2.462	2.756
30	1.310	1.697	2.042	2.457	2.750
40	1.303	1.684	2.021	2.423	2.704
60	1.296	1.671	2.000	2.390	2.660
120	1.289	1.658	1.980	2.358	2.617
∞	1.282	1.645	1.960	2.326	2.576

Source: M. Merrington, "Table of Percentage Points of the *t*-Distribution," *Biometrika* 32 (1941) p. 300. Reproduced by permission of the *Biometrika* trustees.

TABLE 4   Critical Values of the Chi-Square Distribution

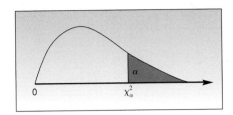

Degrees of Freedom	$\chi^2_{.995}$	$\chi^2_{.990}$	$\chi^2_{.975}$	$\chi^2_{.950}$	$\chi^2_{.900}$
1	0.0000393	0.0001571	0.0009821	0.0039321	0.0157908
2	0.0100251	0.0201007	0.0506356	0.102587	0.210720
3	0.0717212	0.114832	0.215795	0.351846	0.584375
4	0.206990	0.297110	0.484419	0.710721	1.063623
5	0.411740	0.554300	0.831211	1.145476	1.61031
6	0.675727	0.872085	1.237347	1.63539	2.20413
7	0.989265	1.239043	1.68987	2.16735	2.83311
8	1.344419	1.646482	2.17973	2.73264	3.48954
9	1.734926	2.087912	2.70039	3.32511	4.16816
10	2.15585	2.55821	3.24697	3.94030	4.86518
11	2.60321	3.05347	3.81575	4.57481	5.57779
12	3.07382	3.57056	4.40379	5.22603	6.30380
13	3.56503	4.10691	5.00874	5.89186	7.04150
14	4.07468	4.66043	5.62872	6.57063	7.78953
15	4.60094	5.22935	6.26214	7.26094	8.54675
16	5.14224	5.81221	6.90766	7.96164	9.31223
17	5.69724	6.40776	7.56418	8.67176	10.0852
18	6.26481	7.01491	8.23075	9.39046	10.8649
19	6.84398	7.63273	8.90655	10.1170	11.6509
20	7.43386	8.26040	9.59083	10.8508	12.4426
21	8.03366	8.89720	10.28293	11.5913	13.2396
22	8.64272	9.54249	10.9823	12.3380	14.0415
23	9.26042	10.19567	11.6885	13.0905	14.8479
24	9.88623	10.8564	12.4011	13.8484	15.6587
25	10.5197	11.5240	13.1197	14.6114	16.4734
26	11.1603	12.1981	13.8439	15.3791	17.2919
27	11.8076	12.8786	14,5733	16.1513	18.1138
28	12.4613	13.5648	15.3079	16.9279	18.9392
29	13.1211	14.2565	16.0471	17.7083	19.7677
30	13.7867	14.9535	16.7908	18.4926	20.5992
40	20.7065	22.1643	24.4331	26.5093	29.0505
50	27.9907	29.7067	32.3574	34.7642	37.6886
60	35.5346	37.4848	40.4817	43.1879	46.4589
70	43.2752	45.4418	48.7576	51.7393	55.3290
80	51.1720	53.5400	57.1532	60.3915	64.2778
90	59.1963	61.7541	65.6466	69.1260	73.2912
100	67.3276	70.0648	74.2219	77.9295	82.3581

TABLE 4 *(continued)*   **Critical Values of the Chi-Square Distribution**

Degrees of Freedom	$\chi^2_{.100}$	$\chi^2_{.050}$	$\chi^2_{.025}$	$\chi^2_{.010}$	$\chi^2_{.005}$
1	2.70554	3.84146	5.02389	6.63490	7.87944
2	4.60517	5.99147	7.37776	9.21034	10.5966
3	6.25139	7.81473	9.34840	11.3449	12.8381
4	7.77944	9.48773	11.1433	13.2767	14.8602
5	9.23635	11.0705	12.8325	15.0863	16.7496
6	10.6446	12.5916	14.4494	16.8119	18.5476
7	12.0170	14.0671	16.0128	18.4753	20.2777
8	13.3616	15.5073	17.5346	20.0902	21.9550
9	14.6837	16.9190	19.0228	21.6660	23.5893
10	15.9871	18.3070	20.4831	23.2093	25.1882
11	17.2750	19.6751	21.9200	24.7250	26.7569
12	18.5494	21.0261	23.3367	26.2170	28.2995
13	19.8119	22.3621	24.7356	27.6883	29.8194
14	21.0642	23.6848	26.1190	29.1413	31.3193
15	22.3072	24.9958	27.4884	30.5779	32.8013
16	23.5418	26.2962	28.8454	31.9999	34.2672
17	24.7690	27.5871	30.1910	33.4087	35.7185
18	25.9894	28.8693	31.5264	34.8053	37.1564
19	27.2036	30.1435	32.8523	36.1908	38.5822
20	28.4120	31.4104	34.1696	37.5662	39.9968
21	29.6151	32.6705	35.4789	38.9321	41.4010
22	30.8133	33.9244	36.7807	40.2894	42.7956
23	32.0069	35.1725	38.0757	41.6384	44.1813
24	33.1963	36.4151	39.3641	42.9798	45.5585
25	34.3816	37.6525	40.6465	44.3141	46.9278
26	35.5631	38.8852	41.9232	45.6417	48.2899
27	36.7412	40.1133	43.1944	46.9630	49.6449
28	37.9159	41.3372	44.4607	48.2782	50.9933
29	39.0875	42.5569	45.7222	49.5879	52.3356
30	40.2560	43.7729	46.9792	50.8922	53.6720
40	51.8050	55.7585	59.3417	63.6907	66.7659
50	63.1671	67.5048	71.4202	76.1539	79.4900
60	74.3970	79.0819	83.2976	88.3794	91.9517
70	85.5271	90.5312	95.0231	100.425	104.215
80	96.5782	101.879	106.629	112.329	116.321
90	107.565	113.145	118.136	124.116	128.299
100	118.498	124.342	129.561	135.807	140.169

Source: C. M. Thompson, "Tables of the Percentage Points of the χ^2-Distribution," *Biometrika* 32 (1941), pp. 188–89. Reproduced by permission of the *Biometrika* Trustees.

TABLE 5 Critical Values of the *F* Distribution for $\alpha = 0.10$

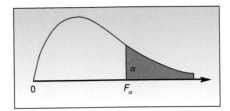

Denominator Degrees of Freedom (k_2)	Numerator Degrees of Freedom (k_1)								
	1	2	3	4	5	6	7	8	9
1	39.86	49.50	53.59	55.83	57.24	58.20	58.91	59.44	59.86
2	8.53	9.00	9.16	9.24	9.29	9.33	9.35	9.37	9.38
3	5.54	5.46	5.39	5.34	5.31	5.28	5.27	5.25	5.24
4	4.54	4.32	4.19	4.11	4.05	4.01	3.98	3.95	3.94
5	4.06	3.78	3.62	3.52	3.45	3.40	3.37	3.34	3.32
6	3.78	3.46	3.29	3.18	3.11	3.05	3.01	2.98	2.96
7	3.59	3.26	3.07	2.96	2.88	2.83	2.78	2.75	2.72
8	3.46	3.11	2.92	2.81	2.73	2.67	2.62	2.59	2.56
9	3.36	3.01	2.81	2.69	2.61	2.55	2.51	2.47	2.44
10	3.29	2.92	2.73	2.61	2.52	2.46	2.41	2.38	2.35
11	3.23	2.86	2.66	2.54	2.45	2.39	2.34	2.30	2.27
12	3.18	2.81	2.61	2.48	2.39	2.33	2.28	2.24	2.21
13	3.14	2.76	2.56	2.43	2.35	2.28	2.23	2.20	2.16
14	3.10	2.73	2.52	2.39	2.31	2.24	2.19	2.15	2.12
15	3.07	2.70	2.49	2.36	2.27	2.21	2.16	2.12	2.09
16	3.05	2.67	2.46	2.33	2.24	2.18	2.13	2.09	2.06
17	3.03	2.64	2.44	2.31	2.22	2.15	2.10	2.06	2.03
18	3.01	2.62	2.42	2.29	2.20	2.13	2.08	2.04	2.00
19	2.99	2.61	2.40	2.27	2.18	2.11	2.06	2.02	1.98
20	2.97	2.59	2.38	2.25	2.16	2.09	2.04	2.00	1.96
21	2.96	2.57	2.36	2.23	2.14	2.08	2.02	1.98	1.95
22	2.95	2.56	2.35	2.22	2.13	2.06	2.01	1.97	1.93
23	2.94	2.55	2.34	2.21	2.11	2.05	1.99	1.95	1.92
24	2.93	2.54	2.33	2.19	2.10	2.04	1.98	1.94	1.91
25	2.92	2.53	2.32	2.18	2.09	2.02	1.97	1.93	1.89
26	2.91	2.52	2.31	2.17	2.08	2.01	1.96	1.92	1.88
27	2.90	2.51	2.30	2.17	2.07	2.00	1.95	1.91	1.87
28	2.89	2.50	2.29	2.16	2.06	2.00	1.94	1.90	1.87
29	2.89	2.50	2.28	2.15	2.06	1.99	1.93	1.89	1.86
30	2.88	2.49	2.28	2.14	2.05	1.98	1.93	1.88	1.85
40	2.84	2.44	2.23	2.09	2.00	1.93	1.87	1.83	1.79
60	2.79	2.39	2.18	2.04	1.95	1.87	1.82	1.77	1.74
120	2.75	2.35	2.13	1.99	1.90	1.82	1.77	1.72	1.68
∞	2.71	2.30	2.08	1.94	1.85	1.77	1.72	1.67	1.63

TABLE 5 *(continued)* **Critical Values of the F Distribution for $\alpha = 0.10$**

Denominator Degrees of Freedom (k_2)	Numerator Degrees of Freedom (k_1)									
	10	12	15	20	24	30	40	60	120	∞
1	60.19	60.71	61.22	61.74	62.00	62.26	62.53	62.79	63.06	63.33
2	9.39	9.41	9.42	9.44	9.45	9.46	9.47	9.47	9.48	9.49
3	5.23	5.22	5.20	5.18	5.18	5.17	5.16	5.15	5.14	5.13
4	3.92	3.90	3.87	3.84	3.83	3.82	3.80	3.79	3.78	3.76
5	3.30	3.27	3.24	3.21	3.19	3.17	3.16	3.14	3.12	3.10
6	2.94	2.90	2.87	2.84	2.82	2.80	2.78	2.76	2.74	2.72
7	2.70	2.67	2.63	2.59	2.58	2.56	2.54	2.51	2.49	2.47
8	2.54	2.50	2.46	2.42	2.40	2.38	2.36	2.34	2.32	2.29
9	2.42	2.38	2.34	2.30	2.28	2.25	2.23	2.21	2.18	2.16
10	2.32	2.28	2.24	2.20	2.18	2.16	2.13	2.11	2.08	2.06
11	2.25	2.21	2.17	2.12	2.10	2.08	2.05	2.03	2.00	1.97
12	2.19	2.15	2.10	2.06	2.04	2.01	1.99	1.96	1.93	1.90
13	2.14	2.10	2.05	2.01	1.98	1.96	1.93	1.90	1.88	1.85
14	2.10	2.05	2.01	1.96	1.94	1.91	1.89	1.86	1.83	1.80
15	2.06	2.02	1.97	1.92	1.90	1.87	1.85	1.82	1.79	1.76
16	2.03	1.99	1.94	1.89	1.87	1.84	1.81	1.78	1.75	1.72
17	2.00	1.96	1.91	1.86	1.84	1.81	1.78	1.75	1.72	1.69
18	1.98	1.93	1.89	1.84	1.81	1.78	1.75	1.72	1.69	1.66
19	1.96	1.91	1.86	1.81	1.79	1.76	1.73	1.70	1.67	1.63
20	1.94	1.89	1.84	1.79	1.77	1.74	1.71	1.68	1.64	1.61
21	1.92	1.87	1.83	1.78	1.75	1.72	1.69	1.66	1.62	1.59
22	1.90	1.86	1.81	1.76	1.73	1.70	1.67	1.64	1.60	1.57
23	1.89	1.84	1.80	1.74	1.72	1.69	1.66	1.62	1.59	1.55
24	1.88	1.83	1.78	1.73	1.70	1.67	1.64	1.61	1.57	1.53
25	1.87	1.82	1.77	1.72	1.69	1.66	1.63	1.59	1.56	1.52
26	1.86	1.81	1.76	1.71	1.68	1.65	1.61	1.58	1.54	1.50
27	1.85	1.80	1.75	1.70	1.67	1.64	1.60	1.57	1.53	1.49
28	1.84	1.79	1.74	1.69	1.66	1.63	1.59	1.56	1.52	1.48
29	1.83	1.78	1.73	1.68	1.65	1.62	1.58	1.55	1.51	1.47
30	1.82	1.77	1.72	1.67	1.64	1.61	1.57	1.54	1.50	1.46
40	1.76	1.71	1.66	1.61	1.57	1.54	1.51	1.47	1.42	1.38
60	1.71	1.66	1.60	1.54	1.51	1.48	1.44	1.40	1.35	1.29
120	1.65	1.60	1.55	1.48	1.45	1.41	1.37	1.32	1.26	1.19
∞	1.60	1.55	1.49	1.42	1.38	1.34	1.30	1.24	1.17	1.00

TABLE 5 *(continued)* **Critical Values of the F Distribution for $\alpha = 0.05$**

Denominator Degrees of Freedom (k_2)	Numerator Degrees of Freedom (k_1)								
	1	2	3	4	5	6	7	8	9
1	161.4	199.5	215.7	224.6	230.2	234.0	236.8	238.9	240.5
2	18.51	19.00	19.16	19.25	19.30	19.33	19.35	19.37	19.38
3	10.13	9.55	9.28	9.12	9.01	8.94	8.89	8.85	8.81
4	7.71	6.94	6.59	6.39	6.26	6.16	6.09	6.04	6.00
5	6.61	5.79	5.41	5.19	5.05	4.95	4.88	4.82	4.77
6	5.99	5.14	4.76	4.53	4.39	4.28	4.21	4.15	4.10
7	5.59	4.74	4.35	4.12	3.97	3.87	3.79	3.73	3.68
8	5.32	4.46	4.07	3.84	3.69	3.58	3.50	3.44	3.39
9	5.12	4.26	3.86	3.63	3.48	3.37	3.29	3.23	3.18
10	4.96	4.10	3.71	3.48	3.33	3.22	3.14	3.07	3.02
11	4.84	3.98	3.59	3.36	3.20	3.09	3.01	2.95	2.90
12	4.75	3.89	3.49	3.26	3.11	3.00	2.91	2.85	2.80
13	4.67	3.81	3.41	3.18	3.03	2.92	2.83	2.77	2.71
14	4.60	3.74	3.34	3.11	2.96	2.85	2.76	2.70	2.65
15	4.54	3.68	3.29	3.06	2.90	2.79	2.71	2.64	2.59
16	4.49	3.63	3.24	3.01	2.85	2.74	2.66	2.59	2.54
17	4.45	3.59	3.20	2.96	2.81	2.70	2.61	2.55	2.49
18	4.41	3.55	3.16	2.93	2.77	2.66	2.58	2.51	2.46
19	4.38	3.52	3.13	2.90	2.74	2.63	2.54	2.48	2.42
20	4.35	3.49	3.10	2.87	2.71	2.60	2.51	2.45	2.39
21	4.32	3.47	3.07	2.84	2.68	2.57	2.49	2.42	2.37
22	4.30	3.44	3.05	2.82	2.66	2.55	2.46	2.40	2.34
23	4.28	3.42	3.03	2.80	2.64	2.53	2.44	2.37	2.32
24	4.26	3.40	3.01	2.78	2.62	2.51	2.42	2.36	2.30
25	4.24	3.39	2.99	2.76	2.60	2.49	2.40	2.34	2.28
26	4.23	3.37	2.98	2.74	2.59	2.47	2.39	2.32	2.27
27	4.21	3.35	2.96	2.73	2.57	2.46	2.37	2.31	2.25
28	4.20	3.34	2.95	2.71	2.56	2.45	2.36	2.29	2.24
29	4.18	3.33	2.93	2.70	2.55	2.43	2.35	2.28	2.22
30	4.17	3.32	2.92	2.69	2.53	2.42	2.33	2.27	2.21
40	4.08	3.23	2.84	2.61	2.45	2.34	2.25	2.18	2.12
60	4.00	3.15	2.76	2.53	2.37	2.25	2.17	2.10	2.04
120	3.92	3.07	2.68	2.45	2.29	2.17	2.09	2.02	1.96
∞	3.84	3.00	2.60	2.37	2.21	2.10	2.01	1.94	1.88

TABLE 5 *(continued)* **Critical Values of the F Distribution for** $\alpha = 0.05$

Denominator Degrees of Freedom (k_2)	Numerator Degrees of Freedom (k_1)									
	10	12	15	20	24	30	40	60	120	∞
1	241.9	243.9	245.9	248.0	249.1	250.1	251.1	252.2	253.3	254.3
2	19.40	19.41	19.43	19.45	19.45	19.46	19.47	19.48	19.49	19.50
3	8.79	8.74	8.70	8.66	8.64	8.62	8.59	8.57	8.55	8.53
4	5.96	5.91	5.86	5.80	5.77	5.75	5.72	5.69	5.66	5.63
5	4.74	4.68	4.62	4.56	4.53	4.50	4.46	4.43	4.40	4.36
6	4.06	4.00	3.94	3.87	3.84	3.81	3.77	3.74	3.70	3.67
7	3.64	3.57	3.51	3.44	3.41	3.38	3.34	3.30	3.27	3.23
8	3.35	3.28	3.22	3.15	3.12	3.08	3.04	3.01	2.97	2.93
9	3.14	3.07	3.01	2.94	2.90	2.86	2.83	2.79	2.75	2.71
10	2.98	2.91	2.85	2.77	2.74	2.70	2.66	2.62	2.58	2.54
11	2.85	2.79	2.72	2.65	2.61	2.57	2.53	2.49	2.45	2.40
12	2.75	2.69	2.62	2.54	2.51	2.47	2.43	2.38	2.34	2.30
13	2.67	2.60	2.53	2.46	2.42	2.38	2.34	2.30	2.25	2.21
14	2.60	2.53	2.46	2.39	2.35	2.31	2.27	2.22	2.18	2.13
15	2.54	2.48	2.40	2.33	2.29	2.25	2.20	2.16	2.11	2.07
16	2.49	2.42	2.35	2.28	2.24	2.19	2.15	2.11	2.06	2.01
17	2.45	2.38	2.31	2.23	2.19	2.15	2.10	2.06	2.01	1.96
18	2.41	2.34	2.27	2.19	2.15	2.11	2.06	2.02	1.97	1.92
19	2.38	2.31	2.23	2.16	2.11	2.07	2.03	1.98	1.93	1.88
20	2.35	2.28	2.20	2.12	2.08	2.04	1.99	1.95	1.90	1.84
21	2.32	2.25	2.18	2.10	2.05	2.01	1.96	1.92	1.87	1.81
22	2.30	2.23	2.15	2.07	2.03	1.98	1.94	1.89	1.84	1.78
23	2.27	2.20	2.13	2.05	2.01	1.96	1.91	1.86	1.81	1.76
24	2.25	2.18	2.11	2.03	1.98	1.94	1.89	1.84	1.79	1.73
25	2.24	2.16	2.09	2.01	1.96	1.92	1.87	1.82	1.77	1.71
26	2.22	2.15	2.07	1.99	1.95	1.90	1.85	1.80	1.75	1.69
27	2.20	2.13	2.06	1.97	1.93	1.88	1.84	1.79	1.73	1.67
28	2.19	2.12	2.04	1.96	1.91	1.87	1.82	1.77	1.71	1.65
29	2.18	2.10	2.03	1.94	1.90	1.85	1.81	1.75	1.70	1.64
30	2.16	2.09	2.01	1.93	1.89	1.84	1.79	1.74	1.68	1.62
40	2.08	2.00	1.92	1.84	1.79	1.74	1.69	1.64	1.58	1.51
60	1.99	1.92	1.84	1.75	1.70	1.65	1.59	1.53	1.47	1.39
120	1.91	1.83	1.75	1.66	1.61	1.55	1.50	1.43	1.35	1.25
∞	1.83	1.75	1.67	1.57	1.52	1.46	1.39	1.32	1.22	1.00

TABLE 5 *(continued)* **Critical Values of the F Distribution for** $\alpha = 0.025$

Denominator Degrees of Freedom (k_2)	Numerator Degrees of Freedom (k_1)								
	1	2	3	4	5	6	7	8	9
1	647.8	799.5	864.2	899.6	921.8	937.1	948.2	956.7	963.3
2	38.51	39.00	39.17	39.25	39.30	39.33	39.36	39.37	39.39
3	17.44	16.04	15.44	15.10	14.88	14.73	14.62	14.54	14.47
4	12.22	10.65	9.98	9.60	9.36	9.20	9.07	8.98	8.90
5	10.01	8.43	7.76	7.39	7.15	6.98	6.85	6.76	6.68
6	8.81	7.26	6.60	6.23	5.99	5.82	5.70	5.60	5.52
7	8.07	6.54	5.89	5.52	5.29	5.12	4.99	4.90	4.82
8	7.57	6.06	5.42	5.05	4.82	4.65	4.53	4.43	4.36
9	7.21	5.71	5.08	4.72	4.48	4.32	4.20	4.10	4.03
10	6.94	5.46	4.83	4.47	4.24	4.07	3.95	3.85	3.78
11	6.72	5.26	4.63	4.28	4.04	3.88	3.76	3.66	3.59
12	6.55	5.10	4.47	4.12	3.89	3.73	3.61	3.51	3.44
13	6.41	4.97	4.35	4.00	3.77	3.60	3.48	3.39	3.31
14	6.30	4.86	4.24	3.89	3.66	3.50	3.38	3.29	3.21
15	6.20	4.77	4.15	3.80	3.58	3.41	3.29	3.20	3.12
16	6.12	4.69	4.08	3.73	3.50	3.34	3.22	3.12	3.05
17	6.04	4.62	4.01	3.66	3.44	3.28	3.16	3.06	2.98
18	5.98	4.56	3.95	3.61	3.38	3.22	3.10	3.01	2.93
19	5.92	4.51	3.90	3.56	3.33	3.17	3.05	2.96	2.88
20	5.87	4.46	3.86	3.51	3.29	3.13	3.01	2.91	2.84
21	5.83	4.42	3.82	3.48	3.25	3.09	2.97	2.87	2.80
22	5.79	4.38	3.78	3.44	3.22	3.05	2.93	2.84	2.76
23	5.75	4.35	3.75	3.41	3.18	3.02	2.90	2.81	2.73
24	5.72	4.32	3.72	3.38	3.15	2.99	2.87	2.78	2.70
25	5.69	4.29	3.69	3.35	3.13	2.97	2.85	2.75	2.68
26	5.66	4.27	3.67	3.33	3.10	2.94	2.82	2.73	2.65
27	5.63	4.24	3.65	3.31	3.08	2.92	2.80	2.71	2.63
28	5.61	4.22	3.63	3.29	3.06	2.90	2.78	2.69	2.61
29	5.59	4.20	3.61	3.27	3.04	2.88	2.76	2.67	2.59
30	5.57	4.18	3.59	3.25	3.03	2.87	2.75	2.65	2.57
40	5.42	4.05	3.46	3.13	2.90	2.74	2.62	2.53	2.45
60	5.29	3.93	3.34	3.01	2.79	2.63	2.51	2.41	2.33
120	5.15	3.80	3.23	2.89	2.67	2.52	2.39	2.30	2.22
∞	5.02	3.69	3.12	2.79	2.57	2.41	2.29	2.19	2.11

TABLE 5 *(continued)*   **Critical Values of the F Distribution for α = 0.025**

Denominator Degrees of Freedom (k_2)	Numerator Degrees of Freedom (k_1)									
	10	12	15	20	24	30	40	60	120	∞
1	968.6	976.7	984.9	993.1	997.2	1001	1006	1010	1014	1018
2	39.40	39.41	39.43	39.45	39.46	39.46	39.47	39.48	39.49	39.50
3	14.42	14.34	14.25	14.17	14.12	14.08	14.04	13.99	13.95	13.90
4	8.84	8.75	8.66	8.56	8.51	8.46	8.41	8.36	8.31	8.26
5	6.62	6.52	6.43	6.33	6.28	6.23	6.18	6.12	6.07	6.02
6	5.46	5.37	5.27	5.17	5.12	5.07	5.01	4.96	4.90	4.85
7	4.76	4.67	4.57	4.47	4.42	4.36	4.31	4.25	4.20	4.14
8	4.30	4.20	4.10	4.00	3.95	3.89	3.84	3.78	3.73	3.67
9	3.96	3.87	3.77	3.67	3.61	3.56	3.51	3.45	3.39	3.33
10	3.72	3.62	3.52	3.42	3.37	3.31	3.26	3.20	3.14	3.08
11	3.53	3.43	3.33	3.23	3.17	3.12	3.06	3.00	2.94	2.88
12	3.37	3.28	3.18	3.07	3.02	2.96	2.91	2.85	2.79	2.72
13	3.25	3.15	3.05	2.95	2.89	2.84	2.78	2.72	2.66	2.60
14	3.15	3.05	2.95	2.84	2.79	2.73	2.67	2.61	2.55	2.49
15	3.06	2.96	2.86	2.76	2.70	2.64	2.59	2.52	2.46	2.40
16	2.99	2.89	2.79	2.68	2.63	2.57	2.51	2.45	2.38	2.32
17	2.92	2.82	2.72	2.62	2.56	2.50	2.44	2.38	2.32	2.25
18	2.87	2.77	2.67	2.56	2.50	2.44	2.38	2.32	2.26	2.19
19	2.82	2.72	2.62	2.51	2.45	2.39	2.33	2.27	2.20	2.13
20	2.77	2.68	2.57	2.46	2.41	2.35	2.29	2.22	2.16	2.09
21	2.73	2.64	2.53	2.42	2.37	2.31	2.25	2.18	2.11	2.04
22	2.70	2.60	2.50	2.39	2.33	2.27	2.21	2.14	2.08	2.00
23	2.67	2.57	2.47	2.36	2.30	2.24	2.18	2.11	2.04	1.97
24	2.64	2.54	2.44	2.33	2.27	2.21	2.15	2.08	2.01	1.94
25	2.61	2.51	2.41	2.30	2.24	2.18	2.12	2.05	1.98	1.91
26	2.59	2.49	2.39	2.28	2.22	2.16	2.09	2.03	1.95	1.88
27	2.57	2.47	2.36	2.25	2.19	2.13	2.07	2.00	1.93	1.85
28	2.55	2.45	2.34	2.23	2.17	2.11	2.05	1.98	1.91	1.83
29	2.53	2.43	2.32	2.21	2.15	2.09	2.03	1.96	1.89	1.81
30	2.51	2.41	2.31	2.20	2.14	2.07	2.01	1.94	1.87	1.79
40	2.39	2.29	2.18	2.07	2.01	1.94	1.88	1.80	1.72	1.64
60	2.27	2.17	2.06	1.94	1.88	1.82	1.74	1.67	1.58	1.48
120	2.16	2.05	1.94	1.82	1.76	1.69	1.61	1.53	1.43	1.31
∞	2.05	1.94	1.83	1.71	1.64	1.57	1.48	1.39	1.27	1.00

TABLE 5 *(continued)* **Critical Values of the F Distribution for $\alpha = 0.01$**

Denominator Degrees of Freedom (k_2)	Numerator Degrees of Freedom (k_1)								
	1	2	3	4	5	6	7	8	9
1	4,052	4,999.5	5,403	5,625	5,764	5,859	5,928	5,982	6,022
2	98.50	99.00	99.17	99.25	99.30	99.33	99.36	99.37	99.39
3	34.12	30.82	29.46	28.71	28.24	27.91	27.67	27.49	27.35
4	21.20	18.00	16.69	15.98	15.52	15.21	14.98	14.80	14.66
5	16.26	13.27	12.06	11.39	10.97	10.67	10.46	10.29	10.16
6	13.75	10.92	9.78	9.15	8.75	8.47	8.26	8.10	7.98
7	12.25	9.55	8.45	7.85	7.46	7.19	6.99	6.84	6.72
8	11.26	8.65	7.59	7.01	6.63	6.37	6.18	6.03	5.91
9	10.56	8.02	6.99	6.42	6.06	5.80	5.61	5.47	5.35
10	10.04	7.56	6.55	5.99	5.64	5.39	5.20	5.06	4.94
11	9.65	7.21	6.22	5.67	5.32	5.07	4.89	4.74	4.63
12	9.33	6.93	5.95	5.41	5.06	4.82	4.64	4.50	4.39
13	9.07	6.70	5.74	5.21	4.86	4.62	4.44	4.30	4.19
14	8.86	6.51	5.56	5.04	4.69	4.46	4.28	4.14	4.03
15	8.68	6.36	5.42	4.89	4.56	4.32	4.14	4.00	3.89
16	8.53	6.23	5.29	4.77	4.44	4.20	4.03	3.89	3.78
17	8.40	6.11	5.18	4.67	4.34	4.10	3.93	3.79	3.68
18	8.29	6.01	5.09	4.58	4.25	4.01	3.84	3.71	3.60
19	8.18	5.93	5.01	4.50	4.17	3.94	3.77	3.63	3.52
20	8.10	5.85	4.94	4.43	4.10	3.87	3.70	3.56	3.46
21	8.02	5.78	4.87	4.37	4.04	3.81	3.64	3.51	3.40
22	7.95	5.72	4.82	4.31	3.99	3.76	3.59	3.45	3.35
23	7.88	5.66	4.76	4.26	3.94	3.71	3.54	3.41	3.30
24	7.82	5.61	4.72	4.22	3.90	3.67	3.50	3.36	3.26
25	7.77	5.57	4.68	4.18	3.85	3.63	3.46	3.32	3.22
26	7.72	5.53	4.64	4.14	3.82	3.59	3.42	3.29	3.18
27	7.68	5.49	4.60	4.11	3.78	3.56	3.39	3.26	3.15
28	7.64	5.45	4.57	4.07	3.75	3.53	3.36	3.23	3.12
29	7.60	5.42	4.54	4.04	3.73	3.50	3.33	3.20	3.09
30	7.56	5.39	4.51	4.02	3.70	3.47	3.30	3.17	3.07
40	7.31	5.18	4.31	3.83	3.51	3.29	3.12	2.99	2.89
60	7.08	4.98	4.13	3.65	3.34	3.12	2.95	2.82	2.72
120	6.85	4.79	3.95	3.48	3.17	2.96	2.79	2.66	2.56
∞	6.63	4.61	3.78	3.32	3.02	2.80	2.64	2.51	2.41

TABLE 5 *(concluded)*　**Critical Values of the *F* Distribution for $\alpha = 0.01$**

Denominator Degrees of Freedom (k_2)	Numerator of Degrees of Freedom (k_1)									
	10	12	15	20	24	30	40	60	120	∞
1	6,056	6,106	6,157	6,209	6,235	6,261	6,287	6,313	6,339	6,366
2	99.40	99.42	99.43	99.45	99.46	99.47	99.47	99.48	99.49	99.50
3	27.23	27.05	26.87	26.69	26.60	26.50	26.41	26.32	26.22	26.13
4	14.55	14.37	14.20	14.02	13.93	13.84	13.75	13.65	13.56	13.46
5	10.05	9.89	9.72	9.55	9.47	9.38	9.29	9.20	9.11	9.02
6	7.87	7.72	7.56	7.40	7.31	7.23	7.14	7.06	6.97	6.88
7	6.62	6.47	6.31	6.16	6.07	5.99	5.91	5.82	5.74	5.65
8	5.81	5.67	5.52	5.36	5.28	5.20	5.12	5.03	4.95	4.86
9	5.26	5.11	4.96	4.81	4.73	4.65	4.57	4.48	4.40	4.31
10	4.85	4.71	4.56	4.41	4.33	4.25	4.17	4.08	4.00	3.91
11	4.54	4.40	4.25	4.10	4.02	3.94	3.86	3.78	3.69	3.60
12	4.30	4.16	4.01	3.86	3.78	3.70	3.62	3.54	3.45	3.36
13	4.10	3.96	3.82	3.66	3.59	3.51	3.43	3.34	3.25	3.17
14	3.94	3.80	3.66	3.51	3.43	3.35	3.27	3.18	3.09	3.00
15	3.80	3.67	3.52	3.37	3.29	3.21	3.13	3.05	2.96	2.87
16	3.69	3.55	3.41	3.26	3.18	3.10	3.02	2.93	2.84	2.75
17	3.59	3.46	3.31	3.16	3.08	3.00	2.92	2.83	2.75	2.65
18	3.51	3.37	3.23	3.08	3.00	2.92	2.84	2.75	2.66	2.57
19	3.43	3.30	3.15	3.00	2.92	2.84	2.76	2.67	2.58	2.49
20	3.37	3.23	3.09	2.94	2.86	2.78	2.69	2.61	2.52	2.42
21	3.31	3.17	3.03	2.88	2.80	2.72	2.64	2.55	2.46	2.36
22	3.26	3.12	2.98	2.83	2.75	2.67	2.58	2.50	2.40	2.31
23	3.21	3.07	2.93	2.78	2.70	2.62	2.54	2.45	2.35	2.26
24	3.17	3.03	2.89	2.74	2.66	2.58	2.49	2.40	2.31	2.21
25	3.13	2.99	2.85	2.70	2.62	2.54	2.45	2.36	2.27	2.17
26	3.09	2.96	2.81	2.66	2.58	2.50	2.42	2.33	2.23	2.13
27	3.06	2.93	2.78	2.63	2.55	2.47	2.38	2.29	2.20	2.10
28	3.03	2.90	2.75	2.60	2.52	2.44	2.35	2.26	2.17	2.06
29	3.00	2.87	2.73	2.57	2.49	2.41	2.33	2.23	2.14	2.03
30	2.98	2.84	2.70	2.55	2.47	2.39	2.30	2.21	2.11	2.01
40	2.80	2.66	2.52	2.37	2.29	2.20	2.11	2.02	1.92	1.80
60	2.63	2.50	2.35	2.20	2.12	2.03	1.94	1.84	1.73	1.60
120	2.47	2.34	2.19	2.03	1.95	1.86	1.76	1.66	1.53	1.38
∞	2.32	2.18	2.04	1.88	1.79	1.70	1.59	1.47	1.32	1.00

Source: M. Merrington and C. M. Thompson, "Tables of Percentage Points of the Inverted Beta (*F*)-Distribution," *Biometrika* 33 (1943) pp. 73–88. Reproduced by permission of the *Biometrika* Trustees.

TABLE 5A   The *F* Distribution for $\alpha = 0.05$ and $\alpha = 0.01$ for Many Possible Degrees of Freedom

Numerator Degrees of Freedom (k_1)

Denominator Degrees of Freedom (k_2)	1	2	3	4	5	6	7	8	9	10	11	12	14	16	20	24	30	40	50	75	100	200	500	∞
1	161 **4,052**	200 **4,999**	216 **5,403**	225 **5,625**	230 **5,764**	234 **5,859**	237 **5,928**	239 **5,981**	241 **6,022**	242 **6,056**	243 **6,082**	244 **6,106**	245 **6,142**	246 **6,169**	248 **6,208**	249 **6,234**	250 **6,261**	251 **6,286**	252 **6,302**	253 **6,323**	253 **6,334**	254 **6,352**	254 **6,361**	254 **6,366**
2	18.51 **98.49**	19.00 **99.00**	19.16 **99.17**	19.25 **99.25**	19.30 **99.30**	19.33 **99.33**	19.36 **99.36**	19.37 **99.37**	19.38 **99.39**	19.39 **99.40**	19.40 **99.41**	19.41 **99.42**	19.42 **99.43**	19.43 **99.44**	19.44 **99.45**	19.45 **99.46**	19.46 **99.47**	19.47 **99.48**	19.47 **99.48**	19.48 **99.49**	19.49 **99.49**	19.49 **99.49**	19.50 **99.50**	19.50 **99.50**
3	10.13 **34.12**	9.55 **30.82**	9.28 **29.46**	9.12 **28.71**	9.01 **28.24**	8.94 **27.91**	8.88 **27.67**	8.84 **27.49**	8.81 **27.34**	8.78 **27.23**	8.76 **27.13**	8.74 **27.05**	8.71 **26.92**	8.69 **26.83**	8.66 **26.69**	8.64 **26.60**	8.62 **26.50**	8.60 **26.41**	8.58 **26.35**	8.57 **26.27**	8.56 **26.23**	8.54 **26.18**	8.54 **26.14**	8.53 **26.12**
4	7.71 **21.20**	6.94 **18.00**	6.59 **16.69**	6.39 **15.98**	6.26 **15.52**	6.16 **15.21**	6.09 **14.98**	6.04 **14.80**	6.00 **14.66**	5.96 **14.54**	5.93 **14.45**	5.91 **14.37**	5.87 **14.24**	5.84 **14.15**	5.80 **14.02**	5.77 **13.93**	5.74 **13.83**	5.71 **13.74**	5.70 **13.69**	5.68 **13.61**	5.66 **13.57**	5.65 **13.52**	5.64 **13.48**	5.63 **13.46**
5	6.61 **16.26**	5.79 **13.27**	5.41 **12.06**	5.19 **11.39**	5.05 **10.97**	4.95 **10.67**	4.88 **10.45**	4.82 **10.29**	4.78 **10.15**	4.74 **10.05**	4.70 **9.96**	4.68 **9.89**	4.64 **9.77**	4.60 **9.68**	4.56 **9.55**	4.53 **9.47**	4.50 **9.38**	4.46 **9.29**	4.44 **9.24**	4.42 **9.17**	4.40 **9.13**	4.38 **9.07**	4.37 **9.04**	4.36 **9.02**
6	5.99 **13.74**	5.14 **10.92**	4.76 **9.78**	4.53 **9.15**	4.39 **8.75**	4.28 **8.47**	4.21 **8.26**	4.15 **8.10**	4.10 **7.98**	4.06 **7.87**	4.03 **7.79**	4.00 **7.72**	3.96 **7.60**	3.92 **7.52**	3.87 **7.39**	3.84 **7.31**	3.81 **7.23**	3.77 **7.14**	3.75 **7.09**	3.72 **7.02**	3.71 **6.99**	3.69 **6.94**	3.68 **6.90**	3.67 **6.88**
7	5.59 **12.25**	4.74 **9.55**	4.35 **8.45**	4.12 **7.85**	3.97 **7.46**	3.87 **7.19**	3.79 **7.00**	3.73 **6.84**	3.68 **6.71**	3.63 **6.62**	3.60 **6.54**	3.57 **6.47**	3.52 **6.35**	3.49 **6.27**	3.44 **6.15**	3.41 **6.07**	3.38 **5.98**	3.34 **5.90**	3.32 **5.85**	3.29 **5.78**	3.28 **5.75**	3.25 **5.70**	3.24 **5.67**	3.23 **5.65**
8	5.32 **11.26**	4.46 **8.65**	4.07 **7.59**	3.84 **7.01**	3.69 **6.63**	3.58 **6.37**	3.50 **6.19**	3.44 **6.03**	3.39 **5.91**	3.34 **5.82**	3.31 **5.74**	3.28 **5.67**	3.23 **5.56**	3.20 **5.48**	3.15 **5.36**	3.12 **5.28**	3.08 **5.20**	3.05 **5.11**	3.03 **5.06**	3.00 **5.00**	2.98 **4.96**	2.96 **4.91**	2.94 **4.88**	2.93 **4.86**
9	5.12 **10.56**	4.26 **8.02**	3.86 **6.99**	3.63 **6.42**	3.48 **6.06**	3.37 **5.80**	3.29 **5.62**	3.23 **5.47**	3.18 **5.35**	3.13 **5.26**	3.10 **5.18**	3.07 **5.11**	3.02 **5.00**	2.98 **4.92**	2.93 **4.80**	2.90 **4.73**	2.86 **4.64**	2.82 **4.56**	2.80 **4.51**	2.77 **4.45**	2.76 **4.41**	2.73 **4.36**	2.72 **4.33**	2.71 **4.31**
10	4.96 **10.04**	4.10 **7.56**	3.71 **6.55**	3.48 **5.99**	3.33 **5.64**	3.22 **5.39**	3.14 **5.21**	3.07 **5.06**	3.02 **4.95**	2.97 **4.85**	2.94 **4.78**	2.91 **4.71**	2.86 **4.60**	2.82 **4.52**	2.77 **4.41**	2.74 **4.33**	2.70 **4.25**	2.67 **4.17**	2.64 **4.12**	2.61 **4.05**	2.59 **4.01**	2.56 **3.96**	2.55 **3.93**	2.54 **3.91**
11	4.84 **9.65**	3.98 **7.20**	3.59 **6.22**	3.36 **5.67**	3.20 **5.32**	3.09 **5.07**	3.01 **4.88**	2.95 **4.74**	2.90 **4.63**	2.86 **4.54**	2.82 **4.46**	2.79 **4.40**	2.74 **4.29**	2.70 **4.21**	2.65 **4.10**	2.61 **4.02**	2.57 **3.94**	2.53 **3.86**	2.50 **3.80**	2.47 **3.74**	2.45 **3.70**	2.42 **3.66**	2.41 **3.62**	2.40 **3.60**
12	4.75 **9.33**	3.88 **6.93**	3.49 **5.95**	3.26 **5.41**	3.11 **5.06**	3.00 **4.82**	2.92 **4.65**	2.85 **4.50**	2.80 **4.39**	2.76 **4.30**	2.72 **4.22**	2.69 **4.16**	2.64 **4.05**	2.60 **3.98**	2.54 **3.86**	2.50 **3.78**	2.46 **3.70**	2.42 **3.61**	2.40 **3.56**	2.36 **3.49**	2.35 **3.46**	2.32 **3.41**	2.31 **3.38**	2.30 **3.36**

TABLE 5A (continued)   The F Distribution for $\alpha = 0.05$ and $\alpha = 0.01$ for Many Possible Degrees of Freedom

Values are given as $\alpha = 0.05$ (top) / $\alpha = 0.01$ (bold, bottom).

Denominator Degrees of Freedom (k_2)	1	2	3	4	5	6	7	8	9	10	11	12	14	16	20	24	30	40	50	75	100	200	500	∞
13	4.67/9.07	3.80/6.70	3.41/5.74	3.18/5.20	3.02/4.86	2.92/4.62	2.84/4.44	2.77/4.30	2.72/4.19	2.67/4.10	2.63/4.02	2.60/3.96	2.55/3.85	2.51/3.78	2.46/3.67	2.42/3.59	2.38/3.51	2.34/3.42	2.32/3.37	2.28/3.30	2.26/3.27	2.24/3.21	2.22/3.18	2.21/3.16
14	4.60/8.86	3.74/6.51	3.34/5.56	3.11/5.03	2.96/4.69	2.85/4.46	2.77/4.28	2.70/4.14	2.65/4.03	2.60/3.94	2.56/3.86	2.53/3.80	2.48/3.70	2.44/3.62	2.39/3.51	2.35/3.43	2.31/3.34	2.27/3.26	2.24/3.21	2.21/3.14	2.19/3.11	2.16/3.06	2.14/3.02	2.13/3.00
15	4.54/8.68	3.68/6.36	3.29/5.42	3.06/4.89	2.90/4.56	2.79/4.32	2.70/4.14	2.64/4.00	2.59/3.89	2.55/3.80	2.51/3.73	2.48/3.67	2.43/3.56	2.39/3.48	2.33/3.36	2.29/3.29	2.25/3.20	2.21/3.12	2.18/3.07	2.15/3.00	2.12/2.97	2.10/2.92	2.08/2.89	2.07/2.87
16	4.49/8.53	3.63/6.23	3.24/5.29	3.01/4.77	2.85/4.44	2.74/4.20	2.66/4.03	2.59/3.89	2.54/3.78	2.49/3.69	2.45/3.61	2.42/3.55	2.37/3.45	2.33/3.37	2.28/3.25	2.24/3.18	2.20/3.10	2.16/3.01	2.13/2.96	2.09/2.89	2.07/2.86	2.04/2.80	2.02/2.77	2.01/2.75
17	4.45/8.40	3.59/6.11	3.20/5.18	2.96/4.67	2.81/4.34	2.70/4.10	2.62/3.93	2.55/3.79	2.50/3.68	2.45/3.59	2.41/3.52	2.38/3.45	2.33/3.35	2.29/3.27	2.23/3.16	2.19/3.08	2.15/3.00	2.11/2.92	2.08/2.86	2.04/2.79	2.02/2.76	1.99/2.70	1.97/2.67	1.96/2.65
18	4.41/8.28	3.55/6.01	3.16/5.09	2.93/4.58	2.77/4.25	2.66/4.01	2.58/3.85	2.51/3.71	2.46/3.60	2.41/3.51	2.37/3.44	2.34/3.37	2.29/3.27	2.25/3.19	2.19/3.07	2.15/3.00	2.11/2.91	2.07/2.83	2.04/2.78	2.00/2.71	1.98/2.68	1.95/2.62	1.93/2.59	1.92/2.57
19	4.38/8.18	3.52/5.93	3.13/5.01	2.90/4.50	2.74/4.17	2.63/3.94	2.55/3.77	2.48/3.63	2.43/3.52	2.38/3.43	2.34/3.36	2.31/3.30	2.26/3.19	2.21/3.12	2.15/3.00	2.11/2.92	2.07/2.84	2.02/2.76	2.00/2.70	1.96/2.63	1.94/2.60	1.91/2.54	1.90/2.51	1.88/2.49
20	4.35/8.10	3.49/5.85	3.10/4.94	2.87/4.43	2.71/4.10	2.60/3.87	2.52/3.71	2.45/3.56	2.40/3.45	2.35/3.37	2.31/3.30	2.28/3.23	2.23/3.13	2.18/3.05	2.12/2.94	2.08/2.86	2.04/2.77	1.99/2.69	1.96/2.63	1.92/2.56	1.90/2.53	1.87/2.47	1.85/2.44	1.84/2.42
21	4.32/8.02	3.47/5.78	3.07/4.87	2.84/4.37	2.68/4.04	2.57/3.81	2.49/3.65	2.42/3.51	2.37/3.40	2.32/3.31	2.28/3.24	2.25/3.17	2.20/3.07	2.15/2.99	2.09/2.88	2.05/2.80	2.00/2.72	1.96/2.63	1.93/2.58	1.89/2.51	1.87/2.47	1.84/2.42	1.82/2.38	1.81/2.36
22	4.30/7.94	3.44/5.72	3.05/4.82	2.82/4.31	2.66/3.99	2.55/3.76	2.47/3.59	2.40/3.45	2.35/3.35	2.30/3.26	2.26/3.18	2.23/3.12	2.18/3.02	2.13/2.94	2.07/2.83	2.03/2.75	1.98/2.67	1.93/2.58	1.91/2.53	1.87/2.46	1.84/2.42	1.81/2.37	1.80/2.33	1.78/2.31
23	4.28/7.88	3.42/5.66	3.03/4.76	2.80/4.26	2.64/3.94	2.53/3.71	2.45/3.54	2.38/3.41	2.32/3.30	2.28/3.21	2.24/3.14	2.20/3.07	2.14/2.97	2.10/2.89	2.04/2.78	2.00/2.70	1.96/2.62	1.91/2.53	1.88/2.48	1.84/2.41	1.82/2.37	1.79/2.32	1.77/2.28	1.76/2.26
24	4.26/7.82	3.40/5.61	3.01/4.72	2.78/4.22	2.62/3.90	2.51/3.67	2.43/3.50	2.36/3.36	2.30/3.25	2.26/3.17	2.22/3.09	2.18/3.03	2.13/2.93	2.09/2.85	2.02/2.74	1.98/2.66	1.94/2.58	1.89/2.49	1.86/2.44	1.82/2.36	1.80/2.33	1.76/2.27	1.74/2.23	1.73/2.21
25	4.24/7.77	3.38/5.57	2.99/4.68	2.76/4.18	2.60/3.86	2.49/3.63	2.41/3.46	2.34/3.32	2.28/3.21	2.24/3.13	2.20/3.05	2.16/2.99	2.11/2.89	2.06/2.81	2.00/2.70	1.96/2.62	1.92/2.54	1.87/2.45	1.84/2.40	1.80/2.32	1.77/2.29	1.74/2.23	1.72/2.19	1.71/2.17
26	4.22/7.72	3.37/5.53	2.98/4.64	2.74/4.14	2.59/3.82	2.47/3.59	2.39/3.42	2.32/3.29	2.27/3.17	2.22/3.09	2.18/3.02	2.15/2.96	2.10/2.86	2.05/2.77	1.99/2.66	1.95/2.58	1.90/2.50	1.85/2.41	1.82/2.36	1.78/2.28	1.76/2.25	1.72/2.19	1.70/2.15	1.69/2.13

Numerator Degrees of Freedom (k_1)

Numerator Degrees of Freedom (k_1)

Denominator Degrees of Freedom (k_2)	1	2	3	4	5	6	7	8	9	10	11	12	14	16	20	24	30	40	50	75	100	200	500	∞
27	4.21 / 7.68	3.35 / 5.49	2.96 / 4.60	2.73 / 4.11	2.57 / 3.79	2.46 / 3.56	2.37 / 3.39	2.30 / 3.26	2.25 / 3.14	2.20 / 3.06	2.16 / 2.98	2.13 / 2.93	2.08 / 2.83	2.03 / 2.74	1.97 / 2.63	1.93 / 2.55	1.88 / 2.47	1.84 / 2.38	1.80 / 2.33	1.76 / 2.25	1.74 / 2.21	1.71 / 2.16	1.68 / 2.12	1.67 / 2.10
28	4.20 / 7.64	3.34 / 5.45	2.95 / 4.57	2.71 / 4.07	2.56 / 3.76	2.44 / 3.53	2.36 / 3.36	2.29 / 3.23	2.24 / 3.11	2.19 / 3.03	2.15 / 2.95	2.12 / 2.90	2.06 / 2.80	2.02 / 2.71	1.96 / 2.60	1.91 / 2.52	1.87 / 2.44	1.81 / 2.35	1.78 / 2.30	1.75 / 2.22	1.72 / 2.18	1.69 / 2.13	1.67 / 2.09	1.65 / 2.06
29	4.18 / 7.60	3.33 / 5.42	2.93 / 4.54	2.70 / 4.04	2.54 / 3.73	2.43 / 3.50	2.35 / 3.33	2.28 / 3.20	2.22 / 3.08	2.18 / 3.00	2.14 / 2.92	2.10 / 2.87	2.05 / 2.77	2.00 / 2.68	1.94 / 2.57	1.90 / 2.49	1.85 / 2.41	1.80 / 2.32	1.77 / 2.27	1.73 / 2.19	1.71 / 2.15	1.68 / 2.10	1.65 / 2.06	1.64 / 2.03
30	4.17 / 7.56	3.32 / 5.39	2.92 / 4.51	2.69 / 4.02	2.53 / 3.70	2.42 / 3.47	2.34 / 3.30	2.27 / 3.17	2.21 / 3.06	2.16 / 2.98	2.12 / 2.90	2.09 / 2.84	2.04 / 2.74	1.99 / 2.66	1.93 / 2.55	1.89 / 2.47	1.84 / 2.38	1.79 / 2.29	1.76 / 2.24	1.72 / 2.16	1.69 / 2.13	1.66 / 2.07	1.64 / 2.03	1.62 / 2.01
32	4.15 / 7.50	3.30 / 5.34	2.90 / 4.46	2.67 / 3.97	2.51 / 3.66	2.40 / 3.42	2.32 / 3.25	2.25 / 3.12	2.19 / 3.01	2.14 / 2.94	2.10 / 2.86	2.07 / 2.80	2.02 / 2.70	1.97 / 2.62	1.91 / 2.51	1.86 / 2.42	1.82 / 2.34	1.76 / 2.25	1.74 / 2.20	1.69 / 2.12	1.67 / 2.08	1.64 / 2.02	1.61 / 1.98	1.59 / 1.96
34	4.13 / 7.44	3.28 / 5.29	2.88 / 4.42	2.65 / 3.93	2.49 / 3.61	2.38 / 3.38	2.30 / 3.21	2.23 / 3.08	2.17 / 2.97	2.12 / 2.89	2.08 / 2.82	2.05 / 2.76	2.00 / 2.66	1.95 / 2.58	1.89 / 2.47	1.84 / 2.38	1.80 / 2.30	1.74 / 2.21	1.71 / 2.15	1.67 / 2.08	1.64 / 2.04	1.61 / 1.98	1.59 / 1.94	1.57 / 1.91
36	4.11 / 7.39	3.26 / 5.25	2.86 / 4.38	2.63 / 3.89	2.48 / 3.58	2.36 / 3.35	2.28 / 3.18	2.21 / 3.04	2.15 / 2.94	2.10 / 2.86	2.06 / 2.78	2.03 / 2.72	1.98 / 2.62	1.93 / 2.54	1.87 / 2.43	1.82 / 2.35	1.78 / 2.26	1.72 / 2.17	1.69 / 2.12	1.65 / 2.04	1.62 / 2.00	1.59 / 1.94	1.56 / 1.90	1.55 / 1.87
38	4.10 / 7.35	3.25 / 5.21	2.85 / 4.34	2.62 / 3.86	2.46 / 3.54	2.35 / 3.32	2.26 / 3.15	2.19 / 3.02	2.14 / 2.91	2.09 / 2.82	2.05 / 2.75	2.02 / 2.69	1.96 / 2.59	1.92 / 2.51	1.85 / 2.40	1.80 / 2.32	1.76 / 2.22	1.71 / 2.14	1.67 / 2.08	1.63 / 2.00	1.60 / 1.97	1.57 / 1.90	1.54 / 1.86	1.53 / 1.84
40	4.08 / 7.31	3.23 / 5.18	2.84 / 4.31	2.61 / 3.83	2.45 / 3.51	2.34 / 3.29	2.25 / 3.12	2.18 / 2.99	2.12 / 2.88	2.07 / 2.80	2.04 / 2.73	2.00 / 2.66	1.95 / 2.56	1.90 / 2.49	1.84 / 2.37	1.79 / 2.29	1.74 / 2.20	1.69 / 2.11	1.66 / 2.05	1.61 / 1.97	1.59 / 1.94	1.55 / 1.88	1.53 / 1.84	1.51 / 1.81
42	4.07 / 7.27	3.22 / 5.15	2.83 / 4.29	2.59 / 3.80	2.44 / 3.49	2.32 / 3.26	2.24 / 3.10	2.17 / 2.96	2.11 / 2.86	2.06 / 2.77	2.02 / 2.70	1.99 / 2.64	1.94 / 2.54	1.89 / 2.46	1.82 / 2.35	1.78 / 2.26	1.73 / 2.17	1.68 / 2.08	1.64 / 2.02	1.60 / 1.94	1.57 / 1.91	1.54 / 1.85	1.51 / 1.80	1.49 / 1.78
44	4.06 / 7.24	3.21 / 5.12	2.82 / 4.26	2.58 / 3.78	2.43 / 3.46	2.31 / 3.24	2.23 / 3.07	2.16 / 2.94	2.10 / 2.84	2.05 / 2.75	2.01 / 2.68	1.98 / 2.62	1.92 / 2.52	1.88 / 2.44	1.81 / 2.32	1.76 / 2.24	1.72 / 2.15	1.66 / 2.06	1.63 / 2.00	1.58 / 1.92	1.56 / 1.88	1.52 / 1.82	1.50 / 1.78	1.48 / 1.75
46	4.05 / 7.21	3.20 / 5.10	2.81 / 4.24	2.57 / 3.76	2.42 / 3.44	2.30 / 3.22	2.22 / 3.05	2.14 / 2.92	2.09 / 2.82	2.04 / 2.73	2.00 / 2.66	1.97 / 2.60	1.91 / 2.50	1.87 / 2.42	1.80 / 2.30	1.75 / 2.22	1.71 / 2.13	1.65 / 2.04	1.62 / 1.98	1.57 / 1.90	1.54 / 1.86	1.51 / 1.80	1.48 / 1.76	1.46 / 1.72
48	4.04 / 7.19	3.19 / 5.08	2.80 / 4.22	2.56 / 3.74	2.41 / 3.42	2.30 / 3.20	2.21 / 3.04	2.14 / 2.90	2.08 / 2.80	2.03 / 2.71	1.99 / 2.64	1.96 / 2.58	1.90 / 2.48	1.86 / 2.40	1.79 / 2.28	1.74 / 2.20	1.70 / 2.11	1.64 / 2.02	1.61 / 1.96	1.56 / 1.88	1.53 / 1.84	1.50 / 1.78	1.47 / 1.73	1.45 / 1.70

TABLE 5A *(concluded)*   The *F* Distribution for $\alpha = 0.05$ and $\alpha = 0.01$ for Many Possible Degrees of Freedom

Denominator Degrees of Freedom (k_2)	\multicolumn{24}{c}{Numerator Degrees of Freedom (k_1)}

k_2	1	2	3	4	5	6	7	8	9	10	11	12	14	16	20	24	30	40	50	75	100	200	500	∞
50	4.03 **7.17**	3.18 **5.06**	2.79 **4.20**	2.56 **3.72**	2.40 **3.41**	2.29 **3.18**	2.20 **3.02**	2.13 **2.88**	2.07 **2.78**	2.02 **2.70**	1.98 **2.62**	1.95 **2.56**	1.90 **2.46**	1.85 **2.39**	1.78 **2.26**	1.74 **2.18**	1.69 **2.10**	1.63 **2.00**	1.60 **1.94**	1.55 **1.86**	1.52 **1.82**	1.48 **1.76**	1.46 **1.71**	1.44 **1.68**
55	4.02 **7.12**	3.17 **5.01**	2.78 **4.16**	2.54 **3.68**	2.38 **3.37**	2.27 **3.15**	2.18 **2.98**	2.11 **2.85**	2.05 **2.75**	2.00 **2.66**	1.97 **2.59**	1.93 **2.53**	1.88 **2.43**	1.83 **2.35**	1.76 **2.23**	1.72 **2.15**	1.67 **2.06**	1.61 **1.96**	1.58 **1.90**	1.52 **1.82**	1.50 **1.78**	1.46 **1.71**	1.43 **1.66**	1.41 **1.64**
60	4.00 **7.08**	3.15 **4.98**	2.76 **4.13**	2.52 **3.65**	2.37 **3.34**	2.25 **3.12**	2.17 **2.95**	2.10 **2.82**	2.04 **2.72**	1.99 **2.63**	1.95 **2.56**	1.92 **2.50**	1.86 **2.40**	1.81 **2.32**	1.75 **2.20**	1.70 **2.12**	1.65 **2.03**	1.59 **1.93**	1.56 **1.87**	1.50 **1.79**	1.48 **1.74**	1.44 **1.68**	1.41 **1.63**	1.39 **1.60**
65	3.99 **7.04**	3.14 **4.95**	2.75 **4.10**	2.51 **3.62**	2.36 **3.31**	2.24 **3.09**	2.15 **2.93**	2.08 **2.79**	2.02 **2.70**	1.98 **2.61**	1.94 **2.54**	1.90 **2.47**	1.85 **2.37**	1.80 **2.30**	1.73 **2.18**	1.68 **2.09**	1.63 **2.00**	1.57 **1.90**	1.54 **1.84**	1.49 **1.76**	1.46 **1.71**	1.42 **1.64**	1.39 **1.60**	1.37 **1.56**
70	3.98 **7.01**	3.13 **4.92**	2.74 **4.08**	2.50 **3.60**	2.35 **3.29**	2.23 **3.07**	2.14 **2.91**	2.07 **2.77**	2.01 **2.67**	1.97 **2.59**	1.93 **2.51**	1.89 **2.45**	1.84 **2.35**	1.79 **2.28**	1.72 **2.15**	1.67 **2.07**	1.62 **1.98**	1.56 **1.88**	1.53 **1.82**	1.47 **1.74**	1.45 **1.69**	1.40 **1.62**	1.37 **1.56**	1.35 **1.53**
80	3.96 **6.96**	3.11 **4.88**	2.72 **4.04**	2.48 **3.56**	2.33 **3.25**	2.21 **3.04**	2.12 **2.87**	2.05 **2.74**	1.99 **2.64**	1.95 **2.55**	1.91 **2.48**	1.88 **2.41**	1.82 **2.32**	1.77 **2.24**	1.70 **2.11**	1.65 **2.03**	1.60 **1.94**	1.54 **1.84**	1.51 **1.78**	1.45 **1.70**	1.42 **1.65**	1.38 **1.57**	1.35 **1.52**	1.32 **1.49**
100	3.94 **6.90**	3.09 **4.82**	2.70 **3.98**	2.46 **3.51**	2.30 **3.20**	2.19 **2.99**	2.10 **2.82**	2.03 **2.69**	1.97 **2.59**	1.92 **2.51**	1.88 **2.43**	1.85 **2.36**	1.79 **2.26**	1.75 **2.19**	1.68 **2.06**	1.63 **1.98**	1.57 **1.89**	1.51 **1.79**	1.48 **1.73**	1.42 **1.64**	1.39 **1.59**	1.34 **1.51**	1.30 **1.46**	1.28 **1.43**
125	3.92 **6.84**	3.07 **4.78**	2.68 **3.94**	2.44 **3.47**	2.29 **3.17**	2.17 **2.95**	2.08 **2.79**	2.01 **2.65**	1.95 **2.56**	1.90 **2.47**	1.86 **2.40**	1.83 **2.33**	1.77 **2.23**	1.72 **2.15**	1.65 **2.03**	1.60 **1.94**	1.55 **1.85**	1.49 **1.75**	1.45 **1.68**	1.39 **1.59**	1.36 **1.54**	1.31 **1.46**	1.27 **1.40**	1.25 **1.37**
150	3.91 **6.81**	3.06 **4.75**	2.67 **3.91**	2.43 **3.44**	2.27 **3.14**	2.16 **2.92**	2.07 **2.76**	2.00 **2.62**	1.94 **2.53**	1.89 **2.44**	1.85 **2.37**	1.82 **2.30**	1.76 **2.20**	1.71 **2.12**	1.64 **2.00**	1.59 **1.91**	1.54 **1.83**	1.47 **1.72**	1.44 **1.66**	1.37 **1.56**	1.34 **1.51**	1.29 **1.43**	1.25 **1.37**	1.22 **1.33**
200	3.89 **6.76**	3.04 **4.71**	2.65 **3.88**	2.41 **3.41**	2.26 **3.11**	2.14 **2.90**	2.05 **2.73**	1.98 **2.60**	1.92 **2.50**	1.87 **2.41**	1.83 **2.34**	1.80 **2.28**	1.74 **2.17**	1.69 **2.09**	1.62 **1.97**	1.57 **1.88**	1.52 **1.79**	1.45 **1.69**	1.42 **1.62**	1.35 **1.53**	1.32 **1.48**	1.26 **1.39**	1.22 **1.33**	1.19 **1.28**
400	3.86 **6.70**	3.02 **4.66**	2.62 **3.83**	2.39 **3.36**	2.23 **3.06**	2.12 **2.85**	2.03 **2.69**	1.96 **2.55**	1.90 **2.46**	1.85 **2.37**	1.81 **2.29**	1.78 **2.23**	1.72 **2.12**	1.67 **2.04**	1.60 **1.92**	1.54 **1.84**	1.49 **1.74**	1.42 **1.64**	1.38 **1.57**	1.32 **1.47**	1.28 **1.42**	1.22 **1.32**	1.16 **1.24**	1.13 **1.19**
1,000	3.85 **6.66**	3.00 **4.62**	2.61 **3.80**	2.38 **3.34**	2.22 **3.04**	2.10 **2.82**	2.02 **2.66**	1.95 **2.53**	1.89 **2.43**	1.84 **2.34**	1.80 **2.26**	1.76 **2.20**	1.70 **2.09**	1.65 **2.01**	1.58 **1.89**	1.53 **1.81**	1.47 **1.71**	1.41 **1.61**	1.36 **1.54**	1.30 **1.44**	1.26 **1.38**	1.19 **1.28**	1.13 **1.19**	1.08 **1.11**
∞	3.84 **6.63**	2.99 **4.60**	2.60 **3.78**	2.37 **3.32**	2.21 **3.02**	2.09 **2.80**	2.01 **2.64**	1.94 **2.51**	1.88 **2.41**	1.83 **2.32**	1.79 **2.24**	1.75 **2.18**	1.69 **2.07**	1.64 **1.99**	1.57 **1.87**	1.52 **1.79**	1.46 **1.69**	1.40 **1.59**	1.35 **1.52**	1.28 **1.41**	1.24 **1.36**	1.17 **1.25**	1.11 **1.15**	1.00 **1.00**

Reprinted by permission from *Statistical Methods*, 7th ed. by George W. Snedecor and William G. Cochran, © 1980 by the Iowa State University Press, Ames, Iowa, 50010

TABLE 6 Critical Values of the Studentized Range Distribution for $\alpha = 0.05$

$n-r$	2	3	4	5	6	7	8	9	10	11	12	13	14	15	16	17	18	19	20
1	18.0	27.0	32.8	37.1	40.4	43.1	45.4	47.4	49.1	50.6	52.0	53.2	54.3	55.4	56.3	57.2	58.0	58.8	59.6
2	6.08	8.33	9.80	10.9	11.7	12.4	13.0	13.5	14.0	14.4	14.7	15.1	15.4	15.7	15.9	16.1	16.4	16.6	16.8
3	4.50	5.91	6.82	7.50	8.04	8.48	8.85	9.18	9.46	9.72	9.95	10.2	10.3	10.5	10.7	10.8	11.0	11.1	11.2
4	3.93	5.04	5.76	6.29	6.71	7.05	7.35	7.60	7.83	8.03	8.21	8.37	8.52	8.66	8.79	8.91	9.03	9.13	9.23
5	3.64	4.60	5.22	5.67	6.03	6.33	6.58	6.80	6.99	7.17	7.32	7.47	7.60	7.72	7.83	7.93	8.03	8.12	8.21
6	3.46	4.34	4.90	5.30	5.63	5.90	6.12	6.32	6.49	6.65	6.79	6.92	7.03	7.14	7.24	7.34	7.43	7.51	7.59
7	3.34	4.16	4.68	5.06	5.36	5.61	5.82	6.00	6.16	6.30	6.43	6.55	6.66	6.76	6.85	6.94	7.02	7.10	7.17
8	3.26	4.04	4.53	4.89	5.17	5.40	5.60	5.77	5.92	6.05	6.18	6.29	6.39	6.48	6.57	6.65	6.73	6.80	6.87
9	3.20	3.95	4.41	4.76	5.02	5.24	5.43	5.59	5.74	5.87	5.98	6.09	6.19	6.28	6.36	6.44	6.51	6.58	6.64
10	3.15	3.88	4.33	4.65	4.91	5.12	5.30	5.46	5.60	5.72	5.83	5.93	6.03	6.11	6.19	6.27	6.34	6.40	6.47
11	3.11	3.82	4.26	4.57	4.82	5.03	5.20	5.35	5.49	5.61	5.71	5.81	5.90	5.98	6.06	6.13	6.20	6.27	6.33
12	3.08	3.77	4.20	4.51	4.75	4.95	5.12	5.27	5.39	5.51	5.61	5.71	5.80	5.88	5.95	6.02	6.09	6.15	6.21
13	3.06	3.73	4.15	4.45	4.69	4.88	5.05	5.19	5.32	5.43	5.53	5.63	5.71	5.79	5.86	5.93	5.99	6.05	6.11
14	3.03	3.70	4.11	4.41	4.64	4.83	4.99	5.13	5.25	5.36	5.46	5.55	5.64	5.71	5.79	5.85	5.91	5.97	6.03
15	3.01	3.67	4.08	4.37	4.59	4.78	4.94	5.08	5.20	5.31	5.40	5.49	5.57	5.65	5.72	5.78	5.85	5.90	5.96
16	3.00	3.65	4.05	4.33	4.56	4.74	4.90	5.03	5.15	5.26	5.35	5.44	5.52	5.59	5.66	5.73	5.79	5.84	5.90
17	2.98	3.63	4.02	4.30	4.52	4.70	4.86	4.99	5.11	5.21	5.31	5.39	5.47	5.54	5.61	5.67	5.73	5.79	5.84
18	2.97	3.61	4.00	4.28	4.49	4.67	4.82	4.96	5.07	5.17	5.27	5.35	5.43	5.50	5.57	5.63	5.69	5.74	5.79
19	2.96	3.59	3.98	4.25	4.47	4.65	4.79	4.92	5.04	5.14	5.23	5.31	5.39	5.46	5.53	5.59	5.65	5.70	5.75
20	2.95	3.58	3.96	4.23	4.45	4.62	4.77	4.90	5.01	5.11	5.20	5.28	5.36	5.43	5.49	5.55	5.61	5.66	5.71
24	2.92	3.53	3.90	4.17	4.37	4.54	4.68	4.81	4.92	5.01	5.10	5.18	5.25	5.32	5.38	5.44	5.49	5.55	5.59
30	2.89	3.49	3.85	4.10	4.30	4.46	4.60	4.72	4.82	4.92	5.00	5.08	5.15	5.21	5.27	5.33	5.38	5.43	5.47
40	2.86	3.44	3.79	4.04	4.23	4.39	4.52	4.63	4.73	4.82	4.90	4.98	5.04	5.11	5.16	5.22	5.27	5.31	5.36
60	2.83	3.40	3.74	3.98	4.16	4.31	4.44	4.55	4.65	4.73	4.81	4.88	4.94	5.00	5.06	5.11	5.15	5.20	5.24
120	2.80	3.36	3.68	3.92	4.10	4.24	4.36	4.47	4.56	4.64	4.71	4.78	4.84	4.90	4.95	5.00	5.04	5.09	5.13
∞	2.77	3.31	3.63	3.86	4.03	4.17	4.29	4.39	4.47	4.55	4.62	4.68	4.74	4.80	4.85	4.89	4.93	4.97	5.01

TABLE 6 *(concluded)* **Critical Values of the Studentized Range Distribution for** $\alpha = 0.01$

$n-r$	2	3	4	5	6	7	8	9	10	11	12	13	14	15	16	17	18	19	20
1	90.0	135	164	186	202	216	227	237	246	253	260	266	272	277	282	286	290	294	298
2	14.0	19.0	22.3	24.7	26.6	28.2	29.5	30.7	31.7	32.6	33.4	34.1	34.8	35.4	36.0	36.5	37.0	37.5	37.9
3	8.26	10.6	12.2	13.3	14.2	15.0	15.6	16.2	16.7	17.1	17.5	17.9	18.2	18.5	18.8	19.1	19.3	19.5	19.8
4	6.51	8.12	9.17	9.96	10.6	11.1	11.5	11.9	12.3	12.6	12.8	13.1	13.3	13.6	13.7	13.9	14.1	14.2	14.4
5	5.70	6.97	7.80	8.42	8.91	9.32	9.67	9.97	10.2	10.5	10.7	10.9	11.1	11.2	11.4	11.6	11.7	11.8	11.9
6	5.24	6.33	7.03	7.56	7.97	8.32	8.61	8.87	9.10	9.30	9.49	9.65	9.81	9.95	10.1	10.2	10.3	10.4	10.5
7	4.95	5.92	6.54	7.01	7.37	7.68	7.94	8.17	8.37	8.55	8.71	8.86	9.00	9.12	9.24	9.35	9.46	9.55	9.65
8	4.74	5.63	6.20	6.63	6.96	7.24	7.47	7.68	7.87	8.03	8.18	8.31	8.44	8.55	8.66	8.76	8.85	8.94	9.03
9	4.60	5.43	5.96	6.35	6.66	6.91	7.13	7.32	7.49	7.65	7.78	7.91	8.03	8.13	8.23	8.32	8.41	8.49	8.57
10	4.48	5.27	5.77	6.14	6.43	6.67	6.87	7.05	7.21	7.36	7.48	7.60	7.71	7.81	7.91	7.99	8.07	8.15	8.22
11	4.39	5.14	5.62	5.97	6.25	6.48	6.67	6.84	6.99	7.13	7.25	7.36	7.46	7.56	7.65	7.73	7.81	7.88	7.95
12	4.32	5.04	5.50	5.84	6.10	6.32	6.51	6.67	6.81	6.94	7.06	7.17	7.26	7.36	7.44	7.52	7.59	7.66	7.73
13	4.26	4.96	5.40	5.73	5.98	6.19	6.37	6.53	6.67	6.79	6.90	7.01	7.10	7.19	7.27	7.34	7.42	7.48	7.55
14	4.21	4.89	5.32	5.63	5.88	6.08	6.26	6.41	6.54	6.66	6.77	6.87	6.96	7.05	7.12	7.20	7.27	7.33	7.39
15	4.17	4.83	5.25	5.56	5.80	5.99	6.16	6.31	6.44	6.55	6.66	6.76	6.84	6.93	7.00	7.07	7.14	7.20	7.26
16	4.13	4.78	5.19	5.49	5.72	5.92	6.08	6.22	6.35	6.46	6.56	6.66	6.74	6.82	6.90	6.97	7.03	7.09	7.15
17	4.10	4.74	5.14	5.43	5.66	5.85	6.01	6.15	6.27	6.38	6.48	6.57	6.66	6.73	6.80	6.87	6.94	7.00	7.05
18	4.07	4.70	5.09	5.38	5.60	5.79	5.94	6.08	6.20	6.31	6.41	6.50	6.58	6.65	6.72	6.79	6.85	6.91	6.96
19	4.05	4.67	5.05	5.33	5.55	5.73	5.89	6.02	6.14	6.25	6.34	6.43	6.51	6.58	6.65	6.72	6.78	6.84	6.89
20	4.02	4.64	5.02	5.29	5.51	5.69	5.84	5.97	6.09	6.19	6.29	6.37	6.45	6.52	6.59	6.65	6.71	6.76	6.82
24	3.96	4.54	4.91	5.17	5.37	5.54	5.69	5.81	5.92	6.02	6.11	6.19	6.26	6.33	6.39	6.45	6.51	6.56	6.61
30	3.89	4.45	4.80	5.05	5.24	5.40	5.54	5.65	5.76	5.85	5.93	6.01	6.08	6.14	6.20	6.26	6.31	6.36	6.41
40	3.82	4.37	4.70	4.93	5.11	5.27	5.39	5.50	5.60	5.69	5.77	5.84	5.90	5.96	6.02	6.07	6.12	6.17	6.21
60	3.76	4.28	4.60	4.82	4.99	5.13	5.25	5.36	5.45	5.53	5.60	5.67	5.73	5.79	5.84	5.89	5.93	5.98	6.02
120	3.70	4.20	4.50	4.71	4.87	5.01	5.12	5.21	5.30	5.38	5.44	5.51	5.56	5.61	5.66	5.71	5.75	5.79	5.83
∞	3.64	4.12	4.40	4.60	4.76	4.88	4.99	5.08	5.16	5.23	5.29	5.35	5.40	5.45	5.49	5.54	5.57	5.61	5.65

r

TABLE 7   Critical Values of the Durbin-Watson Test Statistic for $\alpha = 0.05$

	k = 1		*k* = 2		*k* = 3		*k* = 4		*k* = 5	
n	*d$_L$*	*d$_U$*	*d$_L$*	*d$_U$*	*d$_L$*	*d$_U$*	*d$_L$*	*d$_U$*	*d$_L$*	*d$_U$*
15	1.08	1.36	0.95	1.54	0.82	1.75	0.69	1.97	0.56	2.21
16	1.10	1.37	0.98	1.54	0.86	1.73	0.74	1.93	0.62	2.15
17	1.13	1.38	1.02	1.54	0.90	1.71	0.78	1.90	0.67	2.10
18	1.16	1.39	1.05	1.53	0.93	1.69	0.82	1.87	0.71	2.06
19	1.18	1.40	1.08	1.53	0.97	1.68	0.86	1.85	0.75	2.02
20	1.20	1.41	1.10	1.54	1.00	1.68	0.90	1.83	0.79	1.99
21	1.22	1.42	1.13	1.54	1.03	1.67	0.93	1.81	0.83	1.96
22	1.24	1.43	1.15	1.54	1.05	1.66	0.96	1.80	0.86	1.94
23	1.26	1.44	1.17	1.54	1.08	1.66	0.99	1.79	0.90	1.92
24	1.27	1.45	1.19	1.55	1.10	1.66	1.01	1.78	0.93	1.90
25	1.29	1.45	1.21	1.55	1.12	1.66	1.04	1.77	0.95	1.89
26	1.30	1.46	1.22	1.55	1.14	1.65	1.06	1.76	0.98	1.88
27	1.32	1.47	1.24	1.56	1.16	1.65	1.08	1.76	1.01	1.86
28	1.33	1.48	1.26	1.56	1.18	1.65	1.10	1.75	1.03	1.85
29	1.34	1.48	1.27	1.56	1.20	1.65	1.12	1.74	1.05	1.84
30	1.35	1.49	1.28	1.57	1.21	1.65	1.14	1.74	1.07	1.83
31	1.36	1.50	1.30	1.57	1.23	1.65	1.16	1.74	1.09	1.83
32	1.37	1.50	1.31	1.57	1.24	1.65	1.18	1.73	1.11	1.82
33	1.38	1.51	1.32	1.58	1.26	1.65	1.19	1.73	1.13	1.81
34	1.39	1.51	1.33	1.58	1.27	1.65	1.21	1.73	1.15	1.81
35	1.40	1.52	1.34	1.58	1.28	1.65	1.22	1.73	1.16	1.80
36	1.41	1.52	1.35	1.59	1.29	1.65	1.24	1.73	1.18	1.80
37	1.42	1.53	1.36	1.59	1.31	1.66	1.25	1.72	1.19	1.80
38	1.43	1.54	1.37	1.59	1.32	1.66	1.26	1.72	1.21	1.79
39	1.43	1.54	1.38	1.60	1.33	1.66	1.27	1.72	1.22	1.79
40	1.44	1.54	1.39	1.60	1.34	1.66	1.29	1.72	1.23	1.79
45	1.48	1.57	1.43	1.62	1.38	1.67	1.34	1.72	1.29	1.78
50	1.50	1.59	1.46	1.63	1.42	1.67	1.38	1.72	1.34	1.77
55	1.53	1.60	1.49	1.64	1.45	1.68	1.41	1.72	1.38	1.77
60	1.55	1.62	1.51	1.65	1.48	1.69	1.44	1.73	1.41	1.77
65	1.57	1.63	1.54	1.66	1.50	1.70	1.47	1.73	1.44	1.77
70	1.58	1.64	1.55	1.67	1.52	1.70	1.49	1.74	1.46	1.77
75	1.60	1.65	1.57	1.68	1.54	1.71	1.51	1.74	1.49	1.77
80	1.61	1.66	1.59	1.69	1.56	1.72	1.53	1.74	1.51	1.77
85	1.62	1.67	1.60	1.70	1.57	1.72	1.55	1.75	1.52	1.77
90	1.63	1.68	1.61	1.70	1.59	1.73	1.57	1.75	1.54	1.78
95	1.64	1.69	1.62	1.71	1.60	1.73	1.58	1.75	1.56	1.78
100	1.65	1.69	1.63	1.72	1.61	1.74	1.59	1.76	1.57	1.78

TABLE 7 *(concluded)*   **Critical Values of the Durbin-Watson Test Statistic for** $\alpha = 0.01$

	k = 1		k = 2		k = 3		k = 4		k = 5	
n	d_L	d_U	d_L	d_U	d_L	d_U	d_L	d_U	d_L	d_U
15	0.81	1.07	0.70	1.25	0.59	1.46	0.49	1.70	0.39	1.96
16	0.84	1.09	0.74	1.25	0.63	1.44	0.53	1.66	0.44	1.90
17	0.87	1.10	0.77	1.25	0.67	1.43	0.57	1.63	0.48	1.85
18	0.90	1.12	0.80	1.26	0.71	1.42	0.61	1.60	0.52	1.80
19	0.93	1.13	0.83	1.26	0.74	1.41	0.65	1.58	0.56	1.77
20	0.95	1.15	0.86	1.27	0.77	1.41	0.68	1.57	0.60	1.74
21	0.97	1.16	0.89	1.27	0.80	1.41	0.72	1.55	0.63	1.71
22	1.00	1.17	0.91	1.28	0.83	1.40	0.75	1.54	0.66	1.69
23	1.02	1.19	0.94	1.29	0.86	1.40	0.77	1.53	0.70	1.67
24	1.05	1.20	0.96	1.30	0.88	1.41	0.80	1.53	0.72	1.66
25	1.05	1.21	0.98	1.30	0.90	1.41	0.83	1.52	0.75	1.65
26	1.07	1.22	1.00	1.31	0.93	1.41	0.85	1.52	0.78	1.64
27	1.09	1.23	1.02	1.32	0.95	1.41	0.88	1.51	0.81	1.63
28	1.10	1.24	1.04	1.32	0.97	1.41	0.90	1.51	0.83	1.62
29	1.12	1.25	1.05	1.33	0.99	1.42	0.92	1.51	0.85	1.61
30	1.13	1.26	1.07	1.34	1.01	1.42	0.94	1.51	0.88	1.61
31	1.15	1.27	1.08	1.34	1.02	1.42	0.96	1.51	0.90	1.60
32	1.16	1.28	1.10	1.35	1.04	1.43	0.98	1.51	0.92	1.60
33	1.17	1.29	1.11	1.36	1.05	1.43	1.00	1.51	0.94	1.59
34	1.18	1.30	1.13	1.36	1.07	1.43	1.01	1.51	0.95	1.59
35	1.19	1.31	1.14	1.37	1.08	1.44	1.03	1.51	0.97	1.59
36	1.21	1.32	1.15	1.38	1.10	1.44	1.04	1.51	0.99	1.59
37	1.22	1.32	1.16	1.38	1.11	1.45	1.06	1.51	1.00	1.59
38	1.23	1.33	1.18	1.39	1.12	1.45	1.07	1.52	1.02	1.58
39	1.24	1.34	1.19	1.39	1.14	1.45	1.09	1.52	1.03	1.58
40	1.25	1.34	1.20	1.40	1.15	1.46	1.10	1.52	1.05	1.58
45	1.29	1.38	1.24	1.42	1.20	1.48	1.16	1.53	1.11	1.58
50	1.32	1.40	1.28	1.45	1.24	1.49	1.20	1.54	1.16	1.59
55	1.36	1.43	1.32	1.47	1.28	1.51	1.25	1.55	1.21	1.59
60	1.38	1.45	1.35	1.48	1.32	1.52	1.28	1.56	1.25	1.60
65	1.41	1.47	1.38	1.50	1.35	1.53	1.31	1.57	1.28	1.61
70	1.43	1.49	1.40	1.52	1.37	1.55	1.34	1.58	1.31	1.61
75	1.45	1.50	1.42	1.53	1.39	1.56	1.37	1.59	1.34	1.62
80	1.47	1.52	1.44	1.54	1.42	1.57	1.39	1.60	1.36	1.62
85	1.48	1.53	1.46	1.55	1.43	1.58	1.41	1.60	1.39	1.63
90	1.50	1.54	1.47	1.56	1.45	1.59	1.43	1.61	1.41	1.64
95	1.51	1.55	1.49	1.57	1.47	1.60	1.45	1.62	1.42	1.64
100	1.52	1.56	1.50	1.58	1.48	1.60	1.46	1.63	1.44	1.65

Reproduced by permission from J. Durbin and G. S. Watson, "Testing for Serial Correlation in Least Squares Regression, II," *Biometrika* 38 (1951), pp. 159–78.

TABLE 8   Cumulative Distribution Function: $F(r)$ for the Total Number of Runs R in Samples of Sizes n_1 and n_2

	Number of Runs, r								
(n_1, n_2)	2	3	4	5	6	7	8	9	10
(2,3)	0.200	0.500	0.900	1.000					
(2,4)	0.133	0.400	0.800	1.000					
(2,5)	0.095	0.333	0.714	1.000					
(2,6)	0.071	0.286	0.643	1.000					
(2,7)	0.056	0.250	0.583	1.000					
(2,8)	0.044	0.222	0.533	1.000					
(2,9)	0.036	0.200	0.491	1.000					
(2,10)	0.030	0.182	0.455	1.000					
(3,3)	0.100	0.300	0.700	0.900	1.000				
(3,4)	0.057	0.200	0.543	0.800	0.971	1.000			
(3,5)	0.036	0.143	0.429	0.714	0.929	1.000			
(3,6)	0.024	0.107	0.345	0.643	0.881	1.000			
(3,7)	0.017	0.083	0.283	0.583	0.833	1.000			
(3,8)	0.012	0.067	0.236	0.533	0.788	1.000			
(3,9)	0.009	0.055	0.200	0.491	0.745	1.000			
(3,10)	0.007	0.045	0.171	0.455	0.706	1.000			
(4,4)	0.029	0.114	0.371	0.629	0.886	0.971	1.000		
(4,5)	0.016	0.071	0.262	0.500	0.786	0.929	0.992	1.000	
(4,6)	0.010	0.048	0.190	0.405	0.690	0.881	0.976	1.000	
(4,7)	0.006	0.033	0.142	0.333	0.606	0.833	0.954	1.000	
(4,8)	0.004	0.024	0.109	0.279	0.533	0.788	0.929	1.000	
(4,9)	0.003	0.018	0.085	0.236	0.471	0.745	0.902	1.000	
(4,10)	0.002	0.014	0.068	0.203	0.419	0.706	0.874	1.000	
(5,5)	0.008	0.040	0.167	0.357	0.643	0.833	0.960	0.992	1.000
(5,6)	0.004	0.024	0.110	0.262	0.522	0.738	0.911	0.976	0.998
(5,7)	0.003	0.015	0.076	0.197	0.424	0.652	0.854	0.955	0.992
(5,8)	0.002	0.010	0.054	0.152	0.347	0.576	0.793	0.929	0.984
(5,9)	0.001	0.007	0.039	0.119	0.287	0.510	0.734	0.902	0.972
(5,10)	0.001	0.005	0.029	0.095	0.239	0.455	0.678	0.874	0.958
(6,6)	0.002	0.013	0.067	0.175	0.392	0.608	0.825	0.933	0.987
(6,7)	0.001	0.008	0.043	0.121	0.296	0.500	0.733	0.879	0.966
(6,8)	0.001	0.005	0.028	0.086	0.226	0.413	0.646	0.821	0.937
(6,9)	0.000	0.003	0.019	0.063	0.175	0.343	0.566	0.762	0.902
(6,10)	0.000	0.002	0.013	0.047	0.137	0.288	0.497	0.706	0.864
(7,7)	0.001	0.004	0.025	0.078	0.209	0.383	0.617	0.791	0.922
(7,8)	0.000	0.002	0.015	0.051	0.149	0.296	0.514	0.704	0.867
(7,9)	0.000	0.001	0.010	0.035	0.108	0.231	0.427	0.622	0.806
(7,10)	0.000	0.001	0.006	0.024	0.080	0.182	0.355	0.549	0.743
(8,8)	0.000	0.001	0.009	0.032	0.100	0.214	0.405	0.595	0.786
(8,9)	0.000	0.001	0.005	0.020	0.069	0.157	0.319	0.500	0.702
(8,10)	0.000	0.000	0.003	0.013	0.048	0.117	0.251	0.419	0.621
(9,9)	0.000	0.000	0.003	0.012	0.044	0.109	0.238	0.399	0.601
(9,10)	0.000	0.000	0.002	0.008	0.029	0.077	0.179	0.319	0.510
(10,10)	0.000	0.000	0.001	0.004	0.019	0.051	0.128	0.242	0.414

TABLE 8 *(concluded)*   **Cumulative Distribution Function: $F(r)$ for the Total Number of Runs R in Samples of Sizes n_1 and n_2**

					Number of Runs, r					
(n_1, n_2)	11	12	13	14	15	16	17	18	19	20
(2,3)										
(2,4)										
(2,5)										
(2,6)										
(2,7)										
(2,8)										
(2,9)										
(2,10)										
(3,3)										
(3,4)										
(3,5)										
(3,6)										
(3,7)										
(3,8)										
(3,9)										
(3,10)										
(4,4)										
(4,5)										
(4,6)										
(4,7)										
(4,8)										
(4,9)										
(4,10)										
(5,5)										
(5,6)	1.000									
(5,7)	1.000									
(5,8)	1.000									
(5,9)	1.000									
(5,10)	1.000									
(6,6)	0.998	1.000								
(6,7)	0.992	0.999	1.000							
(6,8)	0.984	0.998	1.000							
(6,9)	0.972	0.994	1.000							
(6,10)	0.958	0.990	1.000							
(7,7)	0.975	0.996	0.999	1.000						
(7,8)	0.949	0.988	0.998	1.000	1.000					
(7,9)	0.916	0.975	0.994	0.999	1.000					
(7,10)	0.879	0.957	0.990	0.998	1.000					
(8,8)	0.900	0.968	0.991	0.999	1.000	1.000				
(8,9)	0.843	0.939	0.980	0.996	0.999	1.000	1.000			
(8,10)	0.782	0.903	0.964	0.990	0.998	1.000	1.000			
(9,9)	0.762	0.891	0.956	0.988	0.997	1.000	1.000	1.000		
(9,10)	0.681	0.834	0.923	0.974	0.992	0.999	1.000	1.000	1.000	
(10,10)	0.586	0.758	0.872	0.949	0.981	0.996	0.999	1.000	1.000	1.000

Reproduced from F. Swed and C. Eisenhart, "Tables for Testing Randomness of Grouping in a Sequence of Alternatives," *Annals of Mathematical Statistics* 14 (1943) by permission of the authors and of the Editor, *Annals of Mathematical Statistics*.

TABLE 9 Cumulative Distribution Function of the Mann-Whitney U Statistic: $F(u)$ for $n_1 \le n_2$ and $3 \le n_2 \le 10$

$n_2 = 3$

u	n_1 1	2	3
0	0.25	0.10	0.05
1	0.50	0.20	0.10
2		0.40	0.20
3		0.60	0.35
4			0.50

$n_2 = 4$

u	n_1 1	2	3	4
0	0.2000	0.0667	0.0286	0.0143
1	0.4000	0.1333	0.0571	0.0286
2	0.6000	0.2667	0.1143	0.0571
3		0.4000	0.2000	0.1000
4		0.6000	0.3143	0.1714
5			0.4286	0.2429
6			0.5714	0.3429
7				0.4429
8				0.5571

$n_2 = 5$

u	n_1 1	2	3	4	5
0	0.1667	0.0476	0.0179	0.0079	0.0040
1	0.3333	0.0952	0.0357	0.0159	0.0079
2	0.5000	0.1905	0.0714	0.0317	0.0159
3		0.2857	0.1250	0.0556	0.0278
4		0.4286	0.1964	0.0952	0.0476
5		0.5714	0.2857	0.1429	0.0754
6			0.3929	0.2063	0.1111
7			0.5000	0.2778	0.1548
8				0.3651	0.2103
9				0.4524	0.2738
10				0.5476	0.3452
11					0.4206
12					0.5000

TABLE 9 *(continued)* **Cumulative Distribution Function of the Mann-Whitney *U* Statistic: *F(u)* for $n_1 \le n_2$ and $3 \le n_2 \le 10$**

$n_2 = 6$
n_1

u	1	2	3	4	5	6
0	0.1429	0.0357	0.0119	0.0048	0.0022	0.0011
1	0.2857	0.0714	0.0238	0.0095	0.0043	0.0022
2	0.4286	0.1429	0.0476	0.0190	0.0087	0.0043
3	0.5714	0.2143	0.0833	0.0333	0.0152	0.0076
4		0.3214	0.1310	0.0571	0.0260	0.0130
5		0.4286	0.1905	0.0857	0.0411	0.0206
6		0.5714	0.2738	0.1286	0.0628	0.0325
7			0.3571	0.1762	0.0887	0.0465
8			0.4524	0.2381	0.1234	0.0660
9			0.5476	0.3048	0.1645	0.0898
10				0.3810	0.2143	0.1201
11				0.4571	0.2684	0.1548
12				0.5429	0.3312	0.1970
13					0.3961	0.2424
14					0.4654	0.2944
15					0.5346	0.3496
16						0.4091
17						0.4686
18						0.5314

$n_2 = 7$
n_1

u	1	2	3	4	5	6	7
0	0.1250	0.0278	0.0083	0.0030	0.0013	0.0006	0.0003
1	0.2500	0.0556	0.0167	0.0061	0.0025	0.0012	0.0006
2	0.3750	0.1111	0.0333	0.0121	0.0051	0.0023	0.0012
3	0.5000	0.1667	0.0583	0.0212	0.0088	0.0041	0.0020
4		0.2500	0.0917	0.0364	0.0152	0.0070	0.0035
5		0.3333	0.1333	0.0545	0.0240	0.0111	0.0055
6		0.4444	0.1917	0.0818	0.0366	0.0175	0.0087
7		0.5556	0.2583	0.1152	0.0530	0.0256	0.0131
8			0.3333	0.1576	0.0745	0.0367	0.0189
9			0.4167	0.2061	0.1010	0.0507	0.0265
10			0.5000	0.2636	0.1338	0.0688	0.0364
11				0.3242	0.1717	0.0903	0.0487
12				0.3939	0.2159	0.1171	0.0641
13				0.4636	0.2652	0.1474	0.0825
14				0.5364	0.3194	0.1830	0.1043
15					0.3775	0.2226	0.1297
16					0.4381	0.2669	0.1588
17					0.5000	0.3141	0.1914
18						0.3654	0.2279
19						0.4178	0.2675
20						0.4726	0.3100
21						0.5274	0.3552
22							0.4024
23							0.4508
24							0.5000

| | | | | $n_2 = 8$ | | | | |
| | | | | n_1 | | | | |
u	1	2	3	4	5	6	7	8
0	0.1111	0.0222	0.0061	0.0020	0.0008	0.0003	0.0002	0.0001
1	0.2222	0.0444	0.0121	0.0040	0.0016	0.0007	0.0003	0.0002
2	0.3333	0.0889	0.0242	0.0081	0.0031	0.0013	0.0006	0.0003
3	0.4444	0.1333	0.0424	0.0141	0.0054	0.0023	0.0011	0.0005
4	0.5556	0.2000	0.0667	0.0242	0.0093	0.0040	0.0019	0.0009
5		0.2667	0.0970	0.0364	0.0148	0.0063	0.0030	0.0015
6		0.3556	0.1394	0.0545	0.0225	0.0100	0.0047	0.0023
7		0.4444	0.1879	0.0768	0.0326	0.0147	0.0070	0.0035
8		0.5556	0.2485	0.1071	0.0466	0.0213	0.0103	0.0052
9			0.3152	0.1414	0.0637	0.0296	0.0145	0.0074
10			0.3879	0.1838	0.0855	0.0406	0.0200	0.0103
11			0.4606	0.2303	0.1111	0.0539	0.0270	0.0141
12			0.5394	0.2848	0.1422	0.0709	0.0361	0.0190
13				0.3414	0.1772	0.0906	0.0469	0.0249
14				0.4040	0.2176	0.1142	0.0603	0.0325
15				0.4667	0.2618	0.1412	0.0760	0.0415
16				0.5333	0.3108	0.1725	0.0946	0.0524
17					0.3621	0.2068	0.1159	0.0652
18					0.4165	0.2454	0.1405	0.0803
19					0.4716	0.2864	0.1678	0.0974
20					0.5284	0.3310	0.1984	0.1172
21						0.3773	0.2317	0.1393
22						0.4259	0.2679	0.1641
23						0.4749	0.3063	0.1911
24						0.5251	0.3472	0.2209
25							0.3894	0.2527
26							0.4333	0.2869
27							0.4775	0.3227
28							0.5225	0.3605
29								0.3992
30								0.4392
31								0.4796
32								0.5204

TABLE 9 *(concluded)*   **Cumulative Distribution Function of the Mann-Whitney *U* Statistic: *F(u)* for $n_1 \leq n_2$ and $3 \leq n_2 \leq 10$**

					$n_2 = 9$				
					n_1				
u	1	2	3	4	5	6	7	8	9
0	0.1000	0.0182	0.0045	0.0014	0.0005	0.0002	0.0001	0.0000	0.0000
1	0.2000	0.0364	0.0091	0.0028	0.0010	0.0004	0.0002	0.0001	0.0000
2	0.3000	0.0727	0.0182	0.0056	0.0020	0.0008	0.0003	0.0002	0.0001
3	0.4000	0.1091	0.0318	0.0098	0.0035	0.0014	0.0006	0.0003	0.0001
4	0.5000	0.1636	0.0500	0.0168	0.0060	0.0024	0.0010	0.0005	0.0002
5		0.2182	0.0727	0.0252	0.0095	0.0038	0.0017	0.0008	0.0004
6		0.2909	0.1045	0.0378	0.0145	0.0060	0.0026	0.0012	0.0006
7		0.3636	0.1409	0.0531	0.0210	0.0088	0.0039	0.0019	0.0009
8		0.4545	0.1864	0.0741	0.0300	0.0128	0.0058	0.0028	0.0014
9		0.5455	0.2409	0.0993	0.0415	0.0180	0.0082	0.0039	0.0020
10			0.3000	0.1301	0.0559	0.0248	0.0115	0.0056	0.0028
11			0.3636	0.1650	0.0734	0.0332	0.0156	0.0076	0.0039
12			0.4318	0.2070	0.0949	0.0440	0.0209	0.0103	0.0053
13			0.5000	0.2517	0.1199	0.0567	0.0274	0.0137	0.0071
14				0.3021	0.1489	0.0723	0.0356	0.0180	0.0094
15				0.3552	0.1818	0.0905	0.0454	0.0232	0.0122
16				0.4126	0.2188	0.1119	0.0571	0.0296	0.0157
17				0.4699	0.2592	0.1361	0.0708	0.0372	0.0200
18				0.5301	0.3032	0.1638	0.0869	0.0464	0.0252
19					0.3497	0.1924	0.1052	0.0570	0.0313
20					0.3986	0.2280	0.1261	0.0694	0.0385
21					0.4491	0.2643	0.1496	0.0836	0.0470
22					0.5000	0.3035	0.1755	0.0998	0.0567
23						0.3445	0.2039	0.1179	0.0680
24						0.3878	0.2349	0.1383	0.0807
25						0.4320	0.2680	0.1606	0.0951
26						0.4773	0.3032	0.1852	0.1112
27						0.5227	0.3403	0.2117	0.1290
28							0.3788	0.2404	0.1487
29							0.4185	0.2707	0.1701
30							0.4591	0.3029	0.1933
31							0.5000	0.3365	0.2181
32								0.3715	0.2447
33								0.4074	0.2729
34								0.4442	0.3024
35								0.4813	0.3332
36								0.5187	0.3652
37									0.3981
38									0.4317
39									0.4657
40									0.5000

$n_2 = 10$

n_1

u	1	2	3	4	5	6	7	8	9	10
0	0.0909	0.0152	0.0035	0.0010	0.0003	0.0001	0.0001	0.0000	0.0000	0.0000
1	0.1818	0.0303	0.0070	0.0020	0.0007	0.0002	0.0001	0.0000	0.0000	0.0000
2	0.2727	0.0606	0.0140	0.0040	0.0013	0.0005	0.0002	0.0001	0.0000	0.0000
3	0.3636	0.0909	0.0245	0.0070	0.0023	0.0009	0.0004	0.0002	0.0001	0.0000
4	0.4545	0.1364	0.0385	0.0120	0.0040	0.0015	0.0006	0.0003	0.0001	0.0001
5	0.5455	0.1818	0.0559	0.0180	0.0063	0.0024	0.0010	0.0004	0.0002	0.0001
6		0.2424	0.0804	0.0270	0.0097	0.0037	0.0015	0.0007	0.0003	0.0002
7		0.3030	0.1084	0.0380	0.0140	0.0055	0.0023	0.0010	0.0005	0.0002
8		0.3788	0.1434	0.0529	0.0200	0.0080	0.0034	0.0015	0.0007	0.0004
9		0.4545	0.1853	0.0709	0.0276	0.0112	0.0048	0.0022	0.0011	0.0005
10		0.5455	0.2343	0.0939	0.0376	0.0156	0.0068	0.0031	0.0015	0.0008
11			0.2867	0.1199	0.0496	0.0210	0.0093	0.0043	0.0021	0.0010
12			0.3462	0.1518	0.0646	0.0280	0.0125	0.0058	0.0028	0.0014
13			0.4056	0.1868	0.0823	0.0363	0.0165	0.0078	0.0038	0.0019
14			0.4685	0.2268	0.1032	0.0467	0.0215	0.0103	0.0051	0.0026
15			0.5315	0.2697	0.1272	0.0589	0.0277	0.0133	0.0066	0.0034
16				0.3177	0.1548	0.0736	0.0351	0.0171	0.0086	0.0045
17				0.3666	0.1855	0.0903	0.0439	0.0217	0.0110	0.0057
18				0.4196	0.2198	0.1099	0.0544	0.0273	0.0140	0.0073
19				0.4725	0.2567	0.1317	0.0665	0.0338	0.0175	0.0093
20				0.5275	0.2970	0.1566	0.0806	0.0416	0.0217	0.0116
21					0.3393	0.1838	0.0966	0.0506	0.0267	0.0144
22					0.3839	0.2139	0.1148	0.0610	0.0326	0.0177
23					0.4296	0.2461	0.1349	0.0729	0.0394	0.0216
24					0.4765	0.2811	0.1574	0.0864	0.0474	0.0262
25					0.5235	0.3177	0.1819	0.1015	0.0564	0.0315
26						0.3564	0.2087	0.1185	0.0667	0.0376
27						0.3962	0.2374	0.1371	0.0782	0.0446
28						0.4374	0.2681	0.1577	0.0912	0.0526
29						0.4789	0.3004	0.1800	0.1055	0.0615
30						0.5211	0.3345	0.2041	0.1214	0.0716
31							0.3698	0.2299	0.1388	0.0827
32							0.4063	0.2574	0.1577	0.0952
33							0.4434	0.2863	0.1781	0.1088
34							0.4811	0.3167	0.2001	0.1237
35							0.5189	0.3482	0.2235	0.1399
36								0.3809	0.2483	0.1575
37								0.4143	0.2745	0.1763
38								0.4484	0.3019	0.1965
39								0.4827	0.3304	0.2179
40								0.5173	0.3598	0.2406
41									0.3901	0.2644
42									0.4211	0.2894
43									0.4524	0.3153
44									0.4841	0.3421
45									0.5159	0.3697
46										0.3980
47										0.4267
48										0.4559
49										0.4853
50										0.5147

TABLE 10   Critical Values of the Wilcoxon *T* Statistic

One-Tailed	Two-Tailed	*n* = 5	*n* = 6	*n* = 7	*n* = 8	*n* = 9	*n* = 10
P = 0.05	*P* = 0.10	1	2	4	6	8	11
P = 0.025	*P* = 0.05		1	2	4	6	8
P = 0.01	*P* = 0.02			0	2	3	5
P = 0.005	*P* = 0.01				0	2	3

One-Tailed	Two-Tailed	*n* = 11	*n* = 12	*n* = 13	*n* = 14	*n* = 15	*n* = 16
p = 0.05	*P* = 0.10	14	17	21	26	30	36
P = 0.025	*P* = 0.05	11	14	17	21	25	30
P = 0.01	*P* = 0.02	7	10	13	16	20	24
P = 0.005	*P* = 0.01	5	7	10	13	16	19

One-Tailed	Two-Tailed	*n* = 17	*n* = 18	*n* = 19	*n* = 20	*n* = 21	*n* = 22
P = 0.05	*P* = 0.10	41	47	54	60	68	75
P = 0.025	*P* = 0.05	35	40	46	52	59	66
P = 0.01	*P* = 0.02	28	33	38	43	49	56
P = 0.005	*P* = 0.01	23	28	32	37	43	49

One-Tailed	Two-Tailed	*n* = 23	*n* = 24	*n* = 25	*n* = 26	*n* = 27	*n* = 28
P = 0.05	*P* = 0.10	83	92	101	110	120	130
P = 0.025	*P* = 0.05	73	81	90	98	107	117
P = 0.01	*P* = 0.02	62	69	77	85	93	102
P = 0.005	*P* = 0.01	55	68	68	76	84	92

One-Tailed	Two-Tailed	*n* = 29	*n* = 30	*n* = 31	*n* = 32	*n* = 33	*n* = 34
P = 0.05	*P* = 0.10	141	152	163	175	188	201
P = 0.025	*P* = 0.05	127	137	148	159	171	183
P = 0.01	*P* = 0.02	111	120	130	141	151	162
P = 0.005	*P* = 0.01	100	109	118	128	138	149

One-Tailed	Two-Tailed	*n* = 35	*n* = 36	*n* = 37	*n* = 38	*n* = 39	
P = 0.05	*P* = 0.10	214	228	242	256	271	
P = 0.025	*P* = 0.05	195	208	222	235	250	
P = 0.01	*P* = 0.02	174	186	198	211	224	
P = 0.005	*P* = 0.01	160	171	183	195	208	

One-Tailed	Two-Tailed	*n* = 40	*n* = 41	*n* = 42	*n* = 43	*n* = 44	*n* = 45
P = 0.05	*P* = 0.10	287	303	319	336	353	371
P = 0.025	*P* = 0.05	264	279	295	311	327	344
P = 0.01	*P* = 0.02	238	252	267	281	297	313
P = 0.005	*P* = 0.01	221	234	248	262	277	292

One-Tailed	Two-Tailed	*n* = 46	*n* = 47	*n* = 48	*n* = 49	*n* = 50	
P = 0.05	*P* = 0.10	389	408	427	446	466	
P = 0.025	*P* = 0.05	361	379	397	415	434	
P = 0.01	*P* = 0.02	329	345	362	380	398	
P = 0.005	*P* = 0.01	307	323	339	356	373	

TABLE 11   Critical Values of Spearman's Rank Correlation Coefficient

n	$\alpha = 0.05$	$\alpha = 0.025$	$\alpha = 0.01$	$\alpha = 0.005$
5	0.900	—	—	—
6	0.829	0.886	0.943	—
7	0.714	0.786	0.893	—
8	0.643	0.738	0.833	0.881
9	0.600	0.683	0.783	0.833
10	0.564	0.648	0.745	0.794
11	0.523	0.623	0.736	0.818
12	0.497	0.591	0.703	0.780
13	0.475	0.566	0.673	0.745
14	0.457	0.545	0.646	0.716
15	0.441	0.525	0.623	0.689
16	0.425	0.507	0.601	0.666
17	0.412	0.490	0.582	0.645
18	0.399	0.476	0.564	0.625
19	0.388	0.462	0.549	0.608
20	0.377	0.450	0.534	0.591
21	0.368	0.438	0.521	0.576
22	0.359	0.428	0.508	0.562
23	0.351	0.418	0.496	0.549
24	0.343	0.409	0.485	0.537
25	0.336	0.400	0.475	0.526
26	0.329	0.392	0.465	0.515
27	0.323	0.385	0.456	0.505
28	0.317	0.377	0.448	0.496
29	0.311	0.370	0.440	0.487
30	0.305	0.364	0.432	0.478

Reproduced by permission from E. G. Olds, "Distribution of Sums of Squares of Rank Differences for Small Samples," *Annals of Mathematical Statistics* 9 (1938).

TABLE 12   Poisson Probability Distribution

This table gives values of

$$P(x) = \frac{\mu^x e^{-\mu}}{x!}$$

| | | | | | μ | | | | | |
x	.005	.01	.02	.03	.04	.05	.06	.07	.08	.09
0	.9950	.9900	.9802	.9704	.9608	.9512	.9418	.9324	.9231	.9139
1	.0050	.0099	.0192	.0291	.0384	.0476	.0565	.0653	.0738	.0823
2	.0000	.0000	.0002	.0004	.0008	.0012	.0017	.0023	.0030	.0037
3	.0000	.0000	.0000	.0000	.0000	.0000	.0000	.0001	.0001	.0001

| | | | | | μ | | | | | |
x	0.1	0.2	0.3	0.4	0.5	0.6	0.7	0.8	0.9	1.0
0	.9048	.8187	.7408	.6703	.6065	.5488	.4966	.4493	.4066	.3679
1	.0905	.1637	.2222	.2681	.3033	.3293	.3476	.3595	.3659	.3679
2	.0045	.0164	.0333	.0536	.0758	.0988	.1217	.1438	.1647	.1839
3	.0002	.0011	.0033	.0072	.0126	.0198	.0284	.0383	.0494	.0613
4	.0000	.0001	.0002	.0007	.0016	.0030	.0050	.0077	.0111	.0153
5	.0000	.0000	.0000	.0001	.0002	.0004	.0007	.0012	.0020	.0031
6	.0000	.0000	.0000	.0000	.0000	.0000	.0001	.0002	.0003	.0005
7	.0000	.0000	.0000	.0000	.0000	.0000	.0000	0000	.0000	.0001

| | | | | | μ | | | | | |
x	1.1	1.2	1.3	1.4	1.5	1.6	1.7	1.8	1.9	2.0
0	.3329	.3012	.2725	.2466	.2231	.2019	.1827	.1653	.1496	.1353
1	.3662	.3614	.3543	.3452	.3347	.3230	.3106	.2975	.2842	.2707
2	.2014	.2169	.2303	.2417	.2510	.2584	.2640	.2678	.2700	.2707
3	.0738	.0867	.0998	.1128	.1255	.1378	.1496	.1607	.1710	.1804
4	.0203	.0260	.0324	.0395	.0471	.0551	.0636	.0723	.0812	.0902
5	.0045	.0062	.0084	.0111	.0141	.0176	.0216	.0260	.0309	.0361
6	.0008	.0012	.0018	.0026	.0035	.0047	.0061	.0078	.0098	.0120
7	.0001	.0002	.0003	.0005	.0008	.0011	.0015	.0020	.0027	.0034
8	.0000	.0000	.0001	.0001	.0001	.0002	.0003	.0005	.0006	.0009
9	.0000	.0000	.0000	.0000	.0000	.0000	.0001	.0001	.0001	.0002

| | | | | | μ | | | | | |
x	2.1	2.2	2.3	2.4	2.5	2.6	2.7	2.8	2.9	3.0
0	.1225	.1108	.1003	.0907	.0821	.0743	.0672	.0608	.0550	.0498
1	.2572	.2438	.2306	.2177	.2052	.1931	.1815	.1703	.1596	.1494
2	.2700	.2681	.2652	.2613	.2565	.2510	.2450	.2384	.2314	.2240
3	.1890	.1966	.2033	.2090	.2138	.2176	.2205	.2225	.2237	.2240
4	.0992	.1082	.1169	.1254	.1336	.1414	.1488	.1557	.1622	.1680

					μ					
x	**2.1**	**2.2**	**2.3**	**2.4**	**2.5**	**2.6**	**2.7**	**2.8**	**2.9**	**3.0**
5	.0417	.0476	.0538	.0602	.0668	.0735	.0804	.0872	.0940	.1008
6	.0146	.0174	.0206	.0241	.0278	.0319	.0362	.0407	.0455	.0504
7	.0044	.0055	.0068	.0083	.0099	.0118	.0139	.0163	.0188	.0216
8	.0011	.0015	.0019	.0025	.0031	.0038	.0047	.0057	.0068	.0081
9	.0003	.0004	.0005	.0007	.0009	.0011	.0014	.0018	.0022	.0027
10	.0001	.0001	.0001	.0002	.0002	.0003	.0004	.0005	.0006	.0008
11	.0000	.0000	.0000	.0000	.0000	.0001	.0001	.0001	.0002	.0002
12	.0000	.0000	.0000	.0000	.0000	.0000	.0000	.0000	.0000	.0001

					μ					
x	**3.1**	**3.2**	**3.3**	**3.4**	**3.5**	**3.6**	**3.7**	**3.8**	**3.9**	**4.0**
0	.0450	.0408	.0369	.0334	.0302	.0273	.0247	.0224	.0202	.0183
1	.1397	.1304	.1217	.1135	.1057	.0984	.0915	.0850	.0789	.0733
2	.2165	.2087	.2008	.1929	.1850	.1771	.1692	.1615	.1539	.1465
3	.2237	.2226	.2209	.2186	.2158	.2125	.2087	.2046	.2001	.1954
4	.1734	.1781	.1823	.1858	.1888	.1912	.1931	.1944	.1951	.1954
5	.1075	.1140	.1203	.1264	.1322	.1377	.1429	.1477	.1522	.1563
6	.0555	.0608	.0662	.0716	.0771	.0826	.0881	.0936	.0989	.1042
7	.0246	.0278	.0312	.0348	.0385	.0425	.0466	.0508	.0551	.0595
8	.0095	.0111	.0129	.0148	.0169	.0191	.0215	.0241	.0269	.0298
9	.0033	.0040	.0047	.0056	.0066	.0076	.0089	.0102	.0116	.0132
10	.0010	.0013	.0016	.0019	.0023	.0028	.0033	.0039	.0045	.0053
11	.0003	.0004	.0005	.0006	.0007	.0009	.0011	.0013	.0016	.0019
12	.0001	.0001	.0001	.0002	.0002	.0003	.0003	.0004	.0005	.0006
13	.0000	.0000	.0000	.0000	.0001	.0001	.0001	.0001	.0002	.0002
14	.0000	.0000	.0000	.0000	.0000	.0000	.0000	.0000	.0000	.0001

					μ					
x	**4.1**	**4.2**	**4.3**	**4.4**	**4.5**	**4.6**	**4.7**	**4.8**	**4.9**	**5.0**
0	.0166	.0150	.0136	.0123	.0111	.0101	.0091	.0082	.0074	.0067
1	.0679	.0630	.0583	.0540	.0500	.0462	.0427	.0395	.0365	.0337
2	.1393	.1323	.1254	.1188	.1125	.1063	.1005	.0948	.0894	.0842
3	.1904	.1852	.1798	.1743	.1687	.1631	.1574	.1517	.1460	.1404
4	.1951	.1944	.1933	.1917	.1898	.1875	.1849	.1820	.1789	.1755
5	.1600	.1633	.1662	.1687	.1708	.1725	.1738	.1747	.1753	.1755
6	.1093	.1143	.1191	.1237	.1281	.1323	.1362	.1398	.1432	.1462
7	.0640	.0686	.0732	.0778	.0824	.0869	.0914	.0959	.1002	.1044
8	.0328	.0360	.0393	.0428	.0463	.0500	.0537	.0575	.0614	.0653
9	.0150	.0168	.0188	.0209	.0232	.0255	.0280	.0307	.0334	.0363

TABLE 12 *(concluded)*   **Poisson Probability Distribution**

	μ									
x	4.1	4.2	4.3	4.4	4.5	4.6	4.7	4.8	4.9	5.0
10	.0061	.0071	.0081	.0092	.0104	.0118	.0132	.0147	.0164	.0181
11	.0023	.0027	.0032	.0037	.0043	.0049	.0056	.0064	.0073	.0082
12	.0008	.0009	.0011	.0014	.0016	.0019	.0022	.0026	.0030	.0034
13	.0002	.0003	.0004	.0005	.0006	.0007	.0008	.0009	.0011	.0013
14	.0001	.0001	.0001	.0001	.0002	.0002	.0003	.0003	.0004	.0005
15	.0000	.0000	.0000	.0000	.0001	.0001	.0001	.0001	.0001	.0002

	μ									
x	5.1	5.2	5.3	5.4	5.5	5.6	5.7	5.8	5.9	6.0
0	.0061	.0055	.0050	.0045	.0041	.0037	.0033	.0030	.0027	.0025
1	.0311	.0287	.0265	.0244	.0225	.0207	.0191	.0176	.0162	.0149
2	.0793	.0746	.0701	.0659	.0618	.0580	.0544	.0509	.0477	.0446
3	.1348	.1293	.1239	.1185	.1133	.1082	.1033	.0985	.0938	.0892
4	.1719	.1681	.1641	.1600	.1558	.1515	.1472	.1428	.1383	.1339
5	.1753	.1748	.1740	.1728	.1714	.1697	.1678	.1656	.1632	.1606
6	.1490	.1515	.1537	.1555	.1571	.1584	.1594	.1601	.1605	.1606
7	.1086	.1125	.1163	.1200	.1234	.1267	.1298	.1326	.1353	.1377
8	.0692	.0731	.0771	.0810	.0849	.0887	.0925	.0962	.0998	.1033
9	.0392	.0423	.0454	.0486	.0519	.0552	.0586	.0620	.0654	.0688
10	.0200	.0220	.0241	.0262	.0285	.0309	.0334	.0359	.0386	.0413
11	.0093	.0104	.0116	.0129	.0143	.0157	.0173	.0190	.0207	.0225
12	.0039	.0045	.0051	.0058	.0065	.0073	.0082	.0092	.0102	.0113
13	.0015	.0018	.0021	.0024	.0028	.0032	.0036	.0041	.0046	.0052
14	.0006	.0007	.0008	.0009	.0011	.0013	.0015	.0017	.0019	.0022
15	.0002	.0002	.0003	.0003	.0004	.0005	.0006	.0007	.0008	.0009
16	.0001	.0001	.0001	.0001	.0001	.0002	.0002	.0002	.0003	.0003
17	.0000	.0000	.0000	.0000	.0000	.0001	.0001	.0001	.0001	.0001

	μ									
x	6.1	6.2	6.3	6.4	6.5	6.6	6.7	6.8	6.9	7.0
0	.0022	.0020	.0019	.0017	.0015	.0014	.0012	.0011	.0010	.0009
1	.0137	.0126	.0116	.0106	.0098	.0090	.0082	.0076	.0070	.0064
2	.0417	.0390	.0364	.0340	.0318	.0296	.0276	.0258	.0240	.0223
3	.0848	.0806	.0765	.0726	.0688	.0652	.0617	.0584	.0552	.0521
4	.1294	.1249	.1205	.1162	.1118	.1076	.1034	.0992	.0952	.0912
5	.1579	.1549	.1519	.1487	.1454	.1420	.1385	.1349	.1314	.1277
6	.1605	.1601	.1595	.1586	.1575	.1562	.1546	.1529	.1511	.1490
7	.1399	.1418	.1435	.1450	.1462	.1472	.1480	.1486	.1489	.1490
8	.1066	.1099	.1130	.1160	.1188	.1215	.1240	.1263	.1284	.1304
9	.0723	.0757	.0791	.0825	.0858	.0891	.0923	.0954	.0985	.1014

					μ					
x	6.1	6.2	6.3	6.4	6.5	6.6	6.7	6.8	6.9	7.0
10	.0441	.0469	.0498	.0528	.0558	.0588	.0618	.0649	.0679	.0710
11	.0245	.0265	.0285	.0307	.0330	.0353	.0377	.0401	.0426	.0452
12	.0124	.0137	.0150	.0164	.0179	.0194	.0210	.0227	.0245	.0264
13	.0058	.0065	.0073	.0081	.0089	.0098	.0108	.0119	.0130	.0142
14	.0025	.0029	.0033	.0037	.0041	.0046	.0052	.0058	.0064	.0071
15	.0010	.0012	.0014	.0016	.0018	.0020	.0023	.0026	.0029	.0033
16	.0004	.0005	.0005	.0006	.0007	.0008	.0010	.0011	.0013	.0014
17	.0001	.0002	.0002	.0002	.0003	.0003	.0004	.0004	.0005	.0006
18	.0000	.0001	.0001	.0001	.0001	.0001	.0001	.0002	.0002	.0002
19	.0000	.0000	.0000	.0000	.0000	.0000	.0000	.0001	.0001	.0001

					μ					
x	7.1	7.2	7.3	7.4	7.5	7.6	7.7	7.8	7.9	8.0
0	.0008	.0007	.0007	.0006	.0006	.0005	.0005	.0004	.0004	.0003
1	.0059	.0054	.0049	.0045	.0041	.0038	.0035	.0032	.0029	.0027
2	.0208	.0194	.0180	.0167	.0156	.0145	.0134	.0125	.0116	.0107
3	.0492	.0464	.0438	.0413	.0389	.0366	.0345	.0324	.0305	.0286
4	.0874	.0836	.0799	.0764	.0729	.0696	.0663	.0632	.0602	.0573
5	.1241	.1204	.1167	.1130	.1094	.1057	.1021	.0986	.0951	.0916
6	.1468	.1445	.1420	.1394	.1367	.1339	.1311	.1282	.1252	.1221
7	.1489	.1486	.1481	.1474	.1465	.1454	.1442	.1428	.1413	.1396
8	.1321	.1337	.1351	.1363	.1373	.1382	.1388	.1392	.1395	.1396
9	.1042	.1070	.1096	.1121	.1144	.1167	.1187	.1207	.1224	.1241
10	.0740	.0770	.0800	.0829	.0858	.0887	.0914	.0941	.0967	.0993
11	.0478	.0504	.0531	.0558	.0585	.0613	.0640	.0667	.0695	.0722
12	.0283	.0303	.0323	.0344	.0366	.0388	.0411	.0434	.0457	.0481
13	.0154	.0168	.0181	.0196	.0211	.0227	.0243	.0260	.0278	.0296
14	.0078	.0086	.0095	.0104	.0113	.0123	.0134	.0145	.0157	.0169
15	.0037	.0041	.0046	.0051	.0057	.0062	.0069	.0075	.0083	.0090
16	.0016	.0019	.0021	.0024	.0026	.0030	.0033	.0037	.0041	.0045
17	.0007	.0008	.0009	.0010	.0012	.0013	.0015	0017	.0019	.0021
18	.0003	.0003	.0004	.0004	.0005	.0006	.0006	.0007	.0008	.0009
19	.0001	.0001	.0001	.0002	.0002	.0002	.0003	.0003	.0003	.0004
20	.0000	.0000	.0001	.0001	.0001	.0001	.0001	.0001	.0001	.0002
21	.0000	.0000	.0000	.0000	.0000	.0000	.0000	.0000	.0001	.0001

TABLE 13   Control Chart Constants

n	For Estimating Sigma		For $\bar{X}$ Chart		For $\bar{X}$ Chart (Standard Given)	For R Chart		For R Chart (Standard Given)		For s Chart (Standard Given)			
	c_4	d_2	A_2	A_3	A	D_3	D_4	D_1	D_2	B_3	B_4	B_5	B_6
2	0.7979	1.128	1.880	2.659	2.121	0	3.267	0	3.686	0	3.267	0	2.606
3	0.8862	1.693	1.023	1.954	1.732	0	2.575	0	4.358	0	2.568	0	2.276
4	0.9213	2.059	0.729	1.628	1.500	0	2.282	0	4.698	0	2.266	0	2.088
5	0.9400	2.326	0.577	1.427	1.342	0	2.115	0	4.918	0	2.089	0	1.964
6	0.9515	2.534	0.483	1.287	1.225	0	2.004	0	5.078	0.030	1.970	0.029	1.874
7	0.9594	2.704	0.419	1.182	1.134	0.076	1.924	0.205	5.203	0.118	1.882	0.113	1.806
8	0.9650	2.847	0.373	1.099	1.061	0.136	1.864	0.387	5.307	0.185	1.815	0.179	1.751
9	0.9693	2.970	0.337	1.032	1.000	0.184	1.816	0.546	5.394	0.239	1.761	0.232	1.707
10	0.9727	3.078	0.308	0.975	0.949	0.223	1.777	0.687	5.469	0.284	1.716	0.276	1.669
15	0.9823	3.472	0.223	0.789	0.775	0.348	1.652	1.207	5.737	0.428	1.572	0.421	1.544
20	0.9869	3.735	0.180	0.680	0.671	0.414	1.586	1.548	5.922	0.510	1.490	0.504	1.470
25	0.9896	3.931	0.153	0.606	0.600	0.459	1.541	1.804	6.058	0.565	1.435	0.559	1.420

Reprinted by permission from T. P. Ryan, *Statistical Methods for Quality Improvement* (New York: John Wiley and Sons, 1989).

TABLE 14 Random Numbers

1559	9068	9290	8303	8508	8954	1051	6677	6415	0342
5550	6245	7313	0117	7652	5069	6354	7668	1096	5780
4735	6214	8037	1385	1882	0828	2957	0530	9210	0177
5333	1313	3063	1134	8676	6241	9960	5304	1582	6198
8495	2956	1121	8484	2920	7934	0670	5263	0968	0069
1947	3353	1197	7363	9003	9313	3434	4261	0066	2714
4785	6325	1868	5020	9100	0823	7379	7391	1250	5501
9972	9163	5833	0100	5758	3696	6496	6297	5653	7782
0472	4629	2007	4464	3312	8728	1193	2497	4219	5339
4727	6994	1175	5622	2341	8562	5192	1471	7206	2027
3658	3226	5981	9025	1080	1437	6721	7331	0792	5383
6906	9758	0244	0259	4609	1269	5957	7556	1975	7898
3793	6916	0132	8873	8987	4975	4814	2098	6683	0901
3376	5966	1614	4025	0721	1537	6695	6090	8083	5450
6126	0224	7169	3596	1593	5097	7286	2686	1796	1150
0466	7566	1320	8777	8470	5448	9575	4669	1402	3905
9908	9832	8185	8835	0384	3699	1272	1181	8627	1968
7594	3636	1224	6808	1184	3404	6752	4391	2016	6167
5715	9301	5847	3524	0077	6674	8061	5438	6508	9673
7932	4739	4567	6797	4540	8488	3639	9777	1621	7244
6311	2025	5250	6099	6718	7539	9681	3204	9637	1091
0476	1624	3470	1600	0675	3261	7749	4195	2660	2150
5317	3903	6098	9438	3482	5505	5167	9993	8191	8488
7474	8876	1918	9828	2061	6664	0391	9170	2776	4025
7460	6800	1987	2758	0737	6880	1500	5763	2061	9373
1002	1494	9972	3877	6104	4006	0477	0669	8557	0513
5449	6891	9047	6297	1075	7762	8091	7153	8881	3367
9453	0809	7151	9982	0411	1120	6129	5090	2053	7570
0471	2725	7588	6573	0546	0110	6132	1224	3124	6563
5469	2668	1996	2249	3857	6637	8010	1701	3141	6147
2782	9603	1877	4159	9809	2570	4544	0544	2660	6737
3129	7217	5020	3788	0853	9465	2186	3945	1696	2286
7092	9885	3714	8557	7804	9524	6228	7774	6674	2775
9566	0501	8352	1062	0634	2401	0379	1697	7153	6208
5863	7000	1714	9276	7218	6922	1032	4838	1954	1680
5881	9151	2321	3147	6755	2510	5759	6947	7102	0097
6416	9939	9569	0439	1705	4680	9881	7071	9596	8758
9568	3012	6316	9065	0710	2158	1639	9149	4848	8634
0452	9538	5730	1893	1186	9245	6558	9562	8534	9321
8762	5920	8989	4777	2169	7073	7082	9495	1594	8600
0194	0270	7601	0342	3897	4133	7650	9228	5558	3597
3306	5478	2797	1605	4996	0023	9780	9429	3937	7573
7198	3079	2171	6972	0928	6599	9328	0597	5948	5753
8350	4846	1309	0612	4584	4988	4642	4430	9481	9048
7449	4279	4224	1018	2496	2091	9750	6086	1955	9860
6126	5399	0852	5491	6557	4946	9918	1541	7894	1843
1851	7940	9908	3860	1536	8011	4314	7269	7047	0382
7698	4218	2726	5130	3132	1722	8592	9662	4795	7718
0810	0118	4979	0458	1059	5739	7919	4557	0245	4861
6647	7149	1409	6809	3313	0082	9024	7477	7320	5822
3867	7111	5549	9439	3427	9793	3071	6651	4267	8099
1172	7278	7527	2492	6211	9457	5120	4903	1023	5745
6701	1668	5067	0413	7961	7825	9261	8572	0634	1140
8244	0620	8736	2649	1429	6253	4181	8120	6500	8127
8009	4031	7884	2215	2382	1931	1252	8088	2490	9122
1947	8315	9755	7187	4074	4743	6669	6060	2319	0635
9562	4821	8050	0106	2782	4665	9436	4973	4879	8900
0729	9026	9631	8096	8906	5713	3212	8854	3435	4206
6904	2569	3251	0079	8838	8738	8503	6333	0952	1641

THE FEDERAL RESERVE DATA SET

The following are monthly observations on six economic variables from September 1981 through April 1995. These data are obtained from the *Federal Reserve Bulletin*, vols. 68 to 74 (Washington, D.C.: Board of Governors of the Federal Reserve System). The variables are defined as follows.

FFR = Monthly average of the federal funds rate (%).

FT = Foreign trade: U.S. exports of domestic and foreign merchandise, excluding grant-aid shipments. Data are in millions of dollars, seasonally adjusted.

IP = Seasonally adjusted U.S. industrial production index (1967 = 100 from September 1981 to August 1984, 1977 = 100 from September 1984 to February 1988, and 1987 = 100 from March 1989 onward).

HS = Number of new-unit private residential housing permits authorized, in thousands of units.

ER = Index of weighted-average exchange value of the U.S. dollar against currencies of 10 industrial nations (1973 = 100).

NSE = New York Stock Exchange common stock price index (1965 = 50).

	Month	FFR	FT	IP	HS	ER	NSE
1981	September	15.87	19,655	151.6	850	107.78	68.37
	October	15.08	19,044	149.2	722	106.34	69.40
	November	13.31	19,153	146.3	743	104.53	71.49
	December	12.37	18,885	143.4	797	105.21	71.81
1982	January	13.22	18,737	140.7	803	106.96	67.91
	February	14.78	18,704	142.9	792	110.36	66.16
	March	14.68	18,602	141.7	851	112.45	63.86
	April	14.94	17,843	140.2	871	114.07	66.97
	May	14.45	18,218	139.2	944	111.03	67.07
	June	14.15	18,822	138.7	929	116.97	63.10
	July	12.59	18,026	138.8	1,062	118.91	62.82
	August	10.12	17,463	138.4	888	119.63	62.91
	September	10.31	17,320	137.3	1,029	120.93	70.21
	October	9.71	16,671	135.7	1,154	123.16	76.10
	November	9.20	15,852	134.9	1,227	124.27	79.75
	December	8.95	16,347	135.2	1,326	119.22	80.30
1983	January	8.68	17,393	137.4	1,447	117.73	83.25
	February	8.51	16,326	138.1	1,479	119.70	84.74
	March	8.77	16,752	140.0	1,467	120.71	87.50
	April	8.80	16,074	142.6	1,536	121.82	90.61
	May	8.63	15,566	144.4	1,635	122.05	94.61
	June	8.98	17,008	146.4	1,761	125.16	96.43
	July	9.37	16,486	149.7	1,752	126.62	96.74
	August	9.56	16,582	151.8	1,671	129.77	93.96
	September	9.45	17,257	153.8	1,540	129.74	96.70
	October	9.04	17,033	155.0	1,650	127.50	96.78
	November	9.34	17,063	155.3	1,649	130.26	95.36
	December	9.47	17,298	156.2	1,602	132.84	94.92
1984	January	9.56	18,326	158.5	1,799	135.07	96.16
	February	9.59	17,212	160.0	1,902	131.71	90.60
	March	9.91	17,727	160.8	1,756	128.07	90.66

	Month	FFR	FT	IP	HS	ER	NSE
	April	10.29	17,521	162.1	1,802	130.01	90.67
	May	10.32	17,950	162.8	1,774	133.49	90.07
	June	11.06	17,633	164.4	1,819	134.31	88.28
	July	11.23	19,442	165.9	1,590	139.30	87.08
	August	11.64	18,036	166.0	1,508	140.21	94.49
	September	11.30	18,210	123.3	1,481	145.70	95.68
	October	9.99	18,411	122.7	1,436	147.56	95.09
	November	9.43	18,395	123.4	1,616	144.92	95.85
	December	8.38	19,142	123.3	1.599	149.24	94.85
1985	January	8.35	19,401	123.6	1,635	152.85	99.11
	February	8.50	17,853	123.7	1,624	158.43	104.73
	March	8.58	18,446	124.0	1,741	158.14	103.42
	April	8.27	17,779	124.1	1,704	149.56	104.66
	May	7.97	17,414	124.1	1,778	149.92	107.00
	June	7.53	17,438	124.3	1,717	147.71	109.52
	July	7.88	17,411	124.1	1,709	140.94	111.64
	August	7.90	17,423	125.2	1,782	137.55	109.09
	September	7.92	17,034	125.1	1,846	139.14	106.62
	October	7.99	17,618	124.4	1,703	130.71	107.57
	November	8.05	17,721	125.4	1,668	128.08	113.93
	December	8.27	16,994	126.4	1,839	125.80	119.33
1986	January	8.14	17,006	126.2	1,861	123.65	120.16
	February	7.86	17,735	125.3	1,808	118.77	126.43
	March	7.48	18,913	123.6	1,834	116.05	133.97
	April	6.99	17,965	124.7	1,885	115.67	137.25
	May	6.85	17,431	124.2	1,788	113.27	137.37
	June	6.92	19,070	124.2	1,792	113.77	140.82
	July	6.56	17,707	124.9	1,759	110.38	138.32
	August	6.17	17,604	125.1	1,673	107.50	140.91
	September	5.89	17,518	125.2	1,603	107.15	137.06
	October	5.85	19,330	125.3	1,565	106.58	136.74
	November	6.04	18,595	126.0	1,613	107.90	140.84
	December	6.91	18,431	126.7	1,910	106.54	142.12
1987	January	6.43	16,421	126.5	1,652	101.13	151.17
	February	6.10	18,660	127.2	1,676	89.46	161.23
	March	6.13	21,776	127.3	1,719	98.99	166.43
	April	6.37	20,496	127.4	1,598	97.09	163.88
	May	6.85	20,784	128.4	1,493	96.05	163.00
	June	6.73	21,126	129.1	1,517	97.78	169.58
	July	6.58	21,008	130.6	1,487	99.36	174.28
	August	6.73	20,222	131.0	1,502	99.43	184.18
	September	7.22	20,986	130.9	1,502	97.23	178.39
	October	7.29	21,752	131.7	1,463	96.65	157.13
	November	6.69	23,799	133.2	1,469	91.49	137.21
	December	6.77	24,801	133.9	1,361	88.70	134.88
1988	January	6.83	22,330	134.4	1,257	89.29	140.55
	February	6.58	23,559	134.4	1,422	91.08	145.13
	March	6.58	29,106	134.7	1,476	89.73	149.88
	April	6.87	26,335	135.4	1,449	88.95	148.46
	May	7.09	27,478	136.1	1,436	89.74	144.99
	June	7.51	26,283	136.5	1,485	92.58	152.72
	July	7.75	26,516	138.0	1,425	96.53	152.12
	August	8.01	27,493	138.5	1,466	98.29	149.25
	September	8.19	27,989	138.6	1,432	97.91	151.47
	October	8.30	27,816	139.4	1,526	95.10	156.36
	November	8.35	27,538	139.9	1,508	91.91	152.67
	December	8.76	28,864	140.4	1,518	91.88	155.35
1989	January	9.12	28,980	140.8	1,486	95.12	160.35
	February	9.36	28,839	140.5	1,403	95.77	165.08
	March	9.85	30,065	107.7	1,230	96.99	164.56
	April	9.84	30,759	108.6	1,334	97.24	169.38
	May	9.81	30,455	108.3	1,347	100.81	175.30
	June	9.53	31,286	108.4	1,323	103.09	180.76
	July	9.24	29,662	107.8	1,281	99.12	185.15
	August	8.99	30,249	108.2	1,334	100.44	192.93

	Month	FFR	FT	IP	HS	ER	NSE
	September	9.02	30,367	108.2	1,310	101.87	193.02
	October	8.84	31,474	107.7	1,362	98.92	192.49
	November	8.55	30,618	108.1	1,364	97.99	188.50
	December	8.45	31,262	108.6	1,416	94.88	192.67
1990	January	8.23	31,372	107.5	1,739	93.00	187.96
	February	8.24	31,576	108.5	1,297	92.25	182.55
	March	8.28	33,266	108.9	1,232	94.11	186.26
	April	8.26	32,058	108.8	1,108	93.51	185.61
	May	8.18	32,774	109.4	1,065	92.04	191.35
	June	8.29	34,221	110.1	1,123	92.43	196.68
	July	8.15	32,125	110.4	1,086	89.68	196.61
	August	8.13	32,515	110.5	1,055	86.55	181.45
	September	8.20	32,231	110.6	989	86.10	173.22
	October	8.11	34,631	109.9	925	83.43	168.05
	November	7.81	33,586	108.3	916	82.12	172.21
	December	7.31	33,570	107.2	854	83.35	179.57
1991	June	5.90	34,975	107.3	956	95.18	207.32
	July	5.82	35,227	108.1	971	95.19	208.29
	August	5.66	34,380	108.0	940	93.47	213.33
	September	5.45	35,283	108.4	974	91.18	212.55
	October	5.21	36,842	108.4	994	90.69	213.10
	November	4.81	37,269	108.1	979	87.98	213.25
	December	4.43	36,053	107.4	1,073	85.65	214.26
1992	January	4.03	35,467	106.6	1,106	86.09	229.34
	February	4.06	37,654	107.2	1,146	88.04	228.12
	March	3.98	37,085	107.6	1,094	90.44	225.21
	April	3.73	36,406	106.3	1,058	89.84	224.55
	May	3.82	35,718	106.7	1,054	88.30	228.55
	June	3.76	38,165	106.0	1,048	85.91	224.68
	July	3.25	37,806	106.8	1,083	82.57	228.17
	August	3.30	35,799	106.6	1,081	80.97	230.07
	September	3.22	37,661	106.2	1,120	81.98	230.13
	October	3.10	38.885	107.5	1,141	85.03	226.97
	November	3.09	37,796	108.4	1,136	90.04	232.84
	December	2.92	39,178	108.9	1,196	90.50	239.47
1993	January	3.02	37,505	109.3	1,157	92.36	239.75
	February	3.03	36,928	109.9	1,141	93.82	243.41
	March	3.07	38,895	110.1	1,034	93.65	248.12
	April	2.96	38,479	110.5	1,101	90.62	244.72
	May	3.00	38,930	110.0	1,121	90.24	246.02
	June	3.04	37,639	110.4	1,122	91.81	247.16
	July	3.06	36,577	110.9	1,169	94.59	247.85
	August	3.03	37,224	111.1	1,234	94.32	251.93
	September	3.09	38,134	111.3	1,265	92.07	254.86
	October	2.99	39,361	111.9	1,298	93.29	257.53
	November	3.02	39,364	113.7	1,363	95.47	255.93
	December	2.96	40,953	114.7	1,474	95.73	257.73
1994	January	3.05	38,533	114.7	1,312	96.54	262.11
	February	3.25	37,425	115.6	1,252	95.79	261.97
	March	3.34	42,065	116.6	1,331	94.35	257.32
	April	3.56	40,378	116.7	1,377	94.39	247.97
	May	4.01	40,276	117.4	1,383	92.79	249.56
	June	4.25	42,028	118.0	1,336	91.60	251.21
	July	4.26	40,101	118.2	1,347	89.06	249.29
	August	4.47	44,054	119.1	1,382	89.26	256.08
	September	4.73	43,485	119.0	1,416	88.08	257.61
	October	4.76	43,289	119.5	1,391	86.66	255.22
	November	5.29	44,814	120.3	1,355	87.71	252.48
	December	5.45	46,490	121.7	1,421	89.64	248.65
1995	January	5.53	44.299	122.2	1,302	88.30	253.56
	February	5.92	45,421		1,287	87.29	261.86
	March	5.98				83.69	266.81
	April					81.81	

INDEX